Microsoft® Windows® Me Millennium Edition Secrets®

Microsoft® Windows® Me Millennium Edition Secrets®

Brian Livingston and Davis Straub

IDG Books Worldwide, Inc.
An International Data Group Company

Foster City, CA ♦ Chicago, IL ♦ Indianapolis, IN ♦ New York, NY

NEW CUMBERLAND
PUBLIC LIBRARY
797 2507

Microsoft® Windows® Me Millennium Edition Secrets®

Published by

IDG Books Worldwide, Inc.

An International Data Group Company
919 E. Hillsdale Blvd., Suite 400
Foster City, CA 94404
www.idgbooks.com (IDG Books Worldwide Web site)

Copyright © 2000 Brian Livingston and Davis Straub. All rights reserved. No part of this book, including interior design, cover design, and icons, may be reproduced or transmitted in any form, by any means (electronic, photocopying, recording, or otherwise) without the prior written permission of the publisher.

ISBN: 0-7645-3493-9

Printed in the United States of America

10 9 8 7 6 5 4 3 2 1

1B/RR/QZ/QQ/FC

Distributed in the United States by IDG Books Worldwide, Inc.

Distributed by CDG Books Canada Inc. for Canada; by Transworld Publishers Limited in the United Kingdom; by IDG Norge Books for Norway; by IDG Sweden Books for Sweden; by IDG Books Australia Publishing Corporation Pty. Ltd. for Australia and New Zealand; by TransQuest Publishers Pte Ltd. for Singapore, Malaysia, Thailand, Indonesia, and Hong Kong; by Gotop Information Inc. for Taiwan; by ICG Muse, Inc. for Japan; by Intersoft for South Africa; by Eyrolles for France; by International Thomson Publishing for Germany, Austria, and Switzerland; by Distribuidora Cuspide for Argentina; by LR International for Brazil; by Galileo Libros for Chile; by Ediciones ZETA S.C.R. Ltda. for Peru; by WS Computer Publishing Corporation, Inc., for the Philippines; by Contemporanea de Ediciones for Venezuela; by Express Computer Distributors for the Caribbean and West Indies; by Micronesia Media Distributor, Inc. for Micronesia; by Chips Computadoras S.A. de C.V. for Mexico; by Editorial Norma de Panama S.A. for Panama; by American Bookshops for Finland.

For general information on IDG Books Worldwide's books in the U.S., please call our Consumer Customer Service department at 800-762-2974. For reseller information, including discounts and premium sales, please call our Reseller Customer Service department at 800-434-3422.

For information on where to purchase IDG Books Worldwide's books outside the U.S., please contact our International Sales department at 317-572-3993 or fax 317-572-4002.

For consumer information on foreign language translations, please contact our Customer Service department at 800-434-3422, fax 317-572-4002, or e-mail rights@idgbooks.com.

For information on licensing foreign or domestic rights, please phone +1-650-653-7098.

For sales inquiries and special prices for bulk quantities, please contact our Order Services department at 800-434-3422 or write to the address above.

For information on using IDG Books Worldwide's books in the classroom or for ordering examination copies, please contact our Educational Sales department at 800-434-2086 or fax 317-572-4005.

For press review copies, author interviews, or other publicity information, please contact our Public Relations department at 650-653-7000 or fax 650-653-7500.

For authorization to photocopy items for corporate, personal, or educational use, please contact Copyright Clearance Center, 222 Rosewood Drive, Danvers, MA 01923, or fax 978-750-4470.

Library of Congress Cataloging-in-Publication Data

Livingston, Brian.
 Microsoft Windows millennium edition secrets/ Brian Livingston and Davis Straub.
  p. cm.
  ISBN 0-7645-3493-9 (alk. paper)
  1. Microsoft Windows (Computer file) 2. Operating systems (Computers) I. Straub, Davis, 1947- II. Title.
 QA76.76.O63 L585   2000
 005.4'469--dc21   00-044951

LIMIT OF LIABILITY/DISCLAIMER OF WARRANTY: THE PUBLISHER AND AUTHOR HAVE USED THEIR BEST EFFORTS IN PREPARING THIS BOOK. THE PUBLISHER AND AUTHOR MAKE NO REPRESENTATIONS OR WARRANTIES WITH RESPECT TO THE ACCURACY OR COMPLETENESS OF THE CONTENTS OF THIS BOOK AND SPECIFICALLY DISCLAIM ANY IMPLIED WARRANTIES OF MERCHANTABILITY OR FITNESS FOR A PARTICULAR PURPOSE. THERE ARE NO WARRANTIES WHICH EXTEND BEYOND THE DESCRIPTIONS CONTAINED IN THIS PARAGRAPH. NO WARRANTY MAY BE CREATED OR EXTENDED BY SALES REPRESENTATIVES OR WRITTEN SALES MATERIALS. THE ACCURACY AND COMPLETENESS OF THE INFORMATION PROVIDED HEREIN AND THE OPINIONS STATED HEREIN ARE NOT GUARANTEED OR WARRANTED TO PRODUCE ANY PARTICULAR RESULTS, AND THE ADVICE AND STRATEGIES CONTAINED HEREIN MAY NOT BE SUITABLE FOR EVERY INDIVIDUAL. NEITHER THE PUBLISHER NOR AUTHOR SHALL BE LIABLE FOR ANY LOSS OF PROFIT OR ANY OTHER COMMERCIAL DAMAGES, INCLUDING BUT NOT LIMITED TO SPECIAL, INCIDENTAL, CONSEQUENTIAL, OR OTHER DAMAGES.

Trademarks: All brand names and product names used in this book are trade names, service marks, trademarks, or registered trademarks of their respective owners. IDG Books Worldwide is not associated with any product or vendor mentioned in this book.

 is a registered trademark or trademark under exclusive license to IDG Books Worldwide, Inc. from International Data Group, Inc. in the United States and/or other countries.

ABOUT IDG BOOKS WORLDWIDE

Welcome to the world of IDG Books Worldwide.

IDG Books Worldwide, Inc., is a subsidiary of International Data Group, the world's largest publisher of computer-related information and the leading global provider of information services on information technology. IDG was founded more than 30 years ago by Patrick J. McGovern and now employs more than 9,000 people worldwide. IDG publishes more than 290 computer publications in over 75 countries. More than 90 million people read one or more IDG publications each month.

Launched in 1990, IDG Books Worldwide is today the #1 publisher of best-selling computer books in the United States. We are proud to have received eight awards from the Computer Press Association in recognition of editorial excellence and three from Computer Currents' First Annual Readers' Choice Awards. Our best-selling ...*For Dummies*® series has more than 50 million copies in print with translations in 31 languages. IDG Books Worldwide, through a joint venture with IDG's Hi-Tech Beijing, became the first U.S. publisher to publish a computer book in the People's Republic of China. In record time, IDG Books Worldwide has become the first choice for millions of readers around the world who want to learn how to better manage their businesses.

Our mission is simple: Every one of our books is designed to bring extra value and skill-building instructions to the reader. Our books are written by experts who understand and care about our readers. The knowledge base of our editorial staff comes from years of experience in publishing, education, and journalism — experience we use to produce books to carry us into the new millennium. In short, we care about books, so we attract the best people. We devote special attention to details such as audience, interior design, use of icons, and illustrations. And because we use an efficient process of authoring, editing, and desktop publishing our books electronically, we can spend more time ensuring superior content and less time on the technicalities of making books.

You can count on our commitment to deliver high-quality books at competitive prices on topics you want to read about. At IDG Books Worldwide, we continue in the IDG tradition of delivering quality for more than 30 years. You'll find no better book on a subject than one from IDG Books Worldwide.

John Kilcullen
Chairman and CEO
IDG Books Worldwide, Inc.

*Eighth Annual
Computer Press
Awards ≥1992*

*Ninth Annual
Computer Press
Awards ≥1993*

*Tenth Annual
Computer Press
Awards ≥1994*

*Eleventh Annual
Computer Press
Awards ≥1995*

IDG is the world's leading IT media, research and exposition company. Founded in 1964, IDG had 1997 revenues of $2.05 billion and has more than 9,000 employees worldwide. IDG offers the widest range of media options that reach IT buyers in 75 countries representing 95% of worldwide IT spending. IDG's diverse product and services portfolio spans six key areas including print publishing, online publishing, expositions and conferences, market research, education and training, and global marketing services. More than 90 million people read one or more of IDG's 290 magazines and newspapers, including IDG's leading global brands — Computerworld, PC World, Network World, Macworld and the Channel World family of publications. IDG Books Worldwide is one of the fastest-growing computer book publishers in the world, with more than 700 titles in 36 languages. The "...For Dummies®" series alone has more than 50 million copies in print. IDG offers online users the largest network of technology-specific Web sites around the world through IDG.net (http://www.idg.net), which comprises more than 225 targeted Web sites in 55 countries worldwide. International Data Corporation (IDC) is the world's largest provider of information technology data, analysis and consulting, with research centers in over 41 countries and more than 400 research analysts worldwide. IDG World Expo is a leading producer of more than 168 globally branded conferences and expositions in 35 countries including E3 (Electronic Entertainment Expo), Macworld Expo, ComNet, Windows World Expo, ICE (Internet Commerce Expo), Agenda, DEMO, and Spotlight. IDG's training subsidiary, ExecuTrain, is the world's largest computer training company, with more than 230 locations worldwide and 785 training courses. IDG Marketing Services helps industry-leading IT companies build international brand recognition by developing global integrated marketing programs via IDG's print, online and exposition products worldwide. Further information about the company can be found at www.idg.com. 1/26/00

Credits

Acquisitions Editor
Andy Cummings

Project Editors
Brian MacDonald
Marti Paul

Technical Editors
Art Brieva
Brian Underdahl

Copy Editors
Chandani Thapa
Dennis Weaver

Proof Editor
Patsy Owens

Project Coordinators
Danette Nurse
Marcos Vergara

Permissions Editor
Carmen Krikorian

Media Development Specialists
Megan Decraene
Brock Bigard

Media Development Coordinator
Marisa Pearman

Graphics and Production Specialists
Robert Bihlmayer
Darren Cutlip
Jude Levinson
Michael Lewis
Victor Pérez-Varela
Ramses Ramirez

Quality Control Technician
Dina F Quan

Illustrators
Rashell Smith
Brian Drumm
Gabriele McCann

Proofreading and Indexing
York Production Services

About the Author

Brian Livingston is the author of IDG Books Worldwide's best-selling *Windows 3 Secrets*; *Windows 3.1 Secrets*, 2nd Edition; *More Windows 3.1 Secrets*; and is coauthor of *Windows Gizmos*, a collection of shareware and freeware tools and games; *Windows 95 Secrets;* and *Windows 98 Secrets*. His books are printed in more than 30 languages. In addition to writing books, Mr. Livingston is a contributing editor of *InfoWorld* magazine and CNET News.com, and has been a contributing editor of *PC/Computing*, *PC World*, *Windows Sources*, and other magazines. He was a recipient of the 1991 Award for Technical Excellence from the National Microcomputer Managers Association.

Davis Straub is the coauthor of *Windows 95 Secrets, Windows 98 Secrets,* and technical editor for *Windows Gizmos*. He previously worked as a Windows multimedia software developer. He is the former president of Generic Software (a successful CAD software company) and Personal Workstations, Inc. (a successful CAD value-added reseller). When not furiously digging for Windows secrets, he spends his time hang gliding.

To Margie Livingston and Belinda Boulter

Contents at a Glance

Contents

Contents

Part IV: Hardware Secrets 1045

Chapter 36: Plug and Play — Device Management 1047

Chapter 37: Disk Tools and File Systems 1077

## Chapter 1

Read This First

In This Chapter

▶ Why a book like *Microsoft Windows Me Millennium Edition Secrets* is needed

▶ Finding the section with the answers to your questions

▶ Brief descriptions of what you will find in each section of the book

▶ How to correctly type Windows Me commands as used in this book

▶ Finding the good parts

▶ Where to get the best technical support

Why *Windows Me Millennium Edition Secrets*

This book is for everyone who uses Windows Me (you will find Millennium Edition referred to as Me in this book) — *and* for everyone who uses Windows 98 and Windows 95, which are easy to upgrade to Windows Me levels of computing.

Windows Me is very similar to both Windows 98 and Windows 95 — *if* you've upgraded your earlier version of Windows 9*x* to the latest release of Microsoft's Internet Explorer browser and other components.

In this book:

■ When we say, "Windows," we mean "Windows Me, or a copy of Windows 98 or 95 that has been upgraded to the latest version of Internet Explorer."

■ When we say, "Windows 2000/NT," we mean "Windows 2000 or a previous version of Windows NT 4.0, 3.5, etc."

It's easy to upgrade Windows 98 or 95 *free* to most of the functionality of Windows Me. Go to the Microsoft Web site and click this link to upgrade to the latest IE, Outlook Express, and other features:

```
http://windowsupdate.microsoft.com
```

You should do this even if you've just acquired a new PC with Windows Me already installed. New upgrades become available from Microsoft all the time. You may find a new component that will improve Windows Me. Or you may just want to bring Windows 9*x* up-to-date with the latest and greatest features. It's up to you.

Once you've upgraded to the latest features available for Windows, you're ready to take advantage of all the secrets we've been able to pack into *Windows Me Millennium Edition Secrets* for you.

But even if you don't upgrade, 90 percent of *Windows Me Millennium Edition Secrets* will still apply to Windows 98 and, to a slightly lesser extent, Windows 95. That's because Windows Me is a minor upgrade — not a major departure — from Windows 98 and Windows 95 (with the addition of Internet Explorer, which originally was a separate product).

Why did we write *Windows Me Millennium Edition Secrets?* Windows Me is a large and complicated piece — actually many pieces — of software with thousands of features and capabilities. Microsoft focused on writing the code for the operating system as its primary task. Documentation was a secondary consideration.

Windows Me is open to a great deal of customization. You have the opportunity to turn it into your personal operating system. *Windows Me Millennium Edition Secrets* provides you with the (often secret) knowledge that you need to take charge of Windows Me and make it behave properly.

Windows Me isn't configured perfectly for you the way it comes out of the box, or on that new computer you just bought with Windows preinstalled. If you don't change it to respond to how you work with your computer, you just aren't going to be as happy with it as you could be. Microsoft has provided many ways to change it. Other programmers have developed tools based on the Windows Explorer extensions that add great functionality. We show you how to find these tools and use them.

How to Use This Book

PART I: If you haven't yet installed Windows Me on your existing computer, turn to "The Setup Process" in Chapter 2.

PART II: If you want to get a feel for Windows Me (assuming that it is already installed) turn to Chapters 4 and 5. These chapters provide a quick look at Windows and a basic tutorial to get you familiar with the Windows Desktop. More detailed information on all aspects of the Windows user interface is provided in Part II. Go to the chapter that addresses the part of the Windows interface that you're most interested in.

PART III: If you want to connect to the Internet and send e-mail, turn to Part III. We discuss how to create a Dial-Up Networking connectoid, hook up with an Internet service provider, and send e-mail using Outlook Express or Windows Messaging.

PART IV: Finally, to get the most out of your hardware, we've included tricks that can help you with disk drives, monitors, printers, mice, modems, and other physical devices. In Part IV, we cover the things you need to know about Plug and Play (what some call "Plug and Pray"). And we describe ways you may need to tweak your memory management and power management settings to get the most out of Windows.

Using the E-Book on the CD-ROM

We hope that you use this book in conjunction with your computer. Open it up and crease the binding so that it stays open to your page. We don't expect you to read this thing like a novel. This is a reference work, so you should hunt and peck around looking for things of interest.

We've included an electronic version of the book on the enclosed CD-ROM. The e-version is in a format that includes the contents of the book, as well as search capabilities. We have found this format to be quite convenient. If you install the e-book on your computer, you will be able to search the book to find information about a particular topic.

The printed book, and of course the e-book, includes hundreds of URLs — *universal resource locators*, or Web addresses. We realize that, by the time this book reaches you, some of our URLs are going to be dead. The Web changes, and there's just no way to keep up with it in a book. If you hit a dead URL, try to go back a ways in the Address field. Delete everything past the last slash and then click the Go button or press Enter. Or delete everything in the address except the domain name (such as `www.microsoft.com`).

We've mentioned plenty of freeware and shareware download sites to visit. We hope that you have a chance to download some of the packages that we recommend. They make an incredible difference in how Windows operates as an operating system.

With this book (and other *Windows Secrets* books we've published in the last two years), we decided not to put shareware on the CD-ROM. With the proliferation of shareware Web sites, it's now easy and cheap to download up-to-the-minute software. We found that we couldn't provide in a book the latest, greatest shareware, as Internet sites can. So we've concentrated on writing the best book we could, instead of assembling a CD of shareware. But we specifically name in our pages the best places where you can get each piece of shareware we recommend, so you won't have to search randomly online.

Getting Commands Right the First Time

You'll be able to use the secrets in this book faster if you know exactly how to type the many Windows commands shown in the text.

Sometimes, the fastest way to accomplish what you want is to click the Start button, then click Run, then type a command. Many commands also work at the command line of the *Windows Me console,* also known as a good old DOS prompt.

Throughout this book, we've indicated many commands like this one, which uses WordPad to print a file without actually opening WordPad and the file:

```
WORDPAD {/p} filename
```

or

```
Wordpad {/p} filename
```

In this command, *filename* is shown in *italics* to indicate that you should change *filename* to the actual name of the file you want to open in the WordPad text editor.

The command /p is shown in curly braces {like this} to indicate that this *command-line parameter* is optional. You should *not* type the curly braces if you decide to add /p to this command. Because Windows often uses square brackets [like this] to indicate the beginning of sections in initialization (ini) files and in the text version of the registry, we do not use square brackets to indicate optional parameters. If you see a line that contains square brackets, you must type the square brackets along with the rest of the line.

If you want to print a file named Readme.txt using WordPad, for example, you could click the Start button on the Taskbar, click Run, and then type this line followed by Enter:

```
Wordpad /p Readme.txt
```

When a command that you should type appears within a paragraph, it is shown in **boldface**. Often, you can enter commands in any combination of uppercase and lowercase — in all lowercase, ALL UPPERCASE, or a mixture of both. However, some command-line parameters, such as /p, are case sensitive. When something you need to type is case sensitive, we let you know.

Whenever you see the term *filename* in italics, you can change it to any form of a valid filename that Windows will recognize, including drive letters and directory names. For example, if C:\Windows\Command is your current folder, any of the following names for the Readme.txt file are valid in this WordPad command:

```
WORDPAD README.TXT
Wordpad Readme.txt
WORDPAD C:\WINDOWS\COMMAND\README.TXT
WORDPAD \WINDOWS\COMMAND\README.TXT
```

We denote special keys on your keyboard with an initial capital letter, like this: Enter, Tab, Backspace, Shift, Alt (Alternate), Ctrl (Control), and Esc (Escape). When you see a phrase such as *press Enter*, you know not to type the keys *e, n, t, e,* and *r,* but to press the Enter key.

If one of the shift keys (Shift, Alt, or Ctrl) should be *held down* at the same time that you also press another key, the two keys are written with a plus sign between them. For example, *press Ctrl+A* means *hold down the Ctrl key, then press the A key, then release both keys.*

If you are supposed to *let up* on a key *before* pressing another one, those keys are separated by commas. If we say *press Alt, F, O,* this means *press and release Alt, then F, then O.* This sequence activates the menu bar of a Windows application, then pulls down the File menu, then executes the Open command. This is the same as saying *click File ⇨ Open.*

We use the character ⇨ to indicate a series of menu choices. For example, saying *click File ⇨ Open* means *click File on the menu bar, then click Open on the File menu.*

In this book, we do not indicate a keyboard-only procedure every time we describe how to do something with your mouse. The phrase *click File ⇨ Open* always means *click the File menu and then click the Open command,* but it can also mean *press the keys on your keyboard to issue the File ⇨ Open command.*

Finding the Good Parts

Each chapter begins with an introduction that gives you a quick idea of the neat tricks in store in that chapter. The summary at the end of each chapter provides a more detailed look at what you can expect to learn in the chapter.

When we discuss a secret, an undocumented feature, a tip, or a set of steps to carry out a specific task, you'll see an icon in the margin of the page. If you want to just hit the high points of this book, you can go from icon to icon, reading the surrounding paragraphs for helpful supporting material.

Secret

The secret icon indicates some useful information that Microsoft would rather that the end user not be aware of. Microsoft feels that the rest of us need to be protected from ourselves, so it would prefer that you didn't mess with the registry, for example.

Tip

Tips are just that — little explanations about how to do a certain task in a particularly nifty manner. Windows gives you lots of ways to do various things, and the documentation from Microsoft misses quite a few of them.

What's the difference between a *secret* and a *tip?* We feel that a secret is any information that isn't included in the documentation you get when you buy Windows. It may be written down somewhere (such as on the Internet), but if it isn't in the box that Windows came in, we consider it not to be in the documentation you purchased, and therefore a secret. We've brought all these secrets together for you into one place.

A *tip,* on the other hand, may be something that is explained somewhere in the Windows help system. But many of these tricks aren't at all obvious. So we point them out to you in this book as we go along.

STEPS

We often give you step-by-step instructions on how to carry out a specific task. One of our goals in creating these steps is to make sure that nobody gets lost. So even if you're unfamiliar with the theory, we include enough details in the steps for you to complete specific tasks. You can breeze through some of the steps as you learn more about Windows.

Getting Technical Support for Windows Me

All Windows programs (and books about Windows programs) have bugs. This includes all retail Windows software, all shareware described in *Windows Me Millennium Edition Secrets,* and all shareware you find on the Internet. Every program, no matter how simple, has some unexpected behavior. This is the nature of software, and existing bugs are usually fixed and new ones introduced with the release of a newer version.

It is not possible for the coauthors or IDG Books to provide technical support for Windows or for the many applications that may cause conflicts in your system.

For technical support for Windows, you will be better off contacting Microsoft directly — or using electronic support (which we describe in a moment).

Microsoft provides telephone technical support for its DOS and Windows products through these numbers:

Type of Support	*Number to Call at Microsoft*
Microsoft Windows Support 90 days of free support starting with your first phone call	425-635-7000 905-568-4494 (Canada)
Microsoft Pay-Per-Call Support ($35/incident)	900-555-2000 (U.S.) or 800-936-5700 (U.S.) 800-668-7975 (Canada)
Microsoft Foreign Pay-Per-Call Support	425-635-3909

Type of Support	Number to Call at Microsoft
Microsoft International Support (for referral to a non-U.S. office)	425-882-8080
Microsoft Windows Environment	425-637-7098
Microsoft Fast Tips — automated touch tone	800-936-4200 (U.S.)

Secret

The best technical support (in our humble opinion) has *never* been provided on phone lines — it has always been provided (this is the secret) on Microsoft's newsgroup server (see the "Accessing Microsoft Support Newsgroups" section later in this chapter).

Online News About Windows

If you don't already have an analog modem, a cable modem, or a digital subscriber line (DSL), we encourage you to get online and start taking advantage of services, newsgroups, and Web sites that specialize in technical support and news.

Here are some good places to seek technical support and read the latest news about Windows:

Where to Get Help	How to Get There
The World Wide Web	`http://support.microsoft.com/support/`
The Microsoft Knowledge Base on the Web	`http://search.support.microsoft.com/kb/c.as`
CompuServe	Type **GO WINNEWS**
AOL	Go to the keyword **Winnews**
Prodigy	Type **Jump Winnews**

In "Windows Home Pages" in Chapter 26, we provide a number of Web addresses for Windows support.

Accessing Microsoft Support Newsgroups

The best place to get Microsoft support is from the Microsoft support newsgroups. These newsgroups combine peer support (for the most part), support from Microsoft volunteers (MVPs, ClubWin, and ClubIE members), and every now and then (depending on the newsgroup), actual support engineers from Microsoft.

Microsoft hosts the newsgroups on its news server, `msnews.microsoft.com`. While some Internet service providers (ISPs) carry the newsgroups, they aren't generally available to other news servers at ISPs. To access the newsgroups, choose `msnews.microsoft.com` as your news server (or as one of a number of news servers) in your newsgroup reader. Outlook Express, the mail and news reader that comes with Windows Me and 98 (and is downloadable free for Windows 95 users), enables you to subscribe to multiple news servers.

Log on to the Microsoft news server after logging on to your ISP. Choose from the long list of product and interest area-specific newsgroups hosted by Microsoft and be prepared for a lot of reading. You can start here: `http://support.microsoft.com/support/news/`. Turn to "Windows Newsgroups" in Chapter 29 for a list of Microsoft Windows support newsgroups.

If you want actual one-on-one contact with Microsoft support engineers, you are pretty much going to have to pay for it on a per-contact or contract basis. You get support for the first 90 days, but after that, it's pay as you go.

If you're really desperate, have read this book, reviewed the newsgroups, and checked out the Microsoft Knowledge Base, and still need help, the coauthor, Davis Straub, makes himself available at `http://www.DavisStraub.com/secrets`. It may not be possible to solve your particular problem, but we want our readers to know that we're trying to give out all the information we possibly can.

Finally, if you've found a solution that could help other readers, Brian is always interested in receiving tips by e-mail. Go to `http://BrianLivingston.com`. From there, you can jump to Brian's latest columns or send in a tip. Brian sends a book free to any reader who's the first to send him a tip he prints in a column.

Technical Support for the CD-ROM

If the CD-ROM disc that comes with this book is damaged, you should, of course, contact IDG Books Worldwide, which is committed to providing you with a CD-ROM disc in perfect condition.

To see changes and updates to this book, and to the e-book that is contained on the CD-ROM, go to IDG Books' Web page, where we will post new information as it becomes available:

`http://www.idgbooks.com/extras`

Summary

▶ Because plenty is missing from Microsoft's documentation, it's difficult to find out how to access all its power.

▶ If you have a question about Windows, use this chapter to find out where you can turn in this book to find the answer.

▶ We tell you how to recognize commands that you need to type from your keyboard.

▶ We describe icons, step-by-step lists, and other shortcuts that will help you find the best parts of the book.

▶ We tell you how to get the best technical support, by phone from Microsoft and electronically through the Microsoft support newsgroups.

Part I

Startup Secrets

Chapter 2

Installing and Setting Up Windows Me

In This Chapter

We discuss how to install and set up Windows Me on your hard disk on a single computer. You can start from a computer with only DOS, a computer with Windows 3.1*x*, or a Windows 98 or 95 computer.

▶ The minimum requirements for installing and running Windows Me

▶ How much free hard disk space you need to run Windows Me

▶ Uninstalling Me

Take a Moment to Reflect

If you've already installed Windows Me — or you bought a computer on which Windows Me was preinstalled — you may feel you can skip this chapter. If so, that's fine, you won't hurt our feelings.

But even people with Windows Me preinstalled will learn some tricks in this chapter that may help them configure Windows to better meet their needs.

In this chapter we discuss how to install and set up Windows Me on a single standalone computer. By *standalone* we mean the computer can (and will) boot Windows Me from its local hard disk without requiring any connection to a network. The standalone computer can be attached to a network and operate as a server on a peer-to-peer network. A standalone computer can stand alone, but is not necessarily unconnected.

Windows Me can also be installed on a network server, allowing network client computers to use and share this single copy of Windows Me. While we don't discuss this type of installation here, you can turn to Chapter 18 for a discussion of networking.

Requirements

Before you install Windows Me, you'll want to take stock of your situation. If you have just bought a new computer and Windows Me is already installed, all you need to do is click the Start button ⇨ Settings ⇨ Control Panel ⇨ Add/Remove Programs icon, and Windows Setup tab to add or remove optional components of Windows Me. If you have an older computer, you need to be sure that it meets the requirements for Windows Me shown in Table 2-1.

Table 2-1   Hardware Requirements for Installing and Running Windows Me

Component	Requirements
Processor	Pentium 166 or greater
Memory	32MB of RAM is required for Windows Me. If you want the Internet Explorer/Windows Me interface to seem responsive, or if you use Windows Messaging, 64MB is much better.
Video	VGA is the minimum, with SVGA recommended by Microsoft. Larger monitors and higher resolution give you more real estate for multiple applications or larger areas for more text, numbers, and so on. Acceel rated display cards make a real difference. We recommend at least 800 × 600 and 256 colors. Almost all new video cards surpass these minimum standards.
Disks	A 1GB hard disk partition is about the minimum you can get away with and still install some Windows applications. According to Microsoft, Windows Me requires 295MB just to install a "typical" upgrade over an existing copy of Windows 95. And in this state, Windows Me is missing a lot of functionality.
	A full install of Windows Me on a new hard disk consumes at least 495MB in its most stripped-down state. This can go as high as 635MB if you select several options during a "custom" installation. (And about 25MB of additional hard disk space is required on drive C: if you install Windows Me to drive D: or some other drive letter.)
	The previous figures can be reduced approximately 10 percent by converting a hard drive from the old 16-bit File Allocation Table (FAT16) to the more efficient FAT32. If you are installing Windows Me over an existing copy of Windows 95 or 98, you can click Start ⇨ Programs ⇨ Accessories ⇨ System Tools ⇨ Drive Converter to convert a FAT16 drive to FAT32 before installing Windows Me.
Others	Windows Me takes advantage of modems, CD-ROM drives, sound cards, midi add-on cards, accelerated video, network cards, joy sticks, and so on

Whether or not you are going to be happy upgrading an existing computer to Windows Me is heavily dependent on whether your hardware is up to the task. As you can see, there are significant hard disk and memory requirements. If you can't come close to meeting them, you might want to leave well enough alone. If this is the case, but you want the power of Windows Me, consider purchasing a new computer.

Unsupported Hardware

The Windows Me CD-ROM comes with a very long list of hardware drivers, but it doesn't come with drivers for everything. There may not be any specific drivers for your particular piece of hardware, so you may need to use your real-mode drivers (those that work with DOS or Windows 3.1x). Otherwise, you will need to get new 32-bit Windows drivers from your hardware manufacturer or from the Windows Update page on the Microsoft Web site (click Start ⇨ Settings ⇨ Windows Update).

Windows Me doesn't support some older CD-ROM drives. You may not be able to access your CD-ROM unless you take specific steps before installing Windows Me. To see a list of which CD-ROM drives had trouble with Windows 95 and 98 (and are likely to cause the same problems with Windows Me), check a Microsoft Knowledge Base article on this subject at `http://support.microsoft.com/support/kb/articles/q131/4/99.asp`.

Making Room for Windows Me

Before you install Windows Me, again carefully consider its hard disk space requirements. If you have a computer with a hard drive smaller than 1GB, Windows Me is going to eat up a big chunk of your hard disk space. You might want to consider a new hard disk or a new computer. The bare bones Windows Me configuration takes up a great deal more hard disk space than older versions, such as Windows 95 or Windows 3.1x. Windows Me is not so much bigger than Windows 98; both versions include Internet Explorer and a great volume of Web-related files. But Windows Me does include some new features that will increase Windows' hard disk "footprint" if you install Me over an existing copy of 98.

When you install Windows Me, you can choose to save your previous operating system, so that you have the option of uninstalling Windows Me. You can then go back to DOS, Windows 3.1x, Windows 98, or Windows 9x. If you do this, your hard disk requirements (for both installation and later) will increase dramatically, depending on your previous hard disk usage.

Just because you can meet the hard disk space requirements detailed above doesn't mean you have enough hard disk space to have a viable system. You'll need additional space for your Windows Me applications, as well as 20 to 40MB for a dynamically sized swap file.

Where to Put the Windows Folder

You can install the Windows Me folder (and all of its subfolders) on any hard drive (or logical drive partition or volume) as long as the disk partition is a FAT16 or FAT32 partition. A few Windows Me files must be installed on your boot drive (usually the C: drive). If you install Windows Me to a different drive letter, such as D:, the Windows Me setup routines will place these special files on C: automatically.

If you already have an existing, older version of Windows installed, and you want to upgrade that copy, you will naturally choose to install Windows Me into the folder that contains the older version of Windows. If not, you can choose any name, but it's common to use the name C:\Windows for this folder.

Upgrading DOS to Windows Me

You can upgrade a computer running just the DOS operating system (version 3.2 or later) to Windows Me if it meets the hardware requirements detailed previously.

You must also have a copy of Windows 98, 95, or 3.1x installed, although not necessarily running, on your hard disk, or a handy Windows 98, 95, or 3.1x setup diskette, if you're installing the less-expensive "upgrade" version of Windows Me.

Windows Me Setup (upgrade version) will prompt you for a CD or floppy from an earlier version of Windows, if you try to install it on a freshly formatted hard drive. It does check the Windows CD-ROM for the following files: WINSETUP.BIN, the two PRECOPYx.CAB files, and all the Windows .CAB files. It is possible to redirect the search for these files to other locations. (Alternatively, it will accept Windows 3.x install diskettes.)

If you have an OEM version of the Windows Me CD-ROM, you can use it to update a DOS computer. This version of the Windows Me CD-ROM doesn't look for your existing Windows files. Microsoft is now discouraging OEMs from providing PC buyers with a separate CD, however. Instead, all the CD files may be located on the hard disk itself to prevent Windows Me from being installed on other computers.

Upgrading Windows 95 to Windows Me

Windows Me is more similar to Windows 98 than it is to the original version of Windows 95. Despite this, however, Windows Me Setup is capable of finding your Windows 95 folder and, with very few questions, replacing your existing Windows 95 system components with their Windows Me counterparts.

Microsoft has incrementally updated Windows 95 ever since it was first unveiled. It has released new Windows CD-ROMs and multiple Internet Explorer versions. Over the last few years, it has made available new versions of the various components of Windows 95 for download from the Microsoft Web site. There is no way the Windows Me Setup can know in advance just what your Windows 95 installation consists of.

The Windows Me CD-ROM updates all of your existing Windows 95 components. If you have a basic Windows 95 installation, the setup routines delete and replace about 25MB of files. Windows Me adds about 110MB over a basic Windows 95 installation.

Installing over a Network or from a CD-ROM

If your computer is connected to a network and the source files are stored on a server, either on a hard disk or a CD-ROM, you can install Windows Me from the server. Unless your system administrator has custom-designed the installation procedures, it is no different than installing Windows Me from a local diskette drive, CD-ROM, or hard disk — with one exception.

Secret

Near the end of the Windows Me installation, Windows Me reboots your computer and grabs further files from the source cabinets. It reboots your computer under Windows Me. If, using the Windows Me network or CD-ROM drivers, it is unable to make the connection to your network server or to your local CD-ROM drive, Windows Me can't continue configuring itself.

Windows Me keeps track of the location of its source installation files. In most cases, this location will be the Windows folder in your CD-ROM drive.

When you make certain changes to your Windows Me configuration, Windows Me searches for the files that it needs in the original location. If it doesn't find these files there, it will ask you where it can find them. If you've installed from the Windows Me CD-ROM, you'll just put it in your CD-ROM drive and continue. If the source files are stored somewhere other than their original location, you can type in this new location when asked.

Windows Me stores the source file location and the source file type (cabinet files or expanded files) in the registry. You can edit your registry, once you've installed Windows Me, to specify a new file location and to change the source file type. (Refer to Chapter 11 to learn more about the Registry Editor.)

STEPS

Changing the Source File Location and Type

Step 1. After you install Windows Me, click Regedit.exe in your \Windows folder.

Step 2. Navigate in your registry to HKEY_LOCAL_MACHINE\ SOFTWARE\ Microsoft\ Windows\ CurrentVersion\ SETUP. Highlight SETUP.

Continued

STEPS

Changing the Source File Location and Type *(continued)*

Step 3.   Double-click SourcePath in the right pane of your Registry Editor. Type a new path for the location of your source files. Click OK.

Step 4.   Double-click SourcePathType. To change it from the expanded NETSETUP value to the cabinet value, type **05 00 00 00**. Click OK and exit the Registry Editor.

Step 5.   If you are changing SourcePathType to the cabinet value, you'll also need to extract the Layout.inf file from the cabinet files and place it in your \Windows\Inf folder. Back up your current Layout.inf file first.

Getting Ready to Start Windows Me Setup

Your installation of Windows Me may choke if you have loaded DOS TSRs into memory or are running Windows utilities, including virus checkers or other add-ons. Microsoft provides a list of TSRs known to cause problems in the file setup.txt, which you will find on the Windows Me CD-ROM. It's a good idea to read this file before starting to install Windows Me.

So many combinations of TSRs and Windows utilities could cause problems that Microsoft would prefer you eliminate as many variables as possible. Most of the support calls that Microsoft receives concern setup issues.

If your computer BIOS includes a virus-checking option, you'll need to turn off this function. Otherwise, Windows Me Setup will freeze. The most common way to access this function is to press a key (usually Delete, F2, or Escape) during your computer's power-on self-test to bring up the built-in BIOS editor.

Windows Me will not install into a disk partition that is compressed. This is true even though Windows 95 and 98 support disk compression. You will need to remove disk compression from the drive you intend to install Windows Me into. Since most people use disk compression because their hard disk is nearing its capacity, this may mean there is no way for you to install Windows Me unless you first delete a large number of files.

If the drive containing an older version of Windows is *not* compressed, but another hard drive letter *is* compressed, you *can* install Windows Me into the uncompressed drive. After installation, however, there will be no way for Windows Me to see or access the files on the compressed drive. This means you should remove all disk compression from all drives before attempting to install Windows Me. If this means you won't have enough free disk space to install Windows Me, you'll probably be better off buying a larger hard drive or a new computer.

Setup Switches

The easiest way to run Windows Me Setup is to start your Windows 9*x* Explorer (or your Windows 3.1*x* File Manager) and then double-click the `setup.exe` file in the root directory of the Windows Me CD-ROM.

However, if you choose to run Setup from the DOS prompt, or if you choose File ⇨ Run in the Windows 3.1*x* File Manager or you choose Start ⇨ Run in Windows 95, you can add some command-line parameters, as shown in Table 2-2.

Table 2-2   Command-Line Parameters for Setup

Switch	Resulting Action
setup /?	Lists some of the setup switches. You get different results depending on whether you do this in a Windows DOS session or in MS-DOS mode. Different switches better work when starting in real-mode DOS than when starting in Windows.
setup /T:*tempdir*	You can name a directory that will store the temporary files that are created and destroyed during the Windows Me setup. If you specify a different disk drive for this directory, you can reduce by 11MB the amount of hard disk space needed on the original drive for installing Windows Me.
setup *script-file*	If you have a batch file that automates the setup process, this is how you run it. The batch file will likely be on a network server, which you will need to log into before you begin setting up.
setup /iq	Doesn't check for cross-linked files.
setup /im	Skips the memory (RAM) check.
setup /il	Loads the Logitech mouse driver instead of the Microsoft mouse driver. Use this option if you have a Logitech Series C mouse.
setup /id	Skips the disk space check. Our tests indicate that it still checks for disk space even with this switch.
setup /in	Setup won't ask about or install network software. If you want to install Direct Cable Connection or Dial-Up Networking (for your Internet connection, for example), don't use this switch.

Continued

Table 2-2 *(continued)*	
Switch	*Resulting Action*
setup /is	Runs Setup without first running ScanDisk. We recommend that you run ScanDisk first. If you get a message that there is not enough free conventional memory to run ScanDisk, and you have freed up as much conventional memory as possible, you can run Setup with this switch. This setting is also required if Windows Me Setup persists in believing that there are errors on your hard drive, when this is not the case.
setup /C	Doesn't load the SmartDrive disk cache. If you don't use this switch, SmartDrive will be loaded to speed the Windows Me setup over DOS or Windows 3.1*x*, or off a CD-ROM with 16-bit drivers.
setup /ie	Doesn't create an Emergency Startup disk.
setup /iq	Skips the check for cross-linked files.
setup /ih	Doesn't run registry consistency checks.
setup /d	Doesn't use the existing version of Windows to run Windows Me Setup. Use this switch only when running Setup from real-mode DOS.
setup /IW	Bypasses the licensing screen (use uppercase letters).
setup /Pf	Creates a new Windows Me registry from scratch, in the case of corrupted registry files.
setup /iv	Doesn't show the Microsoft advertisement graphics as Setup proceeds.
setup /nostart	Copies from the Windows Me source files the minimum Windows 3.1*x* DLLs required to run Windows Me Setup and then exit to DOS.

For further information about setup switches like these, read "Description of the Windows Setup Switches." at http://support.microsoft.com/support/kb/articles/Q186/1/11.asp.

Running Windows Me Setup from DOS

You may wish to run the Windows Me setup process from a DOS prompt. You might do this if Windows Me fails to install under your older, existing version of Windows. Another reason would be that you are installing Windows Me on a new system and you only wish to install an older version of DOS (not a complete install of Windows) so you can then install Windows Me.

You can start DOS from Windows 98 or 95, or you can start DOS manually to choose which drivers to load or not load:

- **Windows 98.** Reboot your PC and hold down the Ctrl key after the memory self-test. This will eventually display the Windows 98 Boot menu, from which you can choose Command Prompt Only.

- **Windows 95.** Reboot your PC, then press the F8 key when you see the message "Starting Windows 95." This will eventually display the Windows 95 Boot menu, from which you can choose Command Prompt Only.

- **DOS 6.x.** When you see the "Starting MS-DOS" message, press the F8 key. You will have the opportunity to load or not load various drivers or bypass running your system files (Config.sys and Autoexec.bat) entirely.

If you boot to DOS in one of the above ways, and your system does not load a real-mode CD-ROM driver, you will not be able to access the Windows Me CD-ROM to install Windows Me. You can solve this by installing the real-mode CD-ROM software that came with your CD-ROM hardware. Alternatively, if you have a Windows Me startup diskette, you can boot from that diskette, which will automatically support most CD-ROM hardware.

Removing Antivirus and Memory-Resident Programs

You should remove any antivirus programs and other memory-resident programs from your Config.sys and Autoexec.bat files before installing Windows Me. Some BIOS programs support antivirus software in read-only memory (ROM). You can disable this by rebooting your PC and pressing a key that will appear on the screen to control "BIOS setup" or similar message.

You can use Windows 98 or 95 to remove anti-virus and memory-resident programs from Config.sys and Autoexec.bat before installing Windows Me. To do this in Windows 98 or 95:

- **Windows 98.** Click Start ⇨ Run, type **sysedit,** then press Enter. Clear the checkboxes at the beginning of each line in Config.sys and Autoexec.bat that loads antivirus and memory-resident programs. Click Apply, click OK, and then restart your PC.

- **Windows 95.** Click Start ⇨ Run, type **sysedit,** then press Enter. Insert the word **REM** at the beginning of each line in Config.sys and Autoexec.bat that loads antivirus and memory-resident programs. Save your changes and then restart your PC.

The Setup Process

You might be getting the idea that setting up Windows Me is no simple matter. Developing its setup software is, indeed, always a complicated process for Microsoft as it must cope with millions of possible variations in existing hardware and software.

But running Windows Me Setup is not that difficult because Microsoft has done so much to make it do the work for you. While we can't cover every step, we do point out some key areas and give you extra guidance about how to proceed.

Most of the dialog boxes that you'll see while Setup runs have Next and Back buttons. You get to choose when you go forward. If you want to go back and make a choice over again, you often have that option.

You can cancel Windows Me Setup at any time, and not disturb your existing Windows or DOS computer. No new files (other than `Setuplog.txt` and a few small hidden files in the root directory) will be installed, and no files will be changed until you click the Next button in the Start Copying Files dialog box at the end of the setup process.

Starting Setup

You can start Windows Me Setup using any one of the three methods described earlier in the section entitled "Setup Switches." The setup routines create a full-screen display with a Welcome dialog box. Click Continue to continue.

Emergency Startup Disk

We strongly recommend that you make a Windows Me Emergency Startup disk. If there is a problem with booting your computer under Windows Me from the hard disk, you have to be able to boot from a diskette. The Windows Me diskette format is different than Windows 98 or 95, and you cannot reliably use a Windows 98 or 95 startup diskette to start a PC that has Windows Me installed.

When the Windows Me setup routine begins the process of making an Emergency Startup disk, be sure to label it properly. Keep the disk in a safe place where you'll be able to find it easily if Windows won't start from the hard drive in the future.

When you boot your computer using the Emergency Startup diskette, a boot menu appears that lets you load real-mode drivers for the most common CD-ROM drives.

Copy Files

Once Setup has gathered the information it needs from you and your computer to successfully configure and install Windows Me, it copies the files that it needs from the Windows Me cabinet source files. You initiate this process by clicking Next in the Start Copying Files dialog box. This is where Windows Me actually starts writing information to your hard drive. If you've decided you don't want to install Windows Me after all, cancel here. Otherwise, proceed and Windows Me will launch into the file-copying process.

Finishing Setup

Copying files proceeds automatically, and at the end Setup will reboot your computer and start up in Windows Me. Unlike the Windows 95 Setup, Windows Me waits until after rebooting your computer before it runs hardware detection. After that, it takes a while for Setup to configure the Windows Me files. If you didn't correctly configure your network card, you will receive a message to that effect, and Setup will tell you that you can make the required changes later.

Next, Windows Me will set up your Control Panel, configure your Start menus, and set up your help files. It will also ask you to choose your time zone setting. In addition, Windows Me will prompt you to set up your printer and your pre-Plug and Play modem, if you have one.

If VGA was chosen for your display adapter during Setup, you can change it after Windows Me starts by clicking the Start button ⇨ Settings ⇨ Control Panel ⇨ Display ⇨ Settings ⇨ Advanced ⇨ Adapter ⇨ Change and choosing a new video adapter.

Adding and Removing Parts of Windows Me

You can revisit the list of Windows Me components you saw in the Select Components dialog box during Setup, and then add or remove parts of Windows Me. Here's how to make changes:

STEPS

Adding or Removing Parts of Windows Me

Step 1. Click the Start button ⇨ Settings, and then Control Panel.

Step 2. Click the Add/Remove Programs icon.

Continued

STEPS

Adding or Removing Parts of Windows Me   *(continued)*

Step 3.   Click the Windows Setup tab. Highlight a category of components and click Details.

Step 4.   You can clear installed components that you want removed, and mark uninstalled components that you want installed.

Secret

A subfolder of Windows Me, named \Windows\Inf, contains the setup information files that guide the installation and removal of Windows Me components (as well as Windows Me Setup). These files have an inf extension.

You can view and edit these files by clicking them. They are all fairly short, so you can edit them with Notepad. If you want to do away with your (or someone else's) ability to easily add or remove Windows Me components, you can delete this folder.

Copying All Your Windows Me Files to a New Hard Disk

You can make a copy of your Windows Me hard disk installation, including all the applications that you have installed, on a new hard disk. This makes the transition to a bigger hard disk a lot easier. Errol Nielson provided the original methods.

STEPS

Copying All Your Windows Me Files

Step 1.   If you are moving to a hard disk that is bigger than your BIOS can handle, you are going to have to use the manufacturer's setup instructions before you follow these steps. You'll either have to upgrade your BIOS, or use a program in the boot tracks of the new hard disk that supersedes your BIOS settings.

Step 2.   Physically install your new hard disk as a slave (setting the correct jumper position) and use your BIOS settings to tell the computer to see it as the secondary drive. We'll refer to the first drive as C: and the new one as D:.

Step 3.   Make sure you have a Windows Me Emergency Startup diskette. If you haven't already created one, click the Start button ⇨ Settings ⇨ Control Panel, and click the Add/Remove Programs icon. Click the Startup Disk tab, and then the Create Disk button.

Step 4. Start Windows Me and click Start ➪ Programs ➪ Accessories ➪ Windows Explorer. Right-click each of the two hard disk icons, and click Properties. Label the C: drive *Old Disk* and the D: drive *New Disk*.

Step 5. Click the Start button ➪ Programs ➪ MS-DOS Prompt. Type **fdisk**, press Enter, and select "Change current fixed disk drive." Select the number that stands for your new drive, usually 2.

Step 6. In Fdisk, select "Create DOS partition or logical DOS drive," and then select and create a primary DOS partition. Exit Fdisk and restart the computer.

Step 7. Click Start ➪ Programs ➪ Accessories ➪ Windows Explorer. Right-click the D: drive (the New Disk drive). Select Format ➪ Full, and Copy System Files.

Step 8. In the Windows Explorer, choose View ➪ Folder Options, click the View tab, and select "Show hidden files and folders."

Step 9. You are now going to copy everything from C: to D:. The one file you don't want to copy is WIN386.swp (located in your \Windows folder on drive C:). You can right-drag all the files and folders from C: to D:, but don't drag the Windows folder because that will copy this file also.

You can also get rid of WIN386.swp by turning off virtual memory and rebooting your computer. If you do this, you can just copy everything from C: to D: without worrying about working around this file. Click the Start button ➪ Settings ➪ Control Panel, click the System icon, click the Performance tab, click the Virtual Memory button, and mark "Let me set my own virtual memory settings," and "Disable virtual memory." Click OK and OK. Reboot.

If you don't disable virtual memory, you'll need to create a new \Windows folder on drive D: and right-drag all the files (except WIN386.swp) and folders in the \Windows folder on C: to the \Windows folder on D:. Turn to "Copying and Moving Files and Folders" in Chapter 7 to see how to copy files using the Explorer.

Be sure to use the right mouse button to drag and drop because if you drag with the left mouse button, Windows Me won't actually copy the executable files. Rather, it will create shortcuts to them on the destination drive. When you right-drag and choose Copy Here from the context menu, Windows Me copies the files themselves.

Step 9a. There is an alternative to right-drag and drop copying. You can click the Start button, click Run, and then type the following:

XCOPY C:\ D:\ /c /e /f /h /r /s

Continued

STEPS

Copying All Your Windows Me Files *(continued)*

Step 10. Right-click your D: drive hard disk icon. Choose Properties, and then click the Tools tab. Click the Check Now button and click the Thorough option button in the ScanDisk dialog box. Click the Start button.

Step 11. When error checking is complete, exit Windows Me and turn off your computer. Unplug or remove the old drive (the C: drive). Reset the jumpers on the slave to turn it into the master.

Step 12. Place your Windows Me Startup diskette in the A: drive. Restart your computer, press the key that gets you into your BIOS editor, change the drive table settings to reflect the changes in the hard disk configuration. Continue the boot process, saving your new BIOS settings to boot off your floppy drive.

Step 13. Type **fdisk** and press Enter. Select "Set active partition." Exit Fdisk, remove the Windows Me Startup diskette from the floppy drive. Restart your computer. You should be running Windows Me off your new hard disk.

Step 14. If everything is working, you can reinstall your original hard disk as your D: drive. Set the jumpers on it to be the slave, exit Windows Me, and turn off the computer. Replug in your old drive. Restart your computer and go to your BIOS settings. Edit the BIOS table to match your current hard disk configuration.

Some computers won't boot with a bootable drive set up as a slave drive. If you find this to be the case, place your Windows Me Startup diskette in your floppy drive, boot to it and use Fdisk to "Delete partition of logical disk drive" on drive D:. Don't do this until you are sure that your new disk drive is working.

There are more automated ways of accomplishing this task. You can find a program designed for system administrators at http://www.ghostsoft.com (it costs $250). Another option is the wonderful program Partition Magic 3.0. This program lets you resize your hard disk partitions without losing all your files and data. It also lets you move all of Windows Me to a new disk. Check it out at http://www.powerquest.com/partitionmagic.

Uninstalling Windows Me

There may come a time that you decide you don't like Windows Me and you want to go back to your previous version of Windows. This is possible *only* if you selected the "Save your system files" option when prompted during Windows Me setup.

If you did select this option, Windows Me created the following hidden files and placed them on your hard disk in case you need them to uninstall later: `W9xundo.dat`, `W9xundo.ini`, and `Winlfn.ini`.

These files must be saved to a local hard disk, not to a removable disk or a network drive. You may, however, select a local hard disk of your choice to save the uninstall files to if two or more local drives have enough space.

If you ever delete the uninstall files, of course, Windows Me will lose the ability to be uninstalled and restore your previous version of Windows. If you want to delete these files in the future (to regain disk space, for example), you shouldn't just delete them. Instead, you should use the Add/Remove Programs control panel, as described below in "Removing Old System Files."

There are some other cases in which you *cannot* revert to a previous version of Windows after installing Windows Me. These may seem pretty obvious, but here we go:

- You install Windows Me into a new directory, not the one the previous version of Windows is in.

- You perform a clean install of Windows Me, and no previous version of Windows is present.

- You install Windows Me over DOS, but it is prior to DOS 5.0.

In any of the above cases, the Windows Me setup won't present you with a choice to "Save your system files," since it would not be possible.

In any event, if you've selected Save Your System Files during Windows Me setup, and you haven't deleted, removed, or damaged the uninstall files, it's pretty easy to uninstall Windows Me and get back to your previous version of Windows:

STEPS

Uninstalling Windows Me

Step 1.   Click the Start button ➪ Settings ➪ Control Panel.

Step 2.   Click the Add/Remove Programs icon.

Step 3.   Click the Install/Uninstall tab. Select Uninstall Windows Millennium Edition, then click Add/Remove.

An alternative to the above steps is to boot up with the Windows Me startup diskette. Then run the command:

```
c:\windows\command\uninstal
```

This is particularly useful if you can't even start Windows Me due to some problem, and you've decided to revert to your previous version of Windows. This also can be used to remove an installation of Windows Me that failed partway through. Running the uninstall command from the hard disk starts the process of reverting to your previous Windows or DOS operating system.

Removing Old System Files

After you've used Windows Me for a while, and you've decided to continue using it, you can easily reclaim the disk space that is consumed by the uninstall files (the "old system files").

Once you've taken the following steps, of course, you can no longer uninstall Windows Me and revert to your previous version of Windows.

STEPS

Removing Old System Files

Step 1.   Click the Start button ⇨ Settings ⇨ Control Panel.

Step 2.   Click the Add/Remove Programs icon.

Step 3.   Click the Install/Uninstall tab. If you are removing Windows 9x uninstall files, select "Remove Windows 9x system files," then click Remove. If you are removing Windows 3.x or DOS uninstall files, select "Old Windows 3.x/MS-DOS system files," then click Remove.

Summary

Lots of little wrinkles come with installing and setting up Windows Me.

▶ Follow our guidelines to determine if your computer can run Windows Me.

▶ If you want to revert to an earlier operating system, you can uninstall Windows Me.

Chapter 3

Customizing Your Windows Startup

In This Chapter

Your computer can start up in all sorts of different configurations. We show you how to set the options for how Windows starts. We discuss:

▶ Getting rid of the Windows startup logo

▶ Using a hot key to start Windows in Safe mode if there is a problem with your hardware

▶ Choosing a startup hardware profile, depending on your computer's hardware configuration

▶ Use the Boot Log Analyzer to see where you might have a problem

▶ Stop Windows from dialing up your Internet service provider when it starts up

Do I Need to Do This?

Do you need to customize your Windows startup? No. Not if all the defaults are just right for you. The Windows Setup program creates all the necessary files and sets up everything invisibly and automatically, so you may not need to worry about anything.

But if you installed Windows in a separate directory from your earlier Windows directory, you'll find the tricks provided here useful. If you want to know the sequence of commands and actions that occur when your computer starts up, you'll find them here. If you want to load DOS real-mode drivers, or work easily with multiple hardware configurations on pre-Plug and Play computers, we'll show you how.

This chapter also outlines the function of the files in your root directory.

How Windows Starts Up

A lot happens between the time you turn on your computer and when the Windows Desktop appears on your screen. The bootup process goes through two phases: power-on self-test and loading Windows.

When you first turn on your computer, it goes through its power-on self-test. The commands stored in your computer's BIOS (and your video card's ROM) chips are carried out. These commands provide low-level drivers for some of your basic hardware (disk drives, ports, video cards, and so on). The last command found in your BIOS is to execute the program that resides in the boot tracks of the boot device (most likely your hard disk).

If you want to learn more about your particular BIOS, check out the following Web sites: http://www.phoenix.com and http://www.ami.com.

The BIOS will find Io.sys (the route to Windows) in the boot tracks unless you have Windows 2000, NT, or OS/2 installed. In these cases, their boot program will be found in the boot tracks. The boot managers that come with these operating systems allow you to go to the Windows Io.sys next, if you desire.

Often, some BIOS settings are displayed on your screen during the power-on self-test. Right after these BIOS settings are displayed, the DOS bootup process begins, and on some computers you see the text message "Loading Windows Me." Not all computers display this message.

Once the BIOS finishes loading, your system begins loading Windows. During this phase, you will see the *splash screen* — a screen announcing Windows Me — while all of the drivers and programs that make up Windows are loaded.

Windows allows you to press and hold the Ctrl key during the power-on self-test. If you hold down this key until you see "Starting Windows," the startup process will bring up the Startup menu. (If your computer doesn't display the "Starting Windows" message, just hold down the Ctrl key for a few seconds during the power-on self-test.) For more information, see the section later in this chapter entitled "Msdos.sys Options."

Secret

Msdos.sys is a configuration file. Io.sys reads this file early on. It determines whether you will see the Windows startup logo or not, whether you can use the startup function keys, and other functions.

You will find Msdos.sys in the root directory (folder) of your boot hard disk, most likely the C drive. In spite of its sys extension, it is a text file. You can edit it with Notepad or Microsoft Edit (Edit.com in the \Windows\Command folder).

Msdos.sys is a hidden, read-only system file. To find and check out the attributes of this file, take the following steps:

STEPS

Viewing the Attributes of Msdos.sys

Step 1. Right-click My Computer on your Desktop and then click Explore.

Step 2. Click Tools ⇨ Folder Options. Click the View tab, and then mark the Show Hidden Files And Folders option button.

Step 3. Remove the check from the Hide Protected Operating System Files option and click Yes. Click OK.

Step 4. Click the hard disk icon in the left pane of the Explorer that represents your boot drive, most likely C. Scroll the right pane until you see Msdos.sys.

Step 5. Right-click Msdos.sys, and then choose Properties.

You can change the attributes of Msdos.sys by marking or clearing the checkboxes in its Properties dialog box. However, you can't change the System property (unless you use the Attrib command in a DOS window). If you want to edit Msdos.sys, clear the Read-Only checkbox.

Msdos.sys File Contents

Your Msdos.sys file may look something like this:

```
[Paths]
WinDir=C:\WINDOWS
WinBootDir=C:\WINDOWS
HostWinBootDrv=C

[Options]
BootMulti=1
BootGUI=1
AutoScan=1
WinVer=4.90.2535
;
;The following lines are required for compatibility with other
programs.
;Do not remove them (MSDOS.SYS needs to be >1024 bytes).
;xxxxxxxxxxxxxxxxxxxxxxxxxxxxxxxxxxxxxxxxxxxxxxxxxxxxxxxxxxxxxxxxxa
;xxxxxxxxxxxxxxxxxxxxxxxxxxxxxxxxxxxxxxxxxxxxxxxxxxxxxxxxxxxxxxxxxb
;xxxxxxxxxxxxxxxxxxxxxxxxxxxxxxxxxxxxxxxxxxxxxxxxxxxxxxxxxxxxxxxxxc
;xxxxxxxxxxxxxxxxxxxxxxxxxxxxxxxxxxxxxxxxxxxxxxxxxxxxxxxxxxxxxxxxxd
```

```
;xxxxxxxxxxxxxxxxxxxxxxxxxxxxxxxxxxxxxxxxxxxxxxxxxxxxxxxxxxxxe
;xxxxxxxxxxxxxxxxxxxxxxxxxxxxxxxxxxxxxxxxxxxxxxxxxxxxxxxxxxxxf
;xxxxxxxxxxxxxxxxxxxxxxxxxxxxxxxxxxxxxxxxxxxxxxxxxxxxxxxxxxxxg
;xxxxxxxxxxxxxxxxxxxxxxxxxxxxxxxxxxxxxxxxxxxxxxxxxxxxxxxxxxxxh
;xxxxxxxxxxxxxxxxxxxxxxxxxxxxxxxxxxxxxxxxxxxxxxxxxxxxxxxxxxxxi
;xxxxxxxxxxxxxxxxxxxxxxxxxxxxxxxxxxxxxxxxxxxxxxxxxxxxxxxxxxxxj
;xxxxxxxxxxxxxxxxxxxxxxxxxxxxxxxxxxxxxxxxxxxxxxxxxxxxxxxxxxxxk
;xxxxxxxxxxxxxxxxxxxxxxxxxxxxxxxxxxxxxxxxxxxxxxxxxxxxxxxxxxxxl
;xxxxxxxxxxxxxxxxxxxxxxxxxxxxxxxxxxxxxxxxxxxxxxxxxxxxxxxxxxxxm
;xxxxxxxxxxxxxxxxxxxxxxxxxxxxxxxxxxxxxxxxxxxxxxxxxxxxxxxxxxxxn
;xxxxxxxxxxxxxxxxxxxxxxxxxxxxxxxxxxxxxxxxxxxxxxxxxxxxxxxxxxxxo
;xxxxxxxxxxxxxxxxxxxxxxxxxxxxxxxxxxxxxxxxxxxxxxxxxxxxxxxxxxxxp
;xxxxxxxxxxxxxxxxxxxxxxxxxxxxxxxxxxxxxxxxxxxxxxxxxxxxxxxxxxxxq
;xxxxxxxxxxxxxxxxxxxxxxxxxxxxxxxxxxxxxxxxxxxxxxxxxxxxxxxxxxxxr
;xxxxxxxxxxxxxxxxxxxxxxxxxxxxxxxxxxxxxxxxxxxxxxxxxxxxxxxxxxxxs
AutoScan=1
WinVer=5.00.xxxx
```

While only three options are listed in this sample file, you can add numerous options to change how your computer starts up. Note that if you have installed Windows onto another hard drive volume or in a different directory, the WinDir folder in your copy of `Msdos.sys` may in fact be named something other than `C:\Windows`.

Msdos.sys Options

The paths you can specify in `Msdos.sys` are listed in Table 3-1. The remaining options are described in the following sections. If an option or path is not listed in the `Msdos.sys` file, `Io.sys` uses its default value. The default value varies depending on the option. Most of the options' default values are 1. The default value for each option is the first value listed after the equal sign.

Caution

Make certain you have a Windows Me startup disk before making any changes to `Msdos.sys`. Some of the options that worked correctly in previous Windows versions can prevent Windows Me from loading properly.

Table 3-1   Path Options for Msdos.sys

Option	Description
HostWinBootDrv	Location of the boot drive root directory
WinBootDir	Location of Windows startup DLLs
WinDir	Location of Windows directory
UninstallDir	Location of uninstall directory

BootMulti

If you recently purchased your computer, the manufacturer may have installed Windows and configured the boot drive on your hard disk as a FAT32 volume. If this is indeed the case, you won't be able to boot between a previous version of DOS or Windows 3.1*x* and Windows Me. DOS and earlier versions of Windows prior to Windows 95 OSR2 don't work with the 32-bit file system, FAT32.

Windows Me, however, can read/write to FAT16 hard disk volumes, and you can use these volumes with previous versions of DOS and Windows. To multiboot to these other operating systems, you'll need to have your boot or C drive configured with FAT16, regardless of where the operating systems reside. Volumes that are configured with FAT32 will not be readable while you are using previous versions of DOS and Windows.

BootMulti=1: You can boot to a previous version of DOS and/or Windows using the Ctrl, F4, or F8 keys.

BootMulti=0: This is the default. You can start only Windows Me. If no reference to BootMulti is found in Msdos.sys, you will not be able to boot to a previous version of DOS or Windows.

If you do not have this option in Msdos.sys and if Io.sys is in the boot tracks of your hard disk, you will not be able to start previous versions of DOS or Windows. If either the Boot Manager for OS/2 or the Windows 2000/NT Boot Loader is in the boot tracks, then these programs control whether you are able to multiboot or not.

Secret

You must be careful when setting up Windows Me if you are upgrading from Windows 3.*x* because the setup routines automatically delete a number of DOS files without telling you. These DOS files have almost exact equivalents to older versions of DOS, but these new files will be stored in the C:\Windows\Command directory and not in your old DOS directory. If your path statements vary depending on which operating system you start up (very likely), you may not have access to your previous DOS functions.

If you want to save existing DOS programs that would otherwise be erased, you need to take some steps before you set up Windows Me.

Copy all your DOS files to a separate directory that is not found in your path statement. The Windows Me Setup program looks for a set of files and uses the path statement to help it find them. Once it finds them, it erases them. For an extra margin of comfort, you might compress this backup copy of your DOS directory.

After Windows Me is set up, you can copy all your DOS files back to your regular DOS directory and erase the temporary directory.

If Windows 2000, NT, or OS/2 controls the boot tracks, and you indicate when prompted by one of their multiboot dialog boxes that you want to boot to DOS and BootMulti=1, you will then have the option of booting to your previous version of DOS or Windows.

If BootMulti is not found in `Msdos.sys`, the F4 function key will not do anything at startup.

The program System Commander from V Communications lets you boot to any operating system set up on your computer and works great with Windows Me. You can also boot any other PC-compatible OS. Call V Communications for more information at 800-648-8266, or go to `http://www.v-com.com`.

BootMenu

BootMenu=1: Display the Startup menu.

BootMenu=0: The default value. Don't display the Startup menu.

The default is to require that you press and hold the Ctrl key during the power-on self-test or press F8 between the power-on self-test and the DOS bootup phase to display the Startup menu. Setting BootMenu=1 forces the menu to appear each time you start up or reboot your computer.

The Startup menu (shown here) provides you with a number of different ways to start up your computer. Some of these mirror the values that you can set in the `Msdos.sys` file.

```
Microsoft Windows Millennium Startup Menu
=================================
    1.    Normal
    2.    Logged (\BOOTLOG.TXT)
    3.    Safe mode
    4.    Step-by-Step confirmation


Enter a Choice: 1         Time Remaining: 30

F5=Safe mode      Shift+F8=Step-by-Step Confirmation [N]
```

BootMenuDefault

BootMenuDefault=_n_: The default value is 1 if the last time you ran Windows you exited normally, 3 if you exited abnormally and don't have a network connection, and 4 if you exited abnormally and do have a network connection. Set the value you want the BootMenu to use without user input.

The Startup menu is not static. Whether certain values appear in this menu depends on the values you set in `Msdos.sys` and `Config.sys`. You may want to choose which value in your menu is the default choice.

BootMenuDelay

BootMenuDelay=*n*: The default value is 30 seconds. This option sets the number of seconds the Startup menu is displayed before the default menu item is acted upon. You can also use TweakUI to set the BootMenuDelay value. You'll find it in the Boot tab.

BootKeys

BootKeys=1: This is the default. The function keys that work during the boot process (F4, F5, F6, F8, Shift+F5, Ctrl+F5, Shift+F8) are enabled.

BootKeys=0: These function keys don't work.

If BootKeys=0, the value assigned to BootDelay is overridden.

You can use TweakUI to determine whether these function keys are available or not. Just mark or clear the Function Keys Available checkbox in the Boot tab.

Logo

Logo=1: The default value. Display the Windows logo screen as Windows boots up.

Logo=0: Leave the screen in text mode.

Some third-party memory managers have trouble when this logo is displayed. Also, it can be annoying in general, and it can prevent you from seeing important messages from real-mode drivers. You can replace `Logo.sys` with another `bmp` file. See the section later in the chapter entitled "Changing the Startup Graphic."

You can use TweakUI to set this value. Mark or clear the Display Splash Screen While Booting checkbox in the Boot tab.

DoubleBuffer

DoubleBuffer=1: The default value.

Secret

The Windows Setup program adds this line above to your `Msdos.sys` file if you have one of these controllers:

- A SCSI controller

- A controller that incorrectly assumes that your computer can only have a maximum total physical memory of 16MB

- A controller that uses its own DMA controller (as opposed to one of the predefined DMA channels on the system board) or whose BIOS lacks support for Virtual DMA Services (VDS)

Secret

Double buffering is used only during the Windows bootup process (or if your hard disk requires 16-bit drivers — compatibility mode). Once the protected mode IDE driver loads, it takes over and handles the DMA buffers directly, with full performance. To see if your hard disk requires 16-bit drivers, turn to the "Real-Mode Disk Drivers" section in Chapter 37.

Setting DoubleBuffer to 1 adds about half a second to your boot time. There is no other performance degradation.

DoubleBuffer=0: You can set the DoubleBuffer value to 0 if you are convinced that it won't corrupt data on your computer. This value is set to 1 in many cases where it is not necessary (because there is so little penalty). If your disk hardware configuration is fast enough to handle the hard disk throughput, you can set this value to 0. You save about 2K of memory space.

Network

Network=0: Set equal to zero as Networking in Safe Mode has been disabled in Windows.

BootFailSafe

BootFailSafe=0: The default value. Windows doesn't boot into Safe mode automatically.

BootFailSafe=1: Forces your computer to start in Safe mode.

AutoScan

The AutoScan default is to run ScanDisk before the Windows desktop appears. (See "ScanDisk" in Chapter 37 for more on details.)

ScanDisk runs if you turned off your computer without going through the standard shutdown procedure, or if Windows doesn't shut itself down properly. While the errors ScanDisk would find are very often not the culprits, Microsoft hopes that a little of this and a little of that will cut down on its support calls.

AutoScan=1: The default. Runs ScanDisk.

AutoScan=0: Don't run ScanDisk.

BootWarn

BootWarn=1: The default value. When BootWarn=1, you see a warning message box when you boot in Safe mode.

BootWarn=0: Don't show the Safe warning message box.

LoadTop

LoadTop=1: The default value. `Command.com` and `Drvspace.bin` or `Dblspace.bin` can be loaded at the top of conventional memory. This is standard.

LoadTop=0: If there is a problem with NetWare or other software, forces these programs not to load at the top of conventional memory.

The Windows Startup Menu

The Windows Startup menu (shown earlier) gives you a set of choices regarding how your computer starts before `Io.sys` carries out its default commands. `Io.sys` reads `Msdos.sys` before the Startup menu appears.

Normal

Starts Windows.

Logged

Same as Normal, but writes out the file `Bootlog.txt`, which tracks the load and startup sequence.

Safe Mode

Starts Windows in Safe mode. Safe mode is a generic Windows startup with VGA graphics, but no networking.

Step-by-Step Confirmation

Same as Shift+F8. Ask for confirmation before carrying out each command from `Io.sys`. Helps to isolate trouble.

What Gets Loaded When

Secret

`Io.sys` carries out a default sequence of commands. You can easily see just what commands `Io.sys` carries out.

The easiest way to get to interactive startup is to hold down the Ctrl key during the power-on self-test, and when the Startup menu appears, choose item 4. You will be asked to confirm if you want various actions to be carried out. Here's how to interpret the questions:

```
Process the system registry [Enter=Y, Esc=N]?
```

If you are actually going to start Windows, you want the registry to be processed.

```
Create a startup log file (BOOTLOG.TXT) [Enter=Y, Esc=N]?
```

The file `Bootlog.txt` is created and a backup of the previous `Bootlog.txt` is written to `Bootlog.prv`.

```
Enable SMARTDRV disk cache [Enter=Y, Esc=N]?
```

Loads the disk caching software to speed up your hard drive access.

```
Load all Windows drivers [Enter=Y, Esc=N]?
```

If you answer yes, you have the option of not loading some drivers, mostly network drivers. If you answer no, you'll start Windows in Safe mode. You may choose not to load some drivers in order to troubleshoot Windows networking problems.

This default load sequence gives you an idea why `Config.sys` and `Autoexec.bat` are not needed in Windows Me. Many of the functions that would be carried out by `Config.sys` are carried out by `Io.sys`, if you let it.

Multiple Hardware Configurations

You can create multiple hardware configurations for one computer. For example, if you have a non-Plug and Play portable computer that is sometimes connected to a docking station, you might want to create a hardware configuration that includes the cards in the docking station and the network connected to the docking station.

The startup sequence for a computer with multiple hardware configurations includes a menu that enables you to choose which hardware configuration you want to use. A sample hardware configuration startup menu is shown in here:

```
Windows cannot determine what configuration your computer is in:
Select one of the following:

    1.    Docking Station with Network
    2.    Disconnected Portable
    3.    None of the Above

Enter your choice:
```

To create multiple hardware configurations, take the following steps:

STEPS

Creating Multiple Hardware Configurations

Step 1.   Click the Start button, point to Settings, and then click Control Panel.

Step 2.   Click the System icon, and then click the Hardware Profiles tab to display the Hardware Profiles list, as shown in Figure 3-1.

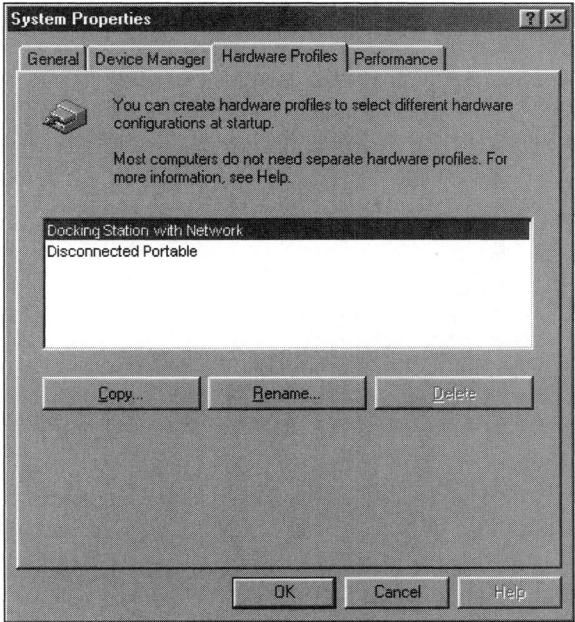

Figure 3-1: The Hardware Profiles list. You can copy, remove, and rename hardware profiles. You define hardware profiles in the Device Manager.

Step 3. Click the Rename button to rename your current profile to something that appropriately describes your current hardware configuration.

Step 4. Click the Copy button, highlight the new hardware profile, and click Rename to rename the new hardware profile.

Step 5. Restart your system and choose the hardware profile you wish to use.

Step 6. Open the System Properties dialog box and click the Device Manager tab. Click the plus sign next to the device types that will vary between hardware profiles.

Step 7. Double-click a device that will be found in one hardware profile but not in the other. Select the "Disable in this hardware profile" checkbox, as shown in Figure 3-2.

Continued

STEPS

Creating Multiple Hardware Configurations *(continued)*

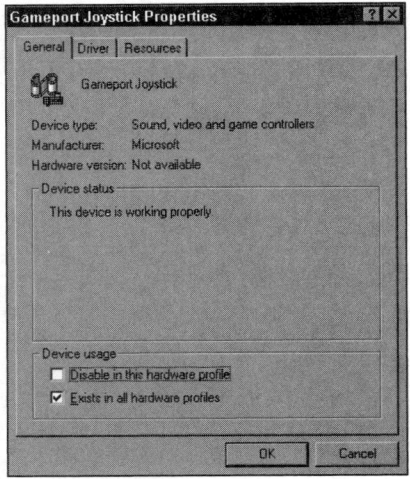

Figure 3-2: Choose which devices go with which hardware configuration.

Your Device Manager may not list all the devices that are available among your various hardware configurations. You have to install device drivers for these devices before you can assign them to your different hardware profiles.

To learn how to add hardware device drivers, turn to Chapter 36.

Changing the Startup Graphic

Before your computer displays the Windows Desktop, you're treated to an animated (640 × 400) Microsoft Windows advertisement. This graphic is embedded in the Io.sys file in your root directory.

Secret

If you have installed Windows Me over an old copy of Windows 95 with Microsoft Plus!, there may be an additional file in your root directory, Logo. sys, which contains a slightly edited version of the original advertisement. In spite of its sys extension, it is a bmp file and can be edited by MS Paint.

You can create your own animated Logo.sys file and replace Microsoft's billboard with your own. You don't have to animate the graphic, but you can if you want to.

If you view an existing `Logo.sys` in MS Paint, you'll notice that it is sized 320 pixels wide by 400 pixels high. The Windows startup routines stretch it out to 640 × 400 when it's displayed. You can create a new graphic at 640 × 400 — or at 533 × 400 if you want to maintain the 4:3 ratio (width to height) that is the standard for video monitors — and then use MS Paint or Paint Shop Pro to shrink the graphic to 320 × 400.

Your `Logo.sys` file must have a color depth of 256 colors (8 bit), and its file size must be 127K. If it is 320 pixels × 400 pixels × 256 colors, it will be 127K in size. The Windows startup routine will reject a `Logo.sys` file that doesn't meet these criteria.

There are lots of animated `Logo.sys` replacements available online. We suggest that you point your browser at `http://www.nucleus.com/ ~kmcmurdo/win95logo.html`. Karl McMurdo, who maintains this site, has collected more animated logos than you'll ever need. You will also find a tool called XrX Animated Logo Utility at the site. This program will help you animate your `bmp` files. The site has complete directions for creating more animated logos.

We also found some nice 3D screens for Windows at `http://mall.lnd.com/ Galitsky/tweaks/tweak24.html` (see Figure 3-3).

Figure 3-3: An oblique view of your logon screen

Secret

If you delete `Logo.sys`, the graphic embedded in `Io.sys` will be used instead. Getting rid of `Logo.sys` doesn't make the graphic go away. But if you set Logo=0 in your `Msdos.sys` file, no graphic will be displayed before the Windows Desktop appears.

Your `\Windows` folder contains an additional graphics file named `Logos.sys`. This is the screen you see when you exit Windows. Just as with `Logo.sys`, you can edit this file or create a replacement for it.

The Startup Folder

When Windows starts, it runs the programs in the Startup folder. Windows knows which folder is the Startup folder because there is an entry in the registry specifying a particular folder, usually `\Windows\Start Menu\ Programs\StartUp`. You can change which folder is used as the Startup folder, as well as which folders are used for other special functions, by editing the entries found in the registry under the following branch:

HKEY_CURRENT_USER\ Software\ Microsoft\ Windows\ CurrentVersion\ Explorer\ shellfolders

Even better, use TweakUI to designate which folders are used for special functions. Click the General tab in TweakUI, choose the folder, and then choose the location.

You may want to load a file and execute it when Windows starts up, but you don't want to place the file (or a shortcut to it) in the Startup folder. You could put it on the load or run line in `Win.ini`. But there is a special set of branches in the registry where calls can be made to start programs without those programs showing up in the Startup folder.

Secret

If you want to know why you can't find the call to Task Scheduler, or if you're curious about other programs that start up without you knowing about it, get out your Registry Editor and check this out:

STEPS

Seeing and Creating Hidden Startup Programs

Step 1.   Click `Regedit.exe` in your `\Windows` folder.

Step 2.   Navigate to either HKEY_LOCAL_MACHINE \ SOFTWARE \ Microsoft\ Windows \ CurrentVersion \ Run or HKEY_LOCAL_MACHINE \ SOFTWARE \ Microsoft \ Windows \ CurrentVersion\RunOnce. You can also check the RunServices or RunServicesOnce keys.

Step 3.   Highlight Run in the left pane. You'll see which programs are currently running when you start up.

Step 4.   To enter a call to a new program to run at startup time (once or always), right-click in the right pane with either Run or RunOnce highlighted. Click New, String Value.

Step 5.   Type any name you want to identify the application that is going to be run at startup.

Step 6.   Double-click this new name. Type the complete path and filename for the application. Click OK.

Step 7.   Exit the Registry Editor.

For more information about editing your registry, turn to Chapter 11.

Temporarily Turn off Startup

You may have some programs that you'd sometimes like to run as part of your Startup group, but not always. A handy solution is to put the shortcuts to these programs in a separate StartUp.Not folder beneath the C:\Windows\ Start Menu\Programs folder (see Figure 3-4). You can then easily drag the shortcuts from the StartUp.Not subfolder to the regular Startup folder when you want to recommence running the applications at startup time.

You can also keep Windows from loading the Startup group at all by holding down the Shift key during the Windows phase of the bootup process.

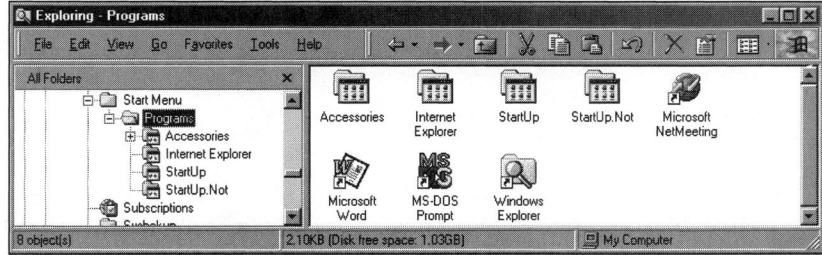

Figure 3-4: The Startup and StartUp.Not folders in the Explorer

Windows Troubleshooting

Microsoft provides troubleshooting guidelines to help you determine what is causing a problem when you can't start Windows in the normal fashion. To access those guidelines, connect to Microsoft's Knowledge Base on its Web site at http://support.microsoft.com/support/kb/articles/q136/ 3/37.asp.

System Configuration Utility

Windows includes a system configuration utility (Msconfig.exe) that gives you much easier and more finely grained control of the Windows startup process. To find it, click Start ➪ Programs ➪ Accessories ➪ System Tools ➪ System Information. In the System Information menu, click Tools ➪ System Configuration Utility.

You can use this utility to choose which files to process during startup, as shown in Figure 3-5.

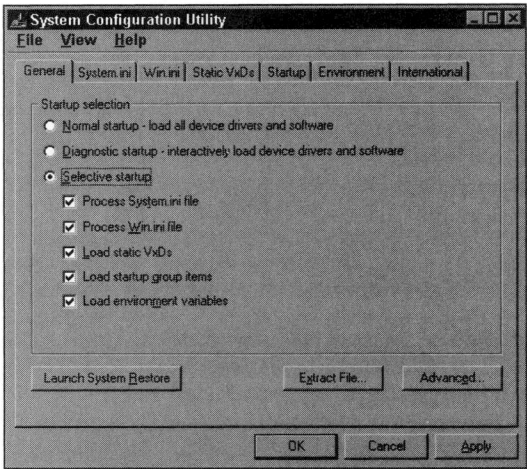

Figure 3-5: The System Configuration Utility dialog box

Other dialog boxes within this utility enable you to choose which lines of which files to process. You can also use it to edit all of the files indicated on the tabs, and to enable and disable items in the Startup folder.

Troubleshoot Windows Startup Problems

Microsoft provides a reasonably comprehensive troubleshooting guide to startup and shutdown problems that you might encounter with Windows. You can read the HTML version online, or download it from the Microsoft Knowledge Base site. You'll find the Knowledge Base article "Troubleshooting Windows Startup Problems and Error Messages" at http://support.microsoft.com/support/kb/articles/q188/8/67.asp. The downloadable version is at http://support.microsoft.com/support/tshoot/default.asp. In addition, if some problem has caused Windows Me to start in Safe mode, the Help and Support application will automatically load to help you troubleshoot the problem.

Manage How Windows Startup Files Start Up

The Windows System Configuration Utility lets you decide whether or not to run any one of the programs in your Startup group when you start Windows. Click Start ➪ Programs ➪ Accessories ➪ System Tools ➪ System Information ➪ Tools ➪ System Configuration Utility ➪ Startup to see how.

If you want to set the order in which the programs run, you can use a batch file, or a little program called DoWinStartup. Download it from `http://www.mrdo.com/dowinstartup/`. It's free.

Pause during Power-On Self-Test

Sometimes you'd like to be able to read the messages that your BIOS is displaying on your screen. While we show you how to get the basic BIOS information from your registry (see "Basic BIOS Info from Your Registry" in Chapter 38), the POST screen is still a convenient place to find some information about your computer.

Some computers allow you to pause during POST. To do so, just press the Pause/Break key.

Keep a Bootlog

Your root directory contains a file that records the steps your computer went through when it booted up. But it won't be a record of the last time that you started your computer, because it isn't created every time.

If you'd like to create a new `bootlog.txt` file that records your next reboot, you can edit the `Msdos.sys` file in your root directory. Because this is a read-only file, you'll need to clear that file attribute first (right-click `Msdos.sys` in your Explorer, click Properties, and clear the Read-only checkbox), edit the file, and then set it again.

The change you need to make to `Msdos.sys` is to add the line `BootMenuDefault=2`. We discuss editing this file in greater depth earlier in the chapter.

Once you've added this line to the `Msdos.sys` file and you've changed the file attribute back to read-only, you can restart your computer. A `bootlog.txt` file will be created.

A handy little freeware utility called the Boot Log Analyzer will display failures or delays in your `bootlog.txt` file (see Figure 3-6). You can download it from `http://www.vision4.dial.pipex.com/`. It doesn't tell you much about how to read the bootlog, but it does point out the problems.

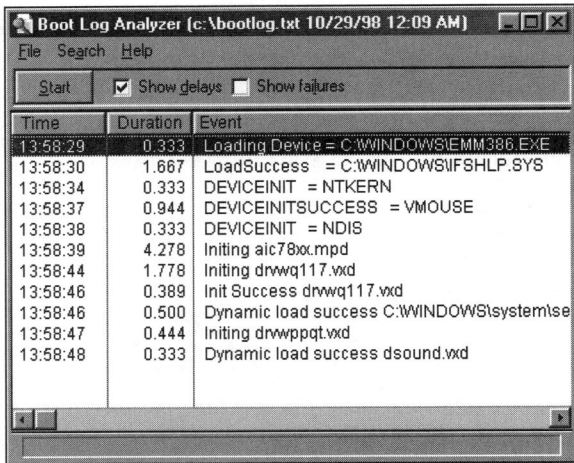

Figure 3-6: Boot Log Analyzer lists the events of this computer's last boot process and their duration. Note that we have marked "Show delays."

Stop Your Modem from Dialing When You Start Windows

It can be quite annoying if every time you start up Windows, a Dial-Up Networking (DUN) connectoid or a dial-up connection dialog box pops up and you hear your modem dialing your Internet service provider (ISP). This annoyance can be caused by a couple of things.

First, if you've installed the Personal Web Server (PWS) that comes on the Windows CD-ROM, its default setting is to connect to the Internet. After all, its job is to publish all these Web pages that you've placed on it.

You can stop this behavior and only connect to the Internet when you desire by running the System Configuration Utility and clearing the MSDTC checkbox in the Startup tab, as described in these steps:

STEPS

Stopping PWS from Dialing

Step 1. Click Start ➪ Programs ➪ Accessories ➪ System Tools ➪ System Information.

Step 2. Choose Tools ➪ System Configuration Utility.

Step 3. Click the Startup tab, and clear the MSDTC (msdtcw-start) checkbox, as shown in Figure 3-7.

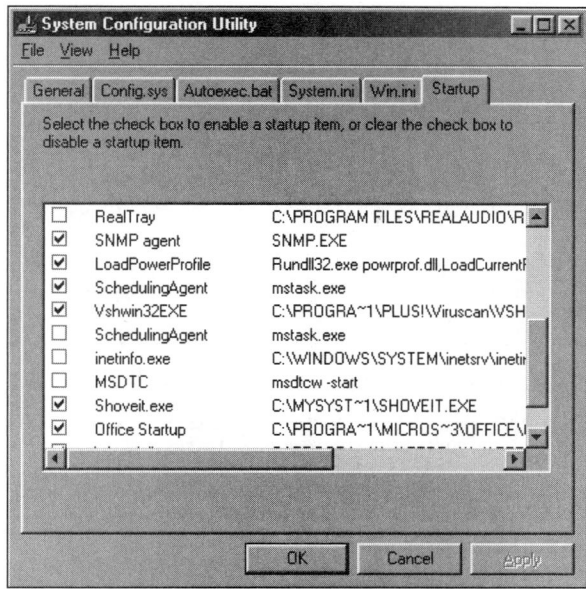

Figure 3-7: Your list on the Startup tab will not be in the same order as this one. Scroll down and look for MSDTC in the middle column.

Step 4.   Click OK. Click Yes when asked to restart Windows.

Thanks to Lance T. Pfeifer for pointing out this tip.

Another possibility is that you have a shortcut to Internet Explorer in your Startup group. When you restart Windows, Internet Explorer wants to connect to display a Web page. This can happen if you have not marked Work Offline in the File menu in the Internet Explorer window, or if you have marked "Always dial my default connection" or "Dial whenever a network connection is not present" under Tools ⇨ Internet Options ⇨ Connections.

To prevent your modem from dialing, you can mark "Never dial a connection," pull the shortcut out of the Startup group, or mark Work Offline in the File menu.

There are yet other reasons why your modem could be dialing when you start up Windows. If you've installed Symantec's WinFAX, you may need to make a change in your registry. Or, you may have a Trojan horse virus.

You can check out the various possibilities using the Microsoft Knowledge Base article "Modem Attempts to Dial When Windows Starts" at http:// support.microsoft.com/support/kb/articles/q175/3/12.asp.

Quit Searching for Floppy Disks

Lots of portable computers don't have floppy disk drives permanently installed. Often, you just plug them in when you need one—which, we are happy to say, isn't that often. You can speed up the Windows startup process by telling Windows not to bother looking for a floppy drive.

STEPS

Ignoring the Floppy Drive

Step 1.   Hold down your Alt key as you click My Computer.

Step 2.   In the System Properties dialog box, click the Performance tab, and click the File System button.

Step 3.   Click the Floppy Disk tab, and clear "Search for new floppy disk drives each time your computer starts," as shown in Figure 3-8.

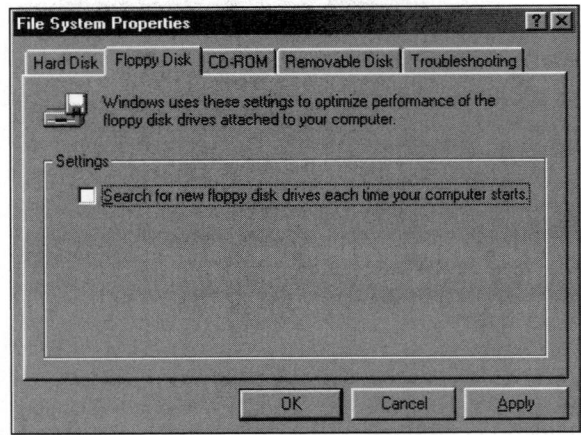

Figure 3-8: Clear the "Search for new floppy disk drives each time your computer starts" checkbox.

Step 4.   Click OK twice.

Thanks to Jamie Sanchez for help on this tip.

Start Up Your Computer with a Dialog Box

If you don't have a blank password, Windows starts up with a Password dialog box. You can add another dialog box if you like (whether or not you have a Password dialog box), although this is not very useful if the computer is your personal computer.

You might want to use this startup dialog box to display a standard message whenever the computer starts, perhaps reminding people to log in as themselves.

To create this message and dialog box, create the following text file. Save the text file with a .reg extension, then right-click it and click Merge to merge it into your registry. After you merge it into your registry, you can edit the text later using your Registry Editor, regedit.exe. (After opening regedit.exe, navigate to the branch indicated below.)

```
REGEDIT4
[HKEY_LOCAL_MACHINE\Software\Microsoft\Windows\CurrentVersion\Winlogon]
"LegalNoticeText"="Your Message"
"LegalNoticeCaption"="Legal Notice"
```

You'll want to edit the "Your Message" and "Legal Notice" text to reflect your message and the name of the dialog box that you want to use. For example, replace "Your Message" with "Bill's Computer," and "Legal Notice" with "Keep Your Hands Off."

Thanks to Mark Dormer for pointing out this secret.

Windows Logs On Nobody

Do you find that when Windows starts up you are logged on as ...? You can tell if you click the Start button and check out Log Off at the bottom of the menu. If three dots follow Off, you aren't logged on. Nobody is logged on.

This is not a good thing. Windows won't remember your passwords, for example. You'll have to log off and log on as yourself—time-consuming.

Secret

There is an errant entry in your registry that is automatically logging on nobody when you start Windows. You need to take these steps to clear up this matter:

STEPS

Stopping AutoLogon

Step 1. Click Start ⇨ Run, type **regedit**, and press Enter.

Step 2. Navigate to HKEY_LOCAL_MACHINE\ SOFTWARE\ Microsoft\ Windows\ Current Version\ Network\ Real Mode Net\.

Step 3.   You can delete the AutoLogon variable in the right pane or rename it xAutoLogn. Either way will work. Close the Registry Editor.

Step 4.   The next time you restart Windows, you won't log on as nobody.

Thanks to Bill Greening who came up with the problem and asked us to find an answer (and to the person on the Windows support newsgroup who actually solved it for him).

Don't Wait Around for Shutdown

It's not such a speedy thing to shut down your computer these days. Not only does it require four mouse clicks (Start ➪ Shut Down ➪ Shut Down ➪ OK), but waiting for Windows to run through its shutdown routine can take quite a while. Here are some products designed to make the process faster and more convenient.

CloseFast 2000 is designed to work in a network environment and includes such features as Internet Based Shutdown, Remote NT Shutdown, and Timed Shutdown. You can also use CloseFast to close all open applications without shutting down, and to manage the windows you have open. You can run it as a small or large toolbar (the large one is shown in Figure 3-9), or in your system tray. CloseFast is very polished and feature-rich freeware. It's available at http://www.rocketdownload.com/Details/Util/closefast.htm.

Figure 3-9: The large CloseFast toolbar

Windows Restart is a fraction of the size of CloseFast at only 350K. It gives you the basic quick shutdown and restart functions shown in Figure 3-10, plus some nice features for managing windows and opening various folders. It runs in your system tray with a spare but functional menu. Windows Restart is freeware. It was created by Jeffrey Carlyle and is available at his web site, http://www.perplexic.com/wr/.

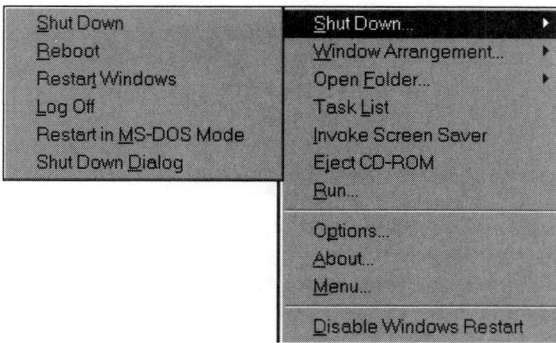

Figure 3-10: The system tray menu for Windows Restart

If you'd like more options for shutting down your laptop, ejecting removable media, or emptying files and folders before shutdown, ShutDown NOW! by Carsten Stratz may be for you. It runs in your system tray and can also run from a command line. The 1MB download is available from `http://www. dworld.de/shdnintern.htm`.

Windows Shutdown Problems

There are a number of different reasons why your computer might have trouble shutting down. You can disable Fast Shutdown and Fast Find (if you have it) to see if these measures clear up the problem. To disable Fast Shutdown, take these steps:

STEPS

Disabling Fast Shutdown

Step 1.   Click Start ⇨ Programs ⇨ Accessories ⇨ System Tools ⇨ System Information.

Step 2.   Click Tools ⇨ System Configuration Utility.

Step 3.   Click the Advanced button and mark the "Disable fast shutdown" checkbox in the Advanced Troubleshooting Settings dialog box, as shown in Figure 3-11.

Continued

STEPS

Disabling Fast Shutdown *(continued)*

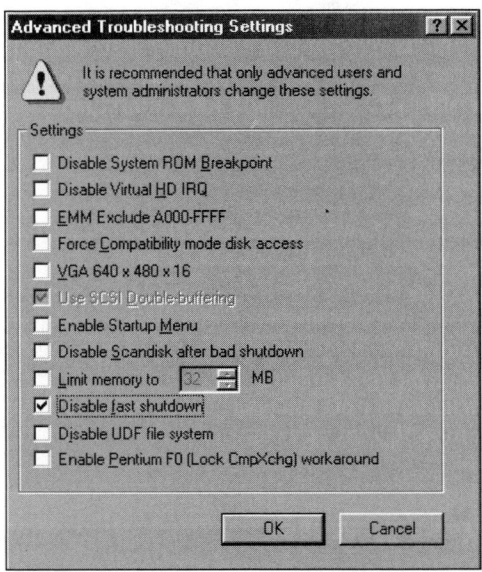

Figure 3-11: The "Disable fast shutdown" checkbox is near the bottom of the dialog box.

Step 4. Click OK. Restart your computer when prompted.

Thanks to Dustin Miller for pointing this out. Dustin responded to an IDG Books Secrets contest at the IDG Books Worldwide Web site, http://www.idgbooks.com.

You can also check out the Microsoft Knowledge Base articles by going to the Personal Online Support Highlights Web site at http://support.Microsoft.com/support/default.asp.

To disable Fast Find, take these steps:

STEPS

Disabling Fast Find

Step 1.   Click Start ⇨ Programs ⇨ Accessories ⇨ System Tools ⇨ System Information.

Step 2.   Click Tools ⇨ System Configuration Utility.

Step 3.   Click the Startup tab.

Step 4.   Clear the checkbox to the left of Microsoft Find Fast, and click OK.

Step 5.   Click Yes when you are prompted to restart your computer.

You can find out more about Fast Find at "OFF97: Overview of Find Fast Indexer" at http://support.microsoft.com/support/kb/articles/ q166/3/02.asp.

Your computer may have other problems that cause Windows shutdown to malfunction. You may have a virus scanner that is looking for a floppy diskette on shutdown. You'll have to track down any virus scanning software that you've loaded.

Your computer may be trying unsuccessfully to disconnect from the network. You'll need to restart the computer without the network to see if this is the source of the problem.

You may have a corrupted Windows swap file. You'll need to restart Windows in Safe mode and then shut down and restart in Normal mode. If that doesn't work, start in DOS mode and delete the Win386.swp file in your \Windows folder. Restart your computer and reboot normally into Windows. Windows will rebuild the swap file.

You may have more than one Windows swap file. Use the Find command to search all your local hard disks for files with the swp extension. Boot to DOS and delete any swap files that are not in the \Windows folder.

Summary

Windows gives you a great deal of control over how your computer starts up. By editing a few files you can control the startup process.

▶ Boot your computer to a DOS 7.1 prompt either by creating an empty `Win.bat` file or by editing `Msdos.sys`.

▶ Start up in your previous version of DOS or Windows either by pressing a function key or by default.

▶ Edit `Msdos.sys` in order to get rid of the Windows logo.

▶ Use function keys to go step by step through the startup process, start Windows in Safe mode if there is a problem with your hardware, or bring up the Startup menu.

▶ Create different hardware profiles and choose between them at startup depending on your current hardware setup.

▶ Develop multiconfiguration `Config.sys` and `Autoexec.bat` files to design your own Windows Startup menu.

▶ Start the startup applets in the order that you want.

▶ Pause before Windows starts.

▶ Disable Fast Shutdown and Fast Find.

Part II

Desktop Secrets

Chapter 4

What's New in Windows Me

In This Chapter

For those who've used Windows before Me came out, we've gathered into this chapter the most significant new features that you need to know about. We discuss the following:

▶ Set your system back to a healthy state with System Restore

▶ No more real-mode DOS in Windows Me — it's a whole new ball game

▶ Image Acquisition and Media Player help you handle digital images from scanners and cameras, and digital media from the Web and other sources

▶ MSN Messenger is a convenient instant messaging package, but we show you how to get rid of it if you don't like having it around

▶ What's up with the universal serial bus (USB), the newer, faster connection for your devices

▶ Some features didn't make it into Windows Me, despite the hopes of many beta testers and Windows users

Get Your System Files Back

System Restore is designed to preserve information about the state of your system at a given moment in time, so that you can restore it to that state if your system becomes damaged. In fact, it automatically creates a whole series of archived restore points so that you can return to an earlier configuration that was known to work. This is different than Backup/Restore, in that only the system files are archived; your work, e-mail, and so on will not be lost, even if you use a restore point that is two weeks old. You now have an added level of security that if something happens to your registry — or some dll goes missing, or some piece of new hardware keeps your old hardware from working, or you were just playing around and now nothing works right — you can get everything back to the way it was without losing that important, urgent e-mail that arrived last night. Not only that, but System Restore is very fast and easy to use. It even runs in Safe mode, when you need it the most.

System Restore requires a minimum of 200MB of free hard disk space beyond that used for Windows Me. If you do not have this amount of space free, System Restore will be disabled (you can enable it later). System Restore saves its archive files in the root directory of the drive or partition where your \Windows folder is stored (usually C:\), and this is not something that you can change. It's worthwhile to have a healthy amount of space in this partition if you can, since 200MB will only let you save two to three days' worth of restore points at best.

System Restore creates a new restore point every 10 hours of time that your computer is running, and at least every day. Restore points are also created automatically as part of the process of installing software with the Windows Install Shield. Auto Update creates a restore point before installing an update. You can also make restore points manually, before you make registry changes or install new hardware or software. You control System Restore by running the System Restore Wizard; it will never restore without your permission.

Tip

Although it can be helpful to go back to a restore point that was made just before an application was installed, System Restore is not the same as uninstalling. Restoring your system may leave behind "harmless" vestiges (folders, shortcuts, and graphics files) of applications that are removed. The best way to uninstall an application is to use the Add/Remove Programs icon in the Control Panel. That way, you are more likely to remove all or most of the files associated with that application, without changing the rest of your system. See "Add/Remove Programs" in Chapter 15 of this book.

Tip

System Restore is no substitute for regular backups. It ignores files with extensions (such as txt, doc, bmp, pdf, zip, and so on) that are commonly used for data. It ignores graphics files even if they are associated with applications. It also ignores the contents of My Documents, your e-mail data store, your Favorites and History, and file types that are not included in the File Types list (to see this list, open the Explorer, click View ⇨ Folder Options, and go to the File Types tab). You must still back up your data files in the usual way.

Tip

If you download software applications in self-extracting files with the extension exe, it is a good idea to back them up on a removable disk. Any exe files that you have added to your hard disk since the last restore point will be removed as part of a restoration, no matter what partition they reside on.

Using the System Restore Wizard

To create a restore point, run the System Restore Wizard. Click Start ⇨ Programs ⇨ Accessories ⇨ System Tools ⇨ System Restore (or click Start ⇨ Help, and under Fix a Problem click Use System Restore), and mark the "Create A restore point" option, then click Next. Give your new restore point a name that will help you to recognize it later (the date and time will be added automatically). Click Next. It may take a minute or two for information to be gathered into the restore point. When the process is complete, a screen will confirm the name and date of the new restore point. Click OK.

To restore your system to a previous state, launch the System Restore Wizard and mark the "Restore My Computer to an earlier time" option, then click Next. A calendar will appear, as shown in Figure 4-1.

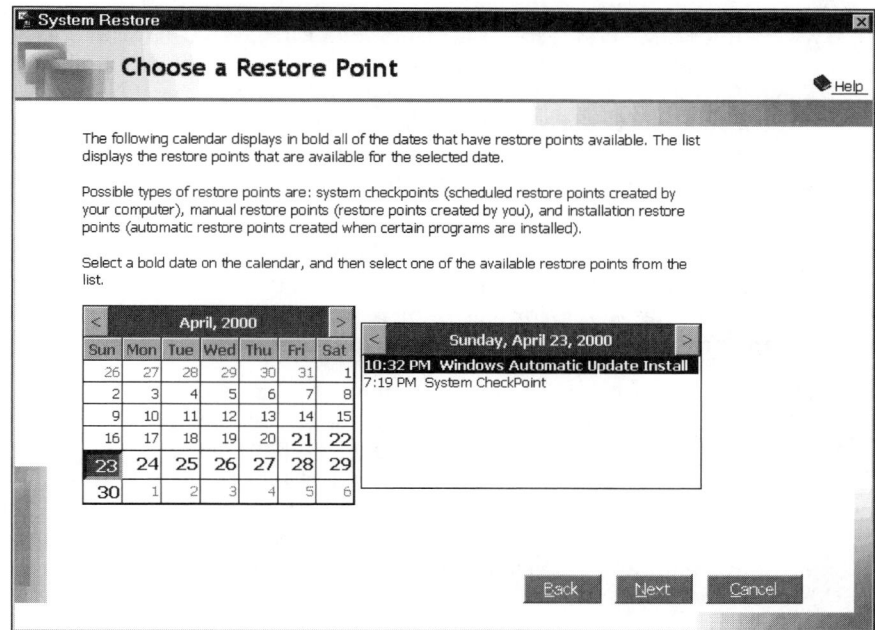

Figure 4-1: Use the calendar in the System Restore Wizard to choose the most recent restore point when your computer was working correctly.

The bold dates in the calendar are those for which there is a restore point. Click the most recent date when you remember your computer working properly; the restore points made on that day are displayed on the right. Select the point you want and then click Next. Save and close any open files and click OK in the warning box, then click Next to actually perform the restoration. Your computer will automatically restart, and you will see a window indicating that the restoration was a success. If any folders were renamed or re-created during the restoration, you will see a "List of renamed folders" link in this window; click it to see this list.

You can also use the System Restore Wizard to undo a system restoration. If you have performed a restoration, when you launch the wizard you will see an option to "Undo my last restoration." Mark this option and click Next. A warning appears to let you close all applications and files; close everything, click OK, and then click Next to undo the restoration and restart your computer.

Your Restore Data Store

The data in each restore point is compressed together in a `cab` archive file, and saved in `C:\_RESTORE\ARCHIVE`. If you can't see this folder, open the Explorer, choose Tools ⇨ Folder Options, click the View tab, mark "Show hidden files and folders," unmark "Hide protected operating system files," and then click OK.

Windows Me creates a `\_RESTORE` folder in every drive and partition (`C:\`, `D:\`, and so on) that it can read and write to, and that is not removable. The `_RESTORE` folder on your `C:` drive contains the primary System Restore information. Folders on other drives and partitions contain one file, simply the identity of that drive. That way System Restore can keep track of any changes in the way your drives and partitions are named, and restore them if necessary.

Tip

If you delete the contents of the `_RESTORE` folder on a drive where Windows Me is not installed, System Restore thinks the drive has been removed and is no longer available for files to be restored to it. It then purges the contents of the primary `_RESTORE` folder, and you will lose all of your restore points.

System Restore works on the principle of first in first out (FIFO). As you build up information and fill up the space allocated on your disk for the Restore Data store, Windows removes earlier files to make room for the new ones, always starting with the oldest file. The smaller the amount of disk space you have set aside, the fewer the number of restore points you will be able to save, and the shorter the distance in time you can reach back to for a working system. Ideally, you'd like to be able to go back a week or two.

To set the amount of hard disk space that is available for the `C:\_RESTORE` folder, right-click My Computer, select Properties, and go to the Performance Tab. Click the File System button, and adjust the System Restore disk space use slider bar in the File System Properties dialog box shown in Figure 4-2. For drives or partitions smaller than 4GB, the maximum is set to 400MB — it is 12.5 percent of the total for larger drives and partitions. If your drive or partition has less than 400MB available, System Restore will recognize that; it will automatically lower the setting on the slider and notify you that you have insufficient disk space. Once you have plenty of disk space to work with, you will be able to set the slider to the level you choose up to the maximum.

Tip

It's a bad idea to manually delete the files in your `_Restore\Temp` folder, because the information Windows Me needs about how and when to make the next `cab` file will be lost. If you have deleted these files by mistake, you should disable System Restore using the following steps. After you have rebooted your system, then you can reenable System Restore. System Restore will start fresh at this point, and earlier restore points will be lost. Thanks to Lewis Umbenhower, Jr. at Microsoft for this advice.

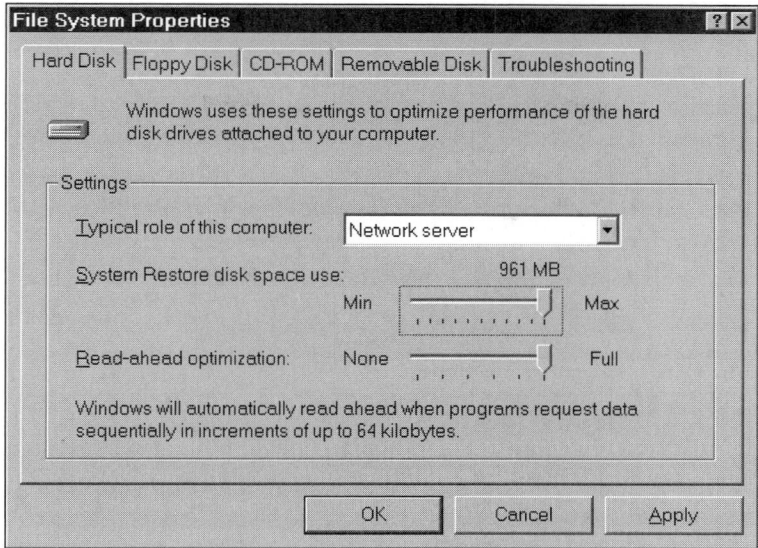

Figure 4-2: Use the "System Restore disk space use" slider bar to adjust the amount of memory allocated for the C:_RESTORE folder.

As the contents of the _RESTORE folder reach 75 percent of the allocated space, or if your hard disk gets full, System Restore stops gathering data. It begins removing files, starting with the oldest, until you are back under 50 percent of your maximum. If this happens you'll have fewer restore points, because you'll have fewer archives to go back to. You may notice this happening if you install software that makes lots of changes to your system.

While you work, Windows Me saves files in the _Restore\Temp folder. Windows Me uses these temporary files as it gathers information about your system; the files change as you work, and the size of the folder grows. When it's time to make a restore point, Windows Me sorts through the files in this folder, compresses the relevant information in a cab file for archiving, and purges the rest. It's normal for the _Restore\Temp folder to be quite large at times, and empty or nearly so at other times.

Disable System Restore

You can delete your _RESTORE directory, but as long as System Restore is enabled, a new empty one will be created the next time you start your computer. If you really want to disable System Restore, follow the steps below, marking the "Disable system restore" checkbox.

If your System Restore disk space use slider bar is grayed out, System Restore has been disabled. To enable it, follow the steps, but *un*check the "Disable system restore" box in Step 3.

STEPS

Disable/Enable System Restore

Step 1. Click Start ⇨ Settings ⇨ Control Panel and click the System icon to open the System Properties dialog box.

Step 2. Go to Performance ⇨ File System ⇨ Troubleshooting.

Step 3. Mark the "Disable system restore" checkbox (or to enable System Restore, unmark this box), then click Apply.

Step 4. You must restart your computer for this to take effect.

After you restart your computer, Windows Me deletes the contents of your _RESTORE directory. You may notice some activity on your hard disk as this occurs.

No More Real-Mode DOS

With the advent of Windows Me, we humans no longer have access to real-mode DOS. This is not the same as saying there is no more DOS, as we shall see. In fact real mode still exists, in the sense that there are still an io.sys and an msdos.sys. You will even see autoexec.bat and config.sys in your root folder; however, you won't be able to use them in the way that you may have up to now. While DOS is still there, it is mostly hidden — and parts of it are inaccessible. We are on the path toward the still-in-development consumer version of Windows 2000, which has no real mode.

When you start your computer, the processor still runs io.sys and msdos.sys, the two DOS hidden files. You still see the power-on self test sequence, and (if you haven't disabled it) the Startup menu. However, you'll notice that the Startup menu offers you fewer choices; you can no longer use it to select "Command prompt only or safe mode command prompt only."

Startup

Another major difference is that you can no longer edit the config.sys or autoexec.bat file to affect your computer's startup sequence. These files still exist in the interest of backward compatibility with software that won't run without them — but their contents are now entirely controlled by the System Configuration utility. If you change or delete these files, Windows Me re-creates them from information in the registry. See "How Windows Starts Up" in Chapter 3 for more specifics about the startup process.

If you select item 4 from the startup menu to run interactive startup, you'll see that the sequence is somewhat different from the one we describe in "What Gets Loaded When" in Chapter 3. For example, the following line is missing:

```
Process your startup device drivers (CONFIG.SYS) [Enter=Y, Esc=N]?
```

Instead, you will see this:

```
Loading and initializing IFSHLP.SYS driver... complete
```

Even in the interactive startup process, you are not given a yes/no choice about this. Decisions about file allocation and memory management are now handled automatically or through the registry.

Other missing lines include:

```
Process your startup command file (AUTOEXEC.BAT) [Enter=Y, Esc=N]?
```

and

```
Load the Windows graphical user interface [Enter=Y, Esc=N]?
```

Autoexec.bat is only there in case some DOS application looks for it, and its contents are no longer read as part of the startup process. You also have no choice about whether to load the Windows interface, since there is no longer an alternative.

If you have occasion to shut down your computer without going through the normal shutdown sequence, you'll also notice that ScanDisk no longer runs during the DOS portion of startup, but now runs in Windows. We have some concerns about the potential for Windows to overwrite corrupted data that might have been recoverable before Windows opened. On the other hand, DOS ScanDisk's propensity to rename files and folders that use long file-names has made life miserable for many.

The DOS Box

The MS-DOS prompt icon is still there in your Start menu (Start ➪ Programs ➪ Accessories ➪ MS-DOS prompt). In fact, the DOS console in Windows has changed very little. This DOS emulation is now your only access to the DOS commands; but Microsoft has not made any real changes to the user inter-face. It's worth noting that the command files (in \Windows\COMMAND) have all been updated—or at least redated.

One nice change is that DOSKEY is now already enabled, so you no longer have to load it separately. See "The Remaining DOS Commands" and "Modifying DOS Commands," in Chapter 20 for more on DOSKEY.

Running DOS Programs

Your old DOS applications that run in virtual mode should still work fine in Windows Me. However, applications that require real mode (that is, they are designed to install as a DOS application before Windows starts) will no longer run.

Your DOS programs may work better if you set the MS-DOS properties to ignore Windows. Do this by opening the DOS console and then clicking the Properties button in the toolbar (it looks like a hand holding a piece of paper). On the Program tab, mark "Prevent MS-DOS-based programs from detecting Windows" and click OK, as shown in Figure 4-3.

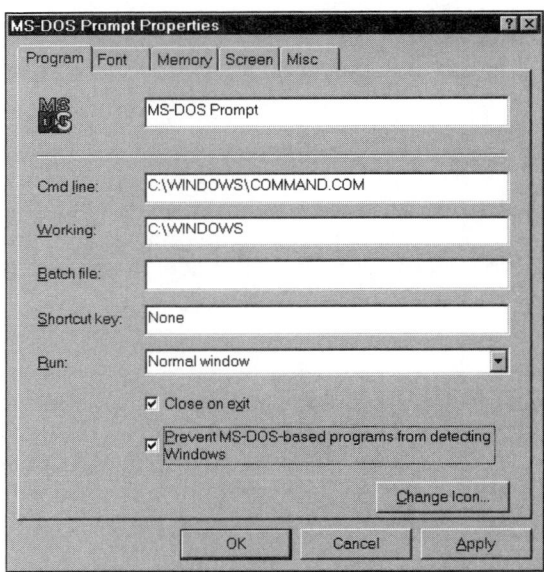

Figure 4-3: In the Program tab of the MS-DOS Prompt Properties dialog box, mark "Prevent MS-DOS-based programs from detecting Windows."

It may also help to make the above changes to the Properties for the `pif` file associated with your application.

Setting Environmental Variables

Some DOS programs require you to set specific environmental variables in order for your video adapter or sound card to work. Instead of editing `autoexec.bat` or `config.sys`, you now set these variables using the System Configuration Utility. To open it, click Start ➪ Programs ➪ Accessories ➪ System Tools ➪ System Information ➪ Tools ➪ System Configuration Utility — or just click Start ➪ Run, type **msconfig**, and click OK.

This dialog box has a new Environment tab for setting environmental variables. For example, if your old DOS program requires a statement such as FILES=x or Country=x, or if you want to modify PATH, you can do that on the Environment tab, as shown in Figure 4-4.

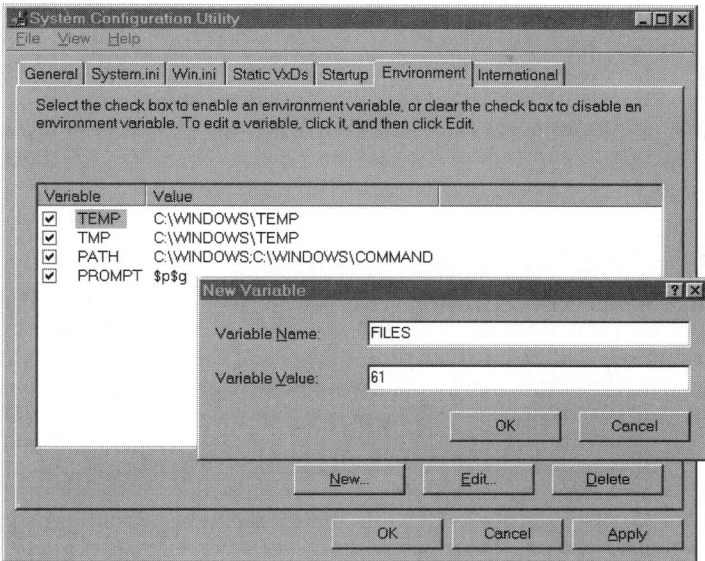

Figure 4-4: Use the Environment tab of the System Configuration Utility to change or add environmental variables.

Emergency Recovery/Bootable Floppies

The old DOS format /s command, which lets you copy basic system files to a disk you are formatting, does not work on floppy disks in Windows Me. In fact, the DOS sys command has been changed and no longer works on any drive except C:. Normally, you would only use sys c: for installing Windows on a new hard disk.

To make a bootable floppy disk without using format /s, start by creating an "Emergency boot disk," either during setup or by using the Startup Disk tab of the Add/Remove Programs dialog box in the Control Panel. Once you have created this disk, you can make a pared down boot disk by deleting everything except io.sys and command.com. There should then be plenty of room to add whatever else you need to this disk—for example, a BIOS update or a hardware installation routine that requires DOS to run.

You can't make a bootable disk just by copying io.sys and command.com onto it; they must be installed using the sys command (now buried in the Emergency Boot Disk utility). Unfortunately, this utility does not support media larger than 1.44MB. So you cannot use your Zip or LS120 drive to make a bootable disk or an Emergency Boot Disk (a lost opportunity, in our opinion).

When you start your computer with this disk in the A: drive, you boot up in real-mode DOS. However, you can only run real-mode DOS from this floppy; if you try to change directories to another drive, you will be firmly redirected to A:.

Rescue disks created by third-party software companies for use with Windows 98 may not work with Windows Me. If you use these products, make sure your disk was made with an updated version designed explicitly for use with Windows Me. Otherwise, it may not be there for you when you need it most.

Dual Booting

People who use more than one operating system on the same computer are put into a somewhat awkward situation by the loss of real-mode access. They have depended on using real-mode DOS to partition their disks and manage their operating systems. If you are dual booting between Windows Me and an earlier version of Windows, you can use the real-mode access in the earlier software to continue working the way you have in the past.

If you are already running Windows NT or 2000, the setup routine for Windows Me Setup adds itself to the Windows NT or 2000 boot menu. You can then use this menu to multiboot between Windows Me and Windows NT or 2000. See the file setup.txt on the Windows Me CD-ROM for a detailed description of how to set up your computer to dual boot between Windows NT and Windows Me.

Many people use third-party software such as Partition Magic to partition their hard disks and manage the multiboot environment. Until recently, these products have required real mode DOS to run; there is, however, a new version of Partition Magic that supports Windows 2000. Powerquest, the makers of Partition Magic, are expected to produce a version that supports Windows Me; check their Web site at http://www.powerquest.com. Until then, only the Partition Magic functions that are accessible from within the Windows environment (without rebooting into DOS) are available in Windows Me. You can always run either the Windows 98 version or the Windows 2000 version, if you are running either of those operating systems.

BeOS requires that you be in real mode in order to boot. You can reportedly boot BeOS from an Emergency Boot Disk, switch to the Be folder, and then use the Be loader (loadbeos.exe). But you are probably better off using Be's own boot floppy.

Look before You Print

Sick of guessing how a Web page will look when you print it out? How many pages will it take? Will it fit on the paper? Do you need to print that last page with all the ads? Finally there's a Print Preview feature in Internet Explorer 5.5. Click Files ⇨ Print Preview to open the Preview window. Better yet, add a Print Preview button to your toolbar. Right-click the toolbar and click Customize; you'll see Print Preview in the list on the left.

When the Print Preview window opens, you see the first page of your document as it will print on paper, in a full-screen view. The toolbar makes it easy to zoom in and out, and to move to a different page. At smaller zoom levels, you see multiple pages, as shown in Figure 4-5.

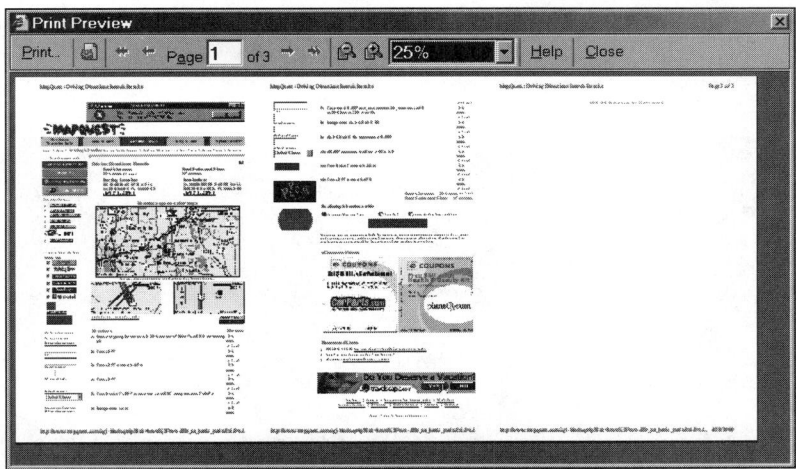

Figure 4-5: Zoom to 25 percent in Print Preview to see several pages at once. Maybe we don't need to print all three pages of this document after all.

An especially nice feature of this Print Preview implementation is the Page Setup button, located on the toolbar next to the Print button. Page Setup lets you adjust margins, change page orientation, and modify or remove page headers before you print. Unlike the Print button on the Internet Explorer toolbar, the Print button in Print Preview first opens the Printer dialog box so you can set the number of copies and number of pages before you print. Click Close to close the Preview window and return to browsing in Internet Explorer.

Tip

If a graphic on the Web page is too big to fit on your paper (because it would be cut off in the middle), it will be moved to the next page. You'll see an empty space on the first page where the graphic would have appeared. You may be able to get the graphic to fit if you use Page Setup to make the top and bottom margins smaller.

Tip

When shopping on the Internet, you often see a generated order confirmation page with instructions to print the page. Generated pages like these won't save properly, even as mht files. Use Print Preview to make sure the page will print correctly, and then choose to print to a file or to Acrobat PDF Writer. That way, you don't waste a piece of paper, but you'll still have the information you need if there's a problem with your order.

Personalized Menus

Windows Me makes extensive use of what are called "personalized" menus. Cascading menus in Start, the Explorer, Internet Explorer, and other places start out showing only a few basic commands. The other commands are there, but to reach them you must click or hover over the double arrows at the bottom of the menu, as shown in Figure 4-6. As time passes and you use the menus, the commands you use most often will appear at the top, and will be faster to get to.

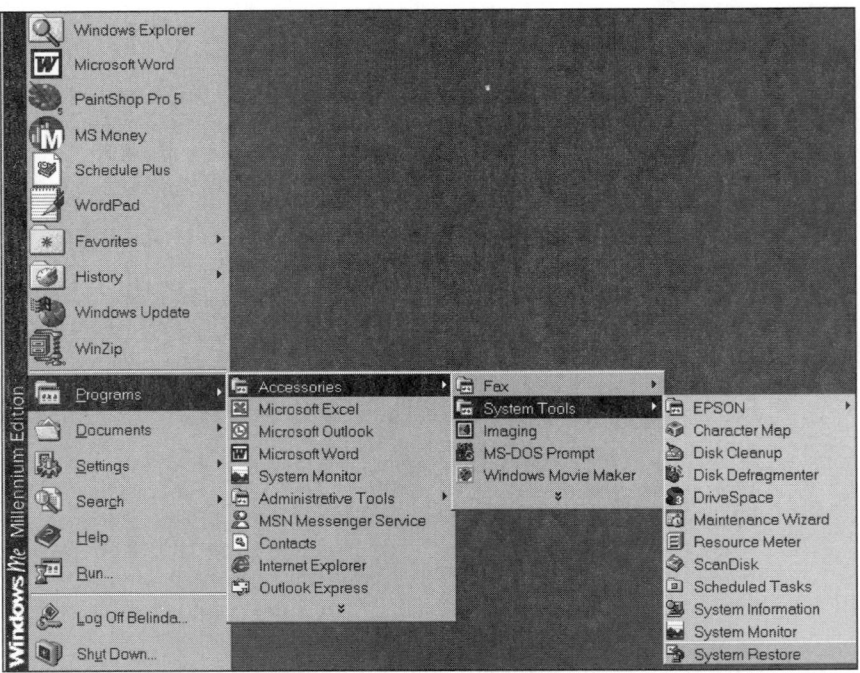

Figure 4-6: The Personalized Start menu. Click the double arrows to see the whole menu. Menu items that appear "raised" appear on the short version.

This feature is supposed to simplify the workspace and make it easier to find what you're looking for, but some people don't like having their menus changed without their permission. If you're among them, it's easy enough to turn Personalized Menus off. Click Start ➪ Settings ➪ Taskbar and Start Menu. On the General tab, unmark "Use personalized menus" and click OK. Now everything is back where it used to be.

Truly Helpful Help

Windows Me comes with a completely revamped HTML-based help system called Help and Support. To launch it, click Start ➪ Help. Right away you'll notice the new look, shown in Figure 4-7. While the HTML takes a few seconds longer to load, it's well worth using the tools that are there. The articles are more detailed, the organization is more intuitive, there are plenty of troubleshooters, and there are links to very helpful online tools as well.

Figure 4-7: The new look of Help and Support. The beauty is more than skin deep.

The Search field is right at the top of the window, so you can type in a keyword and search without any extra mouse clicks. A hierarchical navigation bar horizontally runs just below it, while the links in the left pane take you to specific topics. The Home page of Help and Support lists a number of potential starting places, and includes links to System Restore, Assisted Support, and Online Support. On the right you'll see a list of your recently viewed help topics — a nice touch that makes it easy to get back to what you were working on yesterday, or before you had to reboot. Subsequent pages show links to related topics in the left pane, with the article contents on the right.

The Change Views button lets you toggle between large and small views of Help. Click it to make the Help window smaller, showing you only the article you're reading, without the navigation links in the left pane. To get the links back, click Change Views again. There's also a Print button that lets you quickly print out the article you're reading — properly formatted — so you can refer to it while you work.

You can see by the icon at the beginning of a topic whether it is a Help article, a tour, or a resource located on the Internet. Links with a yellow question mark go to articles on your own computer; links with a little blue Internet Explorer logo lead to resources located online. Some articles from the Microsoft Knowledge Base now also appear locally in Help, so you don't need to go online for them.

Although the new Help and Support Troubleshooters are mostly located on your computer, they have the online symbol because they use the Help and Support Web site to analyze your system and advise you based on the results. You can still see most of the information in a troubleshooter without going online: just leave unchecked any box that says "I want the troubleshooter to investigate settings on this computer." However, if you can work online, leave the box checked to save time and see suggestions that are more relevant to your specific setup.

In Safe mode, if you click Start ➪ Help, you are taken directly to the Safe Mode Troubleshooter. Presumably that's what you need if you're there.

Tip

Help and Support is an easy way to get to your system information and system tools. Open Help and Support, click Assisted Support, and click the System Information link. Your system information appears. Click Tools to see a drop-down list of system information tools. (See Chapter 23 of this book for more on using the system tools.)

If you are planning to use Assisted Support, described in the topic below, it may be a good idea to print out a copy of your system information first. You can only open one session of Help and Support, so if you try to check your system information once you are on the Assisted Support Web site, you will lose whatever you have written there. Assisted Support should upload this information automatically, but if you have a problem (or prefer to do it manually), it pays to be prepared in advance.

Some antivirus software such as Norton Auto-Protect can slow down Help and Support, depending on how it is set up. If the antivirus application is set to check a file every time the file is run or opened, it will slow down a process like Help and Support that reads a lot of files. If a full system scan shows that you have no viruses, you can change your antivirus software to check files only when they are created or downloaded. That way, you'll still be protected, but you won't be checking files needlessly. Thanks to Clayton Macleod at Microsoft for this bit of advice.

Click Assisted Support and you see links to MSN Computing Central forums and message boards, as well as a link to Microsoft's Online Support. We often find that asking other people who use the same product can result in a more informative answer than one from corporate staff — depending on your question, you may want to try the MSN links first. The Online Support link gives you ways to search for online Knowledge Base articles, to ask questions in natural language and receive automated answers, and to submit a question by e-mail to a support professional at Microsoft using Web Response.

Microsoft's Online Support is continually changing and improving, so we won't go into too many specifics here. But we have been greatly impressed by the Web Response support available for some of Microsoft's consumer products. While you fill out an incident report, information about your system is automatically added to the report. This happens on your computer (not Microsoft's), and you can edit the information before submitting your incident. You can also easily attach files such as logs or images that may help in troubleshooting. Within one workday after you submit an incident, you should receive e-mail with a link to the Web location of the response. You reply by creating a supplement, and the back and forth continues until your incident is resolved. In our experience the support staff is knowledgeable, personable, and easy to understand without being condescending — something of a rarity these days.

You are required to have a Passport or a Hotmail account in order to use Web Response. This is a process by which you get a user name and password in exchange for information about who you are and how you can be contacted. Once you have a password, you use it every time you contact Microsoft instead of filling out the same form over and over. People who are concerned about their privacy may balk at having their entire support history linked with their personal profile. But for most of us, the advantages in faster, more accurate technical support outweigh the disadvantages.

Stay Out of DLL Hell

The Windows Me System File Protection feature replaces the System File Checker that came with Windows 98 and takes it a step further. If certain protected system files (such as dll files) are deleted or overwritten, System File Protection automatically replaces the protected file with a clean copy extracted from the system cab files on your hard disk. This means that installing an unruly hardware driver cannot destroy files that are essential for other parts of your system to work properly. You won't be put into a situation where a damaged system file prevents you from opening Windows, even in Safe mode. You won't have to decide which of two conflicting files is the correct one. And you don't have to remember to run System File Protection; it happens automatically.

Microsoft developed the list of protected files based on the experience of its technical support staff — and the staffs of its vendors — helping customers whose systems had been hosed by software that overwrote critical files. To see a list of the files that are protected by System File Protection, use the Explorer to navigate to \WINDOWS\SYSTEM\sfp and open sfpdb.sfp with Notepad. Notice that the protection is for files, not folders; not all of the contents of the \Windows folder are protected, for example.

In the \WINDOWS\SYSTEM\sfp folder, open sfplog.txt to see the actions System File Protection has taken on your behalf. You can see which invalid files were copied onto your system, and where the original file was restored. In most cases, this happens almost instantly. In some cases, you will see that System File Protection has installed new files. Only software that contains a digitally signed and encrypted catalog file, indicating that the newer file meets certain standards, will be allowed to replace system files. At that time, System File Protection backs up the older version in \WINDOWS\SYSTEM\sfp\archive and allows the newer version into the system.

Microsoft has worked with developers and manufacturers to ensure that most software will contain the required Catalog file. It seems unlikely, however, that everyone will comply by the time Windows Me is released. And there will be plenty of older hardware out there, with older drivers to match. If your driver does not meet the new standards, it will probably not install, and you won't be able to use that hardware (this shouldn't be a problem for hardware you already have installed before upgrading to Windows Me). In addition to hardware drivers, games will undoubtedly pose problems in this regard. You will have to contact the manufacturer in question and get an updated driver or a new version of the software before you can use it.

Tip

Even though they don't seem like system files, TWAIN files are protected by System File Protection. This is because several devices may use the same TWAIN driver, which controls communication between the applications and drivers. The TWAIN driver that comes with Windows Me is version 1.7. If your TWAIN scanner or other device requires an earlier version of TWAIN, it will not operate; you must get a new driver for that device that works with the later version of TWAIN.

You cannot configure or disable System File Protection. Microsoft felt this would put people right back in DLL Hell, creating the same support problems they were trying to get away from. It's possible that you may be able to install a noncompliant driver in Safe mode — but you risk making other parts of your system, if not the whole thing, unusable. As frustrating as it might be in the short run, in the long run, System File Protection will save consumers considerable grief.

Put Your Pictures in My Pictures

Windows Me gives you a new, specialized folder called My Pictures, just for storing your images. It's located in the My Documents folder for easy backup. My Pictures is set up by default to display its contents and the contents of its subfolders in Image Preview.

If you are viewing your folders in Web view, Image Preview shows you a thumbnail of the contents of the folder with a full-resolution preview of the selected image file, as shown in Figure 4-8. The preview display is very fast; you only have to hover over an image to see the preview, along with details about the image such as its format and pixel size. Click the buttons at the top of the Preview window to zoom, rotate, or print your image without opening another application, or to see it in a full-screen view.

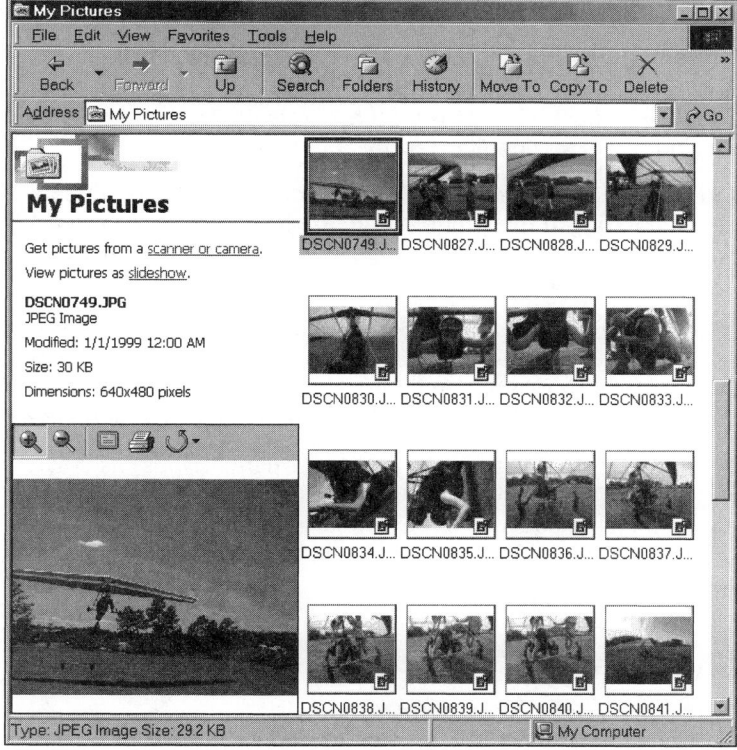

Figure 4-8: The contents of the My Pictures folder are displayed in Image Preview. Use the buttons above the preview to zoom, rotate, or print your image.

To view the contents of your folder as a full-screen slide show, click "View pictures as slideshow" in the left part of the window. Use the controls in the upper right-hand corner to control or exit the slide show. We couldn't find any way to adjust the timing of the slides — they are set to change every ten seconds.

To launch the Scanner and Camera Wizard, click "Get pictures from a scanner or camera" (see "Taking Pictures" later in this chapter for more about this wizard).

If you don't see the preview or the links mentioned in the paragraph above, click Tools ⇨ Folder Options, and mark "Enable Web content in folders under Web view," then click OK. Unfortunately, this will affect the way you view all of your folders. If you don't want to enable Web content in your folders, you can still see thumbnails in My Pictures by choosing View ⇨ Thumbnails. You won't have the preview capabilities or the access to the Scanner and Camera Wizard, though. Kind of a tough decision, we think.

To turn off Image Preview in the My Pictures folder, click Tools ⇨ Folder Options, and under Web View mark "Use Windows classic folders"; then click OK (this will affect all of your folders). Now navigate to My Pictures, click View, and select any choice except Thumbnails.

If you delete a file from My Photos, the thumbnails won't line up automatically. Right-click in the window, and you'll see commands to Arrange Icons, Line Up Icons, and Refresh. Arrange Icons lets you sort by Name, Type, Size, or Date, or Auto Arrange.

My Pictures appears in your Start menu under Documents. To view the contents of My Pictures as a cascading menu instead of a window, click Start ⇨ Settings ⇨ Taskbar and Start Menu, and go to the Advanced tab. Under Start Menu Settings, mark "Expand my pictures" and click OK.

You can delete the My Pictures folder permanently just as you would any other folder. If you decide later that you'd like to get Image Preview back — or if you'd like to use Image Preview in other folders — you can apply those properties to any folder you choose. Follow the steps below:

STEPS

Turn On Image Preview in Any Folder

Step 1. In the Explorer, navigate to the folder you want. Click Tools ⇨ Folder Options, make sure that "Enable Web content in folders" is marked, and then click OK.

Step 2. From the folder, select View ⇨ "Customize this folder." The "Customize this Folder" Wizard launches.

Step 3.   Click Next. Select "Choose or edit an HTML template for this folder." Click Next.

Step 4.   Select Image Preview. Click Next. Click Finish.

Windows Image Acquisition

Windows Image Acquisition (WIA) is both an application programming interface (API) and a device driver interface (DDI) used by Windows Me for devices like scanners and cameras that capture still images. Its purpose is to let you easily add and run multiple cameras and scanners, and to acquire images using fewer steps. WIA is also intended to give hardware developers an easier way to write drivers that will work better in the Windows environment.

WIA is based on the Microsoft Still Image (STI) architecture that was introduced with Windows 98. While the original purpose of that architecture was to support the TWAIN data standard, Microsoft sees WIA as an improvement over (and ultimately a replacement for) TWAIN. Instead of the familiar TWAIN Acquire dialog box launched by imaging applications such as PhotoShop and Paint Shop Pro, when scanning with a WIA scanner you will now launch the Scanners and Cameras Wizard.

When Microsoft refers to "supported" scanners and cameras, it means those for which there is a WIA driver included in Windows Me. Almost without exception, these devices use either SCSI or USB interfaces (some streaming video devices have a kind of WIA wraparound). For these supported devices, Plug and Play should work transparently in Windows Me.

If you are using an "unsupported" scanner or camera, you can still save the image as a file on your hard disk, then open it with editing software — probably the way you do it now. You just won't be able to make photos or scans directly from the Start menu or the My Pictures folder, and you won't be able to link your device to an application.

Installing Scanners and Cameras

Microsoft has elevated scanners and cameras to a new status by giving them their own Control Panel folder in Windows Me. Previously, the icon for this folder only appeared if you had actually installed a camera or a scanner on your system; now it contains a convenient wizard that helps with the installation process.

Like other Control Panel folders, Scanners and Cameras displays the devices you have installed so that you can view and change their properties if needed. However, according to Microsoft's WIA team, this folder "will only list still image devices with certain types of drivers, based on either the STI or WIA standards." To access the properties for other cameras and scanners, click Start ⇨ Settings ⇨ Control Panel. Double-click System, go to the Device Manager tab, and scroll down to Imaging Devices. Right-click the device and click Properties. See "Control Panel Icons" in Chapter 10 to make a shortcut to your Device Manager.

Chances are good that if you are adding a new SCSI or USB device, you won't need to bother with the wizard because it will have a WIA driver. Plug and Play detects scanners and cameras for which drivers are included in Windows Me, and installs them automatically.

Tip

If the SCSI card to which your scanner connects is not detected, the scanner won't be detected. This is true even if the scanner is supported by Windows Me. See "Hardware Detection" in Chapter 36 for more on detecting SCSI cards.

If you are installing a parallel scanner, an older scanner, or a non-USB camera for the first time, you should use the wizard. To launch the Scanner and Camera Installation Wizard, click Start ⇨ Settings ⇨ Scanners and Cameras ⇨ Add Device. Click Next to begin. You will see the list of manufacturers and models shown in Figure 4-9. If your manufacturer is listed, select it and the model and click Next. Click the Have Disk button and follow the directions.

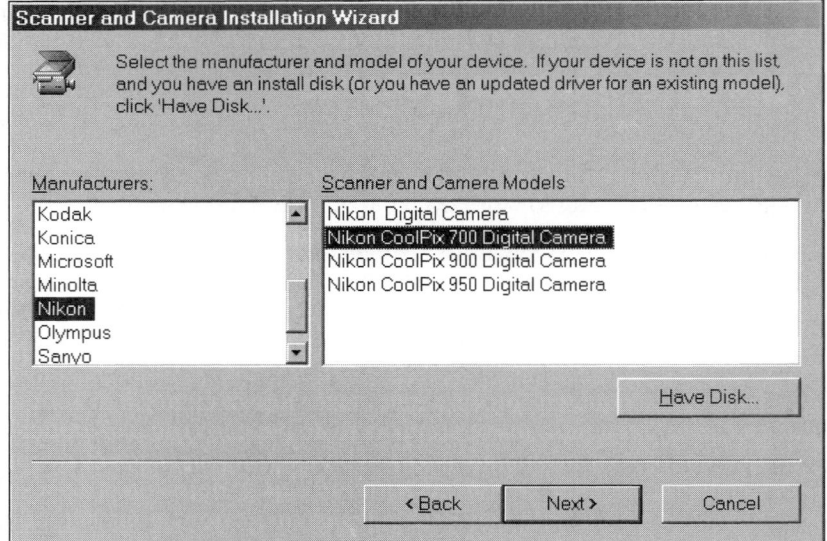

Figure 4-9: The Scanner and Camera Installation Wizard. Select the manufacturer and model of your camera from the list, or click the Have Disk button.

Only USB or Firewire cameras appear on this list (and no scanners); for other devices, you'll need to have a driver (or download one from the manufacturer's Web site), then click the Have Disk button and follow the directions. If a driver for your specific model is not listed, try the generic driver for that manufacturer — for example, Olympus Digital Camera or Epson Digital Camera.

In the next screen, select a port to use and click Next. Give your device a name that will appear in the Scanners and Cameras folder, click Next, and then click Finish.

If you have been using a SCSI or USB scanner, your driver will most likely be replaced by a WIA driver when you update to Windows Me. You will see a new WIA dialog box when you use the device to acquire an image. Some manufacturers offer more functionality in their own drivers than in the WIA drivers they provided to Microsoft. Check your manufacturer's Web site for a newer WIA driver, follow the instructions on the Web site to download it, then run the Scanner and Camera Installation Wizard using the Have Disk button to install the manufacturer's driver. If you install a non-WIA driver for a Windows Me-supported device, it may not work very well — and Plug and Play will probably reinstall the WIA driver next time you start your computer.

Link an Application to a Scanner or Digital Camera

If your scanner or camera supports the WIA standard, you can link it to an application on your computer. This is similar to what happens when you click a data file in the Explorer — you click the file, the linked application begins automatically, and your file opens. Now you can launch an application with your new image displayed by pressing a button on your camera or scanner. Not all applications will work this way, but newer versions of the most popular imaging applications should support WIA functionality.

STEPS

Link Your Camera or Scanner to an Application

Step 1.   Click Start ➪ Settings ➪ Control Panel. If necessary, click "View all control panel options" in the left portion of the pane, then double-click Cameras and Scanners.

Step 2.   Right-click the scanner or camera you want to use and select Properties. Click the Events tab. (If this tab does not appear, this device does not support linking to an application.)

Continued

STEPS

Link Your Camera or Scanner to an Application *(continued)*

Step 3.   In the Scanner Or Camera Events list, click the event that will open the program — for example, pressing the Scan button on your scanner.

Step 4.   In the Run an Application list, click the program that you want to start when this event occurs. Click OK.

Taking Pictures

After a scanner or camera is installed on your system, you can use the Scanner and Camera Wizard to take photos or make scans. Click Start ➪ Programs ➪ Accessories ➪ Scanner and Camera Wizard to launch the Wizard (it won't appear in your Start menu unless you have one of these devices installed) — or navigate to the My Pictures folder and click "Get pictures from a scanner or camera." Select a device from the list and follow the wizard's instructions to crop your picture and change its brightness, then save the new image on your computer.

Chat About Graphics

The MSN Graphics Connection Forum is a combination of articles, artwork, and chat designed to answer your questions about computer graphics and art, provide links to shareware, and feature computer artists and their work. You'll even find reviews of products from other sources than Microsoft. The Message Board seems to be primarily made up of beginners, so don't be shy. You can reach the Connection Forum at `http://www.computingcentral.com/topics/graphics/`

Windows Media Player

Media player is a pretty generic term — any media played by just one software device. Well, at least you know where to go. The problem with this approach is that you get a generic interface that perhaps isn't the best for the particular media type that you are playing. Look around your home and notice the difference between your CD player and your TV.

Version 7 comes with Windows Me and is also available for Windows 98. If you have Windows 98, you can download it from the Microsoft Web site at `http://www.microsoft.com/windows/windowsmedia/en/Download/default.asp`.

The Media Player is also a specialized Web browser that lets you one-button click to Microsoft's radio and media guide sites. Microsoft continues to tie its tools to its Web sites, for obvious reasons.

Playing Your Audio CDs

When we tested the Media Player before Windows Me was released, it had great difficulty identifying any of the CDs that we chose to listen to. It was quite annoying to see the Media Player window announce that we were listening to an unknown album by an unknown artist.

The Microsoft Deluxe CD Player, which was distributed with Windows 98 Plus! in 1998, did a much better job of identifying CDs using databases available on the Web. We assume that the Media Player isn't using those databases because it wants to use Microsoft's partners' databases and thereby allow Microsoft to collect advertising income. Since this is a Web content issue, the results you get may vary over time and are not necessarily contingent on what version of Media Player you have.

You can find CD databases at a number of sites. Check out http://www.cddb.com/. We understand that Microsoft uses http://www.allmusic.com. Perhaps someday it will live up to its name.

You can't install the Microsoft Deluxe CD Player from the Plus! CD-ROM onto your Windows Me system because the Plus! CD-ROM thinks that there is an incompatible version of Windows on your computer and gives you an error message when you try. However, you can copy the /Program Files/Plus!/DeluxeCD folder (and contents) from a Windows 98 computer to your Windows Me computer, and now you have a CD player that is fun to use and that knows who it is listening to.

There are many other nice little CD players available as freeware and shareware on the Web. We are sure that you will have no trouble finding them. For example, http://www.ghlsoftware.com/index.html. You can also check at http://software.mp3.com/software/. We also suggest http://www.winamp.com/getwinamp/. You may also have one that was included with your sound card.

The Media Player does have some advantages over the Microsoft Deluxe CD Player when it comes to playing CDs. The major one is that it can copy (rip) your CDs to your hard disk. As it copies your CDs to your hard disk, it also compresses them so they don't take up as much room.

There was no need for compressing the music on the CD as it has 720MB of room to store all ten or so songs. If you can compress the music and not lose quality, then it makes sense to do so when you store it on your hard disk. You have a choice of how much compression (and loss of quality) to use when you store your CDs.

The Media Player will also check your CDs for certain kinds of errors (scratches, etc.) and try to correct them. Since CDs have a habit of going bad, copying your CDs is one way to help preserve them.

There are, of course, many other products that will let you copy your CDs to your hard disk—for example, `http://www.streambox.com/`. Just click the StreamToolBox button. This one will cost you, so why not go with the free one that Microsoft gives you (unless you have other requirements). Also, check out `http://www.audiograbber.com` and `http://www.poikosoft.com/cdda`.

Microsoft claims that you can listen to your CDs as you copy them. Didn't work for us, even when we did digital copying (the default). Microsoft claims that digital copying is faster and allows visualizations (think of these as your computer on drugs) to beat in time with the music when played off the hard disk. Since visualizations also work when music is played off your CDs, we didn't quite get the difference between analog and digital copying.

If you want to change the format of the music copied to your hard disk, check out the Shuffler Music Converter at `http://www.illustrate.org/music-converter.htm`. You can convert wma (Windows Media Audio) files to mp3 files and vice versa.

Copyright and Copying Music

The Media Player has a built-in license management system, which will let you copy music onto your hard disk and then onto portable music devices that adhere to the music industry standards for licensing music. You can't copy music to these portable devices unless you use the Media Player's license management system.

The default is to "Enable personal rights management," when copying from a CD to your hard disk (see Tools ⇨ Options ⇨ CD Audio). If you clear this checkbox, then you can copy the tracks from the CD onto your hard disk without worrying about a license. You can also copy these wma files to another computer and play them using the Media Player (or other player) on that computer. You won't be able to copy the wma files to another computer unless you uncheck this checkbox.

If you uncheck the "Enable personal rights management" checkbox, you won't be able to copy your copied CD tracks to a portable device that adheres to the SDMI standard.

It is possible to transfer your music licenses between computers. Here's how:

STEPS

Moving Your Music Licenses to a New Computer

Step 1. In the Tools Menu, choose License Management.

Step 2. Change backup directory to a shared folder on the network.

Step 3 Click Backup Now to backup licenses to the shared folder.

Step 4. On a second computer, using either Windows Me or Windows 98 Second Edition, download and install the Windows Media Player 7 Beta.

Step 5. Confirm that you cannot play the Wma files that you stored on your first computer on the second computer by trying to play one of the Wma files.

Step 6. In the Tools Menu on the second computer, choose License Management.

Step 7. Change the backup directory to the same place where you stored the backup License Management files.

Step 8. Click Restore Now.

Step 9. Confirm you can now play the Wma files without error.

Thanks to Robert Rudeseal for these instructions.

Listening to Internet Radio

Click the Radio Tuner button and the Media Player becomes a front end to the http://windowsmedia.com/radiotuner/ Web site. You can visit the site using Internet Explorer, and get the same functionality that you'll find in the Media Player. Actually, we found somewhat better performance from this Web site when we contacted it with the Internet Explorer than when we used the Media Player. Probably just a coincidence.

The Microsoft Media Guide

Click the Media Guide button and you are transported to `http://windowsmedia.com/mediaguide/`, Microsoft's Media Guide Web site. You can also view this site in Internet Explorer, although it looks a bit different. Try `http://windowsmedia.com/MediaGuide/default.asp?page=0&WMPFriendly=true` and it will look the same in Internet Explorer as it does in your Media Player.

Apple's QuickTime Video

If you have `mov` files, video files made with Apple's QuickTime video creator, it is best to play them with the Windows QuickTime player and not the Microsoft Media Player. The Media Player will play QuickTime version 2 files, but this format is now quite old, so recent QuickTime files will not be in this format.

Zach, a Microsoft support technician for the Media Player states, "The Windows Media Player is technically incapable of using most of the Quick-Time v3 or later codecs. It also cannot play QuickTime VR files. The acid test is to attempt to play back any QuickTime file encoded using the Sorenson codec. This will fail in all versions of Windows Media Player."

Windows Media Creation

If you want to create Windows media files for your own use or to place on your Web site, check out the Windows Media Development Center at `http://msdn.microsoft.com/workshop/cframe.htm?949453562292#/workshop/imedia/windowsmedia/default.asp`.

Also, you can download Windows Media Tools at `http://www.microsoft.com/windows/windowsmedia/en/technologies/tools.asp`.

You can use the Windows Media Encoder to create very compact `asf` files from `wav` files. These can in turn be played on the Media Player. The `asf` file will also be much more useful for downloading from a Web site.

Compressing CD Audio

You can use the Microsoft Media Encoder to compress raw CD audio files. One 4-minute song of 44.1K 16-bit stereo is about 42MB. The Microsoft Media Encoder will compress this file to about 1MB or 40:1, and provide almost CD quality.

Compressing `mp3` files at about 20:1 produces files that are larger than the `asf` files produced by the encoder, and of lesser quality.

You can use this encoder with Sound Forge, or with Windows Media Tools.

Save That Streaming Media

If you are listening to streaming audio or watching a streaming video, you may want to capture that media content and save it on your hard disk. Often, the authors of the content don't want you to do this, so that the Media Player won't let you store the content if it is formatted so as not to be storable. To try to store a given stream while you are listening to it, click File ⇨ Add to Library ⇨ "Add currently playing track."

Get Rid of the Little Window in the Lower Right-Hand Corner

You'll notice that if you apply a skin — a different appearance for the Media Player — that gets rid of the boxy Media Player window, that there is now an extra little control window in the lower right-hand corner of your Desktop. This is a convenient control that allows you quickly to get back to the "full" mode of the Media Player.

You can get rid of this pesky little window by clicking (in the full mode, of course), Tools ⇨ Options, clicking the Player tab, and clearing the "When in compact mode, always display anchor window" checkbox. Click OK.

New Skins

You'll be able to download new skins for the Media Player from the media guide as well as at `http://www.microsoft.com/windows/windowsmedia`.

If you want to create new skins, download the software development kit at `http://www.microsoft.com/windows/windowsmedia/en/wm7/SDK.asp`.

DVD and the Media Player

One media player that appears to be missing in Media Player is a DVD player. This normally will come from the manufacturer of your DVD player. Perhaps Microsoft will add this feature in an update.

You Oughta Be in Pictures

Windows Movie Maker (called Media Pad in prerelease versions) is a tool for recording, editing, organizing, and publishing video and sound images — either images that you capture yourself or ones that you import over the Internet. It is designed for people who want to be able to save and play home movies on their computers, post movie clips on their personal Web sites, and e-mail clips to their friends. If you want to do serious video production, even as a hobby, you will probably be happier with the more full-featured commercial software that is already available. Still, this little toy makes a very handy addition to Windows multimedia and capabilities.

Movie Maker requires more computing power than the minimum for running Windows Me. You must have a Pentium II 300MHz computer or better with 64MB of RAM and 2GB of free hard disk space. To make the software really usable, you should also run with a screen resolution of at least 800×600.

To capture original video, you must first install video capture hardware. You can record video outside of Movie Maker using any number of products, save it as an mpg or avi on your hard disk, and import the file into Movie Maker. If you want to record from within Movie Maker, you must use a supported IEEE 1394 digital video camcorder, USB Web cam, or analog video capture card. If you're purchasing hardware to use with Movie Maker, you'll probably have the most success with devices that use an IEEE 1394 connection, also known as Firewire (or Sony iLink). For trouble-free installation, make sure your device is OHCI (Open Host Controller Interface) compliant. Check the Windows Movie Maker Help for a specific list of supported capture products. These products will most likely come with their own video editing software — but you will probably still want to use Movie Maker for publishing your videos because it produces much smaller files and lets you set the video quality.

To achieve this, Movie Maker saves your completed movies in the wmv file format. Using wmv, you can store nearly 23 hours of video per gigabyte of hard drive. A 30-second MPEG clip that we downloaded took up over 8MB in its raw form, but less than 500K as a medium-quality wmv. This makes it practical to e-mail short movies to your friends without crashing their mail servers, and to put home movies on your Web site. You will notice a degradation of resolution at medium quality, but at high quality the same movie was quite acceptable and still only took up a little over 1MB.

Your wmv movies will require Windows Media Player 6.4 or above to be viewed. People not running Windows Me will need to download the new version of Media Player from Microsoft. See "Windows Media Player" in this chapter for details on the latest version.

Claus Martel points out that if you only want to convert an avi file to the smaller wmv format, you can use Microsoft's Windows Media On-Demand Producer. However, Movie Maker gives you more flexibility in choosing the quality of the end product. You can download Media On-Demand Producer from http://www.Microsoft.com/windows/windowsmedia/en/ technologies/tools.asp#Down.

One big complaint about Movie Maker: you don't have a choice whether to install it and can't uninstall it in the normal way. Microsoft intentionally left Movie Maker out of the Windows Setup list in Add/Remove Programs. To permanently delete the Movie Maker executable file, choose Start ➪ Run, type **deltree /y "\program files\movie maker"** and click OK.

Capture the Raw Materials

Click Start ➪ Programs ➪ Accessories ➪ Windows Movie Maker to launch the main Movie Maker window, shown in Figure 4-10.

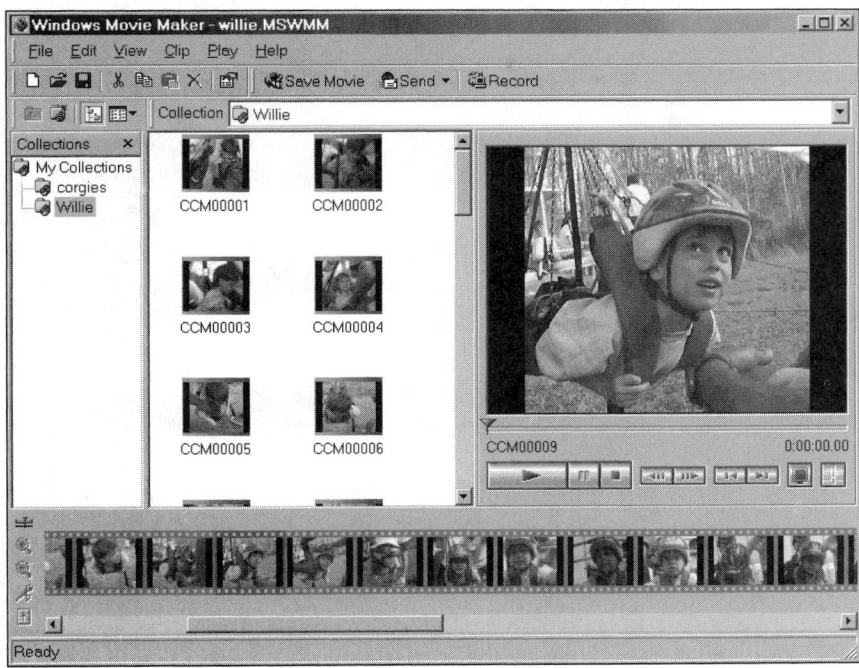

Figure 4-10: The Windows Movie Maker main window. The contents of the selected collection are viewed as thumbnails. The storyboard is visible along the bottom; the selected image is shown on the monitor.

Movie Maker uses collections to organize the raw materials you use to make movies — video, sound, and image files. The files themselves can be stored anywhere on your computer or your network. You can see a list of your collections in the Collections pane; create a new empty collection by right-clicking My Collections and choosing New Collection, or by clicking the New Collection button on the toolbar. Highlight a collection and you see a list or thumbnail of its contents (click the Views button on the toolbar to set how the contents are displayed). You can drag and drop the contents of a collection into another collection, or into the workspace, which runs along the bottom of the window.

Highlight a collection and choose File ➪ Import to import one file or a group of files. You can import and edit video files that use mpg, mp2, and avi formats — but not Apple's proprietary QuickTime mov format. You can also import wav, au, mp3, and other audio formats, and still images in bmp or jpg formats. Use the audio files to give your movie a sound track. Combine a series of still images to make a slideshow movie.

Highlight a collection and click the Record button on the toolbar to launch the Record dialog box, shown in Figure 4-11. This lets you record directly from a Web cam or other video or audio source.

Figure 4-11: The Record dialog box, set up to record video clip

Before you start recording, make sure that you have the correct video and/or audio source shown in the upper left-hand corner — use the Change Source button if you need to select a different device. Set the quality to the highest quality you can conveniently work with; you can save a movie later at lower quality, but you can't go back and improve the quality of your source material.

Tip

To take a still photo from a video source, click the camera icon that appears under the Preview screen. The photo will be saved in jpg format. You can set the length of time this photo will take in View ➪ Options ➪ Set Image Duration, in the main Movie Maker window.

Tip

Video capture performance is very dependent on the speed of your hard disk. If you experience poor-quality video captures, try running Defrag on your hard disk. You may also find that using mono sound settings will improve your video.

If you installed Windows Me as an update and already had video capture software installed, you are probably still using the drivers provided with your hardware manufacturer. This can affect resolution, among other things. Try updating your driver with one from the Windows Me CD-ROM, or check the manufacturer's Web site to see if a Windows Me driver has been developed.

Depending on the features of your video capture hardware, you may be able to adjust saturation and grayscale while you are recording. Not all hardware manufacturers support doing this in software, however. To change these settings, click Change Source ➪ Advanced. Movie Maker does not offer any way to retouch photos or videos after you capture them.

To have Movie Maker divide your video into short clips as it records, check "Create clips" in the lower left-hand corner of the Record dialog box. Movie Maker will detect changes in lighting or background to divide your recording into clips for easier editing. Later, you can use Clip ➪ Combine in the main window to recombine two neighboring pieces of a clip that you didn't want to have divided.

Get the Project Going

Whether you imported a video or captured it, the default is for Movie Maker to divide the content into short clips, based on changes or transitions it detects. The purpose is to make them easier to work with; you can turn off automatic clip creation by choosing View ➪ Options, and clearing the "Automatically create clips" checkbox.

To play a clip, click it in the collections pane or in the Workspace; it appears in the Preview monitor. Click the Play and Pause buttons on the monitor, or use your spacebar to start and stop the preview.

To put individual clips together into a movie, select the clips you want in the collections pane (as you would in an Explorer window), then drag and drop them onto the empty Workspace. To put all the clips from a collection into the storyboard, simply drag the collection's icon from the collection pane into the storyboard (thanks to Steve Weatherford at Microsoft for pointing this out). You will see the first "frame" of each clip (after all, these aren't real movies with real frames). Work you do on clips in the Workspace does not affect your source material; for example, you can delete clips from the Workspace without deleting them from the collection or from your hard disk.

Your source material was saved on your hard disk at the end of your recording, or when you imported it. But to save your clips together in a specific order, you must put them into the Workspace and save them as a project by choosing File ➪ Save Project. Projects are saved with the (rather daring) five-character extension *MSWMM*. A project is still not a movie, but it is a movie-in-progress that you can continue to edit. Unlike a movie, a project can be opened and modified in Movie Maker.

From Project to Movie

You can view the Workspace as either a storyboard or a timeline, depending on the editing you want to do. Use the Storyboard feature to split, combine, and delete clips. Use the Timeline feature to see how long each clip is and how it synchronizes with the soundtrack. To switch between views, click the top icon button at the left end of the Workspace.

To preview your entire project, press Ctrl+A to select all the clips in the Workspace, then press the spacebar or click the Play button in the Preview window to see the action. In the Storyboard view, the current clip is high-lighted while it plays. If you are using the Timeline view, a moving vertical line indicates your progress in time. Click a point on the timeline to preview that image in your movie.

You are actually fairly limited in the kind of editing you can do in Movie Maker. You can add, remove, and rearrange clips in a project by dragging and dropping them in the Workspace. You can split clips and join clips that were recorded next to one another. And, you can trim individual clips.

To trim a clip, it's often easiest if you work in Timeline view. Select the clip you want to trim, and press the spacebar or the Play button to begin playing it; press the spacebar again to pause at the place you want to trim. Select Clip ➪ Set start trim point. Now continue playing the clip and pause at the part you want to trim out — then select Clip ➪ Set end trim point. To clear your trim points, select Clip ➪ Clear trim points. Any trimming you do will only affect your project, not your original clip.

To add a soundtrack to your project, first either import a sound file (a wav, au, or mp3, for example), or use Movie Maker to record and save audio. Your sound file appears in the collections area as an audio clip (if you recorded sound with your video, the audio clip will already appear there). Drag and drop your audio clip onto the Workspace; the view will switch to Timeline if you weren't using it already. You can slide the clip around on the audio bar to match a specific clip or time, and you can drag the trim handles for the clip in the time bar to make it fit your video. To use two simultaneous audio clips (words and music, for example), drag one on top of the other. If you make a mistake, select an audio clip and press Delete to remove it from your Workspace and start over.

Tip

You can record a narration directly into your project. Once you have the video clips the way you want them, click the button with the Microphone icon, located just to the left of the audio bar in the timeline; you can watch a preview of the video while you narrate. Of course, you must have a microphone installed in order to record.

When your movie is complete, you can publish it. To save the movie file on your own computer, select File ⇨ Save Movie. If you want to distribute your movie on the Internet, choose File ⇨ Send Movie To, and select either E-mail or Web Server. Regardless of which you choose, you will see the dialog box shown in Figure 4-12.

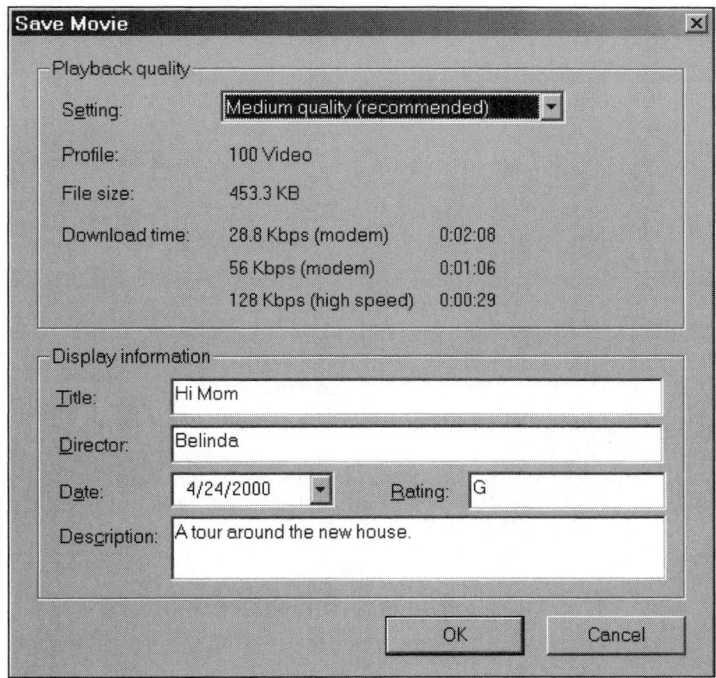

Figure 4-12: The Save Movie dialog box. This is the place where you choose the resolution at which your movie will be viewed.

Use the Setting drop-down list to choose a quality (resolution) for your movie. The dialog box shows you how big your wmv file will be, and how long it will take to download at various modem speeds. If your file is over 1MB, you may not be able to send it by e-mail. You can also save additional information about the content of your movie. The display information that you enter will not appear when you play the movie on your own computer, but it will appear when your movie is played on the Internet.

The Preview window in Movie Maker is designed for editing, not playback — for example, you can't see what your movie will look like at a specific resolution. To see exactly what everyone else will see, save the movie on your computer and use the Media Player to preview your movies before your send them out. (Thanks to Adam Zilinskas for this tip.)

Get Rid of MSN Messenger

Some people love it, some hate it. MSN Messenger Service can be a handy thing to have around if you like to chat in real time with your remote friends. What really bugs people, though, is to be forced to activate MSN Messenger — including signing up for a passport — if all they want to do is get it out of their system trays. If you've already activated MSN Messenger but don't use it, it's easy enough to disable. Open MSN Messenger and click Tools ➪ Options. On the General tab unmark the "Show icon in tray option" and the "Start MSN Messenger automatically" option, then click OK.

To get the MSN Messenger icon out of your tray without activating it first, follow these steps:

STEPS

Disable MSN Messenger Service

Step 1. Click Start ➪ Run, type **msconfig**, then click OK. The System Configuration Utility opens.

Step 2. On the Startup tab, uncheck the box for MSMGS.

Step 3. Click Apply, then OK, and restart your computer as directed. (You must click Apply; this won't work if you just click OK.)

To really, permanently make MSN Messenger go away, use Add/Remove Programs in the Control Panel. On the Windows Setup tab, select Communications and click Details. Unmark the MSN Messenger Service box and click OK twice.

Let Your Computer Hibernate

Hibernate saves everything in RAM to your hard disk, then turns off your disk drive, monitor, and battery if you have one. It is different from Standby, which saves power but doesn't save any documents or settings. It does take longer for your computer to wake up from hibernation. With Hibernate, everything about your current work session is saved, without you having to save and close individual documents — even if the cat goes for a walk on your keyboard while you're gone. When you come back, quickly press the Power button to get back to work.

You can set your computer up to hibernate automatically after being idle for a certain period of time; that way, you're less likely to lose data if you are suddenly interrupted. You control the settings for Hibernate by using the

Power Options in the Control Panel (if you can't see this icon, click "View all control panel options"). If your computer supports Hibernate, you will see a Hibernate tab in the Power Options dialog box.

That's the only problem with Hibernate — it doesn't work with all hardware. If you buy a new computer with Windows Me installed, Hibernate should work fine for you. But you probably won't see a Hibernate tab at all if you purchase Windows Me separately and install it as an update. If you have SCSI devices on your computer, Windows Me detects that and disables Hibernate.

Tip

On an upgrade system, Hibernate is disabled but it's still there. Depending on your system, it may be possible to get Hibernate working. Open the file \Windows\NOHIBER.TXT, and see what it tells you. For example, it may say something like, "Hibernation support has been disabled for the following display adapter:" followed by information about the offending device. Check with your manufacturer to see whether there is a driver update that supports Windows Me for that device. If so, install it, and reboot, then open the Power Options in the Control Panel to see whether you now have a Hibernate tab. If yes, mark the "Enable hibernate support" checkbox and click Enter.

If you're using Internet Connection Sharing, the host computer is prevented from hibernating. This is by design, since a hibernating computer has no Internet connection to share. It's also a bad idea to Hibernate if you're using multiple operating systems.

Help for Internet Connection Sharing

If you've been struggling to get Internet Connection Sharing (ICS) to work on your home network, Tim Higgins may have some help for you. His Web site offers troubleshooting, tips, tutorials, articles, hidden features, and help for special situations such as a particular software application, a firewall, or a cable modem. You'll also find links to some ICS alternatives such as Sygate and WinProxy. You'll find all this at http://www.timhiggins.com/ppd/ics.htm.

Add FTP Servers

Two wizards have been added to My Network Places (what used to be called Network Neighborhood). The Add New Place Wizard lets you specify FTP servers as network places.

The functionality of the wizard was already available in Windows 98 Second Edition, and the wizard was added to make it more obvious how to access this functionality. Using this wizard, you can name an FTP server, and include your user name and password if required. Publicly accessible FTP servers allow you to logon as anonymous.

The FTP connection services provided by Windows are quite limited, but sufficient if you are just logging into public FTP sites. If you wish to use FTP to transfer files to your Web site, it is a much better idea to get another product, like Internet Neighborhood, which we discuss in Chapter 35. Internet Neighborhood integrates with the Explorer and makes it quite easy to manage your remote server.

Internet Neighborhood has been updated since we last wrote about it and now lets you transfer files between FTP servers, not just between your computer and an FTP server. It also is quite a bit more stable and user friendly.

USB 2.0

Windows Me doesn't support the USB 2.0 specification. USB 2.0 has a data transfer rate that is 40 times faster than the USB 1.1 specification that is currently supported. When Windows Me was released, there were very few USB 2.0-compliant devices available.

Microsoft beta support personnel have stated that Microsoft will provide an update to Windows Me after it is released, which will allow it to support USB 2.0 devices and hubs.

Windows 98 and Me have their own USB drivers (or use the drivers found on the manufacturer's diskette). If you are installing Windows Me from DOS, you'll have trouble with your USB mouse if you don't have support for it in your computer's BIOS. The USB BIOS support may be turned off on your computer.

To check your computer's BIOS for USB mouse support, you'll need to go to your computer's hardware setup screen during power-on self test.

Features That Aren't in Windows Me

In addition to USB 2.0 support (see above), there are a few other features that didn't make it into the first release of Windows Me.

Microsoft is expected to include many or all of these in a minor revision to Windows in 2001. Meanwhile, here's a list of features to keep an eye open for:

- **Intel SpeedStep (Geyserville) processor:** These processors shift speeds to respond to different power conditions (wall outlet, laptop running on batteries, and so forth).

- **Intel Willamette:** These processors upgrade the Pentium III line of CPUs.

- **IDE:** Windows Me doesn't include support for native-mode IDE, a fast connection for hard disks and other devices.

- **Bootable Firewire:** Firewire devices (also known as IEEE 1394 or Sony i.Link) that can be booted from as though they were a floppy won't be bootable until some update ships for Windows Me.

- **Swappable ACPI:** The Advanced Configuration and Power Interface (ACPI) has been supported by Windows for some time, but hot-swapping various devices in and out of the bays your computer may provide for them will have to wait for future support.

- **Gaming Control:** Parental control over what games can be played on Windows Me didn't make it into the box. Blast away until the next release.

Information on these and other Windows Me features is posted in Paul Thurott's e-mail newsletter, WinInfo, and on his Web site. Go to http://www.winsupersite.com.

Summary

Windows Me may not be the biggest upgrade in Microsoft history, but it still has some significant new features:

- System Restore provides Windows Me users with important reassurance that a buggy system can be put back right.

- DOS has gone through some major changes, mainly to keep Windows from booting up into real-mode DOS.

- Media support in Windows Me is enhanced with image acquisition software for scanners and digital cameras, and Media Player for streaming audio and video clips.

- MSN Messenger is now integrated with Windows Me, although some people prefer to remove it.

- Several features that many beta testers and others wanted didn't quite make it into Windows Me, but there's hope for future upgrades.

Chapter 5

The Desktop and the Taskbar

In This Chapter

Windows looks like an Internet browser as well as a Desktop with stuff just piled on top of it. It's two, two, two interfaces in one. You get to pick which to use. Here, we discuss the following:

▶ Arranging the icons on your Desktop the way you want them

▶ Replacing existing icons with new ones and fixing corrupted icons

▶ Changing the invisible grid that determines icon spacing

▶ Changing the font and font sizes used for icon titles

▶ Placing new blank documents on your Desktop ready to be opened by an application with a click

▶ Putting the taskbar where it will do you the most good

▶ Adding a Desktop toolbar

▶ Task switching between applications and folders using the keyboard

▶ Changing the appearance of the Start menu

What You See Is a Mess

Your wallpaper is the Desktop with stuff on it. The icons on your Desktop represent different applications and documents, sort of like a regular desktop. The taskbar keeps track of whatever you are currently working on (the icons for active applications now live there, whether the application is minimized or not). The Start button cascades to multiple menus that organize and reveal your applications and documents. The toolbars give you ready access to your favorite documents and applications. The clock . . . well, you can figure that out for yourself.

We discuss the Desktop and the Taskbar and its toolbars in this chapter. We also discuss some aspects of the Start button, but leave deeper details to "The Start Menu" in Chapter 9. Each of the icons on the Desktop has its own chapter — see "The Icons and Items on the Desktop" later in this chapter for more information.

First, Your Password

Before you can use Windows for the very first time, it prompts you to enter your name and password, as shown in Figure 5-1. Windows uses this information to differentiate you from other people who may share your computer and, most importantly, to remember all the other passwords that you will undoubtedly collect as you use this computer. Windows stores all your other passwords in an encrypted file that your other applications can access after you log on to Windows under your name and password. For example, because you log on as you, Outlook Express remembers your e-mail user name and password.

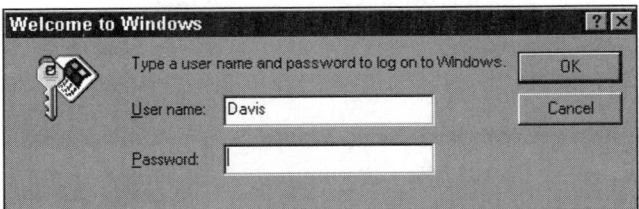

Figure 5-1: The user logon box

If you configure Windows for multiple users, it can remember different profiles for each person, and it uses each person's name and password to determine which configuration to display. If you are on a network, your name and password enable you to log on to network servers.

If you have multiple users on your computer, perhaps other family members, you can configure Windows to present you with a pick box when it first starts up. To log on, you can pick from among the designated users. We discuss the Windows Family Logon in "Logging onto the Network" in Chapter 18.

If you type a name and a nonblank password, this logon box will appear every time you start up Windows. You can make this logon box go away and not reappear the next time you start your computer by typing your name and then clicking the OK button without entering a password. You will be asked to confirm that you want a blank password. Click OK.

Tip

TweakUI lets you bypass the logon box and still enter a nonblank password. The logon box still appears when you first start Windows, but it goes away quickly. The first time you start Windows, enter a user name and a password. Then start TweakUI, click the Network tab, mark "Log on automatically at system startup," and enter your user name and password. (If you don't see TweakUI in your Control Panel, you can install it from the \tools\reskit\ powertoy folder on your Windows CD-ROM.)

While Windows lets you use user names and passwords, it is not a secure system. Other users can get into your computer by simply pressing the Esc key when asked for their name and password. You can, however, use the

System Policy Editor (see "The Icons and Items on the Desktop" section later in this chapter) and third-party software (see "Securing the Windows Desktop" in Chapter 6) to improve the security of Windows computers. Passwords, multiple users, and multiple Windows configurations are discussed in "Whose Desktop Is This Anyway?" in Chapter 6.

The Desktop

Part of the Windows user interface is based on the *desktop* metaphor. Your screen is turned into a graphical desktop with lots of little items on the desktop for you to work with.

In fact, the Windows Desktop doesn't look much like a real desktop, although it doesn't really matter whether it looks like one or not. The primary purpose of the Desktop is to provide a background on which to display graphical objects such as icons and windows. Your open applications and documents appear in separate windows on top of the Desktop.

With the advent of the World Wide Web, the computing world quickly adopted a new *hyperlink* metaphor, which was popularized by the browser software you use to navigate the Web. This metaphor emphasizes the connections (hyperlinks) between documents, both locally and globally.

Even before it released Windows 95, Microsoft realized that it was in its best interest to incorporate this approach into the part of the computer that it owns almost completely, the operating system. Microsoft's Internet Explorer browser is completely integrated into the Windows user interface. The new *Web style* view has expanded and morphed the Windows interface so that it takes on many browser-like characteristics.

For example, many of the same icons that are found in Windows 95 are there, but you can now single-click them instead of double-clicking. As you move your mouse pointer over an icon, it becomes a pointing hand, a familiar shape to anyone who has used a Web browser.

If you right-click an empty part of the Desktop, a context menu appears that lets you control the Desktop. This basic menu — it does change — is shown in Figure 5-2.

Secret

When the context menu is showing, you can only carry out the actions listed on that menu until you left-click (a right-click won't work) the Desktop or click (either left or right) in a window or someplace other than the Desktop. If your taskbar is hidden, it will not pop up as long as the Desktop context menu appears on the Desktop.

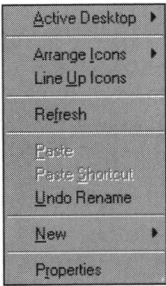

Figure 5-2: The Desktop context menu. Right-click anywhere on the Desktop to bring up the menu.

Click Properties to change many aspects of the Desktop. Move the icons around with Arrange Icons and Line Up Icons.

The Invisible Grid

There is an invisible grid on your Desktop. The icons on the Desktop are centered in the cells defined by this grid and placed on the left side of the Desktop, starting at the top of the screen. You can place the icons in other locations, although most are not as convenient as this default top/left positioning. You can also determine the size of the grid cells.

Arranging the Icons

To align your icons in the center of the grid cells, right-click the Desktop and then click Line Up Icons. Because you can line them up afterwards, you can drag icons to different parts of the Desktop and still have them look orderly when you are finished.

To arrange the icons in one of four predefined orders, right-click the Desktop, point to Arrange Icons, and then choose By Name, By Type, By Size, or By Date. The icons will arrange themselves starting in the upper-left corner and proceeding down to the next cell in the sort order specified. Additional columns of icons will be added to the right if there are more icons than can fit in the first column.

If you want the icons to always place themselves in columns starting at the left-hand side of the Desktop, right-click the Desktop, point to Arrange Icons, and then click Auto Arrange. Auto Arrange is a toggle switch; when it's active, you see a checkmark next to the command. If Auto Arrange is checked, the icons always move back into the columnar arrangement no matter where you move them or where you originally place them.

Secret

Auto Arrange does not sort the icons. When Auto Arrange is checked, you can specify the order for the icons by simply dragging them to new positions in the columns. If you move an icon to the right of the column(s) of icons, it gets placed at the bottom of the rightmost column.

If you turn Auto Arrange off (clear it), you can place icons wherever you like and in any order. If you don't want to be restricted to placing your icons in a particular order or location on the Desktop, don't use the Line Up Icons, Arrange Icons, or Auto Arrange commands. If you don't use these commands, you can drag and drop your icons wherever you like and space them as close together or as far apart as you want.

Changing the Size of the Grid

The grid starts in the upper-left corner of the Desktop. The vertical line that marks the right-hand edge of the first cell is so many pixels to the right of the left edge of the Desktop. The horizontal line that marks the bottom edge of the first cell is so many pixels below the top edge of the Desktop. The invisible grid is revealed in Figure 5-3.

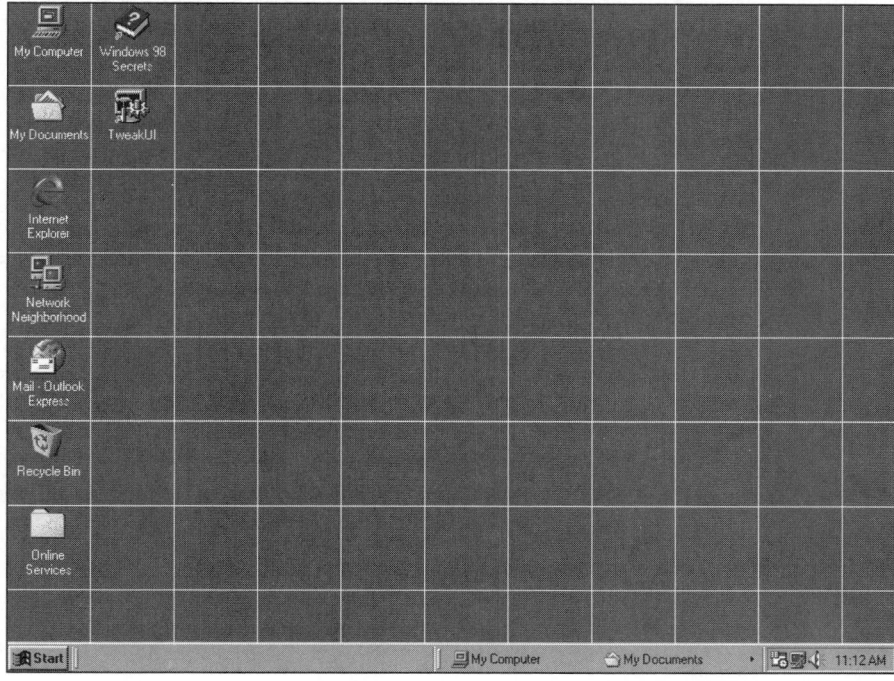

Figure 5-3: A faux icon spacing grid. The size of each cell in the default grid spacing in pixels (assuming a display magnification set at Small Fonts) is 75 pixels high and 75 pixels wide.

Secret

The size of the cells depends on the icon pixel size, icon spacing (both horizontal and vertical), and display magnification (Small Fonts, Large Fonts, or Other). The default cell size (for Small Fonts) is 75 × 75 pixels with a default icon size of 32 pixels and default icon spacing of 43 pixels (32 + 43 = 75). The grid in Figure 5-3 is set at 75 pixels high by 75 pixels wide.

You can change the size of the icon spacing grid by editing the vertical and horizontal icon spacing values. To do this, take the following steps:

STEPS

Editing Icon Spacing

Step 1.   Right-click the Desktop. Click Properties. Click the Appearance tab.

Step 2.   Click the drop-down arrow in the Item field to open up the drop-down list of Desktop items.

Step 3.   Click, one at a time, Icon Spacing (Horizontal) and Icon Spacing (Vertical).

Step 4.   Adjust the size of each — in pixels — using the spin controls in the Size field to the right of the Item field. (Click the up and down arrows or enter a new number value to change the size.) The total vertical size of the cell will be the sum of the icon size plus the vertical spacing. Horizontal size is calculated similarly.

Step 5.   To see what the effect is on icon spacing, click the Apply button when both sizes are adjusted. Keep adjusting icon spacing until you are pleased with the results.

Step 6.   Click OK.

If an icon's title text doesn't fit within the boundaries of the cell, Windows truncates the text and adds ellipses. If you make the vertical or horizontal spacing too small, the icons will overlap — not a good idea.

Secret

If you make the horizontal spacing of the cells too large, you may receive an "Explorer Caused a Divide error in Module Shell32.dll" error message. You'll know then that you've gone too far.

While the Desktop icons are created on a 32 × 32-pixel grid, you can blow them up to a bigger size. This may be useful if you have a high-resolution screen that displays 32 pixels as a very small physical size. Right-click the Desktop, click Properties, click the Effects tab, and mark the "Use large icons" checkbox. Click OK.

Changing the Font and Size of Icon Title Text

By default, the icon titles use the MS Sans Serif 8-point font (at 800 × 600 display resolution—higher resolution displays default to a 10-point font). You have the option of changing the font used to display the icon titles. You can also change the font's point size and make it boldface and/or italic. You can't change the text color to something other than black unless you set your Desktop to a dark color, in which case Windows automatically sets the text color to white.

Tip

MS Sans Serif is a *screen* font, which means that it has been designed to be readable at 96 or 120 pixels per logical inch. You can use any font that you want, including Arial, which looks a lot like MS Sans Serif but is a TrueType font. Check out the various fonts and choose one that you find easy to read.

If you increase the font point size, icon titles get bigger and may not fit in the grid cells.

To change the font used for the icon titles, take the following steps:

STEPS

Changing Icon Title Fonts

Step 1.   Right-click the Desktop. Click Properties. Click the Appearance tab.

Step 2.   Display the Item drop-down list.

Step 3.   Click Icon. You can change the Font and Size fields. You can also use the Bold and Italic buttons (see Figure 5-4).

Step 4.   Click the Apply button when you have chosen a font, point size, and so on, to see the effect of the choices. Keep adjusting these values until you are pleased with the results.

Continued

Editing Icon Spacing *(continued)*

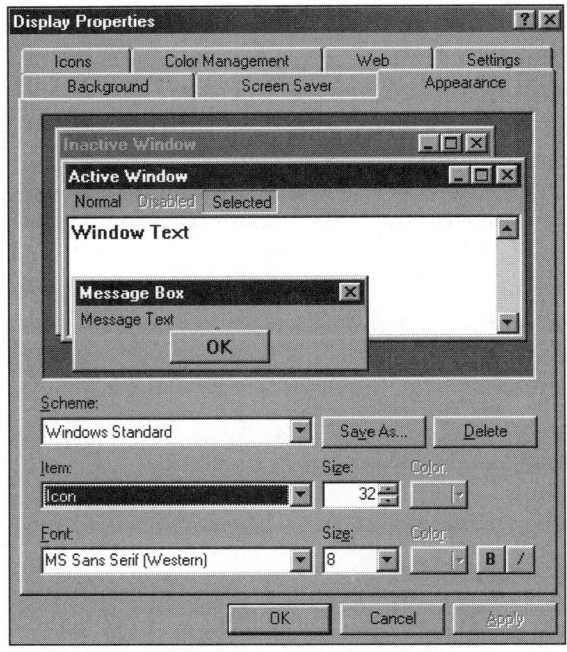

Figure 5-4: The Appearance tab of the Display Properties dialog box. Display the Item drop-down list and then choose Icon. Pick a font style from the Font drop-down list and a point size from the Size field. The B and / buttons stand for bold and italics.

Step 5.   When you are done, click OK.

Putting New Items on the Desktop

It is easy to put new items, represented by icons, on the Desktop. You can place new (empty) folders, new shortcuts, or new (blank) documents on the Desktop. By default, you can create new documents of these types: Internet Document (HTML), Text, WordPad, Bitmap Image, Briefcase, Wave Sound. And if you like, you can add more document types to the list, or remove document types from the list. (You learn how to do this in "Adding Items to the New Menu" in Chapter 12.)

When you create a new shortcut (right-click the Desktop, point to New on the context menu, click Shortcut), a wizard starts that guides you through the process of linking your new shortcut to an application. When you install new applications, they often add their own document type to the New menu. You can edit the list of types in the New menu using the steps detailed in the "Adding Items to the New Menu" section in Chapter 12.

Tip

Placing new blank documents on the Desktop is a pretty nifty feature and contributes to the document-centric character of Windows. When you click a new document icon on your Desktop, Windows brings up the appropriate application and opens the blank document within it so that you can edit the document. To add new document icons to the Desktop, right-click the Desktop, point to New, and then click the document type that you want to add.

The new documents don't necessarily have to be empty or unformatted. You can create forms or certain subtypes of documents, such as "my standard format letter," and use them as a basis for creating new documents.

Pasting and Undoing Actions

The Paste command on the Desktop context menu lets you copy (or move) a file (or application, folder, or shortcut) to the Desktop. For example, if you want to copy a file to the Desktop, you first select a file in a folder window or in the Explorer. Then you right-click the file and choose Copy, which means "copy this file to someplace as soon as I tell you where." Finally, you right-click the Desktop and choose Paste to tell Windows, "this is where I want you to copy the file." (We discuss folder windows, the Explorer, and shortcuts in "Copying and Moving Files and Folders" in Chapter 7, and "Cut and Paste a Shortcut" in Chapter 10.)

Windows includes the Paste command in context menus for a variety of other (yet to be investigated) Desktop icons. As you can see, the Cut, Copy, and Paste commands (and functionality) have made their way out of the word processor and into the operating system.

Your Desktop context menu might include an Undo command below the Paste command. The specific Undo command that appears depends on what actions you have taken in folder windows. If you have just renamed a file, for example, you will see the Undo Rename command. If you have just deleted a file, you will see the Undo Delete command.

The Undo command shows up in the Desktop context menu (and in most context menus) whenever you have taken an action that can be undone. If you remember what it was that you did and you want to undo it (as long as you haven't quit and restarted Windows), here's your chance.

Change the Automatic Font Color

Secret

Here's a Desktop change that also makes a change in your other programs. Right-click your Desktop, click Properties, and click the Appearance tab. In the Item field, scroll down to and highlight Window. You can now set the Fonts color. It is defaulted to black.

This item changes the color of the fonts used in windows. Since Windows uses windows all the time, this is a pretty major change. In addition to changing the font color used in the system windows (Windows windows), programs that use the "automatic" font color use this setting to determine their default font color.

You can check this out by changing the Windows font color and then opening WordPad (Start ⇨ Programs ⇨ Accessories ⇨ WordPad). You'll see that the default font color (that is, the color of the characters you type in the WordPad client window) is the color that you just chose. In WordPad, you can choose another color than the default. This is true in some other programs as well, but not in Notepad. In Notepad, the font in a new document automatically has the new color, and you can't change it.

Unstretch that Wallpaper

Secret

Numerous Windows users have reported trouble getting their wallpaper to stretch, center, or tile. Usually, the Background tab of the Display Properties dialog box (right-click your Desktop, click Properties) has a Display drop-down list in the lower-right corner. Some users don't have this drop-down list.

Dialog boxes are often just user front ends to the registry. If you don't have this particular front end, you can make the changes in the registry yourself.

STEPS

Setting Wallpaper to Center, Tile, or Stretch

Step 1. Start your Registry Editor and navigate to HKEY_CURRENT_USER\Control Panel\desktop, as shown in Figure 5-5.

Step 2. Double-click the WallpaperStyle variable in the right pane of the Registry Editor.

Step 3. Change the value to 0 for centered nonstretched wallpaper, 1 for tiles, or 2 for stretched. Click OK and then close the Registry Editor.

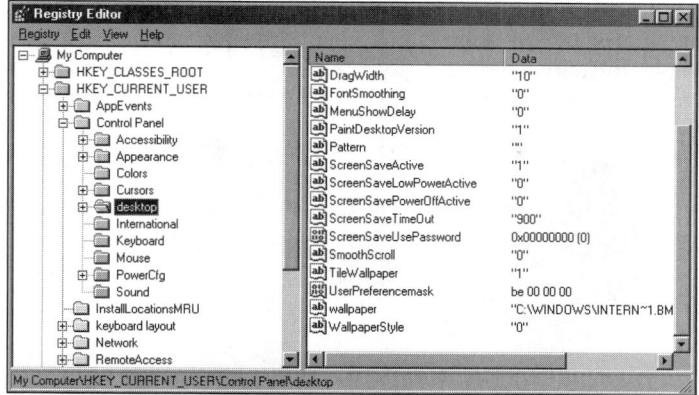

Figure 5-5: The registry location for changing your wallpaper style

Thanks to Penelope Baker for pointing us toward this secret.

Animate Your Desktop

You can place animated gif files on your Desktop and let them play over and over and over again. Animated gif files are graphics files that contain multiple images that are displayed one after another to simulate motion. You can create animated gif files with Paint Shop Pro. You'll find the latest version at http://www.jasc.com. You can also use the GIF Construction Set found at http://www.mindworkshop.com/alchemy/gifcon.html.

To allow your Desktop to play animated gif files, you need to take the following steps:

STEPS

Putting Animated GIFs on Your Desktop

Step 1. Right-click your Desktop, and choose Active Desktop, Customize My Desktop.

Step 2. In the Web tab, mark "Show Web content on my Active Desktop."

Step 3. Click the New button, and then click No.

Step 4. In the New Active Desktop Item dialog box shown in Figure 5-6, click the Browse button and navigate to an animated gif file. We're assuming that you have already stored this file on your computer or network. Click the Open button. Click OK twice.

Continued

Putting Animated GIFs on Your Desktop *(continued)*

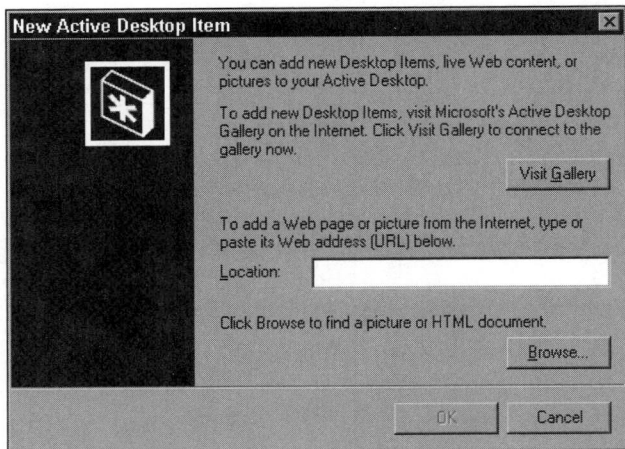

Figure 5-6: Type the name and path of the gif file that you want to put on your Desktop.

Step 5.   Move your mouse pointer over the animated g i f, and when the gray title bar appears, drag it to move the g i f window to the desired spot on the Desktop.

Thanks to Mike Adams for help with this tip.

Your Active Desktop Doesn't Find Its Content

Secret

If you're using the Active Desktop, and your on-the-Desktop Web page or ActiveX components don't show up when you first turn on your computer, it's probably because they're waiting to see if there's an update. They want to go check on the Internet to see if newer information is available. If there isn't a connection to the Internet, they're standing around waiting.

You probably want them to update the Active Desktop based on what's stored in the Internet Explorer cache, since you haven't made the connection to the Internet yourself. You'll have to make a change in the Internet Explorer configuration to get the Explorer to find its Active Desktop content. Here's how:

STEPS

Waking Up Your Active Desktop

Step 1. Right-click the Internet Explorer icon on the Desktop, click Properties, and then click the Connections tab.

Step 2. Make sure the correct dial-up connection is highlighted as the default in the "Dial-up settings" list (see Figure 5-7). To change the default, click the name of the dial-up connection in the list, and then click the Set Default button.

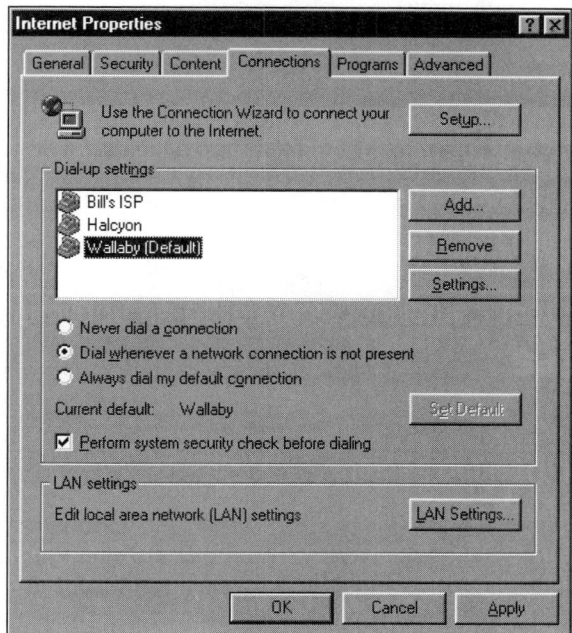

Figure 5-7: Set the dial-up connection that you want to use as the default, if necessary.

Step 3. Mark either "Always dial my default connection" or "Dial whenever a network connection is not present." Click OK.

Change My Documents

The My Documents folder (regardless of its actual name) is a special folder used by Windows as the likely target for storing your files when you open up a File Save dialog box. Of course, you can subdivide this folder into subfolders that reflect documents of particular types, subject matter, or whatever.

Windows puts a My Documents folder icon on your Desktop, giving you a handy way to get to your documents. It's actually a special type of shortcut, called a *shell extension shortcut*, that points to the My Documents folder. Some of you may find this additional Desktop icon a bit annoying, and feel that Microsoft is pushing you to organize your documents in a manner that doesn't match your predilections.

You can do a few things to turn this capability into something more comfortable. It is cool that the operating system wants to help you get to your documents quickly. However, it would be nicer if it did it your way.

Secret

The first change you might make is to rename your My Documents folder. Just right-click your C:\My Documents icon in your Explorer under your boot drive letter designator (not on the Desktop), click Rename, and give it a new name.

To check that the special folder once called My Documents has a new name, right-click the My Documents folder icon on your Desktop, click Properties, and find the new name of the folder in the Target field (see Figure 5-8). Now you can also change the name of the My Documents folder icon on the Desktop; just right-click it and click Rename, and enter a new name.

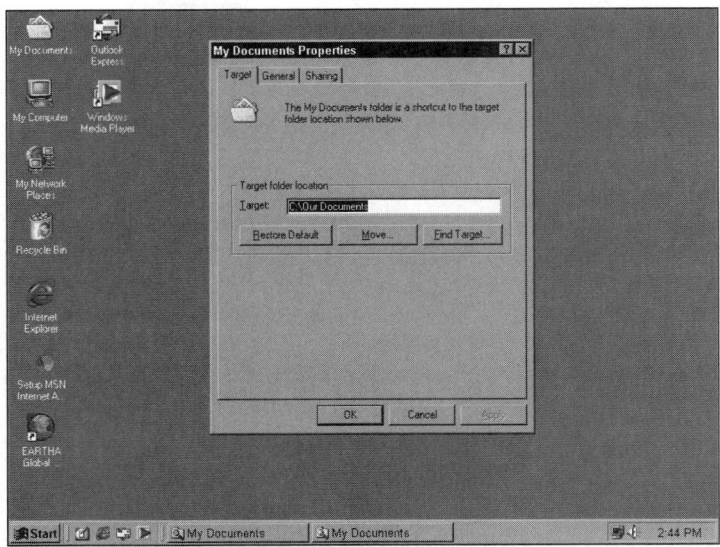

Figure 5-8: After renaming the My Documents folder, its new name appears in the Target field of the Properties dialog box for the My Documents icon on the Desktop.

You may find that some existing shortcuts to documents in your My Documents folder no longer work, but you can edit them to use the new path and filename. Also, previous document paths inside of Word won't work, so you'll have to browse for the previously opened files that were stored in the My Documents folder when it was named My Documents.

Tip

Instead of renaming your existing My Documents folder, you can choose to designate another folder as your My Documents folder. Just use the Target field in the Properties dialog box for the My Documents folder icon to specify the new folder. You can then delete the former My Documents folder in your Explorer. Be sure to move any document files from it first and put them in your newly designated My Documents folder, whatever its actual name.

Get Rid of the ToolTips in Caption Buttons

The caption buttons are the three buttons in the upper-right corner of a window — Minimize, Maximize, Close. So, if you already know what those buttons do, do you need to be reminded again?

If not, click TweakUI in your Control Panel, click the General tab, scroll down the Effects list, and clear the "Mouse hot tracking effects" checkbox.

Write Notes Right on Your Desktop (Sort of)

Take a look at Figure 5-9 and see how the text and the surrounding line are right there on the Desktop. Well, it looks that way anyway.

Figure 5-9: A sticky note without the paper

Screeble (screen + scribble, get it?) takes a shot of your Desktop and then places it right over the Desktop. Now you can paint and type on the Screeble screen. Right-click and click Exit to get back to your Desktop.

You'll find Screeble at `http://village.infoweb.ne.jp/~tek/`.

Tweaking the Windows Desktop

WinBoost allows you to change the name of the Internet Explorer (as displayed on its title bar) to whatever you like. WinBoost can do quite a bit more damage to your orthodox Windows user interface, if you like things your way (see Figure 5-10).

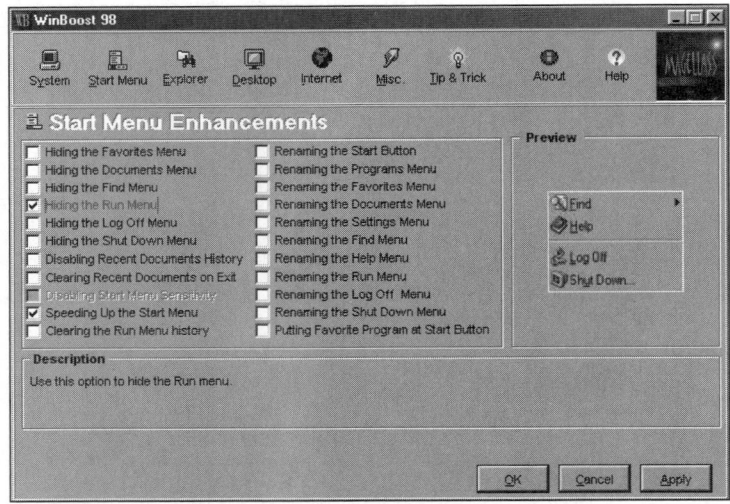

Figure 5-10: The Start Menu Enhancements screen in WinBoost gives you a good idea of its potential for changing things to suit yourself.

The enormous range of tricks the authors of WinBoost have found to tweak Windows is too great to summarize, but here are a few examples of what you can do:

- Hide, disable, or rename various parts of the Start menu, such as Recent Documents (if you don't want people to see the documents you've recently worked on), Favorites, Find, Run, Log Off, and Shut Down.

- Rename the Start button.

- Place a variety of cascading menus on your Start menu, including the contents of Control Panel, Printers, My Network Places, Recycle Bin, My Computer, Fonts, and Briefcase.

- Customize your CD-ROM cache memory (in ways you can't with the Control Panel).

- Optimize your file system for running multimedia applications.

You can also make your Explorer refresh with each change, view nonassociated files with Notepad, and change the Internet Explorer animated logo.

After you've experimented with WinBoost's various productivity improvements, you can play with one of its "nonproductivity" enhancements, a way to cheat at the MS Hearts game included with Windows.

In the Tips and Tricks list, the authors of WinBoost show that Microsoft apparently started to implement something called a DeskBar, but then crippled the feature before shipping Windows. To see this undocumented feature, click Start ⇨ Settings. While holding down your Ctrl key, click Taskbar & Start Menu. In the Taskbar Properties dialog box that appears, you'll see a new DeskBar Options tab. If you click it, however, you'll see that the tab is empty and there is no way to change any settings.

WinBoost 1.24 is a 1.2MB download from the Magellass Corp. at http://www. magellass.com/main.html. It has a 10-day trial period, after which the product is $15 per user or $145 for a site license.

Yet another little tweaker can be found at http://www.windows-help.net/wtt/. Not as powerful or extensive as WinBoost, Tweaking Toolbox for Windows does give you a couple of extra options (see Figure 5-11). For example, you can get rid of some options in the Display Properties dialog box, remove the File System and Virtual Memory buttons from the Performance tab of the System Properties dialog box, edit MS-DOS mode options, and get rid of the Users control panel.

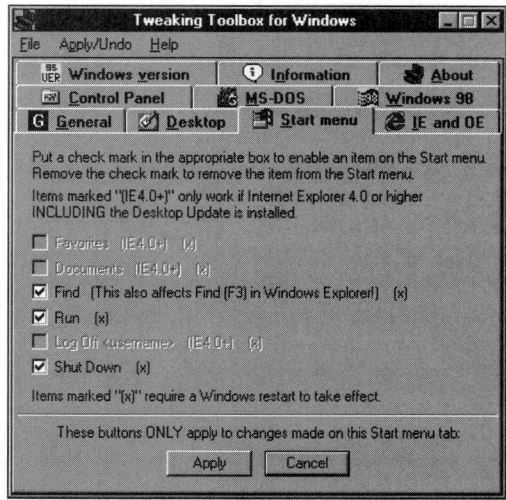

Figure 5-11: The Start Menu tab of Tweaking Toolbox for Windows. Compare its features with those of WinBoost in Figure 5-10.

Virtual Desktops with Desktop Plus

It's hard to get everything on a 15-inch screen, especially when you have multiple applications open. You can press Alt+Tab, you can click the taskbar buttons, or you can set up *virtual desktops* (as though yours wasn't virtual to begin with).

Desktop Plus lets you set up to nine virtual desktops (see Figure 5-12). You can switch between them via hot keys, the Desktop Plus floating toolbar, shortcuts (on the Desktop, Start menu, or Quick Launch toolbar), or icons in your system tray.

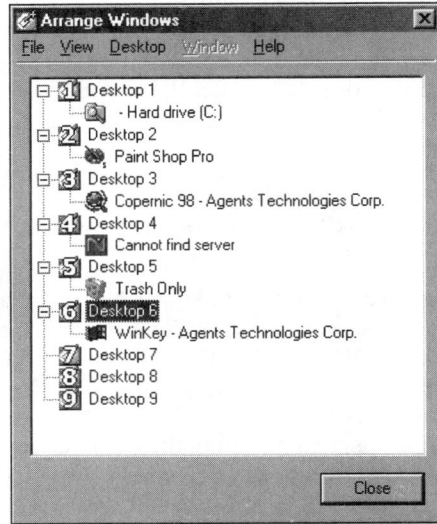

Figure 5-12: Use the Arrange Windows dialog box in Desktop Plus to determine what will be on each of the nine virtual desktops.

You'll find Desktop Plus, where else, but at http://www.desktopplus.com.

TweakUI, the Desktop, and the Control Panel

TweakUI allows you to eliminate extra icons from the Desktop and the Control Panel. It's not particularly hard to do this, and not particularly secret either. But, once you removed some items from these areas, you might forget about the functionality that you've lost. Just a warning.

There are plenty of good reasons to remove icons from the Desktop and Control Panel. For example, the old Windows 98 Service Pack 1 added the Universal Serial Bus icon to your Control Panel, even if you don't have USB installed on your computer. It's kind of irritating to have this useless icon reminding you of its uselessness every time you open up your Control Panel.

To remove any item from the Control Panel (and easily put it back), click the TweakUI icon (for example, in your Control Panel), and then scroll over to and click the Control Panel tab. Clear the checkboxes next to any Control Panel items that you'd rather not see for now, as shown in Figure 5-13.

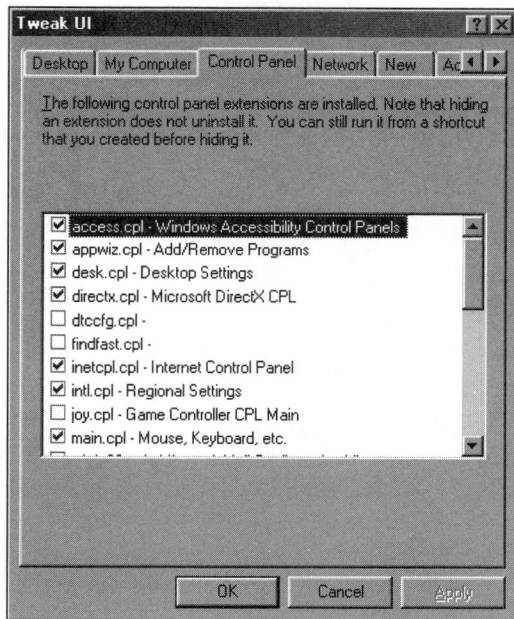

Figure 5-13: The Control Panel tab of TweakUI lets you easily remove and replace Control Panel icons.

The Desktop icons get similar treatment. Click the Desktop tab to display a list of the icons that TweakUI thinks are available to the Desktop. The only problem is that TweakUI may find some that are out-of-date, or doubles of the same one (see Figure 5-14). Don't worry about these discrepancies. Just clear and mark the checkboxes in this dialog box (and click the Apply button) until you see what you want on your Desktop. You can also use TweakUI to fiddle around a bit with the Desktop icons. Right-click any of the items in the Desktop tab to see what you can do. You might rename the Recycle Bin, for example.

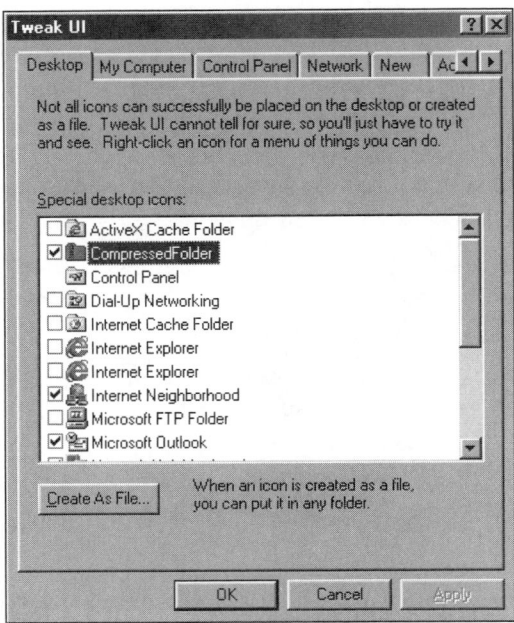

Figure 5-14: In this example, TweakUI displays two copies of Internet Explorer — we've cleared both.

Remember that removing the My Network Places icon from the Desktop removes the associated functionality (why, Microsoft?) from the Explorer also.

Replace the Explorer Shell

Would you like to try a different user interface? Something without shortcuts on the Desktop? Perhaps multiple Desktops? Maybe a pop-up Start menu? X mouse?

You can easily replace the Windows Explorer shell (or Desktop or user interface) with any other shell that folks have a mind to create. The LiteStep development team developed a freeware shell that resembles AFTERSTEP, a Linux shell. It uses a vertical bar called the Wharf to dock your application icons (see Figure 5-15), and a taskbar to hold your system tray and active task buttons (see Figure 5-16). By default, the Wharf is on the right side of the Desktop, and the taskbar is at the bottom.

Figure 5-15: Litestep's Wharf holds application icons.

Figure 5-16: Litestep's Taskbar holds active tasks as well as the system tray.

Right-click one of the squares at the bottom of the Wharf to switch from virtual desktop to virtual desktop. Click an icon on the Wharf to reveal additional program icons. Right-click anywhere on the desktop to get an expanded version of the Start menu (called the PopUp menu).

All of your Windows resources are available (other than the shell), so you can invoke an Explorer window, get to the Control Panel, call any of your applications, and so on. When you install LiteStep, it finds all of the shortcuts on your existing Start menu and puts them on its PopUp menu.

Unfortunately, LiteStep doesn't search your Desktop for shortcuts and add them to the Wharf. And the Wharf includes plenty of icons for software that you may not have on your computer. In addition, we found that the Wharf kept moving over to the left and not sticking to the right edge of the screen. To edit the Wharf, you need to edit the text file Step.rc, unless a user-friendly utility has been developed recently.

To install LiteStep, extract the zip file that you download from http://www.litestep.net into the C:\litestep folder (you'll need to create this folder first). We tried to put it into C:\Program Files\litestep, but even after editing the LiteStep resource file (Step.rc) we couldn't get LiteStep to start from this folder.

You also need to edit your System.ini file in your \Windows folder. The required editing is simple. Just put a semicolon (;) at the beginning of the line shell=Explorer.exe, and type the following line after this line: **shell=c:\litestep\litestep.exe**. Save your System.ini file and restart Windows.

If you get an error message that says you have to reinstall Windows, don't panic. Just click OK, and restart your computer. Insert your Windows Me startup disk and choose Minimal Boot to go to the DOS command prompt. Change directories to your \Windows directory (type **cd\Windows** and press Enter). At the DOS prompt, type **edit system.ini** and press Enter. You can now remove the semicolon in front of the line shell=Explorer.exe and place one in front of shell=c:\litestep\litestep.exe. Save System.ini and restart Windows. This changes your user interface (shell) back to the Windows Explorer interface.

Want to change the look of the Explorer title bar? You'll find eFX, which lets you do just that, at http://www.litestep.net. This site also offers lots of other utilities to change the look of your LiteStep (and standard) interface.

Turn Your PC into a Mac over the Internet

Just for fun, check out http://www.yaromat.com/macos/index.htm. We don't tell you what to expect there because that would spoil the fun. It won't hurt.

If you really do want to make your Windows computer look a lot more Mac-like (and why not), download some of the icons and other things that you'll find at http://www.gjeffrey.com/mac/downloads.html /. This will make those of you who have switched from the Mac to the dark side a bit more comfortable with your choice. Sort of like old home week!

Some folks didn't like the iMac, so they created the iHate iMac site. You can download their iMac Recycle Bin icon and Desktop from `http://www.iamlost.com/imac`.

Replace the Explorer Shell with the Macintosh Interface

If you are interested in using the Macintosh user interface on your Windows computer, you might want to give the freeware MacVision a try. It transforms your Desktop and your taskbar into the Macintosh desktop and Finder bar. Here's what the MacVision Web site claims:

The MacOS Finder bar—MacVision is very useful, since it can replace your taskbar! Instead of using the old Windows taskbar, you can use its fully functional MacOS Finder bar (the bar at the top of the screen on MacOS computers) that has dynamic menus that change with every application. Every aspect of the Finder bar is emulated with great attention to detail—everything looks, works, and acts how it should in Macs, right down to the flickering of the menu items when selected on custom-made MacOS-style menus!

That's just what it did. The author keeps improving it and is working on a MacOS 8.5 version.

You'll find MacVision at `http://members.aol.com/JMB1984/MacVision`. Thanks to Chris Pirillo at `http://www.lockergnome.com` for telling us about it.

Feeling Frustrated?

Has Windows got you down? Share it with others who are probably in the same mood at `http://www.ihatewindows98.com/frames/`.

Pretty much just a long list of rants from the little people, but there are some fun parts (and we wish there were more). Any site with the word *hate* in the name is going to have a tough time being "light." Then, for some folks this is a religious issue.

The Icons and Items on the Desktop

The icons that first appear on the Desktop stand for powerful Windows functions. They are discussed in later chapters. The My Computer icon is discussed in Chapter 8. The Recycle Bin is covered in Chapter 13. The Internet Explorer icon is covered in Chapter 26.

The great thing about the Desktop is that there are icons on it. If you're upgrading from Windows 3.1*x*, you'll notice that the Desktop takes over much of the function of the Windows 3.1x Program Manager. Put up a digitized photograph as your background and the icons hang there in space on your Desktop. In contrast, the Windows 3.1x Program Manager presented a rather boring background for your program groups (unless you had a specialized wallpaper application).

You can put any icon on the Desktop that you want. It is much more natural to put your stuff on the Desktop than it is to be constrained to the confines of the Program Manager. We discuss this in a lot more detail in "Put Your Favorite Files and Programs on the Desktop" in Chapter 10.

You can use the System Policy Editor to get rid of all the icons on your Desktop or to just get rid of the My Network Places icon. (Turn to "System Policy Editor" in Chapter 18 to see how to install the System Policy Editor.) To use the System Policy Editor, take the following steps:

STEPS

Getting Rid of All the Icons on the Desktop

Step 1. Install the System Policy Editor from the Windows CD-ROM. You'll find it in the \tools\reskit\netadmin\poledit folder.

Step 2. Click the Start button, point to Programs ⇨ Accessories ⇨ System Tools, and then click System Policy Editor.

Step 3. Double-click the Local User icon in the System Policy Editor window. Choose File ⇨ Open Registry.

Step 4. Click the plus sign next to the word Shell, and then click the plus sign next to the word Restrictions.

Step 5. Click the "Hide all items on desktop or hide My Network Places" checkbox.

Step 6. Click OK. Choose File ⇨ Save from the System Policy Editor's menu bar. Then choose File ⇨ Exit.

Step 7. Restart Windows.

If you want to selectively choose which icons to display on the Desktop, use TweakUI instead of the System Policy Editor. This is a much preferred method because it allows you to quickly change your mind about which icons you want to display. Click your TweakUI shortcut on your Desktop (or click the TweakUI icon in the Control Panel), click the Desktop tab, and then mark or clear any of the checkboxes.

New Icons for Desktop Items

You can choose new icons to replace the default ones that come with your Desktop. The Windows CD-ROM comes with all the themes that were first released on the old Microsoft Plus! CD-ROM. Each theme includes different icons for the Desktop items in keeping with the theme. For example, the Mystery theme uses a deerstalker cap to represent My Computer. There are also many themes available for downloading on the Internet (lots with copyright infringement warnings written all over them). See http://www.winfiles.com.

If you want to choose your own new icons instead of using the default Windows icons, you need to do manually what the themes application does automatically: You have to edit the registry. Of course, to do this you also have to find a source of new icons.

Icons are stored in some executable files (files with exe extensions), in some dynamic link libraries (files with dll extensions), in icon files (files with ico extensions), and in special icon libraries.

You can change four of the Desktop icons by right-clicking your Desktop, clicking Properties, clicking the Effects tab, highlighting My Computer ⇨ My Documents ⇨ My Network Places or Recycle Bin (full or empty), clicking the Change Icon button, and browsing for icons.

You can also use the File Types tab of the Folder Options dialog box to search an individual file for icons:

STEPS

Looking at Icons

Step 1.   Click My Computer. Choose View ⇨ Folder Options, and then click the File Types tab.

Step 2.   Click any file type in the Registered File Types list. Click the Edit button.

Step 3.   Click the Change Icon button. The icons you see under Current Icon are contained in the file listed in the File Name field. To see icons in other files, click the Browse button. You can now search for another file that contains icons. (For more on searching for a file, turn to "Creating and Editing File Types and Actions" in Chapter 12.)

Step 4.   Be sure to click the Cancel buttons when you are done looking at icons.

To replace the Desktop icons, you can edit your registry as follows:

STEPS

New Icons for Old

Step 1. Click My Computer. Click the drive icon for your hard disk. Click your Windows folder icon. Click Regedit.exe in the \Windows folder. (To find out more about the registry, turn to "The Registry Editor" in Chapter 11.)

Step 2. Using the Registry Editor, click the plus signs in the left pane to navigate to HKEY_CLASSES_ROOT\CLSID. Click the plus sign next to CLSID.

Step 3. To change the My Computer icon, scroll down the left pane of the Registry Editor to {20D04FE0-3AEA-1069-A2D8-08002B30309D}. This is the Class ID for the My Computer object. Click the plus sign next to it and highlight DefaultIcon in the left pane.

Step 4. Double-click Default in the right pane. Type the name of the file that contains the icon you want to use instead of the existing icon. Follow the complete path and filename with a comma and then a number representing the icon's position in the file. (You can determine an icon's position using the "Looking at Icons" steps above. In Step 3, the icons in the Current Icon box are numbered from left to right, top to bottom, beginning with 0 for the upper-left icon.)

Step 5. Click OK, and then exit the Registry Editor.

You can change the icons of the other Desktop items by going to the following Class IDs in Step 3 of the "New Icons for Old" steps:

My Network Places	{208D2C60-3AEA-1069-A2D7-08002B30309D}
Dial-Up Networking	{992CFFA0-F557-101A-88EC-00DD010CCC48}
Printers	{2227A280-3AEA-1069-A2DE-08002B30309D}
Briefcase	{85BBD920-42A0-1069-A2E4-08002B30309D}
Control Panel	{21EC2020-3AEA-1069-A2DD-08002B30309D}
Internet Explorer	{FBF23B42-E3F0-101B-8488-00AA003E56F8)
Outlook Express	{DACF95B0-0A3F-11D1-9389-006097D503D9}
Microsoft Network	{00028B00-0000-0000-C000-000000000046}

Recycle Bin   {645FF040-5081-101B-9F08-00AA002F954E}

Windows Messaging   {00020D75-0000-0000-C000-000000000046}

The Recycle Bin has two icons, one for empty and one for full. Double-click *empty* and *full* in the right pane of the Registry Editor to assign new icons to each of them.

Make Your Own Icons

You can easily make your own icons, just by using MS Paint. Here's how:

STEPS
Making Your Own Icons

Step 1.   Click Start ⇨ Programs ⇨ Accessories ⇨ Paint.

Step 2.   In the Paint window, choose Image ⇨ Attributes. Make the Height and Width 32 pixels, and click OK.

Step 3.   Click View ⇨ Zoom, and then Show Grid.

Step 4.   Click View ⇨ Zoom ⇨ Custom. Choose 800% and click OK.

Step 5.   Create your new icon. Save it as a `bmp` file. You can change its extension later to `.ico`, if you like.

Step 6.   You can now treat this file as a regular icon file. Following the "New Icons for Old" steps in the previous section, you can point to it and use it on your Desktop.

When you replace a Desktop icon with one you made yourself, you don't need to refer to it by anything other than its filename (see Step 4 under "New Icons for Old"). You don't need to use an index number (in this case, 0) because there is only one icon in the file.

High Color icons

While icons were originally limited to 16 colors, you can now have 16-bit (High Color, or 64 thousand colors) or 24-bit (True Color, or 16 million colors) color icons. If you create your own icons with MS Paint, you can choose the color depth.

To display High Color or True Color icons, you need a video card with enough memory at a given resolution. Right-click the Desktop, click Properties, and then click the Settings tab. Check the Color drop-down list to find out what your color depth is. If you have enough memory, you'll see High Color (16 bit) and/or True Color (24 bit) in the list. If you don't see these values, reduce your screen resolution using the Screen Area slider. Then choose either High Color or True Color from the drop-down list and click OK.

Once you've set your color depth to High Color or True Color, you can enable your Desktop to display High Color or True Color icons. Right-click your Desktop, click Properties, click the Effects tab, and mark "Show icons using all possible colors."

If you choose High Color or True Color, you also get gradient fills in the title bars of your dialog boxes.

Get Rid of Unattached Desktop Icons

Secret

If you have icons on your Desktop that you can't get rid of, there is still hope for you yet. We're not talking about My Documents, My Computer, My Network Places, and the Recycle Bin. You can use TweakUI and click the My Desktop tab to take the Recycle Bin and the My Network Places icons off the Desktop. We discuss how to deal with all of these icons in topics throughout this book.

No, we mean icons that got there when you installed a piece of software, and didn't go away when you deleted it. If right-clicking the icons and clicking Delete doesn't work, and you can't see what is creating them, then we've got a spot in the registry where you might just find them.

Open up your Registry Editor and navigate to HKEY_LOCAL_MACHINE\ SOFTWARE\ Microsoft\ Windows\ CurrentVersion\ explorer\ Desktop\ NameSpace. There you'll find a set of Class IDs, as shown in Figure 5-17.

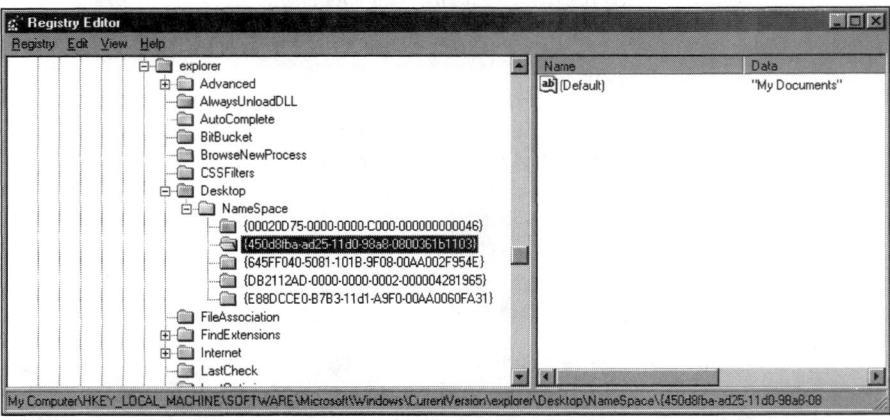

Figure 5-17: The Registry location of the NameSpace Class IDs

Highlight NameSpace in the left pane, and click Registry ⇨ Export Registry File. Enter the name for this text backup of this branch, perhaps **NameSpace**, and click Save. If later you delete something that you'd rather not have deleted, you can get it back by importing this file.

You can highlight each one of these Class IDs and see if there is a corresponding application name displayed in the right pane. If there is a name that corresponds to the software that has been deleted from your computer, you can highlight the Class ID and then delete it.

If you have installed Outlook 98 or 2000, it has a Class ID in the NameSpace for its Desktop icon (the Class ID starts with 00020D75) but no name in the right pane.

If you're considering deleting a Class ID and want to search first to see if there are other instances of it in the registry, you can do that. If you want to find all the instances quickly, use Registry Crawler, as discussed in "Crawl Through the Registry" in Chapter 11.

If you find other instances of this Class ID, you can see if they refer to program executables that are now deleted. If so, you can delete these branches of the registry.

Deleting the Class IDs from the NameSpace will delete the icons from the Desktop.

Thanks to Alex Nichol for pointing out this secret.

Altered Icons

Scrows Icons is a very cool Web site for finding icons to replace those that come standard with Windows. We thought you'd get a kick out of the slightly altered standard icons, as shown in Figure 5-18.

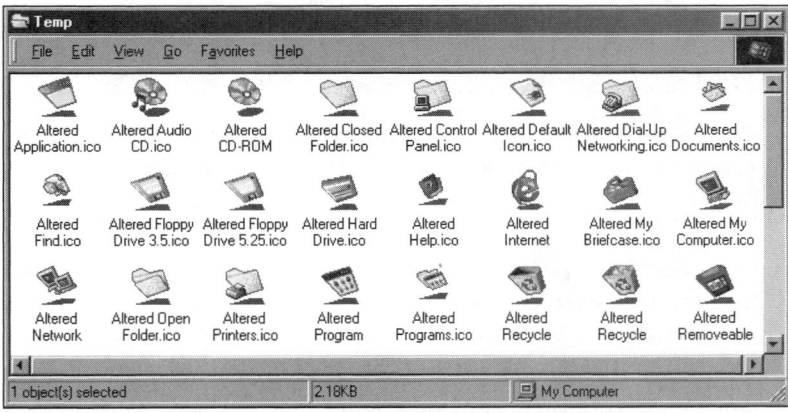

Figure 5-18: No need to use the same old boring icons!

You'll find these icons and many more at `http://members.xoom.com/scrows/`. You can edit the icons using a shareware program such as Microangelo (`http://www.impactsoft.com`) or Microsoft's Image Editor at `http://msdn.microsoft.com/developer/sdk/sdktools.htm`) (you'll have to download the whole set of SDK tools).

An Icon Library that Includes Macintosh Icon Conversion

IconShop is a wonderful icon library generator that is free, small (only 31K to download), and fast. Better yet, it can convert Macintosh icons so that you can use them on Windows computers. To use IconShop, you can just drag and drop a file or folder onto its client window. The icons extracted from the file (or from the files within the folder) will be displayed, as shown in Figure 5-19. You can then save them to an icon library.

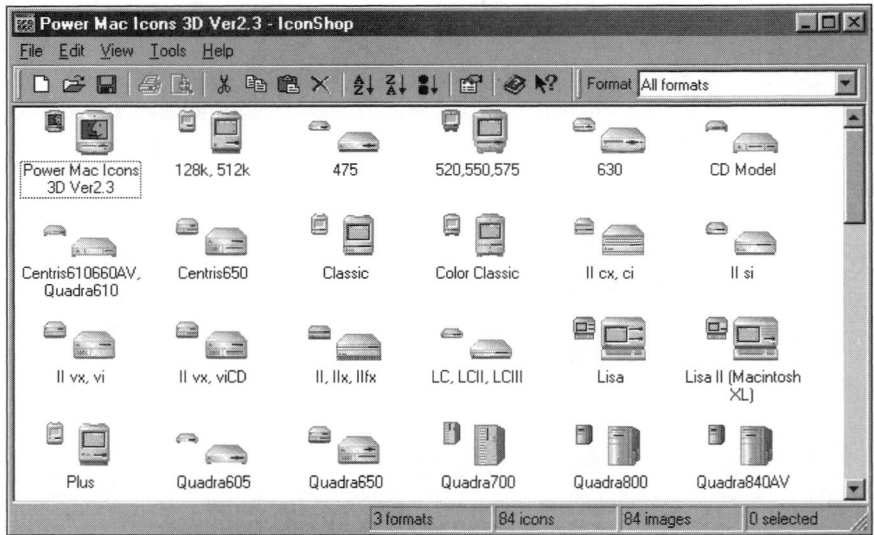

Figure 5-19: IconShop displaying Macintosh icons in All Formats mode, which displays both 16 × 16 and 32 × 32 icons. Only if both sizes of icons are available in the source file are both formats displayed.

Like most icon library generators, IconShop can get bogged down if you try to extract thousands of icons at once. We suggest that you create only a few icon libraries by being selective about which folders you drop on the IconShop window.

You'll find Macintosh icons on the Web — just search for mac icons. You also might try `http://www.iconfactory.com`.

Mac icons often come packed in StuffIt (`sit`) and/or BinHex (`hqx`) format. WinZip can handle `hqx` files, but not `sit` files. You'll need another expander for these ones. Download the free Aladdin Expander for Windows from `http://www.aladdinsys.com/expander/expander_win.html`. To expand your downloaded Mac icons, simply drop them in Expander's client window.

When you first run Aladdin, it asks if it should be the application associated with a number of extensions. You can clear all these extensions and still have it open `sit` files. The Aladdin Expander defaults don't work. Follow the instructions in the IconShop help file (found in the index under *mac icons*) to set up the Expander to correctly expand the Macintosh icons.

Tip

Aladdin also has a shareware product, Aladdin DropStuff, that makes it easy to compress and send files back and forth from a Windows computer to a Macintosh. You'll find it at `http://www.digitalriver.com/AladdinDSWin10/Win`. It's a mere $20.00.

Once you've expanded the Macintosh icon files, they show up as folders in your Explorer. Drag and drop the top folder to IconShop, and then save the icons in an icon library.

You can also use IconShop with the Mac icons found at iconJam. This Web site represents collaboration among icon designers. It also contains lots of links to other Mac icon sites. You'll find iconJam at `http://forthnet.freethemes.com/themeicons/screens/misc/iconjam98.htm`.

Thanks to Chris Pirillo at `http://www.lockergnome.com` for pointers to a few of these sites.

Remove the Block of Color behind the Names of Your Desktop Icons

If you are using wallpaper as the background of your Desktop, you'll no doubt notice that there is a rectangular block of color behind the icon's name. Annoying, isn't it? Well, if you aren't using wallpaper, or if this situation doesn't annoy you, you might as well go on to the next section.

Not sure just what we are talking about? Check out Figure 5-20. The Desktop icon on the left has the colored background, and the one on the right doesn't. You can change the appearance of your icons with a little (and we mean really little) freeware program called Transparent. This tool gives you a surprising amount of control over just how you want your icon names to look. It comes in four versions (all 25K in size). `TransparentW.exe` makes the icon text white, `TransparentB.exe` makes the text black, `TransparentD.exe` lets you set the icon text color, and `Transparent.exe` lets you use a slew of command-line switches.

Figure 5-20: Transparent lets you make your Desktop icons look like the one on the right.

The easiest thing to do is extract the four files from the downloaded Transparent zip file into a temporary folder, move the one that you want to use to your \Program Files\Accessories folder, and then drag this file from the Accessories folder to your \Windows\Start Menu\Programs\ StartUp folder. Because it's an exe file, you won't move the file to the Startup folder; you'll create a shortcut there.

Click the Transparent file after you have moved it to your \Program Files\ Accessories folder and it will immediately take effect. From now on, when you restart Windows it will be called from the Startup folder. It takes up very little memory and CPU resources.

You'll find Transparent at http://www.pobox.com/~jayguerette/ transparent.

Corrupted Desktop Icons

If your Desktop icons get sick, you can refresh them. Windows 98 stores all the icons on the Desktop in a file named ShellIconCache, which is stored in the \Windows folder. It is a hidden file, so be sure to choose View ⇨ Folder Options in your Explorer or My Computer window, click the View tab, and mark "Show hidden files and folders" if you want to see the file listing. Windows caches the shell icons in this file so that it can access them quickly instead of having to search through all the files that hold these icons every time it starts up.

Secret

You can refresh the icon cache by deleting ShellIconCache from your \Windows folder. To do this, first restart your computer in MS-DOS mode or exit to MS-DOS mode. Then type **del ShellIconCache**. (If you type **dir sh*.* /a** at the DOS prompt while in the \Windows folder, ShellIconCache will show up as Shelli~1.) Exit MS-DOS mode and restart Windows. The ShellIcon Cache file is automatically rebuilt from the original icons in their source files.

It's even easier to rebuild your icons using TweakUI. Just click the Repair tab, highlight Rebuild Icons in the drop-down list, and then click the Rebuild Now button.

Increase the Size of Your Icon Cache

Secret

If you find that the icons on your taskbar keep changing, it may be because your icon cache is too small to keep copies of all the icons.

You can increase the size of your icon cache by taking these steps:

STEPS

Increasing Your Icon Cache Size

Step 1. Click Start ➪ Run, type **regedit**, and press Enter.

Step 2. Navigate to HKEY_LOCAL_MACHINE\ SOFTWARE\ Microsoft\ Windows\ CurrentVersion\ explorer. Highlight this key in the left pane of your Registry editor.

Step 3. Right-click the right pane, and choose New ➪ String Value.

Step 4 Rename the string value **MaxCachedIcons**.

Step 5. Double-click MaxCachedIcons in the right pane, type the value **2048**, and click OK.

Thanks to Tom Porterfield for this secret.

Scraps

Some Windows-aware applications can place *scraps* on the Desktop (or in any folder window). You can try this out using WordPad. Open up a WordPad document. Select some text. Drag and drop it onto the Desktop.

An icon with the name Scrap appears on the Desktop. This is a document that can be read by WordPad. It is made up solely of the text that you dropped on the Desktop. Click its icon on the Desktop, and WordPad launches.

Scraps give you an easy way to pile up a bunch of notes or graphics on your Desktop (or in any other folder) and then make something of them later. For example, you might want to put a scrap containing your company logo on the Desktop, and then paste it into documents as you edit them. Scraps give you an alternative to the Clipboard, and the advantage of using them is that you can keep multiple pieces available at one time.

It is also possible to store a bit of boilerplate text in your tray on the taskbar. (See the section entitled "The Tray on the Taskbar" later in the chapter.) You'll need to download a small shareware application to be able to do this. You'll find TrayText at http://www.mjmsoft.com/traytext.htm.

The Taskbar and Its Toolbars

The first time you start up Windows, the taskbar displays little more than the Start button, the Quick Launch toolbar, and a digital clock in the tray. The taskbar is the home of the *active* applications — those applications that you started by clicking a file or an application icon. There is a button on the taskbar (or an icon in the tray) for every major active application or window (it is possible for applications to hide their taskbar icons).

An application or a document needs to be read into memory from the hard disk before it can act or be acted upon. We refer to an application that has been loaded into memory as an *active* application. Applications that are stored on your computer's hard disk but haven't been loaded into memory are *inactive*. A document is loaded into memory with its application. There aren't any stray documents out there in memory without their associated applications.

Some applications don't put buttons on the taskbar or icons in the tray. These "hidden" applications run in the background and aren't looking for any user input. You can hide the taskbar buttons of whatever applications you choose. You can also move taskbar buttons over to the tray, where they are displayed as small icons. To make these changes, you need to use shareware apps. (See "The Tray on the Taskbar" later in this chapter for more information.)

Windows comes with a set of default toolbars. These toolbars resemble the taskbar and are connected to it. Right-click your taskbar, point to Toolbars, and click Address ⇨ Links ⇨ Desktop or Quick Launch to display one of the default toolbars, or click New Toolbar to define your own (see the "Toolbars" section later in this chapter). If you want to hide a toolbar, clear the checkmark next to its name in the Toolbars submenu. (You can't temporarily hide a user-defined toolbar. When you clear its checkmark, the toolbar is removed.)

The Taskbar Buttons

Each taskbar button includes the application's or window's icon and name. If there is an associated document or file with the application, its name is supposed to appear first on the button (according to the Windows software design guidelines). The icons on the taskbar button are smaller versions of the icons you see on the Desktop. They are 16×16 pixels instead of 32×32 pixels.

Windows and multidocument applications place the name of the application first on the taskbar button. For example, if you open a copy of Microsoft Word, you'll see a button labeled Microsoft Word on the taskbar, and you will be hard-pressed to see the name of the open document. If you open the Windows Notepad without a document, Untitled appears as the first name on the taskbar button.

Tip

Every user-interactive active application or window is represented on the taskbar, regardless of whether the application is currently minimized, restored, or maximized. (The only exceptions are applications that run behind the scenes, which don't need taskbar buttons, and those that have icons in the tray instead of taskbar buttons.) *This means that the taskbar is a task switcher.* No matter if the active application has been minimized or is now buried under other application windows on the Desktop, you can bring it to the top by clicking its button (a single click at that) on the taskbar.

The taskbar is one of Window's most fundamental "ease of use" improvements over the old Windows 3.1*x* interface. It is also an advantage that Windows has over the Apple Macintosh. This feature makes it almost impossible to lose track of which documents and programs are open, even when they are stacked on top of each other.

The taskbar takes the place of the minimized active application and window icons that by default were displayed at the bottom of your Windows 3.1*x* Desktop. Because it has a button for every major active application, whether the application is minimized or not, the taskbar has much of the task-switching functionality of the Windows 3.1*x* Task Manager.

Tip

The single-click operation of the taskbar makes it easy to switch between *tasks* — which are simply active applications or windows. Combine this with Windows's enhanced resource management, and it is easy to find yourself using multiple active applications and opening multiple instances of your Explorer or My Computer windows. Windows makes multitasking (defined from the user's perspective as quickly jumping among active applications and windows) easy enough to be useful.

To toggle between minimizing and restoring an application window, just click the application's taskbar button, and then click again. This functionality was added with Internet Explorer 4.0. Therefore, it is available to Windows Me users, Windows 98 users, and Windows 95 users who installed Internet Explorer 4.0 or higher and chose the integrated mode.

Drag and Wait to a Taskbar Button

You can drag a file to a taskbar button and continue to hold down the mouse button after you reach the taskbar button. As you hold the file over the taskbar button, the application associated with that button will spring to life. If it was minimized, it will open into a window on the Desktop. If it was buried under other windows, it will come to the top.

Tip

Once the application window has appeared, you can drop the file icon on it. The application determines what happens next. If the application is a Windows editor or word processor, it will open or insert the dropped file, depending on where you drop it. Drop it on the title bar and the document opens. Drop it in the client window, and the document may be inserted into an existing document.

If the program is a DOS editor, dropping a file will put the name of the dropped file at the insertion point in a DOS file. This behavior isn't all that useful unless you want to build a text document full of filenames.

Specialized Windows 3.1*x* applications that are meant only to be displayed as icons and never expanded into windows do not work with Windows Me.

Hiding the Taskbar

The taskbar has two mode switches: "Always on top" and "Auto hide."

Always on top means always on top of other windows on the Desktop (not exactly *always*, but often enough anyway). Turn on this feature and other windows do their best to stay out of the way of the taskbar. Turn off this feature and other windows don't know that the taskbar is there.

If you turn on "Auto hide," the taskbar disappears (except for a thin line) unless it is the last thing you clicked on. An Auto-hidden taskbar doesn't take up Desktop real estate except when you want to do something with it — such as switch to another task.

When "Auto hide" is on, the taskbar hides itself as soon as you click on another application. To get the taskbar to display itself, move the mouse pointer to the edge of the screen on which you've docked the taskbar. You'll see a 2-pixel-wide line along the edge that is a remnant of the taskbar. When your mouse pointer hot spot gets within 2 pixels of the edge of the Desktop, the pointer becomes a resize arrow, and the taskbar pops up. The mouse pointer then changes back to a normal selection arrow.

Secret

If you move your mouse pointer more than 10 pixels away from the taskbar without clicking it (or one of the taskbar buttons) first, the taskbar disappears. It doesn't disappear instantly. Depending on what is beneath the taskbar, the screen usually takes longer to repaint the Desktop to show what was obscured by the taskbar than it took to pop up the taskbar in the first place. This can be quite a bother.

If you click the taskbar after it pops up, it gains the focus. You can then move the mouse pointer around the Desktop and the taskbar doesn't disappear until you click another window or the Desktop. You have to click directly on the taskbar and not on any of the buttons. Sometimes this is a little difficult, because much of the taskbar itself might be covered by buttons.

If "Auto hide" is on and "Always on top" is off, when the taskbar pops up, it will pop up behind any window that it might have otherwise obscured. You may still be able to have a partial view of the taskbar and be able to switch tasks, and so on.

If "Auto hide" is off and "Always on top" is on, the taskbar sits on top of your Desktop and other windows try to get out of its way. When you maximize a window, it does not cover up the taskbar. The application calculates the maximum window size as the actual screen resolution minus the number of pixels in the taskbar.

If "Always on top" is on, this doesn't mean necessarily that the taskbar will always be on top. Other windows can have this same property. If two windows have this "Always on top" property, whichever window has the focus will be on top.

To change the "Auto hide" and "Always on top" modes, take the following steps:

STEPS

Changing Taskbar Modes

Step 1. Right-click the Taskbar and click Properties to display the Taskbar Properties dialog box, as shown in Figure 5-21. (You can also get to this dialog box by clicking Start ⇨ Settings ⇨ Taskbar & Start Menu.)

Figure 5-21: The Taskbar Options tab of the Taskbar Properties dialog box. Check the "Auto hide" and/or "Always on top" checkboxes to change these taskbar modes.

Continued

STEPS

Changing Taskbar Modes *(continued)*

Step 2.   Click "Auto hide" and/or "Always on top" to change the taskbar modes. Click the Apply button to see the effect of these modes.

Step 3.   When you are done, click OK.

One utility that is absolutely essential if you have your taskbar set to be on the top edge of the Desktop with "Always on top" turned on and "Auto hide" turned off is Shoveit. Shoveit moves misbehaving application windows out from under the taskbar. We discuss it further in the "Which Desktop Edge Is Best for the Taskbar?" section later in this chapter.

Sizing the Taskbar

The taskbar starts out thin, but you can make it bigger. In fact, you can make it as large as one-half of the Desktop.

Move your mouse pointer to the top edge of the taskbar so that the mouse pointer turns into a resize arrow. Hold down the left mouse button and drag the taskbar's edge upward. The taskbar increases in height in button-height increments.

Windows sizes the buttons on the taskbar automatically. All the buttons are the same size, no matter how long the names of the application and its associated document are. If the names are too long to fit in the button, Windows truncates them and places an ellipses after them, if there is room.

You can see the full name of the application and document associated with a given button by placing your mouse pointer over the button and waiting for less than a second. A ToolTip (a small pop-up box with text) appears next to your mouse pointer. This happens only if the full name of the application and its associated document can't fit on the button face.

Secret

As you open additional applications, the taskbar buttons shrink, unless you increase the size of the taskbar. When the buttons become so small that they are just big enough to contain the 16 × 16 pixel icons within them, they get no smaller. If you add more active applications at that point, all the icons will not be displayed at the same time on the taskbar. In this situation, a *spin control* appears on the taskbar. You can spin the control to see icons that are not currently in view.

The taskbar is attached to an edge of the Desktop. If it is on the bottom, you can't narrow it by detaching it from the right or left edge. The resize arrow appears only when the mouse pointer is near the top of the taskbar.

The icons on the Desktop move to avoid the taskbar when you resize it (as long as it isn't in "Auto hide" mode, as explained in the "Which Desktop Edge Is Best for the Taskbar?" section that follows). You have to have quite a few icons on the Desktop to see this effect.

Moving the Taskbar

The taskbar doesn't have to be on the bottom of your Desktop. You can move it to any other edge (the top, bottom, left, or right side of the screen).

To move the taskbar, position the mouse pointer over it, but not over any of the buttons on the taskbar, nor over the line at the left (or top) end of the taskbar button area. Press down the left mouse button and drag toward one of the other Desktop edges. Release the mouse button when the outline of the taskbar is positioned on the desired edge.

Which Desktop Edge Is Best for the Taskbar?

In application windows, the menu bar is at the top of the window, and a scroll bar is often at the right. No doubt you use menus and scroll bars quite often. You are probably used to moving your mouse to the right, top, and bottom of a Windows application client area, in that order of frequency. The left and bottom edges of the screen are the least "natural" areas to point to. You may find yourself doing a lot of extra mousing around if you place the taskbar in these "unnatural" areas.

If you dock your taskbar on the right side, you can get to the buttons on the taskbar with an easy movement of the mouse. If the taskbar is hidden, however, it may be a bit too easy and end up as quite a bother. Here's why: If your document is anywhere near the right edge of your screen and you move the mouse quickly to the right to scroll, you are likely to overshoot the scroll bar and move to the Desktop edge. Up pops the taskbar, which you didn't want. Now you have to move the mouse at least 10 pixels to the left of the taskbar to get the taskbar to disappear — a waste of time.

The advantage of placing the taskbar on the right is that it is easy and natural for you to get to it. And if "Auto hide" is off, the taskbar stays in view so you don't have to worry about making it pop up accidentally. However, there are disadvantages to placing the taskbar on the right as well. If "Auto hide" is turned on, you have to be accurate with your mouse to avoid inadvertently displaying the taskbar. Furthermore, a vertical taskbar with horizontal buttons is most likely fatter than a horizontal taskbar with horizontal buttons, because the buttons have to be wide enough to display the names (although this is only an issue if "Auto hide" is off).

One advantage of leaving the taskbar on the bottom or moving it to the left is that you can have "Auto hide" on and still not accidentally pop up the taskbar so often that it becomes annoying. And if you are left-handed, it might feel natural to attach the taskbar to the left edge of the Desktop. However, docking the taskbar on the left side will probably be a difficult adjustment for most people, and if you place it on the bottom, the Start menu on the taskbar pops up instead of dropping down.

Placing the taskbar on the top edge of the Desktop will make it feel like a menu bar or a toolbar, and moving the mouse to the top of your screen is a "natural" movement for Windows users. The Start menu also drops down from the Start button in a familiar manner. If you have the real estate, put the taskbar on the top edge and keep "Always on top" turned on and "Auto hide" turned off. This option will probably feel comfortable to you. (Just remember that if you turn on "Auto hide," you'll have the problem of mouse overshoot when you choose menu items, although it won't be nearly as bad as if the taskbar is at the right.)

Test out each location to figure out which one works the best for you. Be sure to give yourself a reasonable amount of time to try each one — a couple of days is about right.

Secret

Windows applications may get partially covered by the taskbar if they are at their restored size and the taskbar is attached to the top edge of the Desktop with "Always on top" turned on and "Auto hide" turned off. When Windows applications are maximized, they do not get obscured by the taskbar.

The fact that Windows applications can't seem to find the taskbar when they are at their restored size can be quite annoying. If a window's title bar is covered by the taskbar, you have to use the keyboard to lower the window enough to bring the title bar into view. (Press Alt+spacebar, M, press the down arrow repeatedly to move the window down, and then click once.) You could also just maximize the application's window by pressing Alt+spacebar, X.

A little donation-ware application, ShoveIt (`http://www.phoenixgate.com/shove-it.html`), solves this problem very elegantly. You can choose whether to have it move the application window down from the top of the Desktop (you'd do this if you have the taskbar attached at the top) or from any of the other edges. We find this applet to be absolutely indispensable. ShoveIt is available at numerous shareware Web sites.

Resizing and Moving Windows on the Desktop

Using the taskbar, you can cascade, tile, or minimize all the sizable windows on the Desktop. Right-click the taskbar and choose one of these sizing options.

Minimize All Windows is a very powerful function, because it is paired with Undo Minimize All. (When you right-click the taskbar after choosing Minimize All Windows, the context menu contains an Undo Minimize All command.) You can clear your Desktop with one command, and then place everything back where it came from with the opposite command. This is a very handy feature if you want to get to some icons on your Desktop that are covered up by your application windows.

It is even easier to use the Show Desktop button on the Quick Launch toolbar. This button is also a toggle switch. Click it once to clear your Desktop of all open windows. Click it again to restore them.

The Start Button

We discuss many of the Start button's interesting secrets in "Drop It on the Start Button" in Chapter 9, but here are a few of the high points.

The Start button contains the Stop button, in the form of the Shut Down command. Click the Start button and then click Shut Down to get out of Windows.

Clicking the Start button displays the Start menu. This menu provides a series of cascading menu choices that give you access to much of the functionality of Windows. You can easily change all of the menus that are attached to the Programs menu item to include the menus, folders, files, and applications that you want displayed.

Right-clicking the Start button lets you open and explore your computer and easily change items in the Start menus. You can add items to the Start menu by dragging them over and dropping them on the Start button.

You can rearrange some of icons on the Start menus by using drag and drop as well as by right-clicking them. The Start menu is just a special version of a window.

Ctrl+Esc displays the Start menu, as does the Win key on Windows keyboards.

Toolbars

Toolbars add another way to get at your documents, Web pages, and applications. Applications don't have to be active to be on a toolbar (unlike the taskbar). You can think of toolbars as folder windows with special properties. For the most part, they just contain shortcuts to documents, URLs, and applications. You can leave the toolbars connected to the taskbar, or move them to any location on your Desktop. To display a toolbar, right-click an empty part of the taskbar, click Toolbars, and then click the toolbar.

One of the four default toolbars is the Address toolbar. If you type a URL or a folder name in the Address field of the Address toolbar and press Enter, a window appears on the Desktop displaying the contents of that folder or the Web page associated with the URL.

You can move a toolbar by dragging and dropping it. To do this, move your mouse pointer over the line at the far left (or top) edge of the toolbar. When you see the resize arrow, drag the toolbar to one of the edges of the screen to dock it on that side, or drag it into the middle of the Desktop to make it float. This technique also works to adjust the relative positions of the taskbar and the toolbars if they are sharing the same edge of the screen.

You can create a new toolbar that contains the contents of a folder. One way to do this is to just drag the folder icon (or a shortcut to the folder icon) to the very edge of your Desktop and drop it there. You can do this with My Computer, My Documents, and My Network Places, as well as any icons that represent folders containing documents and/or applications.

Another way to create a toolbar for the contents of a folder is to use the New Toolbar dialog box. To see an example of this, take the following steps:

STEPS

Creating a New Toolbar

Step 1.   Click Start ➪ Programs ➪ Accessories ➪ Windows Explorer.

Step 2.   Click one of your hard disk icons in the left pane of your Explorer. Right-click in a clear area in the right pane of the Explorer.

Step 3.   Click New ➪ Folder, and type My System. Press Enter.

Step 4.   Double-click the My System folder icon in the right pane of the Explorer.

Step 5.   Right-click the right pane of the Explorer, click New ➪ Folder, type **Test**, and press Enter.

Step 6.   Right-click the taskbar, click Toolbars, and then click New Toolbar.

Step 7.   In the New Toolbar dialog box, click the plus sign next to the Hard Disk icon, click the plus sign next to My System, highlight the Test folder icon, and click OK. Your new (as yet empty) toolbar appears at the bottom of the Desktop.

Of course, even though you can create the toolbar out of any existing folder, it is best to use folders that only contain shortcuts. If you want to add shortcuts to the toolbar that you just created (and its corresponding folder), just drag and drop them to the toolbar.

You can also drag and drop shortcuts to the Links toolbar and the Quick Launch toolbar. The Links toolbar appears both on your Desktop and in your Explorer window. Any shortcuts you drag and drop onto it show up on the toolbar in both places.

If you want to remove the toolbar you created in the Creating a New Toolbar steps, right-click the taskbar, click Toolbars, and clear the checkmark next to the toolbar (or right-click the toolbar and click Close). You can't temporarily hide toolbars that you create, unlike the four preexisting toolbars.

Using a Toolbar to Make the Desktop Always Available

The default Windows configuration displays a single toolbar (the Quick Launch toolbar) attached to the taskbar. However, you can display multiple toolbars and place them on any edge of the Desktop (or in the middle of it, if you like).

Tip

For example, you might want to place the Desktop toolbar on the side of your Desktop so that your Desktop icons are always accessible. To do this, take the following steps:

STEPS

Making the Desktop Always Accessible

Step 1. Right-click the taskbar, point to Toolbars, and click Desktop.

Step 2. Point to the vertical bar at the far left edge of the Desktop toolbar (which is now partially covering your taskbar), and drag and drop the toolbar to the left or right edge of your Desktop.

Step 3. Right-click the Desktop toolbar and choose View ⇨ Small.

Step 4. Right-click the toolbar again, and clear Show Text (make sure that you have distinctive icons for every icon on your Desktop).

Step 5. Right-click it again and clear Show Title.

Step 6. Right-click it again and mark "Auto hide." Move your mouse pointer to the edge of the Desktop until the Desktop toolbar appears.

Step 7. Right-click once more and mark "Always on top."

Step 8. Resize the Desktop toolbar to show all your Desktop icons.

Now you have a pop-up Desktop toolbar that gives you immediate access to all your Desktop icons. Of course, you can also use the Deskmenu applet from Power Toys set to put a Deskmenu icon in your Tray. When you download Power Toys, be sure to put it in a folder with no more than eight letters because its installer can't handle long path or folder names. You'll find Power Toys at `http://www.microsoft.com/Windows95/downloads/contents/wutoys/w95pwrtoysset/default.asp?site=95`.

The Tray on the Taskbar

The little indented area on the right edge of the taskbar is called the *tray*. Some applets that start up when Windows starts up put their icons in here. The idea is that by putting small icons in the tray, applets that are always running don't take up as much space on the taskbar as bigger applications, which run only when you choose to start them.

G.L. Liadis Software, publisher of numerous shareware applications for Windows, has come out with WinTray. If you put this 249K application in your Startup folder, you gain the ability to store up to eight icons of your choice in the tray.

Once you've used WinTray's dialog box to select the applications you want in the tray, their icons automatically show up in the tray every time you start Windows. You can configure the icons to launch your favorite apps with a double-click or a single-click (your choice). You can keep WinTray's dialog box open during your Windows session or instruct it to hide. Right-clicking any icon you placed in the tray brings up the WinTray window again so you can reconfigure the program, adding or removing icons from the tray.

The tray is usually used for small system utilities, such as resource monitors and diagnostic tools that you want to frequently check on with a click. For example, the Windows Resource Meter (`C:\Windows\Rsrcmtr.exe`) automatically places itself in the tray when you run it. WinTray lets you store other utilities in the tray as well.

There's no particular reason, however, that you should be limited to putting utilities in the tray. Any major application that you use frequently could be a candidate — your word processor, say, or a favorite game.

You can download an unregistered shareware version of WinTray from the Internet by setting Internet Explorer to `http://www.glliadis.com/`. Click the Utilities keyword to download WinTray or see a listing of many other programs from this prolific shareware author.

Another shareware application, Icon Corral, not only lets you place application icons in the tray, it allows you to remove the space-wasting buttons for these applications from the taskbar itself while they're running. You can download a fully functional version from `http://www.armadillobrothers.com/download.htm`.

Tray Shortcuts is a free program that doesn't remove apps from the taskbar, but does place icons in the tray like WinTray does. You can find `Tscuts.zip` at `http://www.cybermad.com/best/tools.html`.

The Clock

The taskbar has a digital clock. If you rest your mouse pointer over the time, you'll see the date in a ToolTip. If you right-click the time, you can choose Adjust Date/Time in the context menu to display the Date/Time Properties dialog box, as shown in Figure 5-22.

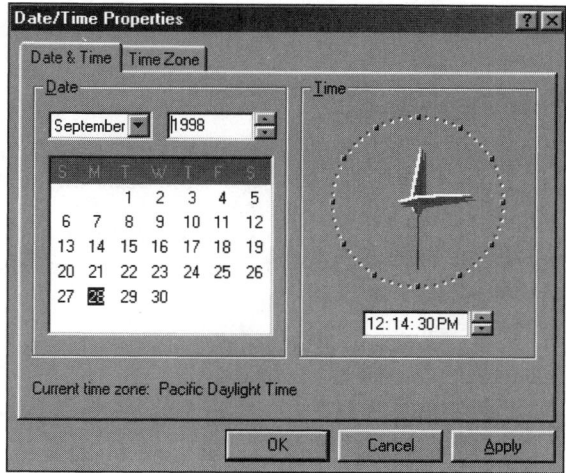

Figure 5-22: The Date/Time Properties dialog box. You can set the date and time by typing new values or clicking the spin controls in the Date and Time fields.

You can change the date by choosing the month from the drop-down list, spinning the Year field, and clicking on a day. You can change the time by typing a new time or by using the spin control. To change the clock to a 24-hour display (instead of AM and PM), take the following steps:

STEPS

Changing the Time Format Display

Step 1. Click Start ⇨ Settings ⇨ Control Panel.

Step 2. Click the Regional Settings icon.

Continued

STEPS

Changing the Time Format Display *(continued)*

Step 3. Click the Time tab.

Step 4. Display the Time Style drop-down list and choose a style with an uppercase H.

Step 5. Click the OK button in the Regional Settings Properties dialog box.

If you want to change the date format, click the Date tab in Step 3 instead of the Time tab.

Secret

If you change the Short Date style, the new style won't be used until you restart Windows.

You can also set your time zone by clicking the Time Zone tab, as shown in Figure 5-23. Check out the world map. This map used to be pretty cool, because you could click an area to illuminate the whole time zone/daylight savings zone. No longer. Too many political entities with disagreements about borders.

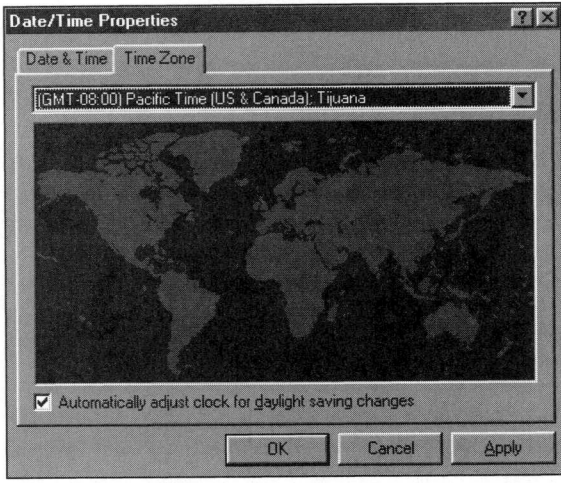

Figure 5-23: The Time Zone map. Click the drop-down list above the map to pick a time zone.

Secret

There are 63 separate entries in the list of time zones (in the original version of Windows 95 there were only 51 — see what an improvement Windows Me is?) even though you might assume that there are only 24 unique time zones. Windows keeps track of the daylight savings time rules for various locations, so, for example, there is a unique entry for Arizona (USA) that doesn't honor daylight savings time. There are also separate entries for Darwin and Adelaide (Australia), both of which are plus 9 ½ hours from Greenwich Mean Time.

When the first day of daylight savings time arrives, you get a message asking if you want to have your computer's clock moved an hour ahead.

The time zone value does have something of a practical value. If you are on a network that crosses time zones — say, your own company's WAN — your computers will use this time zone value to get everyone's time synched to a universal standard such as Zulu, Greenwich mean time, or whatever arbitrary one you choose. Your computers can correctly compare files that are time-stamped on the West Coast with files that are time-stamped on the East Coast.

The Windows Time Zone Editor is a customization tool for those with an abiding interest in the start and end dates of daylight savings time and other time-related policies. You can edit the start and end dates of daylight savings time, create new time zones, and so on. Download Microsoft's Kernel Toys from http://www.microsoft.com/Windows95/downloads/contents/wutoys/ w95kerneltoy/default.asp?site=95. Inside Kernel Toys, you'll find the Time Zone Editor. You will also find it on the Windows CD-ROM, in \tools\reskit\ config.

You can add a date display to the tray. This lets you see the date without having to place your mouse pointer over the time display. You can download TrayDay from http://www.mjmsoft.com.

Task Switching with the Keyboard

Three keyboard combinations let you switch among active applications and folders.

Hold down Alt and press the Tab key. A window that contains the icons of the active applications and folders appears on the Desktop. By pressing and releasing the Tab key you can switch between the active applications and folder windows.

If you want to get back to the Start button, press Ctrl+Esc. This displays the taskbar and the Start menu. You can get to the menu items on the Start menu by pressing the letter key corresponding to the underlined letter in the menu item, or by pressing the up and down arrow keys to highlight the item and then pressing Enter. Menu items in the other menus (ones that cascade off the Start menu) don't have unique assigned letters. However, you can still choose them by pressing the letter key that corresponds to the first letter in the item's name, or by highlighting the item with the up and down arrow keys and then pressing Enter.

Secret

You can get to the icons on the taskbar or the icons on the Desktop with the keyboard. Press Ctrl+Esc to get to the Start menu. Press Esc to put the focus on the Start button and hide the Start menu. Press Tab to put the focus on the taskbar. You can now use the arrow keys to move among the taskbar icons.

Press a second Tab after the first to shift the focus to the icons on the Desktop. You can then use the arrow keys to highlight one icon after another. The Tab key (or the F6 key) toggles the focus between the Start button, the taskbar, any toolbars, and the icons on the Desktop. (The focus must first be on one of these items for this to work.) The Start button doesn't open the Start menu until you focus on it and press the Enter key. If the taskbar is in "Auto hide" mode, it appears when the focus shifts to the Start button or the taskbar and disappears when the focus shifts to the Desktop.

Secret

If you are in a full-screen DOS Windows session, you can return to the Desktop by holding down Alt, pressing the Tab key, and clicking the pop-up window that is displayed when you press Alt+Tab.

You can also switch between tasks by holding down Alt and pressing the Esc key. If the task you switch to is minimized, the only action you will notice is that the task's button on the taskbar is depressed and the title bar of the previously active application changes to its inactive color.

Use a Toolbar to Quickly Get to Your Files

It can be quite time-consuming to navigate around with your Explorer to find the files that you are working on. That's why there is a My Documents shortcut on your Desktop, why you can create shortcuts to any of your documents, and why there is a list of recently opened documents on your Start menu and the File menu in your applications.

Another very clever way to get to your documents and programs, and to almost anything on your computer, is to use menus cascading from a toolbar. To see how this works, open up your Desktop toolbar by taking these steps:

STEPS

Opening a My Desktop Toolbar

Step 1. Right-click your Taskbar, and choose Toolbars ⇨ Desktop.

Step 2. Drag the sizing bar at the left end of the toolbar to move the Desktop toolbar over to the right (assuming you have a horizontal taskbar) so that only the word Desktop and a chevron arrow show.

Step 3. Click the arrow and notice that the Desktop contents are displayed in a menu, as shown in Figure 5-24.

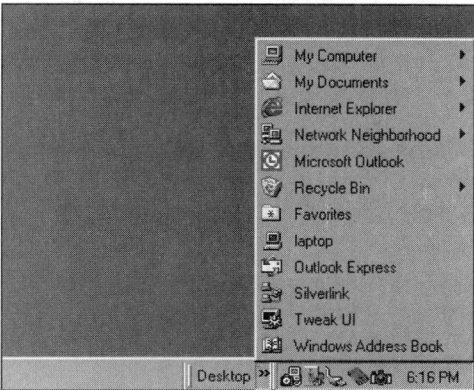

Figure 5-24: The toolbar you have created displays the contents of your Desktop as a menu.

Step 4. Click the My Computer icon in your Desktop menu. The contents of your computer are displayed in a new menu.

Step 5. Click your Hard Drive icon. You get a menu containing the items found in your root directory (except for the hidden files).

Step 6. Continue opening up menus of folders on your hard disk to get to any folder or file that you wish.

You can get to any application or file just by navigating down cascading menus. But there is a way to make this easier.

STEPS

Opening Your Hard Disk Toolbar

Step 1. Right-click your taskbar and choose Toolbars ⇨ New Toolbar.

Step 2. In the New Toolbar dialog box, highlight your main hard disk and click OK.

Step 3. Drag the sizing bar at the end of the new hard disk toolbar to the right so that you see only the name of the hard disk and a chevron arrow.

Continued

STEPS

Opening Your Hard Disk Toolbar *(continued)*

Step 4.   Click the arrow to display the contents of your root directory (minus the hidden files) in a menu, as shown in Figure 5-25.

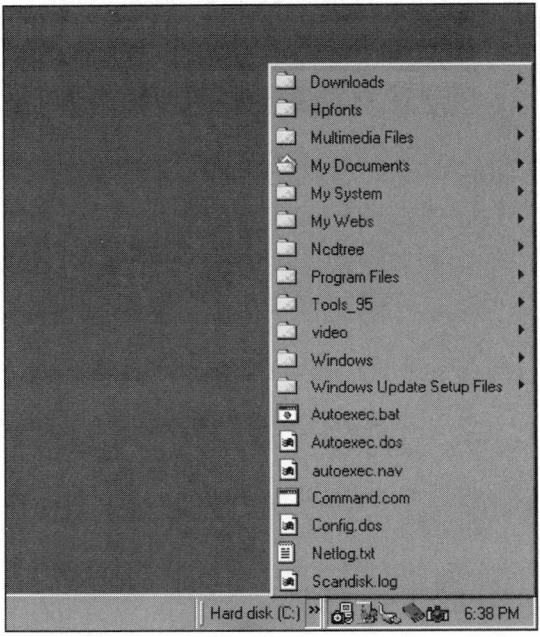

Figure 5-25: Display the contents of your root directory as a menu by creating a new toolbar.

Step 5.   Click a folder on your hard disk menu to display the contents of the folder as a menu.

Step 6.   Click subfolders to display their contents.

You can set up toolbars for multiple hard disks. You can create a toolbar using My Computer instead of your hard disk. In the My Computer toolbar, click Control Panel ⇨ Dial-Up Networking ⇨ Printers ⇨ Web Folders or Scheduled Tasks; the items in these special folders are displayed as menu items.

You can also create toolbars for the Control Panel folder, the Dial-Up Networking folder, and so on. Pretty much any folder can become a menu. These menus are not menus of shortcuts, so you'll need to be careful not to delete items from the menus. If you do, you'll delete the actual thing itself and not just a shortcut to it. For example, if you make a menu of the Dial-Up Networking folder and delete a DUN connectoid from the menu, the actual connectoid is gone.

Thanks to James A. Boyce for his help with this secret.

Move Your Toolbars Quickly to the Right or Left

You'll notice the sizing bar (the vertical bar) at the left end of your toolbars. You can drag the sizing bar to move your toolbar around. If you double-click it, the toolbar will move for you. The sizing bar is a toggle, so keep double-clicking it.

Double-click the sizing bar once to move the toolbar to the left, so that it squeezes the taskbar buttons. Double-click it again to move it back to the right. If you have multiple toolbars, you can get pretty elaborate with these double-clicks. Of course, this also works if you have a vertical taskbar and toolbars.

New Folders for New Toolbars

When you create a new toolbar (right-click your taskbar and choose Toolbars ⇨ New Toolbar) you are not given the opportunity to create a new empty folder, as you can see in Figure 5-26.

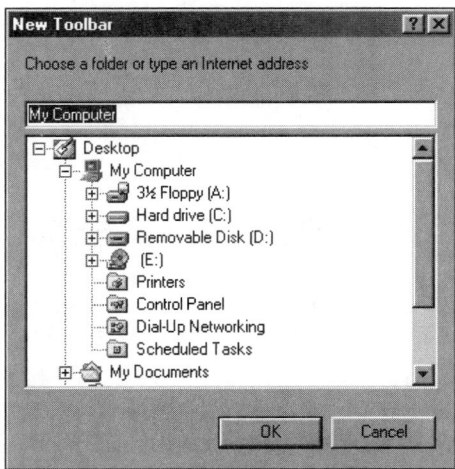

Figure 5-26: The New Toolbar dialog box does not include a New Folder button.

A toolbar can be a convenient place to put shortcuts, especially if you move the toolbar all the way to the right and turn it into a menu of shortcuts. One approach that you might take is to group your shortcuts by common themes and send them to the appropriate toolbar. Then you can get to them easily even if they are also on the Desktop and currently covered up.

A good place to put your toolbar folders is the same location that Microsoft places the Quick Launch toolbar folder. Another option is to put them in your own \My System folder (which we suggest you create to store the files and folders you use to customize Windows).

Take these steps to create your own new toolbar folders and make them easy to get to when creating new shortcuts.

STEPS

Creating New Folders for New Toolbars

Step 1. Using your Explorer, navigate to \Windows\Application Data\ Microsoft\Internet Explorer\ as shown in Figure 5-27.

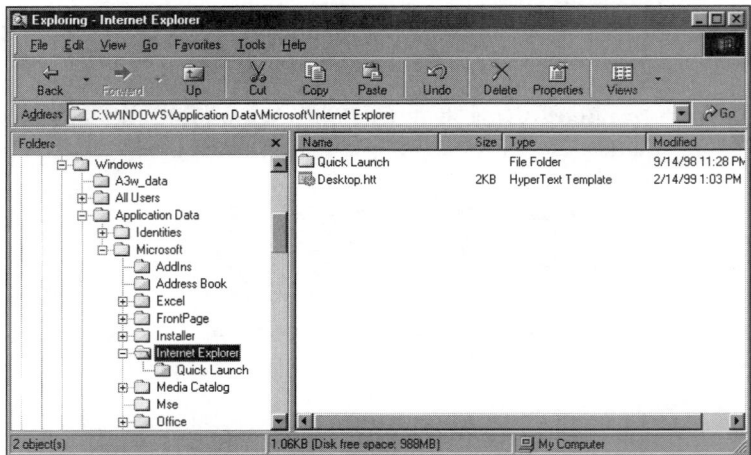

Figure 5-27: Your Quick Launch folder is stored in the location shown here. You could create your toolbar folders here or in the \My System folder.

Step 2. Right-click the Explorer client area, click New ⇨ Folder, and type a short name for the new folder/toolbar. Repeat this step as many times as needed to create the new folders.

Step 3. In the left pane of your Explorer, scroll down to \Windows\SendTo.

Step 4. One by one, right-drag the folders that you just created to `\Windows\SendTo`, and click Create Shortcut(s) Here after you drop each one there.

Step 5. Right-click your taskbar and choose Toolbars ⇨ New Toolbar. Select the first of your new folders, and click OK. Repeat for each new folder.

Step 6. You can now move items off of your Desktop or Start menu just by right-clicking them, clicking Send To, and choosing the appropriate toolbar.

Tip

You don't have to do the Send To portions of this procedure (Steps 3, 4, and 6). Because the items on the Start menu are shortcuts, you can just drag them to any of the toolbars once you open the toolbars. This is part of the improvement of the Windows interface. You can easily move the Start menu items to reflect how you want to work.

Thanks to Martijn Dekkers for pointing out this tip.

Put the Recycle Bin on a Toolbar

If your Recycle Bin is on your Desktop, you can right-drag a Recycle Bin shortcut to a toolbar, and thereby see the Recycle Bin's contents more easily when your Desktop is cluttered up. If you have used TweakUI to take the Recycle Bin off the Desktop, then you won't be able to place a shortcut to it on a toolbar. If you are using the Norton Utilities Protected Recycle Bin, this won't work either.

If neither of those cases is true for you, just right-drag the Recycle Bin icon to a toolbar area and drop it there, and then click Create Shortcut(s) Here. If you don't have a toolbar showing, right-click the taskbar, and choose Toolbars ⇨ Quick Launch. You can right-drag the Recycle Bin icon there to create a shortcut.

Thanks to Mike Brazil for help with this tip.

Toolbars as Web Pages

Because the Windows user shell is an object-oriented program, you'll find that certain items can take on the characteristics of other items even when it doesn't seem that useful. For example, check out the *Windows Secrets* Home Page toolbar shown in Figure 5-28. You can view the whole Web page through the little window in the toolbar.

Figure 5-28: A toolbar can actually contain a whole Web page.

At first glance, this looks rather silly. Indeed, the *Windows Secrets* home page is so big that it is probably not a great choice for a toolbar, but there are other Internet Web pages that may be just right — for example, a stock ticker.

To put a Web page on a toolbar, take these steps:

STEPS

Putting a Web Page on a Toolbar

Step 1.   Right-click your taskbar and choose Toolbars ⇨ New Toolbar.

Step 2.   Type the URL of a local or Internet resource, as shown in Figure 5-29.

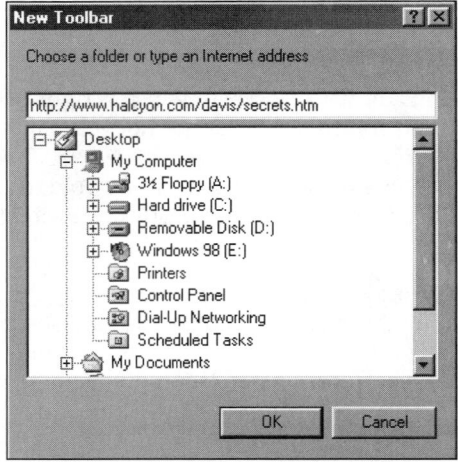

Figure 5-29: Type the complete URL in the New Toolbar dialog box.

Step 3.   Click OK.

Of course, you can resize the toolbar and drag it over to one of the other edges of your Desktop, as shown in Figure 5-30.

Figure 5-30: This toolbar has been resized so that it fits along the side of the Desktop.

Thanks to Roger Wolfson for mentioning this tip.

Tab Through Your Taskbar Buttons

Hold down the Win key as you press the Tab key repeatedly. You'll see your each button on your taskbar appears to be pressed. Press Enter to bring the associated document or application to the foreground.

Use the Address Bar to Run Your Programs

Right-click your taskbar and choose Toolbars ➪ Address to display an Address bar on your Desktop. The Address bar is a toolbar whose main purpose is to call up Internet Explorer when you type or paste in a URL. It looks and works just like the Internet Explorer Address bar, as you can see from Figure 5-31.

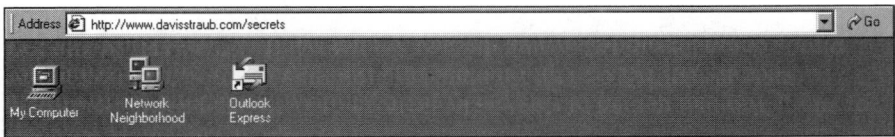

Figure 5-31: The Address bar is a toolbar on your Desktop.

Despite its name, the Address bar is also a command-line processor (oops, here we go back to DOS!). You can type a filename and the associated application will open and display the file. You have to type the complete pathname as well as the filename, and there is no Browse button, as there is in the Start ➪ Run dialog box.

Thanks to Todd D. Perlmutter for this tip.

Put Find on the Quick Launch Toolbar

You can easily put Find on your Quick Launch toolbar. Here's how:

STEPS
Putting Find on the Quick Launch Toolbar

Step 1.   In Explorer, click Tools ➪ Find ➪ Files or Folder.

Step 2.   Make any changes to the Find dialog box necessary to make this your general Find.

Step 3.   Click File ➪ Save Search. This saves the Find settings as a shortcut on the Desktop.

Step 4.   Change the name of the Find shortcut on the Desktop if you like. Otherwise, just drag and drop it onto the Quick Launch toolbar. Delete the shortcut from the Desktop.

Move the Quick Launch Icons Around

You can move the icons in the Quick Launch toolbar just by dragging them to a new location on the toolbar, and dropping them when the black line appears between icons. You can also do this with other toolbars as long as they are folders of shortcuts. You won't be able to do it for a My Computer toolbar. You can do it with a Favorites toolbar.

The order in which the toolbar items appear in these menus is kept in the registry. This is why you can rearrange their order on the toolbar.

While we haven't experienced it, it appears as though toolbar icons can become garbled, especially if you change monitor resolutions. Right-click the sizing bar for any of the toolbars and click Refresh to redisplay the icons.

Thanks to Bo Bickley for pointing out some of these tips.

Restore the Quick Launch Toolbar

Secret

The Quick Launch toolbar contains two icons that may get lost, but are easily restored: Show Desktop and View Channels. If you navigate to \Windows\ Application Data\Microsoft\Internet Explorer\Quick Launch, you'll see these two items. Right-click either of them, click Send To ➪ Notepad, and you'll see that they are text files. (If you haven't put a shortcut to Notepad in your \Windows\SendTo folder, you can open these files by right-clicking them, clicking Open With, and then clicking Notepad.)

If you have accidentally deleted one of these files, you can restore it.

STEPS

Restoring the Show Desktop File

Step 1. Navigate with your Explorer to \Windows\Application Data\ Microsoft\Internet Explorer\Quick Launch.

Step 2. Right-click the right pane in Explorer, and choose New ➪ Text Document.

Step 3. Insert this text into the new document:

```
[Shell]
Command=2
IconFile=explorer.exe,3
[Taskbar]
Command=ToggleDesktop
```

Step 4. Save the file as ShowDesktop.scf.

STEPS

Restoring the View Channels File

Step 1. Navigate with your Explorer to \Windows\Application Data\ Microsoft\Internet Explorer\Quick Launch.

Step 2. Right-click the right pane in Explorer, and click New ⇨ Text Document.

Step 3. Insert this text into the new document:

```
[Shell]
Command=3
IconFile=shdocvw.dll,-118
[IE]
Command=Channels
```

Step 4. Save the file as ViewChannels.scf.

Corrupted Taskbar Icons

Bryan Rockwood reports that Windows has a problem in which icons on the taskbar and the toolbars display garbage icons. This is particularly known to happen when you have changed your display from one resolution to another.

The workaround is to right-click a toolbar and click Refresh in the context menu. (This doesn't work if you don't have a toolbar on your taskbar.)

Keep Running Your System Tray Programs Even After Explorer Crashes

Linus Thorvald has wondered aloud if Windows users have grown inured to their computers crashing. Of course, Linus has a valid point, irrespective of whether his operating system (Linux), highly respected for its resistance to crashes, matches up to user demands in every area. Windows users are used to at least the Explorer crashing, if not the operating system.

Most often, an Explorer crash doesn't cause great harm because it automatically starts again — but you lose your system tray icons. These icons represent running applications, so it sure would be nice to have access to them.

WinResQ to the rescue, sort of. This application keeps a list of running processes, as shown in Figure 5-32. It also sits in the system tray (although its icon disappears). If Explorer crashes, you can invoke WinResQ again. Keep a shortcut to it on your Desktop and click it there. Double-click any process in the WinResQ window that is matched to a missing icon in the system tray to open up that process' main window. (This may not always work.)

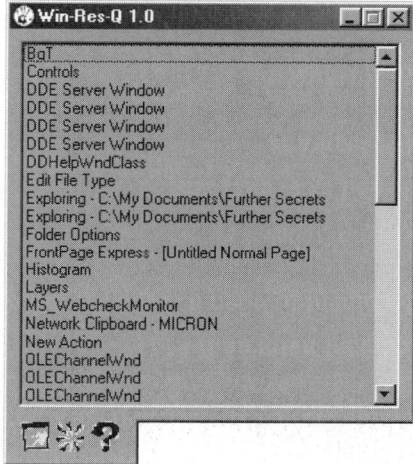

Figure 5-32: A list of currently running processes, viewed using WinResQ

You'll find this little helper at `http://www.magnetiq.com`.

You can also just put shortcuts to the applications that have icons in the system tray on your Desktop. Better still, create a shortcut to a batch file that restarts all the applications with system tray icons.

Foobar, not Toolbar

Foobar is a launch bar with a series of little applets attached to it, as illustrated in Figure 5-33. *Quick* is the key word here — applets that start and end fast, and do a little bit well. Figure 5-34 shows the Reminders applet.

Figure 5-33: Foobar is a collection of helpful little applets that appear as buttons on the launch bar.

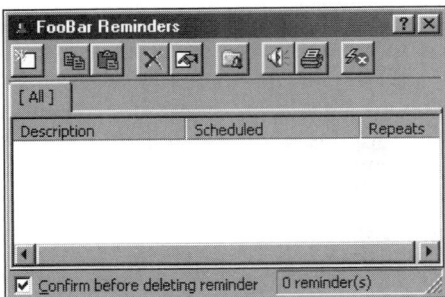

Figure 5-34: The Reminders applet lets you set up reminders that pop up on your screen.

You can keep your passwords (not integrated with Windows), write sticky notes, store a contact list (not integrated with the Windows Address Book), keep track of the time spent on various activities, keep a To Do list, open your favorite documents, run your favorite applications, and set some reminders.

You'll find Foobar at `http://matrixsoftware.com`.

Change Any Time Zone City

You can change the name of the city that appears in any time zone in the Time Zone tab of the Date/Time Properties dialog box (see Figure 5-35). To display this dialog box, double-click the clock in the system tray. Display the drop-down list in the Time Zone tab to display other time zones.

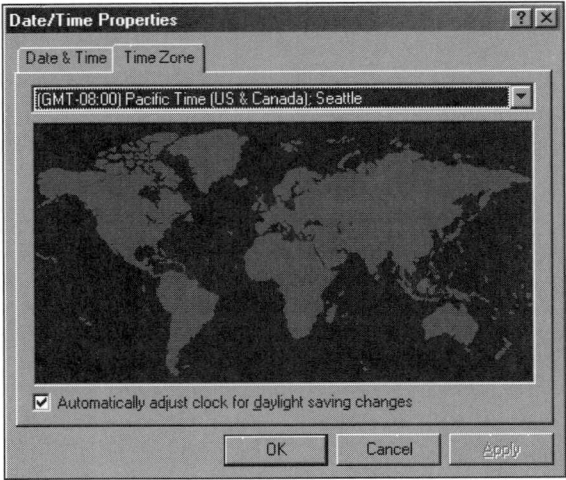

Figure 5-35: The name of a city in the selected time zone appears above the top of the map.

Secret

Earlier in this chapter, we discussed how to download and use the Time Zone Editor that is part of the Windows Kernel Toys. You can use that editor to make this change, but it's also easy to make it using the Registry Editor. Here's how:

STEPS

Changing Your Time Zone City

Step 1. Click Start ➪ Run, type **regedit**, and press Enter.

Step 2. You can either search for the name of a city that you've seen displayed in the Time Zone tab, or you can navigate to HKEY_LOCAL_MACHINE\ SOFTWARE\ Microsoft\ Windows\ CurrentVersion\ TimeZones, and click the key indicating your time zone, as shown in Figure 5-36.

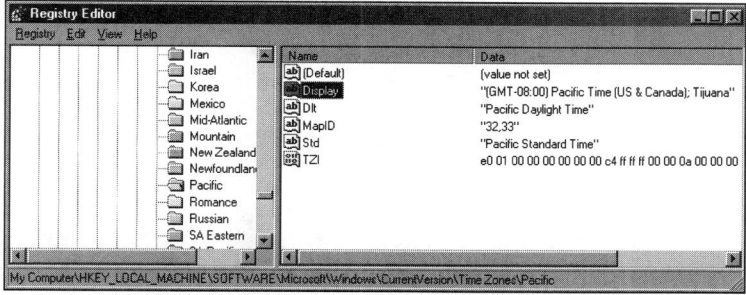

Figure 5-36: In this example, Tijuana is the city associated with Pacific Daylight Time.

Step 3. Double-click Display in the right pane and edit the city name as desired. Click OK and close the Registry Editor.

Controlling the Start Menu

You can also control the items on your Start menu. The following sections show you how to make these changes.

Hide Menu Items

Secret

The Start menu won't display folders, files, or shortcuts that have been marked as hidden. This is a nondestructive way of taking items off of your Start menu without deleting them or moving them. If you decide later that you want an item back on the menu, just unhide it.

STEPS

Hiding Menu Items

Step 1. Click Start ⇨ Programs.

Step 2. Right-click any of the menu items in the Programs folder, click Properties, click the General tab if needed, mark the Hidden checkbox (see Figure 5-37), and click OK.

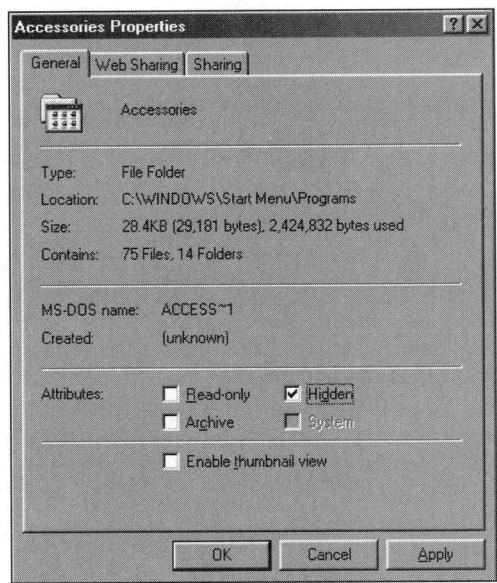

Figure 5-37: The General tab of the Properties dialog box lets you hide a menu item.

Step 3. If you want to unhide a hidden Start menu item, open your Explorer and navigate to \Windows\Start Menu\Programs.

Step 4. Right-click the item in the right pane of the Explorer, click Properties, clear the Hidden checkbox, and click OK.

A number of Start menu items won't let you do this. For example, even if you use your Explorer to mark the Programs or Favorites folders as hidden, they will still show up on the Start menu. If you want to remove the Favorites folder from the Start menu, you can use TweakUI.

Thanks to Byron Hinson, MS-MVP, for help with this tip.

Re-Sorting the Start Menu

Secret

Windows keeps track of the order of the items on your Start menu. This includes the items in the submenus of Programs, Accessories, System Tools, and so on. It does this by creating a variable named *Order* in the registry under the submenu's name whenever you first rearrange the menu from its default alphabetical order.

It's easy to see this in action. Start your Registry Editor by clicking Start ➪ Run, typing **regedit**, and pressing Enter. Navigate to HKEY_CURRENT_USER\ Software\ Microsoft\ Windows\ CurrentVersion\ Explorer\ MenuOrder\ Start Menu\ &Programs\ Menu. You'll see the Order variable in the right pane of the Registry Editor, as shown in Figure 5-38.

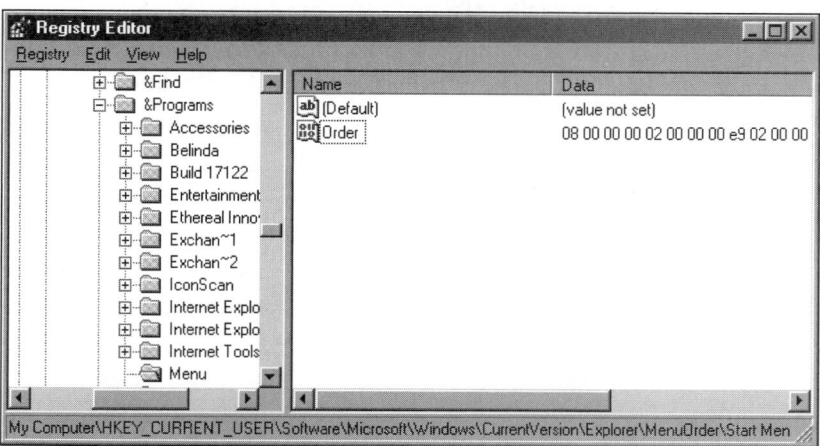

Figure 5-38: The Registry location of the menu order variable.

This Registry item is the menu order variable that remembers the order of the items in the Programs menu. To return the Programs menu to its default alphabetical order, right-click the Order variable in the right pane and click Delete.

You don't need to worry about doing this, because Windows will create the variable again as soon as you reorder anything in the Programs menu. If you don't reorder any items in this menu, it will sort new entries alphabetically and will not create an Order variable.

We found that it was not possible to re-sort the Programs menu correctly without deleting the Order variable in the registry. Right-clicking any of the submenus and clicking "Sort by name" works fine. (This command is new to Internet Explorer 5.)

Other menus have their Order variable stored in a similar location in the registry—under a menu key under their name, or directly under their name. For example, on our computer, the Accessories menu has a menu key, which holds its Order variable, but the system tools key itself holds the system tools' Order variable. Look around a bit in this area of the registry and it's easy to see what's going on.

We'd like to thank Sky King for pointing this out to us.

Redecorate the Start Menu

You can jazz up the Start menu by replacing the icons to the left of your menu items, including Programs, Favorites, Documents, Find, and so on. Not a big change in Windows, but yet another battle in the larger war of user control.

DecoMenu acts like a wizard to step you through the process of creating a graphic that fits in the slot where the icons now stand. It tries to figure out just how big the space is based on what you've still got left on your personalized version of the Start menu. We found that even when we didn't have quite the layout that DecoMenu thought we had, it still worked.

Click the Blank button in the DecoMenu window (see Figure 5-39) to create a blank bmp file and call the associated application. In our case, it's Paint Shop Pro, but it could be MS Paint. Add to the blank bmp file and save it. Now click the Choose button and then the Next button, and you'll have a new Start menu.

If you don't like the effect, you can easily back out of it and go back to the original version of the Start menu icons.

Neil J. Rubenking of PC Magazine wrote DecoMenu, and you'll find it at http://www.zdnet.com/pcmag/pctech/content/17/13/ut1713.001.html.

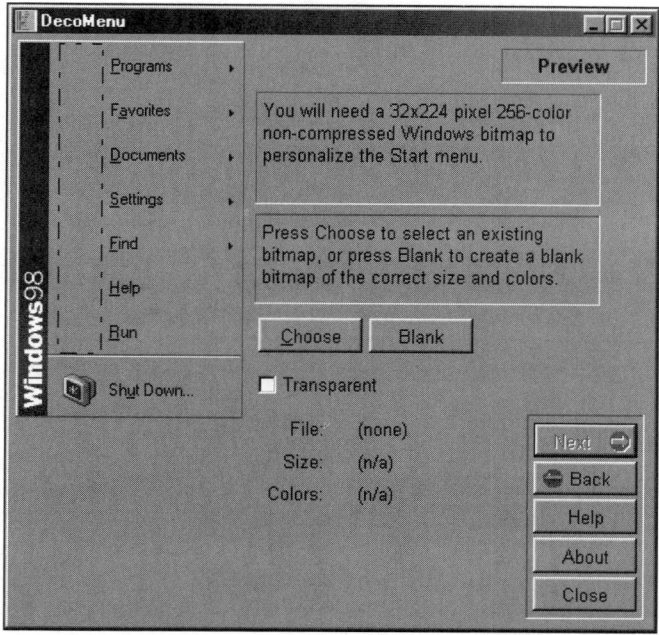

Figure 5-39: DecoMenu functions as a wizard to step you through the process of creating a new look for your Start menu.

The Start Button Is a Window, Too

Secret

Almost everything in Windows is a window. Some windows just look different than others. For example, click your Start button and press Alt+spacebar. You'll see the menu shown in Figure 5-40 appear next to the Start button. Click Close to bring up the Shut Down Windows dialog box.

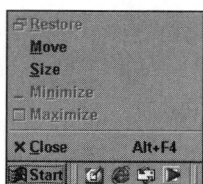

Figure 5-40: Even the Start button contains the standard context menu for a taskbar button.

A Shortcut to a Windows Restart

You can place a little shortcut on your Desktop (or wherever) that lets you quickly restart Windows without going through the Start ⇨ Shut Down ⇨ Restart ⇨ OK routine. Unfortunately, it doesn't restart Windows as fast as this routine does if you also hold down the Shift key when you click OK.

STEPS

Creating a Restart Shortcut

Step 1.   Right-click the Desktop, click New, and then click Shortcut.

Step 2.   Click the Browse button, browse to `C:\Windows\Rundll.exe`, and click Open.

Step 3.   Add a space at the end of the path in the Command Line field, and then type **user.exe,ExitWindowsExec**.

Step 4.   Click Next, and type a new name for the shortcut. We suggest **Restart**.

Step 5.   Click Finish.

An Easy Shortcut

You can use your Start menu to create a hot key to any application without actually creating a new shortcut. The trick is to properly position the application on the Start menu. To see how to do this with a DOS window, take these steps:

STEPS

Creating a Hot Key to DOS

Step 1.   Click Start ⇨ Programs ⇨ Accessories.

Step 2.   Drag the MS-DOS Prompt shortcut all the way to the top of the Programs menu and drop it there (you'll need to drag it from the Accessories menu to the Programs menu).

Step 3.   Press the Win key (or Ctrl+Esc), then the P key, and finally the Enter key (not all together).

Yes, it's cheating, and a bit silly, but why not.

Thanks to Peter Lara for pointing out this trick.

Get Rid of Log Off

If you are the only person using your computer, you can get rid of the Log Off option on your Start menu. Use TweakUI, click the IE tab, clear the Allow Logoff checkbox, Click OK, and reboot your computer.

Fun with Run

Click Start ⇨ Run, type a period (.), and click OK. A folder window containing the shortcuts on your Desktop opens.

Click Start ⇨ Run, type two periods (..), and click OK. A folder window focused on your Windows folder appears on the Desktop.

Click Start ⇨ Run, type a backslash (\), and click OK. A folder window focused on the root directory of your boot drive appears on the Desktop.

Thanks to Byron Hinson, MS-MVP, for help with these tips.

Navigating on the Desktop

Next you'll learn some tricks for making your Desktop a bit easier to use.

Clear the Desktop

You can easily clear the Desktop to get at any of your Desktop shortcuts. Hold down the Win key and press D. This is a toggle, so all your open windows come back when you do it again.

The Win key plus M also works to clear the Desktop, but it isn't a toggle. You have to press Win+Shift+M to bring back the windows.

Quickly Show the Properties of Desktop and Explorer Icons

You ordinarily right-click an icon and click Properties to display its properties. But you can do this even more quickly by pressing the Alt key as you click the icon.

Try this with your My Computer, Internet Explorer, My Documents, and other icons.

Sharing Your Desktop

You can share any of your Windows Me folders on a network. In the following sections you'll learn how to share one of the more useful folders — the Desktop folder.

Put Stuff on Their Desktop

If you're on a network and you share your Desktop, you might come into the office one day to find it piled high with files and documents from your coworkers. Sure, this happens on your physical desk, and maybe that's what you want with your virtual desk also.

If you share your Desktop, other users on the network can send you documents by copying them to an icon on their Desktop. All they have to do to create this icon is to drag your \Windows\Desktop folder to their Desktop and click Create Shortcut(s) Here.

You have to share your \Windows\Desktop folder and allow full or password-controlled access before anyone else can put something on your virtual Desktop. To share your Desktop, right-click your \Windows\Desktop folder and choose Sharing. Then mark Shared As, and mark Full or "Depends on password."

While this might not be a good idea in a large office that may contain a few unruly individuals, hopefully you can trust the people in a small office or at your home.

Thanks to Fred Diether for pointing out this tip.

User Profiles and My Documents

Secret

If you have set up your Windows computer to enable multiple user profiles, you'll find that a My Documents folder gets created for each user under his or her user profile folder — in other words, C:\Windows\Profiles*username*\My Documents. This can be a bit irritating because it makes it somewhat hard to back up everything in the My Documents folder. Fortunately, you can undo the damage that Microsoft has done here.

You'll want to create a folder that will act as a central repository of all the users' My Documents folders. Here's how:

STEPS

Dealing with User Profiles and My Documents

Step 1.   Using your Explorer, navigate to your root directory or the root directory of a secondary partition.

Step 2. Right-click the right pane of your Explorer, click New ➪ Folder, and rename the folder Documents.

Step 3. Right-click the Documents folder and click Explore.

Step 4. Right-click the right pane of your Explorer, click New ➪ Folder, and rename the new folder after the name of one of the users.

Step 5. Repeat Step 4 as many times as needed for all the current users (including yourself).

Step 6. Right-click the My Documents icon on the Desktop, click Properties, click the Browse button, and navigate to the folder that corresponds to your profile (C:\My Documents\username). Click OK.

Step 7. Click Start ➪ Log Off, and log on as one of the other users. Repeat Step 6 for each user, selecting the folder that corresponds to his or her profile.

Step 8. Use your Explorer to copy any files and folders stored in the older My Documents folders into the appropriate new folders under each user's name.

Step 9. Delete the My Document folders under the user names in the C:\Windows\Profiles folder.

There seems to be a problem if one user's folder that is treated as the My Documents folder is a subfolder of another user's folder. Be sure to put all of the folders on the same level.

Thanks to Chuck Rizzio, MS-MVP, for pointing us toward this tip.

Summary

The Desktop, the taskbar, and the toolbars form the core of the Windows user interface. In this chapter we show you how to set them up your way.

▶ We show you how to arrange the icons on your Desktop and change the underlying invisible grid that determines their placement.

▶ It is easy to place empty documents on the Desktop and then click them to bring up applications to edit these documents.

▶ The taskbar can be transformed into a useful tool if you take the time to move and size it for your needs. We show you what kinds of problems you will run into using it in certain configurations and how to find the right edge of the Desktop to use.

▶ Use shareware applets to put taskbar buttons in the tray.

- ▶ Create toolbars from folder shortcuts by dragging the shortcuts to the edge of the Desktop.

- ▶ You can use Alt+Tab, Alt+Esc, and Ctrl+Esc to choose among active applications and folders.

- ▶ Replace your Desktop and user interface with a completely different shell.

- ▶ If you don't have multiple people using your computer, get rid of the superfluous Log Off option.

- ▶ Use the *Windows Resource Sampler Kit* to kill dead links in your Start menu.

- ▶ Clear the Desktop with one keystroke.

- ▶ Set up your screen saver to allow you to view all of your digital photos.

- ▶ Move everyone's My Documents folder to someplace other than a location under the \Windows folder.

Chapter 6

Desktop Strategies—Making Windows Your Own

In This Chapter

Windows is a set of tools waiting for an artist. This is a chance to let your creativity shine. We discuss:

▶ Whose Desktop is it, anyway?

▶ Putting the Start button to work with your heavily used applications

▶ Letting loose and just piling it on the Desktop

▶ Turning a folder window into your program manager and using Explorer as your file manager

▶ How to massage the Context Menu

It Comes with a Start Button

"But, I don't know where to start."

Microsoft went for the uncluttered look in Windows 95. Many of its customers thought the Windows 3.1x Program Manager was ugly. In a reaction to this criticism, Microsoft reduced the Desktop to a taskbar, a Start button, and a few icons.

Along came Windows 98 and the Desktop was suddenly quite cluttered. Microsoft apparently saw all that unused space and decided to fill some of it up. As a result, it designed the Active Desktop to let you display *active windows,* which are narrowly defined applets that can be updated frequently, and *channels,* which you can set up to download specific information off the Internet as it is updated. In addition, Internet Explorer can be set to full screen mode so that the channels provide the working background for all your other application windows.

Microsoft de-emphasized Active Desktop with the introduction of Windows 98 Second Edition (SE). And that de-emphasis continues with Windows Millennium Edition (Me).

You can add Active Desktop elements, however, as part of a basic reality of the new Windows: You have to build your own virtual computer—which, after all, is the real computer—for yourself. Windows provides the tools, but leaves the design up to you.

Windows gives you shortcuts, cascading menus off the Start button, a Desktop that can contain icons as well as "live" channels, folders with properties, a powerful browser in the Internet Explorer, a configurable context menu, a SendTo folder, a configurable connection to the Internet, and a moveable/hideable taskbar with toolbars. We provide a collection of add-on utilities to increase your computer's functionality still further.

A Desktop Strategy

Every one of you would like to set up the Windows Desktop to match your own preferences. In most cases, you can. However, you'll be prevented from making the changes that make your computer your own if a network administrator or system information manager has set up your computer over the network—and enforced a mandatory style (stored on a secure server).

Windows provides a great deal of flexibility—although, of course, there will never be enough to completely please any of us. In this chapter, we present five major strategies for designing a Windows Desktop. You can ignore all our hard work here and go off on your own, or you can start with one of our approaches that most closely matches your own style, and then build on it.

The major considerations in developing a Desktop strategy are getting the tools and putting them close at hand. Windows doesn't include everything that you need in the user interface, so you are going to have to add a number of utilities to make it work for you. We have some of these utilities, and we point out areas where you'll need to get more.

Don't hide the power of Windows under a bushel. Bring it out, make it accessible, make it easy. Take advantage of additional utilities and make them accessible, too.

Whose Desktop Is This Anyway?

When you start Windows for the very first time, you get a logon box similar to the one shown in Figure 6-1. The point of the logon box is to let the computer know who you are and whether you really are who you say you are. Windows, in turn, will let you configure your own Desktop, so even if other people use the computer they won't mess with your Desktop settings (once your system has been configured for multiple users, that is. See "Setting Up Windows for Multiple Users" later in this chapter for more information.).

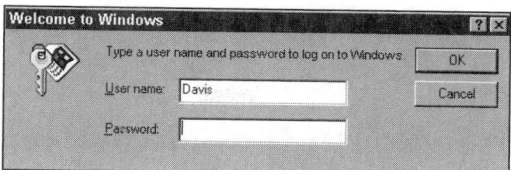

Figure 6-1: The Windows logon box. Type your user name and password to protect your Desktop configuration.

You can configure Windows to make the logon box go away and not come back. If you do this, you are telling Windows that either you are the only user of this computer or that everyone should be treated the same and should get the same Desktop with this computer. You are also saying that you do not want to log onto a local area network at Windows startup.

You must satisfy these three conditions to make the logon box go away:

1. You must have a blank password.

2. You must disable user profiles.

3. You must have Windows configured so that your primary network logon is Windows Logon.

If you meet these conditions (described in the next two sections), Windows won't display the logon box the next time it loads because it won't have any need for your user name and password.

You could also make the logon box go away by simply clicking the Cancel button or pressing the Escape key. However, if you use this method, you only cancel the logon process this one time. The next time Windows starts, it will display the logon box again. Furthermore, if you cancel the logon process and then try to use Windows features that require your account name and password, such as Dial-Up Networking, you'll find that Windows won't remember this information, and you won't be able to save any passwords.

It is possible to log onto your computer and onto a network without typing your user name and password. If you use this method, you don't need to make your password blank, you don't need to disable user profiles, and you can log onto your local area network. To do this, you need to use TweakUI to send your name and password to the logon box.

Click the TweakUI icon in the Control Panel, click the Network tab, fill in your name and password, and mark Log On Automatically At System Startup. You'll see the logon box flash briefly on your Desktop. You don't need to click OK.

If you use this logon method, you won't be able to set Windows to clear the last user's name from the logon box. (You normally set this option by marking the Clear Last User At Logon checkbox in TweakUI's Paranoia tab.) In addition, you won't be able to stop the logon box to enter the name of another user. If you want to log on as another user, you have to log on as the default user (the user specified in TweakUI's Network tab), change the values in the Network tab, and then log on again.

Setting Up Windows for Multiple Users

You can easily configure Windows to allow for multiple users on one computer. Each user can have his or her own settings, including the Desktop, Start menu, Favorites, and so on. Individual settings are determined by *user profiles* (see the steps below) and by *user policies*. We discuss how to set user policies in "System Policy Editor" in Chapter 18.

Windows comes with a wizard that makes it easy to set up new user profiles:

STEPS

Configuring User Profiles

Step 1. Start your computer after installing Windows.

Step 2. When the logon box appears, type a user name and click OK. You have to enter a user name, but you can omit the password. This enters your password as blank.

If you have installed Windows Me over Windows 3.1*x*, you won't necessarily have a logon box. If not, go to Step 3 and finish the rest of the steps. This will configure Windows to call up a logon box the next time you start.

Step 3. Click the Start button, point to Settings, and then click Control Panel.

Step 4. Click the Users icon in the Control Panel to initiate the Multi-User Wizard, as shown in Figure 6-2, and then click Next.

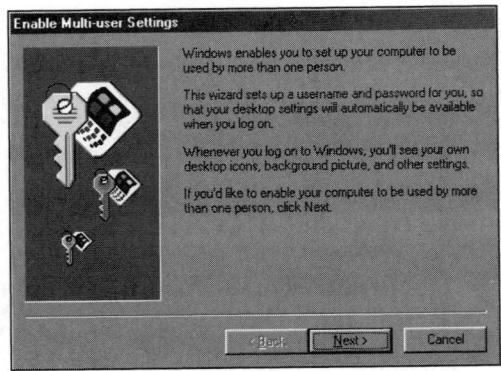

Figure 6-2: The Multi-User Wizard helps you create user profiles for each user name and password.

Step 5.   Enter a user name and password in the next two dialog boxes. You don't have to enter a password for a given user. No password just means it is easier to log on as that user; it doesn't get rid of the logon box because you have still enabled user profiles.

Step 6.   Next, choose among the options shown in the Personalized Items Settings dialog box, as shown in Figure 6-3.

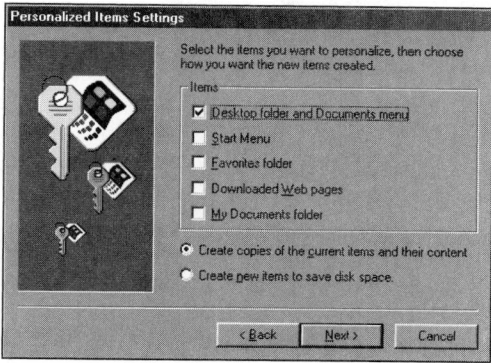

Figure 6-3: Each user can have his or her own Start menu, Favorites folder, temporary Internet cache folder, Internet Explorer history folder, recent documents folder, Desktop, and so on.

Step 7.   Choose whether to create these individual settings from existing folders, or start anew with blank folders. Click Finish.

As soon as you create one new user, Windows enables user profiles and updates the parameters in the User Profiles tab of the Passwords Properties dialog box to the values shown in Figure 6-4. (To display this dialog box, click the Passwords icon in the Control Panel.) The new user's settings, as well as the settings for all the original users, are stored in separate subfolders (one for each user) under \Windows\Profiles.

If you choose to use the same Desktop for all users (by marking the first option button in the User Profiles tab), any changes you make to the current user in the registry and any changes you make on the Desktop or in the Start menus will apply to all users. If you let different users customize their own Desktops and Start menus (by marking the second option button), their changes will apply only to their configuration.

Once you set up one additional user, clicking the Users icon in the Control Panel displays the User Settings dialog box (see Figure 6-5). You can add new user profiles, delete existing ones, and change the passwords or settings for a given user. Of course, any user can change his or her own settings or those of any other user. Only by implementing user policies can you restrict users from altering these settings.

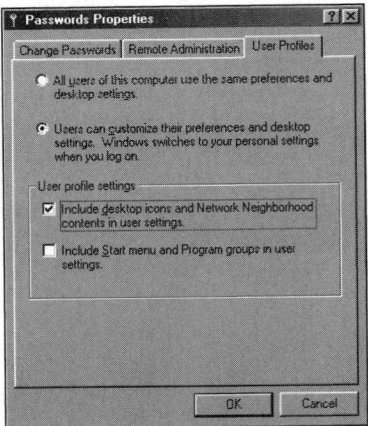

Figure 6-4: The User Profiles tab of the Passwords Properties dialog box. User profiles are enabled as soon as you set up a new user.

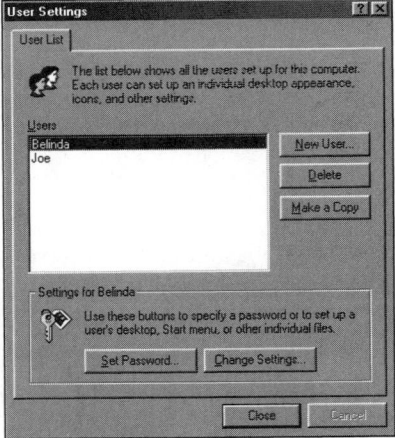

Figure 6-5: The User Settings dialog box. You can add or remove users and change all their settings.

You can also use the Passwords icon in the Control Panel to change your password. In the Passwords Properties dialog box, click the Change Passwords tab and make the desired changes. You can even change your password to blank if you have previously put in another password.

Some settings on your computer apply to all users, and some can be individually determined. Using TweakUI, the System Policy Editor, and user profiles, you can configure individual user settings to some degree, but not completely. Clicking the question mark in the upper-right corner of the TweakUI dialog box and then clicking a setting will tell you if the setting is determined on a per-user or global basis.

Setting Up Your Network Logon Option

To log onto the network when you first start Windows, you have to enter your user name in the logon box. If you want to just get into Windows locally, you don't need to log onto a network, and you can forego the logon box at startup time. To set up your logon options, follow these steps:

STEPS

Configuring Logon Options

Step 1. Click the Start button, point to Settings, and then click Control Panel.

Step 2. Click the Network icon in the Control Panel. Display the Primary Network Logon drop-down list (see Figure 6-6).

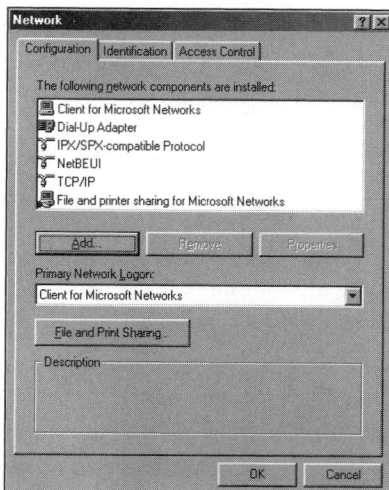

Figure 6-6: The Network dialog box. If you click the Primary Network Logon field, the Description field tells you about the field. To get more detailed information, right-click the field and choose What's This?

Continued

STEPS

Configuring Logon Options *(continued)*

Step 3.   Choose Windows Logon, Client for Microsoft Networks, Client for NetWare Networks, or other possible choices.

Step 4.   Click OK. Restart Windows to have your changes take effect.

If you choose Windows Logon in Step 3, you are saying you don't want to log onto the network, whatever network that might be. If you choose Windows Logon and you've met the first two conditions described in "Whose Desktop Is This Anyway?" earlier in this chapter, the logon box won't appear the next time you start Windows.

You can choose Client for Microsoft Networks in Step 3, and as long as you aren't logging on when you start up Windows, you can still make the logon box disappear. If your network connection is through Dial-Up Networking (DUN), for example, and not through a local area network, you won't have to see the logon box or actively log onto your Windows computer.

Even though you can set up Windows so that you don't see the logon box, this doesn't mean that you haven't logged onto your own computer. If you have a user name and a blank password, you are logged on as your user name when you start Windows, and all your other passwords (for example, your DUN passwords) are stored in your password file.

Securing the Windows Desktop

Windows is designed to be user friendly, not secure. Your Windows computer is not protected from unauthorized use, even if you set up a name and password to protect (sort of) your Desktop configuration. Anyone with physical access to your computer can just log on under a new name and password or press Escape when the logon box appears.

If you want a higher level of access restrictions, you'll need add-on utilities. Passwords and security features are not "friendly," but neither is the experience of discovering that someone has tampered with your computer.

For better security, you can download Clasp97 from http://www.cyberenet. net/~ryan/.

You can find more utilities that provide an additional measure of safety at www.winfiles.com. In addition, if you have enabled user profiles, you can modify Windows to be more secure. Details are available at www.conitech. com/windows/secure.html.

Dealing with a Corrupted Password File

If you have logged onto a Windows computer, Windows creates a password file and saves all your other passwords in this file. You gain access to the additional passwords in this password file by logging onto your computer with your user name and password (which may be blank). Windows will not create and save a password file for you if you have not logged on under your user name (at least once), and it will not let you access that password file unless you are logged on under that user name. If you canceled the logon box, then you aren't logged on, so you won't have access to any passwords and you won't be able to save any passwords.

If you have never seen the Windows logon box, check to see if you have any password (pwl) files stored in your \Windows folder. If not, you can either configure user profiles for multiple users as described in the "Whose Desktop Is This Anyway?" section or install Dial-Up Networking. Either of these actions will let you log in anew.

If you find that other applications are unable to remember their passwords, but their Save Password checkboxes are not grayed out and are checkable, your password file might be corrupted. You will need to either delete or rename it.

If you find that your DUN connectoids no longer have attached passwords, your password file might be corrupted.

Secret

If you get the error message "MPREXE Caused an Invalid Page Fault in Kernel32.dll" while you're trying to access your Internet service provider or when you're using Dial-Up Networking, you most likely have a corrupted password file.

If you suspect that your password file is corrupted, delete or rename your pwl files in your \Windows folder. Restart Windows and let Windows rebuild them. You'll have to enter all new passwords, but now they can at least be saved.

You can look at a number of Microsoft Knowledge Base articles that deal with password issues. Go to http:/support.microsoft.com/support/kb/articles/Q135/1/97.asp or http://support.microsoft.com/support/kb/articles/Q137/3/61.asp or http://support.microsoft.com/support/kb/articles/Q148/9/25.asp

Dealing with the Start Button

If you installed Windows Me over an existing Windows 3.1*x* directory, you will likely find a large number of submenus attached to the Programs menu on your Start button. Windows Me transforms all your program groups into menus (and their corresponding subfolders in the \Windows\Start Menu\Programs folder), and it turns your program items into shortcuts. All these menus add up to a big mess.

Windows Me has its own collection of menus and shortcuts on the Programs menu as well, and these only add to the clutter. You'll probably want to reorganize things soon after you set up Windows Me. You may wonder if you can get rid of some of the menus. You also may not remember the functions of the applications that now have shortcuts in your various new menus.

Tip

One way to deal with all this clutter and still have a manageable set of Start menus is to drag the menu folders out of the \Windows\Start Menu\ Programs folder into a temporary holding folder. Take the following steps to clean up your Start menus:

STEPS

Uncluttering Your Start Menus

Step 1.   Right-click the My Computer icon on your Desktop. Click Explore to display the Explorer window.

Step 2.   Make sure that "Show hidden files and folders" is turned on (choose View ⇨ Folder Options, and click the View tab).

Step 3.   In the left pane of the Explorer window, highlight the drive or folder in which you want to put a folder that will temporarily store some Start menu items.

Step 4.   In the right pane, right-click, point to New, click Folder, and then type a name for the folder such as **TempStart**.

Step 5.   Navigate to the \Windows\Start Menu folder in the left pane.

Step 6.   Highlight the Programs folder, find the menu folders in Programs that you want to temporarily move out of the Start menus, and drag (move, not copy) them from the Programs folder over to the TempStart folder.

You can also temporarily move shortcuts out of the menus; you might want to drag them to a subfolder of the TempStart folder.

You can use the Explorer to rearrange the menu folders under the \Start Menu\Programs folder so that they make more sense to you. Unlike the Windows 3.1x Program Manager, the Start menus in Windows 95, 98, and Me are hierarchical. The hierarchy of folders and subfolders under the Programs menu corresponds directly to the hierarchy of menus and submenus in the Start menu.

You can continue to move folders and subfolders back and forth between TempStart and your \Windows\Start Menu\Programs folder, rearranging their order, pulling shortcuts from one folder to another, and so on.

TempStart gives you a place to store all the extra folders from your old Windows 3.1x configuration until you decide what to do with your new configuration.

The Start Button Itself

You can place shortcuts right on the main Start menu by dragging folder, application, or document icons over to the Start button and dropping them on it. You should only put your most heavily used applications (or folders or documents) on the main Start menu. To start an application that you've dropped on the Start button, all you have to do is click the Start button and then click the application icon (or press Ctrl+Esc, use the down-arrow key to highlight the application icon, and press Enter). This level of convenience demands that you list just the applications (or folders) that deserve it.

There is a cost to this strategy. As the main Start menu gets bigger, it takes longer to draw, and the shortcuts you add make it hard to get to the other items on the Start menus. The icons on the main Start menu are full size (unless you right-click the taskbar, click Properties, and then mark "Show small icons in Start menu"), which means they take up a considerable amount of room. You should restrict the number of icons you place on the main Start menu so that they don't bog you down.

You aren't restricted to placing your shortcuts on the main Start menu. If you drag a shortcut to the Start button and wait until the menu pops up, you can then drag the shortcut up the menu and out onto one of the submenus. (Not all submenus allow you to add shortcuts in this way; two that do are the Favorites and Programs submenus.)

The Menus on the Programs Menu

The Programs menu can contain submenus as well as icons for applications or documents. You can choose how to mix these different elements.

Tip

If you have just one level of submenus in your Programs menu, these submenus will contain the shortcuts to your applications. If you prefer, you can create a hierarchy of two or more levels of submenus. With this type of setup, you could group similar submenus together (for example, all editing and word processing submenus), and then put them under a more general submenu (say, editors), which would be located directly under Programs.

You can use the Programs menu as often or as infrequently as you like. It can take a fair amount of mousing to get to applications in your Programs menu because you may have to navigate through several cascading menus. You might want to use the Programs menu for applications that you use only once in a while. Another idea is to place the applications you use the least out in the most far-flung submenus, and put the programs you use all the time in the main Programs menu.

Multiple Toolbars

Toolbars were first added to the Windows taskbar in Windows 98, or by installing Internet Explorer 4.0 to Windows 95. Windows Me continues this tradition. (To display/hide toolbars, right-click an empty area on the taskbar, point to Toolbars, and mark/clear the check marks next to the toolbars in the submenu.)

These toolbars don't have to stick with the taskbar. They can either connect to the edges of the screen or float freely on the Desktop. To move a toolbar, point to the line at the left (or upper) edge of the toolbar. When the mouse pointer becomes a double-headed arrow, drag the toolbar to an edge of the screen and drop it there, or drop it over the Desktop.

A toolbar can function as a window full of shortcuts to applications and documents. The advantage of a toolbar over a folder window is that you can keep it hidden until you move your mouse pointer to the edge of your screen where it is docked, at which point it slides into view. (To do this, right-click an empty area on the toolbar and mark Auto-Hide.) In addition, you can force it to display even if you are working in another application in a maximized window. (Right-click the toolbar and choose Always on Top.)

You can turn off text labels for the toolbar buttons by right-clicking the toolbar and disabling Show Text. If you also right-click the toolbar and choose View ⇨ Small, you can make the toolbar available but unobtrusive, as shown in Figure 6-7.

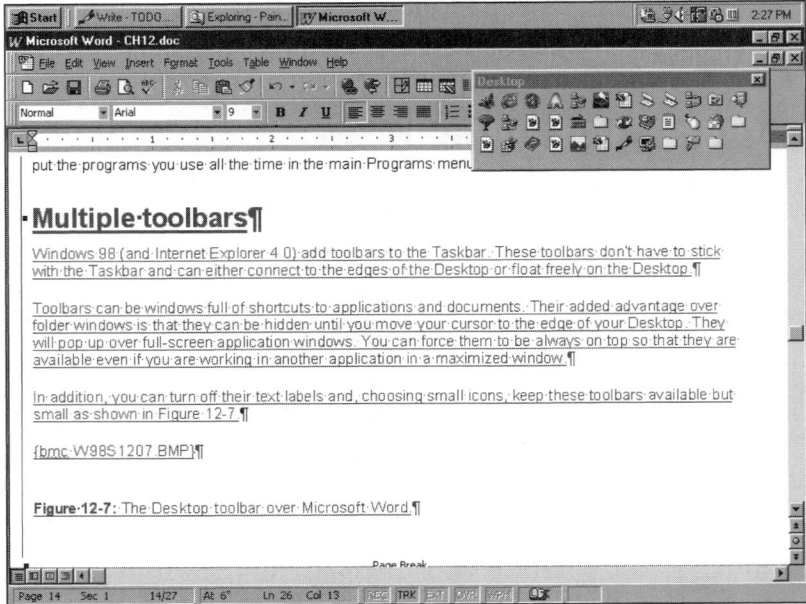

Figure 6-7: The Desktop toolbar over Microsoft Word

Pile It on the Desktop

Your computer Desktop can take it, so why not pile it on? You can throw just about anything that you want on the Desktop, but the best idea is to put shortcuts to applications, folders, and documents there. There is little need to hold back; if you have something that you are dealing with right now, put a shortcut to it on the Desktop.

The Desktop is often easy to get to (especially if you have a large, high-resolution monitor), so you may want to put shortcuts to your most heavily used applications on the Desktop. However, just because shortcuts to your most important applications (in terms of use) end up on the Desktop doesn't mean you should reserve the Desktop for only these high-priority items. You can put just about anything there.

The Desktop is a very convenient temporary storage area. You can right-drag files out of a folder window or the Explorer and drop them there (creating shortcuts when the context menu appears) without having to open another folder window. You can go back later and drag these shortcuts to new locations. Alternatively, you can drop the actual files on the Desktop and move them later.

You can even drag text selections out onto the Desktop from documents created in WordPad or other Desktop-aware word processors. When you use the Desktop this way, it functions like a permanent Clipboard.

It's easy to get things off your Desktop. Just select the icon and press the Delete key, or drag the icon to the Recycle Bin. If the icon is just a shortcut, then no harm is done. You've just removed a link to your application or document. If the icon represents a file, however, you've deleted the whole file. That's why it's a good idea to not put important files and applications on the Desktop, but only shortcuts to them. By doing this, you reduce the risk of deleting something that you wanted.

Tip You can use the Explorer or My Computer to create folders in your \My System folder (if you don't have this folder, you can create it now), and then put shortcuts in them. Then put shortcuts to these folders on the Desktop.

Tip Putting shortcuts to folders on the Desktop is particularly convenient when you're working on a project with many different files in many different folders. You can create a folder to store shortcuts to the files in the project. Put a shortcut to this folder on the Desktop (or on the main Start menu). Now you have a quick way to access all the files in the project.

If the project is divided into recognizable subsets, put the shortcuts to files in each subset into a folder identifying that subset. Put shortcuts to the subset folders into an overall project folder. Put a shortcut to the project folder on the Desktop.

If you have a document that you are working on, drag a shortcut to it onto the Desktop. Click the shortcut, and the document opens in the application you used to create it.

Sometimes you might find it inconvenient to reach the Desktop, especially if you don't have much real estate. For example, you might be running at 640 × 480 on a 14-inch monitor, or maybe you're running your applications in maximized windows. In these situations, you can still use your Desktop. In "The Desktop on the Start Menu" in Chapter 9, we show you how to put the Desktop (the \Windows\Desktop folder) on the main Start menu so that you can always access it, even if it is covered up.

Of course, it's easy to add a Desktop toolbar to your taskbar. Just right-click the taskbar, click Toolbars, and then click Desktop.

Massage the Context Menu

Both the Windows Explorer and My Computer provide navigational windows that give you a view of your computer. Because the Explorer has a folder tree view in the left pane, it has greater navigational abilities, but both can display folders, applications, documents, and Web pages.

If you right-click any of the icons displayed in these views, you get a context menu. You can modify the context menu to make it significantly easier to use. In "Send To Send To" in Chapter 10 and "Creating and Editing File Types and Actions" in Chapter 12, we discuss how to modify the context menu and add destinations — such as a default file opener for all files of unregistered types, Quick View, a file compression program, and your printer — to the Send To menu item. Some of these changes are very easy to make, while others require that you edit the registry a bit.

Summary

Windows is still in the box and waiting for you to assemble it. You might want to add some batteries.

▶ We show you how to dredge up the good stuff and put it where the sun does shine.

▶ We give you a way to clean up the clutter Windows Me created in your Start menus if you set it up over an old Windows 3.1x directory.

▶ We encourage you to use the Desktop as you would any horizontal surface in your office — pile it on. We also show you how you can keep it neat with shortcuts to folders.

Chapter 7

The Explorer

In This Chapter

The Windows Me Explorer has come a long way since its lowly days as the old Windows program called the File Manager. Leaving behind the not-so-friendly confines of your computer, it has merged with the Internet Explorer to become a tool that lets you venture far beyond your own hard disk and local network. We discuss:

▶ Modifying the Explorer on the Start button to act the way you want it to

▶ Putting the Explorer on the Desktop

▶ Using the Explorer to quickly copy and move files and folders

▶ Using keyboard shortcuts to reduce mouse clicking in the Explorer and My Computer windows

▶ Controlling multiple Explorer windows on your Desktop

▶ Learning to use the Explorer to manage all of your files, and much more

▶ Viewing thumbnails of your graphics files

Explorer Basics

To the user, the Windows Explorer first appears as a hierarchical file cabinet or outline view of My Computer — actually *your* computer. It lets you easily understand the file and folder structure of your computer. You can use the Explorer to move, copy, rename, view, and delete files and folders on your computer and on the network. You can also run programs or access documents by clicking files displayed in the Explorer. It gives you a dual-pane view of a folder window.

After Windows is installed, you'll find files and folders have already been stored on your disk drives in a hierarchical structure. Folders divide up your hard drive(s), subfolders divide up folders, and sub-subfolders divide up subfolders. The Explorer makes this upside-down tree organization evident to you, as shown in Figure 7-1.

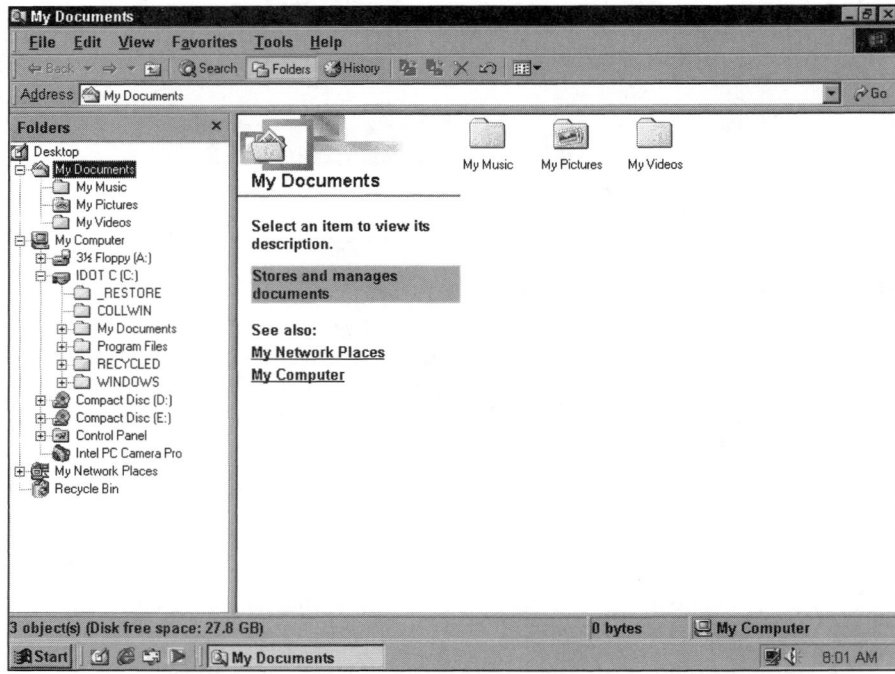

Figure 7-1: An Explorer view of the organization of My Computer. Notice that the hard disk (C:) is connected to and to the right of My Computer. This indicates that it is a part of My Computer. The folder labeled Windows is a part of C:.

Like the Windows 3.1*x* File Manager, the Explorer shows both a tree view and a folder (directory) view. The left pane gives you a hierarchical view of your computer, disk drives, and folders. It also gives you quick access, through special folder icons, to a number of functional areas. The right pane displays the contents of the folder, disk drive, computer, or networked server computer currently selected in the left pane.

Unlike the Windows 3.1*x* File Manager, you can view each branch of the tree in the Explorer by single-clicking the small plus signs to the left of the folder and drive icons. Gone is the need to double-click the icon to expand the branch. A click on the plus sign does not highlight the folder or display its contents in the right pane. This ability to navigate the tree without displaying the contents of folders makes the Explorer easier to use and more versatile than the File Manager.

Tip

You can quickly navigate through your folders and subfolders by clicking the plus signs next to folder names. The Explorer won't try to read the filenames in a folder until you actually select a folder name; therefore, it is much faster than the File Manager.

As you will see in Chapter 8, almost everything regarding the Explorer is applicable to My Computer. All the various ways of copying, moving, renaming, and deleting files and folders are exactly the same for the Explorer and My Computer.

The Explorer Views a Web Page

The Explorer can display Web pages, as can the My Computer window. When you visit a Web page using the Explorer, the Web page's title is shown in the Explorer title bar, as shown in Figure 7-2.

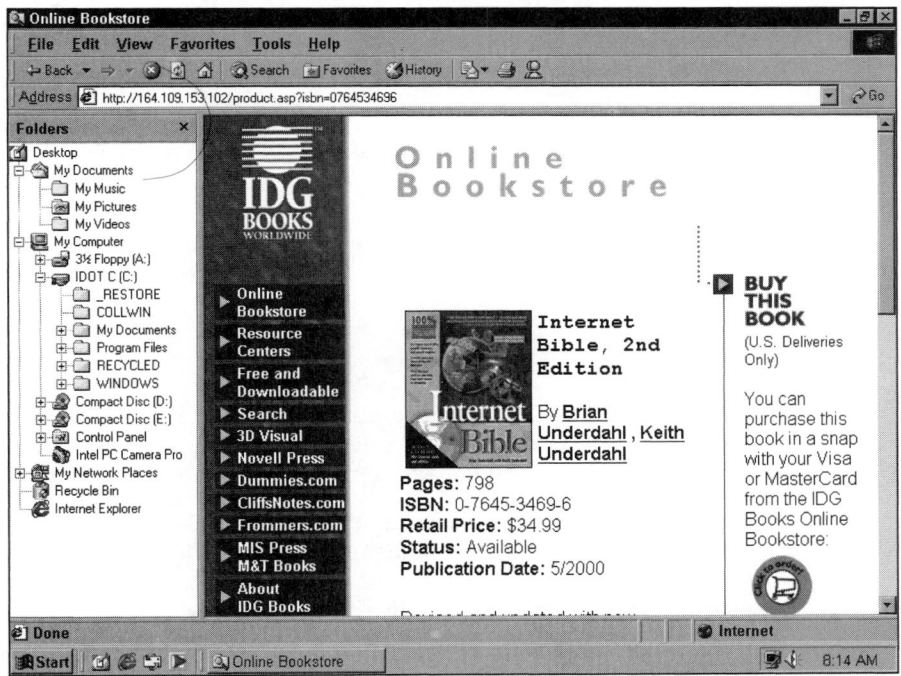

Figure 7-2: An Explorer view of a Web page

The integration of the Internet Explorer with the Windows Explorer means that the Explorer is no longer only capable of displaying folders, filenames, and icons. The Explorer can now display HTML documents because it has gained an integrated HTML-viewing engine.

The Explorer is a dual-pane version of the Internet Explorer. The left pane of the Explorer is called the *Explorer bar*. By default, the Explorer bar appears with the Folders option turned on (View ➪ Explorer Bar ➪ Folders). This option gives you the folder tree. Click the little X in the upper-right corner of the Explorer's left pane to close the Explorer bar, and the Explorer becomes the Internet Explorer.

Secret

Given that the Explorer can view HTML documents, it was an easy step for Microsoft to define a way to view folders as HTML documents. It defined a standard HTML template file (\Windows\Web\Folder.htt) for viewing folders, and it used HTML programming in this file to display the folder icons.

Microsoft also created HTML template files to display the Control Panel (\Windows\Web\Controlp.htt), **My Computer** (\Windows\Web\Mycomp.htt), Recycle Bin, and Dial-Up Networking in new ways. To see an example of this, click the My Computer icon under the Desktop icon in the left pane of an Explorer window. Click a hard disk icon. This HTML view gives you a graphical display of the hard disk size, and the amount of used and unused space on the disk. If you do not see the graphical display, select Tools ⇨ Folder Options and make certain the "Enable Web content in folders" option is selected.

The Explorer, My Computer, and the Internet Explorer are just slight variations on the same thing. All of them give you single- or dual-pane windows through which you view the contents of your computer or the Internet. And all of them can display a Web page or the contents of your computer through the filter of an HTML template file.

Finding the Explorer

Let's check out the Desktop. There's a My Computer icon and an Internet Explorer icon, but there doesn't seem to be an Explorer icon. Could Microsoft have misplaced one of the most important windows of its Windows interface?

Actually, Microsoft is still afraid that you will find the Explorer too difficult, so it gave the Explorer a less prominent place. You'll find it under the Programs ⇨ Accessories menu on the Start button. Hiding the Explorer is Microsoft's way of saying that it's for experts only.

There is a file named Explorer.exe in your \Windows folder, and if you click it, Explorer appears on your Desktop. But surely this isn't how it was meant to be. After all, My Computer sits there in all its glory as the first among icons on the Desktop. Doesn't the Explorer rate something better than a convoluted pathway to Explorer.exe?

If you right-click My Computer, the context menu invites you to Explore. Click Explore and My Computer turns into a dual-pane window view of your computer.

Tip

You can also explore by holding down the Shift key while you double-click the My Computer icon. Just be sure that My Computer is the only icon on your Desktop that is highlighted. Otherwise, you will inadvertently open all the highlighted applications on your Desktop. This happens because Windows interprets the Shift key to mean "select all the icons between the last one highlighted and the My Computer icon." You have to double-click whether you have set single-click or double-click to open an item (Tools ⇨ Folder Options ⇨ Custom ⇨ Settings).

The Explore menu option is available when you right-click the My Network Places icon, the Recycle Bin, the Internet Explorer icon, the Start button, or any folder or disk drive icon. You can view the contents of any of these items in the Explorer view.

The Windows Explorer and the Start Button

The Explorer has its own icon in the Programs submenu of the Start menu.

Click the Start button, point to Programs, and click Windows Explorer in the Programs ⇨ Accessories menu. You can determine just how the Explorer starts up (when you start it from the Programs menu) by editing the properties of this menu item. See the section later in this chapter entitled "Explorer Command-Line Parameters."

Putting the Explorer on the Desktop

My Computer is on the Desktop. You can put the Explorer on the Desktop, too. By doing this, you are saying that the Explorer view is just as important as the My Computer view of your computer. The easiest way to do this is to put a shortcut to the Explorer on the Desktop. To create a shortcut to Explorer, take the following steps:

STEPS

Putting the Explorer on the Desktop

Step 1.   Click Start, point to Programs, and right-click the Windows Explorer icon.

Step 2.   Click Create Shortcut. A new Windows Explorer icon will be added to the menu. Click the down arrow at the bottom of the menu to see it.

Step 3.   Drag the new Windows Explorer shortcut to the Desktop and drop it there.

Step 4.   Right-click the new Windows Explorer icon on the Desktop and click Rename to get rid of the (2) in the name or change the name to Explorer (or whatever you like). Press Enter.

Getting an Overview of Your Computer

The Explorer displays icons arranged hierarchically in its left pane, as shown in Figure 7-3. The topmost icon is the Desktop. At the second level, you'll find My Documents, My Computer, My Network Places, and some additional icons. Floppy-disk drive icons, hard disk drive icons, and folder icons (some with little graphics on them) are attached to My Computer.

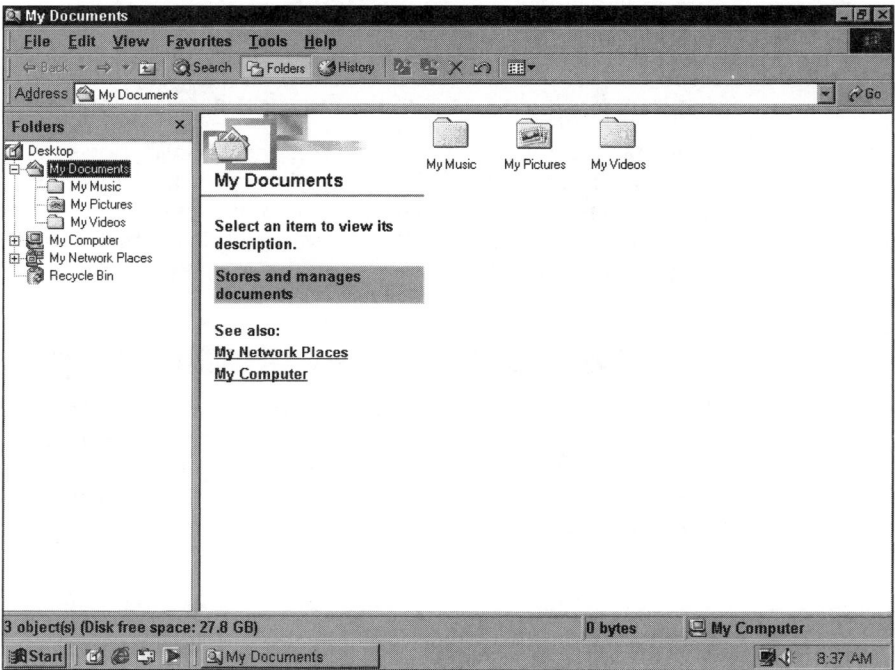

Figure 7-3: The Explorer view. The left pane shows the Desktop and the items that are attached to it.

The view of your computer in the left pane of the Explorer is somewhat strange. It states that everything is part of and contained within the Desktop. But it is clear if we view the contents of the \Windows folder (after marking "Show hidden files and folders," as described in the "Seeing All the Files on Your Computer" section later in this chapter) that the Desktop is a subfolder of your \Windows folder. The \Windows folder is contained within a disk drive that is contained within My Computer. In addition, the Explorer (remember it is Explorer.exe) resides in the \Windows folder.

The Desktop appears at the top and the Desktop appears as a sub-sub-sub-folder of itself, as shown in Figure 7-4. The Explorer appears as a window on top of the Desktop, and at the same time it displays the Desktop (as a folder and as the Desktop) within the Explorer, which is itself a member of the Desktop.

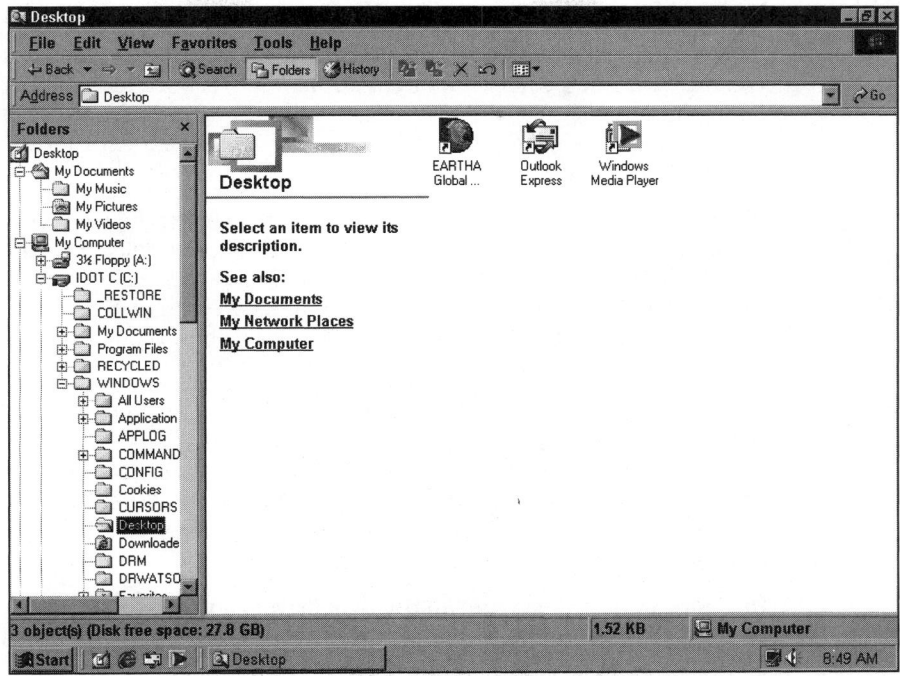

Figure 7-4: Viewing the Desktop as both the icon at the top of the hierarchy and as a folder in the Windows folder.

So making a conceptual leap, you see that My Computer is connected to the Desktop, and that the disk drives — hard and floppy — are connected to My Computer.

The dotted lines are your guides. If a vertical dotted line comes out of the bottom of an icon, the icons connected to that line by horizontal dotted lines are contained within the top icon. My Computer, My Documents, My Network Places, Internet Explorer, Online Services, and Recycle Bin are all contained within the Desktop. The disk drives are contained within My Computer.

The My Documents icon is just a shortcut to your My Documents folder. You can rename this icon and the My Documents folder anything you like and/or change the shortcut to point to any folder. (Right-click the icon, choose Properties, and change the contents of the Target field in the Shortcut tab.) Microsoft is just providing an easy way for you to get to the general area — the folder — that you use to store all your documents. Presumably, you'll divide up the My Documents folder into subfolders.

The My Documents folder has a different folder icon. Since you can name this folder anything you like, you might as well use this folder to store all your documents and data.

The My Network Places icon represents all the computers connected to yours over a LAN. You won't have a My Network Places icon on your Desktop unless you have installed a network or set up Dial-Up Networking or Direct Cable Connection (DCC). You shouldn't remove it from the Desktop (and therefore from the Explorer) with TweakUI unless you are not using DCC or any other networking function, including dialing into the Internet.

My Network Places and Recycle Bin are displayed on the same level as My Computer. Microsoft wants you to think of the network in the same way as you think of your computer. The Recycle Bin spans local hard disk drives (but not floppy drives). In this way, it is indeed equal to My Computer. Also, Microsoft wanted the Recycle Bin on the Desktop permanently.

Shortcuts that you have placed on your Desktop don't appear in the left pane of the Explorer — too much clutter. They do, however, appear in the right pane if you highlight the Desktop icon in the left pane. The Outlook Express, Microsoft Network, and the Inbox icons, even though they are on the Desktop, don't show in the left pane. File icons on the Desktop don't show either. If you place folders on the Desktop, they do show up in the left pane.

Ordinary folders are stored in the disk drives, and the folder icons are connected to the drive icons. Figure 7-3 doesn't show any folder icons attached to the drive icons because the view in the left pane hasn't been expanded to include them. You can see them in Figure 7-4. File icons never show up in the left pane of the Explorer window.

Special Folders

When you install Windows, it sets up a number of preconfigured folders that have special characteristics. These include \My Documents, \Recycled, \Program Files, \Windows\Recent, \Windows\SendTo, and \Windows\ Fonts. In order to work with the Internet Explorer, Windows also creates a \Windows\Favorites folder for Internet Web pages, and a \Windows\ History folder to keep track of the URLs for previously visited Web sites. There are numerous other special or system folders as well.

Some of these folders contain a hidden file called Desktop.ini. This file may have a reference to a dynamic link library (dll) file that defines a particular set of behaviors for the folder. Windows gives these folders the System attribute. Others are just regular folders that Windows uses as default storage locations for certain kinds of files. For example, the default storage location for new applications is \Program Files.

Windows keeps track of some of these folders in the registry. You can edit their entries to point to other locations. This can be useful if you want to move one of these folders to another drive. This doesn't work for the Fonts folder, however.

You can use your Registry Editor (see Chapter 11) to review the settings in HKEY_CURRENT_USER\ Software\ Microsoft\ Windows\ CurrentVersion\ Explorer\ shellfolders. Better still, use TweakUI to make the necessary registry changes. Click the General tab, choose the folder you want to move in the Folder drop-down list, and click the Change Location button.

We suggest that you create another folder under the root directory named \My System. You can use this folder to store files and applications that modify the behavior of your computer, but are specific to your computer alone. Then, no matter how often you update your \Windows or \Windows\ System folders, your still have your original files in \My System.

Two Panes—Connected and Yet Independent

The two panes of the Explorer window are connected. You click an icon in the left pane, and the contents of that drive or folder appear in the right pane.

Much of the power of the Explorer comes from the fact that the two panes, although connected, are also independent of each other. You can view the contents of one folder in the right pane and, without disturbing that view, expand the tree in the left pane to find another folder. This makes it easy to copy or move files and folders from one folder to another.

Think of the right pane of the Explorer window as a folder window. It acts just like a folder window, except that the default action when you click a folder icon in the right pane is to open the folder in the existing Explorer window, rather to open a folder window.

Notice that you do have to click an icon in the left pane to select it. In the right pane, you can hover to select an icon.

The left pane of the Explorer window is now called the Explorer bar (click View ⇨ Explorer Bar).

Click the little X in the upper-right corner of the Explorer bar and the Explorer turns into a folder window.

Previews

You can display preview views of some of the files in a folder. Right-click the right pane of the Explorer window and choose View ⇨ Thumbnails. Preview views of quite a few different types of files are available, including graphics files in bmp, gif, jpg, and tif formats, HTML files (htm or html), and PowerPoint files (ppt). We show an example of previewing a jpg file in Figure 7-5.

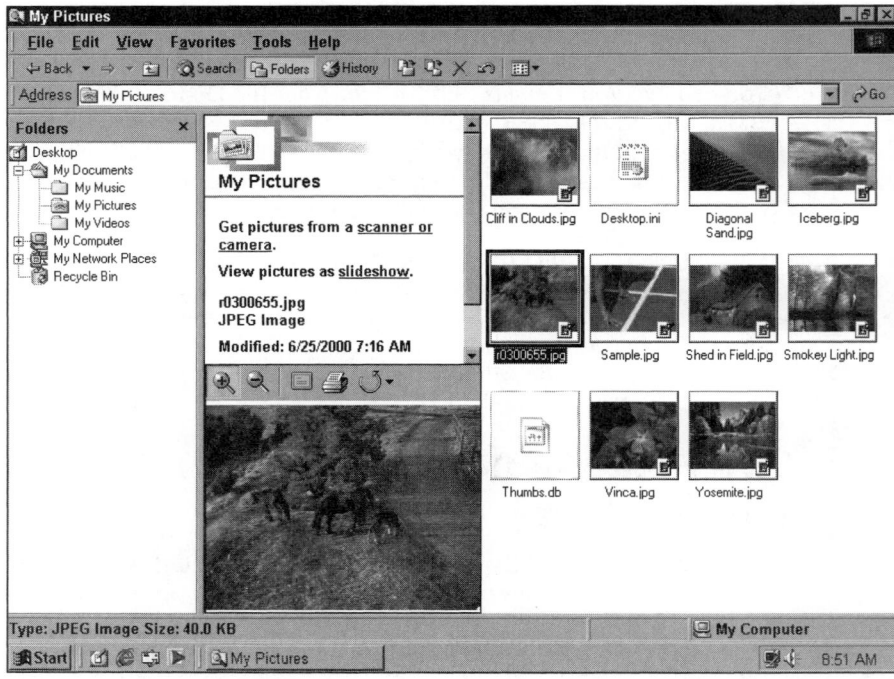

Figure 7-5: The preview of a jpg file

Folder Options

Choosing Tools ➪ Folder Options in any Explorer or My Computer window lets you set a number of Desktop, Explorer, My Computer, and Internet Explorer options. You can also use View ➪ Customize This Folder to open a wizard that enables you to make a number of interesting changes in a folder's appearance.

Windows settings are spread all over the place; Folder Options is just one location of many. This is the dialog box you use to make the basic choice between Web style and Classic style. Web style displays all folders as Web pages. Classic style doesn't display folders as Web pages. This dialog box also enables you to choose between single-click to open and hover to select or double-click to open and single-click to select.

Sticky View Settings

For some users, the improvement to the interface in Windows that they appreciate the most is the fact that each folder can now maintain its own settings. Now you can design each folder window to be the way you like it.

The view settings that you have control over are the icon views in a folder window (Large Icons, Small Icons, List, or Details), the icon order (By Name, By Type, By Size, and By Date), and the widths and order of the columns in Details view.

Now you can display each folder in a manner that is best suited for the contents of that folder. You might display a folder full of shortcuts to applications in Large Icons view sorted by name. If a folder contains pictures, you might choose Thumbnail view so that you can see previews of the files. And if a folder contains documents, you might display it in Details view sorted by date.

To modify how Windows handles view settings, choose Tools ⇨ Folder Options and click the View tab. If you want each folder to remember its view settings, mark "Remember each folder's view settings." To force the view settings for all folders to be the same as the current folder, mark the Like Current Folder button. To force all folders back to the default view settings, click the Reset All Folders button. This process is much easier than it was with the old Windows 95, when you had to change existing views one at a time.

Seeing All the Files on Your Computer

Microsoft is somewhat ashamed of the three-letter file extensions it uses to define file types. It is also a bit embarrassed by its eight-character followed by three-character filenames. It has created a way of doing long filenames (255 characters long) without upsetting its existing disk file structure (FAT, for file allocation table). It wants Windows users to forget about file extensions.

When you first install Windows, it doesn't show files with certain extensions in folder windows or in Explorer windows. And it doesn't show the three-letter extensions for files of registered file types. You can tell Windows to display these missing files and extensions. Here's how:

STEPS

Viewing All Files and File Extensions

Step 1.   Click your My Computer icon.

Step 2.   Choose Tools ⇨ Folder Options, and click the View tab, as shown in Figure 7-6.

Continued

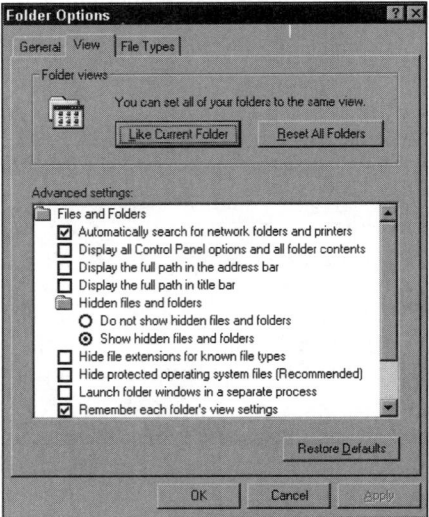

Figure 7-6: The View tab of the Folder Options dialog box

Step 3. Mark the "Show hidden files and folders" option button and clear the checkbox labeled "Hide file extensions for known file types."

Step 4. Click OK.

Seeing Hidden Folders

Secret

If you mark the "Show hidden files and folders" option button, you also get to see more folders contained in the \Windows folder. Microsoft appears to think that less "advanced" users will have a problem with these folders showing up in their folder windows, so it hides them from the view of users who choose to hide files of certain types.

You can see which folders get hidden by opening an Explorer window and expanding the branch connected to your \Windows folder icon in the folder tree. Watch the list of folders change as you switch back and forth between "Show hidden files and folders" and "Hide protected operating system files," clicking the Apply button after each change.

Single-Click or Double-Click

The General tab of the View ⇨ Folder Options dialog box lets you choose between single-clicking and double-clicking to open items. When single-clicking is enabled, you can select icons by hovering your mouse pointer over them. When double-clicking is enabled, you have to click to select icons.

Throughout this book, we assume that you have selected the single-click option.

Navigating with the Explorer

The Explorer is your navigator. It guides you to the files and folders on your computer's disk drives or, if you are connected to a network, on other computers. The Explorer displays, in an expandable tree, your computer's drives and the drives of other computers to which you are networked. You search through the drives by clicking the Explorer tree to expand it. The Explorer also gives you an easy way to copy, move, and link files or folders across disk drives, folders, or the network.

Because the Explorer gives you an overview and a road map of your computer and the server computers you are connected to, you can use it to find your way around computer space. The key to navigating is using the little plus signs to the left of the icons in the folder tree. Clicking a plus sign expands that branch of the tree. For example, clicking the plus sign next to your C: drive icon expands the tree to allow you to see all the folders attached to the root directory of the C: drive.

Click the plus sign next to any of the folders on the C: drive, and you'll see the folders contained within that folder. Each branch of the folder tree gets expanded as you climb out the branches. To collapse a branch, click the minus sign to the left of an icon. The minus sign appears as soon as you expand a branch.

Tip

The folder tree appears in the left pane of the Explorer, which is called the *Explorer bar*. The version of the Explorer bar that shows you the folder tree is called All Folders. (This is the default setting.) You can display other versions of the Explorer bar by choosing View ⇨ Explorer Bar, and clicking Search, Favorites, History, or Channels. These versions let you navigate the Internet in the left pane of the Explorer window. However, most of the time you will probably find it more convenient to navigate the Internet by clicking hyperlinks in a single-pane window (such as a folder window or the Internet Explorer).

You can also navigate by clicking the Back and Forward buttons on the Standard Buttons toolbar. These buttons let you move back to a previously viewed Web page or folder, and then move forward again to the Web page or folder you viewed most recently.

Highlighting a Folder Icon

If you click a folder icon in the left pane, you see the contents of that folder in the right pane. If the contents of the right pane include folder icons, you can expand a branch by clicking one of them. The folder tree in the left pane of the Explorer also expands when you do this.

The default action of clicking a folder icon in the left pane is to display the contents of the folder in the right pane. If you instead right-click a folder icon and choose Open in the context menu, Windows opens a new folder window on the Desktop with the contents of the folder.

Tip

If you click a folder icon in the tree, you both expand the branch at that node and display the contents of the folder in the right pane.

Secret

If you click a folder icon in the right pane of the Explorer, the Explorer view expands to display the contents of that folder in the right pane. By making a change to the folder definition in your registry, you can have this action display the contents of the folder in a new window instead of in the Explorer.

STEPS

Making Single-Pane Views from the Explorer

Step 1. Click Regedit.exe in the \Windows folder. Click the plus sign next to the HKEY_CLASSES_ROOT key. Scroll down to the Folder key.

Step 2. Click the plus sign next to the Folder key and highlight the *shell* key.

Step 3. Double-click Default in the right pane to display the Edit String dialog box. Type **Open** in the Value Data field and click OK.

Step 4. Click a folder icon in the right pane of the Explorer and notice this action now opens a new window. If you click a folder icon in the left pane in the Explorer, the right pane still displays the contents of that folder.

Folder Icons in the Explorer

Double-click a folder icon in the left pane of the Explorer. If this folder has subfolders, clicking it will display them in the folder tree. The double-click is a toggle. If you double-click the folder icon again, the folder tree collapses to hide the subfolders. You have to double-click even if you are using Web style.

Secret

Try this: Drag and hold a file or folder icon from the right pane over a folder icon in the left pane. If the folder in the left pane has subfolders that were previously not displayed (the folder had a plus sign next to it), they are now displayed. This allows you to navigate down the folder tree and find the target subfolder as you are dragging.

Two Versions of the Standard Buttons Toolbar

Windows provides two versions of the Standard Buttons toolbar. One version looks something like the toolbar in the old Windows 95, and the other contains Internet-related buttons. We often refer to this version as the *Internet toolbar*. The Explorer automatically switches to the Internet toolbar if you are using the Explorer to view a Web page.

The Internet toolbar first appeared in earlier versions of the Internet Explorer. Now this toolbar shows up wherever you view Web pages. We discuss this aspect of the Windows user interface in more detail in Chapter 8.

You can increase the height of the Standard Buttons toolbar by pulling down on its bottom edge, if no text labels are showing. If you do this, the toolbar will include text labels as well as icons. You can also right-click a blank part of any of the toolbars and mark or clear Text Labels.

Making the Left Pane Bigger

The two panes of the Explorer window are divided by a vertical bar. You can increase the width of the left pane so that you can see more of its contents as you expand branches of the folder tree. To do this, rest your mouse pointer over the vertical bar. When the mouse pointer turns into a vertical line with two arrows, drag the bar to the right.

Full-Screen Explorer

Windows comes with a full-screen version of the Explorer. (It also has full-screen versions of folder windows and the Internet Explorer.)

To open a full-screen window, press F11 while focused on an Explorer window or hold down the Ctrl key and click the Maximize button at the right end of the Explorer title bar. Your Explorer window will enlarge to cover the Desktop (see Figure 7-7).

You can turn this view into a dual-pane view by moving your mouse pointer to the left. The Folders pane slides into view. Move your mouse pointer back to the right side of this Desktop-sized window, and the Folders pane disappears.

If you want your taskbar to appear over this window, move your mouse pointer to the edge of the screen to which the taskbar is attached.

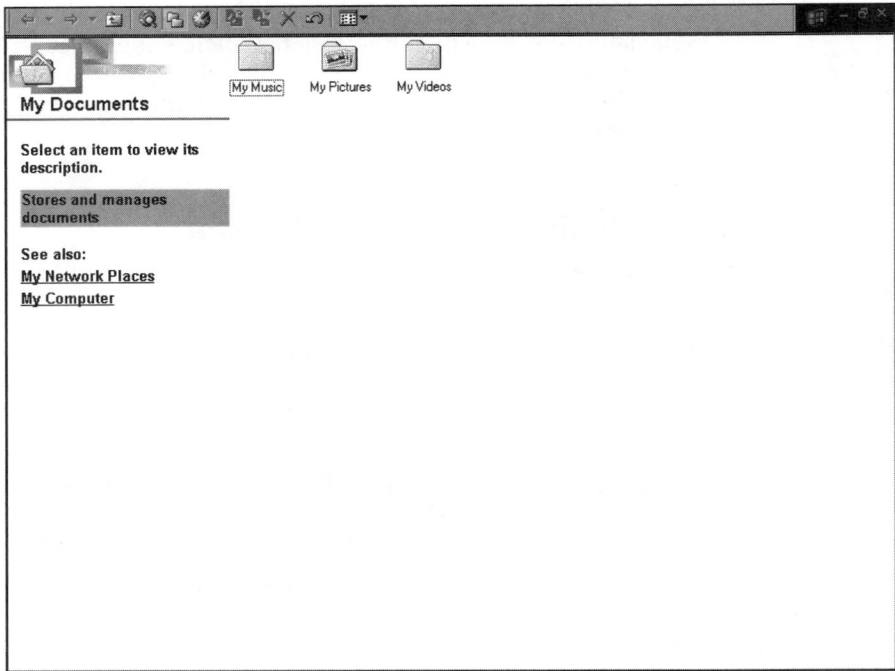

Figure 7-7: The Explorer in full-screen view. Click the Minimize button or press F11 to get your Desktop back.

The My Network Places

The My Network Places icon contains the shared resources of the computers to which your computer is connected. Click this icon to see the disk drives, folders, and printers that are available (shared) to you.

You can expand branches of the folder trees found on other computers just as easily as you can on your computer. Windows treats the networked computers just like My Computer to encourage you to do likewise. You can use the Explorer window to browse networked computers just as you do your own computer.

If you like, you can map a shared folder or disk drive to a drive letter, thereby making it appear as though it is part of My Computer. To do this, choose Tools ➪ Map Network Drive in the Explorer window.

If you want to connect to a shared printer, use the Printers folder (located in the My Computer window).

Using the Keyboard with the Folder Tree

Secret

You can, if you like, expand all the branches of the folder tree at once. To do this, hold down the Alt key and press the asterisk (*) above the number pad. We don't really recommend expanding all branches at once because it can take a long time.

To expand or collapse branches with your mouse, you click the plus and minus signs next to the branches. If you want to use the keyboard instead, press Tab a few times if necessary to bring the focus to the left pane of the Explorer window, use the arrow keys to highlight the branch you want to expand or collapse (or type the first few letters of the folder or drive name), and then press the plus key to expand the branch or the minus key to collapse it.

Secret

Normally, if you collapse a high-level branch when branches underneath it are displayed, the next time you expand the branch, all the branches within it are redisplayed as well. If you want to only see the first level of folders under the branch the next time you expand it, press F5 after you collapse it. Windows "invisibly" collapses the branches under the high-level branch so that they won't show the next time you expand it.

Creating Two Explorer Windows

Using the Windows 3.1*x* File Manager, it was much easier to manage files if you had two child windows open at the same time. Each window had two panes (the directory tree on the left and the directory contents on the right), so when two child windows were open, the File Manager contained a total of four panes.

You could use one child window to display the source directory and the other window to display the destination directory. This made it much easier to copy and move files, or to simply compare the contents of two directories.

Using the File Manager, you couldn't expand the directory tree while maintaining the same contents in the right pane. In contrast, the tree and folder panes in the Explorer are more independent, which allows you to manage files with just two panes.

The File Manager does have an advantage over the Explorer. The File Manager has a multidocument interface. It can contain two child windows within its window border. Microsoft (at least the part of it that isn't producing the Office applications) has decided to drop this interface and have the operating system — not the applications — control the window borders.

As a result of this decision, the Explorer does not have a multidocument interface. So if you want to reduce the amount of scrolling required to find the source and then go to the destination folder when you're moving and copying files, you might find it easier to open two Explorer windows at the same time on the Desktop. This is quite easy to do, because Windows opens a new copy of the Explorer each time you right-click My Computer and click

Explore, or each time you click an Explorer shortcut on the Desktop (see "Putting the Explorer on the Desktop" earlier in this chapter).

Secret

You can open another copy of the Explorer that's already focused on a particular folder by following these steps:

STEPS

Opening a Second Copy of the Explorer

Step 1. In the left pane of an Explorer window, right-click the folder icon you want to Explore. This could be either the source or destination folder.

Step 2. Click Open in the context menu.

Step 3. Right-click the system menu icon (at the left end of the title bar) of the newly opened folder window.

Step 4. Select Explore in the context menu.

Step 5. Click the Close button in the upper-right corner of the folder window you created in step 2.

This will open a new copy of the Explorer with the focus on the selected folder. Once you have two Explorer windows, you can display the contents of the destination folder in one and the source folder in the other.

Tip

You can arrange the Explorer windows like the child windows in the File Manager by right-clicking the taskbar and choosing Cascade, Tile Windows Horizontally, or Tile Windows Vertically. (Before you issue one of these commands, make sure all your other open windows are minimized.) When tiled, the two Explorer windows cover your Desktop completely and look like the two child windows in the Windows 3.1x File Manager when it was maximized.

Secret

If you leave two tiled Explorer windows open when you shut down your computer, they will be ready to go when you start it again. Unfortunately, the two windows won't stay tiled, but will instead be stacked on top of each other. (This is because Window erroneously saves the position of only one Explorer window.) You'll need to right-click the taskbar and choose Tile Windows Horizontally or Tile Windows Vertically to separate the windows again.

Explorer (and My Computer) Keyboard Shortcuts

The Explorer and the My Computer folder windows share a common set of keyboard shortcuts. They are listed in Table 7-1.

Table 7-1	Explorer and Folder Window Keyboard Shortcuts
Key	**Action**
F1	Help.
F2	Rename the highlighted file or folder.
F3	Bring up the Find dialog box.
F4	Display down the list in the Address bar (if any). This is a toggle switch.
F5	Refresh the windows. If the files or folders in a window have changed and have not yet been updated, this will update the display.
F6	Move the focus from left pane, to the Address bar (if you have one), to the right pane, and back to the left pane again. In a folder window, there is only one pane.
F10	Put the focus on the File menu.
F11	Toggle to full screen and back to previous view.
Alt+*	Expand all the branches in the folder tree.
*	Expand all branches below the focused node (folder or drive icon).
Backspace	Move up one level in the folder hierarchy.
Tab	Same as F6; shift the focus between the two panes and the Address bar. This is very useful for navigating the folder tree or picking out files and folders in the right pane.
Arrow keys	Move up and down the folder tree in the left pane or the list of files and folders in the right pane. If you move quickly enough in the left pane, the highlighted folder's contents do not show in the right pane. If you leave the focus on one icon for more than a second, its contents are displayed in the right pane.
Right arrow	Expand the highlighted folder if it isn't expanded already. If it is, go to the subfolder.
Left arrow	Collapse the highlighted folder if it is expanded. If not, go to the parent folder.

Continued

Table 7-1 *(continued)*

Key	Action
Ctrl+arrow keys	Scroll the left or right pane, depending on which pane has the focus. You can use PgUp and PgDn keys also. The focus isn't changed.
Enter	Does nothing in the folder tree. In the right pane, pressing Enter runs the selected file or opens the selected folder, just as clicking would.
Shift+F10	Display the context menu. Same as right-click. Throughout the Windows interface, pressing Shift+F10 is equivalent to clicking the right mouse button.
+	The keypad plus sign. When a folder name is highlighted and the branch below it is collapsed, expand the branch.
−	The keypad minus sign. When a folder name is highlighted and the branch below it is expanded, collapse the branch. When combined with F5, collapse all the branches below.
Alt+spacebar	Open the system menu. This menu allows you to move, minimize, maximize, size, or close the folder or Explorer window.
Alt+Enter	Display the folder's properties.
Ctrl+G	Open the Go To Folder dialog box. This allows you to enter the name of a folder or computer to go to.
Ctrl+X	Cut highlighted item.
Ctrl+C	Copy highlighted item.
Ctrl+V	Paste copied or cut item.
Ctrl+Z	Undo a previous action.
Letter(s)	Jump to the first folder whose name starts with that letter(s). If you type the same letter(s) again, jump to the next folder whose name starts with those letters. You need to type multiple letters quickly or Windows will interpret the second letter as a new first letter.
Alt+F4	Close the application window. Throughout the Windows interface, Alt+F4 closes all applications.

Explore from Here

Later in this chapter we show you how to use the Explorer command line switches to change the Explorer's behavior. One way that you can use switches is to set the top of the Explorer folder list at your current folder and just display the branches shooting out from there.

Secret

If you want to do the same thing without command-line switches, you can add Explore from Here to the context menu that appears when you right-click a folder icon in your Explorer or My Computer window. Selecting it brings up a new Explorer window displaying just the subfolders of the folder you right-clicked. Follow these steps to make this change yourself. Alternatively, you can download PowerToys and use one of its utilities, as described at the end of this section.

STEPS

Adding Explore from Here to All Your Folders

Step 1. Click Start ⇨ Run, type **regedit**, and press Enter.

Step 2. Navigate in the left pane to HKEY_CLASSES_ROOT\ Folder\ shell.

Step 3. Right-click the right pane of your Registry Editor, and click New ⇨ Key.

Step 4. Rename the key something like **fromhere**.

Step 5. Highlight the fromhere key, double-click Default in the right pane, and type **E&xplore from Here** in the Value Data field. The ampersand allows you to use the X key to select this item in the context menu. Click OK.

Step 6. Highlight the fromhere key, right-click the right pane, and click New ⇨ Key.

Step 7. Rename the new key **command**.

Step 8. Highlight the command key, double-click Default, type **Explorer. exe /e,/root,/idlist,%i** in the Value Data field, and click OK.

Step 9. Close the Registry Editor.

You'll now have a new context menu item whenever you right-click a folder icon.

Windows 95/98 PowerToys includes an `Explore.inf` file that does exactly what we have shown you how to do here. You can find it at `http://tucows. hom.net/adnload/dlpowertoy.html`. Extract the PowerToys utilities to a temporary folder, and install Explore from Here by right-clicking `Explore. inf` and clicking Install.

To find out other ways to modify your context menus, see "Add Items to the Context Menu" and the sections that follow it, later in this chapter.

Moving Around Multitabbed Dialog Boxes

Elsewhere in this book, we provide a long list of keyboard shortcuts that work with the Windows user interface. Chris Pirillo reminded us of a couple that we discussed generally, but not specifically, that are very useful when working with multitabbed dialog boxes.

To switch from tab to tab, press Ctrl+Tab. This combination moves the focus on the tabs from left to right. To move it back, use Ctrl+Shift+Tab. To change the focus within the tab, use Tab and Shift+Tab. To mark and clear checkboxes, press the spacebar.

To display drop-down lists, use Alt+up arrow or Alt+down arrow. To then choose an item in the list, use the arrow keys to select it and press Enter. Pressing Enter sends an overall OK if the focus isn't on any other button (even if you aren't focused on the OK button), and closes the dialog box.

It's actually pretty easy to use Windows without a mouse, but you do have to learn quite a few different (and not always consistent) keystrokes.

Get Rid of the Warning About Viewing the Windows Folder

If you have folder options set to display windows as Web pages, you may find that when you click your \Windows folder, you get a display something like that shown in Figure 7-8. This warning tells you to be careful with this folder.

We assume that anyone who is reading this book is capable of viewing and messing with the files in the \Windows folder and all of its subfolders. Not gratuitously mind you, but with a good idea of what you're doing. Therefore, it seems a bit much to ask you to put up with such a warning, at least after you've seen it once.

We also assume that you've chosen to view all file types, by choosing Tools ⇨ Folder Options, clicking the View tab, marking "Show hidden files and folders," and clearing "Hide file extensions for known file types."

Secret

If you now scroll through your \Windows folder, you'll find the folder.htt file. Its Hidden attribute is marked, but it is still visible to your Explorer. This HTML template file contains the code that displays the original warning message and then lets you into the \Windows folder when you click Show Files.

You can either delete this file, or, if that seems too drastic, rename it. Now you'll be able to view your \Windows folder without being asked if you really want to.

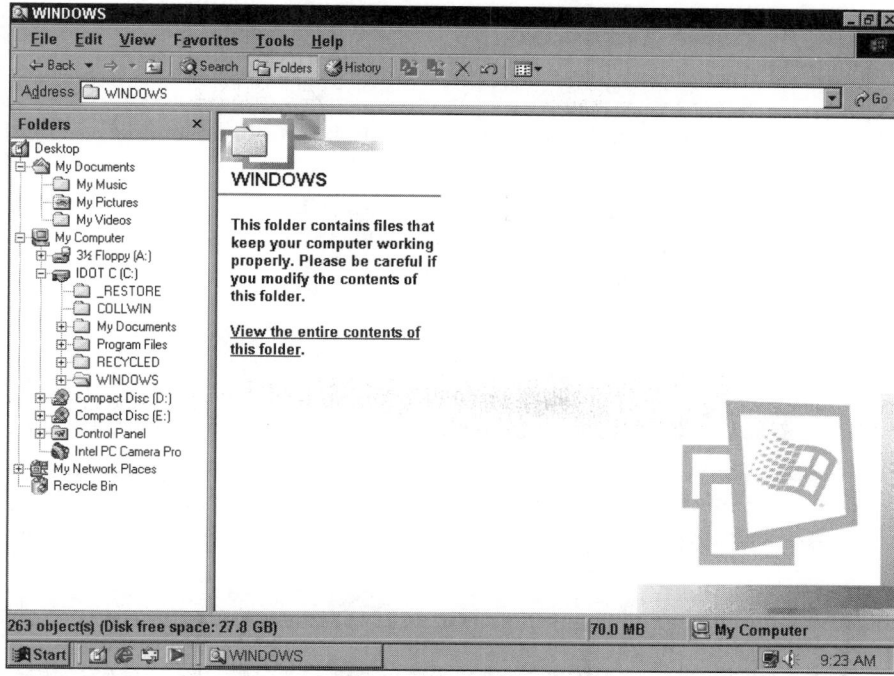

Figure 7-8: The Web Page view of the Windows folder in the Explorer

The Left Pane of Your Explorer Is Missing?

Wow, where did it go? Are you sure that you just didn't click View ⇨ Explorer Bar, and clear the checkmark next to Folders? If you did, just click it again. If not, right-click the Explorer title bar and click Maximize. Is the divider between the two Explorer panes hiding on either the right or left side?

Secret

If these suggestions don't work, you can always edit the registry to return the Folders pane to its default position. Here's how:

STEPS

Recovering the Folders Pane

Step 1. Click Start ⇨ Run, type **regedit**, and press Enter.

Step 2. Navigate to HKEY_CURRENT_USER\ Software\ Microsoft\ Internet Explorer\ Main.

Continued

STEPS

Recovering the Folders Pane *(continued)*

Step 3. Scroll down until you see the ExplorerBar value in the right pane of the Registry Editor.

Step 4. Right-click ExplorerBar, click Delete, and then click Yes. It will revert to its default value.

Step 5. Close the Registry Editor.

Put Two Explorers Next to Each Other

TWinExplorer is a standalone Explorer that combines two Explorers in one window. It's easy to drag and drop files from one folder to another when you can view the source and the target in one window, as shown in Figure 7-9.

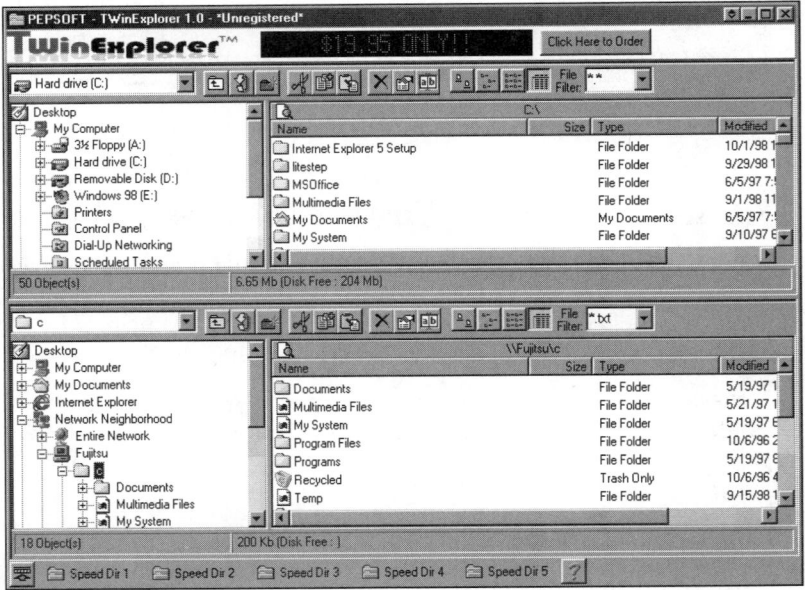

Figure 7-9: TWinExplorer gives you two connected Explorer views for easy dragging and dropping.

TWinExplorer doesn't replace your Windows Explorer; it is a separate application that gives you most of the Windows Explorer functionality while providing two connected Explorer-like views. Those of you who remember

Windows 3.1 with its ability to put up two windows or more in the File Manager will recognize what TWinExplorer is trying to accomplish.

While it can't display HTML pages like the regular Windows Explorer and it doesn't have right-click functionality in the right pane, TWinExplorer can still do some things that the Windows Explorer can't. For example, you can high-light a folder icon in the left pane and click the New Folder toolbar button to create a new folder in the right pane. You can also use the File Filter drop-down list to select which file types to display. And you can define up to five buttons on the status bar that allow you to quickly jump to the assigned folder.

Easy to install and uninstall, you'll find TWinExplorer at `http://www.pepsoft.com`.

Explorer Crashes but You're Still Running

It's not all that hard to crash the Explorer, we say with typical understatement, but it is a quite bit more difficult to understand just went wrong. We're inclined to leave the whys to certain sub-branches of philosophical inquiry. What we want is our system tray icons back—that is, assuming that the system is well enough to teeter onward.

To force the Explorer to refresh these icons, click Start ⇨ Log Off *username* and then click Yes. Of course, this assumes that there is someone else that you can log in as, and then log back in as yourself.

Explorer Command-Line Parameters

Take a moment to look at how the Explorer command-line parameters work:

STEPS

Viewing the Windows Explorer Command-Line Parameters

Step 1. Click the Start button, point to Programs ⇨ Accessories, right-click Windows Explorer, and click Properties.

Step 2. Look at the Target field in the Shortcut tab.

The target for the Windows Explorer shortcut is:

```
C:\WINDOWS\EXPLORER.EXE
```

Change it to:

```
C:\WINDOWS\EXPLORER.EXE /n,/e,C:\
```

With the command-line parameters /n, /e, C:\, an Explorer window you open by clicking Windows Explorer in the Start menu looks like Figure 7-10.

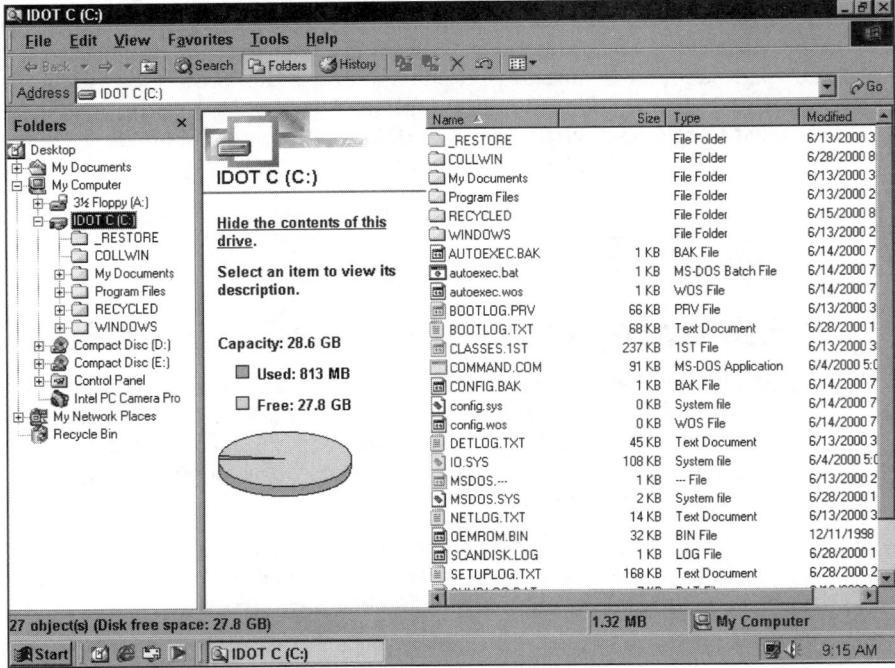

Figure 7-10: An Explorer window focused on the C: drive

The syntax for the Explorer command line is:

```
C:\Windows\Explorer.exe {/n,}{/e,}{options,}{folder}
```

The parameters have the following meanings:

/n,	Opens a *new* Explorer window — by itself, this commands opens a window in folder view
/e,	Opens an *expanded* folder with its contents displayed in Explorer view
options	May be either one of the following: /root, Selects a folder as the *root* of a folder tree or /select, Highlights a folder's parent and displays parent folder's content
folder	May be any folder name or path, such as: C:\ or C:\Windows

Note that you have to use commas between switches on the Explorer command line.

Secret

If there were no command-line parameters after `Explorer.exe`, clicking Windows Explorer in the Start menu would bring up an Explorer window focused on the `C:` drive (where the `Explorer.exe` file is most likely stored).

If you add `C:\Windows` or any other folder name to the Explorer command line, clicking Windows Explorer in the Start menu displays a folder window containing the contents of that folder. Adding a folder name to the Explorer command line turns the Explorer into My Computer.

Secret

If you insert `/e,` (the comma is required) in front of the folder name, clicking Windows Explorer in the Start menu displays an Explorer window focused on the specified folder with the folder expanded and the contents of the folder displayed in the right pane. Putting a folder name in the Target field (command line) takes Explorer out of its default behavior. Using `/e,` restores some of that default behavior; `/e,` means *Explorer view*.

If instead of clicking Windows Explorer in the Start menu, you open an Explorer window and click the shortcut to Windows Explorer found in the `C:\Windows\Start Menu\Program folder`, Windows does not display another Explorer window. Instead, it refocuses your existing Explorer window on the folder in the Target field. To force Windows to create a new Explorer window, you need to add the `/n,` command-line parameter. Adding `/n,` restores the rest of the Explorer's default behavior (except for its focus); `/n,` means *new*.

Secret

When you click Windows Explorer in the Start menu, you get another Explorer window even if you don't use the `/n,` command parameter. The only situation in which you need the `/n,` parameter to get another Explorer window is if you launch the Explorer by clicking the Windows Explorer shortcut within an Explorer window.

You can't replace `C:\Windows` with My Computer or My Network Places. Desktop will work, but it doesn't get you to the top of the hierarchical view of your computer. You might try it to see what we mean.

Secret

The normal topmost icon in the Explorer is the Desktop. This is referred to as the *root* of the folder tree. You can specify a different root if you want. Add `/root,` to the command line and follow it with your new root. The new root could be My Computer, or `C:\Windows`, or whatever you like. Here's an example:

```
C:\WINDOWS\EXPLORER.EXE /n,/e,/root,C:\
```

This example produces an Explorer window that looks like Figure 7-11.

You can use the `/select,` parameter to open a given folder and highlight the folder's parent. Here's an example (see Figure 7-12):

```
C:\WINDOWS\EXPLORER.EXE /n,/e,/select,C:\
```

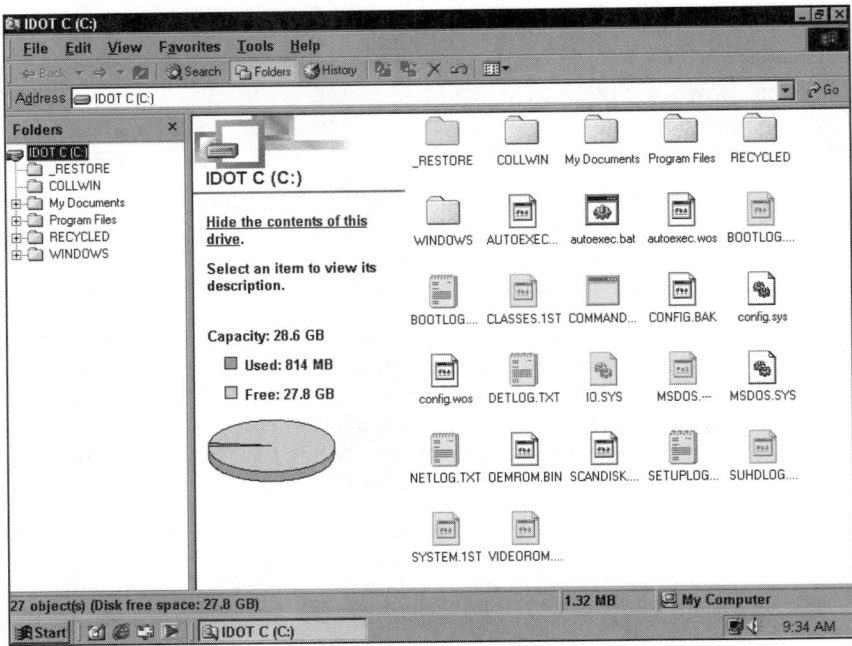

Figure 7-11: An Explorer window with the C: drive as its root (/root,)

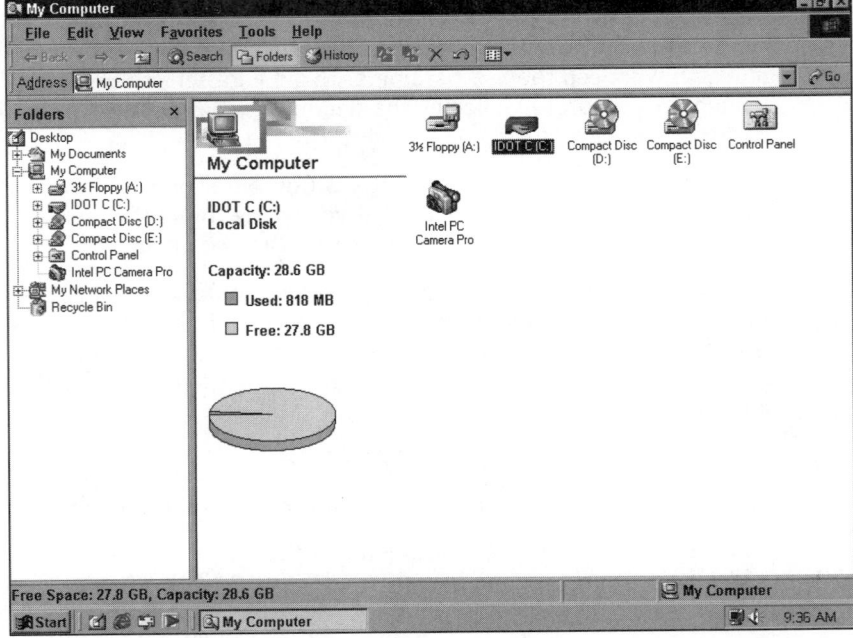

Figure 7-12: An Explorer window focused on the parent of the C: drive, My Computer (/select,)

Notice the differences that these command-line parameters produce by comparing Figures 7-11 and 7-12 with Figure 7-10.

Explorer Thumbnails

Thumbnails are small versions of a graphic image that enable you to see a file's contents without opening or even selecting each file.

Activate Your Thumbnails View

You get two ways to preview your graphics and HTML files with Windows. You can preview them one at a time, or you can build a database of thumbnail views in each folder.

To preview your files one at a time, click the file. You can highlight any gif, bmp, jpg, or HTML file in your folder and view its contents in the preview area to the left of the file list, as shown in Figure 7-13. This is also true of art, dib, jfif, jpe, jpeg, png, ocx, ppt, tif and wmf files.

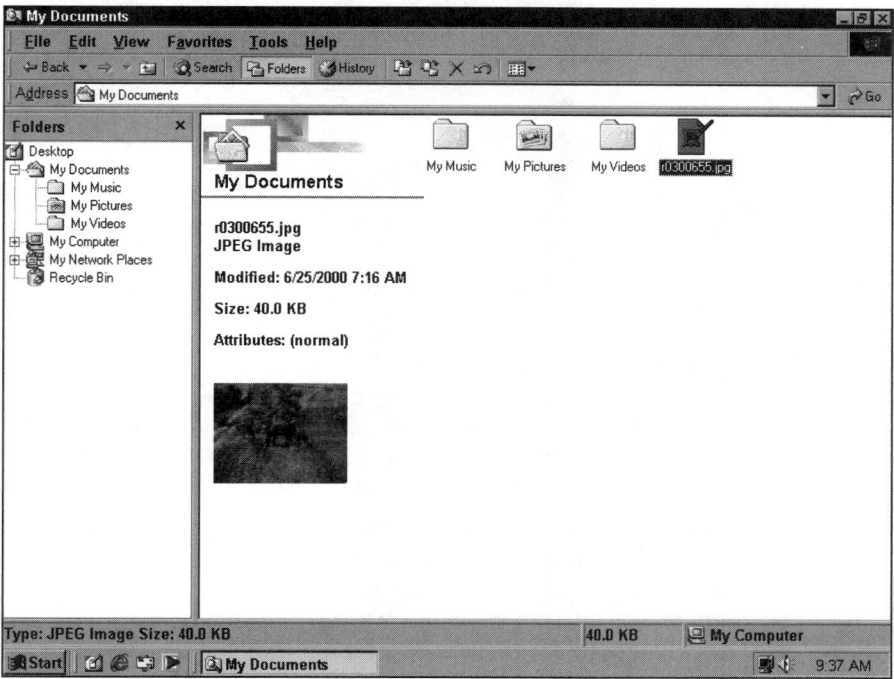

Figure 7-13: You can preview graphics one at a time.

You can also view the files themselves as thumbnails instead of using one of the other views (Large Icons, Small Icons, List, or Details). With Thumbnails view, the thumbnails are the same size as in the preview, but Explorer saves them so you can go back to them quickly, and you can see thumbnails of all the files in the folder at once, as shown in Figure 7-14.

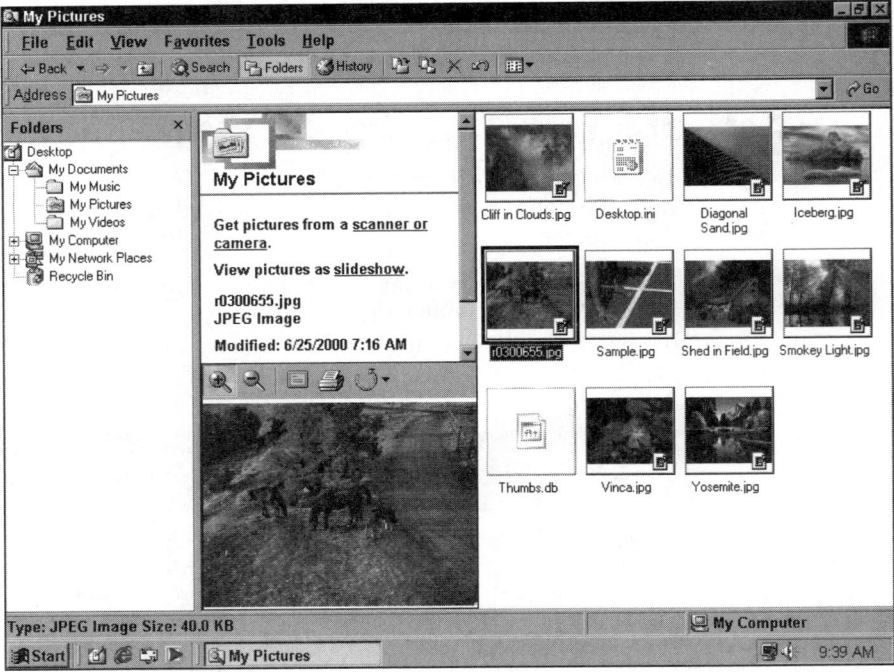

Figure 7-14: Thumbnails view lets you display thumbnails of an entire folder of graphics.

Thumbnails view is designed for folders that contain only or predominantly graphics or HTML files. Windows constructs a database of thumbnails (Thumbs.db) in each folder that you have set to show thumbnails. It does this by creating a hidden desktop.ini file in the folder that specifies which Explorer extension resource is required to display the thumbnails.

To display a folder's contents in Thumbnails view, right-click the folder's icon in your Explorer, click Properties, mark the "Enable thumbnail view" checkbox, and click OK. This action creates the desktop.ini file in the folder. Now right-click the folder's client area in your Explorer, and click View ⇨ Thumbnails, as shown in Figure 7-15.

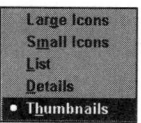

Figure 7-15: Select Thumbnails in the View context menu.

The files that Explorer can display as thumbnails will start to appear as Windows builds a thumbnail database from the files currently visible in the Explorer client area for this folder. As you scroll down, Windows creates additional thumbnails and adds them to the folder's Thumbs.db file. Thumbs. db will only contain thumbnails of *all* the files in the folder if you bring all of the files into view. This allows Windows to forgo the long process of creating a complete database of thumbnails if you just take a look at a couple of the first ones and then switch to another folder.

Tip

Windows updates the thumbnail database every time you add a file to the folder and view that file in the folder's Thumbnails view. If you move to view another folder in your Explorer and then move back, the icons in the folder will no longer be displayed in Thumbnails view. This speeds the display of folder contents within the Explorer. You'll need to right-click the client area for the folder in your Explorer (or folder window) and click View ⇨ Thumbnails again to switch back to this view.

The Explorer's Thumbnails view may not be the best thumbnail viewer for your needs. It appears to have difficulty when there are a lot of graphics files in a folder. It also seems quite a bit slower than dedicated thumbnail databases. We used Paint Shop Pro to manage all of the figures for this book, and we can create thumbnail databases quite easily, and more robustly with it. Other shareware packages are available as well.

Troubles with the Thumbnail Database

When Microsoft added an extension to the Explorer to handle the display of thumbnails, they opened themselves up to a little bit of trouble. They needed a database file that could be stored in the same folders as the graphics files. Once they created that file, any problems with it would cause problems with the Explorer.

Microsoft did this before when they introduced desktop.ini and folder. htt as add-on helper files that are stored in the affected folders. Everything is fine until something happens to these files, or someone erases them.

Secret

If you get one of these error messages when you try to view a folder in Thumbnails view, it's because the Thumb.db file is corrupt:

```
EXPLORER caused an invalid page fault in module THUMBVW.DLL at 015f:799eaee4
EXPLORER caused an invalid page fault in module KERNEL32.DLL at 015f:bff9d709
```

The solution is to delete the Thumbs.db file.

Secret

If you try to empty the Recycle Bin when it contains the contents of a folder that was enabled for Thumbnails view, and you are viewing the contents of the folder (now empty) in Explorer, you'll get another error message:

```
Can not delete Thumbs: Access is denied.
```

While you might be happy that your thumbnails aren't going to be deleted, you can click another folder icon and then empty the Recycle Bin.

Bring Back Your Thumbnails and Previews

Secret

If you are unable to view thumbnails or previews of some of the file types that you previously viewed, it may be because the particular file type is no longer associated with the function that displays the previews and thumbnails.

STEPS

Restoring Previews

Step 1.   Click Start ➪ Run.

Step 2.   Type **regsvr32 /i shdocvw.dll** and press Enter.

If this doesn't work, check in the registry to see if the shell extension that points to this thumbnail and preview display function is properly associated with your graphics file type. Open your Registry Editor and navigate down HKEY_CLASSES_ROOT to .bmp. You should have the same entries as those shown in Figure 7-16.

You can also check any further graphics file extensions that are not being correctly displayed to make sure that they contain this same entry (the same exact alphanumeric codes). All of the following graphics file types should contain this registry entry: gif, bmp, jpg, art, dib, jfif, jpe, jpeg, png, and wmf. If they don't, you can manually add it to them.

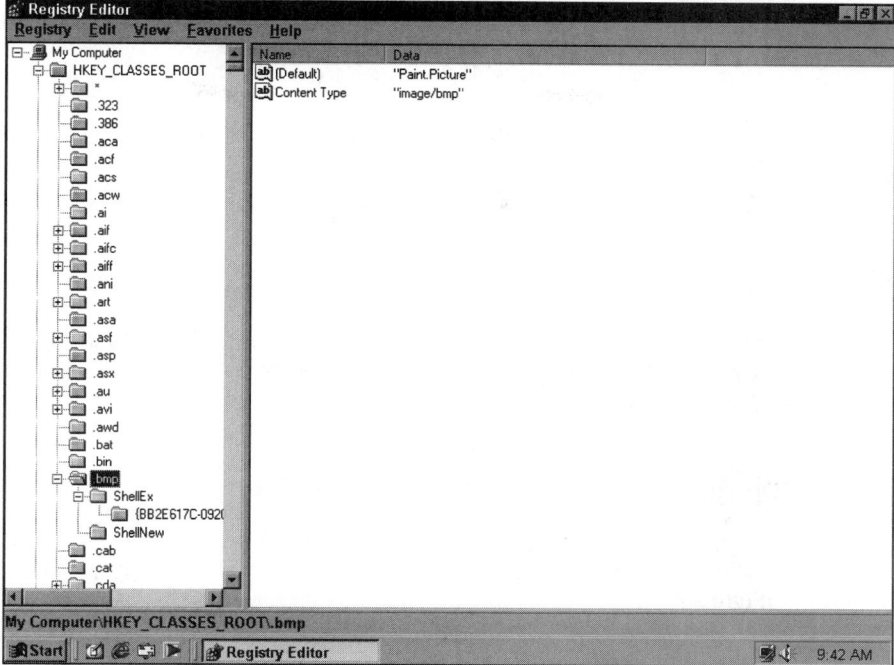

Figure 7-16: The correct registry entries for the shell extension of the bmp file type. Both the right and left panes should match this figure.

Tip

You may find that you are unable to see previews or thumbnails of some `jpg` files, although you can view them when you open the files in MS Paint, Paint Shop Pro, Internet Explorer, or other applications. The functions that display preview and thumbnail views can't handle `jpg` files that use the CMYK format instead of the RGB format. CMYK files are normally created by desktop publishing packages to prepare a file for production on color printing presses. If your `jpg` file is CMYK formatted, it just won't show up in the preview.

If you still can't get previews to work, you can take these steps:

STEPS

Restoring Previews (the Alternate Method)

Step 1.   Click Start ⇨ Run.

Step 2.   Type **regsvr32 actxprxy.dll** and press Enter.

Continued

STEPS

Restoring Previews (the Alternate Method) *(continued)*

Step 3. Click Start ⇨ Shut Down. Mark the Restart option button, and click OK.

Thanks to Adam Vujic for his help with this secret.

This last fix should also restore your ability to open a new Internet Explorer window when you hold down the Shift key and click a link, according to James Geater at Microsoft.

Make Actual Thumbnail Files

Big graphic files in, little graphic files out. This is the way programs used to work. Give them an input folder and wait for the output, as shown in Figure 7-17.

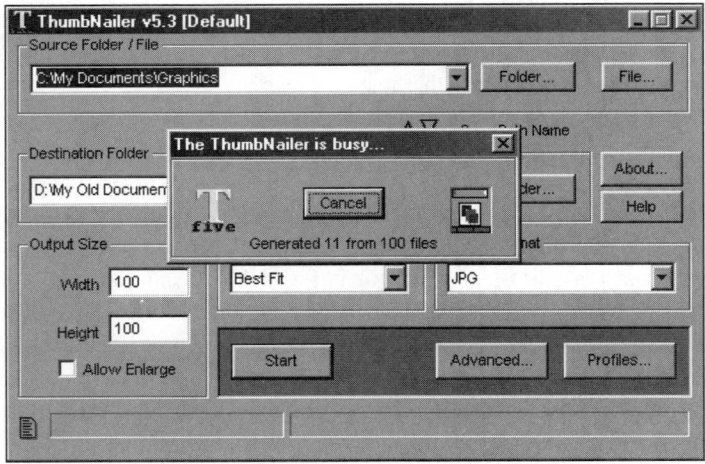

Figure 7-17: Waiting for a thumbnail to generate

Thumbnailer reads your graphics files and converts them into thumbnails — by default, 100 × 100 pixel jpg files at about 3K. These thumbnails are all separate files, not images in a browser, as they are with Paint Shop Pro.

You can use them as thumbnails on your Web pages. Because they are separate files, they are not easy to browse, so they won't help you find out what's in your graphics files.

You'll find Thumbnailer at `http://www.smalleranimals.com` The program costs $25 to register.

Creating New Folders

Windows and your applications create the folders they need during installation. If you want additional folders for your own work, you need to create them yourself. To create folders using the Explorer, take the following steps:

STEPS

Creating a Folder

Step 1. Right-click the My Computer icon on the Desktop. Choose Explore in the context menu.

Step 2. Expand the folder tree in the left pane of the Explorer window until you see the folder in which you want to place your new folder. Click this folder icon to select it. Make sure that the folder name is highlighted and that its name is in the Explorer window title bar.

Step 3. Right-click a blank part of right pane to display a context menu. Point to New, and then click Folder.

Step 4. A new folder icon appears in the right pane, and its name is highlighted. Type an appropriate name for the folder and press Enter.

It would seem natural to right-click a folder or drive icon in the left pane of the Explorer and choose New from a context menu to create a new folder, shortcut, or whatever within the selected folder (or root directory if you right-click a drive icon). Unfortunately, there is no New option on the context menu that appears when you right-click items in the folder tree.

Copying and Moving Files and Folders

You can move and copy files a lot more easily with the Explorer dual-pane window than with a single-pane folder window. You just have to be willing to put up with this dual-pane hierarchical view.

You can view the contents of the source folder in the right pane and independently find the destination folder in the left pane. Once you see both the source and destination, you can copy or move the files and/or folders from the right pane to the left. Instead of dragging and dropping between folder windows, you select icons in the Explorer window's right pane and drop them on folder icons in the left pane.

Secret

You can copy a file into the same folder that contains the original file by pressing the Ctrl key as you drag and drop the file in the right pane of the Explorer.

If you want to move or copy files or folders in the Explorer with Cut and Copy, first select the icons in the right pane. Issue the Cut or Copy command, display the contents of the destination folder in the right pane, and issue the Paste command to move or copy the selected files and/or folders to the new folder.

If you have downloaded Microsoft's PowerToys utility (`http://www.microsoft.com/Windows95/downloads/contents/wutoys/w95pwrtoysset/default.asp?site=95`), you can use Send to any folder to move or copy a file or folder to another folder (see the "Right-Click to a Powerhouse" section in Chapter 10).

Add Hot Links to Your Folders

If you view your folders as Web pages, you can easily add links that show up in the Web Page view of any folder. The links can show up in all folders or just in customized folders. You can create links to files, folders, or Internet resources.

If you want to put your links in all your folders, you'll need to edit the file `folder.htt` (a hidden file) in your `\Windows\Web` folder. If you want to put them in a specific folder, you can edit a file of the same name in that folder. Here's how:

STEPS

Adding Links

Step 1.   Use your Explorer to navigate to a folder that you are willing to view as a Web page.

Step 2. If you're not viewing the folder as a Web page, choose Tools ⇨ Folder Options, and mark the "Enable Web content in folders" option button. Click OK.

Step 3. Right-click the right pane of your Explorer window, and click Customize this Folder to open the Customize This Folder Wizard and click Next, as shown in Figure 7-18.

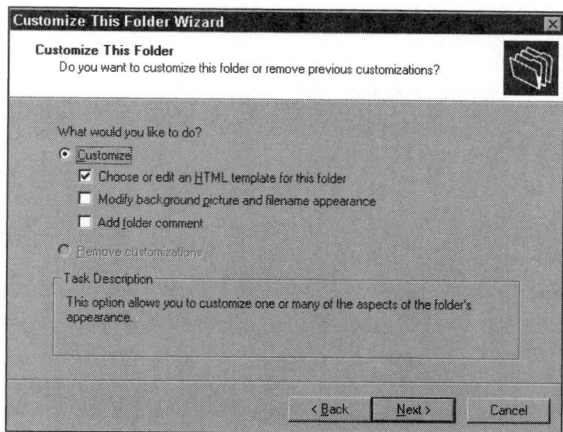

Figure 7-18: The first dialog box of the Customize This Folder Wizard. You should mark the first option button.

Step 4. Click Next, and select the "I want to edit this template" option. Click Next again. This will create a file named folder.htt in your current folder. It will also open up Notepad as your HTML editor and display the contents of the folder.htt file.

Step 5. Scroll down to one page up from the bottom of the file, as shown in Figure 7-19.

Step 6. Make the changes as shown in Figure 7-20. That is, delete the entire "examples commented out" line and the --> below the "Custom Link 2" line to uncomment out the links. Change the links to your own links. We've put in a link to the root directory and a link to a Web site as examples.

Continued

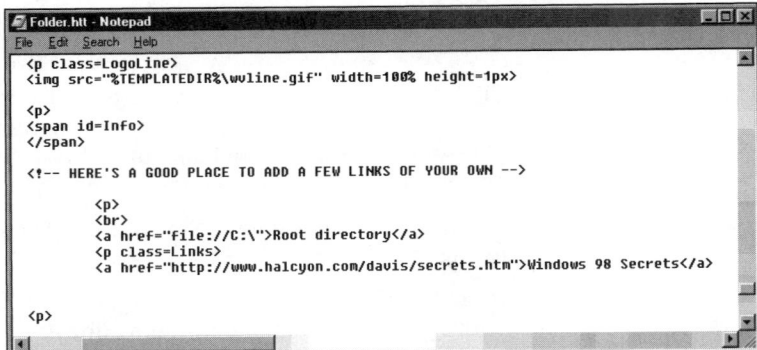

```
Folder.htt - Notepad
File  Edit  Search  Help
        <p class=LogoLine>
        <img src="%TEMPLATEDIR%\wvline.gif" width=100% height=1px>

        <p>
        <span id=Info>
        </span>

        <!-- HERE'S A GOOD PLACE TO ADD A FEW LINKS OF YOUR OWN -->
        <!-- (examples commented out)
                <p>
                <br>
                <a href="http://www.mylink1.com/">Custom Link 1</a>
                <p class=Links>
                <a href="http://www.mylink2.com/">Custom Link 2</a>
        -->

        <p>
```

Figure 7-19: Look for this text near the end of folder.htt telling you where to add links of your own.

```
Folder.htt - Notepad
File  Edit  Search  Help
<p class=LogoLine>
<img src="%TEMPLATEDIR%\wvline.gif" width=100% height=1px>

<p>
<span id=Info>
</span>

<!-- HERE'S A GOOD PLACE TO ADD A FEW LINKS OF YOUR OWN -->

        <p>
        <br>
        <a href="file://C:\">Root directory</a>
        <p class=Links>
        <a href="http://www.halcyon.com/davis/secrets.htm">Windows 98 Secrets</a>

<p>
```

Figure 7-20: This folder.htt file has been edited to add two links.

Step 7. Click File ⇨ Save, and exit Notepad. Click the Finish button to close the wizard. Your folder, when displayed in Web Page view, will change to something like that shown in Figure 7-21.

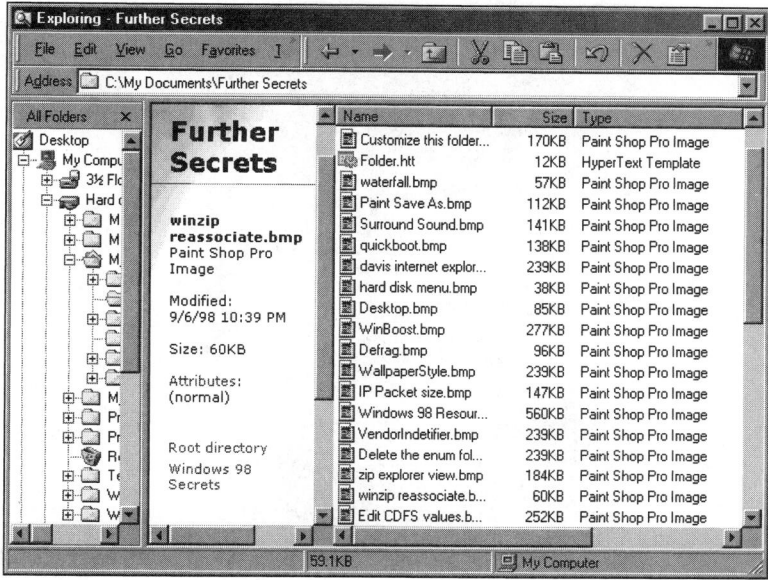

Figure 7-21: You can see the two new links to the left of the file list in the Explorer.

You can use these same steps to edit the `folder.htt` file in your `\Windows\Web` folder. Your edits will then be applied to all folders that don't have their own `folder.htt` files. In other words, if you have followed these steps to edit the `folder.htt` file for a specific folder, that folder will use its own `folder.htt` and not the one in the `\Windows\Web` folder.

Tip You can associate `htt` files with Notepad and easily edit them. Once you've created a `folder.htt` file, you'll want to open it and edit it to revise it, instead of using the Customize this Folder menu item.

If you can't find `folder.htt`, be sure that you can view hidden files by choosing Tools ⇨ Folder Options in your Explorer window, clicking the View tab, and marking "Show hidden files and folders" (see Figure 7-22).

Tip This is just one example of how you can customize your folder view when viewing folders as Web pages in Explorer or My Computer windows. Microsoft uses scripting and ActiveX controls to create these effects, and depending on your level of familiarity with these programming tools, you can add additional features to your folder views.

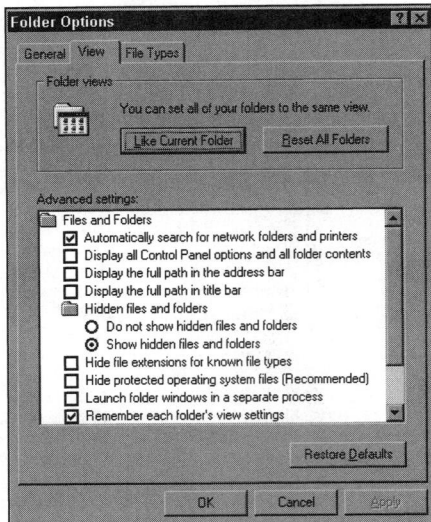

Figure 7-22: Set your folder options so that you can view hidden files.

My Computer Now Has a Folders Pane

Earlier versions of Windows 98 wouldn't let you go from My Computer to My Explorer. If you opened My Computer, you didn't get the View ⇨ Explorer Bar ⇨ Folders option. You could get rid of the left pane if you opened in Explorer mode, but you couldn't add it if you opened in My Computer mode. Happily, that's no longer the case with versions of Windows (including Me) that have Internet Explorer 5 and higher installed.

Uppercase and Lowercase Folder or Filenames

The default action when you type a new name for a folder or a file in the Explorer is to capitalize the first letter and make all the rest of the letters lowercase. So, even if you type all of the letters in uppercase, you only get one uppercase letter. Now for the exceptions.

If you type only lowercase letters, the first letter isn't capitalized. If you type more than eight characters in uppercase or mixed case, they retain their individual cases.

If you include characters that are not allowed in the DOS 8.3 format for file or folder names (such as a space followed by a character, or a comma), the case

of the individual letters is retained. Typing long file or folder names —
anything over eight characters — retains the name as you typed it.

Tip

It's possible to force Explorer to retain the case of letters as you type them for
names of fewer than nine characters. You can make this change in TweakUI. To
use TweakUI to make this change, click the Explorer tab and mark the "Adjust
case of 8.3 filenames" checkbox.

The problem with choosing "Allow all uppercase names" is that all filenames
that are stored as uppercase names will now appear that way in your Explorer.
Names that you thought were nicely subdued with a first letter in uppercase
and the rest in lowercase will now be shouting at you.

For the purposes of identifying files and folder names, the Explorer treats
uppercase and lowercase letters as though they were the same. For example,
the Explorer will not let you create two subfolders within one folder and give
them the same name except for the case. To test this, first turn on "Allow all
uppercase names" and then try creating two subfolders in the same folder,
one called New and one called NEW.

Select All Files and Folders Within a Folder

If you want to copy, move, or delete all files (or all files and folders) within a
folder, use your Explorer to focus on a folder in the left pane and display its
contents in the right pane, and then press Ctrl+A.

This selects the entire contents of the folder. You can now right-click the
highlighted files, drag and drop them, or whatever. If you want to select all
items except for a few, hold down the Ctrl key and click (or hover) over the
ones that you want to remove from the selection. (The hovering works if you
have single-clicking enabled — View ➪ Folder Options ➪ Custom ➪ Settings ➪
"Single-click to open an item (point to select)."

Search for Your Files

Press F3 while your Explorer window has the focus, and up pops the Search
Explorer bar.

Add Items to the Context Menu

Secret

You can add items to the context menu that appears when you right-click
your My Computer icon, Start button, or any folder icon. Sometimes software
manufacturers use this simple and simple-minded method to add their
commands to your context menu. You can use these steps to find out if they
did, and remove their commands if you so choose.

STEPS

Adding New Commands to the Context Menu

Step 1. Open your Registry Editor and click Edit ⇨ Find.

Step 2. Type **{20D04FE0}** in the Find What field to search for {20D04FE0-3AEA-1069-A2D8-08002B30309D} (the Resource ID for My Computer). Click Find Next.

Step 3. Click the plus sign next to {20D04FE0}, and highlight the *shell* key in the left pane of the Registry Editor.

Step 4. Right-click the right pane of the Registry Editor, click New ⇨ Key (see Figure 7-23). Type a short descriptive name for the command you are about to add to the context menu.

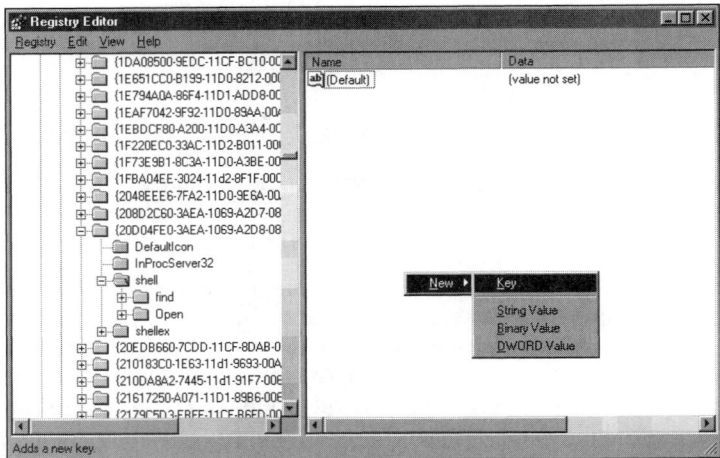

Figure 7-23: Click Key to create a new registry key containing your new context menu command.

Step 5. Double-click Default in the right pane of the Registry Editor and type the new context menu command as it will appear in the context menu. Put an ampersand in front of the letter that you want to designate as the hot key, as shown in Figure 7-24. Click OK.

Step 6. Highlight the new key in the left pane of your Registry Editor, right-click the right pane, and click New ⇨ Key. Rename the key **command**.

Step 7. Highlight your new *command* key in the left pane, double-click Default in the right pane, and type the actual program that you want to call when you click this context menu item, including its pathname (see Figure 7-25). Click OK.

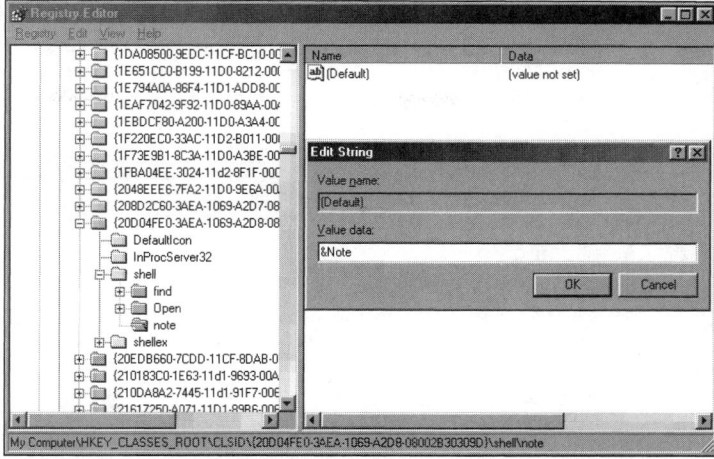

Figure 7-24: Type the command in the Value Data field. Use an ampersand to designate a hot key for your command.

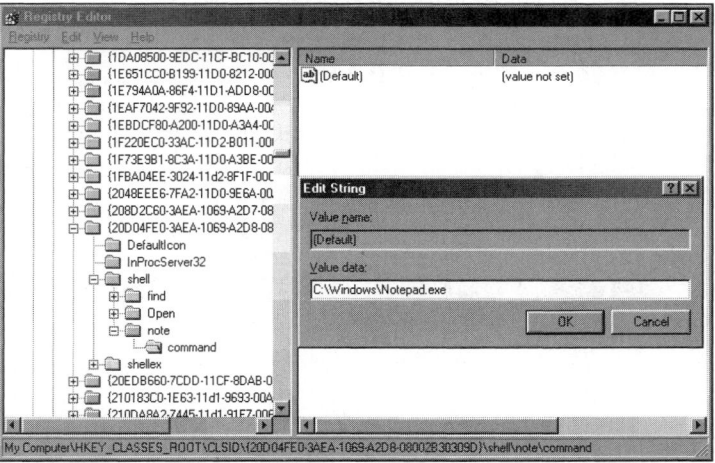

Figure 7-25: Type the program that your command will run, along with its path.

Step 8. Close the Registry Editor and then right-click the My Computer icon on the Desktop to see your new command.

Thanks to Stephen Charles Rea help with this secret.

Secret

Software authors can also use this method to add a menu item to the context menu for all files: Add a key under HKEY_CLASSES_ROOT/ */ shellex/ ContextMenuHandlers. You can see a context menu handler for WinZip in Figure 7-26 because WinZip is installed.

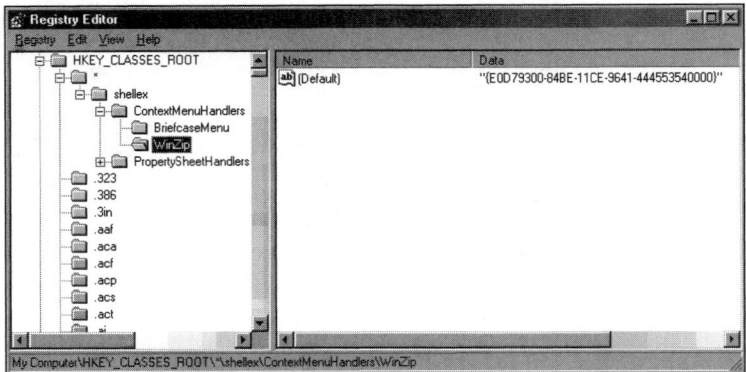

Figure 7-26: The ContextMenuHandlers registry key lists some applications that have added their commands to the context menus for all files.

If you want to delete the context menu items associated with the indicated application (in this case, WinZip), just delete the key under ContextMenu Handlers. You might first highlight the key and click Registry ⇨ Export Registry File to save this registry entry in case you want to put it back in later.

Clear Your Hard Drive Context Menu

When you right-click your Hard Disk icon, you may discover that the context menu items are adding up. Icon Wizard adds a call, as does Sandra. WinZip adds one, too (although it doesn't go into the same place in the registry — see the previous section.

Secret

To remove items that get stuck to your hard drive's context menu, you'll need to edit your registry, as described in these steps:

STEPS

Clearing the Hard Drive's Context Menu

Step 1. Click Start ⇨ Run, type **regedit**, and press Enter.

Step 2. Navigate to HKEY_CLASSES_ROOT\Drive. Click the plus signs next to Drive and next to *shell*. This displays the keys representing the context menu items that have been added to the drive's context menu. Open each of the menu items, highlight the *command* key, and see which applications are called.

Step 3. After viewing the context menu items under *shell*, right-click the keys of the menu items that you want to delete one by one, and click Delete.

If you are not sure, you can save the Drive branch of the registry first; just highlight the Drive key in the left pane, click Registry ➪ Export Registry File, and name this file **Drive.reg**.

Step 4. When you are done, close the Registry Editor.

Change Your Disk Drive Icons in the Explorer

If you don't like the icons that represent your hard disks, you can change them quite easily. All you need to do is add a small text file to the root directory of the hard disk whose icon you want to change. Both the D: and F: drive (which is a CD-ROM drive) icons have been changed in Figure 7-27.

Figure 7-27: You can use different icons for your drives, as in this example.

To change the icon for a disk drive, take these steps:

STEPS

Changing a Disk Drive Icon

Step 1.   In your Explorer, highlight the disk drive icon in the left pane.

Step 2.   Right-click the right pane of the Explorer, and click New ⇨ Text Document.

Step 3.   Rename the text document **autorun.inf**.

Step 4.   Click the new text document to open it. Type the following:

```
[autorun]
icon=d:\otherfolder\youricon.ico
```

Step 5.   Save the new text file and exit Notepad.

Step 6.   Press F5 to refresh the Explorer.

Be sure that the pathname and filename of your icon are correct. We had a problem with the names of some icons that had capital letters near the ends of the prefix. Also, you can reference icons in exe, dll, and other files. You just have to add a comma after the filename, and then the icon's index number.

WinBoost will help you do this also (see "Tweaking the Windows Desktop" in Chapter 5).

Stray Icons in Your Explorer

If you find stray, perhaps blank, icons in your Explorer near the Dial-Up Networking, Control Panel, Printers, and Scheduled Tasks icons, you can get rid of them fairly easily. They are left over from some program that stuck them in this unlikely spot.

Secret

As we discussed in "Get Rid of Unattached Desktop Icons" in Chapter 5, these folders are attached to Class IDs found under the NameSpace key. Open your Registry Editor and navigate to HKEY_LOCAL_MACHINE\ SOFTWARE\ Microsoft\ Windows\ CurrentVersion\ explorer\ mycomputer\ NameSpace.

Highlight each of the Class IDs under NameSpace in the left pane of the Registry Editor and see if there is an associated application name in the right pane. If not, you can use Registry Crawler, as we discuss in "Crawl Through the Registry" in Chapter 11 (or just use the Registry Editor itself) to search for other instances of the Class ID. Use the information found in these other branches to determine whether you should delete the Class ID from the NameSpace.

If the Class ID is not associated with any application, or is associated with a deleted application, then you can remove it. You can also export the NameSpace branch as a `reg` file before you delete any Class IDs, so that you can reimport the `reg` file later if it turns out you got carried away.

Rename Your Files En Masse

Windows has a very limited file rename capability. Users who want to change the names of a bunch of files usually need to open a DOS window and use the REN command. Even this command is limited.

Another option is to use a freeware package, THE Rename, which provides you with plenty of renaming power, as shown in Figure 7-28.

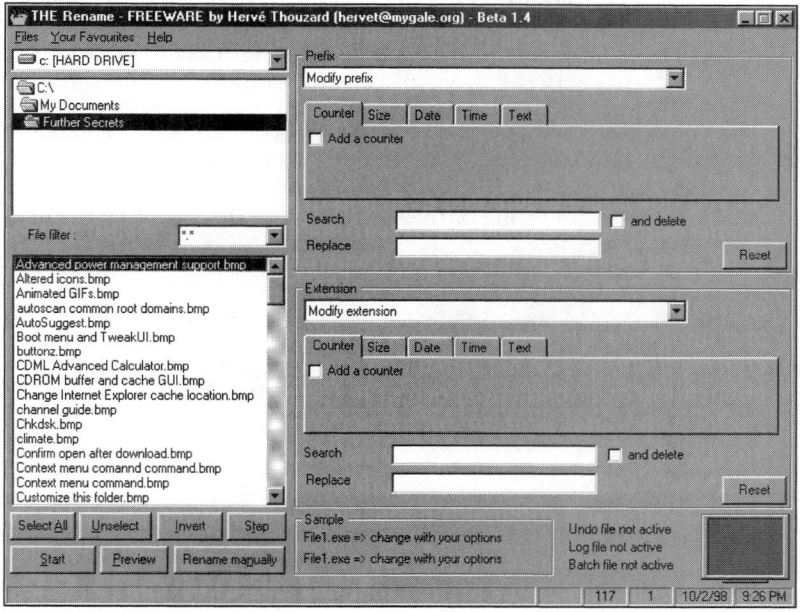

Figure 7-28: THE Rename gives you lots of options for renaming groups of files.

You can use THE Rename to replace filenames with up to the first 25 characters of the file contents, rename files using consecutive alphanumerics, replace the file dates and times, and change all the extensions. You can have THE Rename create a DOS batch file to do the renaming after you decide what results you want.

THE Rename lets you type your own filter — say, to choose all of the files that start with *Belinda*. You can change just the prefixes or extensions, change the case of either, do freeform changes, and see your results before making the changes.

You'll find THE Rename at `http://www.multimania.com/hervet/ index.shtml` .

Keep a Second Copy

Not all backup programs are the same or even similar. We often think of a backup program as something that allows us to restore our hard disk if it crashes, or something that runs overnight.

Second Copy 97 is a bit different. You set it up to run on a schedule to copy files from one device to another, making a second copy. The copied files can be compressed as they are copied. The previous versions of the files to be copied are deleted on the target device, or you can set how many versions deep to keep. You can copy to a floppy diskette, to a Zip drive, to another hard disk, to a network drive, or to another folder on the same hard disk.

You can create multiple sets of Second Copy instructions, called *profiles*, that determine which files are copied, how often, to what folder, and how many versions are kept. See the example in Figure 7-29. You can keep folders in sync, or just copy from source to target. You do all of this through wizards just like the Windows wizards.

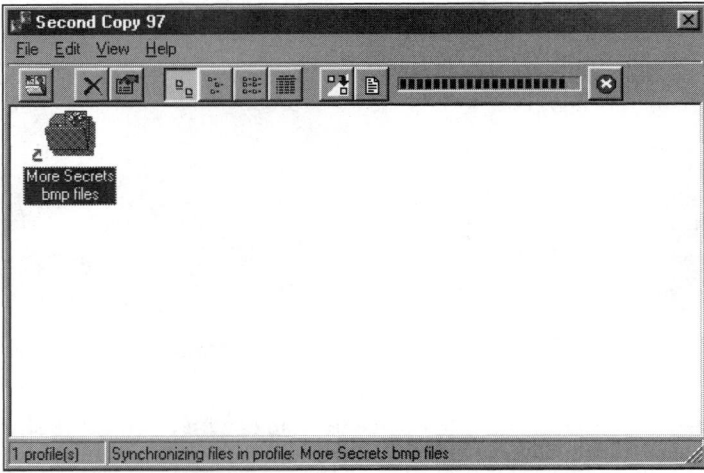

Figure 7-29: In this example, the icon called More Secrets bmp Files represents a *profile*, or set of instructions for making copies of specific files.

Second Copy 97 runs as an icon in your system tray. You can set it to start when you start Windows, and make the first backup at a set time after Windows starts. You can also just use it to backup whenever you tell it to. Even if a file is in use, Second Copy 97 can most likely back it up.

We highly recommend Second Copy 97. It is available for a 30-day trial at http://www.centered.com

Print a Directory of Files in a Folder

Would you like to be able to print a filename listing for any folder? You can use a little freeware package to make the task easy. Directory-2-HTML, shown in Figure 7-30, creates an HTML page from the filename listings for a folder. You can then print out the new HTML page.

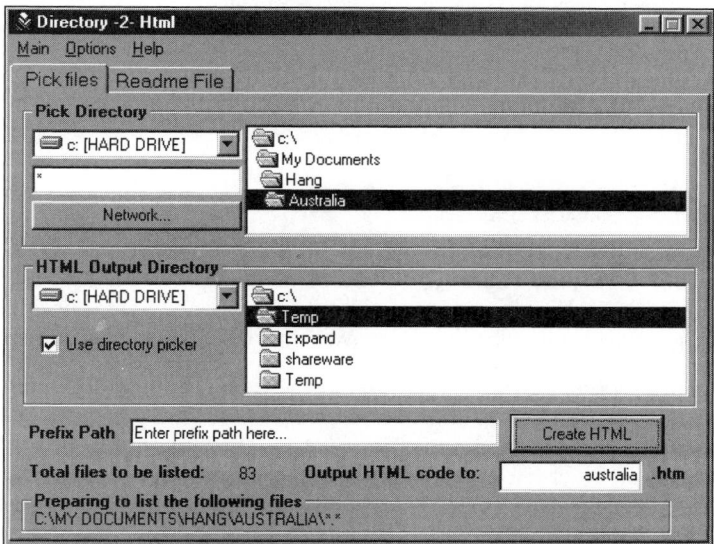

Figure 7-30: The user interface for Directory-2-HTML

You'll find Directory-2-HTML at http://home1.gte.net/billyb99/ dir2html/.

While Directory-2-HTML does a nice job, you might want to try something a little more austere. PrintFolder adds an item to your folder's context menu that lets you print (or copy) a directory listing for any folder, including subfolders if you like. It looks a lot like a DOS directory printout, as shown in Figure 7-31.

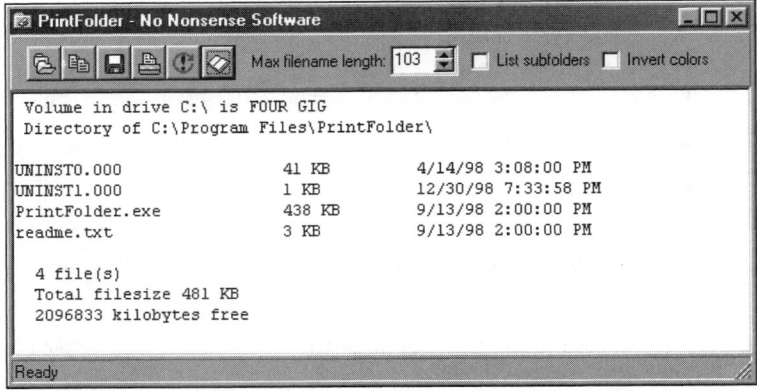

Figure 7-31: PrintFolder is ready to print the directory of files in the PrintFolder folder. You can copy the filename listing to a file, print it, or both.

You'll find this $15 shareware package at `http://no-nonsense-software.com/printfolder/`.

Zip (Compress) Your Files

WinZip has been one of the most downloaded shareware programs of all time. It probably continues to be to this day. Beginning with Plus! 98, and continuing with Windows Me, you'll notice that the basic functionality of WinZip is now built right into Windows, in its Compressed Folders feature.

We wonder why Microsoft hasn't trumpeted this particular feature. It works well and seamlessly, and Microsoft certainly has had a history of adding basic functionality to the operating system, thereby undercutting the competition. Maybe it is because WinZip is so popular and is a shareware package that they didn't want to be seen as destroying the little guy — in this case, Nico Mak.

When you install a version of Windows that supports Compressed Folders, it automatically takes over the zip function from WinZip by changing the action taken on files with `zip` extensions. But the Add to Zip item is still on your context menu (or in a WinZip submenu of your context menu as Add To), and you can reassociate WinZip with `zip` files just by right-clicking a file in your Explorer and clicking Add to Zip. You will be given the chance to make WinZip the default compression program, as shown in Figure 7-32. (This also works with Extract To.)

WinZip
For full access to WinZip's shell and File Manager interface, WinZip must be properly associated with ZIP files. However, WinZip is not currently associated with ZIP files.
Associate WinZip with ZIP files now?
Never display this message
Yes
No
Info...
Help

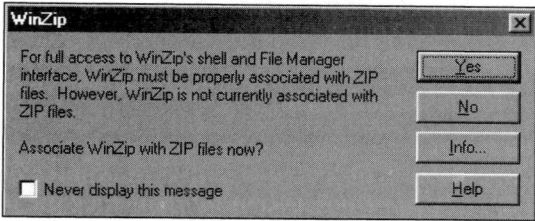

Figure 7-32: To reassociate WinZip with your zip files, click Yes when you see this message box.

If you have the Compressed Folders feature and `zip` files are associated with this Explorer shell extension, you can right-click a file with a `zip` extension and click Explore to see an Explorer-like view of the contents of the `zip` file, as shown in Figure 7-33.

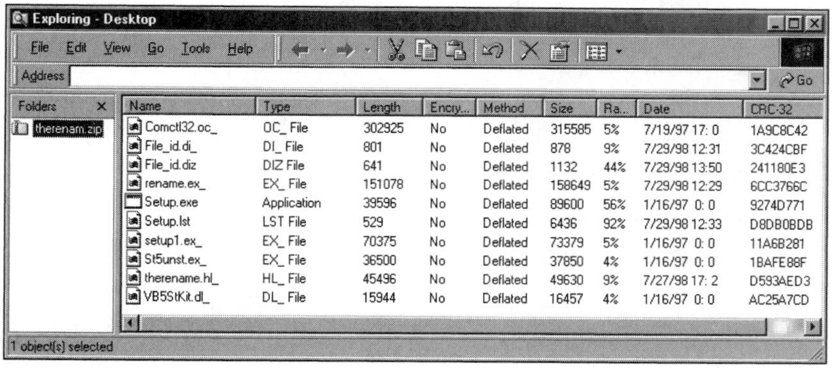

Exploring - Desktop
File Edit View Go Tools Help
Address
Go
Folders
therenam.zip
Name Type Length Encry... Method Size Ra... Date CRC-32
Comctl32.oc_ OC_ File 302925 No Deflated 315585 5% 7/19/97 17: 0 1A9C8C42
File_id.di_ DI_ File 801 No Deflated 878 9% 7/29/98 12:31 3C424CBF
File_id.diz DIZ File 641 No Deflated 1132 44% 7/29/98 13:50 241180E3
rename.ex_ EX_ File 151078 No Deflated 158649 5% 7/29/98 12:29 6CC3766C
Setup.exe Application 39596 No Deflated 89600 56% 1/16/97 0: 0 9274D771
Setup.lst LST File 529 No Deflated 6436 92% 7/29/98 12:33 D8DB0BDB
setup1.ex_ EX_ File 70375 No Deflated 73379 5% 1/16/97 0: 0 11A6B281
St5unst.ex_ EX_ File 36500 No Deflated 37850 4% 1/16/97 0: 0 1BAFE88F
therename.hl_ HL_ File 45496 No Deflated 49630 9% 7/27/98 17: 2 D593AED3
VB5StKit.dl_ DL_ File 15944 No Deflated 16457 4% 1/16/97 0: 0 AC25A7CD
1 object(s) selected

Figure 7-33: The Explorer view of a zip file

Instead of using WinZip's Add to Zip context menu item, you can move files into a compressed `zip` file (known by Windows as a *compressed folder*) by right-clicking the file, and clicking Send To ➪ Compressed Folder. A `zip` file with the same filename is created in the same folder as the original file. You can then drag and drop other files to the compressed folder.

You can extract compressed files from a compressed folder by clicking the `zip` file in your Explorer to open it, and then dragging icons from the compressed folder window into another Explorer window.

To create a new empty compressed folder on your Desktop, right-click the Desktop and click New ➪ Compressed Folder. Type a new name (with the `zip` extension), and then drag files to the folder on the Desktop. Of course, you can do this in any folder in your Explorer, not just on your Desktop.

Summary

The Explorer is the most powerful tool that Windows provides to manage your computer. Unfortunately, much of its power is hidden. Add power to your Explorer with third-party extensions and applications.

▶ Use the Explorer to navigate throughout your computer and the network connected to your computer.

▶ We reveal the hidden command-line parameters that determine how the Explorer behaves.

▶ We show you how to put the Explorer on the Desktop, or just about anywhere that makes sense to you.

▶ If you know how to use the Explorer, you can quickly copy and move files and folders around on your computer.

▶ The Explorer and My Computer come with keyboard shortcuts, and we show you what they are.

▶ We show you how to size and display the Explorer or multiple Explorers on your Desktop.

▶ We compare what the old Windows 3.1x File Manager does with how the Explorer handles the same tasks.

▶ Clear out the warning in Web Page view about viewing the Windows folder.

▶ The Twin Explorer gives you two Explorers side by side.

▶ Explorer can barely rename files. When you need a massive rename, use THE Rename.

▶ Set up Second Copy 97 to make copies of your most important files, even as you work on them.

▶ It's easy to print a directory of files with Directory-2-HTML, a freeware application that creates an HTML version of your filenames.

Chapter 8

My Computer—Folders and Windows

Viewing Your Computer

You need a window, or several windows, to see what is on your computer, your network, or the Internet. This chapter focuses on how to use folder windows (or *single-pane* windows). In Chapter 7, we discuss the Windows Explorer, a *dual-pane* window.

Frankly, we almost never use a single-pane window to view the contents of our computers. It is just too painful. The Windows Explorer, with its hierarchical view of folders, is much more powerful as a navigation device. On the other hand, the single-pane view is just fine for viewing Web documents and navigating with hyperlinks.

To switch from My Computer to the Explorer view, after you open My Computer, click View ➪ Explorer Bar ➪ Folders.

We suggest that you use this chapter to become familiar with how window views work with your computer. You can use almost everything that we discuss here with the Windows Explorer.

Once Is Enough

If you use the new Windows interface (the one in Windows Me and Windows 98), it's possible for you to open an application or document with a single click. Alternatively, you can change this setting to require a double-click if you prefer.

To choose the new way, click the Start button ⇨ Settings ⇨ Control Panel and choose Folder Options. Mark the "Single-click to open an item (point to select)" option button and click OK.

In this chapter and others, we use the term *click* as a stand-in for both methods. When we refer to a click in this book, keep in mind that you can use a double-click instead if you have configured your computer to use the *Classic style* interface (this is the Windows 95 interface). We also state that you can rest your mouse pointer over an icon to select it. If you have chosen the Classic style interface, you'll need to click the icon to select it.

Hovering (resting the mouse pointer over an icon to select it) and single-clicking represent the triumph of the Web browser interface over the previous Windows interface. Microsoft was forced to adopt these options because they are so popular among Web enthusiasts. We applaud anything that reduces the wear on our fingers.

You can also choose between single-clicking or double-clicking in the My Computer window, by choosing View ⇨ Folder Options, and marking either Web style or Classic style. If you mark Custom, you can click the Settings button and choose Single-click.

The My Computer Window

When you first set up Windows, you will see a few icons on the left side of your Desktop. How many you see depends on which options you chose during the Windows setup process, and whether you are updating a Windows 9x computer or have purchased a new computer with Windows Me already installed.

The My Computer icon (and a rather generic-looking computer icon it is) is the first icon on the Desktop — an indication of its importance (as far as Microsoft is concerned) in the hierarchy of items on the Desktop. You can place it somewhere else, if you want. If you arrange the Desktop icons in any of the predetermined sort orders (by right-clicking the Desktop, pointing to Arrange Icons, and choosing any of the sort orders from the submenu), it will again appear in the upper-left corner.

When you click My Computer, a single-pane window much like the one shown in Figure 8-1 appears on your Desktop. In the figure, it's displayed in Large Icons view with the menu bar and the Standard Buttons toolbar showing. The Address bar is turned on, and View ⇨ As Web Page is not checked.

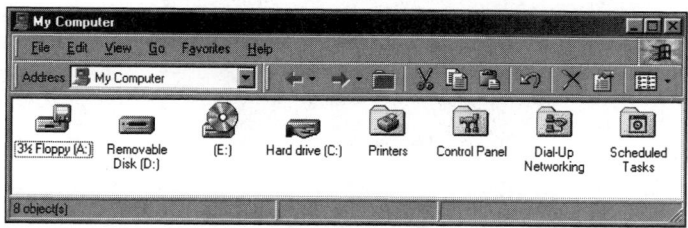

Figure 8-1: The My Computer window. Click the My Computer icon on the Desktop to open it.

Tip

You can also right-click the My Computer icon and then click Open from the context menu. The Open command is at the top of this menu. You can left- or right-click the context menu item — it doesn't care which mouse button you use.

Clicking My Computer opens a window that displays the contents of My Computer. *Open* means to display in a window. If you open an application, it will be displayed in a window. If you open a document, it will also be displayed in a window. Opening an icon such as the My Computer icon means to display its contents within a window.

You don't find windows on real-world desktops — so much for desktop metaphors. You might think of a window as the thing itself plus its edges. A window displays a document on the Desktop, and the edges of the document contain commands that determine how the document is displayed.

The contents that are displayed are not the physical contents of the computer — what you would normally expect to see when you "opened up" your computer — but its logical contents. The My Computer window contains icons that look like physical items: your floppy drive(s) and your hard disk drive(s). The window also has some manila folder icons with graphics on them (*special folders*).

The diskette and hard disk drive icons represent the logical contents — the files, folders, documents, and applications — that are stored on these devices. The special folder icons give you quick access to certain useful functions. For example, the Printers folder (see "The Printers Folder" in Chapter 9) contains the printer drivers. We discuss these particular special folders in much more detail in other chapters. To open and display the contents of any drive or folder icon, click it.

You can also display the contents of My Computer as a Web page (select Tools ⇨ Folder Options and choose Enable Web Content In Folders). In this view, you see something like the My Computer window shown in Figure 8-2.

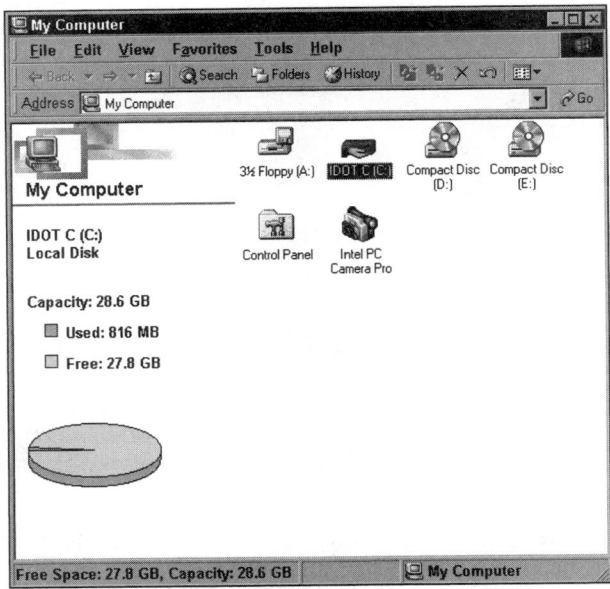

Figure 8-2: The My Computer window displayed as a Web page. Position your mouse pointer over a hard drive icon in this view to display its capacity and free space.

Secret

Microsoft enables you to create your own Web page view for most folders. You do this by right-clicking the client area of the folder window and choosing Customize This Folder, which launches the Customize This Folder Wizard. However, the Customize This Folder command is not available in the My Computer window because Microsoft has already defined My Computer's Web page view. The HTML template file it uses to define this view and its capabilities is \Windows\Web\mycomp.htt.

The Customize This Folder Wizard works for most folders, but it doesn't work on most system or special folders such as the Control Panel, Printers, Downloaded Program Files, Subscriptions, and Tasks folders. The wizard creates a hidden Desktop.ini file in the folder, and this ini file contains pointers to the resources that are used to create the new Web page (HTML) view of the folder. The wizard uses the HTML template \Windows\Web\ folder.htt as its starting point. We discuss this further in the "Customizing This Folder" section later in this chapter.

Folders

Microsoft has replaced the term *directory* (a term from DOS, Windows 3.1*x*, and many operating systems before DOS) with *folder* — a more office-oriented name. Also, folders can do much more than DOS directories. Some special folders, such as the folders in the My Computer window, have additional capabilities. You can place folders (or better yet, shortcuts to folders) on the Desktop, and they can contain folder windows of their own.

You can place a folder icon (or a shortcut to a folder icon) on the Desktop or in a folder window. Folders can contain other folders, just as DOS directories can contain subdirectories. To locate your files, you click a folder icon to display a window containing other folder icons.

If you display the My Computer window as a Web page, you will still see folder icons in the window. Although Web pages out on the World Wide Web could conceivably have folder icons in them, they rarely do. Microsoft is clearly stretching it a bit in its efforts to get the two metaphors (Desktop and World Wide Web) to work together.

Viewing My Computer as a Web page provides more information about the contents of My Computer. For example, if you place your mouse pointer over the Control Panel icon, an explanation about what the Control Panel is appears on the left side of the window.

The Special Folders in the My Computer Window

Secret

The four folders in the My Computer window are unlike most other folders on your hard disk. They have special functions, and their contents are not stored within the folder. For example, the contents of the Control Panel folder are stored in the \Windows\System folder in files with the cpl extension. The other folders are just front ends to information stored only in the registry.

Microsoft made an arbitrary design decision to put these special folder icons in the My Computer window and to put little graphics on the folder icons to remind us that they are special. It placed the special folder icons in the My Computer window because this provides an easy way for you to get to folders that contain useful Windows functions. We have devoted a chapter each to three of these folders.

The Printers folder is introduced in "The Printers Folder" in Chapter 9, the Control Panel folder in "Getting to the Control Panel" in Chapter 15, and the Dial-Up Networking folder in "Dial-Up Networking" in Chapter 19.

You can use the Scheduled Tasks folder to create a list of actions that Windows will perform at a certain time without further input from you. Examples include running ScanDisk, running Defrag, and so on.

My Computer Window Properties

If you right-click an empty area in the My Computer window, a context menu like the one shown in Figure 8-3 appears. This menu is similar to the one you get when you right-click the Desktop, except that it has a View menu item instead of Active Desktop. When you point to View, a submenu appears that lets you change how the icons in the window are displayed. Your choices are As Web Page, Large Icons, Small Icons, List, and Details. Icons on the Desktop are always displayed as large icons.

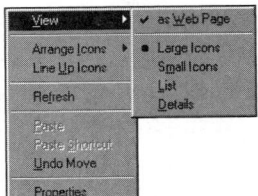

Figure 8-3: The context menu for the My Computer window with the View options showing

Tip

The Properties command displays the System Properties dialog box, which functions as the Windows hardware interface. You can also right-click the My Computer icon on your Desktop and click Properties to get to this dialog box. Turn to "The Device Manager" in Chapter 36 for details on setting system-wide properties.

Drive Properties

When you place your mouse pointer over a drive icon in the My Computer window, a report of its free space and disk capacity appears in the status bar. If you are viewing My Computer as a Web page, this information also appears on the left side of the client window.

To view or change the properties of a drive, right-click the drive icon and click Properties. You can change the drive's volume label, as shown in Figure 8-4. You can also check the drive for errors, back it up, or defragment it by clicking the Tools tab. Check out "A Drive Icon" in Chapter 37 for details.

Type a new volume label for your drive. If you want to check for errors, click the Tools tab. You can share your drive with others on your network by setting your share configuration in the Sharing tab. To compress or decompress your drive, or to change its compression ratio, click the Compression tab. You can also remove files you may not need by clicking the Disk Cleanup button and choosing what to remove.

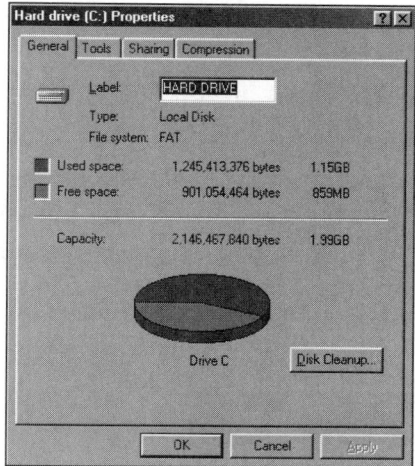

Figure 8-4: The General tab of the Properties dialog box for a disk drive

You can use TweakUI to decide which hard drives are displayed in your My Computer or Explorer window. This is one way to make sure that others don't have the opportunity to see what is on your drives. This is a per-user setting, so if you have multiple users with multiple user profiles on your computer, you can hide different drives for each user. Click the TweakUI icon in your Control Panel, click the My Computer tab, and choose which disk drives to hide. (If you don't have the TweakUI icon, you can install the utility from the \tools\ResKit\Powertoy folder of your Windows CD-ROM.)

Opening a New Window

Click a drive icon in the My Computer window to open a window that displays the contents of the drive. The contents will consist of folder and file icons.

Each icon has an associated window. If you are using the "classic" Windows settings, when you click an icon in one of these windows, you will open yet another window. My Computer has its own window, and all your disk drives have their own windows.

You can continue to click folder icons to move hierarchically through the folders stored on your drive. Folders can contain subfolders, which in turn can contain more subfolders. You can move sideways by returning to a parent folder and then moving to a different subfolder.

If you view your computer's contents through one window, you can also go backward and forward along the path that you have traveled. Click the Back (left-pointing) button to go back to the previous view that you chose. If you've gone back, click the Forward (right-pointing) button to move forward to where you were before you went back. (If you don't see the toolbar, choose View ➪ Toolbars ➪ Standard Buttons.)

Closing a Folder Window

The three buttons in the upper-right corner of a window allow you to minimize, maximize or restore, and close a folder window, respectively, from left to right.

Secret

Hold down the Shift key as you click the Close button to close not only the window with the focus, but all its parent windows as well. If you opened a number of windows to get to the current one, this method gives you an easy way to get rid of all the preceding windows.

Change Your Window View

Many different options are available in Windows 98 under the View menu item, and Windows Me continues this feature. You have multiple toolbars, an Explorer bar, and the ability to view your window as a Web page (View ➪ As Web Page).

You can choose how the drive icons, folder icons, and other icons are displayed in a window by choosing among four views: Large Icons, Small Icons (rows), List (columns), and Details. You can cycle from one view to the next by repeatedly clicking the Views button at the right end of the Standard Buttons toolbar. To switch directly to a particular view, click the down arrow next to the Views button and then click the desired view in the menu. To see how to order your icons, refer to the next section, "Order the Icons."

Windows Me and 98 (unlike Windows 95) allow you to set and maintain unique window display preferences (although not toolbar settings) for every window and every folder. On the other hand, you can force every folder view to be the same. We discuss how to do this in the "Sticky View Settings" section of Chapter 7.

Order the Icons

You can specify the order in which your icons are displayed in a window. Choose View ➪ Arrange Icons and then click the desired option in the submenu that appears.

If you are viewing the top-level My Computer window (you have just clicked the My Computer icon on the Desktop), your choices are by Drive Letter, by Type, by Size, and by Free Space. If you are viewing other drive and folder windows, the choices are usually by Name, by Type, by Size, and by Date. However, the exact set of options you see in the Arrange Icons submenu depends on what kind of folder you are currently viewing.

If you are using Details view, you can also choose which variable to sort on by clicking the heading buttons (Name, Size, Type, and Modified) located at the top of the columns. If you want to toggle between ascending and descending order, click the heading button a second time. You also have the option of displaying an Attributes column to list file or folder attributes, as shown in Figure 8-5. To display this column, right-click the column header and choose Attributes.

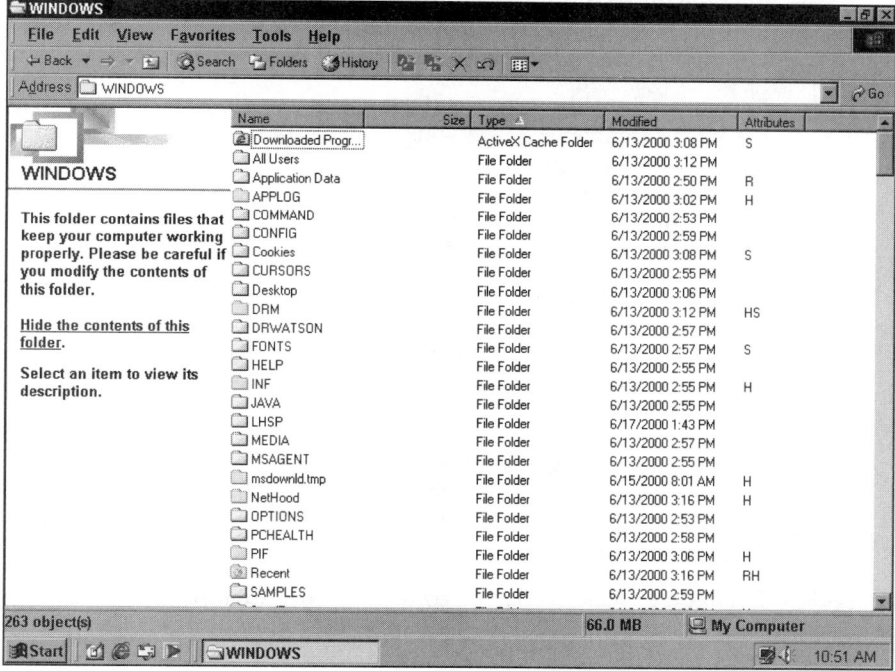

Figure 8-5: A folder window in Details view. Click one of the column heading buttons (Name, Size, Type, Modified, or Attributes) at the top of the client area to order the icons by that variable.

Line Up Your Icons

Secret

If you are not viewing your folder window as a Web page, and if you use the Large Icons or Small Icons view of a window, you can place the icons where you like. They will stay where you put them, even if you switch views, resize the window, or close the window and go back to it. The Large Icons view will mirror the Small Icons view, and vice versa.

As with the Desktop, every folder window contains an invisible grid, although Windows only uses the grid in the Large Icons and Small Icons views. The size of the grid depends on the size of the icons, the font size (magnification), and the display resolution. You can snap your icons to the center of the cells in the grid by right-clicking the client area of the folder window and choosing Line Up Icons.

Changing the Columns in Details View

When you choose the Details view of a folder window (View ➪ Details), heading buttons appear above each column. At the edge of each of these buttons is a black spacer line. When you rest your mouse over the line, the mouse pointer becomes a vertical line with two horizontal arrows.

You can change the order of the columns by dragging a column header to the left or right. Just place your mouse pointer over a heading button, press and hold down the left mouse button, and drag the button to the desired position. For example, we often find ourselves moving the Modified column and putting it just to the right of the Name column to make it easier to see when each file was modified.

You can change a column's width by dragging the spacer line on the right edge of the column's heading button to the left or right. If you drag the spacer line for the Name button to the right, for example, the Name column widens, and the remaining columns shift over to the right.

Tip

If you want to temporarily hide a column in Details view for a given folder window, drag the spacer line on the right edge of the heading button all the way to the left edge of the column. You can redisplay the column — even though you can't see it — by dragging the now-invisible heading button's edge to the right.

Each folder window has its own properties. Before you adjust the width of the columns in a window, they have the default properties. After you change the column widths, Windows retains the new settings and uses them the next time you open that particular folder. This is true even if you open the folder window through My Computer and make changes to it, and then open the same folder in Explorer view (see the next chapter).

Secret

Do you want to adjust a column's width in Details view so that none of the entries in the column are truncated? Rest your mouse pointer over the spacer line and double-click. Windows widens (or narrows) the column just enough to fit the widest entry. This is the same method you use to "AutoFit" columns in Excel and Access.

Windows Toolbars

Back in Windows 95, the My Computer window and Explorer window only came with one toolbar. In Windows Me and 98, these windows come with three toolbars, Standard Buttons, Address bar, and Links. The Standard Buttons toolbar has a standard version and an Internet Explorer version (which we often refer to as the *Internet toolbar*). You can decide which toolbars to display (if any), how they should be positioned, how wide they should be, and whether text will accompany their icons — in short, you have lots of flexibility.

Windows Me and 98 combine the Internet Explorer browser window with the regular Windows 95 windows such as My Computer. Therefore, Microsoft had to come up with a way to combine the toolbars applicable to each window.

If you're used to the Windows 95 interface, Windows Me's plethora of toolbars can be a bit confusing. If you have a small screen (like that on a portable), they can hog a bunch of precious real estate. Thankfully, they are flexible enough that you can decide just how much space to allot to them and how many to use.

To get back to the old, uncluttered Windows 95 look, take the following steps:

STEPS

Going Back to the Windows 95 Look

Step 1.   Click the My Computer icon on your Desktop.

Step 2.   In the View ➪ Toolbars menu, mark Standard Buttons and Address bar, and clear Links and Text Labels.

Step 3.   Point to the vertical line at the left end of the Address bar and drag it to the left edge of the window, directly under the menu bar.

Step 4.   Drag the Standard Buttons toolbar to the right of the Address bar. You should have something that looks like Figure 8-6.

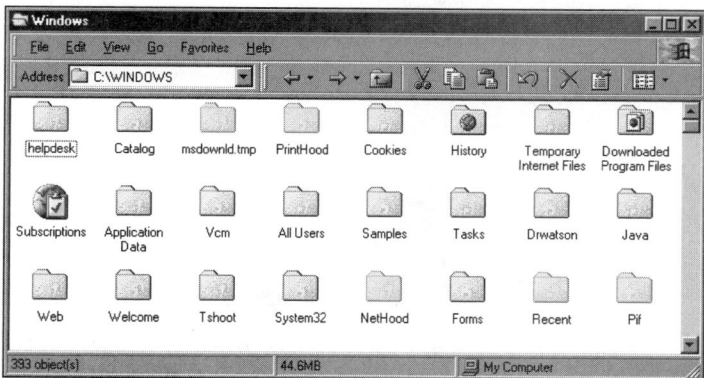

Figure 8-6: A Windows Me folder window made up to look like a Windows 95 folder window

The Address bar lets you navigate to Internet URLs or to folders on your own computer. For example, you could enter `http://www.davisstraub.com/secrets` or `C:\Windows` in this field.

If you want more space and fewer toolbars, right-click a blank area of the Standard Buttons toolbar, and clear the Address bar. Then drag the Standard Buttons toolbar to the right of the menu bar.

Secret

Windows retains the toolbar settings for your My Computer window, so the next time that you open a folder window, you'll see the same toolbars in the same positions. The Windows Explorer and the Internet Explorer windows also retain their own toolbar settings. You can use these three windows interchangeably to perform similar functions, but establish unique toolbar settings in each one.

The Explorer Bar

Choose View ➪ Explorer Bar in a My Computer window and you'll see a submenu. When you mark one of these options, a new pane appears in the My Computer client area. The content of the pane varies depending on which option you choose (Search, Favorites, History, and Folders). Figure 8-7 shows what the My Computer window looks like if you choose View ➪ Explorer Bar ➪ History.

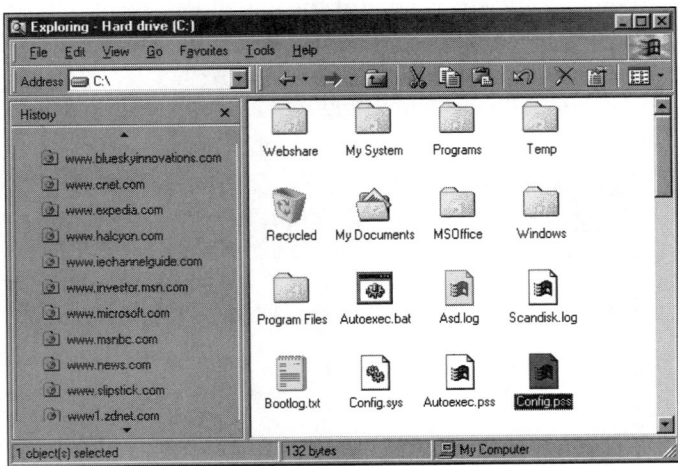

Figure 8-7: A Windows folder window with the History Explorer bar

Customizing This Folder

Windows gives you the option of adding background graphics to your folder and Explorer windows. You can also modify a copy of the HTML template for folders, `\Windows\Web\folder.htt`, to change the Web page view of a given folder. To make either type of change, choose View ⇨ Customize This Folder in the folder whose view you want to modify. In the wizard that appears, mark Modify background picture and filename appearance to add a background graphic, or Choose or edit an HTML template for this folder to modify a copy of the HTML template file, and then continue with the remaining steps in the wizard.

If you select a background graphic, you don't have to view the folder as a Web page in order to see the background. If you modify a copy of the folder template file, Windows places both an edited copy of folder.htt and a hidden Desktop.ini file in your folder. The Desktop.ini file references this copy of folder.htt.

Windows places a hidden Desktop.ini file in the folder whether you choose a background graphic or a customized Web page view. You can easily get rid of the customization by clicking View ⇨ Customize This Folder ⇨ Remove Customization. This erases the Desktop.ini file, and the graphic file and/or the folder.htt file (if present).

Secret

If you customize a folder that already has a Desktop.ini file, Windows updates this file to include the pointers to the new resources. If you remove this customization, your file reverts to its previous version (almost). The changes that were made in this file during the customization and removal process don't affect its operation. However, the Desktop.ini file is no longer hidden, and if the folder had been given the System attribute, the attribute is removed by the customization process.

In the next section, we discuss one reason why you might have a Desktop.ini file in a folder that you haven't yet customized.

Custom Folder Icons

Secret

You can change the little manila folder icons into something a bit more pleasing. You do this by adding a little Desktop.ini file to the folder and marking the folder's System attribute.

You won't be able to use these methods to change the little graphics on the manila folder icons of special folders. You can, however, change those folder icons using the steps detailed in the "New Icons for Desktop Items" section of Chapter 5.

A little freeware program called Icon Wizard adds the Desktop.ini file, marks the System attribute for the folder, and lets you easily choose from its library of folder-like icons. Download the file icwlinst.exe from http://www.winsite.com/info/pc/win95/desktop/cfeicwll.zip/downl.html. The Desktop.ini file that Icon Wizard creates just includes an icon filename and an index to the icon in the file. If there is only one icon in the icon file, the index is zero. If you browse to a file with multiple icons, the index will reflect which icon you choose. You can also manually edit the Desktop.ini file to change the icon yourself.

If you use the Customize This Folder Wizard (see the previous section, "Customizing This Folder") to customize a folder whose icon you've changed, you will lose your System attribute and your icon won't display anymore. You'll need to run the Icon Wizard again to restore the System attribute. When you do this, the changes that you made with the Customize This Folder Wizard will be preserved.

After you use Icon Wizard to change a folder icon, the icon won't be updated in all of the windows in which it's displayed. To get it to update in every window, use TweakUI. Click the Repair tab, choose Rebuild Icons in the drop-down list, and click Repair Now.

Summary

If you want to know how to manage your computer most efficiently, this chapter and the next chapter are the places to look:

▶ We show you how to change the name of My Computer.

▶ The folder window views let you look at your computer in many different ways, and we show you how to change these to suit your needs.

▶ We provide a number of methods you can use to quickly select files and folders in a folder window.

Chapter 9

The Start Button and Finding

In This Chapter

Microsoft paid millions to the Rolling Stones to let it use their song "Start Me Up" back in the days of the rollout of Windows 95. The Start button has met with mixed success ever since. At least with newer versions of Windows (Me and 98), it has gained a bit of badly needed flexibility. We discuss:

▶ Shutting down

▶ Deleting unwanted shortcuts to recent documents from your Documents menu

▶ Adding and removing items from your Start menus

▶ Putting the Desktop on the Start button

▶ Running the Start menus from the keyboard

▶ Creating and saving complex file searches

▶ Using Find to build Start menus and get rid of unwanted files

Starting

In Chapter 5, we looked at the Desktop and the taskbar. The Start button is attached to the taskbar, but there is enough going on with it that it gets its own chapter. It is a primary entry point into Windows. As you change your Desktop to match your needs, the Start button continues to provide useful services.

Secret

If you want, you can change the name on the Start button to something like Panic. The new name has to be five letters to exactly replace Start. You can use a hex editor or a shareware program like WinHacker to edit the Explorer.exe file. To change the name, replace all instances of *Start* in Explorer.exe with your new five letters (after you save a copy of your original Explorer.exe).

WinHacker saves a good copy of `Explorer.exe` as `Explorer.old` in your `\Windows` folder before it makes the change, so you can recover by booting to the DOS prompt and copying the "old" Explorer over the hacked version. You can find WinHacker at `http://www.albert.com/authorpage/000103280/wh95-11r.htm`.

Stopping

We start our discussion of the Start button by talking about the Stop button. The most important function you can find on a computer is how to stop it, how to get it ultimately under your control so that if you have any problems you can just stop the whole thing.

Click the Start button. Click Shut Down, and mark the "Shut down" option button. We're outta here. We know it seems funny that the Start button is also the Stop button, but there it is.

Clicking Shut Down presents you with the dialog box shown in Figure 9-1. This dialog box gives you four choices. If your computer's BIOS has a Windows-compatible Automated Power Management (APM) facility, and you haven't disabled it, the default option (the first time you start the computer) is "Stand by." Your other choices are "Shut down," "Restart," and "Restart in MS-DOS mode."

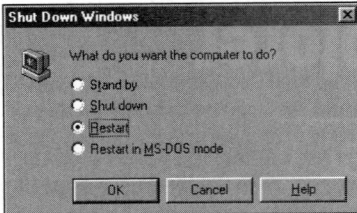

Figure 9-1: The Shut Down Windows dialog box. Make one of four choices.

Windows defaults to the option you chose the last time you made a selection in this dialog box.

You can use the System Policy Editor (see "System Policy Editor" in Chapter 18) to disable the "Shut down" function.

Shut Down

Shut down actually means to shut down Windows. If you have the Windows Advanced Power Management capabilities, and most new computers do, your computer turns off as soon as you choose "Shut down" and click OK.

To keep your computer running after you choose "Shut down," you need to disable APM in your computer's BIOS setup. If you do this, you have to turn off the computer yourself after shutting it down. If you have disabled APM and want to restart Windows after issuing the "Shut down" command, wait until you see the "It's now safe to turn off your computer" screen and then press Ctrl+Alt+Delete.

Secret

The Windows Shut Down screen is a Windows bitmap (bmp) file. Microsoft gave it a sys extension just to keep your prying eyes out of it. If you want to change it, you can edit it with MS Paint. The name is Logos.sys. You'll find it in the \Windows folder.

Restart

If you have had a problem with Windows and just want to start over again, you can choose Restart in the Shut Down Windows dialog box. This option works just like "Shut down" does, but it doesn't require that you press Ctrl+Alt+Delete to restart Windows. It restarts Windows with a warm boot.

Secret

To restart Windows quickly without going through the warm reboot process, mark Restart and then hold down your Shift key while clicking the OK button in the Shut Down Windows dialog box. On some PCs, this quick-restart technique temporarily disables Advanced Power Management. You can check this in the Device Manager tab of the Control Panel's System applet. (If disabled, Power Management will bear a yellow exclamation point under the System Devices tree.) Power Management will be restored the next time you restart Windows *without* holding down the Shift key.

Stand By

Windows 95 displayed a Suspend option in the Start menu on computers that supported APM, as long as APM hadn't been disabled in the BIOS setup. Windows Me and 98 do not have this option; Microsoft wants to encourage you to use Standby mode, so they've now made that the first choice in the Shut Down Windows dialog box. (You won't see this option if you've disabled APM.)

If you put your computer in Standby mode, its power usage is reduced and you can restart it quickly without having to reload all your applications. This would be great if everything worked after your computer spent a night in Standby mode. With a variety of computers, maybe this will be the case, and maybe not. Microsoft wants computers to be perceived as ready to go at a moment's notice. Perhaps most will be, someday.

The Start Menu

Click the Start button and up pops the Start menu, as shown in Figure 9-2. This is the first of the cascading menus.

What is not so great about the Start button is that it takes a lot of mousing to get to where you want to be. One way to cut down on extra mousing is to drag an icon for an application, folder, or document and drop it on the Start button to create a shortcut to the item in the main Start menu. We discuss Start menu shortcuts in more detail later in this chapter.

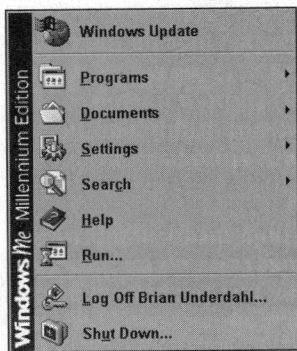

Figure 9-2: The Start menu — your window into the world of Windows

In programmer-speak, the Start menu is a specialized window object. It has specific methods not found in most windows, but it has inherited many of the basic window methods. What this means for you as a user is that you can right-click the items in the Programs, Favorites, and Documents menus and get an appropriate context menu.

Because all of the submenus under the Programs and Favorites menu items are folders (all subfolders of \Windows\Start Menu), their context menus are the same ones that you find when you right-click a folder icon in an Explorer or folder window. By the same token, when you right-click an application or document shortcut in the Start menu, you get the same context menu as you get when you open an Explorer or folder window and right-click the same shortcut in the \Windows\Start Menu folder or one of its subfolders.

You can drag and drop submenu items from the Programs and Favorites menus onto other submenus to rearrange your Start menu. To move items up and down in a menu, just drag and drop them to the desired location.

You can use TweakUI to name other folders as the Start Menu folder, the Programs folder, and the StartUp folder. You should do all three if you want to completely move the Start Menu folder. You might want to make a copy of the Start Menu folder (and all its subfolders) in its new location first, edit it, and then use TweakUI to designate this new folder as the Start Menu folder. Once all that is working, you can delete the original Start Menu folder or switch back and forth between multiple Start Menu folders. We provide more details in the next section.

Programs

Look closely at the Programs icon in the Start menu. It looks like a folder window to remind you that the Programs menu is like a folder window that contains applications. Windows comes with a collection of shortcuts to applications and accessory programs, which it stores in the \Windows\ Start Menu\Programs folder.

If you installed Windows Me into an old Windows 3.1x directory, all the previous program groups are converted to folders and placed in the Programs folder as well. What you see in the Programs menu is the contents of the Programs folder. You aren't restricted to putting just applications in the Programs folder. You can put documents in it too, just as you could with the program groups in the Windows 3.1x Program Manager.

The Programs menu can have multiple submenus. Each submenu can have its own submenus. The submenus are displayed as separate cascading menus in the Programs menu. Of course, the cascading menus can get pretty complicated after a while.

Using tools built into the Start menu, you can easily organize everything in the Programs menu to suit your preferences. You can create a flat or hierarchical structure of submenus. You can rename the application or document icons to anything you want. If you want to move items in the Programs menu, just drag and drop them to new locations in the menu hierarchy. You can also right-click menu items to display a context menu that lets you create new menu items, among other options.

To get to an application, click the Start button, move the mouse pointer over the Programs icon, and follow the cascading menus until you get to the application that you want to run. Click the application once to run it.

Can't find your application? We'll show you how in the "Finding Files or Folders"section later in this chapter.

The \Windows\Start Menu\Programs folder is a special folder. Your registry keeps track of it. Using TweakUI, you can designate another folder as the Programs folder.

STEPS

Naming a New Folder as the Programs Folder

Step 1. Click your TweakUI shortcut on your Desktop (or click the TweakUI icon in the Control Panel), and click the General tab.

Step 2. In the Folder drop-down list, select Programs and click the Change Location button.

Step 3. In the Browse for Folder dialog box, highlight the desired folder, click OK, and then click OK again.

Step 4. You'll have to restart Windows (or at least log off and back on again). Click the Start button, choose Shut Down, mark Restart, and then hold down the Shift key as you click OK to restart Windows without going through a warm reboot.

The new Programs folder (whatever its actual name) won't have very useful menu items in it unless you have carefully constructed it. You can make a copy of your previous Programs folder (\Windows\Start Menu\Programs), edit it, and then use TweakUI to designate this new edited folder as your Programs folder.

You can also use a slight variation of these steps to designate a different folder as the Start Menu folder, and another folder as the StartUp folder. If you paste a copy of your Start Menu folder into a new location (not under \Windows), you can edit it to create the basis for your three new menus.

StartUp Menu

If you have applications that you want to start when Windows starts, you can put shortcuts to them in this menu (which corresponds to the \Windows\Start Menu\Programs\StartUp folder). You can close a program that started when Windows started any time you choose. If you then decide you want to start the program again, click the application in the StartUp menu.

We show you how to put shortcuts in the StartUp folder/menu later in this chapter.

You can use TweakUI to change which folder acts as your StartUp folder; just follow the "Naming a New Folder as the Programs Folder" steps in the previous section and substitute StartUp for Programs in Step 2.

Documents

The last 15 documents that you started by clicking an icon in an Explorer or My Computer window are displayed in this menu. You can restart a document and its associated application by clicking it once in the Documents menu.

For Windows to add a document to this list, you have to have started it from an Explorer or folder window. That way, Windows can grab the document name. If you open a document from inside your application, Windows doesn't know how to put it on the list. However, applications written specifically for Windows Me or 9x can also place their newly opened documents on the Documents list.

The list contains shortcuts to the documents. You can delete all the shortcuts at once (without affecting the documents themselves). Right-click the taskbar, click Properties, click the Start Menu Programs tab, and click the Clear button. All the shortcuts in the Documents menu are gone.

Secret

You can also remove shortcuts individually. Windows puts the shortcuts to your recently opened documents in the \Windows\Recent folder. You can edit these shortcuts or delete them, as you like. You need to be sure that the "Show hidden files and folders" option button is marked in the View tab of the Folder Options dialog box (choose View ➪ Folder Options in any folder or Explorer window). Otherwise, the Recent folder will be hidden from view.

STEPS

Cleaning Up the Documents Menu

Step 1. Open an Explorer window.

Step 2. Click the plus sign next to the \Windows folder. Highlight the Recent subfolder under the \Windows folder.

Step 3. The shortcuts to the documents are displayed in the right pane. You can delete them in any manner you choose.

Clearing the Documents Menu

You can use TweakUI to clear the Documents menu every time you restart Windows. Just click the Paranoia tab and then mark "Clear document history at logon."

To keep recent document shortcuts from ever appearing in the Documents menu (or in the \Windows\Recent folder), click the IE4 tab in TweakUI and clear the "Add new documents to documents on start menu" checkbox. You'll have to restart Windows to have this change take effect.

If you'd like to see the inner workings of a trick like this, you can make the contents of the Documents menu go away without using any utilities by following these steps:

STEPS

Making the Documents Go Away

Step 1. This trick requires that you turn off the Recycle Bin's habit of saving deleted files. To do this, right-click the Recycle Bin icon on your Desktop, choose Properties, and click the Global tab. Mark the "Use one setting for all drives" option button and the "Do not move files to the Recycle Bin" checkbox. Then click OK.

Step 2. Click Regedit.exe in your \Windows folder to run the Registry Editor. Click the plus sign to the left of HKEY_CURRENT_USER, and continue opening subfolders until you display this key:

HKEY_CURRENT_USER\ Software\ Microsoft\ Windows\
Current Version\ Explorer\ Shell Folders

Step 3. Highlight the Shell Folders folder, and look in the right pane for an object named Recent. If this object doesn't exist, create one now by right-clicking a blank space in the right pane, clicking New ⇨ String Value, typing **Recent**, and pressing Enter.

Step 4. Double-click the Recent object. In the Edit String dialog box that appears, replace the value C:\Windows\Recent with the value C:\Recycled. From now on, Windows will immediately send all additions to your Documents menu to the Recycle Bin instead, so they will not appear on the Documents menu. The actual file you accessed will not be affected.

Step 5. Close the Registry Editor.

No Documents or Favorites on the Start Menu

You can use TweakUI to remove the Favorites and Documents menu items from the Start menu. Click your TweakUI shortcut on your Desktop (or click the TweakUI icon in the Control Panel), click the IE4 tab, and clear the "Show documents on start menu" and "Show favorites on start menu" checkboxes.

You'll have to restart Windows to have this change reflected in the Start menu. In addition, you can use the Advanced tab of the Taskbar and Start Menu Properties dialog box to control the display of the Favorites menu (but not the Documents menu).

Furthermore, you can use TweakUI to change which folder acts as the Documents folder. Follow the "Naming a New Folder as the Programs Folder" steps in the "Programs" section earlier in this chapter, and substitute Recent Documents for Programs in Step 2.

Put a Shortcut to Your Recent Documents Folder on the Desktop

Tip

If you want to be able to quickly edit the contents of your recent documents folder, put a shortcut to it on the Desktop. Open the Explorer and focus on the \Windows\Recent folder. Right-drag the Recent folder to the Desktop and drop it there. Click Create Shortcut(s) Here. Edit the name of the shortcut folder icon to Recent Docs or whatever.

Now you can quickly get to the folder of recent documents and remove the documents that you don't care to have there.

Settings

The Settings menu provides access to the folders and dialog boxes that you use to change most of the Windows parameter values. Because there are many different values, and they are spread all over the place, this is a convenient starting point.

The Settings menu contains shortcuts (although not actual Windows shortcuts as described in the previous chapter) to the Control Panel and the Printers folder. It also contains the Taskbar & Start Menu command, which leads to the Taskbar and Start Menu Properties dialog box.

The Control Panel

The Control Panel doesn't exist as an actual folder, so if you use the Explorer to look for a subfolder called Control Panel under your hard disk drive, you won't find one.

You can use the System Policy Editor to keep users out of the Control Panel. (See "System Policy Editor" in Chapter 18.)

The Printers Folder

All the hardware drivers for your currently installed printers are stored in the Printers folder. This folder also contains the Add Printer icon, which lets you add new printers. You can reach the Printers folder through the

Control Panel and the My Computer window as well as the Settings menu. The Printers folder isn't an actual folder, so it only shows up in the left pane of the Explorer window. There are no files associated with the Printers folder (other than printer driver files) — just registry settings. As you add new printers, their properties are stored in the registry.

We cover the Printers folder in Chapter 41.

Taskbar and Start Menu Properties

Clicking the Taskbar & Start Menu item in the Settings menu brings up the Taskbar and Start Menu Properties dialog box. You can display the same dialog box by right-clicking the taskbar and choosing Properties. The first tab in the dialog box is General.

We describe the first two checkboxes in the General tab in "Hiding the Taskbar" in Chapter 5. The "Show small icons in Start menu" checkbox lets you change how the Start menu looks. Mark and clear this box to see which look you prefer. The "Show clock" checkbox lets you choose whether or not to display the clock at the right end of the taskbar.

The Advanced tab is where you will find much of the power to add, remove, clean up, and move menu items (which are just shortcuts) in the various Start menus. This tab is shown in Figure 9-3.

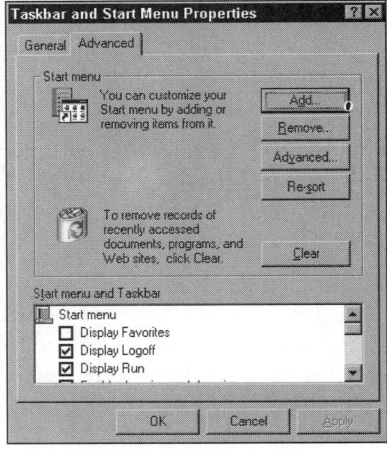

Figure 9-3: The Advanced tab of the Taskbar and Start Menu Properties dialog box

Windows Me and 98 modify the Start menu (as opposed to the way it was in Windows 95) to let you move some menu items from one part of the Start menu to another without invoking the Start Menu Wizard. Just drag a Start menu item from its present location to a new location on the Start menu.

This trick also works on the Favorites menu, both the one displayed on the Start menu and the one in the My Computer and Explorer windows.

Add Start Menu Items

You can use the Advanced tab of the Taskbar and Start Menu Properties dialog box to create shortcuts for applications and then place them on the Desktop or add them to the Start menu, the Programs menu, or the submenus of the Programs menu. Click the Add button to start the Create Shortcut Wizard, as shown in Figure 9-4. This wizard lets you browse for an application, select the menu folder that you want to place the shortcut in (\Windows\Desktop, \Windows\Start Menu, \Windows\Start Menu\Programs, or one of the Programs subfolders), and change the shortcut's name.

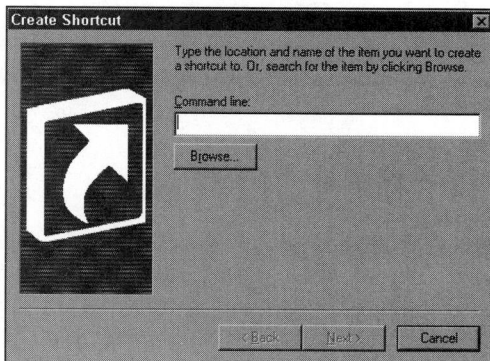

Figure 9-4: The Create Shortcut Wizard

The menu items, which are really shortcuts, don't display the little black arrow in the lower-left corner of their icons. We normally expect to see this black arrow on shortcut icons. Because all menu items are shortcuts, the Microsoft designers felt that there was no need to add the arrow to the icons displayed in the menus. Keep in mind that the menus themselves are not shortcuts, but rather subfolders of the \Windows\Start Menu folder.

Remove Start Menu Items

To remove menu items or entire menus, use the Remove button in the Start Menu Programs tab of the Taskbar and Start Menu Properties dialog box. Be careful—these removals aren't stored in the Recycle Bin for you to put back in place. The Remove Shortcuts/Folders dialog box, which is displayed when you click the Remove button (see Figure 9-5), lets you navigate among the menus/folders to find the items (or folders) that you wish to remove. Of course, the quickest method is to simply right-click the item directly in the Start menu and choose Delete.

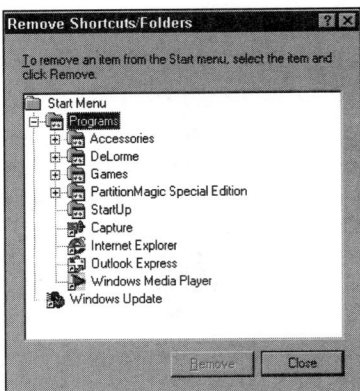

Figure 9-5: The Remove Shortcuts/Folders dialog box. You can highlight the menu item or menu folder that you want to remove. If you remove a menu folder, you also remove (delete) all the shortcuts in that menu.

Edit, Move, Add, and Delete Start Menu Items— the Advanced Button

Click the Advanced button in the Advanced tab of the Taskbar and Start Menu Properties dialog box to open an Explorer view of your Start Menu. This clipped Explorer works like any other Explorer window. (The Start Menu folder is set as the root—see "Explorer Command-Line Parameters" in Chapter 7 to learn how this is accomplished.)

You get all the capability you need to move menu items throughout the Programs menu and in and out of the Start menu. You can right-drag menu items (shortcuts) from another Explorer window and drop them in any menu folder that you like. You can create new menu folders in the Start menu or in any submenu folder.

The Start Menu Explorer, as shown in Figure 9-6, demonstrates very clearly that the Start menu is really a series of folders—special folders, but folders nonetheless. You can manipulate them as you would any other folders.

The menu folders are meant to hold shortcuts. If you want to add a shortcut to a menu folder, the best way to do it is to right-drag an application icon from another Explorer window to the Start Menu Explorer, drop it in the menu folder that you want, and choose Create Shortcut(s) Here.

You can copy or move application icons (and document or folder icons) to the menu folders in the Start menu if you wish, but the menu folders are really intended to hold shortcuts to applications.

The Start Menu Explorer is especially useful for moving menus about. You can't move menus using the Add and Remove buttons.

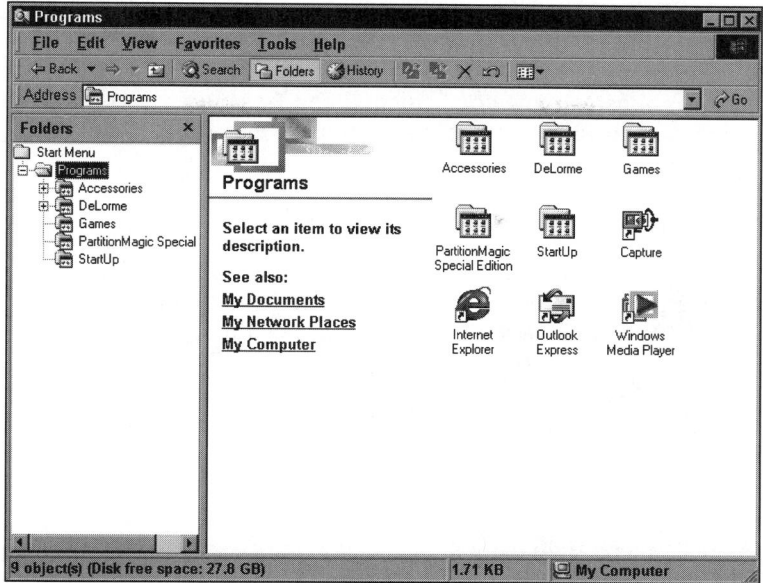

Figure 9-6: The Start Menu Explorer. If you highlight a menu folder icon name in the left pane, the contents of that menu folder appear in the right pane.

Windows has added the capability of dragging and dropping the Programs, Favorites, and Documents menu items around (although you cannot drag items *into* the Documents menu, only out of it). You can also use drag and drop to move items that you've dropped on the Start button. Windows added the drag-and-drop capability because users wanted a quick and dirty way to change their Start menus without having to use the "advanced" Start Menu Explorer.

Folder Options

The Start button provides another way to reach the Folder Options dialog box. This is the same dialog box that you see when you are focused on a drive, folder, or file in the Explorer and click View ⇨ Folder Options. Since the Start button is always easily accessible, this is a quick way to get to these settings. For more on how the Folder Options dialog box works, see "Folder Options" in Chapter 7.

Windows Update

The Windows Update setting is there to help you keep your Windows software and drivers current. Click it, and Windows will connect via the Internet to the Microsoft Windows Update Web site. After asking your permission, this site compares a list of hardware drivers and Windows applications generated on your computer by a Windows applet against a Microsoft list of the latest versions of these drivers and applets. If there are updates available from Microsoft for your software and hardware drivers, you will be notified and you can choose to download any of them. We suggest you use Windows Update periodically to make sure you receive the latest Windows updates.

Search

The Search command is on the Start menu — it's located in the Tools menu in the Explorer window menu, and it's available by pressing the F3 key. We discuss the Search capability later in this chapter.

You can eliminate Search (although not the F3 key version) using the System Policy Editor. (See "System Policy Editor" in Chapter 18.)

Help

The Start menu Help command gets you to the unified help for all of Windows. Click Help and you get the Windows Help window, as shown in Figure 9-7.

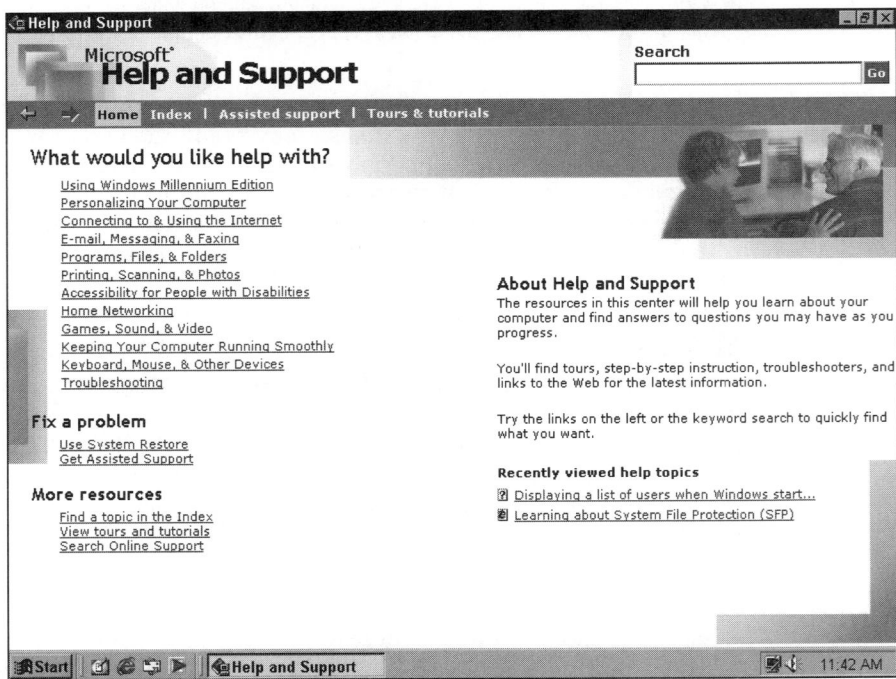

Figure 9-7: The Windows Help window

Because Windows Help is a unified help system, you don't have to search a lot of separate help files to learn about Windows. Windows Help files are stored in the \Windows\Help folder.

The Windows Help engine has been greatly updated since the old version in Windows 95. For example, if you click the Web Help button on the Help toolbar, you can connect to the Windows Update Web site on a Microsoft server. This site is also accessible more directly in the Start menu by clicking Settings ⇨ Windows Update.

Run

This is a command-line interface. If you want to run a program by typing its path and name and perhaps some command-line parameters, then this is the place for you. This is like calling a program from the DOS command line, especially now that you can run Windows programs from the DOS command line.

The Run dialog box (shown in Figure 9-8) keeps a little history in the Open drop-down list. You can bring up previous commands, edit them, and run them again.

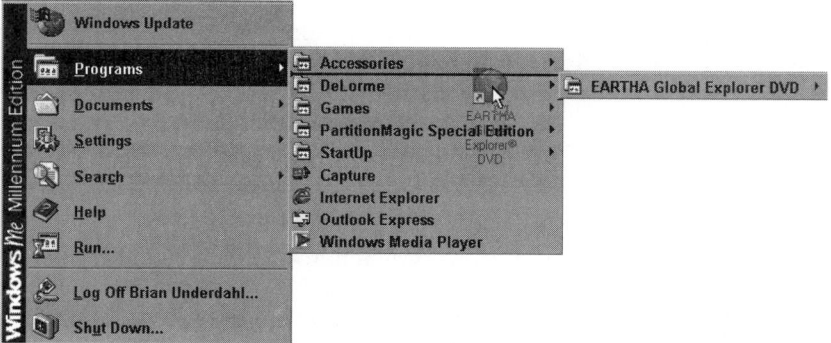

Figure 9-8: The Run dialog box. Type the path and filename of your DOS or Windows application, document, or Internet URL. Put in some command-line parameters, if you like.

You can type the name of a document that has an associated application (as defined in the registry) and run it. For example, you can type the name and path of an ini file. When you click OK, Notepad is invoked, and it displays the ini file in its client window area.

Secret

Want to quickly open a window that displays the files and folders in the root directory of your boot drive? Click the Start button, and then click Run. Type a backslash (\ ) in the Run dialog box and then click OK.

You can use TweakUI to clear the Run history every time that you start Windows. Click the Paranoia tab, and then mark "Clear run history at logon." You can also use the System Policy Editor to hide the Run command.

Log On as a Different User

The option to Log Off (and thereby log on as a different user) appears in the Start menu if you have a network, have installed or used Direct Cable Connection, or have enabled user profiles. If you haven't done any of these things, you won't see it.

Log Off allows you to get out of the current user's setup and into a new user's configuration. Turn to "Whose Desktop Is This Anyway?" in Chapter 6 for more details.

Right-Click the Start Button

You can right-click the Start button and choose Open ⇨ Explore, or Search. Depending on what software you have installed, you may see another option here (such as Add to Zip). Choose Open to display a folder window focused on the Start Menu folder, which is a subfolder of the \Windows folder.

The Start Menu folder contains an icon for the Programs folder. Notice that the icon is the same as the one displayed next to Programs in the Start menu. Clicking the Programs folder icon opens a folder window containing the Accessories folder, the StartUp folder, and other folders and applications. The hierarchy of folders and subfolders in the Start Menu folder corresponds to the cascading menus and submenus within the Start menu.

The Start Menu folder gives you a way of traversing the menus using folders, a different style for those who wish to use it. Because the Start menu is also a folder, you can drag shortcuts into it and its subfolders. You can click icons in the Start Menu folder window to open up other folder windows, and then navigate back up to the parent folders.

When you right-click the Start button and click Explore, Windows displays an Explorer window focused on the Start Menu folder. Unlike the Explorer window that's displayed when you click the Advanced button in the Start Menu Programs tab of the Taskbar and Start Menu Properties dialog box, this is a full Explorer. The folder tree in the left pane will take you anywhere you want to go; it's not restricted to the Start Menu folder and its subfolders.

Finally, right-clicking the Start button and choosing Search opens the Search dialog box. We describe this dialog box in the section entitled "The Search Function" later in this chapter.

Drop It on the Start Button

There is an easy way to add menu items to the Start menu. Drag and drop icons from the Desktop or from a folder or Explorer window to the Start button. When you drag an icon to the Start button, Windows automatically adds a shortcut to it in the Start menu. When you click the Start button to display the main Start menu, any icons you've added in this way appear in their own little section above the Programs command, as shown in Figure 9-9. Better yet, drag and hover over the Start button, and the Start menu opens up; you can now drop your icon onto the Programs or Favorites menu, or one of their cascading submenus.

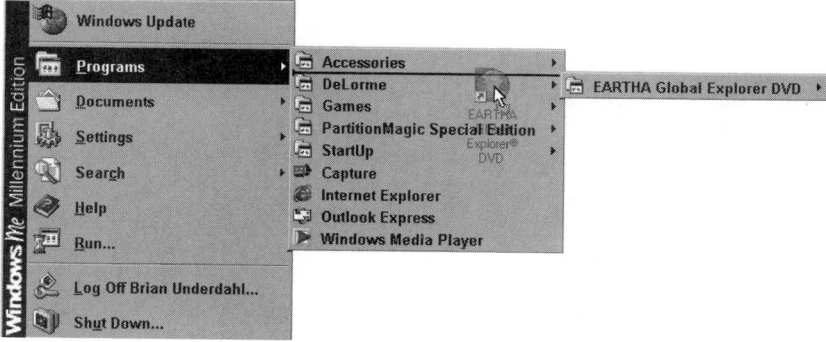

Figure 9-9: The Start menu opens to let you drop an icon into one of the Programs submenus. The icon is translucent while it's being dragged. Notice that, as with other menu items, the shortcuts that were added at the top of the Start menu don't have the little black arrow in the lower-left corner.

These menu items are shortcuts just like the other menu items. The nice thing about them is that the icons are full size, so you can see them more easily. These shortcuts are stored in the Start Menu folder. You can place them in any order that you like. Just drag and drop them to the appropriate location. The shortcuts that originally came on the Start menu can't be moved.

The Desktop on the Start Menu

Secret

A neat trick is to put parts of the Desktop itself on your Start button. Since the Desktop is also a folder, you can drag it from the Explorer onto the Start button. The Desktop folder is located under the \Windows folder.

When you click the Desktop icon on the Start menu, you open a window to your Desktop (minus some crucial pieces). You now have a Desktop window on your Desktop. All the shortcuts that you placed on the Desktop are in the window, along with any documents or folders that you put on the Desktop. This is very handy if the icons on your Desktop are covered with other windows. You just place a window to your Desktop over them.

This trick also comes in handy when you use the keyboard to get to the Start menu. Press Ctrl+Esc to get to the Start menu from anywhere — even full-screen DOS sessions. After the Start menu pops up, you can use your arrow keys to get to the Desktop icon. This gives you a quick way to switch to an inactive application that has a shortcut on the Desktop. The Desktop folder on the Start menu does not contain My Computer, My Network Places, or Recycle Bin.

You can display a separate Desktop toolbar by right-clicking an empty part of the taskbar and choosing Toolbars ⇨ Desktop. The Deskmenu item that comes with Microsoft's PowerToys also lets you easily get to your Desktop. It creates a tray icon called Deskmenu. When you click the icon, a menu of Desktop items is displayed on top of all the windows on your Desktop.

In addition, you might want to try a little shareware application called Tab2Desk. This program allows you to use Alt+Tab to get to the Desktop. Tab2Desk works the same as Minimize All Windows (available when you right-click an uncovered part of the taskbar). When you press Alt+Tab, you can choose the Tab2Desk icon to minimize all open windows on the Desktop. Tab2Desk is available at most Internet shareware sites.

Folders in the Start Menu Folder

If you create a folder in the Start Menu folder, its folder icon includes a little window graphic. The Start Menu folder is a special folder; it automatically adds this window graphic to the icon of any folder stored within it. You can see this by navigating in your Explorer to your \Windows\Start Menu folder. You'll notice that all the subfolders of the Start Menu folder have icons that include this graphic.

At times, it may be more convenient for you to create a new folder in the Start Menu folder than to add a shortcut to a folder. When you click an item in the Start menu for a *shortcut* to a folder, Windows just opens the folder window for you. In contrast, if you add an *actual* folder to the Start Menu folder and then put shortcuts inside the folder (to documents, executables, or other folders), then when you point to the menu item for the folder in the Start Menu, a cascading menu appears with all the shortcuts you placed in the folder.

To do this while in the Explorer view of the Start Menu folder, right-click a blank area of the right pane. Then point to New and click Folder. Type a name for your folder, press Enter, and it's ready to go. You can now right-drag executables, documents, and so on into this new subfolder of the Start Menu folder to create shortcuts. Once you've done this, you can easily pick them from the Start menu.

One other difference between creating a folder in the Start Menu folder versus creating a shortcut to a folder is that a folder containing shortcuts does not change when you add or subtract items in the actual folder. In contrast, a shortcut to a folder is dynamic and always remains up-to-date with the contents of that folder.

Control Panel on a Start Menu

Secret

You normally get to the Control Panel by clicking the Start button, pointing to Settings, and finally clicking Control Panel. The Control Panel is usually displayed in a folder window. However, you can display the Control Panel as a menu and not as a window. To do so, take the following steps:

STEPS

The Control Panel as a Menu

Step 1. Click the Start button, and click Settings ⇨ Taskbar and Start Menu.

Step 2. Click the Advanced tab.

Step 3. Select the Expand Control Panel option.

Step 4. Click OK.

Step 5. Click the Start button. Select Settings ⇨ Control Panel and all the Control Panel icons are listed in a cascading menu attached to it.

The resource ID given in Step 3 is unique to the Control Panel. You can find it by using your Registry Editor and searching for Control Panel. We discuss some additional ways that you can put Control Panel applets on your Start menu in the "Shortcuts to the Control Panel" section of Chapter 15.

You can use the same trick for the Printers folder, Dial-Up Networking, My Documents, and My Pictures.

Keyboard Control of the Start Menus

You can run the Start menus with your keyboard. The most important keyboard combination is Ctrl+Esc, which displays the main Start menu. The Windows key on Windows keyboards also displays the Start menu.

Tip

If you press the Ctrl button while you click the Maximize button in the upper-right corner of a folder or Explorer window, the window expands to full screen and the taskbar disappears. When you have opened a window in full-screen mode, pressing Ctrl+Esc or the Windows key still displays the Start menu.

You can choose menu items on the Start menu by pressing the letter key that corresponds to the underlined letter in the name. If you have added items to the Start menu that begin with the same letter, the letter key will take you to these items first. The letter keys operate in round-robin fashion, going to the first item that starts with that letter, and then the next, until it starts over at the top again.

The letter keys work in all the submenus also. There is no underlined letter in the shortcut names under the Programs menu, so you type the first letter of the item.

The arrow keys can also move you through the menus. The up and down arrow keys move you within a menu. When you get to the bottom of a menu, pressing the down arrow again takes you up to the top. (By the same token, pressing the up arrow when you're at the top of a menu takes you to the bottom.) The right and left arrow keys move you forward and back between the cascading menus. When you reach a menu item that you want to run, press Enter.

Secret

If you press Ctrl+Esc and then Esc, the Start menu disappears, but the focus stays on the Start button. When the Start button has the focus, you'll see the focus rectangle on it. You can confirm the Start button still has the focus by pressing Enter after you've pressed Ctrl+Esc, Esc. The Start menu will reappear.

Once the Start button has the focus, you can press Tab repeatedly to change the focus clockwise from the Start button to other objects on your display. If you have a toolbar immediately to the right of the Start button, the focus will shift there, then to the taskbar, then to any other toolbars, then to the Desktop, then to any of Active Desktop items, and then back to the Start button. If the taskbar is immediately to the right of the Start button, the focus will shift there first.

If the focus is on the taskbar, you can use the arrow keys to move the focus from button to button. To restore an application or bring it to the top of the windows on the Desktop, move the focus to the Taskbar button for that application and press Enter.

If the focus is on an icon on the Desktop, you can use your arrow keys to move among the Desktop icons to focus on the application, folder, or file you want to open. Press Enter when the focus is on the desired icon.

Secret

It's hard to see whether the focus is on the Start button, the taskbar, or the Desktop, and using the Windows default color scheme (called the Windows Standard scheme) makes this even more difficult. If the Start button has the focus, you'll see the typical dotted rectangle around the word *Start*. If the taskbar or the Start button has the focus, and if your color scheme has an Active Window Border color that differs from the 3D Object color (something that is not true of the Windows Standard scheme), you will see a border line around the taskbar.

If the Desktop has the focus, the taskbar border will display the Inactive Window Border color, and an icon on the Desktop will be highlighted.

If you have defined hot keys for the shortcuts on the Start menus, you can start an application immediately without going through the Start button, just by pressing its hot key combination. We describe how to create hot keys in "Hot Keys" in Chapter 10.

Long Start Menus

Windows 95 menus that were too long to fit on the screen produced a second column of menu items. Windows Me and 98 do away with double columns in favor of scroll arrows at the bottom and top of the single menu column. When you point to the scroll arrows, the menu items that are currently hidden scroll into view. The best way to get rid of these long menu columns is to hierarchically divide your menu items.

Secret

You can speed up the display of the hidden menu items by clicking the scroll arrows instead of pointing to them. To further speed the scrolling, hold down the Ctrl key as you point to the arrows or, faster still, hold down the Ctrl key while you click the arrows.

The Search Function

Windows Me includes a real search capability, something that was first introduced with Windows 98.

You can get to this Search function in a number of ways. If you want to search for files or folders, right-click the Start button, the My Computer icon, or any folder icon, and then click Search in the context menu. You can also click the Search button in any Explorer or folder window.

Windows Me and 98 expand the capability of the Search option from what was originally available in Windows 95. You can now search for people using directory services on the Internet or your Windows Address Book. You can also connect to Internet search engines to search for topics, words, or phrases found on Web sites or in newsgroups.

Tip

The easiest way to find a file or folder? Press the F3 key when the focus is on the Desktop, a folder window, an Explorer window, or the taskbar.

Tip

Just because the command is called *Search* doesn't necessarily mean the usefulness of this function is limited to finding things. For example, you can use Search as a filter to list all the executables in a folder or in a set of folders in one window.

Finding Files or Folders

You can find files and/or folders that match the criteria you set in the Search Results dialog box (right-click the Start button and click Search Now). Windows gives you a significant number of options to define your search strategy.

File or Folder Name

Secret

If you are looking for a specific file or folder and you know its name, type the name in the "Search for files or folders named" field, as shown in Figure 9-10. You can search for multiple folders, files, or file types. Just separate their names by commas, as in

```
*.bat, *.sys, *.txt, bill?.*
```

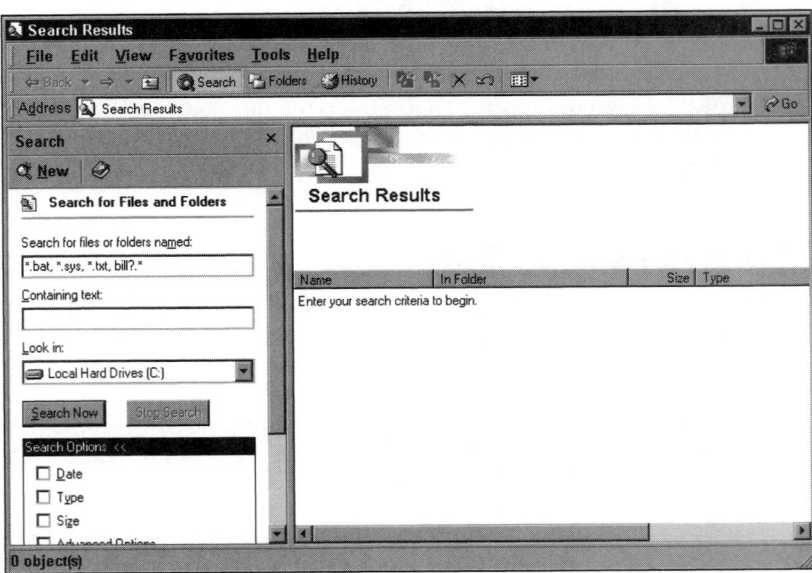

Figure 9-10: Type a file or folder name or partial name. If you know the general area (folder or drive) where the file or folder is located, choose a drive from the "Look in" drop-down list.

Secret

You can type a partial name with wild cards. The wild cards are **?** and *****. The question mark stands for one letter and the asterisk for one or more letters. Table 9-1 shows these and other options. Note that *abc* stands for any three letters.

Table 9-1:   Find Options

Entered in Named Field	*Search Location*
*	All files and folders.
.	All files and folders.
*.	All files.
.	No files or folders. (A file can't be named "dot.")
.exe	No files or folders (because a filename cannot start with a period).
abc	All files and folders with *abc* in name (including extensions).
exe	All files and folders with exe in name or extension; most likely executable files.
*.exe	All files with exe in extension only.
abc	All files and folders with abc in name.
*abc	All files with *abc* as last letters in name (not including extension).
*abc?	All files with *abc* as second to last letters in name (not including extension).
?abc	All files and folders with *abc* as at least second letters in name if not later.
?abc*	All files and folders with *abc* as the second through fourth letters in name.
??abc	All files and folders with *abc* as at least the third letters in name, if not later.
?abc?	All files and folders with at least one letter in front of *abc* and at least one behind in name.
?a?.*	Three-letter filename with middle letter of name given and extension unknown.

Notice that unlike searching in DOS for filenames, you can have an asterisk or question mark in front and still get meaningful results. In fact, the search algorithm is much more flexible and powerful than what was available with DOS or earlier versions of Windows.

In the "Look in" field, enter the general location for the file or folder. If you know a file or folder is on a certain disk drive, choose that drive letter. If you want to narrow it down further, click Browse to choose a folder, or include a path name in the "Search for files or folders named" field.

By default, Windows includes subfolders in the search. You probably want to do a top-down search, so leave the "Search subfolders" checkbox marked unless you know what folder the file is in.

Secret

Search will search for your files in hidden subfolders if you have marked the "Show hidden files and folders" option button in the View tab of the Folder Options dialog box (click Tools ⇨ Folder Options in an Explorer or folder window). Search will not find your fonts in the Fonts folder (which has the System attribute set, but is not hidden) if the "Look in" field in your Find dialog box is set to `\Windows` and not to `Windows\Fonts`.

You may find it convenient to "root" two or more searches at different starting points. In the Look In dialog box, just separate multiple roots with semicolons. For example, you could type **C:\Windows; D:** to start searching at two folders on separate drives. (See Figure 9-11.)

Text String

You can search for files that contain a given text string by typing it in the "Containing text" field. The search method has to search through each file to find out if it contains the string.

Microsoft Office contains its own indexer, called Find Fast, which lets you use the File Open dialog box of any Office application to quickly search for documents based on a text string. If you have installed Microsoft Office, you may want to use this method of searching for text strings in documents instead. Other document indexers are available, such as AltaVista Personal Search, which provides a very powerful means of indexing and thereby quickly finding documents that pertain to your text search criteria. Personal Search recognizes over 200 file formats, including Outlook Express and Windows Messaging, and presents the list of matching files in seconds. It's available for free at `http://altavista.digital.com/av/content/searchpx.htm`.

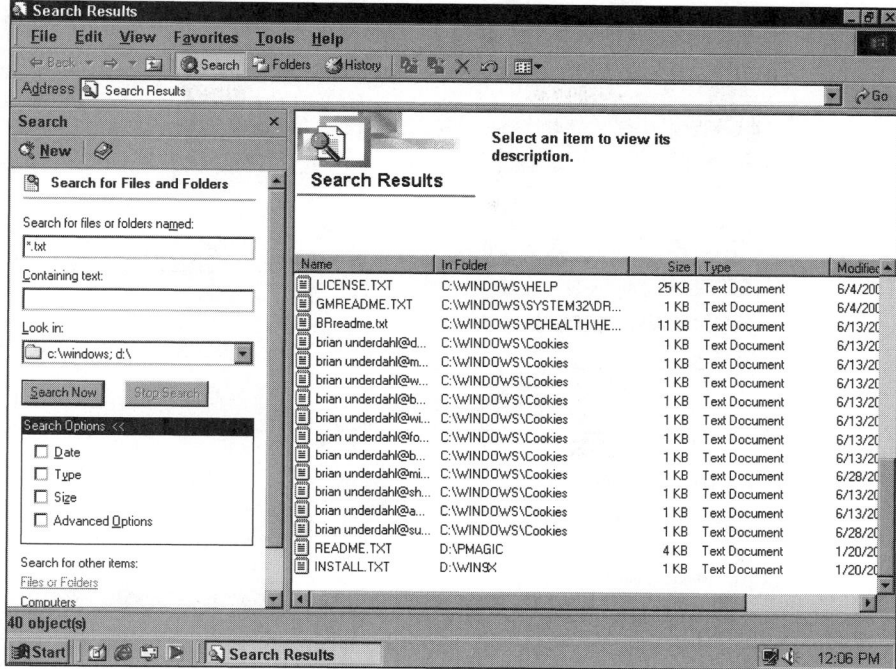

Figure 9-11: Separate drive letters with semicolons to search multiple drives. By indicating the folder to start in, you can make one search start at several different points.

If you leave the Named field blank, Find searches through all the files that match the criteria you set in the "Look in" and "Containing text" fields.

Date

Windows lets you limit your searches based on dates. You can restrict a search to a particular time frame, and you can further restrict the search by specifying whether you're looking for files/folders that were modified during that period. You can also restrict the search to a time period during which the files or folders were created or last accessed.

To set search criteria based on the date, click the Date option (shown in Figure 9-12).

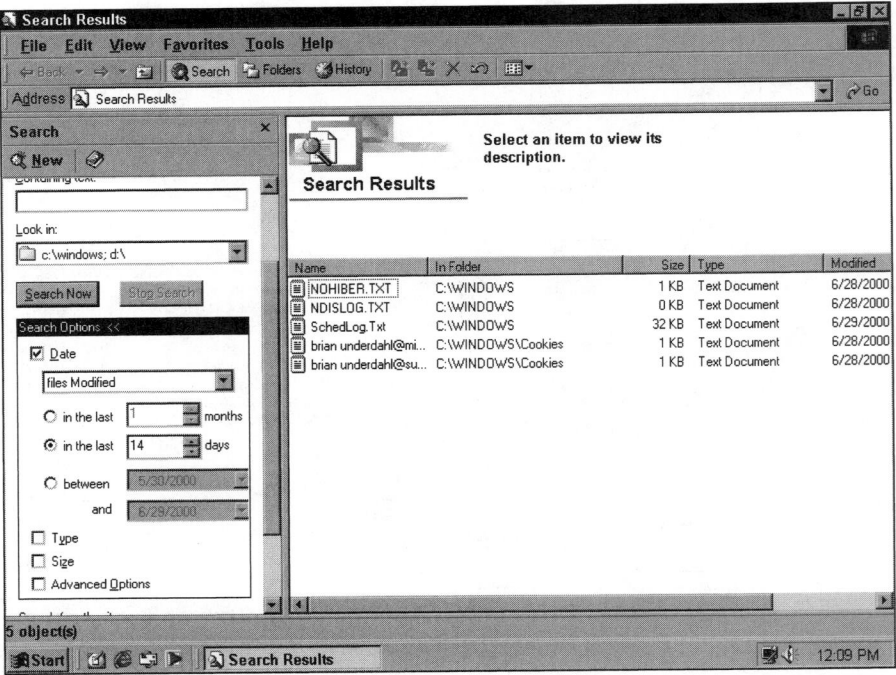

Figure 9-12: The Date options in the Search Results dialog box. You can limit the search for files and folders based on the time/date they were modified, created, or last accessed. If you're looking for a recently changed file, search for files that have been modified in the last few days.

File Type and File Size

You can search for files that are of a certain file type, or are at least as big as or greater than a certain size. Click the Type, Size, and Advanced Options, as shown in Figure 9-13.

You use the Type option to limit the search to files of a certain type—for example, all text files, all Microsoft Word files, or all Quattro Pro files. Moreover, if you have some idea of how large the files you're looking for are, you can use size as a search criterion.

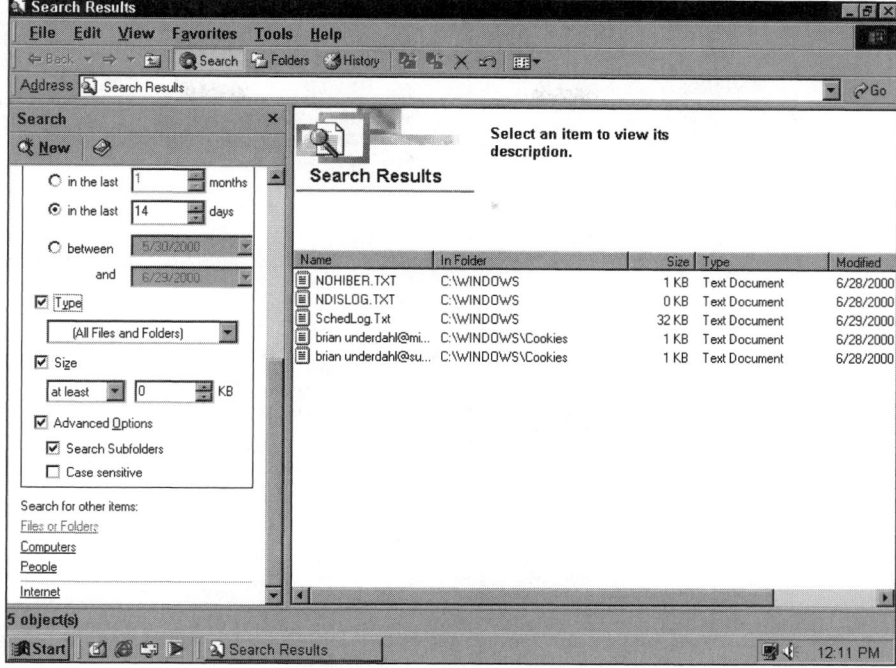

Figure 9-13: The Type, Size, and Advanced Options

Starting the Search

After you have entered all the criteria in the Search Results dialog box, click Search Now. Windows displays the search results in the pane to the right of the search criteria, as shown in Figure 9-14. You can use the View menu to choose among the four standard views (Large Icons, Small Icons, List, and Details).

The results pane looks like a folder window with one exception: When you view the results in Details view, Windows adds a column named In Folder that lists the folder in which each item was found. You can sort the found files and folders by filename, folder name, size, file type, or date modified, in either ascending or descending order.

If you want to go to the folder that contains a file or folder listed in the results pane, select the file or folder and choose File ⇨ Open Containing Folder.

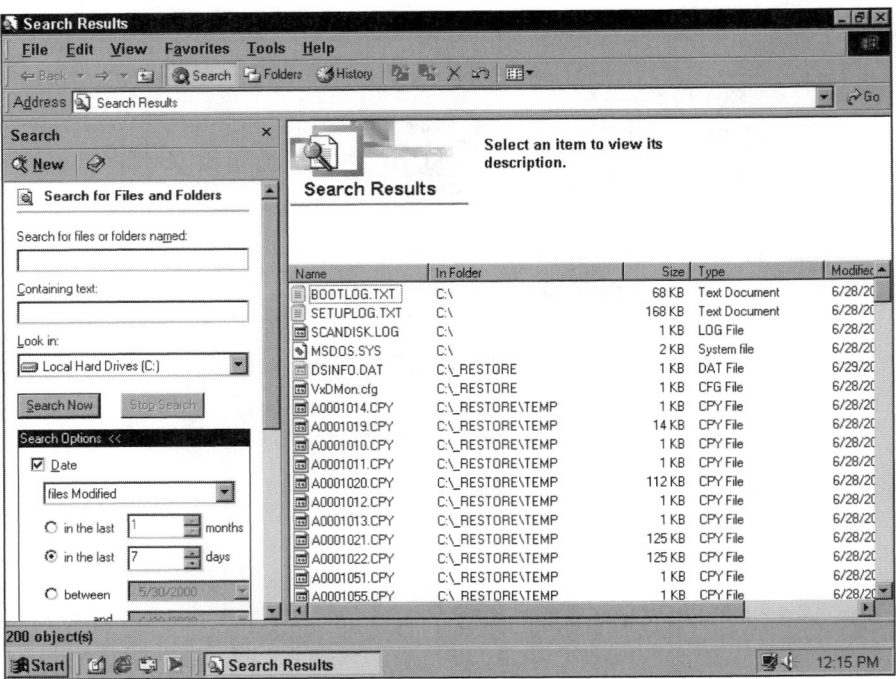

Figure 9-14: The results of the search. You can sort the results in ascending or descending order by filename, folder name, size, file type, or date modified.

Saving the Search

Windows retains your search criteria after you've performed the search. If you don't like the results of a search, you can modify the criteria and do another one. If you want to use a particular set of search criteria as the basis of future searches, you can save it as an icon on your Desktop. To do this, make sure the criteria you want to save is specified in the Search Results dialog box, and choose File ➪ Save Search.

Tip

The saved search will end up as an icon on your Desktop, which is not the best of locations. You might want to create a folder under your \My System folder called Search. You can drag these icons off the Desktop and into this folder, and then create a shortcut to the Search folder on the Desktop.

When you want to perform a search that you've saved as an icon, click the icon (or a shortcut to it). Windows displays the Search Results dialog box with all the search criteria specified. Optionally modify the criteria and then click Search Now to perform the search.

What You Can Do with Search

Tip

You can use Search to locate all the executable files in your games folder and then drag shortcuts to all these games to a newly created games submenu on your Start menu. It is great to be able to see all the executables within the subfolders of a folder that defines a general class of applications. This is especially true if you use Large Icons view in the results pane.

This is a good way to create menus under the Start menu. You can search for all executables on your hard disk and then drag them in groups to new menu folders. You can also create folders or shortcuts to folders on the Desktop, and then drag documents or executables over to these folders.

The Search command really opens up your computer and lets you see what is hiding under the covers. You'll be surprised at what you have ignored.

Tip

Use Search for file management. You can use it to find all the files on your entire hard disk so that you can order them by size or age or file type. You can get rid of all the `tmp` (temporary) files, or all the really old text files. If you have over 10,000 files on your hard disk, you'll have to break this search up by folders.

If you want additional capabilities (such as search and replace) check out `http://home.sprynet.com/sprynet/funduc/` for a complete search-and-replace program that supports regular expressions.

Finding a Computer on Your Network

You can right-click the My Network Places icon on your Desktop and then click "Search for computers." You have to know the exact name of the computer; you can't use wild cards. Needless to say, a find utility isn't worth much if you have to know exactly what it is you are looking for.

If you do use this feature, you need to preface the name of the computer you are looking for with two back slashes (\\ ). This is the universal naming convention for a server — and therefore a computer — name.

Searching the Internet

You can also click the Start button, point to Search, and then click On the Internet. This starts the Dial-Up Networking connectoid that connects to your Internet service provider (if this is how you connect to the Internet). After you connect, the Internet Explorer starts up and displays your default search page.

You can configure which search service you want to use to find things on the Internet. The default service is Microsoft's search page.

You can also search for people's e-mail addresses (found by Web crawlers). Just choose Find ⇨ People. This command also lets you search your local store of e-mail addresses in your Windows Address Book.

Summary

You can use the Start button and the Find function to make your work easier and increase your efficiency.

▶ We show you how to create and modify Start menus to match the way that you work.

▶ We provide a means to trim the unnecessary files from the recently used files list.

▶ If you find that Desktop icons are often covered up, you'll appreciate being able to put the Desktop on the Start menu.

▶ Windows has a very powerful search engine. You can define intricate searches that are quite useful in file management, and you can use searches to build Start menus and create Desktop folders.

Chapter 10

Shortcuts at Home and Abroad

In This Chapter

If it weren't for shortcuts, we wouldn't get anywhere fast. They are an essential means of turning this sow's ear of an operating system into something a bit more personal and friendly. Shortcuts get us around our computers and around the Internet. We discuss:

▶ Putting shortcuts to anything in your computer on your Desktop

▶ Viewing any document with a shortcut to the Quick View file viewers built into Windows

▶ Starting any program when Windows starts

▶ Copying, moving, opening, and viewing files easily with Send To

▶ Starting DOS programs and DOS/Windows batch files from icons

▶ Printing files by dragging and dropping them to an icon on the Desktop

▶ Making the full power of your computer visible

What's a Shortcut?

We want to clear up something right away. We use the word *shortcut* to mean two very different things in this book. When we say something like *keyboard shortcut*, we mean a keystroke that does something that otherwise would have taken a bunch of keystrokes or a lot of mousing around. The *shortcuts* we talk about in this chapter refer to icons that represent, and are linked to, applications, documents, folders, and Internet addresses.

This kind of shortcut is a shortcut in the sense that you don't have to use the Explorer or My Computer windows to find your application, document, folder, or Web page. You can just put a shortcut (a link) to it in a convenient place. Clicking the shortcut is the same as — and sometimes even better than — clicking the original file.

You can create three types of shortcuts:

- Windows shortcut — Links to a Windows application, folder, or document

- URL shortcut — Links to an Internet address

- DOS shortcut — Links to a DOS window, application, or file (also called a pif)

Depending on the type of target, Windows gives you different ways of modifying the shortcut once you've created it.

Shortcuts make your information much more accessible. Microsoft has made shortcuts flexible and powerful. It isn't obvious at first, but you will soon discover that Windows Me shortcuts are a huge improvement over the much older Windows 3.1x interface.

Shortcuts are easily recognizable because the lower-left corner of a shortcut icon has a curved black arrow in a little white box. This "icon on an icon" shows up automatically when you create a shortcut. Take a look at the example in Figure 10-1.

Figure 10-1: A shortcut icon. All shortcut icons have a black arrow in a little white box in the lower-left corner.

You can use TweakUI to change this dark black arrow into a light arrow that is somewhat difficult to see, or even into no arrow at all. Start TweakUI by clicking its shortcut on your Desktop if you have placed one there — we heartily recommend that you do this. (If you don't have a shortcut, click the TweakUI icon in your Control Panel.) Click the Explorer tab. Under Shortcut Overlay at the top of the dialog box, mark the option you want to use. If you have changed the shortcut overlay from the black arrow, you may not be able to tell if an icon represents a shortcut, or the actual application, document, folder, or address.

An important fact to remember is that if you delete a shortcut icon from the Desktop (or anywhere else, for that matter), you have deleted only the short-cut, not the item to which the shortcut points. But if you move an actual file to the Desktop and then delete that file's icon, you have deleted the file.

If you attempt to delete the icon of a program on your computer, you receive this warning from Windows: "The file *appname.exe* is a program. If you remove it, you will no longer be able to run this program or edit some documents. Are you sure you want to delete it?" If you answer yes, Windows sends the program file to the Recycle Bin, unless you held down the Shift key when you pressed Delete or you have configured the Recycle Bin to purge deleted files. In all these cases, the program will no longer be available. So be careful out there.

Shortcuts Are Great (Here's Why)

If it weren't for shortcuts, Windows wouldn't have much to say for itself in the user-friendly interface department. Shortcuts are a powerful means of user customization — a way to fight back against the Microsoft corporate vision. If you use Windows the way it came out of the box, you are not going to be very happy.

Just because a folder is a good place to store something doesn't mean that it's a convenient place to go when you want to get the item you stored. You probably have really good reasons for putting some files or applications in a particular folder, but it also makes perfect sense to give yourself a way to get at them quickly.

Fixed disk drives on new computers have immense storage capacity. The amount of information that can be stored on one can quickly overwhelm the most meticulous person. (If you stack a lot of boxes in a room, you're going to have a hard time getting around in it.)

Our computers are being hooked up ever more tightly to other people's computers, both on local area networks and around the world via the Internet. We're looking for stuff on these other machines and other people on our local area network may be searching for files on ours. A gigabyte here, a gigabyte there, and pretty soon it adds up to real chaos.

Click a shortcut to a Web page and the Internet Explorer will start, dial up your Internet service provider (if that is how you are connected to the Internet) and it takes you to the target Web page. The same thing is true if you are on a local area network and want to get to a page on your Intranet Web server. You can use shortcuts in the Favorites list to quickly get to your favorite Web sites. Shortcuts not only open up your computer and your network, they open up the Internet.

Put Your Favorite Files and Programs on the Desktop

Your Desktop is an icon container, and the perfect spot for shortcuts. You don't really want to put your documents or applications on your Desktop. Keep them in the folders that they share with other similar applications and files. For example, keep all your game applications in subfolders of the Games folder, but put shortcuts to your favorite games on the Desktop.

Tip

Put shortcuts to documents on the Desktop—just the ones that you are currently working on. Working on a set of similar documents? Create a shortcut to the folder that holds them. If the documents themselves are stored in separate folders, place shortcuts to them in a folder, and place a shortcut to that folder on the Desktop.

You can make a group of similar applications available on the Desktop, without letting their icons cover the Desktop. Place a shortcut to a folder on the Desktop and put shortcuts to the applications in the folder.

Want the Explorer on the Desktop? Put a shortcut to `Explorer.exe` on the Desktop, but leave the file `Explorer.exe` where it belongs, in the `\Windows` folder.

If you put a shortcut to your printer on your Desktop, you can drag and drop a document to your printer.

Remember—the Desktop is itself a subfolder of the `\Windows` folder. Its full pathname is `C:\Windows\Desktop`. You usually don't want to *move* files to the Desktop folder. Instead, you want to create *shortcuts* in the Desktop folder, and these shortcuts will appear on your Desktop.

Microsoft has made the fact that the Desktop is a wonderful place for shortcuts less than obvious by placing a bunch of icons on the Desktop that aren't shortcuts and aren't stored in the `\Windows\Desktop` folder. My Computer, Recycle Bin, and Internet Explorer are prime examples. You have to use TweakUI if you want to get these off the Desktop.

You'll have to ignore the fact that Microsoft puts these application icons on the Desktop. Instead of following Microsoft's example and placing your own applications on the Desktop, just put shortcuts to them there.

Automatically Start Programs when Windows Starts

You no doubt have some programs that you want to start when you start Windows. You can put shortcuts to these programs into the StartUp folder, and leave the programs where they are.

Secret

Want to make sure that the programs start in the order that you want them to? It's easy. Create a DOS batch file that is nothing but a series of calls to the programs you want to start, in the order that you want. For example:

```
Winapp1.exe
Winapp2.exe
Winapp3.exe
```

Create a shortcut to this batch file in the StartUp folder, and then delete the shortcuts to the programs themselves.

You can control some aspects of how these Windows programs are displayed by adding the Start command in front of the Windows program names in the batch file and then using one of the Start command's switches. To see how the switches work, click Start ⇨ Programs ⇨ Accessories ⇨ MS-DOS Prompt, and type **Start /?** at the DOS prompt. The DOS Start command is not related to the Windows Start button.

The Start Button Is Full of Shortcuts—Add More

The Start menus cascading across the Desktop are filled with shortcuts. If you install a Windows 3.1*x* application under Windows, its setup program thinks it is creating a program group. In fact, it is creating a folder full of shortcuts to the application and its companion files. Shortcuts in the Start menu make it easy to get to applications. Click the Start button and follow the menus out to the shortcut to the application you want.

The Start menu items under Programs, Favorites, and Documents are shortcuts, and the cascading submenus under these items are just special windows full of shortcuts.

Tip

You can put a shortcut on the Desktop (or in any folder) to a folder that holds the shortcuts to a set of documents or applications—shortcuts within a shortcut to a folder. One way to do this is to copy to the Desktop an icon on the Start menu that represents a set of application icons. Here are the steps:

STEPS

Putting a Shortcut to a Start Menu Folder on the Desktop

Step 1. Click the Start button, point to Programs, and point to Accessories. Accessories is just an example of one folder/menu item you might want to choose; you can pick others.

Step 2. Right-click the Accessories icon in the Start menu and click Copy in the context menu.

Step 3. Click the Desktop and click Paste Shortcut.

You now have a copy of part of your Start menu on your Desktop. You can add or remove shortcuts from this folder with ease just by dragging and dropping. Adding and removing shortcuts from this folder adds and removes the same shortcuts in the associated Start menu.

Shortcuts in Toolbars

Like the Start menu, toolbars are full of shortcuts. To see an example, right-click the taskbar and choose Toolbars ➪ Quick Launch. The Quick Launch toolbar contains shortcuts to the Internet Explorer and Outlook Express (as well as two or more additional icons). The folder that holds these shortcuts is \Windows\Application Data\Microsoft\Internet Explorer\Quick Launch.

Toolbars make excellent locations for shortcuts. They provide another quick way to get to applications, documents, and Web pages. The Desktop toolbar contains both the shortcuts on your Desktop and the icons that Microsoft placed there.

You can create a folder full of shortcuts, and then drag the folder icon from your Explorer or Desktop to the edge of your Desktop to create a new toolbar containing all of the shortcuts in the folder.

Move, Copy, Print, and View Files and Folders Easily

Put shortcuts to the Briefcase, default file opener, Quick Viewer, printer, file compression program, or whatever into your SendTo folder. Then, whenever you right-click a file or folder, you can choose Send To and click one of these destinations to send it there.

Send a file to the shortcut for your default file opener, and the application opens it. Send a file of an unregistered type to the shortcut for Quick Viewer, and the viewer does its best to display the file.

We use the ability to send a file to Notepad all the time. Right-click a file, click Send To, click Notepad, and it opens, ready for editing. To do this, you must first add a shortcut to Notepad in your Send To menu: Right-drag the Notepad icon from the \Windows folder to the \Windows\Send To folder and click Create Shortcut(s) Here. See "Right-Click to a Powerhouse" later in this chapter for more on the Send To menu.

Start DOS Programs by Clicking Icons

Put a shortcut to DOS on your Desktop. There's already one in your Start menu, but it's that much closer if it is on the Desktop (at least when the Desktop isn't covered up).

You can create shortcuts to all your DOS programs. You can use icons from any icon library or from the files that come with Windows. You can treat your DOS programs just like Windows programs. Why not? Most DOS programs run fine in a window.

To see how to create DOS shortcuts, turn to "DOS in Windows" in Chapter 20.

Use a Shortcut to Do More than One Thing at a Time

You can create a shortcut to a DOS batch file that calls a Windows program in addition to calling some DOS functions. If you combine DOS and Windows programs in the batch file, they can all do more together. Here's an example that uses encom and modem, two proprietary DOS utilities that are often provided by portable computer manufacturers:

```
echo off
:: The next line switches COM2 from modem to port
c:\util\encom
:: The next line runs the Direct Cable Connection
:: Start /w is used to suspend the batch file processing
start /w c:\Windows\Directcc.exe
:: This utility switches COM2 back to the internal modem
c:\util\modem
```

The Start command is described in "Windows/DOS Batch Files" in Chapter 20.

Modify How a Windows Program Operates

A shortcut allows you to combine the call to your Windows application with some of its command-line parameters. The Windows Explorer shortcut on the Start ➪ Programs menu is a good example of this (see "The Windows Explorer and the Start Button" in Chapter 7).

If your program has the ability to take command-line parameters, you can create different versions of the command line in different shortcuts to the same program. Who cares if it is just one program behind the scenes (behind the shortcut)? If it acts differently when you call it with one shortcut than with another shortcut, it might as well be a different program.

Use a Different Program to Open a Document

If you have a shortcut to a document, you can change the application that opens or acts on that document. The default shortcut just names the document and its path. Insert the name of the application that you want to act on the document into the definition of this shortcut (in the Target field) to override the file/application association found in the registry.

The properties for such a shortcut are displayed in Figure 10-2. (To display a shortcut's properties, right-click the shortcut and click Properties.) The name of the application and any command-line parameters precede the name of the file. If the pathname to the application includes a space, surround the pathname and filename with double quotes.

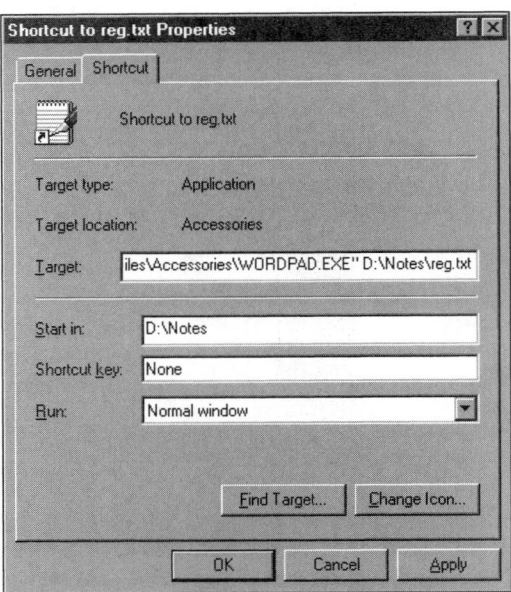

Figure 10-2: The properties for a shortcut to a file ending in the txt extension. By default, Windows associates txt files with Notepad. To override this file association, we have specified that the WordPad application open this file. The file is too big for Notepad.

Put Shortcuts to Parts of Documents on the Desktop

You can copy a paragraph from a document and paste a shortcut to it on the Desktop. Just highlight the paragraph, issue the Copy command, right-click the Desktop, and click Paste Shortcut.

The "scrap" on the Desktop is now a piece of data or text that you can insert into another document. If you click it, Windows invokes the application that created it, and the scrap is displayed in the application's window. The application that opens the document must be OLE-enabled.

Shortcuts to Web Pages and Through the Mail

You can mail a shortcut by dragging and dropping it into an e-mail message. When the recipient receives the message, he or she can access the file or folder that is linked to the shortcut by clicking the shortcut in the mail message. This works with Microsoft Mail on your local area network, with the Microsoft Network (MSN), and with Web pages on the Internet.

You can put shortcuts to Internet addresses in your \Windows\Favorites folder, on your Desktop, or wherever. If you put them in your Favorites folder, they are displayed when you click Favorites in the Explorer menu bar or on the Start menu. If you put them in your \Windows\Favorites\Links folder, they appear on the Links toolbar.

If you want to change the destination that a URL shortcut points to, right-click the shortcut, choose Properties, and edit the contents of the Target URL field in the Internet Shortcut tab. You can use any legitimate URL format in this field, including http://, ftp://, news://, and mailto://.

You can create URL shortcuts in several ways. If you drag and drop the icon at the left end of the Address bar in Internet Explorer to the Desktop, a URL shortcut for the currently displayed Web page is automatically created. If you right-drag and drop a hyperlink in a Web page to the Desktop and choose Create Shortcut(s) Here, a shortcut to the target of the hyperlink appears on the Desktop.

One other way to easily create a shortcut to a Web page is to open the Web page using your Internet Explorer and choose File ➪ Send ➪ Shortcut To Desktop. And you can e-mail the URL shortcut to this Web page by choosing File ➪ Send ➪ Link By E-mail.

Shortcuts to E-Mail Recipients and Newsgroups

Secret

You can easily create a shortcut to a newsgroup or a news server. The shortcut will open Outlook Express (or whatever your default newsgroup reader is) and focus on the newsgroup or news server.

Tom Koch, who provided a lot of help to Outlook Express beta testers, came up with the steps needed to create such a shortcut:

STEPS

Creating a Shortcut to a Newsgroup or News Server

Step 1. Click the Outlook Express icon on your Desktop.

Step 2. In the Outlook Express window, click Outlook Express in the Folder List pane to display the top-level of Outlook Express in the right pane. (If you don't see the Folder List, choose View ➪ Layout, and mark the Folder List checkbox.)

Step 3. Drag and drop any one of the six icons in the right pane to your Desktop.

Continued

STEPS

Creating a Shortcut to a Newsgroup or News Server *(continued)*

Step 4. Right-click the new shortcut icon on your Desktop, and click Properties.

Step 5. In the Target URL field, type **news://**, followed by the name of the news server and the newsgroup, for example, `news://msnews.microsoft.com/microsoft.public.inetexplorer.ie4.outlookexpress`.

Step 6. Click OK.

Step 7. Click anywhere on the Desktop. Press F5 to refresh the Desktop icons and change the shortcut's icon to the newspaper-like icon.

Step 8. Click your new icon to make sure that Outlook Express opens and focuses on your newsgroup. You may want to rename your shortcut with the name of the newsgroup it targets — for example Outlook Express News.

If you want your shortcut to connect to the news server as a whole (and not to a particular newsgroup on that server), don't include the name of the newsgroup. The news server name that you type in the Target URL field must be exactly as you have defined it in the News Account field in Outlook Express (choose Tools ⇨ Accounts, click the News tab, highlight the account, and click the Properties button). The name of the news account may differ from the name of the actual news server, so you have to be careful. Use the name in the News Account field (in the General tab), not the name in the Server Name field (in the Server tab).

Secret

The shortcut may have difficulty parsing the news account name. It turns uppercase letters to lowercase. If you have uppercase letters in your news account name, the shortcut will just create a new news account name and not focus on your existing one. You can avoid this problem by changing the account name to all lowercase before creating a shortcut.

You can also create a shortcut that displays a New Message window. To do this, follow the steps above, but in step 5, type **mailto:** instead the name of a news server or newsgroup. The new shortcut icon on your Desktop will have a Mail icon. Clicking it opens a New Message window without starting Outlook Express. Don't forget to rename your shortcut icon something like Compose New Message so that you remember what it is.

You can also create a New Messages toolbar that gives you easy access to either a new e-mail message or a new newsgroup posting without opening Outlook Express. Take the following steps:

STEPS

Creating a New Messages Toolbar

Step 1. Right-click your My Computer icon, click Explore, and navigate to your \My System folder. If you don't have one, focus your Explorer on your bootable drive, right-click in the right pane, choose New ⇨ Folder and rename the folder **My System**.

Step 2. Click the \My System folder icon in the left pane, right-click the right pane, choose New ⇨ Folder, and rename the folder **New Messages**.

Step 3. Click your Outlook Express icon on your Desktop. Click the Inbox icon in your Folder List pane, click the Compose Message toolbar button, choose File ⇨ Save As in the New Message window, and save the new empty message to the New Messages folder created in the previous step. Name it something like Mail Message (the exact name is not critical). Then close the message.

Step 4. Click a newsgroup in the Folder List pane of Outlook Express. Click the Compose Message toolbar button, choose File ⇨ Save As in the New Message window, and save this message to the New Messages folder with a name that corresponds to the newsgroup you chose (again, the name is not critical). Close your message. Repeat this step for every newsgroup you normally send messages to.

Step 5. Drag and drop the New Messages folder icon from your Explorer to any edge of the Desktop or onto the taskbar.

You have just created a New Messages toolbar. If you want to make it take up less space, right-click it and clear "Show title." (If you only have one shortcut to a newsgroup, you can also clear "Show text" — but if you have more than one, you'll need the text to distinguish among them.) To make the icons smaller, right-click the toolbar again and choose View ⇨ Small.

You can use this toolbar anytime that you want to send a new message. For example, if you are in the midst of reading a newsgroup and decide to send an e-mail message (as opposed to a post to the newsgroup), you don't have to switch to one of the mail folders in Outlook Express to compose your message, and thus lose your place in the newsgroup. Instead, you can just click the e-mail icon in the New Messages toolbar.

The New Message window for newsgroup messages now contains the name of the newsgroup that was highlighted when you created it. You need to change this name if you want to send a posting to another newsgroup.

Creating Shortcuts

The whole point of shortcuts is to put them in convenient places. These include the Desktop, the Start menu, the toolbars, the SendTo folder, folders on the Desktop, and whatever windows you regularly have open on the Desktop. You can put shortcuts wherever you want, but then, what's the point of some of the possible locations?

Drag and Drop to Create a Shortcut

Secret

If you drag and drop a binary executable file to a folder or to the Desktop, Windows automatically creates a shortcut to the file. Executable files have exe, com, or bat extensions. However, bat files are a major exception to this rule. If you drag a bat file to the Desktop, it gets *moved*—a shortcut is *not* created. (Files that end with the pif extension were executable files under Windows 3.1*x*. They are now shortcuts.)

If you left-drag a binary executable file icon from a folder or Explorer window into another window or onto the Desktop, you will see a black curved arrow in the lower-left corner of the transparent file icon. This tells you that Windows will create a shortcut if you release the left mouse button.

Secret

You can choose to create a shortcut when you drag and drop an icon by right-dragging the icon. When you do, you will get a context menu asking if you want to Move Here, Copy Here, Create Shortcut(s) Here, or Cancel the operation. To explicitly create a shortcut with drag and drop, choose Create Shortcut(s) Here.

Name that Shortcut

Tip

You can change the name of a shortcut. It is a good idea to change the name to something meaningful, rather than a short filename. Don't hold back; make the names work for you.

If a shortcut icon is already highlighted, press F2 to invoke the Rename function. If it isn't highlighted, right-click the icon and then click Rename on the context menu. When you see a black box around the name, type the new name and then press Enter.

Give your shortcuts names that are long enough to be meaningful, but not so long that they fill up the Desktop. Windows wraps names to fit in the icon grid on the Desktop. It shortens single words with ellipses.

You can't use these symbols in a shortcut name:

/ * ? .< > |

Get Rid of "Shortcut to"

Do you get tired of seeing "Shortcut to" as the first part of your shortcut's name? TweakUI lets you defeat this behavior. Click the TweakUI shortcut on your Desktop (if you don't have one, click the TweakUI icon in the Control Panel), click the Explorer tab, and clear the Prefix "Shortcut to" on New Shortcuts checkbox.

Cut and Paste a Shortcut

You can create a shortcut whose first location is the same folder as the application or document itself and then move it to the folder that you want. Right-click an icon in a folder window or the Explorer and click Create Shortcut. A shortcut to the file that you right-clicked will appear.

You can then move the shortcut out of this folder to your desired destination by using the Cut and Paste commands. This combined method avoids dragging and dropping.

Create a New "Unattached" Shortcut, then Create the Link

You can create a new shortcut first, and link it to an application or document second. (You can't use this method to create a shortcut to a folder.) To do this, take the following steps:

STEPS

Creating a New Shortcut

Step 1. Right-click the Desktop, a folder window, or the right pane of an Explorer window. Point to New and click Shortcut. This launches the Create Shortcut Wizard, as shown in Figure 10-3.

Step 2. Type the complete path and filename of the program or document that you want to create the shortcut to. Click the Browse button if you would rather find the file instead of typing in the name.

Step 3. Click the Next button. You can type a new name for the shortcut or leave the default name (the name of the file you linked to).

Continued

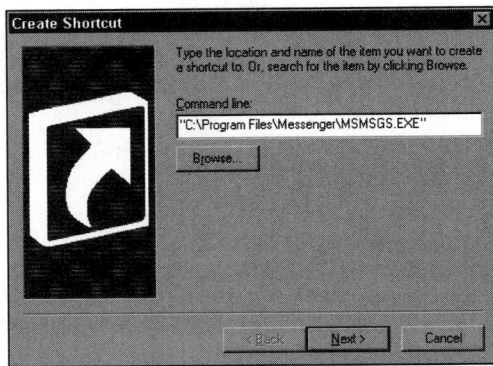

STEPS

Creating a New Shortcut *(continued)*

Figure 10-3: The Create Shortcut Wizard. You can type the path and filename of the application, document, or file that you want to create a shortcut to, or you can click the Browse button to look for the file.

Step 4.   Click the Finish button.

Shortcuts on the Desktop

The Desktop is like any other folder, except that it is always open on the Desktop, so to speak. Drag an application icon from a folder or Explorer window and drop it on the Desktop and you automatically create a shortcut. Right-click the Desktop, point to New, and click Shortcut to create a new shortcut on the Desktop.

Tip

You can create folders on the Desktop and put shortcuts in them. This is a handy way to put a lot of stuff on the Desktop without cluttering it up. To do this, right-click the Desktop and choose New ⇨ Folder. You can change the folder name at any time.

The new folder is now a subfolder of the C:\Windows\Desktop folder. You can use the Explorer to find the Desktop folder. Click the plus sign next to the Windows folder icon in the folder tree and you will see it (if you have configured the Explorer to show all files with View ⇨ Folder Options ⇨ View).

Tip

You can drag and drop shortcuts to the new folder on your Desktop. To do this, click the new folder to open its folder window. Then right-drag icons from other folder windows, drop them onto the new folder window, and click Create Shortcut(s) Here.

Creating a Shortcut to a Folder of Shortcuts

Tip

You don't have to put a folder of shortcuts on the Desktop. Instead, you can put a shortcut to a folder on the Desktop. To do this, use the Explorer to find an appropriate location for a folder that will contain shortcuts. You might, for example, create a Two Person Games subfolder under your Games folder. Or, as the following steps illustrate, you might create a folder called Desktop Folders, and create subfolders of shortcuts within it. You can then put shortcuts to these subfolders on your Desktop. If you click one of the shortcuts on the Desktop, you'll see the contents of the associated subfolder. You can add shortcuts to the subfolders by dragging and dropping icons to the appropriate Desktop shortcut.

STEPS

Creating a Shortcut to a Folder of Shortcuts

Step 1. In the Explorer, navigate to your \My System folder. If you don't have one, highlight the drive icon of your boot drive in the left pane. Then right-click the right pane and choose New ⇨ Folder. Type **My System** as the name for the folder and press Enter. You can use this folder to store files that are particular to your Windows setup.

Step 2. Highlight the \My System folder icon in the left pane of the Explorer, right-click the right pane, and choose New ⇨ Folder. Type **Desktop Folders** as the name for the new folder and press Enter.

Step 3. Highlight Desktop Folders in the left pane of the Explorer, right-click the right pane of the Explorer window, and choose New ⇨ Folder. Type the name of a folder that will hold shortcuts to documents or applications of a certain type — for example, **Graphics**. Press Enter.

Step 4. Right-drag the Graphics folder icon to the Desktop and click Create Shortcut(s) Here.

Step 5. You can now drag and drop shortcuts to graphics files and/or graphics applications to this Graphics folder shortcut on the Desktop. These shortcuts will actually be stored in the \My System\Desktop Folders\Graphics folder, but they will be visible and available via the shortcut to the Graphics folder sitting on your Desktop.

Since you've placed a *shortcut* to the Graphics folder on your Desktop, instead of the Graphics folder itself, you can easily change the icon that represents this folder. Just right-click the Graphics folder shortcut, click Properties, and then click the Change Icon button. You can browse to find new icons.

Shortcuts to Folders, Disks, Computers, Printers, and On and On

You can have shortcuts to items other than files, documents, applications, or URLs. The following sections describe some suggested shortcut opportunities.

Folders

Let's say that you are working on documents you have placed in the C:\JonesAccount\BillsIssues folder. You can right-drag this folder from a folder window or the Explorer onto the Desktop, and then choose Create Shortcut(s) Here in the context menu. Clicking the shortcut to the BillsIssues folder quickly displays the contents of the folder in a folder window.

Disk Drives

Tip

Right-drag a drive icon from the Explorer and drop it on the Desktop. The context menu will let you choose only between Create Shortcut(s) Here and Cancel. You'll find it particularly useful to create shortcuts to mapped drives representing shared resources (folders or drives) located on other peer computers or server computers.

Do you want to know the properties of a hard disk or get quickly to the Scan-Disk, Backup, and Defrag disk tools? Put a shortcut to the hard disk on your Desktop. Right-click the shortcut, click Properties, click the Shortcut tab, click the Find Target button, right-click the target drive icon in the folder window, and click Properties. (You can access the disk tools in the Tools tab.)

Even better, install Target.dll. This utility comes with PowerToys. After you've installed it, right-click the hard disk shortcut icon on your Desktop, and choose Target ⇨ Properties to display the Properties dialog box for the target of the shortcut (in this case, your hard disk), not the shortcut itself. The disk tools will be on the Tools tab. Download PowerToys from http://www.microsoft.com/Windows95/downloads/contents/wutoys/w95pwrtoysset/default.asp?site=95.

Audio CD

Windows comes with an applet called Windows Media Player that lets you play audio CDs (see Figure 10-4). You should be able to find it by clicking Start ⇨ Programs ⇨ Accessories ⇨ Entertainment ⇨ Windows Media Player.

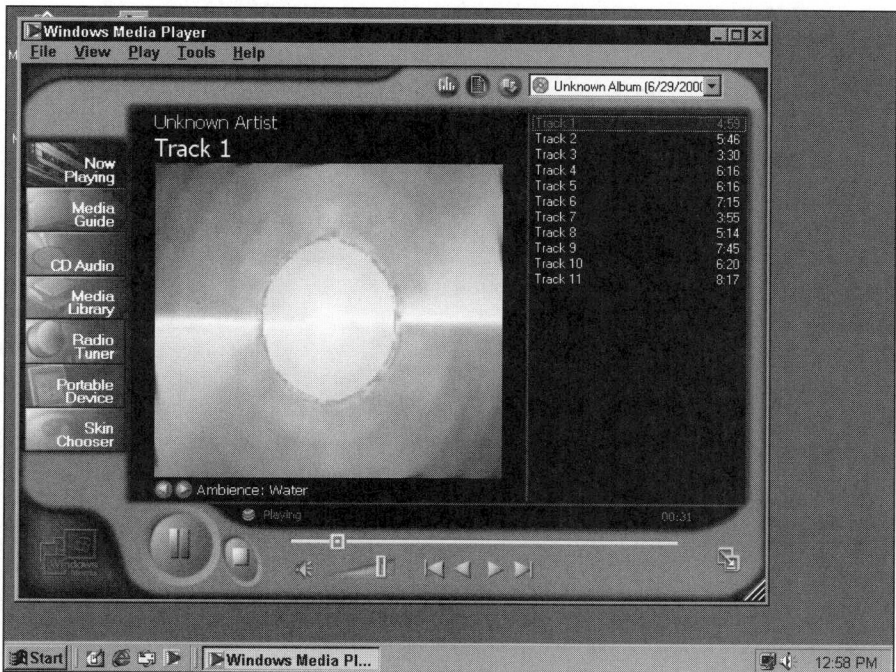

Figure 10-4: Controls for Media Player

Windows Media Player lets you play tracks on audio CDs. If you place an audio CD in your CD-ROM drive and switch to that drive with the Windows Explorer, you'll find a list of files with names like Track01.cda, Track02.cda, and so on (as shown in Figure 10-5). The cda extension stands for *CD Audio*, and indicates a track on a playable compact disk. You can drag one or more of these cda files to your Desktop or Start button, change the shortcut's name to the name of the song or artist, and so on. You can even create hot keys that start and stop your favorite recorded tracks.

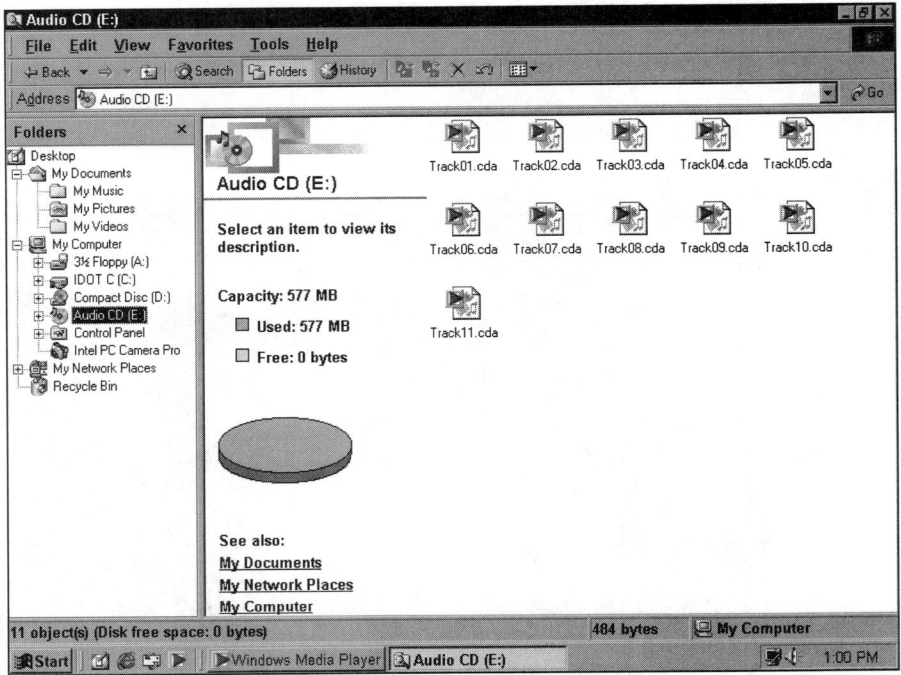

Figure 10-5: Windows Media Player displays tracks as files in an Explorer window.

Computers

You can put a shortcut to an entire computer on the Desktop (or anywhere you like). Right-click the My Computer icon on the Desktop and click **Create Shortcut**. You've got yourself a shortcut on the Desktop to something already on the Desktop (not a very practical idea, but definitely doable).

Secret

A far more useful application of this idea is to create shortcuts to networked computers, even computers that you remotely dial into. Just right-drag them out of My Network Places and onto the Desktop (or another folder window), and choose **Create Shortcut(s) Here**. If you are dialing into the computer through remote access, you can put a shortcut to the computer on your Desktop and initiate the call by clicking the computer's shortcut icon. However, if you're using DCC (Direct Cable Connection), you'll have to make the connection first.

Printers

Right-drag a printer icon out of your Printers folder and drop it on the Desktop. Click **Create Shortcut(s) Here**. Now you can drag and drop files to the printer.

Control Panel Icons

Open the Control Panel (Start ⇨ Settings ⇨ Control Panel). Right-drag one of the icons from the Control Panel to the Desktop, to a folder on the Desktop, or to a shortcut on the Desktop that points to a folder. Click Create Shortcut(s) Here. Now you have immediate access to whatever that icon does. Want to keep changing your mouse properties? You got it.

We would like to thank Matthias Koenig for his great investigative work in finding the following undocumented features.

Secret

To display the Device Manager the "long way," you right-click My Computer, click Properties, and then click the Device Manager tab of the System Properties dialog box. Want to put a shortcut to the Device Manager on your Desktop? Take the following steps:

STEPS

Creating a Shortcut to the Device Manager

Step 1.   Right-click the Desktop, point to New, and then click Shortcut.

Step 2.   In the Command Line field, type

```
C:\Windows\Control.exe Sysdm.cpl, System,1
```

Step 3.   Click Next.

Step 4.   Type **Device Manager** in the Name field. Click Finish.

Secret

You normally display the Settings tab of the Display Properties dialog box by right-clicking the Desktop and choosing Properties (or clicking the Display icon in the Control Panel), and then clicking the Settings tab. How about a shortcut to these properties?

STEPS

Creating a Shortcut to the Display Control Panel

Step 1.   Right-click the Desktop, point to New, and then click Shortcut.

Step 2.   In the Command Line field, type

```
C:\Windows\Control.exe Desk.cpl, Display,3
```

Step 3.   Click Next.

Step 4.   Type **Display Settings** in the Name field. Click Finish.

The format of the above examples is

```
Control.exe {cpl filename} {,applet name} {,tab#}
```

You can find the *cpl filename* of any of the Control Panel icons by searching (using Find as detailed in Chapter 9) for files with the `cpl` extension in the `\Windows\System` folder. The *applet name* you can find by looking in the Control Panel. Click any of the Control Panel icons to figure out the applet's tab number (if any). In the dialog box that appears, count the tabs, starting with 0 for the first tab on the left.

HyperTerminal Connections

Right-drag the desired connection icon out of the HyperTerminal folder (open it from Start ⇨ Programs ⇨ Accessories ⇨ Communications ⇨ HyperTerminal). Drop it on the Desktop and click Create Shortcut(s) Here. Now when you want to call, click the connection's shortcut icon on the Desktop.

Shortcuts to Files Far, Far Away

You can create a shortcut to a document that resides on a computer that you have to dial into with Dial-Up Networking. When you click the shortcut for the file, your modem automatically dials the phone number and makes the connection to the other computer. Once it gets into the other computer, the linked document is displayed on your Desktop. This works for Web pages and for other documents that you access through Dial-Up Networking.

Tip

If you use Direct Cable Connection, you can place shortcuts on the guest's Desktop to resources on the host computer. This is a quick way to navigate to those resources (perhaps a folder that you copy files back and forth from). However, the connection is not automatic — you must start DCC first before the shortcut will work.

Mail Out Shortcuts

You can paste a shortcut to a document into an e-mail message, and send the message over Microsoft Mail on your local area network. The recipient can open the document by clicking the shortcut icon if the document is stored in a shared folder or disk drive. All you have to send by mail is the shortcut, not the document itself. One advantage of e-mailing shortcuts is that you don't overburden the e-mail post office with numerous documents.

You can e-mail shortcuts to other Microsoft Network users by sending shortcuts to Microsoft Network bulletin boards, chat areas, documents, and so on. Users can click the shortcut and go to the targeted area or document.

You can e-mail URL addresses as shortcuts to people over the Internet as long as their mail clients can handle attachments in MIME or UUENCODE format (as Outlook Express can). When the recipient clicks a URL shortcut, it launches his or her browser, which then jumps to the targeted Web page.

(If you have Outlook Express or Outlook, you'll notice that e-mail and Internet addresses in documents are automatically live. You can click on them and immediately call up your e-mail client or Web browser to send e-mail or go to the Web site.)

Paste Shortcuts into Documents

Microsoft has attempted to blur the line between the shell (the Desktop or user interface) and the Windows applications that you use while in Windows. The fact that Cut and Paste are part of the Windows user interface is one example of this.

Another is the fact that you can place shortcuts — which you store in folders for the most part — in documents and e-mail messages. To paste a shortcut into your document, right-click a shortcut in a folder, click Copy, right-click the client window area in your word processor, and then click Paste.

As an example of when this would be useful, you can give someone a document that contains shortcuts to other documents on the Internet. The recipient can then click the shortcuts to access to the latest versions of all the targeted documents. When you click a shortcut in a document, Windows takes the appropriate actions to retrieve that document from wherever it is.

And On and On

Create shortcuts for Direct Cable Connection, Dial-Up Networking, Phone Dialer — whatever you want or need on the Desktop. The idea is to not hold back. Make your computer convenient; put the shortcuts where they do the most good. You should always see if you can make a shortcut to help accomplish a task. It may not work every time, but it's certainly worth trying.

Don't hide your computer under a bushel or in the Explorer. The Explorer is obviously well named: You use it when you have to go exploring for the functionality that you want. Shortcuts can help you reduce this work to a minimum.

Shortcuts to Anywhere

Since shortcuts are so handy, why not make even better use of them by creating some new shortcuts to even more items?

Drag a Shortcut to the Desktop Without Clearing the Desktop

You can create a shortcut to anything just by right-dragging it to your Desktop. However, sometimes your Desktop is obscured. Not to worry.

STEPS

Dragging Shortcuts to Your Covered Desktop

Step 1.   Open your Explorer. Right-drag a folder icon from your Explorer to your taskbar. Be sure that you hover it over a spot on your taskbar that is not occupied by a button. You can hover it over your system tray if you like.

Step 2.   Wait for a second, and all the windows on your Desktop will be closed.

Step 3.   Drag the icon over the now clear Desktop and drop it there. Click Create Shortcut(s) Here.

You can also use this method to move or copy a file or folder to the Desktop. Remember that if you decide not to drop the item on the Desktop, you can just click the other mouse button while dragging. This cancels the command.

Thanks to Joe deSousa for help with this tip.

Create a Shortcut to a Document

Secret

Using Microsoft Word, you can create a shortcut to a document that will open the document at a specific location in the text. Place the shortcut on your Desktop and you can invoke Word, open the document, and have it open at your designated location, all with one click.

STEPS

Creating a Shortcut to a Word Document

Step 1.   Open Microsoft Word, click File ➪ Open, and open a Word document.

Step 2.   Highlight a piece of text within the document.

Step 3.   Right-drag the highlighted text to your Desktop and drop it there.

Step 4. Click Create Document Shortcut Here in the context menu, as shown in Figure 10-6.

Figure 10-6: Click Create Document Shortcut Here in the context menu to create a new shortcut.

Step 5. Save and close your document.

You can now rename the shortcut to be the document name, if you like. When you click this shortcut, you will open the document and the text that you highlighted will be highlighted once again.

When you create this shortcut, an OLE link is created in your Word document in the form of a (nonprinting) bookmark. If you should delete the shortcut, the link will remain. You can use Word's Go To command to find bookmarks called OLE_LINK. To delete a bookmark, click Insert ➪ Bookmark, select the bookmark, click the Delete button, and then click Close.

Thanks to David C. Worthington for pointing out this tip.

Create a Shortcut from a Shell Window

Open up your Internet Explorer, Explorer, My Computer, or any folder window. You can create a shortcut to any item that currently has the focus in the window (the item whose name is displayed in the title bar) by dragging the little control icon at the left end of the title bar to the Desktop.

For example, click the Internet Explorer icon on your Desktop, which will open to your home page even if you are offline. Drag (or right-drag) the aforementioned icon to the Desktop, and you've created a shortcut to your home page. You can do this with any Web page. You can create your own separate Favorites folder in this fashion by putting a shortcut to it on the Desktop and dragging the little control icon to the shortcut every time you open a favorite Web page.

To try this in the Explorer, highlight any of your folders in the left pane, and drag the control icon to your Desktop. (Of course, you can also use the more general method of right-dragging a folder or a file icon from your Explorer to the Desktop and do the same thing.)

Thanks to Holland Rhodes for clueing us into this tip.

Right-Click to a Powerhouse

Secret

Placing shortcuts in the SendTo folder can turn your context menu into a powerhouse. The Send To command is on almost all context menus. And it doesn't really mean *send to*. It means *drop this file on this application or folder*.

However the recipient application or folder deals with drag and drop is how the application reacts when something is sent to it. You can modify the application's behavior using command-line parameters. (See the section later in this chapter entitled "The Target Field".)

Applications in the Send To menu are like commands on the context menu. You can do such things as send files to be compressed in the background, print files, view files, or open files with a particular editor. The difference is that with the Send To menu items, you don't have to associate a file type with an action as you would to create a context menu item. You can just send any file to an application in the Send To menu and let it take the action.

Tip

Use the Explorer to expand your folder tree so you can see the \Windows\ SendTo folder. To see how Send To works, right-drag and drop a Printer icon from your Printers folder to the SendTo folder to create a shortcut to the printer. Now when you want to send a file to the printer, you can right-click the file, point to Send To in the context menu, and click the shortcut to your printer in the Send To submenu.

If you haven't turned off (using TweakUI) the "Shortcut to" text that gets added when you create shortcuts, you'll probably want to edit the names of these shortcuts to get rid of this extraneous text.

You can place other items in the SendTo folder: a shortcut to a folder on a server computer perhaps; a shortcut to an application that you want to use to open files of unregistered types (see "Easiest Way to View/Open an Unregistered File" in Chapter 12), or a shortcut to the Quick Viewer (Quickview. exe in the \Windows\System\Viewers folder).

Secret

When you use Send To, Windows acts as though you used your left mouse button and dragged the file or folder you right-clicked to the application, folder, or object in the Send To menu. For example, say you are using the Send To command to send a file to a folder. If the file is on the same disk drive (or volume) as the folder, it gets moved. If it is on another disk drive, it gets copied.

PowerToys, Microsoft's little user interface fixer-upper, contains a pair of SendtoX files that add four new destinations to your Send To menu: Any Folder, Clipboard as Contents, Clipboard as Name, and Command Line. If you don't like any of these destinations, you can delete them from the SendTo folder. You can download Powertoys.exe from http://www.microsoft.com/Windows95/ downloads/contents/wutoys/w95pwrtoysset/default.asp?site=95.

The Send To Any Folder command allows you to copy or move a file from one folder to any other folder. The Other Folder dialog box, which appears when you choose Send To ⇨ Any Folder, lets you browse to find the target folder, or find it in a drop-down list if it's a previous target.

Send To a Printer

If you have access to two or more printers — whether they are attached to your PC or to your network — you can Send To any of your printers. This is a lot faster than manually changing your current printer every time you want to print a document to one or the other.

One way to get a printer onto your Send To menu is to right-drag its icon from the Printers folder (in the Control Panel) to the `C:\Windows\SendTo` folder.

You can even have the same printer show up twice on the Send To menu with different settings — for instance, draft versus presentation quality. To do this, click the Add Printer icon in the Printers window, then select a printer model you already have installed. When Windows asks if you want to "replace" or "keep" the existing driver, reply "keep" (unless you really do possess an updated driver).

After you finish installing this "new" printer driver, you should have a "Copy 2" icon in your Printers folder. Right-click this icon, click Properties, and configure this copy of your printer driver any way you like. Then right-drag it into the SendTo folder to create a shortcut to it. Your new alternate printer settings will appear on your Send To menu the next time you right-click a file icon.

Other things you may want to add to your Send To menu are the Desktop, the Start menu, and the StartUp folder. To get these in the menu, right-drag the subfolders named Desktop, Start Menu, and `Start Menu\Programs\StartUp` from your `\Windows` folder to the `\Windows\SendTo` folder. When you find a file that you want to put on your Desktop, in your Start menu, or in your StartUp folder, right-click the file, point to Send To, and click the desired option.

There are some caveats. Remember that when you drag a file to a folder in the Explorer, the file is *moved* if the folder is on the same drive, but *copied* if the folder is on a different drive. It works the same way if you send a file to a folder in the Send To menu. Also, if you send an executable file to the Desktop or to any part of the Start menu via the Send To command, the file doesn't get moved. Instead, Windows creates a shortcut to the file (which is actually what you want).

Send To a Menu of Printers

Instead of creating individual shortcuts to each of your printers, you can create a live cascading menu of printers in your Send To menu. This is especially helpful if you have a lot of printer drivers installed, or if you often add or remove printer drivers.

To create the cascading menu, you add the resource ID for the Printers window to your Send To menu. A *resource ID* is a unique, hexadecimal identifier that Windows uses to keep track of each of the many resources available on your computer. The resource IDs are stored in the registry. Because you refer to the resource ID in the shortcut (as opposed to the object itself), every time you make a change in the Printers window, the cascading menu will update automatically.

To add the resource ID for Printers to your Send To list, select the `\Windows\ SendTo` folder in Explorer. Right-click an unoccupied space in Explorer's right pane and choose New ⇨ Folder. In the space where you would name the folder, type the following resource ID — including the period, the two curly braces, the four hyphens, and the hexadecimal codes — and press Enter:

```
Printers.{2227A280-3AEA-1069-A2DE-08002B30309D}
```

Now when you right-click a document and choose Send To ⇨ Printers, you will see the entire contents of your Printers folder. And no matter how often you add or remove printer drivers, this menu will always be up-to-date.

Send To a Computer on the Network

You can also use the Send To menu on your network. This is especially helpful for your associates who may not be "into" computers, don't know how to open shortcuts in their mail clients to see embedded documents, or don't want to figure out how to access files across a network. Since it requires that you have access to your coworker's `\Windows` folder, it is probably most appropriate for smaller networks and workgroups. Thanks to Paul Howell for this idea.

To place a shortcut in your SendTo folder that points to your coworker George's personal Desktop, sharing must first be enabled for George's `C: ` drive, and you must have access to George's `\Windows` folder. Then, on your own computer, open My Network Places, click George's computer, click his `C: ` drive, and click his `\Windows` folder to display its contents. Right-click the Desktop folder and select Copy. Now, in your Explorer, navigate to your own `\Windows\SendTo` folder, right-click in the right pane, and choose Paste Shortcut. You should see a new shortcut named Desktop in the right pane. Press F2 and rename this shortcut George's Desktop, or whatever you like.

Now when you select a document in your Explorer, right-click it, and choose Send To ⇨ George's Desktop, a copy of that document is created on — you guessed it — George's Desktop. All George does is click the icon to view the document.

Send To Send To

You can put a shortcut to the SendTo folder in the SendTo folder.

If you want to browse for executables that you want to put in the SendTo folder as targets, you can send them there easily by right-clicking them, pointing to Send To, and then clicking Shortcut to Send To. A message box appears telling you that you cannot move or copy the executable to this location, and it asks if you want to create a shortcut instead, which you do.

Attempting to right-drag the SendTo folder from the left pane of the Explorer into the SendTo folder in the right pane doesn't work. All you get is Open and Cancel in the context menu that appears — not Create Shortcut(s) Here.

What you need to do instead is right-drag the SendTo folder from the right pane of the Explorer to the SendTo folder in the left pane.

Now browse through your whole system, looking for executable files that would be great targets for sending documents to. When you find one, right-click it and choose Send To ⇨ Shortcut to Send To.

Send To the Desktop

You can create a shortcut to the Desktop folder, which is a subfolder of your \Windows folder. You can even create the shortcut on your Desktop. Then drag this shortcut to the SendTo folder, which is also a subfolder of your \Windows folder. This makes for an easy way to send stuff to the Desktop when it's not visible.

Create Shortcuts to DOS Programs

You can drag and drop a DOS application file to the Desktop or to a folder window just as easily as you can a Windows executable file. You automatically create a shortcut when you drop the file.

You'll probably want to make some changes to a DOS program's shortcut. You might want a different icon than the default MS-DOS icon that you get, and you may need to change some other properties as well. (All shortcuts have properties, which we'll get to in the next section.)

You can create a folder to store the shortcuts to your DOS programs, or you can mix these DOS program shortcuts with your Windows shortcuts. It's up to you.

If you have DOS files, such as files that you edit with the DOS Edit program, you can create shortcuts to these and store them on the Desktop or in a folder. The DOS programs and files can fit right in with the Windows programs and files, as long as they can run in a Windows DOS session.

Tip

You can run a mixture of DOS and Windows programs from a DOS batch file. Windows programs will run from the DOS prompt of a DOS virtual machine, so you can combine commands to run these programs with DOS programs.

You can call a DOS batch file with a shortcut, and the batch file can contain lines that start Windows programs. If you include the following command in a batch file, you can have a DOS batch file run a Windows program and wait for you to quit the Windows program to continue processing the commands in the batch file:

```
Start /w {Windows program}
```

We discuss many aspects of running DOS programs in "DOS in Windows" in Chapter 20.

What's Behind the Shortcut?

To see what's behind a shortcut, right-click it and choose Properties. The tabs and options in the resulting Properties dialog box differ depending on the type of shortcut that you right-clicked. If you are examining a shortcut to a Windows application, folder, or document, you will see a dialog box similar to the one shown in Figure 10-7.

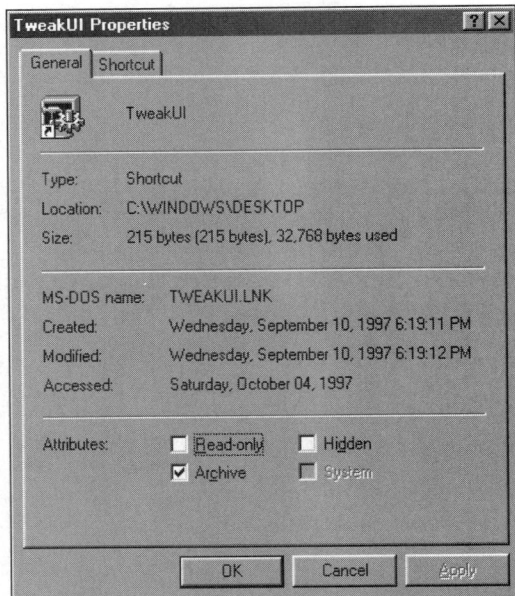

Figure 10-7: The General tab for a Windows shortcut. You can change the file attributes if you like.

The Properties dialog box for a Windows shortcut has two tabs: General and Shortcut. The filename of the shortcut (after all, it is a file) has an lnk extension. A shortcut is a link (or *lnk*) to another file. The only things you can change on the General tab are the file attributes of the shortcut file.

Click the Shortcut tab for a Windows shortcut to view the set of options shown in Figure 10-8.

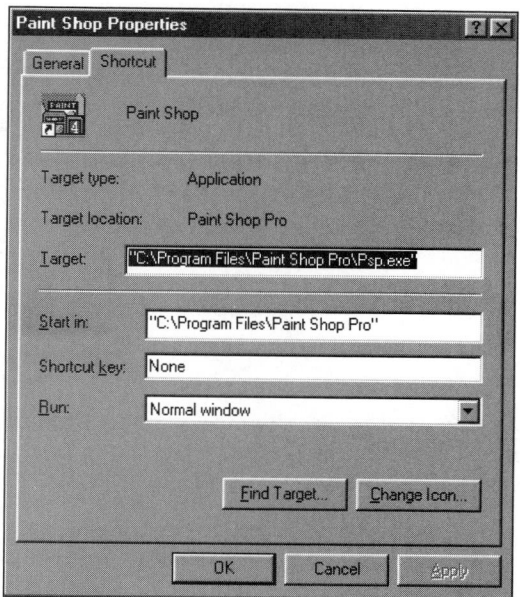

Figure 10-8: The Shortcut tab for a Windows shortcut. The Target field contains the name of the target file. You can change this field in numerous ways. The Change Icon button lets you change the shortcut's icon.

The properties of URL shortcuts are similar to those of Windows shortcuts, so most of the content in the next six sections regarding Windows shortcuts applies to them as well. Where there are differences, we point them out.

We discuss the properties of DOS (pif) shortcuts in detail in "Editing Shortcut Properties" in Chapter 20 and "DOS Shortcut Properties" later in this chapter.

The Target Field

The Target field in the Shortcut tab lists the file that is linked to the shortcut. (The equivalent field for a URL shortcut is the Target URL field in the Internet Shortcut tab.) You can modify this field in many ways. If the target file is an application that accepts command-line parameters, you can include them after the application name.

Tip

If you want to view the document or data file in the Target field with an application other than the one assigned to this file's file type in the registry, you can type the path and filename of the desired application in front of the file's path and filename. In addition, you can add command-line parameters after the application's name to alter its behavior. For example, if you type this entry in the Target field:

```
"C:\Program Files\Accessories\Wordpad.exe" /p D:\Myfolder\Thisfile.txt.
```

The shortcut will print the file `Thisfile.txt` using WordPad.

Secret

The command-line parameters in the Target field won't work if you drag a file to a shortcut. This is also true if you place a shortcut like this in the SendTo folder and then right-click a file and send it to the shortcut. Windows acts as if the command line is as follows:

```
"C:\Program Files\Accessories\Wordpad.exe" %1
```

In this command line, %1 is the name of the dragged or sent file. The /p parameter is ignored.

The Start In Field

The field now labeled *Start In* used to be called the Working Directory in Windows 3.1*x*. (The equivalent field for DOS shortcuts is the Working field in the Program tab.) This field is blank unless you put something in it. You may need to do this if the application in the Target field needs to find some application helper files in another folder and can't do so without help from you.

If the application doesn't require assistance in finding any helper files, you can make the Start In folder the folder that you want to contain the documents that use the application.

Hot Keys

A *hot key*, which we also refer to as a *shortcut key* or an *accelerator key*, is a key combination that runs a shortcut. For example, press Ctrl+Alt+F and up pops FreeCell. Well, not actually, but it could if you defined the hot key for FreeCell. (If you're in Word, it opens the footnote pane.) Hot keys give you a keyboard method of quickly getting to the applications and files you use most often.

Secret

The problem with hot keys is that you have to remember which keyboard combination does what. (You also have to make sure you are not in a program that uses that hot key for another function.) When you use the mouse, the visual user interface gives you feedback that you are headed in the right dir-ection. In contrast, you have to rely exclusively on your finger memory if you want to use hot keys. But then, to each his or her own.

To define a hot key, type the letter in the Shortcut Key field. Crtl+Alt will automatically be added to and precede the letter, making the hot key Ctrl+Alt+*letter*. If you want to use Ctrl+Shift+*letter* instead, then hold down the Ctrl key and the Shift key as you press the letter.

You can also define hot keys for shortcuts to DOS programs. The Shortcut Key field in a pif (the shortcut file to a DOS program) operates somewhat differently than it does in a shortcut to a Windows file.

Run in Which Size Window?

Most of the time you want a shortcut to display the application or document in its normal (restored) window — in other words, a window that is bigger than the button on the taskbar but smaller than the whole Desktop (minus the taskbar). The Run field lets you choose among these three alternatives.

If the shortcut just prints a document, for example, you might as well leave it minimized. If you want the application or document to fill the whole Desktop, then choose Maximized. There isn't an option for full-screen view.

Change the Shortcut's Icon

When you create a shortcut to an application, Windows uses the first icon referenced in the application's executable file. Often this is adequate. If you have different shortcuts to the same application, though, you might want to distinguish them with different icons. You can choose among the icons that may be stored in the application's executable file (not all executable files have icons).

If your shortcut is to a document, Windows chooses the first icon in the associated application's executable file. If a document doesn't have an associated application, then Windows chooses the Blank Document icon. Just how documents get associated with applications is discussed in "Associating Actions with File Extensions" in Chapter 12.

To browse for icons, click the Change Icon button. In addition to looking for icons in the application's executable file, you can look in many other executable files as well. Three files that contain icons are \Windows\Explorer.exe, \Windows\Moricons.dll, and \Windows\System\Shell32.dll.

Tip

Lots of icons are available to use with your shortcuts. You can pick icons from icon libraries distributed as shareware, or from other executable files.

Find that Target

Tip

If you have a shortcut, you can get back to the file linked to the shortcut by clicking the Find Target button. This is helpful if you want to run the application without any of the command-line switches you may have put in the Target field.

When you click the Find Target button, Windows opens a folder window that contains the target. If the Target field contains an application, Windows opens the folder that contains the application, even if the field also contains a document. If the Target field only contains a document, the folder window containing the document opens.

This doesn't apply to URL shortcuts; in fact, the Internet Shortcut tab of the Properties dialog box for a URL shortcut doesn't even have a Find Target button.

DOS Shortcut Properties

If the shortcut targets a DOS window, application, or file (a file whose file type is associated with a DOS application), you'll get a different set of shortcut properties than the ones you get with Windows shortcuts. These properties are so extensive and so interwoven with the workings of DOS programs under Windows that we devote an entire chapter to them. Turn to "Editing Shortcut Properties" in Chapter 20 for further details.

Secret

A DOS shortcut's properties are stored in a file that used to be called a Program Information File, or `pif`. The shortcuts that link to Windows files use the `lnk` extension. The shortcuts that link to DOS files use the `pif` extension. You can see these extensions if you use the File Manager or a DOS window. The `pif` extension isn't visible in the Explorer or in a folder window.

There is a folder named `\Windows\Pif`. This folder can contain the `pif` files that are associated with DOS programs. Anytime you click a DOS program name in the Explorer, you create a default `pif` for it in the same folder as the DOS program unless it can't be created there, in which case Windows places it in the `\Windows\Pif` folder. For example, if the DOS program is in a folder on a CD-ROM, Windows won't be able to place the `pif` file on the CD-ROM (when you click the DOS program), so it will put the `pif` in the `\Windows\Pif` folder. If you drag a shortcut to a DOS file or DOS application onto your Desktop, the `pif` is stored in `\Windows\Desktop`.

All `pif`s are shortcuts. You can open an Explorer window and focus on a folder that contains a `pif` to see that it has the little black arrow in the white box in the lower-left corner of the MS-DOS icon.

Secret

Let's say that you create a shortcut to a Windows file or application. Later you decide to change this shortcut and have it link to a DOS batch file that calls your Windows application after running some other functions. What happens to your shortcut? Windows automatically changes the `lnk` file to a `pif`. Easy as can be.

This doesn't work the other way. If you edit the Target field in a `pif` so that it refers to a Windows file, the `pif` does not automatically change to a `lnk` file.

Shortcuts on the Start Button

We discuss how to put shortcuts on the Start button and in the Start menus in "Drop It on the Start Button" in Chapter 9.

A Shortcut to a Shortcut

In "Creating a Shortcut to a Folder of Shortcuts" earlier in this chapter, we showed you how to make a shortcut to a folder that contains shortcuts. Can you create a shortcut to a shortcut? After all, a shortcut is a file, and if we can have shortcuts to files, why not a shortcut to a shortcut file?

Right-drag one of the shortcut icons that you have created from its source folder and drop it on the Desktop. Click Create Shortcut(s) Here. Now, right-click the shortcut on the Desktop and click Properties. If this is a Windows file shortcut, click the Shortcut tab and examine the Target field. If it's a DOS shortcut, or `pif`, click the Program tab and look at the Cmd line field. If it's a URL shortcut, look at the Target URL field in the Internet Shortcut tab.

Notice that the name in the Cmd Line, Target, or Target URL field is not the name of the shortcut in the source folder, but rather the name of the file that the original shortcut is linked to. A shortcut to a shortcut isn't really a shortcut to a shortcut; it is a shortcut to the original file.

What Happens If I Move or Delete the Linked File?

Shortcuts are linked to a specific item — a file, a folder, and so on. If you move or delete that item, what happens when you click the shortcut?

If you have moved the item, Windows tries to find it the next time you open its shortcut. While Windows is searching, it displays the Missing Shortcut dialog box, as shown in Figure 10-9.

Figure 10-9: The Missing Shortcut dialog box. If you know where you moved the target, you can help out by clicking the Browse button.

When Windows creates a shortcut, it records the creation time and date of the linked file or folder down to a fraction of a second and stores this information in the shortcut file. It is extremely unlikely that any two files or folders would be created at the same time and date to this level of precision.

Using a built-in function, Windows begins searching for the lost file, folder, or object starting at its original location. You may have edited the file or changed its name — Windows doesn't care, because it is searching on the file or folder's creation time/date.

The search method is not foolproof. If you move the target object (say a linked file) from one volume (say the D: drive) to another volume (say the C: drive), it won't find it. If your shortcut is to a file on a mapped networked drive, and the mapping of that drive changes (say from D: to F:), the link to the target is lost.

If you delete the file or folder, then of course Windows won't find it. As it's looking, Windows does keep track of the file or folder that is nearest in time/date to the actual linked item. If it can't find what it is looking for, it gives you the option of choosing the item closest in time, which can provide some weird "matches." You don't have to accept the file that Windows suggests.

Shortcuts to URLs come up short all the time because the Webmasters on Internet are always moving their Web pages around. No big deal — you just get an error message in the Internet Explorer stating that the page can't be found. You'll have to look around for it, or whatever replaces it. You might try clicking in the Address bar, pressing the End key, and erasing the last part of the URL up to the previous forward slash (/). If this shortened URL takes you to the Web page above the one you are looking for, you may be able to travel a link from there to the page you "lost."

Shortcuts in the Help Files

The Windows Help files, which you access by clicking the Start button and choosing Help, are filled with shortcuts that take you to the item that you have a question about. Of course, you may already be there.

The shortcut icon in the help file is a little like the black arrow used to indicate shortcut icons. It is a purple arrow curving to the upper-left corner instead of a black arrow curving to the upper-right corner.

Click the shortcut arrows in the help files to take the action that is explained in the sentence surrounding the arrow icon.

Creating Application-Specific Paths

If you start an application from a shortcut, you may find that it won't work because you haven't correctly identified the location of necessary accessory files in the Start In or Working directory (see "Working directory" in Chapter 20). You might also want to be able to run an application from the Run dialog box (Start ⇨ Run) without specifying the path to the executable file.

Secret

By editing the registry, you can associate a set of folders that house the accessory files an application needs to work correctly. In addition, you can specify the complete pathname to the application. Michael Giroux gave us the basis for these steps:

STEPS

Specifying Paths to Applications in the Registry

Step 1. Click Regedit.exe in your \Windows folder.

Step 2. Click the plus signs in the left pane of the registry to drill down to the following branch:

HKEY_LOCAL_MACHINE\SOFTWARE\Microsoft\Windows\ CurrentVersion\App Paths

Step 3. Right-click the App Paths icon in the left pane, point to New, and then click Key. A new key folder appears in the left pane of the Registry Editor. Type the name of the executable file, including the exe extension.

Step 4. Double-click Default in the right pane while the new folder is highlighted in the left pane. Type the full path to the executable file in the Edit String dialog box. Click OK.

Step 5. You will now be able to type the name of the executable file in the Run dialog box without the pathname and have the application actually run.

Step 6. Define the path to the executable file's associated files by right-clicking the right pane of the Registry Editor while the focus is on the new folder.

Step 7. Point to New and then click String Value. Enter the name **Path** in the highlighted Name field in the right pane of the Registry Editor.

Continued

STEPS

Specifying Paths to Applications in the Registry *(continued)*

Step 8. Double-click Path in the right pane. In the Edit String dialog box, enter the complete path to the folders that contain the associated files. If there is more than one folder, separate the pathnames with semicolons. Click OK.

Step 9. If you have any trouble with these steps, look at the other examples under the App Paths folder. When you are done, exit the registry.

The paths that you entered in step 8 will be added temporarily to your path statement when you invoke the executable file, whether by clicking a shortcut to it, by entering its name in the Run dialog box, or by clicking it in the Explorer or a folder window.

Summary

Windows lets you put links to your applications and files on your Desktop and anywhere you find useful. Shortcuts are an incredibly powerful and convenient means of accessing resources on your computer.

▶ We show you how to use the power of shortcuts to put your most important applications and documents within easy reach.

▶ We guide you through the many ways of creating shortcuts.

▶ We show you how you can drag and drop files to a Desktop file viewer, a Desktop printer, or a default file opener.

▶ DOS and Windows applications can get along much better under Windows Me than under older versions of Windows, and you can even make them appear to like each other.

▶ If you add application-specific paths to your registry, you can run applications from the Run dialog box without specifying their paths.

Chapter 11

The Registry —
The Real User Interface

In This Chapter

Microsoft stores all the goodies in the registry. The registry takes over many of the functions of the `ini` configuration files found in previous versions of DOS and Windows. If you discover the secrets of the registry, you have almost complete control over Windows. Whereas in other chapters we discuss specific registry edits, here we concentrate on the structure of the registry, how to recover from a corrupt registry, and how to use the Registry Editor. We discuss:

▶ `Ini` Files, forever
▶ Registry Monitor
▶ The registry files, keys, and structure
▶ Registry backup and recovery
▶ Recovery
▶ Emergency startup disk and Recovery utility
▶ The Registry Editor
▶ Starting and editing the Registry Editor
▶ Little fixes to the registry
▶ Dealing with file associations
▶ Watching your registry
▶ Safeguarding your registry
▶ The DOS version of the Registry Editor

Ini Files, Forever

In our previous books on Windows, we sometimes assumed that Microsoft wanted to do away with `ini` files and move all user, hardware, and application parameters to the registry. This turns out to be only half true.

There are certainly good reasons for wanting to dispense with `ini` files. Problems caused by relying on these files became apparent with the old Windows 3.1x. Directories throughout the world were filling up with `ini` files. `Win.ini` and `System.ini`, the two files that represent Microsoft's main contribution to this blight under Windows 3.1x, became quite large as some developers took the easy route and used them to store their applications' vital parameters.

This led to a number of difficulties when users and system administrators tried to access configuration information. There were so many different files that no one could keep track of what was where. In addition, there was no systematic distinction between values that were user-specific and those that are machine/software-specific.

In response to these problems, Microsoft introduced the registry (`Reg.dat`) in Windows 3.1 to store file associations and OLE information. Microsoft has greatly expanded the registry since then in Windows NT, Windows 2000, Windows 9x, and Windows Me. The registry is (for the most part) the central repository of user data, application data, and system configuration data.

Despite the advantages of maintaining one central location for configuration data, however, Microsoft programmers still use `ini` files. Indeed, these files are necessary for Windows to operate properly. Just to mention a few `ini` files that are still with us: `Telephon.ini` is maintained in order to retain backward compatibility with 16-bit TAPI applications (the values stored in `Telephon.ini` are also kept in the registry). A hidden `Desktop.ini` file is stored in any folder whose Web view has been customized. DOS real-mode versions of ScanDisk and ScanReg use `ini` files to guide their behavior. `Protocol.ini` is used to store information about the network configuration. And Microsoft retained the `Win.ini` and `System.ini` files to maintain compatibility with Windows 3.1x applications and other previous methods of storing information about system and user configuration. The list could go on.

The `ini` files will continue to be useful in some respects, providing application-specific data that doesn't really need to be in the registry and would just slow startup times. Unfortunately, they will also continue to cause headaches for system administrators who must search for files that users have inadvertently erased.

The Registry Keys and Structure

The registry is a storehouse for configuration values and settings that are used to determine how Windows and Windows applications operate. Of course, for the registry to serve its full purpose, software developers must use it to store their program parameters.

The registry also keeps track of a list of hardware configurations that the Windows setup and hardware-detection routines have discovered. If you change your hardware configuration, the registry is updated.

The *keys* in the registry are similar to the bracketed headings in the Win. ini or System.ini files. Registry keys, unlike ini file headings, can and do contain subkeys. While only text strings are allowed in ini files, values in the registry can consist of executable code.

The registry is a database divided into six main branches, as can be seen in Figure 11-1. Each branch is a *handle* to a different set of key values, hence the names HKEY_CLASSES_ROOT, HKEY_CURRENT_USER, and so on.

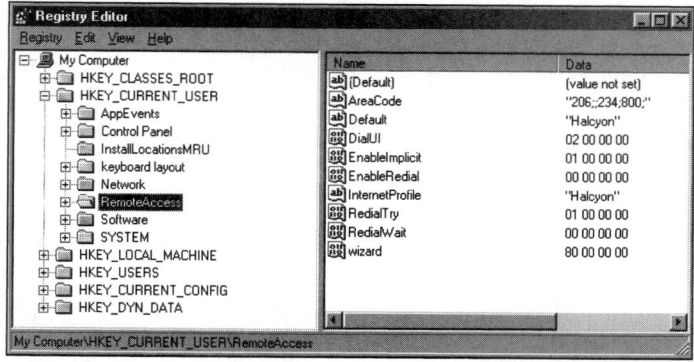

Figure 11-1: The Registry Editor. Click a plus sign to open a branch of the registry.

Each of the six main branches is divided into further branches. Each node is a key. You can follow any of the branches out until you run out of keys and have only data.

Secret

To expand all branches below a node, highlight the node and press Alt+* (that is, press Alt plus the numeric keyboard asterisk). To collapse all the branches below a node, click its minus sign, highlight the node, and press F5.

Much of the registry is not that useful to a user or system administrator. It is maintained by the operating system, configured when you install new software, and often better edited through dialog boxes that you access in the Control Panel and in various other elements of Windows. These dialog boxes serve as front ends to the registry. In addition to using them, you can also customize Windows by using TweakUI. This utility, which we refer to throughout the book, is one of the most powerful registry front ends available. TweakUI dramatically reduces the amount of direct registry editing work required to customize Windows, and we trust that you'll use it as often as we do. (The TweakUI icon is in the Control Panel. If you don't have it, you can install the application from the `\tools\reskit\powertoy` folder of your Windows CD-ROM.)

We have, however, found wide applicability for directly editing the HKEY_ CLASSES_ROOT branch and the HKEY_CURRENT_USER branch of the Registry. You may find that the other branches also provide useful areas for individual customization.

HKEY_CLASSES_ROOT

This branch contains the file extensions and file/application associations as well as OLE data. This branch is an *alias* for HKEY_LOCAL_MACHINE\ SOFTWARE\ Classes. Changes in this area of the registry are discussed in "Creating and Editing File Types and Actions" in Chapter 12.

HKEY_USERS

The information displayed under this key is stored in the `User.dat` file. This includes user-specific Desktop configurations, network connections, and the Start menu. If your computer is configured using user profiles, a separate `User.dat` file is created for each user. When a user logs on to the computer, Windows reads that person's `User.dat` file and integrates it into the registry in memory.

HKEY_CURRENT_USER

This is the portion of HKEY_USERS that is applicable to the current user. If there is only one user, the default user, then HKEY_USERS\Default and HKEY_CURRENT_USER are different views of the same information.

Many of the examples of editing the registry used in this book make the assumption that you are editing the values only for the current user or for the default user. Therefore, many of those changes take place along this branch of the registry.

If you want to make the indicated changes for other users with different login names, you need to track down the appropriate locations in the HKEY_USERS branch.

There are similar values in this branch and in the next one, HKEY_LOCAL_MACHINE. The values in this branch take precedence over the values found in HKEY_LOCAL_MACHINE.

Software developers can store user-specific information in this branch. If they do, their programs will be customized for each individual user. It doesn't matter that one user changes his or her settings. As long as those values are stored here, other users keep their settings. It's up to the software developers to put all their user-specific values in this branch. You'll find this user and application information by looking at:

HKEY_CURRENT_USER\ Software\ *Company Name\ App Name\ Version*

HKEY_LOCAL_MACHINE

This is the branch for computer hardware and its installed software. If the computer can have multiple hardware configurations — such as hooked up to the network or not, or docked or not — the information on each configuration is stored here.

Look down the HKEY_LOCAL_MACHINE branch under SOFTWARE, and you'll find the names of the companies that make the software that you have installed. This branch is meant to be a convenient location for machine-specific information about each company's products. Application programmers don't have to use this area to store various settings, but it sure makes it easy if they do.

This is where you'll find application names, version numbers, application pathnames, and hardware settings — settings that apply to all users. Of course, Microsoft uses this branch to register its software.

Application programmers are also encouraged to store their Windows-compatible uninstall information under this key. You'll find it in:

HKEY_LOCAL_MACHINE\SOFTWARE\Microsoft\Windows\CurrentVersion\ Uninstall.

HKEY_CURRENT_CONFIGURATION

The display settings, certain Internet Explorer settings, and the available printers are here.

HKEY_DYN_DATA

The registry keeps data on Windows performance parameters, and these values are stored here. This information is kept in RAM after Windows loads, and it is updated on an ongoing basis. You can view these statistics using the System Monitor. Plug and Play devices and the software that monitors these devices make use of the information stored here.

Registry Monitor

Not only do the operating system and major applications write information to the registry on startup, but there are many instances in which Windows (or a Windows application) reads the registry during the normal functioning of your system—to look up the value of a setting you've made in the Control Panel, for example. Registry Monitor (Regmon.exe) is a free utility that monitors the registry's keys and the occasions when Windows and Windows applications access them. You can learn many things from watching the use of these keys.

As one example of how you might use RegMon, you can run it while you are installing an application so that you can watch the application's setup routines create keys and fill them with data. RegMon keeps a running list of the changes an application makes to the registry during installation. You can save the output to a disk file and then later open it in WordPad or another text editor to review it more closely.

You can also use RegMon to hunt down program settings in the registry that control important features of the user interface but are not documented in the program's help file or manual. For example, Bill Engels, who first suggested this use of the Registry Monitor, used it to find the cause of a feature that appeared and disappeared from Windows 95 systems at his company. For no apparent reason, the Explorer would suddenly gain the ability to expand folders with a "smooth scrolling" motion instead of expanding them abruptly, which was the Explorer's default behavior. Just as suddenly, Explorer would lose this ability.

Engels finally traced this feature to the installation of beta versions of Internet Explorer 4.0. He tracked down the setting for smooth scrolling by watching RegMon while opening the Windows Explorer. What he found was that the Explorer was looking for a SmoothScroll setting in the registry that didn't exist. By inserting SmoothScroll into the registry and setting it to 1, Engels found he could make the behavior permanent.

Windows itself uses the registry in a variety of different ways. When you make a change in a Control Panel applet or a dialog box, you may be able to locate where such a setting is stored in the registry. This, in turn, may lead you to other settings in the same general area that you want to investigate.

When you start RegMon, it immediately begins displaying accesses to the registry. Figure 11-2 shows a few lines of RegMon output. In the example shown in the figure, a fax job using Symantec's WinFax Pro software was running in the background. When it began a fax transmission, the program queried the registry for all installed printer drivers. The RegMon output displayed these queries in its Request column.

#	Request	Path	Result	Other
47	QueryValueEx	0xC3783708\UserAutoRxMode	SUCCESS	0x0
48	QueryValueEx	0xC3783708\UserAutoRxMode	SUCCESS	0x0
49	OpenKey	LOCAL\System\CurrentControlSet\Control\Print\Printers	SUCCESS	hKey: 0xC3766AAC
50	EnumKey	LOCAL\System\CurrentControlSet\Control\Print\Printers	SUCCESS	WinFax
51	OpenKey	LOCAL\System\CurrentControlSet\Control\Print\Printers\WinFax	SUCCESS	hKey: 0xC3784B70
52	QueryValueEx	LOCAL\System\CurrentControlSet\Control\Print\Printers\WinFax\Port	SUCCESS	"FaxModem"
53	QueryValueEx	LOCAL\System\CurrentControlSet\Control\Print\Printers\WinFax\HPAlreadyAddedToTray	SUCCESS	0x1
54	CloseKey	LOCAL\System\CurrentControlSet\Control\Print\Printers\WinFax	SUCCESS	
55	EnumKey	0xC3766AAC	SUCCESS	Generic / Text Only
56	OpenKey	0xC3766AAC\Generic / Text Only	SUCCESS	hKey: 0xC3784B70
57	QueryValueEx	0xC3766AAC\Generic / Text Only\Port	SUCCESS	"LPT1:"
58	QueryValueEx	0xC3766AAC\Generic / Text Only\HPAlreadyAddedToTray	SUCCESS	0x1
59	CloseKey	0xC3766AAC\Generic / Text Only	SUCCESS	
60	EnumKey	0xC3766AAC	SUCCESS	Delrina MAPI Servic...
61	OpenKey	0xC3766AAC\Delrina MAPI Service Provider	SUCCESS	hKey: 0xC3784B70
62	QueryValueEx	0xC3766AAC\Delrina MAPI Service Provider\Port	SUCCESS	"FaxModem"
63	QueryValueEx	0xC3766AAC\Delrina MAPI Service Provider\HPAlreadyAddedToTray	SUCCESS	0x1
64	CloseKey	0xC3766AAC\Delrina MAPI Service Provider	SUCCESS	

Figure 11-2: The Windows Registry Monitor, a freeware program, shows requests by programs for information from the registry, and the results of those requests.

Looking more closely at Figure 11-2, we can see how the request from the program to EnumKey (or *enumerate key*) results in Windows listing the values underneath a significant key. In the example, the program next sends an OpenKey request, and then queries the value of each item. The program may store the results of these queries in memory for later use.

The names of the keys monitored by RegMon and the abbreviations RegMon uses are listed in Table 11-1.

Table 11-1   Key Abbreviations in Registry Monitor

Key	Abbreviation
HKEY_CLASSES_ROOT	HKCR
HKEY_CURRENT_USER	HKCU
HKEY_LOCAL_MACHINE	HKLM
HKEY_USERS	HKU
HKEY_CURRENT_CONFIG	HKCC
HKEY_DYN_DATA	HKDD

RegMon displays the name of a registry key, such as HKLM\ System\ CurrentControlSet\ Control\Print\ Printers, unless a request involves a key that was first opened before RegMon was started. In that case, RegMon displays the hexadecimal value of the key.

If you want to see how some of your other programs access the registry, add Regmon.exe to your StartUp folder so it will load every time Windows starts. If the display scrolls too fast for you to follow the accesses that programs are making to the registry, choose Events ➪ Auto Scroll and clear the checkmark from this feature. You can then use the scroll bar to scroll at your own pace.

You can download RegMon for Windows or Windows NT from the authors' Web site, http://www.sysinternals.com/regmon.htm.

The Registry Files

System.dat and User.dat are the two hidden, read-only files that make up the registry. Unlike the ini files, they are binary files that can't be read easily with an ASCII file editor. You need the Registry Editor to examine the variables and values stored in the registry.

Actually, you can use WordPad to read the registry, but you need to export it to a text file first. This is an option in the Registry Editor. The resulting file (if you export the whole thing instead of just a branch) is too big to be read by Notepad. You can make changes to the exported registry file and import the altered file back into the registry database, updating the previous registry entries. We discuss this more in the later section entitled "The Registry Editor."

There is only one registry on your computer, but it is made up of two files — System.dat and User.dat. If there is a policy file (a file with the pol extension), it is also with the registry. We discuss policy files and their implications for the registry in the "System Policy Editor" section of Chapter 18. When you invoke the Registry Editor, it displays and treats System.dat and User.dat as one registry.

The registry files have the DOS file attributes of Hidden and Read-Only. This doesn't prevent you from displaying them in the Explorer or a folder window, as long as you have the "Show hidden files and folders" option turned on. (In any Explorer or folder window, choose View ➪ Folder Options, click the View tab, and mark the "Show hidden files and folders" option button.) System.dat and User.dat are by default stored in the \Windows folder. (Remember that while we call our folder Windows, you may have named yours something else, such as Win.) If your \Windows folder is on a compressed drive, these files (and their backups) are stored on the boot drive. Other variations are possible with networked computers.

System.dat stores information specific to a computer and to the software on that computer. System.dat tracks the detected hardware and its configuration as well as Windows and other installed programs that put their information in the registry.

User.dat stores user-specific information, including mouse speed, color scheme, cursor scheme, wallpaper, accessibility settings, icon spacing, fonts, keyboard layout, keyboard delay and speed, regional settings, Explorer settings, and passwords. A user's Desktop icons and network connections are stored in User.dat. If you make the appropriate choice in the User Profiles tab of the Passwords Properties dialog box (click the Passwords icon in the Control Panel), each individual user can have his or her own Start menu and Desktop settings. You can also use the Users icon in the Control Panel to set up new users and their parameters.

What If Bad Things Happen?

Because almost all the vital information about Windows and the Windows applications that you have installed is stored in the registry, it would be a real shame if somehow the files that make up the registry got corrupted. If you edit the registry, you may insert values that later prove to be quite wrong, but you may be unable to determine which values those were. In both of these cases, it would be good to have a copy of the registry files as they existed before things went awry.

If you get an error message when you start Windows stating that there is not enough memory to load the registry or that Windows has encountered an error accessing the system registry, you have a corrupted registry.

It is not that hard to end up with a corrupted registry. Windows reads the registry files off a hard disk, and the disk can have weak areas that weren't marked as such before the files were stored there. Also, the registry is stored in RAM after it is read during Windows startup, and it is often written back to the hard disk as you use Windows. Any memory errors can corrupt the registry, and that corruption is then preserved in the registry files when they are overwritten.

Placing everything in one file and making Windows so dependent on that file means that, of course, it is going to fail. Windows 95 didn't do enough to help you recover your registry when the inevitable happened. We provided some additional means of backing up and recovering your registry files in our previous *Windows 95 Secrets* books, but even those weren't nearly enough.

Windows 95 automatically created backups of your System.dat and User.dat files with the extension da0. These files were created each time Windows successfully started. Windows Me (just as Windows 98 before it) does not create these files. As a consequence, one of our registry recovery utilities from our previous *Windows 95 Secrets* books, Regrecov.bat, won't do anything useful because there are no files for it to operate on.

Windows automatically backs up your registry (and your Win.ini and System.ini files) every day. By default, it keeps the latest five of these backups in your \Windows\Sysbckup folder. It lets you easily create a backup at any time, as described in the next section, "Registry Backup," and it allows you to boot your computer to real-mode DOS and roll back your computer to an earlier registry (and Win.ini and System.ini files), as described in "Registry Recovery" later in this chapter.

The fact that Windows automatically backs up these files every day is the key. Any changes made in your registry during the day are lost if you go back to a previous version of the registry. If you install new software during the day and then roll back to an earlier registry, you will need to reinstall the software. Frankly, this is a small price to pay compared to what you'd have to shell out if you hadn't been making regular backups manually.

Because you most likely will have problems starting Windows normally if you have a corrupted registry, you have to be able to restore your registry another way. That way is to start Windows Me in safe mode and then use the System Restore tool to do the job. Click the Start button and choose Programs ⇨ Accessories ⇨ System Tools ⇨ System Restore to load this tool.

If more than just your registry has gone bad, you may need to boot to DOS from a floppy disk and then gain access to your hard disk. You'll need to create a bootable diskette under Windows to allow this to happen. We discuss this further in the "Emergency Startup Disk" section later in this chapter.

Registry Backup

Windows automatically backs up your registry files, Win.ini, and System.ini every day. It does this by calling the backup and restore program ScanReg (Scanregw.exe /autorun) as part of startup. ScanReg compacts these files and then stores them in your \Windows\Sysbckup folder as cabinet files with the names rb001.cab, rb002.cab, and so on. You can also use Scanreg.exe, a separate DOS real-mode program, to restore a backup after you boot to DOS (see the next section).

If you want to create a backup of the registry yourself while you're using Windows, run ScanReg. Click the Start button and choose Programs ⇨ Accessories ⇨ System Tools ⇨ System Information ⇨ Tools, then click Registry Checker. ScanReg does indeed scan the registry for problems, which is why Microsoft called it ScanReg instead of BackReg. If it doesn't find any errors, it tells you that it has already backed up the registry for the day and asks if you want to back up now.

You have the option of determining whether Windows calls ScanReg at all, how many days worth of backups are stored, where the backups are stored, and what other files are stored with them. You set these parameters in an ini file, Scanreg.ini, which is stored in your \Windows folder.

Scanreg.ini is self-documented. Start the program and follow the instructions it provides for changing how Scanregw.exe and Scanreg.exe work when they create backups. For example, you may want to include other files in your backup, such as Protocol.ini, Autoexec.bat, and Config.sys. You can do this by adding these filenames to Scanreg.ini in the required format. Files you list here will be included in backups made by both Scanregw.exe and Scanreg.exe. Of course, one of the reasons for having a registry is that you shouldn't have to remember just which ini files you need to back up. Oh well!

By modifying Scanreg.ini, you can direct ScanReg to store the backup cabinet file in another folder or on another device. If you direct the backup to a floppy drive, it will be slower than storing the backup file on the hard disk. Even if you store the backups on your hard disk, you can copy them onto removable media on a regular basis. The files are compacted, so they have a chance of fitting on a floppy diskette. Of course, copying the files to another disk isn't automatic, as it is when ScanReg creates them in the first place. And, while having a copy of the backup files on a floppy could be useful if you damage those files, it really won't protect you if your hard disk dies. In that case, you will have to reinstall everything on a new drive anyway. Therefore, it is not such a bad thing if the backup file is only on the hard disk.

Use your Explorer to right-drag Scanreg.ini and Scanregw.exe from the \Windows folder to your Desktop and create shortcuts to them there. These shortcuts will let you quickly make a backup whenever you like and easily change the values in Scanreg.ini.

Scanreg.exe and Scanregw.exe replace Cfback.exe, the Windows 95 registry backup and restore utility. This utility is no longer shipped on the Windows CD-ROM. In addition, because you can configure Scanreg.ini so that ScanReg will back up all your configuration files, there is no need to use the Emergency Recovery Utility, Eru.exe.

Registry Recovery

If your registry goes bad, or if you just want to get back to where you were before you installed some software, you will have to go into real-mode DOS to run Scanreg.exe. You can reboot your computer using your Windows Me startup disk, and choose the Minimal Boot option at the Windows Startup menu. If you type **Scanreg /?** at the DOS prompt, you'll get a listing of options (*switches*) that work with this command, though not all the options are documented there.

You can use the /fix switch to scan and fix an existing registry. Just type **Scanreg /fix**. If you would rather restore a backup of a previous version of the registry, type **Scanreg /restore**. A list of the backup files appears along with their dates, and you can choose which file you want to restore.

You can use the /backup switch to back up your registry at the DOS prompt. Of course, you shouldn't do this if you've just experienced a corrupt registry and that's why you are at the DOS prompt.

ScanReg will automatically trim some empty branches in your registry if it finds over 500K of empty data structures. Since ScanReg is called by Windows as part of startup, it gets a chance to scan for empty data structures whenever you do a warm boot.

Emergency Startup Disk

You may discover that you can't boot your computer from your hard disk. This is not a problem of a corrupt registry, or at least not just a corrupt registry. If you have created a startup disk, otherwise known as an *Emergency Startup Disk* (ESD), you'll be able to boot your computer and perhaps get back to your hard disk.

To create a startup disk, click the Start button, point to Settings, click Control Panel, and click Add/Remove Programs. Then click the Startup Disk tab, click the Create Disk button, and follow the prompts. Of course, you have to do this before disaster strikes.

If you can't boot your computer from your hard disk, place a startup disk in your boot floppy drive and restart your computer. If you can then access your hard disk, you can gain access to the registry backup files and restore the registry if necessary.

Emergency Recover Utility

Microsoft provided another backup and disaster-recovery utility called ERU (Emergency Recovery Utility) with Windows 95, which copies the major user-configuration files, including a compressed version of User.dat, to a boot diskette. We recommend using ScanDisk instead of ERU, since it is run automatically every day—however, if you have an old Windows 95 CD-ROM you can find ERU there. If you upgraded to Windows Me over Windows 95, it will still be on your hard disk.

If you can't start Windows, you can reboot your PC with a bootable floppy disk containing files that ERU placed there. ERU will automatically restore these important files for you.

The Registry Editor

Microsoft has created numerous user interface elements—including the Control Panel, dialog boxes, and TweakUI—that are designed to let you change the values stored in the registry without having to edit it directly. You can find most of these elements by clicking the Start button and pointing to Settings.

If you can make the changes you need without using the Registry Editor, by all means do so. That way, the changes you make are reflected immediately as changes in the behavior of that portion of the operating system affected by the values stored in the registry.

Microsoft hopes that these user interface elements are enough. They aren't.

In many of the chapters in this book, we reveal how to use the Registry Editor to change a value or add a key. Changes you make using the Registry Editor are often not used until the next time you start Windows (when the registry values are read and stored in memory). We have indicated throughout the text when the changes you make take effect immediately versus when you need to restart Windows.

Making changes to registry values using the Windows user interface elements is the safest means of changing these values. If you use the Registry Editor, it is quite possible to delete or alter vital elements of the registry. Some changes may prevent Windows from operating correctly.

One precaution that you can take to recover from such an unfortunate editing session is to make a backup of the registry files before you edit them. The registry scanning utility (`Scanregw.exe`), detailed in the "Registry Backup" section earlier in this chapter, lets you easily and quickly make a backup before you begin editing.

If you engage in a course of action that damages the registry, you still have your automatic backups. If you restart Windows after an editing session that has gotten out of hand, and Windows can't start successfully, you can always go to the backups.

On the other hand, you may have done some damage during your editing session—perhaps made some inadvertent changes that you don't remember and certainly didn't want to make—but the damage is not great enough to prevent Windows from starting the next time. If you have started Windows after one of these rash editing sessions, an intentional backup you did right before your last editing session would be very handy.

Additional Registry Editors and Registry Editor extensions are available on the Internet. One freeware extension, appropriately named Registry Editor Extensions, saves the paths within the registry that you have visited, enabling you to get back to them quickly. You can download the latest version at `http://www.dcsoft.com/ftp/regeditx.zip`.

Registry Editor Extensions also adds some nice user-interface touches. You can display the drop-down list of visited keys by Shift+clicking anywhere in the list box, and you can type or cut and paste a key into the list and instantly navigate there.

Starting the Registry Editor

You'll find the Registry Editor in the `\Windows` folder. Windows Setup does not place it on any of the Start menus. Microsoft is not that eager for the uninitiated to use this tool. The application filename is `Regedit.exe`. Your system administrator may have removed it from your computer.

If you are going to use the editor, it is a good idea to create a shortcut to access it. Place the shortcut on the Desktop or in the Start menus. If you don't know how to create shortcuts, you shouldn't be messing around with the Registry Editor (unless you are following our explicit step-by-step instructions).

Editing with the Registry Editor

Chapters throughout this book contain discussions that point to areas of the registry to be edited. Let's take a minute to see what the editing commands are and how to use them.

To learn how to edit the registry, it helps to get to a location that has some useful keys, constants, and values. We'll use the current Desktop in the following steps as an example of a very fruitful location.

STEPS

Editing the Registry

Step 1.   Click the plus sign to the left of HKEY_CURRENT_USER. Click the plus sign to the left of Control Panel, and then the one next to *desktop*. (The name HKEY refers to the fact that this is a handle to a key. The registry is filled with keys that eventually have data attached to them.)

Step 2.   Highlight the WindowMetrics name next to its folder icon. Notice that the right pane is now filled with constant names (Name) and values (Data).

Step 3.   Right-click in the right pane of the Registry Editor (but not on a constant name or value). A New button, as shown in Figure 11-3, appears. Point to the New button, and a menu appears. You can choose to create a key, a string value, a binary value, or a DWORD value. The key and/or any of the constants will be attached to the WindowMetrics key.

Step 4.   Right-click the *desktop* key in the left pane of the Registry Editor. As shown in Figure 11-4, the context menu will give you the choice of collapsing this expanded branch of the registry; creating a new key, string value, or binary value; finding a text or numerical string in the local branch; or deleting or renaming the key.

It is not a good idea to delete or rename a key unless you know exactly what you are doing. Adding a new key or value (actually a constant that has a value, which the Registry Editor refers to as *Data*) may change the way the Windows operates, but it won't do any damage.

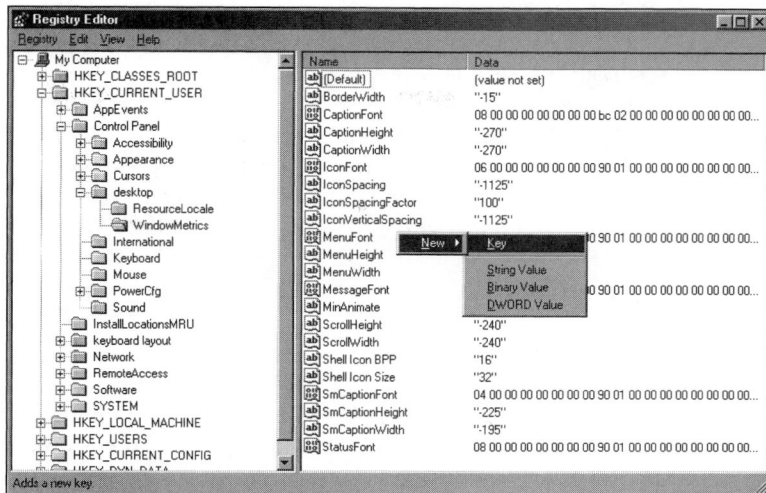

Figure 11-3: Inserting new keys or values in the registry. Right-click the right pane of the Registry Editor to insert new keys or constants.

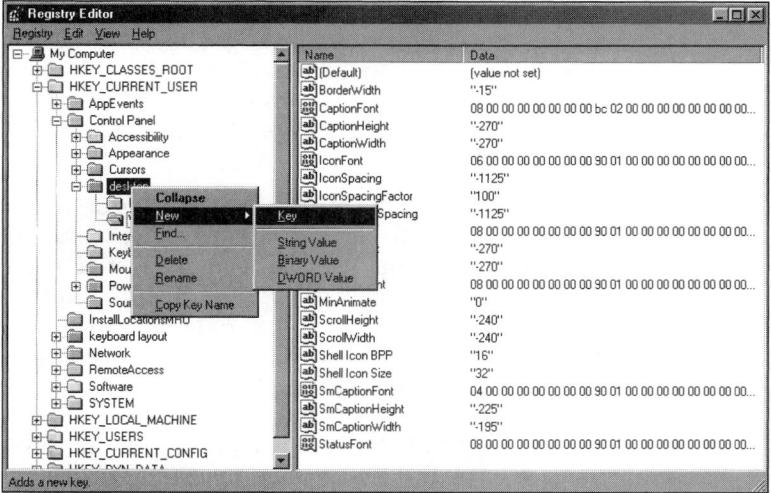

Figure 11-4: Right-click next to a key in the left pane of the Registry Editor to access a context menu.

Step 5.   Right-click a constant in the Name column in the right pane of the Registry Editor. A context menu appears, allowing you to modify the constant's value, delete the constant and its value, or rename the constant.

Continued

STEPS

Editing the Registry *(continued)*

Step 6.   The Edit menu provides similar choices to those that appear on the context menu when you right-click a key or a constant. The Edit menu changes depending on whether you have highlighted a key or a constant. You can't highlight a value (or Data).

Editing the registry consists of adding or deleting keys, adding new constants and their values to be associated with the keys, and modifying those constants and their values — pretty straightforward. The trick is knowing what keys, constants, and values to add, rename, or delete.

Editing the Registry with reg Files

When you upgrade to Windows Me from an older version of Windows, you may lose some of the little fixes to the registry that we've outlined in our earlier books. You can get them back if you create registration files (reg files) that save these changes before upgrading, and then merge them back into your registry after your upgrade. Is it too late for you? Well, you can still save any important personal settings you defined after your upgrade to Windows Me so that they will be available when you upgrade your operating system the next time.

Most often, you edit the registry by changing settings in dialog boxes, without being directly aware that the changes you make are being recorded in the registry. Another way that you can switch between registry settings is to create and use reg files. With this method, you first choose one of the settings you want in a dialog box. You then export the small branch of the registry that contains this setting to a text file and save the file with the reg extension. Next, you use the dialog box to switch to another setting, and then export the updated registry branch to a second reg file. If you now place shortcuts to these two reg files on your Desktop, you can quickly switch back and forth between the settings by clicking these files instead of by interacting with a dialog box.

Crawl Through the Registry

Registry Crawler is a tool that works with the Windows Registry Editor to search for all the instances of a given string, as shown in Figure 11-5. It consolidates all the branches within which the string occurs and lets you more easily edit each of the branches. You'll find it at http://www. 4developers.com/regc.

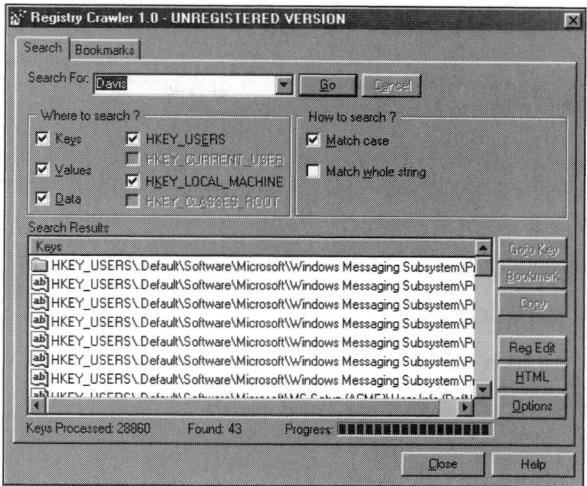

Figure 11-5: In this example, Registry Crawler displays all the places where the string *Davis* appears in Davis' registry.

What we really like about the Registry Crawler is that it is very fast, much faster than searching through the registry with the Registry Editor. And while it is still searching, you can click any found branches to open up the Registry Editor to the indicated location.

Help with Registry Edits

You can download a help file (Regedit.hlp) that provides a bit of help with registry edits for Windows Me, Windows 9*x*, and Windows NT/2000. It includes a registry FAQ, plus lots of little registry edits that help out.

It is not a comprehensive registry help file that thoroughly explains the registry and its deeper branches, so we were a little disappointed. But it may have information you wouldn't otherwise have access to.

You can download this help file from http://www.regedit.com. Check out the Web site for more information about registry edits.

Exporting and Importing the Registry

You can export the registry to an ASCII file with the reg extension. If you do this, Windows writes the keys, constants, and values stored in System.dat and User.dat to an ASCII text file that can be read by WordPad.

You can export the whole registry or just a branch of the registry. To export either, choose Registry ➪ Export Registry File in the Registry Editor. To export a branch, highlight the branch in the left pane of the registry before you choose to export it.

Choosing Registry ➪ Export Registry File displays the common file dialog box with an added modifier extension attached at the bottom, as shown in Figure 11-6. You can choose to export the whole registry or just a branch by clicking one of the two option buttons at the bottom of the dialog box.

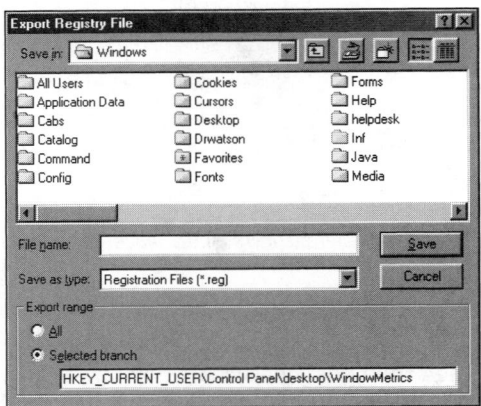

Figure 11-6: The Export Registry File dialog box. You can determine how much of the registry is exported (the highlighted branch or the entire registry) by clicking one of the two option buttons at the bottom of this dialog box.

You should export the registry or a branch of the registry into a file with a reg extension (the default choice in the Export Registry File dialog box). The reg extension will be added automatically if you type a filename. The exported registry is a text file. Using the reg extension makes it easy to merge (import) the registry or its branch later if you edit the exported file.

The exported registry file can be read easily by WordPad. Right-click the exported file and choose Edit on the context menu. Don't click the file, because the default action for a file of this file type is to merge it back into the registry. Figure 11-7 shows how part of an exported registry file looks in WordPad.

Tip

The exported text file encloses the key name, including all preceding key names, in square brackets. The constant names are enclosed in double quote marks. String values associated with the constant names are also enclosed in double quotes. DWORD values (double word in either decimal or hexadecimal format) begin with *dword:*. Binary values begin with *hex:*.

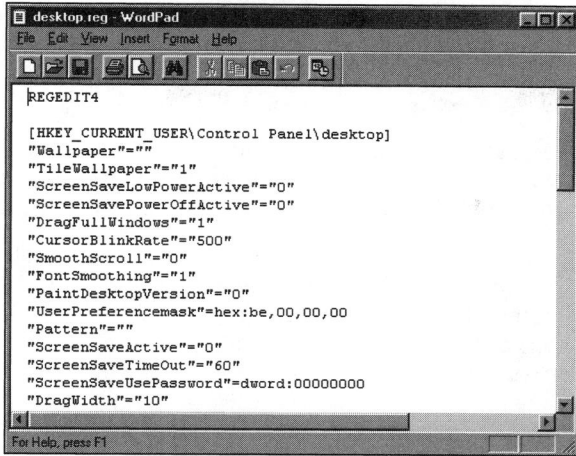

Figure 11-7: The Control Panel\Desktop key area in the registry exported to a text file. The key values are surrounded by square brackets. The constants and their string values are surrounded by double quotes.

Searching an Exported Registry File

One reason to export a registry file is to be able to search it quickly. The Registry Editor has a find facility, but it is slow. You can bring the exported registry text file into WordPad and use its Find toolbar button (the binoculars) to find a text or numeric string much more quickly than you could if you searched in the registry.

This can be quite useful when you're investigating the structure of the registry or trying to find the constant name whose value you want to change. You can have the Registry Editor open on your Desktop, and at the same time have the exported registry file open in WordPad. Search for the constant name in WordPad. Then, in the Registry Editor, click the plus signs next to the registry keys to expand the branch of the registry that contains the constant you are looking for.

Editing an Exported Registry File

Of course, you can edit the registry directly, so why would you export it (or a branch of it) to edit? If you want to make a lot of changes, the editing capabilities of WordPad are much more powerful than those provided by the Registry Editor.

The Registry Editor allows only certain kinds of values to be typed into the fields for keys, constant names, or values. This prevents many of the errors you might make if you edit the exported registry file.

You edit an exported registry file so that you can import (or merge) it back into the registry. If you are not comfortable doing this, then make all of your registry changes either though the Windows user interface elements or directly in the Registry Editor.

Importing or Merging a Text File into the Registry

Once you have exported a branch or all of the registry and edited it, you can put it back in. Now might be a good time to back up the registry using the procedure outlined in the "Registry Backup" section of this chapter.

Merging and importing are the same thing. Click an exported registry file (a file with a `reg` extension), and it is imported (or merged) into the registry. Right-click an exported file, and you will see that the first choice on the context menu is Merge. The values of the keys, constants, and data in the exported text file overwrite or are added to the values stored in the registry.

Of course, you can create a text file with the correctly formatted key, constant name, and data values from scratch and import it into the registry. You will need to review exported files until you understand the format.

You can also import a registry file (actually a text file that has been correctly formatted) by choosing Registry ⇨ Import Registry File in the Registry Editor.

Tip

If you are just importing a branch, then the branch is added to the registry. If the branch is a new version of an existing branch, the values and keys in the imported branch are added to the existing branch. All of the values with the same name (and location) in the existing branch are overwritten by values in the imported branch. No existing keys or values are deleted by the imported branch.

Click to Edit a Registry File

We would rather change the default behavior for exported registry files, so that clicking a registry file chooses the Edit command instead of the Merge command. This way, you don't run the risk of accidentally clicking a `reg` file and merging it into the existing registry when you didn't intend to do so. Once you change the default behavior, you have to deliberately right-click a `reg` file and choose Merge from the context menu if you want to perform a merge. This is safer and more in line with the rest of the Windows interface. To make this change, take the following steps:

STEPS

Making Editing the Default Behavior for Registry Files

Step 1.   Open an Explorer window. Choose View ⇨ Folder Options. Click the File Types tab.

Step 2.   Scroll down the Registered File Types list box to Registration Entries. Highlight Registration Entries and click the Edit button.

Step 3.   Highlight Edit in the Actions box. Click the Set Default button.

Step 4.   Click Close in the Edit File Type dialog box, and then click Close again in the Folder Options dialog box.

Auto-Inserting into Your Registry at Startup

You can insert the data from a `reg` file into your registry when you start Windows. For example, if you want to stop Windows from putting "Shortcut to" at the start of every `lnk` file name, you can create a `reg` file, and then put it (or a shortcut to it) in your `\Windows\Start Menu\Programs\StartUp` folder. This file would contain the following text:

```
REGEDIT4
[HKEY_CURRENT_USER\Software\Microsoft\Windows\CurrentVersion\Explorer]
"link"=hex:00,00,00,00
```

This will only work if Merge is the default action for `reg` files. If Edit is the default action, but you actually want to merge the file, edit the Target field of the shortcut file to include `regedit.exe` followed by the `reg` file's name and extension.

Of course, it is easier to use TweakUI to turn off this particularly obnoxious Windows behavior, but you may think of other reasons why you want to write into the registry at startup.

After Windows runs a `reg` file, it displays a dialog box saying the merge was successful. You can get rid of this dialog box with the RtvReco utility (`http://www.winfiles.com`). Actually, there's a free and easy way around this. The trick is an undocumented switch to RegEdit that J.T. Anderson of Los Angeles was kind enough to point out to us.

RegEdit supports an `/s` switch, which stands for *silent*. When you add this to a RegEdit command line, the switch suppresses the usual "merge was successful" dialog box that you would otherwise have to click OK in to get rid of.

Therefore, if you have a reason to create a shortcut to a `reg` file that you commonly want to merge into the registry, use the `/s` switch on the command line. Instead of creating a shortcut to `Filename.reg`, for example, you would use the following command line in the Target field of the shortcut:

```
Regedit.exe /s filename.reg
```

If you like the way this eliminates the annoying "merge is successful" dialog box, you don't have to limit yourself to eradicating it for a single shortcut. You can suppress this dialog box every time you run RegEdit by editing the default action for RegEdit.

STEPS

Silencing RegEdit

Step 1.   In the Explorer, click View ➪ Folder Options ➪ File Types.

Step 2.   In the Registered File Types list, select Registration Entries, and then click the Edit button.

Step 3.   In the Actions box, select Merge, and then click the Edit button.

Step 4.   In the "Application used to perform action" box, change `regedit.exe` to `regedit.exe /s`. Click OK, and then click Close twice to exit.

This changes the default command line for RegEdit. Of course, changing the command line globally in this way does mean you see no confirmation box when you merge a `reg` file. For this reason, you might want to stick with editing only those shortcuts where you really need the silent treatment.

Changing the Registered Owner

Windows tracks your name and the name of your company. To see this information, choose Help ➪ About in almost any application.

Secret

You can change your name and company settings, which are stored in your registry, using the Registry Editor:

STEPS

A New User

Step 1.   Click `Regedit.exe` in your `\Windows` folder.

Step 2.   Navigate to HKEY_LOCAL_MACHINE\ SOFTWARE\ Microsoft\ Windows\ CurrentVersion.

Step 3.   Double-click RegisteredOwner and/or RegisteredOrganization in the right pane and change the names.

Step 4. Exit the Registry Editor.

Editing the Most Recently Used List

Windows uses the registry to keep track of the devices and folders you use the most frequently to install software. For example, if you install most of your software from your CD-ROM drive, which happens to be drive D:, Windows will default to looking on D: for files that it needs during an installation. If your computer manufacturer has installed the Windows source cabinet files on your hard disk (in \Windows\Options\Cabs), Windows will look there when you make a change to your Windows installation.

If you install software using the Add/Remove Programs icon in the Control Panel, you'll notice that when an installation routine can't find a needed file, a dialog box appears that asks you to browse to a new location or choose from a list. Windows stores this list, called the most recently used (MRU) list, in the registry. It lists the most recent locations you used during an installation, regardless of what you were installing.

You can edit the MRU list to get rid of an incorrect listing. In particular, it is a good idea to get rid of A:\ if you don't install from floppy disks. Clicking the Browse button when A:\ is the first default installation location listed slows the search process substantially. Windows will look in the first location listed, but it doesn't search beyond that location—so the order of the remaining locations in the list is not that important.

STEPS

Changing the MRU List

Step 1. In your Registry Editor, navigate to

HKEY_CURRENT_USER\ InstallLocationsMRU

Step 2. Double-click any of the letters in the right pane of the Explorer, as shown in Figure 11-8.

Step 3. Type a new drive letter and path. Click OK. Repeat this process for any other location you want to change.

Step 4. If you want to modify the order in which the locations are presented, double-click MRUList in the right pane and type a new order. Click OK.

Step 5. Exit the Registry Editor.

Continued

STEPS

Changing the MRU List *(continued)*

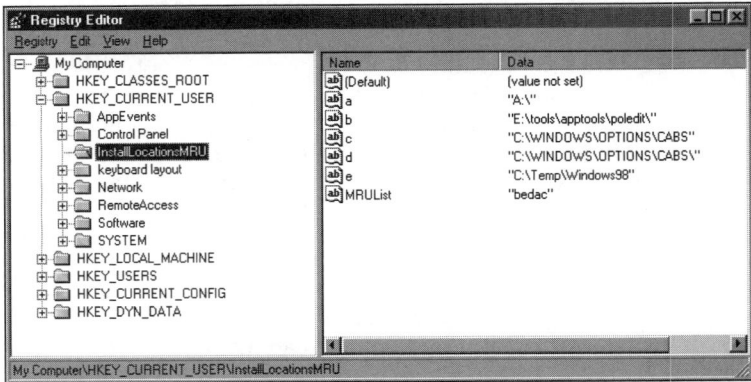

Figure 11-8: There are five locations in the MRU list.

Editing Other People's Registries

The Registry Editor gives you the option of editing registries on other computers that you are networked to over a dial-up line, Direct Cable Connection, or LAN. This feature requires a Windows NT server on your network to provide user-level (as opposed to share-level) network security. In addition, if you are going to let your registry be edited by someone else on your network, you must configure your networking options on your computer to add the Remote Registry Service. Only other users who have user-level access to your computer will be able to edit (or use their Registry Editor to view) your registry.

Setting User-Level Security

If you have a Windows NT server on your network, set your computer to use user-level security by taking the following steps:

STEPS

Setting User-Level Security

Step 1. Click the Start button, point to Settings, and then click Control Panel.

Step 2. Click the Network icon.

Step 3. Click the Access Control tab. Mark the "User-level access control" checkbox. Type the name of the Windows NT server that keeps the list of users, and click OK.

Setting Up a Computer to Allow its Registry to Be Edited

You can set up your computer to be a registry server. That is, you allow people at other computers to edit or view your registry. To do this, take the following steps:

STEPS

Configuring Your Computer as a Registry Server

Step 1. Click the Start button, point to Settings, and then click Control Panel.

Step 2. Click the Network icon.

Step 3. Click the Add button. Double-click the Service icon in the Select Network Component Type dialog box.

Step 4. Click the Have Disk button. Click the Browse button, and browse to the `\tools\nettools\remotreg` folder on your Windows CD-ROM.

Step 5. Click `regsrv.inf`, and then click the OK button.

Step 6. Click OK and then OK again. You will have to restart your computer for this change to take effect.

Using the Registry Editor to Edit Someone Else's Registry

If another computer user on your network has set up his or her computer as a registry server and you have user-level access to that user's computer through a list kept on a Windows NT server, you can edit that user's registry. You'll first need to add `regsrv.inf` to your computer by following the steps in "Setting Up a Computer to Allow its Registry to Be Edited." Then start your Registry Editor, and choose Registry ➪ Connect Network Registry. Type the name of the computer containing the registry you are going to edit. When you are done, choose Registry ➪ Disconnect Network Registry. You can find further details on editing other people's registries at `http:/support.microsoft.com/support/kb/articles/q141/4/60.asp`.

Little Fixes to the Registry

Okay, you've seen a number of very useful things you can do with the registry. Now let's have a look at some little things that are still pretty neat even if they aren't quite so flashy.

Open My Computer in Explorer View

In Chapter 7, we told you how to change My Computer so that it opens with a Folders pane (the two-pane Explorer view). If you've made this change, you can keep it safe by exporting the proper branch of your registry to a reg file. This is the branch you'll want to export:

HKEY_CLASSES_ROOT\CLSID\{20D04FE0-3AEA-1069-A2D8-08002B30309D} \shell\Open

If you haven't made this change yet, or it was overwritten when you upgraded to Windows Me, you can import the following text into your registry.

```
REGEDIT4
[HKEY_CLASSES_ROOT\CLSID\{20D04FE0-3AEA-1069-
A2D8-08002B30309D}\shell\Open]
 [HKEY_CLASSES_ROOT\CLSID\{20D04FE0-3AEA-1069-
A2D8-08002B30309D}\shell\Open\command]
@="Explorer.exe"
```

Make Sure You're the Owner

When you install a new version of Windows, it seems to forget who the computer's owner is. You can restore your rightful ownership by placing this text in a file named Owner.reg and merging it into your registry:

```
REGEDIT4
[HKEY_LOCAL_MACHINE\SOFTWARE\Microsoft\Windows\CurrentVersion]
"InstallType"=hex:01,00
"RegisteredOwner"="Davis Straub"
"RegisteredOrganization"="Windows Secrets"
```

You'll find the Owner.reg file on the accompanying CD-ROM.

Oh yes, be sure to replace "Davis Straub" with your name in quotes, and "Windows Secrets" with your company or organization name, if any.

Your Own Colors

You can keep track of your own Desktop colors and pass them on to friends. Here's an example of one color scheme that we use (a bit greenish). Before you import this color scheme, you'll want to save your present color scheme if it isn't a standard scheme. Right-click your Desktop, click Properties ➪ Appearance ➪ Save As, and enter a name for your present color scheme.

```
REGEDIT4
[HKEY_CURRENT_USER\Control Panel\Colors]
"ActiveTitle"="0 0 128"
"Background"="166 202 240"
"Hilight"="0 0 255"
"HilightText"="255 255 255"
"TitleText"="255 255 255"
"Window"="192 220 192"
"WindowText"="0 0 0"
"Scrollbar"="192 220 192"
"InactiveTitle"="192 220 192"
"Menu"="192 220 192"
"WindowFrame"="0 0 0"
"MenuText"="0 0 0"
"ActiveBorder"="0 0 0"
"InactiveBorder"="192 192 192"
"AppWorkspace"="255 255 128"
"ButtonFace"="0 128 128"
"ButtonShadow"="128 0 128"
"GrayText"="0 0 128"
"ButtonText"="0 0 0"
"InactiveTitleText"="0 0 0"
"ButtonHilight"="192 220 192"
"ButtonDkShadow"="0 0 0"
"ButtonLight"="192 192 192"
"InfoText"="0 0 0"
"InfoWindow"="255 255 225"
"MessageBoxText"="0 0 0"
"MessageBox"="0 128 128"
@="255 255 192"
"ButtonAlternateFace"="184 180 184"
"HotTrackingColor"="0 0 255"
"GradientActiveTitle"="0 128 128"
"GradientInactiveTitle"="128 128 128"
```

You'll find this particular color scheme in the Colors.reg file on the accompanying CD-ROM. To merge it into your registry, right-click the file and click Merge.

Tip

You can also make up your own color scheme (right-click the Desktop, click Properties, click Appearance), and then export the HKEY_CURRENT_USER\ Control Panel\ Colors key. Name the file Colors.reg.

Changing the Default Action for reg Files

We find it a bit unnerving that the default option when clicking a file with the reg extension is Merge (into the registry). This used to be a real problem with Windows 95, because the merge just took place without a question. Now, Windows asks if you want to merge the file contents into the registry.

Still, we'd like a little more deliberation before such a drastic action is taken. We'd like the user to have to right-click the file, and then click Merge. Therefore, we change the default action for reg files to Edit. Put the following text in a file called Regedit.reg and store it in your My System folder:

```
REGEDIT4
[HKEY_CLASSES_ROOT\regfile\shell]
@="edit"
```

You'll find the Regedit.reg file on the accompanying CD-ROM. Merge it into your registry to make this change.

Dealing with File Associations

Windows Me automatically knows how to open many different types of documents because of *file associations*. You can control these associations directly within the registry as shown in the following sections.

Set Your Own File Associations

We're always on the lookout for tools that give you more power over the Windows operating system. One of the most difficult areas to manage — because it is such a massive data structure — is the registry. We've found a few tools that help. One, Freedom of Association, lets you delete orphaned file extensions, reassociate extensions with the applications you prefer, and add extensions to existing file types.

None of your deletions are lost. You can undelete any of them at any time. You can restore any file association that you've changed.

When you first start Freedom of Association, it searches your registry, finds all the file extensions and file types, and displays them as shown in Figure 11-9. If you see a red or yellow mark next to a file extension, you most likely can delete it.

To reassociate a file extension with another file type, highlight the extension in the Extensions tab, click the File Type button, scroll to the file type with which you want to associate this extension, highlight it, click the Extensions tab, and click the Associate W/ button.

Neil J. Rubenking of *PC Magazine* wrote Freedom of Association, and you'll find it at http://www.zdnet.com/pcmag/pctech/content/17/12/ut1712.001.html.

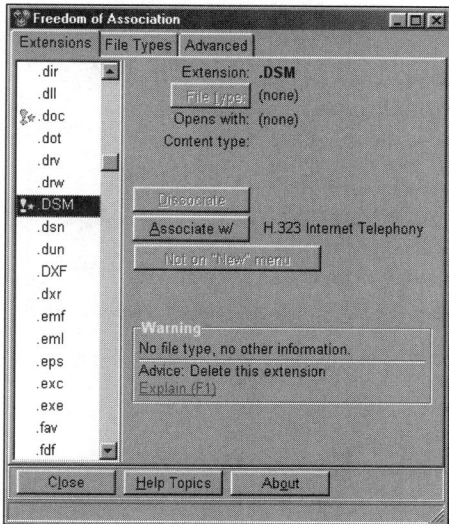

Figure 11-9: The yellow mark makes it easy to see an unassociated file extension.

What Extension Goes with What Application?

If you've forgotten which obscure file extension goes with which long forgotten application, check out the PC Web Encyclopedia, file extension section, at `http://webopedia.internet.com/quick_ref/fileextensions.html`. There is a lot of other useful computer information here as well, especially computer terminology.

Watching Your Registry

Because registry changes can have such a profound effect on your system, you'll probably want to know what changes are being made to it. In these sections you'll see how to track those changes.

Follow the Registry

The Registry Monitor will record and display every read or write to your registry. You can use it to track registry writes during the installation of new software, or to see what might be going wrong when you use a specific piece of software (see Figure 11-10).

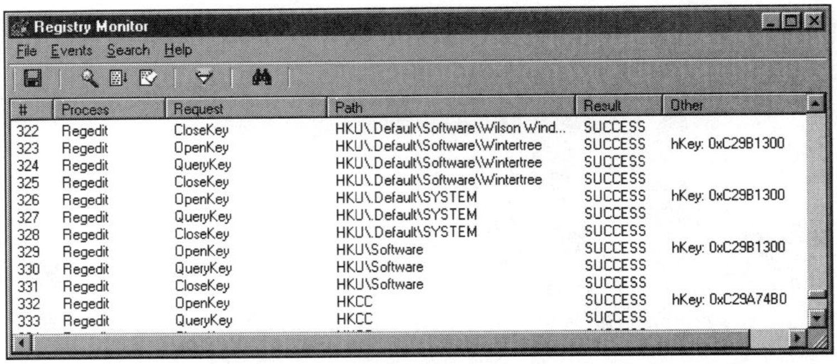

Figure 11-10: The RegMon window lists every process that has called the registry, in the order it occurred.

You'll find a section devoted to the Registry Monitor earlier in this chapter. We mention it here to advise you that there is a new version. You can now filter the output so that the Registry Monitor will only display reads and writes that meet your criteria. You can also limit the number of lines that will be kept in its history. And you can now search the output for a specific string.

You'll find the Registry Monitor at http://www.sysinternals.com.

Monitoring the Files

File Monitor displays any file activity, whether in memory or from the hard disk. You can see how your applications use files or DLLs, as shown in Figure 11-11.

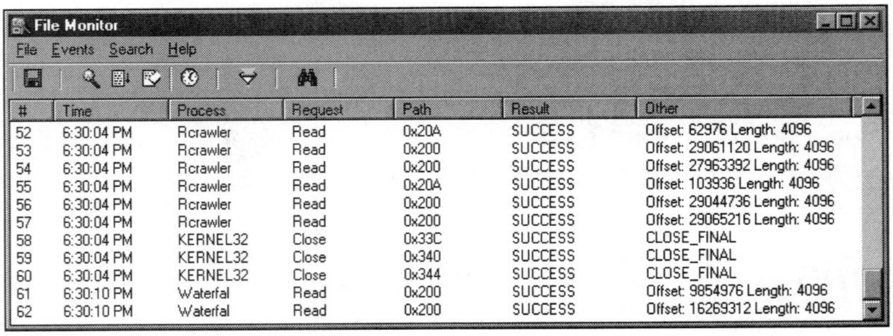

Figure 11-11: The File Monitor user interface

Written by the same folks who wrote Registry Monitor, it provides a similar display of activity, and you get the same kinds of functions for controlling output display and searching.

You'll find the File Monitor at http://www.sysinternals.com.

Safeguarding Your Registry

If you want to run Windows Me on your PC, your system must be able to read the registry properly. It's very important to make certain that your registry is in good condition. The following sections explain how you can do so.

Is Your Registry Damaged?

Have you started up Windows only to receive this scary message?

```
Windows registry is damaged. Windows will restart and try to fix
the problem.
```

While registry damage is indeed a scary proposition, that may not be the problem at all. You may have a faulty memory chip, and because the registry is read into memory during startup, it may fail to be written correctly. When ScanRegistry (Scanregw.exe) scans the registry—it does so automatically at startup unless you configure Windows to skip this step—it finds the badly written part of the registry. The copy of the registry on your hard disk is still just fine. (We discuss how to turn off Scanregw.exe in the "AutoScan" section of Chapter 3.)

Once Scanregw.exe discovers that the registry in memory is damaged because of bad memory, it marks the registry as damaged and runs the real-mode version of Scanreg.exe when it restarts Windows. This may or may not restart Windows normally, because the real-mode version of Scanreg.exe may not find the bad memory location.

You can put new memory chips in your computer to see if that solves the problem, run a memory tester, or limit the amount of memory Windows sees in the hope that the bad chip is beyond your imposed limit.

To test for damage by limiting the amount of memory used to start Windows, take these steps:

STEPS

Limiting the Amount of Memory Used by Windows

Step 1. Restart your computer. Hold down the Ctrl key during the power-on self-test, and when you see the Windows Startup menu, choose to start in Safe mode.

Step 2. Click Start ➪ Programs ➪ Accessories ➪ System Tools ➪ System Information. Then choose Tools ➪ System Configuration Utility.

Step 3. Click the Advanced button to display the Advanced Troubleshooting Settings dialog box shown in Figure 11-12.

Continued

STEPS

Limiting the Amount of Memory Used by Windows *(continued)*

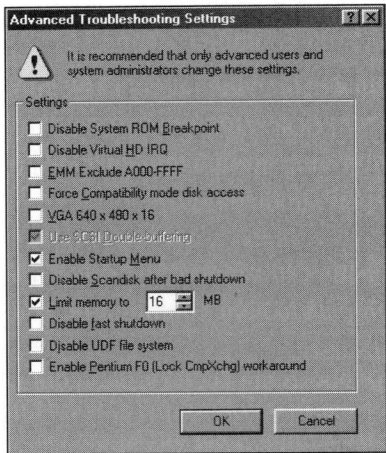

Figure 11-12: Use the Advanced Troubleshooting Settings dialog box to limit memory use for troubleshooting.

Step 4. Mark the "Limit memory to [   ] MB" checkbox, and enter **16**.

Step 5. Click OK. Click OK. Restart Windows.

If your computer restarts Windows and you don't get the error message shown at the beginning of this section, then your registry isn't damaged and you probably have a bad memory chip above the 16MB boundary. If you get the same error message, your bad memory chip may be below the 16MB boundary (if that is the problem). Download the memory test program RAMexam and check.

RAMexam runs in DOS and does a very thorough job of testing your memory. There is a demo version of it, which we found useless, on the company's Web site. The demo is also not a good representation of the program's capabilities. The full version costs $24 and you can download it from the Web, so you're not taking much of a financial risk.

You'll find RAMexam at http://www.qualitas.com.

Back Up Your Registry Once a Day

The Windows ScanRegistry applet scans your registry every time you restart Windows. If you use the Startup tab of your System Configuration Utility (Start ⇨ Programs ⇨ Accessories ⇨ System Information ⇨ Tools ⇨ System Configuration Utility ⇨ Startup), you'll see how it is called up when Windows starts.

ScanRegistry is configured to back up your registry once a day, no matter how many times it is called during the day. However, if you don't shut down your computer at night, ScanRegistry won't run and you won't have a daily backup (for the last five days).

You can add a call to your Task Scheduler to run ScanRegistry at night, so that each day you will have a new registry backup.

STEPS

Calling ScanRegistry at Night

Step 1. Open your Explorer, and click Scheduled Tasks in the left pane. Click Add Scheduled Task in the right pane.

Step 2. In the Scheduled Task Wizard, click Next and wait while your computer goes out and finds registered programs.

Step 3. Click the Browse button (see Figure 11-13), and navigate to Scanregw.exe in your \Windows folder.

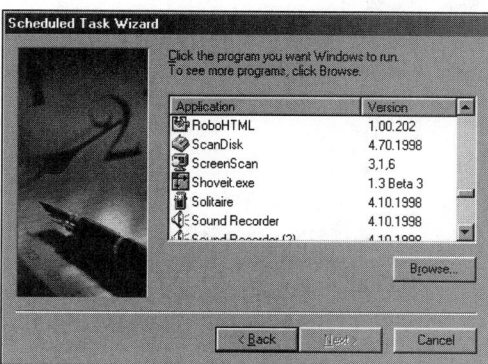

Figure 11-13: You won't find ScanRegistry in the application list, so use the Browse button to navigate to Scanregw.exe.

Step 4. Highlight Scanregw.exe and click Open.

Continued

STEPS

Calling ScanRegistry at Night *(continued)*

Step 5. Click Daily, as shown in Figure 11-14. Click Next.

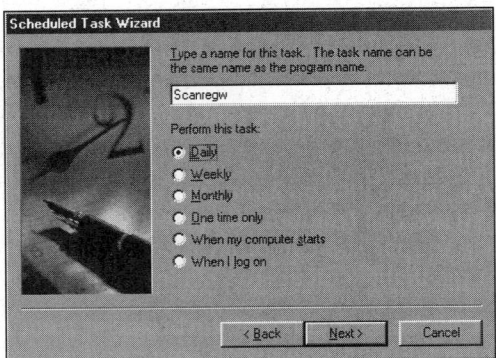

Figure 11-14: Mark the Daily option button.

Step 6. Set a time in the Start time field. Click Next.

Step 7. Mark the "Open advanced properties for this task when I click finish" checkbox, as shown in Figure 11-15. Click Finish.

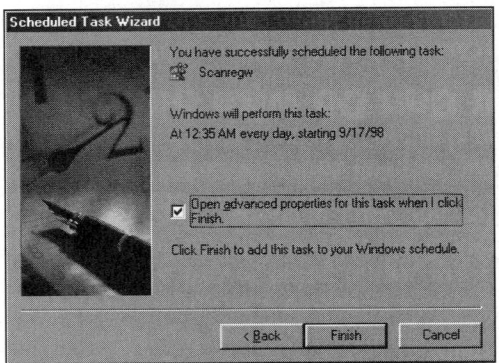

Figure 11-15: Mark the checkbox in the last wizard dialog box before clicking Finish.

Step 8.   Add a space and `/autorun` to the Run field, as shown in Figure 11-16. Click OK.

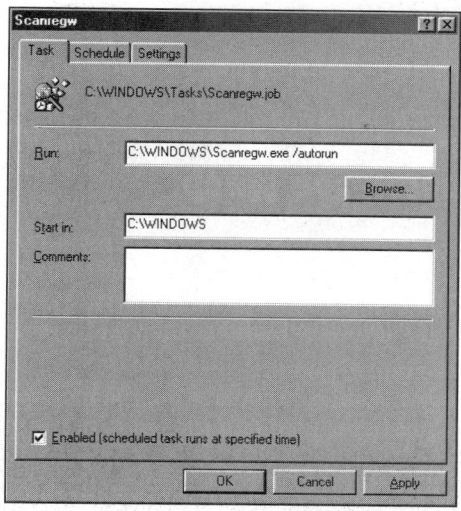

Figure 11-16: Edit the Run field as shown.

Your registry will now be backed up once a day at the scheduled time, presumably when you are not working on the computer.

Thanks to Daniel E. Germann for this tip.

Back Up Your Registry, Plus Other Settings and Files

The Windows registry backup program, `Scanregw.exe`, does an admirable job creating five daily backups of your registry automatically. If you want to create more backups and add additional settings and files to the backup file, check out WinRescue (see Figure 11-17). You can download this shareware from `http://www.superwin.com`.

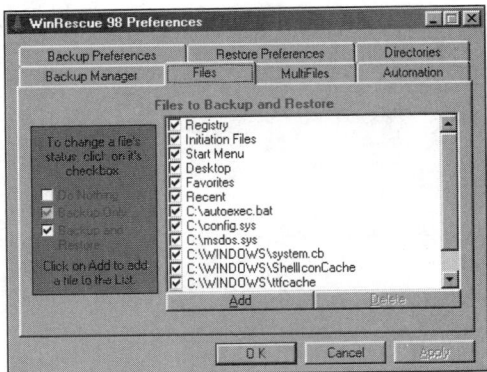

Figure 11-17: Use WinRescue's Files tab to select which files to back up and restore.

Emergency Recovery Utility Doesn't Come with Windows Me

We talk at length in Chapter 15 about backing up and recovering your registry. We also discuss a tool called Emergency Recovery Utility (ERU), which Microsoft included on the old Windows 95 CD. The ERU creates an emergency boot diskette with a copy of your registry and several other configuration files, such as Config.sys. Although in general we recommend using ScanRegistry instead of ERU, there may be times that ERU comes in handy.

You can still use ERU if you have access to a Windows 95 CD-ROM. Read the Eru.txt file found in the \Tools\Misc\Eru folder of your Windows 95 CD-ROM for details. Copy the four files you find in that folder to your \Windows folder, and then create a shortcut for Eru.exe and run it. If you don't have an ERU emergency boot diskette, make one right now. If your hard disk won't boot up (it's only a matter of time), boot from the floppy and you may be able to get your system back to normal.

Registry Key Backup

You can export any branch of your registry to a text file just by opening the Registry Editor, highlighting a key, clicking Registry ⇨ Export Registry File, and typing the name of the reg file that will contain the text version of the branch — simple, but not that powerful.

Suppose you want to export multiple branches into one `reg` file? Or, you want to repeatedly export the same set of branches as you make changes? What you need is a little utility that lets you define different sets of branches to be exported, and then saves these definitions for later use.

This is exactly what Registry Key Backup, a little freeware package, does for you. Click the Add button to open a new blank branches set, and then click the plus (+) button to navigate the registry and add branches to the set, as shown in Figure 11-18.

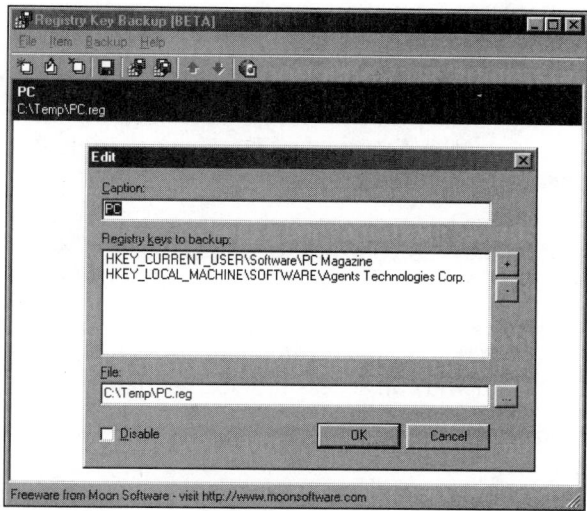

Figure 11-18: Use the + and – buttons along the right side of the Edit dialog box to navigate the registry.

You'll find this handy little tool at `http://www.moonsoftware.com`.

Don't Back Up Your Registry!

Every time Microsoft shows a registry edit in their Knowledge Base, which is plenty of times, they include a disclaimer asking you to back up your registry. They are not the only ones. We see this everywhere, and after a while it begins to look to us like the warning tags on pillows and mattresses that say *do not remove this tag*.

We've edited the registry for over five years, and not once have we backed it up before a registry edit! We've never had a problem.

We'll just bet that if you've done a number of registry edits, you've rarely backed up your registry (other than the automatic backups that happen when you start your computer for the first time each day). Therefore, all the warning messages aside, you're going bare, just like us. A fat lot of good the warning messages did!

There's a reason for this. The warning messages are too extreme. They tell you to do a bunch of work for the slight chance of something going wrong. One of the reasons they do this is to protect their authors' backsides. Just to be clear, we are not telling you to not back up your registry (in spite of the title of this section).

We think that you might want to take a little precaution if you are unfamiliar with registry edits, but this doesn't mean that you should back up the whole blessed thing. Before you make an edit that you are not sure about, export the little branch of the registry that you are working on. To do this, highlight a key above the one you are editing, and click Registry ➪ Export Registry File.

If you decide to undo your edit, you can merge the exported registry branch back in. If you've added keys to your registry, you'll have to delete them, because the merge function doesn't take anything out of the registry.

Of course, you still have a complete registry backup available to you at any time. Windows created it automatically (isn't that what computers are supposed to do?) and you can access it if you get in over your head.

To restore a previous registry, use the steps detailed in "Registry Recovery" later in this chapter.

Cleaning Your Registry

If you didn't uninstall a program correctly, or if the programmer didn't write the uninstall routines correctly for programs that you uninstalled, you left behind dead branches in your registry tree. It is possible for a utility program to check your registry against programs available on your computer (just by going through the folders and seeing if they are there) and determine if it can do a bit of registry pruning.

You have a couple of options. You can download either Perfect Companion, shown in Figure 11-19, from http://www.easydesksoftware.com/index. htm, or Microsoft RegClean from http://support.microsoft.com/support/ kb/articles/q147/7/69.asp. Both utilities work with Windows Me.

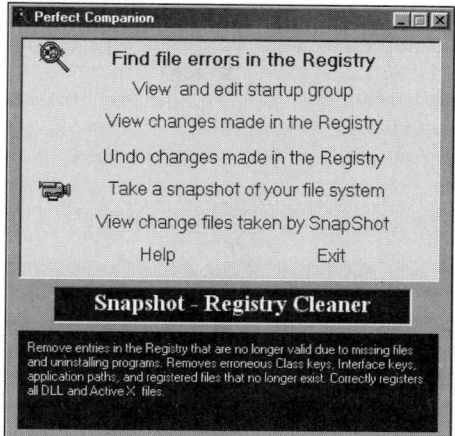

Figure 11-19: The Perfect Companion user interface

The DOS Version of the Registry Editor

You can edit the registry from the DOS prompt. This is useful if you are having difficulties starting Windows. To go to the DOS prompt without starting Windows, reboot your computer using your Windows Me startup disk. Choose the Minimal Boot option in the Startup menu.

Regedit.exe is a program that runs both in real-mode DOS and in Windows, with different behavior. In MS-DOS mode, you use command-line parameters to import and export the contents of the registry files to and from text files. You can also import and export just selected branches or delete a branch from the registry.

Earlier versions of RegEdit had trouble with particularly lengthy branches when running in real-mode DOS. This problem was fixed beginning with the OSR2 version of Windows 95.

If you type **Regedit /?** at the DOS prompt, you will get a little help on how to import and export the registry. You'll need to use the program Edit.com to edit the exported registry. Use RegEdit to import the edited registry file back into the registry.

The DOS RegEdit syntax is as follows:

```
REGEDIT    {/L:system}    {/R:user}    filename1
REGEDIT    {/L:system}    {/R:user}    /C filename2
REGEDIT    {/L:system}    {/R:user}    /E filename3 {regpath1}
REGEDIT    {/L:system}    {/R:user}    /D regpath2
/L:system  Specifies the location of the System.dat file
/R:user    Specifies the location of the User.dat file
```

```
filename1  Specifies the file(s) to import into the Registry
/C filename2    Specifies the file to create the Registry from
/E filename3    Specifies the file to export the Registry to
regpath1   Specifies the starting Registry key to export from
(Defaults to exporting the entire Registry)
/D regpath2     Specifies the Registry key to delete
```

You can export and edit the whole registry or just a branch of it. Don't import a branch back into the registry with the /C (create) option. This will create a registry with only one branch.

Summary

If you can edit the registry, you have complete control of Windows.

▶ We explain how to recover from fatal conditions in the registry.

▶ We show you how to get that extra margin of safety by backing up your registry with ScanReg before you edit.

▶ We describe a number of keystroke shortcuts to help you edit and display the registry more quickly.

▶ We introduce you to editing registries across a LAN.

▶ If there is a real problem starting Windows, we tell you how to edit the registry in DOS.

▶ Compare your registry before and after you make changes to it.

▶ Set the registry scanner to create a new backup of your registry every day, even if you don't turn off your computer at night.

▶ Save registry backup configurations to make it easier to export branches of your registry.

▶ Prune the dead branches of your registry left over from incorrectly uninstalled programs.

Chapter 12

Documents First

In This Chapter

Why have an application in the way of getting to your documents? We show you what you need to know about:

▶ Opening, printing, or taking other useful actions on a file with two clicks

▶ Opening Word files that don't have doc extensions without opening another copy of Word

▶ Creating your own file types and defining convenient actions to take on them without having to first open the application

▶ Making Notepad instead of the slower WordPad the program of choice to edit batch files

▶ Clearing the Documents list on the Start menu

▶ Opening new blank documents on your Desktop

Associating Actions with File Extensions

Like all prior versions of Windows, Windows Me uses file extensions to designate file type. A file with the extension txt can be, and is by default, designated as having the file type of *text*. Your computer can take certain *actions* on files depending on their file type. For example, sound cards can play music files.

Usually, applications perform the actions. For example, a file with the extension cda contains information necessary to successfully play an audio track, but it needs Windows Media Player (or any other application that can read cda files) to perform the action — to actually play the song.

You can choose (and modify) the actions that will be taken on a file from among all the possible actions that are open to you. The available actions depend on what Windows provides and which other applications you have installed on your computer.

File types and their associated actions are defined (registered) in the registry files. Windows defines more than 100 file types (and their associated actions) before you get a chance to define your own.

Where Are These Actions?

If you right-click a file of a registered (defined) file type, a context menu appears. In the top section of the context menu are the actions defined for this file type, including any actions you have added. The action listed in boldface (usually the first choice) is the default action. If you click the file, this action occurs.

It is quite possible for an application to be able to take literally thousands of different actions on a file. Just think of the many different ways that a word processor (with your help) acts on a document. Not all the actions that an application can undertake need to or should be defined in the registry.

It only makes sense to define certain kinds of actions in the registry. Actions that can be taken without significant additional user input come to mind, such as opening, printing, translating the file from one format to another, playing (musically speaking), and updating.

Creating and Editing File Types and Actions

The file type/action association is fundamental to the document-centric character of Windows. Without it, you could not click a filename or file icon on the Desktop or in a window and have it and its application open in a window. You would always have to start an application first, and then search for the document in the application's File Open dialog box.

One of the main purposes of the Windows "Desktop" metaphor is to make applications subservient to the data or document. This metaphor falls down when you can't get to your data without going through an application. If you can right-click a file and choose among associated actions in the context menu, it feels like the file is in charge.

You can change which file extensions are associated with which actions. You can add (or register) new extensions. When you install Windows Me over an existing Windows 3.1x or Windows 9x directory, the Setup program reads your existing Win.ini and registry files and places all your existing file types and their associated actions in the Windows Me registry files.

When you install a new application under Windows, the application stores all its defined file types and their associated action(s) in the registry. The associated action may simply be opening a file.

You can edit or add new file type/action associations in either a My Computer window or an Explorer window. To do so, take the following steps:

STEPS
Viewing File Types

Step 1. Right-click My Computer and choose either Open or Explore.

Step 2. Choose View ⇨ Folder Options to display the Folder Options dialog box, and click the File Types tab (see Figure 12-1).

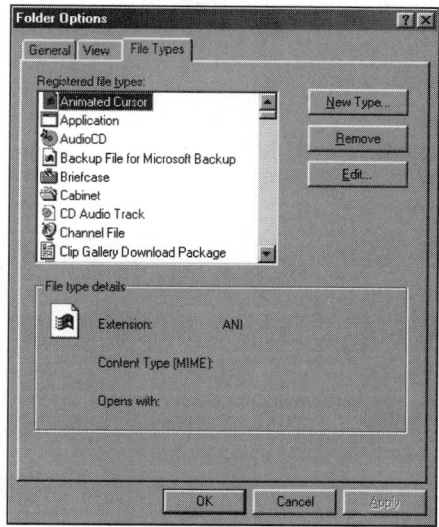

Figure 12-1: The File Types tab of the Folder Options dialog box. Scroll the Registered File Types list to view all registered file types.

Step 3. You can use the New Type, Remove, and Edit buttons to create a new registration for an extension, remove an existing registered extension, or edit the description and associated actions for an existing file type.

Creating a New File Type

New file types are usually created when you install a new application. The application developers designate a set of file extensions that are associated with their application, and they include code in the application setup routine that edits your registry to register their file types and associated application actions.

You can also create your own file types and application actions. While you can do this by editing the registry directly (see "File Associations via the Registry" later in this chapter), you can accomplish the same thing by using dialog boxes. If you only want to define the Open action for the new file type, it's fastest to use the Open With dialog box (see "Multiple Extensions — One Application" later in this chapter). If you want to define actions other than Open, you need to use the Add New File Type dialog box, as described here.

STEPS

Creating a New File Type

Step 1.   If you haven't already done so, follow the "Viewing File Types" steps in the previous section to display the File Types tab of the Folder Options dialog box.

Step 2.   Click the New Type button to display the Add New File Type dialog box (see Figure 12-2).

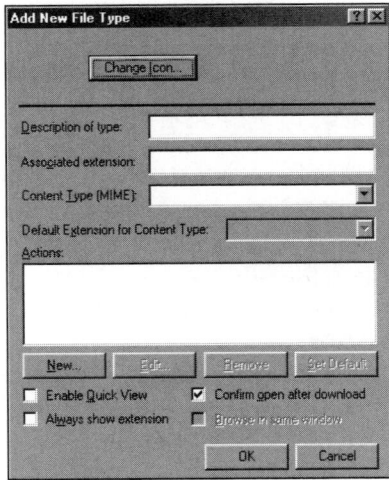

Figure 12-2: The Add New File Type dialog box

Step 3. Press Tab once. Enter a description of the file type in the "Description of type" field. The new file type will be listed in the File Types tab of the Folder Options dialog box in alphabetical order by the first letter of this description. Any name that is relevant to you is okay.

Step 4. Enter the file extension in the "Associated extension" field. The extension should be no longer than three letters if the application can't handle long filenames — that is, an old Win-16 application or one written for Windows 3.1*x*. You don't have to type the period.

You won't be allowed to enter an extension that is already registered. This prevents Windows from having to choose between applications when you click a file.

Step 5. If your file type has a defined content type (such as HTML, GIF, JPF, AVI, or MPEG), select it from the Content Type (MIME) drop-down list. The Default Extension for Content Type field will display the default extension as soon as you choose the content type.

Step 6. Click the New button. The New Action dialog box is displayed, as shown in Figure 12-3. In the Action field, enter an action that you want an application to perform on files of this file type. You might want to begin by defining the default action that an application performs on the file when you click it.

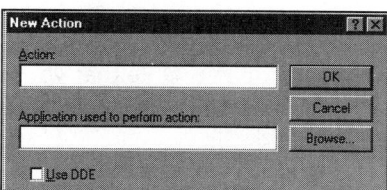

Figure 12-3: The New Action dialog box

You can use any action name you like. You will associate your action name with an action that you define. You can define a number of different actions, and name each one.

For example, Open and Print are possible action names. Windows will use the action names you choose to describe the associated actions, so you should make them understandable.

Put an ampersand (&) in front of the letter that you want to use to select the action from a context menu with the keyboard. For example, &Open underlines the letter O, so you can press the O key and then Enter to execute this action from the keyboard. Capitalize the first letter of the action.

Continued

Step 7. In the "Application used to perform action" field, enter the name of an application that will perform the named action and that is associated with the file type. Type the complete pathname and the application filename. Add to the application name the command-line parameters that will instruct the application to perform the action.

For example, if you want a text file to be printed, you might define the action named Print as **C:\Windows\Notepad.exe /p.** If the application is in a folder with a space in its name, you need to surround the application and its pathname with double quote marks:

```
"C:\Programs Files\Accessories\MSPaint.exe" "%1"
```

This action will open a file (referenced by the parameter %1) using Microsoft Paint.

The possible actions that an application can take on files of this type and the macro language of the application program determine which action names make sense. The default action for most applications is Open. If you put the filename of the application in the "Application used to perform action" field without any command-line parameters, the action it will most likely carry out is to open the file that you right-clicked.

If you put in command-line parameters, don't put double quote marks around them. For example:

```
"C:\Program Files\Accessories\MSPaint.exe" /p "%1"
```

Figure 12-4 shows a way to modify how files with extensions other than doc can be opened by Word for Windows without opening a new copy of Word when it is already active. If you don't use DDE to send a message to Word, another copy of Word is opened when you click a file with an extension other than doc.

Step 8. Click OK when you have finished defining the application's action to return to the Add New File Type dialog box. You can continue defining new actions for a given file type by repeating Steps 6 and 7. The actions you define will be listed in the Actions box in the middle of the Add New File Type dialog box. When you've finished defining actions, select one of the actions in the Actions box and click the Set Default button. This will define the selected action as the action that occurs when you click the file.

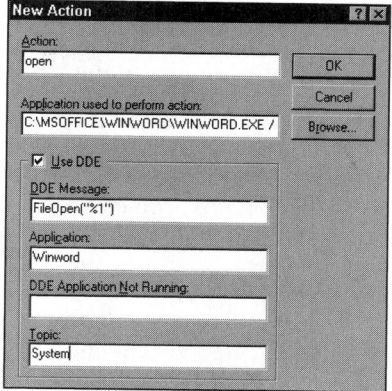

Figure 12-4: Using DDE to modify how a file is opened by Word for Windows.

Step 9.   If you want to change the icon that will represent the new file type, you can do so by clicking the Change Icon button in the Add New File Type dialog box. Optionally mark one or more of the checkboxes at the bottom of the dialog box (see the next four sections for descriptions of these options) and then click OK, and click OK again to close the Folder Options dialog box.

Tip

Windows Me also uses this field to sort files in folder and Explorer windows when you use Details view and order by type. When you order by type, Windows Me and 98 don't sort files by their extension, as was true under Windows 3.1*x*. Rather, they sort files in alphabetical order by the contents of the Description of Type field.

Secret

You can also use Dynamic Data Exchange (DDE) to modify the behavior of the application by passing it a message. If the application has a macro language, you can use that macro language to make the application behave in all sorts of different ways when you choose some action on the context menu. If you want to use DDE to define an action, mark the Use DDE checkbox. Windows expands the dialog box to display additional fields that let you specify how you want to use DDE.

You now have a new file type — a new file extension that is associated with a given set of actions, which most likely originate in one or more applications. All of the actions appear on the context menu that is displayed when you right-click a file of this type.

Confirm Open After Download

If the "Confirm open after download" checkbox at the bottom of the Add New File Type (or Edit File Type) dialog box is marked — the default choice—Windows will ask whether you want to open files of this type after you download them from an Internet site. This is a safety measure to guard against viruses that could be hiding in executable or document files.

Enable Quick View

If you mark the Enable Quick View checkbox at the bottom of the Add New File Type (or Edit File Type) dialog box, you can use Quick Viewers to see files on the Desktop without having to open (or even own) an application that is normally used to open them. Windows ships with more than 20 viewers for some common file types. Application developers can ship their own Quick Viewers with their applications. In addition, Inso Corporation, the maker of Outside In and the Quick View technology, ships Quick View Plus, which contains many more viewers.

Quick View is not installed during the typical Windows setup. If you used our guidelines to select components in Chapter 2 and did a custom setup, you had the opportunity to install Quick View then. If you want to install it now, click the Start button, point to Settings, and click Control Panel. Click the Add/Remove Programs icon, click the Windows Setup tab, click Accessories, and then click the Details button. Scroll down to the Quick View checkbox. Mark it and then click OK twice. You may be asked for your Windows CD-ROM.

You can implement this feature for a file type that has an associated Quick Viewer by marking this box. If you installed the application, it should have marked this box during setup.

Always Show Extension

If you mark the "Always show extension" checkbox in the Add New File Type (or Edit File Type) dialog box, Windows will show the extension for this file type even if the "Hide file extensions for known file types" option is checked in the View tab of the Folder Options dialog box (choose View ⇨ Folder Options in any Explorer or folder window).

Browse in Same Window

ActiveX (or OLE 2) applications such as Microsoft Word can pop up in the Internet Explorer window. If you click a link in a Web page that points to a Word document, for example, you can decide whether the Word document is displayed in the Internet Explorer window or in a separate Word window. Clear this checkbox if you want it to be displayed in a separate window.

Editing an Existing File Type

To edit an existing file type, choose View ⇨ Folder Options (in any Explorer or folder window) and click the File Types tab. Select the file type whose actions, icons, or associated application(s) you want to change and click the Edit button. You will be presented with the Edit File Type dialog box, which, with the exception of the name, looks just like the Add New File Type dialog box.

You can use the Edit File Type dialog box to add new actions, edit or remove existing ones, or declare a different action as the default. You can also change the icon associated with the file type if you like. The steps for editing a file type are very similar to the ones detailed in the "Creating a New File Type" section earlier in the chapter.

One Application Associated with Two File Extensions

Secret

If you scroll carefully through the list of registered file types in the File Types tab of the Folder Options dialog box, you will find some file types that show two file extensions. If you use the New Type button on the File Types tab of the Folder Options dialog box, you will find that you can't create a new file type with two extensions. You also can't add extensions to an existing file type. You can, however, do this using the Registry Editor or the Open With dialog box. (See the section entitled "Multiple Extensions — One Application" later in this chapter.)

File Associations via the Registry

Secret

The File Types tab of the Folder Options dialog box is a front end to the registry — but then so are most of the dialog boxes that you deal with in Windows. You can edit the Registry entries for your file types directly, if you like, using the Registry Editor.

STEPS

Editing File Types in the Registry

Step 1. Go to "The Registry Keys and Structure" section in Chapter 11 if you need to learn more about the registry. If you have put a shortcut to the Registry Editor on your Desktop, click it. Otherwise, click the Start button, select Run, enter regedit, and click OK.

Step 2. Click the plus sign next to HKEY_CLASSES_ROOT to expand this branch of the registry. The first keys shown are the file extensions. They all start with a period. There should be at least 100 keys, all marked with folder icons, as shown in Figure 12-5.

Continued

STEPS

Editing File Types in the Registry *(continued)*

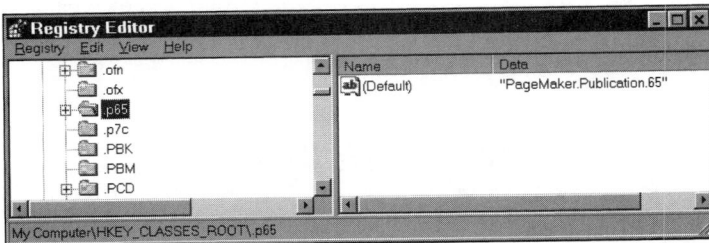

Figure 12-5: The registry listing of file extensions. The selected file extension is associated with Adobe PageMaker.

Step 3. Click any of the keys that are file extensions. A file type name will be associated with each one (listed in the right pane). Look at a few of these names to get an idea of how they are associated with the extension.

Step 4. Scroll down the HKEY_CLASSES_ROOT branch until you pass the extension keys and get to the file type names. Click the plus sign next to a file type name that corresponds to a file type or extension that you previously viewed in Step 3.

Step 5. Click the plus sign next to shell under the file type name. Notice that the action names associated with that file type are displayed. Click the plus signs by those action names and then click the command key, as shown in Figure 12-6.

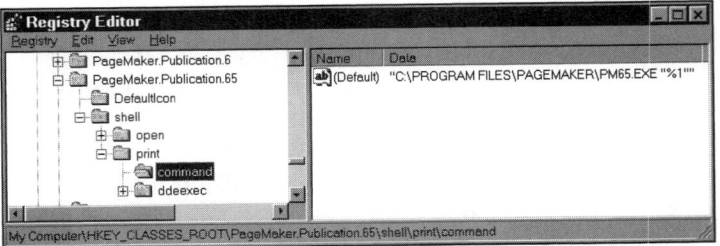

Figure 12-6: The file type names are displayed in the registry, along with the commands required to carry out assigned actions. This is the command key for printing a PageMaker publication.

Step 6. Notice that the action defined in the New Action (or Editing Action) dialog box is defined here. If DDE is used, you will find references to it under whichever action it was defined for.

Step 7.   Use the Registry Editor's New, Delete, and Rename commands (in the Edit menu) to create new file types or edit existing ones, using the models you explored in Steps 1 through 6. You may need to turn to "Editing with the Registry Editor" in Chapter 11 for more information on how to edit these values. When you are done, exit the registry.

You may find old file types and file type names that no longer apply. You can prune them out of the registry if you like.

Change the Edit Application for Batch Files

Tip

If you right-click an MS-DOS batch file (a file with the bat extension) while it is displayed in a folder window, and then click Edit, you will notice that Notepad is used to edit the file. To use WordPad instead of Notepad as the editor for bat files, take the following steps:

STEPS

Editing the Action Associated with Bat Files

Step 1.   Right-click My Computer and choose either Open or Explore.

Step 2.   Choose View ⇨ Folder Options and click the File Types tab.

Step 3.   Select MS-DOS Batch File in the Registered File Types box. Click the Edit button.

Step 4.   Highlight Edit in the Actions field and notice that the Edit button is grayed out. You can't change the application associated with editing a batch file this way. This is why you need access to the registry.

Step 5.   If you have a shortcut to the Registry Editor on your Desktop, click it. Otherwise, find Regedit.exe in the \Windows folder using the Explorer or My Computer and click it.

Step 6.   Click the plus sign next to HKEY_CLASSES_ROOT. Scroll down to batfile. Click the plus sign next to batfile. Click the plus signs next to shell, and then edit.

Step 7.   Select command. Click Default in the right pane of the Registry Editor.

Step 8.   Type **"C:\Program Files\Accessories\Wordpad.exe"** %1.

Step 9.   Exit the Registry Editor.

Multiple Extensions — One Application

Secret

Using the Registry Editor, you can create multiple extensions and associate them with one application. If you have Microsoft Word installed, you will notice that the extensions .dot and .doc in the registry (under HKEY_CLASSES_ROOT) both refer to Word Documents. This is how multiple extensions are associated with one application.

Using the Registry Editor, you can edit an entry for an extension to change the application that the extension is associated with. Highlight an extension entry in the Registry Editor, click Default in the right pane of the Registry Editor, and type a new file type name or the name of an existing file type.

If you created a new file type name, you will then need to create a new key value in HKEY_CLASSES_ROOT by that name. In addition, you will need to define some actions that are associated with that file type. Use the existing keys in this section of the registry as examples.

You can also use the Open With dialog box to associate a new file type with the Open action for an existing application. Unfortunately, when using Open With, the only action you can associate with this new file type and extension is the Open action. Other actions may be associated with the file types that were created when the application was first installed, and you can't use the Open With dialog box to associate these actions with the new file type and extension. However, once you've used Open With to associate a file type with an application, you can edit the file type to associate it with other actions.

To see how the registry is changed when you use the Open With dialog box, take the following steps:

STEPS

New File Types with Open With

Step 1.   Right-click the Desktop, point to New, and click Text Document.

Step 2.   Rename the document **Test.tst**. Click Yes when warned about changing the extension. (Be sure that you are showing your MS-DOS extensions. To do this in the Explorer, choose View ⇨ Folder Options, click the View tab, clear the "Hide file extensions for known file types" checkbox, and click OK.)

Step 3.   Right-click Test.tst. Choose Open With on the context menu. Choose some existing registered application or click Other to specify any other application. Exit the application after Test.tst has been opened.

Step 4. Now open up your Registry Editor, scroll down HKEY_CLASSES_ ROOT to .tst, and find the application name associated with this extension. Scroll further down and find this application name. Notice the associated command for opening a file in the application. Close the Registry Editor.

Editing (Not Merging) Exported Registry Files

Tip

Exporting your registry or a branch of your registry creates a file with a reg extension. The default action for this file type is Merge, as in merge this file back into the registry. We find this a bit dangerous because you could easily make changes to your Registry when you were expecting to view the file contents instead. Fortunately, you can easily change the default action for this file type.

STEPS

Changing the Default Action for an Exported Registry File

Step 1. Open a folder or Explorer window. Choose View ➪ Folder Options and click the File Types tab.

Step 2. Scroll through the Registered File Types list and select Registration Entries.

Step 3. Click the Edit button.

Step 4. Select Edit in the list of actions. Click the Set Default button.

Step 5. Click the Close button twice to close the Edit File Type and Folder Options dialog boxes.

Reassociating RTF Files with WordPad

Tip

If you install Word for Windows after you install Windows, the Open action for Rich Text Format (RTF) files is associated with Word and not WordPad. If you want to open this type of file with WordPad, edit the Open action associated with rtf files so it points to \Program Files\Accessories\ Wordpad.exe instead.

Secret

If you find that your new associations are reverting to their previous association (for example, if after changing the rtf association to WordPad, it goes back to Word), you are the victim of Microsoft's not-too-smart registry association update routines. These go in after you install a new program and update the registry based on what is in the [Extensions] section of the Win.ini file.

If you have an old association of `rtf` with Word in the `Win.ini` file, Windows might use it to "update" your registry and wipe out your new change. A way to get around this is to erase this association in the [`Extensions`] section of `Win.ini`. Unless you are using cc:Mail, you can erase this whole section. You might want to make a copy first, just in case.

Associating More Than One Program with a Given File Type

You can define many actions for a given file type. And you can associate each of these actions with a different application. Each action has to have a unique name. The following example describes one situation in which you might want to associate multiple programs with a single file type.

Tip

Files of the file type screen saver have an `scr` extension. Script files used by many different communications programs (although not by Windows Dial-Up Networking) also use the `scr` extension. You can create an action, which we call Edit Scripts, that is associated with script files. To do so, take the following steps:

STEPS

Associating an Edit Action with the Script File Type

Step 1. Open a folder or Explorer window. Choose View ⇨ Folder Options and click the File Types tab.

Step 2. Scroll through the Registered File Types list and select Screen Saver.

Step 3. Click the Edit button, and then click the New button.

Step 4. Type **Edit Scripts** in the Action field. Browse to `\Windows\Notepad.exe` in the "Application used to perform action" field.

Step 5. Click OK, then Close, and then Close again.

Opening Unregistered File Types

If you click a file that has an extension that is not registered, Windows will not try to open the file. Instead, it will display the Open With dialog box, as shown in Figure 12-7. This dialog box lists all the programs associated through actions to registered file types.

The "Always use this program to open this file" checkbox is marked by default. If, in general, you want files with this extension to be opened by the application that you are about to choose, then leave this box checked. You can also type a description of the file type in the Description of '.*XXX*' Files field. Choose a program to open this file by clicking the program name in the list box or by clicking the Other button to find the program that you want.

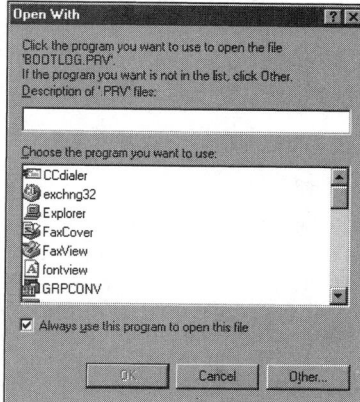

Figure 12-7: The Open With dialog box

If you just want to open this file now and not worry about establishing an association between its file type and an application, clear the "Always use this program to open this file" checkbox and click an appropriate program to open the file.

This method of opening files of an unregistered type gives you a great deal of flexibility, at a cost of having to scroll to find an appropriate application. It also lets you create new file types and associate them with applications without using the File Types tab of the Folder Options dialog box.

Opening a Registered File Type with Another Application

Sometimes, you might want to open a file whose file type is already registered and whose Open action is already associated with an application that you would rather not use this time. If you click the file in the Explorer or a folder window (or right-click the file and choose Open from the context menu), the associated application will open it.

Tip

Hold down the Shift key and right-click the file in an Explorer or folder window. An Open With command is added to the context menu, enabling you to choose an application other than the one already associated with this file type.

When you choose Open With, the Open With dialog box (refer to Figure 12-7) appears, but the "Always use this program to open this file" checkbox is not marked. If you want to change the associated Open action for this file type to the new application, mark this box. (If you only want to use the new application this one time, leave it blank.)

This is a quick way of changing the associated Open action for a given file type. You don't have to go to the File Types tab in the Folder Options dialog box and edit the reference to the application associated with the Open action. When you use the Shift+right-click method, you just change the default Open action, and leave the other actions as they are.

Create a Default File Opener

Secret

You can define a default program that will always open a file of an unregistered type when you right-click the file and choose OpenNote (or a different name of your choosing) from the context menu. This lets you avoid going through the rigmarole of the Open With dialog box. A variation on this method lets you open the file with a click.

STEPS

Defining a Default File Opener

Step 1. If you have a shortcut to the Registry Editor on your Desktop, click it. Otherwise, find Regedit.exe in the \Windows folder using the Explorer or My Computer and click it.

Step 2. Click the plus sign next to HKEY_CLASSES_ROOT. Scroll down the left pane until you find Unknown. Click the plus sign next to the Unknown folder icon. Click shell.

Step 3. Choose Edit ⇨ New ⇨ Key. Type **OpenNote**, and then select OpenNote.

You don't have to name the command OpenNote. You can type any name that will make sense to you as a menu item in the context menu and that corresponds with the action or command that you are about to define.

Step 4. Choose Edit ⇨ New ⇨ Key. Type **command**. Highlight the command folder icon.

Step 5. Click Default in the right pane of the Registry Editor. Enter the filename and path to the application that you want to use as the default file opener. For example, type **C:\Windows\Notepad. exe %1**.

Step 6. Click OK and exit the Registry Editor.

A variation on these steps lets you click to open a file of an unregistered file type with the default file-open application. You need to first examine the *openas* key under the *shell* key described in Step 2 above because you are going to delete it (and the *command* key under it) and then put it back in.

The steps required to do this are the same as the ones given above — but before you take Step 3, examine *openas*, write down the command data, and then delete the *openas* key. After Step 5, use Edit ⇨ New ⇨ Key to put the *openas* key and its *command* key back in as before, but now under OpenNote (or whatever name you chose).

Now when you click a file of an unregistered type in Explorer, it will open the file in the specified program. Both OpenNote and Open With will now be in the context menu when you right-click an unregistered file. You can still use Open With if you want to choose a different program to open the file.

You can substitute other applications instead of Notepad for your default file opener. You might try WordPad. Unlike Notepad, which chokes on nontext files, WordPad can open files of almost any format except executables. If you have a hex editor, use that in this example instead.

General Actions on Any File Type

Secret

You can define a set of actions that will apply to any file type or to any unregistered file type. These actions will then appear in the context menu when you right-click any file or when you right-click any file of an unregistered file type. Matthias Koenig showed us this little gem.

In the earlier section entitled "Create a Default File Opener," we showed you how to use the Registry Editor to create OpenNote, an action that would open unknown file types with `Notepad.exe`. You had to use the Registry Editor to create this action because the "file types" Unknown and All are not displayed in the File Types tab of the Folder Options dialog box.

You can, if you like, display these two "file types" in the File Types tab of the Folder Options dialog box. Once they are there, you can define any actions you care to for them.

STEPS

Defining Actions for Any File Type

Step 1.   Right-click the Desktop, point to New, and then click Text Document.

Continued

STEPS

Defining Actions for Any File Type *(continued)*

Step 2. Rename the text document **All.reg**. Click Yes when asked about the extension change. (Be sure that you are showing your MS-DOS extensions. To do this in the Explorer, choose View ⇨ Folder Options, click the View tab, clear the "Hide file extensions for known file types" checkbox, and click OK.)

Step 3. Right-click the new document icon that you have just created and choose Edit. Type the following text into the document, save, and close it when you are done:

```
REGEDIT4
[HKEY_CLASSES_ROOT\Unknown]
"EditFlags"=hex:02,00,00,00
[HKEY_CLASSES_ROOT\*]
"EditFlags"=hex:02,00,00,00
```

Step 4. Right-click the All.reg document icon, and then click Merge.

Step 5. Open an Explorer or folder window. Choose View ⇨ Folder Options, and then click the File Types tab.

Step 6. The first entry should now be an asterisk (*), which stands for All file types. Scroll down the file types list to find the Unknown file type. You can use the methods described in this chapter to add new actions to these "file types."

Printing Files Using Other Applications

One of the biggest limitations of the Send To menu item is that you cannot configure a Send To command line with parameters. Say you have txt files associated with Notepad, but you frequently want to print txt files with WordPad because you like the fact that WordPad doesn't automatically add headers and footers to the output, as Notepad does. You could try adding /p as a parameter to the Wordpad.exe command line in a Send To shortcut, but it doesn't work. Windows ignores any parameters that follow the executable name in the shortcut. (To see the command line underlying a Send To shortcut, right-click the shortcut in the C:\Windows\SendTo folder, click Properties, and then click the Shortcut tab.)

The best way to get around this limitation is to define a shortcut that will appear on your context menus and do anything you desire. This will let you use your right mouse button to select a file and launch almost any action you can think of.

It's easy to define a new action for all files with a particular extension. Here's how to create a new context menu item that appears when you right-click a txt file in the Explorer or a folder window, and automatically prints text files through WordPad instead of Notepad:

STEPS

Printing a Text File Using WordPad

Step 1. In the Explorer, choose View ➪ Folder Options, and click the File Types tab.

Step 2. In the Registered File Types list, scroll down and select Text Document, click the Edit button, and then click the New button.

Step 3. In the New Action dialog box that appears, type **Print Using WordPad** as the Action. In the "Application used to perform action" checkbox, type the following:

"C:\Program Files\Accessories\WordPad.exe" /p

In this example, the quotes are necessary because one of the folder names contains a space. The parameter /p (which must be lowercase) causes Wordpad.exe to print the txt file.

Step 4. Click OK, and then click Close twice to exit the dialog boxes.

Back in the Explorer window, find a txt file and right-click it. You should see a new Print Using WordPad command on the context menu. Click this choice. You should see WordPad flash for a moment as it reads the file and automatically sends it to the printer.

You can create all kinds of commands for all types of files. Many applications support a variety of command-line parameters that launch different kinds of behaviors on files you open. Word for Windows, for example, supports the parameter /m followed by a Word command. For example, if you use /mFilePrintPreview with doc files, you can open documents in Print Preview mode rather than in Normal view. (In Word, choose Tools ➪ Customize ➪ Commands ➪ All Commands to see other possible commands you can use.)

Viewing a File Without Starting an Application

If you right-click a file icon in the Explorer, you may see Quick View in the context menu (if you don't, see the "Enable Quick View" section earlier in this chapter). You have this option if the file that you right-click is of a registered file type and Windows has a file viewer for that type.

Windows ships with more than 20 file viewers. These viewers know about the file format of the documents of a given file type. They can load quickly, read the document, and display it on your Desktop.

Microsoft encourages application developers to ship file viewers with their applications, so you may have additional viewers stored in the \Windows\System\Viewers folder. Windows Me ships with Quick Viewers for the file types shown in Table 12-1.

Table 12-1   Files Windows Quick Viewer Recognizes

File Extension	File Type
asc	ASCII
bmp	Windows bitmapped graphics
cdr	Corel Draw versions 4 and 5
dib	Windows bitmapped graphics
dll	Dynamic link libraries (application extensions)
doc	Microsoft Word 2.0, 6.0, and 7.0, WordPad, others
drw	Micrographic draw
exe	Executable format
inf	Windows setup files (text)
ini	Windows configuration files (text)
mod	Multiplan versions 3, 4, 4.1
ppt	PowerPoint version 4
pre	Freelance Graphics for Windows
rle	Bitmapped graphics (Run Length Encoded)
rtf	Rich Text Format
sam	Ami, Ami Pro
wb1	Quattro Pro for Windows
wdb	MS Works Database
wk1	Lotus 1-2-3 versions 1 and 2
wk3	Lotus 1-2-3 version 3
wk4	Lotus 1-2-3 version 4
wks	Lotus 1-2-3 or MS Works version 3
wmf	Windows Meta File
wp5	WordPerfect 5

File Extension	File Type
wp6	WordPerfect 6
wpd	WordPerfect demo
wps	MS Works word processing
wq1	Quattro Pro for MS-DOS
wq2	Quattro Pro for MS-DOS version 5
wri	Windows Write
xlc	MS Excel Chart
xls	MS Excel versions 4 and 5

Tip

Many of the applications that Quick View can display are either rarely used or not the latest versions. You can download free, updated Quick Viewers for Word and Excel from the Inso Web site (see last paragraph in this section).

All you have to do is right-click a file of one of the above file types (or with one of the above file extensions) and choose Quick View in the context menu. Quick View will display the file in a view window. If you want to edit the file and you have the associated application, click the Edit button in the view window and Quick View will load that application for you.

Secret

You can create a shortcut on the Desktop for the Quick Viewer, and then drag and drop files to the Quick Viewer from the Explorer or a folder window. If you drag a file to the Quick Viewer that is not associated with any viewer, Quick View will ask if you want to view it with the default viewer.

STEPS

Putting the Quick Viewer on Your Desktop

Step 1. Use My Computer or the Explorer to view the \Windows\System\ Viewers folder.

Step 2. Right-drag Quickview.exe to the Desktop and drop it there.

Step 3. Change the icon name to **Quick Viewer**.

For an even easier and quicker way to view files without a specific viewer, see the next section.

Inso, the manufacturer of Quick View, also offers Quick View Plus, which contains approximately 200 file viewers. Inso's latest version works with the Windows Explorer and Netscape Navigator (as an ActiveX component or as a Netscape Plug-In, respectively) to enable you to view other types of documents while online. You can find Inso at `http://www.inso.com`.

Easiest Way to View/Open an Unregistered File

If you right-click a file in the Explorer or in a folder window, you will see the Send To command in the context menu. When you point to it, a submenu appears, as shown in Figure 12-8. When you first set up Windows, this submenu should contain such items as 3½ Floppy, Desktop as Shortcut, Fax Recipient, Mail Recipient, My Briefcase, and My Documents.

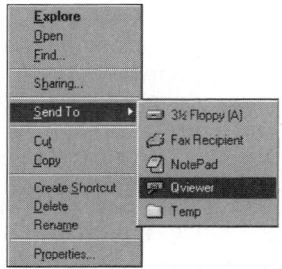

Figure 12-8: The Send To menu

The Send To list contains your common destinations.

You can add shortcuts to the Quick Viewer and your text file opener. Then, when you want to view or open a file of an unregistered type, you can right-click it, point to Send To, and then click either the Quick Viewer or the application you use as your text file opener. Here's how to set up Notepad as a text file-open application:

STEPS

Sending a File to Notepad

Step 1. Open an Explorer window. Make sure you can see all file extensions. If you can't, choose View ⇨ Folder Options, click the View tab, and clear the Hide "File extensions for known file types" checkbox.

Step 2. Navigate to the `\Windows` folder in the left pane and click the plus sign next to it. Then select the Windows folder icon.

Step 3. Scroll down the right pane until `Notepad.exe` is visible. Right-drag `Notepad.exe` to the SendTo folder icon in the left pane and drop it there. Click Create Shortcut(s) Here.

Step 4. Select the SendTo folder icon in the left pane of the Explorer. Select the Shortcut to `Notepad.exe` icon in the right pane and then press F2. Rename this icon **Notepad** and press Enter.

Step 5. Notepad will now be a choice in your Send To menu. You can place a shortcut to `Quickview.exe` in the SendTo folder in a similar manner. (See "Viewing a File Without Starting an Application" earlier in this chapter for more information about Quick View.)

Of course, you don't have to choose Notepad as your text file opener. You can also put numerous other shortcuts in the SendTo folder.

Documents on the Start Menu

If you open a file by clicking it (or by right-clicking it and then choosing Open) in a folder window or an Explorer window, a reference to it will show up in the Documents submenu of the Start menu. The last 15 documents you open this way appear on this list. If you want to work with one of these documents, simply click its name in the Documents submenu. Windows will start the application you used to create the document, and then open the document inside it.

If you open a document within an old-style, 16-bit Windows 3.1*x* application — using the File ⇨ Open command, for example — it does not show up on the Documents list.

You can put a shortcut to `\Windows\Recent` on your Desktop. This is another way to get to these recently opened documents, and it also lets you easily edit the list.

You can clean out the contents of the `Recent` folder every time that you start up Windows using a setting found in TweakUI. Just click the Paranoia tab and then select Clear Document History at Logon.

New Blank Documents

You can create blank documents by right-clicking the Desktop (or an empty part of a folder or Explorer window), pointing to New, and then clicking the desired document type.

Tip

If your desired file type isn't on the New menu, don't worry. Click any file type. When the New Blank Document icon appears, its name is selected. Type a new name with an extension of the registered file type you want. You will get a dialog box asking if you are sure you want to change the extension. You do.

The new file will contain the data associated with the file type you just chose (but not the file type associated with the new extension). If you chose to create a new document of the Text Document file type, but later change the file extension to doc, the file will still contain plain text until you save it in Word for Windows or another word processing document format.

Adding Items to the New Menu

You can use TweakUI to add items to the New menu (or remove them from the menu). It's a simple matter of dragging and dropping a blank document or file of the correct file type onto TweakUI's New tab. The document you drag needs to be associated with an application.

You might have installed an application, but an association with the file extension you want to use for the new blank document has not been created. You can easily create an association by first creating a new blank document in your application. Rename the document with the new extension that you want to associate with this application. Then Shift+right-click the new document in an Explorer or folder window, and choose Open With. Make sure the "Always use this program to open this type of file" checkbox is marked. Click the Other button in the Open With dialog box and browse to your application.

Once you have created an association between the document and an application, you can create a New menu item by dragging the blank document onto TweakUI's New tab.

Secret

You can also edit your registry to manually create the New menu item. This gives you complete control over the process.

If you are going to manually create a New menu item, the first step is to make sure you have registered the document type in the registry. Do this by following the steps in the section entitled "Creating a New File Type" earlier in this chapter.

Next, you need to edit the new file type's entry in the registry. The following steps show you how to do this:

STEPS

Creating an Item on the New Menu

Step 1. Go to "The Registry Keys and Structure" section in Chapter 11 if you need to learn more about the registry. If you have put a shortcut to the Registry Editor on your Desktop, click it. Otherwise, find Regedit.exe in the \Windows folder using the Explorer or My Computer and click it.

Step 2. Click the plus sign next to HKEY_CLASSES_ROOT to expand this branch of the registry. The first keys shown are the file extensions. They all start with a period. There should be at least 100 keys, all marked with folder icons.

Step 3. Click the file extension key that matches the file type you just created.

Step 4. Right-click the right pane of the Registry Editor. Choose New ⇨ Key. Change the name of the key to **ShellNew** and press Enter.

Step 5. Click the new ShellNew key in the left panel of the registry. Right-click the right panel. Choose New ⇨ String Value. Type the name **NullFile** and press Enter.

Step 6. Exit the Registry Editor when you are done.

The file type description for a file with this extension is now added to the New menu. When you select this file type from the New menu, Windows will create a text file, but it will have the extension you just picked in the registry.

Immediately Invoke an Application with a New File

If you want to have an application called immediately when you create a new blank file using the New menu, you can add a command string value to the ShellNew key. To do so, take the following steps:

STEPS

Invoking an Application When You Create a New File

Step 1. Follow the first five steps in the previous section.

Step 2. If it is not highlighted, click the ShellNew key in the left pane of the registry. Right-click the right pane. Click New ⇨ String Value. Type the name **command** and press Enter.

Step 3. Double-click *command*. In the Value Data field, type the path and filename of the application that will be invoked. Include a space and then a **%1** after the filename to allow the new file to be opened by the application. If the application is stored in a folder with a pathname that includes a space, put double quote marks around the combined path and filename of the application, and put double quote marks around the %1.

Continued

STEPS

Invoking an Application When You Create a New File *(continued)*

Step 4. Click OK and then exit the Registry Editor.

Taking Items off the New Menu

Install a bunch of applications and pretty soon your New menu gets unwieldy. You can take document types off the menu and put them back on when you need to. Again, TweakUI comes to the rescue. Just click the New tab and choose which items to keep on the menu.

TweakUI accomplishes its New menu management task by placing a minus sign as the last character in the ShellNew key name associated with the file type extension in the HKEY_CLASSES_ROOT section of the registry. You can use your Registry Editor to examine some of the file extensions listed and see how this works.

Summary

We describe how to make it easy to get to your documents without having to go through your applications first:

▶ The Desktop and folder windows can give you a view of your documents. It is such a bother to have to open an application first to see these documents and work on them. We show you how to get right to the document and let the application take care of itself.

▶ We show you how to create new file types and define actions that can be taken on files of those types — actions that can automate your work.

▶ We use the Registry Editor to change the assigned edit application for MS-DOS batch files from WordPad to Notepad.

▶ We show you how to create new menu choices for the right mouse button so that you can right-click (or click) your files and have something useful happen.

▶ We give you a couple of ways to create shortcuts for opening and viewing files of unknown file types.

▶ We describe how to clear the Documents list on the Start menu and open new blank documents on your Desktop.

Chapter 13

The Recycle Bin—Going Through the Trash

In This Chapter

We reveal the secrets and subtleties of deleting files, folders, and shortcuts, including:

▶ Using the Recycle Bin to store your deleted files and shortcuts until you are sure that you want to get rid of them

▶ Seeing how files are stored in these hidden folders

▶ Deleting (and copying, moving, and renaming) files in the common file dialog boxes

▶ Restoring deleted files and folders or moving the files to new locations out of the Recycle Bin

▶ Deleting files over a network

What's Recyclable About the Recycle Bin?

The Recycle Bin doesn't recycle anything but your disk space. If you want to stretch the analogy a bit, you could say that if you delete unused files, you won't have to go out and buy new hard disks, but that is stretching it.

Our take on the use of this symbol for the trashcan is that Microsoft realized people would rather have a Recycle basket on their Desktop than a trashcan. It is cooler. Right?

So why the Bin part of Recycle Bin? During the early stages of the development of the Recycle Bin—in beta testing of Windows 95 (then code-named Chicago)—its name was Recycle.bin. This is a pun. In a UNIX file system, *bin* is a standard subdirectory where the *binary* files (executable programs) are stored. Combine the trash-receptacle meaning of the word *bin* with its UNIX-world meaning, and the nerds at Microsoft got *.bin* on the Chicago Desktop. An art director or somebody in marketing made them get rid of the period and capitalize the *b*.

You can use TweakUI to rename the Recycle Bin. Click the TweakUI icon in your Control Panel, click the Desktop tab, scroll down to the Recycle Bin icon, right-click it, click Rename, and type a new name. Then click OK. The icon name will update as soon as you activate the Desktop.

The Recycled Folders

The Recycle Bin is an alias (a stand-in) for the special folders labeled Recycled. You can use the Explorer to see these folders — you'll find one on every hard disk and every logical drive on the hard disk. (If you have divided the hard disk into multiple drives, such as C, D, and so on, you will see a Recycled folder on each logical drive.) The Recycle Bin icon is displayed on the Desktop, and it's attached to the Desktop icon in the Explorer, on the same level as the My Computer and My Network Places icons. The Recycled folder icons are attached to the hard disk drive icons along with your other folders. (The Recycled folders are indeed folders, even though they don't have the standard folder icons.) They are designated as file type Recycle Bin.

If you click the Recycle Bin icon or any of the Recycled folder icons, you will find that they all display the same contents. Opening the Recycled folder icon attached to one hard disk will show the files deleted from your other local hard disks as well.

Microsoft made it a point to put the Recycle Bin on the Desktop and make it hard to remove. The Recycle Bin stores all the files that have been deleted from your hard disks. You have to go to only one place to find all your deleted files.

Secret

Want to get the Recycle Bin icon off the Desktop? Use TweakUI to clear it. Don't worry, you can still get to the Recycle Bin by going to the Recycled folders.

Secret

You can change the name of the Recycled folders; it just doesn't do any good. If you change the name *Recycled* to *Wasted*, the next time you start Windows, it creates a new Recycled folder. You end up with two recycle receptacle icons, both of which display the same list of deleted files when you click them.

If you were following along and really created a Wasted folder, now we have to bail you out. You have a Recycled folder and a Wasted folder. How do you erase or get rid of the Wasted folder? It's not so easy.

STEPS

Getting Rid of the 'Wasted' Folder

Step 1. Click Start ➪ Programs ➪ Accessories ➪ MS-DOS Prompt to open a DOS window.

Step 2. Change directories to the \Wasted directory. (You'll find it in the root directory.)

Step 3. Type **dir /a** to see if any files are stored in the Wasted directory. You are going to purge these files, so be sure to restore any that you might want to keep before you take the next step. To restore any of these files, right-click the Wasted folder, click Open, right-click any file that you want to restore, and click Restore.

Step 4. Type **Attrib -r -s -h Desktop.ini**.

Step 5. Type **del *.*** and press the Enter key.

Step 6. Change directories to the root directory of the hard disk partition that contains the Wasted directory (**cd **).

Step 7. Remove the Wasted directory by typing **rd Wasted** at the DOS prompt.

The Recycled folders are system resources. Windows regenerates them if you change the name of a Recycled folder. It doesn't want you to mess with these resources because it needs them to manage deleted files.

Secret

The Recycled folders are indeed folders, but they are special ones. When you display the contents of a Recycled folder in Details view, you'll see an additional column named Original Location. And Recycled folders don't use the folder icon. Furthermore, the Recycled folders are hidden so that you can't see them if you go to DOS and type **dir** (although you can see them if you type **dir /a**).

Windows puts the deleted files in these folders, but it stores them under new names (although you don't see this). Each Recycled folder contains an additional file named Info. Again, you don't see this file (unless you type **dir /a** at the DOS prompt). Windows combines the deleted files and the Info file to create entries that look like the original deleted filenames with the addition of a column that lists their original location.

What is really unusual about these Recycled folders is that their folder windows display the names and icons of all the deleted files, not just the ones stored in that particular folder or deleted from that particular logical disk drive. The files deleted from a particular drive, however, are actually stored in the Recycled folder on that drive. You can see this for yourself by going to the DOS prompt, changing directories to the Recycled folder on a particular drive, and typing **dir /a**.

The code that makes the Recycled folders special is stored in a dynamic link library named Shell32.dll. This file is referenced in the Desktop.ini file.

The Recycle Receptacle Icons

Both the Recycle Bin and the Recycled folders use a recycle bin as their icon. If there are no files in the Recycle Bin, the icon shows an empty bin. If there are any deleted files in the Recycle Bin, the icon displays white paper stuffed into the bin. This bin is for paper recycling only—no cans or bottles.

If you delete a file and the Recycle Bin was previously empty, the Recycle Bin icon on the Desktop changes to its "stuffed with white paper" state. If you click the Recycle Bin icon to open it and then drag a file to the Recycle Bin folder window, the Recycle Bin icon in the title bar changes from the empty state to the "stuffed with white paper" state.

If the Recycle Bin properties have been set to remove files immediately when deleted, a message box with a Shredding Paper icon (as shown in Figure 13-1) will appear when you issue the Delete command. You will be asked for confirmation before the file is purged from the file system. (To check your Recycle Bin's properties, right-click the Recycle Bin icon and choose Properties.)

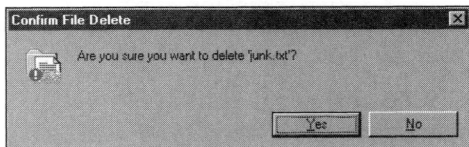

Figure 13-1: The Confirm File Delete message box. If you click Yes, the file is "deleted," in the sense that it is lost to the file management system and its space on the hard disk is free to be written over.

Secret

You can change the icons that represent an empty or a full Recycle Bin. Use your Registry Editor to navigate to HKEY_CLASSES_ROOT\ CLSID\ {645FF040-5081-101B-9F08-00AA002F954E}. Highlight DefaultIcon in the left pane. Double-click first on *empty* and later on *full* in the right pane. Type the path and filename for the files that contain the icons you want to use to represent the Recycle Bin in both states. See "New Icons for Desktop items" in Chapter 5 for more on this subject.

What Does the Recycle Bin Do?

Unless you have configured the Recycle Bin to remove files immediately on delete, the Recycle Bin stores the files (and shortcuts, which are stored as files) that you have deleted from your local hard disks using the Explorer or a folder window.

The deleted files remain in the Recycle Bin until you issue the Empty Recycle Bin command (by right-clicking the Recycle Bin icon and choosing Empty Recycle Bin, or by choosing File ⇨ Empty Recycle Bin in the Recycle Bin window). If you want to restore a file (or files) in the Recycle Bin, you can select it, and then choose File ⇨ Restore (or right-click the file and choose Restore). The selected file is returned to its original folder, even if the folder has been deleted. Windows restores the folder simultaneously.

You'll also see deleted folders in the Recycle Bin. You can restore a folder (and any subfolders it contains) by right-clicking the folder icon in the Recycle Bin and choosing Restore from the context menu. And unlike the pre-Internet Explorer 4.0 version of Windows 95, Windows 98 and Me let you restore empty folders. This is useful, since some transaction software uses empty folders as temporary storage and requires that these folders be always available.

You can send files or folders to the Recycle Bin in several ways. You can select a file/folder in a folder window or the Explorer and press Delete. You can right-click a file/folder and click Delete on the context menu. You can also drag and drop a file/folder to the Recycle Bin icon on the Desktop or in the Explorer, or to the Recycled folder icons in the Explorer and folder windows.

Emptying the Recycle Bin

As you have seen, dropping a file into the Recycle Bin or pressing the Delete key after selecting an icon does nothing more than move the file to the Recycle Bin. It certainly doesn't delete it — unless you chose the "Remove files immediately when deleted" option in the Recycle Bin Properties dialog box (right-click the Recycle Bin icon and choose Properties).

To delete the items in the Recycle Bin, click the Recycle Bin icon on the Desktop and then choose File ⇨ Empty Recycle Bin in the Recycle Bin window. All the files in the Recycle Bin are purged.

If you want to purge only some of the items in the Recycle Bin, select those items first and then choose File ⇨ Delete. Or, you can right-click the items that you want purged and click Delete in the context menu.

Delete Files from Common File Dialog Boxes

You can delete files from the common file dialog boxes that are used by Windows-aware applications. If you choose File ⇨ Open (or File ⇨ Save As) to display the Open (or Save As) dialog box, you can right-click a file and choose Delete from the context menu, or select the file and press Delete. The deleted file is stored in the Recycle Bin.

WordPad, Notepad, and MS Paint use these dialog boxes. The 32-bit versions of Word, Excel, and Access don't use these common dialog boxes, but use similar ones that don't have all their functionality. An example of the common file dialog box is shown in Figure 13-2.

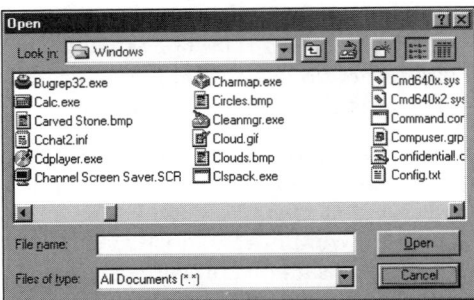

Figure 13-2: The Windows common file dialog box. You can highlight a file listed in this box and delete it by pressing the Delete key. You can also drag and drop files to and from this dialog box.

The Windows common file dialog boxes work a lot like folder windows. You can drag and drop files to and from them. You can rename files. You can create new folders or files. You can't, however, select multiple files or folders.

You can't delete files in the older common file dialog boxes, such as those used by the old Windows 3.1*x* Write. Microsoft now refers to these as *Win-16* common dialog boxes.

Deleted, What Does that Mean?

To *delete* a file means to move it to the Recycle Bin.

The fact that deleted files are stored in the Recycle Bin means that they aren't "really" deleted. They are still taking up space on your hard disk.

What is great about the Recycle Bin is that it allows you to organize and clean up your file system without having to make a decision that you may regret a few minutes later. If you delete something and then realize it's more important than you had thought, you can restore it easily.

The Recycle Bin provides a tradeoff between the safety and convenience of not deleting the file until later and the valuable disk space taken up by these deleted items. It is up to you to decide when to empty it.

Secret

Files that you delete in a DOS session are not sent to the Recycle Bin. Likewise, if an application deletes files without using an Explorer window, folder window, or the new common file dialog boxes, these files are not sent to the Recycle Bin. As far as the Windows or DOS file management system is concerned, the files are deleted. There are some third-party utilities that can still recover these files in some cases.

Do you want the files you delete in a DOS window to go to the Recycle Bin? You can if you use a little freeware application called Delete.exe. You'll find it at http://www.easytools.com/pages/deletex.html.

When you empty the Recycle Bin or delete files in a DOS session, the names of the deleted files are altered so that they don't show up in the file listings in the Explorer, folder windows, or DOS directory lists. The disk space taken up by the files is now available to be written over by new files. If they haven't been written over yet, you can recover these files by using low-level tools. For additional information, see the section entitled "Undelete and Unerase" later in this chapter.

To summarize, there are three levels of delete. If you delete a file in a folder or Explorer window, it is stored in the Recycle Bin. If you delete it from the Recycle Bin or delete it in a DOS window, it is deleted from the file management system. If you use low-level tools to wipe the space on the hard disk that it occupied, it can't be recovered. Still, a slightly earlier version of the file may be intact on the hard disk in some other location — in which case it would be recoverable.

Deleting Shortcuts

If you delete a shortcut, only the shortcut goes to the Recycle Bin, not the target (whether it be a file, application, or folder). The original item stays right where it was and continues to work fine. You are only deleting the shortcut file itself — which has an extension of lnk, pif or url — not the target of the shortcut.

Right- or Left-Drag to the Recycle Bin

There are many ways to delete a file. You can drag the file to the Recycle Bin icon, to a Recycled folder icon, or to an open Recycle Bin or Recycled folder window. If you left-drag the file icon, it is moved to the Recycle Bin. If you right-drag it, you are given the choice to move the file or cancel the move.

You can drag files back out of the Recycle Bin and place them in any folder, not just in their original location. If you right-drag a file out of the Recycle Bin to a folder window, you will be given the chance to move the file or cancel the move.

If you right-click a file icon and click Delete in the context menu, or if you highlight a file icon and press the Delete key, you will be asked to confirm your deletion. It doesn't matter if the Recycle Bin has been set to remove files immediately when deleted or not; you will still be asked for confirmation of the deletion.

If you drag a file (either left- or right-drag) to the Recycle Bin, you will not be asked for confirmation unless you've set the "Remove files immediately when deleted" option. The Windows designers assumed that if you were willing to go to all the trouble of dragging a file to the Recycle Bin, you meant it.

You can turn off the delete confirmation message by following these steps:

STEPS

Turning Off Delete Confirmation

Step 1. Right-click the Recycle Bin icon on your Desktop.

Step 2. Click Properties in the context menu.

Step 3. Click the Global tab (if necessary).

Step 4. Clear the "Display delete confirmation dialog box" checkbox.

Shift+Delete

You can delete files without sending them to the Recycle Bin—in other words, purge them—by highlighting their filenames, holding down the Shift key, and pressing the Delete key. (You can also hold down Shift while clicking Delete in a context menu.) The files won't be sent to the Recycle Bin because by deliberately holding down the Shift key, you are telling Windows that you want these files purged. Don't confuse this use of Shift+Delete with the use of Shift+Delete in word processors to send selected text to the Clipboard. Most word processors also support Ctrl+X to cut to the Clipboard, so if you use this key combination, you won't mix up the meaning of Shift+Delete.

Don't Delete Your Hard Disk

If you right-click a hard disk drive icon in the Explorer or in a folder window, you won't find Delete on the context menu. It's not a good idea to delete a hard disk. You can't. But you can delete—or move to the Recycle Bin—all the files on the hard disk by dragging the drive icon to the Recycle Bin.

We don't suggest you do this, especially if the space taken up by the current files on the hard disk is greater than the space set aside for deleted files in the Recycle Bin. If you delete a hard disk, you are moving all the files on the hard disk to the Recycle Bin. This is not possible if there isn't room for them there.

All this can get quite confusing. The Recycled folders are attached to a hard disk, but they show all the files that have been deleted or moved to the Recycle Bin, no matter which hard disk (or disk partition) they were deleted from. If you drag a hard disk drive icon to the Recycle Bin, are you also deleting the files stored in the Recycled folder? The next section addresses this question.

You Can't Delete My Computer or Other Key Components

You can drag My Computer, My Network Places, and the Recycle Bin and drop them on the Recycle Bin folder window. But when you do, you will just get a beep. Windows won't let you delete these things, thankfully.

The same is true of the Printers folder, the Control Panel, the Fonts folder, and the Dial-Up Networking folder. You just get a beep. You can try deleting one of these folders with a right-drag, which feels safer because right-dragging normally gives you a context menu confirming the move.

You *Can* Delete a Floppy Disk

Files on a floppy disk are not moved to the Recycle Bin when you delete them. (In fact, files you delete from any removable media are not sent to the Recycle Bin.) You can drag the floppy drive icon to the Recycle Bin (icon or folder window), and all the files will be purged after you are first advised of that fact and allowed to change your mind. The message box that appears displays an icon of a file being shredded as a way of indicating that your files will be very difficult to recover if you continue.

If you highlight a file that is stored on a floppy disk and press the Delete key, you will get the same notification. Windows just doesn't provide as much safety for files on floppy disks as it does for files on your local hard disks, although it does ask every time for confirmation of the deletion (purge).

Going Through the Trash — Retrieving Deleted Files

It is easy to get files back from the Recycle Bin. Just click the Recycle Bin icon on the Desktop to open the Recycle Bin folder window, as shown in Figure 13-3. Right-click the item that you want to restore, and then click Restore. The file is restored to its original location. If the folder that it was stored in has been deleted, it is restored also.

You can also just drag the files out of the Recycle Bin and move them to wherever you want. Dragging only moves files in and out of the Recycle Bin, no matter whether you right-drag or left-drag. If you right-drag, you won't see options for Copy, Create Shortcut(s) Here, or any other command you usually see in a context menu when you right-drag and drop.

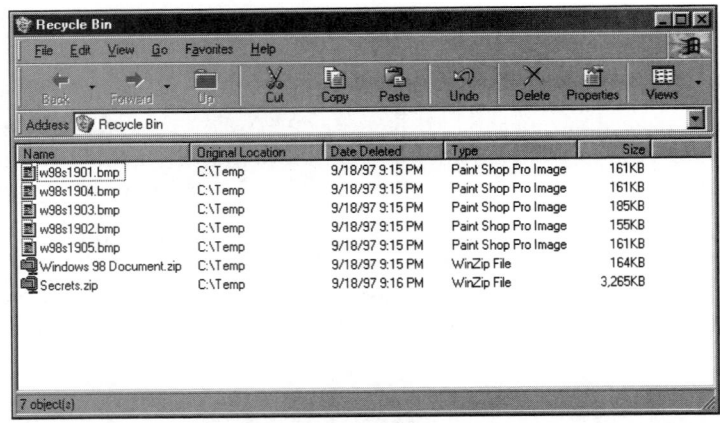

Figure 13-3: The Recycle Bin window. The second column lists the original location (folder) of the deleted file. To restore a file, right-click it and click Restore in the context menu.

Tip

You can use any of the selection techniques discussed in Chapter 8 to choose which files you want to move or restore to their original location. If deleting a file was the last file management action you carried out, you can choose Edit ⇨ Undo Delete in the Recycle Bin window, or right-click the window and choose Undo Delete from the context menu.

Secret

Do you want to check out a graphic or text file that you have already put in the Recycle Bin? Maybe you want to edit it after you deleted it. As long as you haven't emptied your Recycle Bin, you can drag and drop the file from the Recycle Bin onto your application icon. After you're done viewing the file you don't have to worry about deleting it, because it wasn't undeleted in the first place.

If you edited a file that's currently in the Recycle Bin and want to save its new version, save it to another folder. The name of the file in the Save As dialog box will default to its Recycle Bin name, which is not its original name (even though the original name is shown in the Recycle Bin window). This name is used internally by the Recycle Bin to track the deleted files. You may want to change it if you save the edited file to a new folder.

Tip

Unlike moving, copying, or deleting a file, emptying the Recycle Bin is not a recoverable action. You won't find Unempty the Recycle Bin on the context menu. (If the emptied files haven't yet been overwritten by other files, however, you may still be able to get them back with an Undelete utility, as we discuss later in this chapter.)

Remove Files Immediately When Deleted

You can set a Recycle Bin property to remove files immediately when deleted. When you delete a file, it is not moved to the Recycle Bin but is immediately purged from the file system.

When this option is set, if you drag files to the Recycle Bin or highlight them and press the Delete key, Windows confirms the file deletion because now they will be purged. This is also true if you right-click a file and choose Delete.

To set the properties of the Recycle Bin, right-click the Recycle Bin icon or the Recycle Bin folder window and choose Properties. The Recycle Bin Properties dialog box, as shown in Figure 13-4, appears on the Desktop.

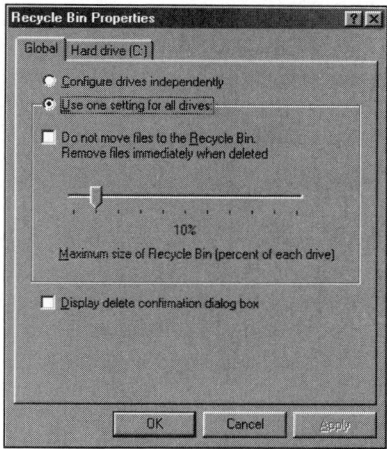

Figure 13-4: The Recycle Bin Properties dialog box. You can choose whether to remove files immediately on delete or not. You can choose the maximum size of the Recycled folders on each hard disk, and you can choose whether to configure the hard disks separately.

The Recycle Bin and Networks

If the Recycle Bin shows you all the deleted files, what if you are connected to a local or wide area network? Are you going to see all the deleted files on all the servers in your Recycle Bin? Nope.

Secret

You see only the files that you deleted from your local hard disks. It doesn't matter if the server resources (a hard disk or folder) are mapped to a local drive letter or not. You can click a Recycled folder on the host or server computer and you still will see only the files that you deleted from your local hard disks.

If you delete a file on the host, it is the same as if you deleted a file from a floppy disk — it is purged. The deleted file is not saved to the Recycle Bin.

Undelete and Unerase

If a file is purged, it is no longer recognized by the Windows file management system. Files are purged when you choose Empty Recycle Bin, when you hold down the Shift key and press the Delete key to delete a selected file, or when you delete a file and the Recycle Bin Properties dialog box has been set to remove files immediately when deleted.

When a file is purged, all that happens is that the first letter of its filename is changed so that it is no longer recognized as a legitimate filename by the file management system. The space taken up by that file is now available for use when other files are written to the hard disk.

DOS 6.x, which was used with Windows 95, came with an Undelete utility. This utility is not available with Windows Me or 98.

Symantec provides Norton Utilities for Windows. These utilities are integrated with the Windows Desktop and user interface, and they include an unerase capability. If you have installed Norton Utilities for Windows, when you right-click the Recycle Bin icon, you'll see some new commands in the context menu. Norton Utilities provides additional backup for deleted files by taking over the functions of the Recycle Bin.

Norton Utilities lets you unerase files that have been purged without having to use the Undelete utility in MS-DOS mode. Unerase has to deal with the same issues as Undelete: The deleted file's name has been altered, so although the hard disk space may still contain the purged file's contents, the space has been marked available. Use Norton Utilities' Unerase as soon as you can after you inadvertently purge a file to increase your chances of recovering it.

Summary

There are three layers of delete. We show you how the Recycle Bin helps you delete files without undue worry:

▶ You can access and manage the Recycle Bin with minimal effort. It is right there on the Desktop.

▶ We show you how deleted files are stored in a special hidden system folder that displays their properties in the Recycle Bin manner.

▶ The common file dialog boxes are like mini folder windows. We show you how to use them to delete files listed in them. You can also copy, move, and rename files listed in these common dialog boxes.

▶ You can move files into and out of the Recycle Bin to or from any location that you please. You can drag with either the right or left mouse button.

▶ If you delete files on a floppy or over a network, they really do go away without going to the Recycle Bin first.

Chapter 14

The Task Scheduler

In This Chapter

The Windows Task Scheduler has improved quite a bit since it was first introduced in the old Windows 95 Plus! package (a Microsoft add-on product). There are a few little gotchas, but we show you how to get around most of them:

▶ Changing the default maintenance schedule so that it works for you, especially if you don't leave your computer on all night, every night.

▶ If you can't add tasks to the Task Scheduler, it may be because you've labeled your boot partition *Windows*. We show you how to fix it.

▶ Stopping the Task Scheduler so that you can clear out its log file.

▶ You can run programs when you quit Windows — you just can't do it with Task Scheduler.

Reschedule Maintenance if Your Computer Doesn't Stay Up All Night

The Windows installation routines automatically set up your Task Scheduler to accomplish various useful tasks while your computer is idle. For example, you have the option of running the Maintenance Wizard, which lets you configure your maintenance tasks to run during the day or at night. The default is to run most of your tasks at night.

If you don't keep your computer on at night, then your Task Scheduler will never have a chance to run, and you'll miss out on the opportunity to have your computer's hard disk scanned and defragmented automatically. Fortunately, you can rework the schedule so that these useful tasks do get accomplished while you're not at the computer.

Secret

If you did a clean install of Windows Me, you may need to run the Maintenance Wizard — Programs ➪ Accessories ➪ System Tools ➪ Maintenance Wizard — to add the system maintenance tasks to the Scheduled Tasks folder for the first time.

If you'd rather not leave your computer on every night, you might want to reschedule most of the tasks to take place once a month, and then remind yourself to leave the computer on that night only. To take this approach, follow these steps:

STEPS

Running Your Tasks Once a Month

Step 1.   Click the Start button and choose Programs ⇨ Accessories ⇨ System Tools ⇨ Scheduled Tasks. Your scheduled tasks will appear as shown in Figure 14-1.

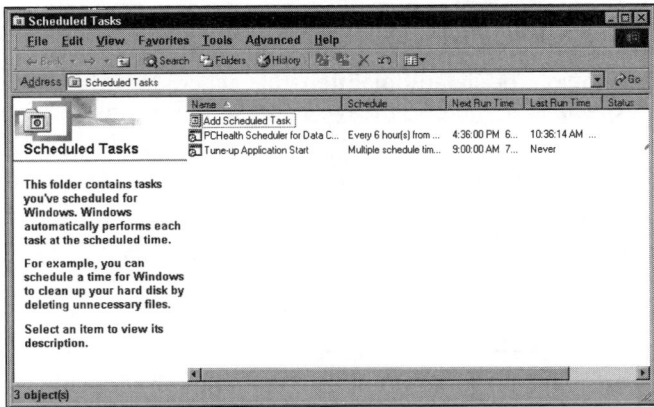

Figure 14-1: The Scheduled Tasks folder contains a list of scheduled tasks.

Step 2.   Click Add Scheduled Task, click Next, and wait a few minutes while the Scheduled Task Wizard searches your registry for registered applications, as shown in Figure 14-2. Highlight ScanDisk, and click the Next button. Continue using the wizard to define the task, and click Finish when done.

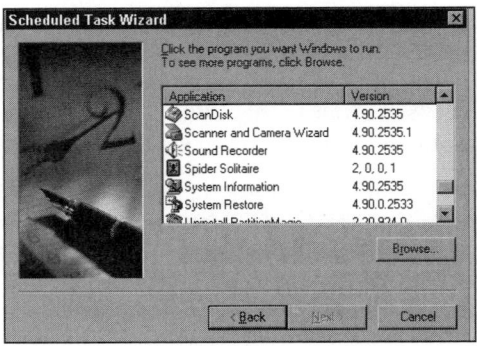

Figure 14-2: The wizard lists applications that you might add to your schedule.

Step 3. Right-click your ScanDisk item, and click Properties. Click the Settings button (not the tab), and make sure that Thorough and "Automatically fix errors" are marked, as shown in Figure 14-3.

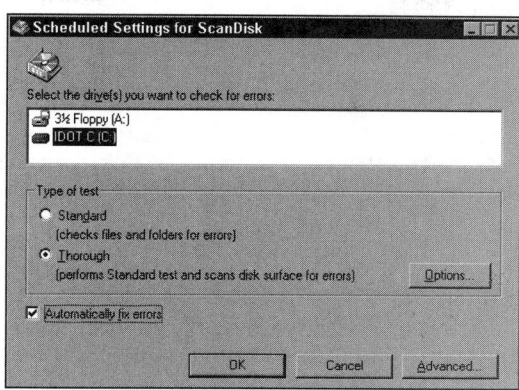

Figure 14-3: Mark the Thorough option button and the "Automatically fix errors" checkbox.

Step 4. Click the Schedule tab, display the Schedule Task drop-down list, and select Monthly. Click the Day option button and then choose a start time for this first task, as shown in Figure 14-4. Click OK.

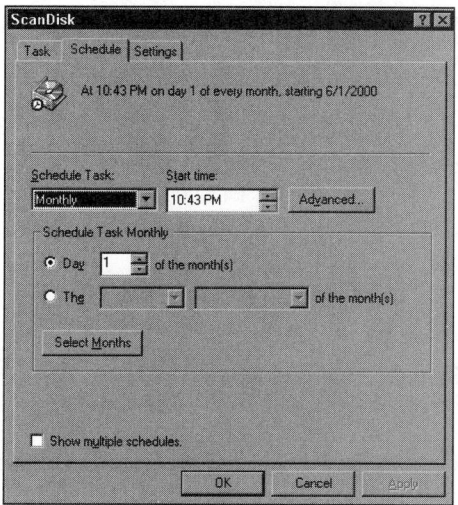

Figure 14-4: The Schedule tab, showing the settings for our example

Continued

STEPS

Running Your Tasks Once a Month *(continued)*

Step 5. Right-click the Maintenance-Disk Cleanup item in the Task Scheduler, if it's present. This task might be called Tune-up Disk Cleanup on your computer — if you're in doubt, check that the Run field on the Task tab says `C:\WINDOWS\CLEANMGR.EXE`. (If you don't see any Disk Cleanup item, follow Step 2 again, this time adding the Disk Cleanup task.) Click Properties. Click the Settings button on the Task tab, and make sure you've selected the files to be deleted automatically, as shown in Figure 14-5. Click OK.

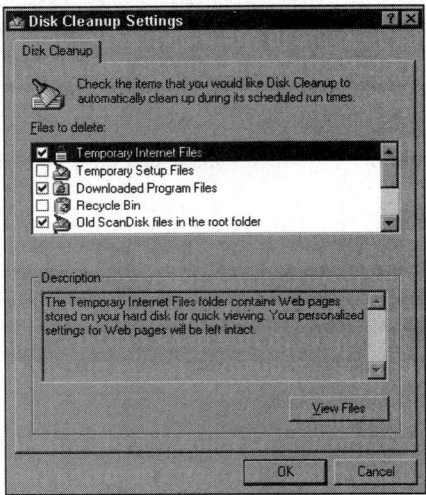

Figure 14-5: The Disk Cleanup tab provides a brief description of each item to help you decide whether to include it for deletion.

Step 6. Click the Schedule tab, and set Disk Cleanup to run an hour later than ScanDisk, but on the same night. Click OK.

Step 7. Right-click the Disk Defragmenter task in the Task Scheduler. (It may also be called Maintenance-Defragment Programs. If you don't see any Disk Defragmenter item, follow Step 2, this time adding the Disk Defragmenter task.) Click Properties. Click the Schedule tab and schedule the Defragmenter to occur on the same day of the month as ScanDisk and Disk Cleanup, but an hour after the cleanup. Click OK.

Tip

Now that you've set up your Task Scheduler to perform these tasks on one day of the month, you'll want to be sure that there are no conflicts between the Disk Defragmenter and your screen savers, power management, or any other applications.

Tip

While you're setting up tasks in the Task Scheduler, be careful not to run intensive disk activities too often. Computer technicians recommend that you don't schedule a thorough scan of your hard disk every night, for example. This can wear out a hard drive more quickly than normal usage will. A scan once a month should take care of most problems that might arise.

Did the Scheduled Tasks Get Done?

Your scheduled tasks are supposed to happen in the background, but your computer may have been turned off when they were supposed to take place. You can keep track of what happened to your scheduled tasks by clicking the Scheduled Tasks icon in the left pane of your Explorer.

Switch to Details view (View ➪ Details) and scroll the right pane to the right until you can see the Status column, as shown in Figure 14-6. If a task was missed, it will say so in this column.

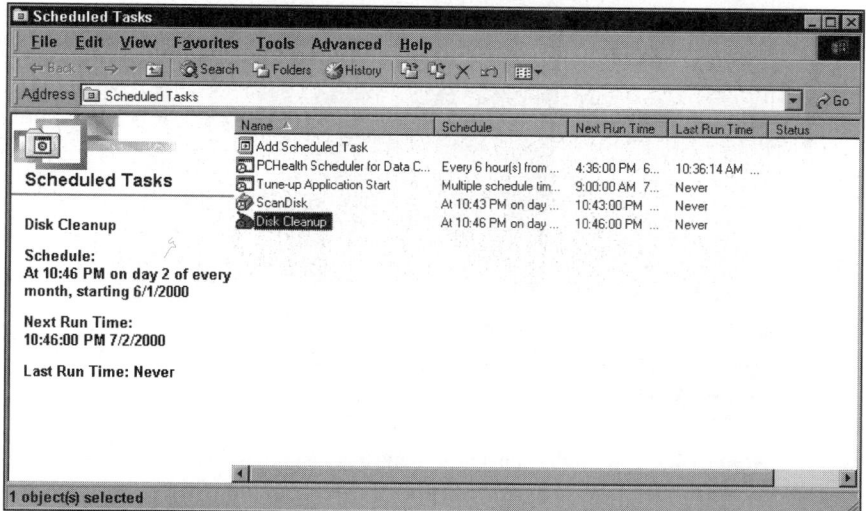

Figure 14-6: The Status column is empty, so in this case all of the tasks were completed. The Last Run Time column tells you when.

If you want to be notified of a missed task when you restart Windows, choose Advanced ➪ Notify Me of Missed Tasks from the Scheduled Tasks menu. This can become a bit bothersome because some tasks happen quite often and you'll get a notice of a missed task every time you restart Windows.

The Task Scheduler doesn't always appear to be aware of whether the tasks got completed. You can interrupt Defrag, for example, and the Task Scheduler log shows that nothing was amiss. If the task ended on its own with an error, the Task Scheduler log displays this problem.

Can't Add Tasks to the Scheduled Tasks?

If you can't add tasks to the Task Scheduler, or if the Task Scheduler will not run at all, it may be because your boot drive is labeled with the same name as your \Windows folder. Weird, huh?

Assuming that your \Windows folder is in fact called Windows, then you want to be darn sure your C drive is not called Windows. In your Explorer, right-click your boot drive hard disk icon and click Properties. If the drive is labeled Windows, as shown in Figure 14-7, rename it in the Label field. Click OK.

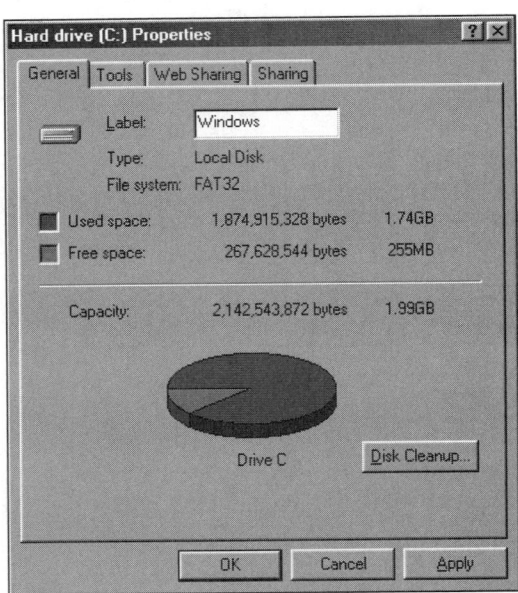

Figure 14-7: Look in the Label field to make sure your C drive is not labeled Windows, as this one is.

Add Antivirus Checking to the Task Scheduler

Many PCs come preinstalled with Network Associates VirusScan or another antivirus program. It may already have been added to your list of scheduled tasks by the maker of your PC. If you don't find Maintenance-Antivirus in the list of scheduled tasks, you can add it in the following way:

STEPS

Creating an Antivirus Scanning Scheduled Task

Step 1. Open your Explorer and highlight Scheduled Tasks in the left pane.

Step 2. Right-click an existing scheduled task and click Copy.

Step 3. Right-click your Desktop and click Paste.

Step 4. Press F2 (while the new item on your Desktop is highlighted) and type **Maintenance-Antivirus** and press Enter.

Step 5. Drag the new icon from your Desktop back into your Task Scheduler.

Step 6. Right-click the Maintenance-Antivirus task icon and click Properties.

Step 7. Change the Run field to read **c:\Program Files\Viruscan\sched.vsc**, as shown in Figure 14-8. You may have your antivirus program located in a different folder, so you might want to check with another copy of your Explorer to make sure where it is.

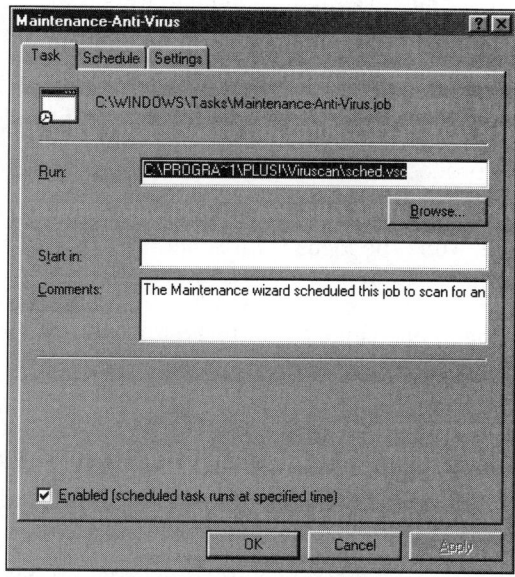

Figure 14-8: This Run field shows one typical path to the VirusScan configuration file.

Continued

STEPS

Creating an Antivirus Scanning Scheduled Task *(continued)*

Step 8. Change the Comments field to reflect the current application.

Step 9. Click the Schedule tab to make any changes to the virus-scanning schedule that you deem necessary. Click OK.

Clear Out the Task Scheduler Log

If you open your Explorer to the Task Scheduler (highlight Scheduled Tasks in the left pane) and click Advanced ⇨ View Log, you'll open a text file (`\Windows\SchedLog.txt`) in Notepad. This file lists the times and application names for applications that have been run by the Task Scheduler.

After a few months, this log file can get a bit long and hard to read. Because it's just a text file, you might get the idea that you can choose Edit ⇨ Select All, press Delete, and then choose File ⇨ Save to clear out the file. Unfortunately, that probably won't work. If you delete the text and then attempt to save the changes with File ⇨ Save, you'll find that the Save As dialog box appears and you're asked to come up with a filename to save the changes to. In other words, you won't be able to save the changes to the `SchedLog.txt` file.

If Task Scheduler is running—and that means `Mstask.exe` is loaded in memory and running—you won't be able to delete the contents of the `SchedLog.txt` file. What you have to do is stop Task Scheduler. You could use the processor killer, WinKill (see "Quickly Kill Any Process or Application" in Chapter 16), but there's an easier way.

In the Explorer, while the focus is on Scheduled Tasks, choose Advanced ⇨ Stop Using Task Scheduler. You can now save the newly empty `SchedLog.txt` file back onto its former self. Once you've done this, click Advanced ⇨ Start Using Task Scheduler to load `Mstask.exe` back into memory and start running Task Scheduler.

Can't View the Scheduled Tasks Log File?

If you open up your Explorer to Scheduled Tasks, click Advanced ⇨ View Log, and find that you can't view the log file, this may be because your plain-text files are associated with an application other than Notepad. Notepad, unlike other text editors, can open files that are currently in use by other applications (in this case, the Task Scheduler). If you have files with the `txt` extension associated with a different application, say WordPad, that application won't be able to open the log file as long as the Task Scheduler is running.

The easiest way to deal with this little glitch is to stop the Task Scheduler by clicking Advanced ⇨ Stop Using Task Scheduler. You can then click Advanced ⇨ View Log to display the log file. Be sure to restart the Task Scheduler after you are done viewing the log file by clicking Advanced ⇨ Start Using Task Scheduler.

You can also reassociate plaintext files with Notepad. We explain how to do this in great detail in Chapter 12.

Run Programs When You Shut Down Windows

There are many tasks you might want to run in Windows at a certain time. For example, you might want to automatically log off a network connection, synchronize your desktop PC with a laptop or palmtop, scan for viruses, run Defrag, or back up your entire system — but only at a certain time of day, such as late at night.

Oddly enough, the Task Scheduler can't schedule a program for the time when you're most likely not to be using your system — when you're quitting for the day and are shutting down. Usually, shutting down means you won't need your computer until the next morning. It's a perfect time to run lengthy processes, but the Task Scheduler can't help you. Fortunately, there are some tools that can take care of this.

WrapUp is a completely updated version of a tool that runs on Windows Me, 98, 95, NT, and 2000. It's produced by Tessler's Nifty Tools, and you can order it from http://www.NiftyTools.com. It's not shareware, but you can download a free evaluation version, and a single-user license of the registered version costs only $39 plus shipping and tax.

Running a program with WrapUp is as easy as dragging a shortcut into the ShutDown folder that WrapUp creates in your \Windows\Start Menu\Programs folder during installation. The program could be a system tool such as Scan Disk, or it could be a batch file or Visual Basic routine that you've written. If there are command-line switches for your program, right-click the shortcut in the Start menu, select Properties, and edit the Target field to add a switch. For example, you can tell ScanDisk to run without user input by adding /n at the end of this field. In addition, you can add a number of command-line switches that help control WrapUp, and these are well documented in its online help. Unfortunately, you can't add or change them from within WrapUp.

WrapUp works best if it has a shortcut in your StartUp folder, so you don't have to remember to start it. It appears on your taskbar (not your system tray, unfortunately) unless you use the /i switch to make it invisible. When you shut down Windows, WrapUp asks you if you want to close all programs and run the items in the ShutDown folder, unless you have configured it to run without asking you for confirmation. If you ever want to shut down

Windows and not have the programs in the ShutDown folder execute (for example, when you just want to restart Windows), it's a simple matter to cancel WrapUp and shut down normally. You can disable WrapUp by pressing its toggle button, as shown in Figure 14-9.

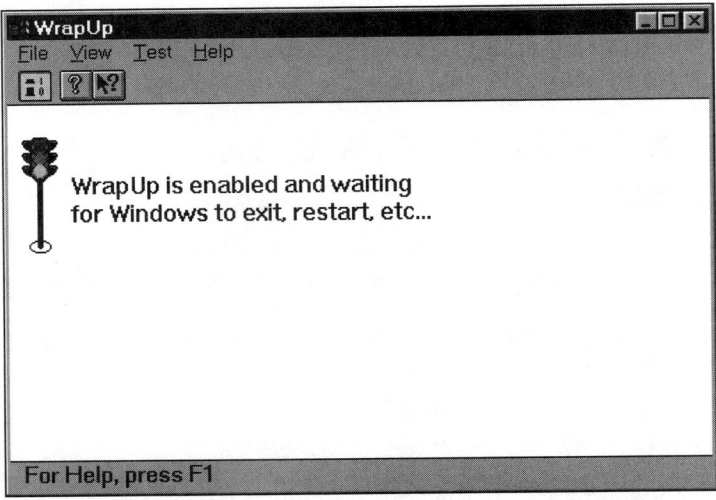

Figure 14-9: The WrapUp user interface. To toggle it on and off, use the button on the left end of the toolbar.

A different approach to this same problem is taken by ShutdownPlus, available from WMSoftware at `http://www.wmsoftware.com`. Again, it's not shareware; the free evaluation version times out after 30 days, after which you must register ($24.95 for a single-user license).

ShutdownPlus replaces the Shut Down Windows dialog box with the one shown in Figure 14-10. As you can see, it allows you to set programs to run on particular days of the week, or to only run once a day. You can use a handy wizard to add standard utilities such as ScanDisk and Defrag or browse to add whatever other programs you like. All of ShutdownPlus' settings are available in its detailed Options dialog box, which you access by right-clicking the icon in your system tray, so there's no messing around with command-line switches.

If you don't need to get too fancy, you might be just as satisfied running a simple batch file. Type the text into an empty Notepad file and save it in your My System folder (which we recommend you create) as something like `Shutdown.bat`. The batch file shown here, written by Jeff Kushen, runs ScanDisk and Defrag on your C and D drives, and then exits Windows:

```
START /W C:\Windows\Scandskw.exe /sagerun:0 C: D:
START /W C:\Windows\Defrag.exe /f c: d:
C:\WINDOWS\RUNDLL.EXE user.exe,ExitWindows
```

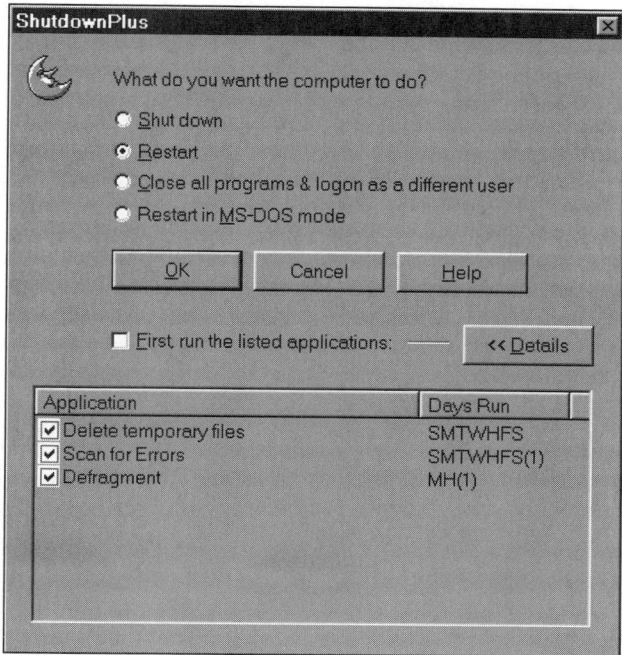

Figure 14-10: The ShutdownPlus Shut Down dialog box

Tip

No matter which of these automated methods you use, your computer will not shut down when you exit Windows unless you have power management enabled. See "Get Standby Back in Your Shut Down Windows Dialog Box" in Chapter 46 to see how to turn it back on if necessary.

None of the programs described in this section can help you with the most obvious maintenance task: backing up your files with Microsoft Backup. This is because you can't specify an individual backup job to run. See the next section for more on this.

Microsoft Backup Doesn't Work with the Task Scheduler

The big problem with a program like Task Scheduler is that it has to run applications on an operating system that is designed to be interactive. If the human isn't there to do something, will these applications perform any useful work?

In most cases, the answer is no. Of course, there are plenty of tasks that could be done with no user interaction if they were just designed to operate that way. The standard way around this is to run programs from the command line and include a few command-line switches that stand in for user input.

Obviously, this is just what you do with a program like ScanDisk, which requires no user input as long as it can use its default settings or you can configure it to use the ones you want.

The Task Scheduler makes this process somewhat easier by including the Settings button. The tasks that you can define via the Settings button previously required that you enter command-line switches in the Run field of the Task tab in the Properties dialog box for the scheduled task.

Secret

Microsoft Backup is still available in Windows Me, but it can be a little hard to find since it is no longer listed on the Windows Setup tab of the Add/Remove Programs dialog box. To install Microsoft Backup, open the \add-ons\MSBackup folder on your Windows Me CD-ROM and double-click msbexp.exe. Follow the on-screen instructions and you'll have Microsoft Backup installed in a few minutes.

The key input that Microsoft Backup requires in order to run a backup is the name of the backup job. Backup jobs are the specifications that tell Backup which files to back up when and where (see Figure 14-11).

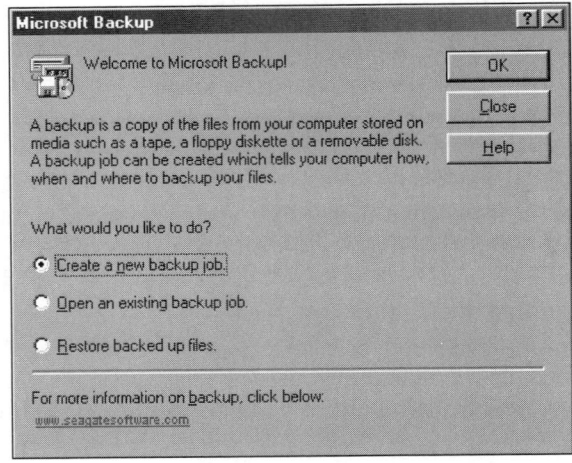

Figure 14-11: The initial screen of Microsoft Backup

Unfortunately, Microsoft and Seagate decided to take out the capability of specifying a backup job name in the Task Scheduler. Therefore, you can't use Microsoft Backup for unattended backup. You have to be there to run it.

Seagate would rather that you buy an upgrade of this basically good program to get this additional feature. You'll find the upgrade at http://www.seagatesoftware.com.

A Replacement for the Task Scheduler

If you want a task scheduler that can much more effectively replace you as an input unit (we're smiling here), you'll want to check out ClockMan or similar shareware packages. What ClockMan brings to the party is the ability to send keystrokes to the programs that it calls. Now you have a way to automate the Microsoft/Seagate Backup program that is too crippled to work with Task Scheduler.

ClockMan also comes with a version of the Windows Interface Language that enables much greater control over hundreds of Windows functions. The batch files that you can create using this language can only be run in ClockMan, unless you have WinBatch (see "Windows Interface Language" in Chapter 16).

ClockMan doesn't have all the finely tuned schedule manipulation power of Task Scheduler, as you can see from Figure 14-12. It also is about as ugly as a Windows program gets, but there is power under the hood.

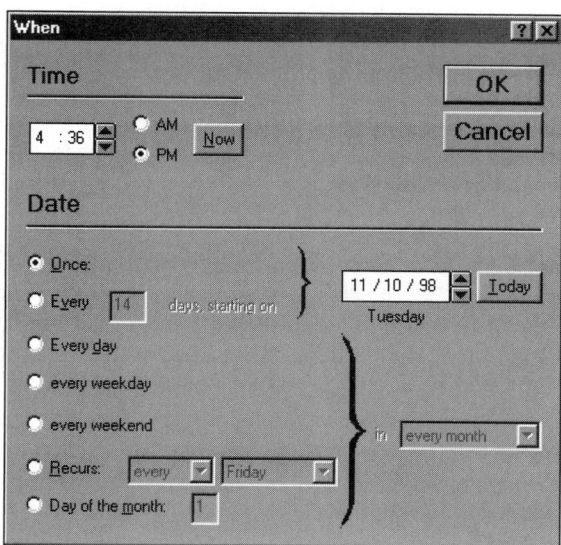

Figure 14-12: ClockMan's scheduling dialog box

You'll find it at http://www.graphicaldynamics.com.

Scheduling with VBScript and JScript

If you install the Windows Scripting Host, you can run VBScript and JScript programs directly from Windows. To do this, click Start ⇨ Run, type the name of the script file, and press Enter, or click the script in the Explorer. You can also create a shortcut to the script and include all the command-line parameters that you want to use with the script.

You can download the Windows Scripting Host from `http://msdn.microsoft.com/scripting/default.htm?/scripting/windowshost`.

You can also have the Task Scheduler, ClockMan, or Alarm++ run a script at an appointed time. Alarm++ comes with a couple of sample scripts that you can run with it. Alarm++ doesn't have its own scripting language, as Clock Man does, but it can easily use JScript and VBScript. Unlike ClockMan, it doesn't internally support sending keystrokes. It will send e-mail directly through Windows Messaging, but not directly through Outlook Express. You'd have to call Outlook Express as you would any other program.

You'll find Alarm++ at `http://www.skst.com/perpetualmotion/`.

Summary

Task Scheduler can run maintenance programs without your intervention. You might want a more powerful option though:

▶ If antivirus scanning didn't get added to your Scheduled Tasks, we show you how to put it there.

▶ If you can't see the Scheduled Task log file, you'll need to reassociate `txt` files with Notepad.

▶ The basic backup program that comes with Windows won't work with the Task Scheduler. You'll need to upgrade.

▶ With VBScript and JScript, you can write scripting programs that carry out many Windows and browser functions, and you can set them to run at an appointed time.

Chapter 15

The Control Panel and Properties

In This Chapter

We cover the Control Panel and general features of properties.

▶ Getting to the Control Panel settings quickly

▶ Installing and removing Windows applications

▶ Controlling your multimedia hardware and drivers

▶ Configuring Windows for your local currency, time, and dates

▶ Associating sounds with Windows events

What Will You Find Where?

Windows has to keep track of itself and the computer it is running on. You need a way to see (and change) your Windows configurations. Thousands of little pieces of information running around in your computer need to be right for everything to work.

In the Control Panel, you'll get a handle on most of your computer's hardware and the software drivers that work with it. In addition, you'll find the Fonts folder (it's also in your Explorer under \Windows\Fonts) and the settings for currency, dates, time, and other location-specific information.

Properties, an innovation that Microsoft first introduced to Windows in Windows 95, provide another means to get at the parameters that define your files, and in some cases, your hardware.

Many of the specific Control Panel settings are described in the chapters in *Part IV: Hardware Secrets*. In this chapter, we discuss the Control Panel settings that aren't described there.

Getting to the Control Panel

It's easy to get to the Control Panel (see Figure 15-1). Just click the Start button, point to Settings, and then click Control Panel. But this isn't the only way to get to the Control Panel, nor is it necessarily the most convenient.

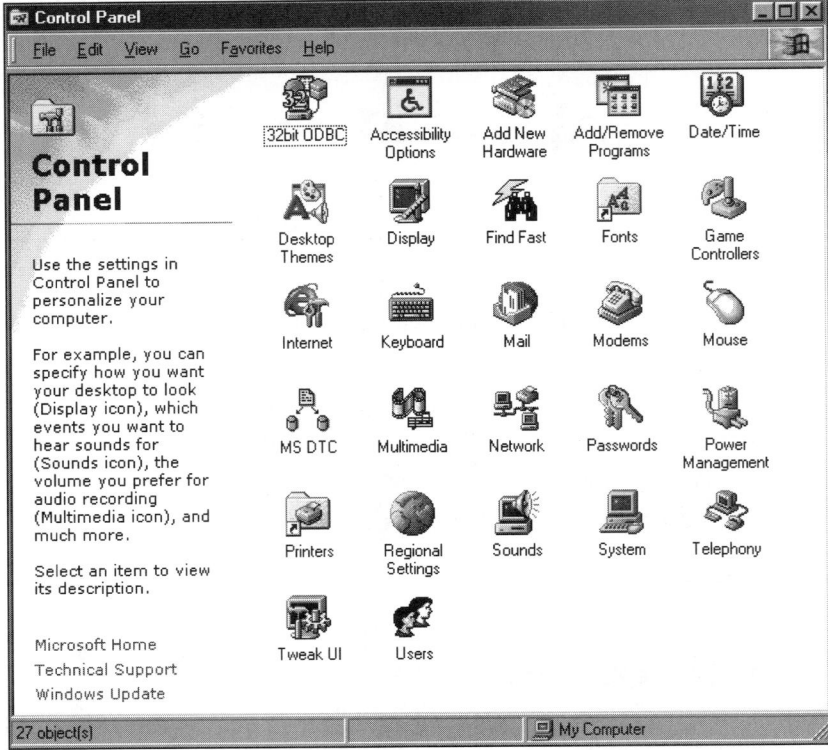

Figure 15-1: The Control Panel. Click any icon to change the settings associated with that icon.

Here are some other ways to get to the items in the Control Panel:

- If you want to use the Display control panel (the Display icon in the Control Panel), right-click the Desktop and click Properties.

- You can get to the Date/Time control panel by double-clicking the clock on the taskbar.

- The Fonts folder is accessible through the Explorer. The Fonts folder is under your C:\Windows folder.

- You can get to the System control panel by right-clicking My Computer and clicking Properties.

- To access a particular modem, right-click a DUN connectoid (not a shortcut to one), click Properties, and then click Configure on the General tab.

- You can also get to a modem by right-clicking My Computer, clicking Properties, choosing the Device Manager tab, selecting Modem, and then double-clicking the desired modem. This method gives you access to additional properties not available through the other methods — for updating the modem driver, for example, and for checking the I/O resources.

- To get the Network control panel, right-click the My Network Places icon on the Desktop and choose Properties.

Shortcuts to the Control Panel

If you want a shortcut to an icon in the Control Panel, open the Control Panel, right-click an icon, and click Create Shortcut. You'll see a dialog box saying you can't create a shortcut in the Control Panel and asking whether you want to place the shortcut on the Desktop instead. You can certainly make that choice.

Shortcuts to Control Panel icons make it easy to get at the specific settings that you want changed. While the Control Panel is a reasonable organizing folder for these items, you may have one or two that you change a lot. Bring them out to the Desktop.

Tip

You can place shortcuts to Control Panel applets on your main Start menu. Even better, create a folder — perhaps under your My System folder — and then drag the folder icon and drop it on the Start button. You can then put all your shortcuts to the Control Panel applets in the new folder. That way, you can determine just which applets you want on the main Start menu, and you can put all the shortcuts in one place. You can name the shortcuts anything you like, and they can point to a certain tab within an applet, such as the Device Manager tab in the System control panel (as described in the next section, "Fine-Tuning Your Control Panel Shortcuts".

Microsoft made the Control Panel much slower in Windows Me, 9x, and Windows 3.1 than it was in the bad old days of Windows 3.0. Starting with Windows 3.1, opening the Control Panel causes Windows to read through every file in your System folder, looking for files with a cpl extension. These cpl files are, of course, Control Panel applets. Making the Control Panel read through all these files enables third-party vendors to add their own applets to the Windows interface, so this delay does have some merit. Independent developers can now install Control Panel applets for multimedia devices, tape drives, and other peripherals.

But sometimes you *don't* want to wait for the Control Panel to assemble its little list of applets. You want fast access to the *one* applet that you use all the time. Perhaps you frequently need to change a setting for your mouse or your keyboard. Or you like to change your Desktop colors or fonts every day. Or you need quick access to the handy Device Manager buried within the System applet. The next two sections teach you how to customize your Control Panel shortcuts to display the exact components you want to access.

Fine-Tuning Your Control Panel Shortcuts

The Control Panel occupies a special place in the Desktop hierarchy. If you look for Control Panel in the Explorer, it doesn't appear as an icon under the \Windows\Start Menu folder, as you might expect. Instead, it appears in the left pane of the Explorer *after* all your floppy drives and hard drives. This implies that Control Panel isn't on any of your disks at all.

This isn't the case, of course. Control Panel is, in reality, a normal executable file stored in your \Windows folder. You can see this by clicking the Start button, clicking Run, and then typing the following command:

```
C:\Windows\Control.exe
```

When you click OK, you see the same Control Panel window appear as you do when you run Control Panel directly from the Start menu (Start ➪ Settings ➪ Control Panel).

If you've visited the Control Panel before, you know it includes icons for changing your keyboard, mouse, and modem settings, and for many other functions of your system. The exact complement of Control Panel applets in your Control Panel window depends on the hardware and software you've installed. But the Control Panel holds a lot of secrets beneath its humble exterior. Control.exe supports a number of parameters that can dramatically speed up your access to the settings in its applets.

For example, let's say you want to change your dialing properties frequently, perhaps because you travel a lot. You could click Start ➪ Run and type the following:

```
C:\Windows\Control.exe Modem.cpl
```

Even better, you can create a command that displays an individual tab of an applet, rather than having to start out at the first one and click your way across to the tab you really want.

For example, you can create a command that takes you directly to the Device Manager, a tab in the System applet. That command should look as follows:

```
C:\Windows\Control.exe Sysdm.cpl, System,1
```

This command causes Control Panel to open Sysdm.cpl, the System applet, and jump to the second available tab. (In programmer-speak, the first tab is numbered 0, the second is 1, and so forth.) You need to specify the applet name in this command line because some applets contain more than one function within them.

What the three examples above have in common is the Control Panel's built-in command syntax. Stripped down to skeletal form, the syntax goes like this:

```
Control.exe {filename.cpl} {,applet-name} {,tab#}
```

If you run `Control.exe` with no parameters, only the Control Panel window is displayed. If you add the correct `filename.cpl`, the first tab of that applet's dialog box is displayed. And if you tack on the correct applet name and tab number, then *that* tab is displayed.

In actual practice (as opposed to theory), there seem to be some quirks in the way Windows processes the tab number for an applet. Some Control Panel applets, particularly Display, dutifully jump to the correct tab when you specify a number in the command line, such as 1, 2, or 3. Other applets refuse to display any tab but the first (tab 0) even if you've used the "correct" syntax. Apparently, some of the programmers at Microsoft didn't know they were supposed to build in this feature, so they didn't. If a particular tab doesn't seem to want to let you "jump to it," the tab simply may not be programmed to do so.

You can place commands like these on the Start menu, on your Desktop, or elsewhere, and access them with a mouse click or a hot key.

Table 15-1 shows some of the `cpl` files available in most Windows systems, and the applet name you'll need in order to jump to a particular tab. (Some applets, such as `Main.cpl`, contain more than one function; these are listed separately below.)

Table 15-1   Control Panel File and Applet Names

Filename	Applet Name
Main.cpl	Fonts
Main.cpl	Keyboard
Main.cpl	Mouse
Main.cpl	Printers
Access.cpl	Accessibility Options
Appwiz.cpl	Add/Remove Programs
Desk.cpl	Display
Dtccfg.cpl	MS DTC
FindFast.cpl	Find Fast*
Inetcpl.cpl	Internet
Infrared.cpl	Infrared
Intl.cpl	Regional Settings
Joy.cpl	Game Controllers
Mlcfg32.cpl	Mail

Continued

Table 15-1 *(continued)*

Filename	Applet Name
Mmsys.cpl	Multimedia
Mmsys.cpl	Sounds
Modem.cpl	Modems
Netcpl.cpl	Network
Odbccp32.cpl	32-bit ODBC*
Password.cpl	Passwords
Powercfg.cpl	Power Management
Sticpl.cpl	Scanners and Cameras
Sysdm.cpl	System
Sysdm.cpl	Add New Hardware
Telephon.cpl	Telephony
Themes.cpl	Desktop Themes
Timedate.cpl	Date/Time
TweakUI.cpl	Tweak UI
Wbemcpl.cpl	WBEM
Wgpocpl.cpl	Microsoft Mail Postoffice

*These applets are only available if you have installed Microsoft Office 97 or 2000.

Now that you know the filenames and applet names to use, let's make sure you never have to type these lines more than once. It's easy to create a shortcut icon on your Desktop that takes you directly to the tab of your choice in a Control Panel applet's dialog box. Here's how:

STEPS

Control Panel Shortcut Icons on the Desktop

Step 1. Right-click an unoccupied spot on your Desktop.

Step 2. On the context menu that appears, point to New and then click Shortcut.

Step 3. In the Create Shortcut Wizard, type a command line such as the following:

```
C:\Windows\Control.exe Desk.cpl, Display,2
```

Step 4. Click the Next button. Type a name for your new shortcut, such as **Display Appearance**, and then click the Finish button. You're done!

You should see a new icon on your Desktop. Click it, and you will be almost instantly transported to (in this case) the Appearance tab of the Display Properties dialog box.

You'll probably want to change the icon for the shortcut, because this method produces one that looks pretty boring. Check out how to do this in the "Change the Shortcut's Icon" section of Chapter 10. You might also want to edit the shortcut's Target field to change the command-line parameters. To do so, right-click the shortcut, click Properties, and then click the Shortcut tab.

Assigning Hot Keys to Control Panel Shortcuts

Once you've put a command for a Control Panel applet in a shortcut and placed the shortcut icon where you want it on the Desktop or your Start menu, you can assign it a hot key combination. This lets you open the dialog box at almost any time by pressing a key combination such as Ctrl+Alt+A.

To assign a hot key to a shortcut icon, right-click the icon (you can right-click the icon on the Desktop or in the Start menu) and then click Properties. Click the Shortcut tab, click in the Shortcut Key field, and then press a letter key on your keyboard. Windows automatically adds Ctrl+Alt to the key you press. For example, pressing the letter *a* assigns the hot key Ctrl+Alt+A to that shortcut. To assign a Ctrl+Shift or Shift+Alt combination, hold down those keys while you press the letter key.

We provide some additional examples of how to make shortcuts to the Control Panel icons in the "Control Panel Icon"section of Chapter 10. You can find further details on how to put the Control Panel on the Start menu in the "Control Panel on a Start Menu" section of Chapter 9.

Control Panel Settings

Most of the Control Panel settings are discussed in other chapters. In this chapter, we discuss those that aren't covered elsewhere.

Missing Files

Accidents do happen, and it's possible for a cpl or dll file to become corrupted. A sign that this might have happened is the following error message, which appears when you exit the Control Panel:

```
FATAL EXCEPTION 0E HAS OCCURRED AT 0028:C07A2B0 IN VXD
IFSMGR(03)+000CF7C.
Run policy editor and restrict Control panel.
```

If this happens, you'll first need to start the Explorer, choose Tools ⇨ Find ⇨ Files or Folders, and search for *.cpl files in your \Windows\ System folder. Open each cpl file individually. At some point, one of them will probably give you an error message. This is the damaged file. Rename it with a different extension, and then open the Control Panel to see if that fixes the problem. To replace a Windows cpl file, you'll need to extract it from the Windows CD-ROM; continue reading to find out how. If the cpl file came from a third party, try reinstalling whatever program put it in the Control Panel.

If you find that the Windows Setup and Startup Disk tabs are missing from the Add/Remove Programs tool in the Control Panel, the cause is most likely a missing or damaged Setupx.dll file. This file should be located in your \Windows\System folder. If you find it there, compare it with the same file on your Windows CD-ROM (in \winme\Precopy2.cab). The dates and sizes of the two files should match.

If the two files don't match, or if yours are missing, first rename the Setupx.dll file (if it exists) in your \Windows\System folder, and then extract a new copy of it from your Windows CD-ROM. After copying it to your \Windows\System folder, you need to restart your computer.

The cpl and dll files are stored in compressed form in cabinet (cab) files on your Windows CD-ROM. A new built-in feature of Windows makes it easy to view the contents of cab files and extract the files you need. Click a cab file (or right-click it and click View) to display its contents in a folder window, and then drag and drop the file you need into your Explorer.

If for some reason you need to work in MS-DOS mode, you can use the Extract program (Extract.exe), which runs from the command line, to extract the file you need. Copy Extract.exe from the \winme folder of your Windows CD-ROM into the root level of your C: drive if it's not there already. To get help with the Extract tool, type **extract /?** at the DOS prompt or read the Microsoft Knowledge Base article about using Extract (http:// support.microsoft.com/support/kb/articles/Q129/6/05.asp).

In most cases, you shouldn't need the cumbersome Extract utility. One situation in which it is useful, however, is if you don't know which cab file contains the file you need. You can tell Extract to examine all the cab files in order and show you the file you're looking for. To do this, click the Start button, choose Programs, and click MS-DOS Prompt. At the prompt, type the following:

```
extract /A /D {drive}:\winme\{first cab file} {file you need} | more
```

For example, if your CD-ROM is drive E:, the first cab file in the sequence is winme_01.cab, and you're looking for modem.cpl, type the following:

```
extract /A /D E:\win98\winme_01.cab modem.cpl | more
```

You will see one screenful of files at a time; to display the next one, press Enter. When you see the file you need, write down the name of the cab file listed above it, type **exit**, and press Enter to return to your Desktop. The easiest way to do the actual extraction is to drag and drop the file from the cab file folder window to your Explorer.

Add/Remove Programs

The Add/Remove Programs control panel lets you perform three tasks:

- Install and remove programs that use the Windows version of Install Shield

- Install and remove programs that are covered by the Windows setup routines or that have inf files consistent with the Microsoft standard for install files

- Create a bootable startup disk, as described in "Emergency Startup Disk" in Chapter 11

These functions are described in the next three sections.

Install/Uninstall

Microsoft has attempted to provide a standard Windows application installation-and-setup procedure, so you don't have to fathom a new set of steps every time you install a new piece of software. By licensing portions of the Install Shield software and integrating it into Windows, Microsoft provides application developers with a tool that will help you install and uninstall their programs.

To install a piece of compatible software, click the Install button, as shown in Figure 15-2.

If you install software using the Install/Uninstall tab, the registry gets updated correctly and Windows retains enough information about the setup so that you can uninstall the software if you choose to later.

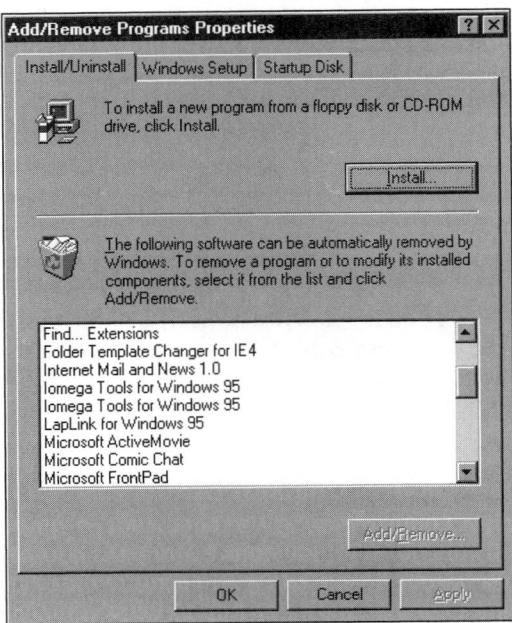

Figure 15-2: The Install/Uninstall tab of the Add/Remove Programs Properties dialog box. Use this tab to install software that uses the built-in Install Shield procedures. Developers of small shareware applications may opt not to use these.

If you want to uninstall a program, it is best to use the Install/Uninstall tab so that you can remove most (if not all) of the bits and pieces of an application that are stored in various parts of your computer. If the application's programmers have written a proper uninstall routine, it will also remove references to the program in the registry.

Microsoft will list a program in the Install/Uninstall tab if that program correctly installs itself *and* if it includes an uninstall routine. (Such programs receive the *Compatible with Windows* logo, which manufacturers display on the box.) The uninstall routine is a small executable file that lies dormant on your hard disk until you're ready to remove the application.

When you select a file from the list and click the Add/Remove button, Windows uses the application's uninstall routine to remove the application files without affecting other programs on your system. That's an important consideration, because removing one program's files may prevent another program from launching. This can occur when applications share files. Common extensions of shared files include dll, vbx, and ocx.

When you install an application, it copies any shared files it needs into your \Windows or \Windows\System folder. It's almost impossible to know whether other applications depend on these files, so it's hard to know whether you can safely delete them. If you delete a shared file that another application needs, when you next try to open that application, you might see an error message such as "Can't find *Shared*.dll." It's also possible that you'll receive a more cryptic error message, or none at all. If you delete a shared vxd (virtual device driver) file, you may get an error message such as "Cannot find a device file that may be needed to run Windows or a Windows application" when you next start Windows.

Before a logo-compliant application installs a shared file, it first checks to see whether a copy of that file is already present on your hard disk. If the file already exists on your system, the application can't copy an *older* version of that file over a newer version (it makes sure this doesn't occur by checking the internal version number stored within the shared file). When an application attempts to install a shared file, a counter kept for that file in the registry is increased by one.

When you uninstall a logo-compliant application, one is subtracted from the value of the counter for each shared file that the application used. A shared file is only deleted when its counter has a value of zero. In other words, if three applications use a shared file, the file won't be deleted it until you have uninstalled all three applications.

Commercial uninstall packages have found a niche because computer users are unsure how to safely delete software themselves. Retail uninstallers claim that they let you remove your old software painlessly, simply by clicking a button. The reality is a different story. Most retail uninstallers come with a database of all the files contained in the most popular applications (such as word processors and spreadsheets), along with the most likely locations for the files. The uninstaller program uses its database to make an educated guess about where to look for the files to be removed. And when a commercial uninstaller encounters a shared file, your guess about how to handle it might be more educated than the uninstaller's. Several programs simply display a dialog box that asks, "Safe to delete this file?"

Commercial uninstaller programs may not contain information about the application you want to remove, and some applications may contain unusual files, such as Control Panel applets, that the uninstaller will not find. If a program comes with its own uninstaller, that's usually the best method to use. An uninstall program, if there is one, is usually located in the application's parent folder (see the next section).

Manual Uninstalling

If you need to uninstall an application that doesn't support the Add/Remove Programs applet, you can safely delete most, if not all of it, manually—with plenty of time and patience. But only use this method as a last resort. To ensure a clean and *total* uninstall, it's best to buy logo-compliant Windows software.

It's not really true, as many retail uninstall packages claim, that new programs install files at random on your disk. Most software actually installs itself into a single new set of folders under one parent folder. Let's call this `C:\Program Files\Myfolder`. In addition, a new program may copy one or more shared files into your `C:\Windows` or `C:\Windows\System` folder.

Beyond this, a Windows application may add a few program-specific lines to the registry.

The truth is, leaving a few leftover files in your System folder or a few unnecessary lines in your registry rarely does your system any harm. You do, however, want to remove the bulk of files located in a program's parent folder and its subfolders, and this you can do manually.

Here's how to safely delete an application's files:

STEPS

Manually Uninstalling an Application

Step 1. Before you delete anything, make an Emergency Startup disk from the Startup Disk tab of the Add/Remove Programs Properties dialog box, and then make sure the startup disk boots up to a `C:` prompt.

Step 2. Once you have restarted Windows Me, open an Explorer window and navigate to `C:\Windows\Start Menu\Programs` in the left pane. Select the folder under the Programs folder that contains the application you want to remove. In the right pane, right-click a few of the shortcut icons stored in this folder, choosing Properties each time. In the Properties dialog box for each shortcut, click the Shortcut tab, if necessary, and check the Target field to locate the application's parent folder — `C:\Program Files\Myfolder`, for example (see Figure 15-3).

Step 3. Once you've identified the folder in which the program resides, use WinZip, PKZip, or another compression program to compress all the files in that folder into a single `zip` file, and then delete the original files. Next, boot up your system and test your other programs. If everything still works, delete the `zip` file or transfer it to a backup disk for later use.

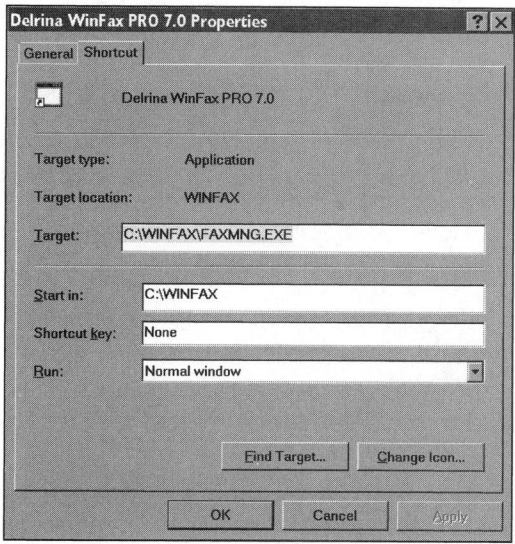

Figure 15-3: The Properties dialog box for a shortcut in a program's Start Menu subfolder may indicate the folder in which that program is stored. This dialog box shows the properties for a shortcut to the executable file for EARTHA Global Explorer DVD. Deleting the C:\Program Files\EARTHA Global Explorer DVD folder (and its subfolders) will remove all of EARTHA Global Explorer DVD's files.

Remember, don't delete an application folder as your first step. Instead, zip its contents first, and then test your system before going any further. Don't try anything you can't undo.

Secret

If you delete an application manually or find that you can't remove an uninstalled program's name from the list in the Install/Uninstall tab, you can use the Add/Remove tab of TweakUI to remove these superfluous entries. (If you don't have a TweakUI icon in your Control Panel, you can install it from your Windows CD-ROM. See the "TweakUI" section later in this chapter.)

You can also remove these entries manually using the Registry Editor:

STEPS

Removing Program Names from the Install/Uninstall List

Step 1.   Click Regedit.exe in your \Windows folder.

Step 2.   In the left pane of the Registry Editor, navigate to this key:

HKEY_LOCAL_MACHINE\ SOFTWARE\ Microsoft\ Windows\ CurrentVersion\ Uninstall.

Step 3.   In the left pane, highlight the name of the application whose name you want to remove from the Install/Uninstall list. Choose Edit ➪ Delete.

Step 4.   Close the Registry Editor.

If You Uninstall Too Much

After uninstalling an application, you might receive this error message the next time you start Windows 98:

■ Cannot find a device file that may be needed to run Windows or a Windows application.

The Windows registry or System.ini file refers to this device file, but the device file no longer exists. If you deleted this file on purpose, try uninstalling the associated application using its uninstall program or setup program.

If you still want to use the application associated with this device file, try reinstalling that application to replace the missing file.

filename.vxd

The name shown in place of *filename* could be any of a number of files (Enable.vxd for example), or the filename may not be specified. When you press any key, Windows may seem to run normally.

This is usually a symptom of a damaged or missing virtual device driver (vxd), or of an invalid or blank value for the driver in the registry. Virtual device drivers are files required by various programs to communicate with your computer's hardware.

You'll need to reinstall the program, and then run the program's uninstall tool if it has one. If it doesn't, and if the program isn't listed in the Control

Panel's Add/Remove Programs Properties dialog box, contact the software manufacturer to find out how to properly uninstall the product. As a last resort, you'll have to remove it by following the advice in the previous section, "Manual Uninstalling."

If the missing file has a 386 extension instead of `vxd`, open your `System.ini` file, locate the line that refers to this device driver, and disable the driver by placing a semicolon (;) at the beginning of the line. For example, if the line referencing the missing device driver reads

```
device=Example.386
```

change the line to read

```
;device=Example.386
```

If the driver is not specifically named in the error message, the problem is probably one of the StaticVXD values in the registry. Use the following steps to locate and delete the value in the registry that refers to the missing device driver. (Be sure to back up your registry before doing this; refer to "Registry Backup" in Chapter 11 for details.)

STEPS

Troubleshooting a Missing StaticVXD Value

Step 1. Click `Regedit.exe` in your `\Windows` folder to start the Registry Editor, and navigate to the following key:

```
HKEY_LOCAL_MACHINE\ System\ CurrentControlSet\
Services\ VXD
```

Click the plus sign next to this key to display the subkeys under it.

Step 2. In the left pane, click each subkey listed under VXD in turn. For each subkey, look for a StaticVXD value in the right pane. See if there is data listed for that value. (The data should be the name of a `vxd` file and should correspond to the subkey.) If you find a StaticVXD value that is blank, contains only spaces, or has odd characters instead of the name of the key, that value is most likely the problem.

Step 3. Determine whether the `vxd` file in question is still on your computer. To do this, open the Explorer and use the Tools ⇨ Find ⇨ Files or Folders command to search for the file. For example, if the StaticVXD value for the PAGESWAP key is empty, search for `Pageswap.vxd`.

Continued

STEPS

Troubleshooting a Missing StaticVXD Value *(continued)*

Step 4. If you find that the vxd file is on your hard disk, you should be able to fix the problem by editing the file's value in the registry. In the Registry Editor, double-click the value with the missing data. In the Value Data field, type an asterisk followed by the name of the vxd file in capital letters (in most cases, this will be identical to the name of the subkey). For instance, in the example above, you would type ***PAGESWAP**. Then exit the Registry Editor.

Step 5. If you cannot find the vxd file on your hard disk, you should extract the original file from your Windows CD-ROM and copy it to the \Windows\System folder on your computer. For more on extracting, refer to the "Missing Files" section earlier in this chapter.

Network Install

If you commonly install software to several PCs in your company, save yourself some shoe leather. You can add a Network Install tab to the Add/ Remove Programs Properties dialog box that lets you or individual users easily install new applications across a network at the click of a mouse.

Let's assume you have a site license to distribute software within your company to all users, or a license to distribute it to a certain number of users. The Network Install tab allows you to install an entire application from another PC — without diskettes or a CD-ROM. (The other PC is usually a network server, but it could be any other PC in a peer-to-peer network.)

To make the Network Install tab appear, you must create the two short text files shown here:

```
Example Contents of Netinst.reg:
REGEDIT4HKEY_LOCAL_MACHINE\ SOFTWARE\ Microsoft\ Windows\
CurrentVersion
AppInstallPath=\\\\Server1\\  Windows\\  Apps.ini
Example Contents of Apps.ini:
[AppInstallList]
Microsoft Internet Explorer=\\  Server1\Apps\  Msie40.exe
Mapped Application=*\\  Server1\  Dummy\  Dumsetup.exe
```

In Netinst.reg, you specify an AppInstallPath. This pinpoints the location of a text file called Apps.ini. In this example, the location is \\Server1\ Windows\ Apps.ini. Notice that you must use *two* backslashes in the AppInstallPath line for every real one in the filename.

You must merge `Netinst.reg` into the Windows registry. To do this, right-click your `Netinst.reg` file and then click Merge. This adds to the registry the two lines below the REGEDIT4 heading.

The `Apps.ini` file is a plaintext file that points to the setup routines for any applications you want to appear on the Network Install tab (what we've shown is only an example). You should put it in a read-only directory on a network server.

The example `Apps.ini` shows lines for the Microsoft Internet Explorer and a "mapped" dummy application. Notice that the "mapped" application, `Dumsetup.exe`, has an asterisk (*) before the double backslash in `\\Server1`. This indicates that `Dumsetup.exe` cannot handle the universal naming convention (UNC) for server names. The setup routine requires a drive letter such as `F:` instead of `\\Server1`. Because of the asterisk, Windows will "map" a drive letter for this server and replace `\\Server1` with `F:` when it runs `Dumsetup.exe`.

Once you have these two files in place and restart Windows, you will see a new Network Install tab in the Add/Remove Programs Properties dialog box.

If `Apps.ini` is later moved or deleted, you'll have trouble opening the Add/Remove Programs icon in the Control Panel. If this happens, use the Find tool in the Explorer to find the folder where `Apps.ini` is stored. Then start the Registry Editor and navigate to this key:

`HKEY_LOCAL_MACHINE\ SOFTWARE\ Microsoft\ Windows\ CurrentVersion\`

Verify that the value for AppInstallPath in this key matches the folder in which `Apps.ini` is stored. You can either edit the path or move `Apps.ini`. If the value points to some place on a network, make sure you can connect to that network location.

Windows Setup

You can install and remove applications that have accompanying `inf` files (control files that install the application without user input) through the Windows Setup tab of the Add/Remove Programs Properties dialog box, as shown in Figure 15-4. Click the Have Disk button to install an application that has an accompanying `inf` file. This is an easy way for a developer to provide for a quick and dirty installation procedure.

You can use the Windows Setup tab to uninstall the optional applications that were installed when you first installed Windows 98. For example, you might want to uninstall games, mouse pointers, and wallpaper, which collectively take up about 3MB of disk space. Or, if you didn't install something when you installed Windows 98 the first time, you can use this tab to install it now. For descriptions of the various Windows 98 components, select the appropriate category in the Components list, and then click the Details button.

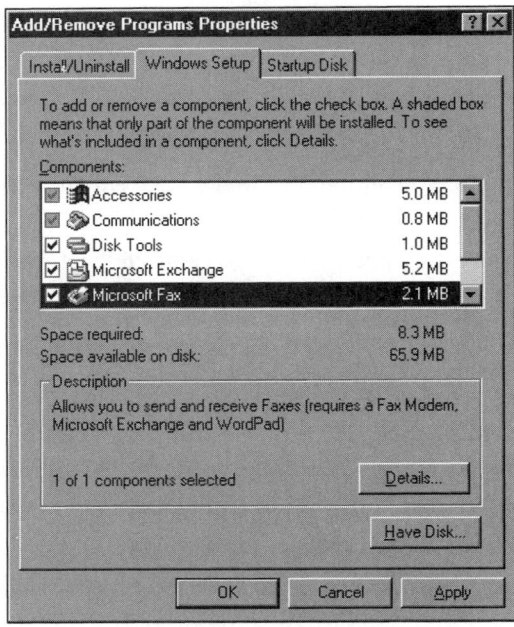

Figure 15-4: The Windows Setup tab of the Add/Remove Programs Properties
dialog box. Click the Have Disk button if your diskette contains an inf file.

The Windows Setup tab displays the amount of disk space required for
the selected category or component, and the space you have available
on your hard disk. However, these values are often inaccurate. In fact, as
you highlight the different components, the values may not change at all.
Microsoft has acknowledged this error. It won't affect your ability to use
Add/Remove Programs, but you shouldn't rely on the numbers as an
indicator of whether you have room to do the installation.

If you are using multiple user profiles on a computer, the Windows Setup
tab will show all the components installed for all users, regardless of whether
they are available to the current user. For example, the EarthLink checkbox in
Online Services may be marked, even though the current user does not have
access to EarthLink.

When you set up a user profile, you can avoid this problem. In the Passwords
Properties dialog box, mark "Include desktop icons and My Network Places
contents in user settings" and/or "Include start menu and program groups in
user settings." See "Whose Desktop Is This Anyway?" in Chapter 6 for more
on user profiles.

If you already have a user profile set up without these options, it is not immediately apparent how to make an installed component available to that user, since the component's checkbox is already marked on the Windows Setup tab. To make a Windows component that was installed by another user available to the current user, follow these steps:

STEPS

Making an Installed Component Available to the Current User

Step 1. Clear the component's checkbox in the Windows Setup tab of the Add/Remove Programs Properties dialog box.

Step 2. Click the Apply button. If you are prompted to restart the computer, click Yes. After the computer restarts, go back to the Windows Setup tab.

Step 3. Mark the component's checkbox.

Step 4. Click the Apply button. If you are prompted to restart your computer, click Yes.

Startup Disk

The Startup Disk tab provides an easy way to make an emergency disk that boots up your system if your hard drive fails. It also gives you a way to recover from problems that can occur when you uninstall applications or they uninstall themselves. We recommend you make a startup disk if you haven't done so already. Insert a blank diskette in drive A: and click the Create Disk button. Windows will copy essential startup files to your diskette. You should test the startup disk to ensure that it actually will boot up your PC successfully. You may need to add some support files, such as any 16-bit drivers listed in your Config.sys or Autoexec.bat files that your system still relies upon.

Make Compatible

A small, undocumented Windows utility called Make Compatible (Mkcompat. exe) can be a lifesaver for anyone who has to work with less-than-perfect Windows software. It can even make some programs work that ordinarily wouldn't work at all. It's not a Control Panel applet; you'll find it in your \Windows\System folder.

Make Compatible lets you modify Windows' behavior when it is running a Windows application that has a slight compatibility problem. You select a filename in Make Compatible and then specify what Windows behavior you want to change. Windows makes the change for that filename only; no other Windows or DOS filenames are affected.

One way Make Compatible can be useful is when Windows 3.1*x* programs won't install properly under Windows Me or 98. For example, when you're installing a Windows 3.1*x* program by running Install.exe or Setup.exe, you might see an error message that reports, "This program requires Windows 3.1 or higher."

What's happening is that the program you're trying to install is checking the version number of Windows incorrectly. The program is checking to see if the version is 3.1 and displaying an error message if it isn't. Of course, what the application should be doing is checking whether the version number is 3.1 *or higher*. Microsoft has published a method to do this for years. But that doesn't help you if you're in this situation.

Microsoft says it knows that programs such as Outpost 1.0, 1.0a, and 1.0b by Sierra On-line and Passport 1.2 by Advantis exhibit this behavior. To resolve this type of incompatibility problem or to fix other similar problems, take these steps:

STEPS

Running Make Compatible

Step 1. Start Make Compatible by clicking Start ⇨ Run, typing **mkcompat**, and clicking OK. (You can also run Make Compatible from the Windows Explorer by clicking Mcompat.exe in your \Windows\ System folder.)

Step 2. Select File ⇨ Choose Program. In the Choose Program dialog box, select the file that you want Windows Me or 98 to treat differently. If you're trying to fix a Windows 3.1*x* program that won't install under Windows Me or 98, select the installation file for that program (it's probably called Install.exe or Setup.exe). Click Open.

Step 3. In the Make Compatible window, mark one or more of the checkboxes in the list. Then choose File ⇨ Save, and then File ⇨ Exit. Changes you have made for a 16-bit application will be written into the [Compatibility] section of Win.ini. Changes for 32-bit applications will be written into the [Compatibility32] section.

If you're fixing the installation problem we discussed previously, mark "Lie about Window's version number" (see Figure 15-5). This option will let you install the affected program because Windows Me or 98 will report to the program that it is running under Windows 3.1.

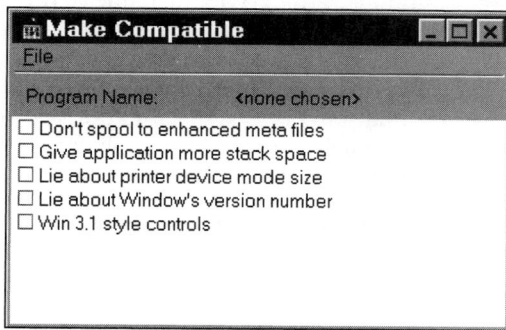

Figure 15-5: To install Windows 3.1 software that looks for the wrong version number, mark the "Lie about Window's version number" checkbox.

Step 4. Unfortunately, Make Compatible applies the changed behavior to all files that have the same filename as the one you selected in step 2. Therefore, if you chose `Install.exe` or `Setup.exe`, Make Compatible will affect the setup routine of any other program whose installation file has the same name. To keep this from happening, run Make Compatible again after you've installed your application. This time, clear the "Lie about Window's version number" option. Then choose File ⇨ Save, and then File ⇨ Exit.

Lying about Windows' version can interfere with the setup routines of programs that are fully compatible with newer versions of Windows, which is why you want to reverse this behavior.

Step 5. If the program name you selected was the main executable of an application (not the installation file) and you marked "Lie about Window's version number," don't clear this option until the application comes out with a new version that is Windows Me–friendly.

You may notice that the Make Compatible menu has no help item. That's because there *isn't* any online help, nor is there any printed documentation. Make Compatible is the essence of simplicity. Its File menu contains only four commands: Choose Program, Advanced Options, Save, and Exit.

To use Make Compatible on a program that's already installed, select File ➪ Choose Program and then type the name of the executable file for the program, or click Browse and browse to the file. If you choose a 32-bit Windows program that is not fully compatible with Windows Me (such as a custom program that uses Microsoft's older Win32 programming libraries), Make Compatible displays a list of options appropriate for 32-bit applications. If you choose a 16-bit application, you'll see a list appropriate for 16-bit applications. These are the five basic options:

- **Don't spool to enhanced meta files** — Some applications cannot print properly when Windows uses a form of data called *enhanced meta files*. This option turns off this performance enhancement and spools data to the printer using a slower method.

- **Give application more stack space** — This option allocates more memory to an application for its program stack. This ensures compatibility with older applications that expect this memory to be available.

- **Lie about printer device mode size** — Older applications may not print correctly if they cannot accommodate newer printer drivers. This option forces Windows to provide information to an application in an older format for compatibility's sake.

- **Lie about Window's version number** — Applications that request the Windows version number are given the answer *3.1*. This corrects some applications that won't run or install unless they see this version number.

- **Win 3.1-style controls** — This option makes the title bar at the top of an application's window, and some other features of the user interface, conform to Windows 3.1 standards. Some applications need this option enabled to display their window correctly.

You can switch to a larger set of options by choosing File ➪ Advanced Options (see Figure 15-6). Issue the same command again to return to the five basic options.

Fortunately, you won't need to use Make Compatible every day. Microsoft has already inserted what it calls *AppHacks* or *Compatibility Hacks* into Win.ini to take care of tested cases it has found where Windows' behavior needs to be modified for a specific application to work smoothly. The [Compatibility32] section of Win.ini lists a few applications that benefit from these hacks, while the 16-bit [Compatibility] section lists well over a hundred such applications (see Figure 15-7).

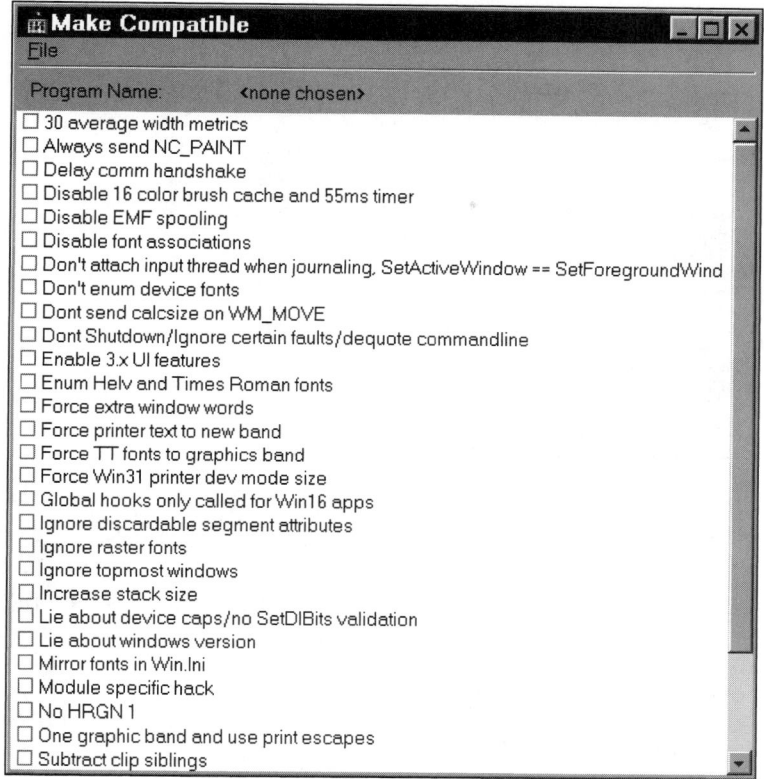

Figure 15-6: Most users will never encounter an application that requires Make Compatible's advanced options. But they're there just in case you do need them some day.

The Make Compatible applet is included with Windows Me and 98 just in case you *do* find an application with slightly weird behavior that Microsoft didn't catch. If you find such a case, first try to resolve it using Make Compatible. If that doesn't work, check with the distributor of the application to see if a new AppHack that can help you has become available.

Multimedia

Audio, video, MIDI, CD music, and advanced settings — the Sounds and Multimedia control panel gives you some control over very basic multimedia parameters, such as volume, size of video playback, MIDI scheme, volume of CD headphone playback, and installed multimedia drivers.

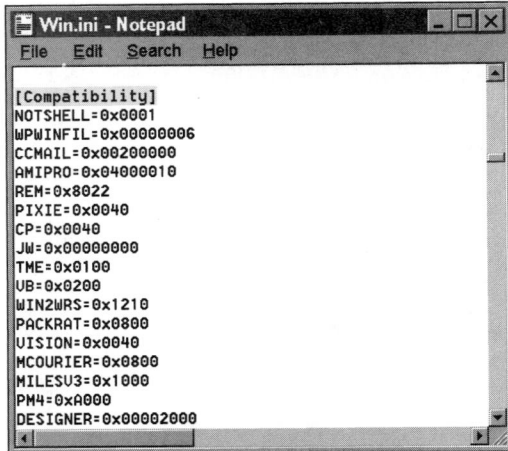

Figure 15-7: The [Compatibility] section of Win.ini lists the names of older Windows application modules that require some modification of Windows' behavior to work smoothly.

Most of the action with multimedia is in the Entertainment submenu of the Start menu (Start ⇨ Programs ⇨ Accessories) or comes from third-party applications that you probably received with your multimedia hardware. Lots of multimedia software or content titles have multimedia applets that control how to play their video clips and listen to their sounds. Most of your interaction with multimedia will take place through the interfaces defined by these applications.

The Sounds and Multimedia control panel lets you associate a given sound with a given Windows event. Windows stores the sounds it uses in files with the wav extension. Windows understands wav files and can "play" them through your sound card.

Windows comes with lots of sounds that you can associate with Windows events (if you installed the sound files). You can also purchase CD-ROMs full of wav files, download sound files from online services or bulletin boards, or get them over the Internet.

The sounds that come with Windows are arranged as "sound schemes," so you can apply them all at once to the designated Windows events. This makes it a lot easier to apply sounds. You can even create your own sound schemes by choosing from among the wav files that are installed on your computer.

You can test the sounds by selecting an event, choosing a sound from the Name drop-down list or browsing for it, and clicking the triangular Play button, as shown in Figure 15-8. If you prefer that an event take place in silence, you can choose (None) instead of a sound from the Name drop-down list.

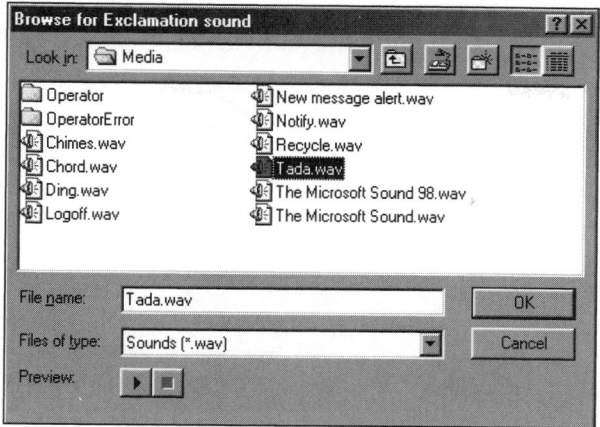

Figure 15-8: The Sounds and Multimedia control panel. Highlight a Windows event, select or browse for a sound, and then click the triangular play button next to Preview.

If you didn't install the sound schemes when you installed Windows, there won't be any listed in the Scheme drop-down list. To install the sound schemes that come with Windows, click the Add/Remove Programs icon in your Control Panel, click the Windows Setup tab, highlight Multimedia, and then click the Details button. Mark "Multimedia sound schemes," click OK twice, and insert your Windows CD-ROM when prompted.

Secret

Desktop themes, which include unnamed sound schemes as well as many other Desktop elements, are available from a variety of sources, including the Internet. The sounds within the themes are associated with Windows events, but no name appears in the Scheme field. If you like, you can name and save a theme's sound scheme. First click the Desktop Themes icon in the Control Panel, choose a theme, and click OK or Apply. Second, open the Sounds applet, click the Save As button, type a name for the new scheme, and click OK.

You've now associated the sounds that came from the Desktop theme that you chose with a sound scheme name. Later, if you choose a new Desktop theme, or no theme, you can still use the sounds associated with the previous theme by applying the sound scheme that you just named.

Applying Sounds to Application Events

Windows comes with sounds and sound schemes that you can apply to various Windows events. Application programmers can also add sounds to events that are specific to their application. If an application doesn't have a sound associated with a particular event, Windows uses the Windows sound that is associated with that event. For example, Windows uses the sound associated with its own Open Program event when you open an application, unless the application has a different sound (or no sound) associated with that event.

Events are organized by application. The first application is Windows. Scroll down the Events list in the Sounds and Multimedia Properties dialog box to see other applications and events.

Secret

Windows users can add sounds to specific applications and specific application events, even if the application programmers neglected to do so. This means that each application can have its own unique sounds for similar types of (or different) events. This requires editing the registry. Here's how:

STEPS

Adding Sounds to Application Events

Step 1. Click Regedit.exe in your \Windows folder.

Step 2. Navigate to this key:

HKEY_CURRENT_USER\ AppEvents\ Schemes\ Apps

Step 3. Highlight Apps in the left pane. Right-click the right pane, and choose New, Key. Type the name of the application's executable file. For example, type **Write** for Windows Write. Press Enter. (If your application is already listed under the Apps key, you can skip this step.)

Step 4. Highlight the key that you just created (or the existing key if your application was already listed) in the left pane of the Registry Editor, right-click the right pane, and choose New ➪ Key. Type one of the following event names:

AppGPFault
Close
MailBeep
Maximize
MenuCommand
MenuPopup
Minimize
Open
RestoreDown
RestoreUp
SystemAsterisk
SystemExclamation
SystemQuestion
SystemHand

You can see more about what these event names mean by navigating to

HKEY_CURRENT_USER\ AppEvents\ EventLabels

and then clicking any one of the event names.

Step 5. Highlight the new key that you just created in the left pane of the Registry Editor, right-click the right pane, and choose New ⇨ Key. Type **.current**.

Step 6. Repeat steps 4 and 5 to name events associated with your application until you have named all the events that you care to. Exit the registry.

Step 7. Click the Sounds applet in the Control Panel. Scroll down the Events list until you find the name of the application that you just named sound events for in the registry. Click a sound event, and select a wav file to associate with that event by selecting it from the Name list or browsing for it with the Browse button.

You can make this all a little easier by exporting the HKEY_CURRENT_USER\ AppEvents\ Schemes\ Apps key from the registry using the Registry Editor. You can use this text file as a basis for creating a reg file that you can merge into the registry. Edit this reg file to duplicate the steps above for each application whose events you want to add sounds to.

To learn more about reg files, turn to the "Exporting and Importing the Registry" section of Chapter 11.

Missing Audio Components

Sounds (wav files) in Windows are played through the Microsoft Audio Compression Manager (MSACM), which is also known as *Wavemapper*. Windows comes with a number of audio compression components, called *codecs*; you can see a list of them by clicking the Multimedia icon in the Control Panel, clicking the Devices tab, and clicking the plus sign next to the Audio Compression Codecs icon. Windows reads each wav file and determines the best codec with which to play it.

If you do not have all of the audio compression components of Windows installed (or if one becomes damaged), you may see one of the following error messages when you try to play sounds in Windows:

```
Your audio hardware cannot play files like the current file.
Mmsystem326
No wave device that can play files in the current format is installed.
Mmsystem296
The file cannot be played on the specified MCI device. The file may be
corrupt, or not in the correct format.
```

Although the last message appears when you try to play an avi file (video clip), the problem is with the file's audio compression.

The first thing to do is make sure you have installed the optional audio compression components of Windows. Open the Control Panel, click Add/ Remove Programs, go to the Windows Setup tab, and double-click the

Multimedia icon. If Audio Compression is not marked, do so and click OK twice.

If the Audio Compression option is marked, it may not be installed properly. To remove it, clear the Audio Compression checkbox and click OK twice to complete the removal. Now follow the directions in the previous paragraph to reinstall Audio Compression. Compressed sound should now play without errors.

The situation is similar with the Volume Control tool, located in the Multimedia section of the Windows Setup tab. If volume control is not available after you install Windows, you need to follow the same procedures for it as you would for Audio Compression.

Windows decides whether to install tools such as Volume Control depending on the hardware that it detects during setup. If your computer contains an ISA Plug and Play device that is not turned on by the BIOS, Windows won't detect it until after setup, so it won't install the related tools.

Keep Video Clips from Disappearing

Perhaps you've been surfing the Web and downloading and playing multimedia files. Perhaps you hate the way these multimedia selections play and then disappear. Thanks to Bart Austin, here's a way to keep those clips open so you can play them again as often as you need.

STEPS

Setting Video Clips to Stay Visible

Step 1.   Start the Explorer and then choose View ➪ Folder Options, and click the File Types tab.

Step 2.   Scroll down the "Registered file types" list until you get to Video Clip, and select this entry. If you have more than one Video Clip entry, select the one with av i as its extension (you can change the other ones later if you wish). The application used to open files of this type is ActiveMovie. (Don't worry if you see RUNDLL32 listed to the right of "Opens with" in the File Types tab—that's just the first part of the path to ActiveMovie.) Click the Edit button.

Step 3.   In the Edit File Type dialog box, click Play in the Actions box, and then click the Edit button.

Step 4. In the Application "Used to perform this action" field, delete the `/close` switch at the end of the command, including the space just before it (since the command will probably be longer than the field, use the End key to make sure you are at the end of the command line). The `/play` switch should now be the last switch on the command line.

Step 5. Click the OK button, and then click Close twice.

You should now be able to download and run `avi` files without having them vanish as soon as they reach the end of their recorded span.

Regional Settings

Where are you and where is your computer?

Regional settings have to do with how date, time, money, and numbers are sorted and displayed. Windows keeps track of which country has which customs regarding these most core symbols of civilization. If the application you are using is smart enough to ask in advance, it can display these values correctly.

You can use the Regional Settings control panel to set the particular configuration yourself (from among many options) if you need to make adjustments.

TweakUI

We mention TweakUI continually throughout this book. It used to be part of the Windows 98 CD-ROM, but now is only available as a separate PowerToys download. Nevertheless, it is not a supported part of Windows, as far as Microsoft is concerned.

You can use TweakUI to "tweak" all sorts of user interface settings. Play with it for a while to see what it can do. (See Figure 15-9.)

TweakUI's Control Panel tab lets you choose which applets are available in the Control Panel. Hiding applets in this way does not uninstall them, but simply protects them from tampering. Similarly, you can use the My Computer tab to hide disk drives from users.

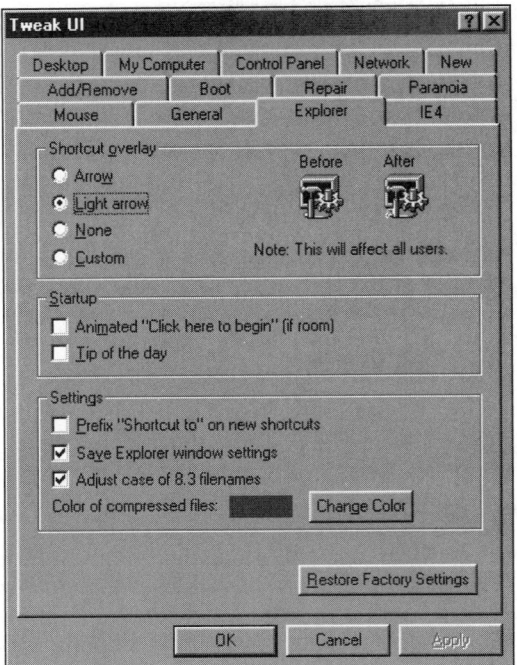

Figure 15-9: TweakUI. Click a tab to find a whole new set of "tweaks."

The Repair tab lets you fix all kinds of problems. Among others, you can rebuild icons that have gotten lost or corrupted, repair file associations, repair the Fonts folder, and repair the Registry editor.

You can also use the Desktop tab to remove or rename special icons such as the Recycle Bin. It's worth exploring TweakUI in advance, so you'll remember it's there when you need it.

Properties

Right-click an object and click Properties. The object's properties are displayed.

Tip

An even quicker way of displaying an object's properties is to hold down the Alt key and click the object's icon. You can also highlight an object, hold down the Alt key, and press Enter.

Pretty much anything you see on your Desktop has properties, except, interestingly enough, the Control Panel icons, which are often properties themselves. For example, the Display icon contains the Desktop's properties.

Every file has properties. Every shortcut to a Windows program has properties, as does every shortcut to a DOS program.

Like the settings in the Control Panel, most properties are discussed in the relevant chapter. We mention properties here because we want to point out that they are a general phenomenon. While they aren't universal—you may run old Windows 3.1x applications that don't use them—they will become more common as developers integrate them into applications.

Summary

The Control Panel settings let you configure hardware and software drivers.

▶ We show you how to quickly get to the different Control Panel settings.

▶ You can install and remove Windows applications through a consistent interface.

▶ You can choose your settings for displaying currency, time, and date.

▶ The Control Panel has a setting for associating sounds with Windows 98 events.

Chapter 16

My System

In This Chapter

This extensive chapter deals with many different system issues, including installing Windows with other operating systems, Windows scripting, and password control. Windows can be complex, and this chapter reflects this.

▶ Your Windows programs run faster if you have configured your computer to make your most frequently used programs the most accessible on your hard disk.

▶ You can set up your hard disk to accommodate multiple versions of Windows as well as other operating systems. We show you how.

▶ Wouldn't it be great if Windows came with a powerful and easy to use scripting or batch language and recorder? It doesn't, but we tell you what's there.

▶ If you want to clear out your user profiles, you'll learn how.

▶ Put your information in where your computer manufacturer did previously.

▶ The Windows Upgrade Web site is supposed to solve problems. It can have a few of its own.

The Different Versions of Windows

You can purchase a Windows CD-ROM in three versions: the complete retail version, the upgrade version, or (with a new computer) the OEM, or Original Equipment Manufacturer version. The full retail version allows you to format and install Windows on a new hard disk without any reference to an existing copy of Windows or DOS. This version can also upgrade your previous version of Windows — it just costs more than the upgrade version.

The OEM version that comes with new PC systems cannot upgrade previous versions of Windows. Microsoft would rather that you didn't try to use it for that function. If you try to use this CD-ROM to upgrade your neighbor's system, you will get an error message.

The next section shows you how to circumvent some of these restrictions.

Undocumented Windows Setup Switches

You can find out about the documented setup switches in Chapter 2 or online in the Microsoft Knowledge Base. Look for articles on Windows setup switches. Table 16-1 lists three undocumented setup switches.

Table 16-1	Undocumented Switches for Windows Setup
Switch	*Resulting Action*
Setup /NTLDR	Bypasses any detection of a previously installed operating system. By default, OEM/VAR versions of the Windows full releases can be installed only on a new computer without any previously installed operating system. This switch allows the Windows setup program to circumvent this restriction.
Setup /Pf	Creates a new Windows registry. All existing settings found in your registry will be lost. You would only want to use this if you are unable to load Windows because of a corrupted registry and you are unable to copy a previously saved version of the registry over your corrupted version.
Setup /nm	Bypasses the detection of your computer's processor. Allows Windows to be installed on computers that do not meet Microsoft minimum requirements (in other words, 386, 486SX, and so on). Also skips the check for the math coprocessor.

Thanks to Anthony Kinyon for pointing out these undocumented features.

Save Your Windows Uninstall Information

Remember back when you installed Windows Millennium (Me) over your previous operating system? You had the option to save system files. If you said yes, then you can uninstall Windows Me later and go back to Windows 98 or 95.

Tip

If you've forgotten whether you saved this information or not, you can check it out by clicking Start ➪ Settings ➪ Control Panel ➪ Add/Remove Programs. If you can find Uninstall Windows Me in your Install/Uninstall program list, then you in fact did save the system files for your previous operating system.

If you should happen to reinstall Windows Me (for whatever reason), these saved system files from your previous operating system are going to be lost, and you won't be able to get back to your previous operating system.

Secret

Before you reinstall Windows Me, you'll want to move the files that contain the backed up system files for your previous operating system to another folder. We suggest that you use your own My System folder.

These files—`Winundo.dat`, `Winundo.ini`, and `Winlfn.ini`—are marked Read-only, Hidden, and System. You'll find them in the root directory of the drive that contains your `\Windows` folder. You can drag and drop them into the My System folder. After you've moved the files, you can reinstall Windows Me.

Check Your Readme Files to Avoid Problems

When most software developers release a product that has last-minute changes—or incompatibilities that appeared after the manual was written—they include a `Readme.txt` file with the program. When Microsoft releases a new operating system, it includes a *dozen* or so of these text files, all with different names.

It's a good idea to read these files, whether you are responsible for maintaining only your own computer or hundreds. A few lines in one of these last-minute files can describe a fix to a problem that could take you hours to figure out yourself.

To find these files, open your `\Windows` folder in the Explorer, and click View ⇨ Arrange Icons ⇨ By Type (or click the Type column heading button in Details view). All the `txt` files should appear together.

If you are running Windows Me, you should examine at least these major files:

- `General.txt`—For problems that affect all computers
- `Hardware.txt`—For specific computers and peripherals
- `Network.txt`—If you have a network
- `Printers.txt`
- `Display.txt`

These files offer a fascinating look at the difficulties that can occur when Microsoft and independent hardware and software developers try to make all of their stuff work together. Here are a few gems:

- USB hubs. Numerous Universal Serial Bus (USB) hubs have problems when powered by a PC bus (rather than a power adapter), or when certain USB devices are plugged in. See `Hardware.txt` for Microsoft's comments on these devices.

- PCI video. Some PCI-based video adapters (Microsoft doesn't say which ones) crash Windows upon first startup, or in 16-color VGA mode, or in Safe mode, because they need different `Vga.drv` and `Vga.vxd` files. Copy these files from the Windows CD-ROM at `\Drivers\Display\Vga\Vga.drv` and `\Drivers\Display\Oldvga\Vga.vxd` to your `\Windows\System` folder, as described in `General.txt`.

- Update your BIOS. You can avoid numerous problems running Windows by upgrading your computer to the latest version of its BIOS firmware. See `Hardware.txt` for Microsoft's recommendations on several specific machines.

- PC Card modems. If you get Modem Not Found or Modem Not Ready messages from your PC Card modem with Windows' power management enabled, you may need to add a short delay to the registry. Click Start ⇨ Run, type **Regedit.exe**, and when Regedit opens, navigate to \HKEY_ LOCAL_MACHINE\System\CurrentControlSet\Services\Class\Modem. Select the key for your PC Card modem. (Click 0000, 0001, or a similar key number and read the modem description in the right pane to determine which modem is your PC Card modem if you have more than one.) Right-click the right pane and choose New ⇨ DWORD Value. Name this value **ConfigDelay**. Double-click ConfigDisplay. In the Edit DWORD Value dialog box, mark the Decimal option button and type **3000** (for a 3-second delay) in the Value Data field. Click OK and close the Registry Editor.

WinAlign Makes Applications Load Faster

One of Windows' biggest performance improvements is that it *aligns* programs. Microsoft has demonstrated that aligned programs load an average of 30 to 40 percent faster than ordinary programs. They also run faster and consume less memory.

When you install Windows Me or 98, its setup routine automatically runs a utility called `WinAlign.dll`. This utility rewrites application programs so that their executable sections begin on 4K boundaries. WinAlign is automatically placed in your Task Scheduler (it's labeled Tune Up Application Start). You should definitely let it run as part of your regular maintenance. (See "Reschedule Maintenance if Your Computer Doesn't Stay Up All Night" and other topics in Chapter 14 for more on scheduling your maintenance.)

Aligned programs benefit from Windows' support of *mapped memory I/O out of cache*. This means that Windows can run a program from cache memory without also copying the program to an equal amount of main memory. This saves RAM and reduces the use of a much slower swap file.

WinAlign gives programs the greatest benefit after you have converted your hard drive to FAT32, a more efficient method of storing information than the file allocation table used by older versions of Windows, FAT16. We discuss the pros and cons of converting to FAT32 in Chapter 37 of this book.

To see a list of which programs have been aligned, open the `Winali.ini` file in the \Windows\System folder (see Figure 16-1). Microsoft Office applications since Office 95 have been made available for alignment, but other software vendors have taken advantage of this option.

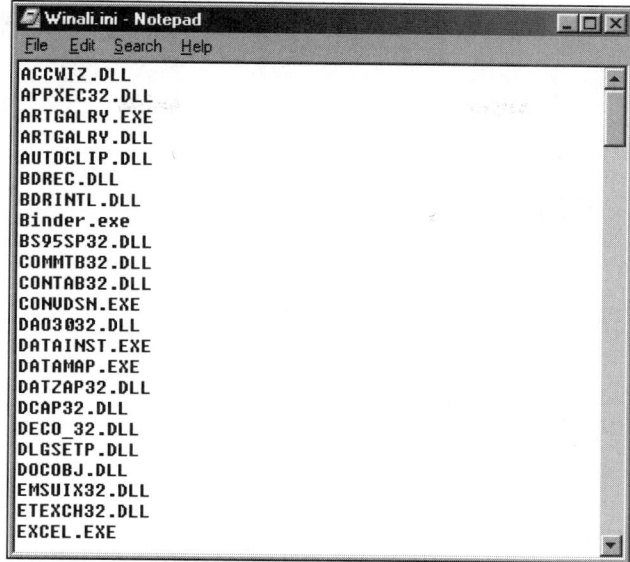

Figure 16-1: A portion of one computer's Winali.ini file, opened in Notepad

Take Advantage of Windows Performance Improvements

Unfortunately, applications don't load more quickly as soon as you install them. To make this happen, you have to do four things:

- You must convert your hard drive to FAT32.

- You must run the WinAlign utility to convert your installed applications to work with the new optimization methods. (See the previous section for more about WinAlign.)

- You must run each of your favorite applications at least four times. This allows a small background process called Taskmon to monitor your applications and log the files they need and the order in which they load.

- Taskmon logs each application the second time you run it and every third time after that. Programs you've run eight times will be optimized first, then programs you've run five times, and so on. You can see Taskmon's logs (lgc files) by using Notepad to open them from the hidden \Windows\Applog folder. Figure 16-2 shows the contents of Winword.lgc, the log file for Microsoft Word.

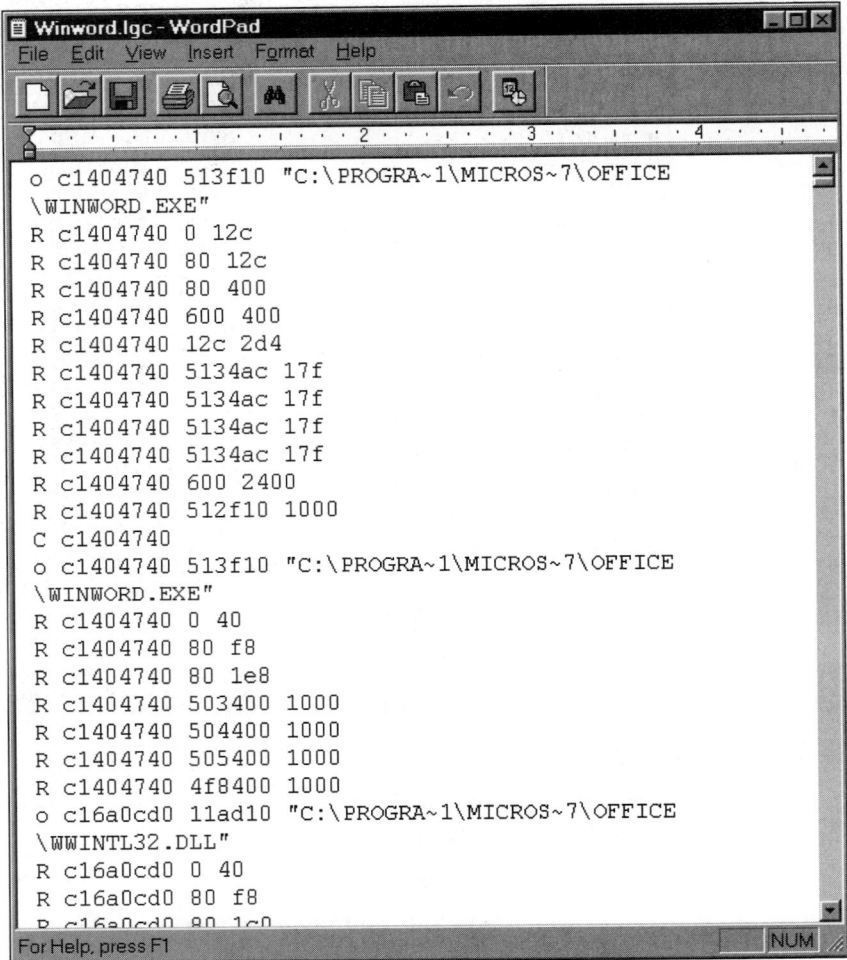

Figure 16-2: A small portion of a Winword.lgc file

■ You must run Defrag. Defrag uses Taskmon's logs to write your program files to disk in the order in which they load fastest.

Microsoft has designed the optimization process to happen over a period of time for all Windows users who convert to FAT32. Eventually, every user will run every installed application four times or more. And eventually every user will run Defrag (or schedule it to be run automatically, a process that the Task Scheduler makes easy). This causes the new, more efficient loading patterns to be written to disk.

But why wait for all of this to take place gradually? If you have just installed Windows Me or 98, and if you decide to convert to FAT32, you might as well get its benefits sooner rather than later by running WinAlign, opening your favorite applications more than four times each, and running Defrag.

Before you implement these features, however, you may want to know how much of a speedup you've gained. To document this, you can perform a simple test using your existing configuration.

STEPS

Measuring Speedup in Opening Applications

Step 1. Create a shortcut in your \Windows\Start Menu\Programs\ StartUp folder for each of your major applications. To do this, find the executable file that launches each application. Right-drag each exe file into the StartUp folder, and click Create Shortcut(s) Here.

Step 2. Shut down Windows and then turn off the power and restart the system. Clock the launch time required by Windows and your suite of applications. You can do this before or after converting to FAT32, which by itself has little or no performance benefit.

Step 3. Now open each of the applications in your test, four or more times apiece, and run Defrag. You may want to do this at the end of your workday, because Defrag can take several hours.

Step 4. Repeat step 2, noting the difference in time to launch your suite of applications. After the test, delete the shortcuts from your StartUp folder.

Running Multiple Versions of Windows (and Other Operating Systems)

You can configure your computer in a number of ways to run multiple operating systems or multiple versions of Windows. One method is built into Windows Me and Windows NT; another requires only the use of batch files; others require additional software.

Rename the Boot Files

Back in 1995, Microsoft made it somewhat easy to switch between DOS (or Windows 3.1) and Windows 95. They thought that this allowed people who worried about their transition to Windows 95 a way to get back to their older applications.

With the release of FAT32, the 32-bit disk file system, Microsoft pulled this dual-boot capability from the newer OSR2 version of Windows 95. This was because DOS couldn't handle FAT32-formatted hard disk partitions. But you can dual boot between Windows Me or 98 and DOS using only the capability that comes with these versions of Windows if your boot partition is formatted as FAT16.

Microsoft accomplishes the feat of dual booting by renaming certain files in the root directory. For example, when dual booting between DOS (or Windows 3.1) and Windows 98, the `Autoexec.bat`, `Config.sys`, `Io.sys`, `Msdos.sys`, and `Command.com` files are given either the `dos` or `w40` extensions, depending on which operating system you are booting to. If you are booting to DOS, the files with the `dos` extension are renamed.

Use the Windows NT, 2000, or Other Boot Loader

You can put Windows NT or 2000 and Windows Me on the same computer and boot to either one using the Windows NT/2000 boot loader. Install Windows Me first and then Windows NT or 2000. Be sure to install each of them into its own partition (Windows Me on `C:`, Windows 2000 on `D:`, for example), and not in the same partition as the other. Windows Me and Windows 2000 can both read partitions that are formatted as FAT32. Windows Me, however, cannot read files on a partition that has been formatted as NTFS (NT File System) by Windows NT or Windows 2000.

Tip

If you've already installed Windows NT, you can still make this work. Check out the Microsoft Knowledge Base article "Setting Up Dual Boot After Installing Windows NT" at `http://support.microsoft.com/support/kb/articles/q153/7/62.asp`.

We discuss OS/2, NT, and other boot loaders in Chapter 3.

Batch Files that Copy Boot Files to the Root Directory

You can use a number of variations on the method described in "Rename the Boot Files" earlier in this chapter to store as many different versions of Windows as you have room for. You can then switch among them after running a batch file and rebooting your computer. The batch file will copy the appropriate versions of the `Autoexec.bat`, `Io.sys`, and other files to your root directory from a folder associated with each version of Windows. You'll find instructions and examples on how to do this at Lee Chapell's site: `http://www.webdev.net/orca/`.

This method works best when you have two completely different operating systems, such as DOS and Windows Me, or Windows 2000 and Windows Me. DOS requires a FAT16 boot partition to be installed on if it's going to be dual booted with Windows Me.

If you want to run Windows 98 and Windows Me, you'll need to also track the Program Files folder. For example, installing Windows Me after Windows 98 would install the newer version of Outlook Express over the Windows 98 version, unless you used batch files to rename the Program Files folder.

Using this method, you can install two different-language versions of Windows Me. This allows you to develop and test programs in two different languages on the same computer.

Partition Your Hard Disk

If you use additional software, it is possible to completely hide one operating system from the other (or multiple others). For example, Partition Magic (http://www.powerquest.com/partitionmagic/index.html) lets you partition your hard disk, switch between active partitions (booting first off one and then the other), and hide partitions from each other. With this method, you can install completely different operating systems in different partitions.

Partition Magic lets you decide which partition is the active partition — the C: drive. You can install one version of Windows on drive C:, change the active partition to another partition, and install another version of Windows on that partition, which also is seen as drive C:.

You'll find details about how disk partitioning works at http://www.users.intercom.com/~ranish/part/primer.htm.

Partition Magic is not the only software that is available to partition your hard disk and allow for multiple operating systems. There is a freeware program, Ranish Partition Manager, available at http://www.users.intercom.com/~ranish/part/. You can see how it works by going to http://www.users.intercom.com/~ranish/part/faq.htm.

Partitioning the hard disk and making first one partition active, then another, can cause lots of problems if you want to keep one e-mail folder, one set of favorites, one set of documents, and so on. You'll probably want to move your My Documents folder, your Favorites folder, your e-mail and newsgroups folders, and even all of your program folders to another partition that can be viewed by both operating systems.

You can use TweakUI to change the location of the My Documents, Favorites, and Program Files folders. Click the General tab, and then click the Change Location button. To see how to move your e-mail, newsgroups, and Windows address book, turn to "Save All Your Documents" in Chapter 27.

Boot from Different Hard Disks

Usually, the switch settings on your hard disks determine which physical hard disk can be used as your boot drive. Some BIOSes allow you to switch between hard drives, but not many. You can, however, use software to switch between hard drives, making one or the other your boot drive.

The program that allows this is BootIt, and it is available at `http://www.terabyteunlimited.com/DIF.HTM`.

Linux Boot Manager

Linux and Windows can coexist on the same hard drive, although in different partitions. If you use the Linux boot manager, you have the option of exiting to DOS and then starting Windows or just continuing on with Linux. You can find out more about how to do this at `http://visar.csustan.edu:8000/HyperNews/get/giveaway/10/3.html` and `http://listas.conectiva.com.br/LDP/HOWTO/mini/Multiboot-with-LILO-1.html`.

Numerous other sites mirror the Multiboot-with-LILO-1.html document. You can receive these and other Linux HowTo documents via e-mail if you fill out a form at any of these mirror sites. Use a Web search engine to find "LDP/HOWTO." (LDP stands for the Linux Documentation Project.)

How About Another Operating System?

While you might be able to go for another word processor, spreadsheet, or database, getting a completely different operating system is a whole other story. Not to mention all the religious issues involved, there are the questions of how to install it, where to put it, how to make it work with your existing operating system, and how to read your existing files and hard disks. Oh, and did we mention, what's the point of all this pain?

Other operating system vendors want to have a life after Microsoft, so those that provide operating systems on Intel hardware have had to accommodate the huge installed base of Windows by providing ways for users to use both their operating system and Windows. For the most part, they have done so only grudgingly, which has only hurt their case and their sales.

On the other hand, if you think of another operating system as just another application that's working in its own unique environment, then it doesn't seem quite so quirky — especially if that operating system has been tuned to provide particular advantages in a well-defined niche.

Linux and BeOS are two operating systems that could find a home on your (large) hard disk, and still let you boot into Windows. There are lots of reasons to use these other operating systems, most of which don't apply to the vast majority of computer users. But since you're reading this book, you can't necessarily count yourself out.

BeOS is aimed at people producing multimedia, whether they be rock bands, video artists, wedding photographers, or the weekend artist. BeOS supports both FAT16 and FAT32 hard drives — always a good first start — and can network on the Microsoft Network (we're talking the local area network, not MSN, although BeOS has a browser that will let you do that, too).

BeOS supports a wide range of hardware (although nothing like Windows), so if you're on its hardware support list, you at least have a fighting chance of getting it up and running. You can find out more about BeOS at its Web site at http://www.be.com, and at http://www.bedepot.com.

Why Not Linux?

Linux has a great reputation among its supporters for reliability. It doesn't have much of a reputation for ease of use, ease of installation, or a consistent, universally supported standard graphical user interface.

Linux appeals to the folks who are interested in a very clean implementation of UNIX on Intel hardware. While that isn't everyone, it certainly is a market. It benefits from the fact that you don't have to feel that you are supporting a monopolist when you purchase or download the software. You're rooting for the little guy, the underdog. All the ambivalent feeling of envy and desire can be set aside.

Linux is supported by anyone and everyone who is interested in supporting it. It's a community as opposed to a corporate support network. Since everyone hates the kind of software support they're used to receiving (although we must admit we've been getting pretty good support lately from corporate support groups), this has definite appeal.

Linux is open source code; anyone who has a very good grasp of C can modify the code to his or her own specifications. This turns a large portion of the geek world into your development department. Many souls can take pride in a shared product.

So, combine its socially redeeming characteristics, its techno-geek panache, and its technically solid base, and you've got an operating system that is at the very least a competitive product. You need the worldwide support of a community the size of the Linux community to compete against a company the size of Microsoft.

You can read the gospel from the prophet's mouth at http://www.linux.org.

Transfer Files from Windows to Linux

If you run Samba using the latest versions of Linux, you can mount a FAT32 volume. You can also access the Linux file system from another Windows computer by running Samba under Linux. Because Windows sends an encrypted password by default, you'll either need to either configure Samba for CHAP or PAP password authentication protocols, or change the Windows registry to send unencrypted passwords. You can see how to do this by reading "Unable to Connect to a Samba Server with Windows" at `http://support.microsoft.com/support/kb/articles/Q187/2/28.asp`.

Windows Scripting

Windows comes with a scripting engine (the Windows Scripting Host) that allows software developers to write little programs, known as *scripts*, to automate various tasks. It is sort of a Windows macro language, but at a higher level, with a longer learning curve and without the built-in capability for macro recording. Scripts can be written in JScript and VBScript.

You can find scripts written with browsing in mind at `http://www.javascriptsource.com/` and `http://www.scriptsearch.com/`. Some of these may be applicable to your Windows Desktop. If you are a developer, you can learn more about how to use scripting languages at: `http://msdn.microsoft.com/scripting/default.htm?/scripting/vbscript/` and `http://msdn.microsoft.com/scripting/default.htm?/scripting/jscript/`.

One very cool site with a long list of FAQs about scripting is located at `http://wsh.glazier.co.nz/frame.htm`. You'll find a chat area there with an archive and links to newsgroups. Also, the PC Tech area of the *PC Magazine* Web site, an excellent source of information on deeper Windows issues, has an article on scripting at `http://www.zdnet.com/pcmag/pctech/content/solutions/uu1714a.htm`.

Chris Pirillo recommends `http://www.infohiway.com/javascript/indexf.htm`. He says, "this particular site covers JavaScript, Perl, CSS and various Plug-ins — and they've got a monthly newsletter, so you shouldn't be more than a few weeks away from getting the latest JavaScript scoop."

Another obvious scripting Web site is `http://www.scripting.com`. It's not really devoted only to scripting, but has plenty of other material regarding Web site development.

If you want a Windows macro program that lets you record not only keystrokes but also mouse movements and clicks, then check out Macro Magic at `http://www.iolo.com`. You can use this macro development program, shown in Figure 16-3, to automate repeated tasks that are carried out while you use either Windows itself or Windows applications.

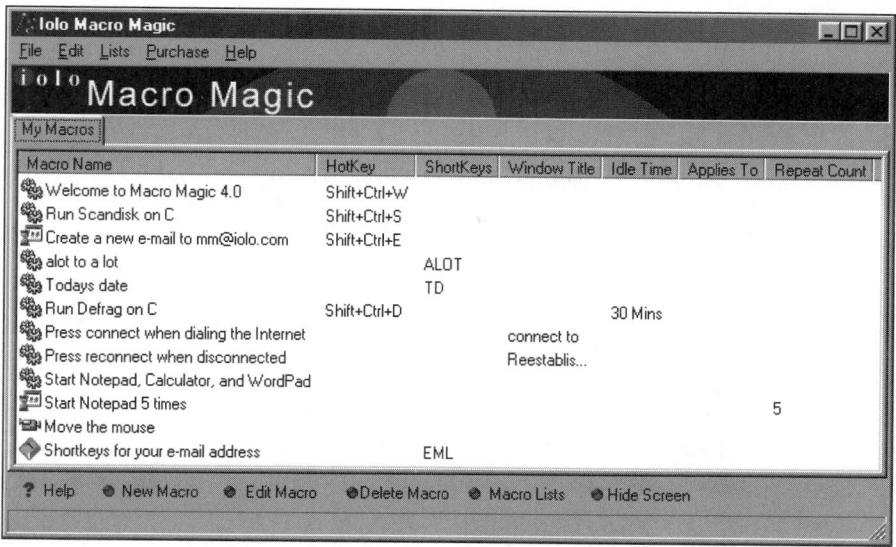

Figure 16-3: Macro Magic lists your macros for quick reference.

While Macro Magic can't automate every Windows task, it does enough to automate many of the simpler functions.

Windows Interface Language

WinBatch has been around forever, and it just keeps growing (at least in the number of Windows functions that it includes). While Microsoft has opened up the Windows scripting market with the ability to use JScript and VBScript, WinBatch uses its own Windows Interface Language (WIL).

WIL is basically a set of function names specific to Windows, along with the associated standard program flow control names. It is a very straightforward language, requiring only that you search for a function in the WIL help file to learn how to use that function. Did you really want to turn into a programmer?

WinBatch doesn't include a recorder to allow you to create a program by just performing the tasks that you want the program to automate. If you just want to send keystrokes to a Windows dialog box, this is essentially a three-line program. Your program can grow from there.

Here is a sample of a WIL program that opens up the Power Management control panel and changes the power scheme setting to the last one in the list of schemes:

```
;Open Power Management Control Panel
Run("C:\Windows\Control.exe", "powercfg.cpl")
```

```
;Wait 5 seconds until the Power Management window displays
WinWaitExist("Power Management Properties", 5)
;Change Power Management setting to the last one on the list and then
close the dialog box
SendKey("{PgDn}{Tab}{Tab}{Tab}{Tab}{Tab}{Enter}")
```

The WinBatch installation has a nasty habit of adding a massive number of commands to your file context menu. You can get these items out of your context menu by editing the registry as follows:

STEPS

Pulling WinBatch out of Your Context Menu

Step 1. Click Start ⇨ Run, type **regedit**, and press Enter.

Step 2. Click the plus sign to the left of HKEY_CLASSES_ROOT*.

Step 3. Continue opening up branches to ContextMenuHandlers.

Step 4. Highlight FileMenu under ContextMenuHandlers in the left pane of your Registry Editor.

Step 5. Click Registry ⇨ Export Registry File. Type **WinBatch FileMenu** and click Save. This saves this small branch of the registry in case you decide that you want these context menu items later.

Step 6. With FileMenu still highlighted, click Edit ⇨ Delete, Yes. Then close the Registry Editor.

Now all of the context menu items associated with WinBatch will be gone from your file context menus.

WinBatch is a shareware program, and you can download it from http://www.windowware.com.

AutoMate

If you're willing to pay for a macro/scripting/recording tool whose basic version costs almost as much as the operating system to begin with, then AutoMate is the program of choice. The $180 professional version lets you write VBA-compatible scripts. AutoMate also works as a scheduler, which allows you to set up tasks to be run at night.

We found that its keystroke and mouse movement recorder worked without any glitches, but AutoMate isn't restricted to just simple tasks. Its front end, shown in Figure 16-4, was a delight to use. An enterprise version of AutoMate sends task instructions over a TCP/IP network.

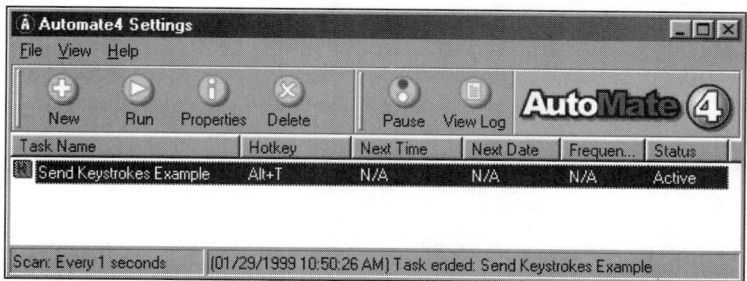

Figure 16-4: The main AutoMate window with one task highlighted

You can order or download AutoMate from `http://www.unisyn.com/automate/`.

Thanks to Chris Pirillo at `http://www.lockergnome.com` for telling us about this program.

Change Your Password when You Don't Have One

If you use a blank password, you have the happy fortune of not having to enter a password when you start Windows, or even to see the Password dialog box. But if you'd like to get this dialog box back, it's easy to do.

Click Start ⇨ Settings ⇨ Control Panel ⇨ Passwords, and click the Change Windows Password button (see Figure 16-5). Press Tab to shift from the Old Password field to the New Password field, leaving the Old Password field blank. Enter the new password twice, the second time in the Confirm New Password field. Click OK.

To change your password back to blank, type your existing password in the Old Password field, Tab through the other fields to the OK button, and press Enter.

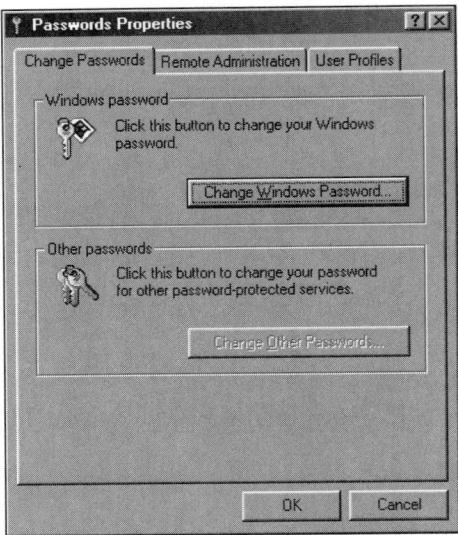

Figure 16-5: Click the Change Windows Password button to enter a new password.

Manage Your Passwords

Windows creates a file that stores various passwords, in an encrypted format, as you accumulate them. The key to this cache of passwords is the password that you use when you start Windows. If you have a blank password, then you don't see the opening User Name and Password dialog box. In this case, all your other passwords are available to you (and anyone else) without the bother of going through a password logon sequence.

A password cache is very powerful because it trades multiple passwords for just one (or, with a blank password, none). As passwords proliferate, especially on Web sites, it would be very inconvenient to keep track of them all manually. The password cache is a pwl file, and you'll find it in your \Windows folder.

Windows comes with a limited password management tool, the Password List Editor. You'll find it on your Windows CD-ROM at \tools\reskit\netadmin\ pwledit. It's a standalone application; you can run it from the CD-ROM by clicking the executable. The installation file, pwledit.inf, just puts a short-cut to it in the System Tools menu on your Start menu and installs it in the \Windows folder.

All that the Password List Editor will let you do is delete previously stored passwords, as shown in Figure 16-6. You can't see what the passwords or user names are. (See the next section to find out about tools that reveal passwords.)

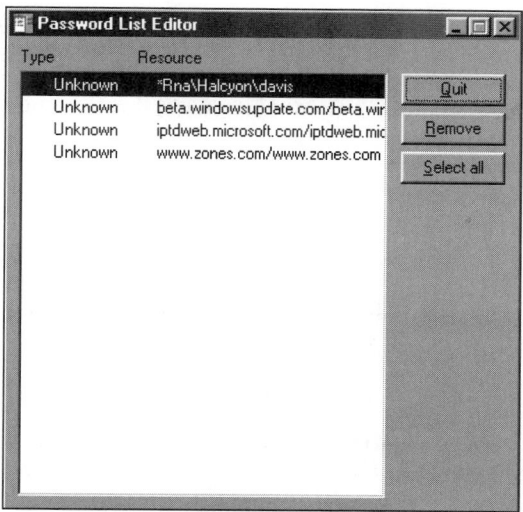

Figure 16-6: The Password List Editor doesn't let you edit, just delete.

Internet Explorer's AutoComplete feature lets you save passwords on the fly as you create them at various Web sites. You can clear the passwords if you like: In the Internet Explorer window, choose Tools ⇨ Internet Options, click the Content tab, click AutoComplete, and click Clear Passwords. The AutoComplete Settings dialog box, shown in Figure 16-7, also lets you decide whether to cache your user names and passwords as you create them.

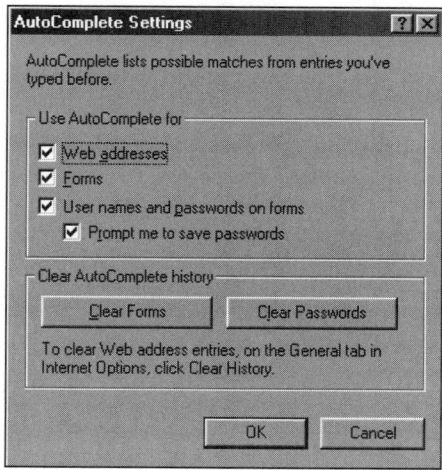

Figure 16-7: You access the AutoComplete Settings dialog box through Internet Explorer's Tools menu.

You can find much more sophisticated password management tools at `http://www.winfiles.com/apps/98/password.html`. The problem with the tools displayed on this Web page is that they are standalone; they don't interact with the powerful and convenient features of the Windows password caching system.

Passwords Revealed

Password Revealer is a little utility that displays your passwords when you move a special mouse pointer over the asterisks in the password field of a dialog box (for example, the DUN Connection dialog box).

You'll find it at `http://user.online.be/jos.branders/revealer.exe`.

Password Revealer comes ready to go; there is no install procedure. The executable you download is the program. Run `Revealer.exe`, and hold down your left mouse button over the Track button. Then drag over any button or field to display its contents. When you move your pointer over a field of asterisks, the underlying password appears.

Thanks to Chris Pirillo at `http://www.lockergnome.com`.

Another freeware package that reveals passwords is appropriately named Revelation. Drag Revelation's little cross, shown in Figure 16-8, across the asterisks in a password field, and the password behind the asterisks is revealed.

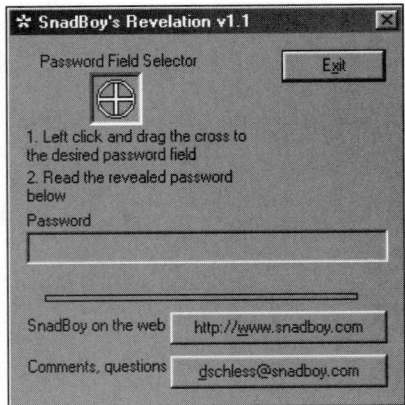

Figure 16-8: Revelation reveals the password behind the asterisks.

You'll find Revelation at `http://www.snadboy.com`.

Get Rid of the Users and Their Profiles

Once you start allowing other folks to use your computer, you'll find that their "stuff" is lying all over the place. You'll be wondering what happened to "one person = one computer." We discuss how to set up your computer for multiple users in Chapter 6.

Of course, there are lots of situations where it isn't *your* computer, but rather a shared resource — a family or business computer. If each person has his or her own user profile, then Windows keeps track of all sorts of individual settings for each user. User profiles aren't required, however, because a large group of people can choose to use the computer with the same settings.

Outlook Express can manage *user identities*, which are different than *user profiles*. One of the main reasons to set up user profiles prior to version 5 of Outlook Express was to separate everyone's e-mail, but you had to reinstall Outlook Express every time you added a profile. Now that identities are available, however, e-mail is no longer much of a reason to use profiles. Outlook Express handles identities in a completely different manner than user profiles — see "Using Identities" in Chapter 27 for a discussion of how to use them.

To delete one or more user profiles, take these steps:

STEPS

Deleting User Profiles

Step 1. Restart Windows and click Cancel at the Windows Logon dialog box. You'll have a Windows Logon dialog box if you have set up user profiles.

To remove a user profile, you need to log in to Windows as either another user or by clicking Cancel at the Logon dialog box. You can't delete a user profile if you are logged on as that user.

If you click Cancel, you aren't logged in as anyone. If you have a previous default user name that isn't used in the user profiles, you can log on as that user later.

Step 2. Click Start ➪ Settings ➪ Control Panel, and click Users to display the User Settings dialog box. If you have user profiles enabled and you have set up some users, they will be listed here, as shown in Figure 16-9. Highlight the user that you want to delete and click Delete.

Continued

STEPS

Deleting User Profiles *(continued)*

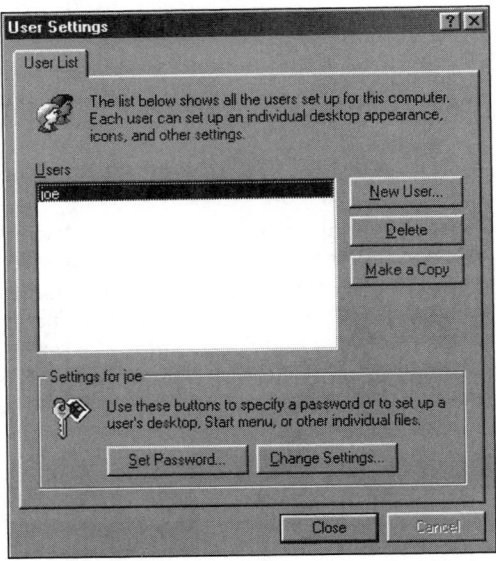

Figure 16-9: Joe is currently the only user enabled on this computer.

Step 3. Continue deleting users until you have deleted all that you want. Click Close.

Deleting a user in this manner does three things. It deletes the user's entry in the profile list in the registry, it deletes the user's profile folder in the \Windows\ Profiles folder, and it deletes the user's password cache file, *username*.pwl. You can check to be sure that these actions have taken place, or you can actually perform manually what the User Settings dialog box lets you do automatically by taking these steps:

STEPS

Deleting User Profiles Manually

Step 1. Open your Explorer and navigate to \Windows\Profiles. Delete any subfolders that have the same name as the user profile that you want to delete.

Step 2. Open your Registry Editor, navigate to HKEY_LOCAL_MACHINE\ SOFTWARE\ Microsoft\ Windows\ CurrentVersion\ ProfileList. Delete any keys under ProfileList that have the same name as the user profile you want to delete. If you want to delete all user profiles, delete the ProfileList key. Close the Registry Editor.

Step 3. In your Explorer, right-click the Windows folder icon, click Find, type the name of the user profile that you want to delete, and press Enter. If and when it appears in the Find results, delete the pwl file whose prefix is the same as user profile name.

This will delete the user's password cache. All of the passwords in the cache will be lost. Users whose pwl files you've deleted will need to know their user names and passwords if they want to access the same resources later. (This does not include the Outlook Express passwords.)

Step 4. The Find command used in step 3 may turn up cookie files associated with the user profile. You can delete these cookies in the Find dialog box by highlighting them there and pressing the Delete key.

All of the unique user settings will be eliminated. This includes all unique Favorites lists, Desktop shortcuts, and so on. Be sure to save these beforehand if you don't want them deleted.

If you've deleted all the user profiles, and checked to make sure that all traces of them are gone, you can now disable user profiles. You could have disabled user profiles first, but then you wouldn't have been able to delete user profiles automatically because the user list wouldn't have shown up in the Users control panel. You can delete user profiles manually even after you have disabled user profiles.

To disable the user profiles capability altogether, take these steps:

STEPS

Disabling User Profiles

Step 1. Restart Windows, and click Cancel at the Windows Logon dialog box. You'll have a Windows Logon dialog box if you have set up user profiles.

You don't need to take this step if you have already started Windows in this fashion when you deleted the user profiles.

Step 2. Click Start ⇨ Settings ⇨ Control Panel. Click Passwords, and click the User Profiles tab.

Continued

STEPS

Disabling User Profiles *(continued)*

Step 3. Mark "All users of this computer use the same preferences and desktop settings," as shown in Figure 16-10. Click OK.

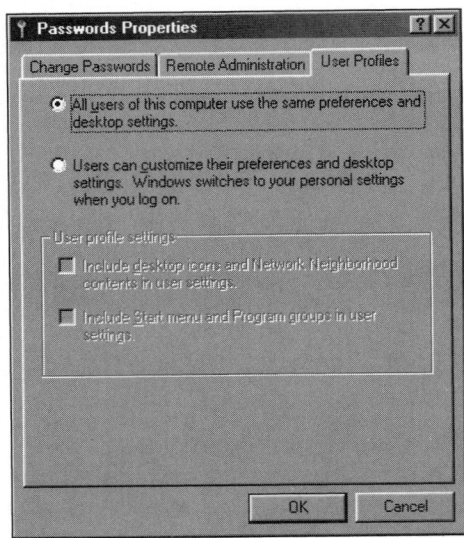

Figure 16-10: Mark the top option button on the User Profiles tab.

Step 4. Restart Windows when prompted.

You will now be prompted to enter your password, and will be provided the user name of the last user that logged on. If you have an original user name that you used before you started adding user profiles, enter this name in the "User name" field (see Figure 16-11). Enter the password associated with this user name, or tab to the OK button and press Enter if the password was blank.

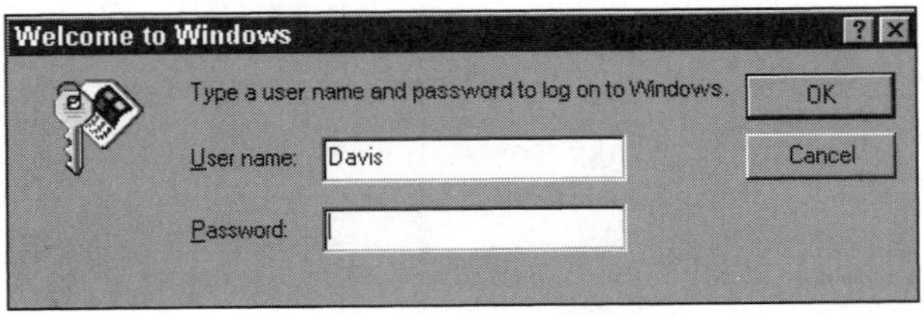

Figure 16-11: If you don't use a password, leave that field blank and click OK.

Windows will restart and use the password cache file associated with the user name that you just entered, *username*.pwl.

On the other hand, you may want to keep and later use a specific user's settings as the default user settings, while you get rid of all the other users and disable user profiles. In this case, you shouldn't delete this user profile from the User list. You can delete all the other user profiles using the "Deleting User Profiles" or "Deleting User Profiles Manually" steps earlier in this section.

Once you've deleted all of the other user profiles and disabled user profiles using the "Disabling User Profiles" steps earlier in this section, you can manually make the other changes required to make this user the default and only user as follows:

STEPS

Changing a User Profile to the Default User

Step 1. Open your Explorer. Navigate to \Windows\Profiles*username*. Move any of the files in the subfolders found under the user name to their corresponding location under the \Windows folder.

For example, copy any of the shortcuts in the user's Favorites folder to the \Windows\Favorites folder. You may want to delete the files and subfolders in the \Windows\Favorites folder first, or just add these favorites to them.

Step 2. Open your Registry Editor, and navigate to HKEY_LOCAL_MACHINE\ SOFTWARE\ Microsoft\ Windows\ CurrentVersion\ ProfileList. Delete the ProfileList key. Close the Registry Editor.

Step 3. Restart Windows and log in under this user name.

Take Over the General Tab of the System Properties Dialog Box

Microsoft lets computer manufacturers (OEMs) have access to the General tab of the Systems Properties dialog box so that they can provide a bit of labeling and some support information. It comes about through the magic of the Oeminfo.ini file in your \Windows\System folder.

You can take over this space for yourself. All you have to do is edit the Oeminfo.ini file and add an Oeminfo.bmp file to your \Windows\System folder, or replace the one that's already there.

STEPS

Editing the Oeminfo.ini File

Step 1.   Using your Explorer, navigate to your \Windows\System folder and find the Oeminfo.ini file.

If you don't have one, right-click in the \Windows\System folder in your Explorer, and click New ⇨ Text Document. Give the new document the name **Oeminfo.ini**.

Step 2.   Open the Oeminfo.ini file in Notepad by right-clicking it and clicking Open. You'll notice that it looks something like Figure 16-12, if you haven't just created it.

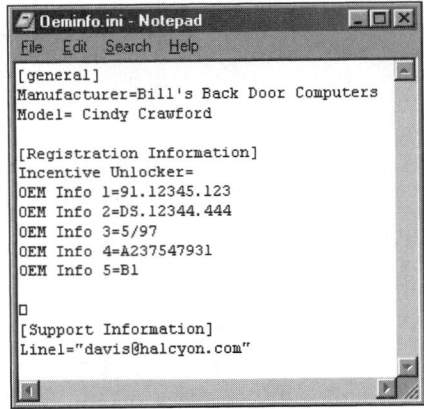

Figure 16-12: A sample Oeminfo.ini file

Step 3.   Change the string after "Manufacturer=" to whatever you like. Do the same after "Model=". If you are creating a new Oeminfo.ini, copy Figure 16-12, adding your own information.

Step 4.   Under [Support Information], add as many lines as you like, starting with **Line1=**, and continuing with **Line2=**, and so on. Put double-quote marks around the text that you are typing in here.

Step 5.   When you're done, click File ⇨ Save.

Step 6.   Open up your System Properties dialog box with Win+Pause/Break (or right-click the My Computer icon on your Desktop and click Properties). You'll notice that the manufacturer and model information you entered is displayed in the General tab. Click the Support Information button to see what you entered in the support information section of Oeminfo.ini.

Now it's time to add a logo.

STEPS

Adding an Oeminfo.bmp File

Step 1. Open up Microsoft Paint or any other paint package that can create a bmp image file. You can start Microsoft Paint by clicking Start ⇨ Programs ⇨ Accessories ⇨ Paint.

Step 2. Create an image 210 pixels wide and 120 pixel high. You can set the height and width of your image in Paint by clicking Image ⇨ Attributes.

Step 3. Save the image as Oemlogo.bmp in the \Windows\System folder.

Open up your System Properties dialog box (right-click the My Computer icon on your Desktop and click Properties). It will now contain your logo, as shown in Figure 16-13.

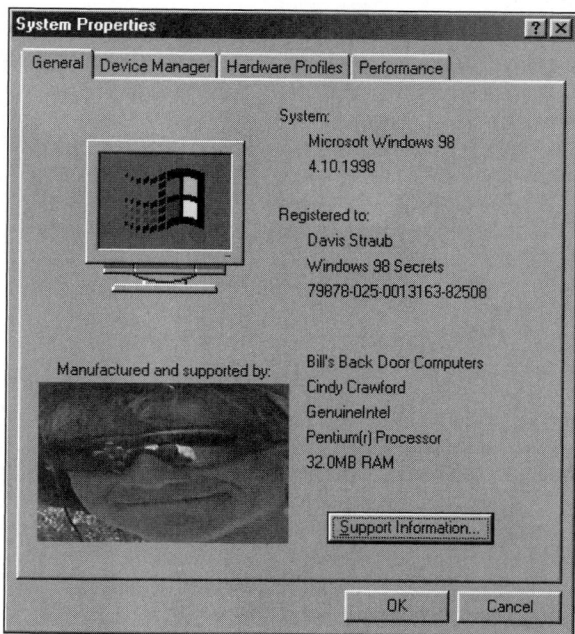

Figure 16-13: Our modified System Properties dialog box includes a photo.

Control the Control Panel

In Chapter 15, we show you how to create shortcuts to any of the Control Panel applications, and how to display specific tabs in multitabbed dialog boxes. Microsoft covers some of the same ground in their Knowledge Base article "How to Run Control Panel Tools by Typing a Command" at http://support.microsoft.com/support/kb/articles/q192/8/06.asp.

Help!

Perhaps, like us, you've found that Windows Help is often not as useful as you would like. We don't mean just the Windows Help files, but all the help files associated with all applications. Fortunately, in Windows Me the situation is greatly improved.

Now Microsoft has two help systems. One is the familiar Winhelp and the other is the new, compiled HTML-based help. The new HTML-based help system is far superior to the old Winhelp.

The full text search is available with both help systems. With full text search, you can display a list of all the topics that include the word that you type in the Search field. You can then click a topic heading to see if the contents of the topic are helpful, as shown in Figure 16-14.

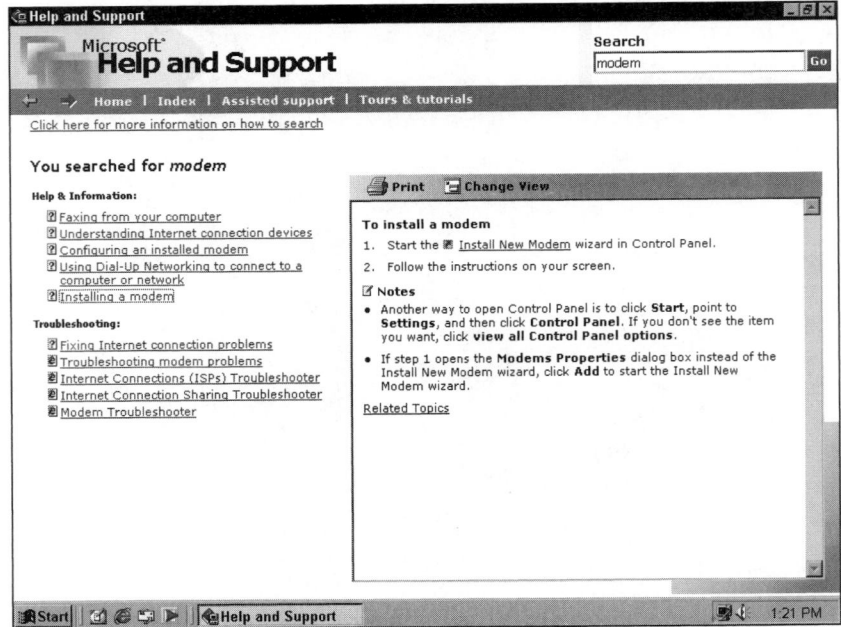

Figure 16-14: With Windows Me Help, you can click a link to choose one of the displayed topics.

The Winhelp full text search is also powerful. You can create a full text search index file that enables you to search for topics that contain the words that you typed, in the exact order that you typed them. You can also search for all topics that contain all the words you typed (an AND condition) or all topics that contain at least one word you typed (an OR condition).

To obtain these powerful full text search features with Winhelp-formatted help files, you need to click the Find tab (see Figure 16-15) or Find button (see Figure 16-16) in the associated help file. If a particular help file doesn't have a Find tab or a Find button, you are out of luck.

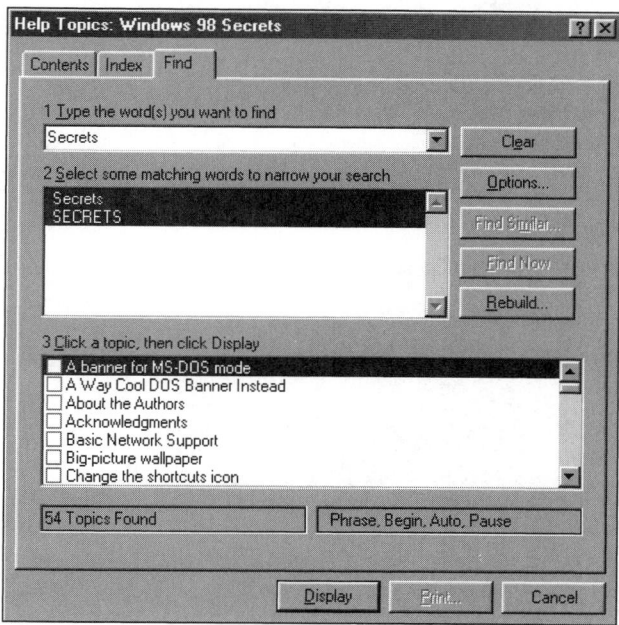

Figure 16-15: Click the Find tab the first time you open a new help file to create a full text search index.

Once you click the Find tab or button, you will be prompted by the Find Setup Wizard to create a full text search index, as shown in Figure 16-17. Click the "Maximize search capabilities" option button to produce the most powerful and flexible search index. This index file will be larger than the minimum produced if you don't click the Maximize button (which is why Microsoft doesn't make it the default choice), but if you have a hard disk whose size is measured in gigabytes, you'll have plenty of room for help-file indices.

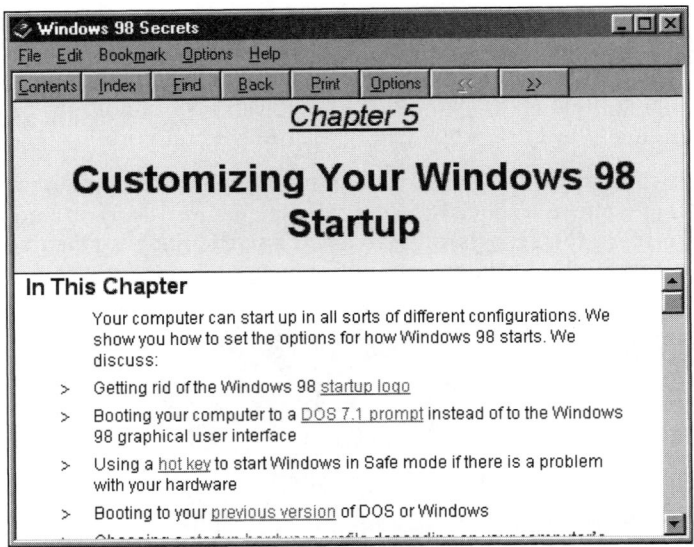

Figure 16-16: It is up to the help-file author to include a Find tab or Find button.

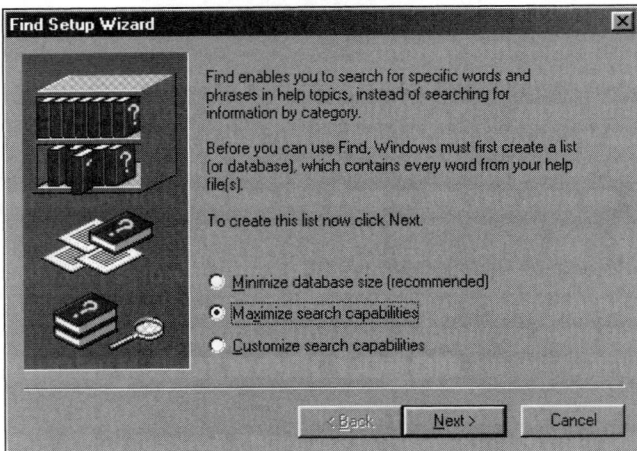

Figure 16-17: Microsoft used to be concerned about creating big help index files. Choose to maximize search capabilities unless you have a very small hard disk.

Once you have created a full text search index, you can determine how help will search the topics by clicking the Options button (see Figure 16-15 earlier in this section). Clicking this button displays the Find Options dialog box, shown in Figure 16-18.

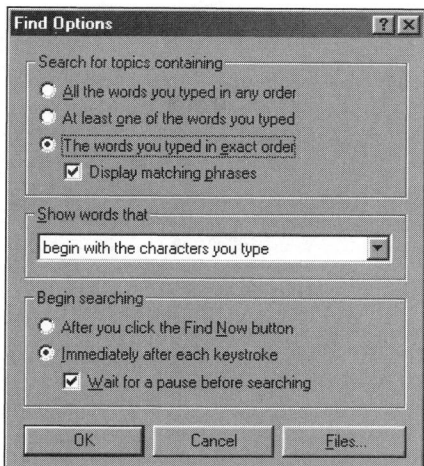

Figure 16-18: We usually search a help file using the option "The words you typed in exact order."

You can customize how HTML help uses the words that you type in the Search field if the help-file author has been kind enough to include this capability. Click the right arrow at the right end of the Search field. You can then click AND, OR, NEAR, or NOT. If there is no right arrow to the right of the Search field, you are out of luck. This appears to be the case with the older Windows 98 Help, for example (as shown earlier in Figure 16-16), although the *Windows 98 Resource Kit Book Online* includes this capability, as shown in Figure 16-19.

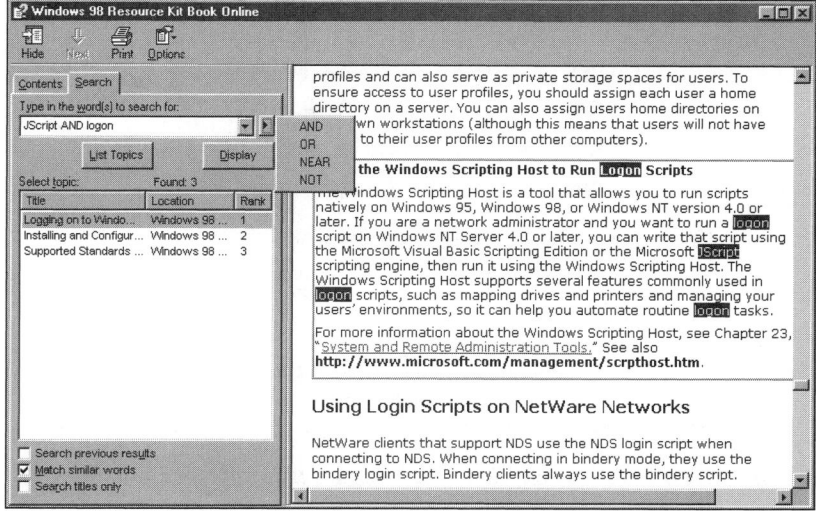

Figure 16-19: Note the pop-up AND, OR, NEAR, and NOT options in this help file.

Not only does Microsoft Office 2000 make it quite difficult to get to the Microsoft Office Help file, it also doesn't include full text search in its HTML help. Now to be fair, the index is very extensive, as shown in Figure 16-20, so you may be OK using just the index to find help. Unfortunately, in most cases we've found that the indexer didn't have in mind what we had in mind.

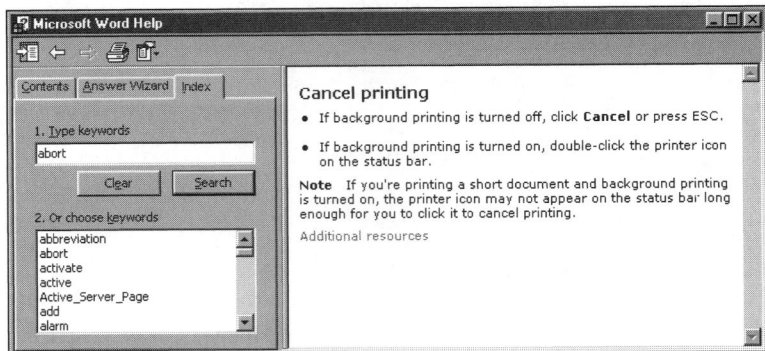

Figure 16-20: The word *abort* isn't actually in the topic, but it is a synonym for the actions described in the help topic.

The Clippy character gets in the way in Office 2000 especially, but you can turn off the little monster.

STEPS

Turning off the Office Assistant

Step 1. Click Start ➪ Programs ➪ Accessories ➪ Systems Tools ➪ System Information ➪ Tools ➪ System Configuration Utility ➪ Startup.

Step 2. Clear the checkbox next to Microsoft Office StartUp. Click OK.

Step 3. Click Start ➪ Programs ➪ Microsoft Word.

Step 4. Click Help ➪ Hide the Office Assistant.

You've turned off the call to start up Office Assistant so that it doesn't start up each time you restart Windows. It is still running in memory until you restart Windows.

Shortly after I wrote this, Peter Deegan, the editor of Woody's Office Watch (http://www.woodyswatch.com) and Woody's Windows Watch (http://www.mcc.com.au/www/index.htm), wrote his "Kill Clippy!" article for ZDNet.

It provides a number of ways to seriously injure (but not actually kill) Clippy. We recommend it to all of our friends, and you'll find it at `http://www.zdnet.com/zdhelp/stories/main/0,5594,2226725-1,00.html`. It includes some great replacement art for damaged Clippies.

Dr. Watson Returns

Dr. Watson is a diagnostic program that was present in Windows 3.1, disappeared in Windows 95, but is back in Windows 98 and Me.

Dr. Watson can be of some help in figuring out why you are having General Protection Fault errors. He is available if you click Start ⇨ Programs ⇨ Accessories ⇨ System Tools ⇨ System Information ⇨ Tools ⇨ Dr. Watson. Dr. Watson runs minimized in your system tray until you need him.

You can also get him to come to the office whenever you start your computer by putting a shortcut to him in the StartUp group. Here is one way to do this:

STEPS

Adding Dr. Watson to Your StartUp Group

Step 1. Right-click your taskbar, click Properties, and click the Start Menu Programs tab.

Step 2. Click the Add button, and enter **C:\Windows\Drwatson.exe** in the Create Shortcut dialog box, as shown in Figure 16-21. Click Next .

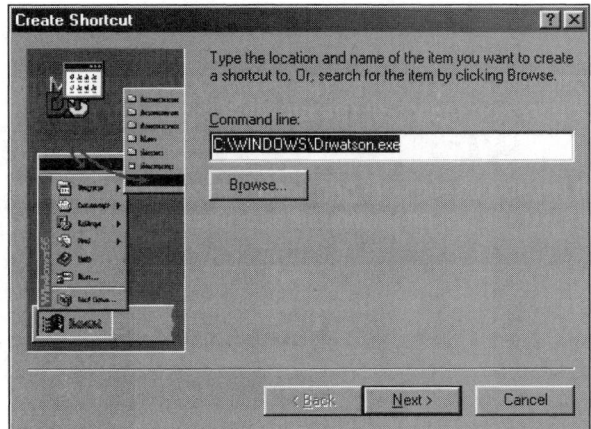

Figure 16-21: Type the path to Dr. Watson in the "Command line" field.

Continued

STEPS

Adding Dr. Watson to Your StartUp Group *(continued)*

Step 3.   Choose the StartUp folder, as shown in Figure 16-22. Click Next and then Finish. Dr. Watson will start the next time you restart Windows.

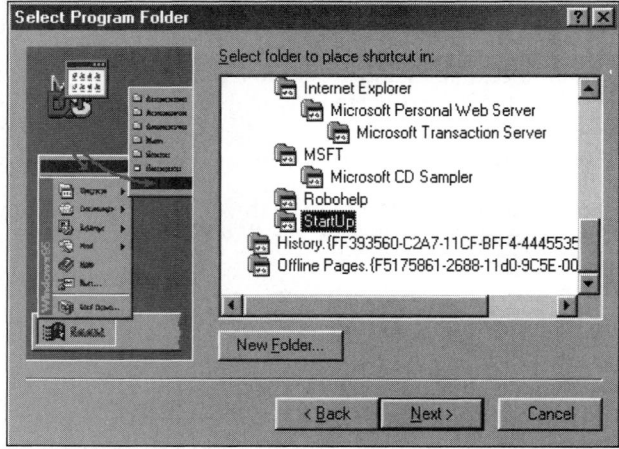

Figure 16-22: The StartUp folder is toward the bottom of the folder list.

Thanks to Daniel P. Cayea for pointing out this tip.

Creating a Windows Boot Diskette

When you install Windows, you are given the option of creating an emergency Startup disk, sometimes referred to as the Windows Startup diskette. You can also create it after installing Windows by clicking Add/Remove Programs in your Control Panel and following the instructions in the Startup Disk tab.

The Windows Me boot diskette will include the generic CD-ROM drivers, so you should be able to boot from it and have access to the CD-ROM drive on your computer. If not, and if you have access to the real-mode CD-ROM driver for your specific CD-ROM, you should copy this driver onto the diskette and edit your Config.sys to call it. This Windows boot diskette will let you boot your computer, access FAT16 and FAT32 formatted drives, and create FAT32 partitions.

CD-ROM God Boot Diskette

Here's what its own Web site has to say about the CD-ROM God:

The CD-ROM God Ver 5.5 is a boot disk that has 50+ CD-ROM drivers. It has basic ATAPI drivers, and model specific drivers. This version unzips drivers to a ramdrive! It has a better, more sleek shareware free menu. This version continues to use DEVICE.COM to load. This way you won't have to re-boot a million times! ISO-9660 CD Support and SMARTDRV.EXE!

If you want to create a Windows boot diskette that includes all the known (to the author) CD-ROM drivers (not just the ATAPI drivers that Microsoft supplies), then the CD-ROM God is the software for you. This solves the very real problem of creating a boot diskette that can give you access to your CD-ROM drive in real mode.

You'll find it at `http://gankish.net/rumblesoft/`. John Staker told Chris Pirillo about this site, and we got it from Chris at `http://www.lockergnome.com`.

Trouble Creating a Startup Diskette

BugNet (`http://www.bugnet.com`) has found that you can't create a Startup diskette if the diskette has ten or more bad sectors. It's a good thing that you can't use a diskette that's this bad, but it sure would be nice to know what was going on.

You can put in a new diskette, or you can check the diskette with ScanDisk and see if the sectors really are bad. If it turns out that this isn't the problem, then turn off any virus scanning software that may be running. The McAfee virus checker that comes with Plus! 98, for one example, doesn't cause any problems, while other antivirus programs do.

If this doesn't do the trick, BugNet says either you've got a tape drive hooked to your floppy controller, you've got a bad floppy drive, or the BIOS setting for your floppy doesn't show a floppy drive.

Get Crash Recovery Help from Your Zip Drive

The Windows setup routines strongly encourage you to create an emergency Startup diskette. You can also go back and create one later from your Control Panel (use Add/Remove Programs).

Iomega and Symantec Corporation provide you with a much-enhanced ability to recover from problems with Windows by offering Zip drive users a free copy of the Norton Zip Rescue program, shown in Figure 16-23. Here's how they describe it:

Figure 16-23: Norton Zip Rescue lets you make a Zip cartridge that will allow you to recover from a system crash.

Norton Zip Rescue is designed to help you keep running in the event of a system crash. Norton Zip Rescue can help you and your computer recover from almost any failure that keeps a PC from starting including:

- Viruses that keep a PC from starting (boot sector and system viruses)
- Windows Registry corruption
- CMOS corruption
- Deleted files
- Disk failures
- Boot sector failures

Norton Zip Rescue does not address applications problems, nor can it fix physical hardware damage, such as a broken hard drive head. However, in the event of a hard drive failure, you may be able to use your Zip Rescue Disk to get into Windows and retrieve undamaged files that have been created or changed since your last backup.

When the user experiences a PC failure where the PC doesn't start Windows properly, the user simply turns off the PC, inserts the Zip

Rescue Disk and floppy, turns the PC on, and Windows will load automatically from the Zip Rescue Disk. The Rescue Wizard guides the user through the rescue, and has the ability to find and fix many problems. Finally, the user is instructed to turn off the PC, remove the Rescue Disk, and turn on the PC. From that point, in many instances, the PC should run properly.

The program creates a bootable floppy in addition to copying a significant portion of your Windows operating system and configuration files onto the Zip drive. This includes your profile files, SendTo folder, Start Menu folder, Favorites folder, system Web pages (found in Windows\Web), and Desktop shortcuts. You can add files, but this is not a backup program, and you can run out of room on your Zip cartridge. This program is meant to allow you to recover your existing Windows 98 configuration, but you may have to use it to copy your important files (such as additional fonts) from your hard disk to be used on a new computer, for example.

To keep the Zip recovery cartridge current with your latest hardware and software installations, updates to your Desktop, Favorites, and so on, you'll need to update it as often as you can manage using Norton Zip Recovery.

Of course, Iomega has enhanced the value of their Zip drives by providing this 8MB program to their new and existing customers. If you currently have a Zip drive, you can profitably download the latest version of this free program from http://www.iomega.com/software or http://www. symantec.com.

How the Recycle Bin Stores Files

If you're curious about how Windows keeps track of the files that you've deleted into the Recycle Bin, you can find out by reading the Microsoft Knowledge Base article "How the Recycle Bin Stores Files" at http:// support.microsoft.com/support/kb/articles/q136/5/17.asp. Essentially, Windows renames files using their source drive letter and the order of their deletion, and it keeps a separate file that links the new name to the old.

This Knowledge Base article also provides a couple of ways to deal with problems that you may encounter with the Recycle Bin.

Stop a Malicious Program

If you happen to run a program that sends a maliciously designed sequence of instructions to your Pentium processor, it can freeze your computer. Windows lets you guard against this particular problem.

STEPS

Enabling the Pentium F0 Workaround

Step 1. Click Start ⇨ Accessories ⇨ System Tools ⇨ System Information.

Step 2. Click Tools ⇨ System Configuration Utility.

Step 3. Click the Advanced button in the General tab and mark "Enable Pentium F0 (CmpXchg) workaround," as shown in Figure 16-24.

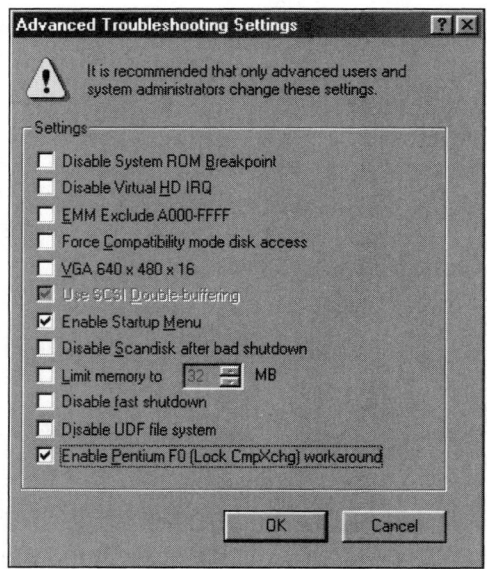

Figure 16-24: Mark the last checkbox to enable a protective workaround for Pentiums.

Step 4. Click OK twice.

Quickly Kill Any Process or Application

WinKill sits in your system tray waiting for you to decide to close an application or kill any process. It will also perform a fast Windows shutdown that fails to notify any ongoing processes that Windows is shutting down, and simply shuts Windows down quickly. Documents whose contents have changed and haven't been saved recently are not updated. You probably don't want to use this capability unless you know that you've saved all your changes, and you just want to quickly close Windows and turn off your computer.

Right-click the WinKill icon, click Kill, and you are presented with a list of current processes, as shown in Figure 16-25. Click a process to kill it.

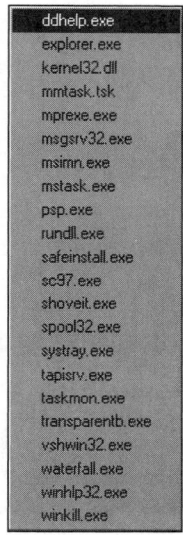

ddhelp.exe
explorer.exe
kernel32.dll
mmtask.tsk
mprexe.exe
msgsrv32.exe
msimn.exe
mstask.exe
psp.exe
rundll.exe
safeinstall.exe
sc97.exe
shoveit.exe
spool32.exe
systray.exe
tapisrv.exe
taskmon.exe
transparentb.exe
vshwin32.exe
waterfall.exe
winhlp32.exe
winkill.exe

Figure 16-25: The WinKill context menu lists the current processes.

If you click the WinKill icon, the mouse pointer turns into a cross. You can then click a window to close it and terminate the underlying task.

WinKill is a freeware applet, and you'll find it at `http://www.softseek.com/Utilities/System/Review_19993_index.html`.

Imm32.dll Error Message

Secret

If you receive this error message when you install or run a program, it may be because you have a corrupted `Mfc42.dll` or `Imm32.dll` file. Your program installation might also have overwritten `Mfc42.dll` with an older version.

Don't panic. This is easy to fix if you have your original source files. Microsoft could have placed copies of these files in the `\Windows\Sysbackup` folder, but they missed the fact that these might be susceptible files. You can place copies there later, after you fix the problem.

You'll find these files in the `\Windows\System` folder. To extract the original versions from the Windows cabinet files, follow the steps detailed in the next section, "Extracting Files from Cabinets."

Extracting Files from Cabinets

Even on the Windows CD-ROM, which has lots of room, the files that make up the Windows source files are packed into cabinet files, which use the `cab` extension. Other programs come packed into cabinet files, too, including updates to Internet Explorer downloaded from the Microsoft Web site.

Most of the time, you let the accompanying setup routines extract files from cabinet files. However, you may want to extract files manually when a file is corrupted, or when you want to retrieve a specific file that the installation program didn't extract.

`Extract.exe` is a command-line-driven DOS program.

You can see how `Extract.exe` works by opening a DOS window (Start ➪ Programs ➪ MS-DOS Prompt), typing **Extract /?**, and pressing Enter.

Use the Windows Update Wizard Without Having to Register

You'll find the Windows Update Wizard on your main Start menu. If it is no longer there, check out Start ➪ Settings ➪ Control Panel ➪ Automatic Updates. When you run the wizard, it checks Microsoft's Web site for new versions of drivers and other Windows components. If it finds newer versions than the ones you have, it offers to update your system for you.

There's a problem that can keep you from using the Windows Update Wizard, however. If you skipped Microsoft's Registration Wizard when you first installed Windows Me or 98, the Windows Update Wizard won't run. Larry Passo of Newport Beach, CA was the first to send Brian a workaround for this foolishness.

Secret

Passo points out that running the Registration Wizard changes two lines in the registry. You can easily make these changes yourself by creating and merging this `reg` file, which you might name `Register.reg`:

```
REGEDIT4
[HKEY_LOCAL_MACHINE\SOFTWARE\Microsoft\Windows\CurrentVersion]
"RegDone"="1"
[HKEY_LOCAL_MACHINE\SOFTWARE\Microsoft\Windows\CurrentVersion\Welcome\
RegWiz]
"@"="1"
```

After you have merged this file into your registry, you can run the Windows Update Wizard without complaint. Brian asked Rob Bennett, group product manager for the original Windows 98, if there was anything else readers should know about this trick. He said, "There is actually some value in registration. It's not just about Microsoft getting name and address info, it's really about helping Windows Update grow over time, so we can learn more about what people are actually doing out there."

Brian also asked whether Passo's patches would have any side effects. Bennett replied, "For now we're going to leave it as-is, but we may do some more stringent checking in the future." If a later version of Windows does turn out to actually check to see if the Registration Wizard was run, you can always run it for real — but we hope that won't be necessary.

Trouble with Windows Update

The Microsoft Windows Update Web site (and command in your Start menu) is supposed to make it easy to upgrade your current Windows installation. Well, two steps forward and one step back. The address for this site, in case you've lost it, is http://windowsupdate.microsoft.com/.

You may run into problems (and as beta testers for the site, we've run into and reported most of them). For example, instead of seeing the Windows Update Web page, you may see a blank page, or you may receive an error message, or, the horror of it all, Windows may hang as it tries to download a file.

Microsoft has identified a number of problems that cause these symptoms. You can check out the latest list in the Knowledge Base article "Troubleshooting Windows Update Connection and Download Problems" at http://support.microsoft.com/support/kb/articles/q193/6/57.asp.

Track Windows System Updates

Microsoft wants to update your computer without bothering to tell you what is going on. Some folks like it this way, others don't. If you're in the second category, check out Windows System Updates before you go to the Windows Update site. You'll find a listing of the recent updates, a description of what they do, a list of all the files, and additional information that will help you decide whether to update. Windows Me also allows you to remove updates that you feel may be causing a problem.

Quick Support from Microsoft

In Windows Me, Microsoft has made it far easier to access online help resources. How easy? Well, just click Start, choose Help, and click the Search Online Support link. Things couldn't be much easier!

Keep Aware of the Latest Windows Betas

You'll find news about the latest beta tests at http://www.betanews.com.

Keep Up on Windows Bugs and Solutions

This is the best list of bugs and solutions that we've found on the Web. Most of the bugs are esoteric. That is, they will only affect a few thousand users, but if you're among that group you will appreciate this site: Bug Alert at `http://www.zdnet.com/zdhelp/bug_help/bugs/bugalert_win98.html`.

Other Sources of Windows Information

Sometimes it seems as though all we talk about are further sources of information. There must be thousands of URLs throughout this book. At least you can be assured of finding some backup to the statements that we make here.

We track Windows information every day by following the discussions on newsgroups, visiting Web sites, and receiving e-zines from knowledgeable sources. One example is WinInfo, from Paul Thurott. This is mostly a sampling of news stories about Windows. It very rarely includes any tricks or secrets, but it is always interesting. You'll find it at `http://www.wininformant.com`.

Then there is Woody's Windows Watch (WWW). Woody Leonard, Barry Simon, and especially Peter Deegan started up this follow-on to the successful Woody's Office Watch (WOW) in November of 1998. Woody and Barry are the co-authors of *The Mother of All Windows 98 Books*.

WWW is a power-packed bundle of Windows information in a beautiful HTML format. It is jam-packed with Windows tips and tricks as well as interesting news and links to other Web sites. I love that fact that it comes from Australia, my favorite country. WOW is also full of Office tips and tricks. You can sign up for WWW at `http://www.woodyswatch.com/windows/` and WOW at `http://www.woodyswatch.com/office/`.

We've mentioned Chris Pirillo's Lockergnome in various places throughout this book. It is a guide to Windows shareware in a good-looking HTML newsletter delivered every working day, with a roundup at the end of the week for the folks with HTML-challenged e-mail clients. Check it out at `http://www.lockergnome.com`.

The CNET Shareware dispatch comes out about once a week and gives you a heads up on the latest shareware for both Windows and the Mac. You can, of course, go to their Web site and search through the archives, but it is nice to have someone looking out for good shareware. You'll find them at `http://shareware.cnet.com/`.

Speaking of CNET, Brian has for some time written a column called "Wired Watchdog" for CNET's News.com site. This column focuses on consumer protection for people who use (or are victimized by) computers. It appears every Friday morning. Go to `http://BrianLivingston.com` and click the link for `News.com`.

The Berst Alert provides daily news about personal computing, Windows, and the computing industry. There is almost always a link to some specific highlighted shareware for the day. You'll also find information on Web site construction, the latest news about Microsoft and its enemies, links to ZDNet's TipZone, and Windows-specific advise. You find it at `http://www. zdnet.com/anchordesk/`.

Bud's Windows Troubleshooter is just a great site. He offers wonderful material on setting up multiple monitors, for example. You can download an antinuke device, stop Windows from searching for a floppy, and fix power management for PC cards. The site deals with Windows 95 and 98, as well as Windows Me, so if you use Windows Me you'll have to weed out the older material.

You'll find it at `http://www.geocities.com/~budallen/`. Thanks to Mark McClure via Chris Pirillo at `http://www.lockergnome.com`.

Note to Shareware/Freeware Developers

We tried out a great deal of freeware and shareware as we've written this book (and all of our previous books). After a while, you get to know what works regarding software installs and what doesn't. If you install software, you might be on the lookout for some of the things that we've noticed. Here's our advice to the developers:

- If you install a shortcut to your software in the `\Windows\Start Menu\ Programs\StartUp` folder, open a small folder window to it at the end of the install to allow us to remove your program from this folder. This is a lot easier than using the System Configuration Utility.

- If you install system files — most likely DLLs in the `\Windows` or `\Windows\System` folder — be sure to check the version numbers of possible duplicates of your DLLs. Only install the latest version.

- Better yet, don't install anything in `\Windows\System`.

- Create a log file of everything that setup does and place it in your folder.

- Ask the user where he or she wants your program to be placed, and don't make the default something two layers deep inside of `\Program Files` with your company name as the first subfolder. We don't care about putting all your company programs together.

- Ask if we want a shortcut in the Start menu, or on the Desktop, or neither.

- Why don't any of you let us put the shortcut on the Start menu anywhere but in the Programs menu at the top level? It never ends up there, since we ideally want it someplace else.

- Don't install a CPL without asking first. Don't install any context menu items without asking first.

■ Don't package your program in an executable that just unzips everything to the current folder in a DOS window.

■ If you put your install executable in a zip file, this is cool because you can include a readme.txt file, which we can read before we decide to install the software. In the readme.txt file, tell us what the program does and why, list your Web site (which may be different from where we downloaded it), tell us if the install program deposits files to any folder other than its own folder, mention whether your software can be uninstalled easily, and tell us who the author is.

■ Always include an uninstall program unless it is really trivial (such as a single file with no registry entries), and in that case be sure to include explicit instructions on how to uninstall.

■ Open a small folder window focused on the new folder at the end of the install. There's no need for a checkbox about the Readme.txt file at the end, because we can click it in the folder window if we like.

■ Use a Windows 32-bit install program that adds an entry to the Add/Remove Programs registry branch.

■ How about displaying your help file before we have to commit to installing your software? We've seen it done, so we know it can be done. This is possible with the standard software installation programs.

Summary

This is a large and diverse chapter that covers many different system elements — from system configuration, to dealing with bugs, to keeping up to date.

▶ Create an Emergency Boot diskette.

▶ Kill any ongoing Windows process.

▶ Install or at least access the Windows Resource Kit from your Windows CD-ROM.

▶ Keep current with the latest list of Windows bugs.

▶ Are you a freeware or shareware developer? If so, check out our note to shareware/freeware developers.

Chapter 17

Laptop to Desktop

In This Chapter

▶ Easily connecting two computers using a serial or parallel cable

▶ Direct Cable Connection — Windows serial/parallel cable networking

▶ What to expect in the way of file transfer rates between Windows computers

▶ Using a serial or parallel cable to give your laptop or other computer direct access to your network

▶ Setting up a parallel cable network that gives you much faster communication speeds than you would expect from ordinary parallel ports

Connecting Two Computers

You can physically connect two computers using a serial or parallel cable, or even infrared transmitters/receivers. Depending on the software you use to drive the connection, the two computers may be limited to just transferring files. With more powerful software, one computer can use the resources (such as hard disk, files, and printers) of the other as though these resources were directly connected to it.

Direct Cable Connection

Windows Me makes it easy to directly connect two computers using a serial or parallel cable. That's because Windows comes with Direct Cable Connection (DCC), which is a serial and parallel port network. DCC is also part of Windows 98 and 95, and you can use it to connect computers running all three flavors of Windows: Me, 98, and 95.

DCC is similar to Microsoft's old DOS-based Interlnk program, but taken to the next level. Like Interlnk (pronounced *interlink*), one computer is the guest — presumably a laptop computer that you've brought into the office — and the other is the host. DCC adds the ability to connect not only to the host but also to the other computers or servers on the network to which the host is attached.

Because DCC is a network, it uses the built-in Windows network protocols to provide the communications link between the guest and both the host and the network connected to the host. You can use NetBEUI (Microsoft's peer-to-peer networking protocol), IPX/SPX (Novell's NetWare protocol), and/or TCP/IP (the protocol used in UNIX networks and/or with dial-up Internet connections). Both IPX/SPX and TCP/IP are routable, so you can communicate across network routing systems to the wider network.

DCC's user interface is a folder window that displays the shared resources (drives, folders, or printers) on the host. You don't have to learn how to use a different set of conventions. The beauty of integrating this kind of capability into the operating system is that you already know how to use it.

When you use DCC, Windows treats other computers and servers networked to your computer like close friends. You can see the files and folders on hard drives that are shared. On your guest computer, you can run programs that reside as executable files on other computers. These programs are loaded into your computer's memory.

Your computer can easily find documents that are stored on other computers. And, of course, you can easily transfer files back and forth, updating older files to the latest versions.

Speed

DCC's speed varies depending on whether you are using serial or parallel port communications. Serial communications can be quite slow, to say the least. If your computer has the older or less expensive serial ports that use the 8250 or 16450 universal asynchronous receiver/transmitter (UART), you are limited to speeds of up to 57,600 bits per second (bps). (A UART is the chip that drives the serial port.) Most new computers come with 16550 UARTs or better. These chips can be driven at up to 115,200 bps.

Unfortunately, DCC can't give you the 14 kilobytes per second (KBps) file transfer speed that the 115,200 bps rate would imply ($115,200/(1024 \times 8)$).

Secret

Parallel ports come in a number of varieties. New computers have incorporated enhanced standards for parallel ports, known as EPP or ECP (see the parallel ports and cables section later in this chapter for a full explanation). EPP/ECP ports can facilitate very high-speed communications between computers — approaching the speed that is available from dedicated networking cards. You can reach speeds of 120 KBps with the appropriate cable and automatic data compression that is built into Windows for parallel ports. At these speeds, networking over parallel cables is about a third as fast as dedicated 10-megabit (Mb) Ethernet cards, without the cost of an Ethernet card.

Although they don't have a reputation for speed, the older parallel ports still have better speed performance than serial ports. Windows has enhanced parallel port software drivers that enable computers with standard parallel ports (4-bit unidirectional and 8-bit bidirectional) connected with a standard bidirectional parallel cable to network at speeds that are often quite acceptable — not just for file transfer, but for data and program sharing, too.

Setup

Direct Cable Connection is not installed unless you did a Custom setup when you installed Windows. Or, you may have installed DCC through the Add/Remove Programs icon in the Control Panel. During a Custom setup, you must choose Communications in the Components dialog box and then specifically mark the Direct Cable Connection checkbox.

If you didn't install Direct Cable Connection when you set up Windows, you can take the following steps to do so now:

STEPS

Installing Direct Cable Connection

Step 1. Click the Start button, point to Settings, and then click Control Panel.

Step 2. Click the Add/Remove Programs icon, and then click the Windows Setup tab.

Step 3. Click Communications, and then click the Details button.

Step 4. Mark the Direct Cable Connection checkbox.

Step 5. Click the OK button in the Communications dialog box and in the Add/Remove Programs Properties dialog box.

If you install Direct Cable Connection, you will also automatically install Dial-Up Networking (DUN) and networking in general. Direct Cable Connection is really just a variant of Dial-Up Networking. It is a dial-up network that doesn't require that you dial up (or have a network card).

DUN is discussed in "Dial-Up Networking" in Chapter 19. Installing DUN during Windows Setup or later from the Add/Remove Programs icon automatically configures the network protocols necessary to run DCC. You can always change these protocols to reconfigure DUN, and thereby also reconfigure DCC.

Secret

The My Network Places icon appears on your Desktop when you install DCC. If you remove it by using TweakUI or the System Policy Editor, or directly by editing the registry, you can no longer use DCC.

The original version of Windows 95 didn't let you keep a DCC connection and a separate DUN connection open at the same time. However, Microsoft has greatly improved Winsock. Winsock versions that come with Windows Me and 98 support multiple connections. Now you don't have to disconnect your modem connection to the Internet in order to open a DCC connection — a big improvement.

Configuration

To access Direct Cable Connection, click your Start button, point to Programs ⇨ Accessories ⇨ Communications, and, finally, click Direct Cable Connection.

The first time you use DCC, the Direct Cable Connection Wizard pops up, as shown in Figure 17-1, and helps you configure DCC.

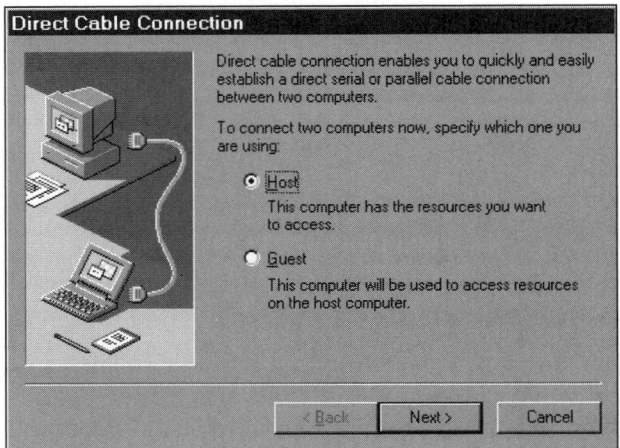

Figure 17-1: Run the Direct Cable Connection Wizard on both computers. Select the Host option button when you run the wizard on your host computer, and select the Guest option button when you run it on your guest computer. You can later change these settings.

The DCC Wizard identifies the serial and parallel ports that are not already in use and can be used for communication, as shown in Figure 17-2. You can pick from among the available ports. If you add ports later, you can rerun the wizard and ask it to check for new ports. This dialog box reminds you to plug in your cable. You don't need to do this for the wizard to complete the configuration, but don't forget to plug it in before you try to connect.

If you are installing the guest computer, click Next and then click Finish. DCC will begin trying to connect; click Close if you're not ready to connect now.

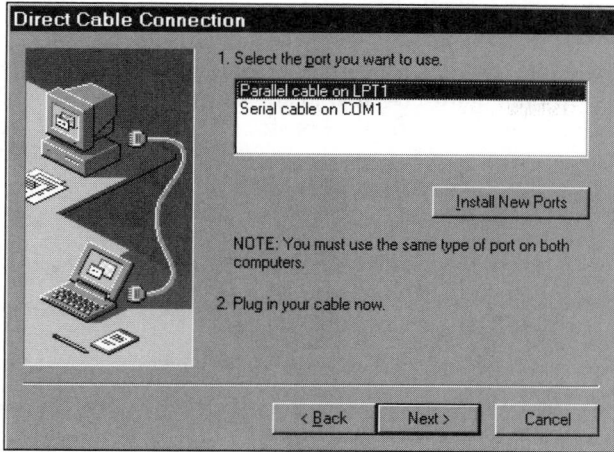

Figure 17-2: Click the Install New Ports button if you have installed new serial or parallel ports since the last time you ran the DCC Wizard.

If you are installing the host, you're not quite done. After you click Next in the dialog box shown in Figure 17-2, the wizard either brings you to the final Wizard dialog box (shown in Figure 17-3), or, if you haven't yet enabled file and printer sharing, it brings you to a dialog box that contains a File and Print Sharing button. Click this button to configure sharing (see the "Sharing Your Resources" section of Chapter 18) and then click Next. (If you click Next without enabling sharing, the wizard warns you that you're setting up DCC without sharing.) In the final Wizard dialog box, you can set a password that is required to connect the guest to the host computer. You can also click Cancel at any time during the process to forget the whole thing.

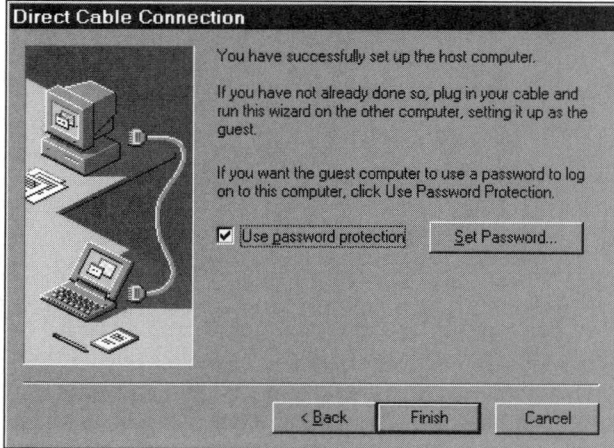

Figure 17-3: Mark the "Use password protection" checkbox to require a password for access to the host computer.

Network Configuration

When DCC is installed, Dial-Up Networking is also installed. The default installation is shown in Figure 17-4. If your host computer isn't connected to a network, you will not need to add other protocols or change this configuration.

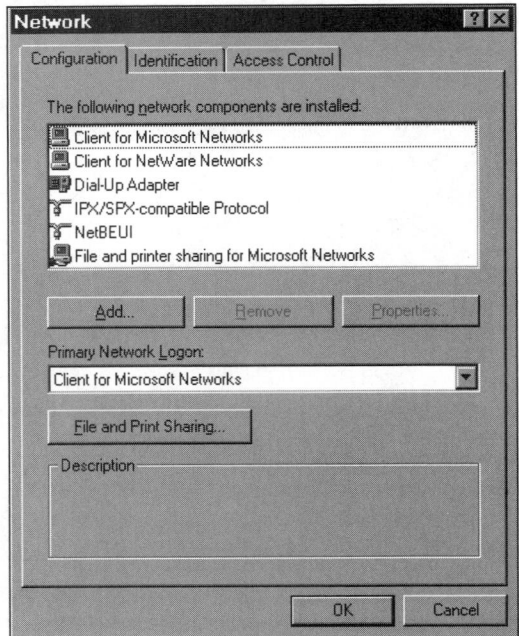

Figure 17-4: The Dial-Up Networking network configuration. All the components of Dial-Up Networking have been installed. The network configuration must be the same on both the guest and the host computer. By default, it will be.

If you want your guest computer to be a full-fledged member of the network to which your host is attached, you may need to add protocols to the Dial-Up Adapter. Turn to the "Network Installation" section of Chapter 18 for instructions on how to do this.

Installing All of the Right Protocols

If you are trying to use DCC to connect a Windows "guest" computer to a Windows "host" computer that is connected to a network, you may experience problems if you haven't bound the IPX/SPX protocol to your Dial-Up Adapter on both the host and guest computer. If you see the messages "Verifying username and password" and then "Disconnect" on the guest computer, the NetBIOS may not have been able to find the computer names on the host. To correct this problem, install and bind the IPX/SPX protocol to the Dial-Up Adapter on both the host and guest computer.

Sharing Comes First

If you want a guest computer to see anything on your Windows host computer or on other computers on the network, you have to share their resources. When the guest computer connects to the host, a folder window displaying the shared resources of the host appears on the guest computer's Desktop.

To enable the host to share its resources, file and printer sharing for Microsoft Networks (or file and printer sharing for NetWare Networks) must be installed. If you do not already have it installed, you should choose to install file and printer sharing for Microsoft Networks when you install DCC.

Furthermore, you must actually share some resources on your host computer. To do this, right-click the folder, drive icon, or printer icon you want to share, choose Sharing from the context menu, choose Shared As in the Sharing tab of the Properties dialog box, and type a name for the shared resource (and an optional comment).

Once you have shared some resources on your host computer, the guest computer will be able to see them.

If the host computer has user-level security (the host computer is connected to a Windows NT or NetWare server that keeps a user database), you need to both share the resources and add to the user list the guest user(s) who will be allowed to access them. To do this, take the following steps:

STEPS

Sharing with User-Level Security

Step 1.   On the host computer, open an Explorer or folder window that contains your shared drive, printer, and/or folder.

Step 2.   Right-click the resource and then click Sharing in the context menu.

Step 3.   Click the Sharing tab in the Properties dialog box for the resource, mark the Shared As option button, type a name (if different) for the resource, and then click the Add button.

Step 4.   In the Add Users dialog box, click the names of the guest(s) who will be allowed to access the resources on the host computer.

Step 5.   Choose the desired access type.

Step 6.   Click OK buttons until you are out of the Properties dialog box for the resource.

Browsing the Host

Secret

By default, the Windows host computer doesn't show up in you're My Network Places if you click the My Network Places icon on your Desktop. You also won't be able to see other computers on the network in My Network Places. If you want to get to them (and their shared resources), you have to type their UNC names in the Find Computer dialog box (Start ➪ Find ➪ Computer).

The capability for DCC (and Dial-Up Networking) to see or *browse* the host or the network may be turned off on your system to keep from slowing DCC down too much. If you browse, your Windows computer must update lots of information about disks, folders, and files that are on the host computer and on the network connected to the host computer.

You can turn the browsing feature back on and see for yourself if it is too slow for you. To do this, take these steps on your host computer:

STEPS

Forcing Browsing with DCC

Step 1. On your Windows 98 host computer, click the Start button, point to Settings, and then click Control Panel.

Step 2. Click the Network icon. In the Component list on the Configuration tab, highlight "File and printer sharing for Microsoft Networks," and then click the Properties button. This will bring up the dialog box shown in Figure 17-5.

Step 3. Highlight Browse Master, choose Enabled in the Value drop-down list, and click OK once.

Step 4. Now click the Identification tab and note the name in the Workgroup field. This name must be the same in both computers. Click OK.

Step 5. Restart your computer for the change to take effect, and start DCC.

Step 6. On the guest, follow Step 1 and click the Network icon. Go to the Identification tab and make sure the name in the Workgroup field is the same as on the host. Click OK and start DCC.

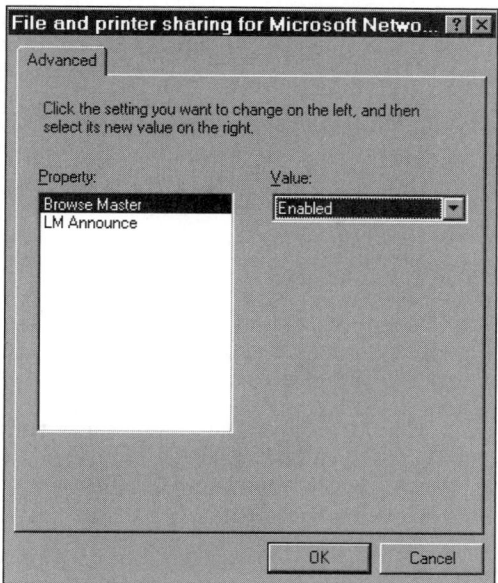

Figure 17-5: The Properties dialog box for file and printer sharing for Microsoft Networks

Now you will be able to "browse" the Windows host and the network from your guest computer whenever you have DCC running. There is one problem, however. If the Windows host is also configured as a Dial-Up Networking server, you can dial in from a Dial-Up Networking client computer, and the host computer will pick up the phone. When you do this, the Browse Master function will still be enabled to let you browse the host and the network, but it will be enabled for a dial-up connection, which is much slower. A serial DCC connection is also slow, but it isn't slow enough to cause a problem with browsing, at least when the Windows host is not connected to another network.

Secret

Although theoretically you can't browse the guest from the host, Tim Craig showed us a way to do it. Connect the two computers normally using DCC. On the host computer, right-click an empty space on the Desktop and select New ➪ Shortcut. In the Command Line field, type the path with the name of the guest computer and the drive or folder you want to browse — for example:

```
\\Laptop\c
```

Click Next, then type a name for your shortcut and click Finish. Now click your shortcut icon, and an Explorer window will open showing you the guest computer's shared resources.

Microsoft has prepared a document to help you troubleshoot your connection to your host computer. You can find it in the Knowledge Base at http://support.microsoft.com/support/kb/articles/Q134/3/04.asp.

Connected to What?

The fact that DCC is a network has manifold implications. While you might be interested in just hooking your laptop to your desktop computer, you can actually accomplish much more.

You can use DCC to connect directly to a computer running Windows. You can also connect indirectly through the network to a NetWare server computer, to a Windows NT server, to other computers running Windows Me, 98, or 95, or to other computers on the network.

If you want to connect through the network to a NetWare server, be sure to bind the IPX/SPX protocol to the Dial-Up Adapter on your guest computer — your laptop, perhaps. IPX/SPX and NetBEUI are the protocols that are initially bound to the Dial-Up Adapter when you install DCC. You will also need the Microsoft Client for NetWare Networks installed.

You can also connect indirectly to a Windows NT or Windows 2000 server through a Windows Me or 98 computer if the Windows computer is connected to the Windows NT/2000 computer on a network. Just use DCC and whatever protocol your Windows host computer is using to talk to the Windows NT/2000 computer — probably NetBEUI, but it could be IPX/SPX.

Running Direct Cable Connection

You run DCC (if you have already set it up) by clicking the Start button, pointing to Programs ⇨ Accessories ⇨ Communications, and then clicking Direct Cable Connection. (If you use DCC a lot, you can easily put a shortcut to it on your Desktop.) Starting DCC displays the Direct Cable Connection dialog box, as shown in Figure 17-6. You can also configure (or reconfigure) DCC in this dialog box, which really means that you can change it from guest to host (or host to guest) and change which port it is using.

Start DCC on both the guest and the host computer. Click the Listen button on the host computer to begin polling for the guest. Click the Connect button on the guest to begin trying to connect to the host. Once the connection is made, the host's shared drives and folders, as well as the shared resources of whatever other network the host is connected to, are available to the guest in the Shared Resources window. Furthermore, if you click the My Network Places icon on the guest's Desktop, you will be able to see the resources available to you if you have set the Browse Master to Enabled on the host computer. (See the "Forcing Browsing with DCC" steps in the "Browsing the Host" section earlier in this chapter.)

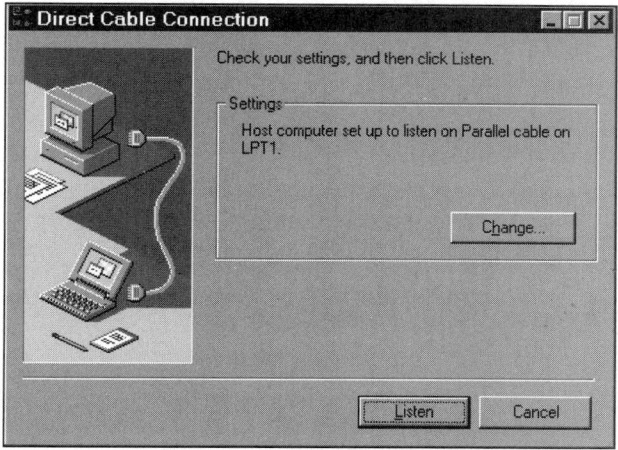

Figure 17-6: The Direct Cable Connection dialog box. On the host computer, the dialog box contains a Listen button. On the guest computer, it contains a Connect button. If you want to invoke the DCC Wizard, click the Change button.

The options you have set in the Explorer's View, Folder Options dialog box will be operative in the Shared Resources window and in the My Network Places window. In other words, these two views will behave like your My Computer window. The one difference is that you won't be able to choose "View as Web page" until you select a folder, file, or shared printer.

The guest is treated as any other node on the network (except for the fact that the host can't ordinarily browse it). The security provisions of the network are enforced, and the guest may be required to provide a password to connect to the Windows host computer.

Accessing the Host

As soon as you make a successful connection with DCC, you will see the host's shared resources in a window on the guest computer. You can click any of the shared folders (or drives) to display the contents of the resource in a folder window.

You won't see drive icons in the Shared Resource window, even if you have shared the whole disk drive on the host. You'll see folder icons used to represent drives instead. This is true even if you browse the host with My Network Places.

Secret

You can map a networked resource (which may be a complete drive or perhaps just a folder) to a local drive letter. A Networked Drive icon will then appear in My Network Places if you enabled Browse Master on the host computer.

Secret

If you disconnect from the host, the folders or folder views of the host that are displayed on your guest don't automatically close. They just aren't connected to anything anymore. As soon as you reconnect to the host, these folders become active again.

You can drag a shortcut to a file, folder, or application from the host to the guest's Desktop or to any folder on the guest computer. Click the Shortcut icon to open its target. If you click the Shortcut icon, but there is no active connection to the host, you won't force DCC to activate and connect to the host. Instead, you will get the message shown in Figure 17-7.

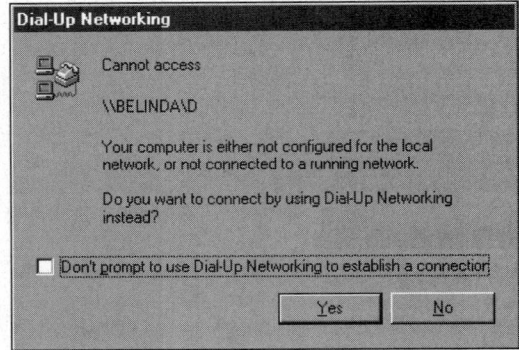

Figure 17-7: The Dial-Up Networking error message. You can see the connection between Dial-Up Networking and DCC. DCC doesn't automatically make the connection.

As soon as you click No, the message shown in Figure 17-8 appears to remind you that you need to make the network resource available.

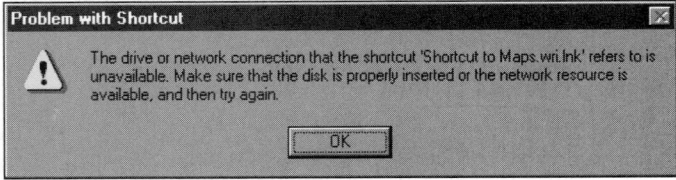

Figure 17-8: The Problem with Shortcut message box. The shortcut can't find the connection to the host.

You can create a shortcut on the host computer that will automatically start listening for a guest (and skip the DCC dialog box). Right-click an empty part of your Desktop and select New ⇨ Shortcut. In the Command Line field, type

directcc.exe connect. Click Next, give your shortcut a name, and click Finish. Notice that the shortcut automatically has a DCC icon. When you click the icon, DCC will automatically start up. Thanks to Jerald R. Haggard for this tip.

You can access the Internet over a DCC connection. Because messages on the Internet are directed to a specific IP address, you need a *proxy server* to interpret the messages and route them correctly. You can use either Internet Connection Sharing, which comes with Windows Me and Windows 98 Second Edition, or use a third-party proxy server. WinGate is a shareware proxy server that can let you do this; you can download an evaluation version from http://www.wingate.deerfield.com.

Serial Ports

You can use DCC with a "null modem" serial cable or a LapLink serial cable. (See Chapter 44 for a discussion of null modem cables.)

LapLink comes with a blue serial cable and a yellow parallel cable. Both of the LapLink cables are about 8 feet long. Traveling Software sells these cables separately or bundled with its LapLink software. You can use them with DCC and InterInk without any problem. You might want to get some longer cables, but they will be heavier to carry around.

Parallel Ports and Cables — One-Third the Speed of 10MB Ethernet

There are five types of parallel ports: 4-bit, 8-bit, semi 8-bit, EPP, and ECP. Most PCs have 4-bit or 8-bit parallel ports. Many portables with the Intel 386 SL chip set have EPP ports. Computers that support the full IEEE 1284 parallel port specification (this includes all new computers) have ECP parallel ports.

- **Standard parallel ports: 4-bit, 8-bit, semi 8-bit.** Almost every PC since the IBM PC-1 has come with an ordinary, 25-pin D-connector parallel port. These low-speed ports are fine for sending output to a printer (which is usually the slowest device in a computer system). But when you're transferring data between two PC parallel ports — using a LapLink cable or something similar — the speed of data transfer varies. While 4-bit ports can output data 8 bits at a time, they can input data only 4 bits at a time, which is about 40 kilobytes per second (Kbps.). Eight-bit ports can output and input 8 bits (80 Kbps or more). Semi 8-bit ports can too, but only with more sophisticated software and peripherals.

- **EPP ports.** The *enhanced parallel port* (EPP) was developed by Intel, Xircom, Zenith, and other companies that planned to exploit two-way communication with external devices. Some laptops built since mid-1991 have EPP ports. One source estimates that 80 percent of Intel 386SL and 486SL portables support EPP version 1.7, the first widely used version.

■ **ECP ports.** At the same time that Intel and others developed the EPP port, Microsoft and Hewlett-Packard were developing a spec called ECP — the *extended capabilities port.* It has about the same high-speed, two-way throughput as an EPP port, but it can use DMA (direct memory access) and a small buffer to provide smoother performance in a multitasking environment, which is why Microsoft supports ECP over EPP.

Both the EPP and the ECP specs were defined by the IEEE 1284 committee in 1993. Chip sets that support 1284 (and therefore can operate in ECP mode or in EPP 1284 mode) started appearing in PCs in 1994.

Four-bit ports are capable of effective transfer rates of 40–80 Kbps (kilobytes per second), while 8-bit ports can handle between 80–150 Kbps. ECP/EPP ports can sustain rates of 300 Kbps. Unfortunately, just because a port can sustain this speed doesn't necessarily mean you will get file transfer rates at these speeds.

If your computers have ECP or EPP parallel ports, they can sustain about one-third of Ethernet link speeds when networked together with DCC. (Standard "10Mbps" Ethernet networks commonly deliver an actual throughput of 350–400 Kbps.) This means that with a proper cable, you may not need to buy Ethernet cards to link together two computers with ECP or EPP parallel ports.

If you have the LapLink cable package (about $20), you already have an 8-foot basic bidirectional parallel cable. This cable is fine for 4-bit ports found on most older computers.

Another type of cable, known as a *universal cable module* (UCM), contains active electronics that speed two-way communications through the ECP/EPP enhanced parallel ports. Because there are several incompatible enhanced parallel ports in the market, the universal cable is key. It detects your port hardware and software and automatically transfers data at the highest available rate.

Microsoft has licensed software code to support the UCM technology from a small firm called Parallel Technologies Inc. and incorporated it into Windows as part of Direct Cable Connection. To purchase Parallel Technologies' UCM cable (called the DirectParallel Universal Cable), contact Parallel Technologies Sales at 800-789-4784 or visit their Web site, `http://www.lpt.com/lpt`. You'll also find lots of helpful information here about using DCC.

Parallel Technologies also offers a free program that will help you check out your Direct Cable Connection setup over a parallel cable as well as measure its throughput. You find the Direct Parallel Monitor (DPM) program (`DPM171b.zip`) at `ftp://ftp.lpt.com/parallel/DPM211b.exe`.

Computers that use the SMC chip set in their ECP ports (the Hewlett-Packard Vectra, for example) may have trouble printing or making a DCC connection through these ports in ECP mode. The data seems to be transferring correctly, but later it turns out to be damaged. This happens if the ECP port didn't initialize properly when you turned on your computer. If you experience this problem, check with your manufacturer for advice on taking one of these actions: configuring the parallel port so it is not in ECP mode; reconfiguring the ECP port so that it will initialize properly (use the SMC setup disk that came with your computer); or getting a newer version of the SMC chip set.

Watch the Interrupts

Secret

DCC over parallel ports uses the interrupts assigned to those ports. LPT1 most often uses Interrupt 7, and LPT2 most often uses Interrupt 5. Parallel printers don't really use these interrupts, so it usually doesn't matter if something else in your computer grabs them first.

Sound cards and CD-ROMs often use these interrupts. Because the parallel ports don't really use them, Windows doesn't report a conflict between the ports and the sound card or CD-ROM if they're using the same interrupts.

If you use DCC over a parallel port and there is a conflict with that port's interrupt, DCC will be slowed down by a factor of three. To prevent this from happening (if you can), you need to be sure that Interrupt 7 is not used by some other card if you are using LPT1 for DCC. The same holds for Interrupt 5 and LPT2.

To find out if there is a conflict, take the following steps:

STEPS

Determining If an Interrupt Conflict Exists

Step 1. Click the Start button, point to Settings, and then click Control Panel.

Step 2. Click the System icon, and then click the Device Manager tab.

Step 3. While Computer is highlighted in the Device Manager, click Properties.

Step 4. From the list of interrupt requests in the Resources tab, you can determine if 7 or 5 is used.

You may be able to change the interrupt used by the card(s) that conflict with DCC. If your card is Plug and Play compatible, you can do this using the Device Manager (see Chapter 36). If not, you may need to change some jumpers on the card or run a piece of setup software from the card's manufacturer.

Sometimes you may find that after you close a DCC connection using a parallel cable, your mouse pointer is jerky and multimedia sound "stutters." This is a symptom of a conflict over the interrupt—the parallel driver doesn't sense that the remote computer has dropped the connection, so it tries to detect whether the connection is still there. In this situation, and if you are forced to live with interrupt conflicts, just wait for 30 seconds or so. The parallel driver will wise up, and your system will go back to normal.

Using the Infrared Communications Driver

You can install the Infrared (IR) Communications Driver on your Windows computer, and run DCC using wireless infrared communications instead of serial or parallel cables. Many popular notebook computers have built-in IR ports. In addition, it's possible to buy an IR adapter and connect it to a serial port. In either case, the IR link is simulating a serial communications link.

For lists of compatible computers and adapters, and for troubleshooting help, read the Microsoft Knowledge Base articles "Infrared Data Association Release Notes, Parts 1 and 2" (at `http://support.microsoft.com/support/kb/articles/Q139/5/42.asp` and `http://support.microsoft.com/support/kb/articles/Q139/5/43.asp`), and "IR Communications Driver 2.0 Release Notes, Parts 1 and 2" (at `http://support.microsoft.com/support/kb/articles/Q149/4/49.asp` and `http://support.microsoft.com/support/kb/articles/Q149/4/50.asp`).

Troubleshooting DCC

If you experience problems getting DCC to work, a Troubleshooter dialog box appears that gives you some guidance on how to proceed. Answer the questions and carry out the actions it suggests based on your answers.

You can invoke the DCC troubleshooter manually by taking the following steps:

STEPS

Getting to the DCC Troubleshooter

Step 1. Click the Start button, click Help, and then click the Contents tab.

Step 2. Click the Troubleshooting book, then the Windows Troubleshooters book.

Step 3. Click the topic Direct Cable Connection, and then click the "click here" link.

Step 4. The Networking Troubleshooter will start. Answer the questions by clicking the gray buttons next to them.

If you see the following message when you try to connect using DCC

```
System seems to connect but can't find the host computer.
```

it may be because both computers have the same name. Check the names by opening the Control Panel, clicking the Network icon, and selecting the Identification tab. The Computer Name field will show you the name, and let you change it if necessary.

It's possible that you may receive one of these two error messages when you are trying to make a connection:

```
Status: Connected via parallel cable on LPT1. Looking for shared
folders.
```

or

```
Cannot find the host computer.
```

If you get either of these error messages, try renaming the `Vredir.vxd` file (if it exists) in the `\Windows\System` folder and then extracting a new copy of `Vredir.vxd` file from your Windows CD-ROM.

If you have trouble with DCC and can't get it to respond, press Ctrl+Alt+Delete, highlight Rnaapp, and click the End Task button. This should allow you to end DCC and start it again.

DCC to Windows NT/2000

Secret

You can use DCC to connect a Windows Me or 98 computer to a Windows NT or Windows 2000 computer. The Windows NT/2000 computer will run Remote Access Server (RAS) and the Windows Me/98 computer will run DCC.

On the Windows NT/2000 computer, use the Null Modem 19200 driver, because DCC defaults to 19200 speed. Windows NT/2000 won't let DCC go any faster than 19,200 bits per second over serial lines. (You can't use a parallel connection between Windows Me/98 and Windows NT, because Windows NT doesn't have a `ParaLnk.VxD` driver.) Windows Me, 98, and 95 computers can communicate with each other using DCC at 115,200 bits per second over serial lines. Either computer can be the guest or the host (referred to as the *server* in Windows NT-speak).

Windows NT and 2000 use user-level security. Your Windows computer needs to log into the NT/2000 domain or workgroup if the NT/2000 computer is the host. If necessary, you can set the NT/2000 domain by clicking the Network icon in the Control Panel, highlighting Client for Microsoft Networks, clicking the Properties button, marking the "Log on to Windows domain" checkbox, and then typing the domain's name.

To connect the Windows computer to the NT/2000 computer, you need to install a null modem driver. For information on this, look at `http://www.mindspring.com/~kewells/net/`.

Administering the Host Computer's Print Queue

Tip

Let's say you are connecting your laptop to your desktop computer using DCC. Let's assume that the desktop computer (the DCC host) has a printer connected to it. You might want to be able to delete or pause print files that you are printing from your laptop onto the desktop's printer. Unfortunately, the desktop computer's print queue isn't automatically available to you on the laptop; you have to move over to the desktop computer and administer the queue there.

To administer the desktop computer's print queue from the laptop, you need to set your desktop computer to permit remote administration. To do this, click the Passwords icon in the Control Panel of the desktop computer, click the Remote Administration tab, and then mark the "Enable remote administration on this server" checkbox. (Note that this tab will not appear unless you have installed either file and printer sharing for Microsoft networks or file and printer sharing for NetWare.)

Summary

- ▶ Windows comes with a built-in network called Direct Cable Connection, which lets you connect two computers with a serial or parallel cable, or through infrared devices.

- ▶ We show you how to configure Direct Cable Connection.

- ▶ We discuss what kinds of network connection speeds you can expect from different serial and parallel ports.

- ▶ We show how Windows has taken the next step toward making the parallel port connection a true networking connection with close to network-standard speeds.

Chapter 18

Networking

Basic Network Support

Windows Me comes with all of the necessary networking software required to:

■ Set up a 32-bit protected-mode Microsoft Windows network of computers running Windows Me and/or Windows 98/95

■ Connect to a network with computers running Windows 2000, Windows NT, LAN Manager, and/or Windows for Workgroups 3.11

Additionally, Windows Me includes a 32-bit protected-mode client for Novell NetWare networks, so your Windows computer can be a compatible client on this type of network as well.

You can configure a Windows computer as a NetWare print and file server on a NetWare network. Windows provides three networking protocols: NetBEUI, IPX/SPX, and TCP/IP. Windows workstations can directly access Windows 2000, NT, and NetWare servers. Multiple (up to 10) 32-bit network clients can be running on your computer at the same time, allowing your computer to access multiple networks and network services simultaneously. For example, your computer could use TCP/IP to access a UNIX server using Internet Explorer while using Client for NetWare Networks to access a NetWare server. Because these network clients run in protected mode, they don't take up conventional (below 640K) memory.

All the networking components developed by Microsoft are 32-bit protected-mode virtual device drivers (VxDs). Because Windows uses protected-mode network components, it doesn't have to switch your processor from protected mode to real mode (a process that wastes too many processor cycles). Therefore, networking speeds under Windows Me/98/95 get much faster (50–200 percent) than under Microsoft's old Windows 3.1*x*.

Real-mode drivers, especially for NetWare, have a nasty habit of causing some programs to lock up your computer — the dreaded "black screen of death." There isn't any way to completely eliminate this problem without using protected-mode drivers. The real-mode drivers create memory conflicts and have unresolved disputes over control of interrupts.

Real-mode network drivers are loaded in conventional memory, although memory managers enable you to partially load these drivers between the 640K and 1MB memory addresses. Network components are particularly large, and if they run in real mode, they reduce the memory resources available to DOS programs to the point that some DOS programs can't run on networked computers. The new protected-mode network components are loaded above the lower 640K area, leaving this memory available for Doom and other mission-critical DOS programs.

Apart from its 32-bit network drivers, Windows can still be a good client for the 16-bit real-mode versions of all of the major networks that are available for PCs. These include:

- Artisoft LANtastic version 5.0 or later
- Banyan VINES version 5.52 or later
- Beame and Whiteside Network File System 3.0c or later
- DEC Pathworks version 5.0 or later
- IBM Data Link Control protocol
- IBM OS/2 LAN Server
- Microsoft Windows Network version 3.11
- MS-Net compatibles
- Novell NetWare 3.11 or later
- Sunselect PC-NFS version 5.0 or later
- TCS 10Net version 4.1 or later

Of course, many of these 16-bit networks have been upgraded to 32-bit, and you can get new drivers from the network manufacturers or the Windows CD-ROM.

Be sure to read `Network.txt` in your `\Windows` folder to learn what Microsoft has to say about networking issues. You can find more extensive coverage of Windows networking in *Windows 98 Networking Secrets* from IDG Books Worldwide.

What Windows Networking Buys You

You network your computers to access resources that are beyond any one computer and to facilitate communication. These resources are shared because they are too expensive to be given exclusively to one user, or because they are a managed resource (for example, a corporate transaction-processing database) that needs to be available to many different users simultaneously.

Windows Me is designed to be a particularly good networking client (and peer-to-peer server). It supports:

- User profiles and system policies that make it possible (with appropriate network administration) for users to log onto any networked Windows computer and have their own Desktop and applications available to them

- Protected-mode networking clients, protocols, and adapter drivers that don't take any conventional memory

- User-level security that is enforced by Windows 2000, NT, or NetWare servers and is centrally administered

- A single Logon box that allows users to log onto their Windows computer (and bring up their user-specific Desktop) as well as onto all the network resources and servers available to them

- Direct Cable Connection (DCC) and Dial-Up Networking (DUN)

- Diskless (or floppy disk-only) workstations connected to shared copies of Windows Me on Windows NT or NetWare servers (including NetWare 4.*x* servers)

- Browsing of shared network resources or resources on network servers through the Explorer, folder windows, common dialog boxes, or My Network Places

- Remote printing and printer administration

- NetWare Directory Services running under NetWare 4.*x*

- Network management through Simple Network Management Protocols (SNMP) using third-party software and a supplied agent

- Simultaneous access to multiple networks and multiple networking protocols

- Multiple 32-bit protected-mode networking protocols: NetBEUI, IPX/SPX, and TCP/IP

- 32-bit protected-mode ATM (Asynchronous Transfer Mode) and DLC (Data Link Control) protocols

- Infrared LAN drivers

- Remote administration and network resource monitoring

Network Installation

If you are going to install Windows Me on a computer that has been running Windows 3.1*x*, and you want it to install the Windows Me client software that will work with 16-bit networks, you should first install the 16-bit real-mode network software from these other vendors. Otherwise, you will have to configure the Windows Me network components yourself, in addition to installing this third-party software.

Click the Network icon in your Control Panel to display the Network dialog box, as shown in Figure 18-1. This dialog box allows you to choose which network client to install, which network adapter to support, which networking protocol to bind to the adapter, and which networking services (for example, peer file and printer sharing) to offer.

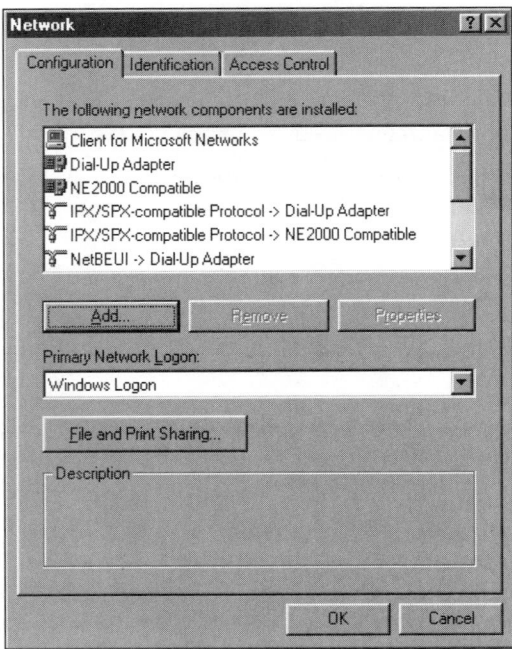

Figure 18-1: The Configuration tab of the Network dialog box. Click the Add button to install additional networking components.

If Windows Me has successfully detected your existing networking hardware and software network components, you don't need to make any changes in the Network dialog box. This is true even if the only network adapter you have installed is a serial or parallel port. Direct Cable Connection (DCC) will use these ports as though they were network adapters. Your modem will be detected as a network adapter and it can then be used by Dial-Up Networking (DUN) to connect to other computers over the phone lines.

There are cases where you will need to make changes to your network configuration, and we discuss them throughout this chapter.

If you add a network card or install networking software for networks other than Microsoft Networks or NetWare after you have installed Windows Me, you may need to use the Network dialog box to install networking support.

A network configuration consists of networking client software, software drivers for a given network adapter, a networking protocol, and networking services. To install any of these components, click the Add button in the Configuration tab of the Network dialog box to display the Select Network Component Type dialog box, as shown in Figure 18-2.

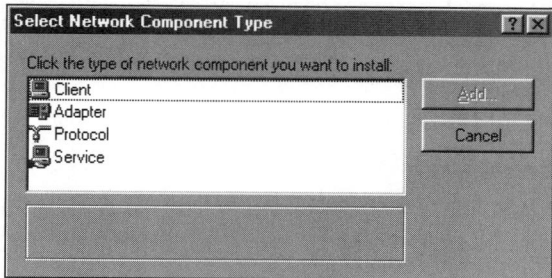

Figure 18-2: The Select Network Component Type dialog box

Choosing a Client

Highlight Client in the list box and click the Add button to display the Select Network Client dialog box, as shown in Figure 18-3. The 32-bit protected-mode clients for Microsoft Networks and NetWare Networks are provided by Microsoft on the Windows Me CD-ROM.

You can install one 16-bit real-mode networking client and up to 10 protected-mode clients. Only two 32-bit protected-mode clients are available from Microsoft — Client for Microsoft Networks and Client for NetWare Networks.

If you install a 16-bit networking client only, you won't need to deal with the other networking components in this dialog box. Instead, you will use the client software to specify how these items are configured.

If you install the Client for Microsoft Networks or NetWare Networks, you can add or change the network adapter, protocol, and network services.

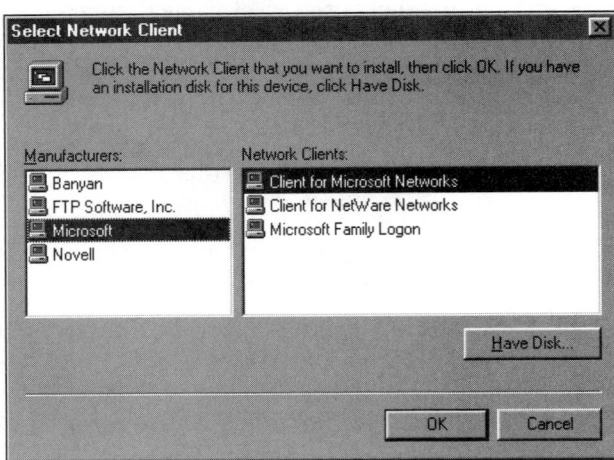

Figure 18-3: The Select Network Client dialog box. You can select a networking client from those provided on the Windows 98 CD-ROM or find a client on another network vendor's diskette.

Choosing an Adapter

Your computer is physically connected to the network through your network adapter (card), your serial or parallel port, or your modem. Windows installs adapter driver software that is specific to your network adapter. If you have installed a Plug and Play network card, the Windows hardware-detection routines should configure it automatically.

Microsoft provides a broad range of adapter drivers that support the Network Device Interface Specification (NDIS) 5 standard. It is this standard that allows for multiple protected-mode networking protocols. Microsoft worked with all the major network adapter manufacturers to include adapter drivers for their cards.

The NDIS 5 specification supports ATM, Ethernet, token ring, FDDI, IrDA, and ArcNet networking cards and hot docking with Plug and Play adapters.

You can also use real-mode NDIS 2.*xx* and ODI (Open Datalink Interface) drivers that come (on diskettes) with pre-Plug and Play adapters if Microsoft hasn't provided a new NDIS 5 driver for your specific adapter.

The Windows hardware-detection routines should correctly determine which network adapter card is installed in your computer and its range of possible interrupt and I/O address settings. This is true for most cards even if they aren't Plug and Play.

If Windows hardware detection didn't get it right, you can configure the adapter driver settings yourself. You may need to click the Add New Hardware icon in the Control Panel first to make Windows find your network card. If you need to add an adapter driver, take the following steps:

STEPS

Adding an Adapter Driver

Step 1. Click the Add button in the Network dialog box.

Step 2. In the Select Network Component Type dialog box, highlight Adapter and click Add.

Step 3. In the Select Network Adapter dialog box, select an adapter manufacturer in the left-hand list and an adapter model in the right-hand list. Click OK twice.

If you use DCC or DUN, you should add Microsoft's Dial-Up Adapter driver. The Dial-Up Adapter is the NDIS 5 driver for your serial or parallel port, or modem. DCC and DUN are real networking options and require full network configuration based on the Dial-Up Adapter.

See Chapters 17 and 19 for more details about these networking options.

Your Plug and Play PC Card Isn't Found

You plug in a Plug and Play PCMCIA network card and find that Windows doesn't detect it. This may be true even if you plug in the card before you turn on your computer.

Often the solution is to remove the PCMCIA socket controller driver.

STEPS

Getting Windows to Detect Your PCMCIA Network Card

Step 1. Remove the card from the slot.

Step 2. Click the System icon in your Control Panel, and click the Device Manager tab.

Step 3. Click the plus sign to the left of the PCMCIA Socket icon. Click the PCMCIA Controller icon.

Continued

STEPS

Getting Windows to Detect Your PCMCIA Network Card *(continued)*

Step 4. Click the Remove button. Click OK. Click OK to restart Windows.

Step 5. The Windows hardware-detection routines will find the PCMCIA controller chip — notice that it is missing from the hardware list — and automatically reinstall the driver for it.

Step 6. Reinsert the PCMCIA network card. Windows should now detect it. If you have a driver for the card that is separate from the drivers provided by Windows (and more recent), be sure to browse to the diskette that contains the install file when asked.

Step 7. If there are any problems detecting the hardware, click the Add New Hardware icon in the Control Panel to force a new hardware detection or to allow you to specify the PCMCIA socket.

Configuring Resources for the Adapter Driver

Once Windows knows which network adapter you have physically installed, it loads the correct driver and determines the current hardware settings for your card. This is where it gets sticky, because Windows may not correctly determine your network adapter's interrupt and I/O address settings if it is not a Plug and Play card. To determine which values Windows has chosen, take the following steps:

STEPS

Determining Network Adapter Resource Values

Step 1. Click the System icon in your Control Panel, click the Device Manager, and click the plus sign next to Network Adapters. Select a network adapter.

Step 2. Click the Properties button to display the Properties dialog box for your network adapter, and then click the Resources tab (see Figure 18-4).

Step 3. Compare the values in the Resources tab with the known values for the adapter card. If you don't know what those values are, you are going to have to accept the values in the dialog box for now.

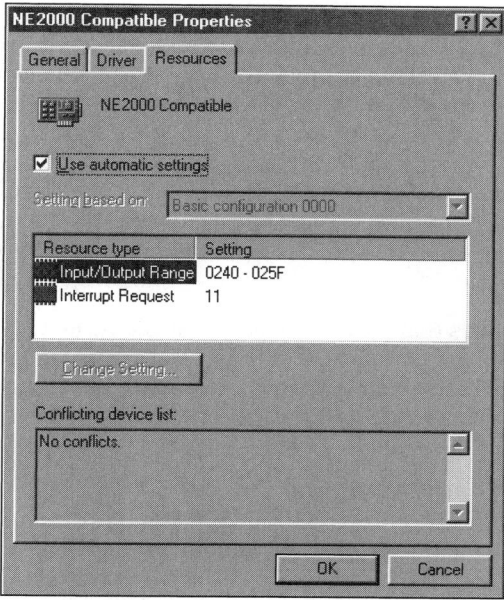

Figure 18-4: The Resources tab in a network adapter's Properties dialog box

If you are going to install Windows Me over an old copy of Windows for Workgroups 3.11, you can find the previous values for your network card by double-clicking the Network Setup icon in the Windows 3.1x Program Manager. The Windows Me setup routines will find these values (in the file Protocol.ini) and correctly configure the adapter driver to conform to the current card settings.

If you have a Plug and Play adapter, Windows will configure it correctly. If you have a pre-Plug and Play adapter, you can change your adapter's settings either by changing jumpers on the adapter or by running configuration software provided by the manufacturer. The Resources tab for these pre-Plug and Play adapters (except for the Intel EtherExpress adapters) displays only possible settings for this adapter, not necessarily the actual current settings for the card. It is up to you to get the possible and the actual settings to match.

Windows chooses possible adapter resource settings that don't conflict with other devices — if it can do this given the set of possible settings for the given adapter. If Windows determines that a conflict exists (because all the possible settings of the adapter card conflict with other devices in your computer), it places an asterisk in the appropriate field in the Resources tab.

Secret

You can't change the resource settings during Windows Me setup, and this can be a source of some difficulty—especially if you are setting up Windows Me over a network and through the adapter to which Windows Me has now assigned the incorrect address or interrupt. For example, the CD-ROM drive that holds your Windows Me CD-ROM might be connected to another computer on the network. In this case, to complete the setup, Windows Me will need to copy files over the network after the computer upon which you are installing Windows Me has been rebooted and is running under Windows Me. But the network will no longer be available to this computer because the network adapter has been incorrectly configured—a little Catch-22.

The source files that may no longer be available include files Windows Me needs to configure your modem and printer. You will have to go back after you have correctly configured your network adapter and install these items separately, using the Printers folder and the Modems icon in the Control Panel.

To get the adapter's settings to match the settings specified in the Resources tab of the Properties dialog box for your network adapter, you need to first complete as much of the Windows Me setup process as you can, and then go back and change either the adapter or the settings in the Resources tab.

To change an adapter that uses jumpers: Turn off your computer, pull the card, move the jumpers to match the settings given in the Resources tab, reinstall the card, and restart Windows Me.

To change an adapter using the manufacturer's configuration software: Open a DOS window when Windows Me restarts after setup, and run the manufacturer's configuration software for the adapter. You'll need to restart Windows after making these changes.

To change the resource settings to match the adapter's current settings, restart Windows Me, follow the "Determining Network Adapter Resource Values" steps earlier in this section, and change the values to match your adapter's values. Then restart Windows again.

Choosing a Networking Protocol

Individual computers have to speak the same language if you want them to talk to each other. The language they speak is the *networking protocol*. Microsoft provides 32-bit protected-mode implementations for three networking protocols: NetBEUI, IPX/SPX, and TCP/IP. You have to bind a networking protocol to the network adapter (or to multiple adapters) for the adapter and the protocol to work together to get the messages across the wire.

- NetBEUI (NetBIOS Extended User Interface) is Microsoft's fast, efficient, workgroup (nonroutable) protocol. It works great between Windows Me/98/95 computers and Windows for Workgroup 3.11, LAN Manager, and Windows 2000/NT workstations and servers.

- IPX/SPX (Internetwork Packet Exchange) is Novell NetWare's protocol, and therefore a standard for small- to medium-sized businesses and department-level networks. You can use this protocol to access both NetWare and Windows NT servers (as well as Windows Me/9x computers). You can configure Windows computers as NetWare file and print servers and address them through IPX/SPX.

- TCP/IP (Transmission Control Protocol/Internet Protocol) is the UNIX and Internet standard protocol. It provides networking support to a broad range of computer operating systems — indeed, to all computers that can communicate over the Internet. Windows includes a set of TCP/IP utilities, as described in "Microsoft's TCP/IP Stack" in Chapter 25. Internet addresses (which are assigned to each computer on the network) can be dynamically allocated because you can configure this version of TCP/IP to use the Dynamic Host Configuration Protocol (DHCP). Microsoft also supplies a Winsock version 2.2 DLL, so Winsock-compliant Internet programs such as FTP Explorer, Netscape Communicator, and Internet mailers can work with TCP/IP.

Windows Me supports 32-bit protocols from other manufacturers in addition to the three provided by Microsoft.

To choose a protocol, take the following steps:

STEPS

Choosing a Protocol

Step 1. Click the Network icon in the Control Panel, and click the Add button.

Step 2. In the Select Network Component Type dialog box, highlight Protocol and click Add.

Step 3. In the Select Network Protocol dialog box, select a manufacturer in the left-hand list and a protocol in the right-hand list. Click OK.

If you have an ATM card, you'll want to install the ATM network drivers:

STEPS

Installing ATM

Step 1. Click the Add button in the Network dialog box. Select Protocol and click Add again.

Continued

STEPS

Installing ATM *(continued)*

Step 2. Select Microsoft, and then ATM Call Manager. Click OK.

Step 3. Repeat for ATM Emulated LAN and ATM LAN emulation client.

Step 4. You also need to add NetBEUI, IPX/SPX, or TCP/IP (or all three). Click the Add button in the Network dialog box, select Protocol, click the Add button, select Microsoft, and select one of these three network protocols. Click OK.

TPC/IP Issues

Windows Me — like Windows 98 but unlike Windows 95 — automatically assigns an IP address to your network card even if your network doesn't have a DHCP server. You can find out more by turning to "Configuring the TCP/IP Stack for a Network Adapter" in Chapter 25. If your IP address isn't assigned (you can check this with Winipcfg.exe), click the Network icon in your Control Panel. Select TCP/IP on your network card, click Properties, mark "Specify an IP address," and enter an address that is unique on your network.

If you have a small network without a DHCP or WINS server, install both NetBEUI and TCP/IP. NetBEUI provides automatic name resolution and browsing through your Explorer.

STEPS

Creating an Lmhosts file

Step 1. Click the Start button ⇨ Programs ⇨ Accessories ⇨ Notepad.

Step 2. On the first line of the new text file, type the IP address of another computer that is on your network. Follow this address by a space, and then the name of that computer (see "Name that Computer" later in this chapter).

Step 3. Follow the name with a space and **#PRE**. Continue doing this for all the computers on your network for which you want to associate a friendly name.

Step 4. When you are finished, save the file in the \Windows folder under the name Lmhosts. You'll have to navigate to it in your Explorer after you save it and rename it to get rid of the txt extension.

The table in Lmhosts associates the friendly computer name with the IP address for these basic TCP/IP utilities. If you are not using NetBEUI or if you have a larger network and your workgroup is connected to other workgroups through a router, this file will be used to associate computer names with IP addresses. Of course, in larger networks, you would be more likely to have a WINS server to resolve for computer names. Then there would be no need for an Lmhosts file.

Choosing Network Services

Most network services — such as the ability to connect to remote computers and browse their disk drives — are available once you've configured your client, adapter, and protocol. Microsoft and other manufacturers provide additional network services. If you use Microsoft's Clients for Microsoft or NetWare Networks, you can configure your computer to share its folders, drives, and/or printers with other users on the network. You can use tape-backup software running on a Windows NT or NetWare server to back up your files, and you can administer HP printers running on NetWare networks.

Microsoft also provides Microsoft Service for NetWare Directory Services. If you install this service, you can log onto NetWare 4.x servers, use NetWare 4.x login scripts, browse the NetWare directory tree using My Network Places, and run 16-bit NDS-aware applications.

To add one or more of these services, take the following steps:

STEPS
Adding Network Services

Step 1. Click the Add button in the Network dialog box.

Step 2. In the Select Network Component Type dialog box, highlight Service and click Add.

Step 3. In the Select Network Service dialog box, select a manufacturer in the left-hand list and the service in the right-hand list. Click OK.

Sharing Your Resources

You make your hard disk drives, folders, and printers available to others on the network by sharing them. Although sharing isn't always easy, in this case it is.

To share your folders or disk drives and printers using the network services provided on the Windows CD-ROM, you need to install either Client for Microsoft Networks or Client for NetWare Networks. In addition, you need to choose Microsoft as the manufacturer in step 3 of the "Adding Network Services" steps in the previous section. Choose either "File and printer sharing for Microsoft Networks" or "File and printer sharing for NetWare Networks" as the network service. For details on sharing a printer, turn to "Sharing a Printer" in Chapter 41.

You have three options for how you want to share your disk drives (or folders): Read-Only, Full, or Depends on Password (if your computer is set for share-level security). Full access allows users at other computers on the network to create files and folders on your drive. They can also delete or edit new or existing files and folders on your drive (or within a specific folder). If you are using user-level security, you can name the users who have access to your resources. (If you are a network administrator with remote administration privileges, you can determine who has access to which resources on a client computer.) We discuss user-level and share-level security in the "Network Security" section later in this chapter.

Read-Only access allows other users to view, but not change, your files or folders. Depends on Password gives them either Full or Read-Only access depending on which of these two privileges you or the network administrator assign to them.

If you share your disk drives or folders with only read-only access, other nonadministrative users cannot delete your files and folders. If you don't share disk drives and folders at all, other users cannot see what you have on your computer.

Once you have chosen to turn on the ability to share, you still need to specify which resources you are going to share. "Sharing a Printer" in Chapter 41 provides details on making your printer available across your network.

To share a folder or disk drive, take the following steps:

STEPS

Sharing a Folder or Drive

Step 1. In an Explorer window, right-click the icon for the drive or folder that you want to share.

Step 2. Click Sharing in the context menu to display the Sharing tab of the Properties dialog box for your drive or folder, as shown in Figure 18-5. (The Sharing option appears in the context menu only if you are on a network, have DCC configured, or have Dial-Up Networking or DUN, which lets you create connectoids to the Internet, MSN, and so on.)

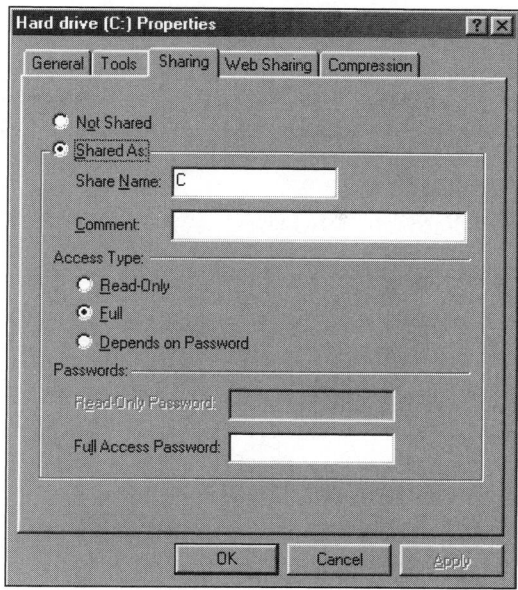

Figure 18-5: The Sharing tab in the Properties dialog box lets you set up share-level security. Choose Not Shared or Shared As. If you have configured your computer for user-level security, you will be able to specify which users can access your computer.

Step 3. To share your drive or folder, click Shared As.

Step 4. You can enter a new name for the resource as well as a comment to help other users understand what resource you're sharing.

If you add a dollar sign to the end of the resource's share name, it is hidden from users who are using My Network Places for network browsing. You might want to do this for your Microsoft Mail post office, which needs to be shared but not browsed.

Step 5. If your computer is configured for share-level security (most likely on a peer-to-peer network), you can set the access type (Read-Only or Full) and the password required to access your resource.

If your computer is configured for user-level security (you have a Windows NT or NetWare server on your network), you can specify who has access to your resources.

Step 6. Click OK.

Primary Network Logon

If you display the Primary Network Logon drop-down list in the Network dialog box (accessed from the Network icon in the Control Panel), you'll see the following choices (if you have installed all the services):

- Windows Logon
- Client for Microsoft Networks
- Client for NetWare Networks

Choose Windows Logon if you are not logging onto a network or are logging onto a peer-to-peer network. Choose one of the two clients if you are logging onto a network with either a Windows 2000 or NT server or a NetWare server and have installed one or both of these clients.

File and Print Sharing

You can decide if you are going to share your printer(s), your folders and drives, or both. Click the File and Print Sharing button in the Network dialog box to make this choice.

Name that Computer

To network your computer, you need to specify its name and the name of your local workgroup. Click the Network icon on your Control Panel, and then click the Identification tab. The *workgroup name*, as shown in Figure 18-6, is a name that a group of computers will share, and it defines them as an entity. Your computer name must be unique on your LAN.

You must give your computer a name and specify a workgroup, no matter which networking software you are using. Your computer name can be as long as 15 characters and can include only alphanumeric characters and these special characters:

! @ # $ % ^ & ( ) - _ ` { } . ~

You can also enter a description of your computer up to 48 characters in length (no commas) to help other users on your network identify your computer.

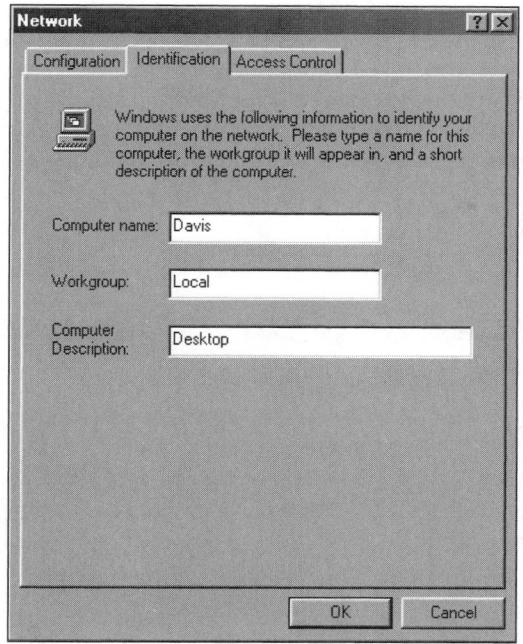

Figure 18-6: The Identification tab of the Network dialog box

Microsoft Networks

You can install Client for Microsoft Networks to connect your Windows Me computer with computers running Windows Me, Windows 98, Windows 95, Windows 2000 or NT, LAN Manager, Windows for Workgroups 3.11, Workgroup Add-On for MS-DOS, as well as other Microsoft Networks–compatible networks. If you configure it as the primary network logon client, you have the option to:

■ Use a Windows 2000 or NT server as a password server, which lets you configure user-level security (as opposed to share-level security, which is standard on peer-to-peer networks) and control it from the server

■ Share your files and printer(s) with other network users

■ Create user profiles, which you can use to set up different network connections and configurations for individual users

■ Allow remote administration of the registry on your computer

If you are installing Windows Me on a computer that is now running Microsoft's old Windows for Workgroups 3.11 networking, the Windows Me hardware-detection routines will automatically install Client for Microsoft Networks. Otherwise, you can install Client for Microsoft Networks using the procedure detailed in "Network Installation" earlier in this chapter, choosing Microsoft as the manufacturer in the Select Network Client dialog box.

If you install DCC and/or DUN, Client for Microsoft Networks and the Dial-Up Adapter are automatically installed.

Configuring Your Computer as Client for Microsoft Networks

If you are connecting your Windows Me computer to other computers using Windows Me, Windows 98, Windows for Workgroups 3.11, or Workgroup Add-On for MS-DOS, you don't need to worry about logging onto a Windows 2000 or NT domain for user-level security. This peer-to-peer networking scheme handles all security by assigning passwords to resources (share-level security). You can choose to reconnect to the resources that are shared on your network at startup time, or later when you actually browse the shared folders on another computer or print to a printer connected to another computer.

If you have a Windows 2000 or NT computer on your Microsoft network, you may need to log onto it if you want to have access to network resources. If the Windows 2000/NT server has been configured to provide user-level security, shared resources on other peer servers (Windows computers that are running file and printer sharing for Microsoft Networks) are available to you after you enter your user password.

To configure your Windows computer to Client for Microsoft Networks, take the following steps:

STEPS

Configuring Client for Microsoft Networks

Step 1. Highlight Client for Microsoft Networks in the Configuration tab of the Network dialog box. Click the Properties button to display the General tab of the Client for Microsoft Networks Properties dialog box, as shown in Figure 18-7.

Step 2. To use a networked Windows 2000 or NT server for logon validation, mark the "Log on to Windows 2000/NT domain" checkbox.

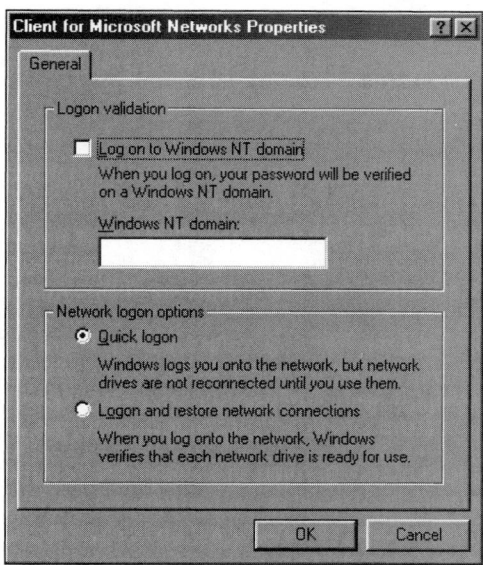

Figure 18-7: The General tab of the Client for Microsoft Networks Properties dialog box

Step 3.   To log onto your Microsoft network and delay connecting to network resources until you need them (if you have previously established a persistent network connection), mark the "Quick logon" option button.

You can establish a persistent network connection for shared folders and disk drives by checking the "Reconnect at logon" checkbox in the Map Network Drive dialog box (choose Tools ⇨ Map Network Drive in the Explorer). For printers, check "Reconnect at logon" in the Capture Printer Port dialog box (right-click a Printer icon, choose Properties, click Details, and click the Capture Printer Port button).

Step 4.   To establish a connection at startup to all the shared network resources with which you have previously specified a persistent connection, mark "Logon and restore network connections."

Step 5.   Click OK.

Configuring a Microsoft Networking Protocol

Client for Microsoft Networks can work with any of the protocols provided by Microsoft. NetBEUI is the default protocol for communication among computers running Windows Me, Windows 98, Windows 95, Windows for Workgroups 3.11, Windows 2000 or NT, LAN Manager, and Microsoft Workgroup Add-On for MS-DOS. However, you can also use IPX/SPX and TCP/IP to communicate with other Windows Me, Windows 98, Windows 95, and Windows 2000/NT computers.

Intranets are based on the TCP/IP protocol. If you are setting up Windows 2000, NT, and/or Windows Me/9x Web servers, then you should use TCP/IP as your networking protocol. You can use multiple protocols over your network, but it will run faster if you stick to one.

Highlight the protocol (or any of the protocols you've selected to work with your network adapter) in the Network dialog box and then click the Properties button. Click the Bindings tab, and then mark Client for Microsoft Networks to bind it to the chosen protocol, as shown in Figure 18-8.

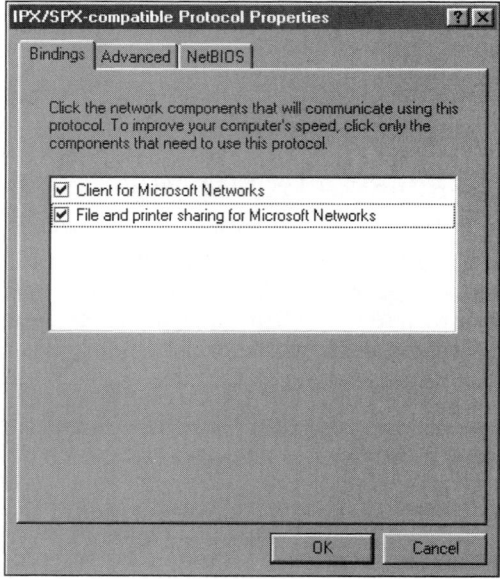

Figure 18-8: The Bindings tab in the Properties dialog box for a protocol. Mark the checkboxes for the network components that you want to bind to this protocol.

Diagnosing Microsoft Networking Problems

If you are having problems communicating from or to a Windows computer that is attached to a Microsoft network, you might check in a few different areas:

1. Make sure that "File and printer sharing for Microsoft Networks" is part of your network configuration by clicking the Network icon in the Control Panel. Click the File and Print Sharing button, and make sure that you have enabled sharing by marking one or both of the File and Print Sharing checkboxes.

2. Highlight File and Printer Sharing for Microsoft Networks in the Network dialog box, and click the Properties button. Set Browse Master to Automatic, and LM Announce to Yes.

3. If you are using the IPX/SPX protocol, highlight that network component in the Network dialog box, click Properties, click the Advanced tab, click Frame, and be sure that the frame type value is set to the frame type that is used on your network. If you are communicating with WFWG 3.11 computers, you may want to set it to 802.3, for example.

4. Click the Identification tab in the Network dialog box, and carefully check your computer name to make sure that it is unique. Also verify that the workgroup name is the same as the workgroup name for the other computers in your workgroup.

5. Make sure that you are actually sharing something. Just because you've enabled the ability to share, doesn't mean you are. Right-click a folder or drive icon in your Explorer and click Sharing.

6. Check your network card setup in the Device Manager. There may be an unrecognized conflict between your network card and I/O port COM 2. Disable COM 2 to check this out. You can change the resources used by the network card later, if you do indeed have a conflict.

You can troubleshoot your network problems by clicking Start ⇨ Help ⇨ Troubleshooting ⇨ Windows Troubleshooters ⇨ Networking. Also check out this Microsoft Knowledge Base article: `http://support.microsoft.com/support/kb/articles/q134/3/04.asp`

Putting a DOS Machine on Your Windows Network

Secret

You don't have to have Windows for Workgroups 3.11 Workgroup Add-On for MS-DOS to connect a DOS computer to your Windows network.

Microsoft charges $55 for this little hummer, but you can download it for free from Microsoft's FTP site. Use FTP Explorer (shareware found at `http://www.winfiles.com`) or Internet Explorer to go to `ftp://ftp.microsoft.com/bussys/Clients/MSCLIENT`. Download the files `DSK3-1.exe` and

DSK3-2.exe into a temporary folder. Copy them from the temporary folder to your DOS machine. Run them at the DOS prompt to expand them, and then run the setup program that shows up.

Novell NetWare Networks

Microsoft doesn't supply the NetWare network operating system software. That is, it doesn't provide the operating system for the NetWare server. That's Novell's job. Microsoft does provide 32-bit protected-mode versions of NetWare-compatible client software, the IPX/SPX-compatible protocol, and NDIS 5 adapter drivers. These drivers allow your Windows computer to connect to a NetWare server. The server can be running Novell NetWare versions 2.15 or later. You won't need to run any of the real-mode software from Novell to turn your computer into a NetWare-compatible client (or NetWare-compatible file and print server).

Novell offers two 16-bit NetWare clients — NETX (for NetWare 3.x) and VLM (for NetWare 4.x). Windows supports these two 16-bit real-mode clients, and you can use them instead of the Microsoft Client for NetWare Networks. There is no benefit to using the NETX client. VLM (Virtual Load Module) provides access to NetWare Directory Services (NDS), an enterprise-wide naming service that makes it simpler for you to manage user access to a wide range of network resources. Microsoft provides NDS access in an updated version of Client for NetWare Networks, which is included in Windows Me.

Novell offers a 32-bit client for IntranetWare and NetWare as well. This client supports DNS. You can download this client directly from Novell at http://www.novell.com/intranetware/products/clients/clientwin95/.

Client for NetWare Networks goes naturally with Microsoft's 32-bit protected-mode IPX/SPX-compatible protocol and NDIS 5 adapter driver. If you choose to install it, these components are automatically configured and installed with it. You can use your existing real-mode ODI adapter drivers and Novell-supplied IPX/SPX protocol stack with Client for NetWare Networks if you want to run TSRs that absolutely require Novell's 16-bit implementation of IPX/SPX.

Because Windows computers can connect to NetWare networks using so many different configurations, you can try different combinations to see what difference the combinations make. It is very easy to go from one to the other, so you don't need to worry about causing problems if you start with something and change it later.

To install Client for NetWare Networks, use the procedure detailed in the "Network Installation" section earlier in this chapter. Choose Microsoft as the manufacturer in the Select Network Client dialog box, and select Client for NetWare Networks in the Network Clients list box.

Configuring Your Computer as Client for NetWare Networks

Client for NetWare Networks is automatically installed and configured if you install Windows in the \Windows folder of a computer configured correctly as a Novell NetWare client. Log onto a NetWare server before you install Windows to make sure that everything gets configured correctly.

To configure your Windows computer for Client for NetWare Networks, take the following steps:

STEPS

Configuring Client for NetWare Networks

Step 1. Highlight Client for NetWare Networks in the Configuration tab of the Network dialog box. Click the Properties button. The General tab of the Client for NetWare Networks Properties dialog box will be displayed, as shown in Figure 18-9.

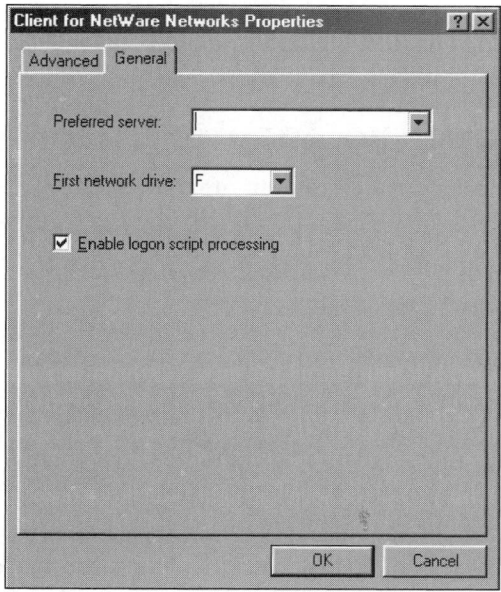

Figure 18-9: The General tab of the Client for NetWare Networks Properties dialog box. Type the UNC name of the NetWare server that you will log onto first.

Continued

STEPS

Configuring Client for NetWare Networks *(continued)*

Step 2. Enter the UNC name of your preferred NetWare server. (See the section "The Universal Naming Convention (UNC)" later in this chapter for information on the UNC.)

Step 3. Enter the volume designation letter for your first network connection.

Step 4. If you want to process a NetWare logon script, mark "Enable logon script processing."

Step 5. Click OK.

Configuring the IPX/SPX-Compatible Protocol

If you are using Microsoft's 32-bit IPX/SPX-compatible protocol, you can configure it (or any of the Microsoft-supplied networking protocols) using the Network dialog box. Just highlight the protocol and click the Properties button.

Configuring the Adapter Driver

Highlight your network adapter in the Network dialog box and click the Properties button. You have the choice of three adapter driver types:

■ Enhanced mode (32-bit and 16-bit) NDIS driver (NDIS 5)

■ Real mode (16-bit) NDIS driver (NDIS 2.*x*)

■ Real mode (16-bit) ODI driver

The default adapter driver selected automatically when you choose Client for NetWare Networks or Client for Microsoft Networks is the NDIS 5 driver. The IPX/SPX-compatible networking protocol will be bound to this adapter. Click the Bindings tab to see which protocols are bound to your adapter.

The adapter's interrupt and I/O address are listed in the Resources tab of the network adapter's Properties dialog box (highlight the adapter in the Network dialog box and click the Properties button). For additional information, see the section earlier in this chapter entitled "Configuring Resources for the Adapter Driver."

The properties displayed in the Advanced tab (if available) of the Properties dialog box for the adapter depend on the specific adapter.

Logging onto the Network

If you are connected to a network using a 16-bit real-mode driver, a network logon prompt appears on your screen in text mode before the Windows Desktop is displayed. You need to log on before Windows starts.

If you have installed Client for Microsoft Networks or Client for NetWare Networks, separate logon boxes appear the first time that you restart Windows. You will also see a Logon box for logging onto your own computer — pretty rude, actually.

If you use the same password in all the logon boxes, the next time you start Windows, you will be presented with one "unified" Logon box. The only way this is going to work is if you have the same password for your logon to your primary NetWare server, to your Windows 2000 or NT server, and to your own computer.

If you are logging onto a Microsoft network without a Windows 2000/NT server (for example, connecting to other Windows Me, Windows 98, Windows 95, and WFWG 3.11 computers), you won't be faced with a Microsoft Networks Logon box. Resources on peer-to-peer networks are protected with passwords that are unique to the resources, not to the users (if the resources are protected at all). You need to configure your logon correctly using the steps outlined earlier in this chapter in the section entitled "Configuring Your Computer as Client for Microsoft Networks."

Passwords for resources that are protected by share-level (peer-to peer) security are encrypted and remembered in the *password cache,* a file stored on your Windows computer. They are retrieved from the password cache after the first time you successfully log onto a shared network resource, so you don't have to enter the password for a resource again. You (or your network administrator) can configure your computer so passwords aren't cached and you have to enter them anew each time you access a resource or server that requires a password.

If you have configured your Windows computer to enable user profiles, you will always have to (at least) negotiate with the Windows Logon box. To enable user profiles, click the Users icon in the Control Panel. Your password can be blank.

You can add the *Windows family logon service,* which allows you to just pick a name from a list of users at logon time. In the Network dialog box, click Add ⇨ select Client, and click Add. Select Microsoft and choose Microsoft Family Logon.

You can log onto the network without seeing a Logon box if you disable user profiles, select Windows Logon as the primary network logon in the Network dialog box, use a blank password, and your passwords for logging onto your NetWare or Windows 2000/NT server are also blank. This is also the case if you are logging onto a Microsoft peer-to-peer network under these conditions.

Windows caches your various passwords. You only need one Logon box to log onto a network (if you do it right), no matter whether it is a peer-to-peer network, a NetWare network, or a Microsoft network with a Windows 2000/NT server.

Your passwords are stored in an encrypted file, *username*.pwl, referred to as a *password cache*. If you delete this file, you lose access to password-protected resources and servers.

You can change some passwords by clicking the Passwords icon in the Control Panel. You can also use the Password List Editor, a utility that comes with Windows Me and 98, to manage your passwords. This utility doesn't let you change passwords, but it does let you delete passwords from your password cache. You might use the Password List Editor to get rid of passwords that you aren't using anymore, or, if you are a network administrator, to disallow access to some resources or servers whose passwords were previously cached.

You'll find the Password List Editor on the Windows CD-ROM in the \ tools\ apptools\ pwledit folder. You can use the Add/Remove Programs icon in the Control Panel to install it. Click the Windows Setup tab, click the Have Disk button, and type the pathname in the Install From Disk dialog box.

Secret

If you like, you can also set the minimum length required for a password to be valid. You'll need to edit the registry to do this.

STEPS

Setting the Minimum Password Length

Step 1.   Click Regedit.exe in the \Windows folder.

Step 2.   Navigate to HKEY_LOCAL_MACHINE\ SOFTWARE\ Microsoft\ Windows\ CurrentVersion\ Policies\ Network.

Step 3.   With the Network key highlighted, right-click the right pane of the Registry Editor and choose New ⇨ Binary Value. Name the binary value **MinPwdLen**.

Step 4.   Double-click MinPwdLen. Give it a value that you want for your minimum password length. Click OK and exit the Registry Editor.

Some network connections will not work if you send an encrypted password to the network server. You can send an unencrypted password if you make a registry change. For details, turn to "Network File System" in Chapter 25.

The My Network Places

The servers and shared resources on the network are made visible through the My Network Places. You can display the My Network Places folder window by clicking this icon on the Desktop or by clicking it in an Explorer window. You'll also find the My Network Places icon in common dialog boxes (such as the File Open dialog box) used by 32-bit Windows-aware applications such as WordPad and MS Paint.

You can click the Map Network Drive button in the Explorer or folder window toolbar (or choose Tools ➪ Map Network Drive in the Explorer) to give a volume drive-letter designation to a server, a shared folder, or a shared drive. You can likewise map a network printer to an LPT port using the Capture Printer Port dialog box, which you access through the Details tab of the Properties dialog box for a network printer. (Right-click a printer icon in the Printers folder, click Properties, click the Details tab, and then click the Capture Printer Port button.)

My Network Places bridges the chasm between your computer and the network. You browse the network in the same manner that you browse your own computer. There isn't a different interface.

Windows integrates your computer and the network by making files and printers on other computers look and feel the same as local resources.

In Windows Me and 9x, unlike in the old Windows 3.1x, you do not have to map a network drive to be able to see and use the files on that drive. As long as the file is displayed in your Explorer or folder window, it is available to you. You can run programs (you may need to make other adjustments in the program's configuration) and edit documents that reside on another computer without mapping that computer's disk drive to a logical drive letter.

The Universal Naming Convention

Every computer and server on your network has a name. You provided a name for your computer when you installed Windows, if you installed any network components.

You refer to other computers and resources on the network by their names. For example, `\\ Billscomputer\ Cdrive\ Mystuff` refers to another computer (Billscomputer) that is sharing a resource, the hard disk drive named `Cdrive` (most likely the `C:` drive on Bill's computer), and the Mystuff folder on that drive.

This way of referring to servers or computers that are sharing their resources is called the *universal naming convention* (UNC). You use two backslashes before the computer's name, a single backslash between the name of the computer and the name of the shared resource (a hard disk drive, in this example), and a single backslash between the name of the shared resource and the folder.

You can also use this convention to refer to networked printers. (You assign a name to each networked printer.) To see how to assign a name to a printer, turn to the "Installing a Printer Driver" section of Chapter 41.

Resource Sharing

The resources on your computer—printers, folders, drives, CD-ROMs—are accessible to other users over your network if you enable file and printer sharing through the Network dialog box. This peer-to-peer resource sharing requires that you use Client for Microsoft Networks, Client for NetWare Networks, or both. Other users on your network who want to access your resources must be running the matching client as well as the same network protocol.

You don't have to share resources that are connected to individual computers with other computers on the network. You could set up the network so that your network servers are the only computers that have resources available to other users.

If your network is a peer-to-peer network—one without a server—then the only way individual users can access network resources is to share them. Not every computer needs to share its resources, and every computer that does becomes a peer server.

Network Security

Security issues affect all aspects of life on a computer network. As a user, you don't want others—whatever authority they hold over you—messing around with your files and programs. If you are a network administrator, you want to be able to allow people to use resources that are available on the network, no matter whose computer they are connected to. You also want to be able to install software on client computers from your computer. Users and administrators alike want to make sure that someone calling in from outside the network can't download private information from their computers or from the network.

You maintain network security by restricting access to network resources. You can restrict access by assigning passwords to resources or by maintaining lists of authorized users (who are assigned passwords). Your computer is quite secure if you:

- Don't share any resources
- Don't enable remote administration
- Don't enable the Windows Dial-Up Server
- Require a logon password to your computer
- Don't allow others physical access to your computer

If you allow any form of access to your computer, you need to provide some security measures to restrict that access.

Windows computers are not completely (or even very) secure. Even if you require a password to access Windows, anyone can press and hold the Ctrl key during the power-on self test to get to your computer's Startup menu. They can then make a choice to go to the DOS prompt.

You can disallow the use of Ctrl key by putting the statement BootKeys=0 in your Msdos.sys file.

Choosing Between Two Kinds of Security

Windows provides two different kinds of security. The first is *share-level security,* which is used on peer-to-peer networks — for example, when you network Windows computers together. The second is *user-level security,* which requires a Windows NT or NetWare server.

You enforce share-level security by attaching passwords to each shared folder, disk drive, and printer. You enforce user-level security by maintaining lists of users on a Windows 2000, NT, or NetWare server. You can mix both types of security on the same network, as long as you have a Windows 2000/NT or NetWare server to maintain user-level security.

Each Windows peer server stores a list of shared resources on that computer, along with the accompanying passwords. The list of users allowed access to shared resources on a particular Windows computer on the network is stored on the Windows 2000, NT, or NetWare server.

A network administrator with the remote administration password can set up the list of users and passwords for shared resources on any of the client Windows computers on the network, as long as they are configured for remote administration.

Share-Level Security

Armed with a remote administration password for each computer and for each shared resource, a network administrator in a share-level security system (for example, a peer-to-peer Microsoft Network with no Windows 2000 or NT server) has some administrative control over the computers on the network. In this type of setup, the network administrator maintains security by managing the peer servers (that is, the Windows 98 computers with shared resources).

In a share-level security system, a remote administration password protects your computer. If someone (an officially designated network administrator or not) has that password, he or she can create, add, or delete shared resources on your computer. If you change the remote administration password, that person loses administrative access until you provide the new password. As a network administrator, you would normally store all the remote administration passwords for the computers that you administer in a cached file on your computer.

If your network does not have a Windows 2000, NT, or NetWare server, your security options are simple — you use share-level security. Share-level security is not available on computers running file and printer sharing for NetWare Networks.

User-Level Security

A network administrator who has been given remote administration authority can grant access to the resources on your computer to other users, and administrative access to other system administrators. The names of the users and administrators are kept on the Windows NT or NetWare server.

Administrators who have remote administration authority over your computer can carry out any of the administrative-access actions detailed later in this chapter in the section entitled "Network Administration." They can edit your registry, customize your computer's configuration and Desktop, edit your password list, and monitor system performance. They can also add or remove other remote administrators.

User-level security is required in order to use the network management tools (other than Net Watcher) that come with Windows, and those available from third parties. The tools that come with Windows are described in the "Network Administration" section.

Setting the Type of Security

It is not a good idea to switch back and forth between share-level and user-level security. Choose one, or follow the guidelines of your network administrator, and stay with it.

STEPS

Setting the Type of Security

Step 1. Click the Network icon in the Control Panel. Click the Access Control tab in the Network dialog box, as shown in Figure 18-10.

Step 2. Mark either "Share-level access control" or "User-level access control".

Step 3. If you choose "User-level access control," enter the name of the server or the domain that stores the list of users who have access to your resources.

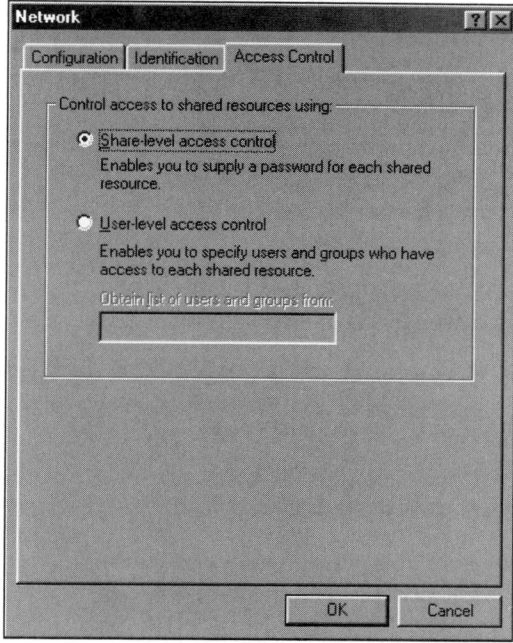

Figure 18-10: The Access Control tab of the Network dialog box

Step 4. Ignore messages about being unable to find the security provider. If you are asked for the authenticator type, enter Server or Domain, depending on which one you are using.

Step 5. Click OK and restart your computer.

Network Administration

Windows comes with four network management tools: System Policy Editor, Registry Editor, System Monitor, and Net Watcher. Only Net Watcher can be used on a peer-to-peer network to remotely administer shared resources on a peer server. The other tools require a Windows 2000, NT, or NetWare server, the designation of user-level security on the computers to be administered, and the installation of Microsoft Remote Registry Service on Windows Client computers as well as on the network administrator's computer.

Using Net Watcher, a network administrator can:

- Determine which clients are connected to any peer server on the network
- Disconnect any clients from any peer server
- View which resources any peer server is sharing
- Change the share attributes of any resource on a peer server
- Start/stop sharing any peer server resource
- Determine which files are open on a peer server
- Close open files on a peer server

Because a network administrator can use Net Watcher to create, add, or change the properties of a shared resource, he or she can edit and delete files, as well as create new ones on any disk drive on your computer — even on drives that you have specified as read-only. The network administrator can install new software on your computer while sitting at his or her computer.

You have the ability to determine which disk drives, folders, and printers are shared on your computer; a network administrator with the remote administration password has the same ability.

A network administrator can use System Policy Editor to change many registry settings and customize the Desktops of remote Windows computers. Of course, you can also use System Policy Editor locally to customize your own Windows computer without having to go through the network.

You can use the Registry Editor locally to edit your own registry, or remotely to edit other people's registries. This is covered in detail in "Using the Registry Editor to Edit Someone Else's Registry" in Chapter 11. If you want to connect to (and possibly edit) a registry on a remote Windows computer, choose Registry ➪ Connect Network Registry in the Registry Editor. Many of the changes you can make to a computer's registry don't take effect until that computer is rebooted.

You can use the System Monitor both locally and remotely to get information about computer performance.

Enable Remote Administration

You can enable remote administration on a computer with either user-level or share-level security. If you have implemented user-level security on your Windows computer, as described in "Setting the Type of Security," remote administration is automatically enabled.

To enable remote administration of a Windows computer, take the following steps:

STEPS

Configuring Your Computer for Remote Administration

Step 1.   Click the Passwords icon in the Control Panel. Click the Remote Administration tab in the Passwords Properties dialog box, as shown in Figure 18-11.

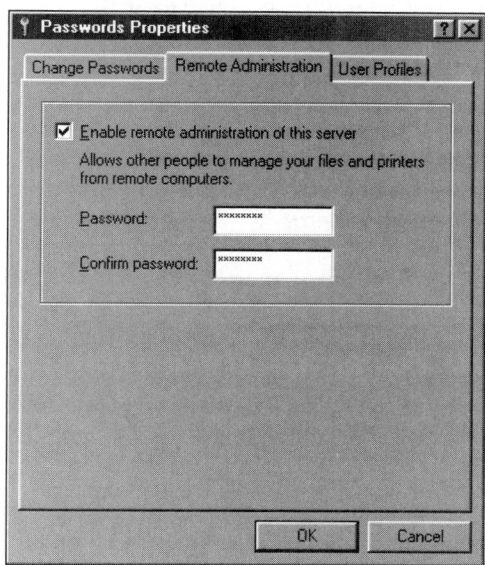

Figure 18-11: The Remote Administration tab of the Passwords Properties dialog box. Mark the "Enable remote administration of this server" checkbox and type a password to allow a network administrator to remotely administer your computer.

Step 2.   Click "Enable remote administration of this server."

Step 3.   If the computer is configured for share-level security, enter a password.

  If, instead, the computer is configured for user-level security, click the Add button and enter the names of the administrators. (The Add button isn't shown in Figure 18-11. If you have enabled user-level security, it will be displayed.)

Step 4.   Click OK.

Install Remote Registry Services

If you are going to allow a network administrator to edit your registry using System Policy Editor and/or the Registry Editor, or allow him or her to monitor the performance of your computer with System Monitor, you need to install Microsoft Remote Registry Service. Of course, if the administrator has your remote administration password, he or she can take these steps for you. You don't need to install Remote Registry Service unless you have enabled user-level security on your computer, because none of these network management tools work with share-level security. To install Remote Registry Service, take the following steps:

STEPS

Installing Microsoft Remote Registry Service

Step 1. Click the Network icon in the Control Panel. Click the Add button, and in the Select Network Component Type dialog box, click Service, and then click the Add button.

Step 2. Click the Have Disk button.

Step 3. Click the Browse button, and browse to the `\ tools\ nettools\ remotreg` folder on the Windows CD-ROM. `Regsrv.inf` will be highlighted. Click OK.

Step 4. Highlight Microsoft Remote Registry and click OK. Restart your computer.

Install Remote Registry Service on the network administrator's computer also. And keep in mind that the administrator's computer and the client computer must share a common networking protocol.

Net Watcher

If you have multiple peer servers on the network, you can run multiple copies of Net Watcher to continuously keep track of them all. You can use Net Watcher to administer all peer servers that have been configured for remote administration, and you can use it to administer your own computer if it is a peer server (that is, if you are running file and printer sharing for Microsoft or NetWare Networks).

If your computer is using share-level security and file and printer sharing for Microsoft Networks, you can use Net Watcher to administer only other computers of the same configuration. If your computer is configured for user-level security and file and printer sharing for Microsoft Networks, you can use Net Watcher to administer other computers running file and printer sharing for Microsoft Networks irrespective of their security scheme. If you are running file and printer sharing for NetWare Networks, you can only administer peer servers that are also running it.

Net Watcher provides three different views of a peer server. The default view is Connections view, which displays the user connections to the peer server. Shared Folders view displays the resources that are shared on the server, and Open Files view displays the files that are open on the server.

You can install Net Watcher using the Windows Setup tab in the Add/Remove Programs Properties dialog box (click the Add/Remove Programs icon in the Control Panel). Click System Tools and then mark Net Watcher. You can also find the Net Watcher install files on your Windows 98 CD-ROM in `\tools\ reskit\netadmin\\ netmon`.

To run Net Watcher after it is installed, click Net Watcher in the Programs ⇨ Accessories ⇨ System Tools menu. When Net Watcher first starts, it is focused on your computer. To administer another peer server, click the Select Server button at the left end of the Net Watcher toolbar (see Figure 18-12).

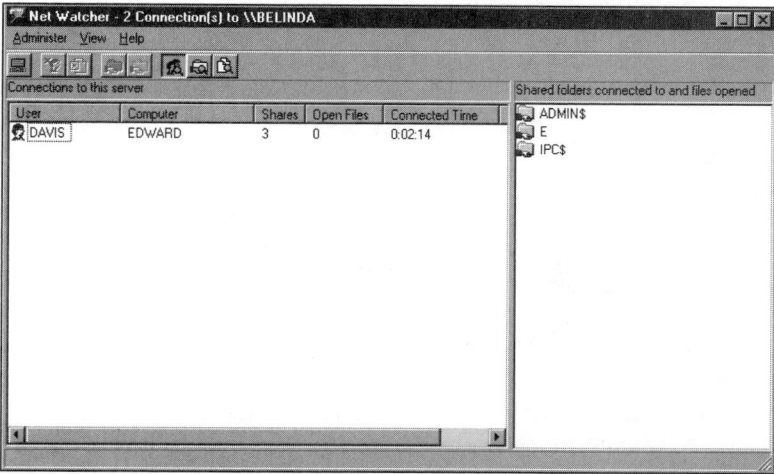

Figure 18-12: The Net Watcher with the default Connections and Details views turned on

Disconnecting Users from a Peer Server

To disconnect a user from a peer server, highlight the user and click the Disconnect User button (the second button from the left) on the Net Watcher toolbar.

Changing or Adding Sharing on a Peer Server

You can share resources that aren't currently being shared on a peer server, change the share properties of an existing shared resource, or quit sharing.

STEPS

Changing Sharing on a Peer Server

Step 1. Click the Show Shared Folders button (the second from the right) in the Net Watcher toolbar to switch to the Shared Folders view. This view displays both shared printers and folders, as shown in Figure 18-13, despite its name.

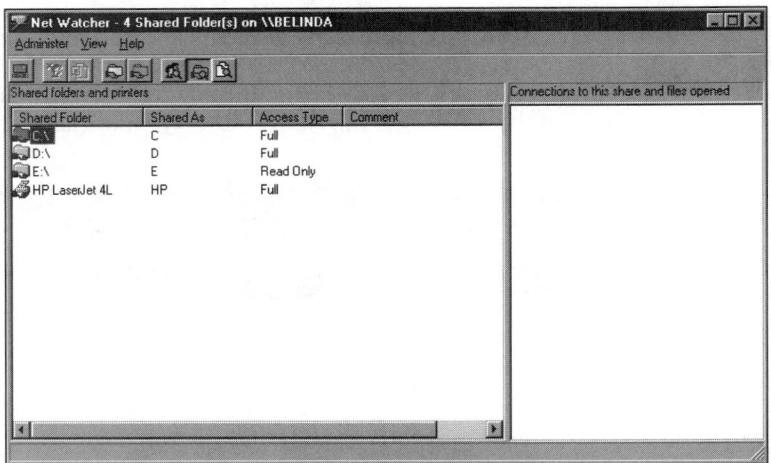

Figure 18-13: Net Watcher in Shared Folders view

Step 2. Highlight the name of the resource whose sharing properties you want to modify.

Step 3. Press Alt+Enter. The Properties dialog box for this resource appears on your Desktop. You can choose Not Shared to quit sharing the resource, change sharing to Full, Read-Only, or Depends on Password, and change the passwords required to access the resources.

If the peer server uses user-level security, you can change the names of the users who can access that resource.

Step 4. Click OK.

You can also stop sharing a resource by highlighting it in the Shared Folders view and choosing Administer ⇨ Stop Sharing Folder.

To turn the peer server into a shared resource, choose Administer ⇨ Add Shared Folder. Click the Browse button in the Enter Path dialog box to display the resources on the peer server.

Dealing with Open Files

You can determine which files are open and close them if you need to. You might want to do this if a client computer is hung with an open file on the peer server.

STEPS

Closing an Open File on a Peer Server

Step 1. In the Net Watcher window, choose View ⇨ By Open Files, or click the Show Files toolbar button (it looks like two pieces of paper and a magnifying glass).

Step 2. Click the file that you want to close.

Step 3. Choose Administrator ⇨ Close File.

Watching a Particular Peer Server

You can set up multiple Net Watcher icons, one for each server.

STEPS

Watching Multiple Peer Servers

Step 1. In an Explorer window, click My Network Places.

Step 2. Click the Entire Network icon, one of your workgroups, or the icon for the computer that you want to administer.

Step 3. Right-click the computer icon for the peer server that you want to track with Net Watcher. Click Properties in the context menu. Click the Tools tab (see Figure 18-14).

Continued

STEPS

Watching Multiple Peer Servers (*continued*)

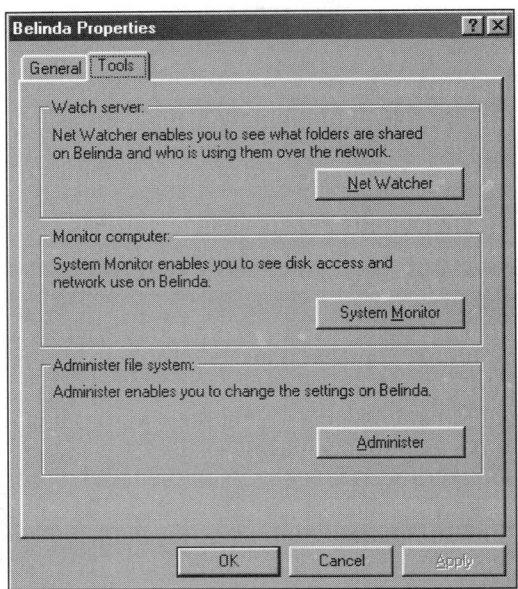

Figure 18-14: The Tools tab of the Properties dialog box for a peer server

Step 4. Click the Net Watcher button.

Step 5. Continue doing this for as many peer servers as you want to track.

You can also browse for a peer server in Net Watcher by choosing Administer ⇨ Select Server.

System Policy Editor

System Policy Editor is a friendly front end to a number of user and computer configuration values stored in the registry. You can use it to perform these tasks, among others:

■ Remove the Shut Down, Settings, and Run commands from user Start menus

■ Get the My Network Places icon off of the Desktop

- Remove a number of Control Panel icons, including System, Display, and Network

- Require validation from a network server for access to the local computer

- Disable password caching

- Disable dial-in from Dial-Up Networking

- Disallow print and/or file sharing

You can define system policies for a given user and computer, or for similar groups of users. You can store these policies on a Windows 2000, NT, or NetWare server, download them at logon time to an individual computer, and use them to modify the registry settings. Storing the system policies on a server protects them from tampering.

You install System Policy Editor (on your computer or on the network administrator's computer) from the Windows CD-ROM. Take the following steps:

STEPS

Installing System Policy Editor

Step 1.   Click the Add/Remove Programs icon in the Control Panel and then click the Windows Setup tab.

Step 2.   Click the Have Disk button, and then click Browse. In the Open dialog box, browse to the folder `\tools\reskit\netadmin\poledit` on your Windows CD-ROM and click OK.

Step 3.   Click the OK button in the Install From File dialog box, and then click the checkboxes next to Group Policies and System Policy Editor in the Have Disk dialog box. Click the Install button.

Step 4.   Click OK.

System Policy Editor is installed and its shortcut is now in the System Tools menu (under Start ⇨ Programs ⇨ Accessories). To use the System Policy Editor to set options for a given user, first log on as that user. In the System Policy Editor menu, click File ⇨ New and open a new policy file. Double-click the User icon to begin choosing policies.

To allow System Policy Editor to create group policies, each client Windows computer needs to have the `Grouppol.dll` file in its `\Windows\System` folder. To put this DLL in the System folder, take the steps above on each client computer, but install only Group Policies.

System policies are by default downloaded from your NetWare preferred server or Windows NT PDC when you log onto your network. You can use the System Policy Editor to cancel this download. Simply choose File ⇨ Open Registry, double-click Local Computer, and click the plus sign next to Network. Then choose Update and clear the Remote Update checkbox.

Registry Editor

To edit the registry that is resident on another Windows computer, choose Registry ⇨ Connect Network Registry in the Registry Editor. You can then browse to find the computer whose registry you wish to edit. The Registry Editor is discussed in detail in "The Registry Editor" in Chapter 11.

System Monitor

The source files for the System Monitor are not stuck in some obscure folder on the Windows CD-ROM. You can install it by clicking the Windows Setup tab in the Add/Remove Programs Properties dialog box (click the Add/Remove Programs icon in the Control Panel). Click System Tools ⇨ Details, and scroll down to System Monitor.

Once it's installed, you'll find the System Monitor in the Start ⇨ Programs ⇨ Accessories ⇨ System Tools menu. To connect System Monitor to another computer (or to connect multiple copies of System Monitor to monitor multiple computers) choose File ⇨ Connect in the System Monitor.

Network Applications

Microsoft still supplies network applications that let you do more than just share resources and administer the network. Windows Messaging lets you send e-mail (and attachments) to anyone on your network. You can also share a fax modem over a network using Windows Messaging (which you'll find on the Windows 98 CD-ROM but not on the Windows Me CD-ROM).

You can install WinPopup—a utility that broadcasts or sends messages and pops up when a job that you have sent to the networked printer is complete. Click Add/Remove Programs in the Control Panel, click the Windows Setup tab, highlight System Tools, click Details, and mark the WinPopup checkbox.

Windows 95 came with WinChat. Windows Me and Windows 98 provide a similar but more powerful program called NetMeeting. You can use NetMeeting to chat, work on the same application at the same time, and speak to and send video to other people on the network. You must have TCP/IP properly configured. You call a computer using its NetBIOS or NetBEUI name. If your network has a NetMeeting directory server, you can use the directory to contact others on the network.

Home and Small Office Networking

If you don't already have a network in your home or small office, it's probably because you haven't gotten around to it quite yet. In the following sections, you'll see how to use the built-in networking capabilities in Windows.

Why a Network?

Sharing is cheaper and more fun (games), uses fewer phone lines for Internet access, and makes life easier when it comes to using peripherals. Sharing used to be too hard to make it worth the trouble. Sharing used to be expensive. Sharing used to use too many resources and degrade the performance of individual machines. Sharing used to cause difficult-to-diagnose problems. Sharing used to mean too much dependence on others or on some expert. Sharing doesn't mean any of those things any more.

A small network is much cheaper than a second printer. A small network is much cheaper than a second phone line and a second Internet service provider (ISP). A small network lets you share an expensive DSL or cable modem connection.

You can share information much easier over a network than by copying it onto a floppy diskette. Floppy diskettes are soon to be all-but-gone. Many portable computers have floppy drives that are external and rarely, if ever, connected.

Printers can be automatically configured over the network, so that any computer can use any printer on the network. No more wheeling the thing around on a cart and then trying to find the driver.

Sharing means that your files can be anywhere. You can use those large hard disks for backup, for making second copies in the background, and for organizing your documents using the whole network as a resource.

All of the software that you need to run a nifty little network comes with Windows, so why not use it? Internet connection sharing provides Internet access through one computer on your small network to every computer on the network. You can also use other third-party software to connect your computers to the Internet.

Setting Up a Small Network Quickly and Cheaply

Given the low cost and ease of installation provided by Windows, it makes a lot of sense to connect two or more computers together in a workgroup with inexpensive networking hardware. If you purchase Plug and Play networking cards (adapters) and install them in computers with Plug and Play BIOSes, Windows will install its networking software and drivers for you.

What's the easiest and cheapest way to set up a network? Buy an Ethernet starter kit and, if you have more computers than there are network cards in the starter kit, a few extra network cards and cables.

Are you going to be able to install it and set it up yourself? Yes — just follow the instructions in this chapter, perhaps backed up with the Web sites we recommend.

What's it going to cost? Fast enough — $85; really fast — $130; more for additional cards and cables. To find a 100Mbps (megabits per second) Ethernet starter kit, check out the kit available from Linksys at http://www.linksys.com. You can also visit the homePCnetwork at http://www.homepcnetwork.com to read their latest recommendations and reviews.

Installing a small network on the cheap requires nothing more than buying an Ethernet starter kit that includes a couple of ISA Plug and Play NE2000-compatible 10-Mbps Ethernet cards, some Category 5 — commonly called Cat 5 — cable with RJ-45 connectors, and a small hub. If you have a portable computer with a Type II PCMCIA slot and card and socket drivers, you need to purchase a separate 10-Mbps Ethernet PC card for it (the kits don't include these PC cards). Plug everything together, turn on the computers, and the network installs itself. (If you want more detailed guidance on setting up your network, see the steps later in this section.)

The incremental cost of going to 100-Mbps Ethernet is now so small that the benefits don't have to be very great to justify the additional expense. The major difference you'll see is that applications and files stored on other computers appear to be stored on your own. When you're using 10-Mbps Ethernet, you notice that it takes a while to pump 100MB of data over to another computer. This might discourage you from backing up as often as you would with 100-Mbps Ethernet.

If your network consists of a portable with the docking station and a desktop computer, make sure that the docking station has a PCI interface and can handle the 100-Mbps Ethernet PCI cards. Otherwise, there is no need to go to the faster network.

Buying a 100-Mbps Ethernet network means buying an Ethernet starter kit with a 100-Mbps hub, PCI network cards, and Class 5 cable with RJ-45 connectors (see the steps below for more about these hardware options). Your network starter kit should come with a manual on how to install the network. Use it!

If you have older equipment, you'll need to give Windows 98 some help in implementing the network. We intermix the details of setting up older equipment with our general networking setup steps:

STEPS

Setting Up a Small Ethernet Network for Home or Business

Step 1.   Purchase an Ethernet starter kit, either 10Mbps or 100Mbps. This will include a hub, a couple of network cards, and the twisted pair (10BaseT) cables needed to hook two computers or more together.

If you need extra cards, buy Plug and Play network cards. (There is no need these days to purchase cards that aren't Plug and Play.) If you are setting up a small network with light networking tasks, you only need 10-Mbps Ethernet cards (at about $19 each) that comply with the IEEE 802.3 and 10BASE-T Ethernet standards.

These are very standard cards, and they are widely available. Most come with RJ-45 connectors. They'll most likely include BNC T connectors. If you are going with 100-Mbps Ethernet, get Fast Ethernet (100 BASE-TX) cards, which handle both 10 and 100Mbps at about $35.

Cards are available for ISA slots as well as PCI slots. The ISA-slot cards are less expensive and perfectly fine for small networks. In the future, computers will not come with ISA slots, so this option will not be available. If you are going to use 100Mbps, use PCI network cards (your only choice, really).

If you need a card that can connect to a portable, you can purchase a PCMCIA 10-Mbps Ethernet card for about $60. One place to look for this type of card is http://www.zdnet.com. Be sure that the connector cable that goes from the card to the RJ-45 and/or BNC jacks is included. PCMCIA cards that handle both 10 and 100Mbps cost about $100.

If your portable connects to the network through a docking station, be sure that it either includes a networking card or purchase an ISA or PCI card that works with the bus in the docking station.

Install the cards in available slots in both of the computers.

Continued

STEPS

Setting Up a Small Ethernet Network for Home or Business

(continued)

Step 2. If you need additional cables, purchase ready-made 25-foot Class 3 cables for 10-Mbps Ethernet. They are available for about $4. One place to check out is `http://www.computergate.com`. Class 5 cables, required for 100-Mbps Ethernet, cost about $7 for 25-foot lengths with the connectors already installed. Connect the hub and Ethernet cards by plugging in the cables.

Ethernet hubs used to be expensive. If you were just hooking two computers together, it was cheaper to go with a coaxial cable. (The problem with using a coaxial cable is that if one computer connection goes down, the whole network goes down, although with two computers this doesn't matter.)

Now you can buy five-port 10-Mbps hubs for around $40. It makes sense to just purchase a hub and plug in Class 3 unshielded twisted-pair wire with RJ-45 jacks. This is a star configuration, with each computer plugged into the hub. If one leg goes down, it doesn't affect the other legs.

Hubs that handle 100-Mbps Ethernet cost a bit less than $100, standalone. If you purchased the Ethernet starter kit, you've got the hub.

If you are never going to have more than two computers networked to each other, you can use a *crossover* Class 3 or 5 twisted-pair cable.

Step 3. T-connectors and terminators come with the cards; use them to connect coaxial cable to the T-connectors, the T-connectors to the cards, and the terminators to the other end of the T-connectors.

If you are using a hub, you don't need to worry about this. Use a hub.

Step 4. If your network cards are Plug and Play, turn off your computer, plug in the cards, plug in the hub, plug the cables into the cards and the hub, turn on the computers, and let your Windows machines find the cards and install the network. Jump down to step 6.

If the cards aren't Plug and Play compatible, run the DOS-based configuration software first to set up their interrupts and I/O addresses. The default values for the cards may be okay, depending on what hardware you have installed in your computers.

To find out which interrupts and I/O addresses are available on your computers, boot them up, click the System icon in the Control Panel, click the Device Manager tab, highlight Computer, and click the Properties button. Click the Interrupt Request (IRQ) option button to see which addresses are already used, as shown in Figure 18-15; used interrupts are listed first.

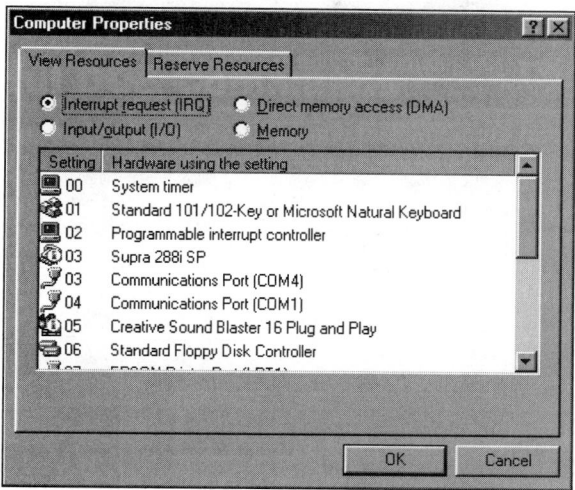

Figure 18-15: The Interrupt Request listing on the View Resources tab of the Computer Properties dialog box

Click Start ⇨ Programs ⇨ MS-DOS Prompt, and run the DOS-based configuration software from the DOS prompt.

Step 5. Click the Add New Hardware icon in the Control Panel on both computers. You can have the Add New Hardware Wizard search for your new adapters, or you can specify what you have. The wizard will load and configure the 32-bit protected-mode NDIS 5 driver for your adapters.

You can check which resources (interrupts and memory) your network card uses. Press Win+Pause/Break (or right-click My Computer and click Properties), click the Device Manager tab, double-click Network Adapters, double-click your network card name, and click the Resources tab, as shown in Figure 18-16.

If there are conflicts with other interrupts, you will need to free up interrupts.

Continued

STEPS

Setting Up a Small Ethernet Network for Home or Business

(continued)

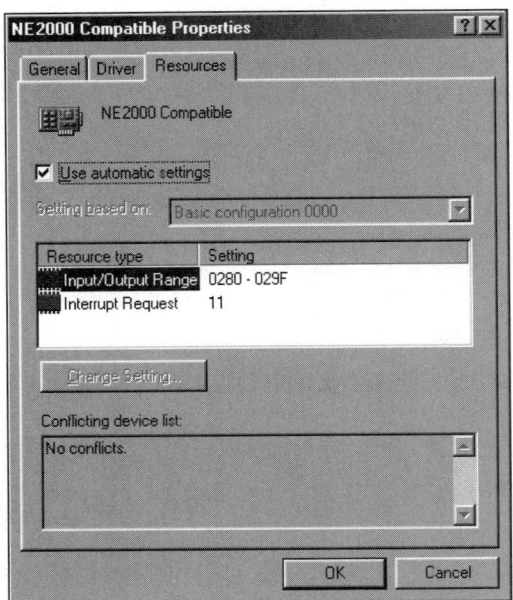

Figure 18-16: The network resources listing

Step 6. If you have a PCMCIA network card, it will undoubtedly be Plug and Play. Be sure that your portable computer supports at least card and socket services. You may have a portable that supports CardBus, a 32-bit connection to the PC Card. If so, you can purchase a CardBus-compatible PC Card that allows for a 100-Mbps Ethernet connection.

You will be asked for your network card drivers after you turn on your computer. Windows may automatically find them on your Windows CD-ROM and install them, although you can direct it toward driver files on diskettes or a CD-ROM supplied by the card manufacturer. There is no need to use the drivers from the manufacturer unless you are sure that they are newer than the ones on the Windows CD-ROM. You can update these drivers later by going to the Windows Update site on the Web.

After you restart your computer (when directed to do so), click the Network icon in the Control Panel. Click the Identification tab in the Network dialog box. Make sure that the two computers have different names but the same workgroup name, as illustrated in Figure 18-17. Click OK.

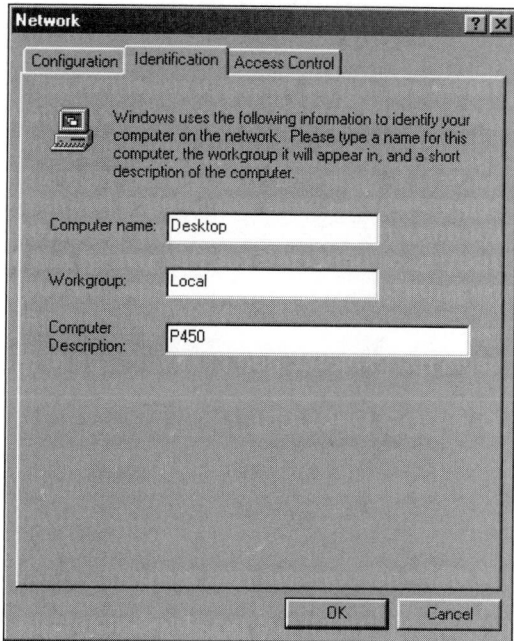

Figure 18-17: This computer is named Desktop, and it shares the Local workgroup with one or more other computers.

Step 7. Click the Network icon in the Control Panel. Highlight your network adapter in the list of networking components. To see which networking protocols have been bound to the adapter, click the Properties button and then click the Bindings tab, as shown in Figure 18-18.

For a small computer network, if you are not going to hook up to the Internet, you'll most likely want to bind NetBEUI and/or IPX/SPX (for playing games). Windows 95 automatically binds these two protocols.

The TCP/IP protocol (and only TCP/IP) is bound to your network card automatically by Windows. This works fine for a small network. There are lots of little software packages that work with it, and you'll need it if you're going to connect to the Internet.

Continued

STEPS

Setting Up a Small Ethernet Network for Home or Business

(continued)

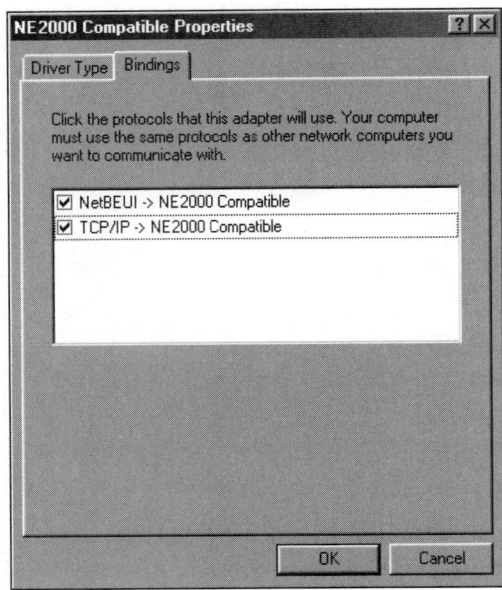

Figure 18-18: In this figure, both the NetBEUI and the TCP/IP protocols have been bound to the network adapter.

If you need to bind a protocol to the list, click OK to close the Properties dialog box, and then click the Add button in the Configuration tab of the Network dialog box. Highlight Protocol in the Select Network Component Type dialog box, click the next Add button, and select the protocol in the Select Network Protocol dialog box (see Figure 18-19). Click OK.

Step 8. Client for Microsoft Networks is added by default during the initial Windows network setup. It is necessary if you want to allow sharing of your resources so that each of the computers can be a peer server to the others. If it isn't listed in the Network dialog box, you need to add it, as well as "File and printer sharing for Microsoft Networks."

To add Client for Microsoft Networks, click Add in the Configuration tab of the Network dialog box, click Client in the Select Network Component Type dialog box, and click Add again. In the Select Network Client dialog box, highlight Microsoft on the left and click Client for Microsoft Networks on the right. Click OK.

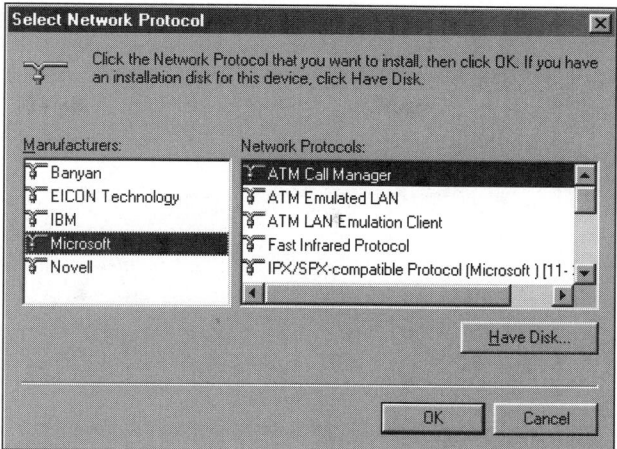

Figure 18-19: Select the manufacturer and the protocol that you want to add in the Select Network Protocol dialog box.

To add file and printer sharing for Microsoft Networks, click Add in the Configuration tab of the Network dialog box, click Service in the Select Network Component Type dialog box, and click Add again. In the Select Network Service dialog box, highlight Microsoft on the left and click "File and printer sharing for Microsoft Networks" on the right. Click OK.

You probably don't want to be file and printer sharing over the Internet, so you can remove this binding to your Dial-Up Adapter. If you forget, you will be reminded the first time you try to access your ISP, and you can remove it then.

To remove it manually, highlight TCP/IP -> Dial-Up Adapter in the Configuration tab of your Network dialog box, click Properties, and click OK when you see the warning shown in Figure 18-20 not to configure your TCP/IP properties for a dial-up connection here. Click Bindings, clear the File and Printer Sharing for Microsoft Networks checkbox, and click OK.

Step 9.   Click the OK button in the Network dialog box and then reboot your computers for all of this to take effect.

You won't have to reboot if you are using Plug and Play cards.

Step 10.   Open Explorer or folder windows on the Desktops of both computers. Right-click resources (disk drives and/or folders) that you want to share, click Sharing in the context menu, and configure the sharing properties. Do the same in the Printers folder for printers that you are going to share.

Continued

STEPS

Setting Up a Small Ethernet Network for Home or Business

(continued)

Figure 18-20: Click OK when you see this warning.

Step 11. Click the My Network Places icon on the Desktop of one of the
computers. You should see the name of the workgroup in the My
Network Places folder window; if not, click the Entire Network icon.
Click the workgroup name to see the names of all the network
computers. Click their names to see the shared resources.

Using these steps, you can install the NetBEUI, IPX/SPX, and/or TCP/IP
protocols and bind them to your network cards. If you are running a small
network, you don't have to run all three protocols. You can use NetBEUI if
you are just sharing printers, disks, and folders, and not accessing the
Internet. You can remove the other protocols in the Network dialog box.

If you want to set up a local Web server or share a modem on the network
to contact your ISP, you can get rid of all the protocols other than TCP/IP.
TCP/IP is, after all, the default networking protocol for Windows.

IP Address Auto Assignment

Windows Me — like Windows 98, but unlike Windows 95 — automatically
assigns each computer on your local network an IP address. This allows
TCP/IP to be the default networking protocol for Windows Me/98 without
further user configuration. Windows Me/98 goes out on the network when
you first start Windows and checks if there is a Dynamic Host Configuration
Protocol (DHCP) server. If not, it assigns an IP address to the local computer.
It then checks to make sure that this is a unique address by checking all the
IP addresses of the other computers on the local network. There is no need
for a DHCP server locally.

To see for yourself how the auto assignment works, click Start ⇨ Settings ⇨ Control Panel ⇨ Network. Highlight the TCP/IP bound to your network card (TCP/IP -> *network card name*), as shown in Figure 18-21, and click Properties.

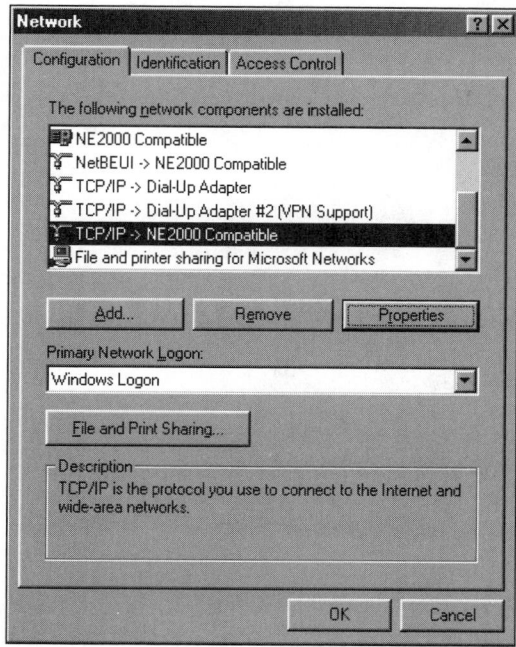

Figure 18-21: Select the TCP/IP bound to your network card in the Configuration tab of the Network dialog box.

Click the IP Address tab, and notice that "Obtain an IP address automatically" is marked by default, as shown in Figure 18-22.

This setting allows Windows to automatically assign each of the computers on your network a unique IP address. If you have a DHCP server on the network, this setting allows the DHCP server to assign each computer its unique IP address.

If you install Sygate, WinGate, or other Internet access software on one of your computers, it will include a limited implementation of a DHCP server that can assign IP addresses to the computers on your network. You should leave "Obtain an IP address automatically" marked if you want to use these mini-DHCP servers.

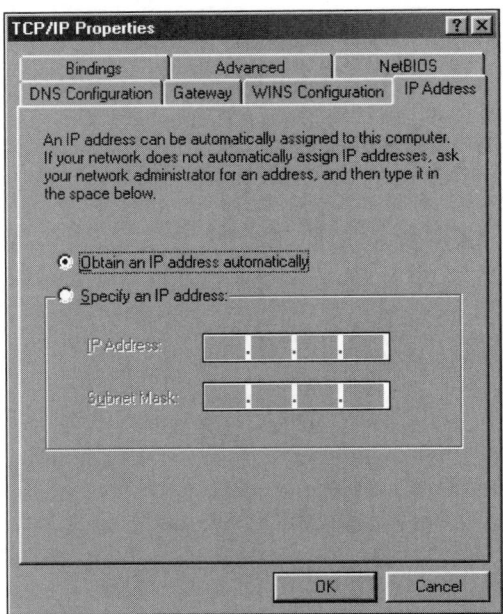

Figure 18-22: The first option is marked by default.

Without a DHCP server, Windows takes a bit of time to assign IP addresses to the computers on your network every time you start up. It has to go out and make sure that each computer has a unique IP address, and assign addresses that don't conflict. You can cut out this automated bit of checking (and reduce the time that it takes to start Windows) by assigning the IP addresses manually.

One way to do this is to let them be assigned automatically at first. Then follow these steps:

STEPS

Setting a Permanent IP Address

Step 1. Find out what IP address and subnet mask have been assigned to your computer by clicking Start ⇨ Run, typing **winipcfg**, and pressing Enter. Display the drop-down list at the top of the dialog box and highlight your network card name. Your computer's IP address will be displayed in the IP Autoconfiguration Address field, as shown in Figure 18-23. Write it down, or keep this window open.

Step 2. Click Start ⇨ Settings ⇨ Control Panel ⇨ Network.

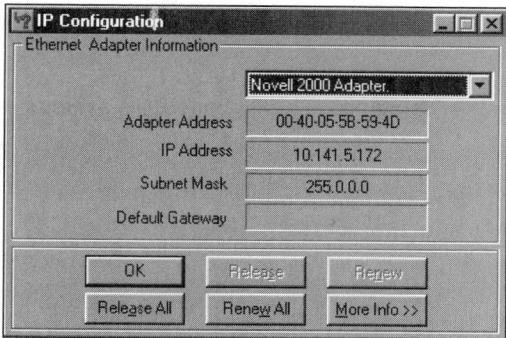

Figure 18-23: The IP Configuration dialog box. The first field should contain your network card name.

Step 3. Scroll down the components list until you see the listing for TCP/IP and your network card, written thusly: TCP/IP -> *network card name*. Highlight this entry and click Properties.

Step 4. Click the IP Address tab if it isn't already displayed. Mark the "Specify an IP address" option button, as shown in Figure 18-24.

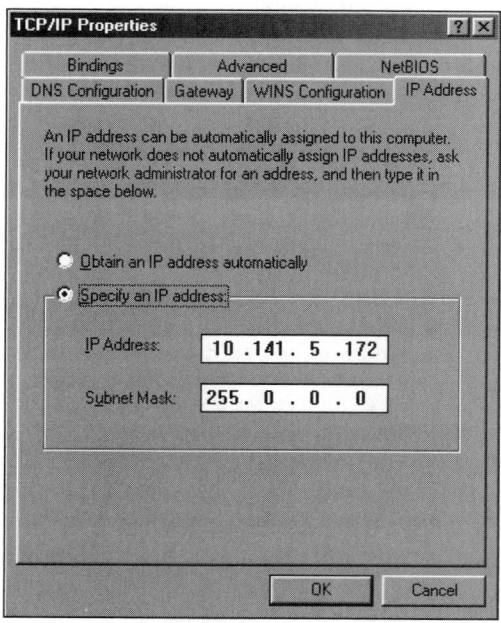

Figure 18-24: Mark the "Specify an IP address" option button.

Continued

STEPS

Setting a Permanent IP Address *(continued)*

Step 5. You can now manually enter an IP address and subnet mask. Type the IP address that you just saw in the IP Configuration dialog box. Enter a submask (typically **255.0.0.0**, but you may need to check your documentation to be sure). Click OK, then click OK again.

Step 6. You may be prompted to insert your Windows CD-ROM and asked to restart your computer. Follow the prompts.

To get each computer on the network to recognize these changes on all the computers on your network, you may need to open your Explorer and press F5 to refresh its view.

You've now taken the automatically assigned IP address for your computer and permanently assigned it to your computer. All computers on the same local network should use IP addresses that start with the same first three numbers.

If you'd like to understand the nature of IP addresses and subnet masks, Microsoft provides a thorough explanation in "Understanding TCP/IP Addressing and Subnetting Basics," which you can find at http://support.microsoft.com/support/kb/articles/q164/0/15.asp.

Make the Network Resources Local

You can get to the resources on the network by using My Network Places, or by entering the UNC (universal naming convention) name of another computer in the Start ➪ Run dialog box or in the Address bar of the Explorer — but this gets old quick. If you had to do this every time you sent a document to a printer connected to another computer, you'd soon be shopping for your own printer.

You'll want to map the available hard disks and folders on other computers as though they were local drives. Of course, this is trivially easy to do. In your Explorer, click Tools ➪ Map Network Drive. If you want this connection to persist (be there the next time you restart your computer), mark the "Reconnect on logon" checkbox in the Map Network Drive dialog box.

If you find yourself doing this a bunch because new network resources keep being added, click View ➪ Folder Options, click the View tab, and mark "Show Map Network Drive button in toolbar" (see Figure 18-25).

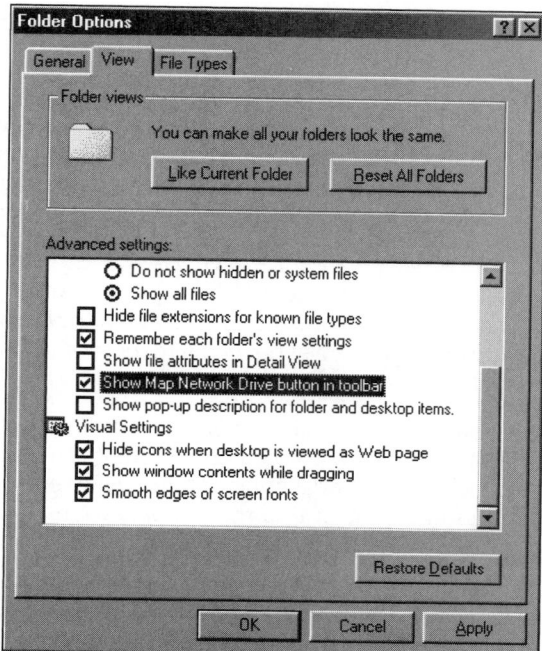

Figure 18-25: In the View tab of the Folder Options dialog box, mark "Show Map Network Drive button in toolbar."

Even better, put shortcuts to shared hard disks and folders right on your Desktop or in your toolbars.

Going Online with a Small Office/Home Network

If you have a small office or home network using the TCP/IP protocol (automatically installed with Windows), it is quite easy to provide a single connection to the Internet through one computer on the network. This means that you only need to have one outside telephone or cable line that will be used to connect everyone on the network to the Internet. You only need to have one account at your ISP. You only need one modem to service the whole network.

There are a couple of downsides. First, the computer that has the modem has to be up and running for everyone else to be able to connect to the Internet. If every computer on the network had its own modem, it would be each user's responsibility to make his or her own connection. If your Internet connection didn't work, well, no skin off anyone else's nose.

Second, all the traffic to the ISP is going to go through one computer and over the local network. As you add client workstations, this can turn the network or the modem server into a bottleneck. You may need to go to a higher-speed Ethernet and/or larger bandwidth access to the service provider.

The computer connection to the ISP can be an analog modem (even a slow one), a cable modem, or a DSL connection through a network adapter (other options are available). With DSL, you'll need two network adapters — one for the local network, and the other for the DSL modem.

Windows Me (and Service Pack 1 for Windows 98) includes Internet connection sharing software that enables you to connect your network to the Internet. In early February 1999, Microsoft bought Nevod, Inc. and its product NAT 1000, and turned it into Internet Connection Sharing.

If you don't like ICS for some reason, there are numerous other ways to make one computer on the network the connecting node to the Internet. A simple solution is provided by SyberGen, Inc. Their Sygate software runs on one Windows computer and turns it into the gateway to the Internet for the network.

Sygate is very simple to install and operates transparently. It has its own mini-DHCP that automatically assigns IP addresses to the rest of the computers on your network and enters a DNS and gateway address in each of the computer's network settings.

Our version of the software didn't come with a help file, but you can download online help by right-clicking the Sygate Manager icon in your system tray and clicking On-line Help. Check the What's New icon on the Sygate Web site to get a better idea of the current configuration.

You'll find Sygate at `http://www.sygate.com`.

WinGate, the Pioneer Internet Gateway for Small Networks

In addition to Internet Connection Sharing and Sygate, discussed in the previous section, you also have other options for getting your small network online. WinGate is the pioneer in this field. WinGate's architecture now includes client software at each computer.

The previous version allowed you to connect two computers to the Internet for no cost, certainly the deal of the year. It didn't have the ability to allow Microsoft NetMeeting traffic, although no one seemed to be able to understand why.

WinGate now costs $40 to have two computers share a modem. You don't have to configure your applications, and your TCP/IP settings are configured automatically for you. You can check out WinGate and download a trial version at `http://www.wingate.com`.

Online Network Resources

Before you purchase a small business or home network, you'll want to check in with the homePCnetwork at `http://www.homepcnetwork.com`. Not only will you find instructions on how to set up a small network, but you'll also find the latest reviews and tests of Ethernet starter kits, network cards, Internet access software, and so on. This site is tightly organized and easy to understand. It concentrates on the small network, so you don't have to wander through lots of extraneous material.

At the other end of the spectrum, with respect to organization, you can check out the sprawling "Windows Networking FAQ" at `http://www.helmig.com/j_helmig/faq.htm`. Presenting a much wider focus and drawing on the developer's history with Windows, this site provides the next level of network understanding as well as a jump up to bigger networks. You can learn about how networks and protocols operate, and explore all the little twists of connecting peer-to-peer networks with computers that aren't running Windows (or are running older versions of Windows).

Be sure to check out "Workgroups Have Limitations" if your network is getting bigger than 15 computers, "Browsing the Network" to see how the My Network Places knows where the resources are, "Your Own Personal Web Server" to learn how to set up Microsoft Personal Web Server, and "Sharing and Mapping a Drive via the Internet" to learn how to use the Internet as though it were a local area network. The FAQ also includes lots of information on connecting to a Novell network, Direct Cable Connection, TCP/IP routing, troubleshooting, and on and on.

The *Windows Resource Kit* has plenty of material on Windows networking. This is a main focus of the book and online manual. We suggest using it as a networking resource, especially for larger network installations.

The articles in the Microsoft Knowledge Base update the *Resource Kit*. Go to `http://support.microsoft.com/support/search/c.asp`. Then select your version of Windows in the "My search is about" field, type **Network** in the "My question is" field, click Go, and choose among the networking articles that appear.

xDSL

You can connect one of the computers on your local network to a DSL modem and get a superfast 24-hour-a-day digital connection to your ISP for an additional $40/month or so. That is, you can if you are lucky enough to be close enough to a central telephone office, and if there is an available port at the office for you.

Exposed on the Internet

If you are about to connect to the Internet and you have bound file and printer sharing for Microsoft Networks to your TCP/IP protocol (the default setting), you will be warned that your TCP/IP is in turn bound to your Dial-Up Adapter. If you don't disable this setting when warned, you should be aware that you may be turning your computer and printer into servers that anyone on the Internet can access.

It's just as though you were treating the Internet as a small local area network. You might share your C: drive locally, but do you want everyone on the Internet to have access to it?

You can immediately disable this setting when warned, or you can disable it manually at another time. To do this, click Start ➪ Settings ➪ Control Panel ➪ Network ➪ TCP/IP -> Dial-Up Adapter ➪ Properties ➪ OK ➪ Bindings, and clear the checkbox next to "File and printer sharing for Microsoft Networks." You can also do this for TCP/IP -> Dial-Up Adapter #2 if you don't want to share your computer or printer on your virtual private network (VPN). (You won't be using VPN on a home network because you need at least a Windows 2000 or NT server.)

Hackers on the Internet can use any of a number of IP address-scanning or port-scanning programs to scan a particular IP address or range of addresses. This process is called *strobing*. If you have file and printer sharing for Microsoft Networks bound to your TCP/IP protocol, this scanning software will display the share names of resources on your network and/or computer.

A hacker can type the command **nbtstat –a *yourIPaddress*** to display your computer name, your workgroup name, and any user account names on your computer. If you open a DOS window on your computer and type this command, replacing *yourIPaddress* with the IP address of a computer on your local area network, you'll see this information. By the way, the *nb* in the DOS command *nbtstat* stands for NetBIOS status.

If you open a DOS window and type **netstat –a –n** and press Enter, you'll get a listing of your current IP address and the ports that are listening. Ports 137, 138, and 139 should be recorded as listening. Password cracking programs direct their attacks at these ports.

The "Forgetting the Password" Problem

A common problem people have with Windows is that it won't allow them to store their passwords in the password cache.

You can check out "The Windows Network FAQ" at http://www.helmig.com/j_helmig/faq.htm and click "Dialup Networking Does NOT Save the Password." Also, see "Can't save your Dial-Up Networking password" in Chapter 44. *PC Magazine* has a long and useful article on passwords (that also deals with Windows) at http://www.zdnet.com/pcmag/pctech/

content/16/21/os1621.002.html. You can find plenty of information in the *Windows Resource Kit* help file on your Windows CD-ROM. Just search on the word *password*.

Synchronize the Clocks on Your Network

We use the little network utility Socket Watch to find the correct time every time we connect to the Internet. You can easily download it from a shareware site such as Tucows at http://www.tucows.com.

Once you've got the correct time on one machine, you might as well share it with the rest of them.

Use Notepad to create a little batch file called something like time.bat. You only need to put one line in the batch file: **net time *thenameofthe computerwithsocketwatch*.** Save the time.bat file in your \My System folder. Drag and drop a shortcut to it into your \Windows\Start Menu\ Programs\StartUp folder. Do this for each of the computers (other than the one with Socket Watch) on your network.

Right-click the time.bat file in your Explorer, click Properties, click Program, and mark the "Close on exit" checkbox.

Get Rid of the Hand Under the Shared Resource Icon

Secret

If you share a resource, a Hand icon appears under the icon of the shared resource. You can eliminate this Hand icon by taking these steps:

STEPS

Ridding Yourself of the Blue-Sleeved Hand

Step 1. Click Start ➪ Run, type **regedit**, and press Enter.

Step 2. Navigate to HKEY_CLASSES_ROOT\ Network.

Step 3. Highlight the SharingHandler key in the left pane of your Registry Editor, as shown in Figure 18-26.

Step 4. Double-click the Default value in the right pane.

Step 5. Delete the value **msshrui.dll** in the Value Data field in the Edit String dialog box. Click OK and exit the Registry Editor.

Step 6. Restart Windows for this to take effect.

Continued

STEPS

Ridding Yourself of the Blue-Sleeved Hand *(continued)*

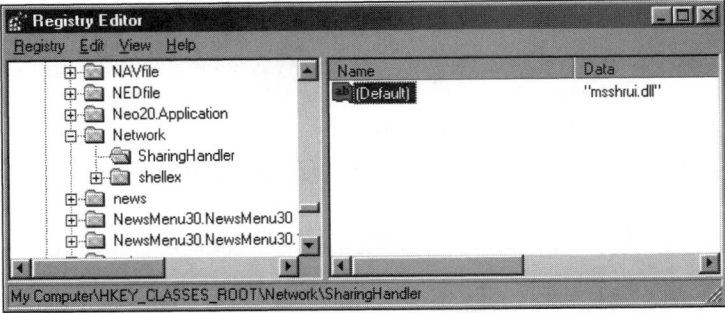

Figure 18-26: Highlight the SharingHandler registry key.

To restore the hand, repeat these steps, but in step 5, define the default value as **msshrui.dll**.

Let Me See Those DHCP Errors Again

Windows gives you plenty of opportunities to never again see certain dialog boxes. If you received a DHCP error message and marked the checkbox in the DHCP error dialog box requesting not to see these error messages again, that's it — you won't. But in case you change your mind, you can take these steps:

STEPS

Seeing DHCP Errors Once Again

Step 1. Click Start ➪ Run, type **regedit**, and press Enter.

Step 2. Navigate to HKEY_LOCAL_MACHINE\ System\ CurrentControlSet\ Services\ VxD\ DHCP.

Step 3. Double-click PopupFlag in the right pane of the Registry Editor and press Delete.

Step 4. Type **01**.

Step 5. Click OK and exit the Registry Editor.

See the Other Players in a Multiplayer Game

Lots of multiuser games use the IPX/SPX networking protocol to support communication among players. Sometimes one player can't see the other players. What's missing is a commonly agreed *frame type*. To get everyone in sync, take these steps:

STEPS

Setting the IPX/SPX Frame Type

Step 1. Click Start ➪ Settings ➪ Control Panel, and click the Network icon.

Step 2. Highlight IPX/SPX-compatible Protocol -> *your network adapter or modem*.

Step 3. Click the Properties button, click the Advanced tab, and highlight Frame Type, as shown in Figure 18-27.

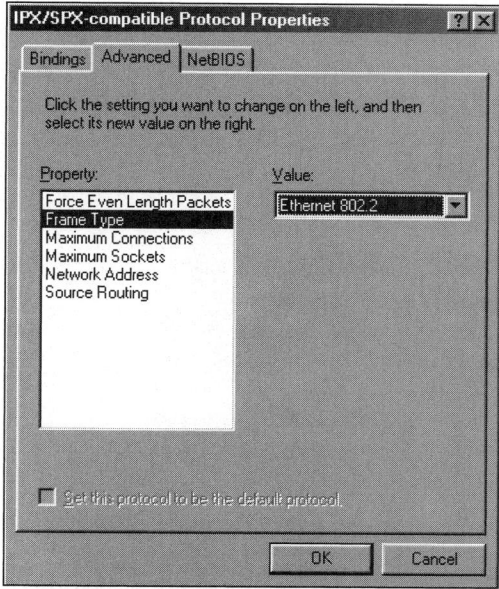

Figure 18-27: Frame Type is in the Property list. Use the Value drop-down list to set the type.

Step 4. Display the Value drop-down list, select Ethernet 802.2 or Ethernet 802.3 (whichever is used on your network), and click OK.

All of the other players should also do this with their computers.

Copy from Machine A to Machine B

Imagine three people with Windows computers, all working on a project together in a small office. They want to ship paragraphs and bits of documents or graphics between computers on their small network. What should a group like this do?

One option is to create Desktop or Start menu shortcuts to documents stored on another computer. Then they could copy and paste text to and from those documents by invoking the shortcuts and saving the edits. It works, but it isn't always that convenient to get to the shortcuts, the shortcuts can easily proliferate, and you've got to have the document on your own computer as well as one on the other one, in case the other computer isn't on.

Another option is to use NetMeeting. NetMeeting is nice as a communications tool, but it is a bit of overkill for just sending little pieces of documents.

What we need is a Clipboard that actually works. A clipboard that lets you share your Windows Clipboard with other users — a network clipboard.

That's just what you get with Network Clipboard. Install Network Clipboard on a few computers that are connected together with a local area TCP/IP network (basically the default for Windows), click its icon on the Desktop, and the other computers will show up in your Active Users list, as shown in Figure 18-28.

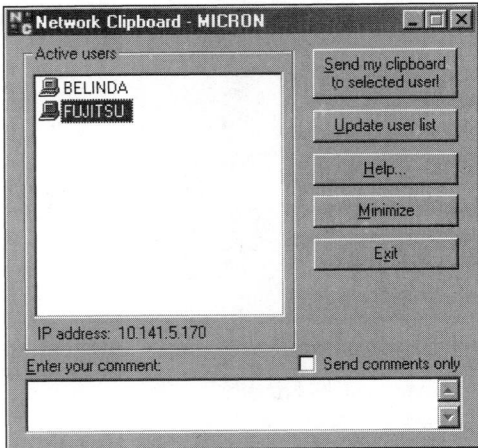

Figure 18-28: The Active Users list on a three-computer network. (The computer you are using isn't listed).

If your network consists of one person with two computers, and you log on as yourself on both computers, you won't be able to copy between computers. You need to use two slightly different logon names.

The Network Clipboard lets you send your Windows Clipboard to one of the listed users. He or she can choose to accept it or not. There is no provision for multiple Clipboards. Users can assign their own hot keys to bring up the Network Clipboard window (right-click the icon in the system tray and click Options), and can decide whether they want a beep when a Clipboard comes their way. By default, Network Clipboard places itself in each user's StartUp group.

You use your regular Copy command (Ctrl+C or Ctrl+Ins) to copy something to your Windows Clipboard. You then use the Network Clipboard to send whatever is in your Clipboard to another computer. It overwrites the material in the other computer's Clipboard.

Network Clipboard is shareware, but it's pretty cheap at $15 for five users. You'll find it at `http://www.geocities.com/SiliconValley/Network/7846/netclip.html`.

Another option is the Polar MultiClipboard . It appears to let you share multiple Clipboards, as indicated by the tab shown in Figure 18-29. Unfortunately, when we tried it, Polar Clipboard didn't recognize any of the users on our network.

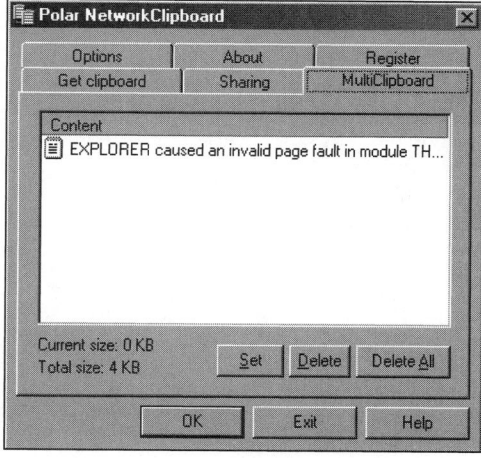

Figure 18-29: Polar NetworkClipboard's MultiClipboard tab

We include Polar NetworkClipboard because, if it works for you, it adds that extra dimension of multiple Clipboards.

Polar NetworkClipboard, unlike Network Clipboard, works on the Get model as opposed to the Put model. If you want something from someone's Clipboard, they have to be willing to share it with you first.

You'll find Polar NetworkClipboard at http://www.polarsoftware.com/ products.asp.

Direct Cable Connection with TCP/IP Only

When you install Dial-Up Networking with Windows, TCP/IP is the only networking protocol installed (unless you are installing Windows Me over Windows 95). You can also install Direct Cable Connection (DCC) if you want to connect your portable to your desktop computer with a serial or parallel cable. You may find that when you start DCC, you will be asked for the host computer's name. If the host computer is on a network, its name, as far as DCC is concerned, is its IP address.

After you start DCC, you may see a dialog box such as the one shown in Figure 18-30, which asks for the host's name after it can't find the shared files and folders. DCC has already made the connection from the guest to the host. The host will verify that the guest has the correct name and password, if any, and then the guest will display this dialog box to prompt for the host name.

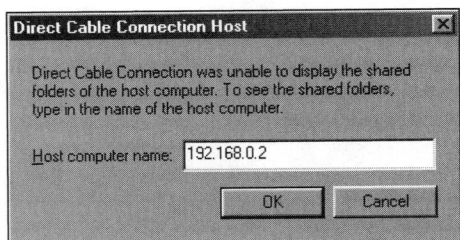

Figure 18-30: Enter the host's IP address.

Our experience is that if the host computer has a network card installed, and TCP/IP is the network protocol configured for the network card, DCC will not accept the host's name (its UNC name, otherwise known as the computer name) as its name, but only the host's IP address.

If you are using TCP/IP as your only networking protocol, then that is what DCC also uses. If the host doesn't have a network card installed (and therefore doesn't have an IP address), DCC will accept the host's name (as configured in the Identification tab of the Network dialog box).

Summary

▶ We show you how to turn your Windows computer into a networking client or peer server so that it can share resources with other computer users on your network.

▶ Windows will work with your existing 16-bit real-mode network.

▶ Windows comes with 32-bit protected-mode networking clients, protocols, and adapter drivers, which reduces the load on conventional memory.

▶ It is a lot easier to configure pre-Plug and Play network adapters using built-in Windows hardware detection and the Device Manager.

▶ You can configure Windows as a protected-mode peer server on either a Microsoft network (with or without a Windows 2000 or NT server) or a NetWare network.

▶ You can use different networking protocols to connect to multiple networks simultaneously.

▶ Windows comes with a raft of network management tools and the ability to interact with third-party network management SNMP tools.

▶ You can configure your computer to allow remote administration.

▶ You can build a great little two-computer network for 100 bucks.

▶ Connect your network to the Internet to save money and speed up access.

▶ Find online networking help resources.

▶ Synchronize the clocks on all your computers on the network.

▶ Get rid of that little sharing icon if it bothers you.

▶ Share your Windows Clipboard to copy and paste across the network.

▶ You don't have to map networked printers or drives to local logical ports or drive letters to access them using the universal naming convention.

Chapter 19

Dial-Up Networking

In This Chapter

Windows includes the capability to dial up another computer. This computer can be your Internet service provider's server or any computer running Windows Me, 98, 95 Windows NT or 2000, LAN Manager, NetWare, or UNIX. In Chapter 25, we discuss using Dial-Up Networking to connect to the Internet. Here, we discuss:

▶ Calling and connecting over a modem to a computer running Windows Me, Windows 98, Windows 95, Windows NT/2000, UNIX, or NetWare

▶ Setting up a Windows computer to receive modem phone calls from another Windows or other computer

▶ Setting up your Windows computer as a guest and calling into other computers

▶ Configuring the Windows Dial-Up Adapter for the correct protocols

Networking? Over a Modem?

Those of you who can remember back to the days before the World Wide Web was the next big thing can probably picture this typical scenario: You started some communications software, perhaps the Terminal emulator software that came with the old Windows 3.1. You used it to dial into a bulletin board, a commercial online service such as CompuServe, or an Internet service provider (using a dial-up shell account). Once connected, you downloaded files, used a UNIX server-based e-mail package, cruised the forums, or looked at the newsgroups. This terminal-based way of interacting with a remote computer is still with us in Windows Me.

Many of you have also used software that allows you to connect two computers in close proximity, either through a serial or parallel cable. You run software such as LapLink on both computers, which facilitates file transfer between the computers using a point-and-click interface.

And if your computer is connected to a local area network, you have experienced high-speed communications with other computers located in your general vicinity. Clicking the My Network Places icon in Windows gets you quickly to the shared resources available to you on the network. You can print your files on printers connected to other computers or servers on the network. You can quickly copy files, send e-mail, chat, and so on over the LAN. (Turn to "Basic Network Support" in Chapter 18 for more details.)

Dial-Up Networking (DUN) is a mixture of all three of these communications modes — using a modem to dial into another computer, network, or Internet service provider (ISP), connecting two computers in close proximity (through Direct Cable Connection, which uses DUN), and sharing resources with other computers as though you were networked to them.

DUN lets your computer at home or on the road use a modem to access the resources of a computer at work and/or the resources of the network connected to a computer at work, including shared disk drives, folders, printers, NetWare servers, NT/2000 servers, and much more. You can also use DUN to connect your home computer to the Internet and the World Wide Web through an ISP.

DUN enables your computer to communicate with a network (or a computer on a network) as though it were on the network directly, even though it's in fact only connected to the network through a modem and another computer (or modem server) on the network. The one difference is that a DUN connection is slower than a direct network connection through a dedicated network card or port.

Secret

You can use DUN in a whole host of ways. You can get your e-mail from work. You can send a file from your computer at home to a printer at work. You can send out fax files from your computer at home using the fax/modem on the computer at work. You can run programs that are stored on the computer at work on your computer at home. You can copy and update files between computers. You can copy programs from work. You can be a client of a client/server application running on a computer at work.

With DUN, you get what the computer business calls *remote access*. In other words, you have access to the resources on the remote, or dialed-up, computer or network. You don't have *remote control*, which is the ability to run your computer at the office as though you were typing on its keyboard while you are sitting in front of your computer at home.

Once you get everything set up (which is somewhat tricky), DUN is actually easy to use. It's easy because it uses standard Windows user interface objects such as Explorer and folder windows.

In this chapter, we'll use *computer at work* and *computer at home* to cut down on the level of abstraction that you have to deal with. By *computer at work*, we mean any computer that you dial into, and by *computer at home* we mean the computer that does the dialing. You can, of course, substitute anything that makes more sense to you — computer A and computer B, computer connected to a network and remote computer, desktop computer and portable computer, host and guest, server and client, remote and mobile, or ISP and user.

Dial-Up Networking

In order to dial into another computer, you need to configure your Windows computer at home as the Dial-Up Networking *client*. You learn how to do this in the "Setting Up Your Computer at Home As a Guest" section later in the chapter.

If you are calling into a Windows computer at work, you need to configure that computer as a Dial-Up Networking *host*. We show you how in "Setting Up Your Windows Computer at Work As a Host."

To make the connection between the two computers you need:

1. Properly configured computers at home and work

2. A shared dial-up protocol (to establish the connection)

3. A shared network protocol (to allow communication between the two computers)

Dial-Up Servers

You can connect your Windows computer at home over the phone lines to another computer or server running:

- Windows Me, 98, or 95 Dial-Up Networking Server

- Windows NT or Windows 2000 Remote Access Server (RAS) or PPP

- Windows for Workgroups 3.11 RAS

- Microsoft LAN Manager

- NetWare Connect

- UNIX with SLIP or PPP protocols

- TCP/IP with PPP protocol (especially for connections to the Internet)

You can also connect to a dedicated modem server such as the Shiva LanRover or a compatible device, or to an ISP (if you have a SLIP or PPP account).

Network Protocols

Windows supports in native 32-bit mode the following network protocols:

- NetBEUI (Microsoft's networking protocol)
- IPX/SPX (Novell's NetWare protocol)
- TCP/IP (the UNIX, Internet, and Intranet standard protocol)

Dial-Up Protocols

To connect to the computer at work, the Windows DUN client can use any one of the following dial-up protocols:

- PPP (Point-to-Point Protocol)
- NRN (Novell NetWare Connect)
- RAS (Windows NT/2000 and Windows for Workgroups 3.11 Remote Access Server using Asynchronous NetBEUI)
- SLIP (Serial Line Internet Protocol)
- CSLIP (SLIP with IP header compression)

Point-to-Point Protocol is the default dial-up protocol used by Windows Me, 98, 95, and NT/2000 computers. You can use PPP to connect to a network or computer running any one of the three network protocols included with Windows. Many ISPs also use PPP. You can also use PPP to call into NIX, Windows, or NT/2000 servers.

Novell NetWare Connect allows you to dial into a NetWare Connect server.

RAS allows a Windows computer to call into an NT/2000 computer running RAS or into a computer running Windows for Workgroups 3.11, and vice versa.

SLIP is an older dial-up protocol, but it is still used by some ISPs, and it is used on some UNIX servers as well.

Setting Up Your Windows Computer at Work As a Host

If you have a significant network at work, you will want to provide dial-up services through a Windows NT/2000 server, which can handle up to 256 dial-up connections, a LAN modem server, a NetWare Connect server, or perhaps a UNIX computer. Another option is the Shiva LanRover, which is built for handling large-scale dial-in communications in conjunction with a corporate-sized NetWare, NetBEUI, or TCP/IP local area network.

If your network isn't that big (maybe it just consists of your desktop computer) and only a few people need dial-up access, then calling into a Windows Me/98/95 computer at work may fit the bill. The Windows Dial-Up

Networking Server (DUN Server) can take calls from and connect to Windows Me, 98 or 95 clients, computers running RAS on Windows for Workgroups or Windows 3.1, and other computers running the PPP dial-up protocol.

Secret

You can set up your Windows computer at work as a Web server using Microsoft's Personal Web Server. You can connect to this Web server from home using Dial-Up Networking and Internet Explorer. You can also connect to it directly with a serial or parallel cable using Direct Cable Connection (which relies on DUN).

Secret

You can call out with other TAPI-aware programs, such as DUN, while DUN Server is running. No one can call in while you are using the line, but once you have completed your call, DUN Server will pick up incoming calls.

We are going to assume that you want to call in from home — or from a hotel when you are on the road — to your Windows computer (and your network) at work. You must do three things to set up your Windows computer at work as a host:

1. Install a modem driver (this may have occurred if you had your modem installed when you set up Windows).

2. Install the Microsoft Dial-Up Adapter and the accompanying network software/drivers (this may also have occurred during setup).

3. Set the Windows Dial-Up Networking Server to allow caller access.

Secret

The Dial-Up Adapter will be automatically installed (if it is not already) the first time you choose Connections ➪ Dial-Up Server from the menu bar of the Dial-Up Networking folder window. If you do this and you haven't yet installed your modem, you will be prompted to do so. You can separately install the Dial-Up Adapter (see the section entitled "The Dial-Up Adapter" later in this chapter) and the modem before you install the Dial-Up Networking Server.

STEPS

Setting Up a Windows Computer As a Host for Dial-Up Networking

Step 1. If your modem isn't already set up, do so now using the Modems icon in the Control Panel. Click the Add button in the Modems Properties dialog box, and then follow the steps in the Install New Modem Wizard. You will be prompted to set up your modem if you take steps 4 and 5 first.

Step 2. If you haven't yet installed Dial-Up Networking, click the Add/Remove Programs icon in your Control Panel, and click the Windows Setup tab. Select the Communications component, click the Details button, mark the Dial-Up Networking checkbox, and click OK twice.

Continued

STEPS

Setting Up a Windows Computer As a Host for
Dial-Up Networking *(continued)*

Step 3. If you haven't already done so, set up the Dial-Up Adapter by clicking the Network icon in the Control Panel. Click the Add button, highlight Adapter in the "Select Network Component type" dialog box, and click the Add button. For details, see the steps in the section entitled "The Dial-Up Adapter" later in this chapter. This will happen automatically if you take steps 4 and 5.

Step 4. Click the Dial-Up Networking folder icon in the Explorer, or choose Dial-Up Networking from the Start ➪ Programs ➪ Accessories ➪ Communications menu.

Step 5. Choose Connections ➪ Dial-Up Server on the menu of the Dial-Up Networking folder window. The Dial-Up Server dialog box will pop up, as shown in Figure 19-1.

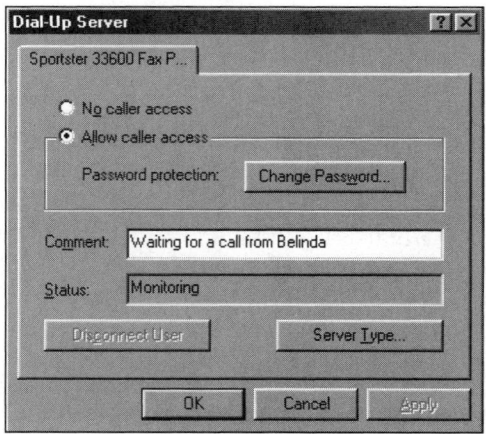

Figure 19-1: The dial-in options in the Dial-Up Server dialog box. You need to allow caller access.

If you don't have Dial-Up Server on your Connections menu, click the Add/Remove Programs icon in your Control Panel, click the Windows Setup tab, highlight Communications, click the Details button, mark the Dial-Up Server checkbox, and click OK.

Step 6. Mark the "Allow caller access" option button. You want people (perhaps just yourself) using other computers to be able to call into your host computer (the Windows computer at work).

Step 7. To require a password to access your computer at work, click the Change Password button.

Step 8. Click the Server Type button if you want to change the dial-up protocol used when the server answers the phone. We suggest that you leave it on Default, which starts with PPP and switches to RAS if PPP fails. This makes it easy for computers with Windows Me, Windows 98, Windows 95, Windows for Workgroups, Windows 3.1 RAS, Windows NT, and Windows 2000, as well as other operating systems that support PPP to call into your server.

Step 9. Click Apply or OK to begin monitoring for phone calls. (Apply leaves the dialog box on the Desktop. OK minimizes the dialog box.) The computer at the office will now pick up the phone line attached to its modem when that line is called. You don't have a way of telling it how many rings to wait until it picks up the line.

You now have a computer at work that will respond to calls from your computer at home. You need to set the computer at work into this answer mode before you can call into it. You will normally want to leave it in this mode when you are away from the office.

Remember to share some resources (disk drives, folders, printers) if you want to be able to access these resources on your computer at work when you call in.

As you can see from the steps above, it requires a few steps to activate the DUN Server. Once you set it though, it will stay set. If you shut down your computer and restart, the DUN Server reloads.

A little freeware application, RunServe, will let you easily start and stop the DUN Server. You can place a shortcut to it on your Desktop. You'll find it at it `http://www.frontiernet.net/~enderw`

Disallowing Dial-In Access

You (or your system administrator) can determine whether a Windows computer has the capability of serving as a host. You can use the System Policy Editor to permanently disable dial-in to Dial-Up Networking. If you do this, the "Allow caller access" option button in the Dial-Up Server dialog box will be grayed out. Obviously, if you only want to temporarily prohibit people from calling in, you can just choose the "No caller access" option button.

Security

Security is an issue because anyone with the right password (if even that is required) can gain access to a company's network by calling into its Windows DUN Server. System administrators are justifiably wary of allowing users to configure their computers as servers because it leaves the whole network vulnerable.

If the Windows DUN Server is on a network that includes NetWare or Windows NT/2000 servers, the system administrator can use (and may already be using) the NetWare or NT/2000 servers to provide user-level, centrally controlled password protection.

Setting Up Your Computer at Home As a Guest

If you want to set up your computer at home to make the phone call and initiate the modem communications, you need to make sure that:

1. Your modem driver is configured.

2. You have set up your Dial-Up Adapter.

3. You have set up a specific dial-in connection (or *connectoid*) for your computer at work.

Secret

You don't have to set up the modem driver first. If it is not set up yet, a wizard will guide you through the setup process.

STEPS

Setting Up Your Computer at Home

Step 1. Choose Dial-Up Networking from the Start ⇨ Programs ⇨ Accessories ⇨ Communications menu.

If you haven't installed Dial-Up Networking, you need to do so now. Click the Add/Remove Programs icon in your Control Panel, click the Windows Setup tab, highlight Communications, click the Details button, and mark Dial-Up Networking. Click OK twice.

Step 2. Click the Make New Connection icon in the Dial-Up Networking folder window.

Step 3. The Make New Connection Wizard will start. If you have not set up your modem driver yet, the Install New Modem Wizard will pop up on top of the Make New Connection Wizard and ask that you do this first. Follow the steps in the Install New Modem Wizard.

Step 4. In the first Make New Connection Wizard dialog box, enter a name for the computer that you will be dialing into, such as **Computer at Work**. Click Next.

Step 5. Type the area code and number for the computer at work. Click Next.

Step 6. Click Finish.

Step 7. If you do not have a Dial-Up Adapter set up in your network configuration (or you have no network configured), you will be asked to install it now.

Step 8. The Dial-Up Adapter will now be installed, along with the network protocols and network support software, if they have not already been installed.

You can install NetBEUI and IPX/SPX protocols and bind them to your Dial-Up Adapter if you are going to use Direct Cable Connection or if you will connect to a Windows network or a NetWare network. If you are going to connect to an intranet at work or the Internet, you should be sure to leave the Microsoft TCP/IP protocol bound to your Dial Up Adapter. This is discussed in "Bind TCP/IP to Your Dial-Up Adapter" in Chapter 25. The TCP/IP protocol should also be bound to the Dial-Up Adapter on your computer at work if you are going to access the Personal Web Server on it. If you are dialing into a standalone DUN Server, NetBEUI and IPX/SPX are sufficient.

An icon for the new connectoid will appear in the Dial-Up Networking folder window with the name you entered in step 4 above. It represents your connection to the computer at the office. When you click the connectoid, the Connect To dialog box (shown in Figure 19-2) appears to let you initiate the phone call.

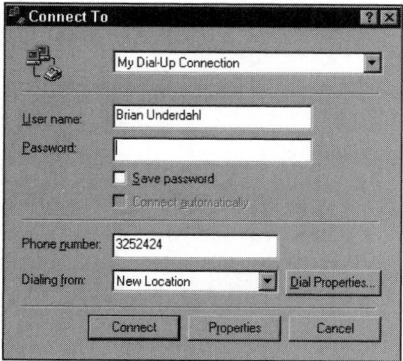

Figure 19-2: The Connect To dialog box for your Dial-Up Networking connectoid. To initiate the phone call, type your password, if necessary, and then click the Connect button.

If you have changed your general Dial-Up Networking settings to not prompt for information before dialing (Click Connections ⇨ Settings in the Dial-Up Networking folder window), you will not see this Connect To dialog box and you will not have to click the Connect button.

To end the connection, right-click the Modem Status icon in the tray and click Disconnect.

Secret

If your "Save password" checkbox is grayed out in the Connect To dialog box for your Dial-Up Networking connectoid, check to make sure that you have installed Client for Microsoft Networks. You can use the instructions provided in "Network Installation" in Chapter 18.

To change the server type and other properties associated with this connectoid, right-click it in the Dial-Up Networking folder window, select Properties, and click the Networking tab (shown in Figure 19-3).

Secret

The settings for logging onto the network, making your connection automatic, and storing your user name and password have been moved to the Security tab. If you don't log onto the network, you won't have access to the resources shared by other servers on the network.

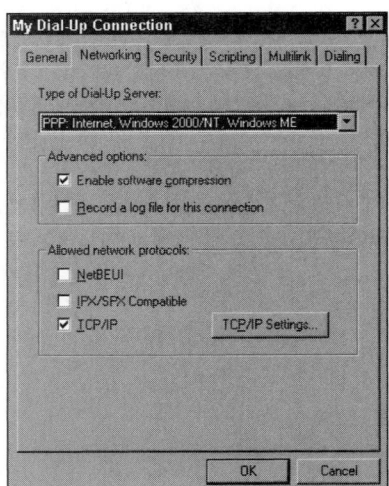

Figure 19-3: The Networking tab

PPP is the default dial-up protocol, and if you set your Windows host computer at work to use this protocol, both computers will be in sync. In the "Allowed network protocols" area of the dialog box, you can clear any of the protocol checkboxes for protocols that you don't use. See "Dialing into Another Operating System" later in this chapter for further guidance.

Your Windows client computer uses your modem as a network interface card. You should make sure that the proper networking protocols are bound to the Dial-Up Adapter. If you are calling into a UNXI or Windows NT/2000 TCP/IP server, be sure that the TCP/IP protocol is bound to the Dial-Up Adapter. To see how to do this, check out "Bind TCP/IP to Your Dial-Up Adapter" in Chapter 25.

If you have any problems with these instructions, you can find additional help in the Microsoft Knowledge Base (of course, that assumes that you can connect to it, which is likely the problem to begin with). If you can connect to the Internet, find "How to Connect to a Remote Server" at http://support. microsoft.com/support/kb/articles/q145/8/43

General Connectoid Settings

You can set your connectoids to redial automatically if they don't make a connection on the first try. In the Dial-Up Networking folder window, right-click your connection and choose Properties. Then click the Dialing tab of the dialog box, as shown in Figure 19-4. This dialog box lets you choose how often to try and how long to wait between tries.

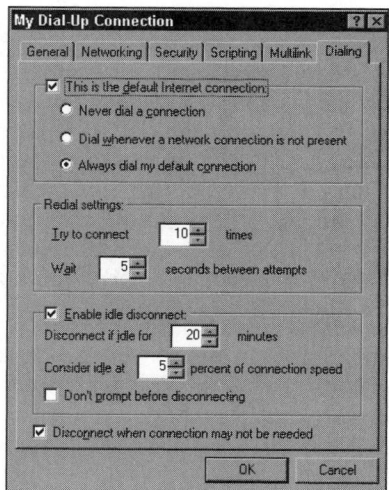

Figure 19-4: The Dialing tab of the Dial-Up Networking dialog box

Secret

To eliminate the need to click the Connect button in the Connect To dialog box, select the "Connect automatically" checkbox on the Security tab. You can also get rid of the Connection Confirmation dialog box and the Modem Status icon in the tray. If you do not ask DUN to show the Modem Status icon in the tray after connecting, you won't be able to disconnect by right-clicking this icon and clicking Disconnect.

Tip

Other applications that call and use the DUN connectoid (Internet applications, for example) may have their own buttons or icons that can accomplish the disconnect function. If you want to call DUN only through these applications, you can dispense with putting the Modem Status icon in the tray.

Mark the "Prompt to use Dial-Up Networking" option button if you want a network connection to be reestablished through Dial-Up Networking. For example, assume you have a shortcut icon on your Desktop that links to a folder on another computer. You normally connect to this computer over your modem using Dial-Up Networking. If you click this icon, you will be asked (the first time) which DUN connectoid to use to make the connection (if you have marked "Prompt to use Dial-Up Networking").

Secret

Once you have chosen a DUN connectoid, the next time you click this icon, the DUN connectoid is invoked and dialing begins. If you mark "Don't prompt to use Dial-Up Networking," you won't be prompted, and a DUN connectoid will not be associated with this shortcut. You will need to connect to the computer at work first before you can click this icon and access the folder.

Secret

Direct Cable Connection, which uses Dial-Up Networking, but without a DUN connectoid, cannot use this capability. You have to start DCC on both computers first before you can click the icon on the guest's Desktop to successfully access resources on the host.

Preparing for Server Dial-Back

The server that you are dialing into may need to call you back before you can properly connect to it. This is a security feature. If server dial-back is implemented, each user has an assigned phone number (his or her home phone, for example). The server dials the phone number of the person who supposedly just tried to log in. If someone else is using your name and password, you still get the phone call at home, not the other person. Of course, this does make things difficult if you are in a hotel.

Secret

Windows Dial-Up Networking wasn't built with the server dial-back feature in mind, but you can kludge it in if you're using the PPP protocol to communicate with the server. You'll need to create an additional modem string to properly set the state of your modem when making the connection.

STEPS

Configuring DUN for Dial-Back Servers

Step 1. Click the Start button, point to Settings, and click Control Panel. Click the Modems icon.

Step 2. Highlight your modem and click the Properties button.

Step 3. Click the Connection tab, and then click the Advanced button.

Step 4. In the Extra Settings field, enter **&C0 S0=1**. Click OK twice, and then click Close.

If there are already settings in the Extra Settings field, just add the new string to the end of the existing ones.

The &C0 setting keeps the PPP client active. The S0=1 setting sets your modem to auto-answer after one ring.

Dialing into Another Operating System

Dial-Up Networking lets you connect over the phone to a whole variety of networks, including the Internet. You can call into a computer running Windows NT/2000 Server, which allows up to 256 connections and supports IPX/SPX, NetBEUI, and TCP/IP protocols. You can also call into computers running UNIX and the SLIP or PPP protocols.

If you are calling into a Windows nt/2000, NetWare, Shiva Netmodem/ LanRover, Windows for Workgroups, LAN Manager, or UNIX server instead of a Windows Me, 98, or 95 computer, you may need to change the server type associated with your DUN connectoid. Right-click the new DUN Connectoid icon in the Dial-Up Networking folder window, click Properties, and then click the Networking tab.

You get to choose from these options:

- CSLIP: Unix Connection with IP Header Compression
- NRN: NetWare Connect Version 1.0 and 1.1
- PPP: Internet, Windows NT/2000 Server, Windows Me, or 9x
- SLIP: Unix Connection
- Windows for Workgroups and Windows NT 3.1

Your UNIX computer server (in some cases a remote UNIX server at an ISP) will use either PPP or SLIP. You need to find out which protocol it uses from your computer support staff (or ISP).

You can use Dial-Up Networking to connect to the Internet if you are calling into a dial-up ISP. See "Dial-Up Connection to Your Service Provider" in Chapter 25 for more details.

If you want to just connect to the computer that you are calling into and not to a network that the computer may be connected to, clear the "Log on to network" checkbox in the Server Types dialog box. This goes for Internet servers also.

Few servers required encrypted passwords, so you can clear this checkbox also unless you know that the computer you are dialing into requires one.

A given connection may require only one or two networking protocols. Clear the checkboxes for the unnecessary protocols. If you are dialing into an ISP, clear the NetBEUI and IPX/SPX checkboxes. If you are dialing into a NetWare server, clear NetBEUI and TCP/IP.

SLIP Server Type

To connect to a server using the SLIP dial-up protocol, you need to be sure that the TCP/IP protocol is bound to your Dial-Up Adapter. To do so, take the steps in the "Bind TCP/IP to Your Dial-Up Adapter" section of Chapter 25.

After you have checked to make sure that the TCP/IP protocol is bound to your Dial-Up Adapter, you need to create a SLIP connection. Here's how:

STEPS

Creating a SLIP Connectoid

Step 1. Click the Dial-Up Networking folder icon in the Explorer, or choose Dial-Up Networking from the Start ➪ Programs ➪ Accessories ➪ Communications menu.

Step 2. Click the Make New Connection icon in the Dial-Up Networking folder window.

Step 3. The Make New Connection Wizard starts. Give the computer that you will be dialing into a name, perhaps something like **Internet**. Click Next.

Step 4. Type the area code and phone number for the SLIP computer. Click Next.

Step 5. Click Finish.

Step 6. Right-click the new connectoid and select Properties. Click the Configure button to display the Properties dialog box for your modem, and then click the Options tab.

Step 7. Mark the "Bring up terminal window after dialing" checkbox. This allows you to log onto your SLIP account. You will need to type your name and password when you log on. (You can avoid having to enter your name and password if you use Windows's scripting facility, as described in "Automating Your DUN Logon" in Chapter 25.) Click OK.

Step 8. Click the Networking tab and display the "Type of dial-up server" drop-down list.

Step 9. Highlight either SLIP or CSLIP depending on the capabilities of your Internet service provider or UNIX server.

Step 10. If you want to change the static IP address of your computer (or change how it is obtained), click the TCP/IP Settings button. See "Multiple TCP/IP Settings for Multiple Connections" in Chapter 25 for more details.

Step 11. Click the OK buttons until you are back to the Dial-Up Networking folder window.

Refer to "Installing an Internet Dial-Up Connection" in Chapter 25 to learn more about the properties of TCP/IP and connectoids to the Internet. You need to bind to the Dial-Up Adapter the protocol appropriate to the network that you are dialing into. If you are dialing into different networks, you may need to bind all three protocols—IPX/SPX, NetBEUI, and TCP/IP.

Setting Up Your Basic Telephone Information

Windows can keep track of telephone information for multiple locations. For example, for each location you dial from, it can remember whether you have to dial an access number to get an outside line, whether your phone has call waiting, and whether the connection is local or long distance.

To edit this location-specific information, click the Modems icon in the Control Panel, and click the Dialing Properties button to display the Dialing Properties dialog box.

Your Modem

Your modem was originally set up by the Install New Modem Wizard. This most likely happened automatically when you first set up Windows, when you set up your computer at home as a guest, or when you clicked the Modems icon in the Control Panel, but if you need to, you can change the properties for your modem now.

Right-click your Connectoid icon in the Dial-Up Networking folder window, and choose Properties. Click the Configure button to display the Properties dialog box for your modem.

The Dial-Up Adapter

To call into your computer at work over your modem, you need to have the Dial-Up Adapter set up on both computers. It is automatically set up on your home computer when you create a new connection. It is also automatically set up on your Windows computer at work when you configure it as a host.

After you have installed your adapter, go back to the Control Panel and click the Network icon. Highlight the Dial-Up Adapter and click the Properties button. You'll see the Dial-Up Adapter Properties dialog box, as shown in Figure 19-5.

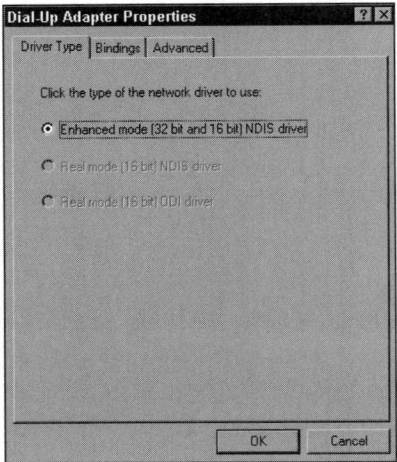

Figure 19-5: The Dial-Up Adapter Properties dialog box

Secret

Microsoft has written an NDIS (Network Driver Interface Specification) 5 level driver for the modem/serial port. This is a low-level driver most often associated with network cards. The Dial-Up Adapter treats the modem as though it were a network card using this driver. NDIS 5 allows multiple protocols to run on a network interface card (or, in this case, a modem) simultaneously.

The default protocol of the Dial-Up Networking communication between two Windows computers is TCP/IP. The protocols were installed when you set up the Dial-Up Adapter and are bound to it. *Bound* means that they are used to carry out the communication between the two computers. You can find out whether one or more of the protocols are bound by clicking the Bindings tab. Which protocol is actually used depends on the configuration of the computer at work.

If you don't find a protocol or find that it isn't bound to the Dial-Up Adapter, you can add it. To see how, turn to "Configuring the Adapter Driver" in Chapter 18.

Dialing into the Office

After you have connected your home computer's modem to your phone line, you can dial into the computer at work. Of course, the computer at work could actually be a networked modem server that acts like a Windows Me or 98, Windows NT/2000, or NetWare Connect server set up as a host.

STEPS

Dialing In from Home

Step 1. Click the Dial-Up Networking folder icon in an Explorer window, or choose Dial-Up Networking from the Start ⇨ Programs ⇨ Accessories ⇨ Communications menu.

Step 2. Click the connectoid for your computer at work in the Dial-Up Networking folder window. If you call work often, you might want to right-drag this icon onto the Desktop or Start button and choose Create Shortcut(s) Here from the context menu. That way, you will have a convenient way of accessing the computer at work.

Step 3. The Connect To dialog box appears (unless you have turned off this option, which is not a good idea if you're making a connection for the first time). Type your name and password if you have set up a password on the computer at work. Mark the "Save password" checkbox if you don't want to type your password every time you connect.

If you are unable to make a successful connection, your password will not be saved. This can be a bit annoying. You just have to keep trying until the first successful connection.

Step 4. If necessary, you can click the Dial Properties button to edit your (at home) location information at this point. There are other entry points for editing this information, but this is as good as any. See the previous section entitled "Setting Up Your Basic Telephone Information" for more on this.

Step 5. Click the Connect button.

Your computer will dial your modem and attempt to make a network connection across the phone lines to your computer at work. If all goes well, you will be networked to your work computer.

If you have chosen the "Log on to network" option (right-click the connectoid for your computer at work, choose Properties, and click the Networking tab), you will also be logged onto the network that is connected to the server you dialed into. In this case, you can access other servers on the network by following the steps in the "Accessing Shared Resources" section later in this chapter.

Dialing In Manually

You can dial into the host computer manually. Once you make the connection, perhaps through an operator or using your credit card, you turn over the phone line to your computer. You might want to do this if you are having trouble defining an automated dialing procedure in a new location. For this to work, the phone must be connected to the same line as your computer.

STEPS

Dialing In Manually

Step 1. Choose Dial-Up Networking from the Settings menu.

Step 2. Right-click the connectoid for your computer at work in the Dial-Up Networking folder window. Click Properties.

Step 3. Click the Configure button, and then click the Options tab.

Step 4. Mark the "Operator assisted or manual dial" checkbox. Click OK twice.

Step 5. Click the connectoid. You will be prompted to pick up the receiver and dial the number.

Step 6. When you hear the tone from the computer, click Connect and then hang up the phone.

DUN Command-Line Parameters

The easiest way to start a DUN connection is to click a shortcut of a DUN connectoid that you have placed on your Desktop. You can also invoke a DUN connectoid by using the following command-line parameters:

```
rundll rnaui.dll,RnaDial My Connection
```

Replace *My Connection* with the name of one of your connectoids. You can create a shortcut and place the above syntax in the Target field (right-click the shortcut and choose Properties). Furthermore, you can type this syntax in the Run dialog box (Start ⇨ Run) to start the connectoid.

Networking over a Modem

Once you have made the connection, you are another node (albeit a slow one) on the network at work. If you are just hooking two computers together, then they are networking over the modem, and that is the only network.

Accessing Shared Resources

You access the shared resources of the computer at work (folders, printers, and drives on the host computer) by explicitly naming the resource. Once you're connected, click the Start button, and then click Run. Type the name of the computer at work followed by the shared resource name, using the universal naming convention (UNC) — \\WorkComputer\C, for example. (When you attempt to access a shared resource, you might be required to enter a password if it is not already stored in the user-password cache on your computer, or if this is the first time you have accessed a resource that is protected by a password.)

If you want to find the name of a computer, you'll need to click Start ⇨ Settings ⇨ Control Panel ⇨ Network ⇨ Identification tab. You have to do this on the computer whose name you need to check.

For this method (or any method) of accessing a shared resource to work, you first need to share your resources on the host computer.

The UNC enables you to access resources by name, without having to map them to a drive letter on your computer. It uses two backslashes before the name of the server, host, or computer at work, and a single backslash before the resource name.

A folder window containing the resource you specified will open up on the Desktop of your home computer. You can then browse the resource to find the files or programs that you are interested in. To access other computers connected by a network to your computer at work, you can type their UNC names in the Run dialog box.

You can create shortcuts on your computer at home to these shared resources on your computer at work. For example, create a shortcut to a folder on the computer at work by dragging to your Desktop a folder from an open folder window that is displaying the folder icon. The UNC name is captured in the shortcut.

You can map a networked resource (a folder or a drive) to a drive letter by clicking Tools ⇨ Map Network Drive in the Explorer menu on your computer at home. You normally map a networked resource to a drive letter, not a Dial-Up Networked resource. Unless you have a very fast dial-up connection, accessing this resource through your Explorer could make it repaint quite slowly.

In the Path field of the Map Network Drive dialog box, you just type two backslashes, followed by the name of the networked computer, followed by a single backslash and the name of the shared resource. You can also map a network drive if you are using Direct Cable Connection, which uses DUN.

Monitoring Your Calls

Secret

DUN works with System Monitor to let you see the speed of your uploads and downloads. System Monitor (Windows 95 and higher) has an Add Item dialog box that contains a Dial-Up Adapter item for this purpose.

The System Monitor is a great place to display incoming and outgoing data transfer rates. If it's already installed, you'll find it under Start ⇨ Programs ⇨ Accessories ⇨ System Tools ⇨ System Monitor. If you haven't installed it yet, you should do so now. Click the Add/Remove Programs icon in your Control Panel, click the Windows Setup tab, highlight System Accessories, click the Details button, and mark the System Monitor checkbox. It's a good idea to place a shortcut to the System Monitor on your Desktop.

To monitor your data transfer rates, choose Edit ⇨ Add Item in the System Monitor window, and select Dial-Up Adapter in the Add Item dialog box. Choose Bytes Received/Second and Bytes Transmitted/Second (see Figure 19-6).

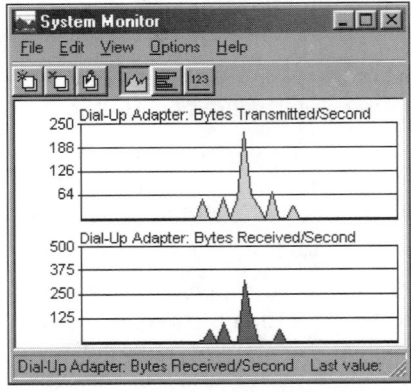

Figure 19-6: Monitoring bytes transmitted and received in System Monitor

As you can see in the list on the right side of the Add Item dialog box, the System Monitor lets you monitor additional parameters for Dial-Up Adapter. Here is a quick run down of what they mean:

■ Frames Received/Second and Frames Transmitted/Second measure *frames*, which are packets of many bytes. These two technical measurements will probably not be as useful to you as Bytes Received/Second and Bytes Transmitted/Second.

■ Framing Errors and Incomplete Frames indicate frames that arrive with a smaller or larger number of bytes than expected. These errors can impede the throughput of your modem. They can be caused by incompatibilities between your modem and the modem of the computer at work, which may not be reliably capable of sending data as fast as it appears to be.

- CRC Errors indicate that something, probably line noise, has corrupted a few bits as they were being transmitted. The acronym stands for *cyclical redundancy check*. This means that a CRC code at the end of several bytes no longer matches the data received. In this case, the modems usually retransmit and re-receive the data so that good data is ensured. But these errors can slow down your throughput. If you see CRC errors, it may be best to hang up and call again to see if a faulty line in the telephone company was causing too much noise for reliable communications.

- Timeout Errors occur when no data has been transmitted during a normal waiting period for your end of the communications. This is the opposite of Overrun Errors or Buffer Overruns, which occur when more data has been sent than your modem can process. Modems are supposed to let each other know how fast to send data, so overruns may indicate an incompatibility between your modem and the modem of the computer at work (or your ISP).

- Alignment Errors indicate possible incompatibilities among the hardware and software used by both ends of the communications link. Trying different speed settings or modems may isolate this problem.

Connecting to a Personal Web Server

Your Windows computer at work can serve as a Web server if it is running the Microsoft Personal Web Server software. You can then call in from your computer at home and access the Web pages on your computer at work. This also works with Direct Cable Connection.

We discuss the issues related to connecting to Web servers on the Internet in "Installing an Internet Dial-Up Connection" in Chapter 25.

To connect to your own Web server directly (and not necessarily through the Internet), you need to configure both computers to allow the computer at work to serve up Web pages to the computer at home. Take the following steps:

STEPS

Serving Personal Web Pages

Step 1. Install Personal Web Server. To do this, use your Explorer to navigate to \add-ons\pws on your Windows CD-ROM. Click setup.exe. Once you have installed the Personal Web Server, you will find the Publish shortcut on your Desktop.

Continued

STEPS

Serving Personal Web Pages *(continued)*

Step 2. Be sure the TCP/IP protocol is bound to the Dial-Up Adapters in both your computer at work and your computer at home (see "Bind TCP/IP to Your Dial-Up Adapter" in Chapter 25).

Step 3. On your computer at home, create a DUN connectoid that connects to your computer at work. Be sure to include the TCP/IP protocol. You won't need NetBEUI or IPX if you are using this DUN connectoid just to connect to the Web server running on the computer at work.

Step 4. Start the DUN Server on the computer at work.

Step 5. Click Start ⇨ Run, type **winipcfg**, and click OK. This starts the Windows IP Configuration utility, which lets you monitor your IP address. You'll need this address later. You can drag a shortcut to Winipcfg.exe from your \Windows folder onto your Desktop.

Step 6. Click your DUN connectoid for the computer at work on your computer at home and establish a connection. Click the Renew All button in your IP Configuration window on your computer at work. Note the IP address (for your computer at work).

Step 7. Start Personal Web Server on the computer at work. Start Internet Explorer on the computer at home.

Step 8. In the Address bar of Internet Explorer, type **http://**, followed by the IP address that you noted in the IP Configuration window on your computer at work, followed by **/homepage.htm**.

Step 9. On the computer at work, click the Network icon in the Control Panel, click the Identification tab, and note the value in the Computer Name field.

Step 10. On the computer at home, navigate with the Explorer to the \Windows folder. Right-click the right pane of the Explorer and choose New ⇨ Text Document.

Step 11. In the first line of the blank text file, enter the value from the Computer Name field from step 9, press the Tab key, enter the IP address from step 6, press the Tab key, and type **#PRE**.

Step 12. Save and close the text file. Rename it Lmhosts with no extension. You will now be able to access the Personal Web Server on your Windows 98 computer at work using its name instead of its IP address.

Step 13. In the Internet Explorer window on your computer at home, choose File ➪ Send ➪ Shortcut To Desktop. This creates a shortcut to the Web page on your computer at work. You can edit this shortcut (right-click it and click Properties) to change the address in the Target field from the IP address to the computer name.

Personal Web Server is the same Web server that runs on NT/2000, with a few limitations. You can access its Web pages on a network, over DUN, or using Direct Cable Connection. If the Windows computer is connected to a LAN at work using the TCP/IP protocol, the address assigned to this computer may be determined by a WINS or DNS server. If you call into the network instead of directly into the Windows computer, you'll use these services to resolve the name of the computer at work instead of the Lmhosts file.

DUN Troubles

Dial-Up Networking is not bulletproof. There are a few areas that require your attention if you run into problems.

If you clear the "Use area code and dialing properties" checkbox in one DUN connectoid, it may force you to enter the phone number to dial in other DUN connectoids. The solution is to not clear this checkbox to begin with. If you do clear the checkbox, you'll lose the dialer's ability to set call waiting and to use area codes when needed.

When you invoke a DUN connectoid, you also load Rnaapp.exe (Remote Network Access Application). If you click a DUN connectoid and it is unable to connect to the remote computer, you may find that you aren't able to immediately try again. You can wait for a few more seconds, or you can press Ctrl+Alt+Del, highlight Rnaapp, and click End Task to clear Rnaapp out of memory. You'll then be able to start your DUN connectoid again.

Clearing Rnaapp out of memory can make little communication problems go away. It is designed to hang around for a little while so that you don't have to load it every time you start a new communications application. Unfortunately, this behavior seems to cause more problems than it is worth.

Summary

You can call into a server computer over a modem from your computer at home or on the road. The server can be a Windows Me computer, a Windows 98 computer, a Windows 95 computer, an NT/2000 computer, a LAN Manager server, a NetWare server, a UNIX computer, an ISP, or a dedicated networked modem server. We show you:

▶ How to set up a Windows computer as a host at work so you can call into it from home

▶ How to set up your computer at home so you can call into various servers, including your Windows computer at work

▶ How to access and use shared resources on the network with Dial-Up Networking

▶ How to configure a Web page server and connect to it directly using DUN Server and a DUN connectoid

▶ How to use your computer at home to print on your printer at work

Chapter 20

DOS Is Still in There

What DOS Does

Windows Millennium doesn't start out in character-mode DOS, and then switch to graphical-mode DOS, as previous versions of Windows do. But you can still open a DOS window within Windows Millennium and run some, but not all, DOS programs. And the DOS command line is still the fastest (and sometimes the only) way to accomplish certain system-management tasks.

The Remaining DOS Commands

DOS character-mode commands have been updated to work with Windows Millennium. They have been changed to work with long filenames, with the VFAT (Virtual Fat Allocation Table), and with FAT32. All of the previous internal DOS commands (the ones that are within the command interpreter and are not separate .com or .exe files) are also available and have themselves been updated.

Table 20-1 lists the DOS external commands that come with Windows Millennium.

Table 20-1   DOS External Commands in Windows

Filename	Definition
Attrib.exe	Show or change file attributes
Chkdsk.exe	Check disk and provide status report (use ScanDisk instead)
Choice.com	Accept user input in a batch file
Cvt.exe	Convert Fat16 to Fat32
Deltree.exe	Delete tree (directory and subdirectories)
Diskcopy.com	Make a full copy of diskettes
Doskey.com	Edit command lines, recall them, create macros
Edit.com	A character-mode file-editing application
Extract.exe	Extract files from a Windows Cabinet (.cab) file
Fc.exe	Compare two files
Fdisk.exe	Low-level disk partitioning and configuration utility
Find.exe	Find text in a plaintext file
Format.com	Format a disk
Iextract.exe	Extract a file from a backup file
Label.exe	Label a disk
Mem.exe	Display memory use
Mode.com	Mode of port or display, or code page (character set)
More.com	Pause for output one screen at a time
Move.exe	Move files (copy and delete original)
Mscdex.exe	Real-mode CD-ROM extensions
Scandisk.exe	Fix disks. Parameters to control it are found in Scandisk.ini
Scanreg.exe	Registry backup, restore, and scanner
Share.exe	File locking
Sort.exe	Sort the contents of a plaintext file
Start.exe	Run a Windows program
Subst.exe	Substitute a drive letter for a directory
Sys.com	Create a system disk
Xcopy.exe	Extended file and directories copy
Xcopy32.exe	Improved version of Xcopy.exe, which is called by Xcopy.exe

The most popular internal DOS commands (internal to the Command interpreter) are:

CD and CHDIR	PATH
CLS	PROMPT
COPY	RD and RMDIR
DATE	REN and RENAME
DEL and ERASE	SET
EXIT	TIME
MD and MKDIR	VER

You can learn how to use almost all of these commands by typing the command and adding **/?** before pressing Enter.

DOS Edit

Windows Millennium ships with DOS Edit. Written by a contractor to Microsoft, Emory Horvath, it is a nifty little editor, and it's quite useful for dealing with text and batch files.

You can easily create a shortcut to it and put it on your Start menu or your Desktop (see "Create Shortcuts to DOS Programs" in Chapter 10). You'll find Edit.com in your \Windows\Command folder.

Secret

Edit can load up to nine files and can have two windows open at any one time. It can use up to 5.5MB of virtual memory to load and manage files, handling files of up to 64,000 lines. The maximum line length is 1,024 characters. It doesn't require Windows to run, and it should run on any processor equal to or greater than a 286. It requires only 160K of conventional memory.

Edit is great for looking for text in binary files, and it has a switch in its File Open dialog box to give you that option. The Edit command's File Open dialog box defaults to opening files with any extension—a big improvement over older versions, especially if you use it to edit Windows batch (.bat) files.

Secret

The Edit command doesn't recognize a mouse double-click setting in the registry. If you have set your middle mouse button on a Logitech mouse to double-click (as described in "Double-Clicking with the Middle Mouse Button" in Chapter 43), it won't work with Edit. You'll have to remember to double-click with the left mouse button.

Wonderful DOS Commands

Windows is great, but there are still some tasks that are handled more efficiently at the DOS command line. For example, if you want to rename a set of files in Windows, you have two choices: either the Windows Explorer (and its common File Open dialog box in many applications) or the faster DOS Ren command. To compare files, Fc.exe does so in a way that still isn't a feature of Windows Millennium.

While you're in a DOS window, you can navigate up the folder tree using just dots as names for grandparent and great-grandparent folders. The dots are stand-ins for the various folders as follows:

.	The current folder
..	The parent folder
...	The grandparent folder
....	The great-grandparent folder

You can use these stand-in dot names in place of the actual names in DOS commands. For example:

Copy *thisfile.ext* ...	Copies *thisfile.ext* to the grandparent folder
CD	Changes the current folder to the great-grandparent folder

Modifying DOS Commands

You can modify the default behavior of some DOS commands so that they do just what you want them to. You do this by setting the value of certain environmental variables. For example, if you want to change the default behavior of the DIR command, you can add the following line to a batch file that you configure to run every time you start a Windows DOS session:

```
set dircmd=/p /l /o:-d
```

This line modifies the DIR command to pause after each screen full of listed files, display the filenames in lowercase, and order the filenames in descending date order.

You can modify the Copy command by setting the value of *copycmd*.

How do you know which modifiers to use when changing these commands? They are the same ones you could type in manually when you enter the command. Type **copy /?** or **dir /?** at the command prompt and press Enter to see the available modifiers.

Doskey lets you define macros, so you can redefine any of the DOS internal or external commands. You run the commands after loading Doskey and the macro definitions (most likely in your Autoexec.bat file or in a batch file that is run when you start a Windows DOS session). For example, if you want to redefine the Mem command to pause after each page of information, add the following to your batch file:

```
c:\Windows\Command\Doskey
Doskey mem=mem.exe $* /p
```

The Mem command is now changed to mean "Mem with the page pause modifier." The symbol **$*** means "include whatever is typed after Mem on the command line." For more information on Doskey, type **doskey/?** at the command prompt.

Shortcuts to DOS Commands

You can make further modifications to DOS commands by using shortcuts to MS-DOS programs (also known as pifs) to call the commands. Some of these are carried out automatically. To see what we mean, take the following steps:

STEPS

Creating a Shortcut to Mem.exe

Step 1. Using your Explorer, navigate to the C:\Windows\Command folder. Right-click Mem.exe. Click Properties.

Step 2. Click the Program tab. Notice that the "Cmd line" field has the following entry:

```
C:\WINDOWS\COMMAND\MEM.EXE /c /p
```

This entry modifies the Mem command to display greater details about memory allocation, and to pause after displaying one page of information. These commands were automatically added to the command line.

Step 3. Click OK (or Cancel).

Step 4. Press the F5 key to refresh the Explorer window. Scroll through the Command folder until you find the MS-DOS icon labeled Mem. It will be right below the Mem.exe file (if you are using Details view and Name order) and its type is listed as Shortcut to MS-DOS Program.

Step 5. Click the shortcut to the Mem icon. Pretty cool, huh?

Clicking the shortcut to the Mem icon opens a Windows DOS session, displays the memory details, and then pauses, waiting for you to press another key. You will want to edit this shortcut so that it doesn't close on exit (right-click the Shortcut icon, click Properties, click the Program tab, and clear the "Close on exit" checkbox).

You can create a Windows shortcut for any of the DOS commands. You can put these shortcuts anywhere that makes sense to you — on your Desktop, in the Start menus, in a DOS folder that has a shortcut on your Desktop. In this way, the DOS commands become Windows programs.

Secret

If you create a shortcut that can't be added to the same folder, Windows will put it in the \Windows\Pif folder. You'll notice this, for example, if you create a shortcut to a DOS command in the \other\oldmsdos folder on your Windows CD-ROM.

If you use DOS that support parameters or filenames that change, you can add a space and a question mark after the DOS command name in the command line, as in **Edit ?**. This will cause a dialog box to open when you start that command in Windows. The dialog box will ask you to type the parameter or filename, then click OK. The command will automatically use what you typed. This is a good way to remind yourself or others to include a parameter or filename if one is needed before starting the program.

DOS Commands You Shouldn't Run

There are a few DOS commands and applications that you must *never* run while in a Windows DOS session.

Don't ever run any disk utilities that haven't been updated to work with long filenames, unless you have saved your long filenames. Note that earlier disk utilities usually will refuse to work on any FAT32 drives or partitions if they weren't designed to support them.

You won't be able to run Chkdsk /f, Fdisk, Format C: (but Format A: and Format B: are fine), or Sys C: while in a Windows DOS session.

Don't ever run a disk optimization package other than Defrag (which comes with Windows) if it hasn't been updated for long filenames. Don't run programs that change your hard disk interleave from a Windows DOS session.

Windows has a built-in disk cache. Don't run third-party disk cache programs that aren't specifically designed for Windows.

Don't ever run utilities that undelete files unless they have been specifically designed for your current version of Windows. You *can* use the DOS 6.*x* version of Undelete using the steps provided in "Undelete and Unerase" in Chapter 13.

The Path and Windows Applications

The default path that is set if you don't have an `Autoexec.bat` file is

`C:\Windows;C:\Windows\Command`

This assumes, of course, that your Windows folder is called Windows and that it is on the `C:` drive. If not, then the path statement will be automatically changed to the correct values.

You can add more folders than this to the path, if you like. You can also change the path in a batch file that you run when you open a DOS window. For example, the first line of your batch file could read:

`path=C:\Windows;C:\Windows\Command;C:\MyFolder`

Secret

Windows applications can set a pointer to the folder that contains their executable files. The reference is stored in the registry at HKEY_LOCAL_MACHINE\ Software\ Microsoft\ Windows\ CurrentVersion\ AppPaths.

When a Windows application starts, the shell looks at the entry at this location and appends the referenced folder(s) to the path.

You can set up references at this location in the registry so you don't have to type the full pathname in front of an executable file's name when you use the Run menu item to run a program. This also works with the Start command in DOS batch files.

Use the Registry Editor to add folder references, patterned after the ones already in the registry at the above location, for your own Windows applications that don't know about this Windows feature. You can then reference the applications in Start commands without using their full pathname.

DOS in Windows

If your DOS programs run in Windows DOS sessions, by all means run them there. Windows creates a "virtual machine" for each Windows DOS session. As far as your DOS program is concerned, it is running in its own computer.

Each Windows DOS session is its own virtual machine. Each virtual machine can be different. You can run a number of them at once. Each is preemptively multitasked. This means no one session can hog all of your computer's resources.

You can set a number of virtual machine operational parameters. You determine what the computer looks like to the DOS program by editing the Windows DOS session properties found in Program Information Files (`pifs`).

The easiest way to run a DOS program in Windows is to click its icon in a folder window or the Explorer. In many cases, the DOS program will just run and that's all there is to it. You can create shortcuts to DOS programs (pifs) and documents, and treat them just as you would shortcuts to Windows programs and documents. (Pifs have been enhanced since their first use in the old Windows 3.1*x* to take on the function of shortcuts to DOS programs.)

You can also run a DOS program from the Run command in the Start menu. Click the Start button, and then click Run. Type the full name of the program, including its path. Type any command-line parameters after the program's name.

Secret

If you want to run the DOS internal commands such as Copy, from the Run command, you need to use something like the following syntax:

```
command /c copy filename lpt1
```

The /c switch loads another copy of the DOS command processor and allows you to run internal DOS commands.

Tip

If you have an application that writes a PostScript file to disk, and later you want to send that PostScript file to the printer, there is no "Windows" command to do this. You have to copy the file to the printer port, as shown in the previous example — one good reason to keep DOS around. (Note that the previous example will not eject the last page of text files from laser printers; you must do this manually.)

Windows Millennium provides Windows DOS sessions with 32-bit file access to the hard drive as well as disk caching. This significantly speeds hard disk access by DOS programs. DOS programs have full mouse functionality (if they are designed to use a mouse) without having to load a 16-bit mouse driver. You don't need 16-bit sound card drivers, CD-ROM drivers, or network drivers, because these services are provided by Windows 98 32-bit drivers.

You can run DOS programs in a window or full screen. To switch a DOS session between windowed and full-screen modes, press Alt+Enter. To switch between DOS sessions, press Alt+Tab. You can copy data in a DOS window and paste it into a Windows window.

Your Start submenus contain an MS-DOS Prompt menu item. Click the Start button, point to Programs, and click MS-DOS Prompt. This starts a generic Windows DOS session. You can run a DOS program in the Windows DOS session from the DOS prompt. You can open multiple Windows DOS sessions by choosing this Start menu item. You can edit its parameters by right-clicking the MS-DOS Prompt icon on the Start menu and clicking Properties.

Given all the features you get when you run your DOS programs in a Windows DOS session, you might conclude that Windows Millennium provides a better DOS than DOS. If all DOS programs were able to take advantage of the DOS box, this would surely be the case.

DOS in a Box

You can either display a DOS program that's running in a Windows DOS session in a window on the Windows Desktop, or full screen. A DOS window can have a toolbar just like any respectable Windows program (see Figure 20-1). If your DOS window doesn't have a toolbar, click the system menu icon on the left end of the DOS window's title bar and choose Toolbar.

```
MS-DOS Prompt                                              _ □ ×
Auto    ▼  [icons]  A

 Volume in drive C is HOMEBASE
 Volume Serial Number is 4071-1CD5
 Directory of C:\WINDOWS

.              <DIR>         12-16-96   9:10p .
..             <DIR>         12-16-96   9:10p ..
SYSTEM         <DIR>         12-16-96   9:10p SYSTEM
COMMAND        <DIR>         12-16-96   9:10p COMMAND
OPTIONS        <DIR>         12-16-96   9:10p OPTIONS
CONFIG         <DIR>         12-16-96   9:10p CONFIG
CURSORS        <DIR>         12-16-96   9:10p CURSORS
DESKTOP        <DIR>         12-16-96   9:10p DESKTOP
FORMS          <DIR>         12-16-96   9:10p FORMS
HELP           <DIR>         12-16-96   9:10p HELP
JAVA           <DIR>         12-16-96   9:10p JAVA
MEDIA          <DIR>         12-16-96   9:10p MEDIA
WAVEMIX  INI            54   09-30-97   2:02p WAVEMIX.INI
WANGSAMP       <DIR>         12-16-96   9:10p WANGSAMP
WORDVIEW       <DIR>         12-16-96   9:16p WORDVIEW
TEMP           <DIR>         12-16-96   9:17p TEMP
SYSTEM   INI        2,203    10-01-97  12:02a SYSTEM.INI
MSAPPS         <DIR>         12-16-96   9:20p MsApps
ADDLFNPR REG          115    08-24-96  11:11a ADDLFNPR.REG
Press any key to continue . . .
```

Figure 20-1: A Windows DOS session. Notice the toolbar. The title bar is at the top of the window. The system menu icon is at the left end of the title bar.

You can use the DOS window toolbar to:

■ Change the DOS font size and thereby the DOS window size

■ Mark, copy, and paste text to and from the DOS window and the Clipboard

■ Expand the DOS window to full screen

■ Change the properties of the shortcut to the DOS application

■ Choose to not suspend the DOS program when it is in the background (doesn't have the focus)

DOS Window vs. DOS Screen

There is a difference between a DOS *screen* and a DOS *window*. In full-screen mode, there is no DOS window, and the DOS screen is the same as your computer's screen. A DOS screen on the Desktop is contained in a DOS window. In Figure 20-1 in the previous section, the DOS screen is the area underneath the toolbar and inside the edges of the DOS window.

You will frequently want to see the whole DOS screen inside the DOS window, because DOS programs are designed with the assumption that you can see the entire screen. If you can't see the complete DOS screen in the DOS window, it may be more difficult to run the program effectively.

The DOS window is smaller than the DOS screen if you can see a horizontal and/or vertical scroll bar in the DOS window. In this case, the DOS window only shows you a part of the DOS screen at any one time.

Sizing and Locating the DOS Window

You can change the size of a DOS window and/or a DOS screen in three ways:

- Set the DOS font size to Auto and drag the edge or corner of the DOS window
- Change the DOS font size
- Set the DOS font size to a fixed size and drag the edge or corner of the DOS window

Drag a DOS Window with Font Set to Auto

First, set the font size to Auto in the Font Size box at the left end of the DOS toolbar. You should be able to see the whole DOS screen. If you can't, click one of the corners of the DOS window. The DOS window and screen will shrink to fit.

Now, stretch or shrink the DOS window by dragging one of its corners. The whole DOS screen stretches and shrinks along with the DOS window. The DOS font changes size to match the changing DOS screen size (after you release the mouse button).

Dragging the DOS window will not smoothly resize it. The DOS window resizes in increments that correspond to multiples of the available font sizes.

Tip

You can drag a side of the DOS window, but it is quite a bit easier to drag from a corner. Because the DOS window's width and height jump in increments that are multiples of the fixed ratios of font pixel width to height, the window may get a lot shorter all of a sudden or not expand at all in another direction. Dragging by the corner opens up possible moves along both axes, making dragging somewhat smoother.

If you have clicked the Maximize button in the DOS window title bar, you won't be able to resize the DOS window. In fact, the resize arrows won't appear if the DOS window has been maximized. The DOS window is already maximized anyway if the whole DOS screen is visible and the font size is fixed. That is the meaning of the "maximum" DOS window size (with fixed font size) — the whole DOS screen is visible.

If the font is set on Auto, maximizing the DOS window enlarges the font size, and consequently, the DOS screen. The DOS window will be the largest it can be and still be within the boundaries of the Desktop.

As you adjust the DOS window size, you are adjusting the size of a full DOS screen. Everything on the DOS screen is displayed in the window. Nothing is scrolled. There is no window on a DOS screen that enables you to see only part of the DOS screen at a time.

Size the DOS Window by Changing the Font Size

The DOS window and the DOS screen will automatically resize themselves if you change the font size. Just pick a new font (other than Auto) in the Font Size box on the left end of the DOS window's toolbar.

The DOS screen must be completely visible — no scroll bars. If there are scroll bars and you make the screen smaller, the DOS screen and window will shrink to the new size, and the scroll bar may disappear if you shrink it enough.

If you call for a larger font and the DOS window is smaller than the DOS screen, the DOS screen and the font will increase in size, but the DOS window will not. The scroll bars will stay right where they are.

Drag the DOS Window Edges or Corner

Set the DOS fonts to a fixed size. You can shrink the DOS window so that only part of the DOS screen shows. The resize arrows move the DOS window edges smoothly. When you release the mouse button, the scroll bars appear. You now have a window on your DOS screen.

If the DOS window is maximized, the resize arrows do not appear.

Relocate the DOS Window

To relocate the DOS window, drag its title bar. The DOS window remembers its new size and location. This information is stored in its pif. The next time you start this DOS application, the window will be located in the same place with the same font at the same size.

Choosing the DOS Display Fonts

Windows provides 25 different fonts for displaying text in a DOS window. Sixteen of the fonts are fixed-pitch TrueType fonts (Lucida Console), and nine are bitmapped Terminal fonts.

Windows makes Lucida Console the default DOS font instead of Courier New. You can see the differences between these two fonts if you move Lucida Console out of the Fonts folder. Your DOS windows will automatically use the Courier font if the Lucida font is not found. In fact, the only way you can use Courier New is by moving Lucida Console.

Secret

You won't be able to move Lucida Console unless you restart Windows, press the Ctrl key during the power-on self-test, and boot to the command prompt. You can then use the DOS Move command to move Lucida Console to another folder.

These fonts aren't used when DOS is displayed at full-screen size. The font built into your computer's ROM is used instead.

You can choose the font size and type (TrueType or bitmap) for displaying DOS commands and programs in a window in two ways. The first is as follows:

STEPS

Choosing a DOS Font, First Method

Step 1. If your DOS application is displayed at full-screen size, press Alt+Enter to get DOS into a window.

Step 2. If the DOS window does not have a toolbar, click the System Menu icon in the upper-left corner of the DOS window and select Toolbar.

Step 3. Click the arrow on the Font Size combo box at the left end of the toolbar.

Step 4. Use the scroll bar on the Font List box to review the choices.

Step 5. Choose a font size and type.

The second method is as follows:

STEPS

Choosing a DOS Font, Second Method

Step 1. Click the Font button (the button with an *A* on its face) at the right end of the DOS window toolbar.

Step 2. Choose a font from the Font Size list, as shown in Figure 20-2. A preview of the DOS window size appears along with a preview of the font itself.

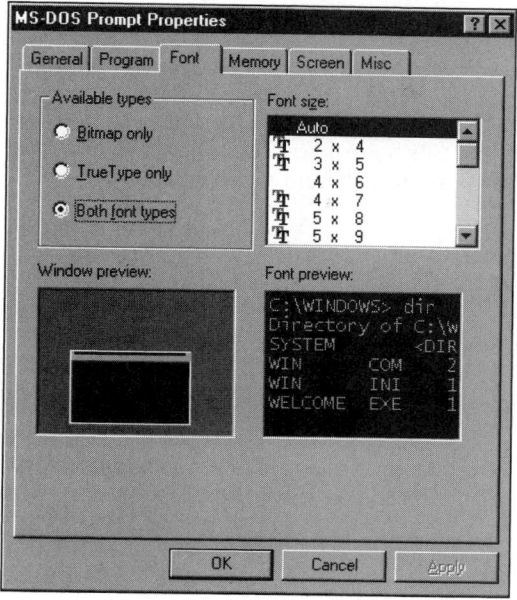

Figure 20-2: The Font tab of the MS-DOS Prompt Properties dialog box. When you choose a font from the list in the upper-right corner, the result is displayed in the two preview boxes.

Step 3.   Click OK.

Secret

If the "Both font types" option is marked in the "Available types" area, only 23 fonts are shown, in addition to Auto. This is in spite of the fact that 25 fonts are available (16 TrueType and 9 bitmapped). There is an overlap of the 4 × 6 and 7 × 12 TrueType and bitmapped fonts. Only the bitmapped fonts for these sizes are shown when this box is checked.

To choose the TrueType font for these two font sizes, mark the "TrueType only" option button. These fonts of the same size look quite a bit different.

Auto Font

If you want the font to change based on the size of the DOS window, set the font size to Auto. As you drag the window, Auto will choose the font size that best fits your DOS window size from among 23, 18, 16, or 9 fonts (depending on your choice of available fonts).

Mark, Copy, and Paste Text or Graphics to and from the DOS Window and the Clipboard

The toolbar in a DOS window makes it easy to mark and copy data and text to and from the Clipboard. You can copy data and text into DOS documents from Windows documents and vice versa.

STEPS

Copying DOS Data to the Clipboard

Step 1. To start marking data (graphics or text), click the Mark button (it shows a dotted square) on the left side of the toolbar.

Step 2. Move your mouse pointer to anywhere just outside the area that contains the data or text that you want to copy to the Clipboard.

Step 3. Press and hold the left mouse button.

Step 4. Drag until the rectangle you are dragging with your mouse pointer completely covers the desired data or text.

Step 5. Release the mouse button.

Step 6. Click the Copy toolbar button (it shows two pieces of paper) or press Enter.

To paste text or graphics from the Clipboard into your DOS (or Windows) document, position your cursor in the document and click the Paste toolbar button (it shows a clipboard), located to the right of the Copy button.

Changing Directories in a DOS Window

Secret

Here's a cool trick from Kaleb Axon, a Windows beta tester. It is an interesting way to change directories in a DOS window.

STEPS

Changing Directories in DOS

Step 1. Open a DOS window by clicking Start ⇨ Programs ⇨ MS-DOS Prompt.

Step 2. Open an Explorer window by right-clicking My Computer, and then clicking Explore. Navigate in the Explorer to any folder or subfolder.

Step 3. Type **cd** at the DOS prompt in the DOS window. Press the spacebar.

Step 4. Drag and drop a folder icon from the Explorer window to the DOS window.

Step 5. The folder name now appears on the DOS command line.

This is an example of a general class of behaviors. Drag and drop works with DOS, sort of. While you can't drag and drop text from a Windows application into a DOS application, you can drag and drop filenames to the command line of a DOS application. (If you do need to drag and drop text from a Windows application, you can copy it to the Clipboard and then paste it into a DOS text-editing application.)

Connecting a DOS Window to the Explorer

Secret

Want to quickly open a DOS window into the current directory while you are navigating about your hard disk in the Explorer? This makes it easy to use dir to look more closely at the files in that folder.

STEPS

DOS Windows and Folder Together

Step 1. Open an Explorer window.

Step 2. Choose View ⇨ Folder Options, and click the File Types tab.

Step 3. Click File Folder in the Registered File Types list, and then click the Edit button.

Step 4. Click the New button.

Step 5. In the Action field, type **MS-DOS Prompt**.

Step 6. In the "Application used to perform action" field, type **C:\Command.com /k cd**.

Step 7. Click OK, click Close, and then click Close again.

Step 8. Right-click any folder icon in the Explorer window, and click MS-DOS Prompt in the context menu.

You now have a new context menu command, MS-DOS Prompt, associated with any folder. This always works, regardless of whether you right-click a folder icon in the right or left pane of the Explorer, a folder icon in a folder window, or a shortcut to a folder on the Desktop (or in any other folder). The DOS window opens up with its current directory equal to the folder that you right-clicked. This gives you a quick way to open a DOS window on any current folder in the Explorer.

You can use `Doshere.inf`, a file in Microsoft PowerToys, to do this automatically. `Doshere.inf` edits your registry to insert the command shown in step 6 above. It puts the words *Command Prompt Here* in your context menu. If you'd rather have `Doshere.inf` add the words *MS-DOS Prompt*, you can edit it by opening it in Notepad. Download PowerToys from `http://www.winmag.com/windows/win98/software.htm`.

Expand the DOS Window to Full Screen

You can run DOS in a DOS window or you can run it at the full-screen size. It's easy to switch back and forth. Press Alt+Enter to switch between the two modes. If you have the toolbar displayed, you can switch to full screen by clicking the Full Screen toolbar button (the button with four arrowheads).

Change the Properties of the Shortcut to the DOS Application

Click the Properties button in the DOS window toolbar. It is the fourth button from the right, and it shows a hand holding a sheet of paper. We discuss the effect of changing these properties in the "Editing Shortcut Properties" section later in this chapter.

Background Button

Click the Background button on the DOS window toolbar to *not* suspend the DOS application while it is in the background; that is, when the DOS application doesn't have the focus. (This button is turned on by default.) See the "Background" section later in this chapter.

Closing a DOS Application

Under normal circumstances, you exit your DOS application by whatever means the developer of your DOS program provided. If you mark the "Close on exit" checkbox in your DOS application's `pif`, the DOS window will also close when you exit your application.

If you are unable to exit normally, you can exit by clicking the Close button (the X) at the right end of the DOS window's title bar. You will get a warning message if the "Warn if still active" checkbox is marked in the DOS application's `pif`.

Using the old Windows 3.1*x*, you exited from the DOS command prompt in a Windows DOS session by typing **exit** and pressing Enter. Starting with Windows 95/98 and continuing in Windows Millennium, you can now just click the Close button. Placing an `X.bat` file on your path that contains the single line `exit` also gives you an easy way to end a DOS session. If you do this, you can simply press the letter *X*, and then press Enter to exit.

Creating a Virtual Machine for DOS Programs

Windows creates a "virtual machine" for every DOS program you start from Windows (every Windows DOS session). You have the option of designing this "virtual machine." Instead of interacting with your computer hardware (the real machine), the DOS program interacts with something that it "sees" as a real machine: the virtual machine.

Secret

If you start your DOS programs from MS-DOS Prompt in the Start menu, they will run in the virtual computer associated with that MS-DOS prompt. This virtual machine is defined by properties stored in the MS-DOS Prompt shortcut in the `\Windows\Start Menu` folder. You can edit these properties to redefine the virtual machine associated with the Start menu's MS-DOS Prompt.

Secret

When you click an icon that represents a DOS program in a folder window, or the Explorer, you automatically create a shortcut. This is also true if you choose Run from the Start menu. This shortcut to a DOS program is stored in the same folder the DOS program is stored in. If a shortcut is already there, a new one isn't created.

Secret

If you delete or move the shortcut, clicking the DOS application's icon in the Explorer creates a new shortcut in the folder that contains the DOS application, unless you moved the shortcut to the `\Windows\Pif` folder. If the DOS program doesn't execute, the shortcut won't be created.

These shortcuts to DOS programs are like shortcuts to Windows programs. However, the properties of a shortcut to a DOS program, a `pif`, are different from those of a shortcut to a Windows program because the properties of a shortcut to a DOS program define a virtual machine.

Click a shortcut to a DOS program and the program starts. You can move and copy these shortcuts. You can place them on your Desktop or on your Start menus. You can have multiple shortcuts for one DOS program, just as you can have multiple, and different, shortcuts for Windows programs or documents.

Shortcuts to DOS can be associated with documents instead of programs, just like Windows shortcuts. You can associate the DOS applications that open these documents with the documents' extension. See "Creating and Editing File Types and Actions" in Chapter 12 for details on how to associate applications with document extensions.

Secret

While the task of identifying the needs of each and every DOS program is too daunting for Microsoft to attempt, Windows comes with Apps.inf, which is stored in the \Windows\Inf folder. Apps.inf provides the basic virtual machine configuration for over 300 DOS applications. You don't have to do anything to access this file; Windows automatically uses it to help create shortcuts for the DOS programs referenced in it.

In many cases, the default shortcut that is created when you click a DOS application icon works just fine.

Secret

Many DOS software developers include pifs with their DOS applications. You can place them wherever they are appropriate for your work.

Secret

When a shortcut is created automatically, it has the same name as the DOS program, but a different extension: pif. You won't see this extension even if you have chosen View ⇨ Folder Options ⇨ View in the Explorer and cleared the "Hide file extensions for known file types" checkbox. (Likewise, you won't see the lnk extension used for shortcuts to Windows programs.) You will see the file type Shortcut to MS-DOS Program.

Secret

There is a difference between starting a DOS program at the MS-DOS prompt within a Windows DOS session and clicking the DOS program icon in a folder window.

■ If you start the DOS program from the MS-DOS prompt in a Windows DOS session, no shortcut is created.

■ If you click the DOS program icon (or run the DOS program by choosing Run from the Start menu), a shortcut is created.

You can also create a shortcut by right-clicking a DOS program icon and clicking Create Shortcut.

Creating Multiple Shortcuts

You can create multiple shortcuts that are all associated with the same DOS program. By setting different properties in each shortcut, you can start the DOS program in different configurations by clicking the different shortcuts. Here's how.

STEPS

Creating Multiple Shortcuts

Step 1. Click a DOS program's executable icon in the Explorer (or in a folder window).

Step 2. Exit the DOS program.

Step 3. Use the Explorer to display the folder that contains the DOS program.

Step 4. Highlight the shortcut associated with your DOS program. Press F2.

Step 5. Type a new filename for the shortcut and press Enter.

Step 6. Right-click the shortcut, then choose Copy. Right-click the right pane of the Explorer and choose Paste.

Step 7. Click the new shortcut and press F2. Type a new name for this shortcut and press Enter.

Step 8. Repeat steps 6 and 7 to create new shortcuts associated with the same DOS program.

Step 9. Edit each of these shortcuts for different properties, as detailed in the following sections. You can move these shortcuts to different folders or onto the Desktop or Start menus.

Opening Program Information Files (pifs)

Windows Millennium has no Pif Editor to edit pif files, as old versions of Windows did. Good riddance.

In its place, you can easily change the properties that are stored in a DOS program's shortcut. The shortcut stores these changes. We show two ways to display these properties. Our sample DOS application is Command.com. Here's the first method:

STEPS

Displaying a DOS Application's Properties

Step 1. Use the Explorer to view the \Windows folder.

Step 2. Right-click the Command.com icon and then select Properties. A shortcut to Command.com is created.

If a shortcut has already been created for a DOS application, you can use the Explorer, perhaps in conjunction with the Find tool, to find the shortcut. Once you have found it, right-click it and choose Properties. You can open the shortcut associated with any DOS program in this same manner.

The following steps describe another method:

STEPS

Getting to a DOS Shortcut

Step 1.   Using the Explorer, find Command.com in the \Windows folder. Click Command.com.

Step 2.   Click the System Menu icon at the left end of the DOS window's title bar, or right-click the title bar. (If you are using a full-screen Windows DOS session, press Alt+Enter to switch to a windowed DOS session.)

Step 3.   Choose Properties from the menu.

Step 4.   You can now change the properties of the virtual machine. The properties will be stored in the shortcut.

You can use this method whenever you are running a DOS program in a window. If the toolbar is displayed, you can also click the Properties toolbar button.

Editing Shortcut Properties

There are seven tabs associated with a DOS program. The first one, the General tab, is for any DOS or Windows file or folder. You won't see this tab if you have the DOS window open and you click the Properties toolbar button, or click the System Menu icon (or right-click the title bar) and choose Properties.

Program Properties

The Program tab is the meat of the matter. Take a look at Figure 20-3 to see what we mean. The Program tab contains the command line for the DOS program, its working directory, an optional startup batch file that runs before the DOS application, a hot key definition, a window configuration, and buttons to change the associated shortcut's icon and define MS-DOS mode. You'll find a big chunk of DOS program functionality here.

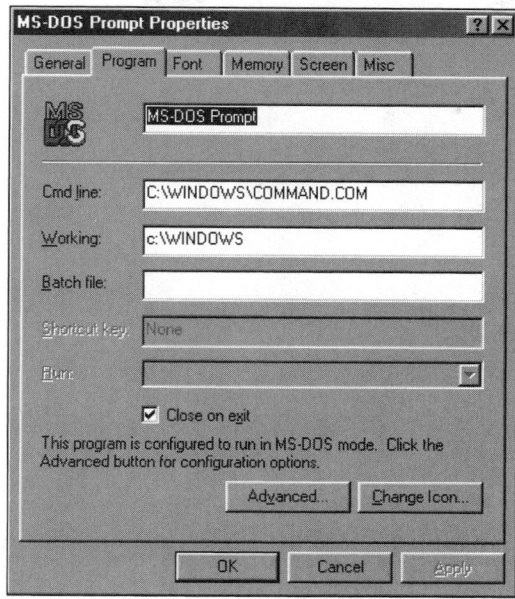

Figure 20-3: The Program tab. Define the title of the application, its command line, working directory, startup batch file, shortcut key combination, state of the DOS window, and icon. Also specify whether the application needs to run in MS-DOS mode or not.

The Program tab for a shortcut to a DOS program is a lot like the Shortcut tab associated with Windows programs. Figure 20-4 shows the similarities. Where there are differences, we point them out.

Notice that the Program and Shortcut properties have titles, command lines ("Cmd line" and Target), working directories (Working and "Start in"), Shortcut Key and Run fields, and Change Icon buttons. For more on shortcuts, see "DOS Shortcut Properties" in Chapter 10.

Title

The title is displayed on the left side of a DOS application's title bar, which appears when the application is running in a window (not in full-screen mode). The title is also displayed on the taskbar button for the window. By default, Windows uses the name of the shortcut for the title, but you can change it by typing a new title in the field at the top of the Program tab.

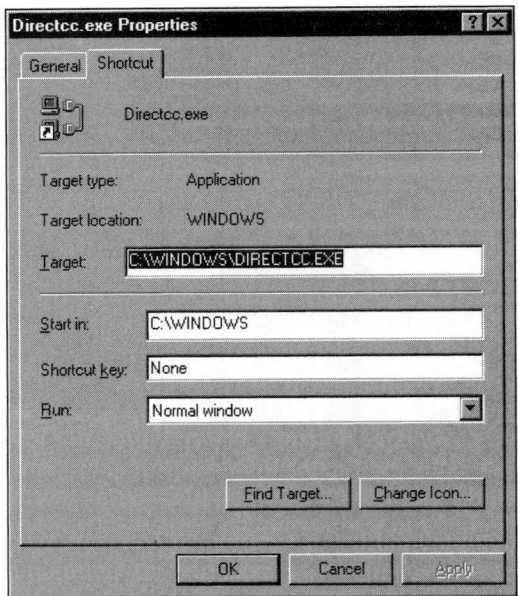

Figure 20-4: The Shortcut tab for a Windows shortcut. The Target field is like the "Cmd line" field in the Program tab. The "Start in" field is similar to the Working field. Both tabs have Run and Shortcut Key fields, and both have Change Icon buttons.

Command Line

When you start a DOS program for the first time by clicking its icon in a folder window, you automatically create a shortcut that contains the complete pathname of the DOS application in the "Cmd line" field. The command line can contain the driver letter, folder name, filename, extension, and any command-line parameters.

You can set the values for what are referred to as *environmental variables* in your Autoexec.bat file and other DOS batch files. You do this with a Set command. You can use these variables in the "Cmd line" field in the Program tab to insert their associated values in the command line. You use the following form:

%variablename%

For example, if you entered the command Set location = ABC in your Autoexec.bat, you could then enter the command line c:\%location%\ Myprog.exe in the "Cmd line" field to run the program Myprog in the ABC directory.

Secret

If you move the DOS program, or if you want the shortcut to refer to another program, you can edit this command line. Unlike shortcuts to Windows applications or documents, a shortcut to a DOS program or document will not go looking for the associated DOS program or document if you move it. You have to edit the command line to give it a new location.

The Shortcut tab has a Find Target button. There is no such button in a shortcut to a DOS program. You have to navigate to the DOS application's folder by yourself, using the Explorer or a folder window.

If your DOS program can accept different command-line parameters and you want to be able to type them whenever you start the DOS program, you need to add a space and a question mark at the end of the command line string. You only need to type one question mark, no matter how many parameters your DOS program can accept. If you make this modification to your command line, the MS-DOS Prompt dialog box, shown in Figure 20-5, will appear each time you start the DOS program to let you enter your parameters.

Figure 20-5: If you enter a question mark after the program name in the command line of a DOS shortcut, you get to specify the command-line parameters every time you start this DOS application.

If you use the same command-line parameters every time you start a DOS application, just type them in the "Cmd line" field after the program's pathname. You can create multiple shortcuts associated with one DOS program, each with different command-line parameters, and perhaps one with a question mark.

Secret

When you run a shortcut from the Run command on the Start menu, any parameters you type after the shortcut name *override* the parameters that you specified in the "Cmd line" field on the shortcut's Program tab. For example, doing a command such as Run Myapp.lnk /abc forces your app to use the parameter /abc instead of whatever command line you defined in the short-cut. This is one way to use one set of switches to start the application most of the time, and use a different set occasionally.

Secret

The command line can contain a DOS application name and a filename, something like C:\Windows\Command\Edit.com C:\Windows\Temp\ New.txt, for example. The shortcut will be a shortcut to the document, just like a Windows shortcut to a document.

Secret

If the DOS application is associated with a file extension, you can easily create a `lnk` shortcut to a DOS document. Right-click a document with that extension and click Create Shortcut. This creates a Windows shortcut, a file with the `lnk` extension, not a `pif`. You have to create the association between the file extension and the DOS program first. Turn to "Associating Actions with File Extensions" in Chapter 12 for details.

Secret

You can change a `lnk` file to a `pif` just by adding the DOS application name in front of the document filename in the Target field of the Shortcut tab. For example, assume you have a shortcut to a text file that is normally associated with Notepad. You can edit the command line in the Shortcut tab for this document to use `Edit.com` instead. When you do, the `lnk` file turns into a `pif`.

You can't create a `lnk` shortcut from a `pif`. If you right-click a `pif` and choose Create Shortcut, you'll create another `pif`.

Working Directory

The working directory is the folder meant to contain files that work in conjunction with your DOS application or the data or text files you edit with the DOS application. The DOS program will search the directory you enter in the Working field for any files it needs. Whether an entry is needed here or not depends on the DOS program.

Tip

For example, one of the authors runs the DOS program Doom (don't so many misguided souls?). The Doom shortcut is stored in `\Windows\Desktop`. The command line for Doom is `d:\games\doom\doom.exe`. The working directory for Doom is `d:\games\doom`. If the Working field is blank, Doom 1.2 won't run when you click the Doom shortcut icon. Heretic, another product from id Software, the developers of Doom, doesn't require an entry in the Working field.

Batch File

You can run a DOS batch file before your application starts up.

This is one way to set certain environmental variables for a DOS application before you run it. For example, put the following line in this batch file:

```
Set Mydir=C:\thisone
```

Alternatively, you can load TSR programs in the batch file before your primary DOS application starts. You then can access the TSR from within that DOS application—without using memory in every DOS session by loading that TSR prior to starting Windows.

Hot Key(s)

You can type an entry in the hot key field (it's labeled Shortcut Key) to define a set of keys that you press at the same time to start a DOS application. Hot keys work for shortcuts that are in the Start menus or on the Desktop.

Hot keys let you start an application from the keyboard without mousing around. People who use DOS applications in full-screen mode and want to quickly start and switch between applications are particularly fond of them.

While the name of the field, Shortcut Key, is singular, it is best to assign a *set* of keys to be pressed together as one hot key. That way, you can define three keys that probably won't be used for something in another application that might be open at the time you press these three keys. For example, you could define Ctrl+Alt+D to start the MS-DOS Prompt window.

If you use the Ctrl, Alt, and/or Shift key, it is easy to press and hold down one or two of these keys while you press the last key, most likely a letter key. These keys are modifier keys, and usually your applications won't react to them until you press another key. This makes it easier to press three keys at once.

Even if another application has the focus and you are in full-screen DOS mode, the hot key will work. The hot key takes precedence. If you define a hot key combination that was originally used in another application, that application loses the ability to use that combination, even if it has the focus. The keyboard combination opens the application for which you defined the hot key instead.

Tip

For example, if you define a hot key as Shift+D without Ctrl or Alt, you will be unable to type a *D* (uppercase *d*) in your word processor. Or, if you define a hot key as Ctrl+Shift+D and that combination is used in your spreadsheet for some function, the spreadsheet will not be able to see that combination, because Windows will grab it before the spreadsheet can get a hold of it — even if the spreadsheet has the focus.

Secret

Your hot key should (by convention) include either an Alt or Ctrl key, plus a function key or printable key. The Windows Help files say it has to, but it doesn't. You can include the Shift key in the combination, but not the keys Backspace, Enter, Escape, Print Screen, Spacebar, or Tab. Ctrl+Shift or Ctrl+Alt plus a letter key is often a good combination. Windows applications often leave combinations with these keys undefined so you can define macros with them.

Something else to try is Ctrl or Alt in combination with the punctuation keys (period, comma, and so on). Windows applications rarely use these combinations.

If you just want to switch to running applications, an easier way to do this is to press Alt+Tab. This allows you to switch to any running application, DOS *or* Windows. You can also use Ctrl+Escape to get to the Start menu.

Tip

If you set a hot key for a shortcut and later want to get rid of it, you can't just delete the key combination from the Shortcut Key field and then save the shortcut. The previous key assignment isn't actually deleted unless you succeed in entering None in the box. And you can't just type the word *none* — you must place your insertion point in the field and press Backspace to specify None.

Secret

The Shortcut tab of a `lnk` file also has a hot key definition field. While hot keys work the same way with both types of shortcuts (`pif` and `lnk`), entering keystrokes into the hot key field works differently. If you type the d key in the Shortcut Key field of the Program tab for a `pif` file, it gets entered as a d. In contrast, if you type a d in the same field of the Shortcut tab for a `lnk` file, Windows automatically adds Ctrl+Alt+ before the d.

It is not a good idea to redefine function keys, such as F1 (help), as hot keys. This reduces the functionality of Windows. Many applications also use the combinations Ctrl+F1, Ctrl+Shift+F1, and so on.

Run — Normal, Minimized, Maximized

In what size window do you want to start your DOS application?

If your font size is set to Auto, you can maximize the DOS window so that it fills up the Desktop as much as possible. DOS windows are sized based on the height-to-width ratio of the DOS font you're using, and their size is limited by the size of the Desktop. If you choose Maximized with Auto font sizing, you'll get a large DOS window.

If you have a fixed DOS font size, the Maximized setting will display a DOS *window* that encompasses a whole DOS *screen* at the set DOS font.

If you choose Normal, you will get a DOS window that is the restored size. If the maximized and restored size are the same because you are using a fixed DOS font size, and the DOS window is big enough to display the whole DOS screen, the only difference between Normal and Maximized may be the location of the window.

If you choose Minimized, the DOS application opens as a button on the taskbar. This is great for running DOS programs that don't require any interaction with the user (as is true of many batch files).

Close on Exit

The "Close on exit" checkbox is a very nice feature. If you want to run a quick DOS batch file, you can have it show up only as a button on your taskbar and make it go away as soon as it carries out its work.

In many cases, you will want the DOS window to close after you have completed working with the DOS application or document. This is the way all Windows programs work; nothing is left open after you quit them. The only reason you would want to leave the DOS window open is if you wanted to run another DOS program after you finished working on the one that you are currently running.

You can open a DOS window with just the DOS prompt, as you do when you click the MS-DOS Prompt item in the Start menu. Even with "Close on exit" checked, the DOS prompt is there ready for you to run the next DOS program. You don't exit the command prompt DOS window until you type **exit** at the prompt or click the Close button (the X) in the upper-right corner of the DOS window.

Tip

If your DOS program does some work, writes some output to the DOS screen, and then quits, you won't be able to see what the output was if you mark "Close on exit." Lots of DOS programs do this, so clear this checkbox if you want to see their output.

If you quit a DOS application and the DOS window is still on the Desktop, the title bar of the DOS window states that the application is inactive. To get rid of the DOS window, click its Close button.

Change Icon Button

The Change Icon button is pretty straightforward. You are given a choice of icons contained in C:\Windows\System\Pifmgr.dll, as shown in Figure 20-6. If your current icon is contained in another file, the icons in that file are displayed. You can choose a new icon from among those displayed, or browse through other files for other icons.

Figure 20-6: Choose an icon. Use the scroll bar to move to the right or left and then double-click the icon you want. If you want to get an icon from another file, click Browse.

The Browse button brings up the common File Open dialog box. You use this dialog box to find the file that contains the icons you want to use.

Advanced Button

Clicking the Advanced button in the Program tab displays the Advanced Program Settings dialog box shown in Figure 20-7.

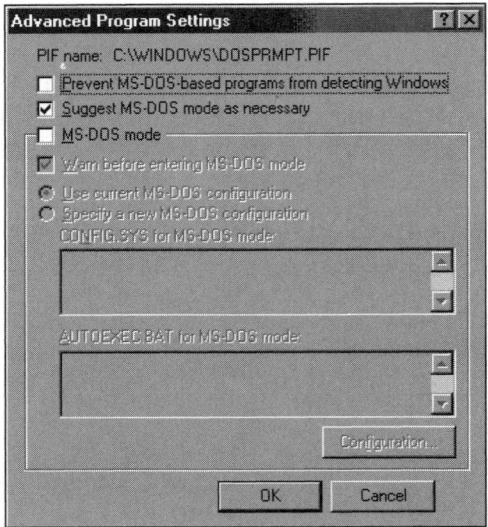

Figure 20-7: The Advanced Program Settings dialog box

Mark the "Prevent MS-DOS-based programs from detecting Windows" checkbox if you want the DOS box to try to fool any program that checks to see if it is running under Windows by telling the program that it isn't. If you mark the "Suggest MS-DOS mode as necessary" checkbox, Windows will see if the DOS program you're running could better use MS-DOS mode. The third checkbox turns on MS-DOS mode. If you click a DOS program icon that has this checkbox marked, your computer is switched to MS-DOS mode.

Tip

If you have a Windows-unfriendly program that can, in fact, run in the Windows DOS session, you can send a message to it when it asks if it is running under Windows telling it that it is not (when, of course, it is). This allows it to run in a Windows DOS session (hopefully) successfully. You send this message by marking the "Prevent MS-DOS-based programs from detecting Windows" checkbox.

By default, you can run Windows programs from the DOS prompt of a Windows DOS session. If you mark the first checkbox in the Advanced Program Settings dialog box, Windows will no longer be able to recognize that you typed the name of the Windows program at the DOS prompt, and Windows programs will not run from a Windows DOS session.

Windows checks to see if there are incompatibilities in a DOS program that will most likely prevent it from running successfully in a Windows DOS session. If you leave the "Suggest MS-DOS mode as necessary" checkbox marked (the default), Windows tells you if it finds such incompatibilities. If you clear this checkbox, you run the risk of running a badly behaved DOS program in your Windows DOS session.

If you mark the "MS-DOS mode checkbox and mark the "Specify a new MS-DOS configuration" option button, the lower portion of the Advanced Program Settings dialog box becomes active, and you can edit the "CONFIG.SYS for MS-DOS mode" and "AUTOEXEC.BAT for MS-DOS mode" fields.

If you clear the "MS-DOS mode" checkbox, the rest of the dialog box doesn't apply and is dimmed.

Font Properties

For details on the Font tab, see the section earlier in this chapter entitled "Choosing the DOS Display Fonts."

Memory Properties

The amount of memory available to a DOS program running in a Windows DOS session depends on the configuration of the `Autoexec.bat` and `Config.sys` files (if you have them), and whether DOS TSRs and 16-bit drivers are loaded in conventional memory or in the upper memory blocks (UMBs). You can find further details in Chapter 39.

Windows can provide DOS programs with expanded, extended, and/or DOS protected-mode memory (DPMI, for DOS Protected Mode Interface). The DOS programs must comply with Windows expanded, extended, and/or DPMI memory specifications in order to be able to use this memory.

Because Windows makes extensive use of 32-bit protected-mode drivers that do not use conventional memory or UMBs, it can provide up to 612K of conventional memory for DOS programs that run in Windows DOS sessions.

The Memory tab in the Properties dialog box, as shown in Figure 20-8, is divided into four sections, one for each type of memory available to DOS programs. You can use these sections to set the amount of each type of memory that's available to your DOS program.

The default setting is Auto, which means, "let the DOS programs determine how much they need or want." Some DOS programs don't do a good job of restraining themselves and need to be limited in their memory acquisition.

Conventional Memory

The maximum amount of conventional memory available is about 612K under the best of circumstances. DOS games and other large programs will likely take all they can get. The only reason to limit the amount of conventional memory available to a DOS program is to let the program load slightly faster. This may help on slower computers, but won't be noticeable on faster ones.

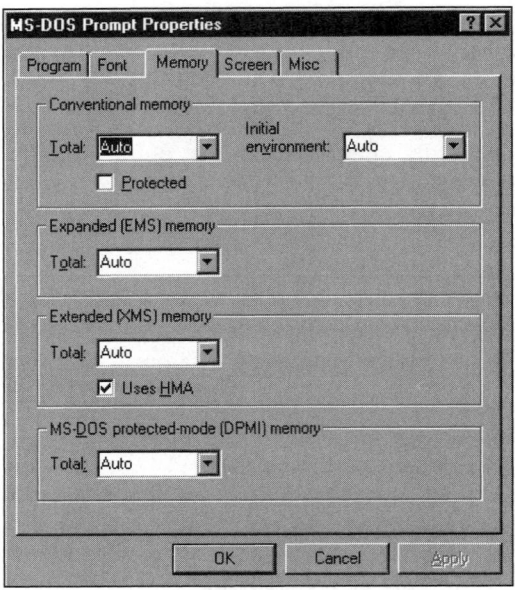

Figure 20-8: The Memory tab. You can set the amount of available conventional, expanded, extended, and/or DPMI memory.

Tip

You could create a separate shortcut, for example, for "small" DOS sessions in which you plan to run only DOS commands such as DIR, Del, and so on. Setting conventional memory at 160K would be adequate for these tasks. This would conserve physical memory for other applications while a "small" DOS session is running.

Protected

Does your DOS program contain a bug? Does it write to memory in areas that it shouldn't? If so, click the Protected checkbox to help protect Windows from crashing because of bugs caused by your DOS application.

When the Protected checkbox is marked, the MS-DOS system memory area is write-protected so your DOS application can't write into this area and corrupt it.

Environment

If you are running a batch file to set environment variables before your DOS application runs, you might want to expand the size of the environment that stores these variables. You may have a smaller environment size in your common Config.sys file. Use the "Initial environment" drop-down list to set aside a larger environment for environment variables that are particular to your DOS application.

Expanded (EMS) Memory

If a DOS program makes use of expanded memory that meets the LIM 4.0 specification, Windows itself can provide it with expanded memory. Windows includes its own expanded memory manager separate from Emm386.exe. DOS games such as Xwing use expanded memory for handling sound effects and music. Some DOS spreadsheets also use expanded memory.

You can set the value for expanded memory to Auto if you want the DOS program to determine how much it needs, or you can limit its appetite. Some DOS programs don't know when they have had enough, so you'll have to tell them.

If you have a Config.sys file with a line calling the MS-DOS expanded memory manager (Emm386.exe), and if the parameter noems is on that line, expanded memory will not be available to DOS programs running in Windows DOS sessions. The Memory tab will be altered to show this state of affairs, as shown in Figure 20-9.

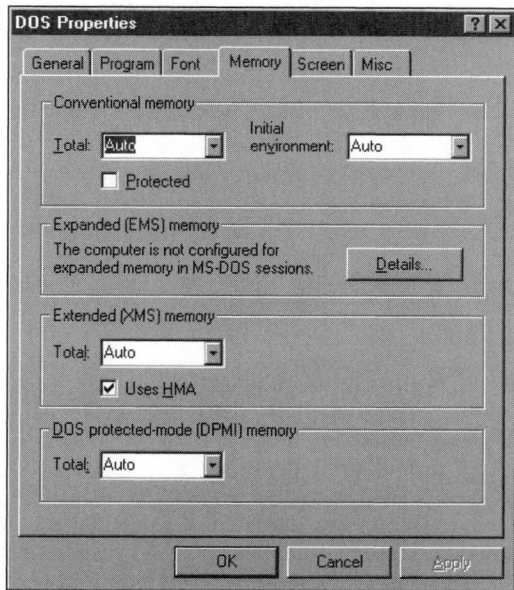

Figure 20-9: The Memory tab with no expanded memory available. If you have a line such as Device=Emm386.exe noems in your Config.sys file, there will be no expanded memory available to your DOS programs.

For most DOS programs, you can set expanded memory equal to zero. If you have any DOS programs that use expanded or extended memory, you should give these programs their own shortcuts.

Extended (XMS) Memory

If your DOS application makes use of extended memory in a way that is compatible with running under Windows, the XMS memory settings allow you to specify the amount of available extended memory.

Applications that use DPMI (DOS Protected Mode Interface)—which Microsoft prescribes as the correct way to access extended memory under a multitasking environment—can use this extended memory. (DPMI applications obtain extended memory through Himem.sys or other "XMS managers.")

HMA

If DOS or other 16-bit drivers are loaded high in your Config.sys file, marking the Uses HMA checkbox doesn't do anything. Otherwise, you can use this memory like extended memory.

The High Memory Area (HMA) is the first 64K of extended memory. It is the only part of extended memory that an application running under DOS can access while still in real mode. Very few DOS applications currently use this memory area. This is unfortunate, because if they did, they would be able to add almost 64K to the amount of conventional memory available to them (unless the line DOS=High is in your Config.sys file). The Windows memory manager, Himem.sys, and all other compatible memory managers make this 64K area available to Windows or any other program that requests it.

The rule for the Uses HMA checkbox is: If you start two shortcuts under Windows—both using the HMA—Windows will switch this memory between them in turn, so they can both benefit from using it.

If you turn *off* the Uses HMA checkbox, an application started from that shortcut cannot access any HMA from within Windows, even if it would otherwise be capable of doing so.

If, however, DOS or a DOS application claims the HMA *before* you start Windows, then no Windows application or shortcut to a DOS program can ever use it.

DOS applications that can use the HMA generally make this fact very well known in their publicity and documentation. You can leave this checkbox marked unless you know that two particular applications using it at once would conflict. In that case, turn it off for the application that requires less memory.

DOS Protected-Mode (DPMI) Memory

Some DOS programs use this specification for turning extended memory into something that DOS programs can use.

Screen Properties

The default setting for a new shortcut is to run your DOS application windowed on the Windows Desktop. This makes DOS programs look and feel more like Windows programs, which is a nice touch.

Tip

MS-DOS programs that run in VGA graphics mode can run in a window on the Desktop. DOS games that rely on hand-eye coordination, however, will probably run too slowly in a window. You'll want to run them at full-screen size.

You can always switch between full-screen and windowed views with Alt+Enter.

Starting a Windows DOS session in a small window takes slightly more memory than starting it full screen. So if your application won't start in a window, mark the "Full-screen" option button in the tab of the Properties dialog box (see Figure 20-10).

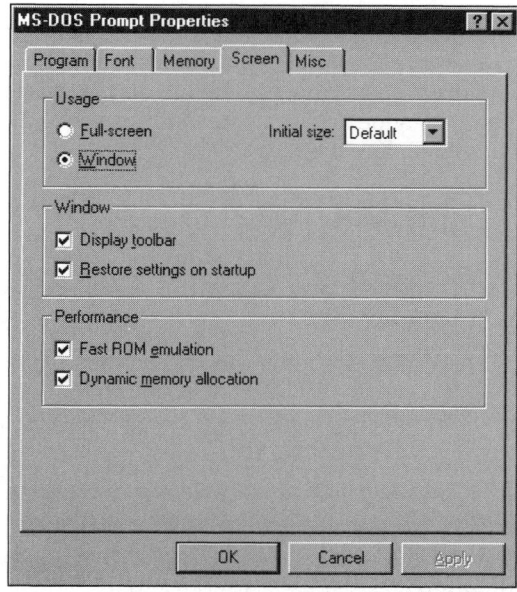

Figure 20-10: The Screen tab. Choose how your DOS program will be windowed.

Initial Size — Number of Lines Displayed

If your video display driver can provide support for more than 25 lines of DOS text in a DOS window or full-screen display (and most VGA or higher-resolution systems can) the "Initial size" drop-down list will be active. You can change the number of lines displayed in the first box.

This works great for a windowed DOS session, even one that merely displays the good old DOS C:\> prompt. When you configure Windows for a number of screen lines greater than 25 — let's say 50 — DOS commands *know* that the screen now contains that many lines. For example, the command dir /p, which halts a directory listing at the end of each screen page, now stops scrolling the display after showing 50 lines instead of 25.

DOS applications themselves vary in their support for higher-than-25-line screens. Some applications automatically adjust to the number of lines in effect when they start up. Other applications, presuming that no one would ever have a display with more than 25 lines, are hard-coded to force themselves into that mode every time.

No matter how many DOS screen lines you configure Windows for, Windows won't open a windowed DOS session any taller than your screen will allow. If you specify a number of lines that would make a windowed DOS session extend beyond the top and bottom of your screen (with the DOS screen font you're using), Windows creates a window only the height of your physical screen — with scroll bars so you can see the rest.

Most VGA adapters support 25-, 43-, and 50-line modes, although if yours doesn't, this setting won't change anything. A 43-line display takes up less room on your display than a 50-line display, while still giving you a lot more information than the bad old 25-line display.

Restore Settings on Startup

You can change your font, window size, and position while running your DOS application. If you want your original values to be used the next time you start the application, mark the "Restore settings on startup" checkbox.

If this checkbox is cleared, Windows retains the values you used in your last session. For example, if you exit your DOS application and close the DOS window while you are in full-screen mode, the next time you start this application it will come up in full-screen mode.

Fast ROM Emulation

Applications that display text run faster if you mark the "Fast ROM emulation" checkbox. This allows Windows to use faster routines in RAM if the application normally uses standard ROM BIOS calls to write text to the screen. You must turn off this setting if garbage appears on the application's screen or if you lose control of its mouse when you run it under Windows.

Dynamic Memory Allocation

If your DOS application switches back and forth between text and graphics modes or starts in text mode and switches later to graphics mode, you need to be sure always to have enough memory for the graphics mode. In these cases, you'll want to clear the "Dynamic memory allocation" checkbox. Otherwise, you can release this memory for other programs if they start in graphics mode and then switch to text mode. This switch appears to be written in the most part for Microsoft Word for MS-DOS.

Check this box if you want to let other programs use the small amount of extra available memory when the DOS application goes into text mode.

Misc Properties

Microsoft had no other place to put these properties of the DOS virtual machine, so it created a Misc tab, as shown in Figure 20-11. Not too original, but what the heck.

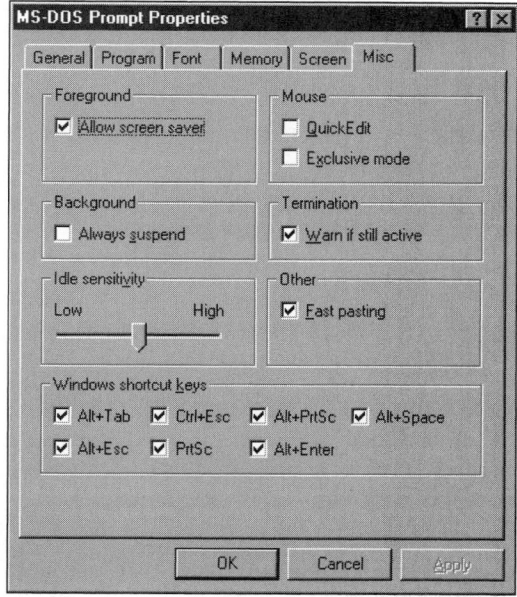

Figure 20-11: The Misc tab. This is the grab bag of the DOS properties. Whatever didn't fit elsewhere is here.

Allow Screen Saver

Screen savers can be pretty unruly. If you want to allow your screen saver to start up even though you are in full-screen DOS mode, mark the "Allow screen saver" checkbox.

Screen savers can interfere with DOS communications or terminal emulation programs, which is the biggest reason to clear this checkbox.

Background

Background refers to the time when an application doesn't have the focus. If the DOS application is running in full-screen mode and you can see it, it has the focus. If it is running in a window and its title bar is highlighted, it has the focus.

If your program is a DOS communications application that runs in the background, clear the "Always suspend" checkbox so that it can download files and do other tasks for you as you're working in another application in the foreground. You don't want to suspend communications programs when they are in the background, because they are productive even when they don't have the focus.

Other DOS applications don't do anything if they don't have the focus, so for these programs, you might as well mark the "Always suspend" checkbox to give all the computer's resources to the foreground task.

Idle Sensitivity

When you turn the idle sensitivity to high, Windows can stop giving DOS applications any time slices if it determines that the application is doing nothing but waiting for you to press a key. This cutoff can make foreground Windows applications run faster when a DOS session that needs no time slices is running in the background.

Whether Windows *correctly* determines that a DOS application is idle, however, varies from application to application.

Newer DOS applications can detect when they are running under Windows and send it a message whenever they are merely waiting for a keystroke. This makes your whole system run faster, since Windows doesn't have to give time slices to that application until you start using it again.

Tip

The "Idle sensitivity" option is intended for older kinds of DOS applications. The rules for using it with the newer DOS programs are not intuitive. You should set this option according to one of the following three rules:

1. If the application is an older one and does not do *anything* in the background that is important, turn idle sensitivity to high.

2. If the application does something once a second, or intermittently when a certain event occurs (such as midnight), turn idle sensitivity to low.

3. If the application is a newer, Windows-aware type, turn idle sensitivity to low. Your applications will all run a little faster if Windows gets the "idle" message directly from these applications and does not have to test for it.

Unfortunately, it is difficult to determine whether a particular DOS application does or does not send this "idle" message to Windows. If the documentation doesn't mention this feature, you have to assume that it hasn't been added to the program.

Mouse

Don't mark the QuickEdit checkbox if your DOS application uses a mouse. Marking this checkbox makes it easier to use your mouse to mark, copy, and paste selections to the Clipboard, but it does this at the cost of disabling the mouse for other actions.

Normally, if you want to mark a selection to copy to the Clipboard from a DOS window, you have to click the Mark toolbar button before you start dragging to select the text (or graphics). If you mark the QuickEdit checkbox, you don't have to do this. As soon as you begin to drag, Windows turns on the Mark button for you.

This setting is useful if you are copying and pasting a great deal of data from your DOS application to Windows or to other DOS applications.

If you check "Exclusive mode," you lose your Windows mouse pointer while this DOS application is in the foreground. The only reason to do this is if your DOS program won't use the mouse correctly unless it exclusively controls it.

Tip

To get your Windows mouse pointer back while this DOS application is in the foreground, press Alt+spacebar, P. This is the keyboard shortcut to display the Properties dialog box. You can then use the mouse to click the Misc tab and clear this checkbox.

Termination

You can exit your DOS application in a number of ways. If your DOS application is Command.com (the DOS prompt), you can type **exit** and press Enter. If you are in some other DOS application, you exit that application in the fashion determined by the application. If you have chosen "Close on exit" in the Program tab, the DOS window closes.

You can also close a DOS window just by clicking the Close button (the X) in the upper-right corner of the window. If you are at the DOS prompt, the DOS window closes without further ado. If you are in a DOS program, you may want to close this DOS program first before you close the DOS window. This way, you can be sure you have saved any unsaved data to your disk.

If you want Windows to remind you to close your DOS application before you close its DOS window, mark the "Warn if still active" checkbox.

Other

Some old DOS programs can take input only so fast. They expect you to be typing, not piping stuff over from some Windows file. If you paste data into your DOS application and it has trouble with it, clear the "Fast pasting" checkbox.

Windows Shortcut Keys

Windows has a defined set of what we call *hot keys*, which it refers to as *shortcut keys*. It grabs them first whenever you press them. If your DOS program wants these keys for its own uses, you have to configure a shortcut for that application that tells Windows to back off and let the keystrokes go to the DOS application.

Table 20-2 lists these hot keys and their definitions.

Table 20-2 Windows Hot Keys	
Hot Key	***Definition***
Alt+Tab	Tab from one active application to another. Switch to graphics mode if DOS is in full-screen text mode. This is the "cool switch." Windows 3.1x has a text-mode version of the cool switch that doesn't switch to graphics mode when you switch between full-screen DOS applications.
Alt+Tab+Click	If your DOS application is in full-screen mode and you press and hold the Alt+Tab key combination, clicking any mouse button brings up the Desktop.
Ctrl+Esc	Switch to graphics mode, if necessary, from full-screen DOS, display the Desktop and the taskbar, and click the Start button.
Alt+Print Screen	Copy the active window to the Clipboard. If the DOS application is in a DOS window, copy it as a graphic; if the DOS application is in full-screen text mode, copy it as text.
Alt+spacebar	Click the System Menu icon.
Alt+Esc	Switch to the next active application.
Print Screen	Copy the complete Desktop, including all windows, to the Clipboard. In full-screen DOS text mode, copy all the text to the Clipboard.
Alt+Enter	Switch between full-screen and DOS window.

To let the DOS application use any of these keystrokes while it has the focus or is in full-screen mode, clear the checkbox associated with the appropriate keystrokes.

If you clear the PrtSc checkbox and the Windows DOS session is in full-screen mode, the Print Screen key sends the current DOS screen to the printer in the same way it would under the DOS operating system.

Secret

Pressing Alt+Enter toggles between the Window and Full-Screen option buttons in the shortcut's Screen tab. You may want your DOS application to come up the same way you set it the first time and not the way you left it the last time. To preserve the settings in a shortcut's properties, you can set the shortcut's file attribute to Read-Only. Right-click the Shortcut icon, click Properties, and then mark the Read-Only checkbox in the General tab.

Creating a Distinct Prompt for DOS

You can create a prompt for Windows DOS sessions that is different than the DOS prompt that is the default. You can also create a different prompt for each MS-DOS mode shortcut.

Windows prevents you from starting another instance of itself, for example, if you type **win** at a DOS prompt while in a Windows DOS session. (If you try, it just displays a warning message.) But you still might find it desirable to remind yourself — in full-screen DOS sessions — whether you are running a Windows DOS session.

There is a good reason to have a reminder that you are in a DOS session under Windows. While it is safe to turn off your PC while in an older version of DOS (without Windows installed), it is not such a good idea when you're at a DOS prompt in a full-screen Windows DOS session.

DOS Prompt for Windows DOS Sessions

Tip

You can alert yourself to the fact that you are in a Windows DOS session by adding a line to your Windows batch (.bat) files. This line might look like the following:

```
SET PROMPT=Press ALT+ENTER or type EXIT to return to Windows.$_$_$P$G
```

The $_ symbols insert blank lines between your message and the normal path and greater-than signs used in the default prompt. (PG means path and greater-than sign.) Be sure to make this all one line in your batch file.

When you run a batch file with this as the first line, you should see your new prompt inside a Windows DOS session.

If you type **set** by itself in a Windows DOS session, you can see what's happening. The Set command displays the contents of the DOS environment. Set Prompt is equal to your longer message.

Windows/DOS Batch Files

DOS batch files are no longer just DOS batch files. They can now contain the Start command, which allows them to start Windows programs. You can run Windows programs and use their internal macro languages to carry out further commands. Batch files can pause until the Windows program has completed its work.

The Start command has the following format:

```
START {options} program
START {options} document.ext
```

The options are as follows:

/m	Run the new program minimized (in the background).
/max	Run the new program maximized (in the foreground).
/r	Run the new program restored (in the foreground). The default.
/w	Wait. Do not return until the other program exits.

A batch file can run Windows programs, it can run in a minimized window so it doesn't open a window that looks like DOS, it can start from a shortcut icon, and it can run Windows application macros. DOS batch files are now Windows batch files.

Commands You Can Use in Batch Files

A number of DOS commands work only in batch files. These mostly control the flow of the execution of the commands in the batch file. They are as follows:

Call	If
Choice	Pause
Echo	Rem
For	Shift
Goto	

Launching Batch Files from Macro Languages

In other cases, you might want to start a DOS batch file from within a Windows application. For example, you could command a Windows application to start a batch file in order to send a listing of the current directory to your printer — a common task that almost no Windows application can perform.

To do this, you would create a macro within your Windows application, assuming it has something like Visual Basic or its own macro language. For example, in versions of Excel prior to Excel 97, a macro to start a batch file named `Mybatch.bat` (from a shortcut) would look like the following:

```
RunMyBatch
=EXEC("mybatch.bat")
=RETURN()
```

In Visual Basic for Applications (used for macros in Excel 97 and Word 97), this same action would appear something like this:

```
SUB MAIN
SHELL "mybatch.bat", 3
END SUB
```

These examples illustrate a good reason why you should define shortcut files to run all your batch files (or define a single, master shortcut file that you rename over and over for each of your batch files). Make sure that the shortcut for a batch file you run from a Windows macro language has the "Always suspend" checkbox (in the Misc tab of the Properties dialog box) cleared, or Windows may switch away from the batch file before it is finished carrying out its tasks. This would return control to the Windows application that launched the batch file *prior to the batch file's completion*. This could lead to errors that might be hard to diagnose.

Finding the Windows Folder

A full-blown Windows program can always find the folder that contains Windows (for example, `C:\Windows`) by asking Windows through a published application programming interface (API) call. But what about a batch file?

The developers of Windows created an environmental variable specifically to meet this need in batch files. If you open a Windows DOS session and type **set** by itself (no parameters), you'll see the current DOS environment strings. One of them should be something like `windir=c:\windows`. This variable's value is the directory that contains Windows — the directory `C:\Windows`, in this case. Of course, if the Windows folder were always `C:\Windows`, there would be little point in having this environmental variable.

Unfortunately, this variable is of little use in its original form. This is because batch files always treat the names of environmental variables as ALL CAPS. You might try to use the *windir* variable in a batch file, as in this line:

```
COPY A:\MY.DLL %WINDIR%\MY.DLL
```

DOS looks for a variable named *windir*, which should have the value
c:\windows. But Windows names its *windir* variable in all *lowercase*.
Therefore, there is no match. A DOS batch file can't *see* the variable at all.
But you *can* write a batch file that uses the value of *windir* correctly.

The following batch file (Wintest.bat) tests for the existence of the string
windir= in the environment, and jumps to the label *nowin* if it isn't found:

```
@Echo off
SET|FIND "windir=">C:\TEMP_1.BAT
COPY C:\TEMP_1.BAT C:\TEMP_2.BAT
IF NOT EXIST C:\TEMP_2.BAT GOTO :NOWIN
C:\TEMP_2.BAT
:NOWIN
DEL C:\TEMP_1.BAT
ECHO Windows, where are you?
```

The first line pipes the output of the Set command into Find, which is case-
sensitive. Find writes the line it finds into a temporary file. If no line contains
windir=, this will be a 0-byte file. This will be the case if you booted Windows
98 to the command prompt. It will not be true if you are in a Windows DOS
session.

The second line copies the temporary file to a new name. Due to a feature
of Copy (which thousands of batch files now rely upon), if the first file is a
0-byte file, the second file will not be created.

The third line, therefore, tests for the existence of the second file. If there is
none, no *windir=* was in the environment.

If the batch file was run in a Windows DOS session, however, temp_2.bat
will contain a single line:

```
windir=C:\WINDOWS
```

Running temp_2.bat executes this line, which runs a file (which you must
create) called windir.bat and feeds it a single parameter: the directory
name. (DOS considers a single equals sign to be a blank, so this line looks
like windir c:\windows to DOS.)

windir.bat does your *real* work, as follows:

```
@echo off
SET WIN-DIR=%1
DEL C:\TEMP_2.BAT
```

The replaceable parameter %1 has the value c:\windows. This is just what
you want. This batch file leaves an environmental variable, %WIN-DIR%,
available for future use (until this DOS session is terminated or the PC is
rebooted).

You can then create and use any batch file that uses the environmental
variable %WIN-DIR%.

Using the Clipboard in DOS Sessions

The Windows Clipboard is an extremely useful area of memory for Windows applications. To add Clipboard Viewer after you install Windows, click Start ⇨ Settings ⇨ Control Panel. Click the Add/Remove Programs icon, click the Windows Setup tab, highlight Accessories, click the Details button, and mark the Clipboard Viewer checkbox. You can also choose Clipboard during setup in the Select Components dialog box under Accessories (unless you are setting up Windows Millennium over Windows 95).

DOS Applications Recognize the Clipboard/Clipbook

In Windows applications, highlighting some text and then pressing Ctrl+Insert copies the text into the Clipboard. Pressing Shift+Delete has the effect of *deleting* the text from the application while moving it to the Clipboard. In either case, moving the insertion point to another location or another application and then pressing Shift+Insert pastes the text into the new location. You can perform the same operations with a mouse by choosing Edit ⇨ Copy, Edit ⇨ Cut, and Edit ⇨ Paste — choices that appear in the menu bar of almost all Windows applications. After performing any of these actions, you can view the contents of the Clipboard memory area by running the Clipbrd.exe program that is included with Windows. This program is actually a *viewer* of the Clipboard, not the Clipboard itself. The Clipboard memory area can contain many types of data other than text — bitmapped graphics, Windows metafile graphics, and so on.

DOS applications vary widely in their support for the Windows Clipboard. Many DOS apps (such as Edit.com) can't use it directly. But other programs, such as Microsoft Word for DOS, have choices right on their menus for copying to and pasting from the Clipboard. (This assumes that Windows is running and, therefore, a Clipboard exists.)

You can copy text *from* a DOS application *into* the Clipboard; simply use the Mark and Copy toolbar buttons in the DOS window. If you are in full-screen text mode in a Windows DOS session, press the Print Screen key to copy text to the Clipboard. If you are in a window, Alt+PrtSc prints your DOS window in graphics mode to the Clipboard.

To paste text *from* the Clipboard *into* a DOS application, run the DOS application in a window and click the Paste toolbar button. The text is pasted at the location of the cursor in the DOS application.

If the text that appears in your DOS application is missing a few characters, the program may not be able to receive keystrokes as fast as the Clipboard is capable of sending them. In this case, you need to change the DOS application's shortcut to clear the "Fast pasting" option (click the Misc tab in the Properties dialog box).

End Runs Around the Clipboard

If you have major problems making a DOS application accept material from the Windows Clipboard (and you've tried the method explained above), there may be a formatting conflict. All three applications involved in a copy-and-paste — the source of the material, the Clipboard, and the recipient of the material — must have *some* format in common in order for the transfer to work.

To get around this, you may have to first save the material into a file on your hard disk. You can then merge this file into your DOS application to transfer the material. You can save text into a plaintext file on disk using the Windows Notepad. If you want to save textual material that has *formatting* you don't want to lose, such as boldface and italic type or different type sizes, try saving it with Windows Write as a Microsoft Word format file. Many DOS programs can import Microsoft Word files, complete with formatting.

A possibility for getting graphics into your DOS application is to save the graphic in a `pcx` format on disk using MS Paint or another format using Paint Shop Pro. Then try to open this file in your DOS application.

Using the Print Screen Key in DOS Sessions

We want to emphasize that you can Print Screen to the printer when you're running a DOS application (or `Command.com`). If you clear the PrtSc checkbox in the shortcut associated with the DOS application (located in the Misc tab of the Properties dialog box), your text (or graphics) goes to the printer instead of to the Clipboard.

Getting a Directory Listing

It's hard to print out a directory (folder) listing from Windows. You can focus on a folder using your Explorer or a folder window. You can send this view of your folder to the Clipboard by pressing Alt+PrtSc. You can then print this view by pasting it into a new empty MS Paint file and printing from MS Paint.

This will work only if your whole folder view is visible in one screen (unless you wish to do this multiple times).

DOS gives you a better way.

STEPS

Printing a Directory Listing from DOS

Step 1. Click the Start button, point to Programs, and then click MS-DOS Prompt.

Step 2. Use the CD, or *change directory*, command to move to the folder or directory whose file listing you are interested in printing.

Step 3. Type in the command **dir > dir.txt** and press Enter. If you have redefined your DIR command to pause for each page, type this instead: **dir /-p > dir.txt**. This transfers the directory listing to a file that can then be printed.

While you can print the directory listing directly to the printer with dir > lpt1:, this method will fail to eject the last page from a laser printer.

Step 4. Navigate using your Explorer to the directory whose listing you have just printed. Right-click dir.txt to select this file in the Explorer. (If you can't find dir.txt, press F5 to refresh your file listing in your Explorer.)

Step 5. Click Print on the context menu.

If you have created a quick way to the DOS prompt using the methods detailed in the "Connecting a DOS Window to the Explorer" section of this chapter, you'll be able to skip the first two steps above.

Secret

While the above method is a good ad hoc way of printing a directory of a given folder, you might want to create a permanent method that will always reside in the context menu. You can do this by creating a directory-printing batch file and editing your registry to connect this file to your folders. Here's how:

STEPS

Printing a Directory Listing from the Context Menu

Step 1. Using Notepad, create a file with the following two lines:

```
cd %1
dir>lpt1
```

Step 2. If you have modified your DIR command, you should change the second line as described in step 3 of the "Printing a Directory Listing from DOS" steps above. If you print to a port other than LPT1, you need to substitute the name of that printer port in step 1.

Step 3. Save the file as Printdir.bat.

Continued

STEPS

Printing a Directory Listing from the Context Menu *(continued)*

Step 4. Using the Explorer, right-click `Printdir.bat`, click Properties, and then click the Program tab. Mark the "Close on exit" checkbox, and choose Minimized in the Run drop-down list. Click OK.

Step 5. Start your Registry Editor (`Regedit.exe` in the `\Windows folder`). Navigate to HKEY_CLASSES_ROOT\ Directory\ shell, highlighting *shell* in the left pane.

Step 6. Right-click the right pane, and choose New ⇨ Key. Type **Print** as the name of the new key and then press Enter.

Step 7. Highlight Print in the left pane, right-click the right pane, and choose New ⇨ Key. Type **Command** as the new key name and press Enter.

Step 8. Double-click Default in the right pane, and type **C:***the folder where you saved the file***\Printdir.bat**.

Step 9. Close the Registry Editor. The changes take place immediately.

These steps add a new Print command to the context menu. When you right-click a folder, you can choose this command to print the contents to your printer.

Check the DOS Filenames

There is one option in the ScanDisk Advanced Options dialog box that is not explained when you click the Help button (the question mark in the upper-right corner of the dialog box) and then click the option "Report MS-DOS mode name length errors." To display this dialog box, shown in Figure 20-12, click Start ⇨ Programs ⇨ Accessories ⇨ System Tools ⇨ ScanDisk ⇨ Advanced. Windows saves filenames in both long and DOS-compatible versions. The DOS-compatible version consists of eight characters and a three-character extension. Marking this option tells ScanDisk to check this 8.3-format version of the filenames and report any problems.

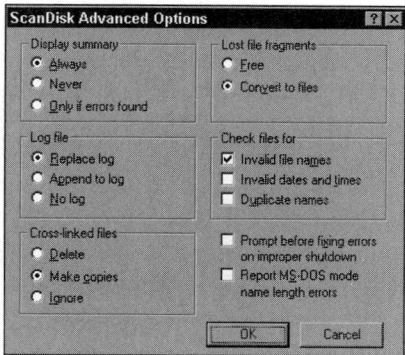

Figure 20-12: The ScanDisk Advanced Options dialog box. The checkbox for reporting name length errors is in the lower-right corner.

DOS Understands Server Names on the Network

You can use UNC-style server names with DOS commands in a DOS window. For example, if there is a server called Brian on the network, typing **dir \\Brian\C** and pressing Enter will display the contents of the C: drive on the Brian computer, if the C: drive is shared (as C:).

Tip

Not all of the DOS commands work. DIR, MD, RD, COPY, MOVE, and REN do, while CD does not.

Run DOS Batch Files with Long Filenames

Windows DOS includes an internal DOS command that allows you to use long filenames in DOS batch files. In particular, you can use long filenames with the IF, FOR, DO, ERRORLEVEL, and GOTO batch file commands.

The command LFNFOR sets a mode switch to permit the use of long filenames. At the DOS prompt, type **lfnfor** and press Enter to see the current state of LFNFOR mode, as shown in Figure 20-13. You can use the command in a batch file to turn on this mode, or put it in your Autoexec.bat to turn it on automatically. By default, it is turned off.

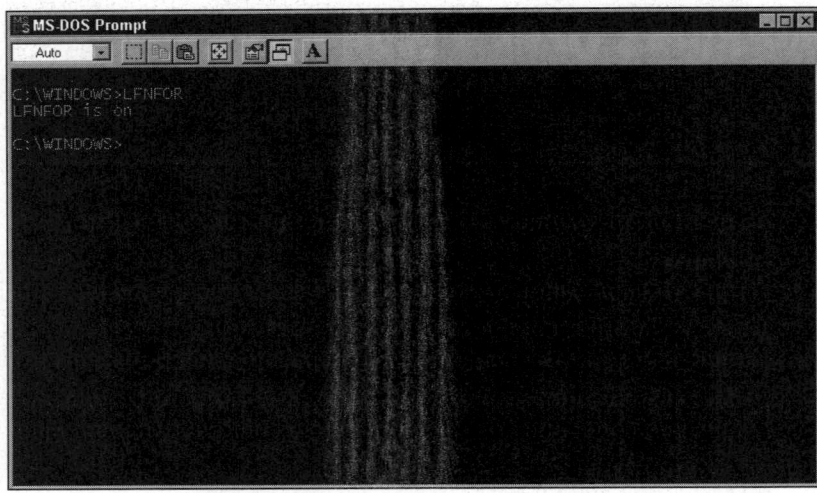

Figure 20-13: Type **LFNFOR** at the DOS prompt to see its current state.

Thanks to Anthony Kinyon for help with this tip.

Not Enough Memory for DOS Programs in a DOS Window

If you don't have enough memory to run a DOS program in a DOS window, it may be because Windows didn't unload the real-mode DriveSpace compressed disk driver when it started. When Windows loads, it is supposed to replace the real-mode version of DriveSpace and DoubleSpace with its own 32-bit protected-mode version that doesn't use conventional memory.

You can find out if this is your problem by checking the amount of memory available in the DOS window. Click Start ➪ Programs ➪ MS-DOS Prompt. At the DOS prompt, type **mem /d/p** and press Enter. Press Enter again. Check the output of mem to see if Drvspace.bin is loaded into conventional memory (see Figure 20-14). If it is loaded, it should be listed right above BUFFERS=12 in the rightmost column.

If you find DriveSpace loaded in conventional memory in a DOS window, you can take a number of steps to make sure that it is unloaded when Windows starts. The steps are detailed in the Microsoft Knowledge Base article "DriveSpace Real-Mode Driver May Not Be Removed from Memory." You'll find it at http://support.microsoft.com/support/kb/articles/q134/3/64.asp.

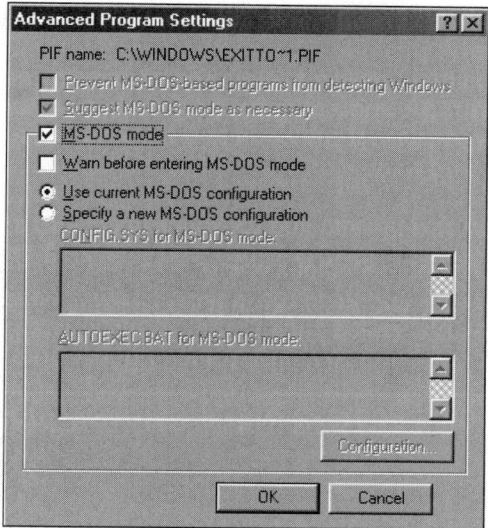

Figure 20-14: If Drvspace.bin is loaded, it will appear in the rightmost column, just above the line BUFFERS=12. In this example, it's not there.

Summary

Windows Millennium doesn't boot to DOS and then switch to Windows (like previous versions do) but it does provide a better virtual machine for DOS programs. Lots of DOS programs can run in Windows DOS sessions.

▶ Windows provides a DOS window for the DOS screen. The DOS screen has access to 20 different fonts and can be extensively manipulated by the DOS window.

▶ DOS programs can have shortcuts to them just like Windows programs. These shortcuts also define the virtual machine that surrounds the DOS program.

▶ If you can't run the DOS program in a Windows DOS session, you should be able to run it in MS-DOS mode (real-mode DOS). Each program can have its own Autoexec.bat and Config.sys files.

▶ Batch files now work with both DOS and Windows programs, so you can use DOS batch files for Windows programming.

Chapter 21

Fonts

In This Chapter

We discuss how text is displayed on the screen and printed on the printer. We show:

▶ The different fonts available in Windows

▶ How to view, install, and uninstall fonts using the Windows Font Installer

What Are Fonts?

Text is displayed on your screen or printer through the medium of typefaces or fonts. The characters look different depending on which typeface or font you use to display the text.

A *font* is a set of character shapes of a given size, weight, style, and design. For example, Courier New 12-point regular or Times New Roman 12-point bold are different fonts. A *font family* or *typeface* is a family of fonts of a similar design with different sizes and weights, including italic, bold, bold italic, and sometimes condensed and expanded versions of the same design. In Windows terminology, *font* is often used to mean a font file or a typeface. Following the Windows convention, we use *font* in this book to mean font or typeface, interchangeably.

Most of the fonts available for Windows use the Windows ANSI character set. Five of the TrueType fonts that come with Windows (Lucida Console, Lucida Sans Unicode, Symbol, Wingdings, and Webdings) are exceptions that use their own character sets. If you want to use unusual characters, you may need to purchase additional fonts that include those characters. If you install Multilanguage Support, your Arial, Courier New, Tahoma, Times New Roman, and Verdana fonts will use a 652-character set. You can find more details on character sets in "Windows Character Sets" in Chapter 42.

Using Fonts in an Application

Windows applications have access to a common font dialog box. You can see what the font looks like in the Sample area of the dialog box, as shown in Figure 21-1.

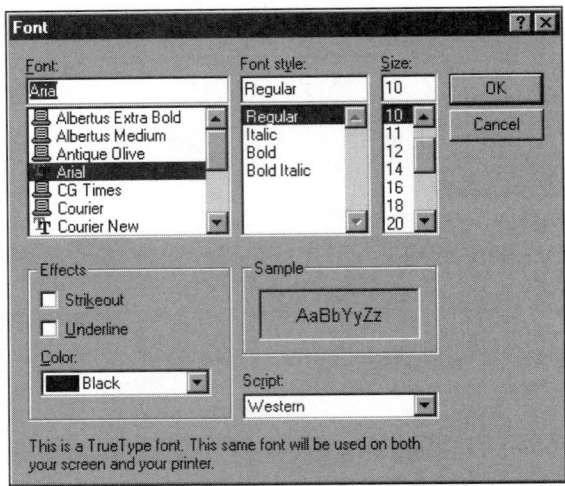

Figure 21-1: The Font dialog box. This dialog box is used by WordPad and can be used by other applications to make it easy to choose a font.

WordPad, a word processing applet that comes with Windows, uses the Font dialog box to allow the user to change font style. Choose Format ➪ Font in WordPad to bring it up.

The Script field shown in Figure 21-1 lists the character set used by the font. Western refers to the Windows ANSI character set, DOS/OEM to the IBM PC-8 character set, and Symbol to one of many nonstandard character sets. Turkish, Cyrillic, Central European, Greek, Baltic, and so on, refer to other character sets. These designations appear only if you have installed fonts that support these additional characters, which you can do by installing Multilanguage Support. See "Windows Character Sets" in Chapter 42.

You can configure the Fonts folder so that applications do not have access to screen or printer fonts.

Where Are the Fonts Installed?

To see what fonts you currently have installed, click the Start button on the taskbar, point to Settings, and then click Control Panel. Click the Fonts folder icon to display the Fonts folder window (shown in Figure 21-2). This folder window displays the extended font names and font file icons of the fonts that come with Windows.

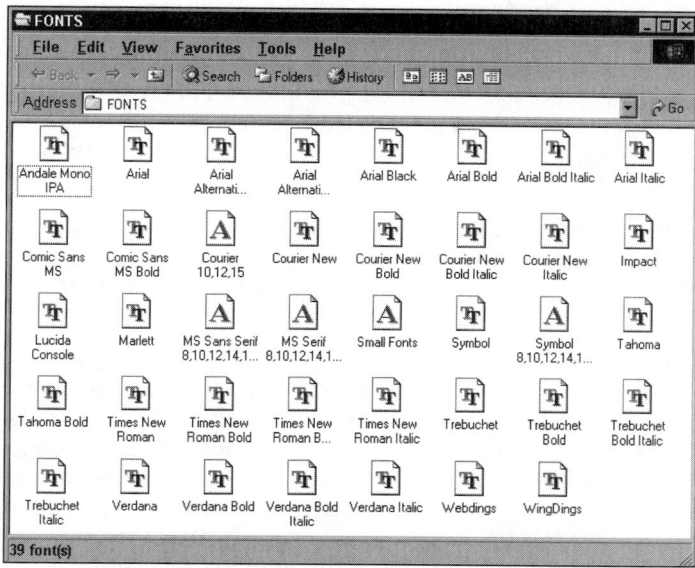

Figure 21-2: The Fonts folder window showing the standard screen (raster) and TrueType fonts that come with Windows

All of the fonts that come with Windows are stored in the \Windows\Fonts folder. When you view this folder in the Explorer, they are shown with their filenames and font icons in the right pane. The font files stored in the \Windows\Fonts folder are displayed differently than font files that you may have stored in other folders. The Large Icons view of the \Windows\Fonts folder (shown in Figure 21-2) displays the font's long font name. In Details view, the first column shows the long font name, the second the filename, the third the size, and the fourth the date.

It can be a little confusing to see exactly what fonts you have, because there is a separate file for each variation in a font family. For example, the Century Gothic Bold and Century Gothic Italic font files are both part of the Century Gothic font family. To see a display of only the font families (Century Gothic, Times New Roman, and so on), choose View ⇨ Hide Variations (Bold, Italic, and so on) while viewing the \Windows\Fonts folder. Note that some variations — Arial Black, for example — will still be visible, because they have been set up by their developers as standalone products.

While the font files themselves are in the \Windows\Fonts folder, a listing of all the fonts is stored in the registry. In fact, if any TrueType font information is later added to the Win.ini file, Windows will move it to the registry the next time it starts up. PostScript font information, on the other hand, is still installed and kept in the `Win.ini` file. The old Microsoft TrueType Font Assistant, which looks for font information in the `Win.ini` file, does not work with Windows Me or Windows 98.

Secret

Not all the font files stored in the `\Windows\Fonts` folder are displayed in a folder or Explorer window, even if you have set View ⇨ Folder Options ⇨ View to "Show hidden files and folders". If you use the Find tool to search for `*.fon`, you'll see several additional fonts, including `8514sys.fon` and `Vgasys.fon`. Windows defines one of these fonts as the System font, depending on your screen resolution.

Fonts don't have to be physically stored in the `\Windows\Fonts` folder to be displayed in that folder (and therefore "installed"). You can install fonts stored in other folders by simply placing shortcuts to them in `\Windows\Fonts`.

For example, you might want to place fonts in your own fonts folder, and place shortcuts to your fonts in the `\Windows\Fonts` folder. If you have created a folder called `\My System` (as we suggest in the "Special Folders" section of Chapter 7), you can create a subfolder called Fonts and place your additional fonts there. That way, you know what fonts you have installed, and you can protect them from being written over by other applications. Using this method also lets you uninstall your fonts without removing them from your hard disk (see "Uninstalling Fonts" later in this chapter).

Secret

If you accidentally move a file that is not a font file into the `\Windows\Fonts` folder, it will not be displayed in a folder or Explorer window focused on `\Windows\Fonts`. To check if there are any misplaced files in this folder, use the Tools ⇨ Find ⇨ Files or Folder command in the Explorer window, or open a DOS window with the DOS prompt at `\Windows\Fonts` and display the directory using the `dir` or `dir/p` command. (It is difficult to inadvertently move a file to the `\Windows\Fonts` folder, because the Explorer won't allow you to cut and paste or drag and drop a nonfont file to this folder.)

Installing Fonts

When an application running under Windows installs a TrueType font, the font is by default copied to the `\Windows\Fonts` folder. Even though there is only one special `\Windows\Fonts` folder, you can store font files in any folder on your hard disk.

You can use the Windows font installer to install new fonts (that is, make them visible to Windows applications). The font installer lets you copy the font files you're installing into the `\Windows\Fonts` folder or leave them where they are and place shortcuts to them in `\Windows\Fonts`.

To install new fonts, take the following steps.

STEPS

Installing TrueType Fonts

Step 1. Click the Start button, point to Settings, and then click Control Panel. Click the Fonts folder icon in the Control Panel.

Step 2. Choose File ⇨ Install New Font in the Fonts folder window to display the Add Fonts dialog box, as shown in Figure 21-3.

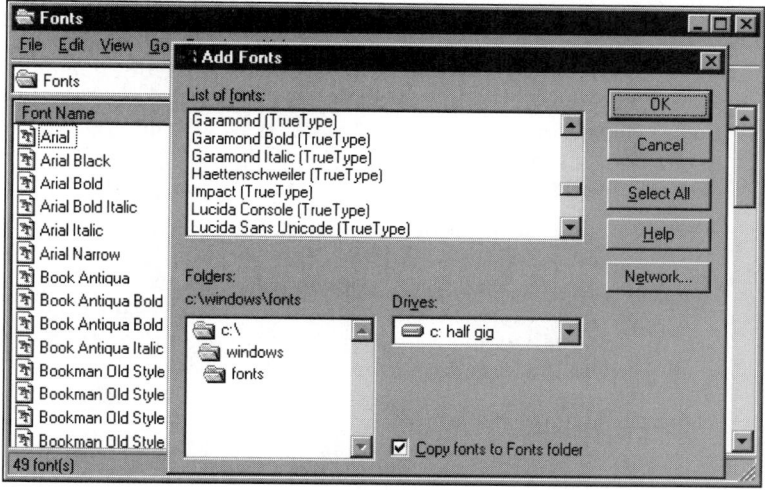

Figure 21-3: The Add Fonts dialog box

Step 3. The default action is to place a copy of the font file in the \Windows\Fonts folder. The "Copy fonts to Fonts folder" check-box is automatically marked every time you display the Add Fonts dialog box. If you copy the font to the \Windows\Fonts folder and it was previously stored in another folder on your hard disk, you might want to delete it from its original location. You probably wouldn't want to do this if it came from a network hard disk or from your original diskettes. Clear the "Copy fonts to Fonts folder" checkbox if you want to leave the font file where it is (on your hard disk or on a network server's hard disk) and just place a *shortcut* to it in your \Windows\Fonts folder.

Step 4. Use the Add Fonts dialog box to browse to find the location of the fonts that you want to install. Select the fonts that you will be installing from the list box and click OK.

If you cleared the "Copy fonts to Fonts folder" checkbox, you will notice that only shortcuts are added to the \Windows\Fonts folder.

You can also drag and drop fonts to install them. Copy a series of fonts from diskettes or CD-ROMs to your \My System\Fonts folder (or another folder you've created to store your fonts). Right-drag the fonts to \Windows\Fonts in your Explorer. Click Create Shortcut(s) Here. This method installs the fonts and makes them immediately visible to applications that use fonts, while leaving them in your own fonts folder.

Limits on the Number of Fonts Installed

There is a limit to the number of TrueType fonts you can install. The total number depends on the length of the font names, but it is about 1,000 fonts — fewer if the average length of the font names is greater than ten characters. This is because all font names are stored in the registry, and the maximum size of a registry key is 64K. Fonts that are installed somewhere other than the \Windows\Fonts folder have their full path shown in the registry, considerably increasing the length of their names.

There is no limit to the number of installed fonts you can use and print at one time.

As you install more fonts, your computer takes longer and longer to boot. Font management becomes a problem, and applications have to access unwieldy Font drop-down lists. If you have a large number of installed fonts, you should consider using more sophisticated font-management tools, such as those available as shareware on the Internet. (You should also read the section entitled "Font Cataloging" later in this chapter.)

Uninstalling Fonts

If you delete a font file that is stored in the \Windows\Fonts folder, it is both uninstalled (the font is no longer available to Windows applications) and deleted (the font file is moved to the Recycle Bin). If you delete a shortcut in the \Windows\Fonts folder for a font file that is stored in another folder, the font is uninstalled but the font file is not deleted.

To uninstall a font by deleting its font file stored in the \Windows\Fonts folder, click Start ➪ Settings ➪ Control Panel. Click the Fonts folder icon, right-click the font you want to uninstall, and select Delete from the context menu. If you have another copy of the font file stored in another folder, you can later reinstall it using the "Installing TrueType Fonts" steps in the "Installing Fonts" section earlier in the chapter.

To uninstall a font by deleting its shortcut in the \Windows\Fonts folder, highlight the font's shortcut and press Delete. Answer yes to the message asking if you want to uninstall the font. The original font file is not deleted, but the font is no longer available to be used by Windows applications and is not displayed in the \Windows\Fonts folder.

Viewing Fonts

You can see a sample "printout" of a font by double-clicking its icon in any folder window or in the \Windows\Fonts folder. Figure 21-4 shows what Arial Bold looks like.

Figure 21-4: Sample "printout" of the Arial Bold TrueType font. Double-click a font icon in a folder window to see what the font looks like at various point sizes.

Secret

A font's icon appears in the \Windows\Fonts folder if it is installed. If a font is not installed, you can still view it by opening the folder window where the font is stored and double-clicking its icon. You can produce the same "printout" by double-clicking a font file wherever it is stored.

Most text editing and word processing applications only list TrueType or printer fonts in their font lists. To keep these font lists manageable, you should install only the fonts that you use. You can use Windows 98's built-in font viewing capability to decide whether you want to install a particular font.

Tip

Numerous more sophisticated font viewers and font managers are available from other vendors.

Font Cataloging

If you use Windows TrueType fonts (and who among us doesn't?), the time eventually comes when you want to use a font other than Times Roman and Arial. And when that time comes, you want to look at your potential typefaces with something more powerful than the plaintext drop-down list of font names that you can display in most Windows applications.

There are dozens of freeware and shareware programs that will merely catalog and print the TrueType fonts that are installed in your \Windows\Fonts folder. The tricky part is to find programs that will do the same thing for fonts that you haven't installed into Windows yet.

A good program should be able to catalog fonts that are located anywhere on your hard drive, a network drive, or a CD-ROM. It's much more convenient to keep collections of fonts in a separate location and install them into Windows only as needed. For one thing, scrolling through a drop-down list containing the names of hundreds of typefaces is our least favorite way to choose a specific one for use in a document.

We have evaluated four shareware font-management packages for this task:

- FontFinder by Maverick Land & Cattle Co., http://radio.wustl.edu/~alan/fntfnd/fntfnd10.zip.

- FontFinder32 (no relation to FontFinder) by Sunshine Software, http://www.alliance.net/~fasttrax/sunshine/fontfinder.html.

- Printer's Apprentice by Lose Your Mind Development, http://www.igi.net/~btkinkel. (This program also requires Visual Basic 4.0 runtime files, available from http://www.igi.net/~btkinkel/zipfiles/vbrun4.zip.)

- TTFPlus by Watermark Software, http://www.wmsoftware.com.

- FontLister, at $5.00, is just the basic step up for the right price. It doesn't manage thousands of fonts, but if you have a hundred or two, it will help you manage them. You'll find FontLister at http://www.theill.com/fl/. You can register it online.

The winner, in our opinion, is a venerable standard: Printer's Apprentice. It's easily worth the $25 registration fee requested, and you get a 15-day free trial period during which it's fully functional.

An additional source of font-management utilities is QualiType Corp. Their FontHandler lets you view, preview, print, and manage both TrueType and Adobe Type 1 fonts, installing and uninstalling them individually or by special font groups. QualiType's Font Sentry utility can install fonts for you on the fly, as they are needed by programs or documents. It also gives you control over the font list in your application programs, and lets you access uninstalled fonts from within your applications.

While FontHandler and Font Sentry are not shareware, they are reasonably priced at $79 and $89 each, or bundled together with 150 TrueType fonts for $99. Free demos of these and other font utilities are available from QualiType's Web site at http://www.qualitype.com. (The QualiType Web site is worth visiting anyway, for its informative "Fonts 101" primer.)

All the Characters, All the Time

We've been looking for a tool like this for a long time, and were amazed to find ourselves unsuccessful. Perhaps you've found such a tool, and wonder what took us so long. Yes, we've wanted to find a font lister that shows *all* of the characters in a font. We want to see not just the Western character set, but all the characters in the Unicode fonts as well.

Microsoft has supported Unicode for a long time. They ship out plenty of fonts that use the Unicode character sets. So what's the problem?

With the help of Windows Office Watch (http://www.woodyswatch.com/office//), we finally had our wishes answered. We can now see the complete set of characters in the extended fonts, as shown in Figure 21-5.

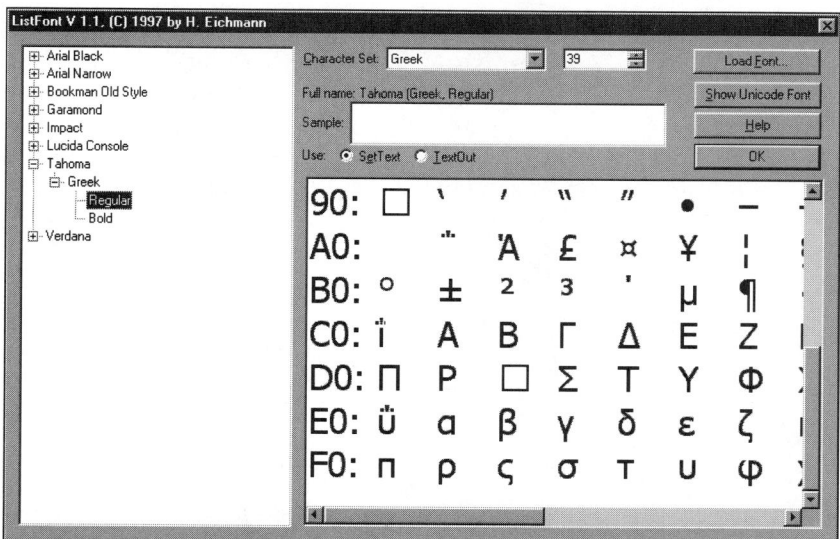

Figure 21-5: You can open up a font in the left pane, and pick a language and a style within it.

Choose a character set in the Character Set field in ListFont, and all of the fonts that you have installed that include that character set are displayed. Click the Show Unicode Font button to display a complete list of all characters in a given font.

You'll find Heiner Eichmann's freeware ListFont at `http://www.heiner-eichmann.de/software/listfont/listfont.htm`. It's very small and very fast.

There's a Euro in the Fonts

The fonts that come with Windows Me, Windows 98 (with Service Pack 1 or OEM Service Release 1), and Windows 2000 include the euro currency symbol in the 128th slot. If you have Windows NT, Windows 95, or the original Windows 95, you'll need to update your fonts to include the euro.

What does the symbol for the euro look like? As specified by the European Commission, it looks like a lower-case *e*, but with two horizontal bars similar to an equals sign, like this: .

You can download the original euro symbol file in Windows Metafile format at `http://europa.eu.int/euro/html/dossiers/00203/html/index-EN.html`. Click "Download of a vector image without constructions" to get the euro symbol discussed in the previous paragraph. If you have trouble opening this file, try starting a blank Word document and inserting the file by clicking Insert ⇨ Picture ⇨ From File, and entering the filename.

Microsoft has placed free, updated font files for Windows 95 users that contain the euro symbol on its "Fonts for the Web" page, at `http://www.microsoft.com/typography/fontpack/default.htm`. This page offers the "core fonts" — Arial, Times New Roman, and Courier New — as well as several sophisticated new free fonts that display well on Web pages, such as Georgia, Verdana, and Trebuchet. Windows Me and Windows 98 users will want to download these Web fonts, since they're free and well designed for both displays and printers.

Microsoft's type designers have made an excellent translation of the symbol into Arial. The symbol is slightly condensed from its original, circular design. This is desirable, because it allows the symbol to align with numerals in spreadsheet columns.

Microsoft's versions of the symbol in Times and Courier however, are pathetic. The horizontal lines are too light and will disappear at small point sizes. The euro in these two typefaces looks like an uppercase *C* with super-imposed faint lines. The result hardly resembles an *e* at all.

Details on Microsoft's euro symbol downloads — and a FAQ on application support for the euro symbol — are available at `http://www.microsoft.com/typography/faq/faq12.htm`. This page also contains numerous links to other free fonts, such as three free type families from Adobe.

Once you've installed the updates, users of U.S. keyboards can insert the euro character in their documents by typing Alt+0128. (Use Alt+0163 for pounds [£], and Alt+0165 for yen [¥].) Microsoft's FAQ describes several ways to insert a euro on most other countries' keyboards, usually RightAlt+e. Try it — impress your friends!

Completely ClearType?

As we write this, there is plenty of controversy about whether Microsoft has invented anything new with its ClearType font-rendering technology. Many font technophiles are claiming that the basic idea has been around since the start of the Apple II.

Our old buddy, Steve Gibson, is right in the thick of things. He's making very substantial claims that Microsoft has no right to patent this technology. You can check out his Web page on the topic at http://grc.com/cleartype.htm.

To get the other side of the story, consult Microsoft's ClearType Web page at http://www.microsoft.com/typography/cleartype/default.htm.

Sources of TrueType Fonts

When you're ready to move beyond the fonts that come with Windows, one of the best bargains in truly professional fonts is the Bitstream 500 Font CD-ROM for Windows. This collection is exactly what it sounds like: 500 different typefaces, most of them useful for normal business correspondence (as opposed to novelty, headline typefaces), in both TrueType and PostScript formats. The CD-ROM lists for $49.95. Contact Bitstream at 800-522-FONT or 617-497-6222, or online at http://www.bitstream.com/.

There are great font resources online. Check out http://www.fonthead. com/, and be sure to download GoodDogCool.ttf.

If you really want to go nuts with free fonts, you can keep yourself busy for a long, long while by perusing the sites listed at http://www.yahoo.com/ Arts/Design_Arts/Graphic_Design/Typography/Typefaces. This is Yahoo's index of Web sites with downloadable fonts or links to fonts.

An extensive source of information about fonts and typography is Norman Walsh's Frequently Asked Questions About Fonts (http://www.rzg.mpg. de/rzg/text/comp.fonts/cf_toc.htm). This comprehensive site includes lots of links to font publishers, discussions of font terminology, a history of typography, online sources for font software, and much, much more. If you find fonts at all interesting or puzzling, you should not miss this site.

Microsoft itself has put together a very useful resource on the subject of typography, with an emphasis on developing font technology and electronic publication. This is a good place to keep up with developments in the

OpenType initiative and font embedding, for example. You can also download free fonts designed for use on the Web, all with editable embedding (and some with installable embedding). You'll find the Microsoft Typography site at `http://www.microsoft.com/typography/web/embedding/weft/weft0.htm`.

Summary

▶ We show you how to use the font installer that is built into Windows to view both installed and uninstalled fonts, as well as to install and uninstall them.

▶ We examine some shareware programs that will let you view your fonts.

▶ We discuss where to obtain more free and low-cost fonts.

Chapter 22

Accessories

Text Editors

Chances are, you use a text editor more than any other application on your computer. It sure is nice to tweak such applications so that they work the way you want them to.

Open Word 97 and Word 2000 Documents in WordPad

The version of WordPad that comes with Windows Me and 98 has been upgraded to enable it to read Word 97 documents — and because Word 2000 uses the same format, WordPad can read its files also. (To find WordPad if you installed it with Windows, click Start ➪ Programs ➪ Accessories ➪ WordPad. If it's not installed, use the Windows Setup tab of the Add/Remove Programs control panel to install it from the Windows CD-ROM.)

WordPad doesn't necessarily read .doc files correctly if they use lots of Word's more esoteric features. But WordPad at least gives you a good chance of seeing the text in Word files, even if you don't have Word.

Tip

If you don't have Word and need to read Word documents, you can also download the latest Word reader from the Microsoft Web site at `http://www.microsoft.com/office`.

Thanks to Adam Vujic for pointing this out.

A Little Word Secret

We usually don't give out a lot of Word secrets, leaving that to other authors who concentrate on that particular piece of software. However, we received one secret from Galah Nuga, via Chris Pirillo at `http://www.lockergnome.com`, that we thought was too cool not to share.

Have you noticed that dragging the scroll box in the vertical scroll bar on the right side of your document in Word 97 doesn't actually scroll the document until you release your mouse button? Give it a try. Notice that this is not the behavior exhibited by Notepad, WordPad, or Word 2000.

Now the nice thing about dragging the scroll box is that Word 97 does display the page number that you have scrolled to if you are viewing a multipage document. Still, it would be nice to actually see the text as you scroll.

Secret

You can force the text to scroll as you drag the scroll box by making this change to your registry:

STEPS

Forcing the Scroll Bar in Word 97 to Scroll

Step 1. Click Start ➪ Run, type **regedit**, and press Enter.

Step 2. Navigate to HKEY_CURRENT_USER\ Software\ Microsoft\ Office\ 8.0\ Word\ Options.

Step 3. Right-click the right pane of your Registry Editor, click New ➪ String Value.

Step 4. Type the name **LiveScrolling** for the string value and press Enter.

Step 5. Double-click LiveScrolling. Type **1** in the Data Value field. Click OK. Exit the Registry Editor.

Step 6. Start up Word 97 and see if this works for you.

Make WordPad Write

WordPad has improved quite a bit since its initial release in Windows 95. It is now quite fast, and you can make it look very much like Microsoft's older Windows Write applet. WordPad can even save files with `wri` extensions in Write format. This last feature is important if you want to invoke WordPad instead of Word when you click a file.

You'll want to change some of the default settings for WordPad, and you can do this by creating a template file on which new documents will be based. We'll show you how to do this, also.

STEPS

A WordPad-to-Write Makeover

Step 1.   To make WordPad work more like the older Windows Write, click Start ➪ Programs ➪ Accessories ➪ WordPad. You'll see a program that looks a lot like a stripped-down version of Word, as shown in Figure 22-1.

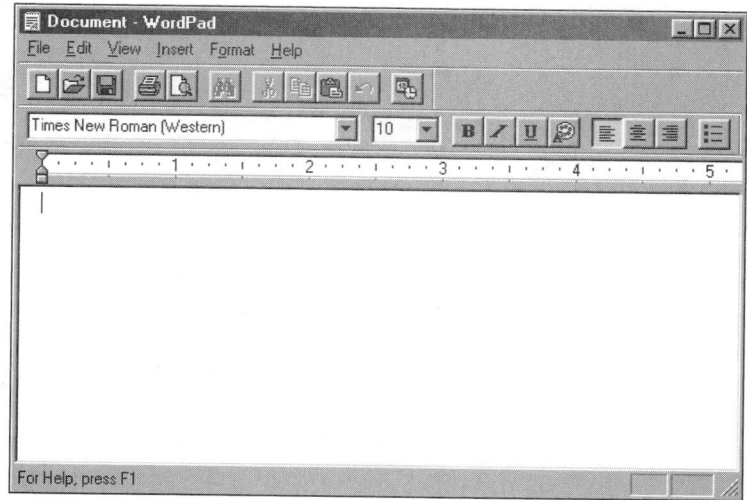

Figure 22-1: WordPad looks a lot like Word.

Step 2.   Click View, and clear the checkmarks next to Toolbar, Format Bar, and Ruler.

Continued

STEPS

A WordPad-to-Write Makeover *(continued)*

Step 3. Click View ➪ Options. Click the Word tab, clear the Toolbar, Format Bar, and Ruler checkboxes, and mark the "Wrap to window" option button. Take these same steps in the Write tab, and then click OK.

Step 4. Now, with WordPad looking pretty much like it does in Figure 22-2, choose File ➪ Save.

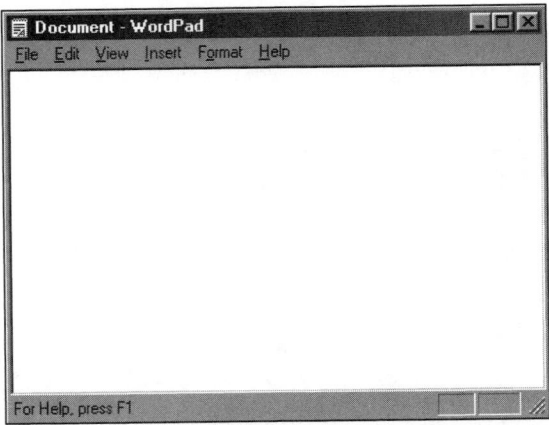

Figure 22-2: After your changes, WordPad should look more like Write.

Step 5. As you can see from Figure 22-3, WordPad will save the document in Word format by default. Click the Up One Level toolbar button a few times until Desktop appears in the "Save in" field (or simply display the "Save in" drop-down list and click Desktop).

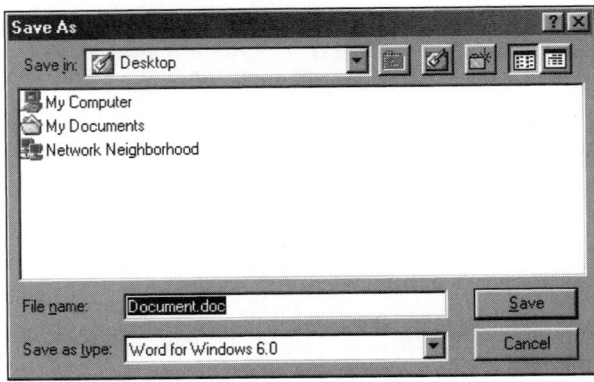

Figure 22-3: Save your document to the Desktop.

Step 6. In the "File name" field, replace the default filename Document. doc with the name WordPad.wri. Click the Save button.

Step 7. To exit WordPad, choose File ⇨ Exit.

Step 8. Click the TweakUI icon on your Desktop (assuming you put it there — if you haven't, click it in the Control Panel). Click the right arrow in the upper-right corner of the dialog box until the New tab appears. Click the New tab.

Step 9. Drag and drop the WordPad.wri icon from your Desktop to the middle of the TweakUI dialog box to add the Write Document file type to the New tab, as shown in Figure 22-4. You will now have a new item on your New menu. Click OK to close TweakUI.

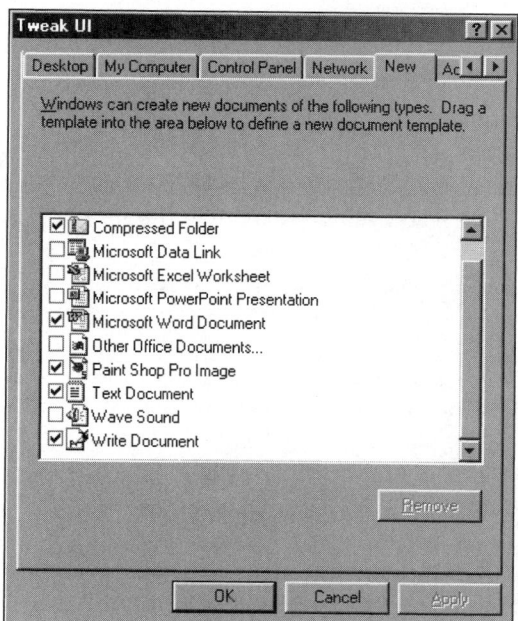

Figure 22-4: It's easy to put WordPad on your New menu.

Step 10. To create a new Write document that opens with WordPad, right-click your Desktop, click New, and then click Write Document. You can delete the WordPad.wri file from your Desktop, although you might want to use it in the next set of steps.

While these steps get you a blank WordPad document with the minimal settings for the Format bar, toolbar, and so on, they don't change the default font to something other than Times New Roman. To do this, you need to make a slight change in WordPad.wri (or to any other new file with a wri extension).

STEPS

Setting a New Default Font for WordPad

Step 1. Click WordPad.wri on your Desktop. Type a period in the blank document.

Step 2. Press the Home key, and then press Shift+End to highlight the period.

Step 3. Click Format ⇨ Font. Choose a font, font style, size, color, and script in the Font dialog box. Click OK.

Step 4. Choose File ⇨ Save and exit WordPad.

Step 5. Drag the newly edited WordPad.wri file to the New tab of TweakUI (see step 8 in the preceding set of steps if you need help getting there). You will be asked if you want to replace your existing file. Click Yes, and click OK.

Now when you right-click your Desktop, click New, choose Write Document, and then click the new Write Document.wri, WordPad's client area defaults to Times New Roman, but then gets the message that it should type a period using your selected font style, and so on.

You may find that the New menu says WRI Document and not Write Document. If this is the case, or if you click the new document that you just saved and WordPad doesn't open it, you can fix this problem. You can also use this next set of steps to create another file type that WordPad will open.

STEPS

New Document Types Associated with WordPad

Step 1. Click Start ⇨ Programs ⇨ Accessories ⇨ WordPad.

Step 2. Click File ⇨ Save As. Choose Text Document in the "Save as type" field. Give the file a new name with the extension that you want (perhaps wri). Navigate in the "Save in" field to the Desktop.

Step 3. Click the Save button. Click Yes if warned that you will lose any formatting when you save this file as a text document. Close WordPad.

Step 4. Right-click the new document on your Desktop. Click Rename and remove the txt extension if it is added. Press Enter.

Step 5. Shift+right-click the new document. Click "Open with," and scroll down to WordPad. Highlight WordPad and click OK.

You can make any other changes that you like in the File Types tab of the Folder Options dialog box. In your Explorer, click View ⇨ Folder Options, and click the File Types tab. Scroll down to your new file extension (or to wri). Highlight the file type and click the Edit button. You can change the description of the file type, and make other changes as well. We go into more depth about this in Chapter 12.

Use Fonts with Notepad

While it is quite hard to believe, Microsoft has updated Notepad (click Start ⇨ Programs ⇨ Accessories ⇨ Notepad) to be able to display and print its text using a font of your choosing. You wonder why they would modify this venerable and rickety plaintext editor, but there you have it. Perhaps they decided to make it easier for all of those users who had edited their registries to choose a new font for Notepad.

To set the default font for all documents, just click Edit ⇨ Set Font.

Thanks to Adam Vujic for pointing this out.

Replace Notepad

The easiest way to increase the power of Notepad is to replace it with Notepad+, written by Roger Muers. This program has been around since 1996, and it is still a winner. It includes a multiple document interface, bigger files, search and replace, and fonts. It uses the same filename as Notepad. exe, so rename Notepad.exe to something like NotepadOld.exe, then copy Muers' program into your C:\Windows folder.

You'll find Notepad+ at http://pcworld.com/fileworld/file_ description/0%2C1458%2C3953%2C00.html. If this site doesn't work, click the Search toolbar button in your Internet Explorer and look for npplus.zip. This file is available at a number of download sites.

Use Notepad as an Unformatter

Notepad just doesn't remember formatting (except its default font), so you can strip formatting out of a document by cutting and pasting it to Notepad first. Next, cut it out of the Notepad document and paste it into your target message or document. The formatting that your text had in the original document will be gone.

Thanks to Carmen Knowles for helping us with this tip.

MS Paint

MS Paint is pretty basic, but you can use it for a number of graphics file types that you wouldn't likely guess it could handle.

Convert Graphics Files with MS Paint

The Windows version of MS Paint (Start ➪ Programs ➪ Accessories ➪ Paint) has been upgraded to enable you to convert among `bmp`, `gif`, and `jpeg` file formats if you have Microsoft Office installed. Just open a `bmp`, `gif`, or `jpeg` graphics file, and click File ➪ Save As. Display the "Save as type" field (see Figure 22-5), and choose the desired file type.

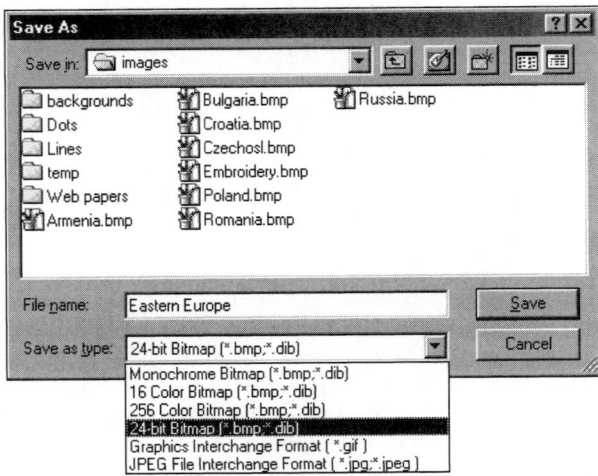

Figure 22-5: Use the "Save as type" field to choose a different file type for the document you're saving.

Thanks to Adam Vujic for this tip.

Icons from MS Paint

In Chapter 5, we show you how to use MS Paint to create your own icons. If you set the image size to 32 by 32 pixels and save the file as a bmp file, you're all set.

Secret

You don't have to give the file the bmp extension. You can give it the ico extension so that it can be recognized as an icon file. You can still drag and drop this file into MS Paint, or associate the ico extension with MS Paint, and Paint will have no trouble opening it.

PowerToys Work with Windows Me

Secret

Some of the Windows 95 PowerToys can be used with Windows Me and 98 to good effect. The most powerful toy, a new version of TweakUI, is found on your Windows Me and 98 CD-ROM at \tools\reskit\powertoy. It is an absolutely essential component for many Windows users.

The other PowerToys aren't on the Windows Me or Windows 98 CD-ROMs, but you can download them from http://www.microsoft.com/Windows95/downloads/contents/WUToys/W95PwrToysSet/Default.asp. A number of these utilities have been superceded — they were essentially incorporated into Windows 98 and continue to exist in Windows Me. Nevertheless, you may want to install the others. They come as a package, but once you extract them, you can install one at a time.

Send To X

Send To X adds a number of items to the Send To menu, as shown in Figure 22-6. These include Any Folder, Clipboard as Contents, Clipboard as Name, and Command Line. To get to this menu, right-click any file or folder and click Send To in the context menu.

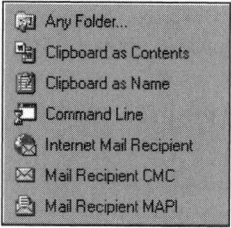

Figure 22-6: A Send To menu, with additional items courtesy of Send To X

The Send To ⇨ Any Folder item lets you build a history of folders. Clicking Any Folder displays the Other Folder dialog box (see Figure 22-7). To add items to the history, click the Browse button.

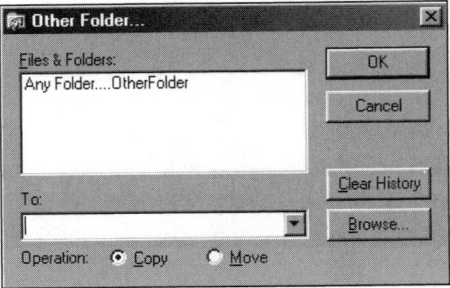

Figure 22-7: The Other Folder dialog box lists the previous folders to which you have copied or moved files, and lets you add more by browsing. In this example, there is no history yet.

Send To X also includes Mail Recipient CMC and Mail Recipient MAPI. You may already have a Send To, MAPI item, so you can delete this new one. They both work, although they use different DLLs. The Mail Recipient CMC command is supposed to send mail to an Exchange Server or other mail server that handles the Common Messaging Calls protocol. Unfortunately, this item adds a bug, which you'll probably want to fix.

Download the PowerToys executable and place it by itself in a temporary folder. When you click the executable file, it opens up a DOS window and extracts all the files that make up the PowerToys into the same folder. To install any of the PowerToys, right-click the associated `inf` file in the Explorer and click Install in the context menu.

Installing Send To X overwrites a registry entry that associates the Send To ⇨ Desktop (Create Shortcut) menu item with the DLL containing the function that actually does create a shortcut and place it on the Desktop. Instead, Send To X associates the Desktop (Create Shortcut) menu item with the `Sendtox.dll` file. You lose the ability to create shortcuts to items on the Desktop through the Send To menu. The icon for this item also changes to become a little yellow envelope.

Secret

Fortunately, you can get this functionality back after you install Send To X. All you have to do is merge a `reg` file called `Sendto Desktop shortcut.reg` into your registry. The Desktop (Create Shortcut) menu item will be back functioning correctly.

You can create this `reg` file yourself. Start a new text file and insert these commands into it (there should be four lines when you are finished — the `REGEDIT4` line, and the three lines each beginning with `[HKEY]`):

```
REGEDIT4
[HKEY_CLASSES_ROOT\CLSID\{9E56BE61-C50F-11CF-9A2C-00A0C90A90CE}]
@=""
[HKEY_CLASSES_ROOT\CLSID\{9E56BE61-C50F-11CF-9A2C-
00A0C90A90CE}\InProcServer32]
@="C:\\WINDOWS\\SYSTEM\\SENDMAIL.DLL"
```

```
"ThreadingModel"="Apartment"
[HKEY_CLASSES_ROOT\CLSID\{9E56BE61-C50F-11CF-9A2C-
00A0C90A90CE}\DefaultIcon]
@="C:\\WINDOWS\\explorer.exe,-103"
```

Rename the file to give it a `reg` extension, and then right-click it in the Explorer and click Merge.

The Desktop (Create Shortcut) icon will also change back to the Desktop icon, as shown in Figure 22-8. If it doesn't, click your TweakUI icon on your Desktop (or in the Control Panel), scroll the Repair tab into view, and click Repair Now.

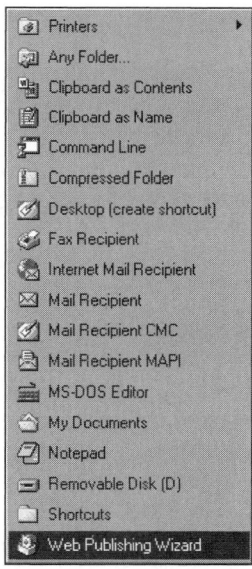

Figure 22-8: The Desktop (Create Shortcut) icon has been restored in this sample Send To menu. It is the seventh item from the top.

Unfortunately, you lose the functionality of the Mail Recipient CMC item. This functionality can be retrieved by associating the CMCSend extension with the `Sendtox.dll`. This associates the Mail Recipient CMC menu item with the functions in this dynamic link library.

Other PowerToys that Are Still Useful

Round Clock, DOS Prompt Here, Explore from Here, Shortcut Target Menu, Telephone Location Selector, and Fast Folder Contents all work in Windows Me and Windows 98 as they did in Windows 95.

PowerToys that Are No Longer Needed

DeskMenu is a system tray item that displays the icons on the Desktop as a menu when you click it. Of course, the Desktop toolbar in Windows Me/98 does the same thing. In addition, the Show Desktop button in the Quick Launch toolbar of Windows Me/98 clears the Desktop of windows (or redisplays them). Therefore, DeskMenu is not as necessary as it once was. However, you may still want to use it if you don't use the Quick Launch or Desktop toolbar.

Cabfile Viewer and QuickRes are now built into Windows Me and Windows 98, and X-Mouse is built into Windows Me and Windows 98's TweakUI.

Summary

There's life in these standard accessories, if you just put them to use—no need to download shareware alternatives and learn new programs.

▶ WordPad is actually a very useful editor, and is small enough to load quickly. It is flexible enough to take on different file formats, and you can set it up to work with a range of file extensions.

▶ You can create icons with MS Paint. Just save the files in `bmp` format, and then rename them with the `ico` extension.

▶ With Screen Rip32, you get a freeware screen capture program that adds to the capabilities built into Windows.

Chapter 23

System Tools

In This Chapter

Windows Me supports a larger number of system tools than the ones available with older versions of Windows, such as Windows 95. We show you how to make them easier to get to and how to work around a couple of problems.

▶ Put your System Configuration Utility on your Desktop

▶ Fix some problems that get in the way of using System Information Utility

▶ You'll want to know more about your computer than your System Information Utility tells you

Access System Configuration on the Desktop

Windows Me and Windows 98 come with a utility that lets you see what programs are loaded when you start up Windows. This utility also makes it easy for you to stop these programs from loading the next time you start Windows. You'll find the System Configuration Utility (Msconfig.exe) in your \Windows\System folder.

To get easy access to it, drag Msconfig.exe to your Desktop to create a shortcut to it. You can also find it by clicking Start ➪ Programs ➪ Accessories ➪ System Tools ➪ System Information, and then choosing Tools ➪ System Configuration Utility. Microsoft decided to put it in a galaxy far, far away, but we find it so useful that we've put a shortcut to it on our Desktop.

When you install new software, you'll often find that a new, related utility is loaded without your permission. The System Configuration Utility can help you find out what is loaded, and then you can decide whether or not you want that to happen.

Click your new System Configuration Utility shortcut, and then click the Startup tab to see what programs are loaded when Windows starts (see Figure 23-1). Clear the checkboxes next to any programs that you're sure you'd rather not start. You can also check out your Autoexec.bat and Config.sys files by clicking the tab related to each.

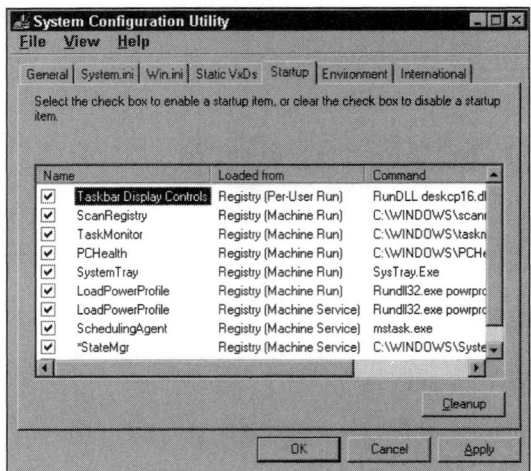

Figure 23-1: Look on the Startup tab to see and control what will be loaded at Startup.

While you're at it, you might as well drag some other useful programs onto the Desktop to create shortcuts to them. If you've installed the *Windows Resource Kit*, drag the Tools Management Console to the Desktop. One way to do this is as follows:

STEPS
Dragging the Tools Management Console to the Desktop

Step 1.   Click Start ⇨ Programs ⇨ Windows Resource Kit.

Step 2.   Right-click Tools Management Console, and click Create Shortcut. A shortcut appears in the Windows Resource Kit menu.

Step 3.   Drag the new shortcut onto the Desktop. Select it, press F2, and get rid of the (2) in the name.

You can also place the System Information Utility (`Msinfo32.exe`) and the System Tools folder on your Desktop. The Tools menu in the System Information Utility is a gateway to a bunch of other utilities, including Dr. Watson and Version Conflict Manager. One easy way to get access to all of these utilities is to put the System Information Utility on the Desktop.

STEPS

Putting the System Information Utility on the Desktop

Step 1. Click Start ➪ Programs ➪ Accessories ➪ System Tools.

Step 2. Right-click System Information. Click Copy.

Step 3. Right-click your Desktop. Click Paste Shortcut.

To put a shortcut to the System Tools folder on your Desktop, take these steps:

STEPS

Putting the System Tools Folder on the Desktop

Step 1. Click Start ➪ Programs ➪ Accessories.

Step 2. Right-click System Tools. Click Copy.

Step 3. Right-click your Desktop. Click Paste Shortcut.

You'll notice that the System Tools icon that you just created on your Desktop is a Start menu folder icon. It is a shortcut to the Start menu folder \Windows\ Start Menu\ Programs\ Accessories\ System Tools. This folder is a folder of shortcuts.

Use the Advanced Features of System Configuration Utility

The Advanced button of the System Configuration Utility provides access to a variety of troubleshooting settings that previously required detailed knowledge of System.ini or the registry.

Within the Advanced Troubleshooting Settings dialog box, shown in Figure 23-2, you can configure Windows to boot up in a variety of safe, safer, and safest modes to eliminate potential startup problems. For example, you can force Windows to start up in plain-vanilla 640 × 480 VGA mode or disable the automatic ScanDisk routine to avoid delays if you need to reboot frequently to test your system. You can limit the amount of memory available to Windows to test for faulty memory chips. You can also disable Windows' fast shutdown features to determine whether they conflict with your software.

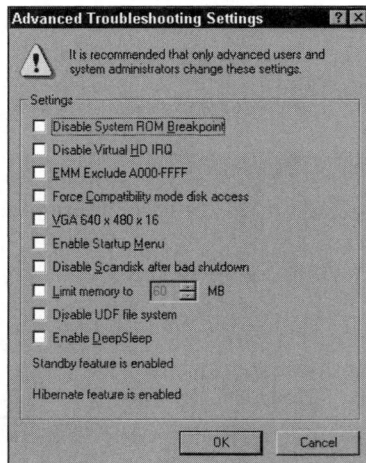

Figure 23-2: The Advanced Troubleshooting Settings dialog box of the System Configuration Utility

Unfortunately, the help available within the System Configuration Utility provides even less information about the Advanced options than you get by simply looking at the dialog box itself. We don't propose that you start changing the Advanced Troubleshooting Settings at random to see if they improve Windows. But if you manage several Windows computers — or even if you just have to keep your own computer working — knowledge of these options may be a lifesaver some day.

You can find Microsoft's explanation of the options in the Advanced Troubleshooting Settings dialog box at `http://support.microsoft.com/support/kb/articles/q181/9/66.asp`. This document explains the symptoms of problems you may experience with Windows and why you might change various settings to troubleshoot the situation. The page also links to descriptions of little-known `Win.com` and `Msdos.sys` options that let you start Windows in troubleshooting modes.

Disabled Startups

If you use the System Configuration Utility to clear some of the checkboxes next to the startup applets that you don't want to run on startup, you might want to know just how this bit of magic is achieved. Also, the list of unused startup applets can get pretty long if, like us, you install hundreds of pieces of shareware. If you're in this situation, you'll want to clean up this list.

Secret

You'll find part of the secret in the registry. The System Configuration Utility moves the calls to many of the startup applets to a new key whose name is the same as the old key, but now followed by a minus sign. The three keys are:

```
HKEY_CURRENT_USER\Software\Microsoft\Windows\CurrentVersion\Run-
HKEY_LOCAL_MACHINE\SOFTWARE\Microsoft\Windows\CurrentVersion\Run-
HKEY_LOCAL_MACHINE\SOFTWARE\Microsoft\Windows\CurrentVersion\RunServices-
```

If you compare the cleared boxes under the Startup tab in the System Configuration Utility with the variables stored under these keys in your registry, you'll find a number of your applets. You can clear out old startup calls to old applets by deleting their values in the registry. Right-click a variable name in the right pane of your Registry Editor while you are focused on one of these three keys and click Delete.

The rest of the startup applets are found in the \Windows\Start Menu\ Programs\StartUp folder. Usually, you'll just find shortcuts to startup applets here. You can use the System Configuration Utility to move these shortcuts to the Disable Startup Items menu folder.

You can delete from the Disabled Startup Items folder any items that you no longer want. You can also delete the complete Disabled Startup Items menu item if you like. You'll have to create your own startup menu shortcuts if you later restore some calls to startup applets.

Trouble with the System Information Utility

If you find that your System Information Utility (Start ⇨ Programs ⇨ Accessories ⇨ System Tools ⇨ System Information) is not providing much information, it may be because some driver is blocking it. Navigate to the System Information Utility, click Components in the left pane, click Multimedia, and click Sound Device. You may also want to click View ⇨ Advanced to adjust the level of detail that will appear in the right pane (see Figure 23-3). If you only get a date and time for the driver, you've got trouble.

If no information is displayed, then something is blocking your System Information Utility.

Secret

Ironically, it could be Microsoft's IntelliMouse software that's getting in the way. Here's how you can figure out what it is. Use the WinKill freeware utility or the Close Program dialog box (displayed by pressing Ctrl+Alt+Del) to kill any ongoing processes you think might be interfering with the System Information Utility. You'll find information about WinKill in "Quickly Kill Any Process or Application" in Chapter 16.

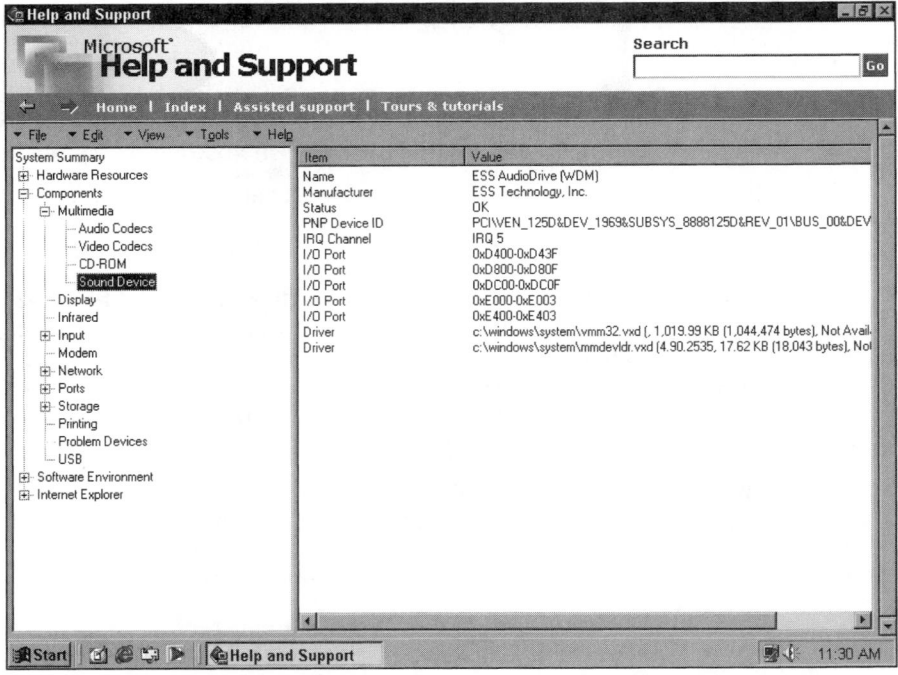

Figure 23-3: The System Information Utility shows detailed information on your PC.

If you are running an IntelliMouse, you can kill the Point32 process. Press Ctrl+Alt+Del, highlight Point32, and click End Task.

Now, close down and run the System Information Utility again. See if that solves the problem. If not, kill other processes, or stop other programs from running. You will want to keep Explorer and Systray running, but you can close down everything else. Keep checking to see what is getting in the way of the System Information Utility.

Thanks to Don Lebow for this secret.

Add to Your System Info

The Microsoft System Information Utility just doesn't quite do it when it comes to providing information about your computer. For example, try to get it to tell you how much video memory you have. You can improve on this utility with many others out there. One that we liked was InfoPro. The display information is shown in Figure 23-4. You can download this utility from `http://members.xoom.com/easternd/index.html`.

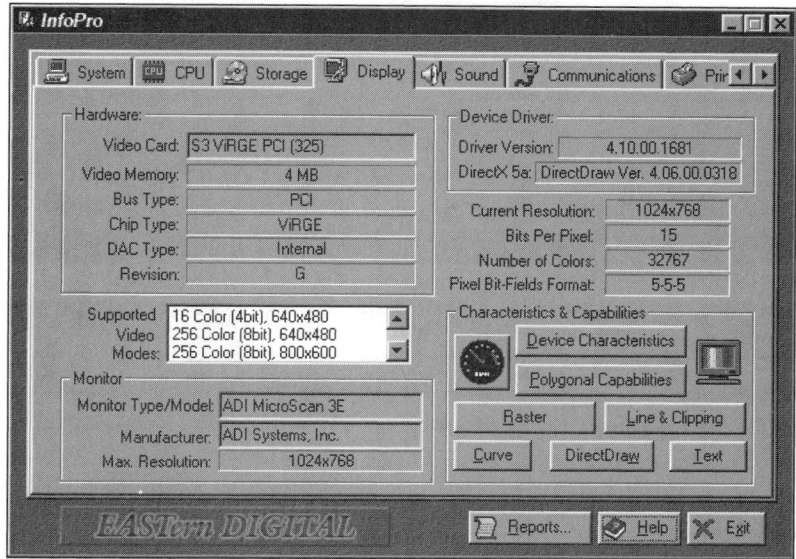

Figure 23-4: The Display tab in the InfoPro window

Another full-fledged utility that we couldn't quite make up our minds about was SiSoft's Sandra (see Figure 23-5). This is a very professional package from a programming outfit that definitely knows its way around Windows. The standard version is free, but it is really just a way to get you to buy the whole package. Nothing wrong with that, mind you, but it was always disappointing to click one of Sandra's icons only to be told that you needed to buy the professional package to get the capability behind the icon.

When the Basic version of Sandra is installed, it not only finds its way onto your Start menu and Desktop, but also into the Control Panel, and onto various context menus. Makes it pretty convenient to use; still, this program puts itself in more places than any other we've ever used. Perhaps there should be a switch that lets you tell it to be a little less aggressive.

There is a lot to like about Sandra. It provides detailed information about your hardware and software settings, in addition to a number of useful benchmarks that compare your computer against others. The authors include a plethora of useful hints, and the help is quite extensive. For example, the memory information module, shown in Figure 23-6, warns you if your swap file is too big.

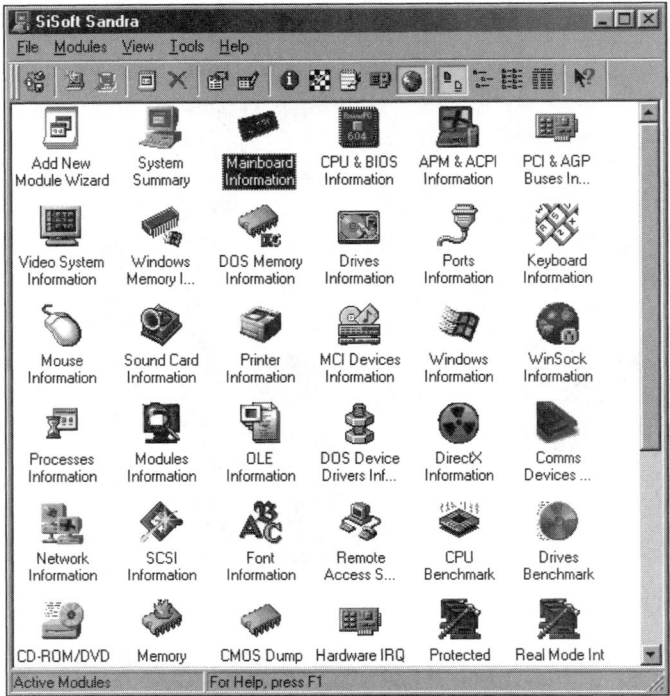

Figure 23-5: The Sandra user interface includes icons for features in both the Basic and the Professional versions.

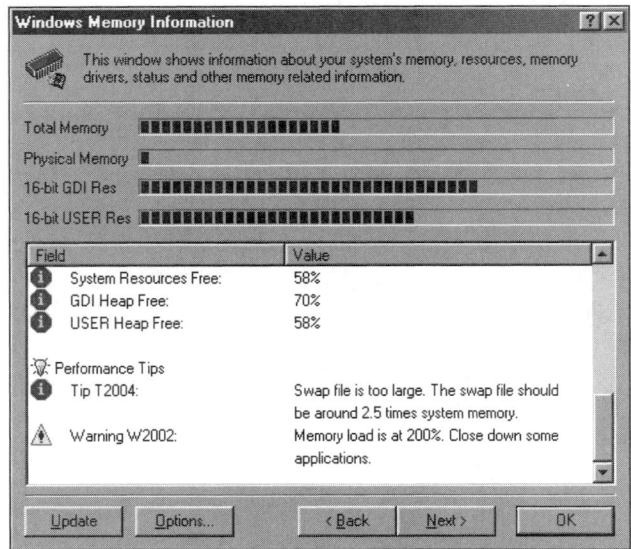

Figure 23-6: One of Sandra's Performance Tips tells us that the swap file is too large, while the yellow exclamation point warns us of memory overload.

One question we've had of all add-on system information utilities: Can they tell us which device is on which IDE controller? Sandra didn't answer that question (and none of the others we've checked have). So far, none of these utilities is perfect, but Sandra provides a lot of power, even at the cost of a bit of aggravation.

You'll find Sandra at `http://www.sisoftware.demon.co.uk/sandra`.

Undo Your Policy Mistakes

Don't our political leaders wish they had this option? While they don't, you do. If you chose the option "Only run allowed Windows applications," and then forgot to place all your applications on the list of allowed applications, you'll want to go into the Policy Editor and add to the list. Oops. What if you forgot to put the Policy Editor on the list of allowed applications?

You've got a couple of options. If you have multiple user profiles, and you haven't set this option for everyone or for Default User, log in as one of the users that isn't restricted and reset the option.

If you set this option for Default User, you can also restart your computer, hold down the Ctrl key during the power-on self-test, and choose Safe mode when the Windows Startup menu comes up. When the Safe-Mode Desktop is displayed, click Start ⇨ Run, type **poledit**, and press Enter. You can then change this option.

Secret

If you happen to have put the Registry Editor on the allowed applications list, you can navigate in your registry to HKEY_CURRENT_USER\ Software\ Microsoft\ Windows\ CurrentVersion\ Policies\ Explorer. You can then delete the Explorer key to get rid of all your policies, and then start again.

If you can get to the User Profiles tab in the Passwords Properties dialog box in your Control Panel, mark "All users of this computer use the same preferences and desktop settings" and click OK. Then restart your computer, run the Policy Editor (Start ⇨ Programs ⇨ Accessories ⇨ System Tools ⇨ Policy Editor), and change the setting for allowed applications. You'll have to go back to your Passwords Properties dialog box, mark "Users can customize their preferences and desktop settings," and click OK.

The *Windows Resource Kit* has other options. Search for Only Run Allowed.

Stealing Text from Dialog Boxes

If you happen to be writing a book about Windows or doing beta testing for Microsoft Internet Explorer, there will be plenty of times when you'll want to do a screen capture to take a "photo" of the latest error message. SnagIt is the screen capture program that we used for *Windows Me Millennium Edition Secrets*, and it is slick and easy to work with. SnagIt can also often capture the text displayed on your screen; you just have to set it for text capture, as shown in Figure 23-7.

Figure 23-7: Click the Text Capture button to switch capture modes. SnagIt maintains separate settings for each mode.

In some cases (with the text in the Internet Explorer About dialog box, for example) SnagIt cannot capture text, and you're left wondering what to do. Kleptomania is a powerful text capture package that uses OCR technology, as well as a constructed database of your installed fonts, to capture text on your screen and place it on the Clipboard as text. You can then paste the text into any text editor. This is yet another way to print out a directory listing, for example.

You'll find SnagIt at http://www.techsmith.com. Kleptomania is available at http://www.structurise.com/kleptomania.

Summary

The system tools do help out some, and if you add a couple more, things get even better. You can't ever have too much control over your system.

▶ Use the advanced features of the System Configuration Utility.

▶ Keep the Critical Update Notification at bay.

▶ Fix your Policy Editor mistakes.

Chapter 24

Fun

In This Chapter

Here's where we put all the stuff that didn't fit anywhere else, but then it turned out that this stuff was pretty cool. We can't always be serious, so we thought we'd let you in on some neat things we've found.

▶ Metric versus English, and all sorts of other conversions

▶ Print your own graph paper

▶ Keep track of the weather without going to the weather channel

▶ Not creative? Download these answering machine greetings

Unit Conversion

Until we found Convert, we had not been impressed with the many unit conversion programs available as shareware or freeware. They've all been way too weak, with silly front ends. Convert converted us.

Convert has an extensive array of unit conversion ratios and can convert just about anything, as you can tell from Figure 24-1. As long as we live in the worst of all possible worlds (that is, one in which there are two widely used measurement systems), Convert is an absolute necessity.

Convert is freeware, and you'll find the latest version at http://www.joshmadison.com/software.

Lo and behold, we did find another conversion program that we liked, not that its shareware nag screens were all that pleasant. Tek Converter II uses a cute version of the Explorer interface to let you choose the units that you'll convert between. Just drag and drop each unit from the right pane of the Tek Explorer down to the boxes at the bottom of the window, as shown in Figure 24-2.

While its interface was, well, cute, what we really liked was the fact that you can add any conversion units that you like and group them in any manner that makes sense to you. You can also get rid of conversion units that you would never use.

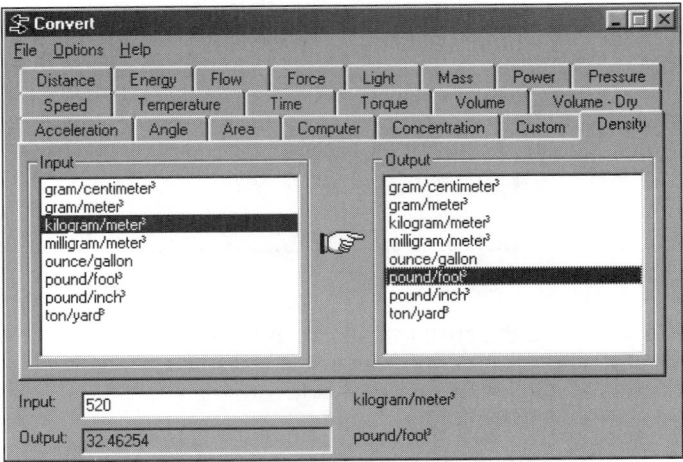

Figure 24-1: Conversion from metric to English units of density using Convert

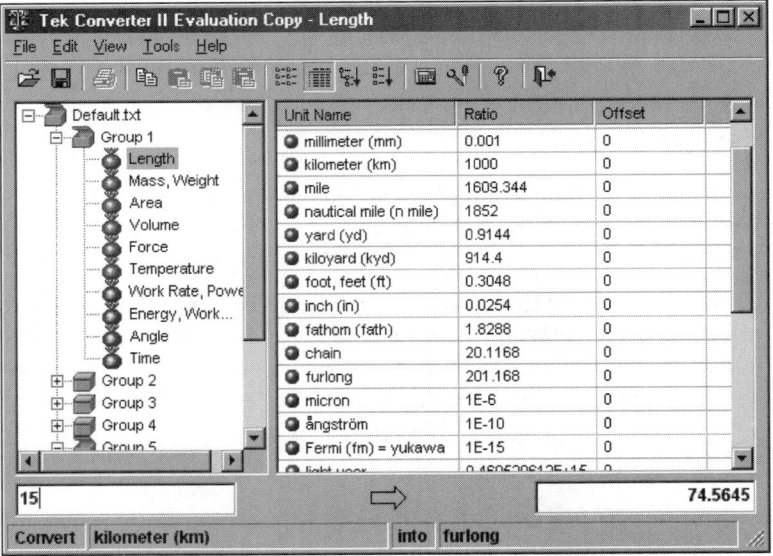

Figure 24-2: The Explorer-like interface of Tek Converter

Tek Converter II is shareware, but there is a freeware version available at the same site. You'll find it at `http://village.infoweb.ne.jp/~tek/index.htm`.

Calculator with Paper Tape and Unit Conversions

There are plenty of shareware calculators available on the Web. If you are looking for something special, you should conduct a search and check out a number of different ones.

You might take a look at the CDML Advanced Calculator, shown in Figure 24-3. It has three nice features: a paper tape, a financial calculator, and a unit converter. This is not a scientific calculator, but it does calculate net present value, annuity payments, double-declining balance depreciation, and other financial functions.

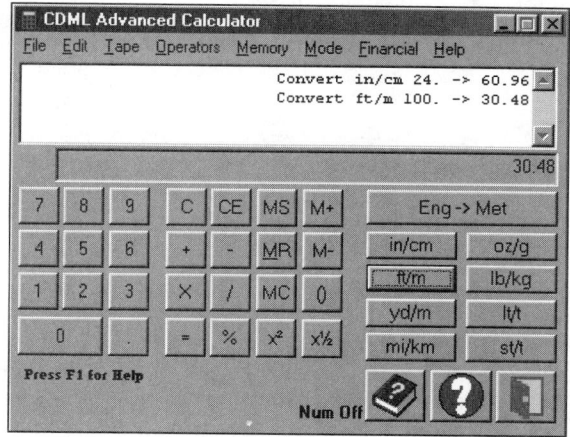

Figure 24-3: The CDML Advanced Calculator offers lots of functions and a "paper tape."

You'll find it at `http://www.cdml.com/`.

Print Graph Paper

You can't keep every type of graph paper on hand. Graph Paper Printer prints a sheet (or more) of graph paper for you, based on your settings. How about log paper with 16 sets, as shown in Figure 24-4? Or just a linear one-millimeter scale on the abscissa and the ordinate? Perhaps a polar graph? You get to choose a scale that is linear, logarithmic, quadratic, or gaussian.

All of these types of graph paper, and many more, are available in this freeware package. You'll find it at `http://perso.easynet.fr/~philimar`.

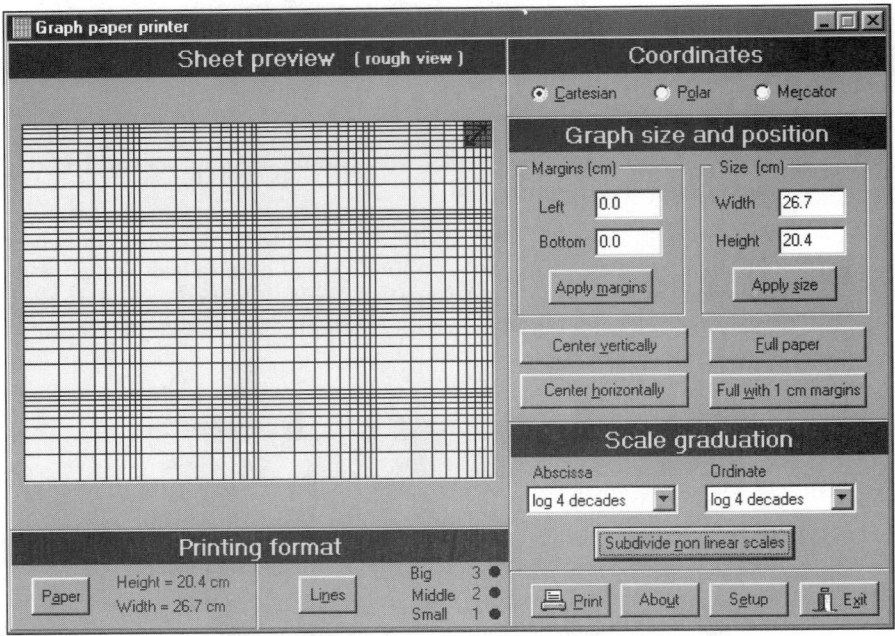

Figure 24-4: Graph Paper Printer lets you print more kinds of graph paper than you might have known existed.

The program consists of one executable file, and its installation doesn't add any DLLs to your System folder. Uninstalling Graph Paper Printer consists of deleting the program, its folder, and any shortcuts to it that you may have created.

Know What's Going on Outside

While you're pressing your nose to the computer screen, it might be nice to know what is going on outside, and maybe what will be happening over the next few hours or days. While it is not exactly a Windows secret, Cli-Mate is a handy little piece of shareware that sits in your system tray and periodically goes out on the Internet and updates itself with the latest weather.

You can choose which weather server to use. It shows current conditions (see Figure 24-5), and you can click it to display the NOAA forecast and the extended forecast. It can keep track of multiple cities as well as the radar. It doesn't provide everything that some of us weather fanatics want, but for painless weather data gathering (without having to open your browser), it works great.

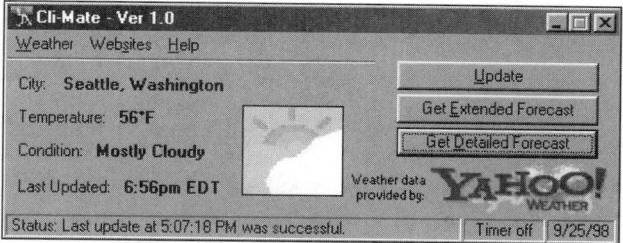

Figure 24-5: Double-click Cli-Mate in your system tray to see an updated overview of the weather. You can choose your preferred weather server.

You'll find it at http://users.nac.net/splat/climate/index.htm.

You can also get the weather e-mailed to you. You get an HTML-formatted e-mail message every morning (and afternoon, if you like) with a basic three-day forecast. Click one of the links and get detailed current conditions, a five-day forecast, and radar and satellite images. The server is much quicker than other weather sites. Bob Kaplan told Chris Pirillo about this site: http://www.weather24.com.

Look Back at Earth

While there is an endless variety of themes available on the Internet, this one is especially cool, as you can see from Figure 24-6.

Figure 24-6: A Desktop view of the Earth View theme

You can find the Earth View theme at `http://www.digitaldaze.com/steves-web/`.

Download an Answering Machine Greeting

Another of the endless possibilities of the Web. You can go to The Answering Machine Web site (see Figure 24-7) and download any of their long list of answering machine greetings. Courteous or not, that's up to you.

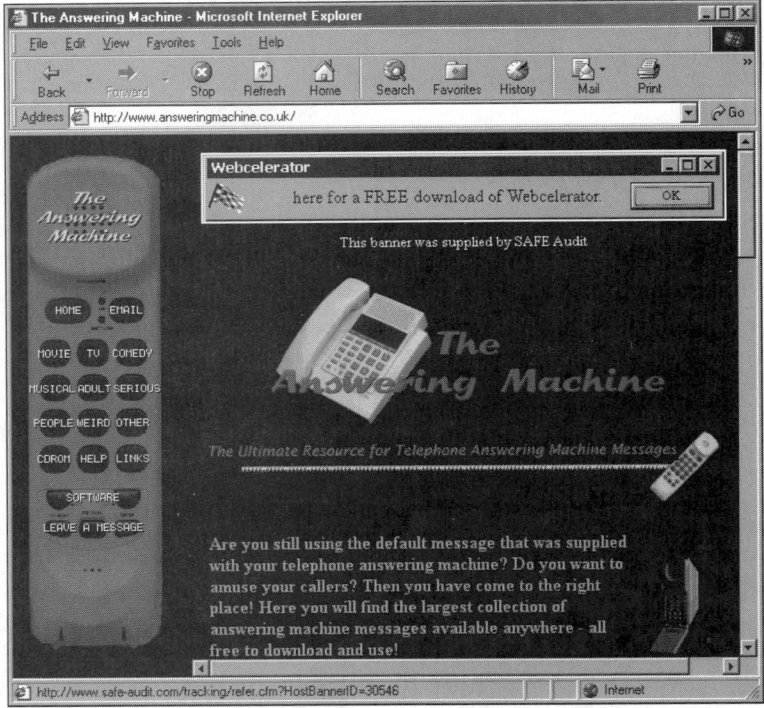

Figure 24-7: The Answering Machine Web site

The files come in the `wav` format. You can play them into your answering machine or use them on your computer-based voice mail system.

You'll find The Answering Machine at `http://www.answeringmachine.co.uk`.

Buy Low

How about a little comparison shopping made easy? If you know what you want, you can find it cheap on the Web. It's always nice to have a little Web page front end to do that dirty work for you, too. One place to check out, and there are many, is Bottom Dollar. You'll find it at `http://www.bottom dollar.com`.

There are other sites, such as `http://www.pricewatch.com`. Because of its wealth of online supporting articles, I like Ziff-Davis' Computer Shopper at `http://www.zdnet.com/computershopper/index1.html`. You'll want to go there if you need to figure out what you want to buy. One other really inexpensive place to buy computer equipment on the Web is `http://www.buycomp.com`.

The Home of Freeware

Programming is fun, or at least it can be. Software authors like to get their programs out there so that others can use them and recognize the authors for their technical brilliance. Let's see, any other good reasons for the availability of freeware?

There is a huge amount of freeware that can be downloaded from the Web, and many sites supply it in addition to shareware. While we've covered a number of freeware and shareware products, we could never even come close to covering them all.

You'll find the Freeware Home, obviously a site that specializes in freeware (and makes its income from advertising), at `http://www.freewarehome.com`.

Easter Eggs, Anyone?

"Easter Eggs" are secret lists of the names of the programmers who developed Windows or a Windows application. For some reason, Easter Eggs aren't usually available through a choice on the Help menu. They require a secret key combination or set of steps, and you have to seek them out. No, they don't go bad, even though some of them are a bit old. Rather than print them all here (more are discovered every week), we're recommending the best Web site we know of that documents them. To get the latest, turn to the Easter Egg Archive at `http://www.eeggs.com/`.

Summary

We show you where to look on the Web for fun stuff.

▶ Freeware in one place.

▶ Easter Eggs, for those who want to know.

▶ The Web is a reference source if you can find the right sources.

Part III

Internet Secrets

Chapter 25

Connecting to the Internet

In This Chapter

Want to get on the Internet? We show you how to do it using the tools built into Windows Me. Windows comes with a TCP/IP stack and a dialer to connect your computer to an Internet service provider (ISP).

▶ Getting the right kind of account (PPP, SLIP, or TIA) from your ISP

▶ Asking your service provider for the right information about your account

▶ Setting up Dial-Up Networking (DUN) to make the connection to your service provider

▶ Getting your TCP/IP stack and your Dial-Up Adapter to work together

▶ Connecting to your service provider

▶ Verifying that you've got a good connection

Your First Point of Internet Attachment

There are two fundamentally different ways to gain access to the Internet from your computer — retail and wholesale. You can call through the analog modem, cable modem, or DSL router connecting your computer to a local or national Internet service provider. Or you can communicate over your local area network (LAN) to a server that is connected by a phone line to an ISP. The connection can vary from a dial-up 28.8-Kbps service to a fast, dedicated leased T1 line.

Service providers that offer call-in modem access to the general public are a relatively new phenomenon. Before 1994, most Internet users accessed it through UNIX workstations on a college campus or on the job at defense contractors. They didn't have to worry about how to get access. The system administrator took care of those details. Once the rest of us were allowed to join the party, *we* became the system administrators for our own computers.

CompuServe, America Online, Prodigy, and other early online services have turned themselves into Internet service providers (although not completely) while maintaining some or all of their online services. These national online services have offered connections to Internet mail (although not connections to Internet mail POP3 and SMTP servers) since 1993, and in 1997 they began providing almost full Internet access, like their ISP competitors.

When Microsoft offered MSN with Windows 95 in 1995, it also purchased partial interest in a nationwide service provider named UUNET. MSN provides a connection to Internet mail (but it didn't install a direct connection to POP3 and SMTP Internet e-mail servers until late in 1997). And it provided full access to Internet newsgroups with an NNTP news server (although it didn't provide access to Internet news servers outside of MSN until early 1997). As a nationwide service provider, MSN provides dial-up access that supports both the Internet TCP/IP protocol and the MSN networking protocol.

Tip

If you use an analog modem, you should look for a service provider that has enough phone lines so you won't get a busy signal too often. The Internet works best at the highest speed you can afford. If the service provider has 56-Kbps modems and so do you, great. Some service providers are very small and may not have adequate technical support to keep their lines up and functioning. Move on to another one if this is the case.

Some service providers let you connect with DSL through the local telco. See if your telephone company will install a DSL line to your home or business. If so, they will also provide the hardware necessary to connect your computer, and soon you'll be ready to really cruise the Internet.

Microsoft's TCP/IP Stack

Windows comes with tools that allow you to access the Internet either over a modem or through a network. At the lowest level, Microsoft provides a TCP/IP stack. TCP/IP (Transfer Control Protocol/Internet Protocol) is the Internet protocol (or language). It can be spoken over your modem, network card, or through Windows' Direct Cable Connection (see Chapter 17 for more on DCC).

You can associate (bind) the TCP/IP stack to your Dial-Up Adapter and/or your network card. If you bind it to your Dial-Up Adapter, you can use Windows' Dial-Up Networking to call your service provider and connect to the Internet using TCP/IP. If you install Dial-Up Networking under Windows, TCP/IP is bound automatically to your Dial-Up Adapter.

If you bind the TCP/IP stack to your network card, and your network is connected to a UNIX server or Windows 2000/NT server, or to a Windows Me/9x computer, you can communicate with that server using Internet (or Internet-related) applications compatible with Winsock. The server can provide the gateway to the Internet. (The Windows Me/9xcomputer requires a third-party program to act as a gateway to the Internet for other computers on a LAN.)

If you use the TCP/IP protocol on your local area network, your network becomes an intranet. (An *intranet* is a local area network that uses Internet standards.) If you do this, you can configure Windows Me, Windows 98, Windows 95, Windows 2000/NT, NetWare, and, of course, UNIX servers as Web servers and POP3 and SMTP e-mail servers.

Installing an Internet Dial-Up Connection

To gain Internet access through your modem, you need to carry out the following tasks:

- Install and configure your modem

- Sign up for an Internet account with your service provider or online service

- Obtain from the service provider the information you need to successfully connect your computer to their computer

- Install Dial-Up Networking on your Windows computer

- Check to see that the Windows TCP/IP stack is bound to the Dial-Up Adapter (your modem).

- Define and configure a Dial-Up Networking connection for your service provider.

- Configure the TCP/IP settings specific to your service provider using the information they provide.

- Write a connection script if your ISP doesn't provide PPP with CHAP or PAP.

Windows Me includes the Internet Connection Wizard, which can help you create a dial-up connection to your ISP. We discuss how to use this wizard a little later in this chapter.

Installing and Configuring Your Modem

We discuss how to install and configure your modem in "Configuring Your Modem" in Chapter 44. The Windows Setup program's hardware detection routines may already have correctly identified your modem and installed the appropriate driver for it. Even if you installed your modem after you installed Windows, similar hardware-detection routines may have correctly detected it and installed the right driver.

To check if your modem has been detected, click the Modems icon in your Control Panel to display the Modems Properties dialog box. If your modem has been detected, it will be listed in the General tab of the dialog box. You can also click the Dialing Properties button to review or edit the properties that characterize your calling location. If your modem driver isn't yet installed, you can do so at this point by clicking the Add button.

An Internet Service Provider Account

To connect to the Internet, you need an account with an ISP. Service providers give you access to the Internet through their computers, which are connected to fast, dedicated telephone lines. The service provider maintains a bundle of dial-in phone lines attached to racks of modems, which are in turn attached to the service provider's computer(s).

Tip

If you are opening a new account, you should obtain a PPP (Point-to-Point Protocol) account from the service provider. If you already have a different type of account, you should change it to a PPP account. In addition, you should find a service provider that provides either PAP (Password Authentication Protocol) or CHAP (Challenge-Handshake Authentication Protocol), if possible. If your account supports PAP or CHAP, you don't have to type your logon name and password after you connect to the service provider. If your PPP account doesn't have one of these types of authentication, you have to either type your logon name and password each time you connect or create a script file (using a scripting utility that comes with Windows) that enters this information for you.

When you connect to the Internet, your computer is assigned an IP address to identify it to other computers. Most ISPs assign IP addresses dynamically — that is, at logon time. In some cases, you can obtain a static IP address. If you have a SLIP (Serial Line/Internet Protocol) account instead of a PPP account, and you have a dynamically assigned IP address, your SLIP script will need to capture the dynamically assigned IP address and send it back to the service provider.

Some service providers don't offer PPP or SLIP accounts directly, but require that you first connect to a shell account, and then send a message once you're online to switch to a PPP or SLIP connection. A *shell account* is the most basic account type available from a service provider. It treats your expensive computer as a dumb terminal and requires that you run UNIX software on the service provider's computer to do anything on the Internet. You can use your script to send a command to switch from the shell to SLIP or PPP.

Most Internet service providers today have already upgraded to all the standards we recommend here. But it doesn't hurt for you to know about these standards, so you're able to discuss them intelligently when you're setting up a new ISP account.

Tip

If you just want to maintain a low-level shell account, you can use Hyper-Terminal to call into your service provider. HyperTerminal doesn't come with scripting to automate the logon process, but it will still work fine as a tool for connecting to a UNIX computer.

Tip

Your service provider may offer a TIA (The Internet Adapter) account, which allows you to switch to a SLIP-type account after you log on in your shell account. The Windows 98 scripting utility works with TIA accounts to switch to SLIP.

Service Provider Account Information

The first step, of course, is to find a service provider. If you live in a metropolitan area, you should be able to find at computer stores a free local computer newspaper that lists service providers.

A local service provider will have a local number and perhaps an 800 number. A national service provider will provide local numbers, an 800 number, or a number in the closest town. You can find ads for national service providers in national computer magazines or in national newspapers such as the *New York Times* (especially the Tuesday "Science Times" section). If you have access to a friend's Internet account, you can check out online databases of service providers such as `http://www.thelist.com` to find ISPs in your area. Go to their home pages and check them out. You should be able to sign up with a service provider online by filling out a sign-up form on their Web site.

You need some specific information from your service provider. The staff at local service providers much prefer to talk to other people (sometimes known as customers) by way of their computers. This can be quite difficult when you don't have an e-mail account (which is one of the reasons that you're trying to contact the service provider to begin with). If you already have an e-mail account with a national online service such as AOL or CompuServe, you can use that account to send e-mail to a local service provider, assuming you can find their e-mail address.

You can always just call an ISP on a voice line, but it is often difficult to reach anyone. You can fax them your questions, and hope that they fax you back the answers. This poor "out-of-the-box" experience with some service providers has been a major bottleneck in their growth. Many are very small companies run by one or two technically minded people; no glad-handing sales types are allowed. On the other hand, ISPs are independent businesses with a self-interest in serving their local customers, so some do indeed make every effort to give you the assistance you need.

The major online services and MSN are attempting to simplify the process of getting online. Microsoft is very smart to make it so easy to connect to MSN (although some would say it is unfairly using its monopoly position).

You need the following information from your service provider to configure your Windows TCP/IP stack:

- Dial-in phone number you'll use to connect to the service provider's modems

- Account type

- If it is a SLIP account, whether it is compressed SLIP (CSLIP) or not

- If it is a PPP account, whether it has either PAP or CHAP

- If it is a PPP account without PAP or CHAP, whether it supports software compression and encrypted passwords

- User name (or *logon name*), for example, something like *billsmith* or *nancyf*

- Password

- Your host name (which can be the same as your user name)

    You can think of your host name as your computer's name, or as your name on the Internet. It will be appended to the service provider's domain name to become your address on the Internet.

Since this will become your address, you should tell the service provider what you want as a host name, and see if they can swing it without any conflicts.

- The service provider's domain name (for example, `netters.com`)

  Your Internet address will be a combination of your host name and the service provider's domain name, as in `billsmith.netters.com`. Your e-mail address will be `billsmith@netters.com`. You can have as many different e-mail addresses on the Internet as you have accounts.

- Domain Name System (DNS) server's IP (Internet Protocol) address

  DNS servers translate (from a lookup table) the somewhat user-friendly domain names into the underlying IP addresses (for example, 207.182. 15.50). Get the IP address of the DNS server that you'll be automatically accessing when you use your service provider's services. Your service provider may automatically assign the IP address of the DNS server, in which case you won't have to get this address.

  You can also register your own domain name and have it translated by a DNS server. You'll need to set up a Web server (or rent a spot on a virtual server at an ISP) to take advantage of the name. The address for your Web site will be something like `www.yourname.com`, and people will be able to send you e-mail at `yourname@yourname.com`. Talk to your service provider about registration and costs.

In most cases, your service provider will assign a different IP address to your computer every time you log on. When other people use your Internet address to contact your computer, your service provider will automatically translate your Internet address into this dynamic IP address.

It can be quite useful to have a fixed IP address. It's almost like having your own domain name. Also, if you have a fixed IP address, you can publish Web pages from your own Windows computer, using Personal Web Server. People will be able to access your pages when you're connected to your service provider over your modem or router.

Of course, the Internet routers won't have a way of finding your computer by looking for a domain name such as `www.yourcomputer.com` (instead of your fixed IP address) if you haven't registered one. And if you aren't online pretty much all the time, putting a Web site on your own computer, while technically feasible, wouldn't be that useful. It's a better idea to put your Web site on the service provider's computers because they are online 24 hours a day, they have a fast connection to the Internet, and you won't be bothered with people connecting to your computer while you're using it.

Windows includes the Personal Web Server, which allows you to publish HTML pages and make them available to others on your local area network or over the Internet. If you want to publish them over the Internet, you'll have to establish an Internet connection. (See "Connecting to a Personal Web Server" in Chapter 19.)

The above information is all you need to be able to connect to your service provider. To be able to access e-mail and newsgroups, you'll need the following information:

- Your e-mail address (most likely the combination of your host name and the service provider's domain name)
- POP3 mail server's address
- SMTP mail server's address
- News server's address
- Mail gateway's address (needed only for some mail readers)

Your service provider should have no problem giving you this information (assuming you can actually talk to someone). In fact, many service providers have all of the information compiled into one document, which they can fax or mail to you. Alternatively, if you have access to a computer connected to the Internet, they can send it in an e-mail message or you can download it from their Web site.

Some ISPs will tell you that you have to use their custom software to configure your connection and access the Internet. This is absolutely not the case. We strongly suggest that you do not use the software provided by the Internet service provider, but instead use the capabilities built into Windows, as described in this chapter. Politely and firmly tell the ISP that you don't need their software, you just need the pieces of information listed in this section. Sooner or later, you will find someone who is willing to give you the information that you need.

The Internet Connection Wizard

The Internet Connection Wizard can help you set up an account with an Internet service provider. And for select providers, it can actually set you up with an account automatically. As you step through the wizard, it asks you a series of questions. You can find all of the information you need to answer these questions by reading the relevant topics in this chapter.

Microsoft allows other ISPs a place in a folder called Online Services on the Desktop in exchange for their commitment to promoting Internet Explorer as their preferred Internet user interface. You can sign up automatically for AOL, AT&T World Net, Prodigy, or CompuServe, as well as MSN.

The Internet Connection Wizard will also call into Microsoft's Internet Referral Server and download the latest information about ISPs that offer service in the area defined by your area code and the first three numbers in your phone number. This list is limited to those service providers who have agreements with Microsoft to provide Internet Explorer as their preferred browser.

If you want to sign up with another national or local ISP, you have to manually provide to the Internet Connection Wizard the information that the wizard supplies automatically for the favored service providers. In addition, if you connect to your service provider using a SLIP account, you may have to manually edit a script file.

We give you all the information that you need to create a connectoid to your service provider either manually or by using the Internet Connection Wizard in this chapter and in "Setting Up Your Computer at Home As a Guest" in Chapter 19.

The Internet Connection Wizard automatically starts the first time you run Internet Explorer. If you want to run it again, you'll find it in your Start menu, under Programs ⇨ Internet Explorer ⇨ Connection Wizard. The executable file for the Internet Connection Wizard is `icwconn1.exe`, and it's stored in the `\Program Files\Internet Explorer\Connection Wizard` folder. You can also right-click the Internet Explorer icon on your Desktop, click Properties, click the Connection tab, and then click the Connect button.

Dial-Up Networking

If you installed Direct Cable Connection (DCC) during Windows Setup, Dial-Up Networking (DUN) is already installed. You may also have chosen to install DUN if you ran a Custom setup.

To find out if DUN is installed, click the Start button, point to Settings, and then click Control Panel. Click the Network icon in the Control Panel and see whether Dial-Up Adapter is listed in the Configuration tab of your Network dialog box.

If it isn't, you can install DUN by taking these steps:

STEPS

Installing Dial-Up Networking

Step 1.   Click the Start button, point to Settings, and then click Control Panel.

Step 2.   Click the Add/Remove Programs icon. Click the Windows Setup tab.

Step 3.   Highlight Communications, and then click the Details button.

Step 4.   Mark the Dial-Up Networking checkbox, and click the OK button in the Communications dialog box.

Step 5.   Click the OK button in the Add/Remove Programs Properties dialog box. You may be asked to insert your Windows CD-ROM. DUN is now installed.

Bind TCP/IP to Your Dial-Up Adapter

Adding Dial-Up Networking to your Windows configuration may not add the TCP/IP stack to the list of protocols bound to the Dial-Up Adapter. This is especially true if you are installing Windows Me over a Windows 95 configuration that doesn't include TCP/IP. If you don't find TCP/IP listed in the Configuration tab of your Network dialog box, take the following steps:

STEPS

Binding Your TCP/IP Stack to Dial-Up Adapter

Step 1. Click Start ➪ Settings ➪ Control Panel.

Step 2. Click the Network icon. Click the Add button.

Step 3. Highlight Protocol in the Select Network Component Type dialog box and click the Add button.

Step 4. In the Select Network Protocol dialog box, highlight Microsoft in the Manufacturers list, and highlight TCP/IP in the Network Protocols list. Click the OK button.

Step 5. Click OK in the Network dialog box. You may be asked to insert your Windows CD-ROM.

You now have a TCP/IP stack and a dialer, both of which will be encompassed in your DUN connectoid. After you configure your connectoid for your service provider account, you will be able to make an Internet connection. The default TCP/IP settings are described in the next section.

You can choose which networking protocols work with a given DUN connectoid, so there is no need to uninstall them or unbind them from the Dial-Up Adapter.

Configuring the TCP/IP Stack

These are the default settings for the TCP/IP stack:

- Obtain an IP address automatically
- Use DHCP for WINS resolution
- No gateways
- NetBIOS over TCP/IP
- Disable DNS

You shouldn't change these settings if you are going to connect to the Internet only through a dial-up ISP and you don't use TCP/IP on a local area network. You should set the TCP/IP settings that are specific to your service provider when you create a DUN connectoid, as shown in the "Dial-Up Connection to Your Service Provider" section later in this chapter.

You might need to change the TCP/IP settings if you connect to a LAN using the TCP/IP protocol bound to a network card. If you have a LAN network adapter and a Dial-Up Adapter displayed in the Configuration tab of your Network dialog box along with the TCP/IP protocol, you will see separate entries for TCP/IP -> LAN and TCP/IP -> Dial-Up Adapter. This makes it appear as though there are two separately configurable TCP/IP stacks. Not so.

In spite of the fact that the Network dialog box shows two different TCP/IP components, setting values in the TCP/IP -> LAN card component sets those same values in the TCP/IP -> Dial-Up Adapter component. If you try to set the TCP/IP values in the TCP/IP -> Dial-Up Adapter component, you will be warned that you should set these values in the DUN connectoid. You won't get a similar warning if you try to set the TCP/IP values in the TCP/IP -> LAN card component, although you should.

For instructions on setting up TCP/IP for your network adapter, turn to "Configuring the TCP/IP Stack for a Network Adapter" later in this chapter.

If you have both a LAN TCP/IP connection and a DUN TCP/IP connection, you need to make other provisions to deal correctly with routing. Turn to "Setting Up Your Own Routes" later in the chapter.

Multiple TCP/IP Settings for Multiple Connections

You can provide different TCP/IP settings for different connections if you have multiple Internet service providers.

These are the only TCP/IP settings that can be specific to a given connection to an ISP:

- Your IP address (fixed or dynamically assigned)
- IP address for DNS or WINS server (fixed or dynamically assigned)
- Use IP header compression or not
- Use default gateway at Internet service provider or not

Follow the steps in the next section to set these TCP/IP settings for each of your connections.

Dial-Up Connection to Your Service Provider

Now that you have installed DUN and bound the TCP/IP stack to the Dial-Up Adapter, you are ready to create a DUN connection (a connectoid) that will call your service provider and establish the connection to your account. To do this, take the following steps:

STEPS

Creating a Service Provider Connection

Step 1.   Click Start ⇨ Programs ⇨ Accessories ⇨ Communications ⇨ Dial-Up Networking. (You can place a shortcut to DUN on your Desktop or in any other folder if you like. For details on creating and using shortcuts, see "Creating Shortcuts" in Chapter 10.)

Step 2.   Click the Make New Connection icon in the Dial-Up Networking folder window. Enter the name of your service provider in the first dialog box of the Make New Connection Wizard. If you want to change the modem-specific characteristics for this connection, click the Configure button to display the Properties dialog box for the selected modem, make the desired changes, and click OK. Click the Next button, and enter the phone number your modem will dial to connect to the ISP. Click Next again, and then click Finish.

Step 3.   Right-click the new connectoid in the DUN folder window. Click Properties to display the Properties dialog box for your connection to this service provider.

Step 4.   Click the Security tab, as shown in Figure 25-1.

You don't need to mark the "Log on to network" checkbox in a connectoid for an ISP unless you are logging onto a Windows network over the Internet. Otherwise, it just slows things down.

If you mark the "Require encrypted password" checkbox, your computer sends an encrypted password directly to your server provider's computer. The ISP has to be able to decode the password before you can connect, and your password doesn't go out on the Net (where passwords can be stolen).

"Require encrypted password" only works with PPP. Many service providers can't deal with encrypted passwords, so check with yours before you mark this checkbox.

Continued

STEPS

Creating a Service Provider Connection *(continued)*

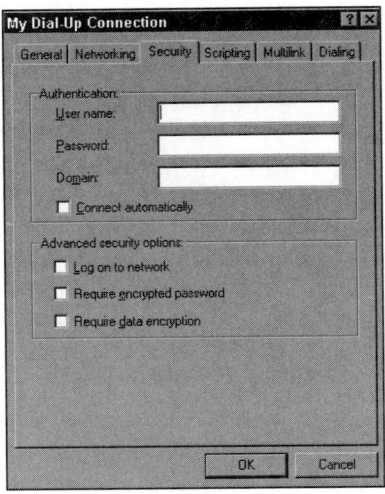

Figure 25-1: The Security tab of the Properties dialog box for your connection to the service provider

Step 5.   Click the Networking tab and choose the server type (from the Type of Dial-Up Server drop-down list at the top of the dialog box) that describes your account. If you have a SLIP account, you need to select either "CSLIP: Unix connection with IP header compression" or "SLIP: Unix connection," depending on which type of SLIP account you have.

Checking "Enable software compression" tells your connection software to negotiate compression with the remote computer. If your modem already handles hardware compression, then you don't really want to do this. Your modem may have already negotiated hardware compression with the server's modem (most do), so adding software compression slows things down.

Step 6.   Clear the NetBEUI and IPX/SPX Compatible checkboxes under "Allowed network protocols." You only need TCP/IP to connect with your service provider, and clearing these boxes will speed things up a bit at connect time.

If you choose SLIP or CSLIP, these checkboxes will be grayed out. You only use the TCP/IP protocol to communicate to a UNIX server.

Step 7. Click the TCP/IP Settings button to set the specific TCP/IP settings for this connection. The values that you enter in the TCP/IP Settings dialog box (see Figure 25-2) are those that you received from your ISP.

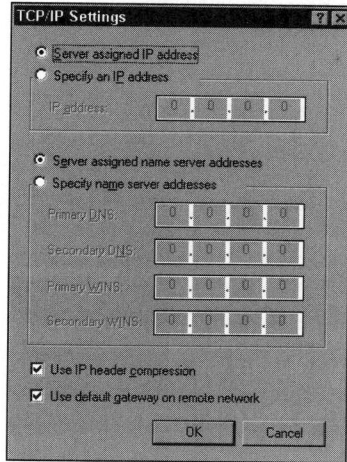

Figure 25-2: The TCP/IP Settings dialog box. These settings are specific to this connection to an individual ISP.

Step 8. If your computer's IP address is fixed, mark the "Specify an IP address" option button, and then type your IP address in the "IP address" field. If your IP address is dynamically assigned, mark the "Server assigned IP address" option button. (If you have a TIA account, your IP address will be fixed. If you have a PPP account, it will be dynamically assigned. If you have a SLIP account, it could be either fixed or dynamically assigned.)

Step 9. If your service provider gave you one or more IP addresses for their DNS or WINS server(s), mark the "Specify name server addresses" option button, and enter the IP addresses in the four fields in the middle of the dialog box. If your service provider dynamically assigns the IP addresses of their servers, mark the "Server assigned name server addresses" option button.

Step 10. If you have a TIA account, clear the "Use IP header compression" checkbox. Click OK in the TCP/IP Settings dialog box. Click OK again in the Properties dialog box.

Step 11. Click the Configure button in the General tab of the Properties dialog box for your service provider. This brings up the Properties dialog box associated with your modem and this connection. Click the Options tab, as shown in Figure 25-3.

Continued

STEPS

Creating a Service Provider Connection *(continued)*

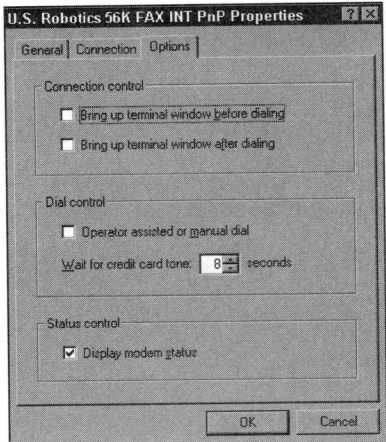

Figure 25-3: The Options tab of the Properties dialog box for your modem and connection

Step 12. If your service provider requires that you manually log in before you start your session, you will need to check "Bring up terminal window after dialing." This will be the case if you have a SLIP account or a PPP account without PAP or CHAP and you are not using the scripting utility.

If you are going to use the scripting utility, you normally want to leave this checkbox cleared because the scripting utility doesn't need the terminal window opened by this setting. However, when you are opening a new account at a service provider that requires a manual log on, you might want to mark this checkbox temporarily. That way, you can make sure that the commands that you enter are correct before you try using the script that you have edited to contain these commands.

Step 13. Make any other changes you think are necessary in the Properties dialog box associated with the modem and this connection. Then click the OK button, and click OK again to close the Properties dialog box for the service provider connection.

You are now ready to connect to your service provider. If you have a SLIP account or a PPP account without PAP or CHAP and you want to automate the connection with the scripting utility, you still have a little bit of work to do. See the section entitled "Automating Your DUN Logon" later in this chapter.

Saving Your DUN Connectoid Passwords

You may find that the "Save password" checkbox is grayed out when you click a DUN connectoid. This means that you can't save your password for this service provider connection, so you have to type your password every time you call them up. This can be quite irritating.

There are four possible causes for this problem:

1. You haven't installed either Client for Microsoft Networks or Client for NetWare Networks.

2. Your Windows startup is configured to ask you for a password (to identify you to the computer), and you clicked Cancel or pressed the Escape key when the logon box was displayed.

3. You have a corrupted password file.

4. You haven't enabled share-level access.

The cure to the first problem is easy. Install one of the above-named clients using the Network icon in your Control Panel. (Click the Network icon, and click the Add button. In the "Select network component type" dialog box, highlight Client, and click the Add button. In the Select Network Client dialog box, highlight Microsoft on the left side of the dialog box, highlight Client for Microsoft Networks or Client for NetWare Networks on the right, click OK, and then click OK again.)

Regarding the second problem, Windows won't save your DUN passwords unless it knows who you are. If you log on with a Cancel, it won't save your passwords. You should log on as yourself — that is, type a user name in the logon box — then press Enter.

The solution to the third problem is more complicated. If you think your password file is corrupted, rename the pwl files in your \Windows folder, and then shut down and restart Windows. You will have to build your list of passwords from scratch. As an example of the type of problem that can cause this, the earliest version of the Windows 95 Service Pack 1 corrupted password files. You can also check Don Lebow's Generic DUN Password Saving Advice Web page at http://www.maui.net/~dml/dunpass.html for the latest approach to the problem.

To fix the fourth problem, click the Network icon in the Control Panel, click the Access Control tab, and mark the "Share-level access control" option button.

Calling Your Service Provider

Now that you have created a connection to your service provider, you are ready to make the connection.

STEPS

Connecting to Your Service Provider

Step 1. Click the new connectoid in your DUN folder window. The Connect To dialog box appears on your Desktop, as shown in Figure 25-4. If you like, you can make this dialog box disappear by choosing Connections ⇨ Settings in the Dial-Up Networking folder window and clearing the "Prompt for information before dialing" checkbox.

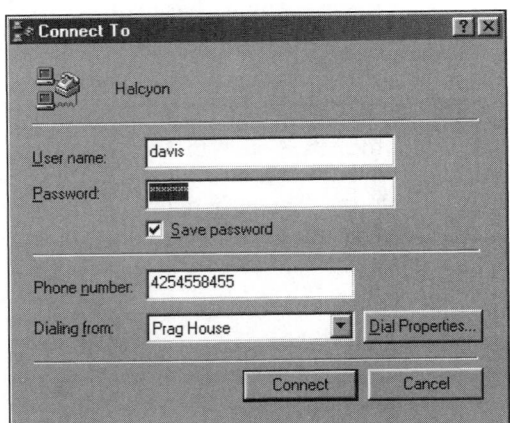

Figure 25-4: The Connect To dialog box. You don't need to use the "User name" and Password fields unless you have a PPP account with PAP or CHAP. Click the Connect button to have the modem start dialing up your service provider.

Step 2. Enter your logon name and password and click the "Save password" checkbox if you would rather not type your password every time. User names and passwords are case sensitive. Be sure you type them correctly.

Step 3. Click the Connect button to direct your modem to dial into your service provider and make a connection. Once the connection is made, you are on the Internet and ready to run Winsock-compatible Internet applications. If your account requires that you manually log in, a terminal window will be displayed first, as shown in Figure 25-5.

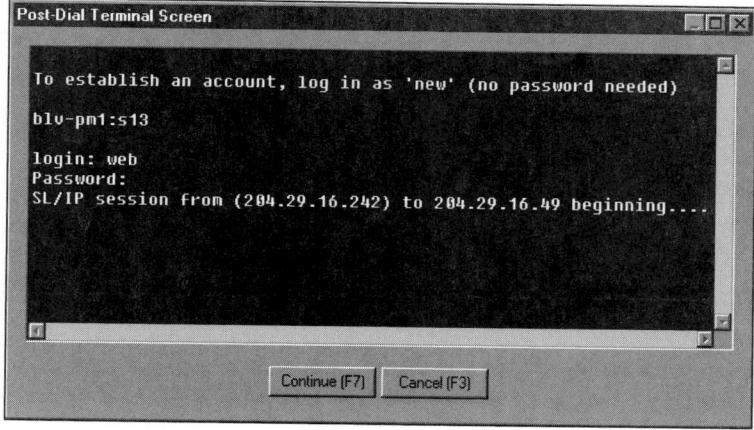

Figure 25-5: The Post-Dial Terminal Screen. Type **PPP** or **SLIP** and press Enter if your service provider requires that you first specify your account type. Type your logon name and password when prompted. If you have a SLIP account, wait for your dynamically assigned IP address to be displayed and write it down so that you can remember it for a few seconds.

Step 4. If you need to specify your account type to your service provider, type **PPP** or **SLIP** and press Enter. When prompted by your service provider's computer, type your logon name and password. Again, your logon name and password are case sensitive. If you have a TIA account, you will log on first and then type **TIA** at the shell prompt.

Step 5. If you have a SLIP account with dynamically assigned IP addresses, your IP address will appear. Write it down; you will need it in the next step, and this terminal window is going to disappear. Click the Continue button or press F7.

(If you configured your TCP/IP stack for a fixed IP address that matches the first two or three numbers of your dynamically assigned one, you will only have to worry about typing the last number or two in the next step.)

Step 6. If you have a SLIP account, the dialog box shown in Figure 25-6 will be displayed after step 5 to let you enter your IP address. Make sure you type your IP address exactly as it was displayed in the terminal window. If you get it wrong, your Winsock-compatible Internet applications will not work.

Continued

STEPS

Connecting to Your Service Provider *(continued)*

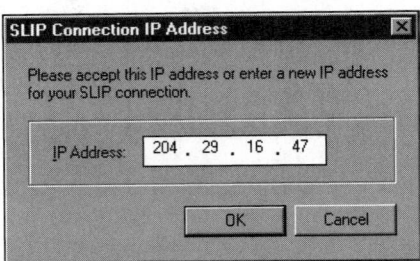

Figure 25-6: The SLIP Connection IP Address dialog box. Type your dynamically assigned IP address exactly as displayed in your terminal window.

Step 7.   If you have a TIA account, you will see the dialog box shown in Figure 25-6. If you earlier specified a fixed IP address in the TCP/IP Settings dialog box, this address will be displayed here. You need to change this IP address if you were prompted to do so after you typed **TIA** in the terminal window.

If you are using the scripting utility, you can omit steps 4 through 7.

If you are using Outlook Express, you can make the connection with your service provider just by clicking the Outlook Express icon on your Desktop.

You can configure Microsoft Internet Explorer, Netscape Navigator, Microsoft Outlook Express, NetMeeting, and other Internet-specific applications to automatically call your service provider by invoking your DUN connectoid. To do this, click the Internet Options icon in the Control Panel, and click the Connection tab in the Internet Properties dialog box. Highlight a specific Internet connection, click "Dial whenever a network connection is not present," and then click OK twice.

Notice in step 3 above that you had to click the Connect button. Once you have everything set up, you can eliminate this box altogether. In the Dial-Up Networking folder window, choose Connections ⇨ Settings to display the General tab of the Dial-Up Networking dialog box and clear the "Prompt for information before dialing" checkbox.

Automating Your DUN Logon

The Windows scripting facility can run a script that you create for a specific connection. This script can send your logon name, password, and account type. It can also capture a dynamically assigned IP address and send it back to your ISP.

To edit a script, right-click a DUN connectoid, click Properties, click the Scripting tab, and then browse to find the script file. Sample script files are stored in your `\Program Files\Accessories` folder. You can edit a copy of one of these script files (they have an extension of `scp`) to meet the requirements of your ISP. Just click the Edit button in the Scripting tab after you have chosen a script file.

Secret

Notice that Microsoft doesn't use the `scr` extension for its script files, as everyone else in the world does. This is because it already uses this extension for its screen saver files. Windows creates an association with the `scr` extension and the screen saver tester. Click a script file with an `scr` extension, and Windows will try to play it as a screen saver. (In "Creating and Editing File Types and Actions" in Chapter 12, we show you how to solve this problem for any script file you have that ends in `scr`.)

Making Sure You Have a Good Connection

It's easy to check out your DUN connection to your service provider (just click its DUN connectoid). If you are having connection problems, you can try a few things in the Server Types tab of its Properties dialog box (right-click the connectoid and click Properties). Make sure you have the correct account type specified in the drop-down list, disable software compression, and, if you have a SLIP account, switch from CSLIP to SLIP or vice versa.

You can also try using the `ping` command. `Ping` sends out a request to see if a certain computer at a given address is indeed there. After you have dialed up your service provider, open a Windows DOS session. Type **ping 198.105.232.1.** This is the IP address for `ftp.microsoft.com` (the FTP server at Microsoft). If `ping` works, your TCP/IP stack and connection to the Internet is working. Note, though, that since IP addresses can and do change, this IP address may no longer be valid when you try it. As an alternative, you may want to `ping` your DNS server — if you know the correct IP address, that is. Your ISP can provide you with the IP address for one of their servers, if necessary.

Tip

You can also use `ping` to test your DNS server connection. To do this, try to ping to an IP address, and then `ping` the name that goes with that IP address. For example, type **ping 198.105.232.1** and, if that works, type **ping ftp.microsoft.com.** If both pings work, you know that you are correctly connected to a DNS server.

If the first case works but the second doesn't, then your DNS is set up wrong. If the first fails, either you are not talking to the network or the network doesn't know who you are.

Creating a Connection Log File

You can generate a log file that will record the progress of your attempt to connect to your service provider. This file can help pinpoint problems. To generate a log file, take the following steps:

STEPS

Creating a Connection Log File

Step 1. Click the Start button, point to Settings, and then click Control Panel.

Step 2. Click the Network icon, highlight Dial-Up Adapter, and click the Properties button.

Step 3. Click the Advanced tab, highlight "Record a log file" in the Property list, and choose Yes in the Value field.

Step 4. Click OK in both the Dial-Up Adapter Properties dialog box and the Network dialog box.

Step 5. Click your connectoid in the Dial-Up Networking folder window.

A file named Ppplog.txt will be created in your \Windows folder when you take step 5. You can review this file after you attempt to make your connection. Place a shortcut to this file on your Desktop so that you can get to it easily.

Disabling IP Header Compression

If you have a PPP account, you might experience connection problems that you can cure by disabling IP header compression. To do this, take the following steps:

STEPS

Disabling IP Header Compression

Step 1. Click Start ⇨ Settings ⇨ Control Panel.

Step 2. Click the Network icon, highlight Dial-Up Adapter, and click the Properties button.

Step 3. Highlight "Use IP header compression" in the Property list. Choose No in the Value field.

Step 4. Click both OK buttons.

Other Problems with DUN TCP/IP Connections

You may receive the error message, "Dial-Up Networking cannot negotiate a compatible set of protocols..." Michael Santovec, a regular contributor to the Microsoft Windows newsgroups, created this list of possible causes for the problem and recommended actions:

1. Your Internet service provider may be experiencing temporary problems. You should try again later.

2. Some ISPs can't handle software compression. Right-click your connectoid in the Dial-Up Networking folder window. Click Properties, click the Server Types tab, and clear the "Enable software compression" checkbox.

3. Make sure that your connectoid only uses TCP/IP to connect to your ISP. Right-click your connectoid in the Dial-Up Networking folder window. Click Properties, click the Server Types tab, and make sure that only the TCP/IP checkbox is marked under "Allowed network protocols,"

4. Make sure that your modem uses hardware flow control rather than software flow control. Right-click your connectoid in the Dial-Up Networking folder window, click Properties, and then click the Configure button in the General tab. Click the Connection tab, click the Advanced button, and mark the Hardware (RTS/CTS) option button.

5. If you have an external modem and don't have a 16550 UART chip in the COM port that the modem connects to, then you should not use FIFO. (This doesn't apply to internal modems, since they have the 16550 UART built in.) Also, if you do have a 16550 UART and have FIFO enabled, adjusting the buffer sizes may help. To disable FIFO or adjust the buffer sizes, right-click your connectoid in the Dial-Up Networking folder window, click Properties, and then click the Configure button in the General tab. Click the Connection tab, and then click the Port Settings button. In the Advanced Port Settings dialog box, clear the checkbox to disable FIFO, or drag the sliders to adjust the buffers.

Check out Michael's Windows help Web site at `http://pages.prodigy.net/ michael_santovec/techhelp.htm` for links to other helpful Web pages.

If you want keep abreast of the latest problems and fixes for Microsoft TCP/IP connections to the Internet, check out `http://www.technotronic.com/ microsoft.html` .

Internet Through Your LAN

As we mentioned at the beginning of this chapter, you can also access the Internet through your local area network. In fact, you can have UNIX, NetWare, Windows Me, Windows 98, Windows 95, and Windows 2000/NT servers on your LAN and access them through your TCP/IP stack — no need to dial them up. Your LAN becomes an intranet.

Tip

You can place a World Wide Web server on a local server and publish your own home pages internally. Computer users throughout your business can surf the local net, using copies of Internet Explorer or Netscape Communicator to access local home pages that are updated to provide corporate information. If you install a POP3 and SMTP mail server, you can handle e-mail as though it were any other Internet mail.

Of course, your system administrator can provide access to the Internet (in addition to the intranet) through a server over any level of telephone access to some type of ISP. (When companies do this, they often set up a firewall to keep overly inquisitive outsiders from accessing internal corporate information.)

You or your system administrator will configure your computer in a manner similar to that described earlier in this chapter in the section entitled "Installing an Internet Dial-Up Connection." If you have a LAN connection, your TCP/IP stack is bound to your local area network card. Your system administrator can set up a local DHCP server to provide IP addresses. You won't need a Dial-Up Adapter, except for Direct Cable Connection.

Tip

A Windows computer set up as a Dial-Up Networking server can't route TCP/IP. So you can't call in from home (to this computer) by using the TCP/IP protocol bound to your Dial-Up Adapter at your home computer and expect to be able to connect over TCP/IP to your intranet on your LAN at work.

A Windows 2000 or NT server set up as a RAS (or DUN) server can take your TCP/IP call and connect you to your company's intranet, and, through one of your company's servers, to its Internet service provider.

Configuring the TCP/IP Stack for a Network Adapter

If you have a LAN connection over a network card to a TCP/IP network, you should turn to "Choosing a Networking Protocol" in Chapter 18 for additional information on local area networks.

You can configure the TCP/IP stack for a LAN connection using the following steps:

STEPS

Setting the Default TCP/IP Properties for a LAN Connection

Step 1.   Click Start ➪ Settings ➪ Control Panel.

Step 2.   Click the Network icon. Highlight TCP/IP in the Network dialog box and click the Properties button.

Step 3. Click the DNS Configuration tab (shown in Figure 25-7). If your LAN has a DHCP server that dynamically supplies the DNS IP addresses, don't change anything under this tab. Otherwise, mark the Enable DNS option button, and then type your host name, your service provider's domain name, and the IP address of the DNS server you will use. Click the Add button to put the DNS server's IP address in the list. If you have multiple addresses, enter them in the order that you want them searched. Be sure to click the Add button after you type each one.

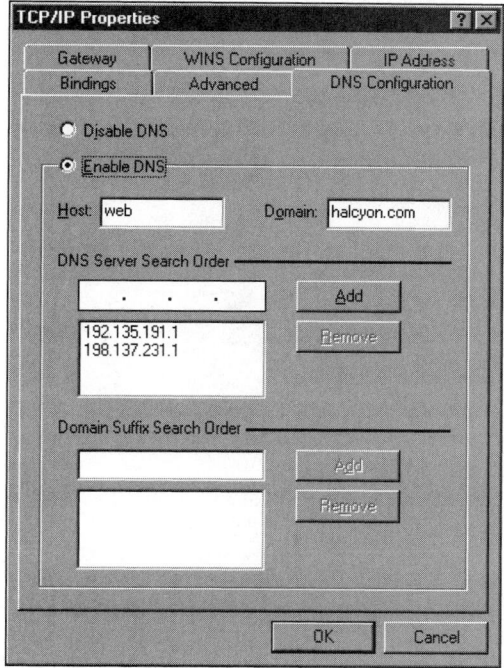

Figure 25-7: The DNS Configuration tab. Fill in the fields for your host name, your service provider's domain name, and the DNS server's IP address.

Step 4. Click the IP Address tab (shown in Figure 25-8). Mark the "Obtain an IP address automatically" option button if your network has a DHCP server that provides you with a dynamic IP address. If you have a fixed IP address, mark the "Specify an IP address" option button, and enter the IP address and the subnet mask.

Step 5. If you have a fixed IP address, click the Gateway tab, enter your gateway IP address, and click the Add button.

Continued

STEPS

Setting the Default TCP/IP Properties for a LAN Connection *(continued)*

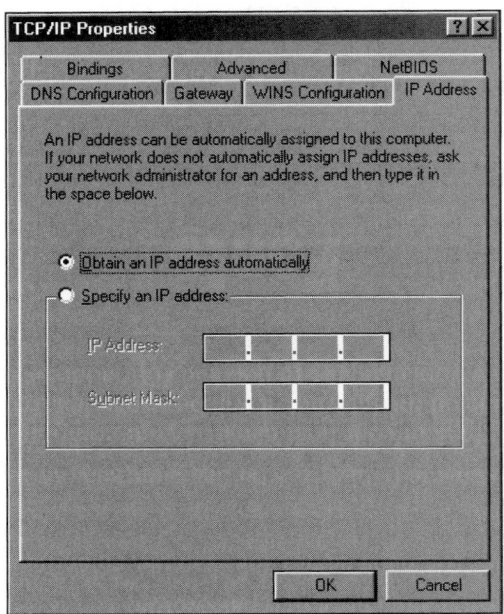

Figure 25-8: The IP Address tab. Mark "Obtain an IP address automatically" if your network has a DHCP server.

Step 6. Click the WINS Configuration tab and make sure that the "Disable WINS resolution" option button is marked unless your network has a WINS server. If you have a WINS server, but not a DHCP server, mark "Enable WINS resolution" and type the IP address for your WINS server. If you have a DHCP server, mark the "Use DHCP for WINS resolution" option button.

Step 7. Click OK to close the TCP/IP Properties dialog box.

Step 8. Restart your computer.

If your local area network uses a DHCP server to assign IP addresses for your DNS server and for users, you really don't have to make any changes in the TCP/IP settings. This gives you the most flexibility, because addresses can be dynamically assigned regardless of how your computer connects to the Internet or intranet.

Windows will automatically and by default assign an IP address to the network card in your computer. This allows you to connect to your intranet when you first plug in the cable to the network card. You don't need an assigned static IP address, or a DHCP server to provide a dynamically assigned one.

TCP/IP will automatically assign an IP address unless you reconfigure its settings. (Click the Network icon in your Control Panel, select TCP/IP, click the Properties button, and click the IP Address tab.) The way it does this is to first search for a DHCP server on your network. If it doesn't find one, it assigns an IP address and then checks for conflicts, changing the address if it finds any. This allows you to get up on the network without having to assign IP addresses first. If your computer later finds a DHCP server, it will use the dynamically assigned IP address.

TCP/IP Conflicts Between the LAN Card and the Dial-Up Adapter

If you normally connect your portable to your TCP/IP LAN at your office, and then you take your portable home and call in to your office network, your computer at home may try to send the network traffic out the network card and not over the modem. This occurs if you have configured your TCP/IP settings to use the DHCP server at the office to resolve IP addresses.

To solve this problem, you can run Winipcfg (see "Displaying Your TCP/IP Settings" later in this chapter) after you have made the connection with your office network, and click the Release All button to release assigned IP addresses. If this doesn't work and your network adapter is a PC card, pull it out of its slot on the side of the portable.

If you have an internal network card, you'll need to disable the network card by marking the "Disable in this hardware profile" checkbox in the General tab of the Properties dialog box for your network adapter. (To display this dialog box, right-click your My Computer icon and click Properties. Click the Device Manager tab, click the plus sign next to Network Adapters, and double-click your network adapter card icon.)

If you do this, you will have to enable the network card the next time you connect to the network. A way around this is to set up two hardware profiles (one for home and one for the office). You can then disable the network card in the home profile.

Hardware profiles are not supposed to be necessary if you have Plug and Play hardware (both cards and the system board). In this case, it doesn't quite work out. To see how to set up multiple hardware profiles, turn to "Hardware Profiles" in Chapter 36.

Setting Up Your Own Routes

If you connect to a TCP/IP network locally through a network card, and at the same time you call out through a modem to an ISP, you now have two routes and Microsoft's TCP/IP stack can only handle one at a time. The route assigned to the last connection made is the active route.

If your LAN network resources are behind a firewall, you lose the ability to see them if you make a connection with a service provider after connecting to the LAN. You can use the route add command (discussed in "TCP/IP Utilities" later in this chapter) to create a table of resource locations (IP addresses) that are associated with the IP address of the LAN gateway. If you do this, you'll still be able to access your LAN resources.

STEPS

Associating a Resource Address with a Gateway Address

Step 1. Connect your computer to your intranet. Choose Start ⇨ Run, type **Winipcfg** (see "Displaying Your TCP/IP Settings" later in this chapter), and click OK. Read the default gateway value, and leave the IP Configuration dialog box open.

Step 2. Open up a new text file and add the following line to it:

```
Route add gateway-IP-address DNS-IP-address
```

The *gateway-IP-address* is the value that you read in step 1, and the *DNS-IP-address* is the address of the DNS service on your local area network. If you don't have a DNS server, use a DHCP server IP address instead.

Step 3. Save the file, and then rename it with a bat extension. Click it to run it.

Step 4. Dial into an Internet service provider on the same computer. Click the Renew All button in the IP Configuration dialog box to confirm that your IP address and gateway IP address have changed and are now the same value.

Step 5. Open a DOS window and use the ping command to access a LAN resource. For example: ping www.localintranetserver.com

Connecting a Windows Network to the Internet

You can configure a peer-to-peer network of Windows Me computers to connect to the Internet without using a Windows 2000/NT, UNIX, or other type of server. One of the Windows Me computers acts as the Internet connection server. This is an inexpensive way to connect a small network through one phone line to an ISP.

Windows Me (and also Windows 98 Second Edition) comes with Internet Connection Sharing, which allows you to accomplish this task without the use of third-party software. If you do not have Second Edition, you can use other software as detailed in Chapter 23.

TCP/IP Utilities

Microsoft ships some low-level TCP/IP utilities with Windows. Most of these utilities are DOS-based — which is kinda weird. Well, UNIX and DOS are text-based, and TCP/IP is down there below the user interface, so it makes some sense. Microsoft also provides one Windows-based TCP/IP utility.

Table 25-1 lists the TCP/IP utilities you get with Windows.

Table 25-1	TCP/IP Utilities
Command	*What It Does*
DOS Utilities	
Arp	Displays and modifies the IP-to-physical (Ethernet card) address translation tables used by address resolution protocol (ARP). If you're dialing into the Internet over your own modem, you won't be using this utility.
Ftp	File Transfer Protocol. Enables you to log onto other computers on the Internet (perhaps as anonymous) and download or upload files. Much better Windows-based FTP programs are available on the Internet at shareware sites.
Nbtstat	Displays protocol statistics and current TCP/IP connections using NBT (NetBIOS over TCP/IP).
Netstat	Displays protocol statistics and current TCP/IP connections.
Ping	Checks for a connection to a remote computer. For example, type **ping ftp.microsoft.com**. We suggest you use FTP Explorer, or Internet Neighborhood, as discussed later in "Network File System" instead.

Continued

Table 25-1 *(continued)*	
Command	**What It Does**
DOS Utilities	
Route	Manually controls network routing tables. Routes added to the table are dynamic and need to be reestablished every time you reboot the computer. You can create a batch file with the proper commands and then put a `pif` file that points to it in your StartUp folder.
Tracert	Displays the route taken to a remote computer. For example, type **tracert ftp.microsoft.com**. If you aren't connected, your default DUN connectoid is called.
Windows Utility	
Winipcfg	Displays current TCP/IP network configurations. You don't use it to change these configurations; for that, you go to the TCP/IP Properties dialog box (accessed through the Network icon in the Control Panel).

To find out how to use the DOS-based TCP/IP applications, open a DOS Windows session and type the command name followed by `-?`. Winipcfg is stored in the `\Windows` folder. You can create a shortcut to it and put the shortcut in a folder that you use for Internet utilities. (You can also do this for the DOS-based utilities. You'll find them in the `\Windows` folder as well.)

Displaying Your TCP/IP Settings

You can easily use Winipcfg to display your current TCP/IP configuration. `Winipcfg.exe` is by default stored in your `\Windows` folder. If you haven't created a shortcut to it, just run it by clicking your Start button, clicking Run, typing **Winipcfg**, and clicking OK. The results are shown in Figure 25-9.

Your adapter address is a number hard-coded into a network card if your TCP/IP protocol is bound to a network card. If your TCP/IP protocol is bound to your Dial-Up Adapter (your modem, in other words), the number is meaningless because modems don't have an address hard-coded in.

If your IP address is dynamically assigned, this field and the Subnet Mask field will be filled with zeros. If you have a dynamically assigned IP address from a DHCP server, you can get a new one by clicking the Renew All button.

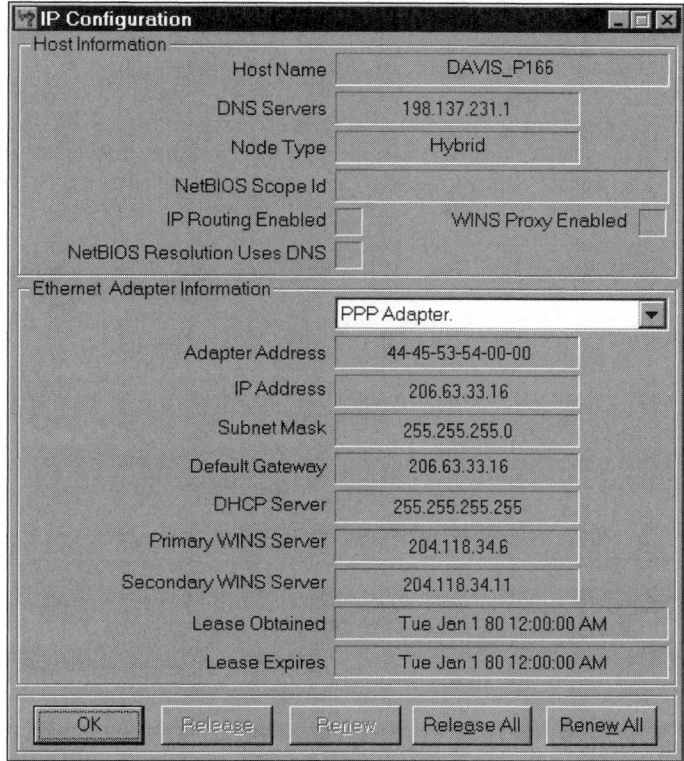

Figure 25-9: The IP Configuration dialog box

As soon as you make a DUN connection (even with DCC), you are assigned an IP address. To find out what it is, run Winipcfg and click the Renew All button.

Telnet

Windows comes with a reasonably good Telnet client. Telnet lets you log onto a remote computer (or even your service provider's computer) as a terminal (like HyperTerminal). You can then run the UNIX software running on that remote computer.

This might seem like a step backwards, but it is handy at times to be able to get the Internet out of the way of talking to a specific computer. Telnet.exe is stored in the \Windows folder. Create a shortcut to it and place it in an Internet folder.

Network File System

Tip

Windows doesn't include a network file system (NFS) such as the installable file system for UNIX. The directories and file systems on UNIX computers don't look like the file systems on Windows computers. It's nice to have a translation layer that both makes them look like the Windows file system, and adds drag-and-drop between file systems. That way, you can just drag a file from a remote UNIX computer and drop it in your local folder. You can use Internet Neighborhood, found at http://www.knowareinc.com/in32.html, to provide some of this functionality.

A no-cost program called Samba that runs on a Sun server enables Windows computers to access the files on the Sun server as though they were FAT-type files. You can get information about Samba at http://www.samba.org.

By default, a Samba server can't work with encrypted passwords. The Windows SMB redirector does not send an unencrypted password unless you add a registry entry to enable unencrypted passwords. This can cause problems connecting to Windows share-mode servers if the share in question has no password. To enable the Windows client to send an unencrypted user password, use your Registry Editor to add a new value to the registry key HKEY_LOCAL_MACHINE\System\ CurrentControlSet\ Services\ VxD\ VNETSUP. Right-click the right pane of the Registry Editor after you have navigated to this key, click DWORD, and name the value **EnablePlainText Password**. Double-click this name and give it a value of 1 (default is 0).

You might also try ICE NFS, which provides a virtual drive for Windows. It enables Windows to mount drives on other machines. You'll find it at http://www.jriver.com/ice.nfs.html.

If you want an FTP client that is fully integrated into the Explorer, check out Internet Neighborhood. It is a Windows shell extension for browsing remote FTP sites as if they were folders and files on your computer. You'll find it at http://www.knowareinc.com/in32.html.

This shareware program, available in a single-user registered version for $26.50 from KnoWare Inc. of Baltimore, Maryland, integrates itself into the Windows Explorer and makes file transfers intuitive. Unlike other FTP programs that use their own interfaces, Internet Neighborhood uses the Windows Explorer window as a built-in interface. FTP sites show up as folders underneath an Internet Neighborhood icon in your My Computer tree. Since Internet Neighborhood is a 32-bit shell extension to the Explorer, it is loaded into memory by Windows when needed.

Just as Microsoft's My Network Places icon shows subfolders for any computers that reside on a network with your PC, Internet Neighborhood shows folders for FTP sites. You can drag and drop files from an FTP site to your hard drive, and do the same to upload your files to an FTP site (if you have access rights). This process works in exactly the same way as dragging any files in the Explorer.

There's little or nothing to learn. You can also use the Windows Clipboard to upload and download files. Just like files on your hard drive, files on an FTP site can be copied and pasted where you want them. For large files, Internet Neighborhood displays an estimate of the time it will take to complete the transfer, including the percentage completed and number of bytes transferred.

Internet Neighborhood includes an FTP Wizard to make it simple to add FTP sites. For example, if you want to download files from `ftp.netscape.com`, specifying this site in the FTP Wizard immediately makes it available from within the Explorer window. Internet Neighborhood works with firewalls, if your company has one. The FTP Wizard includes settings to access your company's type of firewall, to establish a connection to the firewall computer, and to run a "User without login" command.

In addition to single-user licenses, Internet Neighborhood is also available in a 50-user license for $295, and an unlimited-user site license for $495. In case you happen to need to uninstall Internet Neighborhood, read the uninstall directions at `http://www.knowareinc.com/uninstall.html`.

Summary

▶ Windows supports three networking protocol stacks, one of which is TCP/IP (the protocol used by the Internet).

▶ Combine TCP/IP support with Dial-Up Networking, and Windows gives you the tools you need to connect to the Internet.

▶ We help you secure the right kind of account with an Internet service provider.

▶ You need to get the right information from your service provider; we tell you what to ask for.

▶ We explain each of the steps for setting up your Windows computer for Dial-Up Networking and TCP/IP support.

▶ We show you how to connect to your service provider and make sure that you've got a good connection.

Chapter 26

Internet Explorer

The Windows User/Browser Interface

Internet Explorer, the World Wide Web browser provided by Microsoft, has gone through quite an evolution to reach its current status in Windows Me.

When Windows 95 was first released in 1995, it didn't include an Internet browser. Microsoft sold Internet Explorer (IE) at that time as a separate product from Windows, in a separate box.

In December 1995, Microsoft chairman Bill Gates announced at a well-publicized press conference (which both of your *Windows Secrets* coauthors attended in Seattle) that Internet Explorer would henceforth be given away free. The browser was soon integrated into Service Release 1 (SR1) of Windows 95, which PC manufacturers were required by Microsoft to install on all new PCs.

Despite a court order against doing so (which was later reversed by an appeals court), Microsoft melded Internet Explorer into Windows 98 in such a way that IE couldn't easily be removed. The rest is history. As this book is written, Microsoft has been found guilty of anticompetitive behavior, but penalties have not yet been imposed.

No matter what happens in court, it's unlikely to affect Windows Me users, who will continue to find Internet Explorer bundled with the operating system, just as it was in Windows 98.

As far as this chapter is concerned, it doesn't matter whether you have:

1. Windows Me with its bundled Internet Explorer

2. Windows 98 or Windows 95 (SR1) with their bundled Internet Explorer

3. The original Windows 95, to which you've installed a standalone version of Internet Explorer

The user interfaces for Internet Explorer under Windows Me, Windows 98, and Windows 95 (with IE installed) are almost identical.

From the beginning, the Internet Explorer icon has appeared on both the Desktop and in the Control Panel. However, starting with Windows 98 (and continuing in Windows Me), a browser-friendly toolbar appears in any Windows Explorer or My Computer window as soon as it's needed. For example, it appears as soon as you type a URL in the Address bar and press Enter. Any Explorer or My Computer window can now look like what Internet Explorer used to look like when it was a standalone application.

Microsoft will continue to develop Internet Explorer. You will undoubtedly be able to upgrade your Explorer by downloading a newer version from the Microsoft Web site. Microsoft will also continue to develop and support Internet Explorer for other operating systems, such as the Mac and Windows 3.1.

If you have an older version of Internet Explorer that came with Windows 98 or 95, you should download the latest version of the Internet Explorer from `http://www.microsoft.com/windows/ie/default.htm`. This will help to make your browser consistent with the discussion we'll lead you through in this and other chapters.

On the other hand, if you really, really want to get rid of Internet Explorer in Windows Me, you can do so with a $25 product called 98lite III. It adds Internet Explorer and many other components of Windows Me and 9*x* to the Add/Remove Programs control panel. You can then remove IE or other components and then add them back whenever you like.

To download 98lite III, go to `http://www.98lite.net` (*not* `98lite.com`, which is an adults-only site with a similar name).

Starting the Internet Explorer

Click the Internet Explorer icon on your Desktop to start the Internet Explorer. You can also start the Internet Explorer by clicking the Start ⇨ Favorites, and then clicking a favorite Web site.

Secret

If you don't see the Favorites option on your Start menu, select Settings ➪ Taskbar and Start Menu to display the Taskbar and Start Menu Properties dialog box. Click the Advanced tab and choose the Display Favorites option. Click OK.

In a My Computer window, click Favorites in the menu bar, and choose a favorite Web site. You can also do this in an Explorer window. Both windows will turn into the Internet Explorer, and the Standard Buttons toolbar will change into its Internet version, which we refer to as the *Internet toolbar*.

Type a Web address (a URL) in the Address bar in an Explorer window and press Enter. The Explorer becomes the Internet Explorer.

When you open up the Internet Explorer, display the Tools menu. Notice that the Internet Explorer window doesn't have a Folder Options command in this menu; it has an Internet Options command instead. The Internet Options dialog box allows you to set a number of Internet Explorer parameters.

You can take the Internet Explorer icon off of your Desktop. Right-click the Internet Explorer icon on your Desktop, click Properties, and click the Advanced tab. Clear the "Show Internet Explorer icon on the desktop" checkbox. Click OK.

The Internet Explorer is a version (or an extension) of the Explorer/My Computer window. You can transform either the Explorer or a My Computer window into the Internet Explorer. You can also transform the Internet Explorer into either the Explorer or a My Computer window.

New Link, New Window

If you want to open a new window when you jump to a new site, hold down the Shift key when you click the link. (If you prefer, you can right-click the link, then click "Open in new window" to do the same thing without using the keyboard.) You'll then be able to see both the target site and the source page in different Internet Explorer windows.

ActiveX Documents

Drag and drop a Word document, Excel spreadsheet, or any other OLE 2-enabled document from My Documents or the Explorer onto the Internet Explorer Address bar or menu bar.

The document is displayed in an Internet Explorer window. It looks just as it would inside the associated application (see Figure 26-1), toolbars and all. You can edit the document in the Internet Explorer just as you would in the application itself.

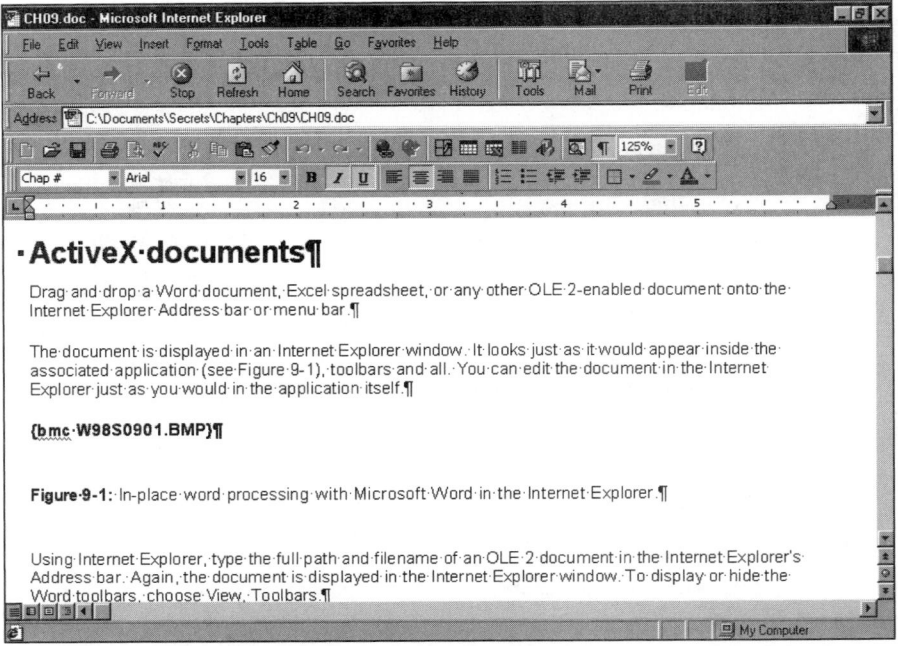

Figure 26-1: In-place word processing with Microsoft Word in the Internet Explorer

Using Internet Explorer, type the full path and filename of an OLE 2 document in the Internet Explorer's Address bar. Again, the document is displayed in the Internet Explorer window. (However, if you select the document from the Address bar's drop-down list, it will open in its own application.) To display or hide the Word toolbars, choose View ➪ Toolbars.

If you are an intranet Webmaster, you don't have to convert all the documents you want to put up on the intranet into HTML. People will be able to view the original documents quite easily in the Internet Explorer window. To view them, they'll need the OLE 2 application or a viewer such as Microsoft Word Viewer installed on their computer.

You can create Web pages that have links to Word documents. When you click this type of link, the Word document opens in your Internet Explorer. If you want to open the Word document in a new window, hold down the Shift key when you click the link.

You can also change the default so that Word documents automatically appear in a separate Word window instead of in the Internet Explorer window. To do this, click Start ➪ Settings ➪ Folder Options, and click the Files Types tab. Scroll to and highlight Microsoft Word Document in the Registered File Types list. Click the Edit button, and clear the Browse in same window checkbox.

Internet Explorer Web Accessories

Microsoft programmers write a few little programs to help out as they create the big applications. The Windows project managers have been willing to round up these little gems and put them in a downloadable package of unsupported applets. Not everyone needs all their functionality, but if one of these little applets works to solve your problem, hey, that's what it's all about.

To give you two examples of the applets in Web Accessories, the Image Toggler is a button that appears on your Links toolbar. You click the button to quickly turn Web graphics on or off — great when you want to switch frequently between "fast" text-only mode and slower graphics and text. The QuickSearch feature lets you type a line in your Address bar to launch a particular search engine with a specific keyword. For example, typing **av software** launches the AltaVista search engine with *software* as the keyword. You can download Internet Explorer Web Accessories from `http://www.microsoft.com/Windows/IE/WebAccess/default.asp` or `http://www.microsoft.com/Windows/IE/WebAccess/ie5tools.asp`.

Connecting to the Internet with the Internet Explorer

Internet Explorer (in Windows Me and 98) comes with the Internet Connection Wizard, which automates many of the steps required to create an Internet connection (as explained in "The Internet Connection Wizard" in Chapter 25). You can use the wizard to create a connection, and then go back and manually check what the wizard did by following the steps we detail in Chapter 25.

The Internet Connection Wizard creates a Dial-Up Networking connectoid for you if you connect to the Internet through a dial-up connection to an Internet service provider (ISP). This connectoid is automatically associated with the Internet Explorer, and it is called every time you click the Internet Explorer icon on your Desktop, or place an Internet address in the Address bar of an Explorer window.

The wizard also installs and configures the Internet Options icon in your Control Panel. Clicking this icon displays the Internet Properties dialog box. The Dial-Up Networking connectoid that the Internet Connection Wizard created for you is specified in the Connections tab of this dialog box. If you have another connectoid that you want to use to call another ISP instead of the one you originally created using the Internet Connection Wizard, you can specify it in this dialog box by highlighting it in the Dial-up Settings window. Mark "Dial whenever a network connection is not present" and click the Set Default button.

You can also right-click the Internet Explorer icon on your Desktop and click Properties to display the Internet Options dialog box. Then click the Connections tab and choose another DUN connectoid. To start the Internet Connection Wizard from the Internet Options dialog box, click Connections and then Setup.

If you set up your computer at work and find that when you take it home you can't browse the Internet, this may be because your computer is still trying to use the domain name server located at work. This domain name server is unavailable to you at home when you call through a dial-up ISP.

To allow your Internet Explorer to find sites on the Internet while you are at home, you will want to disable the connection to the domain name server at work. Follow these steps:

STEPS

Disabling a Domain Name Server

Step 1. Click Start ⇨ Settings, and click Control Panel.

Step 2. Click the Network icon. Scroll down to TCP/IP ⇨ Dial-Up Adapter. Click Properties.

Step 3. Click the DNS Configuration tab. Mark the Disable DNS option button, and click OK twice.

Step 4. You will be asked to restart Windows. Click OK.

We assume that you have correctly created a Dial-Up Networking connectoid for your local ISP. The TCP/IP settings associated with this connectoid include a DNS setting, as detailed in "Service Provider Account Information" in Chapter 25.

Internet Explorer, the 128-bit Version

Internet Explorer comes in two flavors. One supports 40-bit (or weaker) encryption, and the other supports 128-bit (very strong) encryption. U.S. government regulations, until fairly recently, restricted the export of products that incorporate 128-bit encryption. For this reason, you may have a version of IE that Microsoft shipped with only 40-bit encryption. If that's the case, you can download the 128-bit version from the Microsoft Web site (http://www.microsoft.com/windows/ie/download/128bit/intro.htm).

If you want to find out more about 40-bit versus 128-bit encryption, check out the information from Wells Fargo Bank at `http://wellsfargo.com/per/services/security/encryption/`.

In versions of Internet Explorer shipped after June of 1997, Microsoft obtained special U.S. government permission to incorporate, in a limited fashion, 128-bit encryption into the versions of its products that it ships overseas, including Internet Explorer. This 128-bit encryption is enabled (switched on) in the Internet Explorer only when you connect to a bank's Web site, *if* the bank has a digital certificate on its server. Banks obtain their digital certificates through a third-party organization.

Only transactions with certified banks will be protected with 128-bit encryption if you are using this older version of Internet Explorer. In this case, if your bank isn't certified, your transactions will be encrypted using a less-secure method.

The Microsoft Web server checks to see if you have an IP address in Canada or the United States. before it will download certain products (including, until recently, the 128-bit version of the Internet Explorer). If it does not get a valid DNS address return from its query of your ISP, it may not let you download restricted software. You'll know that this is what's happening if the DNS entry on the query form is blank.

Secret

Many ISPs keep their domain name servers behind firewalls for security reasons. The service provider's domain name server may not send your IP address to Microsoft's Web server when requested. If you have this problem, contact your service provider and ask them to reconfigure their firewall to permit DNS address queries, using a method that won't compromise their security.

Commands to Connect to the Internet

Secret

You can start the Internet Explorer and connect to the Internet just by typing the address of the place you want to go in the Run dialog box. Click Start ➪ Run. Type a location such as the following:

```
ftp://ftp.microsoft.com
```

or

```
http://BrianLivingston.com
```

Secret

You don't need to type the `http://` or the `ftp://`. If the resource is stored in your cache, an Internet Explorer window will open and you can cancel your dial-up Internet connection and display the resource from the cache.

Secret

If you want to log in to an FTP site with your user name and password, type:

```
ftp://username:password@address/
```

For example, you could type **ftp://davis:straub@davisstraub.com**.

Tip

Want to send e-mail while you're using the Internet Explorer? Click in the Address bar (or click Start ➪ Run). Type the following:

`mailto:davis@davisstraub.com`

Then press Enter.

This will start Outlook Express, Windows Messaging, or whatever your default e-mail program is and open a New Message window addressed to the person whose e-mail address you typed after `mailto:`.

You can send a friend a document that contains the shortcuts to your favorite places on the Internet. You can put shortcuts in Word or WordPad documents, and you can send these documents as e-mail attachments. You can also put URL shortcuts in Windows Messaging or Outlook Express e-mail messages. Just copy and paste or drag and drop them from your Favorites folder.

Managing Downloads from the Internet

Internet Explorer provides only basic functions for downloading files from Internet servers. Internet Explorer for the Mac comes with a slick download management system. If you don't like the features of IE for Windows, you can add a download manager for your Windows version by going to any one of the following sites:

Find FileHound at `http://www.fortunecity.com/roswell/divination/702/filehound.html` or Getright at `http://www.headlightsw.com/`, or check out the download manager at `http://www.download.com`.

Secret

Want to find out where the Internet Explorer will download files from the Internet? Open RegEdit and go to HKEY_CURRENT_USER\ Software\ Microsoft\ Internet Explorer. Double-click Download Directory in the right-pane. Change it to a new folder name.

You can also just download a new file from the Internet and save it to a new location. This will update the Download Directory value.

Creating Custom Versions of the Internet Explorer

Microsoft makes *its* version of the Internet Explorer. You can make *your own* version. Download the Internet Explorer Administration Kit (IEAK). With this program, you can set up the default start and search pages, the pages for the Quick Links in the Links toolbar, the logos and title bars, and so on. How about your own animated icon in the upper-right corner? To download the IEAK or apply for the IEAK CD-ROM, see `http://www.microsoft.com/windows/ieak/en/download/default.asp`.

You can customize your links and your home page without having to use the IEAK. By making these adjustments, you can actually make these links useful and not just ways for Microsoft to draw you into its fold.

A system administrator using this kit can create a list of friendly names that correspond to the unfriendly URLs where useful information is stored, on an intranet or otherwise. For example, users could type **401K** in the Address bar to reach a document that had a URL of http://benefits/employee/401K. Thanks to Ray Sun at Microsoft for pointing this out to us.

To change your links, open your Windows Explorer to \Windows\Favorites\ Links. Drag and drop shortcuts to URLs from your other Favorites folders into the Links folder. Delete any shortcuts in the Links folder that you no longer want to use as links.

To replace the Globe icon, you'll need to add two strings to your registry. Navigate to HKEY_CURRENT_USER\ Software\ Microsoft\ Internet Explorer\ Main, and add the string values BrandBitmap and SmBrandBitmap to this key. Give these two values the path and filenames of the bmp files that contain the replacement graphics.

Underlining Hyperlinks

By default, hyperlinks on Web pages are displayed as underlined in most Web browsers. And if you have chosen single-clicking (Start ⇨ Settings ⇨ Folder Options), you will notice that as you move your mouse pointer over the icons on your Desktop, they also are underlined, mimicking hyperlinks in Web pages.

You can determine when file and folder names, shortcuts, and so on are underlined in the right pane of the Explorer, in a My Computer window, and on the Desktop. To get this to work, you need to make changes in two separate dialog boxes — another triumph of user-interface engineering.

Because underlining Desktop items can depend on how you view hyperlinks in Internet Explorer, you'll first want to set how underlining will work when you are using Internet Explorer to view a Web page or an HTML document. In Internet Explorer, you can choose to have hyperlinks always underlined, never underlined, or underlined only when you rest your mouse pointer over them. (This last option is called *hover.*)

STEPS

Setting Up Underlining

Step 1. Click the Internet Explorer icon on the Desktop, choose Tools ⇨ Internet Options, and click the Advanced tab. Scroll down to Underline Links.

Continued

STEPS

Setting Up Underlining *(continued)*

Step 2. Mark the option button for the type of underlining that you want for Web pages. Click OK.

Step 3. Click your My Computer icon on the Desktop.

Step 4. Choose View ⇨ Folder Options, mark the "Custom, based on settings that you choose" option button, and then click the Settings button.

Step 5. In the Custom Settings dialog box, mark "Single-click to open an item (point to select)" and either "Underline icon titles consistent with my browser settings," or "Underline icon titles only when I point at them." Click OK.

If you choose "Single-click to open an item (point to select)" and "Underline icon titles only when I point at them," it doesn't matter what your browser settings are. You can have no underlining on a Web page, but you'll have hover underlining on the Desktop and in the right-pane of the Explorer when viewing files and folders. This is true even if you are viewing your files and folders as a Web page (in an Explorer or My Computer window, click View ⇨ As Web Page).

If you choose "Underline icon titles consistent with my browser settings," and you have chosen to always underline hyperlinks in the Internet Explorer, all your file and folder names will always be underlined. You might think this over a bit.

Edit on the Internet Explorer Toolbar

You get the Internet toolbar when you start the Internet Explorer. See the previous section, "Starting the Internet Explorer."

Secret

If you have installed FrontPage or other Microsoft HTML editors, you'll notice that the Internet toolbar has an additional button — the Edit button. If you click this button, you can edit the page that you are currently viewing in the Internet Explorer.

If you don't have the Edit button and wish you did, here's how to get it:

STEPS

Putting the Edit Button on the Internet Toolbar

Step 1. Click My Computer on the Desktop. Choose View ⇨ Folder Options, and click the File Types tab.

Step 2. Scroll down to Microsoft MHTML Document. Click the Edit button, and then click the New button.

Step 3. In the Action field, type **&Edit**. In the "Application used to perform action" field, either click the Browse button or type the path to your HTML editor. If you don't have one, type **C:\Windows\ Notepad.exe**. Click OK and close the Folder Options dialog box.

Step 4. Click the Internet Explorer icon on the Desktop. You'll see the Edit button in the Internet toolbar.

If you are using Notepad to edit HTML documents and you install FrontPage or FrontPage Express, it will change the action associated with the Edit button. You can switch it back to Notepad using the steps above.

If you install Netscape Communicator, you may lose your Edit button. You can get it back using the above steps.

Make History a Quick Link

Microsoft includes a few of its Web sites as Quick Links — that is, buttons on the Links toolbar. You can display the Links toolbar in the Internet Explorer window or on the Desktop. Right-click any of the toolbars (including the menu) in an Explorer, Internet Explorer, or My Computer window. Click Links.

If you display the Links toolbar on the Desktop, you can connect it to the taskbar or let it stand alone as a floating toolbar. If the Links toolbar isn't already displayed, right-click the taskbar, click Toolbars, and click Links. To move it away from the taskbar, place your mouse pointer at the left edge of the Links toolbar and drag the toolbar to anywhere on your Desktop.

You can decide what buttons go on the Links toolbar. They can be links to Internet URLs or to local files or folders. You can drag and drop shortcuts to the Links toolbar or right-click existing items to delete or cut them.

One quick way to get to your History folder is to put it on the Links toolbar. To do so, take the following steps:

STEPS

Putting History on the Links Toolbar

Step 1. Click the Internet Explorer icon on your Desktop.

Step 2. Type **c:\windows\history** in the Address bar and press Enter.

Continued

STEPS

Putting History on the Links Toolbar *(continued)*

Step 3.   Right-click the taskbar and click Toolbars (or right-click the Internet Explorer menu or toolbar), and click Links if it isn't already checked.

Step 4.   Drag the history folder icon at the left edge of the Address bar to the Links toolbar and drop it there.

If you haven't used TweakUI to turn off "Shortcut to...," you'll find this prefix in your new History button on the Links toolbar. To keep this from happening in the future, click your TweakUI shortcut on your Desktop (or in the Control Panel), click the Explorer tab, and clear the "Prefix 'Shortcut to' on new shortcuts" checkbox. You'll have to rename the History button in the \Windows\Favorites\Links folder.

You'll find the shortcuts on the Links toolbar at \Windows\Favorites\Links. You can use the Explorer to move any shortcut into and out of this folder. (In general, toolbars should just contain shortcuts. You could put anything you like in the Links toolbar, but it's really designed to store shortcuts to documents, folders, and Web sites.)

Stop Dialing Up My Internet Service Provider

If you normally connect to the Internet through one of your Dial-Up Networking connectoids, you will automatically start up the connectoid that is associated with your Internet Explorer whenever you choose to browse the Internet. This happens when you click the Internet Explorer icon on your Desktop or click the Start button and choose any of the Internet Web pages in the Favorites submenu.

You can turn off this capability if you'd rather connect to the Internet manually by clicking the appropriate connectoid when you want to connect. To disassociate the connectoid from the Internet Explorer, take the following steps:

STEPS

Disconnecting the Connectoid from the Internet Explorer

Step 1. Right-click the Internet Explorer icon on the Desktop, click Properties, and then click the Connections tab.

Step 2. Mark the checkbox labeled "Never dial a connection."

Step 3. Click the OK button.

Now when you want to connect to the Internet, do so by clicking your DUN connectoid. Once you are connected, you can use your Internet Explorer to browse the Internet.

Navigating Internet Explorer

Internet Explorer has a number of features that automate many common tasks. The following sections show you how to take advantage of these.

The Complete AutoComplete

Internet Explorer has a feature called AutoComplete that helps you complete your entry in the Address bar as soon as you type in the first few letters. For example, type **www.davis**, pause for a few seconds, and you'll get a drop-down list of sites you have previously visited that start with www.davis, including www.davisstraub.com/secrets. Even if there is a long list of URLs that start with the same letters that you've typed, you can easily use your mouse or arrow keys to scroll to and highlight an entry in the list, and then press Enter or Tab to jump to the site.

If you press Alt+down arrow or F4 when the Address bar is active, Internet Explorer displays a drop-down list of complete addresses you've recently typed in the Address bar. This is a totally different list than the AutoComplete drop-down list; it is the same list that appears when you click the down arrow at the right end of the Address bar.

To enable or disable AutoComplete, choose Tools ⇨ Internet Options, click the Content tab, and click the AutoComplete button. In the AutoComplete Settings dialog box, you can choose whether to use AutoComplete for Web addresses, forms, and/or user names and passwords (see Figure 26-2). (We discuss using AutoComplete for forms in the next section.)

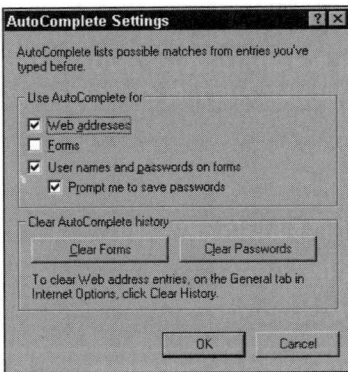

Figure 26-2: You can control the AutoComplete settings.

Tip

You can save time when typing Web addresses by making Internet Explorer automatically preface your entry with www. and end it with the suffix .com. Just type the domain name in the Address bar and then press Ctrl+Enter. For example, type **brianlivingston**, press Ctrl+Enter, and you get http://www.BrianLivingston.com. This is different from actually searching on the Internet for the address; see "Autosearch for a Web Address" later in this chapter for more on that.

Fill in Forms by Clicking a Button or Two

According to a Microsoft Intelliform developer document, when you submit a form on a Web page, Internet Explorer encrypts and saves on your computer the name of each text field with the value you have entered in that field. The next time you visit a Web page and begin typing in a text field of the same name, AutoComplete will prompt you with a list of previously used data.

So, if the name of the field on a Web page form is Address, the next time you run into a Web page form with a field named Address, your previous input value will be displayed in a drop-down list. You can then choose to enter it or not.

While it's really great that Microsoft built in the AutoComplete capability, it is also nice to enter text by clicking a single button. The great thing is that you can do either or both.

TypeItIn is a simple — and simple-minded — utility that puts a toolbar on your Desktop (see Figure 26-3). You can define and name up to 50 buttons. Click a button, and the associated text is squirted into the active window at the current location of the insertion point.

You can add, edit, rearrange, and delete buttons. A right-click lets you undo an erroneous entry. You can also use TypeItIn to insert the current date and time, or use it as a Start menu to start programs. Keep it always on top or not. TypeItIn stays in the system tray so you can call it up at any time. It's very fast, and it handles special characters.

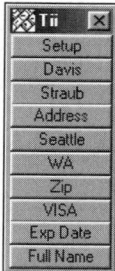

Figure 26-3: The TypeItIn toolbar inserts the associated text when you click one of its buttons.

In addition to the freeware version, you can get a professional version that lets you group your buttons — by application, for example. You'll find TypeItIn at `http://www.wavget.com/typeitin.html`. Nothing fancy, but very functional.

Finding Web Sites

Do you want to find a specific Web site, or text from a specific Web page?

In an Internet Explorer window, click in the Address bar, type **find**, **search**, or **?**, type a space, and then type the name of the company or organization whose site you want to find. If the name has a space in it, forget typing the **find**, **search**, or **?**, and just put double quote marks around the name. You can also just type in any word, and the search function will be started.

This will automatically start a search for the company, word in a Web page, or organization on MSN. You can customize your Address Bar search functions, by clicking Tools ⇨ Internet Options, clicking Advanced, and scrolling down to "Search from the Address Bar."

Autosearch for a Web Address

Internet Explorer will automatically search on the Internet for a Web address if you ask it to. Type a fragment of an address in the Address bar, press Enter, and Internet Explorer will treat the fragment as a search term. After a minute or two, you'll see a list of URLs containing the text you typed, and Internet Explorer will navigate to the site that is the most likely match according to its criteria, as shown in Figure 26-4.

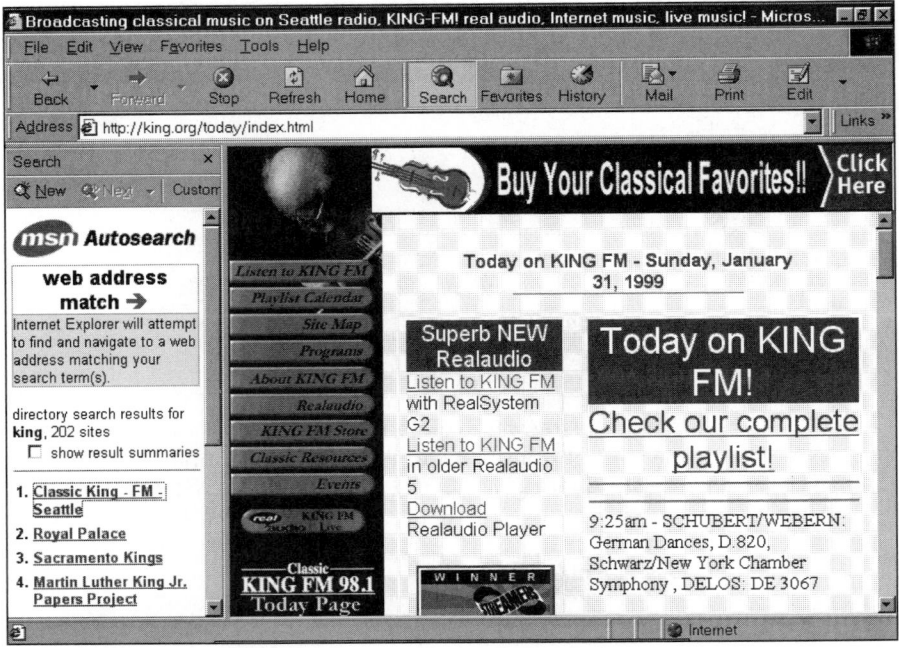

Figure 26-4: The results of an Autosearch for a Web address containing the word *king*.

You can choose to turn this feature off or change how it functions by taking these steps:

STEPS
Changing Your Autosearch Settings

Step 1. Click Tools ⇨ Internet Options in your Internet Explorer.

Step 2. Click the Advanced tab and scroll down to "Search from the Address bar."

Step 3. Mark the option button that you prefer, and click OK (see Figure 26-5).

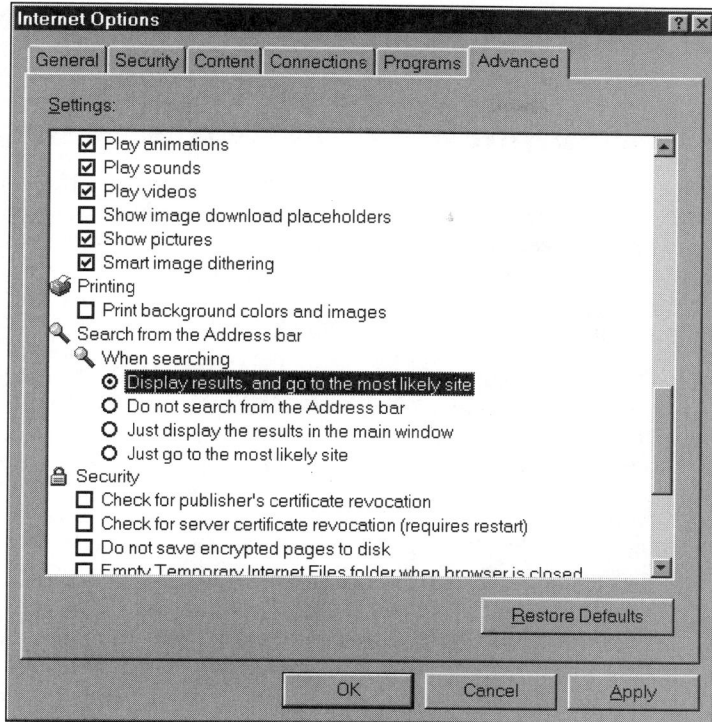

Figure 26-5: Select an option button to turn off Autosearch or to change the way it behaves.

The Search Pane

Click the Search toolbar button, and the Search pane opens on the left side of the Internet Explorer window.

Microsoft's search feature doesn't search with all the Web search engines, just the first one on the list you create in the Customize Search Settings window. Mark the search engines that you want to have available in the Search pane, and then use up and down arrows to change the order of the engines in the list. This will be the order they are used for searching.

Because Customize Search Settings doesn't provide any information about the individual search engines, it may be hard for you to choose which one to use. You may need to run a sample search or two, starting with the default search Web site. Once you have tried a search with it, you can use the Next button at the top of the Search pane to try each search engine in the order listed and see how it handles your queries. There are many more search engines than the ones shown in the Customize Search Settings window.

You can still search the old-fashioned way, by typing the Web address of a search engine in your Address bar. Or, you can use a search engine front end that searches multiple search engine sites for you. We discuss Copernic and Express, which do just that, in the next section.

Search Multiple Search Engines at Once

It may seem a bit redundant to search the search engines, but there are some advantages that aren't clear at first. First, local agent software on your computer can manage searches more effectively than the front ends of the search engines. For example, you can more easily save the results of previous searches so that you can go back later and review them. You can organize and group the search results into categories that you find helpful.

Also, a package such as Copernic can keep track of up to 130 search engines, which would be a bit of a pain for you and me. You can organize the results by rating, date found, address, and so on. You can browse the results and create a Web page from them. Send the Web page of results to a friend.

You'll find Copernic at `http://www.copernic.com`. The freeware version is somewhat limited in the number of search engines it will search; the professional version will search through 130 of them.

Express is another freeware tool that performs searches using multiple search engines at once, then retrieves only those Web pages you say are the most relevant. It retrieves data from up to seven search engines you specify and combines the ratings from all these engines into a single ranked list.

Express is a free download from Infoseek, itself a major search engine. To its credit, Infoseek doesn't seem to get any preference in the ranking of the listings, although Express doesn't let you control this yourself. Express is free, but it does present a lot of advertising, including ads from the other sites its listings come from (this is apparently intended to give something back in exchange for the use of those databases). Express also manages to place itself in every conceivable menu, toolbar, and nook and cranny of your Windows user interface to a level that we found annoying.

The professional version of Copernic offers far more in the sheer number of search engines it can manage, and much better flexibility in saving, managing and using past searches.

Express is available for download at `http://express.infoseek.com`. It requires 10MB of disk space, an 800 × 600 display, and Microsoft Internet Explorer 3.0 or higher or Netscape Navigator 3.0 or higher.

If you prefer your search listings without advertising, you need to buy a different software package that eschews ads. Danny Sullivan's Search Engine Watch contains a page that briefly reviews such products as BullsEye, Copernic, Mata Hari, and WebFerretPro. See `http://www.searchenginewatch.com/`. A good comparative review of five commercial search utilities (plus the free Express utility) is available at Chris Sherman's Mining Co., `http://websearch.miningco.com/library/weekly/aa100998.htm`.

Standardizing Search Engines

Search engines often return far too many results to find the one item you want, and different search engines refine their searches in completely different ways. Now someone is doing more than just complaining about this. Danny Sullivan, the editor of Search Engine Watch, an Internet analysis service, has a goal to bring together major search engine executives so users need learn only one set of search techniques that will work across all engines. For details, see `http://searchenginewatch.com/standards`.

By "major" search engines, Sullivan means AltaVista, AOL NetFind, Excite, HotBot, InfoSeek/Go, Google, GoTo, LookSmart, Lycos, MSN Search, Netscape Search, Northern Light, Snap, WebCrawler, and Yahoo. All of these engines exist because no single engine can fill all users' needs.

Choosing which engine to use for a particular task is daunting even for experienced data miners, much less occasional users. Sullivan's project to standardize search procedures may help users who must jump from engine to engine to find the information they need.

Most queries return thousands of hits, and narrowing your search becomes a painful but essential step. Fortunately, there are many little-known ways to make fine-tuning easy. And this is exactly where Sullivan's standards project may be able to help.

One fast way to narrow your focus is to search only the titles of Web sites. This eliminates many sites that have mere passing references to your subject. AltaVista, HotBot, InfoSeek, GoTo, MSN, Snap, and Northern Light allow you to do this with the prefix "title:" (as in title: windows bugs). But Yahoo uses the prefix "t:" and Lycos makes you go to an "advanced search" page.

If you are still getting too many hits, you can narrow your search to a single Web site that has many relevant pages. The syntax for this type of search is even less standardized, however. AltaVista uses the prefix "host:" (as in *host:infoworld.com windows bugs*). InfoSeek uses "site:". HotBot, GoTo, MSN, and Snap use "domain:". And other engines don't yet support this useful refinement (though some do on "advanced search" pages).

Even the most basic searches, such as *windows bugs*, aren't foolproof. Most engines treat this entry as *windows OR bugs*, but HotBot, Lycos, MSA, and Northern Light treat such entries as though you typed *windows AND bugs*. AltaVista and Google default to *"windows bugs"* (they treat it as a phrase).

A complete description of all these rules can be found at `http://searchenginewatch.com/facts/powersearch.html`. A handy chart summarizing the rules is available at `http://www.davisstraub.com/secrets/searchenginerules.htm`.

By looking at the "grey" cells in this chart (which indicates features we consider desirable), you can see that AltaVista has a lot of special features we like, while LookSmart has few. But any search engine may have a particular feature that makes it the best one for your needs. We appreciate Search Engine Watch's efforts to at least standardize the way users access special features in different search engines.

Another Web site, `http://www.searchengines.net`, makes it easy to quickly review different search engines. If you have a Web site and want to place a link on one of your Web pages to a search engine, this site makes that easy. Many search engines provide small forms that you can incorporate into your site, thus allowing your visitors to do a quick, perhaps specialized, search of the Net from your site. You'll find all the forms here.

Jump to a Site Without Searching

If you had a database that associated a company name with its Web site address, it would be a bit easier to find the company's Web site (assuming you knew the company's name). 1jump is an Internet Explorer add-on that comes with just such a database.

1jump is another example of the continuous growth in Web services. Take an address format that only technicians could love, and put a user-friendly front end on top of it. Type the name of the company, its stock symbol, or a brand, and click the Jump button to open up its Web site (see Figure 26-6).

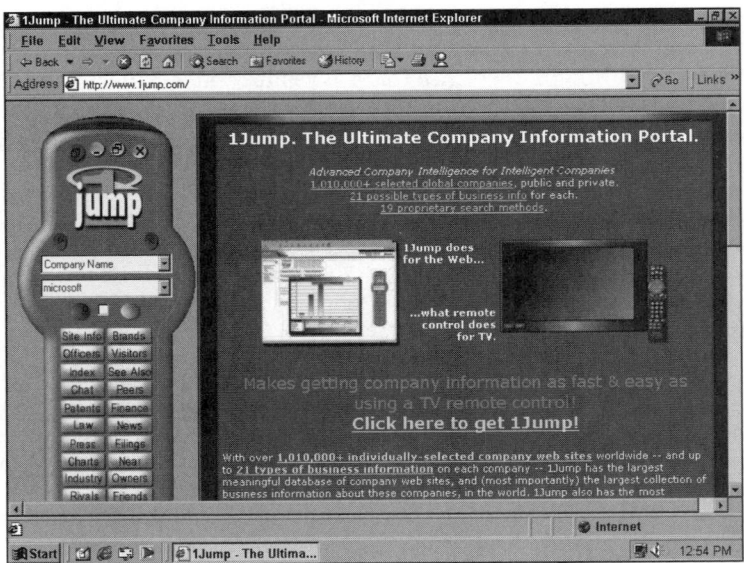

Figure 26-6: Use 1jump to jump to a company's Web site even if you don't know its address.

You can download 1jump from `http://www.1jump.com`.

Placeholder for Images on Web Pages

Tip

It isn't the default, so you might miss it. Internet Explorer will not put in placeholder borders for images yet to be downloaded. If you want this feature turned on so that the text can wrap around the images as yet unseen, you can turn it on in your Internet Options dialog box. Choose Tools ⇨ Internet Options, click the Advanced tab, and scroll down to Multimedia. Mark the "Show image download placeholders" checkbox. Click OK.

Clear the Frames

Sometimes you just want to get rid of the menu frame on the left side of a Web page. One of those times is when you click a link to another Web site and the frame from the old one remains in the browser window.

A quick way to get rid of the frame is to drag the link of the page you're viewing to the Address bar and drop it there. This sends you to the URL associated with the link, whether it is to another site or just to another Web page at the same site. In either case, the menu frame goes away.

Thanks to Chris Pirillo at `http://www.lockergnome.com` for this tip.

png Graphics

Internet Explorer can display a graphics format known as png. You probably haven't seen any graphics files using this format, but perhaps you will in the future. Check out `http://www.w3.org/Graphics/PNG/Inline-img.html` for an example.

The PNG format is described by the World Wide Web Consortium (W3C) as "an extensible file format for the lossless, portable, well-compressed storage of raster images. PNG provides a patent-free replacement for GIF and can also replace many common uses of TIFF." Many users of graphics files have avoided GIF (the Graphics Interchange Format) because of patent rights that sometimes necessitate license payments to use the format. PNG, by contrast, is an open standard.

Copy and Paste Links

Wherever there's a hot link, there's a way to cut and paste it. If you receive an e-mail message in Outlook Express that contains a link, you can of course just click it to invoke an Internet Explorer window (if it's a link to a Web site or an FTP address).

You can right-click a link and click Copy Shortcut. Then paste this URL into the Address bar, into a text file, onto the Desktop—whatever you like. You can also click Add to Favorites instead of Copy Shortcut.

Right-click a Web page name in your History Explorer bar, and you can click Copy or Add to Favorites. You can do the same with a Web page name in search results displayed in the Search Explorer bar.

Copy and Paste URLs

Internet Explorer saves Web pages as URL shortcuts. You'll find lots of them in your \Windows\Favorites folder. You can easily copy and paste these shortcuts into e-mail messages, other folders, to and from your Desktop, and so on.

Sometimes you don't want to copy the shortcut, you just want to copy the URL embedded in the shortcut. CopyURL, a freeware applet, makes this easy. It adds three items to the context menus associated with URL shortcuts. Right-click a URL shortcut, perhaps on your Favorites menu, and you will see the three additional options, as shown in Figure 26-7.

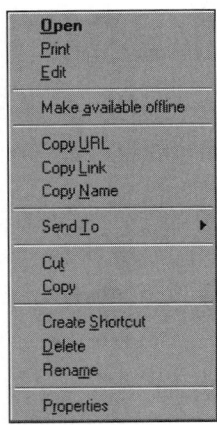

Figure 26-7: This context menu has been modified using CopyURL. The three new commands are in the third section of the menu.

The Copy URL command lets you copy just the URL — for example, http://www.davisstraub.com/secrets.

The Copy Link command lets you copy the URL as a link — for example, <A HREF="http://www.davisstraub/secrets">Windows Millennium Secrets</A>. This text with HTML tags is ready to be inserted in an HTML document.

Finally, the Copy Name command lets you copy the URL along with the title of its Web page — for example, Windows Me Secrets: http://www.davisstraub/secrets. This gives you a handy way to create a list of names and URLs if you highlight and copy a whole bunch of shortcuts at once (the other two commands also work with multiple selected shortcuts).

Extract the CopyURL zip file to a temporary folder. Right-click `CopyURL.inf` and click Install. You can then delete the files in the temporary folder.

You'll find this little hummer at `http://www.moonsoftware.com/`.

Stay Online

Does your Internet service provider (including AOL and Prodigy) kick you offline after a period of inactivity? Would you like to have an applet that simulated user input and kept your connection open even when you are away from the computer?

StayOn Pro will randomly ping URLs on its list to simulate user input over a PPP connection to an ISP. If you are on AOL, it will let you stay online by helping you identify the dialog box that AOL sends out requesting that you respond.

StayOn Pro isn't pretty, and it doesn't do much, but if you need what it does, it does it.

You'll find this at `http://rclabs.simplenet.com`.

Protect Your E-Mail Address

One thing we don't like is people sending us commercial e-mail when we haven't requested it. The Internet's popular SendMail program has recently been revised to give Internet service providers more tools to stop "spam relay," such as refusing to deliver messages that have bogus return addresses. And vigilant ISPs continue to find new defenses against the tide of junk e-mail from lists we can't seem to get removed from.

Still, there are ways that Web sites can capture your e-mail address without your knowledge. Some Web sites can make your browser silently download a tiny file using FTP. To start the FTP download, your browser sends your e-mail address.

The scam doesn't work with newer versions of Internet Explorer, which send Web sites a generic e-mail address such as `ieuser40@` (the "@" sign fools the Web site script). You can increase Internet Explorer's resistance to other similar tricks, however. To do so, choose Tools ⇨ Internet Options, click the Security tab, click the Custom Level button, scroll down to Logon under User Authentication, and mark either "Anonymous logon" or "Automatic logon only in Intranet zone."

In our opinion, it's unethical for commercial entities to collect personal information from you or about your computer without your consent. Closing this loophole won't stop all spam. But it's one step toward more privacy on the Web.

Toggle Internet Explorer Between Full-Screen Mode and Restore

Open up Internet Explorer and press the F11 key. If you weren't before, you are now in full-screen mode. If you were maximized before, hitting F11 again will get you back there.

Did we say Internet Explorer? Because Windows integrates Internet Explorer and Explorer, you can use the F11 toggle switch to "blow up" your Windows Explorer, too, as well as My Computer, Control Panel, or any folder window.

Thanks to Dave Adams and Jason Nadal for these tips.

Internet Explorer Shortcut Keys

Microsoft Help actually does a pretty good job of listing IE's shortcut keys. We'll point out in Table 26-1 a few keys that are of special interest, and you can look in Internet Explorer help for more.

One that we think is pretty cool is Ctrl+F5. This key combination forces Internet Explorer to download and refresh the current page, even if it thinks it has the latest version in the cache. This is useful for pages that change constantly, such as news sites.

Tom Pipinich at Microsoft pointed this out to us.

Table 26-1   Keyboard Shortcuts for Internet Explorer

Key or Combination	*Effect*
Enter	Goes to the highlighted link
Backspace and Shift+Backspace,	Same as Back and Forward arrow buttons on the Internet toolbar
Alt+Left Arrow and Alt+Right Arrow	Same as Back and Forward arrow buttons on the Internet toolbar
Shift+F10 or Ctrl+B	Displays a context menu for a page
F5	Reloads the current page from the server
Esc	Stops downloading a page
Ctrl+O or Ctrl+L	Goes to a new location (URL)
Ctrl+N	Opens a new window
Ctrl+S	Saves the current page
Ctrl+Shift+Tab	Cycles between frames
Tab and Shift+Tab	Cycles between links on a page

Key or Combination	Effect
Ctrl+D	Adds current Web page to Favorites (immediately and silently)
Ctrl+R	Reloads the current page (F5)
Ctrl+W	Closes the active Internet Explorer window
Alt+D	Jumps to the Address bar
Ctrl+F	Brings up the Find dialog box
Ctrl+P	Brings up the Print dialog box
Ctrl+Shift+Tab	Moves backward among frames
Ctrl+Tab	Moves forward among frames
F4 (or Alt+down arrow)	Displays the Address bar history
F6	Jumps to the Address bar
F11	Toggles full-screen mode
Page Down	Scrolls down, one screen at a time
Page Up	Scrolls up, one screen at a time
Spacebar	Scrolls down, one screen at a time

Tip

One thing that's cool about Tab and Shift+Tab is that they highlight the active areas on an image map. An *image map* is a (usually large) graphic on a Web page. The graphic is generally divided into active areas that point to different URLs. When you press Tab (to highlight the active areas) or Shift+Tab (which highlights in reverse order), you can see an outline around each area.

A Key Resource for Keystrokes

It's often a lot faster to press a little-known key combination than to accomplish the same thing with multiple mouse clicks. An expert at this named Michael Maardt, a Danish writer/publisher, decided to publish English versions of his best-selling booklets (in Scandinavia) to get them out to more users and build interest in his efforts among a wider audience. The books are free in the PDF format. To view the files, you need to download the free Acrobat reader from Adobe Systems at `http://www.adobe.com/supportservice/custsupport/LIBRARY/acrwin.htm`.

We found his *Escape from the Mousetrap* booklet to be quite well done and useful. It was originally written for Windows 95, so it doesn't have all the latest Internet Explorer 5 and Windows 98 keystrokes. But it does have the ones that Windows 95 and 98 share in common.

He has a few other booklets online that you can download for friends who are just beginning to use Windows. Michael encourages users to ignore their mouse and use their keyboards to accomplish all their Windows tasks.

You'll find his booklets at `http://www.knowwareglobal.com/index.htm`. Alan Eldredge told Chris Pirillo at `http://www.lockergnome.com` about this site, and that's how we found out about it.

Customizing Internet Explorer

Internet Explorer 5.5 gives you more ways than ever to customize the user interface. Here are some secrets for making it look and act the way you want it to.

Do Away with the Go Button

Microsoft added the Go button to the Internet Explorer because the folks who they brought in from the real world would sit back after they typed a URL in the Address field and wait for the Web page to display. It sometimes took quite a while for people to figure out that they had to press Enter to "go" to the site — hence, the Go button.

If you've been trained to press Enter to execute a command, you'll find the Go button a bit much. To banish the offending helper for the less-than-initiated, do this: In Internet Explorer, choose Tools ➪ Internet Options, click the Advanced tab, and clear the "Show Go button in the Address bar" checkbox. Notice how high up this item is in the list of checkboxes in the Advanced dialog box — makes it real easy to get rid of.

Rename Internet Explorer

Secret

You can use the Internet Explorer Administration Kit described earlier in this chapter to rename the Internet Explorer window. But if you'd rather not use this kit, you can manually rename Internet Explorer with a little registry editing. Here's how:

STEPS

Changing Microsoft Internet Explorer to a New Name

Step 1. Open your Registry Editor and navigate to HKEY_LOCAL_MACHINE\ SOFTWARE\ Microsoft\ Internet Explorer\ Main.

Step 2. If the value Window Title doesn't exist in the right pane, right-click the right pane, and click New ➪ String Value.

Step 3. Give the string value variable the name **Window Title**. Press Enter.

Step 4. Double-click Window Title. In the Edit String dialog box, type the name you'd like to see instead of Microsoft Internet Explorer (see Figure 26-8). Press Enter. Exit the Registry Editor.

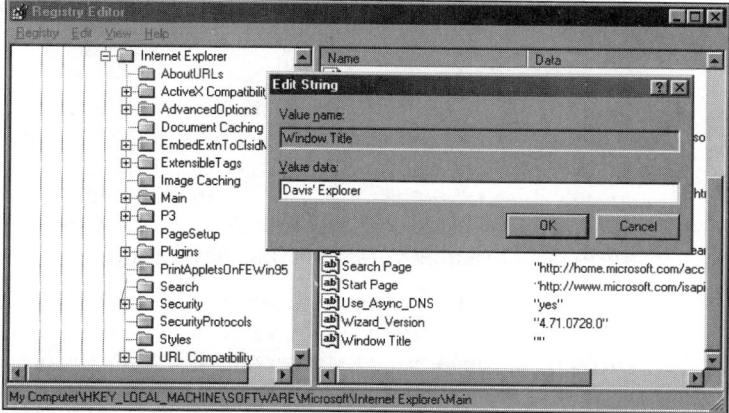

Figure 26-8: In this example, Internet Explorer will now be called *Davis' Explorer*.

The next time you open Internet Explorer, it will use your new title in the title bar.

Thanks to Peter Lara and many others for this tip.

You can also use the little freeware program IE Tweakin' Tool to accomplish this task and a few others. You'll find it at http://www.digitalspider.co.uk/tweak.

Clear Out the Internet Explorer Brands

Some computer suppliers and Internet service providers put their own brand logos in the copies of Internet Explorer that they provide. They may substitute their own logo for the animated Internet Explorer logo in the upper-right corner of the window, or even add an additional logo pane in the Internet Explorer window. If you prefer to do without the third-party branding, you can clear out these brands and put in your own.

Tip

The easiest way to do this is to use WinBoost, discussed in "Tweaking the Windows Desktop" in Chapter 5. Click WinBoost's Internet toolbar button, and then mark "Changing IE and OE logo animation and putting text in Internet Explorer title bar." You can decide whether to change the values or get rid of existing values to go back to the Internet Explorer defaults.

Instead of using WinBoost, you can edit your registry directly. If you want to remove a brand name from the title bar, use the steps in the previous section and delete the Window Title entry.

To delete the animated icons of other companies that may run in your Internet Explorer window, use the Registry Editor to navigate to HKEY_CURRENT_ USER\ Software\ Microsoft\ Internet Explorer\ Toolbar. You can delete the string values labeled BrandBitmap and SmBrandBitmap if you see them in the right pane of the Registry Editor. (You won't see them if you don't have a third-party branded version of Internet Explorer.)

Secret

If you want to change these values (and add them to this key), you can also do that. Just be sure to specify the value of a correctly sized graphics file. To fit correctly in the Internet Explorer window pane, the file that is associated with BrandBitmap should be 30 pixels wide and 38 pixels high for each image. A file that is 38 × 722 × 256 (colors) allows for 19 frames in an animation sequence. The graphics file associated with SmBrandBitmap should be 22 pixels wide and 22 pixels high for each image.

If you have a branded Internet Explorer, you can find the existing graphics files by looking in the registry at the branch given above, and then edit the files with MS Paint, if you like.

Ask to Open Media Files

Secret

Normally, Internet Explorer automatically opens and plays media files when it downloads them from the Internet. These files include sound files in the wav format and video clips in avi, mov, and qt formats. You can force Internet Explorer to ask whether you want to open or save the files, instead of just playing them. This gives you the option of saving media files under recognizable filenames in your designated locations.

STEPS

Confirming Open After Download

Step 1. In your Explorer window, choose View ⇨ Folder Options, and click the File Types tab.

Step 2. Scroll down the Registered File Types list to the media type that you want to change — Wave Sound, for example.

Step 3. Highlight the media type and click the Edit button to display the Edit File Type dialog box.

Step 4. Mark the "Confirm open after download" checkbox, as shown in Figure 26-9.

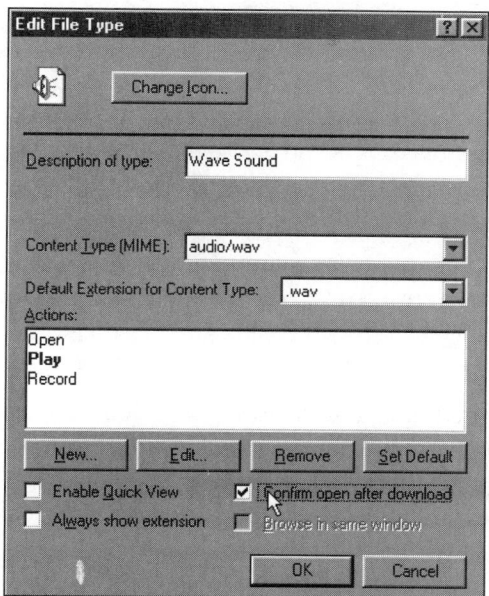

Figure 26-9: The "Confirm open after download" checkbox is in the lower-right corner of the Edit File Type dialog box.

Step 5. Click OK.

Step 6. Repeat this process for other media file types, and then click OK to close the Folder Options dialog box.

Add History to Your Start menu

Secret

Accessing your history menus through the History button on the Internet Explorer toolbar is a bit of a pain. You can access them as a toolbar off your taskbar (create a toolbar for the \Windows\History\History folder), but that requires that you hold down the Ctrl key when you click the button for any given week to get a menu of the previously visited sites (otherwise, clicking the button opens a folder window).

It is possible to put the History folder directly on the Start menu and access all the sites easily as menu items. Follow these steps to do this:

STEPS

Getting Quickly to Your Internet Explorer History

Step 1. Right-click the Start button, and click Open. If you want to have the History menu item on the main Start menu, stop here. Otherwise, continue to open up windows of menu items until you open the menu folder where you want it stored.

Step 2. Right-click an open area of the window. Choose New ⇨ Folder.

Step 3. The temporary name New Folder is highlighted so that you can type over it with a new name. Type the following text exactly as we have printed it here:

```
History.{FF393560-C2A7-11CF-BFF4-444553540000}
```

Step 4. Press Enter, and the New Folder icon is replaced with the History icon.

Step 5. Click the Start button. The History icon appears as a menu item, and all the Web sites stored in the History folder are listed in a cascading menu attached to it.

We feel that this is an absolutely necessary change to be able to run history effectively. The history function is much improved in recent versions of Internet Explorer, and it is well worth your effort to be able to get to it easily and often.

Tip

We also suggest that you greatly expand the range of your history file, far beyond the 20 days that are standard. Choose Tools ⇨ Internet Options. In the General tab of the Internet Options dialog box, increase the number of days to keep pages in the History folder.

Restore Open in New Window

Secret

Internet Explorer lets you open a new Internet Explorer window by right-clicking a link in a Web page and clicking Open in New Window. It is possible to lose this capability.

You can restore your ability to open new windows from links by taking these steps:

STEPS

Restoring Open in New Window

Step 1. Click Start ⇨ Run.

Step 2. Type **regsvr32 shdocvw.dll** and press Enter.

Step 3. Click Start ⇨ Shut Down, click Restart, and click OK.

Thanks to Adam Vujic for this secret.

Set Work Offline Before You Open Internet Explorer

Secret

By changing your registry settings, you can make a pair of shortcuts that let you switch between online and offline mode before you open Internet Explorer. This is useful if you have marked "Always dial my default connection in the Connections tab of the Internet Options dialog box. If you have done this and you use a home page that is not stored in your Temporary Internet Files folder, Internet Explorer will try to dial a connection as soon as you open it, and you'll have to cancel the dialing. It's much easier if you can set your system to offline mode before this happens.

These steps walk you through the creation of two files, Online.reg and Offline.reg.

STEPS

Setting Online/Offline Status

Step 1. In Notepad, start a new text file and type the following:

```
REGEDIT4
[HKEY_USERS\.Default\Software\Microsoft\Windows\
CurrentVersion\InternetSettings]
"GlobalUserOffline"=dword:00000000
```

Save your file as Online.reg (if you have created a My System folder as we suggest elsewhere in this book, that's a good place for it), and then close it.

Continued

STEPS

Setting Online/Offline Status *(continued)*

Step 2.   Start another text file and type the following:

```
REGEDIT4
[HKEY_USERS\.Default\Software\Microsoft\Windows\
CurrentVersion\InternetSettings]
"GlobalUserOffline"=dword:00000001
```

Save this file as `Offline.reg` in the same folder you used for the file in step 1, and close it.

Step 3.   You can make shortcuts to your two new files on your Desktop. Better yet, put the shortcuts on a toolbar so they'll always be handy. See "New Folders for New Toolbars" in Chapter 5 to learn how to make a new toolbar for shortcuts like these. Drag the toolbar's sizing bar to the right until only the toolbar's name is visible, and click the arrow to display your shortcuts, as shown in Figure 26-10.

Figure 26-10: You can put your Online and Offline shortcuts on their own toolbar. We put the toolbar just to the left of the Quick Launch toolbar.

Step 4.   Click the `Offline.reg` shortcut. You will be asked if you want to add the information in `Offline.reg` to your registry. Click Yes. When you see a confirmation that the registry has changed, click OK again. Now open Internet Explorer, and notice that it will not try to make a connection. When you click File, you should see a checkmark next to Work Offline. Click File ⇨ Work Offline to remove the checkmark and switch to online mode.

If Internet Explorer is closed and you want to switch to online mode, click the `Online.reg` shortcut, click Yes and then OK, and reopen Internet Explorer.

To eliminate the warning and confirmation in step 4, right-click the icon for each shortcut (in the Explorer, not on the toolbar) and select Properties. At the beginning of the Target field, type **regedit /s** followed by a space in front of the path to the target, and then click OK. You'll find more on this in "Auto-Inserting into your Registry at Startup" in Chapter 11.

Thanks to Tom Koch for this secret!

You might find it easiest to download InkSwitch, a small Windows Me/9*x*/NT/ 2000 program available from Inkland. InkSwitch indicates whether you are working online or offline, and lets you change the status by clicking its icon. You can put it in your system tray, and set Windows to always start in offline or online mode. You can even define hot keys for it. InkSwitch is freeware, and it's available at http://www.inkland.f9.co.uk/.

Replace the Internet Explorer Shell

You can think of the Internet Explorer as just a user interface to built-in Windows capabilities. Microsoft certainly has made the case that the Windows operating system and the Internet Explorer browser are "integrated." This means that they consist of dynamic link library files that can be called by any other program.

Neoplanet is an Internet browser front end that takes advantage of the Internet services provided by Windows, as illustrated in Figure 26-11. It uses the online service SNAP as its organizer and portal, although you can change that if you like.

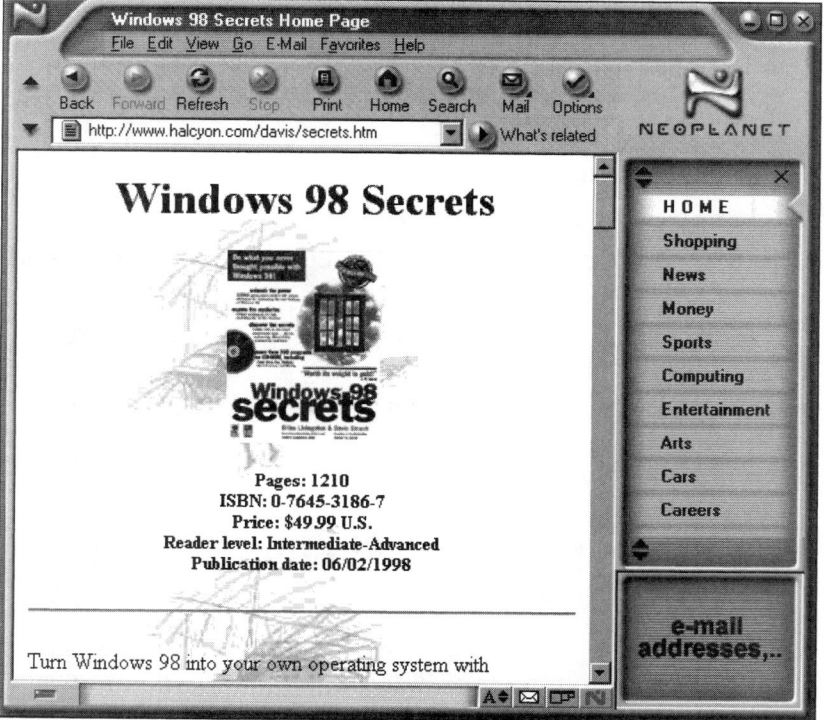

Figure 26-11: The Neoplanet user interface

We like Neoplanet's look and feel, especially the buttons. You can run it at the same time that you run Internet Explorer. It comes with its own integrated e-mail, and you can import your Outlook or Outlook Express settings to it automatically. It uses your existing Favorites folder.

Is it competing or cooperating with Microsoft? Yes.

You'll find it at `http://www.neoplanet.com`.

Internet Explorer Opens Partially Off-Screen

Secret

If you open an Internet Explorer window only to find that most of it is off your Desktop, it may be because you have bad values stored under window placement in your registry. It's best just to delete the relevant keys and then let them get rebuilt.

STEPS
Clearing Your Window Placement Keys

Step 1. Use your Registry Editor to navigate to the following key:

HKEY_CURRENT_USER\ Software\ Microsoft\ Internet Explorer\ Main

Step 2. Right-click Window_Placement in the right pane, and then click Delete.

Step 3. Navigate to the following key:

HKEY_CURRENT_USER\ Software\ Microsoft\ Internet_Explorer\ Desktop\ OldWorkAreas

Step 4. If you see OldWorkAreaRects in the right pane, right-click it and then click Delete.

Step 5. Exit your Registry Editor and restart Windows.

Keep the Browser Window Behind the Current Window

Wouldn't it be great if when you clicked a link, the browser window didn't pop up over what you are currently doing? We realize that this wouldn't be a good thing for new users because they would wonder what happened to the Web site that they just tried to invoke, but it sure would be good for the rest of us.

We'd sometimes like to keep the browser window in the background, filling in from our little wire going to our ISP. After a decent interval, we could click the browser window and see what's up. Meanwhile, we could continue reading the material in the current window.

Here's a solution that, while not perfect, works well enough. TopIt! allows you to designate windows that stay on top. If you want your Outlook Express window to stay on top when you click a link to a Web site in your e-mail, just make sure that your Outlook Express window is set to stay on top.

One caveat: If you've set the Outlook Express window to stay on top, you can't click a window underneath it and have that window go to the top. You have to minimize Outlook Express. Outlook Express will now stay on top of any other window unless the other window is also marked to stay on top.

You can download this $5 program from Cloud Nine Software at http://members.tripod.com/cybertech_software/.

Microsoft's Tweaks to Internet Explorer

Microsoft has released its own add-ons and tools that help you change and use Internet Explorer. You can zoom in and out on images, customize your searches, open a frame in a new window, paste URLs, and more.

All of these tools are available from the Web Accessories page on the Microsoft Web site at http://www.microsoft.com/windows/ie/webaccess/default.asp.

Favorites and Offline Web Pages

A URL (Uniform Resource Locator) is a unique identifier for a Web page or other resource on the Internet. Windows maintains a list of the URLs for your favorite sites. Your *favorites* are actually shortcuts stored in the \Windows\Favorites folder.

You can store whatever you like in the Favorites subfolders, but we suggest limiting what you put in these folders to shortcuts (either to URLs or to other folders or documents). You can put copies of URL shortcuts on your Desktop and start your Internet Explorer by clicking a shortcut's icon. You can also create shortcuts to URLs on the fly as you're browsing. See "URL Shortcuts" later in this chapter for more information.

Secret

You can drag and drop (move) your Favorites folder wherever you like (say, onto a drive other than the drive that contains the \Windows folder), and the Internet Explorer will track its location. The current Favorites folder location is stored in the registry at HKEY_CURRENT_USER\ Software\ Microsoft\ Windows\ CurrentVersion\ Explorer\ Shell Folders and at HKEY_CURRENT_USER\ Software\ Microsoft\ Windows\ CurrentVersion\ Explorer\ User Shell Folders, if you move it.

To create a shortcut to your favorites, open an Explorer window and navigate to \Windows\Favorites. Right-drag and drop your Favorites folder onto your Desktop. Choose Create Shortcut(s) Here.

You can get to your favorites from the Start menu, the My Computer menu, the Internet Explorer menu, and the Explorer menu. You'll also find a Favorites button in the Internet toolbar. This button opens a Favorites pane on the left side of the client area of the Internet Explorer. If you click View ⇨ Explorer Bar ⇨ Favorites, this same Favorites pane appears. You can right-click the favorites in this pane to open their associated context menus.

Organizing Your Favorites

You can divide your Favorites folder into subfolders organized around common topics, and then place shortcuts to your favorite sites in these subfolders. To create Favorites subfolders, choose Favorites ⇨ Organize Favorites in an Explorer window and click the Create New Folder button.

Tip

You can also open a window to display the contents of your Favorites folder by holding down the Shift key when you click the Organize Favorites command. Unlike the Organize Favorites window, this is a regular folder window focused on one of the Favorites subfolders.

You can create subfolders for your Favorites folder in any Explorer window. You can move these folders around (after all, they are just folders containing shortcuts), but if you want them to show up under the Favorites menu item, you need to leave them stored under the Favorites folder. You can subdivide the Favorites folder's subfolders, and you can drag shortcuts from folder to folder. You can also rename shortcuts. This is helpful because the default name of a shortcut is often not that meaningful. (The default name is whatever the Webmaster came up with for the document at the specific URL to which the shortcut is linked.)

Tip

You'll notice that your Favorites list contains a shortcut to your My Documents folder. This shortcut gives you a way to use the Favorites menu item to navigate to your My Documents folder. Of course, you can add other shortcuts to local files or folders to your Favorites folder as well. Just open an Explorer window, navigate to the file or folder that you want to create a shortcut for, and choose Favorites ⇨ Add to Favorites. You can also right-drag the file into the \Windows\Favorites folder or a subfolder, and choose Create Shortcut Here.

You can have multiple lists of favorites. One way to do this is to drag and drop a copy of your \Windows\Favorites to a new location. Rename the new folder, and then edit the contents of both folders. You can then use TweakUI to switch back and forth between folders, first designating one as your Favorites folder, and then the other. To switch the Favorites folder, click the TweakUI icon, click the General tab, and choose Favorites in the Folder drop-down list. Click the Change Location button, and then browse to the new favorites folder.

URL Shortcuts

The Internet Explorer keeps track of Web sites using shortcuts to URLs. These shortcuts have an extension of url instead of the standard lnk extension for Windows shortcuts.

URL shortcuts store more information about the URLs than just their values. (See Figure 26-12.) Internet Explorer uses this additional information to help you manage your shortcuts as well as to let you view Web sites offline.

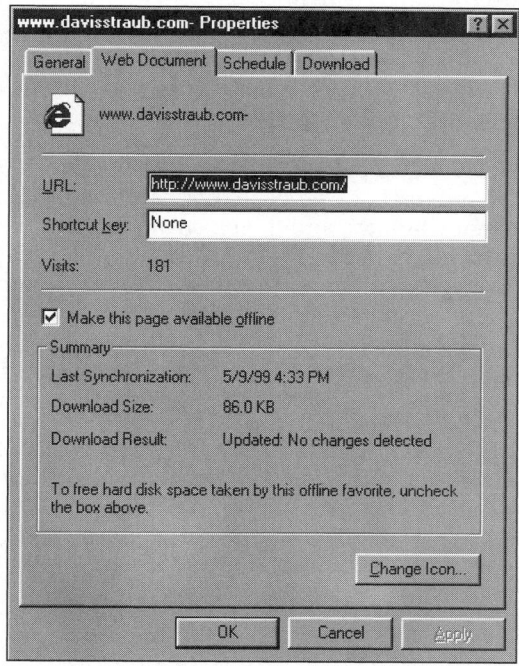

Figure 26-12: The Properties dialog box for a URL shortcut. Notice the tabs for additional properties.

You can create a URL shortcut to a Web site just by displaying the site in an Internet Explorer window, and choosing Favorites ⇨ Add to Favorites. If you want to place the shortcut in an existing or new subfolder of the Favorites folder, click the Create In button. To use an existing subfolder, just select it and then click OK. To create a new subfolder, click the New Folder button.

If you would rather put the shortcut directly on the Desktop, right-click an area on the Web page that doesn't include a graphic or a link to another location and choose Create Shortcut from the context menu. Or, click File ⇨ Send ⇨ Shortcut To Desktop.

You can also drag the icon at the left end of the Address bar to the Desktop to create a shortcut to the Web page.

Tip

To create a shortcut to a link (a jump to another URL) in a Web page, drag the link to the Desktop. You can later click this shortcut to open an Internet Explorer window and go to the indicated location on the Web.

Tip

You don't have to put URL shortcuts in the Favorites folder or one of its subfolders. If you do, then the shortcuts are accessible from the Favorites toolbar button or menu item in an Explorer window. But you are free to put them wherever you like. You can create many folders of URL shortcuts, and place shortcuts to these folders on your Desktop.

Capturing URLs in a Frame

Normally when you display a Web page or site, its URL appears in the Address bar. However, if you open a Web page that uses frames (panes within the Internet Explorer client window), and then navigate within the main, or largest, frame to a page on another site, the Address bar will not update to show you the URL for the page you're currently viewing. This happens because Web designers often use frames as a way to let you view other people's pages without leaving their own site. This allows them to keep their text, logos, navigational buttons, and graphics in view (in smaller frames around the main frame) even as you're viewing pages at other locations.

Secret

You may want to know the new URL for a page you're viewing in a frame, if for no other reason than to get out of the frame at the original site and onto the new site of the page you're viewing. Here's how to capture the URL:

STEPS

Finding the URL for a Site That's Been "Framed"

Step 1. Right-click an open spot in the frame that contains the Web page whose URL you want to know. Select Properties.

Step 2. You'll now see the URL. If you want to jump to the site, highlight the URL and press Ctrl+C to copy it.

Step 3. Click in Internet Explorer's Address field, press Ctrl+V to paste the URL, and then press Enter.

Deleting Typed URLs in the Address Field

If you type a URL in the Address field in Internet Explorer, you can go back later and choose that URL from a drop-down list attached to the Address field. This list lets you scroll through previously typed URLs to pick the one you want. (Sometimes URLs that you didn't type are put on this list — they get "typed in" automatically.)

Secret

You can edit this list or delete it using your Registry Editor. Just navigate to HKEY_CURRENT_USER\ Software\ Microsoft\ Internet Explorer\ TypedURLs. You'll notice a list of URLs in the right pane of the Registry Editor. To delete an entry, select it (click its url*x* name in the Name column) and press Delete. To edit an entry, double-click its url*x* name.

Converting Netscape Navigator Bookmarks to Favorites

If you've installed Netscape Navigator on Windows, and you later want to convert your Netscape bookmarks to Internet Explorer favorites, you can do it either one step at a time or in batch mode.

STEPS

Converting Navigator Bookmarks — the Manual Method

Step 1.   In the Explorer, navigate to your Netscape folder (in the Program Files folder) and find the file `Bookmark.htm`.

Step 2.   Click this file to open it.

Step 3.   Right-click a bookmark in the Bookmark file, and then click Add To Favorites on the menu that appears.

Step 4.   Repeat step 3 for each bookmark you want to convert.

Secret

If you want to convert *all* your Netscape Navigator bookmarks at once, you can use the Internet Explorer Import/Export Wizard. Choose Files, Import and Export to launch the wizard, then follow its instructions to indicate what you wish to import. You can also use this wizard to export your favorites as a `bookmark.htm` file that Netscape can read.

Internet Explorer Drag and Drop Links

It's easy to save links and graphics files as you browse the Web if you open up Internet Explorer with two panes. You can do this by right-clicking the Internet Explorer icon on your Desktop, and choosing Explore. Starting Internet Explorer this way adds the Folders option to the View ⇨ Explorer Bar submenu and automatically selects it, so you see your folders listed in the left pane.

As you browse Web sites in the right pane, you can drag and drop links — either to Web pages or to files you want to download — and graphics into appropriate folders in the left pane. Links are stored as URL shortcuts. If you later click a shortcut for a link to a Web page, Internet Explorer takes you to the linked Web site. If you click a shortcut for a link to a file you want to download, you start the download process. Graphics files are copied from your cache and stored in the folder into which you drag them.

Drag and Drop Images

If you are displaying a Web site or HTML document in your Internet Explorer, you can drag an image on the Web page to the title bar or Address bar to display the image by itself. This is not the same as a Web page *thumbnail*, which is a small version of an image that leads to a larger, more detailed version when you click it.

Secret

This doesn't work if you are viewing a page constructed using the Microsoft HTML format (MHTML), which includes graphics in the same file as the text file that makes up the Web page. These files have the mht extension.

You'll can also drag links or mail addresses from the displayed page onto the title bar or Address bar as a way to command Internet Explorer to go to the linked page or to open your default e-mail client. Of course, you can also just do this by clicking the links on the Web page.

Saving Graphics off the Internet

Do you want to save a Web-based graphic that you are viewing in Internet Explorer? Right-click it, choose Save Picture As, and then give it a path and a name. If you don't save a graphics file as you're viewing it, you can save it later from the cache. When Internet Explorer first downloads a graphics file, it automatically caches (saves) it in the \Windows\Temporary Internet Files folder. You can find the file in this folder and save it permanently by copying it to another location.

If you want to turn a graphic in a Web page into wallpaper on your Desktop, right-click the graphic and choose Set As Wallpaper.

Favorites off the Start Menu

The Windows Start menu includes the Favorites folder. When you click Favorites on the Start menu, you'll notice that the URL shortcuts to your favorite Web sites are displayed in a menu fashion (as opposed to folder window fashion).

You can also get to your favorites by clicking the Favorites button on the Internet Explorer toolbar, or the Favorites menu item in your Explorer or Internet Explorer. If you don't use the Favorites Start menu item very frequently and would like to remove it from your Start menu, you can do so with TweakUI. (In TweakUI, click the IE tab, clear "Show favorites on start menu," and click OK.)

If you've removed the Favorites item from your Start menu, you can create an alternate method of getting to your Favorites folder by right-dragging the folder \Windows\Favorites to your Desktop and choosing Create Shortcut(s) Here. You can also create a Favorites toolbar by following these steps:

STEPS

Creating a Favorites Toolbar

Step 1. Right-click your taskbar, click Toolbars ⇨ New Toolbar, browse to \Windows\Favorites in the New Toolbar dialog box, and click OK.

Step 2. Drag the sizing bar at the left edge of the Favorites toolbar over to the right until only the word *Favorites* is still visible.

Step 3. Click the arrow next to the word *Favorites* to display a vertical menu of Favorites, as shown in Figure 26-13. Click a menu item to open a folder window of Favorites.

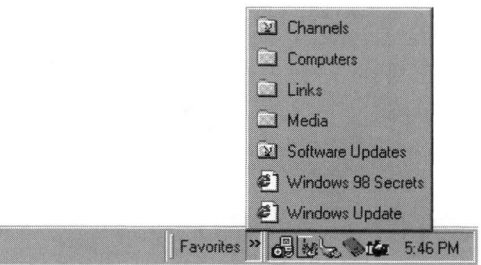

Figure 26-13: The Favorites menu, as displayed on a Favorites toolbar

Easy Access to Your Offline Web Pages Folder

Speaking of favorites, it can be a bit difficult to get to your Offline Web Pages folder if you've removed the Favorites item from your Start menu. You can get easy access to this folder in a couple of ways.

One option is to right-drag the \Windows\Offline Web Pages folder to your Desktop and create a shortcut to it there. You can also right-drag the folder and drop it on your Start button. (In this case, you can also left-drag to create the shortcut, but this is not standard behavior when you left drag a folder.)

Secret

If you use the Offline Pages resource identifier when dragging the Offline Web Pages folder to the Start menu, you can create a cascading menu instead of opening a folder window, as described in these steps:

STEPS

Easing Access to Your Offline Web Pages

Step 1. Right-click the Start button and click Open. If you want the Offline Web Pages item to appear on the main Start menu, stop here. Otherwise, continue to open up windows of menu items until you open the menu folder that you want to contain it.

Step 2. Right-click an open area of the window and choose New ⇨ Folder.

Step 3. The temporary name New Folder is highlighted so that you can type over it with a new name. Type the following text exactly as we have printed it here:

Offline Web Pages.{F5175861-2688-11d0-9C5E-00AA00A45957}

Step 4. Press Enter, and the New Folder icon is replaced with the Offline Web Pages icon.

Step 5. Click the Start button. The Offline Web Pages icon appears as a menu item, and all of the offline Web sites are listed in a cascading menu attached to it (see Figure 26-14).

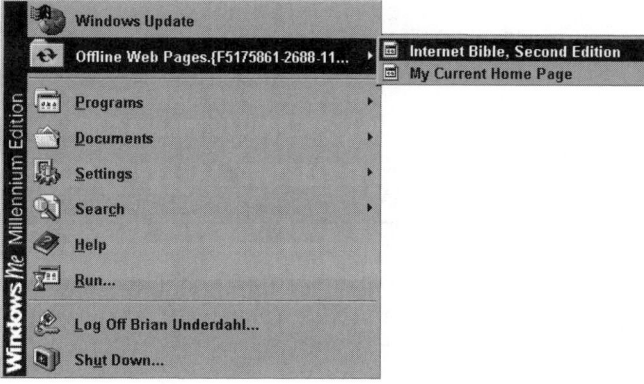

Figure 26-14: The offline pages are now available on the main Start menu.

Download Web Sites for Later Perusal

Assuming that you've created a shortcut to your \Windows\Offline Web Pages folder on your Desktop, click it to display your offline Web pages, as shown in Figure 26-15.

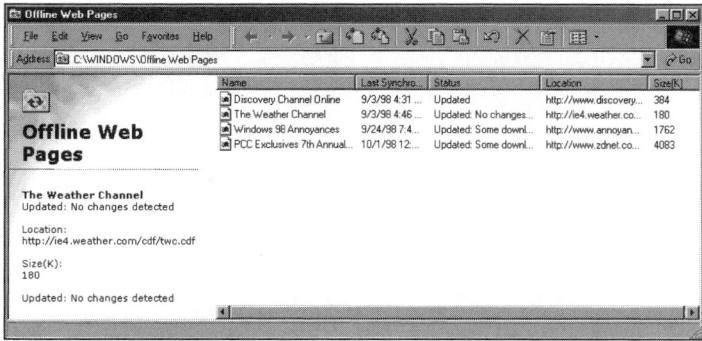

Figure 26-15: The Web pages you download for offline viewing are displayed in the Offline Web Pages folder.

The toolbar at the top of the Offline Web Pages folder contains two buttons, Sync and Sync All. These buttons are located just to the left of the Cut (scissors) button. You can use them to download a Web page or site immediately.

Clicking the Sync or Sync All button will by default download only one page of a Web site, unless the Web site publisher has specified other pages. If you want to go deeper, you can let Internet Explorer download a pretty complete set of HTML documents from a Web site—up to three links deep starting from any Web page that you choose. To do so, take these steps:

STEPS

Downloading a Web Site

Step 1.   Connect to the Internet and use your Internet Explorer to navigate to a Web page on a Web site that you want to view offline. If you have already added this page to your Favorites, you don't need to go online—right-click it in the Favorites, click "Make available offline," and go to step 4.

Step 2.   Navigate to a central page of the Web site that provides links throughout the site to information that you are interested in.

Step 3.   Click Favorites ⇨ Add to Favorites. In the Add Favorite dialog box that appears, mark the "Make available offline" checkbox, and select a Favorites folder for saving the shortcut. Than click the Customize button.

Step 4.   This brings up the Offline Favorite Wizard shown in Figure 26-16. (If you haven't run the wizard before, you will see an introductory screen that tells you about the wizard. You can choose not to show this again.) Click the Yes option button, choose how deep to delve into the Web site by selecting 1, 2, or 3, and then click Next.

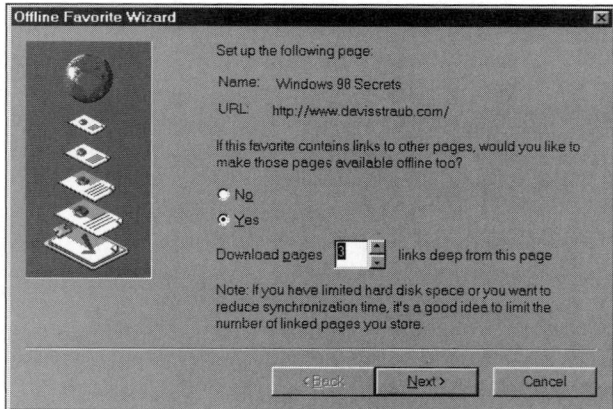

Figure 26-16: The Offline Favorite Wizard

Step 5.   The wizard now asks how often you want to update (synchronize) the Web page/site. Unless you already have a schedule set up, click "Only when I choose synchronize from the Tools menu," as shown in Figure 26-17. Click Next.

Step 6. If the site doesn't require a password, click the Finish button. Otherwise, enter your user name and password (twice), click Finish, and then click OK to close the Add Favorite dialog box.

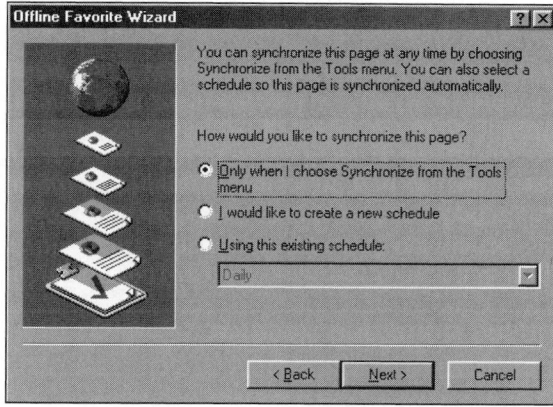

Figure 26-17: Mark the first option button in this Offline Favorite Wizard dialog box unless you have established a schedule for downloading.

Step 7. Internet Explorer will attempt to download (synchronize) the site right now. You can do this now, or wait until after you've refined your synchronization schedule using the remaining steps. To wait until later, click the Stop button shown in Figure 26-18.

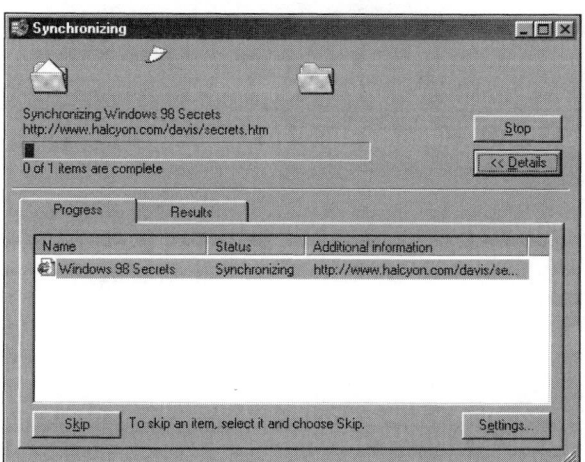

Figure 26-18: Click the Stop button if you want to refine your schedule before synchronizing.

Continued

STEPS

Downloading a Web Site *(continued)*

Step 8.   Click your Offline Web Pages shortcut on your Desktop or in your Start menu, or navigate to \Windows\Offline Web Pages. Right-click the shortcut to the offline Web page that you just created, and click Properties. Click the Download tab in the Properties dialog box, as shown in Figure 26-19.

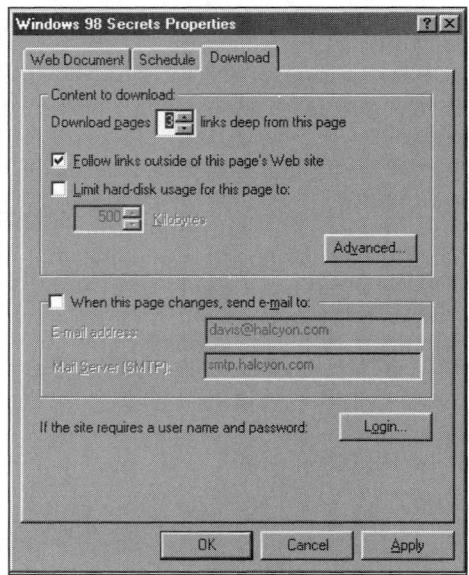

Figure 26-19: The Download tab of the Properties dialog box for the Windows 98 Secrets offline Web page

Step 9.   Adjust any of the parameters in the Download tab. If you want to exclude graphics files, sound, video, ActiveX controls, or Java applets, click the Advanced button.

Step 10.   To set up a regular schedule to update your downloaded Web site/page at a time while you're asleep or away from your computer, click the Schedule tab, shown in Figure 26-20. You can select a daily, weekly, or monthly schedule, or create a custom schedule. Highlight the schedule you want and then click the Edit button.

Step 11.   Click the Schedule tab in the dialog box for your schedule, display the Schedule Task list, and choose a frequency for synchronizing the Web site, as shown in Figure 26-21. Depending on what you have selected, you may also need to choose a time or specify other information.

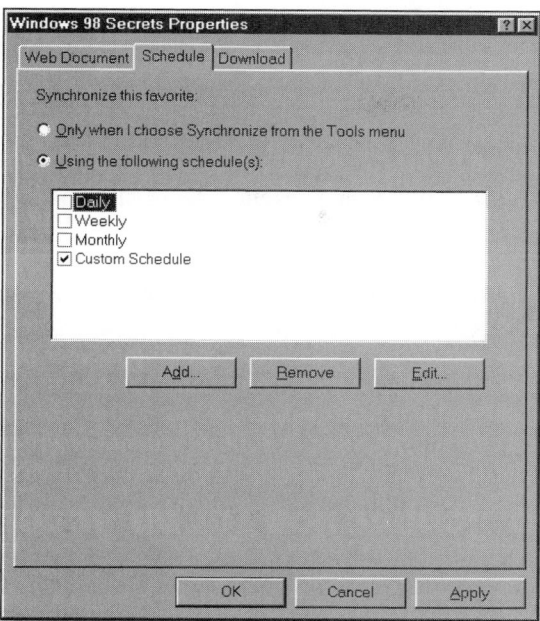

Figure 26-20: Select one of the preset schedules, or set up a custom schedule.

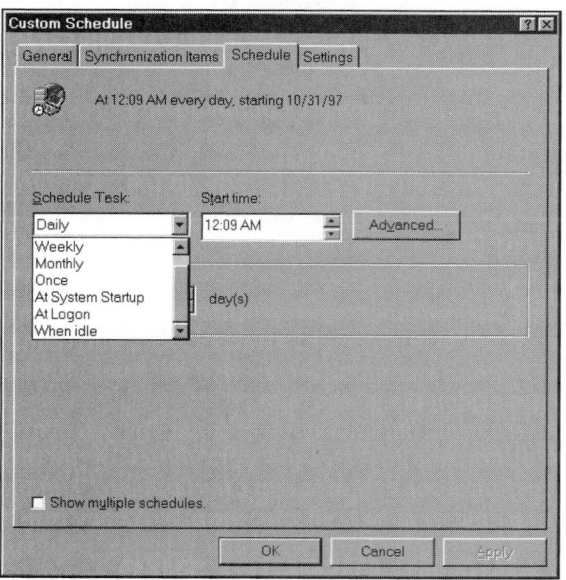

Figure 26-21: Select a frequency for synchronizing from the Schedule Task drop-down list.

Continued

STEPS

Downloading a Web Site *(continued)*

Step 12. If you chose Weekly or Monthly in step 11, click the Advanced button. In the Advanced Schedule Options dialog box, choose a start date for your schedule, as shown in Figure 26-22. Then click OK twice.

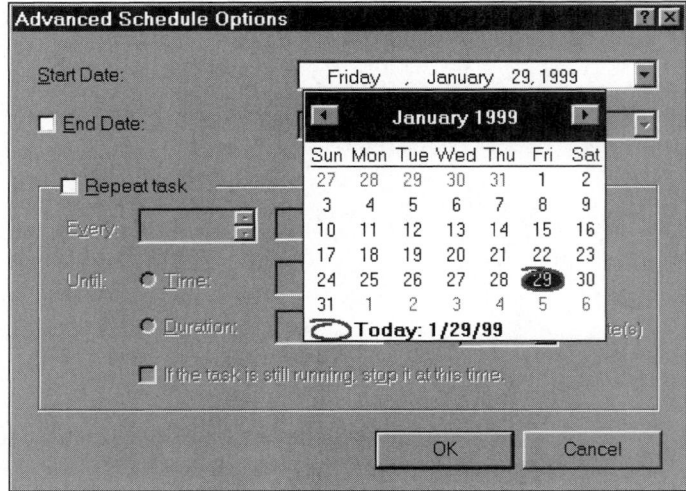

Figure 26-22: You can set your weekly or monthly schedule to start today.

Your Web page/site will now be downloaded at the date and time that you've chosen, as long as you have your computer on at that time. During synchronization, the icon for the Synchronization Manager will appear in your system tray. Later, you can click your Offline Web Pages shortcut on your Desktop or in your Start menu, and click the new Web page to view it. If your computer tries to go online, click File ⇨ Work Offline in the Internet Explorer window.

If you find that the download has missed a page or two (hey, it's a jungle out there on the Web), just go online and click the links that seem to be missing.

Internet Explorer will go out on the schedule you have set up, and will check whether a page has been changed since the last synchronization. It won't download the page to your offline Web page store again if it hasn't changed.

If your Web page is a channel, the Offline Favorite Wizard won't give you the option of choosing how many pages deep to download. The channel operator is limiting access to the site. The Download tab of the Properties dialog box for a channel gives you two options: download the content specified by the channel operator, or just download the home page and a table of contents. Channel operators have recommended schedules, which show up in the Schedule tab of the Properties dialog box. You can choose their schedule if you like, but you can't edit it. You can also choose another schedule.

Windows tracks the offline Web pages separately from the temporary Internet files. You can manage them with the Disk Cleanup applet (Start ⇨ Programs ⇨ Accessories ⇨ System Tools ⇨ Disk Cleanup), as shown in Figure 26-23. Notice that this applet can distinguish between the two types of files.

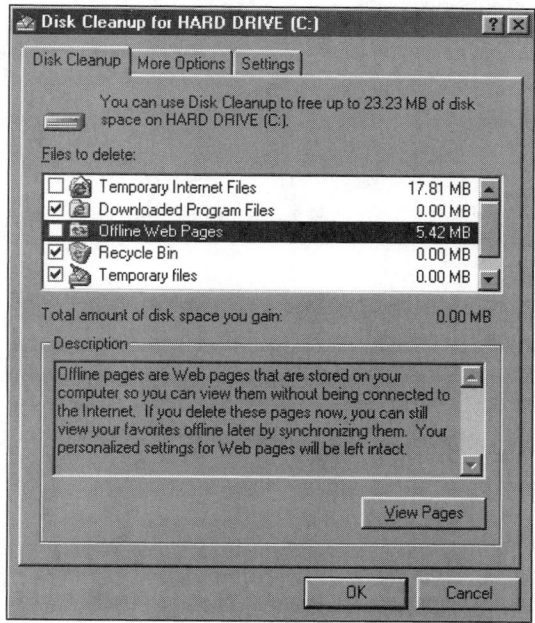

Figure 26-23: The Disk Cleanup dialog box. You can delete the temporary Internet files while leaving the offline Web pages intact.

Deeper Offline Viewing

The Internet Explorer offline viewer limits your Web page gathering to three levels starting from any given page. If you want to go a little deeper and have a bit more control and flexibility, check out SiteSnagger, a freeware package from Steven Sipe via *PC Magazine*. SiteSnagger lets you follow the links up to 20 jumps away from the original page. (Be careful: If each page has 10 unique links, 20 jumps will theoretically encompass 11,111,111,111,111,111,110 pages [10 on the first page + 100 on the first jump + 1,000 on the second jump, and so forth]. This is probably more pages than you have disk space for!)

You can set SiteSnagger for the maximum number of Web pages, whether or not you'll download GIFs, JPEGs, and other multimedia or non-HTML files, and whether to follow the links to another server.

SiteSnagger stores all the pages and multimedia files associated with the site in a separate subfolder for each site (or user-defined project), as shown in Figure 26-24. You can have SiteSnagger create an HTML table of contents that just lists the names of the Web pages, but it's not really as useful as the pages and their own links.

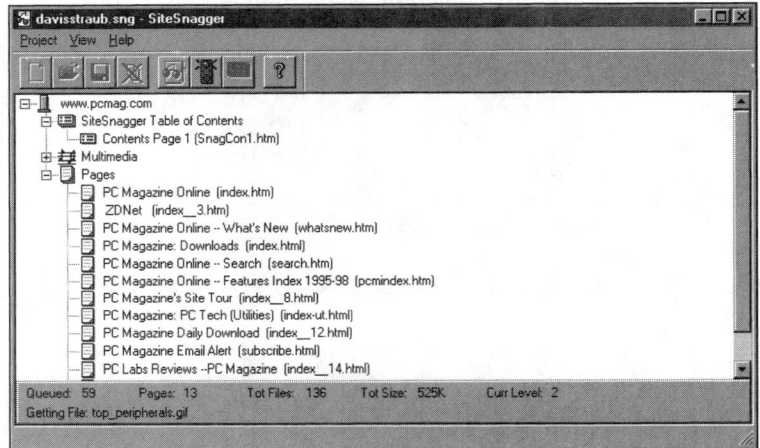

Figure 26-24: SiteSnagger makes it easy to navigate among the pages you've downloaded from a Web site.

SiteSnagger is easy to use and reassuring in that it saves all the pages and accompanying files in a subfolder that is easy to control. On the other hand, the Internet Explorer offline Web pages feature checks each Web page to see if the local copy needs to be updated before it downloads a new one, and SiteSnagger does not.

Web site authors can use tags that limit Internet Explorer's ability to crawl through a site. If an author has set these tags specifically for Internet Explorer, SiteSnagger will ignore the tags.

You'll find SiteSnagger at `http://www.zdnet.com/pcmag/pctech/content/17/04/ut1704.001.html`.

Save Complete Web Pages

Saving a Web page as an HTML file in Internet Explorer usually saves only the text and layout of the page — the graphics are saved separately as links. However, Internet Explorer does have the ability to save a Web page as a single document. The Microsoft HTML (.mht) file format incorporates both the graphics and the HTML text on a Web page into one file. The graphics are encoded using MIME (and Uuencoding), so everything is stored in e-mail-capable, 7-bit ASCII text characters. But Internet Explorer can decode the file on the fly and display the graphics.

This feature greatly expands the power of the Internet. If a document is displayed as one Web page, you can download it and all of its associated graphic files, and save everything in one very convenient document. If you do this, you don't have to save the document as an offline page to keep it readily available.

All you do to save a Web page in this format is click File ⇨ Save As, and choose "Web Archive for E-mail" in the "Save as type" field. This secret isn't hidden, but it sure is powerful. It turns the Web into something that you can actually use as a publishing arena.

Tip

You can see the entire underlying text file if you open a file with an mht extension in WordPad. If you click View ⇨ Source in the Internet Explorer when viewing an mht file, you'll only see the HTML code, and not the encoded graphics that are in fact there in the file.

Internet Explorer also lets you save a document as a "complete" Web page (click File ⇨ Save As, and choose Web Page ⇨ Complete in the "Save as type" field). In this case, the graphic files are not included in the HTML source text. Instead, Internet Explorer creates a subfolder in which it saves the downloaded graphics files. It rewrites the saved Web page to reference the graphics files in this subfolder, and enters the Web page's URL as a comment at the top of the page. We wish Save As ⇨ Web Archive for Email saved the Web page's URL as a comment.

Turn Your Favorites into a Web Page

The Favorites menu and submenus are fine for starters, but sometimes it is a bit of a drag to search repeatedly through all these menus. How about creating a single Web page of all your favorites? Or separate Web pages for different subsets of favorites?

Internet Explorer includes the Import/Export Wizard, which can export your favorites or cookies. It writes them to your disk in a format that Netscape can read. You can also use the wizard to import cookies and favorites from Netscape. The wizard writes out your favorites as an HTML file. This makes it easy to look through your favorites with Notepad and edit them if you like. You can also use the HTML file as a page in Internet Explorer, from which you can easily jump to any site on your list.

Choose File ⇨ Import and Export to run the wizard.

Move Favorites to Links

We're not big fans of the Favorites Explorer bar you can turn on. It occupies space on the left side of the Internet Explorer window. You might like to have a way to get to your Favorites other than the Internet Explorer menu itself.

One way out of this dilemma is to move your Favorites subfolder into the Links subfolder. Before you do this, you might create an additional subfolder for all of your existing links, and store the subfolder under the Links folder. Now you'll have a Links toolbar that contains menu items for your favorites as well as your links. This process is detailed in these steps:

STEPS

Moving Your Favorites to Your Links

Step 1. Open your Explorer and navigate to \Windows\Favorites\Links.

Step 2. Right-click your right pane, click New ⇨ Folder, and rename the new folder **Links**.

Step 3. Drag all of the shortcuts in your \Windows\Favorites\Links folder to your \Windows\Favorites\Links\Links folder.

Step 4. Drag the rest of your Favorites shortcuts and subfolders into your \Windows\Favorites\Links folder.

Step 5. Position your Links toolbar in your Internet Explorer window so that you can see all of your favorites on the toolbar, as shown in Figure 26-25.

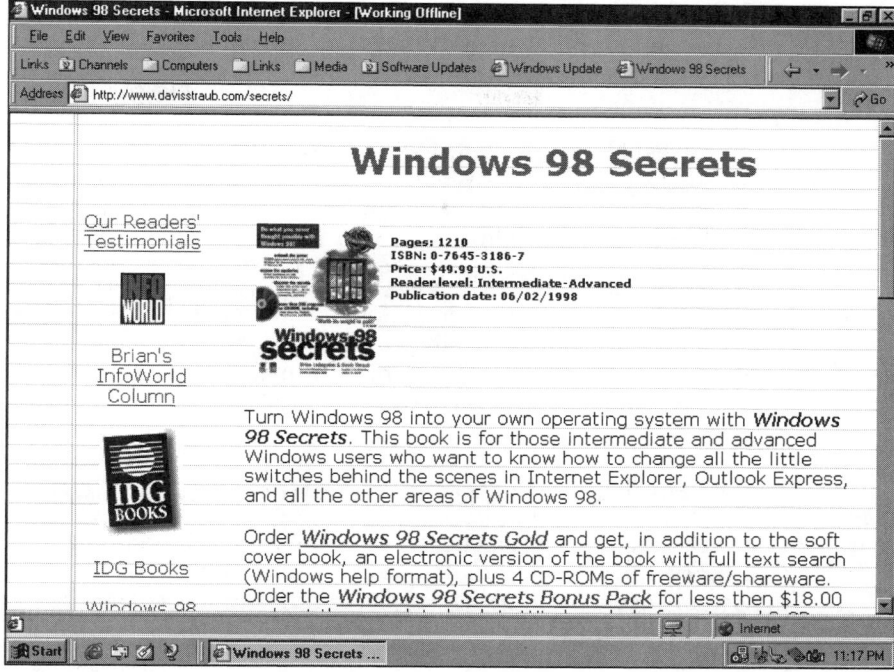

Figure 26-25: The new Links toolbar appears at the top of the window, just below the Address bar.

Now you can use the Links toolbar to get to your favorites.

Thanks to Jim Schott for this tip.

Internet Security

Internet Explorer's "security levels"—designed by Microsoft to protect you from the Internet as you surf the World Wide Web—have caused consternation among many Windows users. In some ways, the default settings aren't secure enough to be safe. But many people also want to keep security warning messages from popping up every time they move from one Web site to another.

If you know where you're going on the Internet—and you don't need a "Net nanny"—follow the advice in the next three sections and you'll see far fewer dialog boxes interrupting your journeys.

Some Web sites also provide extra forms of security. If you see a little padlock on the right side of your status bar, you know that you're on a site that has some sort of security. If you want to know just what sort, hover your mouse over the padlock.

You can get Microsoft's latest word on security at `http://www.microsoft.com/windows/ie/security/default.asp`. However, you might also try the Unofficial Microsoft Internet Explorer Security FAQ at `http://www.nwnetworks.com/iesc.html` .

If you've looked at the `\Windows\Temporary Internet Files` folder, you'll notice the random names for the four subfolders. This is a security feature you're seeing. It's theoretically possible for someone to embed a destructive program in a Web page and then run it from the cache, but only if he or she has the exact pathname. This is not as easy with four random subfolder names.

Internet Explorer's Security Options

In the Internet Explorer, choose Tools ⇨ Internet Options, and click the Security tab. Select Internet Zone in the Zone drop-down list, click the Custom Level button to display the Security Settings dialog box, as shown in Figure 26-26.

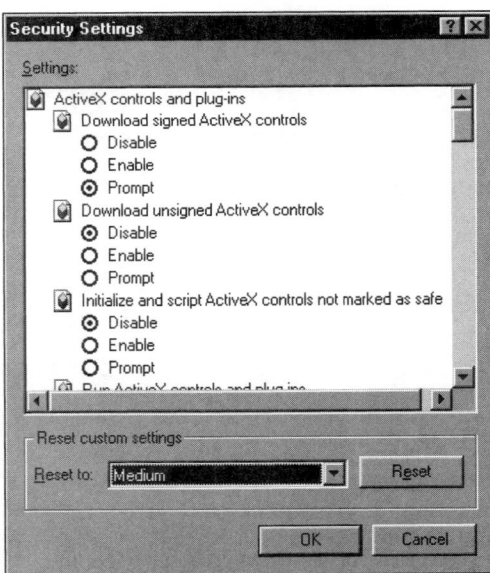

Figure 26-26: Security settings for the Internet Explorer

In this dialog box, you can see some of the assumptions Microsoft has built into Windows. If you select the Medium default settings, these are the values you get. All types of data are acceptable to Internet Explorer under these defaults, except ActiveX controls that are not "signed" or are not marked "safe."

Microsoft's security model divides Internet sites into four different types, or *zones*:

1. Local Intranet Zone — Web sites within your own company

2. Trusted Sites Zone — Sites you expect won't contain a computer virus or harmful code

3. Restricted Sites Zone — Sites that *do* contain the potential risk of viruses and antisocial behaviors

4. Internet Zone — Everything else

The View ⇨ Internet Options dialog box enables you to set a different level of security for each zone: High, Medium, Low, or Custom. You will need to add the Web sites by name in the first three zones for this security system to work.

You may find it easier to simply pick the set of security rules you think you can live with and configure the Internet Zone accordingly. All of the sites you visit will be subject to those rules. If you find that these rules are too tight or too loose for particular sites, you can add sites individually to the Trusted or Restricted categories.

Beneath Your Level

Choosing the security level you're comfortable with isn't too hard. Table 26-2 shows the choices you're making when you adopt a High, Medium, or Low security setting.

Table 26-2   Internet Explorer's Security Settings

	High	*Medium*	*Low*
Run ActiveX controls and plug-ins	Disable	Enable	Enable
Download signed ActiveX controls	Disable	Prompt	Enable
Download unsigned ActiveX controls	Disable	Prompt	Prompt
Script ActiveX controls not "safe"	Disable	Prompt	Prompt

Continued

Table 26-2 *(continued)*			
	High	*Medium*	*Low*
Java permissions (security level)	High	Medium	Low
Active scripting	Enable	Enable	Enable
Scripting of Java applets	Disable	Enable	Enable
File downloads	Disable	Enable	Enable
Font downloads	Disable	Prompt	Enable
Submit nonencrypted form data	Prompt	Prompt	Enable
Launching applications and files	Disable	Prompt	Enable
Installation of Desktop items	Disable	Prompt	Enable
Drag and drop or copy and paste files	Prompt	Enable	Enable

Generally, you'll want fairly restrictive rules for sites. But if you feel fairly confident about your ability to notice when a rogue Web site is messing around in files it should not be getting into, you may want to set your security level to Low. This enables all behaviors of Web sites, except that Internet Explorer will still prompt you with a dialog box prior to acting on ActiveX controls and scripts that are unsigned or not marked as safe — in other words, the ones that do not carry an "electronic certificate" acting as a kind of Good Housekeeping seal.

You can even turn off the warnings for suspect ActiveX controls by resetting all defaults to Low. To do this, click the Custom Level button, choose Low Security in the Reset To drop-down list, click the Reset button, click Yes, and then choose Enable under "Download unsigned ActiveX controls" and "Initialize and script ActiveX controls not marked as safe." But with these two cases, it probably makes sense to remain on the Prompt security level, since the whole premise of electronic certificates is to distinguish between ActiveX controls developed by reputable sources and those that might not be so reputable.

In addition to the security settings in the Security tab of the Tools ⇨ Internet Options dialog box, there are others to be found in the Advanced tab of the same dialog box. Scroll down to the Security heading to display the choices shown in Figure 26-27.

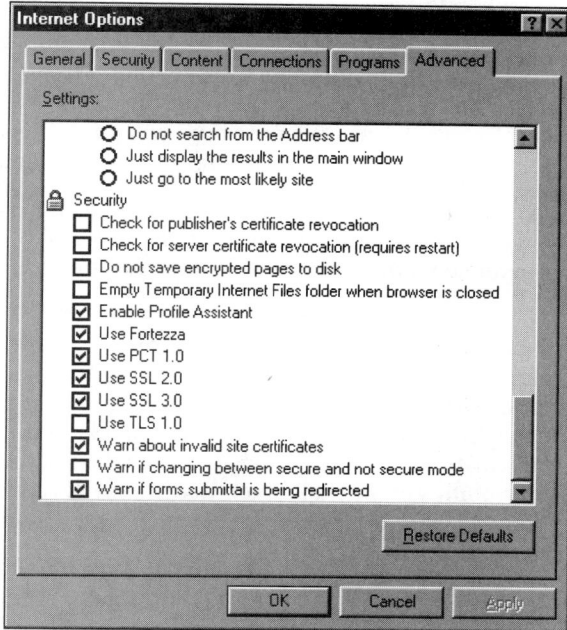

Figure 26-27: Advanced security settings

PCT and SSL refer to Private Communications Technology and Secure Sockets Layer. These are two encryption standards that let you enter sensitive information such as credit card numbers in Web page forms. There's little reason to turn these settings off unless you want to send out your credit card numbers as plaintext.

"Do not save encrypted pages to disk" turns off some of Windows' caching, which could hurt your Internet browsing performance.

We recommend clearing "Warn if changing between secure and not secure mode," unless you've turned off PCT or SSL for some reason. We suggest that you keep "Check for publisher's certificate revocation" turned off, and keep "Warn about invalid site certificates" turned on.

Where Are the Cookies?

The companies that Webmasters work for want to keep track of who visits their sites and just what it is that they look at or do there. One way Webmasters can do this is to store a little bit of information on your hard disk that is accessible to them the next time you come around. If you fill out a form when you are at a site, the information goes into the company's transaction-processing database, but some or all of it might also get placed back on your computer, in the form of a *cookie*.

Tasty bits of data, or cookies, are stored on your computer, ready and able to be used by the companies and individuals that own the Web sites you visit. Microsoft likes to cite its MSN Web site as an example of a Web page that is customizable. It can present you with the types of information you have selected (from a rather anemic menu) the next time you go to the site. MSN does this by storing your preferences on your computer as a nice big cookie.

Where's the cookie jar? `\Windows\Cookies`. The cookie filenames are usually your host name followed by an @ symbol, and then the name of the Web site. The files have a `txt` extension and they are readable, but they don't make much sense.

If you have your Internet Explorer set to warn you about incoming cookies, you'll get a cookie alert message. You can choose whether to take the cookie or not. If you want to just take the cookies, you can turn off this warning mechanism by choosing Tools ⇨ Internet Options, and clicking the Custom Level button on the Security tab. Under Cookies, enable the "Allow cookies that are stored on your computer option. If you don't want to have any cookies on your computer, mark Disable.

If you want more cookie control, check out Cookie Pal, available from `http://www.kburra.com`. Cookie Pal is free for 30 days, after which it's $15.

Corrupted Files in the Internet Cache Folder

Tip

The Internet Explorer caches quite a bit of the material you gather off the Internet. This makes it faster to go back to a Web page you've recently visited, because Internet Explorer can open it from your disk instead of retrieving it from the Internet again. The Internet Explorer always checks to see if it has the latest version of a Web page in its cache before it opens it. If it discovers that the page has been updated on the Web site since it was cached, it retrieves the updated version instead of using the cached copy. To make sure that you have the latest information from a site, you can force the Internet Explorer to retrieve a new copy of a Web page instead of using a copy from the cache. Just choose View ⇨ Refresh or press the F5 key.

You can determine whether Internet Explorer refreshes a Web page every time you view it, just when you start the Internet Explorer, or not until you press F5. In an Internet Explorer window, choose Tools ⇨ Internet Options, click the General tab, click the Settings button, and choose the desired option at the top of the Settings dialog box.

You can also set the size of the Internet cache folder (`\Windows\Temporary Internet Files`) in the Settings dialog box. Slide the slider under "Amount of disk space to use" to a percentage of the hard disk that you are willing to use for caching these Internet files.

Want to view what is in your cache? Click the View Files button in the Settings dialog box. If you order the files by Internet address, all the files from the same site will show up next to each other. Right-click an empty part of the window, choose Arrange Icons, and choose By Internet Address.

If some of the files in your Internet cache are corrupt, this can lead to a number of different error messages and Internet Explorer crashes. These include errors indicating cross-linked files and Kernel32.dll errors. If the errors are not so bad that you can't start your Internet Explorer, click the Internet Explorer icon, choose Tools ⇨ Internet Options, and click the Delete Files button in the General tab. You should also click the Clear History button.

If you still have similar error messages, take the following steps:

STEPS

Deleting the Internet Cache Files

Step 1. Click Start ⇨ Shut Down, select Restart in MS-DOS Mode, and click OK.

Step 2. At the DOS prompt, type **Attrib -s c:\Windows\Tempor~1** and press Enter.

Step 3. At the DOS prompt type **Deltree \Windows\Tempor~1** and press Enter.

Step 4. Type **exit** and press Enter.

This will delete the cache files folder. This folder will be re-created when you restart Windows.

You can tell Internet Explorer to store its cached files in a different folder. This might be a good idea if you have limited space on the drive that contains the \Windows folder.

To specify a different folder for your cached Web pages, right-click the Internet Explorer icon on your Desktop, choose Properties, click the General tab, click the Settings button, and then click the Move Folder button. In the Browse for Folder dialog box, highlight the desired folder and click OK. You have to restart Windows for the change to take effect. Note that when you specify a new cache folder, the Internet Explorer deletes all the cached files from the original folder.

Corrupt History Folder

Secret

If you open your History folder (click the History button on the Internet toolbar) and find that there are no URLs listed, you have a corrupt History folder (unless you haven't yet started exploring the Internet with the Internet Explorer). To solve this problem, click Start ⇨ Run, type **Regsvr32.exe/u C:\Windows\System\cachevu.dll**, and click OK. Next, click Start ⇨ Run, type **Regsvr32.exe C:\Windows\System\cachevu.dll**, and click OK.

Secret

If you get error messages stating that there is not enough memory when you try to view the History folder, you might have too many entries for the Internet Explorer to handle correctly. If clicking your Clear History button (Tools ⇨ Internet Options ⇨ General ⇨ Clear History) doesn't get rid of these error messages, take the following steps:

STEPS

Fixing a History Folder That Is Too Big

Step 1. Click Start ⇨ Shut Down, select Restart in MS-DOS Mode, and click OK.

Step 2. At the DOS prompt, type **Attrib -s c:\Windows\Tempor~1** and press Enter.

Step 3. Type **Deltree \Windows\Tempor~1** and press Enter.

Step 4. Type **Attrib -s c:\Windows\History** and press Enter.

Step 5. Type **Deltree \Windows\History** and press Enter.

Step 6. Type **exit** and press Enter.

Step 7. Click Start ⇨ Run, type **Regsvr32.exe/u C:\Windows\System\cachevu.dll** and click OK.

Step 8. Click Start ⇨ Run, type **Regsvr32.exe C:\Windows\System\cachevu.dll**, and click OK.

Regsvr32 registers applications in your registry. It finds the target code in Cachevu.dll. It creates the History and Temporary Internet Files folders if they are not present, and then initializes them by creating a copy of Desktop.ini with the proper pointer to the registered objects. It also creates the history index files (Mm*.dat).

After you run Regsvr32, you might discover that the Desktop.ini file in your History folder has been deleted. As a precaution, you might want to put a copy of it in your personal \My System folder (see "Special Folders" in Chapter 7) before you run Regsvr32. To create a copy of the Desktop.ini file that's stored in the History folder, use Notepad to create a text file with the following contents:

```
[.ShellClassInfo]
UICLSID={FF393560-C2A7-11CF-BFF4-444553540000}
CLSID={FF393560-C2A7-11CF-BFF4-444553540000}
```

Save this file as History Desktop.ini. When and if you need to put it back in your History folder, copy it there, rename it as Desktop.ini, and set its attribute to Hidden.

Defrag Hangs

Secret

If you have URLs in your History folder whose names are longer than 256 characters, Defrag may choke. ScanDisk won't find any problems. You can get around this problem by deleting the History folder, as detailed in the previous section.

Filling in Forms Gives Me an Error

If you get an error message when you click the Submit button on a simple Web-based form, you've run into an incompatibility between Netscape Navigator's extensions and those used by Internet Explorer. The Web site author used a Netscape Navigator extension that allows Netscape Navigator to send e-mail disguised as a form.

Presently, there isn't a way around this other than to tell the Web site designer to quit using this extension. Of course, it's tough to tell the author unless he or she gives you an e-mail address, which is specifically what the author is trying to hide with the use of this extension. You can find more information on this problem at http://support.microsoft.com/support/kb/articles/Q154/8/64.asp.

Slow Browsing

If you have enabled the Content Advisor rating system, you may find that your Internet Explorer is taking its own sweet time downloading Web sites. Check to see if you can speed up your browsing by disabling ratings.

In the Internet Explorer, choose Tools ⇨ Internet Options, click the Content tab, and click the Disable button.

Err Msg: MPREXE caused an invalid page fault in Kernel32.dll

Numerous problems with the Windows interface can be traced to a corrupt password file. If this happens, you may get this error message: "MPREXE caused an invalid page fault in module Kernel32.dll." If you get this message, delete or rename the files in the \Windows folder with the extension pwl. You can find out more about this problem in the "Dealing with a Corrupted Password File" section in Chapter 6.

The Trouble with Web sites

The Internet Explorer will give you an idea if there is something amiss on the other end of the line. To see the kind of information that Internet Explorer can supply, go to a site that has a Web page with misplaced tags, such as http://logan.creek.net/ie/index.html. With this particular page, you'll notice that nothing shows up. Instead you'll see Internet Explorer's explanation of the problem.

Can't Find an Internet Site

If you are trying to view your own start page, and you get an error message stating that Internet Explorer can't find the site, you may have an old, missing, or corrupt Url.dll file. One source of the problem: If you uninstalled earlier beta versions of Netscape Navigator, they didn't restore the original Url.dll file.

STEPS

Fixing Url.dll

Step 1. If you can find Url.dll file in the \Windows\System folder, remove or rename it.

Step 2. Type the following command at a DOS prompt and then press Enter:

copy C:\Windows\Sysbckup\Url.dll C:\Windows\System

Step 3. Click Start ⇨ Shut Down, choose Restart, and then click OK.

File Download Dialog Box

By default, the Internet Explorer displays the File Download dialog box when you access a file on the Internet. This dialog box gives you the option of opening the file or saving it to your hard disk to be opened later. If the file is a graphics file, to open it is to view it. If it is an executable file, to open it is to run the program.

For every file type, the Windows registry keeps track of whether it should display the File Download dialog box when you start to download a file of that type from the Internet.

The first time you download an executable file, Internet Explorer displays the File Download dialog box with the "Always ask before opening this type of file" checkbox marked. If you clear this checkbox, you will not be asked whether you want to save or open executable files in the future. They will automatically be opened.

Secret

If executable files (files with exe extensions) are opening automatically and you want to regain the option to save them instead, use the Registry Editor to navigate to exefile in HKEY_CLASSES_ROOT. Highlight *exefile* in the left pane, and double-click EditFlags in the right pane. Change **d8 07 01 00** to **d8 07 00 00**. Click OK. The File Download dialog box will now display when you begin to download an executable file.

To turn off the File Download dialog box for file types other than executable files, take the following steps:

STEPS

Turning Off the File Download Dialog Box

Step 1. Click Start ⇨ Settings ⇨ Folder Options, and the Files Types tab.

Step 2. Scroll down to and highlight the file type that you want to change.

Step 3. Click the Edit button. Clear the "Confirm open after download" checkbox to eliminate the File Download dialog box for this file type. Mark it to display this dialog box.

Step 4. Click OK twice.

Tip

One way to download a file that always lets you choose whether to open or save is to right-click the filename, and then click Open or Save Target As in the context menu.

Browser Wars

Netscape would like you to set its browser as the default browser. Microsoft wants you to choose its browser. At least they both give you a choice.

In the Internet Explorer, choose Tools ➪ Internet Options, and click the Programs tab. If you mark the "Internet Explorer should check to see whether it is the default browser" checkbox at the bottom of this dialog box, the Internet Explorer will check to make sure that it is the default browser every time you start it up. If you have installed Netscape Navigator and made it the default, the Internet Explorer will ask if you want to set Internet Explorer as the default browser.

If you don't mark this checkbox and Netscape Navigator is your default browser, it will open when you click an HTML page. Windows does all of this through file type associations in the registry. Click Start ➪ Settings ➪ Folder Options, and the File Types tab. Scroll down to and highlight Microsoft HTML Document or Microsoft MHTML Document to see which browser is associated with HTML files.

You can make changes in the File Types tab if you like, but to make them permanent, you need to issue commands in Netscape to tell it whether it is the default browser and whether it should check if it's the default, just as you do in the Internet Explorer.

Windows Web Pages

As long as you're on the Internet, you might as well use it to learn more about Windows. Table 26-3 lists some interesting Windows-related sites you can visit on the Web:

Table 26-3   Windows-Related Web Sites

Site	Address
Windows Secrets	`http://www.davisstraub.com/secrets`
Brian's Home Page	`http://BrianLivingston.com`
IDG Books	`http://www.idgbooks.com`
Brian's InfoWorld Columns	`http://www.infoworld.com/livingston`
Brian's News.com Columns	`http://www.news.com/Perspectives/Column/Archive/0,194,9,00.html`

Site	Address
Microsoft Downloads	`http://support.microsoft.com/support/downloads/default.asp`
Microsoft FAQs	`http://support.microsoft.com/support/default-faq.asp`
MS Internet Explorer Start page	`http:// www.msn.com /`
Microsoft Knowledge Base	`http://support.microsoft.com/support/`
Microsoft Newsgroups	`http://support.microsoft.com/support/news/default.asp`
Outlook Express	`http://www.microsoft.com/windows/oe/`
Winfiles.com (shareware library)	`http://www.winfiles.com`
Windows Annoyances	`http://www.creativelement.com/win95ann/index.html`
The Microsoft Exchange Center	`http://www.slipstick.com/index.htm`
Ed Tiley's Windows Home Page	`http://www.supernet.net/~edtiley/win95/`
Dale's Desktop Themes Page	`http://dale.bitshop.com/mainbody.asp`
Windows Startup Logos	`http://www.nucleus.com/~kmcmurdo/win95logo.html`
Download.com	`http://www.download.com/`
Software for the Internet	`http:// www.tucows.com`
Microsoft's Windows Games Pages	`http://www.zone.com/`
Windows Tip Sheet	`http://www.cs.umb.edu/~alilley/win.html`
ClubWin	`http://www.clubwin.com/`
The 32-bit Software Archive	`http://www.32bit.com/software/index.phtml`
Windows & IE Resource Page	`http://www.chipcom.net/reskit.htm`

Summary

Internet Explorer is integrated into the Windows Desktop. This chapter is devoted to helping you make this integration work for you.

▶ With the Internet Explorer Administration Kit, you can create your own Internet Explorer browser.

▶ You can start the Internet Explorer in lots of different ways.

▶ Search the search engines with third-party add-ons.

▶ Do away with the Go button.

▶ Restore your Internet Explorer to the default version by getting rid of your third-party brands.

▶ Replace the Internet Explorer shell, but not the underlying functionality.

▶ The Internet Explorer has lots of keyboard shortcuts.

▶ You have plenty of options for organizing your favorite Web sites.

▶ You don't have to translate your documents into HTML to view them over an intranet.

▶ There are plenty of Web sites devoted to Windows.

## Chapter 27

Using Outlook Express

In This Chapter

Outlook Express 5.5 uses a new data structure and offers lots of new features. We show you some of the most important changes and how to really take advantage of them.

▶ Move all your mail and news documents to one place where they're easy to back up

▶ Use multiple identities to handle several users on one computer

▶ Schedule sending and receiving mail

▶ Access your Hotmail account with Outlook Express

▶ Put a shortcut to a New Message window on your Desktop

Get the Latest Outlook Express

If you're using a version of Windows previous to the Millennium Edition, you can always download the latest version of Outlook Express from Microsoft's web site at http://www.microsoft.com/windows/ie/download/windows.htm.

Outlook Express is Configurable

Outlook Express is one of those programs that many people use without ever realizing its full potential. One reason for this is that most people tend to use it as is — without bothering to consider all of the configuration possibilities that are available. In the following sections you'll learn how to make Outlook Express better fit your needs.

Configuring Outlook Express

If you are connected to the Internet through a dial-up connection, you'll need to properly configure a Dial-Up Networking (DUN) connectoid as described in Chapters 19 and 25. To use Outlook Express mail, you need to get the names of the SMTP and POP3 servers at your Internet service provider, as well as your e-mail address and e-mail password, your account name (user ID), and your logon password. In the Outlook Express window, choose Tools, Accounts, Add, Mail to start a version of the Internet Connection Wizard that will help you create an entry for your Internet mail account.

By default, the Windows Me Internet Explorer uses Outlook Express as the mail tool when you click an e-mail address while viewing a web page. If you want to use another e-mail client (such as Microsoft Outlook or Eudora) you can change this default behavior. Right-click the Internet Explorer icon on your Desktop, click Properties, click the Programs tab, and then display the E-mail drop-down list. If you have another e-mail program installed on your computer, you can choose it here.

To read the articles (also called *messages* or *postings*) in newsgroups, you need to connect to a news server. Your Internet service provider probably maintains a Usenet news server. You can also connect to other news servers. The most likely name for your service provider's news server is news.*serviceprovidername*.com. We discuss newsgroups in greater detail in Chapter 29.

To connect to a news server, choose Tools, Accounts, Add, News to start a version of the Internet Connection Wizard that will help you set up a news server account.

Changing Outlook Express Options Right Away

We don't like the default configurations for Outlook Express — especially for the first-time user. We suggest that you make a number of changes along with us.

When you first open Outlook Express, the focus is on the Outlook Express folder and a welcome message is displayed in the message pane. Scroll to the bottom of this pane and mark the When Outlook Express Starts, Go Directly to My Inbox checkbox. Unfortunately, you can't set Outlook Express to open in a folder other than the main folder or the Inbox. You can create a shortcut to your newsgroups, however; see "Shortcuts to Outlook Express" later in this chapter.

Choose Tools, Options. Click the Read tab, and mark the Automatically Expand Grouped Messages checkbox, as shown in Figure 27-1. Click OK. Now you won't have to click the plus symbol repeatedly to follow a conversation thread, at the slight cost of seeing multiple entries in a thread that you might not be particularly interested in.

Tip

Choose Tools, Options, and click the General tab. Clear the Check for New Messages Every [   ] Minutes checkbox if you use a Dial-Up Networking connectoid and are only online for a limited amount of time during any one session.

If you have a dial-up connection, it is a bother to have Outlook Express dial up your Internet service provider every time you invoke it. You can work offline and then force a dial-up connection when you connect to the mail server to send and/or receive mail, or connect to a news server. Choose Tools, Options, and clear the Send and Receive Messages at Startup checkbox on the General tab.

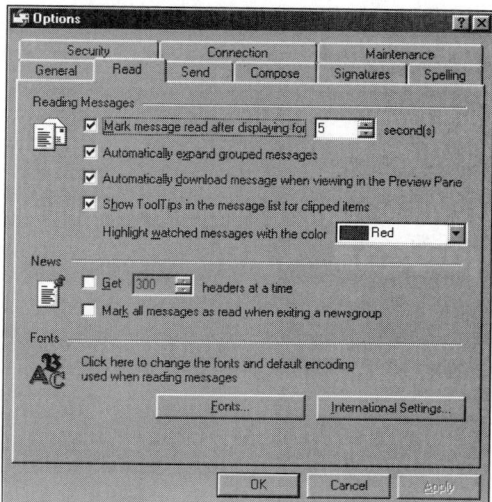

Figure 27-1: The Read tab of the Options dialog box in Outlook Express

Tip

Choose Tools, Accounts, Add, News to add additional news servers to your list. You'll want to add the msnews.microsoft.com news server. This is Microsoft's support news server. You'll find a basic level of supervision from Microsoft support personnel, peer-to-peer support, and help from Microsoft volunteers. The microsoft.public.inetexplorer.ie40.outlookexpress newsgroup provides the latest information about Outlook Express.

You can choose which news server is the default, or first-accessed server, by choosing Tools, Accounts, News, highlighting your news server account, and clicking the Set As Default button.

If you want people to contact you directly from your postings in newsgroups, type your e-mail address in the E-mail Address field in the General tab of the Properties dialog box for the news server. To do this, choose Tools, Accounts, highlight the news account, and then click the Properties button.

When a news folder has the focus, you will find a Reply to Sender button on the Outlook Express toolbar. This lets you send a response directly to the author of a message when you don't feel the need to respond on the newsgroup. You won't be able to send a private message if the author hasn't placed his or her e-mail address in the E-mail Address or Reply Address field. If you leave your Reply Address field blank, the address in your E-mail Address field is used. If you send mail from one address but want replies to go to another, then enter the second address in the Reply Address field.

Secret

If you don't want your address picked up by Usenet bots that scan Usenet newsgroups for addresses, then put a fake address in the Reply Address field, such as fakename@fakenet.net.

Choose Tools, Options, and click the Signatures tab. Enter at least a rudimentary "signature"—your name at least—in this dialog box (see Figure 27-2). You can make additional signatures and get more elaborate as discussed later in this chapter, but we suggest that you don't get carried away. Mark the Add Signatures to All Outgoing Messages checkbox. You can choose Insert ⇨ Signature in a New Message window to insert your default signature when you write a message, but if you usually use the same signature it's easier and more consistent to let the computer do it for you.

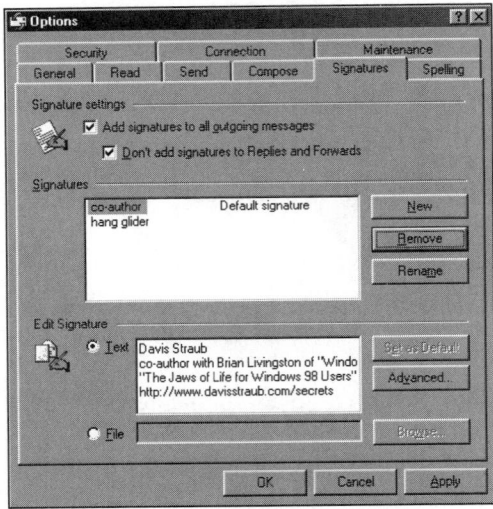

Figure 27-2: Mark the Add Signatures to All Outgoing Messages checkbox to add a signature to your e-mail messages.

If you often select among different signatures, leave the Add Signatures to All Outgoing Messages checkbox blank. Instead, add an Insert Signature button to the toolbar of the New Message window. To do this, open a New Message window, right-click the toolbar and choose Customize. In the left-hand column, highlight Insert Signature and click the Add button. Once on your toolbar, this button includes a drop-down list of all the signatures you have defined. You must customize the New Message window toolbars separately for news and for mail.

To automatically associate a particular signature with a mail or news account, highlight it in the Signatures list and click the Advanced button. In the Advanced Signature Settings dialog box, check all the accounts for which this signature is to be the default. For these accounts only, doing so will override the general default signature setting.

A vCard (virtual business card) is a standard format for all your personal contact information. Outlook Express can import the information contained in vCards into its address book. Other software packages can read and write vCards, which allows users to exchange contact information easily.

If you want to include a vCard in e-mail messages, first open the Address Book and make an entry for yourself. Now choose Tools, Options, and click the Compose tab, mark the Mail checkbox (see Figure 27-3) and choose an address book entry from the drop-down list. Use the Edit button to make any additions or changes. It's probably not a great idea to send your vCard to a newsgroup. If someone would like your contact information, he or she can send you an e-mail message, and you can respond with your vCard.

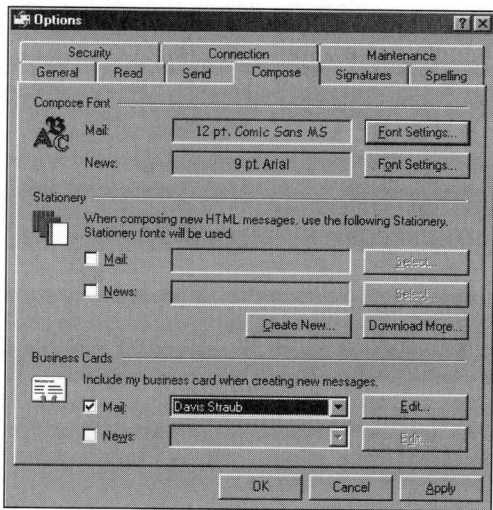

Figure 27-3: Mark the Mail checkbox and select from the list to add a business card to your e-mail messages.

Make sure that the Send Messages Immediately checkbox in the Send tab (Tools, Options) is marked if you work online or want to have messages sent as soon as you finish writing them. If you work offline, clear this checkbox, and choose Tools, Send and Receive when you're ready to send your mail. You can also just click the Send and Receive button in the Outlook Express toolbar to send mail from your Outbox to the mail server.

If you are browsing the Internet online and click an e-mail address on a web page to send a message, that message will not go out right away unless the Send Messages Immediately checkbox is marked. Instead it will wait in your Outbox until you click the Send and Receive button in Outlook Express.

More Outlook Express Changes

The Outlook Express window is by default divided into four panes. The message header pane (the one on the top right) lists the message headers, and the preview pane (the one on the bottom right) displays the contents of whatever message you have selected in the message header pane. You can arrange these two panes either horizontally or vertically. To do this, choose View, Layout, Below Messages or Beside Messages (actually below or beside message headers).

By default, Outlook Express displays its folders in a large pane on the upper left, called the Folder List. It displays the contents of your address book in a pane on the lower left, called the Contacts pane. You can turn off either of these panes by choosing View, Layout and clearing the Folder List and/or the Contacts checkbox (see Figure 27-4). You can also easily switch these panes on and off by placing the Folder List and/or Contacts button on your Outlook Express toolbar. To do this, right-click the toolbar and click Buttons in the context menu.

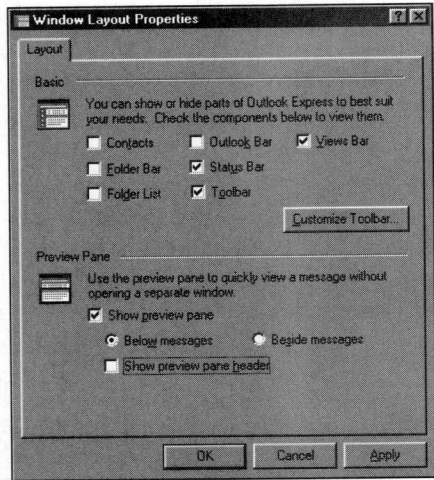

Figure 27-4: Clear the Folder List and the Contacts checkboxes in the Window Layout Properties dialog box to hide the Folder List and Contacts panes.

When you single-click a message header, you can view its contents in the preview pane. This works just fine most of the time. If you want to view a message in a new (and bigger) window, double-click the message header. If you want to get rid of the preview pane and only view messages in separate message windows, choose View, Layout and clear the Use Preview Pane checkbox. On low-resolution video cards with small monitors, this may be the way you want to go.

Tip

If you want news messages to appear in the preview pane as soon as you select them, choose Tools, Options, click the Read tab, and mark the Automatically Download Message When Viewing in the Preview Pane checkbox. When this option is turned off, you have to press the spacebar after selecting a message to display its contents in the preview pane.

If you don't like the column order in the message header pane, drag the gray column header buttons to the desired position. You can also change the width of the columns by resting your mouse on the spacer line between column header buttons and dragging to the right or the left. To sort your messages by a particular column (the Subject column, for example), click the column header button. To sort by the same column in reverse order, click the button again. To add or remove columns, right-click the column header and choose Columns, then check or clear the boxes for the columns you want to display.

Tip

If you're using the preview pane to view your messages, you can get a little extra room by hiding the header bar at the top of the preview pane. To do this choose View, Layout, Show Preview Pane Header. The tradeoff is that you lose the ability to quickly open or save attachments by clicking the paper clip button in the header bar.

If you right-click the Outlook Express toolbar and choose Customize, you'll notice that you can change its content and appearance. The toolbar gets a lot thinner if you make the icons smaller (choose Small Icons from the Icon Options list) and take out the text under the buttons (choose No Text Labels from the Text Options list), but then it also gets less understandable (although you do get ToolTips to replace the text). If you have a low-resolution video card on a small monitor, you may want to reduce the size of the toolbar. You can also get rid of it altogether by choosing View, and clearing the checkmark next to Toolbar. Unfortunately, beginning with version 5 you no longer have the ability to put your toolbar any place you want—at the side of the window, for example.

Tip

There are actually several sets of buttons on the Outlook Express toolbar. One set is for mail, another for news, a third for Outlook Express in general, plus there are separate sets for the New Message window in both mail and news. The set that appears changes automatically depending on which part of Outlook Express you have activated, either via the Folder List or the Outlook bar. The mail buttons appear when you click a mail folder (such as the Inbox, Outbox, or Sent Items), the news buttons appear when you click a news folder (either a folder for a news server or a newsgroup), and the general buttons appear when you click Outlook Express at the top of the Folder List or Outlook bar. The New Message window buttons appear when you start a new message from either a mail or a news folder. To customize any set of buttons, activate a folder or window of the appropriate type, right-click the toolbar, and choose Customize in the context menu.

We added Mark All, Mark Conversation, Reply All, and Next Conversation to the news buttons. We got rid of Forward and Reply to Sender. If you don't use the Outlook bar or the Folders pane, it's also handy to put an Inbox icon on your news toolbar. To customize the mail buttons, you might want to add the Print and Save As buttons and remove the Delete button (you can simply press Delete to delete messages instead). You'll also want to add buttons for any panes you have chosen not to view (using View, Layout).

To make more space for the buttons you've added, drag the Views bar up to the right of the Menu bar. You can remove it by right-clicking the toolbar and unchecking Views Bar, but we find it to be a pretty handy item to keep around. For more about setting the view and creating custom views, see Chapter 8.

If you want to do without the Folder List, you might choose View, Layout, and mark Outlook bar instead. The Outlook bar displays all of the Outlook Express system folders as icons. This really cuts down on the amount of space used by the Outlook Express window. You can add other folders and newsgroups by dragging them onto the Outlook bar.

When you're viewing a newsgroup message, if you choose Compose, Reply to Newsgroup and Author (or click the Reply to All button if you have added this button to the toolbar) to reply to a posting in a newsgroup, your message gets sent to the newsgroup and to the author of the message to which you are replying. By default, a copy of the message to the author is stored in the Sent Items folder. If you want to disable (or enable) this feature, click Tools, Options, click the Send tab, and clear (or mark) the Save Copy of Sent Messages in the "Sent Items" Folder checkbox. If you clear Save Copy of Sent Messages, your outgoing e-mail messages won't get saved in the Sent Items folder either.

If you need to view mail or news articles in a foreign language, you may need to use other character sets. Turn to "Multilingual e-mail" in Chapter 42 for details.

The Views Bar

Right-click your toolbar and you'll see a new menu item—Views Bar. Click it to display a handy drop-down list of views, as shown in Figure 27-5. Now you can easily see whether you've chosen Show All Messages, Hide Read or Ignored Messages, or perhaps a custom viewing filter. You can drag the Views bar up to the same row as the menu bar and toolbar. If there's not enough room to display the down arrow to the right of the Views list, you can click the currently selected view to display the list instead.

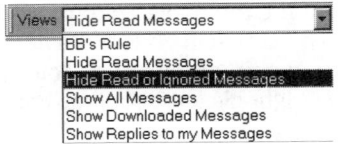

Figure 27-5: The Views bar makes it easier to see and select your view.

The Folders List

The Folder bar is a thick gray stripe under the toolbar that lists your current message folder and identity. When the Folders pane is not displayed, you can use the Folder bar to verify which folder you're in and navigate to another. Click the name of the current folder in the Folder bar to display a drop-down Folders list, as shown in Figure 27-6. The Folders list works similarly to the Folders pane, in that you can right-click folders in it, and use it to drag and drop.

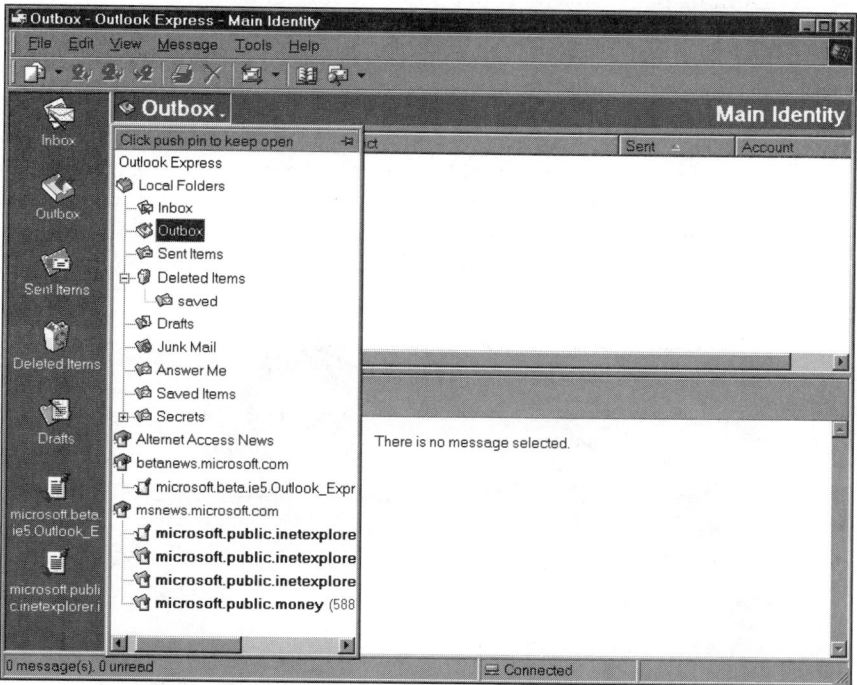

Figure 27-6: Click the name of the current folder in the Folder bar to see a drop-down list of message folders.

You may decide not to display the Folders pane, and to use the Folders list instead. This gives you a wider Preview pane and makes it easier to read messages without opening them. To turn off the Folders pane, click the Close Window button in the upper-right corner of the pane — or choose View, Layout, clear Folder List, and then click OK.

If you prefer to display the Folders pane, you might find that the Folder bar takes up too much real estate in your Outlook Express window. To turn the Folder bar off, choose View, Layout, and clear the Folder Bar checkbox. If you do this, you may want to put the Folder List button on your toolbar so you can toggle the Folder List pane on and off without using the Folder bar.

The Outlook Bar

The Outlook bar, a popular feature of Outlook 98, is new to Outlook Express. It contains shortcuts to message folders. The Outlook bar appears on the left side of the Outlook Express window, where many of us used to keep our toolbars.

You might prefer to use the Outlook bar for navigation instead of the Folders pane, especially if space is at a premium. Right-clicking a blank area of the Outlook bar displays a context menu for controlling the Outlook bar's appearance. To switch from large icons to small ones (or vice versa), choose Large Icons or Small Icons. To hide the Outlook bar, choose Hide Outlook Bar. If you want to add a new shortcut to the Outlook bar, choose New Outlook Bar Shortcut and select the desired folder in the New Shortcut dialog box (see Figure 27-7). Another simpler way to add a shortcut is to drag and drop the icon for the desired folder from the Folders pane or the Folders list onto the Outlook bar (or right-click the icon and click Add to Outlook Bar). To rearrange the order of the shortcut icons, just drag and drop them to suit yourself. To remove a shortcut icon from the Outlook bar, right-click it and choose Remove from Outlook Bar.

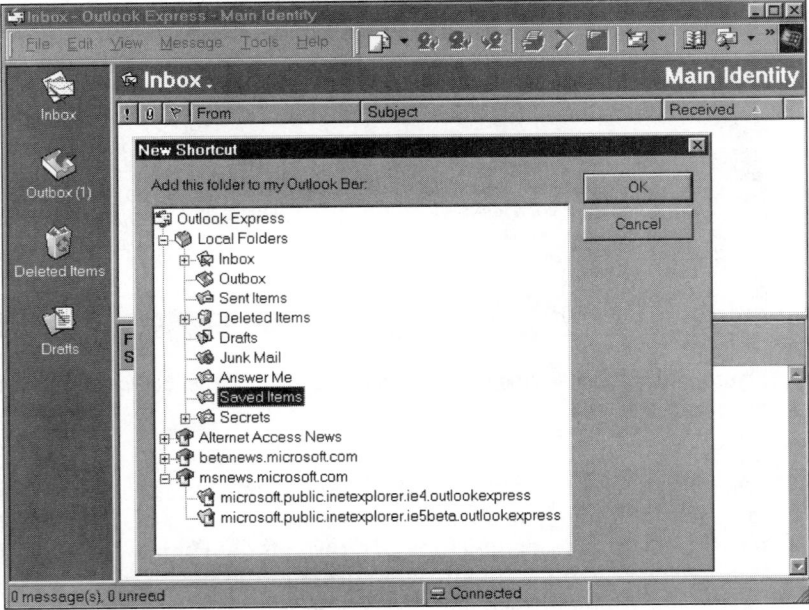

Figure 27-7: Browse to add a shortcut to your Outlook bar — the dark gray vertical bar on the left.

If you don't have an icon for a folder in your Outlook bar, and you don't have your Folders pane open, you won't be able to tell if you have unread mail in that folder. For example, you might have something new in your Junk Mail folder that's not really junk (this happens all too frequently). You can always see which folders have unread mail in the Folders list, but you have to remember to display the list to look there.

If you right-click a shortcut on the Outlook bar and choose Find Message, the Find Message dialog box opens, allowing you to search for and open a message from any folder without opening the folder itself. So, for example, if you're reading a large newsgroup, you can search for and read a message in your Sent Items folder without losing your place in the newsgroup. You can also empty the Deleted Items folder by right-clicking its icon in the Outlook bar and choosing Empty Deleted Items Folder. Right-click and select Properties to see the properties of the folder itself (not the shortcut), with a quick summary of the number of files in that folder, the number unread, and the location where the folder is stored.

Start a Message from the Contacts Pane

Right away you'll notice a pane in the lower-left part of the Outlook Express 5.5 window that displays the entries in your address book. If you prefer not to see the Contacts pane, click the Close Window button in the upper-right corner of the pane. To get it back, choose View, Layout, and mark the Contacts checkbox.

To send a message to someone in your address book, simply double-click the name or group and a New Message window will open. This works even while you are using the newsreader, and without making you lose your place — answering a long-time request from Outlook Express newsgroup members.

The Contacts Pane Is Not the Address Book

Although the Contacts pane in the Outlook Express window is handy for quickly picking a name out of your address book, it does not have all the address book features. For example, you do not have the ability to sort other than by first name.

The Outlook Express 5.5 address book lets you organize your contacts in folders and share them with other identities (see "Folders and groups" and "sharing an address book" in Chapter 32). But in the Contacts pane, you cannot add a new group or address book folder, add a contact to any folder other than the main Contacts folder, or even see your other folders, for that matter. In the Contacts pane, the contents of all folders, including your Shared Contacts folder, are shown in one alphabetical list, with addresses and phone numbers not visible.

You can access the full address book properties for a contact by right-clicking it in the Contacts pane and choosing Properties. You can add a new contact by choosing New Contact from the Contacts drop-down menu at the top of the Contacts pane. And to open the real address book from the Contacts pane, right-click any name and choose Address Book.

Rename Outlook Express

Secret

Some versions of Outlook Express include the words *provided by Microsoft* in the title bar at the top of the window. If you'd rather have your window without the additional advertising—or if you'd like it to say something more personally meaningful, you can change it. Here's how:

STEPS

Changing the Outlook Express Title Bar

Step 1. Open your Registry Editor and navigate to HKEY_CURRENT_USER\ Identities\{*your identity number*}\Software\Microsoft\Outlook Express\5.0. If you aren't sure which identity number is the right one, click a number and you'll see the associated user name in the right pane. If you only have one identity set up in Outlook Express, you'll only see one number.

Step 2. If the value WindowTitle doesn't exist in the right pane, right-click the right pane, click New, and choose String Value.

Step 3. Give the string value variable the name **WindowTitle**, and press Enter.

Step 4. Double-click WindowTitle. In the Edit String dialog box, type the name you'd like to see in the title bar, as shown in Figure 27-8. Press Enter, and close the Registry Editor.

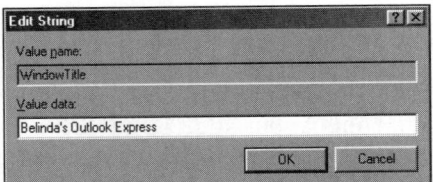

Figure 27-8: In this example, Outlook Express will now be called *Belinda's Outlook Express*.

The next time you open Outlook Express, it will use your new title in the title bar.

Thanks to Marc Butenko and many others for this tip.

Disable the Info pane

If you have a "branded" version of Outlook Express — that is, one that carries the logo of a third party such as a computer vendor — you will see an additional pane in the Outlook Express window when you first open it. This is called the Info pane. In fact, even if you have uninstalled the branded version, the old Info pane may still be displayed when you open Outlook Express. You may feel you have a better use for that real estate.

Secret

To temporarily disable the Info pane, open Outlook Express, choose View, Layout, and clear the Info Pane checkbox. To permanently disable the Info pane, you must edit the Registry, as described in these steps:

STEPS

Permanently Disabling the Outlook Express Info Pane

Step 1.   Start with Outlook Express closed.

Step 2.   Open the Registry Editor (regedit.exe) and navigate to HKEY_CURRENT_USER\Identities\ *{your identity number}*\ Software\Microsoft\ Outlook Express \ 5.0.

Step 3.   Find the string called BodyBarPath and delete it. Press F5 to refresh your Registry, and close the Registry Editor.

Step 4.   Open Outlook Express, and choose View, Layout. You will no longer see the Info Pane checkbox.

Secret

You can create your own Info pane if you like.

STEPS

Creating Your Own Info Pane

Step 1.   Create artwork using MS Paint or another pixel-painting application. A good dimension is 720 pixels wide by 72 pixels high. Save your image as a *bmp* file.

Step 2.   Close Outlook Express.

Step 3.   Open the Registry Editor and navigate to HKEY_CURRENT_USER\ Identities\ *{your identity number}*\ Software\Microsoft\ Outlook Express \ 5.0.

Continued

STEPS

Creating Your Own Info Pane *(continued)*

Step 4. If you already have a string called BodyBarPath (because you have a branded version of Outlook Express), double-click it. In the Value Data field, enter the path and filename of the *bmp* file you created in Step 1 and click OK.

If you don't have BodyBarPath, right-click the right pane of the Registry Editor, and click New, String Value. Rename the value to **BodyBarPath**. Then double-click it and, in the Value Data field, enter the path and filename of the *bmp* file you created in Step 1. Click OK.

Step 5. Find the DWORD called ShowBodyBar and look at its value. If the last digit is set to 0, double-click ShowBodyBar, type **1** in the Value Data Field, and click OK. Close the Registry Editor.

Step 6. Now open Outlook Express. You should see your new image in the Info pane at the bottom of the window, as shown in Figure 27-9.

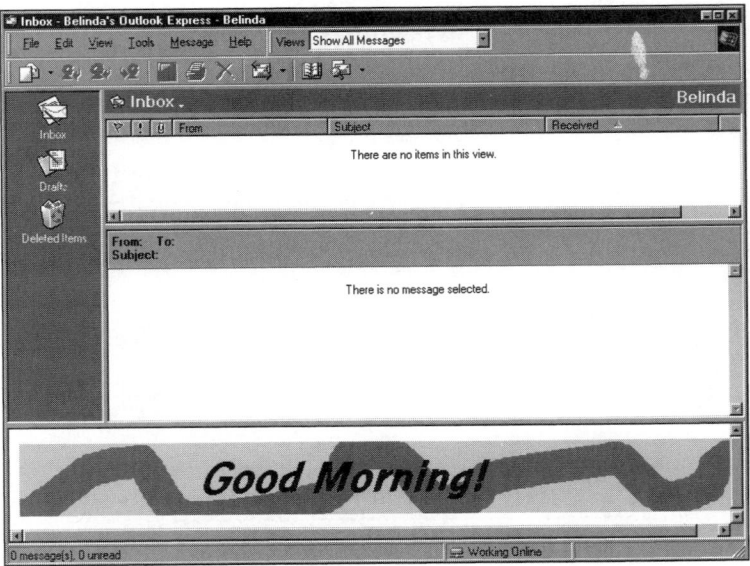

Figure 27-9: You can put your own artwork in the Outlook Express Info pane.

You can change your artwork as often as you like without editing the Registry. Just save it with the same name and path you entered in Step 4. You must close Outlook Express and reopen it to see the change.

Spell checking

Outlook Express uses Microsoft's Office 95 or Office 97 spell checker.

Secret

Outlook Express looks in the Registry to find the dictionary and the spelling engine. It goes to HKEY_LOCAL_MACHINE\ Software\ Microsoft\ Shared Tools\ Proofing Tools\ Spelling\ *languageID*\ Normal. The *languageID* is a four-digit number. For example, U.S. English is 1033, Australian is 2057, and British English is 3081. You'll find two string values under the Normal key that name the dictionary and the engine.

Tip

The spelling files mssp2_en.lex, mssp232.dll, and custom.dic should be stored in the folder C:\Program Files\ Common Files\ Microsoft Shared\ Proof. If you are having trouble enabling spell checking, use your Windows Me Explorer to search for these files and make sure that they are stored in this folder.

If you still are having trouble getting spell checking to work, check out Eric Miller's "Outlook Express User Tips" at http://www.activeie.com/oe to find explicit help on enabling spell checking.

Where to Find More Help

You can download the latest version of Outlook Express from Microsoft's web site at http://www.microsoft.com/windows/ie/download/windows.htm.

Check out Eric Miller's "Outlook Express User Tips" at http://www.okinfoweb. com/moe/. Microsoft provides its help for Outlook Express at http://www. microsoft.com/windows/oe/Support/.

Working with Outlook Express Data Files

Any messages you send or receive, any contacts you create, or any news items you download in Outlook Express are stored on your hard drive. The following sections explain how to work with these Outlook Express data files.

The Outlook Express Data Structure

The Outlook Express message folders and their contents are referred to collectively as the *message store*. Earlier versions of Outlook Express used separate file formats for the mail (*mbx* and *idx*) and news (*nch*) portions of the message store, and stored them in separate folders. These were replaced in Outlook Express 5 by a new *dbx* file type for both news and e-mail messages. The new structure is designed to be faster and to eliminate what Microsoft felt were design limitations of the old one.

The *dbx* files for both mail and news are now all stored together—the default location is \Windows\Application Data\Identities\{*your identity number*}\ Microsoft\Outlook Express. Your identity number will be a long hexadecimal string, something like {6DAF96CE-A1A7-11D2-87AD-0040055B596B}. If multiple Outlook Express identities are set up on your computer, you will see a different Outlook Express message store for each one. See "Using identities" later in this chapter for more on what identities are and how to use them. See "Save all your documents," also in this chapter, to learn how to tell which identity belongs to you.

In your message store folder, you'll see a separate file for each message folder and newsgroup, identified by its familiar name. So, for example, the file containing your Inbox data is called Inbox.dbx. This makes it easy to selectively back up message files.

Mark Lium, Outlook Express Beta Support Engineer at Microsoft, described the key files in this folder:

- *Pop3FolderName*.dbx: Contains the index and the messages contained in the POP3 folder.

- *newsgroupname*.dbx: Contains the index, headers, and messages contained in the indicated newsgroup.

- *ImapServerName-FolderName*.dbx: Contains the index, headers, and messages contained in the indicated folder on the indicated IMAP4 server.

- **Offline.dbx:** Contains all of the IMAP4 actions you carry out while offline. Upon reconnecting to the IMAP4 server, these actions are carried out on the server.

- **Folders.dbx:** Contains the list of all newsgroups and IMAP4 folders available, the newsgroups and IMAP4 folders you're subscribed to, and the folder hierarchy of your store. You can actually rename or delete this file while troubleshooting and it will rebuild itself based on the files in the store. If you do this, your newsgroup list will need to be re-downloaded and your folders will all be placed on the top level of the hierarchy.

- **Pop3uidl.dbx:** Contains the list of POP3 messages you've already downloaded. It is used primarily if you choose to leave a copy of messages on the server so that Outlook Express doesn't download the messages more than once.

- **Cleanup.log:** Contains a log of compaction activity.

To find out the name and location of a particular item such as your Inbox, right-click its icon in the Folders pane, the Folders list, or the Outlook bar, and select Properties. The Properties dialog box for that item will show you the filename and its path (see Figure 27-10). The path will most likely be too long to fit in the dialog box. Click the path and use your right arrow key or End key to scroll the rest of the path into view.

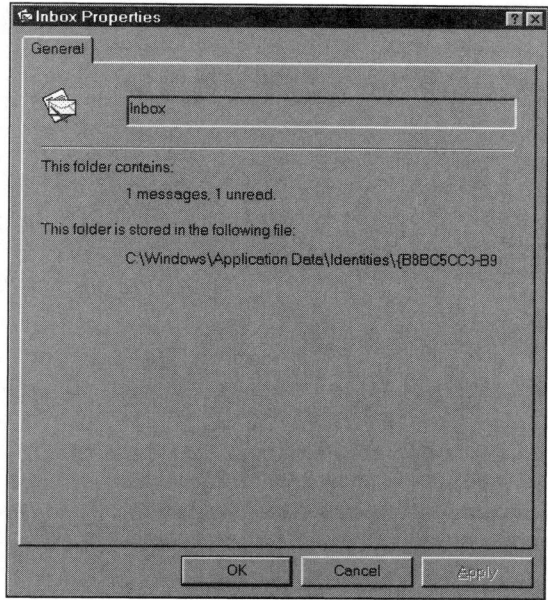

Figure 27-10: The Properties dialog box shows the path and filename of the Inbox.

If you delete a message folder in Outlook Express, you will still see its *dbx* file in your Explorer as long as it is in the Deleted Items folder. Once you permanently delete the message folder, its *dbx* file will disappear from the Explorer.

Save All Your Documents

One of the convenient features of the My Documents folder is that it organizes all your documents into one place for easier backup. Unfortunately, Windows Me places all e-mail and news messages and your address book — very important documents indeed — someplace else.

On the other hand, it is now much easier to move your messages to subfolders under your My Documents folder, as described in these steps:

STEPS

Moving Your Outlook Express E-mail

Step 1. Using your Explorer, navigate to My Documents. Right-click the right-pane of your Explorer, and choose New, Folder. Name the new folder **Outlook Express**.

Continued

STEPS

Moving Your Outlook Express E-mail *(continued)*

Step 2. In the Outlook Express window, choose Tools, Options, click the Maintenance tab, and click the Store Folder button. The current location of your message store appears in the Store Location dialog box, as shown in Figure 27-11. If you can't see the whole path, click inside the path field and press your End key to scroll to the end.

Figure 27-11: The Store Location dialog box shows where your messages are stored.

Step 3. Click the Change button to display the Browse for Folder dialog box (see Figure 27-12). Navigate to the folder you created in Step 1, highlight it, click OK three times, and then restart Outlook Express.

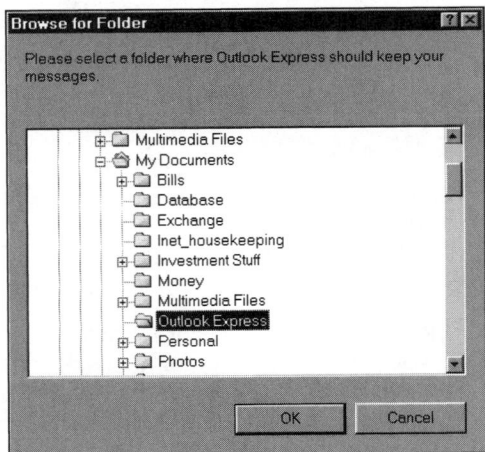

Figure 27-12: Navigate to your new folder.

Step 4. When you restart Outlook Express, you will see a message stating that your message store is being moved. Use your Explorer to verify that your messages have moved to their new location.

If you have trouble with these steps for any reason (or just like the challenge of doing it the hard way), you can move your message folders by making a couple of changes in the Registry to show Outlook Express where everything is stored. This is also still the only method for moving your Windows address book.

STEPS

Editing the Registry to Move Your Outlook Express E-mail

Step 1.   Exit Outlook Express.

Step 2.   Start your Registry Editor, navigate to HKEY_CURRENT_USER\
Identities\ {*your identity number*}\ Software\ Microsoft\ Outlook
Express\ 5.0, and locate Store Root in the right pane.
(See Figure 27-13.)

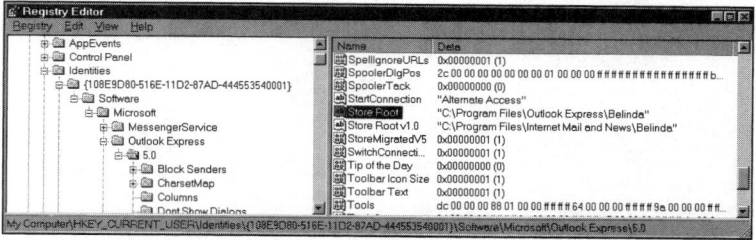

Figure 27-13: The Registry location of Store Root

As you can see from Figure 27-13, identities are listed in the Registry by their hexadecimal numbers (see "Using identities" later in this chapter for more on what identities are). If you have more than one identity set up on your computer, you can easily tell which one is which. Select an identity in the left pane of the Registry Editor, and you'll see Username in the right pane, listing the user name associated with the identity, as shown in Figure 27-14:

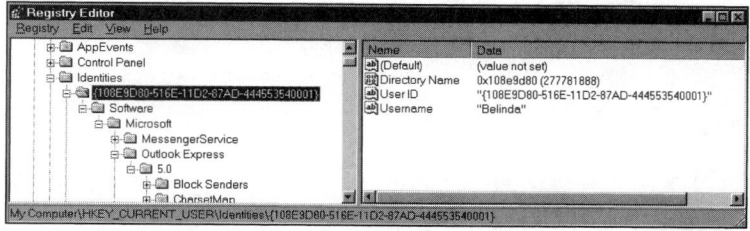

Figure 27-14: Select an identity to see the associated user name.

Continued

STEPS

Editing the Registry to Move Your Outlook Express E-mail *(continued)*

Step 3. Double-click Store Root in the right pane of your Registry Editor. In the Edit String dialog box, change the folder where the message folders are stored to C:\My Documents\Outlook Express, as shown in Figure 27-15. If you have multiple profiles set up on this computer, the path should instead be **C:\Windows\Profiles*Username*\\My Documents**. (See "User profiles and My Documents" in Chapter 5 for more on this.) If your My Documents folder is on some other drive, or if you've changed its name, use those values instead.

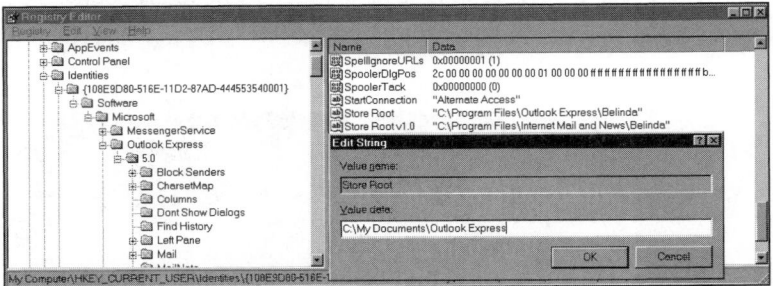

Figure 27-15: Type a new location for your message store.

Step 4. Click OK, and close the Registry Editor.

Step 5. Using the Explorer, navigate to My Documents. Right-click the right pane of your Explorer, and choose New, Folder. Name the new folder **Outlook Express**.

Step 6. Navigate to the current location of your Outlook Express message store. It may be in your \Program Files\Outlook Express folder, under your user name. If so, drag the folder with your user name to \My Documents\Outlook Express and drop it there.

If your Outlook Express folder is \Windows\Application Data\ Microsoft\Outlook Express, drag that folder to \My Documents and drop it there.

Secret

Now that you've moved your message folders, you need to move your address book.

STEPS

Moving Your Windows Address Book

Step 1. Exit Outlook Express.

Step 2. Start your Registry Editor, and navigate to HKEY_CURRENT_USER\ Software\ Microsoft\ WAB\WAB4\ Wab File Name.

Step 3. Double-click Default in the right pane of the Registry Editor, and type the new location and address book filename in the Edit String dialog box — for example, **C:\My Documents\Outlook Express\ Belinda.wab** (see Figure 27-16).

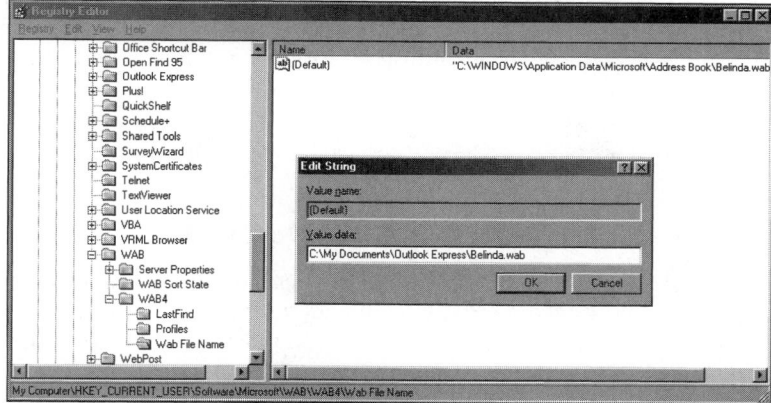

Figure 26-16: Type a new location for your address book.

Step 4. Click OK and close the Registry Editor.

Step 5. Using the Explorer, navigate to the current Windows address book location at \Windows\Application Data\Microsoft\Address Book.

Step 6. Drag the address book (*wab*) file from this location to \My Documents\ Outlook Express.

Recover from corrupted messages

If you're having trouble opening your Inbox or reading its contents, it's possible that you have downloaded a corrupted message, or a message with an attachment that's so big it's causing problems. You can recover from these situations by having Outlook Express rebuild your Inbox.

STEPS

Recovering from Corrupted Messages in Your Inbox

Step 1.   In the Outlook Express Folders pane or Folders list, right-click Local Folders and select New Folder. Name the new folder something like **Temp**. If you have any messages in your Inbox that you want to save, drag and drop them into your new Temp folder.

Step 2.   In the Explorer, navigate to the message store (the default location is \Windows\Application Data\Identities\{*your identity number*}\Microsoft\Outlook Express). Rename Inbox.dbx to Inbox.old. When you see the warning, click OK.

Step 3.   Now when you open Outlook Express, it will automatically create a new Inbox folder. You can drag the messages you saved in Step 1 back into your Inbox if you like. If everything is working properly, you can now delete the Inbox.old file.

Background Compaction

Although you can still compact individual newsgroups, Outlook Express now automatically compacts your entire message store in the background. Normally you should not even notice that this is happening.

According to Mark Lium, Outlook Express Beta Support Engineer at Microsoft, compaction begins thirty seconds after you open Outlook Express, and by default reoccurs every thirty minutes while Outlook Express stays open. Background compaction is not applied to a folder where there is activity such as downloading, copying, or deleting.

To enable or disable background compaction, choose Tools, Options, and click the Maintenance tab (see Figure 27-17). Mark or clear the Compact Messages in the Background checkbox.

You can change the frequency with which background compaction occurs by changing the number in the Compact Messages When There Is [   ] Percent Wasted Space. A smaller number in this box (5 for example, as shown in Figure 27-17) will cause compaction to occur more frequently.

To see a record of compaction activity, close Outlook Express and use Notepad to open the Cleanup.log file in your message store folder (the default is \Windows\Application Data\Identities\{*your identity number*}\Microsoft\Outlook Express). This file is emptied when it reaches 64K and then starts over, so as to take up a minimum of space on your hard disk.

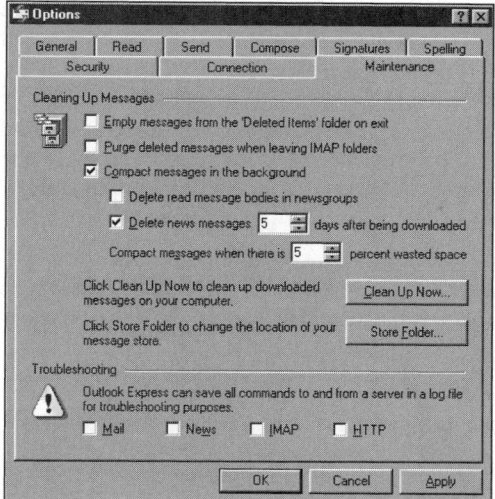

Figure 27-17: Mark the Compact Messages in the Background checkbox to enable background compaction.

Tip

When Outlook Express compacts your messages, it creates temporary files with the *dbt* extension. These should automatically disappear when the compaction process is complete. If there is a problem, however, they may not be deleted, and they may be quite large. If you notice that your hard disk is suddenly full, check for any *dbt* files in your message store folder, and delete them.

When Outlook Express Won't Open

If something in your message store becomes corrupted, you may not be able to open Outlook Express at all. You may see an error message such as:

```
Outlook Express could not be started. The application was unable to
open the Outlook Express Message Store. Your computer may be out of
memory or its disk is full. (0x800C0069, 8).
```

Secret

This error message means that Outlook Express could not start because the Msoe.dll file could not be loaded into memory (probably because it could not be found). Despite the message's wording, lack of memory or a full disk are not probable causes of this problem. A more likely cause is that Outlook Express is not installed correctly. This is a side effect of having everything in one big message store. Still, it's possible to recover.

STEPS

Recovering When Outlook Express Won't Open

Step 1. In the Explorer, create a new temporary folder. Then navigate to the folder that contains your Outlook Express message store. The default location is \Windows\Application Data\Identities\{*your identity number*}\Microsoft\Outlook Express.

Step 2. Move the contents of the message store folder (*dbx* files) to the temporary folder you created in Step 1. If you have a *wab* file in this folder, leave that where it is.

Step 3. Now open Outlook Express. When it doesn't find your message store files, it will rebuild your Inbox and other system folders. Your mail accounts, news accounts, and other settings should be intact.

Step 4. Choose File, Import, Messages to launch the Outlook Express Import Wizard. Choose Microsoft Outlook Express 5 in the first wizard dialog box, and click Next.

Step 5. The Import From OE5 Wizard appears. Click Import Mail from an OE Store Directory, and click OK.

Step 6. In the Location of Messages dialog box, click the Browse button and navigate to the temporary folder where you moved your *dbx* files. Mark All Folders, and Click Next. After your message store is reimported into Outlook Express, click Finish.

You may lose the hierarchical structure of your message folders during this process. You will certainly lose all your newsgroup subscriptions and their contents. But at least you will be back in business.

Recover Deleted Message Folders

In earlier versions of Outlook Express, if you deleted a message folder by accident, there was no way to recover it or its contents. But in Outlook Express 5, when you delete a message folder it is moved into your Deleted Items folder, as shown in Figure 27-18. It won't be permanently deleted unless you delete it from the Deleted Items folder or empty the Deleted Items folder.

Figure 27-18: You can now recover a deleted message folder and its contents.

To recover a deleted folder and its contents, use the Folders pane to drag it from the Deleted Items folder to another place under Local Folders.

Get Those Dialog Boxes Back

Lots of Outlook Express dialog boxes include a checkbox that says Don't Ask Me This Again. It's possible that you might mark one of these checkboxes and later wish that it *would* ask you again. Luckily, the Registry settings for these dialog boxes are all neatly stored in one place. Open the Registry Editor and navigate to HKEY_CURRENT_USER\ Identities\ *{your identity number}*\ Software\ Microsoft\ Outlook \ 5.0\ Don't Show Dialogs. You'll see a list of the warning dialog boxes in the right pane, as shown in Figure 27-19. A value of 0 means the box is turned off; double-click the one you want and set its value to 1 to reactivate it.

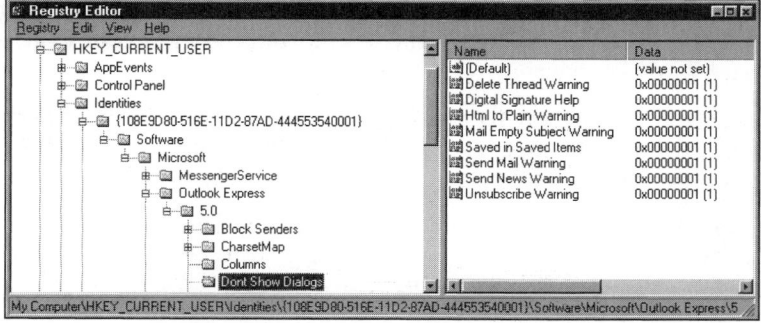

Figure 27-19: The Registry location of the Don't Show Dialogs key

Transferring Message Rules to a New Computer

Message Rules, formerly called Inbox Assistant, are a part of Outlook Express designed to help you filter and organize your mail and news, based on rules you set up in advance. To find this feature choose Tools, Message Rules, then choose either Mail, News, or the Blocked Senders List. Message Rules have been greatly enhanced in Outlook Express; Chapter 30, "Rules for Mail and News," discusses their use in detail.

The rules that you define for you are stored in your Registry. You can export the rules branches of the Registry into a text file, which you can then import into the Registry of another computer.

You'll find the Inbox Assistant rules at HKEY_CURRENT_USER\ Identities\ {your identity number}\ Software\ Microsoft\ Outlook Express\ 5.0\ Rules\. This branch contains sub-branches for View filters, Mail, News, and Junk Mail, so you can select the Rules branch itself to export them all or select only one of these folders. These Registry entries will only contain values if you have created some rules.

Notice that each rule is numbered, starting with Rule0000 (if you haven't deleted your first rule previously). You'll want to edit these numbers in the exported text file if they conflict with rule numbers of rules already on the target computer.

First export each of these branches by using RegEdit and choosing Registry, Export Registry File. Then edit the rule numbers, and import the files into the Registry of the target computer.

Corrupted Passwords

You may you find that you are repeatedly asked to enter your account name and password when connecting to a news or mail server. Outlook Express doesn't keep its passwords (which are different than your Internet service provider logon password) in the *pwl* file, but rather in your Registry. These passwords are encrypted in RSA RC4 format.

If instead you are having problems with your DUN user name and password when trying to connect to the Internet with Outlook Express, turn to "Saving your DUN connectoid passwords" in Chapter 25.

The first step in fixing the Outlook Express password problem is to create a new news or mail account and then check to see if Outlook Express remembers the password for it.

STEPS

Repairing Outlook Express Password Problems

Step 1. Choose Tools, Accounts, Add, News or Mail to invoke the Internet Connection Wizard. Follow the steps in the Wizard to create a new account.

Step 2. Check to see if the new password was saved correctly by choosing Tools, Accounts, highlighting the account name, clicking the Properties button, and clicking the Server tab. Check if there are asterisks in the Password field. If the field is blank, Outlook Express isn't remembering the password to the server.

Step 3. If your Password field is blank, open a DOS window. (Click the Start button, point to Programs, and click MS-DOS Prompt.) At the DOS prompt, type **cd \Windows\System** and press Enter to change directories to your \Windows\System folder.

Step 4. Type **pstores -install** and press Enter. Type **exit** and press Enter to return to Windows.

Step 5. Enter a new password in one of your mail or news accounts. Click the Connect button in Outlook Express to see if you can successfully connect to that server without being asked about your password.

Beware of Sharing with Outlook

Outlook is a Microsoft personal information management product that is completely different from Outlook Express, though it bears a similar name. These two products have a history of causing problems for each other. Although by the time you read this the problems may have all been fixed, one in particular has been so widespread that we thought it worth mentioning.

Secret

When you install Outlook, it will offer to import your messages and address book from Outlook Express, as shown in Figure 27-20. If you do this, your messages and address book will no longer be available to Outlook Express (even if you uninstall Outlook). At the very least, you'll have to reimport them into Outlook Express, and some people have had to reinstall Outlook Express to get it to work again. We recommend waiting until you are certain that you want to migrate to Outlook before you import messages into Outlook from your Outlook Express.

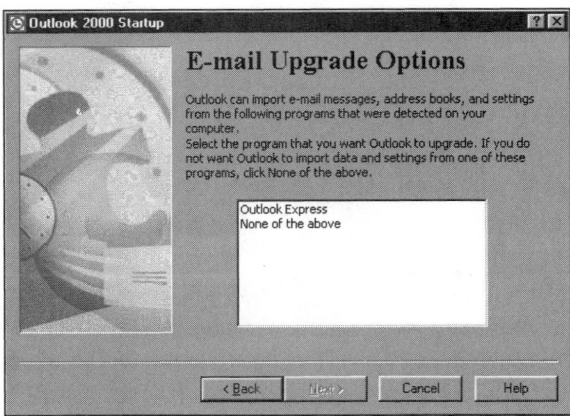

Figure 27-20: Outlook will offer to import your Outlook Express messages and address book.

Who Am I?

In Outlook Express you can store your personal information — your *identity* — to make using e-mail far easier. The following sections show you how to use identities in Outlook Express.

Signatures

The Signatures tab of the Tools, Options dialog box lets you create several signatures for different uses (see Figure 27-21). You can create signatures for specific mail and news accounts and set up a separate set of signatures for each identity.

STEPS

Creating a New Signature

Step 1.   Choose Tools, Options, and click the Signatures tab.

Step 2.   In the Signatures area, click the New button. The words *Signature #1* appear in the Signatures list, and your insertion point jumps to the Edit Signature box. You can type the text for your signature in the box, or click the File option button and type or browse to a file that contains your signature. Your signature can be a text file, an HTML file, or an animated *gif* file. However, there is a 4K size limit on signature files, so it's best to keep your ego in check.

Step 3. To give your signature a short name so that you'll remember which one it is, click it in the Signatures list. Now click the Rename button, type the new name, and press Enter.

Step 4. To set a signature as your default, select it in the Signatures list and then click the Set As Default button next to the Edit Signature box.

Step 5. If you want to associate your signature with an Outlook Express account, select it and click the Advanced button. In the Advanced Signature Settings dialog box, select the account(s) and click OK. You can only associate one signature with a particular account.

Step 6. To automatically insert your signature in all messages, mark the Add Signatures to All Outgoing Messages checkbox at the top of the Signatures tab. If you prefer to insert your signature at the time you compose a message, clear this checkbox. Click OK to close the Options dialog box.

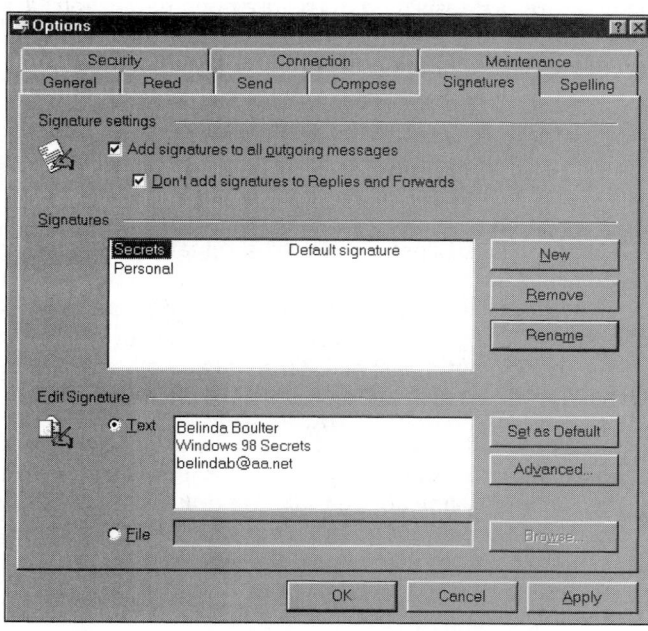

Figure 27-21: The new Signatures tab lets you create and manage multiple signatures.

To insert a signature in a message as you're composing it, make sure your insertion point is in the text area of the message (not the header), choose Insert, Signature, and click the one you want. To replace a signature, highlight it before inserting the new one.

If you marked Add Signatures to All Outgoing Messages in Step 6, and if you have multiple mail accounts going into the same Inbox, the signature for your default mail account will be the default. The exception is that if you reply to a message sent to a non-default account, the signature inserted will be the one for that account. If you have not associated a signature with your default mail account, the default signature will be inserted. If you are sending a message from a news or IMAP folder, the signature associated with that account will be inserted, or the default signature will be used if none is associated with that account.

You can add a Signature button to the toolbar of your New Message window (but not to the main Outlook Express toolbar). To do this, start a new message, right-click an empty spot on the toolbar, and choose Customize. In the Customize Toolbar dialog box, double-click the Insert Signature toolbar button, and then click Close. You'll need to do this separately for mail and news. After you've added this button to your toolbar, you can click it to insert the default signature (as described in the previous paragraph). If you have created more than one signature, you can select the signature you want from a drop-down list attached to the button.

Tip

If you don't have any signatures defined, you may find that extra blank lines are being added in your messages where the signature would otherwise be. To fix this, choose Tools, Options, click the Signatures tab, and make sure that Add Signatures to All Outgoing Messages is cleared.

If you have set up Outlook Express to insert a signature automatically, it will do this for all messages and all accounts, both mail and news. What if you only want to sign newsgroup postings, not mail messages? You can't set up an empty signature and assign it to an account. But you can set up a signature that consists of nothing but one space. This will add a blank line to your message, so it's not the ideal solution, but you might be able to live with it.

In keeping with a generally accepted standard on many newsgroups, Outlook Express precedes signatures in newsgroup messages with two hyphens on a line above, with an empty line above that. You don't need to add the hyphens or the line; Outlook Express inserts them automatically. So, for example, a signature for a news account might look like this:

```
--
Belinda
```

This is not the case with signatures in mail messages, however. No hyphens, no extra line. If you want them, you'll have to create a different signature for use in mail messages and put them into that signature yourself.

Using Identities

Identities make it a lot easier for several people to use the same computer to get their mail and read their favorite newsgroups. Unlike profiles, which affect all of your Windows Me settings, *identities* affect only Outlook Express. You can easily add or remove identities at any time. Each identity has its own accounts, newsgroup subscriptions and maintenance, signatures, and Options settings. You have to set up all of these items separately for each identity. When you first install Outlook Express, you have only one identity, called Main Identity, and it is set as the default.

Because it's easy to switch among different identities, you may find it convenient to use multiple identities for yourself. For example, you might use your laptop on a local area network at the office, and then take it home to follow your favorite hobby newsgroups on a dial-up account. Or you might have one identity with a password and one without. Maintaining a different identity for each situation makes it easy to globally switch all of the settings that change with each environment.

STEPS

Adding a New Identity

Step 1. In the Outlook Express window, choose File, Identities, Add New Identity.

Step 2. In the Type Your Name field of the New Identity dialog box, type a name for your identity (different from all other identity names). Click OK, and click Yes in the Identity Added dialog box to switch to your new identity. Outlook Express will close, and after a few seconds it will reopen along with the Internet Connection Wizard.

Step 3. If you have already set up an Internet mail account in Microsoft Exchange, Windows Messaging, or Outlook (not Outlook Express, however), you can import it into this identity by marking Use an Existing Internet Mail Account and clicking Next. The wizard will step you through to confirm the settings.

To set up a new mail account for this identity, mark Create a New Internet Mail Account and click Next. The wizard will step you through the settings for a new account.

If you want, you can click Cancel to exit the wizard. Your identity will have a name, but will have no accounts or other settings. You can then import an account that you have first exported from another Outlook Express identity by following the steps in the next section.

Continued

STEPS

Adding a New Identity *(continued)*

Step 4. If you have a message store from Microsoft Exchange, Windows Messaging, or Outlook, the Outlook Express Import Wizard now prompts you to import the messages and/or address book from that application. You can choose Cancel here and do it later if you like by choosing File, Import in the Outlook Express window for this identity.

Step 5. After you have finished or canceled the wizards, Outlook Express closes and reopens at the Welcome screen, with the name of your new identity displayed at the right end of the Folder bar. Choose File, Identities, Manage Identities to display the Manage Identities dialog box, as shown in Figure 27-22. If you want to make your new identity the default, highlight it in the Identities Names list and click the Make Default button.

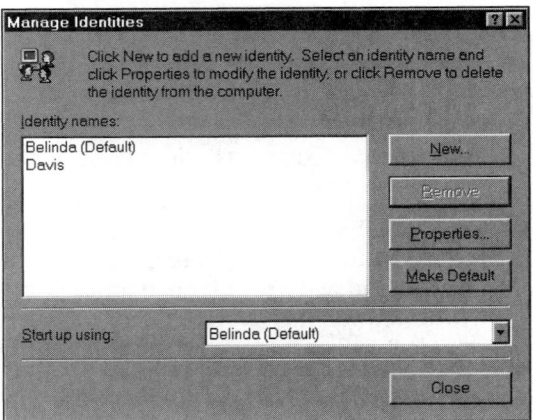

Figure 27-22: The Manage Identities dialog box

Step 6. To always start Outlook Express in your new identity (regardless of whether it is the default), select it in the Start Up Using list. If you want to be prompted for an identity when you open Outlook Express, choose Ask Me.

Step 7. To add password protection for this identity, click the Properties button, and mark the Ask Me for a Password When I Start checkbox in the Properties dialog box. Type your password (twice) in the Enter Password dialog box, click OK twice, and then click Close in the Manage Identities dialog box.

Adding password protection to your identity is a simple way to protect your e-mail messages and newsgroups from the prying eyes of your co-workers or family members. It does not protect anything on your system outside of Outlook Express, and it offers only a basic level of security — a truly malicious, computer-savvy person could most likely get around it. For more robust security, you'll need a more "corporate" program such as Outlook 2000 (and likely a secure mail server such as Exchange Server).

You will only be prompted for your password when you switch identities, or if you log off your current identity before closing Outlook Express. To log off your identity, choose File, Identities, Logoff *YourIdentityName*. The next time you open Outlook Express, you will have to enter your password to use this identity.

As you go about your business under this new identity, you will quickly notice that all settings are set to the default, *not* to what you had for your original identity. For example, you'll need to create new signatures for your new identity, you'll need to set up the toolbars and panes the way you like them, and you'll need to set up all new newsgroup accounts. In essence, it's as though you had just installed a new copy of Outlook Express.

Import an Account for Your New Identity

When you first create an identity, the Internet Connection Wizard opens to help you set up a new Internet mail account. Although the wizard can import an account from a Microsoft Exchange client such as Outlook, it cannot import an account directly from another Outlook Express identity. But it's very likely that you will want to do just that. Luckily, you can export an account from the first identity as an *iaf* file. Then you can import it into your new identity.

STEPS

Exporting and Importing a Mail Account

Step 1. In the old identity, choose Tools, Accounts, and click the Mail tab.

Step 2. Highlight the account that you want to use in the other identity, and click the Export button (see Figure 27-23).

Continued

STEPS

Exporting and Importing a Mail Account *(continued)*

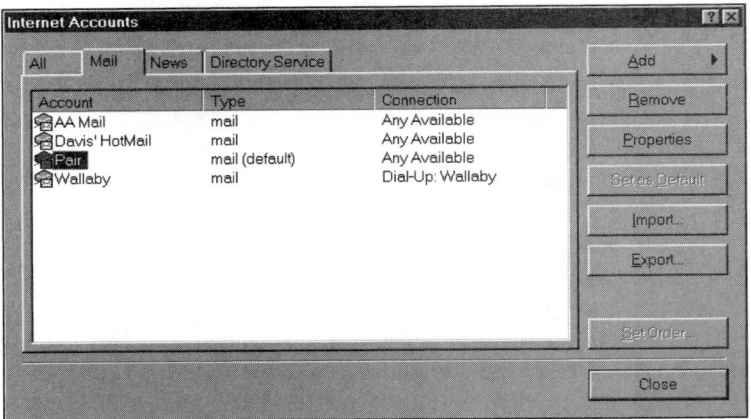

Figure 27-23: Click the Export button to export your mail account.

In the Export Internet Account dialog box that appears, navigate to the place where you want to save this *iaf* file — your default Outlook Express folder is a good choice — and click Save. Then click Close in the Internet Accounts dialog box.

Step 3. Choose File, Switch Identity. Select your new identity in the Switch Identities dialog box, and click OK. Outlook Express closes and reopens in your new identity.

Step 4. Choose Tools, Accounts, click the Mail tab, and click the Import button. The Import Internet Account dialog box opens to the default Outlook Express folder. Select the *iaf* file you saved in Step 2, and click Open. This account now appears in the Internet Accounts dialog box. Click Properties if you need to change the e-mail address or other information, and then click Close.

These steps describe exporting and importing a mail account, but the process is the same for news accounts. If you import a news account, it will not have any subscriptions; it will just contain the server information.

Import Messages from Another Identity

It may seem odd to import messages from one identity to another, because one of the reasons to use identities is to keep one set of messages separate from another. But maybe you've just set up a new identity, and previously your messages were all mixed up with someone else's in the same Inbox. You can move your messages to a different mail folder, and then import only that folder from the other identity.

To import messages from another identity, choose File, Import, Messages, select Microsoft Outlook Express 5 in the Select Program list, and click Next. Mark the Import Mail from an OE5 Identity option, select the identity from which you want to import messages (*not* your current identity), and click OK. You will see the message store location for the identity you have chosen; click Next if it is correct. In the Select Folders dialog box shown in Figure 27-24, mark the Selected Folders option button and highlight the folder(s) that contain the messages you want to import. Click Next, and then click Finish. Your imported folders should now appear in the Folders pane. These folders and messages have not been moved from the other identity, only copied.

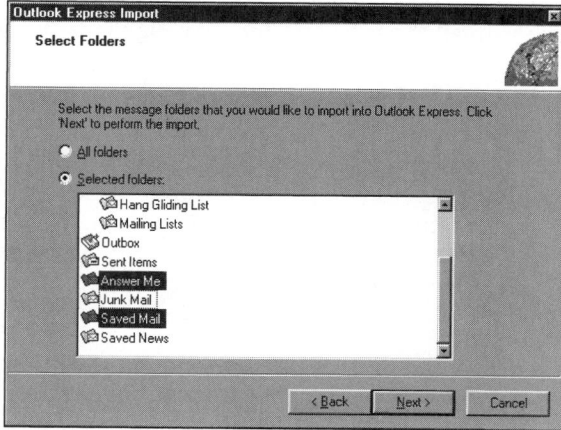

Figure 27-24: Use your Shift and/or Ctrl keys to select multiple folders to import.

Create an Identity to Import a Single Message Folder

The File, Import, Message command in Outlook Express is designed for importing a whole message store, not an individual message folder. But you may wish to do just that. For example, you may have archived a group of messages in a message folder on one computer and now need to read them on another. You can do this using Identities.

STEPS

Importing a Single Message Folder

Step 1.   Using the Explorer, create a new empty folder and into it move the message folder you want to import. (It doesn't matter where you put this folder since it's only temporary.)

Step 2.   In Outlook Express, create a new identity and call it Temp. Click Yes when asked if you wish to switch to Temp now. Cancel out of the Internet Connection Wizard and the Import Account wizard and the Import Messages and Address Book Wizard.

Step 3.   Choose Tools, Options, Maintenance and click the Store Folder button. Click Change and navigate to the folder where you stored the message folder in Step 1. Click OK twice. The message folder you wish to import should appear in the folders list. Delete the welcome message from your new Inbox. Close Outlook Express.

Step 4.   Open Outlook Express and if necessary switch to the identity where you want to import the message folder. Choose File, Import, Messages, highlight Microsoft Outlook Express 5 and click Next. Mark Import Mail From An OE5 Identity, highlight Temp in the list of identities, and click OK. Your message folder should now appear in the folders list.

A copy of the message folder you imported now appears in the message store for the identity into which you imported it. Once you're sure everything is working, you can delete the temporary folder you created in Step 1. You can also delete the Temp identity you created in Step 2.

Shedding Old Identities

To remove an identity, you must first switch to a different identity — click File, Switch Identity and select an identity other than the one to be removed. Now click File, Identities, Manage Identities. Highlight the identity to be removed and click the Remove button, click Delete, and then click Close. Although that identity will no longer appear in the Manage Identities dialog box, its folder and data still appear in your Explorer. You'll need to delete this folder manually.

Identities are stored at \Windows\Application Data\Identities. The folders have hexadecimal numbers for names. This makes it very hard to tell in the Explorer which identity is which, so you'll have a hard time figuring out which folder you can safely delete.

Secret

To sort this out, start the Registry Editor and navigate to HKEY_USERS\.
Default\Identities. Click the folder for an identity in the left pane, and you'll
see a Username string in the right pane. The value of this string is the name
of your identity. Only current identities appear in the Registry. Make a note
of the number, and now go back to the Explorer and delete the folders for
the identities that no longer appear in the Registry.

Connecting with Outlook Express

You need to connect to the Internet to send and receive e-mail with Outlook
Express. In the following sections you'll learn the ins and outs of connecting
with Outlook Express.

Connecting with the DUNs

If you connect to the Internet through a dial-up connection, you'll want to
customize just how and when that connection is made. Outlook Express uses
the Internet Explorer connection settings, which you can reach from within
Outlook Express by choosing Tools ⇨ Options ⇨ Connection and clicking the
Change button. To override these settings for a specific account, choose
Tools, Accounts, highlight a news or mail server, click Properties, and then
click the Connection tab (see Figure 27-25).

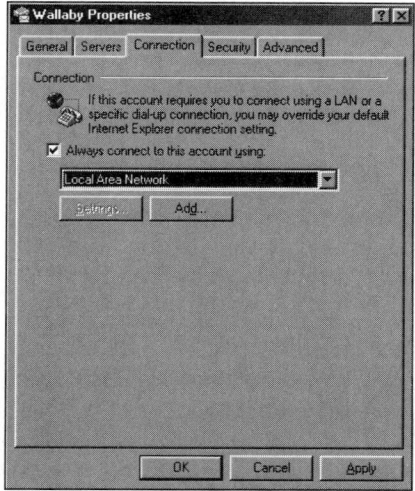

Figure 27-25: The Connection tab of the Properties dialog box for a news or mail account

If you leave the box on this tab unchecked, Outlook Express will assign Any
Available as the connection for this account. If you prefer to connect to the

Internet first by clicking your Internet service provider's DUN connectoid, this will let you choose your connection on an ad hoc basis. However, it also means Outlook Express will not initiate an Internet connection on its own.

Outlook Express will not automatically hang up after carrying out the requested task (such as sending and retrieving e-mail). You can change this behavior by choosing Tools, Options, clicking the Connection tab, and marking the Hang Up After Sending and Receiving checkbox. You can also mark or clear this box by clearing the Hang Up When Finished checkbox in the message box that appears when you initiate an Outlook Express command that requires a connection to the Internet.

You can set up Outlook Express to automatically retrieve new mail. Choose Tools, Options, and click the General tab. Mark the Check for New Messages Every [ ] Minute(s) checkbox.

If you are working offline and want to remain offline until you specifically ask Outlook Express to dial in to your Internet service provider, choose File, Work Offline. You can also toggle back and forth by double-clicking Working Offline or Working Online in the status bar at the bottom of the Outlook Express window. This setting affects both Outlook Express and Internet Explorer. If you open a message (most likely an HTML-formatted one) that contains HTML code referencing a resource of the Internet (in other words, the HREF tag and a URL), Windows will invoke the Internet Explorer but will give you the option to continue working offline.

POP3, SMTP, and XOVER required

Outlook Express requires that your Internet service provider (or your local area network) have an SMTP server if you want to send mail, and a POP3 server if you want to receive mail. Some service providers use only an SMTP server to send and receive mail. This configuration won't work with Outlook Express.

Secret

You can send mail with Outlook Express even if you don't have a POP3 server to receive mail. Just choose Tools, Options, click the Send tab, and mark the Send Messages Immediately checkbox. This way, Outlook Express won't check for incoming mail.

If you don't have a POP3 server, you can put a bogus entry in the POP3 server field (choose Tools, Accounts, click the account in the Mail tab, click the Properties button, and click the Servers tab). If you set up a bogus POP3 entry and have mail in the Outbox, don't click Tools, Send and Receive. Just click Tools, Send.

You can also choose to skip an account that doesn't have a POP3 server by removing it from the list of accounts that are checked for incoming mail. Choose Tools, Accounts, highlight the account in the Mail tab, click Properties, and clear the Include This Account When Receiving Mail or Synchronizing checkbox.

Your Internet service provider's news server must support the XOVER extension of the NNTP protocol (Network News Transfer Protocol). Most likely it does. If not, give your service provider a call or find a new provider.

Multiple Accounts for the Same Server

You can name each account that you create, which lets you keep track of different accounts that use the same mail or news server. This is quite handy. For example, during the early beta testing period for Internet Explorer 4.0 and Windows 98, Microsoft included the two beta newsgroups on the same beta-news.microsoft.com news server. Each beta required that you log on to the same news server with a different password and beta ID. By setting up two news accounts, we were able to place two different sets of IDs and passwords in the Properties dialog box for each account. (Choose Tools, Accounts, click the News tab, highlight the account, click the Properties button, click the Server tab, mark the This Server Requires Me to Log On checkbox, and then enter the account name and password.) We could then log on sequentially to the same news server, but under different beta identities.

You can also use this method to make two separate mail accounts that log on to the same mail server, but through different DUNs. In this way, you can use one account to log on to get your e-mail when you are away from home and using a national service provider, and another for when you are at home. If you log on at the office over a LAN and at home over the phone lines, you can set up two mail accounts for the same mail server.

If you are setting up different mail server accounts with different DUNs or LAN connections, you will probably have to have a different SMTP outgoing mail server in each of them, even though the POP3 mail server may be the same. Turn to "Choose which account to send your messages through" in Chapter 28 for more details.

Different Service Providers for Internet Explorer and Outlook Express

Outlook Express lets you connect to multiple mail and news servers through different Internet service providers (or LANs) or through one provider. You can have multiple DUN connectoids stored in your Dial-Up Networking folder. If you use a dial-up connection to the Internet, you can set Internet Explorer to call using any one of your DUN connectoids, and it doesn't have to be one that's used by Outlook Express. We've got ourselves a little management job here.

If you have connected to the Internet using Outlook Express and you display a message (most likely an HTML-formatted message) that contains a reference to an Internet resource (using the HREF tag and a URL), Windows will try to connect to that resource using Internet Explorer. If Internet Explorer is configured to call up through a different Internet service provider, it will conflict with your current Internet connection and kick you off the connection. A similar behavior could happen if you have multiple messages in your Outbox, each associated with a different account.

To prevent this, choose Tools, Options, and click the Connection tab. Mark the Ask Before Switching Dial-Up Connections checkbox. Now when you request a resource that is associated with a different DUN, you will be given the option of trying to locate the server on the current connection. This almost always works just fine.

Sending Messages Now or Later

You have the option of sending messages immediately (as soon as you click the Send or Post button) or storing them in the Outbox to be sent later. Even if they are sent immediately, they do go by way of the Outbox.

If you choose Tools, Options, click the Send tab, and mark the Send Messages Immediately checkbox, your messages go quickly to your mail or news server, especially if you are already online or connected to a LAN. If you are working offline, Outlook Express calls your Internet service provider and sends your message from your Outbox to the server as soon as it makes the connection. If you have marked Hang Up When Finished Sending, Receiving, or Downloading in the Dial Up tab of the Tools, Options dialog box, the Internet connection is severed after the message is delivered.

If you are working offline, you probably want to store up a few messages before you batch them off to the server, so you'll likely want to clear Send Messages Immediately.

Working Online or Offline

Unlike earlier versions of Outlook Express that used a separate (and sometimes competing) dialer to make dial-up connections, Outlook Express 5 now shares the Internet Explorer dialer. This eliminates lots of previous problems, such as Outlook Express hanging up a connection that was initiated by another application. It also makes for a more consistent user interface. In fact, you can now access the Internet Explorer connection properties from Outlook Express. To do this, choose Tools, Options, click the Connection tab, and click the Change button. The changes you make here also affect Internet Explorer.

Because Outlook Express now uses Internet Explorer's connection management system, the concept of working online or working offline has become considerably more significant. If you have a constant Internet connection, you can work online all the time without worrying about it.

But if you dial up to connect to the Internet, you sometimes need a way to use communications applications such as Outlook Express and Internet Explorer without trying to communicate with the server.

For example, when you move from your Inbox to a news folder, Outlook Express attempts to connect to that news server if you are working online. This might also happen when you highlight the header of an e-mail message that links to a web site. If you just want to look at the messages without connecting, first switch to working offline. This setting is global for all of your applications that use it, so if you are offline in Internet Explorer, you are also offline in Outlook Express.

If you have chosen Never Dial a Connection in the Connections tab of the Internet Properties dialog box (click Tools, Options, click the Connection tab, and click the Change button), you might think that this would keep Outlook Express from trying to make a connection. But choosing that setting only makes Outlook Express assume that you have already established a connection (perhaps over a network). If you are set to work online and you go to a news folder, Outlook Express will still attempt to connect to that news server, but will fail to find the server because there is no Internet connection. You should choose an Internet Properties setting that is appropriate for the way you connect to that mail or news account in general, and use the work online/work offline settings to tell Windows 98 how you want to work at the moment.

The standard way to change your work online/work offline setting is by choosing File ⇨ Work Offline in either Outlook Express or Internet Explorer. But Outlook Express offers two other ways to both see and change your current state. One is a button that you can add to your mail and/or news toolbar, shown in Figure 27-26. When you are working offline, it appears to be depressed. The button's icon and text show you what will happen if you click it, *not* your current state. Some of us find this confusing.

More convenient than the toolbar button is the status bar at the bottom of your Outlook Express window, shown in Figure 27-27. Not only does the status bar clearly indicate your current online/offline state, but in Outlook Express it toggles on and off with a simple double-click. If you don't see a status bar in Outlook Express, choose View, Layout and mark the Status Bar checkbox. (The Internet Explorer status bar only shows you an icon if you are working offline; it looks slightly different and is only a status indicator, not a toggle button.)

You can also make a pair of shortcuts that let you set your Registry directly to work in online or offline mode. See "Set Work Offline before you open Internet Explorer" in Chapter 26 for the steps.

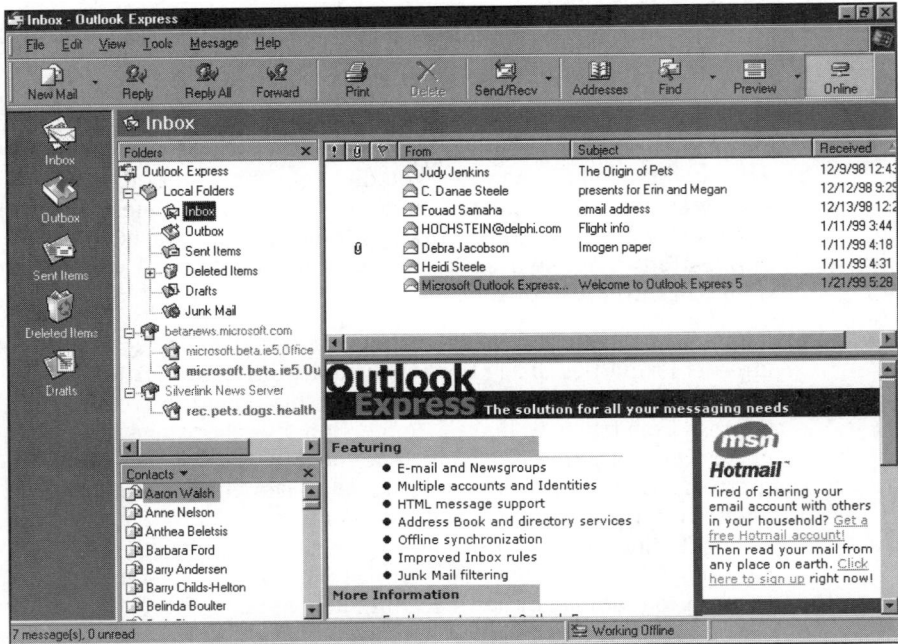

Figure 27-26: The toolbar button is depressed when you are working offline. The text and icon indicate the state you would switch to if you clicked it, *not* your current state.

Figure 27-27: The status bar clearly indicates that we are offline at the moment.

Disable the Disconnect Message

Normally, when you close an Internet application and there are no others running, you will be prompted to disconnect from your dial-up account. This is a useful reminder if you are paying by the minute for access. However, if you switch applications often and like to leave your connection open, this little warning can get very old.

The easiest way to disable this message is to mark the Don't Use Auto Disconnect check-box in the Auto Disconnect message box itself, shown in Figure 27-28.

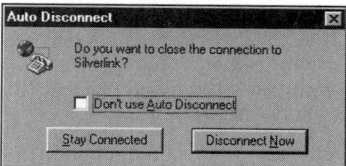

Figure 27-28: When the Auto Disconnect message appears, you can disable it by marking the checkbox.

There is another, longer way to do this that doesn't require you to go online. Choose Tools, Options, click the Connection tab, and click the Change button. In the Connections tab of the Internet Properties dialog box, highlight your dial-up account, click the Settings button, and then click the Advanced button under Dial-Up Settings. In the Advanced Dial-Up dialog box, clear the Disconnect When Connection May No Longer Be Needed checkbox, as shown in Figure 27-29. Click OK four times to close all the dialog boxes.

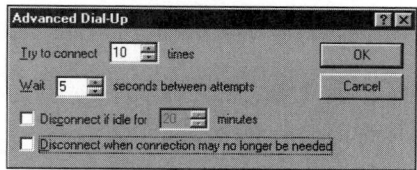

Figure 27-29: Clear the Disconnect When Connection May No Longer Be Needed checkbox to disable the disconnect warning.

Using a Non-default Mail or News Account

If you have set up more than one mail account, when you start a new mail message you will see a From field at the top of the New Message window displaying your default mail account. If you reply to a mail message, the From field in your reply will display the account to which the original message was sent. News messages include a News Server field in the message header. This field displays the news server for the newsgroup that you are currently reading.

It's really easy to choose a different mail account or news server for your message. Click the down arrow to the right of the From (or News Server) field in the message header and select from the list of active accounts. Once a message is in your Outbox, you can look in the Account column to see which account it will use. (If you don't see that column, right-click a column header, click Columns, mark the Account checkbox in the Columns list, and then click OK.)

Set the Connection for an Account

If you need to always use a specific connection for a particular mail or news server, you can set that up. For example, many Internet service providers refuse access to their news servers if you dial in from another service, so you need to associate that news account with the correct dial-up connection. If you need to always use a local area network to access a certain server, you also need to be able to specify that. Designating a specific connection in this way overrides the default connection.

To associate a connection with a mail or news account, choose Tools, Accounts, highlight the account in question, click the Properties button, and click the Connection tab. Mark the Always Connect to This Account Using checkbox (see Figure 27-30), and then select the dial-up connection in the drop-down list.

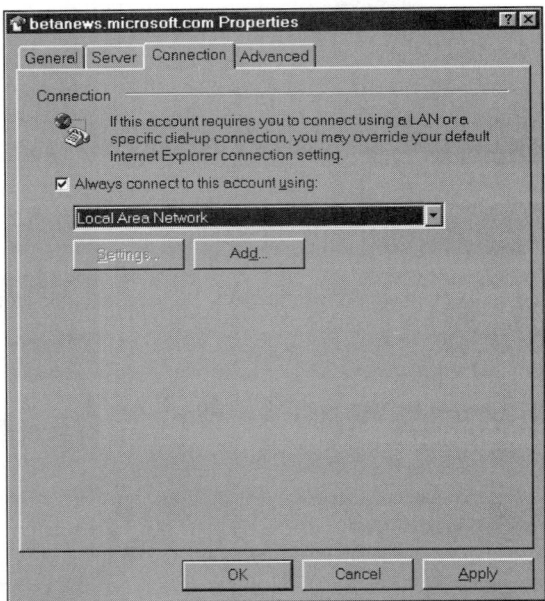

Figure 27-30: If you need to use a specific connection with a mail or news account, specify the connection in the Connection tab of the Properties dialog box for the account.

Your Outbox can contain messages associated with several different mail and news accounts, each associated with a different connection. When you click the Send and Receive button, Outlook Express uses the default dial-up connection to connect with the Internet. When it comes to a message in the Outbox that is set to use a different connection, Outlook Express will either hang up and dial the other connection or it will prompt you with the message shown in Figure 27-31. You control this by marking or clearing the Ask Before Switching Dial-Up Connections checkbox in the Connection tab of the Options dialog box.

Usually it works just fine to use the current connection to look for the other server. In fact if you travel, this is a good way to access your mail server back home while using a dial-up connection that's a local call from the place you're visiting.

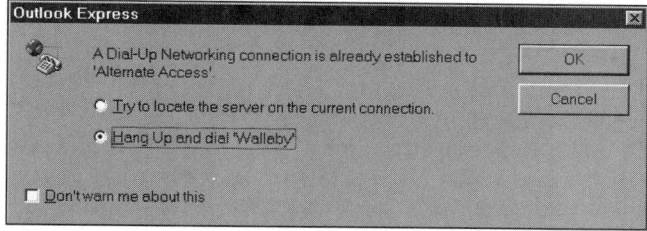

Figure 27-31: You'll see this warning if you try to use a different dial-up connection.

Tip

In the lower-left corner of this dialog box, you can mark the Don't Warn Me About This box to avoid getting this warning in the future. But beware: If you mark this box, in the future Outlook Express will automatically choose the second option, always disconnecting and establishing a new (possibly long distance?) dial-up connection. To restore the original setting, choose Tools, Options in the Outlook Express window, click the Connection tab, and mark the Ask Before Switching Dial-Up Connections checkbox.

Scheduling the Mail

Secret

You can use the Task Scheduler that comes with Windows 98 to automatically open Outlook Express and retrieve your mail at a set time every day, as long as your computer is running.

STEPS

Scheduling Send and Receive

Step 1. In Outlook Express, choose Tools, Options.

Step 2. In the General tab, mark Send and Receive Messages at Startup.

Step 3. On the Connection tab, make sure that Hang Up After Sending and Receiving is marked. Click OK and close Outlook Express.

Continued

STEPS

Scheduling Send and Receive *(continued)*

Step 4. Click Start, Programs, System Tools, Scheduled Tasks. In the Scheduled Tasks folder window, click Add Scheduled Task. In the Scheduled Task Wizard that appears, click Next and be patient while the Task Scheduler examines all the applications on your computer. When the wizard presents you with a list of programs, Highlight Outlook Express and click Next. (If for some reason you don't see Outlook Express, click the Browse button and navigate to \Program Files\Outlook Express. Click msimn.exe and click Open.)

Step 5. Type **Outlook Express** at the top of the next dialog box if it's not already there. Mark the Daily option button, and click Next. Set the start time and start date. Then indicate whether you want to do this every day, just weekdays, or at a particular interval of days, and click Next. (If you want to test your task now, enter a time in the next couple of minutes — it's easy to change later.) Mark Open Advanced Properties for This Task When I Click Finish, and click Finish.

Step 6. The Properties dialog box for your task opens. On the Settings tab, mark the checkbox next to Stop the Scheduled Task If It Runs for [ ] hour(s) [ ] Minutes(s), and set the length of time to something like 5 or 10 minutes — long enough to make a connection and do a Send/Receive. Click OK, and minimize the Scheduled Tasks folder window.

Step 7. Once you are satisfied that your scheduled task works, restore the Scheduled Tasks folder window and click the Outlook Express task to open its Properties. Go to the Schedule tab and enter the correct time when you want Outlook Express to open (for example, midnight, or 7 AM). Click OK, and close Scheduled Tasks.

Remember to leave your computer turned on with Outlook Express *closed* in order for this to work!

What's That Pushpin For?

You may have noticed a pushpin icon in the lower-right corner of Outlook Express' Send and Receive dialog box (shown in Figure 27-32). Or you may never have noticed it. The purpose of the pushpin is to tell you how the dialog box will behave. Normally, the "point" of the pushpin points to the left. This indicates that the dialog box will close automatically after your e-mail messages are downloaded. But if you click the pushpin, it will appear as though it's sticking into the screen, indicating that now the dialog box will stay visible after the download is complete. That can be useful if you want to review the tasks Outlook Express went through in sending and receiving messages. If Outlook Express encounters any errors, the dialog box stays visible with the Errors tab in front, even if the pushpin is "out." In either case, you can just click the Hide button to send the dialog box away.

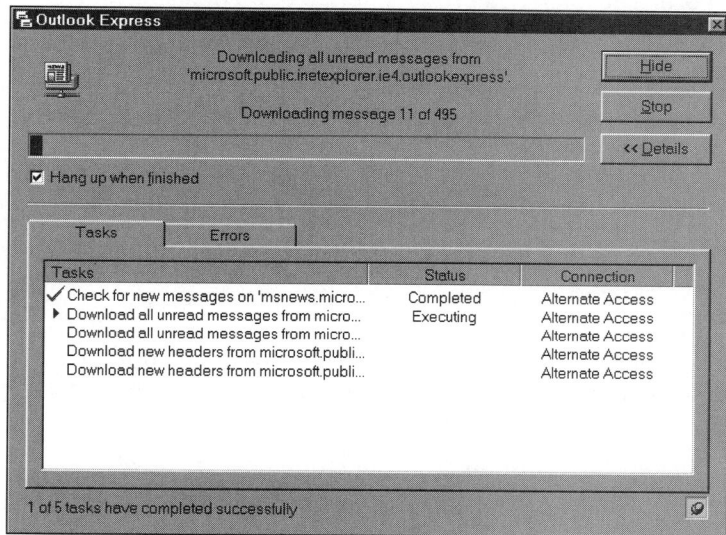

Figure 27-32: This pushpin appears to be "pushed in." The dialog box will continue to be displayed after the download is complete.

Previewing Your Mail

If you want to be able to look over your message headers and choose which messages to download, you might want to try something like Magic Mail Monitor. This small, fast, freeware program sits in your system tray, checks for incoming mail, and lets you view message headers and even delete messages without downloading their bodies. This is great if you occasionally receive files with large attachments that take too long to download or cause your dial-up connection to time out. Check out the Magic web site for more details and to download the software: http://www.geocities.com/SiliconValley/Vista/2576/magic.html.

A similar (though much larger) freeware product is POP3 Scan Mailbox, available at http://www.netcomuk.co.uk/~kempston/smb/.

Monitor Web-based E-mail

If you are using Juno, Yahoo, or some other web-based e-mail system, you have to remember to check if you have new mail. If you have multiple accounts, this can be a bit much. One solution is to use a program that checks all your accounts for you.

Ristra Mail Monitor may be just the ticket for you. It will check your web-based e-mail account at a pre-set interval or on demand, and let you know if you have new mail. You'll find it at `http://ristra.hypermart.net/`.

Access Your Hotmail with Outlook Express

Many people would like to be able to access their web-based e-mail accounts using Outlook Express. It's nice to be able to read your mail offline and to save it on your computer. Outlook Express now has the built-in ability to do this for users of Hotmail, a service of Microsoft's MSN online service.

To set up a new Hotmail account from within Outlook Express, choose Tools, New Account Signup, Hotmail. The Setup Hotmail Account Wizard launches, initiates a dial-up connection, and walks you through the account setup sequence online. It also creates a new mail account on your computer for Hotmail and a new Hotmail folder in your Folders list.

If you already have a Hotmail account, don't use the New Account Signup command. Instead, click Tools, Accounts, Add, Mail. After entering your name, click Next. In the next wizard dialog box, mark I Already Have an E-mail Address That I'd Like to Use, enter your Hotmail address, and then click Next. Outlook Express recognizes that you have entered a Hotmail account and sets the defaults accordingly. Continue through the wizard to enter your password, click Finish, and click Yes to download your Hotmail folder.

Your new Hotmail folder contains its own Inbox and Sent Items folders, separate from the main Outlook Express Inbox and Sent Items folders. These will only be created when they have contents. The Hotmail folder actually behaves more like a newsgroup server than like e-mail, as you can see in Figure 27-33. The synchronization settings work the way they do in a newsgroup. Messages that you download reside on your hard disk, while those you don't download remain on the Hotmail server.

Instead of choosing the synchronization setting All Messages, you might prefer to use Headers Only (select the Hotmail folder in the Folders pane, click the Settings button in the right pane, and choose Headers Only). Then you retrieve only the messages you want by right-clicking their headers and selecting Download Message Later. In fact, you may find this method of mail management to be a reason for using Hotmail instead of standard e-mail.

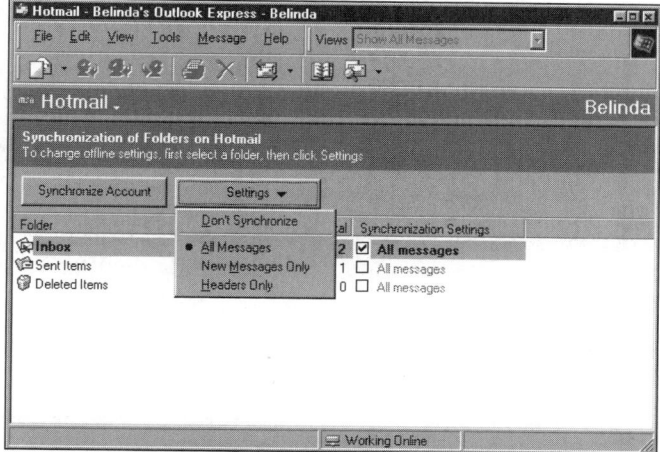

Figure 27-33: The Hotmail folder lets you choose synchronization settings as you would for a newsgroup.

If you prefer to have your Hotmail messages go into your regular Inbox and be managed in the same way as your other e-mail, you might want to try a shareware package called Hotmail Express from C-WebMail. Hotmail Express gives you POP3 access to your Hotmail account, letting you download messages using any POP3 e-mail software. It even gets rid of the advertising messages. And you can still get your mail by logging onto the web when you are using a different computer.

Shortcuts in Outlook Express

Shortcuts are always welcome. Anything that makes your life a little simpler is worth learning. The following sections describe several ways to make using Outlook Express easier.

Shortcuts to Outlook Express

You can start Outlook Express by clicking the Outlook Express icon on your Desktop or on your Quick Launch toolbar. You can also start it from a command line, or from a DOS prompt for that matter.

Another flexible and convenient way to start Outlook Express is to create a shortcut for it. If you do this, you can then modify the shortcut to invoke Outlook Express in any number of special ways. (Once you create your own shortcut, you may want to remove the Outlook Express icon from your Desktop by right-clicking it and clicking Delete.)

To create a shortcut, right-click `msimn.exe` in the `\Program Files\ Outlook Express\` folder and click Create Shortcut.

To open Outlook Express in mail, right-click the shortcut that you just created (it will be in the same folder), click Properties in the context menu, and modify the contents of the Target field in the Shortcut tab to look like this:

```
"C:\Program Files\Outlook Express\msimn.exe" /mail
```

You can also force Outlook Express to start in mail by choosing Tools, Options in the Outlook Express window, and marking the When Starting, Go Directly to My 'Inbox' Folder checkbox in the General tab.

```
To open Outlook Express to your default news server, make sure that
the Target field looks like this:
"C:\Program Files\Outlook Express\msimn.exe" /news
If you want to open Outlook Express from the DOS command prompt, type
this:
start "C:\Program Files\Outlook Express\msimn.exe"
```

If you want to start an Outlook Express New Message window without starting all of Outlook Express, you can click the Start button, click Run, and type **mailto:*someone@aserviceprovider*.com**. The e-mail address will appear in the To field of the New Message window. If you just type **mailto:**, a New Message window appears with a blank To field. Outlook Express must be your default e-mail program for this method to work.

Adding Outlook Express Messages to the New Menu

Secret

In other chapters, we have discussed ways to add items to the New menu. If you like, you can create a New menu item for Outlook Express. Here's how:

STEPS

Placing Outlook Express Mail Messages on Your New Menu

Step 1. Right-click your Desktop, point to New, and click Text Document.

Step 2. Rename the text document **New.eml**. Click Yes.

Step 3. Click the Start button, point to Settings, and click Control Panel. Click your TweakUI icon. Click the New tab.

Step 4. Drag and drop `New.eml` into the New tab. You'll notice that there is now a new checked entry on the list of new documents in TweakUI: Outlook Express Mail Message.

Secret

Do you want to add an item for Outlook Express news postings to the New menu? Follow these same steps, but in Step 2, rename the new text document New.nws. Or, instead of following Steps 1 and 2, click the New Post button while you're using Outlook Express and focused on a newsgroup, click the Save As button in the New Message toolbar, and save the blank news document with the name New.nws on your Desktop. Then continue with Steps 3 and 4.

Dragging and Dropping Messages

You can drag and drop messages from one Outlook Express folder to another, except for the Outbox folder. Outlook Express prepares messages to be sent over the Internet before placing them in the Outbox folder. It does this when you click the Send (or Post) button in the New Message window.

Outlook Express could have been programmed to allow you to drag and drop into the Outbox folder, but the Microsoft developers chose not to add this code to the standard drag and drop function.

If you drag and hold a message icon over a folder in the Folder List pane that contains subfolders, the list expands and the subfolders are displayed. This makes it possible to drag and drop to subfolders. And if you drag a message to the top or bottom of the Folder List pane, the list scrolls up or down to let you drop the message on a folder that was originally hidden.

Shortcut to the New Message Window

If you want to be able to write e-mail messages quickly, you can create a shortcut to the Outlook Express New Message window. Place the shortcut on your Desktop or drag it to a toolbar.

STEPS

Creating a Shortcut to the New Message Window

Step 1. Right-click an empty part of your Desktop and click New, Shortcut.

Step 2. Insert the following text into the Command Line field of the Create Shortcut dialog box, as shown in Figure 27-34:

"C:\Program Files\Outlook Express\Msimn.Exe" /mailurl:%1

Continued

STEPS

Creating a Shortcut to the New Message Window *(continued)*

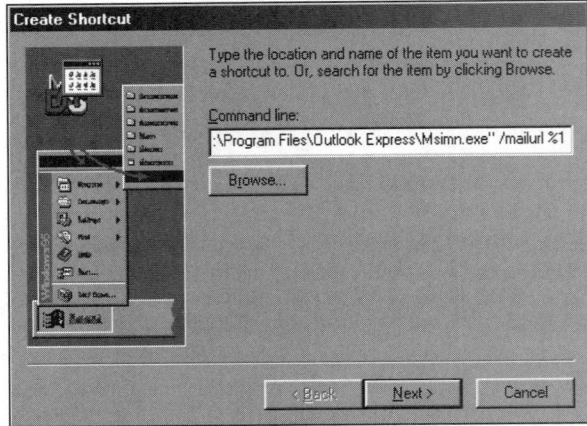

Figure 27-34: Insert the command to open the Outlook Express New Message window in the Command-Line field.

Step 3. Click the Next button, rename the shortcut **New Message**, and click the Finish button.

Step 4. You can now drag the shortcut to a toolbar and drop it there. After dropping it on a toolbar, right-click the shortcut on the Desktop and click delete to get rid of it from the Desktop.

Thanks to Ryan Coe for this tip.

When you click your shortcut icon, a New Message window opens without opening Outlook Express. After you've composed your message, when you click the Send button, the message will be put in your Outbox unless you have marked Send Messages Immediately in Tools, Options, Send. In that case, you will still need to open Outlook Express and do a Send and Receive in order to send the message.

Copy a Shortcut from a Message

Right-click an e-mail address or URL in a message and click Copy Shortcut. The message needn't be open; you can do it from the Preview pane. Now you can paste this shortcut into the To field of an outgoing message, paste it as a live link in a message body or an HTML document, or paste it into your Address bar and press Enter to open a New Message window or a web site. If you paste it onto your Desktop (right-click your Desktop and click Paste Shortcut) you will create a URL shortcut, which you can use over and over, as described in the next section.

Creating a Command-Line Shortcut

A URL shortcut is like a shortcut to a web page, but instead of starting with http: to indicate a web address, it starts with the Internet mailto: command. With a URL shortcut, you can pre-specify the contents of all the header lines, and even the message body. This is useful if you frequently send mail messages to the same person or group of people, or if you frequently send the same short message to various people. You must have Outlook Express set up as the default MAPI client for this method to work.

If you have received the address in an Outlook Express message, you can skip the Creating a Mailto Shortcut steps below. Just right-click the link, click Copy Shortcut, and then right-click your Desktop and click Paste Shortcut. If you want to add some command-line parameters, as discussed later in this section, right-click the shortcut on your Desktop, click Properties, add the parameters to the end of the Command Line field, and click OK.

Another way to make this type of shortcut is to type your mailto: command in the Address bar (in the Internet Explorer or on your Desktop). Click the Go button, close the New Message window that opens, and then drag the icon from the Address bar onto your Desktop (see Figure 27-35).

Figure 27-35: Drag the icon for your mailto: command onto the Desktop to create a shortcut.

Here's how to create a mailto shortcut from scratch:

STEPS

Creating a Mailto Shortcut

Step 1. Right-click an empty part of your Desktop and click New, Shortcut.

Step 2. In the Command Line field of the Create Shortcut dialog box, type **mailto:**. You can add an e-mail address (for example, **mailto:davis@halcyon.com**) or one or more other fields using the syntax described in a moment. Click Next.

Step 3. Type a name for your shortcut and click Finish.

Secret

If you want more of the message to be filled in automatically than just the To field, you can add more parameters to the command line for your shortcut. To do so, right-click the shortcut and click Properties. In the Web Document tab of the Properties dialog box for the shortcut, you'll see the URL field containing your mailto: command line. Make your edits here, using these guidelines:

- Precede the first parameter with a question mark (?).
- Separate fields with an ampersand (&).
- Separate addresses within fields with a semicolon (;).
- Separate the name of the field from its contents with an equal sign (=).
- If a field contains only one address, you can type a name as it is displayed in your address book — if there are two people in that field, you must type their actual addresses.
- The fields that can have parameters are subject, CC, BCC, and body.
- The total number of characters in your command line must be fewer than 457 characters; otherwise you'll get an error message and your shortcut won't work. Keep this in mind if you are planning to include body text or a whole lot of addresses; it's best to keep it short.

Here's an example of a command line using lots of parameters; the results are shown in Figure 27-36.

```
mailto:davis@halcyon.com?subject=Hi
There&CC=mom@ix.netcom.com;joe@eskimo.com&BCC=
belindab@aa.net&body=Hello everyone!
```

The next time you click the shortcut, the changes you made to the command line will be reflected in the message. The New Message window opens without opening Outlook Express. After you've composed your message, when you click the Send button, the message will be put in your Outbox unless you have marked Send Messages Immediately in Tools, Options, Send. In that case, you will still need to open Outlook Express and do a Send and Receive to send the message.

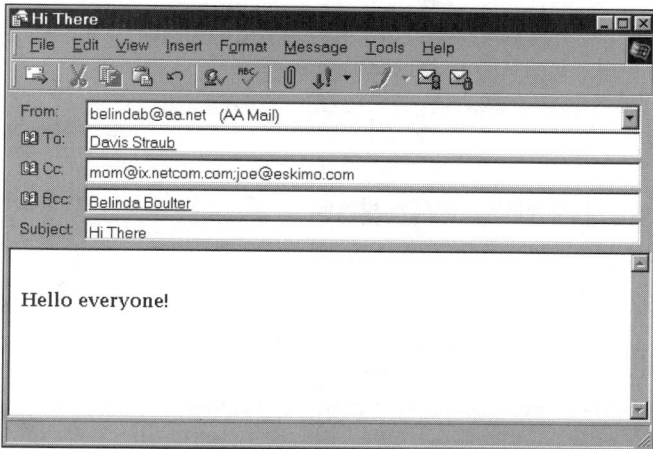

Figure 27-36: You can use parameters to fill in more of the message if you like.

Drag and Drop to an Outlook Express Message

If you want to send a new message containing some text from another message or document, all you have to do is drag and drop. Outlook Express must be open for this to work, but it can be minimized.

STEPS

Dragging Text to a New Message

Step 1. Highlight the text that you want to send. If the text is in an Outlook Express message, you can highlight it in either the message window or the Preview pane. If it's in another document, such as a text file or a Microsoft Word document, highlight it there.

Step 2. Drag and drop the highlighted text onto any message folder except the Outbox. If Outlook Express is minimized, hover over its Taskbar button until it opens. If the Folders pane is not displayed, hover over the folder name on the Folder bar until the Folders list appears. Drop onto a mail folder for mail, or onto a news folder for news.

Continued

STEPS

Dragging Text to a New Message *(continued)*

Step 3.   A New Message window appears containing only the text you highlighted. No header information appears in the new message, and no quote characters are included.

Shortcut to the Windows Address Book

You can also create a shortcut to the Windows address book. Keep it on your Desktop, or drag it into your Quick Launch toolbar. The shortcut makes it easy to add or update contacts without waiting for Outlook Express to open. You can compose a new message directly from the address book by right-clicking a contact and choosing Action, Send Mail. With the address book's new telephone dialing capabilities (see "The address book does more than e-mail" in Chapter 32), it makes even more sense to keep your address book as handy as possible.

STEPS

Creating a Shortcut to Your Address Book

Step 1.   Right-click your Desktop and click New, Shortcut.

Step 2.   Click the Browse button. In the Browse dialog box, choose All Files in the Files of Type field.

Step 3.   Navigate to `\Windows\Application Data\Microsoft\Address Book` to find your address book, unless you've moved it to your My Documents folder, or you have multiple user profiles. In this latter case, you can find your address book by using the Find command (Start, Find, Files or Folders) to search for `*.wab`.

Step 4.   Click your Windows address book name, click Open, and then click Next.

Step 5.   Rename the shortcut **Windows Address Book** and click the Finish button.

Because the `wab` file contains the address books for all the identities set up in Outlook Express on your computer, when you open the `wab` file from outside of Outlook Express, the focus is on the Shared Contacts folder. Unless you have shared some contacts, it will appear empty. To make your own contacts appear, mark View, Folders and Groups in the Address Book window. In the left pane that appears, highlight the folder for your identity's contacts (or Main Identity's Contacts if you haven't set others up). You should now see the contents of your address book. While your shortcut will now always open with the Folders and Groups pane open, it will unfortunately still open with the focus on Shared Contacts.

Keyboard Shortcuts for Outlook Express

In addition to the standard Windows keyboard shortcuts, there are a number of shortcuts more or less unique to Outlook Express. Most are listed in Table 27-1:

Table 27-1   Keyboard Shortcuts in Outlook Express

Action	Key
Go to Inbox	Ctrl+I
Go to the Newsgroup Subscriptions dialog box	Ctrl+W
Send and Receive	Ctrl+M
Download all (news)	Ctrl+Shift+M
Open a New Message window	Ctrl+N
Forward a message	Ctrl+F
Reply to author	Ctrl+R
Insert signature	Ctrl+Shift+S
Send	Ctrl+Enter or Alt+S
Next message	Ctrl+Shift+>
Previous message	Ctrl+Shift+<
Next unread message	Ctrl+U
Next unread news thread	Ctrl+Shift+U
Next unread newsgroup	Ctrl+J
Mark as read	Ctrl+Enter or Ctrl+Q
Mark all news messages as read	Ctrl+Shift+A
View full header and body	Ctrl+F3
Edit HTML source	Ctrl+F2

Summary

Outlook Express 5.5 is even more configurable than previous versions. You can set it up to look and act the way that works best for you.

▶ You can make your mail and news files much easier to back up by moving them to My Documents.

▶ The Contacts pane and the additional toolbars make navigation more flexible. We recommend changing things around to gain as much message-reading space as possible.

▶ Identities are an important new tool that let multiple users share a computer for e-mail.

▶ It can be helpful to work offline to minimize unwanted dialing. We show you how to toggle back and forth between online and offline mode more easily.

▶ You can make a Desktop shortcut that lets you start composing a new message without opening Outlook Express.

Chapter 28

Mail and News Messages

In This Chapter

Reading, composing, and saving mail and news messages is the heart of Outlook Express. We show you how to make your everyday communication look the way you want it to.

▶ Send a message as a web page

▶ Publish an Outlook Express e-zine

▶ Finding

▶ Install on Demand

▶ Associating a message with an account

▶ Remove hyperlinks from HTML text

▶ Use the wizard to design new stationery

▶ Get back to plain text

▶ Read attachments without opening the message

▶ Add URLs to your favorites without going online

▶ Saving GIFs

▶ ASCII Art

▶ Talking e-mail

Outlook Express Mail

Outlook Express switches to mail mode when you highlight a mail folder in the Folder List pane or the Outlook bar. The toolbar changes to the mail toolbar, and any changes that you make to the toolbar only affect the mail toolbar. The menu items change also. For example, Catch up does not appear on the Edit menu, and there are fewer commands for synchronizing on the Tools menu.

Multiple E-mail Accounts

Secret

Outlook Express allows you to create multiple e-mail accounts that you can contact through one or multiple Internet connections. You can log on to any Internet service provider where you (or an associate) have an account, and get your e-mail from any Internet standard e-mail server upon which you have a valid e-mail account.

It is possible to have Outlook Express call up one Internet connection after another and access each e-mail account. You can also access each account through one Internet connection, going one at a time to each e-mail server.

To set up an e-mail account in Outlook Express, choose Tools, Accounts, Add, Mail. Use the Internet connection Wizard to enter the appropriate server, account, and password information. Click Finish. Go through this process again for the next account.

Secret

Many Internet service providers won't let you send e-mail through your e-mail account with them if you are logged onto another service provider. They do this in order to keep SPAMers from using their server to send out their "offerings." This actually doesn't present you with a problem. You can send e-mail out the SMTP outgoing mail server provided by the service you are connected to and receive mail through the POP3 incoming mail server at another provider. Just configure each e-mail account to use the SMTP server of the connection it is intended to use.

If you have multiple e-mail server accounts, you can poll a single account for e-mail manually. Just choose Tools, Send and Receive, and then choose the account from the submenu that appears. You can choose which e-mail accounts are polled when you click the Send and Receive button (which does the same thing as Tools, Send and Receive, All Accounts). Just click Tools, Accounts, highlight a mail account, click the Properties button, and mark or clear the Include This Account When Receiving Mail or Synchronizing checkbox. This also works to choose which accounts Outlook Express polls automatically.

Replies to your messages will still go to your stated e-mail address (the reply address you indicate in the General tab of each account's Properties dialog box) even though you don't necessarily send out your e-mail through the SMTP server at your e-mail address location.

Choose Which Account to Send Your Messages Through

If you have multiple e-mail server accounts, the New Message window gives you the ability to choose which account the message will be delivered through. This is true even if you are replying to a message that may have been delivered through a different account. Each account has a specific SMTP outgoing mail server. To associate a specific account with a message, use the drop-down menu button at the right end of the From field.

If you don't specify an account, Outlook Express sends the message through your default mail server account. Because each account can have a separate Internet connection, and because you can stack mail in your Outbox, it is quite possible to click the Send and Receive button and have Outlook Express call up multiple Internet service providers and send out mail through each of them.

Duplicate Messages Downloaded from the Mail Server

You can set Outlook Express to leave copies of your incoming messages on your mail server. (Choose Tools, Accounts, highlight a mail server account, click the Properties button, click the Advanced tab, and mark the Leave a Copy of Messages on Server checkbox.) If you have done this, Outlook Express is supposed to know which messages you have already downloaded to your computer and which are new messages. Turn to "Leaving mail on the server" later in this chapter for more details.

If you click Send and Receive and get your already received e-mail messages all over again, you probably have a corrupted pop3uidl.dat file. This can occur if Outlook Express crashes at a crucial moment. You'll find pop3uidl. dat in your \Program Files\Outlook Express*yourusername*\Mail folder. You should delete this file.

After you delete pop3uidl.dat, you need to download all the messages on your mail server once again with the Send and Receive button. After you do this, Outlook Express should remember which messages you've already received, at least until it crashes again.

Outlook Express as the Default Mail Program

When you install Outlook Express, it sets itself up as the default e-mail client. If you install other e-mail clients or somehow mess up your settings, Outlook Express may not appear when you click e-mail addresses embedded in web pages. To get it back, you'll want to check out your system.

Choose Tools, Options, and click the General tab. Make sure that the tab says This Application is the Default Mail Handler; if not, click the Make Default button. (To do the same for news, click the lower Make Default button.)

You get the same results by right-clicking the Internet Explorer icon on the Desktop, clicking Properties, and clicking the Programs tab. Make sure that Outlook Express is selected in both the Mail and News drop-down lists. This also allows you to click the Mail toolbar button in Internet Explorer to invoke Outlook Express.

Outlook Express is not a full MAPI client. You can't use it to send faxes, for example. It is a simple MAPI client, and if you are willing to disable Windows Messaging or Outlook, you can use it in conjunction with Word, Excel, and PowerPoint. If you click File, Send in any of these programs, the current document is sent to a new message in Outlook Express as an attachment.

Sending Messages to a Group

Outlook Express lets you create groups of e-mail recipients from among those listed in your Windows Address Book. It does this to let you send one message to a group of folks.

Secret

If you just put the name of the group in the To field, then everyone gets a message starting with a long list of names. That's no fun. To keep this from happening, insert the group name in the BCC field of your message and put your own name in the To field (assuming you have your own name in your address book).

Corrupted Folders

Secret

If you get error messages complaining about your Outbox, Inbox, Deleted Items, or Sent Items folder, you're going to have to delete the corrupted folder. Outlook Express will construct a new, clean, empty folder for you if it is one of the standard folders. (If the corrupted folder is one you created, you'll have to create it again.)

First exit Outlook Express. Use your Explorer to navigate to \Windows\ Application Data\Identities*{youridentitynumber}*\Microsoft\Outlook Express. Delete the *dbx* file associated with the corrupted folder—for example, Outbox.dbx. Restart Outlook Express. This will delete all the text of the messages in your Outbox, so you'll have to recreate the messages. Although corrupted message folders are no longer the common occurrence they once were, it is still a good idea to save important messages in a separate local folder, and to avoid letting your Inbox fill up with several weeks' worth of messages.

Waving when the Mail Arrives

You can make your computer play a tune (play a *wav* file) when your mail arrives. To do this, choose Tools, Options, click the General tab, and mark the Play Sound When New Messages Arrive checkbox. This only makes sense if you have marked Check for New Messages Every [   ] Minute(s) in the same tab.

If you dial up to your Internet service provider, download your mail, and then disconnect, there's no point in doing this. Outlook Express must be running for the tune to play. (And if you receive your mail from the Internet and not an Intranet, you have to be connected to the Internet as well.)

You can, if you like, set your own sound to play when new messages arrive. Use the steps detailed in the "Applying sounds to application events" section in Chapter 15. Find the New Mail Notification event under the Windows events, and choose among the listed *wav* files, or browse for another one.

When Outlook Express is running and you're connected to the Internet (or your Intranet), an envelope appears in your Tray when mail arrives. Be sure to turn on your speakers.

Leaving Mail on the Server

If you are traveling, you might want to leave mail messages on your mail server until you get back, even though you want to read them now. That way, you can download them to your office computer when you return.

To do this, choose Tools, Accounts, highlight your mail server, click the Properties button, click the Advanced tab, and mark the Leave a Copy of Messages on Server checkbox.

You can take a copy of your address book with you on your portable just by copying your *username.wab* file from the \Windows\ Application Data\ Microsoft\ Address Book folder on your desktop computer onto your portable computer. We are assuming that you have already set up Outlook Express on your portable and that the *wab* files have the same name and location on your portable and desktop computer. You are just overwriting your portable's version with your desktop's version.

Secret

You need to make sure that both computers use the same location for the Windows Address Book. Open your Registry on both computers and go to HKEY_CURRENT_USER\ Software\ Microsoft\ WAB\ WAB4\ Wab File Name to find the path.

Converting the Mail

You can import Eudora, Netscape, Microsoft Exchange, Windows Messaging, or Outlook e-mail messages into Outlook Express format. In Outlook Express, just choose File, Import.

To see how to import Pegasus messages, check out Eric Miller's "Outlook Express User Tips" at http://www.activeie.com/oe/.

You can find out more about Eudora, which uses the same message format as Outlook Express, at http://mango.human.cornell.edu/kens/MoreFAQ. html. Go to Qualcomm's web site at http://www.eudora.com/, where you can also download a freeware version of the program.

Reading and Managing Messages

Electronic messages differ from other types of messages in several ways, but one of the most significant is the ease in composing and sending messages electronically. This ease contributes to the absolute flood of messages that many people send and receive on a regular basis. Fortunately, Outlook Express offers several ways for you to deal with all of these messages — as you'll see in the following sections.

Did You Receive the Message?

When you send an important letter the old fashioned way, you can ask the post office to notify you when the letter is delivered. It's possible for e-mail to work the same way. Actually it's not quite the same, because there's no friendly postal carrier to hand the letter to the addressee and ask him or her to sign the receipt. Still, you can ask to be notified when someone opens a message you have sent. In the New Message window, select Tools, Request Read Receipt. You can set this globally for all messages you send by choosing Tools, Options, Receipts and marking Request A Read Receipt For All Sent Messages. But before you mark this box, consider: do you really want to clutter up your Inbox with all those receipts?

If you receive a message with a receipt request, Outlook Express will ask whether you wish to send a receipt. You can set it to Always Send A Read Receipt or to Never Send A Read Receipt by marking the appropriate box on the Receipts tab of the Tools, Options dialog box. If you decide to always send a receipt, you will probably want to make an exception for mailing lists by marking the checkbox shown in Figure 28-1.

If you frequently send or receive digitally signed messages, it can be very helpful to verify that the message arrived free of security errors. You set the behavior for secure receipts separately from the non-secure kind, using the same Tools, Options, Receipts dialog box.

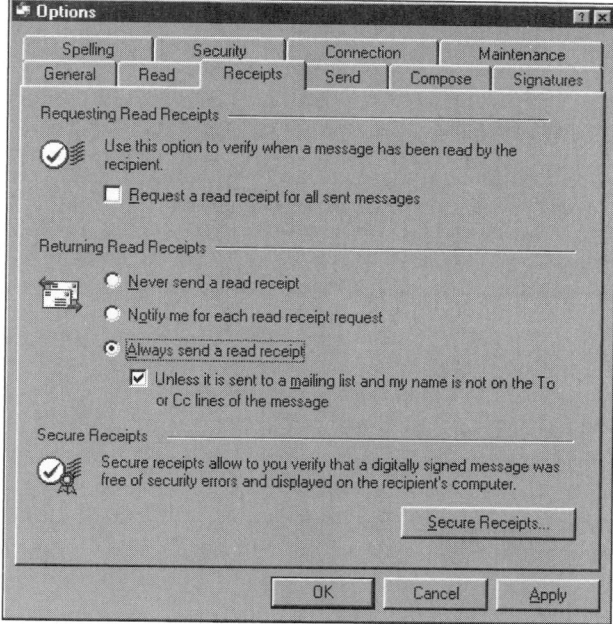

Figure 28-1: The Receipts tab of the Tools, Options dialog box. Avoid sending receipts to mailing lists by marking the checkbox shown.

UUENCODE or MIME

A basic e-mail client will let you send messages as plain text — that is, no characters beyond the first 128 (7-bit) US ASCII; no underlining, italics, boldface, fonts, pictures, or attachments. Outlook Express, which is quite a bit more than a basic e-mail client, supports HTML formatting of the text in your message. It also lets you include pictures in your message and add attachments to it.

Because the Internet e-mail standard only supports 7-bit ASCII characters, formatted messages and attachments need to be encoded by the e-mail client into ASCII characters and decoded by the recipient's e-mail client when they arrive. Outlook Express supports the MIME and UUENCODE encoding/decoding standards.

If you are sending e-mail messages to recipients who have powerful e-mail clients, then you'll want to select HTML formatting and MIME encoding. This will allow you to format your messages to your heart's content.

Tip

If you send messages to recipients with Unix e-mail readers, to Unix-based mailing lists, or to news servers that don't support formatted messages (which includes most news servers), then you'll want to ignore MIME altogether and set encoding at UUENCODE. (This will not encode the message text but will encode attachments with UUENCODE.)

To change your encoding scheme, choose Tools, Options, click the Send tab, and then click the Settings button for the selected format, HTML or Plain Text. If you choose MIME in the HTML Settings or Plain Text Settings dialog box (the only option with HTML), you can select None, Quoted Printable, or Base 64 from a drop-down list. These options only apply to the text portion of your message and not to the attachments. The attachments are coded in MIME at Base 64.

Tip

If you choose None, then your message is not encoded at all, although any attachments will be encoded in MIME (Base 64). Your message text will be sent as unencoded 8-bit characters. This may cause a problem because your message has a very slight chance of being forwarded through a machine that can't handle 8-bit characters. The advantage of choosing None is that even a recipient who doesn't have a MIME-capable e-mail client can easily read your text.

Secret

If you choose Quoted Printable and send your message to a recipient who can't handle MIME, he or she will find equal signs (=) at the end of the lines in your message. This is your clue to stop sending messages formatted with MIME to this recipient.

Outlook Express makes it easy to switch back and forth between sending formatted (HTML) and plain messages. You set the default in the Send tab of the Options dialog box. Then when you're composing a message, you can change the setting for just that message by clicking Format, Rich Text (HTML) or Plain Text in the New Message menu. This lets you set your default for HTML and then switch to plain text when sending to less capable recipients. (For more on HTML-formatted messages, see "Messages Formatted in HTML" later in this chapter.)

Tip

You can also choose to send only plain text to a given recipient by marking the Send E-mail Using Plain Text Only checkbox in the Personal tab of the recipient's Properties dialog box in your Windows Address Book. This is really the best way to be sure that you don't send badly formatted or unreadable text to a mailing list or to a recipient with an inadequate e-mail client.

Outlook Express automatically encodes and decodes attachments. It can't decode some types of encoded messages, and you may find that an attachment isn't decoded properly. If this is the case, you can use another program such as WinZip to decode the attachment.

You'll find WinZip at http://www.winzip.com. To make the attachment available to WinZip or to other decoding programs, you need to save it as a separate file. Use the methods described in "Saving attachments" later in this chapter. If you need to decode an e-mail or news message, you can also use File, Save As to save it as a separate file and then decode it with a separate application.

One encoding method that Outlook Express doesn't handle very well is BinHex, a popular Mac standard. Outlook Express 5.5 will decode some forms of BinHex, but not all. You can see if a message or an attachment is encoded with BinHex by right-clicking it, selecting Properties, and then Details. You'll need to save the message or attachment as a separate file and then decode it with a BinHex decoder. WinZip can handle BinHex.

You can read more about encoding and decoding in Outlook Express at Eric Miller's site at http://www.activeie.com/oe. Be sure to look under "Issues Affecting both Mail and News", "Encoding Information."

You can find encoders and decoders at http://www.winfiles.com or ftp://ftp.andrew.cmu.edu/pub/mpack/ for munpack (MIME decoding), http://www.tucows.com for Wincode (UUdecoding), and http://www.aladdinsys.com/ for StuffIt (BinHex).

Make Messages and Threads Easier to Find

You can flag mail and news messages that are important or that you want to find easily later. Either highlight the message header in the Message pane and click Message, Flag Message, or simply click next to the message header in the Flag column, as shown in Figure 28-2. A little flag icon appears next to the header of a flagged message, and when you open the message you'll see a flag icon and the note "This message is Flagged" in the header.

The Flag column is turned on by default in mail message folders, but in news folders it is turned off. To see the Flag column when you are reading news, right-click a column header button at the top of a column and select Columns. In the Columns dialog box, mark the Flag checkbox and click OK. The Columns setting can be different for each message folder.

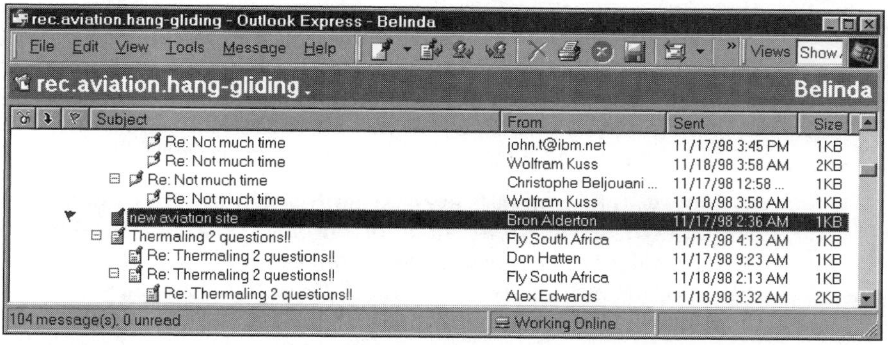

Figure 28-2: It's easy to flag messages for later reference.

You can also flag a message header that appears in the Find Message dialog box (Edit, Find, Message), so that you'll be able to locate it later in the Message pane. Just click in the Flag column as you would in the Message pane.

A similar tool for tracking conversations in a newsgroup is the Watch/Ignore icon (a pair of glasses or a red X), which you can use to mark threads that you want to watch or ignore (see Figure 28-3). To mark or unmark a thread, choose Message, Watch Conversation or Message, Ignore Conversation—or simply click next to a message in the Watch/Ignore column. Your first click marks the thread to be watched, your second click marks it to be ignored, and your third click unmarks it. You only have to select and mark one message to mark the entire thread. As you download headers for new messages in a thread, they will also be marked. When you open a watched or ignored message, you see the glasses or X icon and a note saying either "This message is being Watched" or "This message is being Ignored."

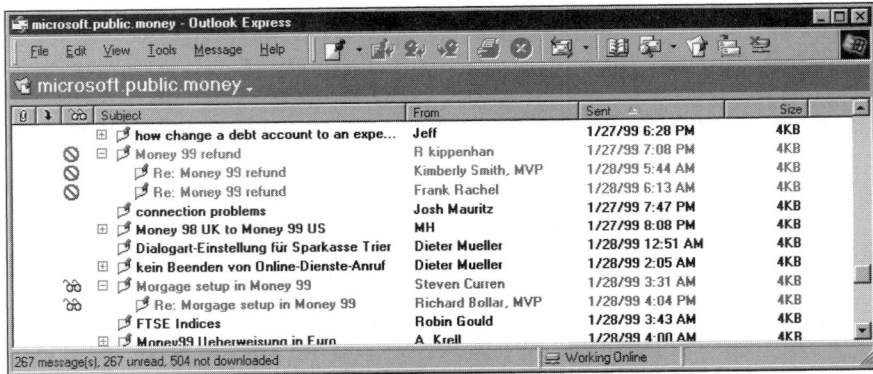

Figure 28-3: It is easier to keep track of what's going on in a large newsgroup if you mark conversations that you want to watch or ignore.

Threads now function in mail as well as in news, but the Watch/Ignore column is not turned on by default for message folders. You might want to use this if you save messages in a message folder over a period of time, or if you have a very high volume of messages. To turn on the Watch/Ignore column, right-click a column header button at the top of a column and select Columns. In the Columns dialog box, mark the Watch/Ignore checkbox and click OK.

To make watched threads even easier to see, they are by default highlighted with red. To select a different color, choose Tools, Options, click the Read tab, and select the color you want from the Highlight Watched Messages with the Color drop-down list. (To turn off color highlighting, select Default from the drop-down list.) Not only will watched threads be highlighted in color, but folders containing unread watched messages will be highlighted in the Folders pane (see Figure 28-4).

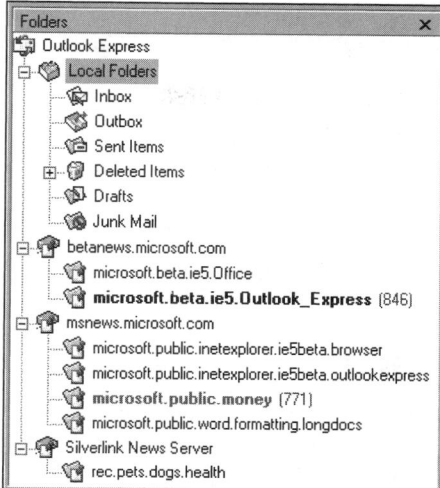

Figure 28-4: The red folder contains watched messages.

A big advantage of flags and watch/ignore icons is that you can sort by them. Just click the column header button (the flag or glasses icon) at the top of the column to bring the flagged or watched messages to the top of the list. While the author sets the priority of a message, the reader gets to flag it or mark it to be watched.

If you have chosen Hide Read Messages in the Views bar (or View, Current View, Hide Read Messages), you won't be able to see a message you have read even though you have flagged it or marked it to be watched. But if you have collapsed a thread you're watching so that you only see the first message, that message will appear to be unread as long as there is at least one unread message in the thread.

Depending on your settings, Outlook Express may still download headers for ignored threads, but you can choose not to view them by choosing Hide Read Or Ignored Messages in the Views bar. Outlook Express will only download the body of an ignored message if you select the message header while online. If you clean up your newsgroups, as we describe in "No need to keep messages forever " in Chapter 29, Outlook Express may delete flagged or watched messages. For messages you really want to keep, it's still best to create a local folder and drag those messages into it.

What Are Those Little Arrows?

The icons for messages in the Message pane change to indicate if a mail or news message has been forwarded or replied to. The open envelope icon next to a message you've read shows a little red arrow pointing to the left if you've also sent a reply, and a blue arrow pointing to the right if you've forwarded it (see Figure 28-5). No more trying to remember whether you've responded, or hunting through your Sent Items folder!

Figure 28-5: The first message has been replied to. The second message has been forwarded.

Choose Your Columns

You can choose which columns to display in the Message pane. To do this, right-click any column header button and click Columns (or choose View, Columns). In the Columns dialog box, mark the columns you want to see and clear those you don't. Use the Move Up button and the Move Down button to set the order in which columns will appear (or you can drag the column header buttons to position them). Each message folder can have different column settings.

For example, if you find the Flag and Watch/Ignore columns aren't useful and are just taking up space, you can turn them off. While you will still be able to flag a message or mark a thread to watch or ignore, you won't see the icons in the Message pane and will be unable to sort by flag or by thread state.

Tip

If you have more than one incoming mail account, you might want to view the Account column. That way, you can easily see where a message came from without bothering with message rules. The Account column can also be very helpful in your Outbox.

Finding

Outlook Express' find utility offers two different search approaches. To scan through the current folder for messages that contain a certain piece of text, choose Edit, Find, Message in This Folder. Type your text in the Look For field (see Figure 28-6), and click Find Next. The header of the first message that contains your text appears highlighted with gray in the Message pane. To see the next message, press F3 — in this way you can quickly scan through a folder to find the message you want, viewing the contents in the Preview pane.

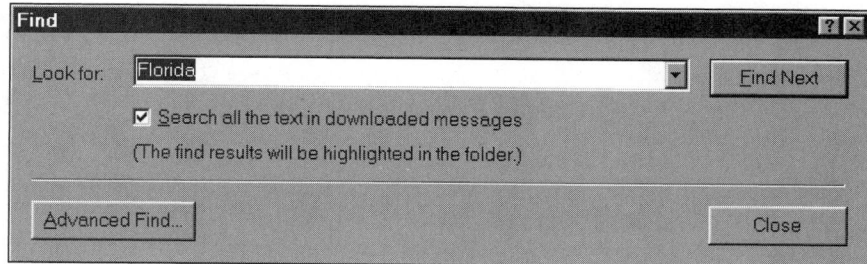

Figure 28-6: Mark Search All the Text in Downloaded Messages if you want to search the message body as well as its header.

The other approach gives you much more flexibility in designing your search, and it displays the results differently. You can initiate this type of search in a number of ways: Click the Advanced Search button in the Find dialog box shown in Figure 28-6; choose Edit, Find, Message; or right-click a folder in the Folders list, the Folders pane or the Outlook bar, and click Find. You can also go to the Outlook Express Welcome screen (click Outlook Express at the top of the Folders pane) and click the Find A Message button. Any of these actions will bring up the Find Message dialog box, shown in Figure 28-7.

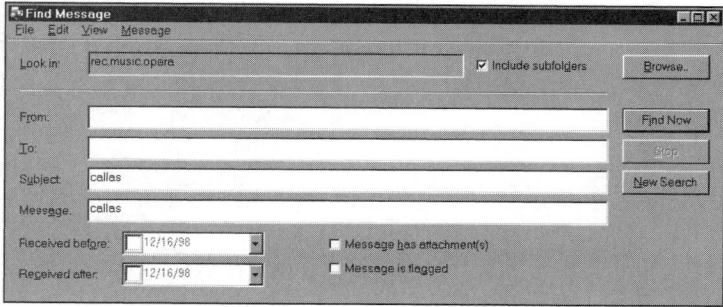

Figure 28-7: The Find Message dialog box offers more flexibility in searching.

You can search for a text string in the bodies of messages, as well as in their headers. You don't need to type the complete name or subject, just a partial name or a keyword. For example, if you type **msn.com** in the From field, you'll retrieve all the messages from everyone who sent e-mail using MSN.

By default, the search starts from the current folder or the folder you have right-clicked. If you start from the Welcome screen, the search by default includes all of your mail and newsgroup folders. To change the folder or folders that will be searched, click the Browse button in the Find Message dialog box.

Secret

The search results appear at the bottom of the Find Message dialog box, as shown in Figure 28-8. You can open the messages in the results by double-clicking their headers in the list. To sort them, click the column header buttons. You can add a flag to a message by clicking next to it in the Flag column. The flag will also appear next to the message in the Message pane of the Outlook Express window, allowing you to easily locate the message later without doing another search. Right-click the message header to access the same context menu you see in the Message pane. You can save a copy of a message to an Explorer folder without opening it — just drag it directly into the Explorer.

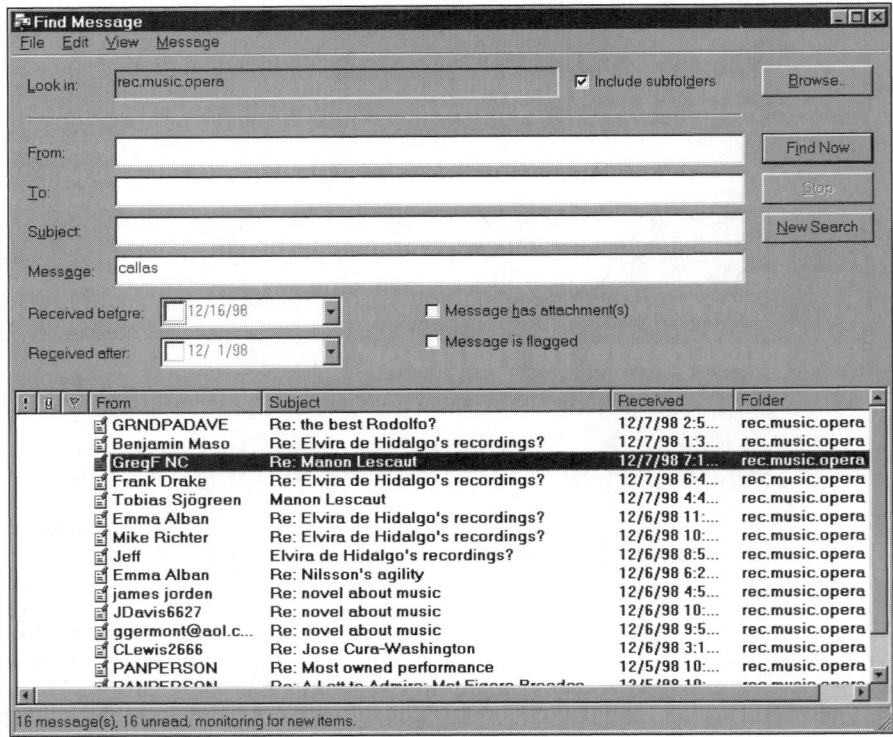

Figure 28-8: The results of an advanced search are listed at the bottom of the Find Message dialog box.

Sending Web Addresses

You can include Internet URLs (locations of Internet resources) in your messages. Outlook Express changes the address' font color and makes it clickable. If you click an address in a message, your Internet Explorer displays that web page or other resource.

Your Desktop (and other folders) can also display clickable URLs. Instead of changing the font color, Windows designates these URLs as shortcuts and adds an icon to the URL's name.

Windows Me makes it easier to send URLs and shortcuts to URLs to your recipients. They can then drag a URL's shortcut to their Desktop for easy access. There are a number of ways to do this.

You'll find a Mail button on the Explorer toolbar when you're viewing a web site. Click this button and choose Send a Link to mail the URL of the current web page along with its shortcut. The URL shortcut is sent as an attachment. If you want to send the whole HTML formatted page instead of just the link to the page, choose Send Page.

If you are viewing a web page in Explorer, you can right-click anywhere in the Address field and click Copy. Then in Outlook Express, click the New Mail or New Post button, right-click in the body of the message, and click Paste to place the URL in the message. The URL is clickable, but there is no URL shortcut added to the message.

If you want to send one of the URLs from your Favorites list, click the Start button, point to Favorites, navigate to the favorite, and drag and drop it into the body of your new message. The shortcut is added as an attachment to the message.

More than Meets the Eye

Outlook Express doesn't display much of the message header information in the preview pane or the separate message window. Most of this information is really only used by e-mail clients or newsgroup readers to correctly format the message, and it's not all that useful to us. Nonetheless, sometimes you need this information to help troubleshoot a problem or find out an e-mail address.

To see the complete message header, press Ctrl+F3, or right-click the message header in the message header pane, click Properties, and click the Details tab (see Figure 28-9). If you click the Message Source button, a new window opens up and you can cut and paste text from the complete message.

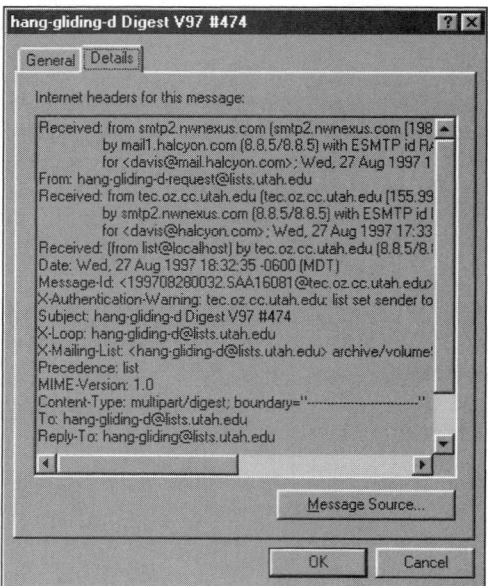

Figure 28-9: The source code for a message is displayed in a separate window.

Time Stamps on E-mail

Occasionally, you may find that the time and date shown in the header of a mail or news message is different (earlier or later) than what you expect. The header might even indicate that the message was sent at a time later than when you received it. While the time stamp isn't actually controlled by Outlook Express, it's interesting to understand.

If you highlight a message header in the Message pane and press Ctrl+F3, the complete header information for that message appears in a separate Message Source window, as shown in Figure 28-10.

Notice that there are a number of time stamps in the header shown in Figure 28-10. The time on the second line (Fri Sep 4 10:30:47 1998) is the time that Belinda's computer retrieved this message from her Internet service provider's POP3 mail server. You have to go down to line seven to see when the message was received by her service provider's SMTP mail server (Fri, 4 Sep 1998 06:00:21 –0700). This is the time displayed in the Received column in the Outlook Express Message pane. Both of these time/date stamps were put there by the Internet service provider's servers — if the clock in one of the servers was wrong, the time shown will be incorrect. The very last time/date stamp (Fri, 4 Sep 1998 08:28:05 –0400) was put there by the author's computer when she clicked her Send button. This time is displayed on the Date line in the message header when the recipient opens the message. In between are stamps from all the servers that this message passed through on its way.

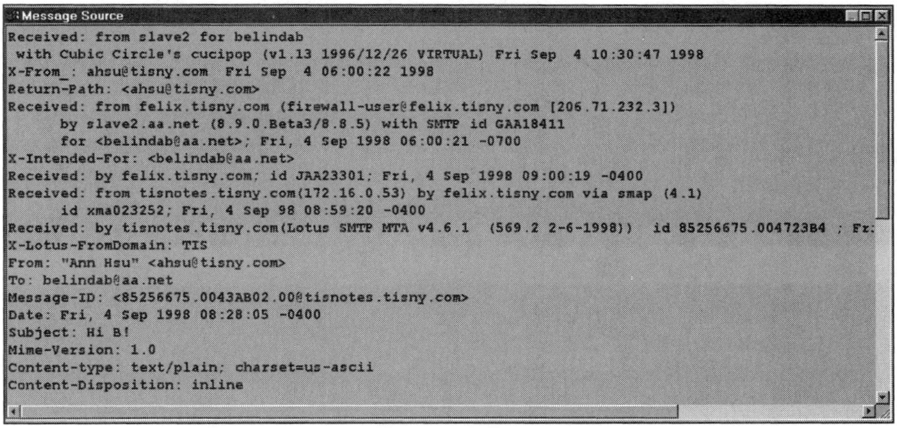

```
Message Source
Received: from slave2 for belindab
 with Cubic Circle's cucipop (v1.13 1996/12/26 VIRTUAL) Fri Sep  4 10:30:47 1998
X-From_: ahsu@tisny.com  Fri Sep  4 06:00:22 1998
Return-Path: <ahsu@tisny.com>
Received: from felix.tisny.com (firewall-user@felix.tisny.com [206.71.232.3])
 by slave2.aa.net (8.9.0.Beta3/8.8.5) with SMTP id GAA18411
 for <belindab@aa.net>; Fri, 4 Sep 1998 06:00:21 -0700
X-Intended-For: <belindab@aa.net>
Received: by felix.tisny.com; id JAA23301; Fri, 4 Sep 1998 09:00:19 -0400
Received: from tisnotes.tisny.com(172.16.0.53) by felix.tisny.com via smap (4.1)
 id xma023252; Fri, 4 Sep 98 08:59:20 -0400
Received: by tisnotes.tisny.com(Lotus SMTP MTA v4.6.1  (569.2 2-6-1998))  id 85256675.004723B4 ; Fr:
X-Lotus-FromDomain: TIS
From: "Ann Hsu" <ahsu@tisny.com>
To: belindab@aa.net
Message-ID: <85256675.0043AB02.00@tisnotes.tisny.com>
Date: Fri, 4 Sep 1998 08:28:05 -0400
Subject: Hi B!
Mime-Version: 1.0
Content-type: text/plain; charset=us-ascii
Content-Disposition: inline
```

Figure 28-10: Display the complete message header to see all of its time/date stamps.

At first, it looks as though this message was sent three hours before it was received. The author was in the U.S. Eastern time zone and the recipient was in the U.S. Pacific time zone, and the times are local for each computer. You can see time zone codes in two of the time stamps above: -0700 indicates that the recipient's server was seven hours earlier than Greenwich Mean Time (GMT), and –0400 indicates that the sender's server was only four hours earlier than GMT. (GMT doesn't recognize Daylight Savings Time.)

While some messages may show a time zone code (for example, PDT for Pacific Daylight Time), the international standard is GMT. If Outlook Express comes across a time zone code that it doesn't recognize (most non-U.S. codes are in this category), it will treat it as GMT. In addition, if the time stamp doesn't contain the expected number of characters and spaces, Outlook Express may not recognize it, and will treat the stamp as 00:00:00 GMT. In either of these cases, the times displayed by Outlook Express could be several hours off. If the time doesn't look right, check the original message header by pressing Ctrl+F3 to see what might be going on.

Thanks to Eric Miller for his insight into these issues.

Install on Demand

With older versions of Outlook Express, if someone sent you a message using a character set that you had not installed—Hebrew, for example—you would see what appeared to be gibberish, with no easy way to find out how to fix it. Now, if you open a message that uses a language or other component you don't have, the Internet Explorer Install on Demand dialog box appears and offers to download the components you need, as shown in Figure 28-11.

Figure 28-11: In the example shown here, a language pack is required to read the message. Install on Demand offers to download and install it.

To download and install the necessary component, click the Download button. Outlook Express initiates a dial-up connection if necessary, downloads the component from Microsoft, and installs it for you. If you don't want to download the component, just click Cancel.

Install on Demand applies not only to languages, but to other components that you might need to see animation or hear sounds. You no longer need to worry about whether to install everything in advance, because you'll be able to get what you need easily whenever you need it.

Install on Demand should be enabled by default. If it is not, choose Tools, Options, click the Connection tab, and click the Change button. In the Internet Properties dialog box, click the Advanced tab, and mark Enable Install On Demand.

The Character Issue

To select the character set to use for viewing a message, click View ➪ Encoding (see Figure 28-12).

Secret

If you leave Auto Select marked (see Figure 28-12), Outlook Express uses the message's header information to apply what seems to be the most appropriate character set. But you might come across some messages that contain odd characters or symbols. If you click View ➪ Encoding, you may discover that the Western European (Windows) character set is marked. Try selecting Western European (ISO) instead — it should clear up the problem. Of course, this assumes that the message was written using a Western alphabet — you might need to apply non-Western encoding instead.

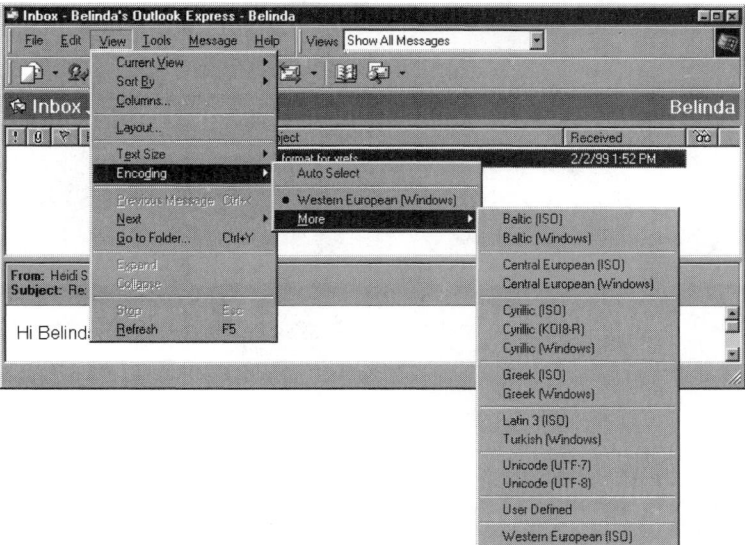

Figure 28-12: The Encoding menu lists all the available character sets on this system.

Composing and Sending Messages

Outlook Express 5.5 offers more flexibility in how you compose and send your messages. Some features are more intuitive than others — here are some suggestions for getting the mail out.

Associating a Message with an Account

You can associate a new mail message with a specific account at the time that the message is composed. This is especially helpful if you have multiple users with different accounts on the same computer.

STEPS

Associating a Message with an Account

Step 1. Open a New Message window by clicking Message, New Message.

Step 2. Click the down arrow at the right end of the From field to display a list of your accounts (see Figure 28-13).

Continued

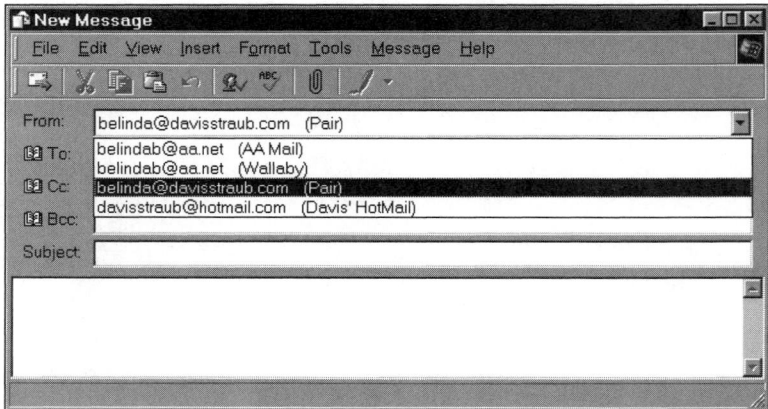

Figure 28-13: Select your account in the From drop-down list.

Step 3.   Select the mail account you want to use when sending the message.

What's the Drafts Folder For?

The Drafts folder is a place to keep messages that you're not yet ready to
send. When you are composing a message and you choose File, Save, your
unfinished message is automatically stored in the Drafts folder. If you close a
New Message window without sending the message and click Yes when asked
if you want to save it, the message will be stored in Drafts. To finish editing
a message stored in the Drafts folder, double-click the message to open it.
When you click the Send button, Outlook Express moves it from the Drafts
folder to the Outbox.

Quoting in Replies and Forwards

When you reply to an e-mail message, it's helpful if you can distinguish the text
you write from the message text you are replying to. In plaintext messages, the
standard is to place a > symbol in front of each quoted line of text. To make
this happen automatically, follow these steps:

STEPS

Automatic Quoting in Plain Text Replies

Step 1. Choose Tools, Options in the Outlook Express window, and click the Send tab.

Step 2. Make sure that the Include Message in Reply checkbox is marked. (This is the default.) If this option is deselected your replies will be much harder to understand since they will not include a copy of the original message.

Step 3. On this same tab, click the Plain Text Settings button under Mail Sending Format. Make sure Indent the Original Text with [ ] When Replying Or Forwarding is marked (see Figure 28-14). If you like, you can use the drop-down list to choose : or | as your quote character instead of >.

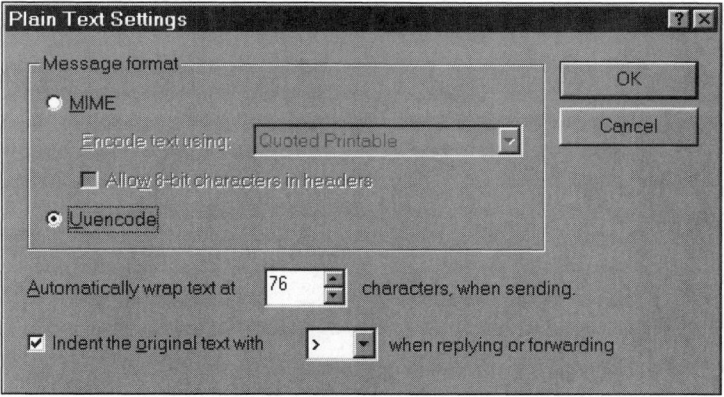

Figure 28-14: Use the Plain Text Settings dialog box to automatically insert a reply character in plaintext messages.

Step 4. Click OK.

So far so good. But this kind of quoting only works as long as you are replying to a message sent using plaintext. Messages sent using MIME/Quoted Printable (such as HTML-formatted messages) don't insert line endings, so there are no line beginnings for Outlook Express to mark with >. Instead, the text is formatted in paragraphs. Even if you tell Outlook Express to reply in plaintext, it will still not place a > at the beginning of quoted lines if they weren't originally composed in plaintext. See "UUENCODE or MIME" in Chapter 19 of *Windows 98 Secrets* for a fuller discussion of message encoding formats.

If you reply in HTML format, you can use the BLOCKQUOTE paragraph tag to mark paragraphs. However, this is not one of the paragraph styles available via the Paragraph Style toolbar button in the New Message window. To be able to use it without editing the HTML source, you must choose Tools, Options, and click the Send tab. Click the HTML Settings button under Mail Sending Format, and mark Indent Messages on Reply in the HTML Settings dialog box. Now your quoted HTML text will be indented with a vertical bar along its left side, as shown in Figure 28-15.

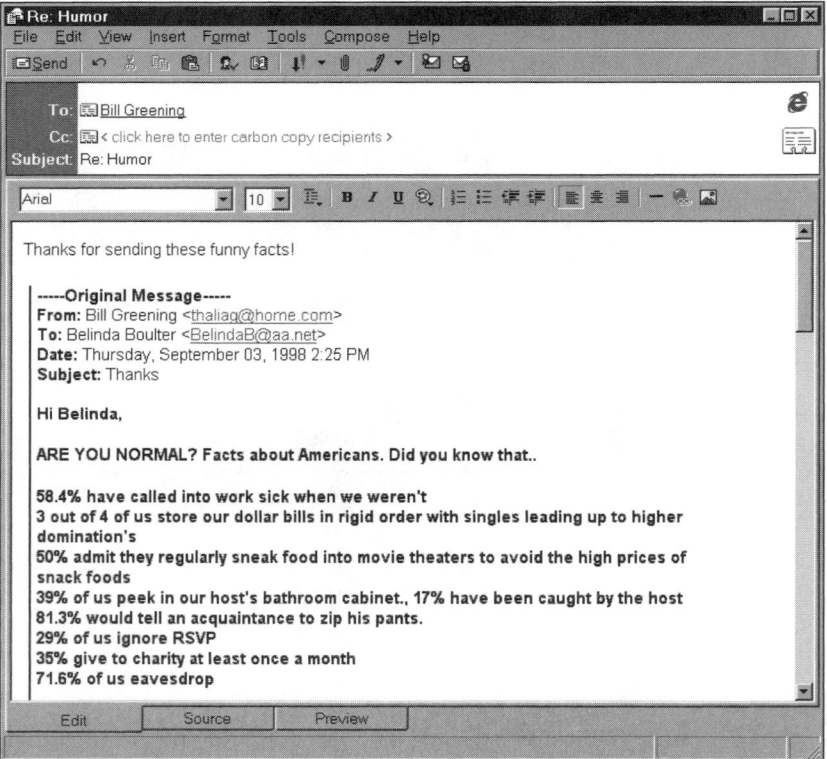

Figure 28-15: In this reply to an HTML-formatted message, the quoted text is indented with a vertical bar.

Secret

There is a downside to marking Indent Messages on Reply, however, if you like to intersperse replies with quoted text to simulate a conversation. If you insert your reply after a section of quoted text, you'll find the new text is also indented with the vertical bar. To get rid of the indent and the bar, first place your insertion point in the quoted text where you want to insert your reply text and press Enter — this inserts a line break. Then with your insertion point in the new paragraph, click the Paragraph Style toolbar button and click Normal. Even though the drop-down list shows that the current paragraph is already Normal, this will work. Your new text will be flush left and will not have a vertical bar.

Send a Message as a Web Page

You can use Outlook Express to e-mail a web page from the Internet without having to open your browser.

STEPS

Mailing a Web Page from Outlook Express

Step 1.   In Outlook Express, choose Message, New Message Using, Web Page (or click the down arrow next to the New Message toolbar button and choose Web Page).

Step 2.   In the Send Web Page dialog box, type the Internet address of a web page and click OK. Outlook Express will initiate a dial-up connection if necessary. The address must start with http. Even if the web page is available offline, you can't send it without actually going to it on the Internet.

Step 3.   A New Message window opens, displaying the web page you have indicated. You can click in the page and insert additional text if you like. You can also do more extensive HTML editing by choosing View, Source Edit and then clicking the Source tab at the bottom of the page.

Step 4.   Address your message, add a subject, and click the Send toolbar button to send it to your Outbox.

You can send an HTML file that resides on your hard disk by opening it in Internet Explorer, saving it in Web Archive for E-Mail (*mht*) format, and then sending the *mht* file as an attachment. (See "Save complete web pages" in Chapter 26 for more on the *mht* file format.) However, if you use this method the web page will not appear in the body of your message.

Remove Hyperlinks from HTML Text

While composing a message, if you type a sequence of characters that looks something like an e-mail address or a URL, Outlook Express automatically makes it into a clickable hyperlink. Sometimes, however, what you've typed might not be a real link, or there may be some other reason why you'd rather not have a link associated with that particular text.

To remove a link from an HTML message, click anywhere in the link, and then choose Edit, Remove Hyperlink. The text remains in your message, but it is no longer highlighted and will not produce a clickable link when the message is sent. The Remove Hyperlink command only works with HTML-formatted messages; it's dim for plaintext messages, even though these messages can still contain links.

Break up Large Messages

You can tell Outlook Express to automatically break apart messages larger than a certain size. This is a courtesy to your recipient, and may be necessary depending on your ISP. When Outlook Express receives mail files that have been broken apart, it will combine and decode them automatically. For newsgroup files you must do this by choosing Message, Combine and Decode.

STEPS

Breaking Up Large Messages

Step 1. In Outlook Express, choose Tools, Accounts. Highlight the name of the account you will use to send large files, and click the Properties button. In the Properties dialog box for that account, click the Advanced tab.

Step 2. Under Sending, mark the Break Apart Messages Larger Than [　] KB box, as shown in Figure 28-16. Enter a file size, or keep the default of 60K, and click OK. Then click Close.

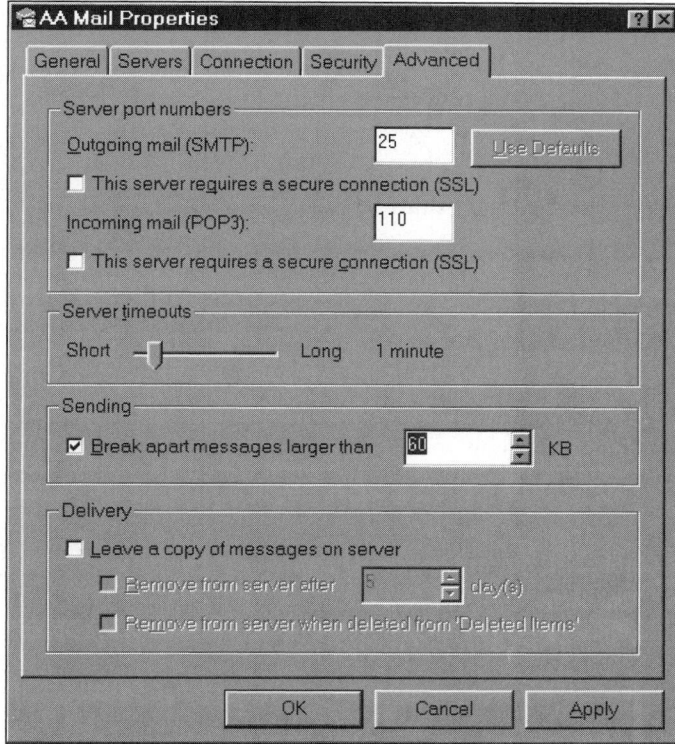

Figure 28-16: Outlook Express will automatically break apart files that are larger than the size you enter in the Advanced tab.

Step 3.   Send the large file using the usual method. It will look normal in your Outbox. But when you do a Send and Receive, you will see that the message is being broken into two or more messages.

Tip   Outlook Express often has difficulty combining HTML files, so it's best to send files with big attachments as plaintext in MIME/Quoted Printable in case they have to be broken up.

Messages Formatted in HTML

Outlook Express allows you to format your e-mail messages and newsgroup posts using HTML. Choose Tools, Options, and click the Send tab. You'll find the option to set the default format for messages as HTML.

You can always override the default setting for the current newsgroup post or e-mail message. Just choose Format in the New Message window, and click Rich Text (HTML) or Plain Text. If you're using HTML, you get a formatting toolbar that lets you choose the font, font size, font color, and so on.

Tip

Lots of newsgroup and e-mail clients aren't able to display HTML-formatted text. If they can't, your correspondents will see the HTML tags embedded in the plaintext of your messages — something that they might not appreciate.

HTML-formatted messages are always sent as MIME-structured, and by default, Quoted Printable encoded messages. In order for them to be properly displayed, your recipient has to have an e-mail client that can display HTML-formatted messages, and his or her Internet service provider has to have an e-mail server that correctly handles MIME.

If your recipient's e-mail client cannot read HTML, but can read MIME documents, then he or she will receive a text version of your message and an attached HTML version that can be read by a browser.

Outlook Express's default setting is to reply to messages using the same format as the message. If you want to use your own settings instead, clear the Reply to Messages Using the Format in Which They Were Sent checkbox under Tools, Options, Send.

Secret

Outlook Express displays all messages using HTML. This is true even if you create a message in plaintext. The reason for this is that Outlook Express uses an HTML display engine, so it has to add HTML tags to non-HTML-formatted messages in order to display them correctly.

You can see this by double-clicking a message header to open a separate message window and then pressing Ctrl+F2. A new window opens to display a plaintext version of the message with its HTML tags.

Outlook Express doesn't include these HTML tags when it sends a message that you have formatted as plaintext. It just adds these tags on the fly to allow the message to be displayed correctly. You can see the actual content of the message by pressing Ctrl+F3 or by right-clicking the message header, clicking Properties, clicking the Details tab, and clicking the Message Source button.

The HTML display engine also looks for e-mail addresses and URLs contained within messages. If it finds them, it highlights them to indicate that they are clickable — you can click an e-mail address to send a message to that address, click a URL to view a web site, and so on.

Editing HTML Messages

Outlook Express has a simple HTML-capable WYSIWYG editor built in. You can set the font, font style (boldface, italic, underline), font size, font color, and background color. You can format paragraphs as bullets or numbered lists and align them left, right, or center. You can insert a *gif* picture or use one as a background. Microsoft provides a small selection of *gif* files in the \Program Files\Common Files\ Microsoft Shared\Stationery folder.

Microsoft also provides a more sophisticated HTML editor/generator called FrontPage 2000. You can edit the body of a message in FrontPage 2000 and insert the HTML text using the Insert, Text from File command. Because Outlook Express uses the capabilities of the Internet Explorer to display its messages (all of which it formats for display using HTML), you can create and receive all manner of multimedia messages. You can order a 45-day trial version of FrontPage 2000 for $6.95 from http://www.Microsoft.com/frontpage/trial/default.htm.

Of course, you can send Web pages as attachments, but as long as your recipients have Outlook Express or a similar e-mail client, they can view the page as part of (or all of) the message (just paste it in). They won't have any need to open a separate browser window.

Stationery

The HTML tag BACKGROUND lets you create a stationery-like effect for your messages. You can configure Outlook Express to automatically start a new blank message with your chosen background color, background image, font, and margins. You can choose from among the existing stationery files, create new stationery, create stationery that is just a background color, or download new stationery from Microsoft.

You need to format your message with HTML in order to be able to use stationery (click Tools, Options, Send, and mark the HTML option button under Mail Sending Format). To pick a default stationery type, choose Tools, Compose, mark the Mail or News check- box under Stationery, and click the Select button. You get to preview the stationery before you select it. Once you have chosen a stationery type, clicking New Mail or New Post will open a New Message window with that stationery already included in the message.

Secret

Press Ctrl+F2 to see that the source code of the *htm* file that Outlook Express uses to create the stationery has been inserted into your new message, including the name of the associated *gif* file. In addition, at the top of this HTML view of your message, you'll find a reference pointing to the folder that holds the stationery's *gif* file.

If you want to create a message with something other than the default stationery, click the down arrow to the right of the New Mail or New Post button. You can pick which *htm* file to use as stationery, or choose no stationery at all.

Secret

Outlook Express includes the associated *gif* file as an attachment when it sends out a message with stationery. You can verify this by first creating a new test message with stationery.

Click File, Save. Your message will be saved in the Draft folder. (The Draft folder is used to store messages that you save with the File, Save command. The messages remain in this folder until you click Send.) Now choose Tools, Options, Send, and change the Mail Sending Format to Plain Text. On the same tab, clear the Reply to Messages in the Format in Which They Were Sent checkbox. Highlight the message header in your Draft folder in Outlook Express and click the Forward button on the toolbar. You'll see the associated GIF file in the Attach field of the New Message window that appears.

We converted the message to plaintext in order to make the attached *gif* file apparent. Outlook Express doesn't show this as an attachment as long as you are formatting an HTML-formatted message.

Outlook Express creates stationery by using a very small *gif* file and an *htm* file that contains at least the BACKGROUND tag and maybe more. You can view the source code for the stationery files that Microsoft includes with Outlook Express by opening the *htm* and *gif* files in the \Program Files\ Common Files\Microsoft Shared\Stationery folder. Check out the Chicken Soup *htm* file as an example of a more complicated stationery file (see Figure 28-17).

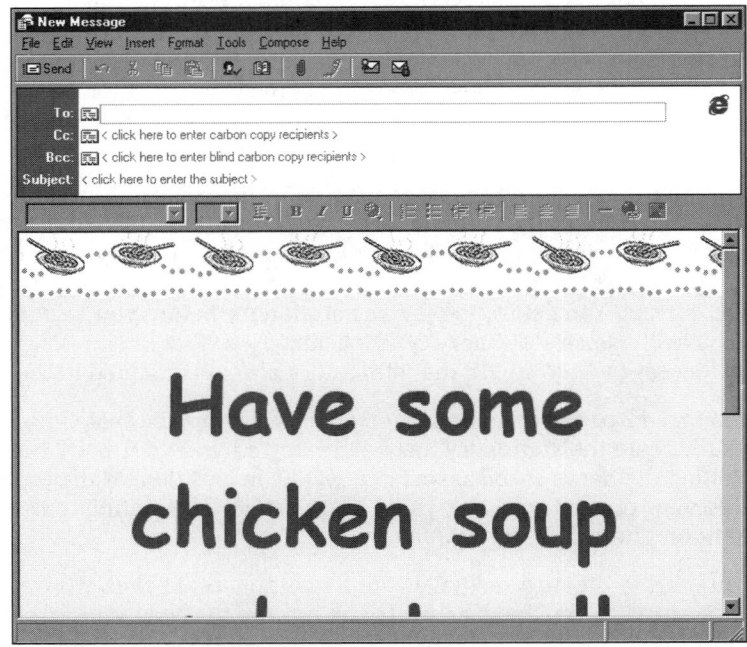

Figure 28-17: The Chicken Soup stationery is actually a template. Change the text to match your needs.

You can create your own stationery using copies of the *htm* files and just editing or replacing the *gif* files. You can also click the Create New button on the Compose tab (Tools, Options) to launch the Stationery Setup Wizard, which will walk you through the creation of stationery. To keep your messages small, make sure that you use very small *gif* files (under 500 bytes) that can be displayed as a repeated pattern on the recipient's computer.

Tip

You can capture stationery from an incoming message. Just double-click the message header and choose File, Save As Stationery. In spite of what *Save As Stationery* sounds like, the whole message is not saved as stationery, just the stationery part of the message.

If you're familiar with HTML, you can make any changes you like in your stationery files, including changes to fonts. You should use a plaintext editor instead of FrontPage Express to edit these files. FrontPage Express places header information in a file when you save it that makes that file unusable as stationery. You may find it easier to start over from scratch using the Stationery Setup Wizard.

If you reference a font in your stationery that isn't widely found on your recipients' computers, your message will be displayed with their default font (found on their computers in Outlook Express under Tools, Options, Read, Fonts).

Tip

When you create an HTML-formatted message that uses stationary, you might want to apply a background color to the message that approximates your stationery color. If you do this, then in the event that your stationery *gif* doesn't get through, the background color will be used instead. This will ensure that your recipients can read your message, since the font color you used over your stationery will also be legible with this background color. To apply a background color, choose Format, Background, Color in the New Message window.

You can easily select a background color for your new messages each time you start one by choosing Format, Background, Color. If you want a default color for message backgrounds, you can set up a stationary file that includes a background color by using the Stationery Setup Wizard (choose Tools, Options, click the Compose tab and the Create New button).

Tip

Another easy way to create stationery that contains a background color is to create a blank HTML-formatted message, choose a background color, and then send the message to yourself. When you receive it, click File, Save As Stationery.

Microsoft makes more stationery available at its web site. Click Tools, Options, Compose, Download More. Figure 28-18 is an example of what is possible.

If you want to reply to a message using your own stationery, click Format, Apply Stationery in the reply message window.

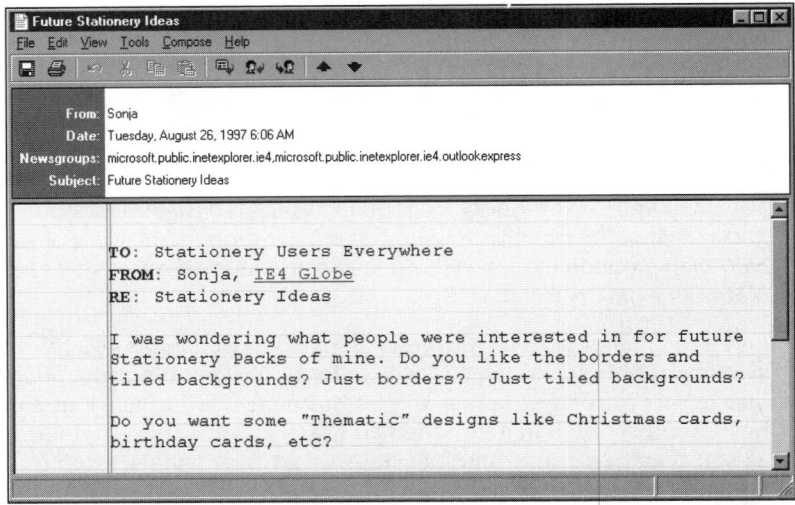

Figure 28-18: This notebook stationery incorporates a margin in its design.

Fancy Signatures

Most people hate to receive fancy signatures, especially in newsgroups. Such an ego trip. If you must create an HTML-formatted signature with a bouncing name, perhaps you can just use it on messages that you send to your Mom.

Tip

You can create a fancy signature using FrontPage Express or any other clever HTML editor and save it as a file. To designate this file as your signature, choose Tools, Options, click the Signatures tab, mark the File option button, and then click the Browse button.

Of course the easiest way to create a new signature is to rip-off someone else's and put your name in there instead — easy to do when these things get shipped around the Internet.

The Compose tab of the Options dialog box lets you designate your vCard from your entry in your Windows Address Book. There really is no need to send your vCard out every time, so you might refrain from marking the Include My Business Card When Creating New Messages checkboxes. When you want to attach your vCard to an individual message, use the Insert, Business Card command.

Pictures and Text

Because Outlook Express implements the MHTML format, it includes any picture files (*bmp, gif,* and *jpg*) that you place in HTML-formatted messages (including stationery) as attachments when it sends your message. The default setting is to include pictures, so you'll find the Format, Send Pictures with Message command marked in the New Message window. To change the default, choose Tools, Options, click the Send tab, and then click the HTML Settings button next to the Sending Format option buttons for both news and mail.

If the Tools, Send Pictures with Message command is not marked when you send a message that references a local picture file, this file gets left behind. The recipient will find a reference in his or her message pointing to your hard disk folder where the picture file is stored, but no picture—and, of course, no way to get it.

If you happen to send a reference to a picture file that is stored on your A drive and Send Pictures with Message is turned off, then when your recipient opens your message, his or her computer will try to find the picture on the A drive.

If you receive a message with references to resources located on the Internet— for example, a picture file stored on a web server—your Internet Explorer will try to connect to the resource, download it in background, and display it in your message. If you are connected to the Internet as you read the message, you may not notice this happening, although there may be some delay if the resource is large or the Internet is busy (as always).

If you are not connected to the Internet, Internet Explorer will try to connect to download the resource. This can make offline reading a bit tedious. If you cancel the connection and the resource is in your Internet cache (perhaps you previously viewed that resource or it was referred to in an earlier message from the same source), it will be displayed in your message.

Tip

If you are sending a message with stationery that references a picture file stored at an Internet server and not included with your message, you may want to set your background color equal to or close to the color of the stationery. This is especially true if you have set the color of your text to show up against your stationery (for example, white text and black stationery).

If your recipient doesn't get your stationery's picture file and is forced to read white text on a default white background, he or she is not going to know why you sent a message with no text. Since you don't know what the default color of your recipient's background is, it's a good idea to include the background color in any stationery file that includes references to web-based pictures.

Secret

If you communicate often with one person, you can forego sending that person your stationery every time. If you are sending non-standard stationery, you only have to send it once as an attachment. If the recipient stores it in his or her stationery file using the same path as yours, Outlook Express will be able to find it the next time you send a message that just includes the reference to the stationery file (clear the checkmark next to Tools, Send Pictures with Message in the New Message window).

This also works for all standard stationery files, as long as your recipient has them stored under the same path as you do. You are just sending the path and filename to your stationery in the message.

Use the Wizard to Design New Stationery

A stationery style is more than just the background you see in a message. It also defines the font, font color, sounds, and images that make up the total "look and feel" of your message (everything but the content, that is). All of these parameters are defined in an HTML document that you can store and apply to HTML messages.

Although you can use the stationery samples that come with Outlook Express, you don't need to be an HTML programmer to define a new stationery style. To do so, choose Tools, Options, click the Compose tab, and click the Create New button. In the Stationery Setup Wizard that opens, click the Next button to move to the dialog box shown in Figure 28-19.

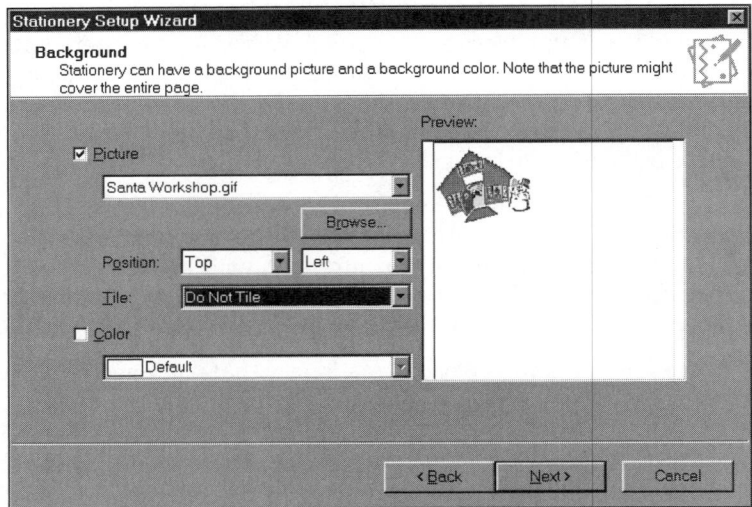

Figure 28-19: The Stationery Setup Wizard walks you through the design of a new stationery style.

The wizard contains a drop-down list of *gif* files you can use in your background, or you can use the Browse button to point to a different one — the Preview area lets you see what you'll be getting. After you have set the information about background graphics for your stationery, click Next to display a dialog box for selecting the font that will be part of this stationery. The information you set here only applies to this stationery. When you're done, click Next. The next dialog box lets you set margins (in pixels). Use the Preview area to see how the text and graphic will work together. Click Next when you've defined the margins. Now give your stationery a name, and click Finish. Outlook Express saves your stationery with the other stationery; the default location is \Program Files\Common Files\Microsoft Shared\ Stationery.

To make your new stationery the default for mail or news messages, mark the Mail or News checkbox under Stationery on the Compose tab of the Tools, Option dialog box, and click the Select button to select your stationery. If you mark the Mail or News check- box, your default format will be HTML, regardless of what you have marked on the Send tab — see "Get back to plain text" later in this chapter.

If you only use stationery occasionally, you can apply it to an individual message by choosing Format, Apply Stationery in the New Message window (this command is only active when Format, Rich Text (HTML) is marked), or by clicking the down arrow next to the New Message toolbar button and selecting the stationery from the drop-down list, as shown in Figure 28-20. The stationery you used most recently appears at the top of the list.

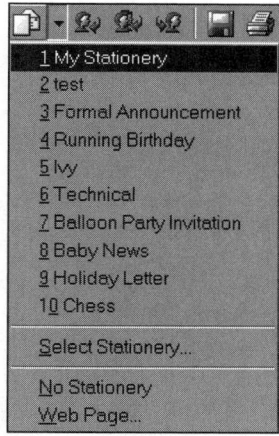

Figure 28-20: Select stationery from the New Message drop-down list for occasional use.

Change the Default Font for Your Stationery

In earlier versions of Outlook Express, the default Compose Font settings shown in Figure 28-21 (Tools, Options, Compose) affected your message regardless of whether you applied stationery, as long as the stationery did not contain font information. That is no longer true; these settings now only apply to HTML messages in which you have not applied stationery. You may find that your old stationery now uses Times Roman instead of the font you used to use.

You can edit an individual HTML message in the New Message window by clicking View, Source Edit, and using the Source tab. But of course you don't want to do that every time. You can also (theoretically, at least) access an application that will let you edit stationery from within Outlook Express. (To do this, choose Tools, Options, and click the Compose tab. In the Stationery area, mark the Mail or News checkbox, and click the associated Select button.

In the Select Stationery dialog box, select your stationery and click the Edit button.) However, doing this may not work for you.

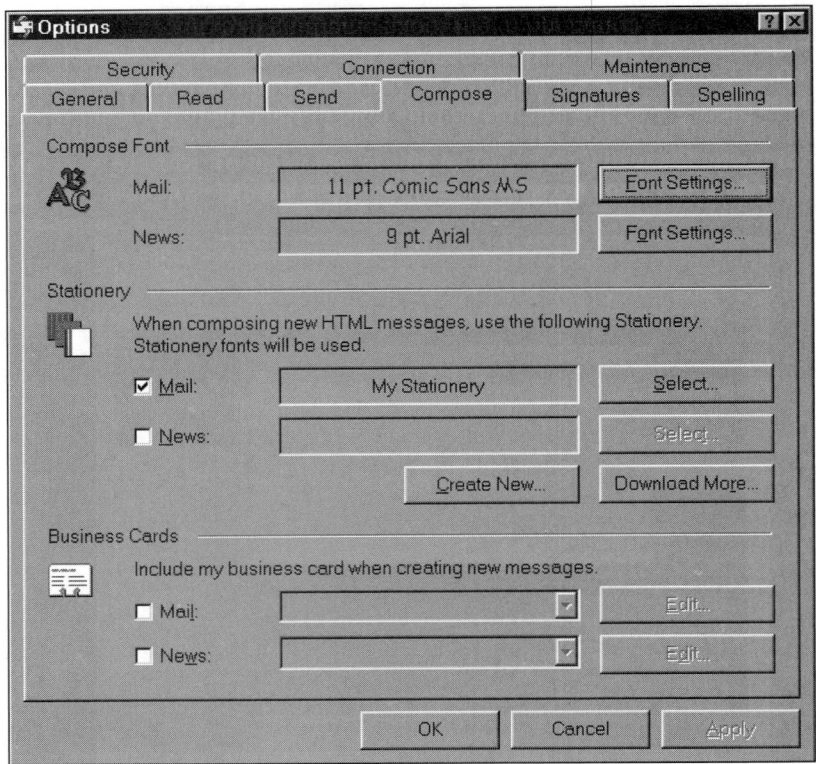

Figure 28-21: The Compose Font settings no longer affect messages that use stationery.

Secret

Unless you have set things up otherwise, the default application associated with editing HTML files (including stationery) is most likely Front Page Express. Unfortunately, the header information placed in a file by Front Page Express when you save it will make that file unusable as stationery. You must use a plaintext editor such as Notepad for editing stationery instead. While it's possible to change the file association so that the Edit button in the Select Stationery dialog box opens Notepad (see "Creating and Editing File Types and Actions" in Chapter 12), it's probably easier just to open Notepad and edit the HTML file for your stationery from there.

If you are planning to change the default font color, you will need to know the HTML hexadecimal code for the color. If you have Paint Shop Pro 5, it's easy to find this information. Open Paint Shop Pro 5, click the color that you want to use in the Color Palette, and then click the foreground color box at the bottom of the Color Palette. The Color dialog box appears with the hexadecimal code for the color listed at the bottom of the dialog box. If you don't have Paint Shop Pro 5, you'll find an HTML color chart at `http://desktoppublishing.com/color-codes.html`, `http://www.btinternet.com/~paulr/color/msie4/index.htm`, and numerous other places.

If you are unfamiliar with editing HTML code, you may want to save a backup copy of your stationery file before you edit it. Open Notepad, choose File, Open, and browse to the stationery file that you want to edit (the default location is \Program Files\Common Files\Microsoft Shared\Stationery). Figure 28-22 shows part of the HTML code for one of the stationery samples that come with Outlook Express. Notice that within the <STYLE> tag, the font attributes for various paragraph styles are listed. You can edit the font family and other characteristics for each paragraph style, and then save your stationery file when you're done. Now test your stationery in Outlook Express by opening a New Message window using the stationery you edited. Use the Paragraph Style toolbar button to change your current style if necessary.

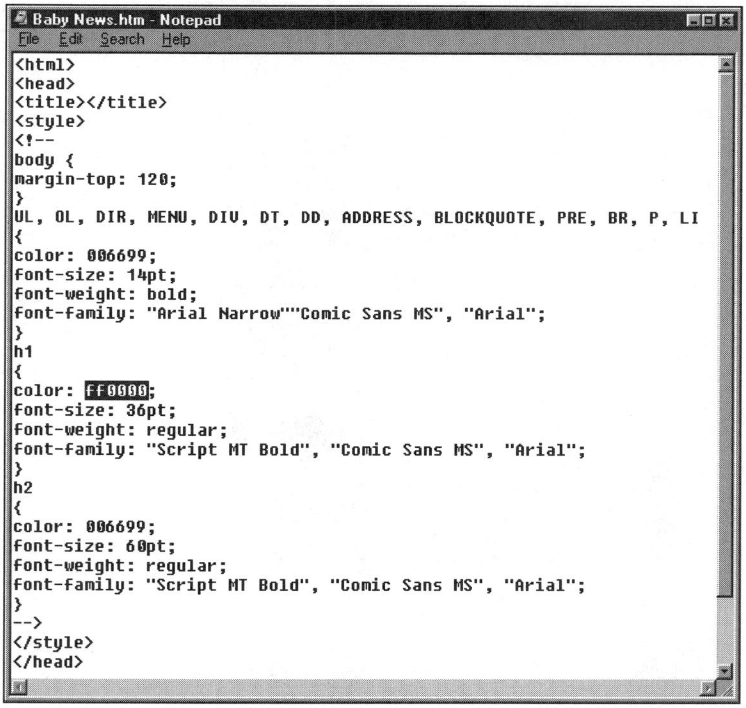


```
<html>
<head>
<title></title>
<style>
<!--
body {
margin-top: 120;
}
UL, OL, DIR, MENU, DIV, DT, DD, ADDRESS, BLOCKQUOTE, PRE, BR, P, LI
{
color: 006699;
font-size: 14pt;
font-weight: bold;
font-family: "Arial Narrow""Comic Sans MS", "Arial";
}
h1
{
color: ff0000;
font-size: 36pt;
font-weight: regular;
font-family: "Script MT Bold", "Comic Sans MS", "Arial";
}
h2
{
color: 006699;
font-size: 60pt;
font-weight: regular;
font-family: "Script MT Bold", "Comic Sans MS", "Arial";
}
-->
</style>
</head>
```

Figure 28-22: In this stationery sample we have changed the color of the H1 paragraph style from blue to red.

We find it much easier to just start over fresh using the New Stationery Wizard.

Get Back to Plain Text

If you mark the Mail or News checkbox under Stationery in the Compose tab of the Tools, Options dialog box (see Figure 28-23) and select a stationery to use for your mail/news messages, your new messages will always start in HTML. This happens even if you have marked Plain Text under Mail Sending Format or News Sending Format on the Send tab (see Figure 28-24). In other words, if you have set a default stationery style, it will be your default for *all* messages. If you prefer to use plaintext as your default, clear the Mail or News checkbox. Then when you want to use stationery, choose Format, Apply Stationery in the New Message window, or choose the stationery from the drop-down list attached to the New Message toolbar button in the Outlook Express window.

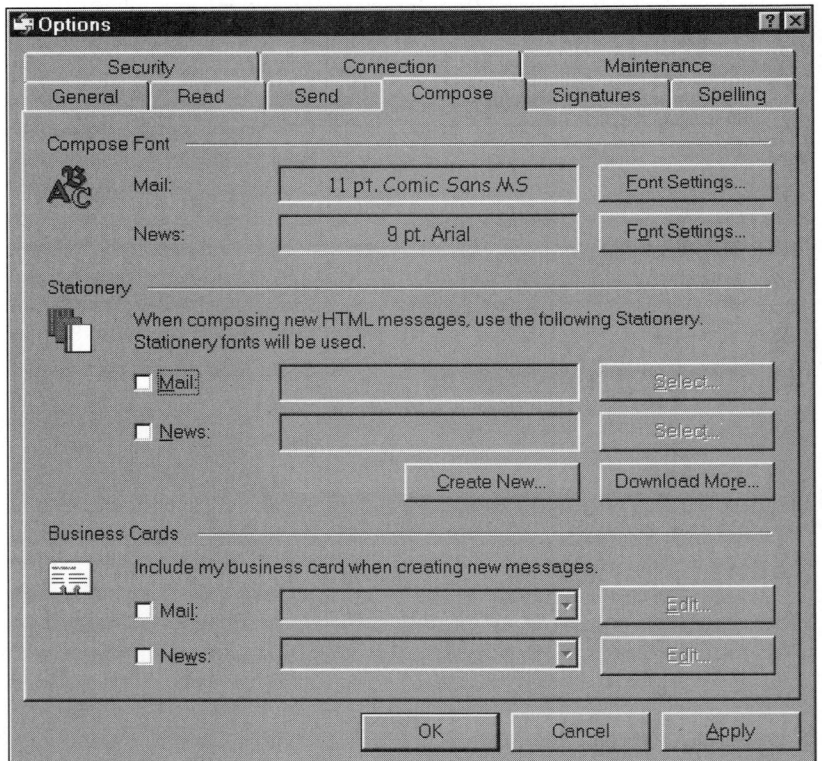

Figure 28-23: Clear the Mail or News checkbox under Stationery to get your plaintext back.

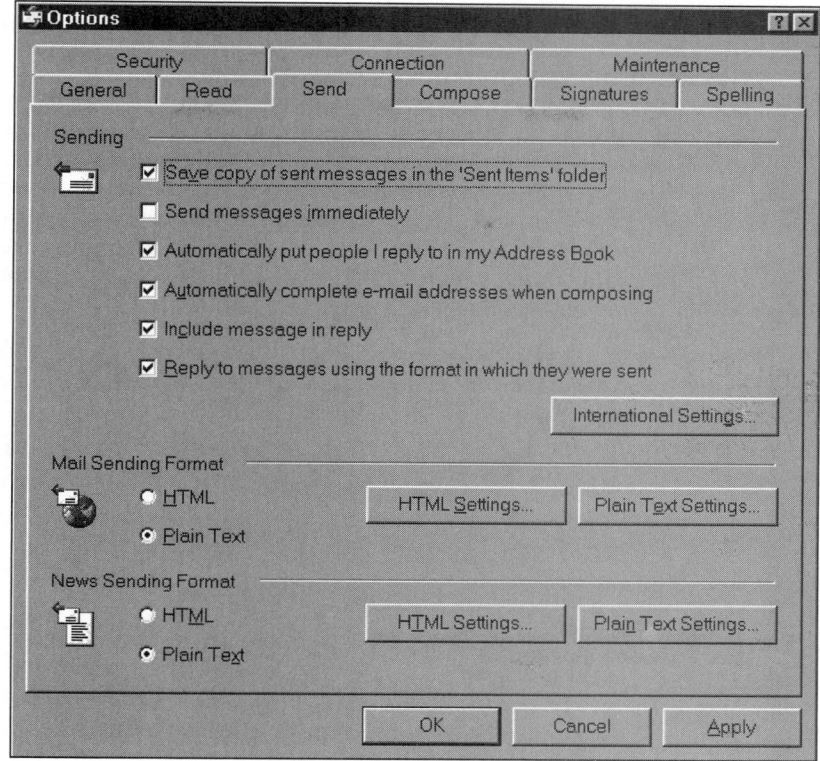

Figure 28-24: Even if you set Plain Text as the default in the Send tab, your setting will be overridden if you have marked the Mail or News checkbox under Stationery in the Compose tab.

Move Your Stationery Folder

Secret

If you've spent a lot of time developing stationery files, you might want to put them some place that's easier to back up — under My Documents, for instance. To do this, you need to edit the Registry. If for some reason you find you have two Stationery folders, you can use the following Steps 1 and 2 below to determine which is the default. Then move into the default folder anything from the other one that you want to save, and delete the non-default folder.

STEPS

Moving Your Stationery Folder

Step 1.   Open the Registry editor.

Continued

Step 2. Navigate to HKEY_LOCAL_MACHINE\SOFTWARE\Microsoft\ Shared Tools\Stationery. Highlight Stationery in the left pane. In the right pane, you'll see Backgrounds Folder and Stationery Folder, with the current default location for each. The default is for backgrounds and stationery to be stored in the same folder, so they most likely have the same string value in the Registry (you can change this if you like).

Step 3. Double-click Stationery Folder. In the Value Data field, change the location for your Stationery folder, and then click OK. Do the same for Backgrounds Folder. Close the Registry editor.

Step 4. In the Explorer, navigate to the Stationery folder (in its old location) and drag it to the location you gave it in Step 3. If you have set a different location for the Backgrounds folder, you'll need to create the new folder and drag the background files into it.

No Default Stationery for Replies

Even if you have set Outlook Express to always send in HTML and to always use stationery, you will find that you cannot use your default stationery automatically in a reply.

Of course, if the original message contains stationery, you can use that in your reply. If you have set HTML as your default for sending mail, or if you have marked Reply to Messages in the Format in Which They Were Sent on the Send tab of the Options dialog box, the stationery of the original message will be the default for your reply.

If you want to use your default stationery in a reply, click Format, Apply Stationery and select it from the submenu that appears.

More Stationery

If you're sick of stationery that looks like notebook paper, try Kenja's Stationery at http://www.kenja.com/stationery/. Kenja has created quite a variety of colorful stationery that you can download as a zip file for personal use.

David Guess of Bowling Green, Kentucky, has created a web site in which he reveals ways to insert scrolling messages, sounds, and marquee backgrounds into Outlook Express messages. His "Majik's Stationery Help Page," `http://www.mindspring.com/~majik/docs.htm`, is packed with tricks to make your e-mail distinctive.

To find a host of other sites with stationery files and how-to information, take a tour of the OE Stationery Web Ring at `http://www.webring.org/cgi-bin/ webring?ring=oestationery;list`.

And for lots of ideas and help in designing your own stationery, don't forget the Outlook Express stationery newsgroup at msnews.microsoft.com\microsoft. public.inetexplorer.ie4.outlookexpress.stationery. This is a very active group with lots of large files, so don't try downloading the whole thing at once!

Publish an Outlook Express e-zine

Because Outlook Express can produce and read HTML-coded text, you can use it to produce an HTML-formatted newsletter or e-zine that contains all of the formatting possible with HTML. If your readers have HTML-based e-mail clients, they'll be able to read the formatted version of your newsletter or e-zine.

Originally, HTML was used to format decent looking web pages. Early on, Outlook Express incorporated an HTML display engine to display HTML-formatted text in e-mail. Once HTML-compatible e-mail clients became widespread, it became practical to publish e-mail-delivered e-zines using HTML-formatting.

You can use Outlook Express as a low-end HTML editor. It's easy to design stationery that includes a background and font information specifically for your newsletter. If you combine Outlook Express with Front Page Express (which comes with Windows 98) or FrontPage 2000 (which, as mentioned earlier, is available for a 45-day trial), you can post the newsletter on your web site after you've sent out copies by e-mail.

There are plenty of HTML-formatted newsletters already available for you to sample. For example, you can subscribe to Jesse Berst's Email Alert, a daily fix of computer news, at `http://www.zdnet.com/anchordesk/`, or Chris Pirillo's Lockergnome, a daily Windows shareware review (see Figure 28-25), at `http://www.lockergnome.com`.

Unfortunately, incompatibilities continue to exist among various implementations and definitions of the advanced features of HTML. It is precisely these advanced features that you will want to use to make your e-zine as attractive as possible. One way of dealing with these incompatibilities is to use the agreed upon HTML standards in tricky ways to make your text look good.

A good example of an advanced feature is in-line graphics — pictures inserted directly into the body of your e-mail messages. This is a great option that really adds to the power of your e-zine. (To keep your e-zine small, be sure to send out only *gif, jpg,* or similarly compact graphics files.)

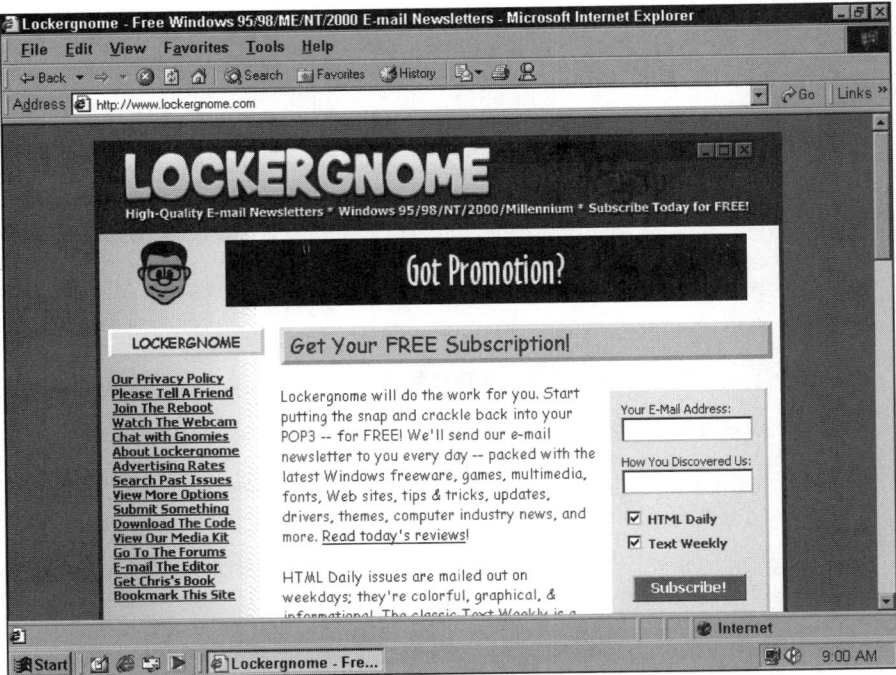

Figure 28-25: Lockergnome is a good example of an HTML-formatted e-mail newsletter.

Standard HTML doesn't support the inclusion of a graphic file in the same file as the HTML text. This is exactly what you want to do though — send the pictures and the text as one file. Fortunately, Outlook Express lets you do this. It places a pointer and a resource ID at the inserted location of the graphic and adds the graphic, encoded in text, at the end of the message file.

However, not all e-mail clients can read in-line graphics. Jesse Berst, Chris Pirillo, and other publishers get around this problem by not inserting graphics files, and instead inserting links to graphics files located on the publishers' web servers. When you receive and display one of these newsletters, the graphics are updated from files on the author's web site and stored in your Temporary Internet Files folder. This technique also gives the authors the opportunity to place continuously updating banner ads in their newsletters.

If you go offline before you display one of these newsletters, you'll find that there are only placeholders where the graphics would normally be displayed. Because you went offline before you displayed the newsletter, no commands were sent to the web server to download the graphics files.

Once you have viewed the newsletter online — and thereby downloaded the graphics files — the files will be in your Temporary Internet Files folder so that Outlook Express can find them after you go offline.

You can see the difference between these two methods of handling graphics files by looking at the underlying HTML source text. To display the HTML source of an e-mail message, double-click it in Outlook Express and press Ctrl+F2.

For example, here is a portion of Jesse Berst's newsletter:

```
<CENTER><A href="http://ads.zdnet.com/cgi-bin/accipiter/aamr.exe/
RGROUP=r128"><IMG src="http://ads.zdnet.com/cgi-bin/accipiter/aami.
exe/RGROUP=r128"></A>
```

You can see that the reference to a graphic file is a reference to the Ziff Davis web server.

Here is a pointer to a graphic that is contained within the Outlook Express e-mail message:

```
<P><IMG align=baseline src="cid:011b01bdeb2e$8ddf8160$aa058d0a
@fujitsu"></P>
```

Notice the resource ID — the string of letters, numbers, and punctuation that identifies the graphic. This graphic is stored at the end of the e-mail message that contains it.

If you include in-line graphics and the recipients of your e-zine use Outlook Express or a compatible e-mail client, they'll be able to view your e-zine with the graphics files located where you inserted them when you composed the message. If the recipients use e-mail clients that don't support in-line graphics, the pictures will either not show up at all or will be displayed as file attachments. These readers will have to click the attachments to display them.

If you want a separate web page that displays the contents of your e-zine, you can copy the contents of your e-zine into a blank Front Page Express file. Front Page Express doesn't know what to do with the pointer to the enclosed graphics files and will display broken references to them. You will have to copy the graphics files into the folder where you store your local copy of the new web page, and edit the web page to refer to the external graphics files. Just right-click each broken graphics symbol in Front Page Express, select Image Properties, and use the Browse button to enter the filename and path for each image.

If you used stationery when creating your e-zine, you'll need to copy the stationery graphic over to the new folder that contains the web page. You'll most likely find the stationery in \Program Files\Common Files\Microsoft Shared\Stationery.

We often find when we have copied text from Outlook Express into a new blank Front Page Express file that the text styles are forgotten. Hopefully Microsoft will fix this. You'll have to select all the text in Front Page Express, click Format, Font, and choose the font again. Similarly, the background color may be altered; to fix this, choose Format, Background, and change the background color.

You can create a template file that you can then reuse to create new issues of your e-zine. It should include any background or stationery, and any repeated text. This could be nothing more than the last issue of your e-zine, saved in an Outlook Express Local Folder. To use it as a template, you simply delete the existing content and add the new content.

You might want to include a comment in the HTML source that warns people if their e-mail client is unable to display HTML. Here is an example of the kind of comment that you can add:

```
<META HTTP-EQUIV="Content-Type" CONTENT="text/html;charset=Windows-
1252">
<!-- ***
This is Lockergnome's Daily HTML Newsletter, not the Text Weekly one.
If you can see this paragraph, then you are not using an HTML compliant
e-mail client. Don't worry, you may remove yourself from the Daily
(and still retain the Classic Text Weekly Lockergnome) at: http://www.
lockergnome.com/options.html or e-mail removehtml@lockergnome.com --
Sorry for any inconvenience this may have caused you.
*** -->
```

Attachments

Here's how to handle all those incoming e-mail attachments.

Saving Attachments

To save an attachment to a message you have received, double-click the message header in the message header pane to display the message in a separate window. Then drag and drop the attachment icon from the Attach field into a folder or onto the Desktop. You can also right-click the attachment icon and click Save As.

To save an attachment without opening a separate message window, click the message header, and then click the yellow paper clip icon in the upper-right corner of the preview pane (the Show Preview Pane Header checkbox must be marked in the View, Layout dialog box). A menu listing the names of the attachments in the message appears. Click the name of the attachment you want to open or save. You can then choose to open it or save it to a folder. If you instead choose Save Attachments from this menu, you can browse to a folder for saving more than one at a time. If, when you click attachments of a particular type, you find that they open automatically and you'd like the option of saving them instead, you need to edit the file type. See "Confirm open after download" in Chapter 12 for details.

You can also just highlight the message header and choose File, Save Attachments.

You can send graphic files in *gif* and *jpeg* format (as well as other formats) as attachments to Outlook Express messages. Outlook Express encodes the graphics in UUENCODE or MIME format. After you receive a message with a *gif* or *jpeg* attachment and it is decoded (Outlook Express does this automatically) you can read the file using the helper application with which it's associated. (To check what applications are associated with *gif* and *jpeg* files, choose View, Folder Options in the Explorer, click File Types, and look through the Registered File Types list for these file types.)

Read Attachments without Opening the Message

Sometimes a message is nothing but attachments. For example, some mailing list digests arrive as an empty message with a bunch of text files attached. The easy way to deal with attachments is to use the big paper clip icon that appears at the right end of the preview pane header of the message. If this header isn't visible, click View, Layout, and mark Show Preview Pane Header. (You must of course also have Show Preview Pane marked.) Click the paper clip to display a list of all the attachments, as shown in Figure 28-26.

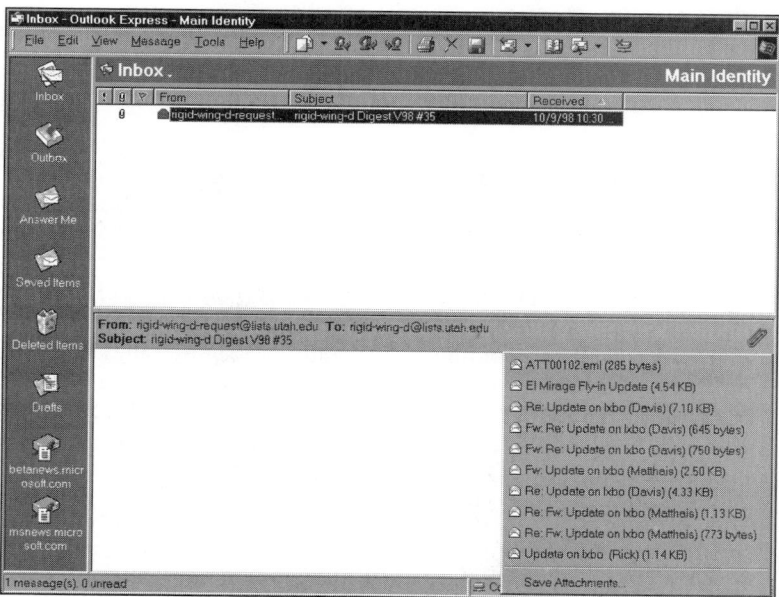

Figure 28-26: This mailing list digest contains a series of attached messages.

Click an attachment in the list to open it. Alternatively, you can choose Save Attachments at the bottom of the list (or choose File, Save Attachments) to display the Save Attachments dialog box, and then save any or all of the attachments to disk.

Unfortunately, you can no longer save an attachment by dragging its little paper clip icon out of the Message pane. Now if you do that, you'll save a copy of the whole message.

Strange Attachments

Occasionally you may receive attachments that you can't seem to view or open. They may have a *dat* or *doc* extension. Usually these are files that were saved in Rich Text Format (RTF) — it's likely they were sent by someone using Windows Messaging or Outlook 9*x*. RTF is not an Internet standard and cannot be decoded using Outlook Express. Your only option is to ask your correspondent to re-send the attachment as a plaintext file.

On the other hand, Outlook Express can now read many attachments encoded using Binhex, a popular Macintosh format. This decoding is transparent; you shouldn't have to do anything special to read these files. If you do receive one that doesn't open, you can decode it using Wincode, available as shareware on the Internet from `http://www.jumbo.com`, `http://www.hotfiles.com`, and many other shareware sites (be sure to get version 2.7.3A or later).

For an interesting, fairly technical discussion of encoding and decoding, see Michael Santovec's article, "Decoding Internet Attachments" at `http://pages.prodigy.net/michael_santovec/decode.htm`.

Why All Those Little Envelopes?

Maybe you've had the experience of opening a mail message to find no text, but only an attachment that looks like a little envelope in the message's Attach field. When you open the attachment, you discover that it contains nothing but another attachment, and maybe even the next one is the same. Finally you open an attachment containing the actual message. This is a common experience with humor that gets passed on from person to person. This is not a behavior of Outlook Express at all; instead, each reader has chosen to forward the message as an attachment (this is called *redirecting* in some mail applications). Many users of other mail software such as Netscape don't even realize they are doing this.

Tip

In fact, there may be times when you do want to redirect, or forward a message as an attachment. For example, you might want to do it if you are forwarding a message to a mailing list, troubleshooting a problem message, or complaining to an ISP about junk mail. To forward a message as an attachment, highlight the message header in the Outlook Express window, and choose Message, Forward As Attachment. You will see the message's icon in the Attach field of the New Message window that appears.

Save Messages without Attachments

Some people keep copies of all the messages they send for their records. But attachments can take up a lot of hard disk space, especially since you have probably already saved the file somewhere else.

After sending a message, open it from your Sent Items folder, and then use File, Save As to save it as a *txt* file. The attachment will be stripped out in the process. You can then delete the message from your Sent Items folder.

Put Sound in Your Messages

HTML-formatted messages can include sound as well as graphics. To add a *wav* file to a new HTML message, click Format, Background, Sound to open the Background Sound dialog box shown in Figure 28-27. Use the Browse button to select a file, and then click Open. You can choose whether to play the sound only once or continuously (hope it's something very pleasant if you choose the latter). After you click OK, you'll get a preview of the sound, continuous or not depending on what you have chosen, in the New Message window.

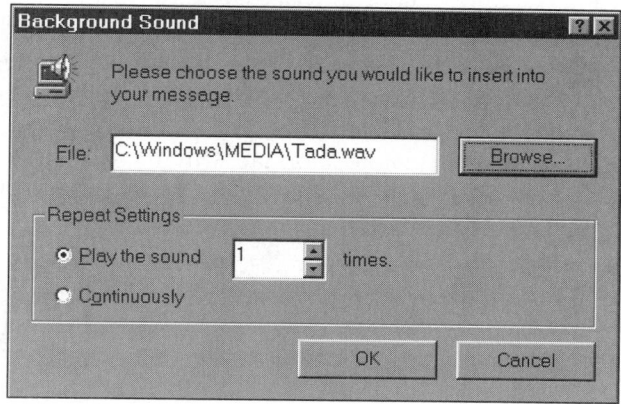

Figure 28-27: The Background Sound dialog box lets you select a sound to include in your message.

Add URLs to Your Favorites without Going Online

If someone e-mails you a link to a URL, you don't need to connect to the Internet to add the site to your Favorites. This works for any URL that functions as a hyperlink in Outlook Express. Just right-click the link and choose Add to Favorites.

Unfortunately, at the time we tested this it wasn't working quite right. You could choose Add to Favorites, but you weren't prompted to add it to a Favorites subfolder or to give it a name. After saving the shortcut you had to go to the \Windows\Favorites folder in the Explorer to name it something other than "Favorites from Outlook Express" and to move it to a subfolder. We hope that by the time you try it things have improved.

Saving GIFs

It's fun to collect the animated *gifs* you see in newsgroup postings or messages from your friends. But if you try to save a file by right-clicking and choosing Save Picture As, your only choice is to save it as a *bmp* file, thus losing the animation. Here's a way to save a *gif* as a *gif*:

STEPS
Saving Animated GIF Files

Step 1. In Outlook Express, choose Tools, Options, click the Send tab, and under Mail Sending Format, mark Plain Text. Clear Reply to Messages Using the Format in Which They Were Sent. Click OK.

Step 2. Highlight the header of the news message containing the *gif* file you want to save, and click the Forward button. The message should come up in plaintext format, with the original *htm* file and any included *gif* files shown as attachments in the Attach field (as shown in Figure 28-28).

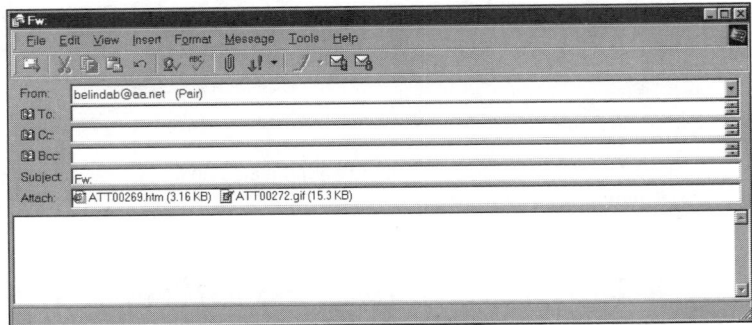

Figure 28-28: The gif file is shown as an attachment when you forward a message in plaintext format.

Step 3. Right-drag the icon for the *gif* file you want to save directly into your Explorer and choose Copy Here.

ASCII Art

If you read your e-mail with a fixed space font, you get to see the ASCII art signatures. While HTML e-mail provides much more artistic power than that available to plaintext messages, ASCII art is a fun way to turn dots, dashes, letters, and punctuation marks into art. Give an artist a limit and it's still art.

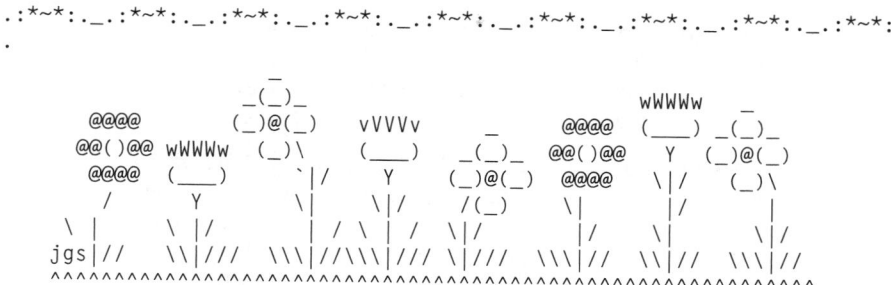

This example came from Joan Stark's ASCII art gallery at http://www. geocities.com/SoHo/7373/.

There is an easy way to convert existing graphics files (in *bmp* format) to ASCII art. You'll want to use an appropriate graphics file that translates well. Also, if you are going to use the ASCII graphic as a signature, you'll want to resize the graphics file so that after it is translated it is small enough to look good in an e-mail message. Each pixel in the graphics file is translated to a character, so a 600 x 480 graphics file is going to look really big. You might try 15 x 15 pixels.

ASCII Pic is the freeware program that will do the conversion, and you'll find it at http://5679soft.virtualave.net/asciipic.html. Thanks to Chris Pirillo at http://www.lockergnome.com.

Message Helpers

There are lots of tools available online to help you get your message across. Here are a few we've tried.

Spell Check Help

Outlook Express uses the Microsoft Office spell checker. But what if you don't use Microsoft Office? Speller for Microsoft Internet Products is shareware produced by CompuBridge. They also make spell checkers for Microsoft Office and WordPad, and they make AutoSpell for other e-mail products such as Netscape and Pegasus. A main benefit of Speller is spell checking in multiple languages, such as Danish, Dutch, French, German, Italian, and Spanish, as well as a couple flavors of English. CompuBridge is promising to support spell checking of the Subject line in Outlook Express messages — a helpful touch.

You can download free evaluation copies of Speller for Microsoft Internet Products from `http://www.spellchecker.com`. Registration (gets rid of the nag screen) is $14.95.

Talking E-mail

Now you can have a pleasant voice announce the arrival of your e-mail and read your messages to you (up to 30 lines each). Choose a friendly animated cartoon character to do the talking (see the example shown in Figure 28-29). The registered version gives you a choice of characters and voices.

Developed by 4Developers, Talking E-mail is shareware that uses Microsoft's advanced text-to-speech technology. It works with your standard mail account, and leaves messages on your mail server so you can download them later with Outlook Express. No special hardware other than a sound card is required. You can download Talking E-mail at `http://www.4developers.com/talkmail/`

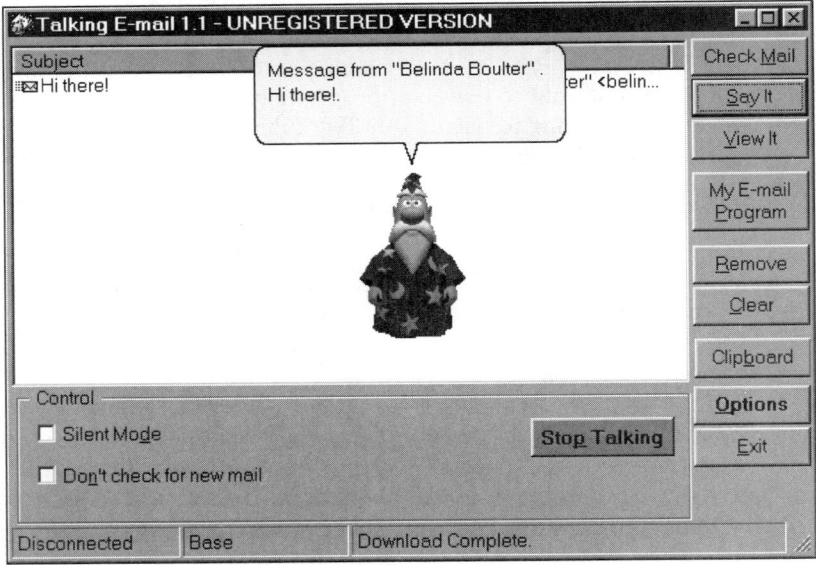

Figure 28-29: The cartoon character reads your e-mail to you while you do something else.

Jazz up Your Mail Announcement

If you're looking for something a bit more entertaining to announce the arrival of mail, check out this page: `http://wso.williams.edu/~eudora/eudora-3-0-spam-sounds.html`. They have *wav* files for announcing the arrival of spam (including the entire Monty Python Spam Song) — it might as well be good for something, after all.

Outlook Express can use any *wav* file to announce mail, so even though this site is geared toward users of Eudora the files will work fine. Right-click the link to the file you want and choose Save Target As, and then save the file in your \Windows\Media folder or some other place where you keep sound files. Click the Sounds icon in your Control Panel to associate this file with the New Mail Notification action. For specifics on using *wav* files to announce mail, see "Waving When the Mail Arrives" earlier in this chapter and "Applying Sounds to Application Events" in Chapter 15.

Another good source of sounds is G-Man, `http://gman.simplenet.com/email`.

Summary

Outlook Express gives you a lot of tools for composing and managing mail and news messages.

▶ You can use Flag, Watch, and Ignore to make it easier to see the messages you really want. Use them with Find so you only have to find them once.

▶ Quoting in HTML files works better than before, or you can send plaintext with customized quote characters.

▶ The Stationery Setup Wizard will help you design your own stationery. You can use the stationery to publish an illustrated e-zine.

▶ The preview pane header lets you open an attachment without opening the message.

▶ You can save an animated *gif* graphic from a message by forwarding it to yourself.

Chapter 29

Keeping Up with the News

In This Chapter

The Outlook Express news reader is your link to the thousands of Usenet newsgroups on the Internet. We show you how to sort through the clutter and make newsgroups work for you.

▶ Set the synchronization to download the messages or headers you want

▶ Design a custom newsgroup view to sort your messages

▶ Put a shortcut to your favorite newsgroup on your Desktop or toolbar

▶ Save a whole thread at once and preserve its order

▶ Add a custom header to your news messages that can help protect your privacy

▶ Forward a mail message

▶ Keep old news from filling up your hard disk

Synchronizing and Subscribing

Keeping up with newsgroup messages can be very easy if you let Outlook Express do most of the work for you. The following sections show you how.

Reading News with Outlook Express

Highlight a news server account in your Folder List pane or Outlook bar and Outlook Express turns into a newsgroup reader. Notice the various changes on your toolbar and in your Tools menu.

Tip

Even if you use another e-mail client, you can still use Outlook Express as your news reader. To clear out the mail-related clutter, choose Tools ➪ Accounts, and delete any mail accounts. Choose Tools ➪ Options, click the General tab, and clear the "Make Outlook Express my default e-mail program" checkbox. Finally, you can rename the Outlook Express icon on your Desktop to News (highlight the icon and press F2).

Sync One Newsgroup or the Whole Shebang

Outlook Express uses the term *synchronize* to refer to downloading a newsgroup. It's true, you are synchronizing the header list on your computer to the one on the newsgroup server. But all those folks who have wasted time looking for the "download" command are wondering if the change was really necessary. To avoid confusion, though, we'll stick with Microsoft's terminology.

You determine what synchronization entails for each newsgroup in the Synchronization pane for the newsgroup's news server (see Figure 29-1). Highlight the server in the Folders pane or the Folders list to display its Synchronization pane. In the Synchronization pane, highlight a newsgroup or use the Ctrl and Shift keys to highlight several at once, and then click the Settings button and select the desired option from the menu that appears. You can change the synchronization settings for a single newsgroup by right-clicking it in the Folders pane or the Folders list and choosing Synchronization Settings. This brings up the same menu as the one that's displayed when you click the Settings button in the Synchronization pane (see Figure 29-2).

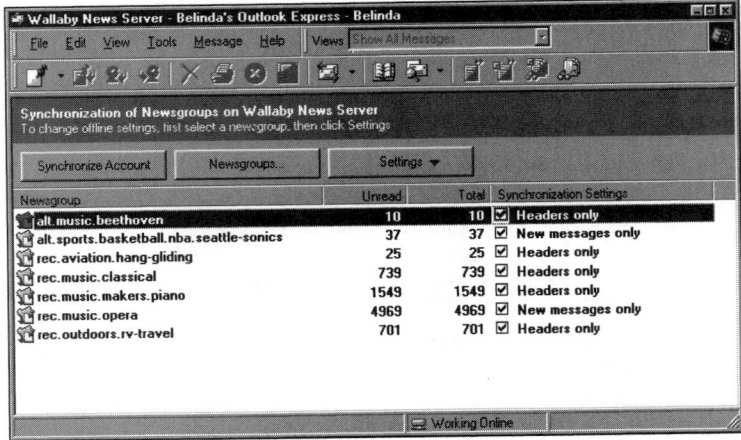

Figure 29-1: Use the Synchronization pane to control the synchronization of all the newsgroups on a news server.

Here is a description of the commands in the Settings menu:

- **All Messages:** Outlook Express first downloads all of the headers for this newsgroup that aren't already downloaded, and then downloads all of those messages. This can take quite a while if there are thousands of messages (often the case).

- **New Messages Only:** Outlook Express retrieves the headers and messages for a predetermined number of the newest messages (see the next section for how to set this number).

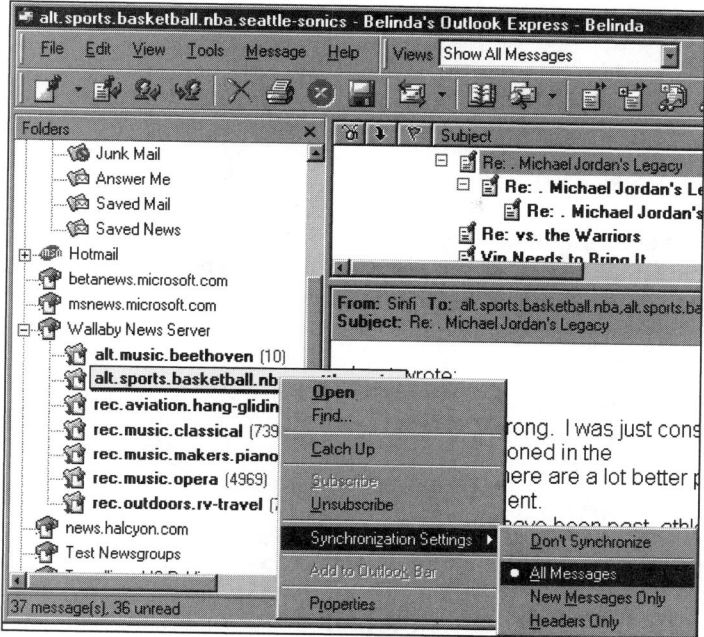

Figure 29-2: The menu for changing your synchronization settings

- **Headers Only:** Outlook Express downloads only the headers. You can then mark the headers that look interesting (right-click the message header and choose either "Download message later" or "Download conversation later" — or click in the "Mark for offline" column if you have it displayed) and download only those messages the next time you synchronize (this will automatically be added to the tasks that will be carried out during a Send and Receive). A blue arrow appears next to the message in the Mark for Offline column if you have this column displayed.

- **Don't Synchronize:** Outlook Express skips this newsgroup when it synchronizes the others. (You can also clear the newsgroup's checkbox in the Synchronization pane.)

To synchronize all of your newsgroups on all news servers, choose Tools ➪ Synchronize All. This action performs a Send and Receive for your e-mail at the same time. You'll see all of the tasks listed in the Outlook Express dialog box. While you can stop the whole process by clicking the Stop button, there's no way to skip a task and continue with the others once the process begins. Put a Synchronize All button on your news toolbar if you use this command a lot.

You can synchronize a single newsgroup or a single news server (which could include numerous newsgroups). To do this, highlight the newsgroup or account in the Folders pane and then choose Tools ➪ Synchronize Newsgroup if you've highlighted a newsgroup, or Tools ➪ Synchronize Account if you've highlighted a server.

Connecting to a News Server

Outlook Express updates the unread message count automatically when you highlight a newsgroup. The message count is quite useful because it tells you whether there are new messages in a given newsgroup.

Secret

To force Outlook Express to go out and check the news server and update the unread message count, choose Tools ⇨ Options, click the General tab, and mark "Check for new messages every [ ] minutes." Also, choose Tools ⇨ Accounts, highlight your news server, click the Properties button, click the General tab, and mark "Include this account when checking for new messages." Then click the Connection tab in the same dialog box and mark "Automatically connect to this server."

Tip

If you are reading news postings online and writing responses, you may at times get disconnected from the news server (but not necessarily from your Internet server provider). Press F5 or click View ⇨ Refresh to reconnect.

Some news servers require secure connections through the Secure Socket Layer protocol. If your news server requires this type of connection, choose Tools ⇨ Accounts, highlight your news account, click the Properties button, and then click the Advanced tab. Mark the "This server requires a secure connection (SSL)" checkbox. The port number in the field above the checkbox will change to 563.

When you are downloading a newsgroup, the status bar lists the number of messages on the server, the number that have been downloaded, and how many of those you have read. But sometimes the numbers seem to be inaccurate. Steve Serdy, a Microsoft Outlook Express Developer, wrote about this:

> Most, if not all, newsreaders suffer from problems like this. The problem stems from the fact that the message count information we can get quickly from the news server are all *estimates*. Based on that, OE comes up with the estimated number of messages we're going to download so that we can show some approximate progress. Depending on the sparseness of the data in the newsgroup, this number can be fairly accurate or not even close.
>
> I've spent an enormous amount of time over the last few years trying to come up with some better algorithm to make this number more accurate, but I haven't been able to without significantly increasing the amount of data we'd have to download from the server. Obviously increasing the download time is not acceptable.

Despite what Steve says, we believe we have seen some improvement in this area. If you are having a consistent problem, make sure you have set the view filter to "Show all messages" — you may have hidden some. And remember that if you have chosen Edit ⇨ Catch Up, there will be messages on the server that you can't download because they have been marked as read. See "Catch Up" later in this chapter for more about this.

Tip If you have a newsgroup with wildly inaccurate message counts, try resetting it. To do this, right-click the newsgroup in the Folders pane or the Folders list, click Properties, click the Local File tab, and click the Reset button. If that doesn't help, unsubscribe from that newsgroup and then subscribe again. Of course, the work you put into downloading and sorting messages you've already read may make the cure worse than the disease.

Reading the News Offline

News readers (that is, human ones) who reside outside the United States often have to pay what appear to U.S. residents as exorbitant hourly rates to connect to the Internet. These people, and the few remaining U.S. citizens who don't have nearby Internet service providers (ISPs) with fixed monthly fees, will find it much cheaper to take their reading offline. Outlook Express gives you this option.

Outlook Express keeps on your computer a threaded list of message headers for each subscribed newsgroup. When you go online and browse a newsgroup, Outlook Express updates the threaded list of message headers in that one newsgroup. The message headers are downloaded when you click the newsgroup's name in the Folder List pane.

If you click each of your subscribed newsgroup names in your Folder List pane, you capture all of the message headers currently on the news server. You can then go offline and, by clicking message headers, choose which messages to download later when you go back online.

Alternatively, you can download the message headers in a set of newsgroups (see the next paragraph) and then go offline. You can then browse through the list of headers by highlighting the name of the newsgroup that you want to peruse in the Folder List pane. As you highlight various headers (you can use Shift and Ctrl to choose multiple headers), you can mark the ones whose messages you want to download. To do this, choose Tools ⇨ Mark for Offline, and then select Download Message Later, Download Conversation Later, Download All Messages Later, or Do Not Download Message from the submenu that appears. You'll also find the first two of these choices on the context menu that appears when you right-click a message header. Once you have marked the messages you want to download, choose Tools ⇨ Synchronize All. Outlook Express will download the marked messages from the news server.

If you want to download all the message headers from a number of newsgroups at once, it is easiest to specify which newsgroups' headers you want to download while you are offline, then connect and have Outlook Express automatically update the headers for each newsgroup. While you're offline, highlight the desired news server account in the Folder List pane, and then highlight the desired newsgroups in the message header pane. (If you want to download the headers from all the newsgroups on a given news server, highlight that server in your Folder List pane, highlight any newsgroup, and choose Edit ⇨ Select All.) Then click the Settings button and choose Headers Only. Finally, choose Tools ⇨ Synchronize All.

You can now go through the headers and mark those whose associated messages presumably merit downloading (right-click each message, and choose Download Message Later). Choose Tools ⇨ Synchronize All to go online and get the marked messages. To unmark a message, click the Download icon (downward pointing arrow) that appears next to it in the Message pane.

If you choose to download both the headers and the messages at the same time, you obviously don't need to go back and download the messages later. Of course, the initial download takes a bit longer than if you just get the headers, and you'll get a lot of messages that aren't of interest to you.

To do this, select the news server account in the Folders list. Select the newsgroups whose messages you wish to download in the message header pane, click the Settings button and choose New Messages. You can also right-click individual newsgroups in the Folders list and choose Synchronization Settings ⇨ New Messages.

Outlook Express knows which headers you already have stored on your computer, so it won't download any old ones. Even if you download both the headers and the messages at the same time, you don't have to worry about Outlook Express going out and downloading messages associated with headers you have previously stored.

If you do want to download messages associated with headers that you already have stored on your computer, you can mark those headers for download individually or by using Select All. Or, you can right-click the newsgroup name in the Folder List pane and choose Synchronization Settings ⇨ All Messages. Then click Tools ⇨ Synchronize Account.

Tip

One problem with choosing to download all messages is the chance that there will be some long messages that take an inordinate amount of time to download. You can use Tools ⇨ Message Rules ⇨ News to reject all messages greater than a selected number of lines. Click the Add button in the Newsgroup Filters dialog box, mark the "Where the number of lines in the message is more than lines" checkbox in the Conditions area, and check the "Mark it as read" checkbox in the Actions area. Click the blue underlined word *Lines* and indicate the number of lines. Finally, give your rule a name.

Get More (or Fewer) than 300 Headers at a Time

By default, Outlook Express downloads 300 headers at one time, starting with the most recent ones. To get the previous 300, choose Tools ⇨ Get Next 300 Headers.

You may feel this is too many headers to digest at once, or it may not be enough to suit you. To change the number of headers that Outlook Express downloads, choose Tools ➪ Options, and click the Read tab. Under News, either clear the "Get [ ] headers at a time" checkbox, or set the number higher, as shown in Figure 29-3. The highest number you can enter is 1,000. If you clear the checkbox, you'll get all of the headers.

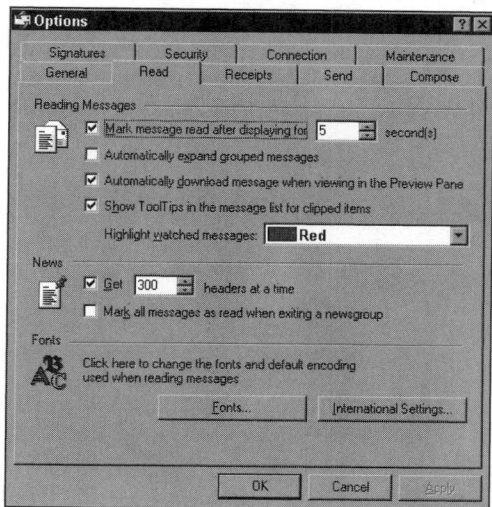

Figure 29-3: Clear the "Get [ ] headers at a time" checkbox, or increase the number of headers.

If you prefer to download headers in small batches, you'll probably want to take advantage of the Headers button on your toolbar. This button is the equivalent of the Tools ➪ Get Next *X* Headers command.

Tip

If you have Outlook Express set to download a set number of headers at a time, you may occasionally find that when you go to a newsgroup it downloads another, previous group of headers — without prompting. To stop this behavior, use the Catch Up command, described in "Catch Up" later in this chapter.

Read Messages Without Sync-ing

When you switch from mail to news or switch to a newsgroup on a different news server, and you are working in online mode, Outlook Express will begin downloading message headers. This happens regardless of what your synchronization settings are. In fact, you never really need to synchronize at all if you have a continuous Internet connection or don't mind staying connected while you read the news. Each message will be downloaded individually when you highlight its header.

Secret

If you read newsgroups this way and have the Preview pane displayed, you will notice that it can take a moment for a message to download. It's easy to select a header by mistake, when you really didn't want to read that message. If you like, you can tell Outlook Express to download a message only when you tell it to.

To do this, choose Tools ➪ Options, click the Read tab, and clear the checkbox labeled "Automatically download message when viewing in the Preview Pane." Now when you highlight a header, you'll see the message shown in Figure 29-4 in the Preview pane.

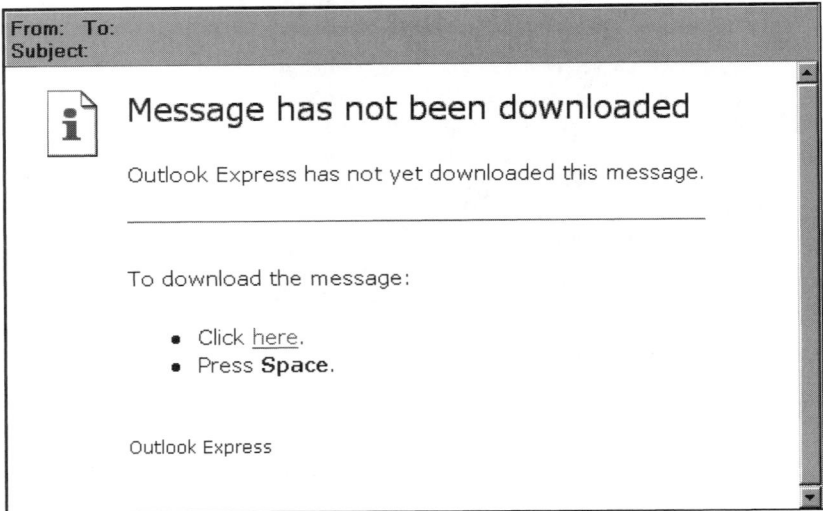

Figure 29-4: You'll see this message in the Preview pane if the message has not been automatically downloaded. Press the spacebar to download the message.

Keep the Downloads Coming

If you frequently use Synchronize All to download lots of big newsgroups, you know how frustrating it can be to get disconnected in mid-download when you were away from your computer. (For that matter, it's a pain if you often receive very large e-mail attachments.) If this is a frequent problem, you might want to try InLook 1.03 for Outlook Express 4 and 5.

During synchronization, InLook checks every minute for the Reestablish Connection dialog box. If it's there (meaning you've been disconnected), InLook reconnects for you and starts another Synchronize All. This lets you go off and have lunch or go to bed instead of babysitting your computer.

InLook only works over a dial-up connection. You must have already made the connection and have your Inbox open for InLook to work (so you can't use it with the Task Scheduler to schedule a synchronization, for example).

InLook is freeware, available from Edgemeal Software at `http://edgemeal.homepage.com/inlook107.zip` .

Add a News Account to Send and Receive

You can have Outlook Express check your news server as part of the standard Send and Receive operation or an automatic poll (Tools ⇨ Options ⇨ General ⇨ "Check for new messages every [ ] minutes"). To do this, choose Tools ⇨ Accounts, click the News tab, highlight the account you want to add, and click the Properties button. In the Properties dialog box for this account, mark "Include this account when checking for new messages," as illustrated in Figure 29-5.

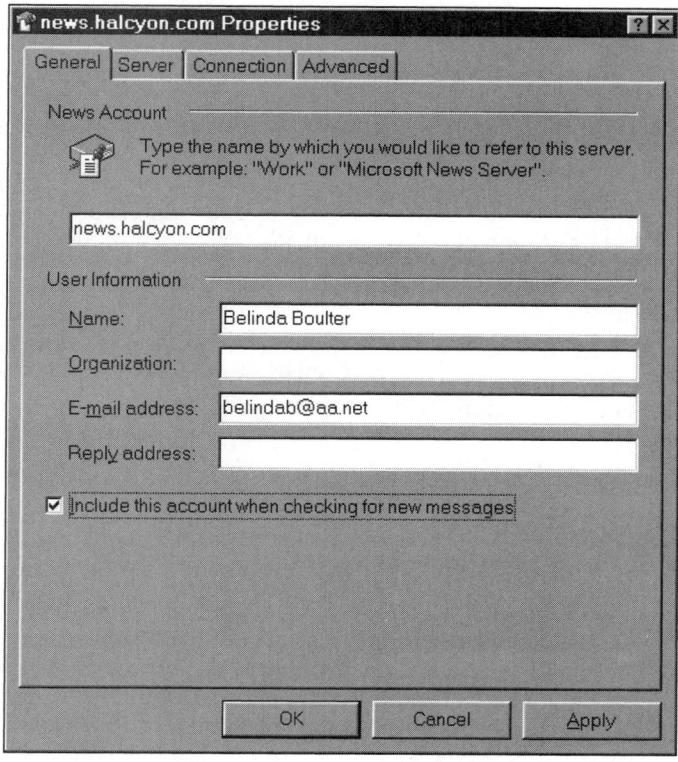

Figure 29-5: Mark the "Include this account when checking for new messages" checkbox to include this news server in a standard Send and Receive operation.

You might think that this means Outlook Express will synchronize the newsgroups on this server when you perform a Send and Receive. So, for example, you might expect to see new headers or new messages after the process is complete. However, all that actually changes is the message count. In other words, when you go to a newsgroup on this server, you'll be able to see if there are unread messages, and how many there are. At this time there is still no way to automatically download unread headers or messages.

You Don't Need to Subscribe to Read

If you're just curious about a newsgroup, you don't need to subscribe to it. Right-click the newsgroup's server in the Folders pane or Folders list, and choose Newsgroups. In the Newsgroup Subscriptions dialog box, highlight the newsgroup in the list, and click the Go To button. If you like, you can browse through the messages one by one online. If you'd rather work offline, you can still right-click headers of interest and choose Download Message Later or Download Conversation Later. Then, later, click Tools ➪ Synchronize Newsgroup to download the message bodies. You cannot set synchronization settings for a nonsubscribed newsgroup, and the newsgroup will not appear in the Synchronization pane for the server to which it belongs. If you choose Synchronize All, this newsgroup will not appear in the list of Send and Receive tasks (although individual messages you've marked to download will).

When you leave the newsgroup, you will be asked if you want to subscribe. If you click No, the newsgroup will still appear in your Folders pane, and the messages and headers will still be available, but only until you close Outlook Express. If you mark the "Don't ask me this again" checkbox, the button that you click (Yes or No) will govern future behavior for this situation.

Earlier problems with removing unsubscribed newsgroups in Outlook Express have been resolved. So if you think you'll want to go back to a newsgroup, there's no harm in subscribing to it — you can easily unsubscribe whenever you like.

Force Plaintext for an Account

Secret

Even if your default message format is HTML, you can force Outlook Express to send messages for a particular news account using plaintext. To do this, choose Tools ➪ Accounts, double-click an account, and go to the Advanced tab. Mark the "Ignore news sending format and post using" checkbox, and then mark the Plain Text option button, as shown in Figure 29-6. This overrides whatever option you have chosen under News Sending Format in the Send tab of the Tools ➪ Options dialog box.

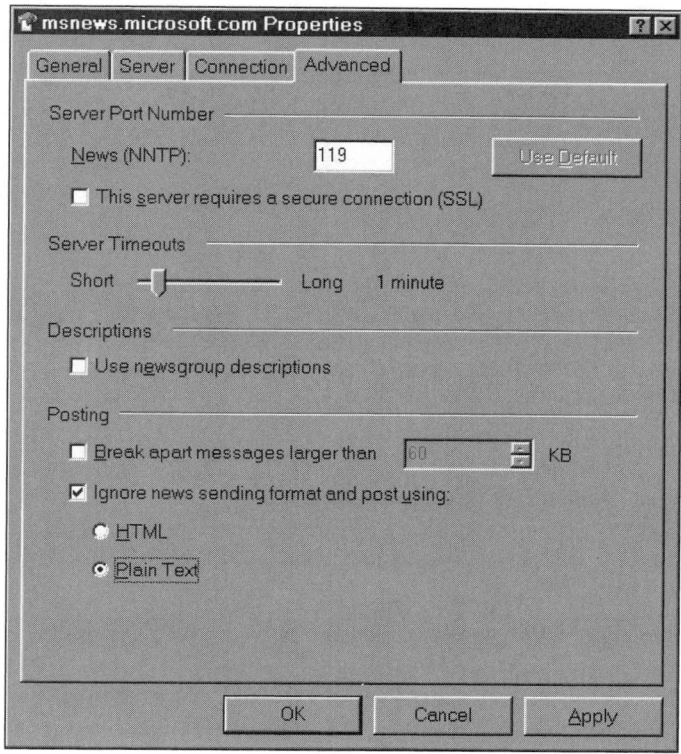

Figure 29-6: You can override your default sending options for a news account and send plaintext messages.

Reading the News

There are literally thousands of newsgroups, and many of them include thousands of messages. Finding and reading the messages that interest you would be nearly impossible without effective methods of navigating the newsgroups.

Moving Around in a Newsgroup

When you go to a newsgroup and you're in online mode, Outlook Express automatically tries to download headers. If you don't have a connection, you will be prompted to connect. Select a header, and the message will be downloaded. If you like, you can read the whole newsgroup this way without ever synchronizing.

When you click a newsgroup in the Folders pane or the Outlook bar, Outlook Express takes you to the first unread message. To see the next unread message, conversation, or folder, choose View ➪ Next, and select from the menu shown in Figure 29-7. Because this is a bit cumbersome to do constantly, you may want to add a button to your news toolbar for one or all of these commands. Or, just use the keyboard shortcuts shown in the menu: Ctrl+U for the next unread message, Ctrl+Shift+U for the next unread conversation, and Ctrl+J for the next unread folder.

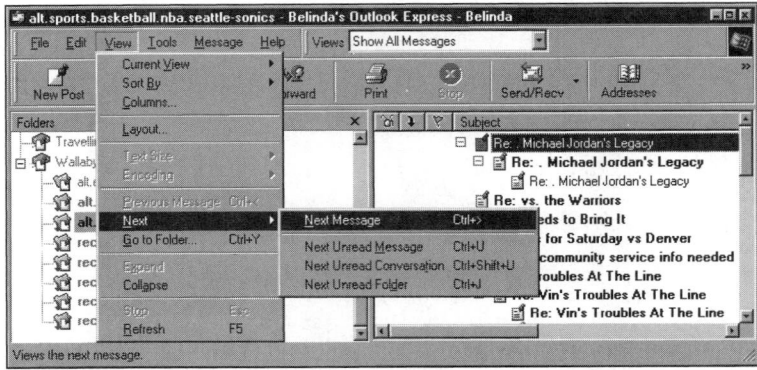

Figure 29-7: Choose the next unread message, conversation, or folder in the View ➪ Next menu.

When you reach the bottom of the Message pane, the Next Unread command cycles the focus back to the top if there are still unread messages in this newsgroup. If you have read all of the messages and click the Next Unread Message button, you will be prompted to go to the next news folder with unread messages (see Figure 29-8).

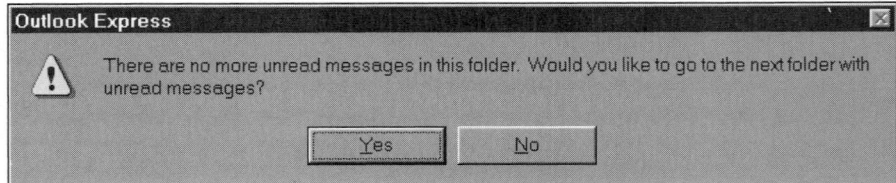

Figure 29-8: Click Yes to go to the next news folder with unread messages.

You may have unread messages in a thread where the first message has been read. If you have not marked "Automatically expand grouped messages" on the Read tab of the Options dialog box, these will be hidden. In this situation, the top message will be shown in bold type as if it were unread. When you press Ctrl+U, the thread will automatically expand, and the unread message will be selected.

Next Unread Conversation (Ctrl+Shift+U) takes you to the first message in a conversation containing an unread message, regardless of whether the first message is read. Use Next Unread Message to expand the thread if necessary and go to the unread message.

Setting the View

It's a good thing we have the Views bar, because the current view is now set individually for each newsgroup and mail folder. You can set the view to "View all messages" in a smaller newsgroup, but "Hide read or ignored messages" in a group with lots of flame wars. When you move to a newsgroup, the view setting changes to what it was when you were there last. You'll soon develop the habit of glancing at the Views bar to check the current view.

Tip

If your Views bar isn't showing, right-click the Outlook Express toolbar and click Views Bar. You can drag the Views bar up next to the menu bar to get it out of the way. Now you have a handy drop-down list of all the View settings, including the custom views you design yourself (see Figure 29-9).

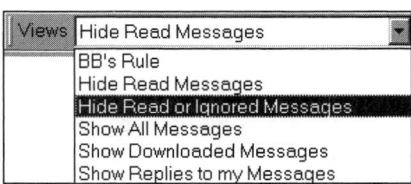

Figure 29-9: The Views bar is a boon to newsgroup addicts.

Design a Custom View

You can design a custom view and save it to use whenever you read newsgroups. For example, sometimes you might want to see just the news messages from particular people (the ones whose comments you find most helpful, maybe, or the ones with the best gossip). Or you might set up a different view for each of several subject keywords, so you can read the messages for each subject as a group. Because it's easy to switch views, you can get to just the part of the newsgroup you're interested in at the moment without having to wade through the rest.

The easiest way to create a custom view is to modify the one you're currently using. Select the view that most closely matches the one you want, and then choose View ⇨ Current View ⇨ Customize Current View. (You will still be able to change any part of the view definition, so the view you start with is not critical, but it can be helpful.) The Customize Current View dialog box appears (see Figure 29-10), showing the definition of the current view.

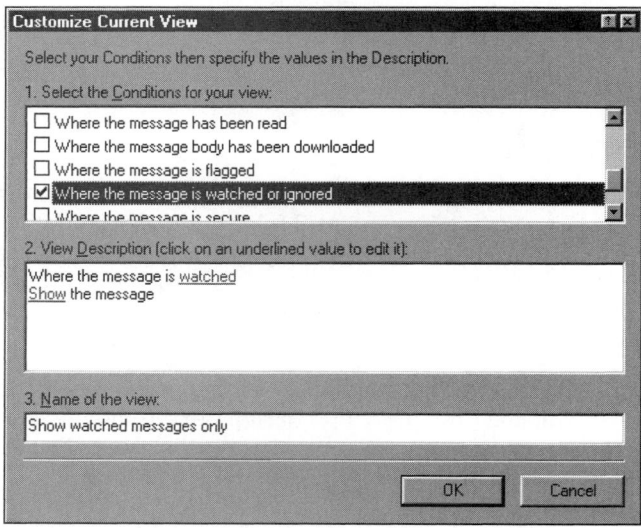

Figure 29-10: The current view in this example is Show Watched Messages Only.

The Conditions area lets you change or add conditions to describe the messages that you want to show or hide. You do this by marking or unmarking the checkbox for that condition. When this dialog box first appears, the conditions for your current view will be marked, but you can clear them if you want. These conditions are very general. For example, you can specify that the From line must contain people. Later you get more specific about which people. You can mark more than one condition, and later specify whether the messages must match all of the conditions or any of them.

As you select conditions, you will see a summary of all your choices in the View Description area. This is where you make each of your conditions specific. Click each blue underlined word or phrase in the Description area to display a dialog box that lets you define it or change the definition. The dialog boxes vary depending on what you are selecting, be it people, subject words, or something else. For example, the Select People dialog box, shown in Figure 29-11, lets you use the Address Book button to browse for people you want to select, or type their addresses and click the Add button — you can add as many people as you like. Other dialog boxes may contain only a drop-down list or option buttons.

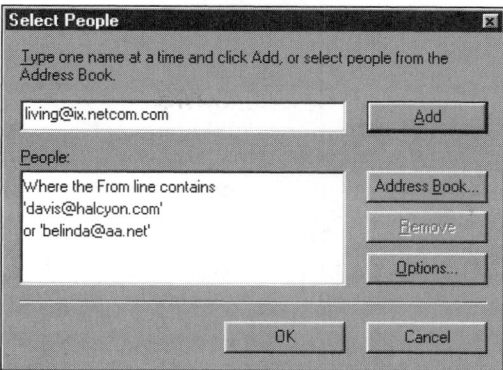

Figure 29-11: The Select People dialog box lets you select one or more people whose messages you will choose to show or hide.

Secret

You can further refine your selection by clicking the Options button available in some of the dialog boxes that appear when you click a blue underlined word or phrase in the Description area. The Rule Condition Options dialog box, shown in Figure 29-12, lets you change your condition in either of two important ways. The first pair of option buttons lets you select by *exclusion* rather than by *inclusion*—in other words, you can set the condition to view all messages that do *not* contain the keywords or addresses you have indicated. The second pair of option buttons lets you change the OR operator to AND—so that a message must contain *all* of the keywords or addresses you have indicated in order for the condition to be met.

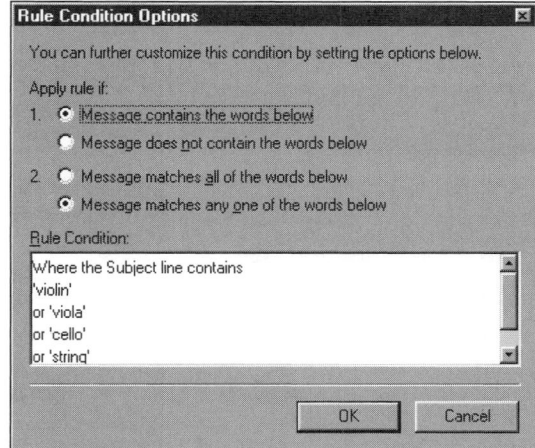

Figure 29-12: You can use the Rule Condition Options dialog box to change the way your condition will work.

Any changes you make in the Rule Condition Options dialog box affect only that one condition. If you have set multiple conditions by marking more than one checkbox in the Conditions area, the blue underlined word *And* appears between each condition listed in the Description area. This means the messages must match all of the conditions you have set. To change the And to Or, click the *And*. In the And/Or dialog box that appears, mark the "Messages match any one of the criteria" option button and click OK.

When you have finished editing all of the values in the View Description area, type a name for your view in the Name of the View field, click OK, and your view will be added to the Views bar and to the Current View menu.

Tip

While a custom view may seem similar to a news message rule, there are some significant differences. Message rules offer more possible actions than simply showing or hiding. And views do not affect what is downloaded, only what you can see at the moment. You can set up lots of views and quickly switch from view to view as you read, while message rules are designed to operate all or most of the time. For more on message rules, see "Setting Up Message Rules" in Chapter 30.

If none of the existing views is similar to what you want, or if you're planning to set up several views at once, you might prefer to start from scratch instead of basing your custom view on the current one. That way, you don't have to clear all of the existing conditions before marking the ones you want. This method also lets you edit a view without actually having it current. Click View ➪ Current View ➪ Define Views. You will see a list of all the views, along with their descriptions. You can add a new view definition or modify an existing one in the same way we have just described.

After you've defined a new view, you must still apply it to a message folder, normally by selecting it from the Views bar. To apply your new view to your current folder (or globally to all your Outlook Express folders), while your view is still highlighted in the Define Views dialog box, click the Apply View button (and if you want, mark the "All of my folders" option button, as shown in Figure 29-13). You might also find this a convenient way to reset all of your folders to "Show all messages."

A Shortcut to a Newsgroup

Secret

You can't set Outlook Express to open anywhere except the Inbox—but you can create a shortcut on your Desktop to a favorite newsgroup.

STEPS

Creating a Newsgroup Shortcut

Step 1.   On an empty part of your Desktop, click New ➪ Shortcut.

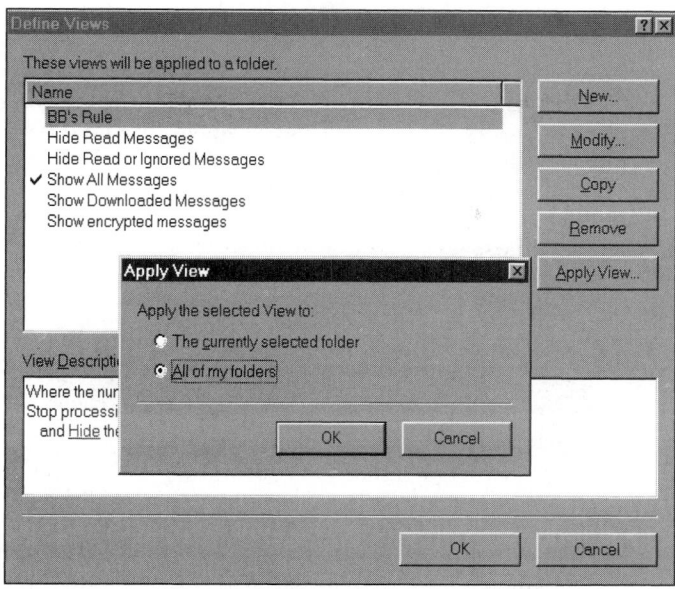

Figure 29-13: You can apply a view to all of your folders.

Step 2. In the Command Line field of the Create Shortcut dialog box, type **news://** followed by the exact name of your news server, a forward slash, and the name of the newsgroup. For example, your command might look something like this:

```
news://msnews.microsoft.com/microsoft.public.opk.Me
```

Use the full server and newsgroup names listed in the Synchronization pane for that news server. Click Next.

Step 3. The Select a Title for the Program dialog box appears. Type a name for your shortcut and click Finish.

Step 4. Click your new shortcut to go directly to your newsgroup.

Tip

If you have a bunch of newsgroups, you could make a newsgroup toolbar. Make a shortcut to each newsgroup, and then create a new folder called Newsgroups (perhaps under your \My System folder) and move all of the shortcuts from the Desktop to the folder. Now right-click the taskbar, click Toolbars ⇨ New Toolbar, navigate to your Newsgroups folder in the New Toolbar dialog box, and click OK. Drag the sizing bar at the left end of the new toolbar to the right, so you only see the name of the toolbar. Then, click the toolbar name to display a menu of your newsgroup shortcuts, and click the one that you want to open.

Threads

You can sort both mail and news messages by subject. These subjects are called *conversations* in Outlook Express, but they're known as *threads* in the wider Internet community. To see your messages in threaded order, choose View ➪ Current View ➪ Group Messages by Conversation. Unlike the current view, this setting applies to either all your news folders or all your mail folders, depending on whether you are in a news or mail folder when you choose it. Grouping messages in this way helps to make sense of the responses and counter-responses as a newsgroup discussion develops. An example of a long thread is shown in Figure 29-14.

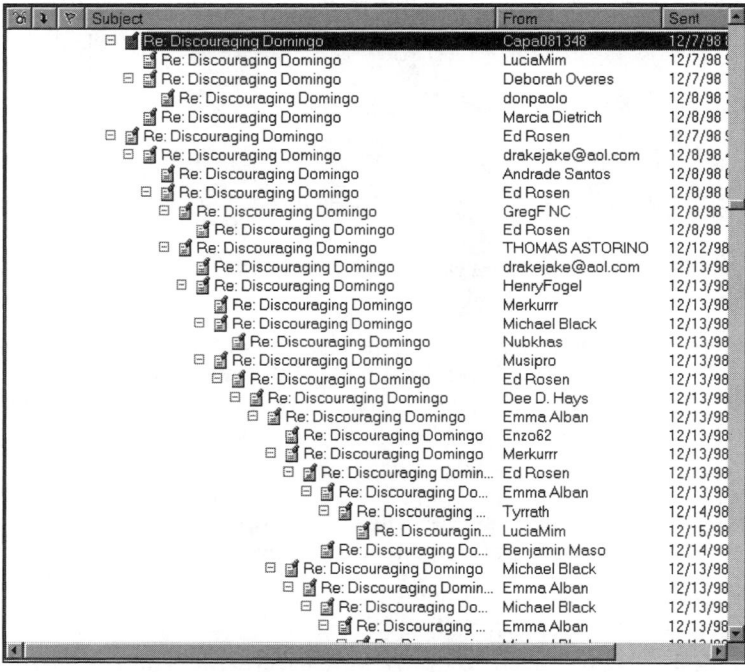

Figure 29-14: An example of a thread (conversation) taken from the rec.music.opera newsgroup.

According to Steve Serdy, a Microsoft Outlook Express Developer, Outlook Express uses the References line in a message's header (placed there automatically by the sender's news software) to decide whether it belongs in a thread. But because many news clients don't use this header, Outlook Express then does a secondary sort by subject. Although this means that some messages will be added to threads where they don't belong, at least all of the messages that do belong will usually be grouped together.

If you're contributing to an ongoing discussion, it's helpful to preserve the threading so that your message doesn't end up a disconnected orphan. To do this, highlight the message to which you're replying and click the Reply to Group button (*not* the New Post button or the Reply to Sender button). This will add the appropriate References line to your message's header, with a pointer to the message that you're replying to. You can see this line once your message is in your Outbox by highlighting the message and pressing Ctrl-F3.

If you have quoting enabled (Tools ➪ Options ➪ Send ➪ "Include message in reply"), you will also see a reference to the original message at the beginning of the quoted portion of the body of your message, for example:

```
Somebody <somebody@isp> wrote in message
news:#wa0#RgK#GA.193@uppssnewspub04.moswest.msn.Net...
```

You can set whole threads to be watched or ignored. For more about this, see "Make Messages and Threads Easier to Find" in Chapter 28.

You can save a whole conversation (or any group of messages) together in an Outlook Express folder. Highlight the messages and click Edit ➪ Copy to Folder — or right-click and click Copy to Folder in the context menu. In the Copy dialog box, select or create a folder for saving the messages, and click OK. The threading information in the message headers will be preserved in the new folder.

Secret

If you save the messages to an Explorer folder, the threading information will not be preserved. Not only that, but because the default filename is the subject, if all the messages in the group have the same subject (the usual case) you'll have to save each message individually and rename each one. A much easier way to save a thread, and a way that preserves the order of the messages, is to save them in one file. Here's how:

STEPS

Saving a Group of Messages As One File

Step 1.   In the Message pane, highlight the headers of plaintext messages you want to save by using Shift+click (for consecutive messages) or Ctrl+click (for nonconsecutive messages).

Step 2.   Click Message ➪ Combine and Decode.

Continued

STEPS

Saving a Group of Messages As One File *(continued)*

Step 3. The Order for Decoding dialog box, shown in Figure 29-15, appears. Use the Move Up and Move Down buttons to select the order of the messages, or just drag the messages up and down the list with your mouse (a little black arrow appears on the left to indicate where the message will be dropped). When you're finished, click OK.

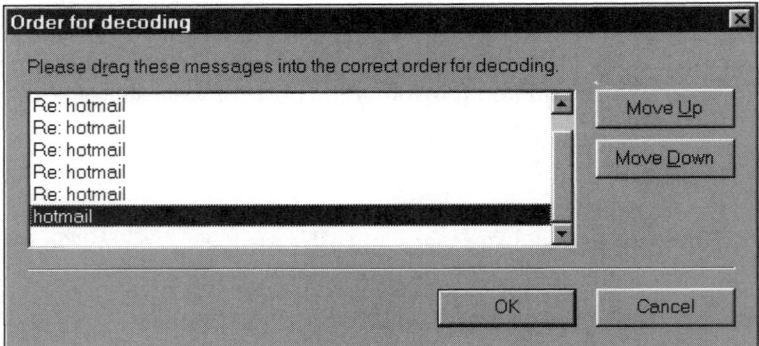

Figure 29-15: The Order for Decoding dialog box

Step 4. The text of all of the messages appears in one message window. Now click File ⇨ Save As to save your file to a folder outside of Outlook Express. You can choose to save it in either mail (eml) or text (txt) format.

Combine and Decode now works on mail as well as news. It works best if the messages are in plaintext format, because otherwise you see all of the HTML code along with the message. We have heard that using Combine and Decode with an HTML message can cause Outlook Express to crash, but we have not experienced it. The only other drawback with this method is that header information is only preserved for the first file.

Tip Saving a batch of messages to a txt file is a good way to print a batch of messages at once. In fact, with the new message store structure, it's now the only way.

Posting to Newsgroups

You aren't really a full newsgroup participant until you join in and add your own messages. The following sections provide information on posting newsgroup messages.

Track Replies to Your Postings

It can be hard to find your own posts among the hundreds of messages on a newsgroup. To see only your messages and the replies to them, choose View ⇨ Current View ⇨ Show Replies to my Messages. But you can also set up a message rule to watch threads containing your messages. This way, they'll be highlighted regardless of the current view. For a more detailed discussion of message rules, see "Setting Up Message Rules" and the other topics in Chapter 30.

STEPS

Watching Your Own Posts

Step 1. Click Tools ⇨ Message Rules ⇨ News. In the Message Rules dialog box that opens, click the New button.

Step 2. In the New News Rule dialog box, set up the rule following the example in Figure 29-16. Use your own address in the Rule Description field. (Mark the two checkboxes in the Conditions and Actions fields. You will see a *contains people* link in the Rule Description field. Click this link, type your address in the Select People dialog box, click the Add button, and click OK. Then click the *watched or ignored* link, mark Watch Message in the Watch or Ignore dialog box, and click OK.) Make sure to name the rule at the bottom of the New News Rule dialog box. When you're finished, click OK.

Step 3. Move this rule to the top of the list in the Message Rules dialog box, and click OK.

Continued

STEPS

Watching Your Own Posts *(continued)*

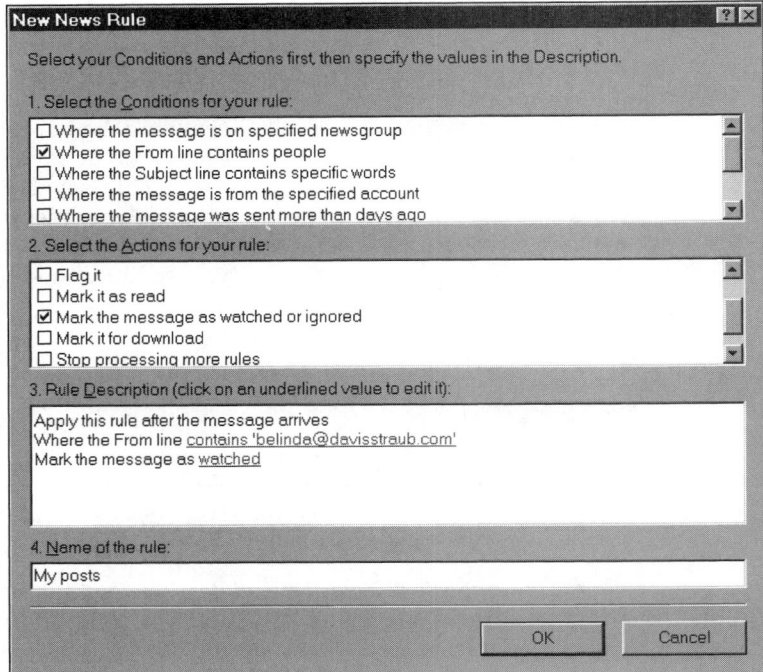

Figure 29-16: Follow this example for setting up the message rule, using your own address.

Now your messages and the threads they appear in will be marked as "watched." The headers will appear marked with glasses and highlighted with red. If you prefer to mark only your own posts, you can set up the Action field in the rule to flag your messages instead of watching their threads. A big advantage of using the thread state ("watch" or "ignore") or the flag is that you can easily reverse them. If you instead choose the "Highlight it with color" action in the rule definition, it can be a chore to change the colors of all those headers when you decide that lime green is hard to read.

Beware of Cross Posters

If you single-click a newsgroup message to view it in the Preview pane, you might not notice if it has been posted to multiple newsgroups. You may assume that it has only been posted to the newsgroup that you are currently reading. This might give you the feeling you're part of a little community, and that you're only interacting with the people on this one newsgroup. This can be a false reading.

People can (and do) post messages to many different newsgroups at once. Sometimes this is legitimate; the person who posted the message is simply trying to get help wherever he or she can find it. Sometimes it's just spam. If you reply to a message that was posted in multiple newsgroups, your reply will by default get posted in all the newsgroups, not just the one you're currently participating in.

Secret

If you want to respond in just one newsgroup, highlight the message header and click the Reply to Group toolbar button. Click the icon to the left of the Newsgroups field, as shown in Figure 29-17, to display the Pick Newsgroups dialog box. Here, you can remove newsgroups and/or add others.

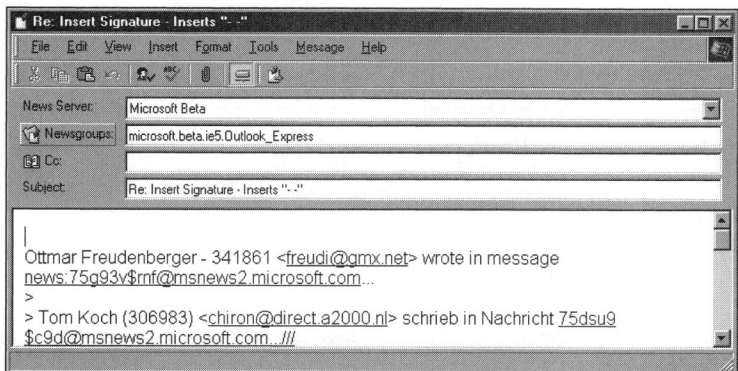

Figure 29-17: Click the icon on the left side of the Newsgroups field to tailor the list of newsgroups on which your message will be posted.

You can also click the Newsgroups icon when you're writing new messages if you want to send them off to other newsgroups.

Outlook Express always has a current news server. When you click a newsgroup on a different news server, the current news server changes. When you click the Newsgroup icon, the Pick Newsgroups dialog box only lists newsgroups available on the current news server.

Secret

If some of the newsgroups to which a message has been posted aren't present on the news server you are currently logged onto, you'll get an error message stating that the newsgroup name can't be resolved. This is particularly true with the Microsoft's news server because it only lists its own newsgroups. If you see this error message, you know without even double-clicking the message header that a cross poster sent the message.

Handling Cross-Posted Messages Independently

Secret

Outlook Express has the normally very useful feature of automatically marking cross-posted messages (messages sent to more than one newsgroup) as read. That way, if someone has posted the same message to every newsgroup on your server, you only have to read his or her spam once. Still, some people find that a message they overlooked in one newsgroup is more useful in the context of another. If this applies to you, you can disable this feature with a simple registry change.

STEPS

Handling Cross-Posted Messages Independently

Step 1. Open your Registry Editor (`regedit.exe`) and navigate to HKEY_CURRENT_USER\ Identities\ {*your identity number*}\ Software\ Microsoft\ Outlook Express\ 5.0\ News.

Step 2. In the right pane, locate MarkXPostsRead, as shown in Figure 29-18, and double-click it.

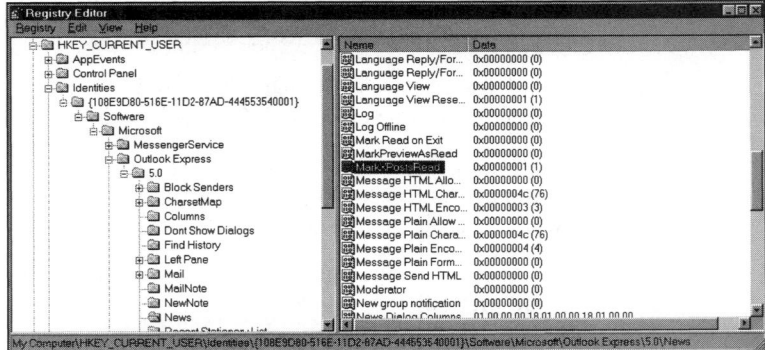

Figure 29-18: Double-click the MarkXPostsRead DWORD.

Step 3. In the Edit DWORD Value dialog box that appears, change the Value Data field from 1 to 0. Click OK and close the Registry Editor.

Thanks to Eric Miller for this tip.

Which Group to Reply to?

Cross posting is generally frowned upon because it is so abused. Nobody wants to read messages that have no relevance to the newsgroup they are reading, and that have been sent to a hundred other off-topic groups as well. But occasionally you may feel that your message is of genuine interest to more than one newsgroup, so you choose to send it to two or three.

If you do this, you'll want to indicate in the message header a newsgroup where people should send their replies, as described in the steps below. This helps to keep conversations from spreading all over by putting all the replies in one place, so there's less duplication and it's easier for you to keep track of replies. Even if someone reads your message in a different newsgroup, the reply will automatically go to the one you indicate.

Just as Outlook Express will only let you cross post to newsgroups on the same server, it only lets you designate a follow-up newsgroup on the same server as the one to which you are posting.

STEPS

Setting the Follow-Up Newsgroup

Step 1. From one of the newsgroups to which you want to post a message, open a New Message window by clicking the New Message toolbar button or by choosing Message ➪ New Message.

Step 2. In the New Message window, click View ➪ All Headers. Your message header changes to include additional lines, including a Followup-To line, as shown in Figure 29-19.

Step 3. Click the Followup-To label at the beginning of that line to open a list of the newsgroups you have subscribed to on this server (see Figure 29-20). To see all of the newsgroups available on this server, click the "Show only subscribed newsgroups" button to disable it. Double-click the newsgroup where you want to have replies sent, and click OK. Although you can select multiple newsgroups in this dialog box, doing so pretty much defeats our purpose in this case.

Continued

STEPS

Handling Cross-Posted Messages Independently *(continued)*

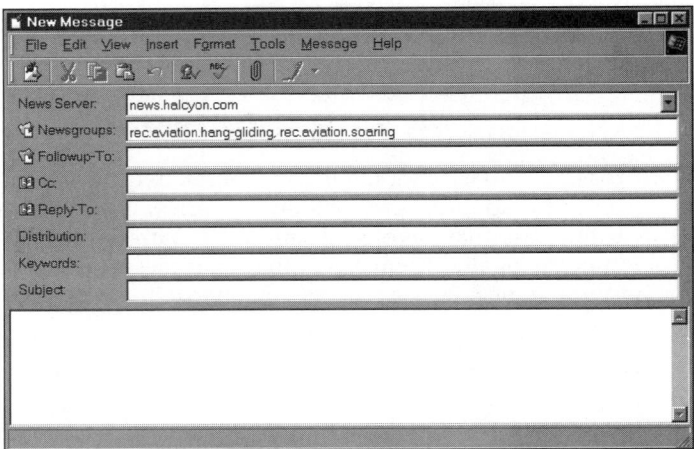

Figure 29-19: Choose View ⇨ All Headers to display additional header lines in your New Message window.

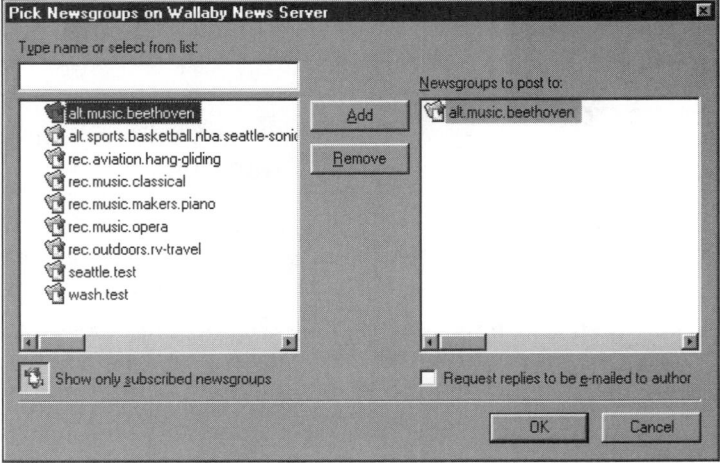

Figure 29-20: Select from the list of newsgroups in the left column to designate where follow-up messages should be posted.

If you also want to have replies sent to you as e-mail, mark "Request replies to be e-mailed to author." This places the word *poster* in the Followup-To line. (You could also just type this word in that field instead of designating a newsgroup.) When someone replies to your message, you will automatically be sent a copy. This doesn't prevent the person from also replying to the group; it's more an indication of your preference.

Reply To

Another line that appears when you click View ➪ All Headers (see step 2 in the previous section) is the Reply To field. Ordinarily, if someone replies directly to you instead of to the newsgroup, his or her message goes to your default e-mail address. But you can use the Reply To header line to direct replies to a different address if you like. This can be very useful if you send a message from work (or from someone else's computer) but want replies to come to your home address.

The Reply To line in a news message header is controlled by the properties for the news server associated with that newsgroup. To see this, choose Tools ➪ Accounts, click the News tab, and double-click the name of your news server. The contents of the "Reply address" field, shown in Figure 29-21, control the Reply To line for messages you compose for this server. If the field is empty, or if it is the same as your default e-mail address, the Reply To line will be empty in messages that you compose. But if you put something different here, that address will be used in your message header.

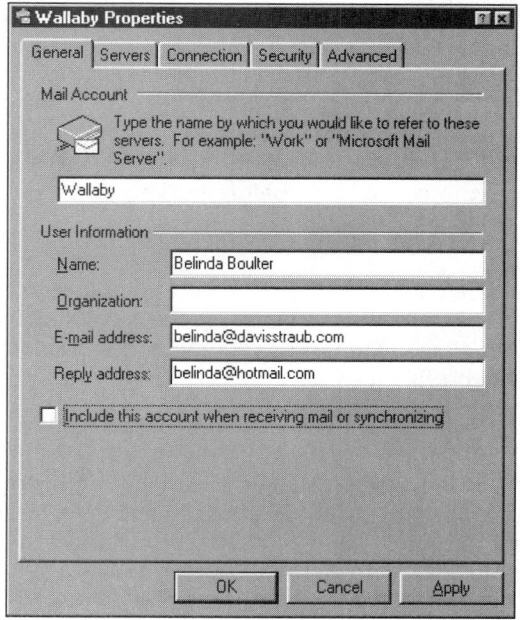

Figure 29-21: The "Reply address" field controls the content of the Reply To line in message headers.

Thanks to Sky King for help with this topic.

Anti-Spam

Spammers build e-mail mailing lists from the addresses they find in postings to newsgroups.

Secret

If you don't want your address picked up by Usenet bots that scan Usenet newsgroups for addresses, then put a fake address in the "E-mail address" field, such as `fakename@fakenet.net`. (Choose Tools ⇨ Accounts, highlight a news server, and click the Properties button.) Also, make sure that you don't have your correct address in the "Reply address" field. Unfortunately, if you put a fake address in the "E-mail address" field, newsgroup readers who want to reply to your postings with an e-mail message directly to you will not be able to; they'll have to send their responses only to the newsgroup. If you have different news server accounts, you can have different fake names for each account, and you can use your real e-mail address for your mail account.

Tip

If you want to indicate to other newsgroup subscribers that your indicated e-mail address is not your actual address, you can change your posted name to something like Spammers Beware. To do this, choose Tools ⇨ Accounts, highlight a news server, click the Properties button, and change the name in the Name field.

You can also use the Message Rules to avoid some of the incoming spam. Choose Tools ⇨ Message Rules ⇨ Mail, and click the New button. In the Conditions area, check the "Where the Subject line contains specific words" checkbox. In the Actions area, mark the checkbox for an appropriate action, such as "Do not download from the server." In the Rule Description area, click the blue underlined phrase "Contains specific words," and type a word or phrase that you only see in the subject headings of spam messages and click Add (see Figure 29-22). You can add additional words and phrases before clicking OK. Give your rule a name before clicking OK.

For more detailed discussion with examples of Message Rules, see Chapter 30.

Another option for avoiding Usenet bots is to add an asterisk to your "E-mail address" field. You can then put a note in your signature pointing out the asterisk and asking respondents who want to contact you to remove the asterisk from the To field of their reply message.

If you want to let people respond easily while avoiding the spammers, you can also put your e-mail address in your signature. Respondents can just click on your address to create a new message. The disadvantages of this method are that they lose the indented original message (if they have configured their e-mail client to include it in replies), they have to type a subject in the new message, and they can't just click the Reply to All button.

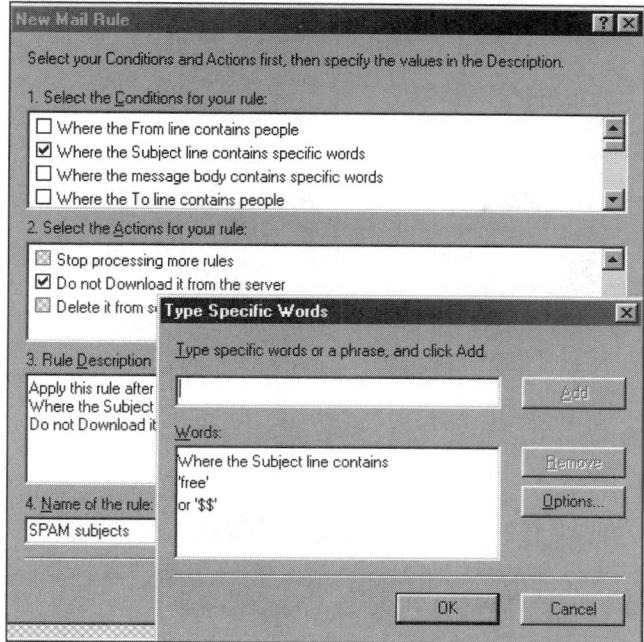

Figure 29-22: Type a word that only appears in the subject of spam messages.

Replying Politely

Some newsgroups include a lot of pictures and sound. For example, `microsoft.public.inetexplorer.ie4.outlookexpress.stationery` on the `msnews.microsoft.com` news server is specially designated as a place for people to share their multimedia stationery. Many of these files are quite large. On the other hand, in most newsgroups it's the information that people want, and they don't appreciate having to download a big file for only a few lines of text. Newsgroups are international, and in many places people have to pay by the minute for Internet access. Newsgroup participants who are in this situation appreciate receiving smaller messages.

It's possible to set Outlook Express so that if you are replying to a message that uses stationery, your reply will use the same stationery. In fact, this is the default setting for HTML mail messages. It's a very good idea *not* to use this setting for news, however, because a whole thread of messages using the same stationery can get big fast. If you find that your replies to newsgroup postings include the original stationery, choose Tools ⇨ Options, and click the Send tab. Click the HTML Settings button under News Sending Format, and then clear the "Send pictures with messages" checkbox, as shown in Figure 29-23.

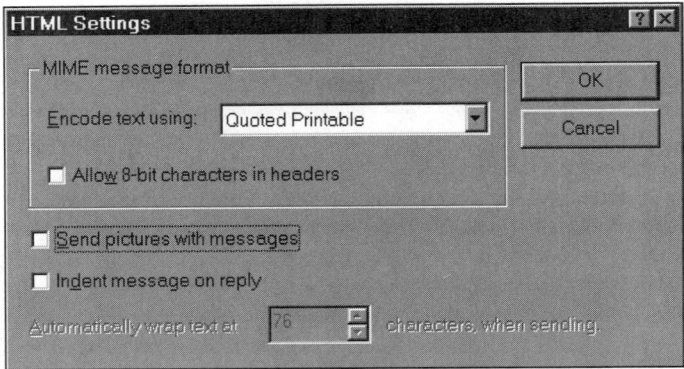

Figure 29-23: Clear the "Send pictures with messages" checkbox to avoid sending stationery with your news reply.

Custom Headers in News Messages

Click View ➪ All Headers in a New Message window, and you'll see some additional header lines appear. But there are some header lines used in Internet newsgroups that are not normally available in Outlook Express. One of these keeps your message from being archived indefinitely on Usenet archiving servers such as deja.com. Once a message has expired from the news server you sent it to, archiving servers are supposed delete it if the header contains the line X-No-Archive: Yes. This helps protect your privacy somewhat by keeping someone from seeing every message you have ever posted to any newsgroup.

Secret

Although it's not particularly easy, you can insert X-No-Archive: Yes in your news message headers.

STEPS

Adding X-No-Archive: Yes to Your News Headers

Step 1.   While in a news folder, open a New Message window. Click View ➪ All Headers if you haven't already done so.

Step 2.   In the Keywords field, type **World** and press Enter. On the new line, type **X-No-Archive: Yes** (see Figure 29-24).

Step 3.   Finish composing your message and post it without opening it in the Outbox. You might want to post the message on a test newsgroup before you send it to your regular group.

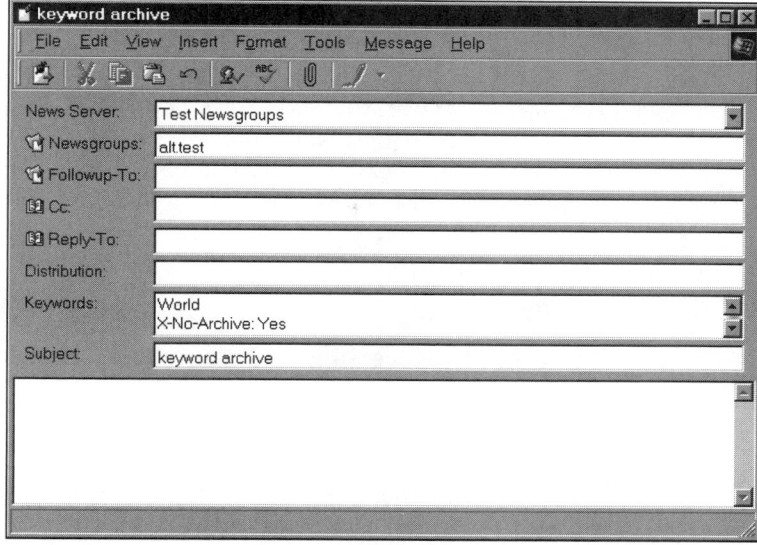

Figure 29-24: The Keywords line in your message header should look like this example.

Step 4. When you see your message in the newsgroup, press Ctrl+F3 to view the full header. You should see the text you added in the header, as shown in Figure 29-25.

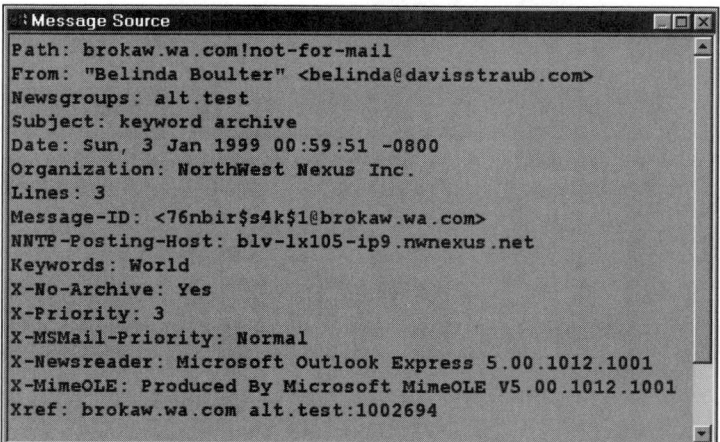

Figure 29-25: The full header of the message shown in Figure 29-24 after posting it to a test newsgroup.

Thanks to Eric Miller at `http://www.okinfoweb.com/moe` for pointing us in the right direction.

You might like to know about another custom header line that's used mostly by newsgroup moderators. (See "Start Your Own Newsgroup" at the end of this chapter for resources on becoming a moderator.) This line adds a stamp of approval to your message header, indicating that as the moderator you have approved it for posting.

STEPS

Adding an Approved Line to Your News Headers

Step 1. While in a news folder, open a New Message window. Choose View ⇨ All Headers if you haven't already done so.

Step 2. In the Keywords line, type **World** and press Enter. On the new line, type **Approved: *username@yourisp.com***, using your own e-mail address.

Step 3. Finish composing your message and post it without opening it in the Outbox. You might want to post the message on a test newsgroup before you send it to your regular group.

Step 4. When you see your message in the newsgroup, press Ctrl+F3 to view the full header. You should see the text you added in the header.

Thanks to the pseudonymous mcwebber for this variation.

Tip

To automatically add the Approved line to the headers of all your newsgroup postings, you can make a simple change to the registry. Open the Registry Editor and navigate to HKEY_CURRENT_USER\Identities\{*your identity number*}\Software\Microsoft\Outlook Express\5.0\News. In the right pane, scroll down to the Moderator dword, double-click it, and change the Value Data field to 1.

Now when you open a New Message window from a mail folder, the message header will include the line Approved: *username@yourisp.com*. The only drawback to doing this is that it adds this line to *all* of your news posts, regardless of newsgroup or server, and it cannot be edited from the New Message window. To make use of this feature, you'll probably need to set up a separate identity for your moderator persona (see "Using Identities" in Chapter 27).

Forwarding a Mail Message to a Newsgroup

You might receive a private e-mail message that you'd like to forward to a newsgroup. (Of course, courtesy dictates that you would first get permission from the author.) Although there's no obvious way to forward a mail message to a newsgroup, it's actually very simple. Just drag the message from the Message pane and drop it onto the name of the newsgroup in the Folders pane or the Folders list. A New Message window opens, addressed to that newsgroup and with the body of the mail message in the body of the new message (no quote marks). You can add a subject, plus comments to indicate the original author before clicking Send.

Troubleshooting News

There's a lot to keeping up with the news. The following sections show you how to deal with a number of situations you might encounter.

Catch Up

If you have just subscribed to a very active newsgroup or if you've just come back from vacation, it can be quite overwhelming to deal with downloading thousands of messages. The same is true if you need to reset a newsgroup when you have already read all the messages. The Catch Up command lets you start fresh by marking everything on the news server as "read," including the messages you haven't yet downloaded.

To catch up on a newsgroup, right-click it in the Folders pane or the Folders list, and select Catch Up — or click Edit ⇨ Catch Up while the newsgroup is selected. Now if you synchronize this newsgroup, you'll see something like "0 message(s), 0 unread, 1607 not downloaded" in the status bar. The messages on the server are not downloaded because Outlook Express believes they are already read.

Secret

You might wonder about the difference between Catch Up and Mark All Read. The latter command only affects messages you've already downloaded, not those still waiting on the server.

Keeping Newsgroup Messages

Only a few of the many newsgroup messages are worth keeping around for any length of time. If you have Tools ⇨ Options ⇨ Maintenance ⇨ "Delete news messages [   ] days after being downloaded" or "Delete read message bodies in newsgroups" marked, then your newsgroup messages are going to go away when automatic background compaction occurs, or when you click the Clean Up Now button on this same Maintenance tab. This tab also lets you control compaction by setting the amount of wasted space that will automatically trigger it.

There is no way to mark individual messages within the newsgroups as keepers. If you want to preserve them for a while, you are going to have to move them to a folder. Drag and drop works great for this. You can also place the Copy To button on your news toolbar to facilitate moving newsgroup messages.

No Need to Keep Messages Forever

After you have been reading a newsgroup for a while, its folder can get pretty big. Because no hard disk is infinitely large, and most messages have only ephemeral value at best, you'll want to limit their stay on your system. To do so, choose Tools ➪ Options and click the Maintenance tab (see Figure 29-26).

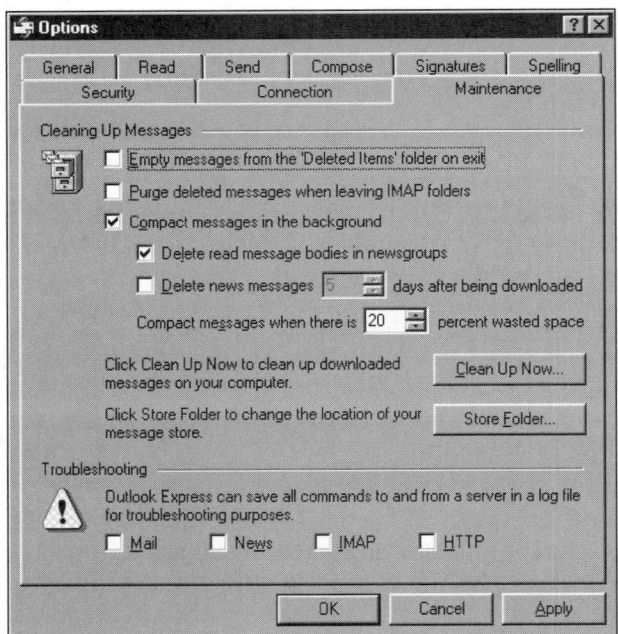

Figure 29-26: The Maintenance tab lets you clean up all your newsgroups.

If you work with very large newsgroups and are especially concerned about disk space, you might want to set "Delete news messages [ ] days after being downloaded" to three days or less instead of the default five days. Remember that this only deletes the message bodies from your computer — message headers are removed as part of the synchronization process, when those messages are no longer available on the newsgroup server (the length of time varies with the newsgroup). To get rid of old messages even faster, you can mark "Delete read message bodies in newsgroups." If you do this, be sure to save messages you might want to see again in a separate folder.

In addition, you can reduce the setting for "Compact messages when there is [   ] percent wasted space" from the default 20 percent to 10 percent. Compaction occurs automatically in the background unless you clear the "Compact messages in the background" checkbox. See "Background Compaction" in Chapter 27 for more on how this works.

For more newsgroup maintenance options, click Clean Up Now. This takes you to the Local File Clean Up dialog box discussed in the next section.

If you haven't been on a newsgroup for a while, you may see lines through many of your headers (see Figure 29-27). These messages have been removed from the newsgroup server, but their headers are still on your computer. These headers will be removed from your computer automatically the next time you open or synchronize the newsgroup.

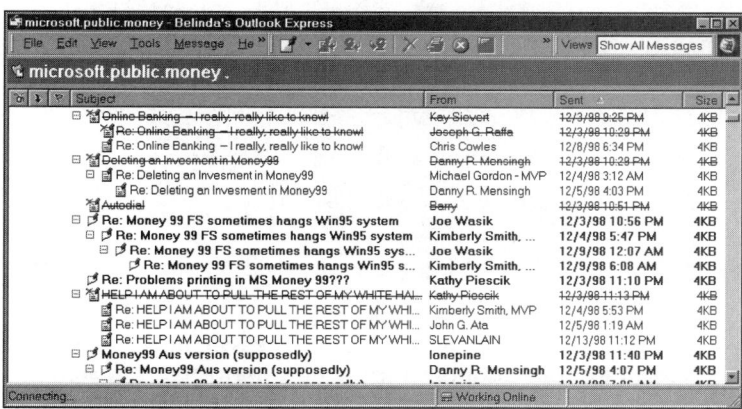

Figure 29-27: If a header has a red X and a line through it, its message is no longer on the newsgroup server.

Tidying Up

Right-click a newsgroup in the Folders pane or the Folders list, click Properties, and then click the Local File tab, shown in Figure 29-28. This is the place for tidying up that particular newsgroup folder. (You can reach a similar dialog box by choosing Tools ⇨ Options, clicking the Maintenance tab, and clicking Clean Up Now. In the Local File Clean Up dialog box, you can select individual newsgroups or an entire news server for cleanup.)

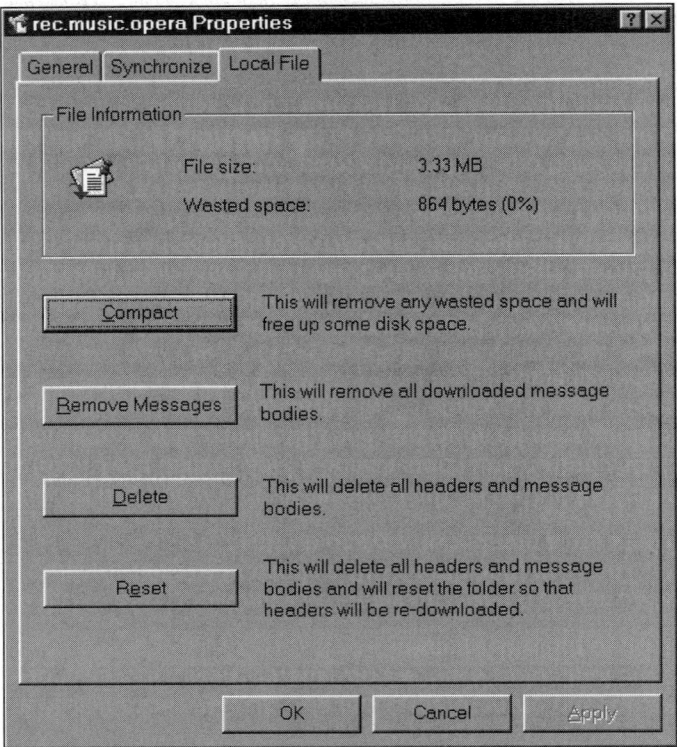

Figure 29-28: The Local File tab is part of the properties of a specific newsgroup.

If you have plenty of room on your hard disk, you may never need to use the Compact button. Outlook Express now performs compaction in the background while you are reading your mail or doing other things, so you really don't need to manually compact your newsgroups at regular intervals. See "Background Compaction" in Chapter 27 for more about this.

If you find that you're short on disk space, one way to regain it is to use the Remove Messages button. Outlook Express keeps the message headers, but deletes all the message bodies you have downloaded for that newsgroup. Keep in mind that most news servers delete messages after a certain amount of time, so you may not be able to redownload the message bodies later if you decide you need them after all. For messages you really want to save, it's best to save them in a separate folder.

The Delete button removes not only the message bodies, but their headers as well. However, the index for this newsgroup will still remember what has been downloaded and what hasn't, so you will not be able to retrieve deleted messages later even though they might still be on the newsgroup server.

Once you've removed or deleted the messages, you won't see a change in the file size until you click the Compact button. It's no longer necessary to compact everything after unsubscribing from a newsgroup — the disk space will be reclaimed immediately after you unsubscribe.

If you want to both delete the messages *and* reset the index (or to just reset the index after you've deleted messages), click the Reset button. You would most likely want to use this if you had a corrupted file that prevented you from opening this newsgroup. Reset starts everything fresh, as though you had never downloaded any messages from the newsgroup. Of course, it will also remove any record of what you have read, so when you go back to this newsgroup, you will end up downloading lots of messages that you have already seen. You can use Catch Up after resetting to mark all the messages on the server as read and keep them from being downloaded, or you can download the headers and sort through them manually.

You can't remove or delete individual messages from your newsgroup folder. If you don't want to see them, mark them as read or ignored, and set the view filter to "Hide read or ignored messages."

ROT 13 in the News

Some newsgroup messages come in ROT 13 format. If you find a message that looks scrambled, double-click its header to open a separate message window, and then choose Edit ⇨ Unscramble (ROT13). This command makes messages formatted with ROT 13 readable by rotating the letters and numbers. It rotates the letters by 13 characters and the numbers by 5. For more information, check out http://support.microsoft.com/support/kb/articles/q153/9/31.asp.

Multipart Files

In some newsgroups, you might come across postings that are in fact large files, most likely binary files. These files are often broken into several parts that are identified as such. In order to discover the contents of these files, you need to recombine them and decode them. You can use Outlook Express to do just that.

Holding down your Ctrl key, click each message header that indicates it is a part of the larger file. Next, choose Tools ⇨ Combine and Decode (or right-click the highlighted headers and choose Combine and Decode from the context menu). You will be asked to select the proper order in which to reassemble the individual messages back into the larger file. Once you have moved the message headers up and down to get the proper order, click OK and a new window will open with the decoded file.

You can also use this method to combine several postings into one file and print or save it as a separate file.

Corrupted Newsgroups

A number of symptoms have a similar cause: The file that stores the messages and message headers for a given newsgroup is corrupted. These symptoms include losing newsgroups from the list of newsgroups associated with a given news server, finding all new message headers mistakenly marked as read, or having Outlook Express fail to respond when a newsgroup is highlighted (requiring you to abort with Ctrl+Alt+Delete).

If you can carry this out, the first line of defense is to reset the newsgroup. (This may not be possible if Outlook Express crashes when you highlight the newsgroup.) Right-click any newsgroup with a problem, click Properties to display the Properties dialog box for that newsgroup, and click the Local Files tab. Then click the Reset button.

In a case where the new message headers are marked as read when they are updated, you can try to solve the problem by choosing Tools ⇨ Options, clicking the Read tab, and clearing the checkbox labeled "Mark all messages as read when exiting a newsgroup." Also clear the checkbox labeled "Message is read after being previewed for [ ] second(s)."

If none of these remedies work, you can delete the dbx file (the file that contains the headers and, if downloaded, the messages) for the offending newsgroup. You'll find them in a folder under your news account's name in the \Windows\Application Data\Identities\{youridentitynumber}\ Microsoft\Outlook Express folder.

If you delete an offending newsgroup file (or all of them), when you reconnect to the news server you'll probably want to download all the message headers currently stored on the news server and start over. If things get so bad that you delete everything in the news account's folder, or even everything under the News folder, you'll have to add your news servers again and resubscribe to your newsgroups.

Can't Get News Through the Firewall

If Outlook Express can't access newsgroups on your local area network, the problem could be that your firewall uses the SOCKS proxy, which is not supported by Outlook Express. Luckily, you can use SocksCap to get around it. SocksCap is freeware that intercepts the networking calls from WinSock applications such as Outlook Express, and redirects them through your SOCKS server. You can download SocksCap from http://www.socks.nec.com/sockscap.html.

Thanks to Mike Santovec for this tip.

Use Test Groups for Testing

Sometimes you need to post a message to a newsgroup to test something about the way your news reader is set up. But newsgroup members can become quite irate about test files cluttering up the group — and who can blame them? That's why most news servers carry test newsgroups.

To find a test newsgroup, go to the Synchronization pane for your news server and click the Newsgroups button. In the "Display newsgroups which contain" field at the top of the Newsgroup Subscriptions dialog box, type **test** to search for newsgroups with the word *test* in their names. You should see a list such as the one in Figure 29-29. Subscribe to one of these and post to your heart's content — nobody reads anything but their own posts on these newsgroups.

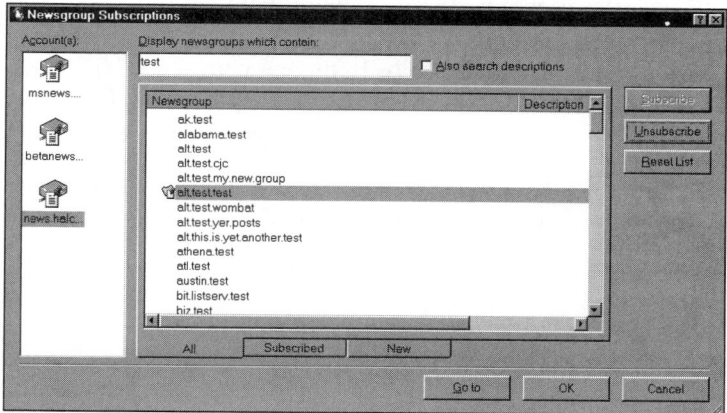

Figure 29-29: Search for a newsgroup with *test* in the name.

Access to Public News Servers

If your Internet service provider does not have a news server, check out these Web sites for listings of other news servers:

Site	Address
deja.com	http://www.deja.com/usenet
eGroups	http:// www.egroups.com /

Windows Me Newsgroups

The following is a list of newsgroups pertaining to Windows. The first newsgroups are hosted on the Microsoft support news server at `msnews.microsoft.com`. The others are Usenet newsgroups, and you should be able to find them on your Internet service provider's local news server.

You might be able to subscribe to some of the Microsoft newsgroups on your local ISP's news server — your service provider decides which newsgroups it will carry. Microsoft does not officially support sending its newsgroups to other ISP's news servers. You can subscribe to the Microsoft newsgroups directly by choosing Tools ➪ Accounts ➪ Add ➪ News and designating `msnews.microsoft.com` as the news server on the account.

Be sure to configure Outlook Express to access a news server before you try to subscribe to that news server's newsgroups.

Undoubtedly, many new newsgroups have become available since this list was developed. Some newsgroups that dealt with Windows 98 will continue to cover Windows Me topics, while other completely original newsgroups will also emerge. When you subscribe to msnews or any other news server, you will be asked if you want to download the list of newsgroups available on that news server. Click Yes. You can search for Windows-specific newsgroups by choosing Tools ➪ Newsgroups, and typing **Win** in the "Display newsgroups which contain" field.

```
http://support.microsoft.com/support/news/default.asp
news:microsoft.public.internet.mschat
news:microsoft.public.internet.netmeeting
news:microsoft.public.internet.personwebserv
news:microsoft.public.internet.explorer.ieak
news:microsoft.public.internet.explorer.java
news:microsoft.public.java.activex
news:microsoft.public.java.cab
news:microsoft.public.news.server.lists
news:microsoft.public.win98.general.discussion
news:microsoft.public.win98.apps
news:microsoft.public.win98.comm.dun
news:microsoft.public.win98.comm.modem
news:microsoft.public.win98.fat32
news:microsoft.public.win98.internet
news:microsoft.public.win98.internet.active_desktop
```

```
news:microsoft.public.win98.internet.browser
news:microsoft.public.win98.internet.netmeeting
news:microsoft.public.win98.internet.outlookexpress
news:microsoft.public.win98.internet.windows_update
news:microsoft.public.win98.multimedia
news:microsoft.public.win98.networking
news:microsoft.public.win98.performance
news:microsoft.public.win98.power_mgmt
news:microsoft.public.win98.printing
news:microsoft.public.win98.setup
news:microsoft.public.win98.shell
news:microsoft.public.win98.webtv
news:comp.os.ms-windows.announce
news:comp.os.ms-windows.networking.windows
news:comp.os.ms-windows.networking.tcp-ip
news:comp.os.ms-windows.apps.misc
news:comp.os.ms-windows.apps.winsock.misc
news:comp.os.ms-windows.apps.winsock.news
news:comp.os.ms-windows.apps.winsock.mail
news:comp.os.ms-windows.apps.comm
news:comp.os.ms-windows.networking.ras
news:comp.os.ms-windows.misc
```

Start Your Own Newsgroup

Mike Santovec pointed out four resources that can help you start a new newsgroup or just answer your questions about how they work:

- "So You Want to Create an Alt Newsgroup" at `http://www.visi.com/~barr/alt-creation-guide.html`
- "All About Newsgroups" at `http://www.learnthenet.com/english/html/26nwsgrp.htm`
- Deja News at `http://www.deja.com`
- Usenet Info Center at `http://sunsite.unc.edu/usenet-i`

Summary

Newsgroups can be overwhelming, but if you manage them well, you can find truly useful information.

▶ The synchronization settings can help you control the flow of messages that you download.

▶ You can create custom views to look at only some of your messages at one time.

▶ You can use a rule or a view to keep track of replies to your posts.

▶ Threads let you follow a newsgroup conversation over time. You can save a whole thread together to preserve its order.

▶ You can use a line in your message headers to specify the reply path, and add a custom line requesting that your message not be archived.

▶ The Maintenance tab of the Options dialog box and the Local File tab of the Properties dialog box for a newsgroup contain important features for controlling the size of your newsgroup folders.

▶ We show you how to make Outlook Express a lot easier to use and more powerful by making a few quick changes to its configuration.

▶ You'll find out where to turn to on the Web for additional help using these programs.

▶ You can create fancy signatures and your own stationery using the built-in HTML capability in Outlook Express.

▶ You can fix corrupted Outlook Express folders.

▶ We tell you where Microsoft and others are providing newsgroup support for their products.

Chapter 30

Rules for Mail and News

In This Chapter

Outlook Express lets you set up rules for both incoming mail and newsgroup messages. We show you how to make them work to your advantage.

▶ Get your rules in the right order so they'll work properly

▶ Cut down on unwanted mail messages

▶ Set up automatic e-mail replies

▶ Sort your Sent Items folder

▶ Back up your rules

Make Up Your Own Rules

You can create your own rules for handling messages in Outlook Express. When you do, Outlook Express will apply those rules whenever you receive new messages.

Setting Up Message Rules

The user interface for editing mail message rules is now simpler and more explicit, compared with previous versions of Outlook Express, and you now have a similar dialog box for creating news message rules. If you have set up Inbox Assistant rules in an earlier version of Outlook Express, they will be preserved as mail rules and displayed in the Mail Rules tab of the Message Rules dialog box (Tools ➪ Message Rules ➪ Mail), as shown in Figure 30-1.

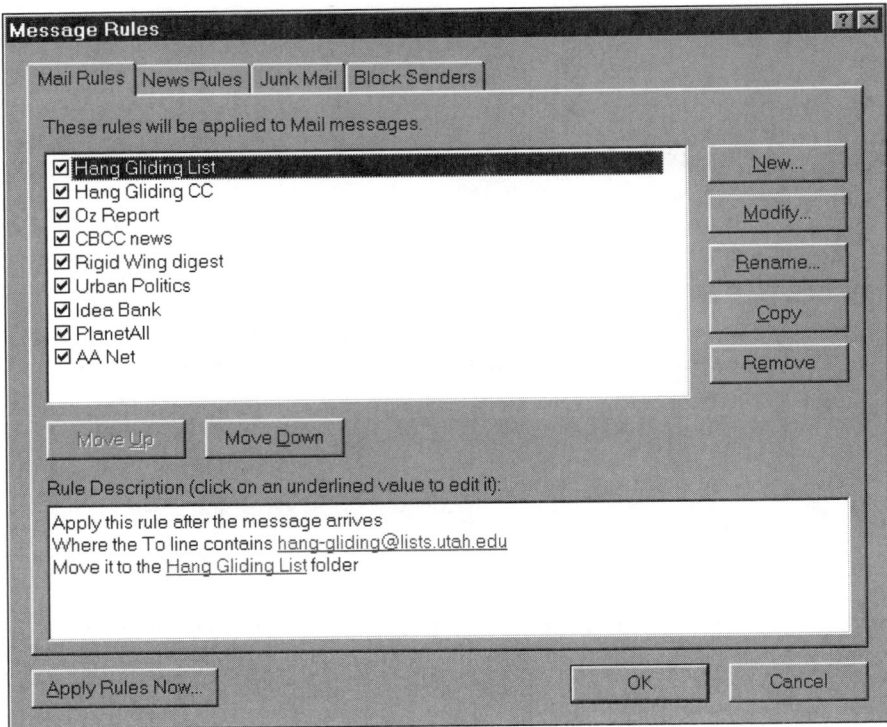

Figure 30-1: The Mail Rules tab of the Message Rules dialog box

To define a new rule that applies to incoming mail messages, use these steps:

STEPS

Designing a New Mail Rule

Step 1. In Outlook Express, choose Tools ⇨ Message Rules ⇨ Mail. The Mail Rules tab of the Message Rules dialog box appears. Click the New button to open the New Mail Rule dialog box, shown in Figure 30-2.

Step 2. In the Conditions area, select one or more conditions that will cause this rule to be applied to a message. For example, mark "Where the To line contains people" if this rule is based on the contents of the To line. Don't worry yet about what the actual content will be (you'll specify it in step 4). As you select conditions, they will appear in the Rule Description area.

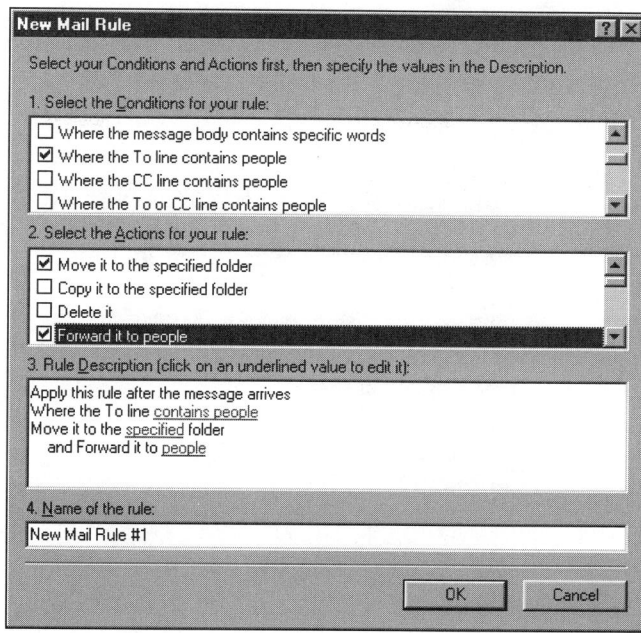

Figure 30-2: The New Mail Rule dialog box gives you a step-by-step approach to setting up or changing message rules.

Step 3. In the Actions area, mark one or more actions that will be applied to messages that meet the conditions of this rule. For example, you might want the message moved to a specific Outlook Express folder, or forwarded to a different address. You can mark more than one action here — both "Move it to the specified folder" and "Forward it to people," for example.

Step 4. In the Rule Description area, you define the specifics. Click each piece of highlighted text to define what it will mean. For example, click the word *people* to enter one or more e-mail addresses in the Select People dialog box, as shown in Figure 30-3. For a folder, click the word *specified* and you'll see a Move dialog box with a folder tree. Click the phrase *contains specific words* to list one or more keywords in the Type Specific Words dialog box.

Step 5. The Select People dialog box and the Type Specific Words dialog box contain an Options button. Clicking this button displays the Rule Condition Options dialog box, in which you can further refine your selection (see Figure 30-4). You can change your condition in two important ways. The first pair of option buttons lets you select by *exclusion* rather than by *inclusion* — in other words, you can set the rule to act on all messages that do *not* contain the keywords or addresses you have indicated. (The default is inclusion.)

Continued

Designing a New Mail Rule *(continued)*

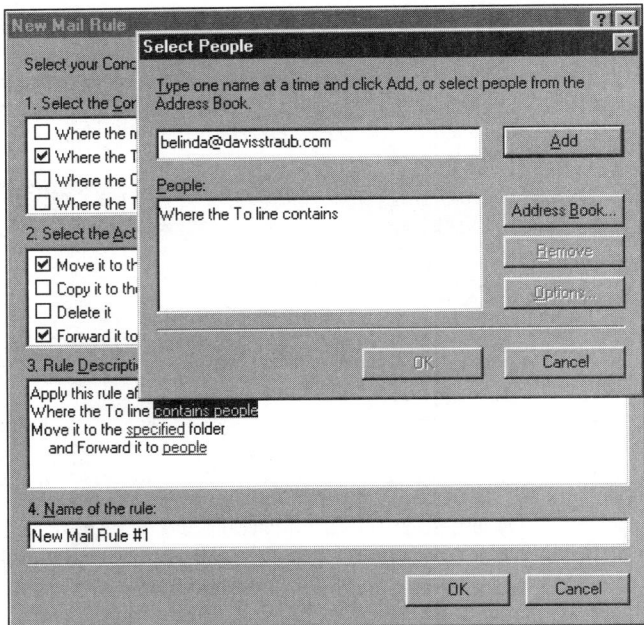

Figure 30-3: Type an address in the Select People dialog box, then click Add. Or, use the Address Book button to copy names or a group from the address book.

The second pair of option buttons (active if you have entered more than one address or keyword) lets you change the OR operator to AND—so that a message must contain all of the keywords or addresses you have indicated in order for the condition to be met. (The default is OR.)

Any changes you make in the Rule Condition Options dialog box will affect only that one condition. You don't need to bother with the Options button if you want to use the default settings.

Step 6. If you selected more than one condition in step 2, a highlighted *and* will connect each condition in the Rule Description area. Click it, and the And/Or dialog box appears, giving you a choice between having messages match *all* of the criteria (AND) or *any* of the criteria (OR).

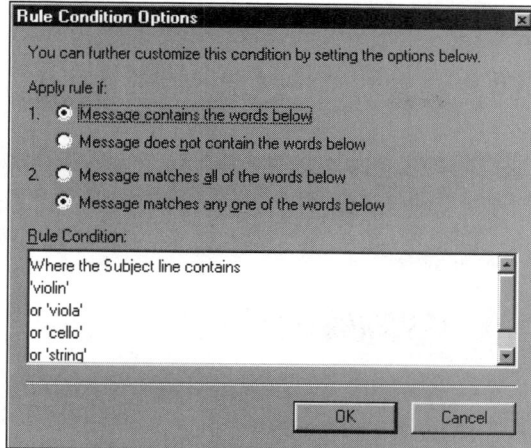

Figure 30-4: You can use the Rule Condition Options dialog box to change the way your condition will work.

If you don't set up a definition for each highlighted word in the Rule Description area, you will see a warning and the undefined phrases will be highlighted in red.

Step 7. Enter a descriptive name for your rule in the Name field at the bottom of the New Mail Rule dialog box. When you are done defining your rule, click OK. Your new rule appears in the Mail Rules tab. Highlight it and use the Move Up and Move Down buttons to put it in the correct spot. (The reasons why rule order matters are explained immediately after these steps and later in this chapter.)

Step 8. If you have messages in your Inbox and you want to apply your new rule to them, click the Apply Now button to open the Apply Mail Rules Now dialog box (see Figure 30-5). Select your new rule and click the Apply Now button, wait for the filter to work, and then click Close. Click OK.

You can also use the Apply Mail Rules Now dialog box to apply a rule to a folder other than the Inbox. (In fact, this is the only way you can apply a rule to a folder other than the Inbox.) The settings you apply here are used on a one-time only basis, and do not become part of the rule definition. See "Sorting Your Sent Messages" later in this chapter for another way to use this feature.

Continued

STEPS

Designing a New Mail Rule *(continued)*

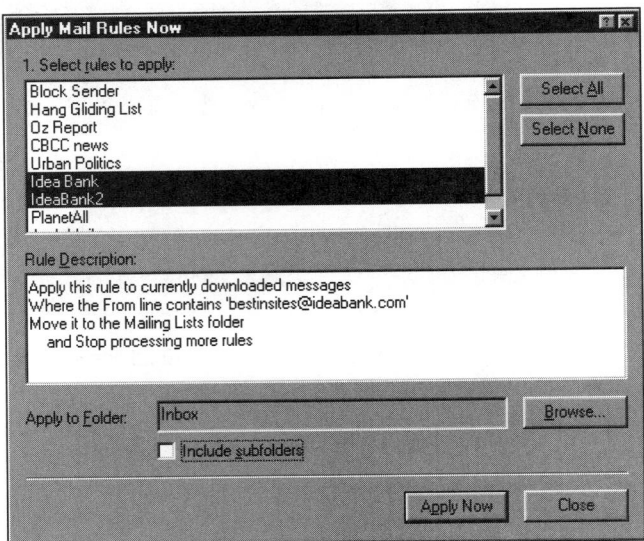

Figure 30-5: The Apply Mail Rules Now dialog box

Outlook Express carries out message rules in the sequence they are listed in the Message Rules dialog box. Giving each of your rules a meaningful name helps you keep them in the correct order. See "It's All in the Order" later in this chapter for more on why this is important.

Tip

You can temporarily disable a rule without deleting it by clearing it in the Message Rules dialog box. Then mark it when you want to enable it again. This can be especially helpful in troubleshooting, when you think one rule might be affecting the rules below it. And it's essential for some rules — for example, the ones we discuss in "Sorting Your Sent Messages" later in this chapter.

To set up rules that apply to newsgroups, click Tools ⇨ Message Rules ⇨ News. The news rules work in the same way as the mail rules, but you choose from a slightly different set of conditions and actions. You might want to set up a news rule to flag messages from a certain newsgroup member, as shown in Figure 30-6.

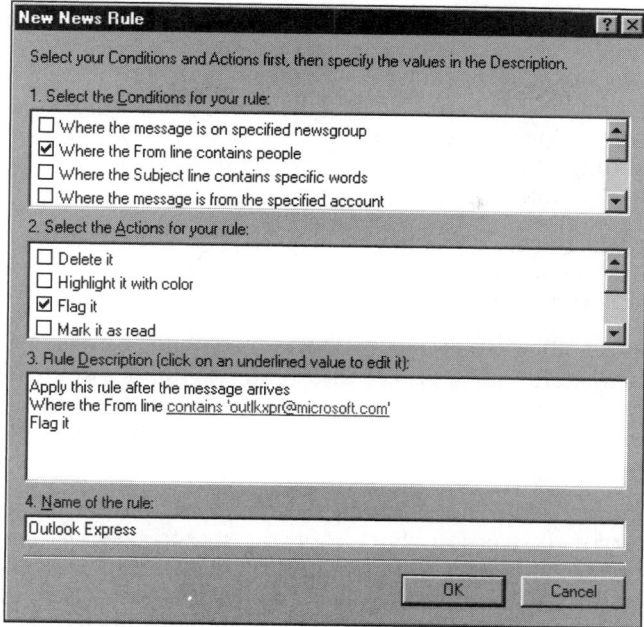

Figure 30-6: A sample news rule that will flag newsgroup messages from a specific address

Play by the Rules

If you highlight a rule in the Mail Rules (or News Rules) tab of the Message Rules dialog box, you'll see its description in the Rule Description area. To change one of the values specified in the rule, click the value in this area and change it in the dialog box that appears. To change a condition or action for a rule, double-click the rule to open the Edit Mail Rule (or Edit News Rule) dialog box.

Read through the list in the Conditions area to make sure you select the most accurate one for your rule. For example, to capture messages where an address is contained in *either* the To line *or* the CC line (a common occurrence), mark "Where the To or CC line contains people." That way, you don't have to make one rule for the To line and another rule for the CC line.

Notice also that you can select "Where the message body contains specific words." This could be much more powerful than depending on messages to have particular keywords in their subject lines. On the other hand, you will be more likely to catch unrelated messages.

Secret

You can enter an address book group when setting the values for a rule involving people. Click the highlighted phrase *contains people* to bring up the Select People dialog box, click the Address Book button, double-click your group name, and then click OK. The members of your group will appear in the People list — you don't have to type their addresses individually. You might use this in setting up a rule where the action is to forward certain messages to a number of people at once.

Rule values are not case sensitive. So, if you set up a rule that looks for *Birds* in the subject line or the message body, it will also apply to messages where the subject contains *birds*.

Only the basic ASCII character set will work in defining values. ASCII Extended characters — such as accented letters, graphics characters, and special symbols — cause Outlook Express to skip that rule and go on to the next. (This could have dire consequences if the next rule involves deleting messages.)

Wild card characters are not allowed either, but you don't really need to use them. If you type the word or characters you want to select for, any string containing those characters will meet the conditions. So if you have several e-mail addresses, each containing the string *yourname*, just use *yourname* as the value in the rule description and the rule will apply to messages containing any of your addresses.

If you move a folder that is used by a rule, Outlook Express adjusts the rule so that your messages will still be sent to that folder. This will happen even if you move the folder to the Deleted Items folder. If you permanently delete the folder, the rule will be disabled and marked with a big red X in the Message Rules dialog box.

It's All in the Order

Outlook Express carries out rules in the order in which they are displayed in the Message Rules dialog box. Changing the order can often affect the results, so plan carefully and test before you set up a rule that deletes messages you haven't seen.

Once a message has been acted upon by a rule, other rules further down the list can still apply to it. For example, one rule might move a message to a folder based on the person who sent it, while a later rule changes its color (or even deletes it) based on a keyword in the message's Subject line. If you want to prevent this, select the "Stop processing more rules" action as an additional action in the last rule that you want to apply.

Actions within a rule are carried out in the order listed in the Actions area, and you can't change their order. For example, if you mark both "Move it to the specified folder" and "Copy it to the specified folder," the message will be moved out of your Inbox before it can be copied. This makes it difficult to use message rules to distribute messages to more than one user.

Secret

If you define a rule that creates an "endless loop," it will be skipped. For example, if you wanted to forward a file to yourself as a test, that would create an endless loop of forwarding the file again and again every time you receive it. In that case, Outlook Express ignores your rule (and your test appears to fail). If you find your rules aren't working as you expected, this could be a cause.

When you are defining rules, it may be helpful to set up only one or two at a time. This makes it easier to detect problems with individual rules, or with their order, as your mail comes in. Don't set up an action such as "Delete it" or "Delete it from server" until you are sure everything is working properly. Instead, have those items moved to a different subfolder so that you can see what you will be deleting, until you're sure it's really all junk.

Secret

If you are having trouble understanding why a certain rule fails or behaves differently than expected, try setting up a rule just above it with the condition "For all messages," and the action "Move it to a specified folder" (a folder you create). You may find that the real trouble is a rule further upstream. For example, you may have set up an action to copy messages when you should have moved them, with the unintended consequence that they are still there for the next rule to act on.

Create a Rule from a Message

The easy way to create a new rule with a condition based on the From line is by using a message as an example. This works with both mail and news messages. Simply select the message header and choose Message ⇨ Create Rule from Message. The New Mail Rule (or New News Rule) dialog box appears with the "Where the From line contains" condition set to the address of the person who sent the message. Although you may have different criteria in mind, more often than not this will at least give you a helpful head start. Then follow steps 2 through 8 in the "Setting Up Message Rules" section earlier in this chapter to finish your rule.

Get Rid of Unwanted Mail

Not all e-mail messages are welcome. Many messages could simply be deleted by Outlook Express without cluttering up your Inbox. The following sections show you how.

A Do-it-Yourself Spam Filter

One of the most popular uses for message rules is to filter out unsolicited mail. Because new spam techniques are being invented every day, this is never going to be 100-percent effective. But many people have reasonable success using the principle that most of the unsolicited e-mail you receive has something other than your own address in the To or CC line.

Secret

To the delight of many users, the regular message rules now allow for exclusionary searching, which lets you leave the "good" mail in your Inbox where it belongs. You can set the action to send the unwanted mail to a junk mail folder you've created in the Local Folders, where it's easy to delete permanently.

To define such an additional rule, choose Tools ➪ Message Rules, and click New. In the Conditions area of the New Mail Rule dialog box, mark "Where the To or CC line contains people." In the Actions area, mark "Move it to the specified folder." In the Description area, click the highlighted phrase *contains people*. In the Select People dialog box, enter your own address (or addresses if you have more than one) and click Add, and then click the Options button. In the Rule Condition Options dialog box, mark the "Message does not contain the people below" option button, and then click OK to return to the Select People dialog box (see Figure 30-7). Click OK. Also in the Description area, click the highlighted word *specified*. In the Move dialog box, highlight the folder where you want to stash junk mail, and click OK. Give your new rule a name, and click OK.

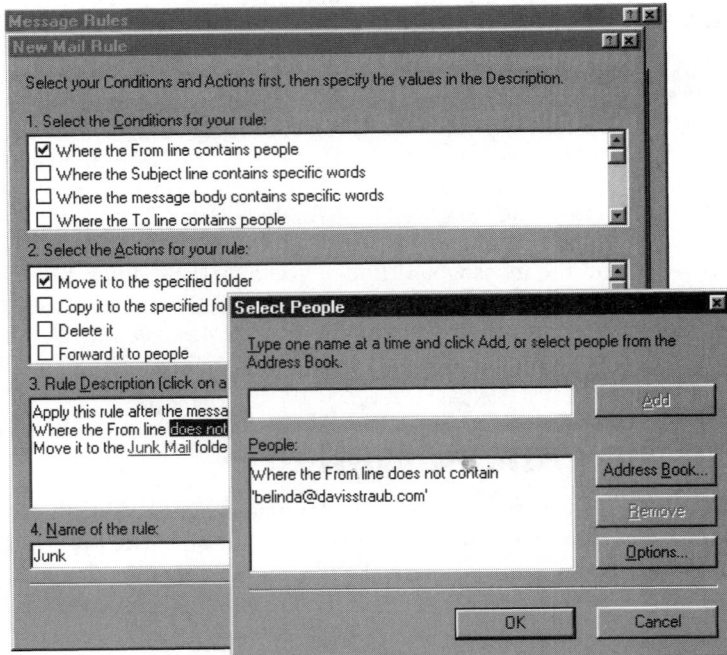

Figure 30-7: A sample rule to separate mail addressed to you from that which is not

This rule should go below any other rules you may have set up. If you subscribe to a mailing list or newsletter that does not place your address in the To or CC field (most do not), you'll need to add a rule above this rule that specifically addresses those messages — otherwise, they'll be treated as junk.

Anti-Spam Software

A rule such as the one described in the previous section can be a helpful step in the battle against unwanted e-mail. Still, if you get a lot of the stuff, you may want to take a more active approach to the problem.

SpamEater (Standard and Pro versions), from High Mountain Software, checks your e-mail on your POP3 server and determines if it is coming from a known spammer. You can have it just check for spam or check and eat the spam, as shown in Figure 30-8. You can also create a list of acceptable e-mail addresses. Only messages addressed to these addresses will be allowed through. SpamEater's database of 5,000 known spammers is upgradable from the program's menu bar.

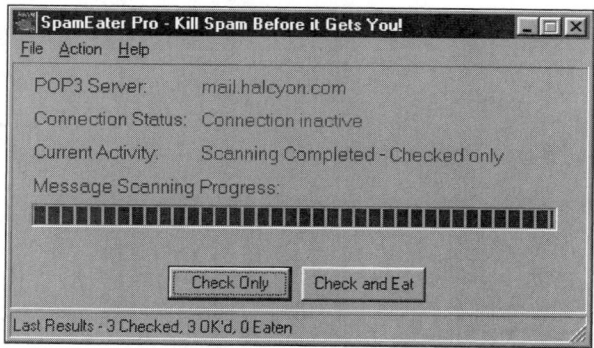

Figure 30-8: SpamEater Pro's status bar tells you how many messages it's scanned and eaten.

Because it can take a while to scan your e-mail headers on the server, you may want to have SpamEater run in the background and then call Outlook Express to get the uneaten mail. Unfortunately, SpamEater doesn't call your DUN and dial in to your Internet service provider (ISP).

This is a thoroughly professional package. The Standard version is freeware and is only missing a few of the nicer features of the Pro version. We are quite impressed with the shareware/freeware products by High Mountain Software. We also discuss their iSpeed software in "Test Your Download Rate" in Chapter 44. You can find more details about SpamEater and download it at http://www.hms.com/default.asp.

Your ISP may have installed filters that do essentially what SpamEater Pro does. Northwest Nexus, an ISP we use in Seattle, has installed anti-spam filters, and we rarely receive any. If your service provider isn't providing this service, perhaps they should.

Blocking Senders

You don't have to set up a rule just to avoid mail from a specific address. Instead, you can use the Blocked Senders tab of the Message Rules dialog box, shown in Figure 30-9. The Blocked Senders tab works on both mail and news, so if someone from a newsgroup starts sending you abusive personal mail, you can more or less avoid seeing any of it.

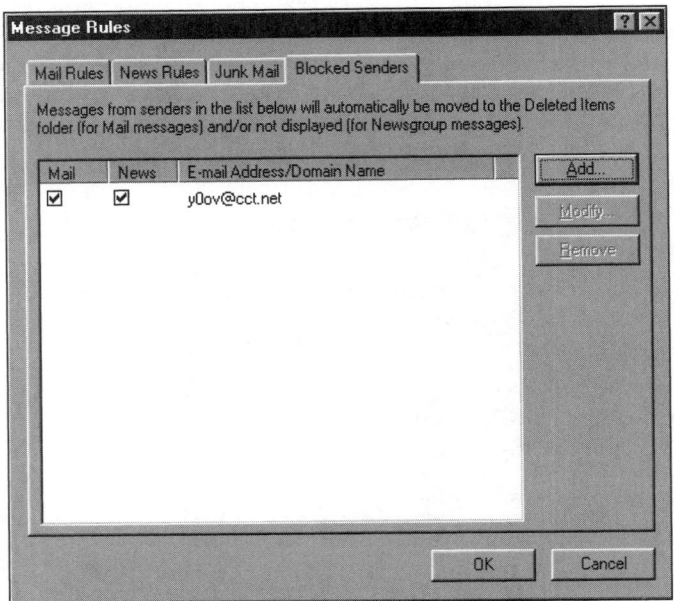

Figure 30-9: To add a sender's address, click the Add button. At least one of the checkboxes must be marked for an address to remain on the list.

You still can't avoid downloading mail messages or news headers from these addresses. But the mail messages will be moved automatically to your Deleted Items folder, and news messages will be marked as read. To completely avoid seeing blocked mail messages, you should mark "Empty messages from the 'Deleted Items' folder on exit" in the Maintenance tab of the Tools ⇨ Options dialog box. To avoid seeing headers for blocked news messages, set your current view to "Hide read or ignored messages." If you're having a real problem with mail, you might prefer to use a mail rule with the action "Delete it from server" to delete messages from that address. You can't delete a message from a news server, however — you can only tell Outlook Express to ignore it.

Mail Filtering Strategies

Of course, there are many different ways to handle e-mail messages. Developing an effective filtering strategy will enable you to more effectively deal with varying situations.

Big Messages

In addition to filtering messages based on their To, From, or Subject lines, you can also restrict them by size. That way you won't get stuck spending 15 minutes downloading some misguided person's 750K `jpeg` file — just mark the condition "Where the message size is more than size" and the action "Do not download it from the server." Of course, you might miss some cute pictures of your sister's new baby that way — and there's no way in Outlook Express to download just the message headers so you can see who sent the messages.

If you frequently receive large files and really want to know what they are before downloading them, you might want to try something like Magic Mail Monitor. This small, fast freeware program sits in your system tray, checks for incoming mail, and lets you view message headers and even delete messages without downloading their bodies. It has lots of other convenient features, too. Check out the Magic Web site for more details and to download the software: `http://www.geocities.com/SiliconValley/Vista/2576/ magic.html`. A similar (though much larger) freeware product is POP3 Scan Mailbox, available from `http://www.netcomuk.co.uk/~kempston/smb`.

Mailing Lists

Secret

Subscribing to a mailing list can be a great way to keep up with the news on a particular topic. But popular mailing lists can generate dozens of messages a day (or more!), making it hard to find the more urgent messages in your Inbox. You can't always tell from the message header that a message is from a mailing list. While some lists are available in digest format, this isn't true for all — and digests can be hard to browse. As an alternative, you can easily set up a message rule using Message ⇨ Create Rule from Message that will put messages from the mailing list's server into a separate Outlook Express folder. Make sure that you set your criteria to use the line where the server's address appears — it may be the To line, as shown in Figure 30-10, but this is not always the case.

Setting Up Automatic Reply Rules

You can set up a rule to automatically reply to messages that meet certain criteria. For example, if people send you messages with a certain subject or send messages to a certain address, you can send them an automatic prewritten message or file in response. This is a great way to distribute a Frequently Asked Questions document, a current price list, or your résumé.

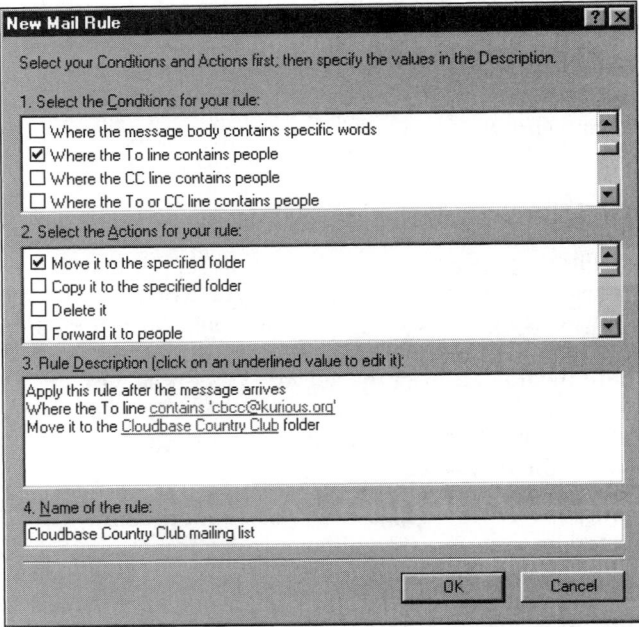

Figure 30-10: An example of a rule that sends messages from a mailing list to their own folder

STEPS

Setting Up an Automatic Reply Rule

Step 1. In Outlook Express, choose Tools ⇨ Message Rules ⇨ Mail. The Mail Rules tab of the Message Rules dialog box appears. Click the New button to open the New Mail Rule dialog box.

Step 2. In the Conditions area, mark "Where the Subject line contains specific words."

Step 3. In the Actions area, mark both "Reply with message," and "Move it to the specified folder" (or mark "Delete it" if you don't want to keep the incoming messages).

Step 4. In the Rule Description area, click the underlined text *contains specific words*. In the Type Specific Words dialog box that appears, type the text that people should put in the subject line of their messages in order to receive your reply, as shown in Figure 30-11. It doesn't matter if you use capital letters or not. Click Add, and then click OK.

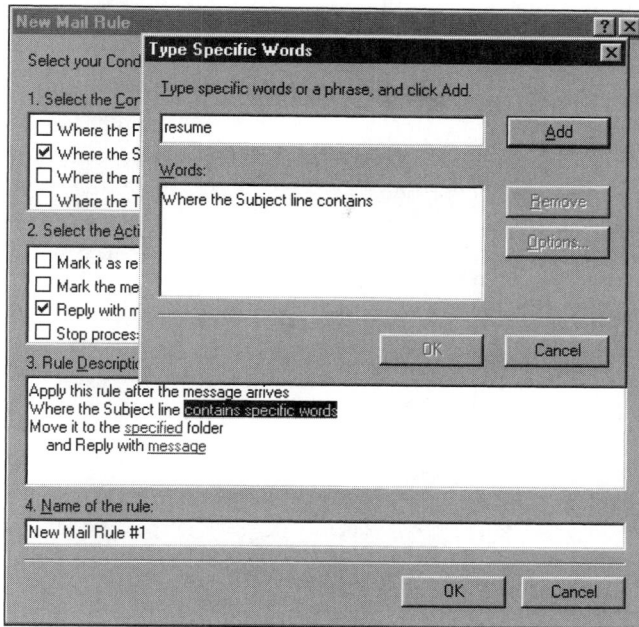

Figure 30-11: In the Rule Description area of the New Mail Rule dialog box, click the underlined words to define them.

Step 5. In the same area, click the underlined word *specified*. If you did not mark the action "Move it to the specified folder" in step 3, this text won't appear. If that's the case, go on to step 6. In the Move dialog box that appears, select the mail folder that will be the parent of your new folder, and click New Folder. In the New Folder dialog box, type a name for the mail folder — for example, **Resume Requests**. Click OK, and then click OK again to close the Move dialog box.

Step 6. Also in the Rule Description area, click the underlined word *message*. The Open dialog box appears to let you browse to the file that you want people to receive as your reply. Double-click to select the file you want to use, as shown in Figure 30-12. You can send news (nws), mail (eml), HTML (htm), or ASCII text (txt) files. If you want the file to appear in the body of the reply, choose txt or htm. If you want it to appear as an attachment, choose nws or eml. Select your file, and click Open.

Continued

STEPS

Setting Up an Automatic Reply Rule *(continued)*

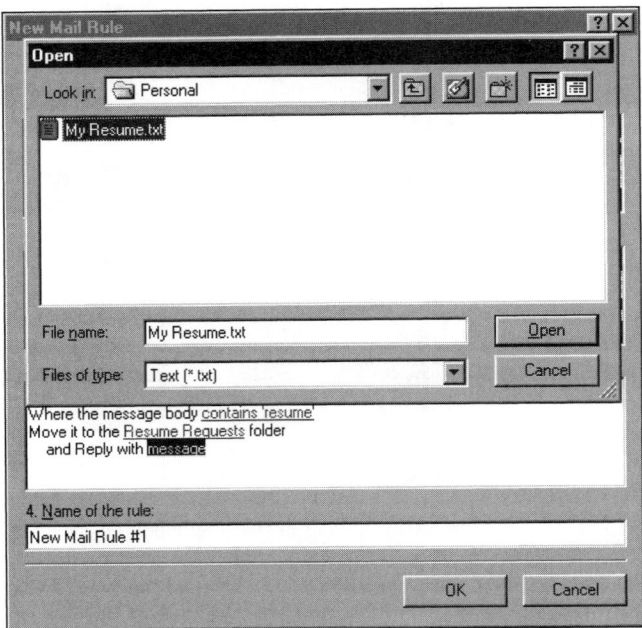

Figure 30-12: You can browse to select the file you want to use as your automatic response.

Step 7. Type a name for your rule in the Name field. When you are finished defining your rule, click OK.

If you have forgotten to define any values in steps 4, 5, and 6, the New Mail Rule dialog box stays open and Outlook Express displays a message box telling you that some information is missing or incorrect and asking you to correct the highlighted items. Click OK. A similar message appears at the top of the Rule Description area, and the problem is highlighted in red. When you've entered the information, click OK again, and you'll be back at the Message Rules dialog box.

Step 8. Your new rule appears in the Mail Rules tab. Highlight it and use the Move Up and Move Down buttons to put it in the correct spot in the list. You will probably want to put your autoreply rules at or near the top of the list, where the other rules can't affect them.

Step 9. If you have messages in your Inbox and you want to apply your new rule to them, click the Apply Now button. In the Apply Mail Rules Now dialog box, select your new rule and click the Apply Now button, and then click Close. Click OK.

Now when a message comes in with the word you have specified in its Subject line, a reply message will be created automatically and sent to your Outbox, where it will wait for the Send and Receive command to be issued.

If you have set Outlook Express to save copies of your sent messages, your automatic replies will also be saved. There is no automatic way to filter *outgoing* mail, so your autoreplies will be mixed in with your other replies in the Sent Items folder (see the next section for a nonautomatic solution). If you don't want to save *any* replies, automatic or otherwise, choose Tools ⇨ Options, click the Send tab, and clear "Save copy of sent messages in the 'Sent Items' folder." Any other options you have set in the Send tab, such as the mail sending format or including the original message with a reply, will also apply to your automatic responses.

You may find that after people receive your automatic response, they reply to it without changing the Subject line in their message. For example, you might get messages with the subject *Re: Resume* from people who received your résumé. You don't want these messages (job offers?) to get caught by your autoreply rule, because the senders already received your résumé once. But Outlook Express doesn't offer an obvious way to limit a condition to an exact match. You must set up a separate rule that goes before your autoreply rule to move these replies to a different folder. You might try setting the condition with a colon before the phrase (for example, **: Resume**) because replies in any language will use a colon. Thanks to Tom Koch for pointing out this solution.

Secret

Another way to use the automatic reply is to send a kind of "receipt" to people who send you mail. Outlook Express doesn't have the capability to request confirmation that a message has been received—and such a confirmation wouldn't really guarantee that anyone had read it, only downloaded it. However, if you correspond with someone who needs to know you've received a message, even though you're too busy to answer at the moment, you can use the automatic reply to send that person—or everyone—a notice that you've downloaded their messages. If you're one of those people who must cope with hundreds of incoming messages each day, this gives you a way to respond politely and still get your regular work done.

Secret

You might also think of using an automatic reply to let people know when you're on vacation. Remember, though, that you must be able to download your e-mail for this to work. This requires that you leave your computer running, and that you set up a schedule for automatically sending and receiving mail. If your circumstances allow this, it might be worth a try. See "Scheduling the Mail" in Chapter 27 for details on the scheduling aspect. And remember to disable this rule by clearing it in the Message Rules dialog box when you get back.

Sorting Your Sent Messages

Secret

Outlook Express' message rules feature is designed to only apply to incoming messages, not the ones you send. It would be nice, though, to be able to sort certain messages from your Sent Items folder into their own separate folder, so you could easily see everything you've sent on a particular subject or to a particular person. While you can't do this automatically, you can use message rules to sort messages in your Sent Items folder after the fact. Tom Koch showed us how.

STEPS

Sorting Your Sent Items

Step 1.   Choose Tools ⇨ Message Rules ⇨ Mail. Click the New button to display the New Mail Rule dialog box.

Step 2.   In the Conditions area, set the condition for the messages you want to sort into their own folder. For example, this might be "Where the To line contains people." In addition, be sure to set the condition "Where the From line contains people."

Step 3.   In the Actions area, set the action "Move it to the specified folder."

Step 4.   In the Rule Description area, enter your own address for the From line and one or more addresses for the To line. Click the highlighted *and*, mark "Messages match all of the criteria in the And/Or dialog box," and click OK. Click the highlighted word *specified* to define a folder where these messages will be sent (you can create a new folder if you like), and click OK. Name your rule and click OK. Set up additional rules that will apply to other folders, if you like.

Step 5.   In the Mail Rules tab, click the Apply Now button. In the Apply Mail Rules Now dialog box, click the Select None button, and then select only your new rules (Shift+click to select sequential rules, Ctrl+click to select nonsequential ones). Click the Browse button next to the Apply to Folder field and select your Sent Items folder.

Click OK. Now click the Apply Now button, wait while your messages are sorted, and then click Close.

Step 6. Clear the checkbox for this rule in the Mail Rules tab, and click OK to close the Message Rules dialog box.

Tip

You can only target a folder other than your Inbox if you use Apply Now, so be sure to leave your rule cleared during normal use. Then, when you want to sort your Sent Items, open the Mail Rules tab of the Message Rules dialog box, mark your sorting rule, and repeat steps 5 and 6.

Using News Rules

Newsgroup rules are helpful for gleaning the messages you find relevant from the large mass of messages contained in a large newsgroup. These rules are different from the news viewing filters that we discuss in "Setting the View" in Chapter 29, though they work in similar ways and overlap somewhat in functionality. Here are some examples of ways you might use news rules.

You can define a rule so that messages on a specified newsgroup and posted more than a certain number of days ago are marked as read. Then you can set that newsgroup's synchronization to download All Messages and still only get the newest ones. This could be a very good alternative to getting a batch of 50 or 100 at a time. Instead, you get all of the messages that are one or two days old, and only those messages.

You subscribe to rec.music.opera and are primarily interested in baroque opera. You can set up conditions with keywords in the subject line for your favorite composers, performers, or names of operas (one rule for each). Set the action to highlight these messages with a different color for each composer.

You have posted a question on microsoft.public.money, and you don't want to miss any of the responses. Set a condition with specific words in the Subject line (the Subject line of your message), and set the action to move all those messages (the thread of your subject) to a separate folder for saving.

There are one or two regular contributors to your favorite newsgroup whose postings you especially enjoy. Set up a rule for each one, to flag his or her postings. Then, after you download, you can sort the view by flag to read their postings first.

Secret

If your favorite newsgroup occasionally contains messages on a subject that you never want to see, you can mark messages with that word in the Subject line as read. In this way, you avoid downloading the message headers as well as the bodies.

Backing Up Your Rules

Secret

To back up the rules you have created, open the Registry Editor and navigate to HKEY_CURRENT_USER\ Identities\ {*your identity number*}\ Software\ Microsoft\ Outlook Express\ 5.0\ Rules\. This branch contains sub-branches for Mail, News, and Junk Mail, so you can select the Rules branch itself to export them all or select only one of these folders. Now click Registry ⇨ Export Registry File, navigate to where you would like to save your backup, give it a name (the extension should be reg), and click Save. (You can see the name associated with an identity in the registry by highlighting the number in the left pane and looking under Username in the right pane.)

You can move the reg file to a diskette or another computer if you like. If you should need to restore your rules, close Outlook Express, and then double-click the registry backup file. Now start Outlook Express again; your rules should be restored.

If you use this process to move rules to a different computer that already has rules set up, the two sets of rules will be merged. After you merge two sets of rules, you'll need to adjust the rule order to make sure they still work.

Summary

The Outlook Express rules act as filters to control what you see and download to your computer from your mail and news servers, and what happens to those messages.

▶ It's easy to set up one or more rules using the Message Rules dialog box, or to create a rule from a mail or news message.

▶ You can develop a rule or take advantage of shareware to help minimize unwanted mail messages.

▶ You can set up a rule to send an automatic mail reply to messages that request it.

▶ You can use a rule to sort the contents of your Sent Items folder, but it's not automatic.

▶ News rules operate similarly to mail rules and can be helpful for wading through large newsgroups.

▶ You can back up your rules by exporting a branch from your registry.

Chapter 31

Secure E-mail

In This Chapter

Outlook Express supports certificates and encryption, important tools that can help ensure privacy in e-mail. We show you how to send and receive digitally signed and encrypted messages.

▶ Tell Outlook Express to automatically verify that a digital signature is still valid

▶ Set the level of trust for a certificate or for the organization that issued it

▶ Archive your certificate or move it to a new computer

▶ Enable Outlook Express to read the encrypted messages you send

Using Digital Certificates

Certificates are a digital means of verifying someone's identification. Since virtually all contact via the Internet is done at a distance, certificates provide you with some level of assurance that people are who they say they are.

Outlook Express Security

All the Windows Internet applications that come from Microsoft share the same security settings. You can see this if you choose Tools ➪ Options, click the Connection tab, click the change button, and go to the Security tab. You can also get to these settings by right-clicking the Internet Explorer icon on your Desktop, clicking Properties, and clicking the Security tab.

It's possible for someone to send you an ActiveX control or a Java applet in an e-mail message or over a newsgroup (one that supports this level of content) that could potentially cause some damage to the files on your com-puter. To tailor Outlook Express (and all other Windows Internet applications) to check these controls and warn you if they are not from trusted sources, click the Custom Level button on the Security tab. You can then choose which types of controls to download, which to prompt for before downloading, and which to block.

Now that you have determined the security level for one or more security zones, you can set which zone will be in effect for Outlook Express. To do this, choose Tools ⇨ Options, click the Security tab, and mark the option button for either the "Internet zone" or the "Restricted Sites zone."

Certificates — What's the Point?

Certificates, also called *digital IDs* and *digital signatures*, serve two different but related functions in Outlook Express. First, a certificate gives your correspondents some level of assurance that a message you send is actually from you. Second — and much more importantly — a certificate contains the information required for sending and receiving encrypted messages. This information includes a *public key*, a *private key*, and a *digital signature*. (Public and private keys are discussed further in "Public-Key Encryption" later in this chapter.)

You can always receive messages that are digitally signed. But you can't receive encrypted messages from someone unless that person has a copy of your certificate. Likewise, in order to send an encrypted message, you must first have a copy of your correspondent's certificate.

Certificates are issued by third-party certification authorities such as VeriSign or BelSign, and are also sometimes issued by individuals or companies for internal use. Each certificate is associated with a specific e-mail address. Outlook Express lets you look at the certificate's source information, so you can decide how trustworthy you think it is.

Receiving Digitally Signed Mail

A digitally signed message is indicated by a Red Ribbon icon in the Message pane. Highlight the message header and you will see a button with the Red Ribbon icon in its preview pane header, as shown in Figure 31-1. And after you have opened the message, a red ribbon appears on the message header. Encrypted messages also show a Padlock icon in these locations.

The first time you receive a message with a digital signature, you will see a special help screen in the Preview pane. If VeriSign or another organization recognized by Microsoft issued the sender's certificate, the screen will simply indicate that the message was digitally signed, as shown in Figure 31-2. If you like, mark "Don't show me this Help screen again" before clicking Continue. As soon as you click Continue, the message itself appears in the Preview pane.

If the issuer was a source unknown to Microsoft, or if the certificate has expired or has another problem, you will see a help screen such as the one shown in Figure 31-3. You can still open and read the message by clicking the Open Message button in the help screen. And you can still reply to it once it is open. But you should not reply with sensitive or confidential information until you have resolved the security issues. If you try to send an encrypted reply, you will see an error message such as the one shown in Figure 31-4.

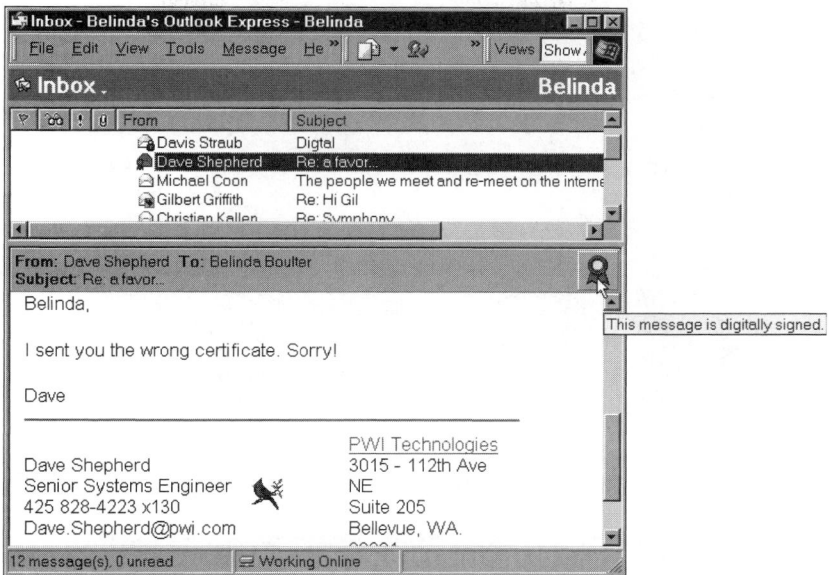

Figure 31-1: The Red Ribbon icon indicates that this message has been digitally signed.

Figure 31-2: This screen indicates the message has been digitally signed with a certificate you haven't seen before.

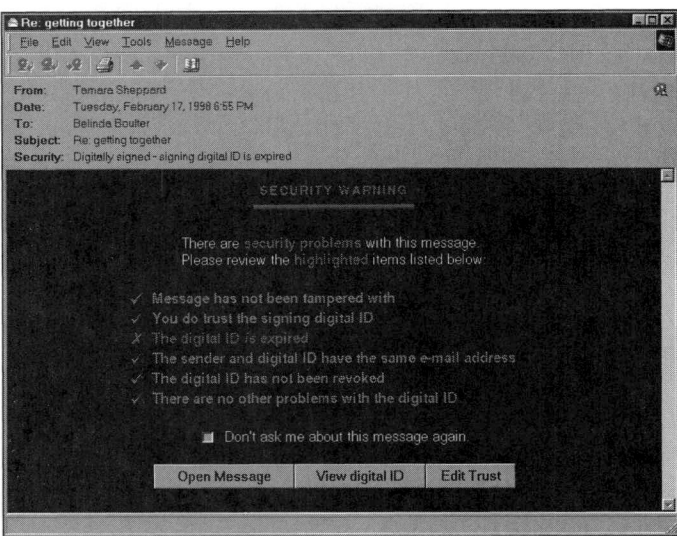

Figure 31-3: The Security Warning screen indicates what the problem might be.

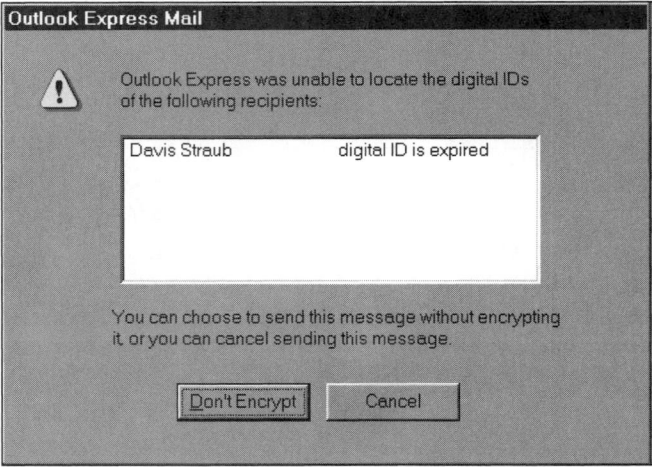

Figure 31-4: If you try to send an encrypted reply to an expired certificate, you'll see this warning.

Setting the Level of Trust

One reason you might see the Security Warning screen is if you haven't set the level of trust. You can tell Outlook Express how much trust you have in a particular certificate. Ordinarily, though, it makes more sense to set the level of trust for the agency or company that issued the certificate, and apply that to the individual certificate.

STEPS

Setting the Level of Trust for a Digital Certificate

Step 1. If you are looking at a Security Warning screen, click the Edit Trust button in that screen. Otherwise, highlight a message signed with this certificate in your Outlook Express Inbox. In the message's preview pane header, click the Red Ribbon icon and choose Edit Trust. This opens the Trust tab of the Signing Digital ID Properties dialog box, shown in Figure 31-5.

You can also edit a certificate's trust level by editing the properties of its owner in your address book. Right-click the sender's name, select Properties in the context menu, click the Digital IDs tab, highlight an ID, and click the Properties button, and then click the Trust tab in the Certificate dialog box. This Trust tab functions the same as the one in the Signing Digital ID Properties dialog box.

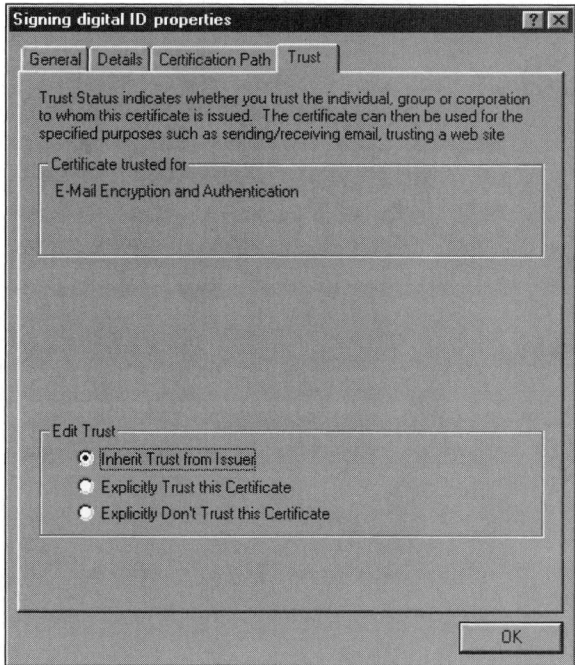

Figure 31-5: The Trust tab of the properties for a sample certificate

Continued

STEPS

Setting the Level of Trust for a Digital Certificate *(continued)*

Step 2. In most cases, you will base your trust for the individual certificate on the organization that issued it (if you don't want to do this, skip to step 5). For example, looking at Figure 31-5, if I believe that a certificate issued by PWI Certificate Authority is valid, then anyone who sends me one of their certificates should be trusted to be who they say they are. To see where the certificate came from, go to the Certification Path tab, shown in Figure 31-6.

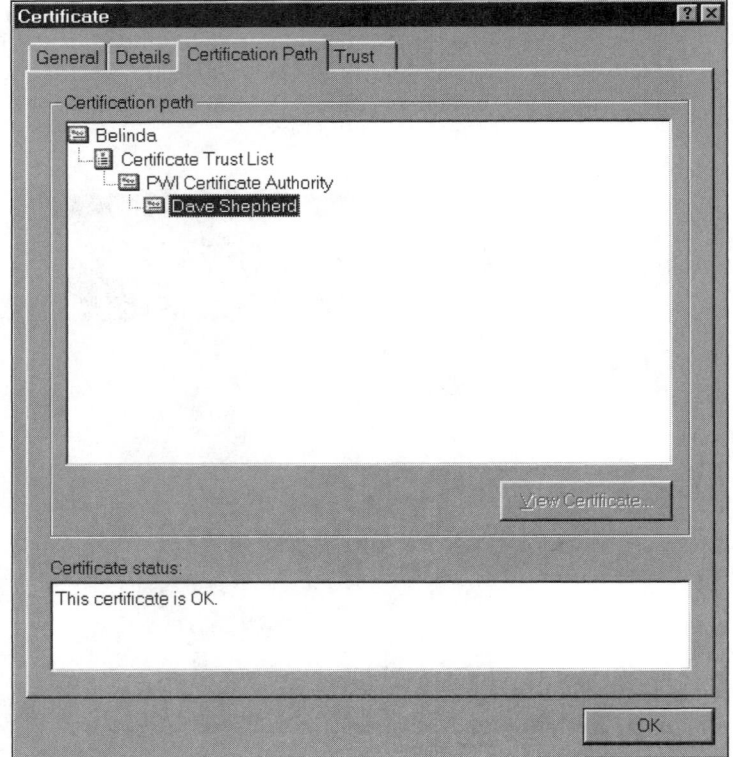

Figure 31-6: The Certification Path tab shows the hierarchy of trust for a specific certificate.

Step 3. If the issuer of the certificate was not VeriSign or another group automatically trusted by Microsoft, you may need to set a level of trust for the issuer before you can pass that trust along to the individual certificate. To do this, highlight the issuer's name in the Certification Path tab and click View Certificate. A new Certificate dialog box opens for the issuing authority. Check the General and Details tabs for information about the issuer, and then click the Trust tab. Highlight the issuer's name in the hierar-chical list, either mark Explicitly Trust this Certificate or Explicitly Don't Trust this Certificate (see Figure 31-7), and click OK.

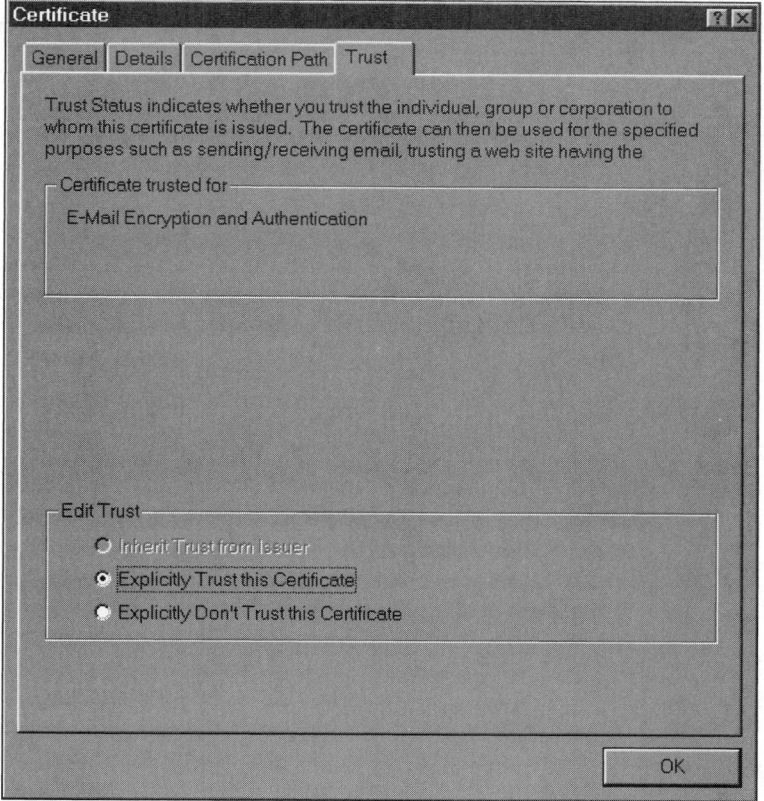

Figure 31-7: The Trust tab for the issuing authority is similar to the one for a certificate, only the first option button is dimmed. (If the issuer is automatically trusted by Microsoft, all of the buttons will be dimmed.)

Continued

Setting the Level of Trust for a Digital Certificate *(continued)*

Step 4. Now go back to the Trust tab for the individual certificate, mark the Inherit Trust from Issuer option button, and click OK twice.

Step 5. If this certificate has no issuer to inherit from, or if for some reason you want to treat this certificate differently from others issued by that organization, you can set its level of trust individually. In that case, skip steps 2 through 4 and mark either Explicitly Trust this Certificate or Explicitly Don't Trust this Certificate on the Trust tab. Your choice will depend on what you know about the certificate and its source — you can use the information on the certificate's General and Details tabs to help decide. After you've marked the Trust tab, click OK, and then click OK again and close the address book if you opened it.

If you mark Explicitly Don't Trust this Certificate, you will not be able to send encrypted e-mail to the certificate's owner, or to the owners of any certificates whose trust is inherited from this one.

Secret

To see and edit a list of issuers that are trusted by default, choose Tools ⇨ Options, and click the Security tab. Click the Digital IDs button to launch the Certificate Manager, and click the Trusted Root Certification Authorities tab (see Figure 31-8). Highlight an authority and click the View button to see information about its certificate. You can remove an authority from this list by highlighting it and clicking Remove (but if you do this, certificates issued by this body will not be trusted).

Saving a Certificate

Outlook Express lets you save a digital ID in your address book along with its owner's address. This is necessary if you want to send encrypted e-mail to the certificate's owner.

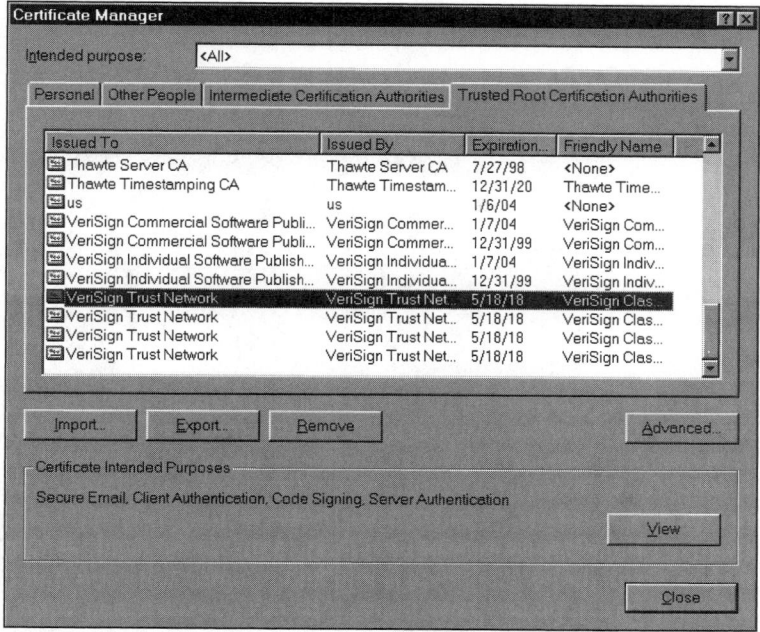

Figure 31-8: The Trusted Root Certification Authorities tab shows the certification authorities that are automatically trusted by Outlook Express.

STEPS

Saving a Digital ID in Your Address Book

Step 1. Highlight the digitally signed message in your Inbox. In the message's preview pane header, click the Red Ribbon icon and choose View Security Properties. Or, highlight the message, choose File ⇨ Properties, and click the Security tab (see Figure 31-9). This tab shows you the security status of this specific message — you will only see it if the message is digitally signed.

Continued

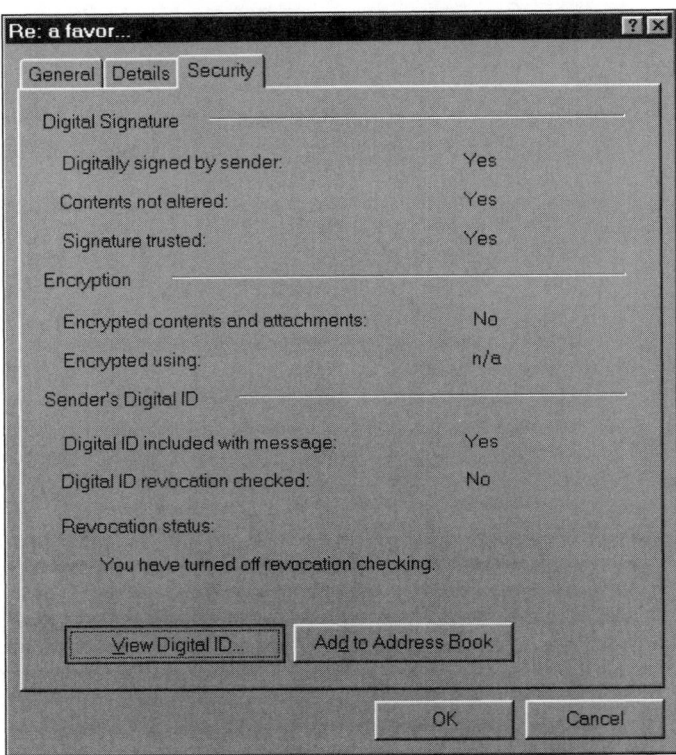

Figure 31-9: The Security tab is part of a digitally signed message's Properties dialog box.

Step 2.   If you want more detailed information about this certificate, click the View Digital ID button to open the Signing Digital ID Properties dialog box, and click the Details tab (see Figure 31-10). Here you can see what organization issued the certificate, along with the certificate's serial number, expiration date, and public key. Click OK when you're finished viewing the information.

Step 3.   In the Security tab of the Properties dialog box for the message (refer back to Figure 31-9), click the Add to Address Book button, and then click OK twice.

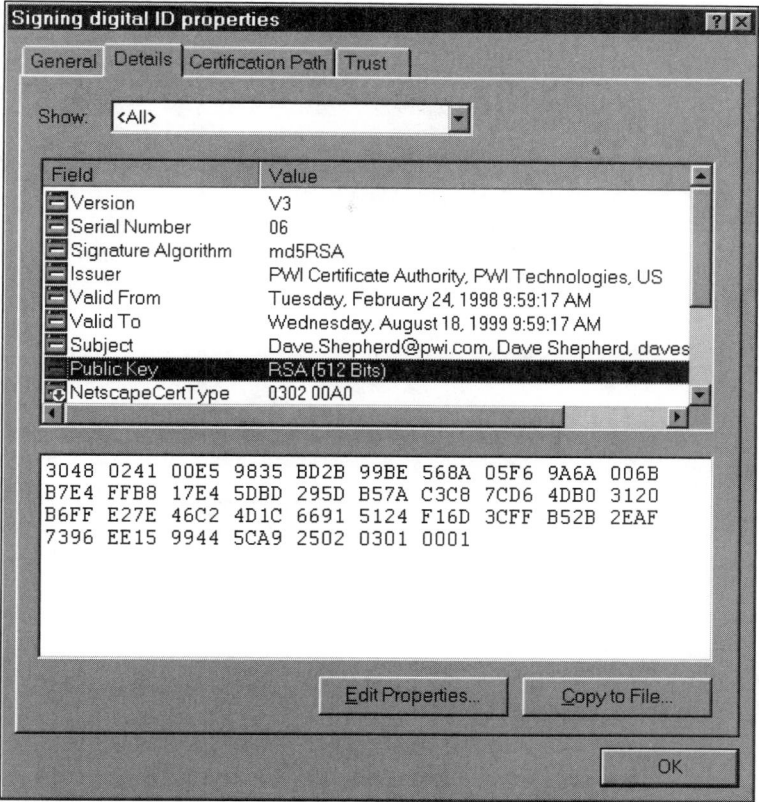

Figure 31-10: The Details tab of the Signing Digital ID Properties dialog box

The next time you receive a message with this person's certificate attached, Outlook Express will recognize it as valid. In addition, you have stored the digital signature and public key you need to send an encrypted message to the certificate's owner.

Address book entries for people with certificates appear with a Red Ribbon icon in the address book and in the Contacts pane. You can view and edit the digital ID for anyone in your address book by right-clicking his or her name in the Address Book window or your Contacts pane, choosing Properties, and going to the Digital IDs tab (see Figure 31-11). Select the ID and click the Properties button to open the Certificate dialog box.

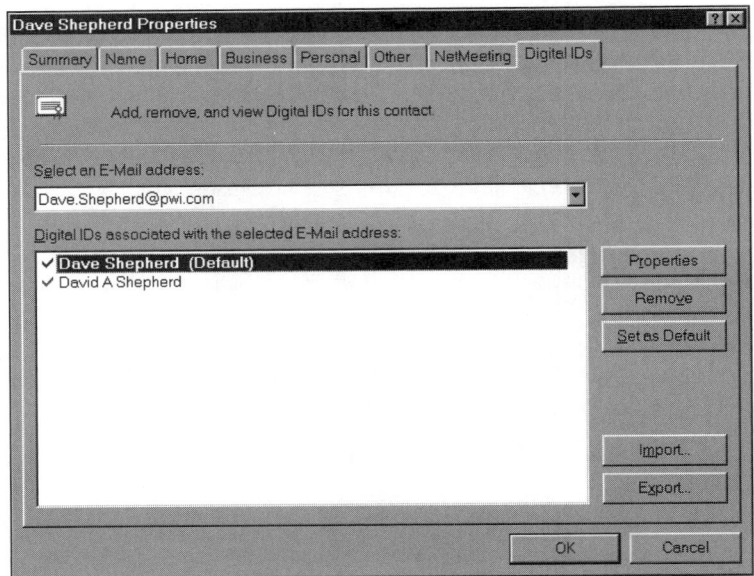

Figure 31-11: To view or edit information about a certificate, select it and click the Properties button. The person in this example has certificates from two different issuers.

Secret

To see and manage a list of all the digital IDs stored in your address book, open the Certificate Manager by clicking Tools ⇨ Options, clicking the Security tab, and clicking the Digital IDs button. Click the Other People tab to see a list of certificates such as the one in Figure 31-12. As you can see, this is a handy place to import, export, and remove certificates (see "Exporting and Importing Certificates" later in this chapter for more on what this means). Use the View button to check the certification path and details for a digital ID.

Tip

It's possible that someone might send you e-mail without digitally signing it, but with a certificate sent as an attached file. The certificate looks like an ordinary file with the extension p7c or cer. To verify the trust level and add the certificate to your Windows Address Book, click the file attachment to open it, and then follow the "Saving a Digital ID in Your Address Book" steps earlier in this section.

Revocation Checking

Certificates contain an expiration date, so Outlook Express knows when a certificate has expired. Still, a person's certificate may be revoked before the expiration date if he or she switches jobs or changes e-mail addresses. How can you verify that a certificate is still good before you send that person a sensitive or encrypted message? Outlook Express can do this for you if you tell it to.

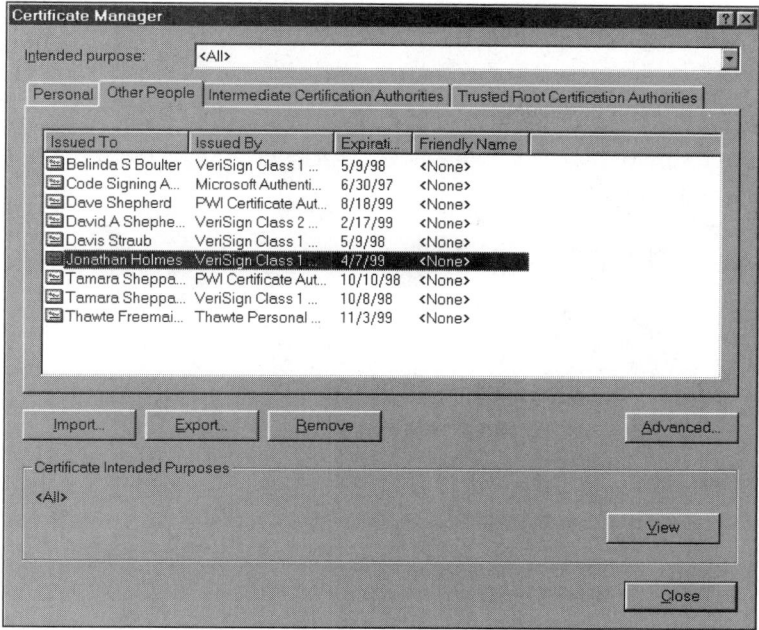

Figure 31-12: The Certificate Manager lets you see a list of all the certificates you have stored, including their expiration dates.

Secret

To enable revocation checking, choose Tools ⇨ Options, click the Security tab, and click Advanced. In the Advanced Security Settings dialog box, mark the "Only when online" option button (see Figure 31-13), and then click OK twice.

Now if you open a digitally signed message while you are online, Outlook Express will automatically send a message to the issuer of the certificate to verify that the certificate is still valid. If you are not online, you can read the message, but its certificate will not be verified.

Getting Your Certificate

To send messages with your own digital signature, you must first register with a certification authority and receive a certificate from them. (The certification authority will most likely charge a fee for this service.) Your digital signature lets other people send encrypted messages to you by sharing your public key — it does not contain any sensitive or private information about you, so you can feel fine about sharing it.

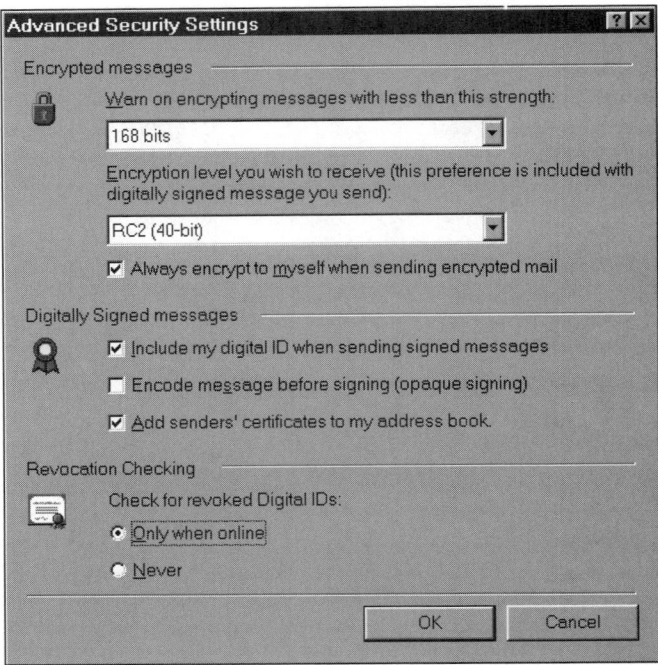

Figure 31-13: Mark the "Only when online" option button to enable revocation checking.

The easiest way to find a certification authority is to choose Tools ⇨ Options in the Outlook Express window, click the Security tab, and click the Get Digital ID button. (You can also get to this button by clicking Tools ⇨ Accounts, highlighting a specific account, clicking the Properties button, and clicking the Security tab.) The Get Digital ID button launches Internet Explorer and takes you to a Microsoft Web site with links to the Web sites of some certification authorities. There you will find detailed information on security levels, pricing, and steps for buying and downloading your certificate. You may also find useful technical information about data encryption and Internet security. Some additional certifying authorities include:

GlobalSign	http://www.belsign.be	(Based in Belgium)
Compusource	http://www.compusource.co.za/id	(Based in South Africa)
UniCert	http://www.baltimore.ie/cert	(Based in Ireland)
BT Trustwise	http://www.trustwise.com	(Based in Great Britain)

Because the process of registering your certificate will vary with the certification authority, we can only provide general information here. At a minimum, you will be asked for your name and e-mail address. These will be permanently associated with this certificate, so make sure they are correct. You will only be able to use this certificate with this e-mail address; if you get a new address or change your name, you will probably have to apply for a new certificate. Depending on the level of security you require for your certificate, you will be asked for more information about yourself, and you may even need to submit to a credit check.

When you are asked to select a cryptography provider, be sure to choose the MS Base Cryptographic Provider v1.0 — otherwise, Outlook Express won't be able to find your private key.

After you register, the certification authority will send you e-mail (confirming that the address you gave is correct) with directions for completing the certificate download. During this process, a private key, which is required for you to be able to read the encrypted messages you receive, will be generated on your computer.

Your private key will be stored in the registry in encrypted form. Windows sets a default security level for access to your private key, as shown in Figure 31-14. To change the security level, click the Set Security Level button, mark the High, Medium, or Low option button (see Figure 31-15), and click Next to continue through the wizard. These security levels have nothing to do with the level of encryption; they are for controlling access to your digital certificate in case someone else might use your computer. If you choose High, you will have to enter a password in order to encrypt a message.

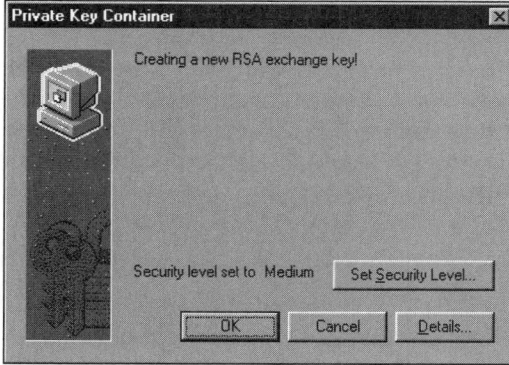

Figure 31-14: To choose a security level other than the default indicated, click the Set Security Level button.

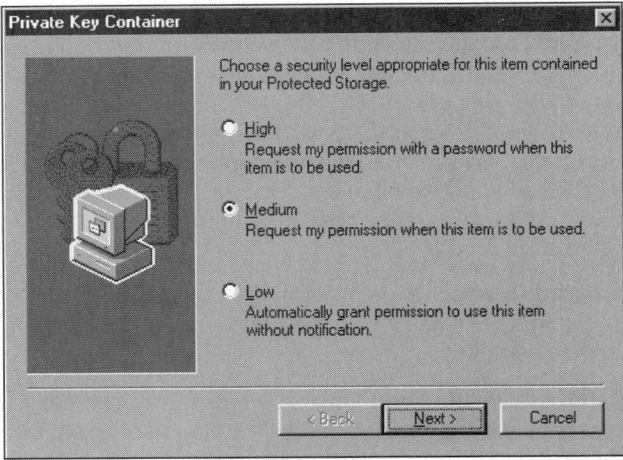

Figure 31-15: Select a level of security for use of your digital ID.

Using Your Certificate

Secret

Once you have registered and installed your digital ID, if you have more than one e-mail account set up in Outlook Express, you must associate your certificate with the appropriate account, as described in these steps. (If you have only one account, there's no need to do this.)

STEPS

Associating Your Digital Certificate with Your E-mail Account

Step 1. In the Outlook Express window, click Tools ⇨ Accounts. Highlight the account that you want to associate with this certificate (the one for the address you gave to the certification authority) and click the Properties button.

Step 2. Click the Security tab and mark the "Use a digital ID when sending secure messages from" checkbox, as shown in Figure 31-16.

Step 3. Click the Digital ID button, highlight the certificate you want to use in the Select Certificate dialog box, and click OK.

Step 4. Now click the General tab and remove any entries in the Reply Address field (this field must be blank for encryption to work). Click OK, and then click Close.

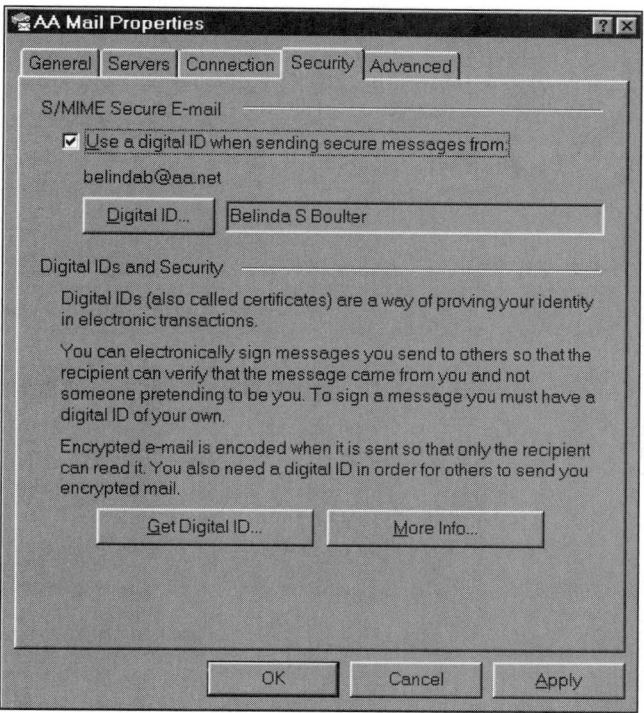

Figure 31-16: Mark the "Use a digital ID when sending secure messages from" checkbox to associate your certificate with a mail account.

Secret

It's a good idea to add your certificate to your own address book. You can do this by sending yourself digitally signed e-mail, and then following the "Saving a Digital ID in Your Address Book" steps in the "Saving a Certificate" section earlier in this chapter. Now when you send an encrypted message to someone else, you will be able to read your copy of it.

To attach your digital ID to an outgoing e-mail message, follow these steps:

STEPS

Sending a Digitally Signed Message

Step 1. In Outlook Express, click Tools ➪ Options, click the Security tab, and then click the Advanced button.

Continued

STEPS

Sending a Digitally Signed Message *(continued)*

Step 2. In the Advanced Security Settings dialog box, mark "Include my digital ID when sending signed messages." This will include the public-key portion of your digital ID with your digital signature, so that others can reply with encrypted mail if they wish. See "Public-Key Encryption" later in this chapter for more on keys and encryption.

Step 3. Open a New Message window and choose Tools ⇨ Digitally Sign (or click the Digitally Sign Message toolbar button). Compose and send your message as usual.

If you want to attach your digital ID to *all* of your outgoing messages, choose Tools ⇨ Options, click the Security tab, mark the "Digitally sign all outgoing messages" checkbox, and then click OK.

It's possible to send your certificate as a file attachment, without using it to sign the message. To do this, you would export your certificate without including your personal key (see "Exporting and Importing Certificates" later in this chapter for more on exporting). The certificate is saved as a p7c or cer file, depending on the format you choose during export. However, this method seems like a lot of trouble, with no real advantage over simply digitally signing a message.

Get Rid of Old Certificates

Prior to Windows 98, Outlook Express did not give you a way to remove old certificates from your system without editing your registry. Now it's easy, as described in these steps:

STEPS

Removing a Digital Certificate from Your Address Book

Step 1. Open your Address Book window and right-click the name of the owner of the certificate that you want to delete. Click Properties and go to the Digital IDs tab.

Step 2. Click the Remove button and click OK.

Step 3. Notice that the address book listing no longer has the Red Ribbon icon associated with it. Close the Address Book window.

Exporting and Importing Certificates

Until recently, a certificate could only be used on one specific computer. Although Outlook Express now makes it easy to export your certificate to another computer — the one you use at work, for example — when you download your certificate, you should use the computer that you want to primarily associate with it. Because the whole point of using a certificate is to verify your identity for security purposes, and because it contains your private key for reading encrypted messages, you should be cautious about putting your certificate on other computers.

It's a good idea to keep a backup copy of your digital ID in case you ever have to reinstall Windows or Outlook Express, or in case your hard disk becomes damaged. It will save you the trouble and expense of reapplying for a new ID. For security reasons, your digital ID is not accessible as a file, or directly through your registry, so you must export it in order to back it up. While you might have occasion to export other people's certificates — to pass one along to a friend, for example — it's not necessary to back them up because they are stored as part of your address book. (See "Save All Your Documents" in Chapter 27 for how to make your address book easier to back up.)

If you change your e-mail software after you have installed a certificate, you must either get a new ID or export it from the old application and import it into the new one. For example, if you originally installed your ID using Netscape, you must export the ID from Netscape and import it into Outlook Express in order to use it there. (If you simply upgrade Outlook Express, your certificate is automatically preserved.) This ability to import and export is a relatively recent feature of both Netscape and Outlook Express, so you may need to download and install the most current version of Netscape before you can export the ID. Other e-mail applications may not give you the ability to export; in that case, you must apply for a new certificate.

STEPS

Exporting a Copy of Your Digital ID to a Floppy Disk

Step 1. In Outlook Express, choose Tools ➪ Options, and click the Security tab. Click the Digital IDs button to launch the Certificate Manager, shown in Figure 31-17.

Step 2. Insert a disk into your floppy disk drive. Then highlight the certificate that you want to export and click the Export button. Your own certificates are listed on the Personal tab, while other people's certificates are on the Other People tab.

Continued

STEPS

Exporting a Copy of Your Digital ID to a Floppy Disk *(continued)*

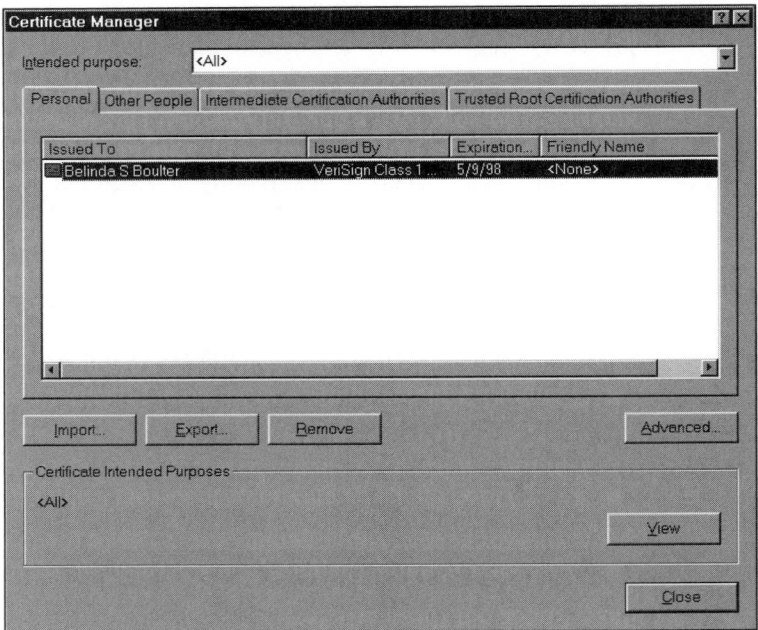

Figure 31-17: The Certificate Manager enables you to manage certificates belonging to yourself and others.

Step 3. The Certificate Manager Export Wizard opens to walk you through the export process. Be sure to mark the "Yes, export the private key" option when you are asked, unless you are exporting this certificate to send to someone else. This will include assigning a password that you use only for importing and exporting this certificate. The wizard will export your certificate with the pfx extension to your floppy disk (or to another location of your choosing). After you have completed the wizard, click Finish to save your new pfx file.

Step 4. Click OK to confirm the security level, and then click OK again to acknowledge that the export process is complete. Close the Certificate Manager dialog box.

To import a `pfx` certificate, click it in the Explorer. The Certificate Manager Import Wizard opens and guides you through the import process.

For directions on exporting from Netscape, see `http://digitalid.verisign.com/chngsw.htm`. Then, use these steps to import the certificate into OE. You can learn more about exporting and importing from your certification authority. For example, VeriSign has helpful information at `http://www.verisign.com/support/index.html`.

Public-Key Encryption

Encryption is the process of encoding a message (and any attachments) so that it must be decoded with a *key* before it can be read. The purpose of encryption is to ensure that your messages remain private; this can be extremely important if you are exchanging sensitive personal or financial infor-mation. Outlook Express has some encryption capabilities built in, and if you live in the United States, more capabilities are available in the form of upgrades and plug-ins.

These days, the most commonly used encryption scheme is *public-key encryption*. This involves two keys, a *private key* that you use for reading encrypted messages sent to you, and a *public key* that lets other people encrypt messages for you to read. Anyone can obtain your public key, either when you send him or her a digitally signed message or a message with your certificate attached, or by downloading it from your certification authority. But only you have access to your private key.

Encryption Protocols

Until recently, the strongest encryption legally available in the United States was 40-bit encryption, a relatively weak level of encryption. (The more bits, the harder the code is to crack.) Outlook Express automatically supports the "RC2 (40-bit)" encryption protocol. Residents of the United States and Canada can now download and install a 128-bit upgrade for Internet Explorer (available from `http://www.microsoft.com/ie/download/`). The upgrade allows you to send and receive the DES, RC2 (128-bit), and 3DES encryption protocols in addition to RC2 (40-bit). All of these protocols use the S/MIME algorithm created by RSA Data Security and licensed to Microsoft and many others. Both the sender and the recipient must have installed the 128-bit upgrade to use this higher level of encryption. Otherwise, the message will be sent in the RC2 protocol (but Outlook Express will still be able to encrypt it).

Outlook Express can tell from the certificate what protocol to use when sending encrypted e-mail. If you want to see what protocol was used to encrypt a message in your Inbox, Outbox, or Sent Messages folder, highlight the message in the Message pane, click the encryption (Padlock) icon in the preview pane header, and choose View Security Properties. You will see the protocol shown under Encrypted Using (see Figure 31-18).

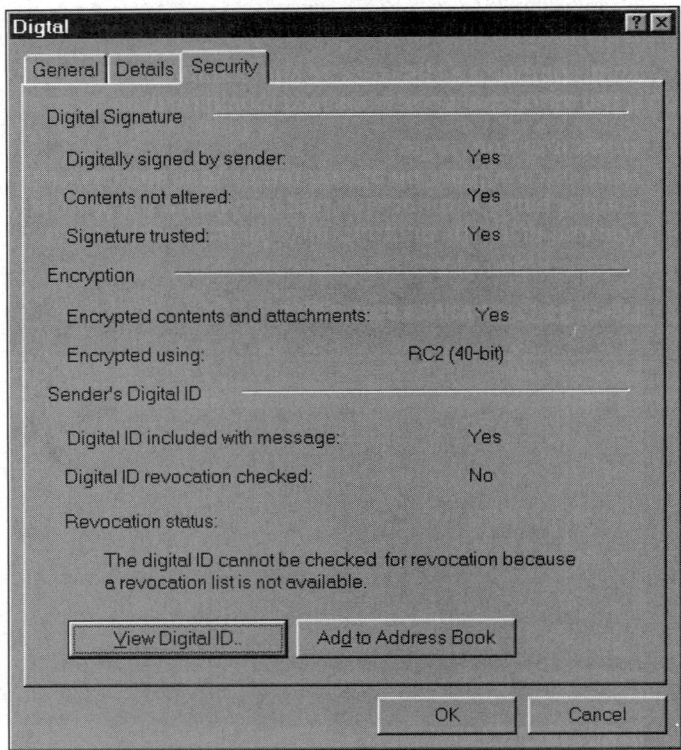

Figure 31-18: The Security tab of the Properties dialog box for this message shows that it was encrypted using the RC2 (40-bit) protocol.

Secret

To see the protocol preference associated with a certificate in your address book, open your Address Book window, right-click the name of the certificate's owner, click Properties, click the Digital IDs tab, and click the Properties button. In the Certificate dialog box, look on the Details tab for the Signature Algorithm. You will see the associated preference in the Value column, as illustrated in Figure 31-19.

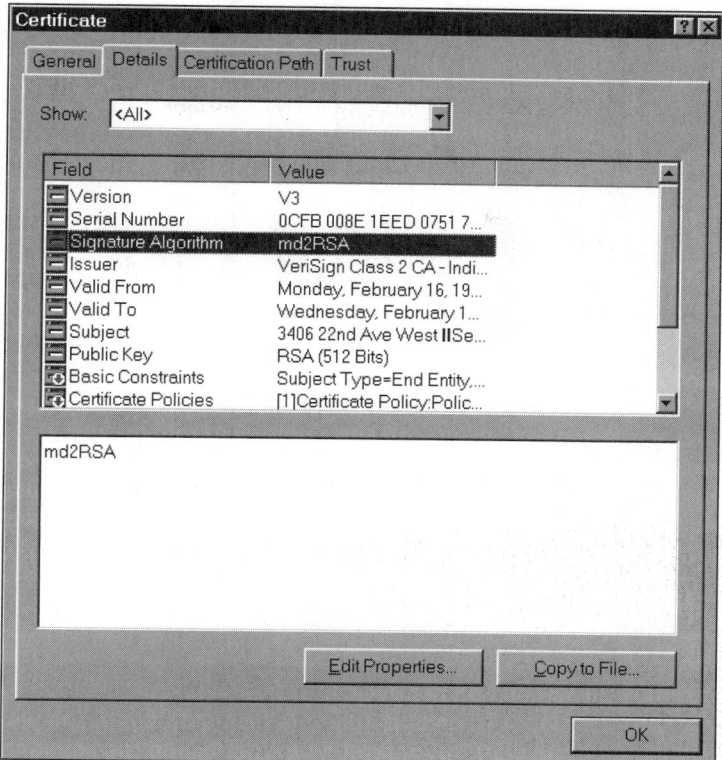

Figure 31-19: The Details tab for this digital ID shows that it is set to use md2RSA encryption.

Sending an Encrypted Message

Say, for example, that you want to send an encrypted message to your friend Joe. To do this, you must first have a copy of Joe's digital certificate, which contains Joe's public key, stored in your address book. Joe's certificate also contains information about the encryption protocol that he prefers to receive. Outlook Express will automatically encrypt your message to Joe using the preferences contained in his certificate (*not* the preferences you set up for your own certificate). When Joe receives your message, his e-mail software will use his private key (stored in his registry) to decode the message.

Because you don't have Joe's private key, you won't automatically be able to read (decrypt) the message you sent to Joe, even though you wrote it. When you send an encrypted message to Joe, you will see the error message shown in Figure 31-20. You will still be able to send the message, but you won't be able to read it in your Sent Items folder. To be able to read the encrypted messages you send, follow these steps:

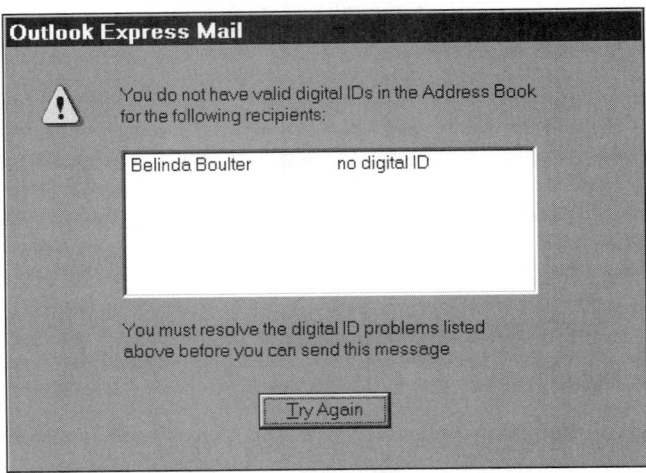

Figure 31-20: This message appears if you haven't added your own public key to encrypted messages you've sent.

STEPS

Reading Encrypted Messages You Send to Others

Step 1.   Register for your own digital ID with a certification authority, and add your certificate to your own address book. (See "Using Your Certificate" earlier in this chapter for more about this.)

Step 2.   In Outlook Express, choose Tools ⇨ Options, click the Security tab, and then click the Advanced button.

Step 3.   Under Encrypted Messages, mark "Always encrypt to myself when sending encrypted mail," as shown in Figure 31-21. Click OK twice to close the dialog boxes.

Now when you send an encrypted message to Joe, Outlook Express will make a second encrypted message using your public key and put it in your Sent Items folder, where you will be able to read it with your private key.

When you receive an encrypted message for which you already have the public key, Outlook Express will display a dialog box asking if you want it to automatically decrypt the message. You don't have to do anything else to read it, just click OK.

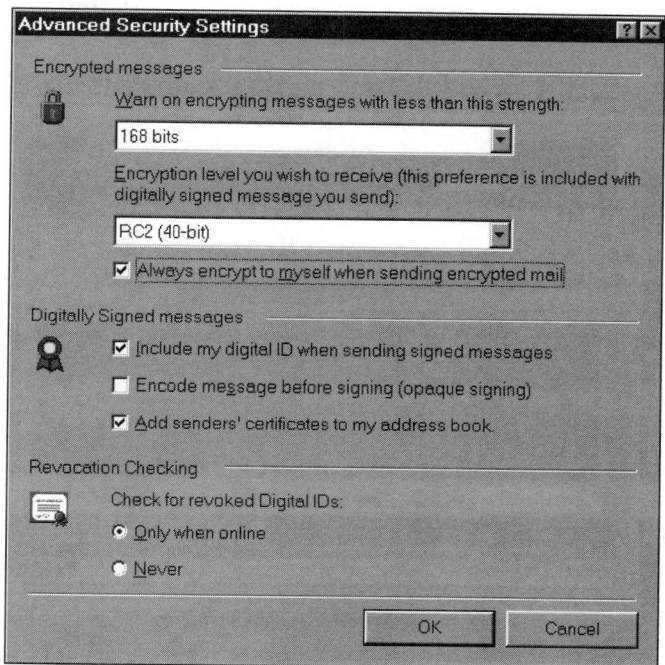

Figure 31-21: Be sure to mark "Always encrypt to myself when sending encrypted mail" if you want to be able to read the encrypted messages you send.

If you want all of your messages to be either digitally signed or encrypted (or both), click Tools ⇨ Options in the Outlook Express window, and click the Security tab. Under Secure Mail, mark "Digitally sign all outgoing messages" and/or "Encrypt contents and attachments for all outgoing messages." If you have 128-bit encryption, click Advanced and select the algorithm you prefer in the Preferred Encryption Algorithm drop-down list. Click OK, and then click OK again to close the Options dialog box.

Tip If you save an encrypted or digitally signed message in your Drafts folder without sending it, the security settings will be lost. In Outlook Express 4, there was no warning — version 5 at least gives you a warning when you save the message. Be sure to re-add the encryption and/or the digital signature before sending the message. Thanks to Eric Miller for pointing this out.

Learn More About Encryption

You can learn a lot about cryptography at RSA's Web site: `http://www. rsasecurity.com/`. For more on S/MIME and how it works, see "S/MIME Capabilities" and "Troubleshooting Enhanced Encryption" on Eric Miller's Web site: `http://www.okinfoweb.com/moe/smime/encrypt/index.htm`.

Another popular encryption protocol is Pretty Good Privacy (PGP), originally written by Philip Zimmermann and available in both commercial and freeware versions. PGP and S/MIME are not compatible; a message encoded using S/MIME cannot be decoded using PGP, and vice versa. You and your correspondent need to agree in advance on a protocol before you can exchange encrypted messages.

PGP Inc. is now part of Network Associates, at `http://www.pgp.com/ asp_set/products/tns/intro.asp`. They offer a plug-in for Outlook Express that's designed to make OpenPGP somewhat integrated with your regular e-mail. The plug-in and PGP freeware are available from the Network Associates site; the freeware is also available from the MIT PGP distribution Web site, `http://web.mit.edu/network/pgp.html`. Some excellent articles about OpenPGP are located at `http://www.cnet.com/Content/ Features/Howto/Encryption`.

If you are having trouble sending encrypted messages to someone who is not S/MIME enabled, take a look at Eric Miller's article "Sending DIDs to Non-S/MIME Readers" at `http://www.okinfoweb.com/moe/smime/DIDs/ did_011.htm`.

Summary

A certificate contains information you need to send encrypted messages to its owner, and it assures you that its ownership is valid.

▶ You can set the level of trust for an individual certificate or for the organization that issued it.

▶ Revocation checking tells Outlook Express to automatically verify on the Internet at the time of receipt that a certificate is still valid.

▶ If you obtain your own certificate, you can receive encrypted messages from people you send it to.

▶ You can export and import certificates for backup purposes.

▶ If you send an encrypted message, you won't necessarily be able to read it. You can read the encrypted messages you send if you have your own certificate.

Chapter 32

The Windows Address Book

In This Chapter

The Windows Address Book is coming closer to being a truly useful contacts manager. We show you how to take advantage of some little-used or new features.

▶ Use address book folders to organize your contacts and share them with other identities

▶ Use multiple address books on one computer

▶ Dial your phone from your address book

Making the Most of Your Address Book

The Windows Address Book stores information that can be used in many different programs — including Outlook Express. By storing all of your contact information in the Windows Address Book, you make it easy to reuse that same information in the future. You don't, for example, have to constantly retype e-mail addresses because you can simply use the information directly from your Windows Address Book.

If you use more than one computer you might have separate address books on each of those systems. Rather than reentering the same information in each separate address book, you'll probably find it's far less work to simply merge the information that you've added to one address book into the others. You can also take this a few steps further and integrate data from someone else's address book or even from another application.

Merging Windows Address Books

Because you can import and export data from your Windows Address Book, you can merge data from one or more address books into an existing (or new) address book.

STEPS

Merging a Windows Address Book from Another Computer

Step 1. Open the address book on one computer, choose File ⇨ Export ⇨ Address Book, select Text File (Comma Separated Values), and click the Export button. In the CSV Export Wizard, set the target file extension as csv and mark every field if you want to export everything in the address book. Then click Finish.

Step 2. Copy the file to a folder holding temporary files on the target computer.

Step 3. Open the address book on the target computer. Choose File ⇨ Import ⇨ Address Book, select Text File (Comma Separated Values), and click the Import button. In the CSV Import Wizard, browse for the exported filename. You can choose which fields to import and where they go. Click Finish.

Step 4. You will be notified of any duplicate names as they are about to be imported, and you will get to choose whether to overwrite the existing names or not. If you choose not to overwrite, you will end up with multiple entries for the same name. You'll need to go back and remove the redundant entries manually.

You can also create a new blank Windows Address Book and merge names from other address books into it using these steps. To create a new blank Windows Address Book, click Start ⇨ Run. Type **wab /New**. Enter the path and filename for the new blank address book.

If you want to see what else you can do with the wab command, try typing **wab /?**.

Add New Entries to Your Address Book

It's easy to add addresses to your Windows address book from messages you've received. Just right-click a message in the Message pane and choose Add Sender to Address Book. You can also right-click an address in the body of a message (or in the Preview pane), or in the header of an open message window, and choose Add to Address Book.

Secret

In the toolbar of an open mail or news message, click Tools ⇨ Add to Address Book. In the submenu that appears, choose Sender, or Everyone on To List, or select individual addressees. The Everyone on To List option is an easy way to capture a whole group of addresses at once. For example, if you get a message that's been circulated to everyone working on a certain project, you can add them all with one command. Unfortunately you can't specify a folder or a group, so if you want to keep the addresses together, you'll have to go into the address book, hunt each address down individually, and drag it into a group or folder.

If you get mail from someone new, you can automatically add him or her to your address book when you send a reply. In Outlook Express, choose Tools ⇨ Options, click the Send tab, and mark "Automatically put people I reply to in my Address Book." If you don't reply to a message, the new address will not be added unless you specifically add it.

The only drawback to using this option is that if you have already entered this person with a slightly different name (Bob instead of Robert, for example), Outlook Express will create a second entry for the new name. If your correspondent has not bothered to enter a "friendly name" in his or her account setup, you will see an e-mail address instead of a name in your address book. You are pretty much forced to live with the name the way your correspondent has it set up, or else have a lot of duplicates in your address book.

We thought that using the Nickname field would get around this, and it almost does. The Nickname field is illustrated in Figure 32-1. If you give someone a nickname for which the first few letters are unique in your address book, you can type those letters in the To field and Outlook Express will enter the e-mail address. But if another entry starts with those letters, you can type the whole nickname and it will still not insert the person's address. So, for example, in our address book the nickname Goofy works fine as an alias for a contact whose first name is Robert, but Bobby does not work because we already have a couple of other names starting with Bob. You may want to test this out for yourself, because it may work better in future versions.

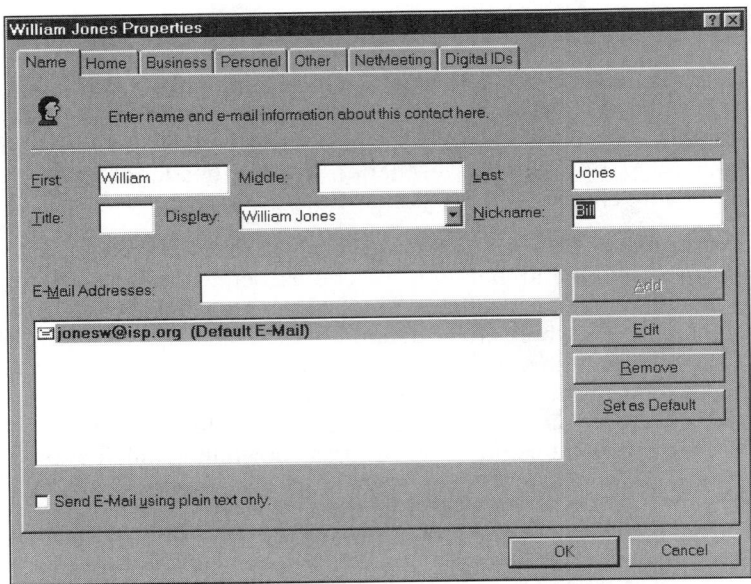

Figure 32-1: You can add a nickname that's different from a contact's name.

Folders and Groups

A *group* is a set of pointers to address book entries, not the entries themselves. If you regularly e-mail information to the same people (people in your department at work, distant family members, or fellow hobbyists, for example), you can put all of their addresses into a group. If you do this, you can avoid having to enter each contact individually in the To line every time you send a message to these people. A contact can belong to multiple groups.

A *folder*, on the other hand, is a way of subdividing actual address book entries to make them easier to find and manage. A contact can belong to only one folder. All folders must be part of either the Shared Contacts folder or your identity's main Contacts folder. (These two permanent folders are explained further in the next section.)

Secret

If you open your address book and don't see any entries, it's most likely because the focus is on the Shared Contacts folder instead of your main Contacts folder. To see your Contacts folder, along with subfolders and groups you have created in the address book ➪ click View ➪ Folders and Groups. A left pane opens in the Address Book window, as shown in Figure 32-2.

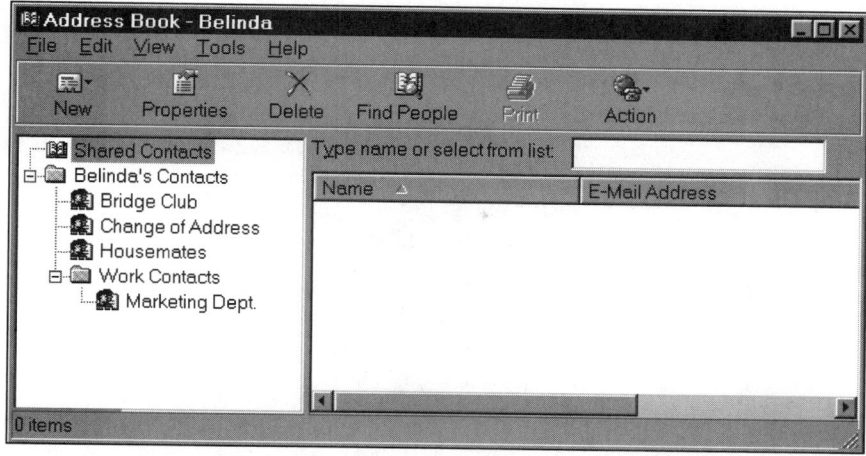

Figure 32-2: The hierarchy of folders and groups is visible in the left pane. Because the focus is on the Shared Contacts folder, and because we haven't shared any contacts, the right pane is empty.

You can't copy contacts, groups, and folders between folders — only move them. You can move a group to another folder without affecting the folder locations of the contacts in the group. You cannot move or copy a folder from one computer to another; if you need this kind of portability, you'll need to create a separate address book (see "Multiple Address Books" later in this chapter).

Secret

To make a contact appear in more than one folder, create a new group, add the contact, and then drag and drop the group into the other folder(s). Now if you open the group, you can see that contact.

If you double-click a group to view its Properties dialog box and click Select Members, you will see a list of all the contacts in the main Contacts folder, as shown in Figure 32-3. Add any of these contacts to the group by highlighting them and clicking Select, and then click OK. To add contacts from another folder to this group you must drag and drop them. (The contacts will be copied, not moved.) To remove a contact, highlight the name in the right pane and press your Delete key (the contact will only be removed from the group, not from your address book).

When you right-click an address book folder, you'll notice there's no Rename menu option. Instead, to rename a folder, select Properties. The folder name is the only value in the Properties dialog box. You can't change the name of your main Contacts folder (or remove it, for that matter). We can only surmise that this is to prevent two identities from accidentally giving their main folders the same name.

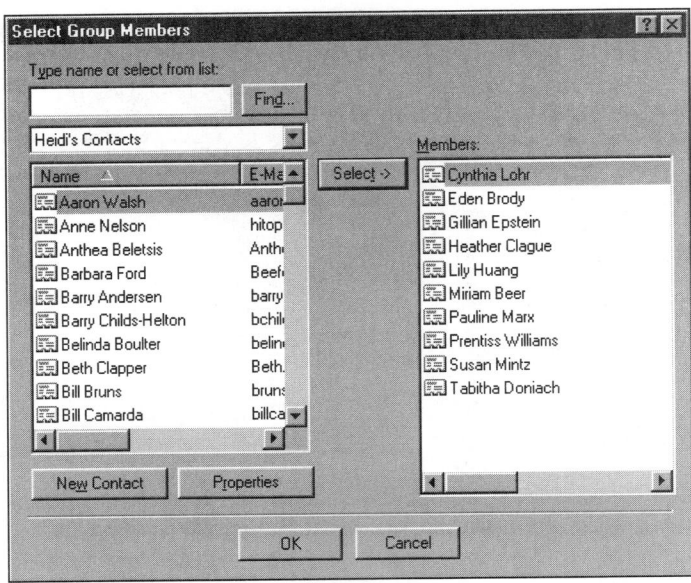

Figure 32-3: The Select Group Members dialog box lets you add members to a group, or remove them.

You can type a contact directly into a group or a folder. Simply select the group or folder before clicking New ⇨ New Contact. This is different from the behavior of the Contacts pane, where you can only add contacts to your identity's main Contacts folder. You cannot import contacts from another address book directly into a folder or group, you must first import them into your identity's main Contacts folder (File ⇨ Import ⇨ Address Book [WAB]), and then move them to a folder or add them to a group individually.

Sharing an Address Book

Every address book contains at least two permanent folders — one for each identity, and one called Shared Contacts. No matter how many identities there are for a particular user profile, there is only one default address book (wab) file, named for the current user. (Remember that profiles are different from identities in that they govern your entire system, not just Outlook Express.) Ordinarily you can only see the entries for your identity's main Contacts folder, plus the Shared Contacts folder.

When you add a contact to your address book — for example, by right-clicking an address and choosing Add to Address Book — that information is stored in the Contacts folder for the current identity. To share a contact or group with other identities, drag the icon for that item into the Shared Contacts folder in the left pane, as shown in Figure 32-4. That contact or group will now appear in the Shared Contacts folder (and thus the Contacts pane) of every identity on this computer, instead of in your main Contacts folder. If you use a lot of shared contacts, it's probably desirable either to keep the Contacts pane open in Outlook Express (View ➪ Layout ➪ Contacts) or to add the Contacts icon to your Outlook Express toolbar.

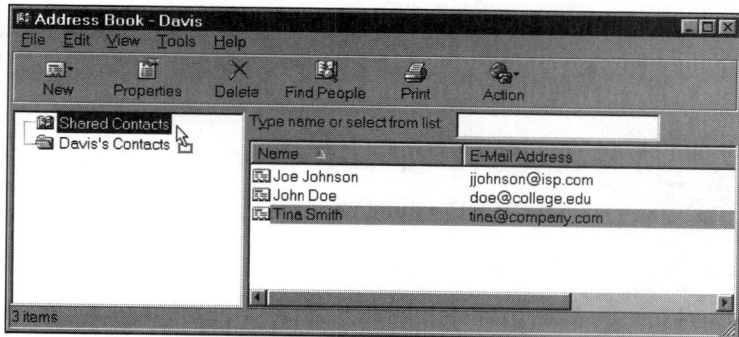

Figure 32-4: Drag the contact into the Shared Contacts folder to share it with other identities.

Multiple Address Books

Now that the Windows Address Book can contain multiple folders, the need for multiple address book files is significantly decreased. Address book folders are certainly easier to set up and use. But you can still have multiple address books if you choose, and this may be the best option if you need to move a subset of your address book between computers.

You can have as many wab files (address books) as you want, but only one default wab file. The default wab is the one you see in the Contacts pane, and the one used when you click To in the header of a New Message window. The path to the default wab is stored in your registry (see "Save All Your Documents" in Chapter 27 for instructions on moving your default address book).

Secret

To create a new address book, click Start ➪ Run, type **WAB /New**, and press Enter. Browse to the place where you want to keep your new address book (probably the same folder where you keep your other one). Then type a name for your new address book and click Open (see Figure 32-5). A new, empty address book appears.

You can open the nondefault wab files by clicking them in the Explorer. You can easily make shortcuts to them on your Desktop, on a toolbar, or in the Start menu. Or, you can make shortcuts to registry files that will automatically change the default wab. To see how this is done, take a look at "Using Multiple WABs" on Eric Miller's User Tips Web site, http://www.okinfoweb.com/moe/wab/wab_015.htm.

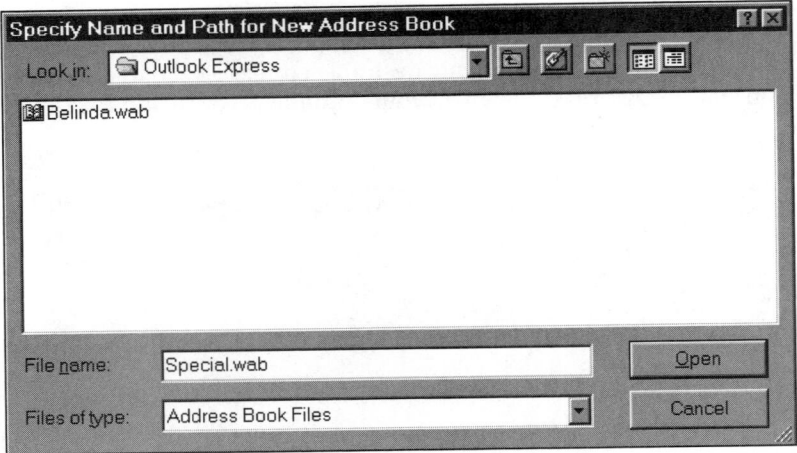

Figure 32-5: In this example, the new address book will be called Special and will be stored in the same folder as Belinda's default address book.

Tip

It's easy to copy address book entries from one wab file to another. Just open both address books side by side, select one or more contacts to be copied (you can use the Shift and Ctrl keys to select the ones you want), and drag them into the other address book. This makes it quick to add multiple contacts from your address book at the office to the one on your computer at home, for example.

The Address Book Does More Than E-Mail

You don't have to open Outlook Express to send mail to someone in your address book. From the address book, highlight the person's name, click the Action toolbar button, and click Send Mail. A New Message window opens with that person in the To line.

You can also use your address book to dial the telephone or initiate a NetMeeting conference. You must first have entered the information to do this, of course. To dial the telephone, highlight a contact for which you have entered a phone number, click the Action toolbar button, and click Dial. This launches the Windows Phone Dialer applet (discussed in "Phone Dialer" in Chapter 45). A New Call dialog box opens, as shown in Figure 32-6. Click Call to dial the phone, pick up your receiver, and then click the Talk button in the Call Status dialog box before you start to talk. The Phone Dialer remains open but minimized after you end the call and click the Hang Up button.

Figure 32-6: Click the Call button to dial the number you have selected.

To start a NetMeeting conference, double-click a contact to open its Properties dialog box, and then click the NetMeeting tab to enter Internet conferencing information for a contact. (This tab will be called Conferencing if you have not installed NetMeeting.) Enter the server and address information in the appropriate fields (see Figure 32-7), and then click Add. To initiate a conference, click Call Now.

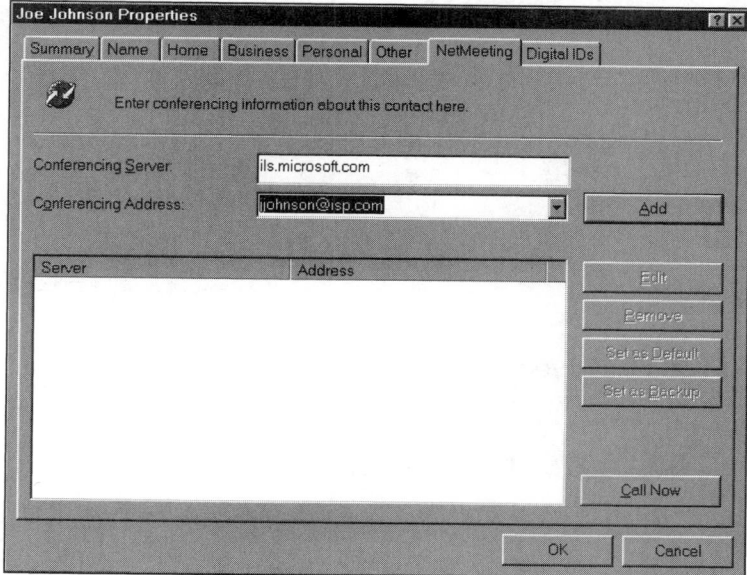

Figure 32-7: The NetMeeting tab will be called the Conferencing tab if you have not installed NetMeeting.

See "Connecting to Other NetMeeting Users" in Chapter 33 for more on how to use NetMeeting.

Print a Phone List

If you click the Print button in the Address Book toolbar, you'll see a dialog box such as the one shown in Figure 32-8. What makes it different from a normal Print dialog box is the choice of print styles. The Memo option prints all of the contact information for your contacts, Business Card prints the information on the Business tab, and Phone List produces a nice alphabetized phone list that you can carry with you. With all three print styles, you can print the information for all of the contacts in your address book or only for the selected ones. On the downside, you don't have much control over the layout, and you're stuck with printing on 8½ × 11 paper.

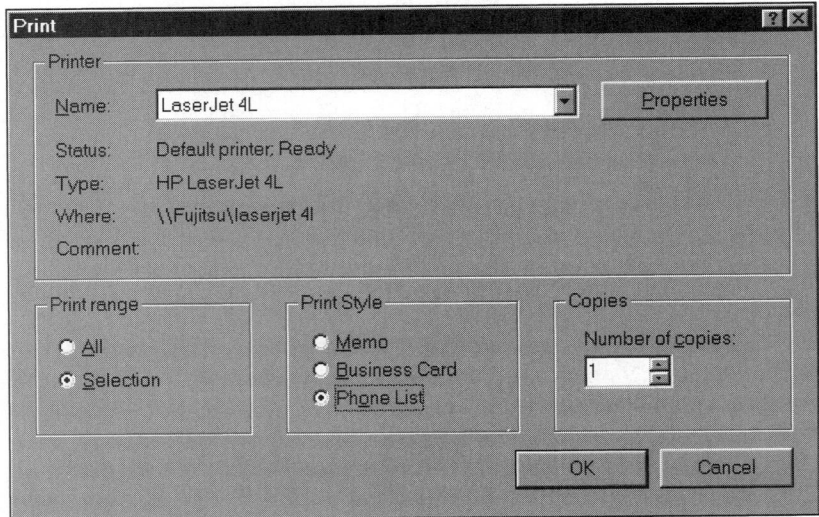

Figure 32-8: The address book's Print dialog box lets you select a print style.

Copy a Contact into Word

Although you can't do anything as sophisticated as mail merging with your address book, you can at least get contact information into a Microsoft Word document pretty easily. Just drag and drop one or more contacts from your address book into a Word document, or right-click to copy and paste in the normal way.

If you do this, you'll find that all the nonempty fields for the contacts are pasted into your document — you'll need to delete the extraneous stuff if all you want is the mailing address. Still, it's better than typing.

If you have a lot of names and you want to do a full-scale mail merge, you'll need to export your address book to a comma-separated value (CSV) text file.

You have to open this file in Microsoft Excel and save it in Microsoft Excel Workbook (xls) format before Word can use it as a mail merge source. Kind of a project, but again, better than typing.

To create the csv file, choose File ⇨ Export ⇨ Other Address Book, select Text File (Comma Separated Values) in the Address Book Export Tool dialog box, and then click Export. The CSV Export Wizard opens. Browse to a location for saving, enter a name for your file, click Save, and then click Next. You can select the fields to export by marking their checkboxes, as shown in Figure 32-9. When you're done, click Finish, and then click OK when the export is complete.

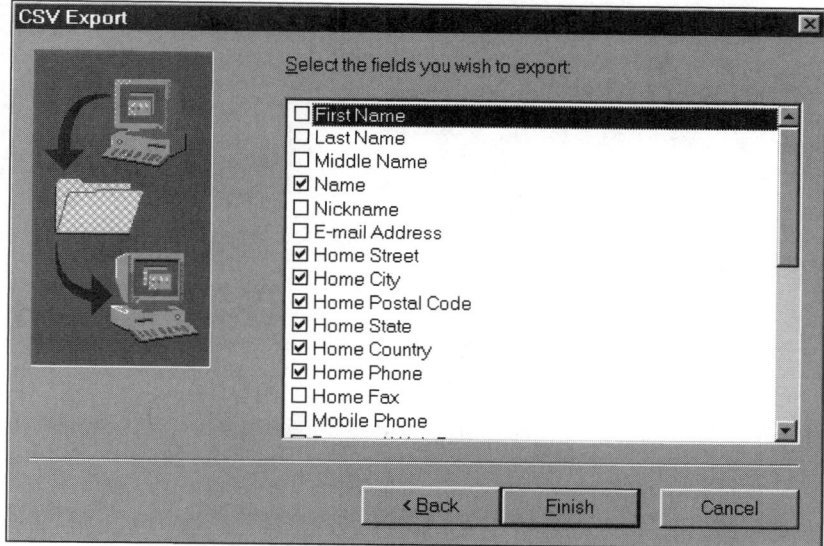

Figure 32-9: Mark the checkboxes for the fields that you want to export.

Converting Between Address Book Formats

Outlook Express lets you import address book files from Eudora, Netscape, and several other formats (click File ⇨ Import ⇨ Other Address Book). But if you have some format that Outlook Express doesn't handle, or if you want to convert from Outlook Express to another format, you may find the InterGuru's E-Mail Address Book Conversions Web site helpful. The conversion page is shown in Figure 32-10. This is a shareware service that performs the conversion for you online, and also offers links to some other helpful sites. Please note that we have not tested this conversion service. You'll find it at http://www.interguru.com/mailconv.htm.

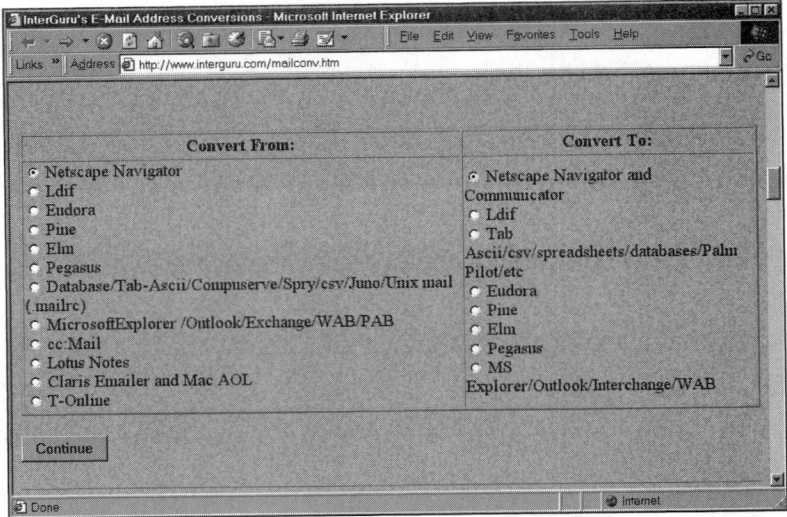

Figure 32-10: The conversion table at InterGuru's Web site lists the possible conversion combinations.

Summary

The Windows Address Book has added some tools for managing your contacts. While the method leaves a lot to be desired, you can export contact listings into Microsoft Word.

▶ You can easily share address book contacts among identities if you put them in the Shared Contacts folder.

▶ You can use the address book to initiate a telephone call or an Internet conference.

## Chapter 33

NetMeeting

In This Chapter

Microsoft will not leave an Internet stone unturned. To keep the Internet from becoming the operating system, they need to turn the operating system into the ultimate Internet client. NetMeeting lets you use the Internet as a video phone line, a chat room, a whiteboard, and a place to share applications.

▶ NetMeeting is an Internet phone, but you've got to make sure your audio doesn't echo

▶ The capabilities of your sound card and driver determine whether NetMeeting acts like a phone or a two-way radio

▶ Fix your microphone and sound card so that NetMeeting can detect them

▶ How to contact the other guy

▶ Use NetMeeting as an answering machine

▶ Explore NetMeeting-related Web sites

Audio and Video Issues

You cannot send audio and video information between NetMeeting users unless they are connected via a TCP/IP network. The Internet is such a network, as are properly configured local area networks, as well as Direct Cable Connection. NetMeeting will work over IPX and NetBEUI networking protocols, but it will lack the audio and video features.

In addition to the help provided in this chapter, you can find assistance on audio problems at the Microsoft Knowledge Base. Check out these articles:

- "Participants Cannot Hear During Audio NetMeeting Conference" at http://support.microsoft.com/support/kb/articles/q174/6/11.asp

- " Audio Quality Problems in NetMeeting " at http://support.microsoft.com/support/kb/articles/q165/6/22.asp

- "Audio May Echo with Microsoft NetMeeting" at http://support.microsoft.com/support/kb/articles/q166/0/38.asp

- "Must Take Turns Speaking in NetMeeting" at http://support.microsoft.com/support/kb/articles/q155/0/24.asp

Feedback and Echo

It is possible to test NetMeeting using two computers connected to each other through a null modem cable or over a TCP/IP network. If these computers are close to each other and if both sound cards are operating in full-duplex mode, you'll find that the audio output from one computer can register as the input to the other, creating unpleasant feedback.

In addition to feedback, you may find that both microphones pick up what one person is saying. This produces an echo because both computers' speakers broadcast what is being said, with a slight delay. To reduce echo, you can reduce the volume on the speakers in NetMeeting, or use an antiecho or noise-canceling microphone. You'll find them at `http://www.andreaelectronics.com`.

Tip

Some computers also produce feedback on their own when output from their speakers is picked up by their own microphones. To avoid both forms of feedback, turn down the volume on the speakers or the level on the microphone, so that the microphone does not pick up output from the speakers. The best option is to plug headphones into your sound card to cut the feedback loop.

Why Do I Have to Stop Talking Before My Friend Can Talk?

NetMeeting uses your sound card to both send out your voice when you speak and to play the voice of the person with whom you are speaking. In some cases, your sound card may only be able to support *half duplex*—that is, only one speaker at a time.

Half duplex is like two-way radio communication. First one person transmits, then the other. Unlike radio, NetMeeting doesn't require that you push the Push-to-Talk button. NetMeeting automatically senses your voice when you speak and also senses when the other person isn't speaking. This automatic sensing capability can be a source of problems (see the next section).

Sound cards with full-duplex capability enable you to speak and listen in the same manner that your phone allows. These sound cards can transmit your voice at the same time as they play the voice of the person to whom you are speaking.

If either you or your friend's sound card does not have full-duplex capabilities, you'll each have to wait for the other to quit speaking before you commence to speak. For a full-duplex conversation to occur using NetMeeting, both parties must have full-duplex sound cards and drivers. You may both have to upgrade if this is not the case and you want this capability.

You can determine whether your sound card has full-duplex capabilities by starting NetMeeting and taking these steps:

STEPS

Checking for a Full-Duplex Sound Card

Step 1. Click the Start button ➪ Programs ➪ NetMeeting. (If you've never run NetMeeting before, you will see the NetMeeting Wizard and then the Audio Tuning Wizard. Follow both wizards to set basic options, and then continue with these steps.)

Step 2. In NetMeeting, choose Tools ➪ Options, and click the Audio tab.

Step 3. If either your sound card or your sound card driver doesn't support full-duplex audio, the first checkbox will be dim, as shown in Figure 33-1. If this is the case, you will not be able to use full-duplex audio.

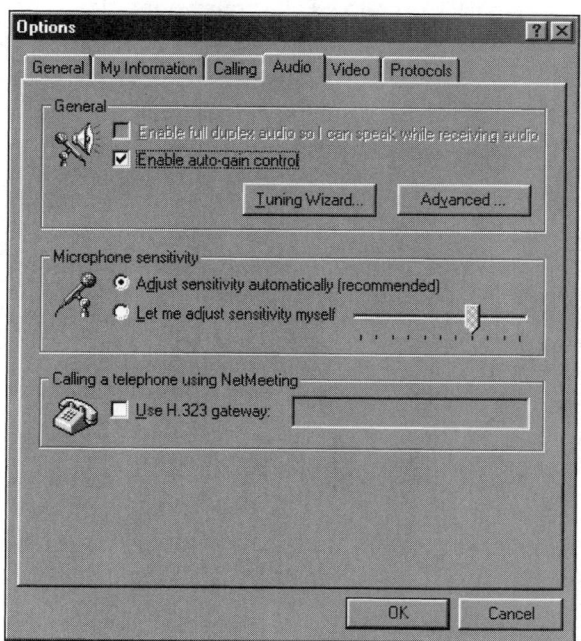

Figure 33-1: The Audio tab of the Options dialog box. The first checkbox is dim if your sound card or its driver doesn't have full-duplex capability.

Tip

You may be able to get an updated driver for your sound card that provides full-duplex operation. Click Start ➪ Settings ➪ Windows Update to connect to the Microsoft Windows Update site through the Internet. It will download and install a new sound card driver if one is available.

To turn on full-duplex capabilities for Sound Blaster drivers (the industry standard), take these steps:

STEPS

Turning on Full Duplex

Step 1. Click Start ➪ Settings ➪ Control Panel, click System, and click Device Manager.

Step 2. Click the plus sign next to Sound, Video and Game Controllers. Highlight Creative Sound Blaster Plug and Play.

Step 3. Click the Properties button. Then click the Settings tab, and mark the "Allow Full-Duplex operation" checkbox, as shown in Figure 33-2. Click OK, then click OK again.

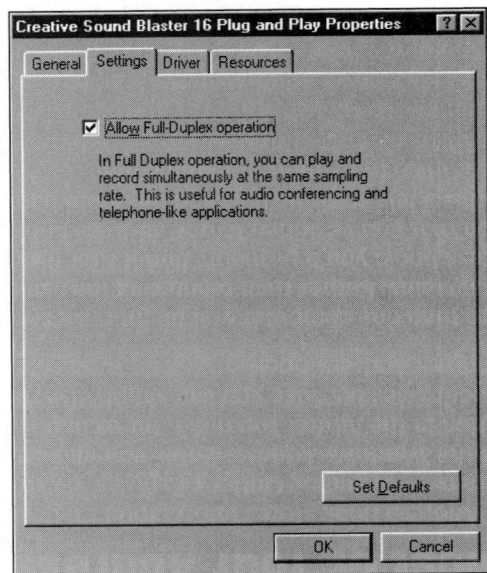

Figure 33-2: The Properties dialog box for a Sound Blaster driver

Step 4.   Restart your computer and NetMeeting to allow these changes to take effect.

Why Can't I Hear the Person I'm Talking To?

If you are running NetMeeting with a half-duplex sound card and/or driver, you may have difficulty receiving audio from the people with whom you are connected. This may be because your microphone is picking up sounds in addition to your voice, and blocking the incoming audio.

To correct this problem, turn down your microphone level in the NetMeeting window. This prevents NetMeeting from switching to the mode it uses to send audio from your computer (Transmit Audio mode). You can also get a directional or antiecho microphone. You'll find them at `http://www.andreaelectronics.com`.

NetMeeting also can have trouble with DirectSound (Microsoft's sound drivers). You can turn off DirectSound using NetMeeting Super Enhancer. See where to get it in "How Can I Log on to a New NetMeeting Directory Server?" later in this chapter.

Have the person you are trying to hear check to see that his or her microphone is working by clicking Start ➪ Programs ➪ Accessories ➪ Entertainment ➪ Sound Recorder. Your friend should be able to click the Record button (the red dot), and record and then play back his or her voice. If your friend can't record and hear the playback, check out the suggestions in the next section.

The Audio Tuning Wizard Doesn't Find My Microphone

The first time you start NetMeeting, the Audio Tuning Wizard runs automatically. You can also run it after you start NetMeeting (click Tools ➪ Audio Tuning Wizard).

If you run the Audio Tuning Wizard, you'll get to the dialog box that tests your microphone, shown in Figure 33-3. If nothing shows up on the decibel meter (the horizontal green line just above the volume slider that moves to the right as you speak louder), it may be because your microphone is muted.

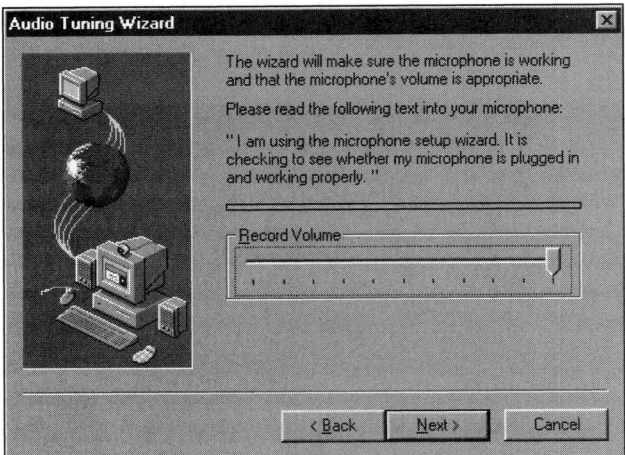

Figure 33-3: The Audio Tuning Wizard. This dialog box displays your microphone volume as you speak into your microphone. If you don't see a green line, NetMeeting isn't receiving any input from your mike.

To check out your mike, take these steps:

STEPS

Checking Your Microphone

Step 1. Right-click the Volume icon in your system tray and click Adjust Audio Properties. Or, click Start ⇨ Settings ⇨ Control Panel, then click Multimedia, and click Audio.

Both of these methods display the Audio control panel (see Figure 33-4).

Step 2. Click the icon directly under Recording to display the Recording control panel (see Figure 33-5).

Step 3. If the Select checkbox in the microphone control is not marked, the Audio Tuning Wizard won't find your mike. Be sure to mark this checkbox, and click OK.

Step 4. If you don't find the Microphone column on your Recording control panel, you can add it by choosing Options ⇨ Properties to display the Properties dialog box shown in Figure 33-6.

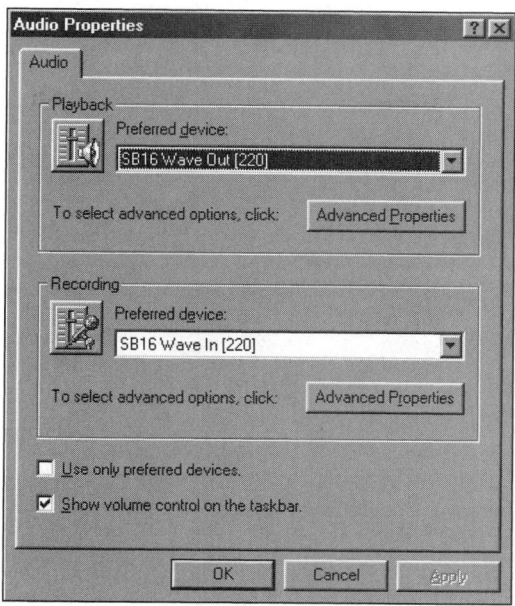

Figure 33-4: The Audio control panel. Both the Volume and Recording control panels are accessible from here.

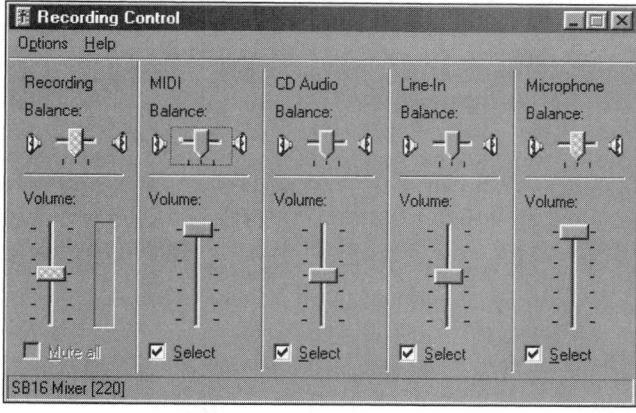

Figure 33-5: The Recording control panel

Continued

STEPS

Checking Your Microphone *(continued)*

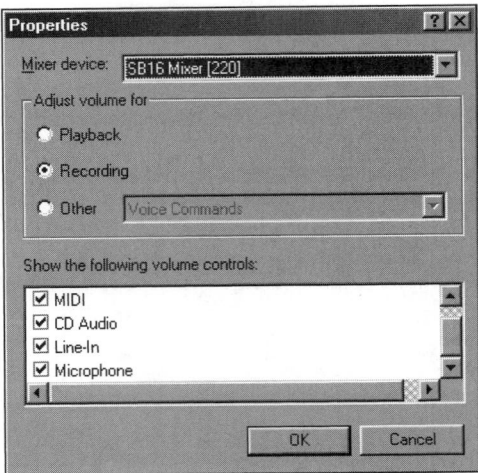

Figure 33-6: The Properties dialog box for the Recording control panel

Step 5. Scroll down the Volume Control list and mark Microphone. Click OK.

As soon as you mark the Select checkbox for the microphone in the Recording control panel, the microphone will be available to the Audio Tuning Wizard. You can take these steps while you are running the wizard.

While you're adjusting your mike, you should also check out its volume setting in the Volume control panel. To do so, take these steps:

STEPS

Adjusting Microphone Volume

Step 1. Right-click the Volume icon in the system tray and click Open Volume Controls. Or, click Start ➪ Settings ➪ Control Panel, click Multimedia, click Audio, and then click the icon below Playback. (A third option is to click Start ➪ Programs ➪ Entertainment ➪ Accessories ➪ Volume Control.)

Step 2. The Volume control panel, shown in Figure 33-7, doesn't have the microphone volume control by default. To display it, click Options ⇨ Properties. Scroll down to the Microphone checkbox, mark it, and click OK.

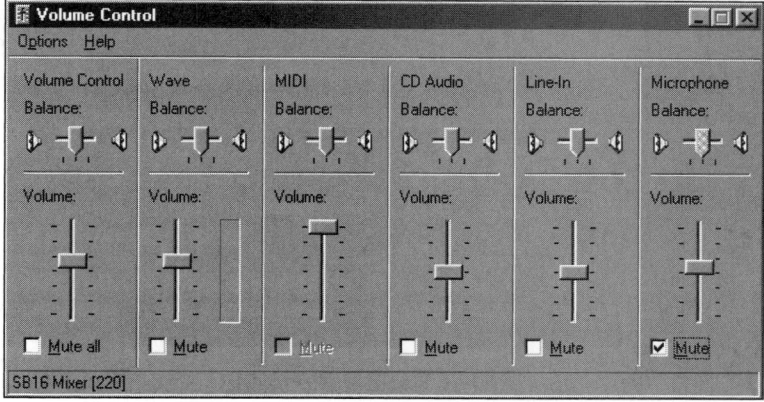

Figure 33-7: The Volume control panel

Step 3. You can mark the microphone's Mute checkbox in the Volume control panel without affecting NetMeeting. If Mute is marked, your voice will not be played out of your speakers when you speak into your mike.

If the Mute checkbox is cleared, you'll hear yourself speak through your computer's speakers as you communicate using NetMeeting.

You may find that your computer's speakers put out a fair bit of electronic noise if the microphone volume isn't muted. We found that marking the Mute checkbox provides the most pleasant experience with NetMeeting.

Secret

You can have the Volume control panel, the Recording control panel, and the Audio Tuning Wizard all visible and running at the same time, if you have enough real estate on your monitor. You'll notice that as you adjust the microphone volume control in any one of these panels, the volume slider in the other panels is also adjusted. This lets you know that all of these controls are working together.

Different sound cards and drivers have different capabilities. Some sound cards don't support microphone volume control, so the microphone volume control in the Recording control panel doesn't do anything.

The Audio Tuning Wizard Has Trouble with My Sound Card

If you run the Audio Tuning Wizard and you get the error message "Microsoft NetMeeting may not able to use audio correctly," this could be due to an outdated audio driver. You can run the Windows Update Wizard (Start ⇨ Settings ⇨ Windows Update), or you can check at the sound card manufacturer's Web site to find the latest driver updates.

For example, for the latest Sound Blaster drivers, go to `http://www.creaf. com/support/files/download.asp` .

NetMeeting may have trouble with your DirectSound drivers. You can turn off DirectSound using NetMeeting Super Enhancer. See where to get it in "How Can I Log on to a New NetMeeting Directory Server?" later in this chapter.

In NetMeeting Super Enhancer, click File ⇨ Disable DirectSound. You can store NetMeeting Super Enhancer in the `\Program Files\NetMeeting` folder. Place a shortcut to it on your Desktop or in the Start ⇨ Programs ⇨ Internet Explorer menu (the `\Windows\Start Menu\Programs\Internet Explorer` folder). In fact, if your NetMeeting shortcut is in your Programs menu, you may consider moving it to the Internet Explorer menu as well, so that you keep all of your Internet Explorer–related applications in one place.

Can a Group of NetMeeting Users Share Audio Together?

You can address your audio to more than one listener if you log onto a NetMeeting server that provides these capabilities. Use your Web browser to check out `http://www.cuseeme.com/` . The site provides a publicly available server.

You can also download server software for Windows 2000 or NT from the first two sites. This software allows you to configure your own NetMeeting server with these enhanced capabilities. Thanks to Jeffery Durham, Robert Scoble, and Roger Tragin for pointing out these sites.

There are other software packages that do multiparty video and audio. You can find them at `http://www.ivisit.com` and `http://www.cuseeme.com/`. Thanks to Robert Scoble at `http://www.vbits98.com` for reminding us about these other sites.

Neither Audio nor Video Works

If you can't get an audio and video connection, click Tools ⇨ Switch Audio and Video, and select your correspondent. NetMeeting has a bit of a problem if either you or your friend is using an Internet service provider (ISP) that doesn't support header compression, and one of you has enabled it. You'll need to right-click your DUN connectoid, click Properties ➪ Server Types ➪ TCP/IP Settings, and clear Use IP Header Compression.

You can find additional help on video problems at the Microsoft Knowledge Base. Check out these articles:

- "My Video Window Displays Black Screen" at `http://support.microsoft.com/support/kb/articles/q166/1/14.asp`

- "Poor Video Image Quality in or Incorrect Colors in NetMeeting Video Window" at `http://support.microsoft.com/support/kb/articles/q165/7/78.asp`

- "Cannot Exchange Audio and Video at Start of Conference" at `http://support.microsoft.com/support/kb/articles/q174/5/94.asp`

No Local Audio or Video When Connected to Your Internet Service Provider?

If you are connected to a local area network and you use your modem to call your ISP, most likely you won't be able to contact anyone else with audio and video on your LAN using NetMeeting. This is because your local TCP/IP services are stopped automatically when you start using TCP/IP remotely. Microsoft does this to keep your Windows computer from serving as an IP router.

At least that is what many others have experienced, and what happened when we tested NetMeeting under these circumstances. When our technical editor tested NetMeeting on a two-computer TCP/IP network, this configuration *was* able to transmit audio locally while connected to an ISP. Go figure. Perhaps it will work for you.

Your local area network may consist of just a few computers at your home, and may use other networking protocols as well. These protocols are not affected when you connect to your ISP. If your LAN uses other protocols in addition to TCP/IP, you will still be able to chat, use the whiteboard, and so on. But TCP/IP is required to share audio and video data.

I Can't Hear Anyone Through My Router

NetMeeting requires a direct connection over a TCP/IP network for audio and video to work. Some routers incorporate a network address translation (NAT) table to translate local IP addresses to an address that will work on the Internet at large. Some implementations of NAT don't pass dynamic UDP (Internet standard for a packet type used for audio and video) properly, and thus you're not able to get audio or video at all.

Make sure that you are not behind a firewall that uses a NAT if you want to have audio and video work when you're connected to someone on the other side. If you're running a NAT on a Windows Me, 98, or 95 server, you can switch over to Sybergen (http://www.sygate.com), which can handle NetMeeting, or WinGate (http://wingate.deerfield.com/). Note: Versions 2.*x* of WinGate didn't work with NetMeeting.

If you are running Windows 2000 or NT with their proxy server, you'll want to learn how to configure it to allow Windows Me/98 clients to receive NetMeeting calls. There is a Web site dedicated to the proxy server at http://proxyfaq. networkgods.com/downloads.htm. Here's the Windows 2000 or NT registry change that you want to make:

```
REGEDIT4
[HKEY_LOCAL_MACHINE\Software\Microsoft\Internet Audio\NacObject]
"DisableWinsock2"=dword:00000001
```

Thanks to Doug Thews for this secret. This is one that we haven't tested.

You can find out more about firewalls, port numbers for TCP/IP connections, and UDP in the *NetMeeting Resource Kit*, at http://www.microsoft.com/ netmeeting/reskit/.

Connecting to Other NetMeeting Users

Unlike using a phone, you can't just call up anyone using NetMeeting. Your friend's computer must be turned on, and he or she must be connected to your network, or you both must be connected through the Internet for you to be able to connect at all. Even if your friend is connected to your network or the Internet, you have to know this person's current address (which may be just his or her computer name).

How Do I Find Out the Address of the Person I Want to Talk To?

The short answer is that you should write an e-mail message and ask your friend for his or her Internet address or listing on a NetMeeting directory server (an ILS server).

The problem with Internet or IP addresses is that in many, if not most, cases they aren't static (that is, fixed). Most often, they are dynamically assigned when the user connects to his or her server or ISP. It's hard to keep track of someone's address if it is always changing. You don't even necessarily know your own IP address after you connect to your ISP, for example, unless you check.

NetMeeting directory servers are one way of dealing with this problem. If you log onto a directory, your current IP address is captured and associated with your fixed directory listing. All you have to do is notify your associates of this listing (which you may choose not to have displayed on the directory server), and whenever you are logged onto the directory, they can connect to you. If you'd prefer to solve this problem by getting a fixed IP address, see "Your Own Dynamic IP Address and Static Domain Name" in Chapter 35.

You may be wondering: if you can have a stable e-mail address, why can't you have a fixed IP address that NetMeeting can use? With a fixed e-mail address, it is relatively easy to let others know how they can get hold of you by e-mail — just write them a note. Unfortunately, this is not always possible with a real-time communications package such as NetMeeting.

E-mail is a store-and-forward system. Messages are mailed to an e-mail server (POP3 or IMAP4 are the Internet standard e-mail server types) that is connected full time to the Internet. This server has a fixed address. When you want to get your e-mail, you use your e-mail client — Outlook Express, for example — to interrogate the e-mail server and have it download the messages.

NetMeeting creates a real-time connection among the various parties communicating with each other. In order to do this, it needs to know where to send the packets of voice, video, and data. It can't send these packets to a server and let you connect to the server at your convenience.

Computers on the Internet or an intranet connect by using IP addresses. Every computer participating in a NetMeeting needs to know the IP address of all the other computers with which it is communicating. You can't connect to someone with NetMeeting unless that person is online and running NetMeeting also.

If you are using NetMeeting to connect to someone else over an intranet (that is, a local or wide area network that uses the TCP/IP protocol), you can keep a copy of their IP address (or computer name) in your NetMeeting SpeedDial list and connect to your associate's computer at any time. In this case, you have no need for a directory.

If you are NetMeeting with someone else, you can find out his or her IP address. Click Start ➪ Run. Type **netstat -n 30** and press Enter. A DOS window opens and displays an updated network status every 30 seconds, including the IP addresses of those computers to which you are connected (see Figure 33-8). The IP address is on the left side of the colon. The TCP/IP port addresses that NetMeeting is using are to the right of the colon. Each TCP/IP application uses a different port address.

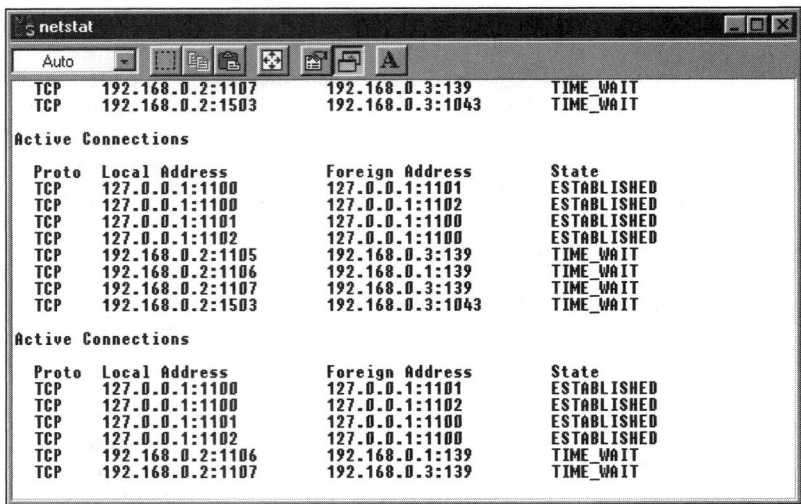

Figure 33-8: The netstat results are displayed in a DOS window.

To stop netstat, click the Close button in the upper-right corner of the DOS window, and then click Yes.

Create a SpeedDial Listing to Send to Others

One convenient way to send people your address (and have them send their address to you) is to create a SpeedDial listing shortcut. You can create it using the following steps:

STEPS

Creating Your Own SpeedDial Listing

Step 1. Click Start ⇨ Programs ⇨ Accessories ⇨ Communications ⇨ NetMeeting.

Step 2. To open the Create SpeedDial dialog box shown in Figure 33-9, click Call ⇨ Create SpeedDial.

Step 3. Type your address or directory listing in the Address field. Your default address will be the combination of your default NetMeeting directory server and your e-mail address.

If you have a fixed IP address, you can type it in — for example, **10.141.5.170**.

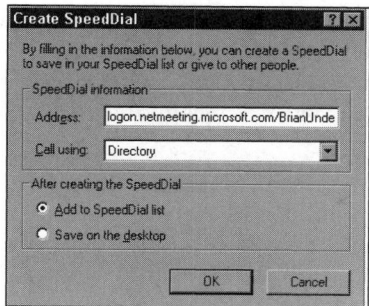

Figure 33-9: The Create SpeedDial dialog box. Enter your address and the method used to find that address.

You can also type your computer's name (you'll find it in the Control Panel ⇨ Network icon ⇨ Identification tab).

You can type the name of a NetMeeting directory server that you want to use, followed by a slash and then your e-mail name, as shown in Figure 33-9.

Step 4. Display the "Call using" drop-down list and choose the method that NetMeeting will use to find the address.

If you are on an intranet (any local network using the TCP/IP protocol) without a NetMeeting directory server, choose Network (TCP/IP).

If you are on the Internet and want to connect through a NetMeeting directory server, choose Directory Server.

Step 5. Mark the "Save on the desktop" option button. Click OK, and then click OK again. You've now created a NetMeeting shortcut on your Desktop. It is a file with a `cnf` extension.

Once you have created this SpeedDial listing, you can send it around to anyone who asks for it. If you send e-mail to someone asking for his or her SpeedDial listing, you might ask your associate to follow these steps and send the shortcut to you. To send a SpeedDial listing, right-click its icon on the Desktop, click Send To ⇨ Mail Recipient, type the e-mail address of the person to whom you're sending the listing in the To line of the New Message window, and send the message.

Tip

If you want to put the SpeedDial listing in an e-mail message as you create it, Choose Send To ⇨ Mail Recipient in step 5 above. You can Ctrl+drag the SpeedDial listing from the Attach line of the e-mail message to the Desktop to place a copy of it there before you send the message.

To find out your IP address (whether you have a fixed one or one that was just assigned to you), click Start ⇨ Run and type **Winipcfg**. In the IP Configuration dialog box that appears, your IP address is listed in the IP Autoconfiguration Address field. If you're asking for an IP address from someone on a Windows NT workstation, have him or her click Start ⇨ Run and type **Ipconfig**. (You can also see your address when you run netstat, as detailed in the previous section.)

You'll find Winipcfg in your \Windows folder. You can place a shortcut to it on your Desktop. You may have to choose the correct network adapter in the drop-down list at the top of the dialog box.

You can also open a DOS window by clicking Start ⇨ Run, and typing **ping yourcomputername** where *yourcomputername* is replaced by the name you have given your computer in the Identification tab of the Network dialog box (click the Network icon in the Control Panel).

If you use a fixed IP address in step 3, this address will become the name of the SpeedDial listing shortcut. It won't be very helpful to receive or send out such an attachment. You can change the name of the shortcut to your name (right-click it, click Rename). The IP address will still be used, but the listing will have a much friendlier name. If you use your computer's name in step 3, you might also want to rename the shortcut to your own name.

You can keep as many of these SpeedDial listing shortcuts on your Desktop as you like, but they may crowd out other icons that vie for that space. Drag them into another folder; better yet, drag them into the \Program Files\ NetMeeting\SpeedDial folder in an Explorer window. If you do this, they will appear in SpeedDial view in the NetMeeting window.

To drag and drop a SpeedDial listing to your NetMeeting SpeedDial folder, take these steps:

STEPS

Adding a SpeedDial Shortcut to the List

Step 1.   Click Start ⇨ Programs ⇨ Accessories ⇨ Windows Explorer.

Step 2.   Navigate to \Program Files\NetMeeting\SpeedDial.

Step 3.   Drag and drop a SpeedDial listing shortcut from your Desktop to this folder in the Explorer window.

Step 4.   Click Start ⇨ Programs ⇨ Accessories ⇨ Communications ⇨ NetMeeting.

Step 5.   Click View ⇨ SpeedDial. You'll see your new listing.

Step 6.   If you don't see your new listing, press F5. If that doesn't work, exit NetMeeting and restart.

Tip

If, when you create a new SpeedDial entry, you click the "Add to Speed Dial list" option button in the Add SpeedDial dialog box, the new entry is automatically added to the \Program Files\NetMeeting\SpeedDial folder. If you receive a SpeedDial entry as a cnf file attachment in an e-mail message, you can just save it to this folder.

How Do I Know If Someone Is Online?

In order to use NetMeeting, all of the participants in a meeting have to be online. This isn't a problem if you are connected together through an intranet, or if your computer is always connected to the Internet and you are running NetMeeting (perhaps in the background).

If you are permanently online, you'll most likely have a fixed IP address, and it will be easy for your associates to contact you. They'll just click your name in their SpeedDial folders.

If you go online at irregular intervals, your associates will either have to contact you (say by e-mail) to make arrangements to NetMeet at a certain time, or wait to contact you when you do go online. One way to do this is to use a notification service such as ICQ that works with NetMeeting. ICQ provides the option of holding a NetMeeting whenever you find that one of your buddies (that is, someone on your Buddy list) is online. You'll find ICQ at http://web.icq.com/.

If your correspondents register with a NetMeeting directory server (an ILS server), you can see if they are logged onto their server by keeping their name and address in your SpeedDial list. NetMeeting regularly checks your SpeedDial list to see if one of your buddies is online. You get to set the interval (click Tools ⇨ Options, click the Calling tab, and click "Automatically refresh SpeedDial list every [   ] minutes").

They can also send you e-mail when they go online, telling you their IP address or sending you a SpeedDial listing.

Can NetMeeting Act Like an Answering Machine?

The problem with NetMeeting is that you have to be online and running the program for anyone to be able to connect to you using NetMeeting. It is possible to run NetMeeting in the background so that it can recognize when someone is calling you and alert you to start a NetMeeting.

You can have NetMeeting start automatically or only when you decide to start it. You can also have NetMeeting track who else has tried to contact you with NetMeeting while you were away or not responding for other reasons.

To set these options, take these steps:

STEPS

Putting NetMeeting in the Background

Step 1. Click Start ➪ Programs ➪ Accessories ➪ Communications ➪ NetMeeting.

Step 2. Choose Tools ➪ Options, and click the General tab. Two check-boxes let you configure NetMeeting to work in the background (see Figure 33-10).

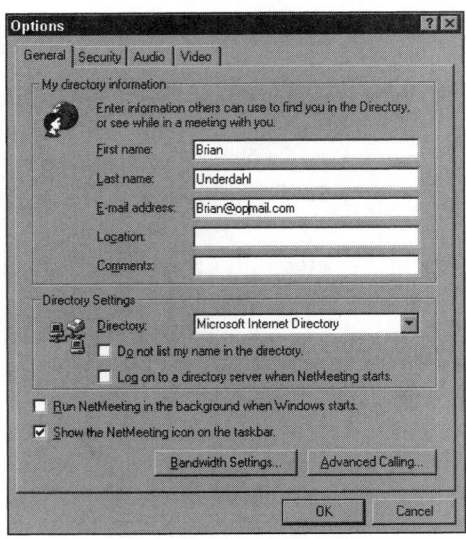

Figure 33-10: The General tab of the Options dialog box

Step 3. Mark "Show the NetMeeting icon on the taskbar." This actually puts the NetMeeting icon in the system tray. If the icon is in the system tray, you can start NetMeeting by double-clicking the icon or by right-clicking it and clicking Open.

If NetMeeting is running (you'll know that this is the case because its button will appear on the taskbar), you can also click the icon in the system tray and choose among four NetMeeting functions: Share Application, Start Collaborating, Chat, and Whiteboard.

Step 4. Mark "Run NetMeeting in the background when Windows starts." This puts a command in your startup sequence that runs NetMeeting in background mode (it doesn't put a button on the taskbar).

To get this mode to start, you'll need to click OK in the Options dialog box, and then choose Call ⇨ Exit to stop NetMeeting. To start NetMeeting again, double-click its icon in the system tray.

You can see that this option has in fact set up NetMeeting to start in background mode by clicking Start ⇨ Programs ⇨ Accessories ⇨ System Tools ⇨ System Information, and clicking Tools ⇨ System Configuration Utility ⇨ Startup. You'll find Microsoft NetMeeting in the list of startup items.

Step 5. Click OK.

If you want to use NetMeeting to communicate with others on a regular basis, you'll need to have it running at least in background mode pretty much all the time. You'll also have to be connected to at least an intranet as much as possible, if not continuously. Otherwise, you will have to send e-mail to your associates to arrange a time for your NetMeetings, or use a notification service such as ICQ.

How Can I Log on to a New NetMeeting Directory Server?

Secret

A list of NetMeeting directory servers is kept, where else, in your registry, under HKEY_CURRENT_USER\ Software\ Microsoft\Conferencing\ UI\ Directory. You can add or subtract servers from your list of directory servers either by editing the list in your registry or by using the NetMeeting Super Enhancer shown in Figure 33-11. You'll find NetMeeting Super Enhancer at http://www.netmeet.net.

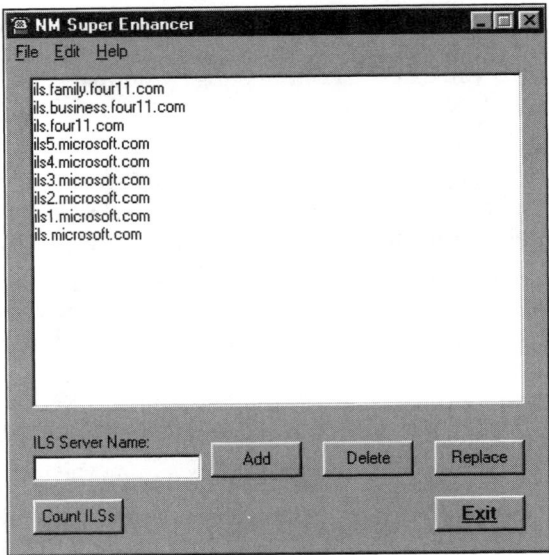

Figure 33-11: NetMeeting Super Enhancer

You can add (but not subtract) a server listing in NetMeeting by typing its name in the Server Name field. Choose Call ➪ Change My Information to display the Options dialog box, click the Calling tab, and type a server name in this field.

If you are on an intranet with a directory server, you'll want to add it to your list. You may want to get rid of other directories from this list, especially if you are a system administrator and don't want users on your network trying to access outside servers.

To choose a directory to log onto, choose Tools ➪ Options, click the Calling tab, and select a server name in the "Server name" field, as shown in Figure 33-12.

Thanks to Tom Lake for pointing out where the list of servers is kept.

You can find a list of the NetMeeting directory servers available on the Internet at http://www.netmeet.net/bestservers.asp.

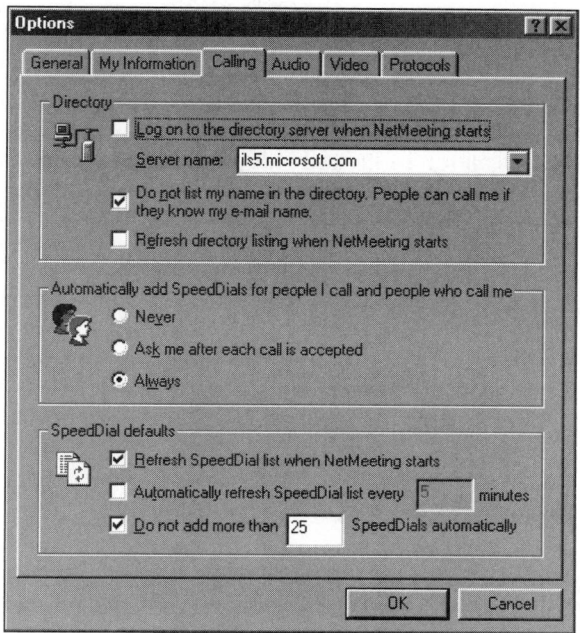

Figure 33-12: Use the Calling tab of the Options dialog box to choose a directory to log onto.

How Can I Use NetMeeting to Contact Others Outside My Corporate Firewall?

James Rice helped us out with this one. Have your system administrator configure your firewall so that the ports listed in Table 33-1 are not blocked.

Table 33-1   Firewall Settings for NetMeeting Users

Port Number	Protocol
ULS server	LDAP. Port 389 TCP and UDP
1503	T.120 (TCP)
1720	H.323 call setup (TCP)
1731	Audio call control (TCP)
Dynamic	H.323 call control (TCP)
Dynamic	H.323 streaming (RTP over UDP)

The H.323 call setup protocol (over port 1720) dynamically negotiates a TCP port for use by the H.323 call control protocol. Both the audio call control protocol (over port 1731) and the H.323 call setup protocol (over port 1720) dynamically negotiate UDP ports for use by the H.323 streaming protocol, called the *real-time protocol* (RTP). In NetMeeting, two ports are determined on each side of the firewall for audio and video streaming. These dynamically negotiated ports are selected arbitrarily from all ports that can be assigned dynamically.

Can I Use NetMeeting to Talk with AOL Users?

You can if they have installed AOL 3.0 or later and are running Windows Me, 98, or 95. They have to connect to AOL using a 32-bit version of TCP/IP. Earlier versions of the AOL client software used 16-bit connections.

Why Can't My Friend Accept My NetMeeting Calls?

There are several reasons why the person you are trying to contact may be unavailable even if both of you are logged onto the same NetMeeting directory server and see each other's name in the directory.

The directory server's list of names is not immediately updated if someone logs off. Therefore, while it may appear that the person is there, he or she may in fact have already left.

If the person you are trying to access is connecting to his or her ISP through a nonstandard protocol — perhaps a PPP emulator — NetMeeting won't be able to establish contact. If the person is behind a firewall or a server/router that converts IP addresses, NetMeeting won't be able to find it's way through.

If your friend's computer has the TCP/IP protocol bound to the network card and the Dial-Up Adapter, the NetMeeting directory server may have associated the wrong IP address with your friend's directory listing. Your friend has to unbind the TCP/IP protocol from his or her network card temporarily. To do this, have your friend take these steps:

STEPS

Releasing a Network Card's TCP/IP Address

Step 1.   Click Start ➪ Run, type **winipcfg**, and press Enter.

Step 2. Display the drop-down list at the top of the IP Configuration dialog box and choose the network card.

Step 3. Click the Release button, and click OK. (To later rebind the TCP/IP protocol to the network card, your friend will need to restart his or her computer.)

On the other hand, your friend may not want to be disturbed and may have clicked Call ➪ Do Not Disturb.

Can I Call into My Computer at Work and Use NetMeeting?

You can configure your computer at work as a Dial-Up Networking server. You can then call in from your computer at home, and as long as you are running the TCP/IP protocol over your Dial-Up Adapter, you can run NetMeeting and pass audio and video information.

You'll first need to install Dial-Up Networking on both computers. If you haven't done this already, you can follow the steps in Chapter 19. In particular, review the sections "Setting Up Your Windows Computer at Work As a Host" and "Setting Up Your Computer at Home As a Guest." You can also follow the steps in the *Windows Resource Kit* on your Windows CD-ROM.

Once you have installed Dial-Up Networking and the Dial-Up Adapter, take these steps to configure your computers to enable a connection between them:

STEPS

Setting Up Your Computers to Allow NetMeeting Calls

Step 1. On your computer at work, click Start ➪ Settings ➪ Control Panel, click the Network icon, and click Configuration. Scroll down to and highlight TCP/IP -> Dial-Up Adapter, as shown in Figure 33-13. Click Properties.

Step 2. You will be warned that setting the TCP/IP properties in the Network dialog box is not a good idea, and that you should set them in the dial-up connectoid (see Figure 33-14). Click OK.

Continued

STEPS

Setting Up Your Computers to Allow NetMeeting Calls *(continued)*

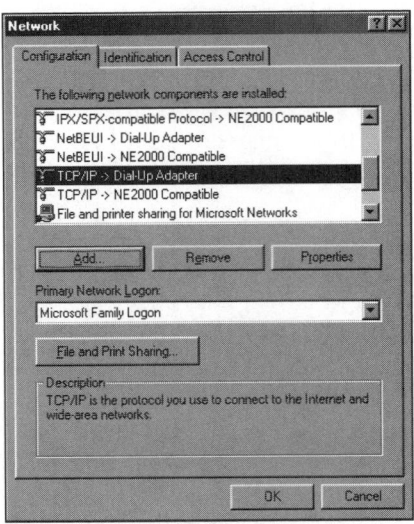

Figure 33-13: The Configuration tab of the Network dialog box

Figure 33-14: The TCP/IP Properties Information dialog box

You are only going to set the IP address for the DUN server. This will be overridden if you dial into the Internet with a DUN connectoid using the computer at work.

Step 3.   In the TCP/IP Properties dialog box, click the IP Address tab, and mark "Specify an IP address." Type **192.168.0.1** for the IP address, and for the Subnet Mask, use **255.255.255.0**, as shown in Figure 33-15. Click OK, and then click OK again. You will have to restart the computer when prompted.

Step 4. After your computer restarts, click Start ⇨ Programs ⇨ Accessories ⇨ Communications ⇨ Dial-Up Networking. In the Dial-Up Networking folder window, choose Connections ⇨ Dial-Up Server.

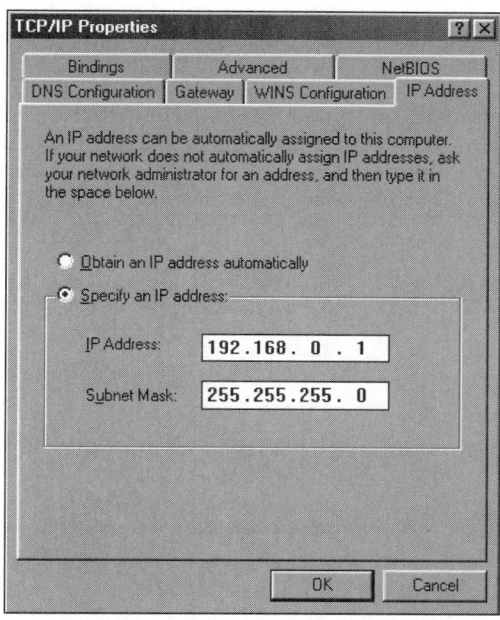

Figure 33-15: The IP Address tab of the TCP/IP Properties dialog box

Step 5. In the Dial-Up Server dialog box, mark "Allow caller access" (see Figure 33-16). Click OK.

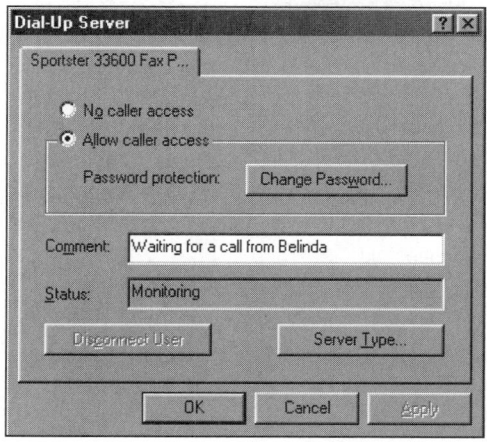

Figure 33-16: The Dial-Up Server dialog box

Continued

STEPS

Setting Up Your Computers to Allow NetMeeting Calls *(continued)*

Step 6.   On your computer at home, click Start ⇨ Programs ⇨ Accessories ⇨ Communications ⇨ Dial-Up Networking. In the Dial-Up Networking folder window, click the Make New Connection icon.

Follow the steps in the Make New Connection Wizard, giving your DUN connectoid a new name and entering the phone number for the phone line connected to the computer at work.

Step 7.   Right-click this new connectoid. Click Properties, and click the Server Types tab.

Step 8.   Under "Allowed network protocols," clear NetBEUI and IPX/SPX Compatible, and leave TCP/IP marked (see Figure 33-17). Click the TCP/IP Settings button.

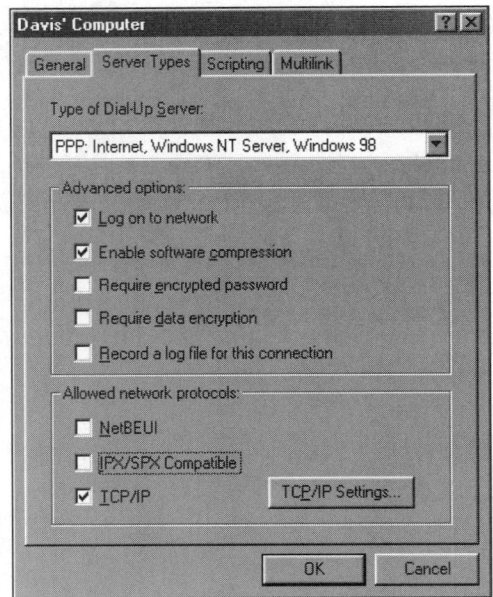

Figure 33-17: The Server Types tab of the Properties dialog box for your new DUN connectoid

Step 9. In the TCP/IP Settings dialog box, mark "Specify an IP address" and type **192.168.0.2**, as shown in Figure 33-18. Click OK. Click OK again.

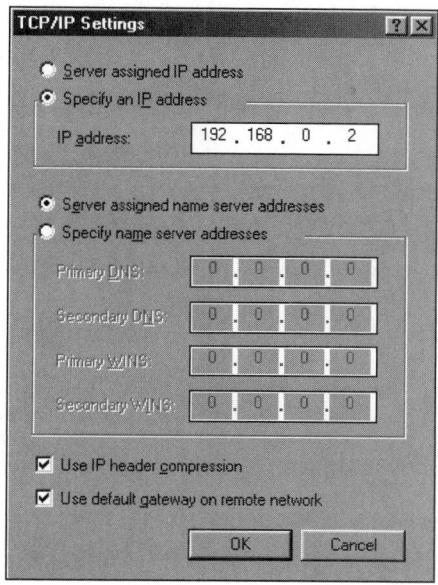

Figure 33-18: The TCP/IP Settings dialog box

Step 10. On both computers, in an Internet Explorer window, click Tools ⇨ Internet Options. Click the Connections tab. Mark "Never dial a connection." Click OK.

Step 11. On both computers, in a NetMeeting window, choose Tools ⇨ Options, and click the Calling tab. Clear "Log on to the directory server when NetMeeting starts." Click OK.

Step 12. On the computer at home, click the DUN connectoid that calls up and connects to the computer at work. When the connection is successful, click Call ⇨ New Call, and enter the TCP/IP address of the computer at work, as given in step 3.

Step 13. Choose Network (TCP/IP) in the "Call using" field, and click the Call button.

Your NetMeeting session should now begin. Thanks to Mark Andres for tips on some of the more obscure steps.

Let People Contact You Through Your Web Site

You can put a call button on your Web site and ask folks to contact you by going to your Web site and clicking the Call button. If they have NetMeeting and they click the Call button on your Web site, their copy of NetMeeting will open. You have to be online to take the call, and they have to use Internet Explorer as their browser to be able to use the Call button.

Here is an example of some HTML code that you could add to your Web page to add a Call button:

```
You can contact me using NetMeeting at <A HREF="callto:ils5.microsoft.com/
davis@davisstraub.com"> ils5.microsoft.com/davis@davisstraub.com</A>.
```

If you have a fixed IP address, you can substitute it for the NetMeeting directory server address. You can also use a graphical button if you like, instead of the text shown in the example.

Connect a Few Computers Together to Use NetMeeting

If you have a small local area network, you can configure your network in a very simple fashion to enable NetMeeting to work between computers. If you want to exchange audio and video, you will have to bind the TCP/IP protocol to your network card. You can see how to do this in Chapter 18.

Each computer on your local area network will have a unique name. To connect to any one of them, click Call and type the name of the computer. (You can assign a unique name to a computer in the Identification tab of the Network dialog box—see Chapter 18 for more information.)

If you assign an IP address to each of the computers on the network, you can call that unique address just by including it in your SpeedDial. You can assign such an address by clicking the Network icon in your Control Panel, highlighting TCP/IP on your network card, clicking Properties, and then clicking the IP Address tab. Click "Specify an IP address," and type an IP address (mine is 10.141.5.170) and a submask (mine is 255.0.0.0).

Using NetMeeting to Talk on the Telephone

Here's an inappropriate use of technology: use a $2,500 computer as a $50 telephone. Well, it is almost worth it. Of course, it's harder than just using the phone.

You can connect to other NetMeeting users who are online and talk to them. Your voice is carried as packages of data that are reassembled and played when they get to the person you're calling. You can also (theoretically) use NetMeeting to call a telephone number and speak to the person who answers the phone as though you were using a phone (sort of).

This is different than Microsoft Phone (or other H.324-compliant software). Microsoft Phone uses a voice-capable modem (V.80) and/or sound card to turn your computer into a phone. You dial through your computer and it acts just like a phone.

To use NetMeeting as a phone, you need to connect to a server that will convert the NetMeeting data stream into a regular analog audio stream as well as place the call that you have dialed. What is cool about this capability is that you can use the cheap Internet backbone to get to a server close to the location that you want to call, and then have the server place a local call. It cuts down on the cost of long-distance calls by using the Internet to get most of the way.

The problem is that you need to be able to connect to a server that provides this IP-to-audio switcheroo — an H.323 gateway. There may soon be publicly available servers that you can use to make these kinds of calls. We expect that they will figure out how to bill you.

You have to provide the IP address of the H.323 gateway. In NetMeeting, choose Tools ⇨ Options, click the Audio tab, mark the "Use H.323 gateway" checkbox, and type the IP address in the field on the right.

Want to learn more about H.323? Visit `http://www.netmeet.net/`.

Net2Phone

Net2Phone is not a part of NetMeeting, but an alternative to it for certain functions.

If you want to use a solution that is really available now to use your computer as a phone and to call up a telephone, you can use Net Phone at `http://www.net2phone.com`. Net2Phone turns your microphone, sound card, speakers, and computer into a telephone that can call any telephone in the world. You use the Net2Phone software and Net2Phone's Internet servers to place the telephone call. The advantage is that you may be able to make inexpensive long-distance or international phone calls, partially through the Internet and partially over the local phone company at the receiving end.

You need to sign up with Net2Phone after you download their client software in order to place phone calls. You can check out their rates and determine if they are any less expensive than using your regular telephone. The big advantage comes from calling back into the U.S. Your international call from China to the U.S. might only cost you the price of the local call to an ISP in China, plus $0.10/minute for the long-distance connection in the US.

You use Net2Phone just like a regular phone, punching in the numbers on the keypad or using the speed dial (see Figure 33-19).

Figure 33-19: Net2Phone gives you a familiar user interface.

Connecting to other Conferencing Systems

You can use NetMeeting to connect to similar systems that exchange audio, video, and textual information. For example, you can connect to Pictel at an H.320/H.323 gateway. Check out `http://www.picturetel.com/` for more details.

A number of video conferencing software systems comply with the H.320 standard. They require high throughput to work at all and are often based on ISDN modems.

NetMeeting Makes a Call to an Invalid DLL

Secret

Installing Windows Me over Windows 98 or 95 should update all dynamic link libraries to the latest versions — and if you have the latest version of NetMeeting, then all should be well. That said, time marches on, and things change. If you get the error message, "Program Error - Your program is making an invalid dynamic link call to a .DLL file," you may have an out-of-date video or Direct Sound driver.

You can update your Windows NetMeeting setup by clicking Start ➪ Settings ➪ Windows Update.

NetMeeting Freezes Your Computer When Starting

Secret

There are a couple of reasons this might happen. NetMeeting enumerates and sorts all your fonts when it starts up so that they can be used for application sharing. If some of your font files are corrupted or you've previously installed Hewlett Packard's "Fonts for the Family," then NetMeeting will hang your computer. You can find out which fonts come with the HP set by reading the Microsoft Knowledge Base article "NetMeeting Hangs When Starting" at http://support.microsoft.com/support/kb/articles/q156/0/94.asp.

NetMeeting may also be conflicting with a remote control application such as PC Anywhere, which installs a virtual display driver. When NetMeeting attempts to interact with the "real" display driver, the computer freezes. You may need to uninstall any remote control software. Check the manufacturer's Web site first to see if they have a solution.

Thanks to Roman Deeds for this secret.

Cameras and Video Capture Cards That Work with NetMeeting

Purchase an inexpensive charged couple diode camera as an input device to the video card, or get a card that attaches to your existing video camera. You also have to buy a video card to process the video input. Without it, your computer's CPU would be bogged down processing the video signal.

You'll want to check out http://www.winnov.com. You'll find cards both for desktop and portable computers there.

You might find that NetMeeting incorrectly states that you have video capture hardware already installed. Some software, such as Microsoft Camcorder, emulates video devices and will be detected by NetMeeting. To eliminate this false video capture detection, click Start ➪ Settings ➪ Control Panel, click Multimedia, click Devices, and click Video Capture Devices. Disable any device found there. (Thanks to Bill Schneider for this secret.)

Want to create a videogram (an audio/video clip) and send it off as e-mail? You can do this directly with Outlook Express. Just insert the video clips in your e-mail and send them out. The Microsoft Media Player should play them.

NetMeeting Web Sites and Newsgroups

NetMeeting is changing. Anything we say in this book could be out-of-date. New versions of NetMeeting are released all the time, sometimes even without a version number change.

If you are going to keep up with the changes, you need to visit the sites listed in Table 33-2 and browse the NetMeeting newsgroups every so often.

Table 33-2   Useful NetMeeting Web Sites

Description	URL
Video capture	http:/ / www.winnov.com
Standard Scoble Advice	http:/ / www.netmeet.net
NetMeeting FAQ	http://support.microsoft.com/support/ netmeeting/faq/
NetMeeting Resource Kit	http://www.microsoft.com/netmeeting/ reskit/
ITU standard H.320	http://www.itu.int
Microsoft ILS server	http://www.microsoft.com/netmeeting/ils/
Meeting by Wire	http://www.meetingbywire.com
PlanetExchange's Conference Center for Microsoft NetMeeting	http://ilscenter.com
ILS list	http://www.netmeet.net/bestservers.asp

The following is a list of the NetMeeting support newsgroups on msnews.microsoft.com:

> microsoft.public.internet.netmeeting
>
> microsoft.public.internet.netmeeting.beta
>
> microsoft.public.inetexplorer.ie5beta.netmeetingchat
>
> microsoft.public.win98.internet.netmeeting
>
> microsoft.public.inetexplorer.ie4.netmeeting

Summary

Yet another Internet facility built into the operating system, NetMeeting lets you share with others.

▶ Use an Internet-based server to share audio and video with multiple conference participants.

▶ Send your own SpeedDial listing to your friends.

▶ Have your system administrator properly configure your corporate firewall to allow NetMeeting packets in and out.

▶ Configure a Windows server to allow incoming NetMeeting calls.

▶ Use NetMeeting to make a phone call.

▶ Find a video camera that will put the least strain on your computer's resources.

Chapter 34

Chat

Chatty Microsoft

Since 1995, Microsoft has been in a panic to make sure that it doesn't miss any boat, or even canoe, that may be leaving the Internet dock. Therefore, they gave a few programmers in the backroom the task of providing an Internet chat client.

There were plenty of Internet Relay Chat (IRC) clients available when Microsoft first introduced Microsoft Comic Chat 1.0, so they added the twist of displaying little two-dimensional characters that could express a limited array of "emotions." It took a special Comic Chat server, which Microsoft also developed, to display these different faces to the other comic chatters.

Microsoft now provides Microsoft Chat and operates publicly available online Internet chat servers. You'll find these http://webchat.msn.com/.

Microsoft operates other free chat servers at other URLs. They are all part of the irc.msn.com chat network. In addition, there are plenty of other chat servers, operated by other entities. See "Chat Servers" later in this chapter for some of their addresses.

There are plenty of other IRC clients. You might try mIRC at http://www.mirc.co.uk, and Pirch at http://www.pirchat.com.

Starting a Conversation

Once you're online and connected to a chat server, you can look around. You don't need to respond to anyone, and you can enter rooms that are open without having to chat, whisper, accept files, open NetMeeting chats, or interact in any fashion whatsoever.

You'll find all the basics covered in Microsoft's online help files for Chat. You can check these out offline before you enter any room populated by other chat users (as well as a few chat bots). There is usually a help room available for questions about the chat network or your chat client. Just ask a question of the host.

Microsoft maintains a FAQ about its chat network. You'll find it at `http://computingcentral.msn.com/help/howtochat.asp`. If you're a new chat user, we suggest that you check out a couple of introductions to chat at `http://www.mirc.co.uk/irc.html` and `http://www.mirc.co.uk/ircintro.html`.

Who Are You?

Chat clients let you mask a bit of your identity. This is part of the appeal of chat. You get to pretend. Of course, if you are on an intranet chat, there may be some restrictions on how much anonymity, if any, you are allowed.

Chat encourages you to enter some information about yourself — your real name and e-mail address, for instance — but you are not required to do so. You can leave these fields blank or make imaginary entries. You are required to enter a nickname (which can be your real name). This is the limit of your identity, almost.

Others can find out this information about you by double-clicking your nickname when you are in a chat room. They also see your user ID. The user ID contains a *masked* version of your current IP address. While your IP address is masked to other users in your chat room, the chat room's host gets to see the whole thing.

This comes in quite handy if you behave badly. The host can ban anyone using the miscreant's Internet service provider (ISP) from entering his or her chat room. Because in most cases IP addresses are assigned dynamically, it would do no good to ban a given IP address. It would be a simple matter for the person who has behaved inappropriately to just log off his or her service provider and then log on again to receive a new IP address.

The host or system operator may therefore decide to ban the ISP by choosing to disallow a range of IP addresses (those dynamically provided by the ISP). The ban may occur for a few hours or days. It is then up to the service provider to deal with the user who has now inconvenienced all of the ISP's other users who may have wanted to enter that same chat room.

Given that we could be easily talking about America Online as the service provider, you can see how this could become a major hassle very quickly.

So, even if you are playing the game of hiding your identity, it isn't hidden from all those who may be in a position to make your life a little bit harder. Hassle a chat room operator, and you may pay a heavy price (get kicked off your ISP).

Is Someone Hassling You?

You go into a chat room to chat with someone else. It may turn out that you don't want to chat with a person who wants to talk to you, and he or she just can't take a hint. If you are using Chat, right-click the name of the offensive individual and click Ignore to ignore the pestering.

This works unless the person is persistent or obsessive—a modern fear if there ever was one. When computer communication makes reaching out and touching someone so easy, the flip side is that it is realistic to fear getting hounded by one of the millions of thoughtless boors who inhabit the cyber planet.

Ignoring only works as long as the person doesn't change his or her name. Changing a nickname doesn't work because the chat server tracks users by their user IDs. Unfortunately, the person can easily change his or her user ID by briefly logging off the chat server and changing names.

You can ask the room host to ban the unpleasant individual. The host may do so, and he or she may ban all the users from that ISP. You then have the opportunity to contact the service provider and ask them to take action against the offender. The service provider now has a definite interest in fixing the problem, because all of their users are being banned from the chat room.

If the harasser has decided to nuke you—that is, send ICMP packets to your computer with various error messages in them—you have arrived at the next level of Internet irritation. ICMP is the acronym for Internet Control Message Protocol. This protocol reports errors and provides other information relevant to IP packet processing. It's documented in RFC 792 (use a search engine on the Internet to find out more about this if you like). If the IP address and port numbers in the ICMP packets match your connection to the chat server, your connection will be terminated.

There are a number of ways to deal with the nuker. First, Windows incorporates Winsock 2.2, an upgraded layer of the multilayered Internet protocols. Winsock stands between your Internet application and the network. Winsock 2.2 successfully combats many of the ICMP attacks.

Second, you can contact the attacker's service provider to ask that this person be dropped as a customer. You can protect yourself by installing firewall software, even if you are a standalone computer.

You can find out more about these types of denial-of-service attacks at http://www.irchelp.org/irchelp/nuke/.

Chat Commands

You're just chatting away until you enter a slash (/) as the first character, and then you are sending a command. Chat's friendly user interface makes many of these commands unnecessary. In addition, these clients come with keyboard shortcuts that let you react quickly as you chat.

Still, the command interface is available to you, and you may use other IRC clients that use it exclusively. You can find out about the standard and extended IRC commands at http://www.mirc.co.uk/ircintro.html.

Chat clients may not implement all (or even most) of the commands. You can give each of them a try and see what's available.

If you are having trouble joining a chat room, you can use the /list command to what chat rooms meet your criteria. Table 34-1 lists some ways to use this command:

Table 34-1   Common /List Commands

Command	Type of Room
/listx R=1	Registered rooms
/listx R=0	Dynamic rooms
/listx N=*comic*	Rooms with the word *comic* anywhere in the name
/listx T=*help*	Rooms with *help* in the topic
/listx >25	Rooms with more than 25 members
/listx <20	Rooms with fewer than 20 members

You can then use the /join *roomname* command to join a chat room. An interested party makes up dynamic rooms on the spot. Registered rooms have a more permanent status.

Chat Servers

In addition to the Microsoft irc.msn.com chat network, there are plenty of other chat servers out there on the Internet.

The irc.msn.com network goes by many names and has many servers. You can connect to it using any of these server names:

```
mschat.msn.com
mschat2.msn.com
mschat3.msn.com
mschat4.msn.com
irc.msn.com
irc2.msn.com
irc3.msn.com
irc4.msn.com
comicsrv.microsoft.com
comicsrv2.microsoft.com
comicsrv3.microsoft.com
comicsrv4.microsoft.com
204.255.245.172:6667
204.255.245.173:6667
204.255.245.174:6667
```

MSN has its own chat server restricted to MSN users. You'll find it at chat. msn.com.

TalkCity at `http://www.talkcity.com/` runs an extensive schedule of chats. You'll even find the authors of *Secrets* books chatting away over there from time to time. Check out the IDG Books Worldwide Web site at `http://www.idgbooks.com` for more information and author chat schedules.

Tip

You can add a new server to your list of chat servers just by typing its name in the Server field of the Chat Connection dialog box, which appears when you start up Chat, or under Room ➪ Connect in either chat client. You can remove names from the chat server list by editing your registry. Find out more about how to do this in Chapter 11.

Tip

If you are trying to connect to irc.msn.com from AOL, you might want to try irc.msn.com:7000 instead. The default is port 6667, but this address may work better for you.

Internet Chat Newsgroups and Resources

It is a bit funny when you think about it, but there are newsgroups about chat. Of course, if you have a question, you can just go to the help room on your chat network and ask one of the system operators. Then again, they really don't answer questions about the chat clients, so you'll have to check out the newsgroups.

Microsoft provides newsgroups for its chat clients and chat server, as well as for its chat network. Table 34-2 lists some of them.

Table 34-2   Newsgroups for Microsoft Chat

Newsgroup	URL
Help with Microsoft's chat network	`news://publicnews.msn.com/msn.irc.support`
Help on Chat	`news://msnews.microsoft.com/microsoft.public.internet.mschat`
Help on Chat	`news://msnews.microsoft.com/microsoft.public.inetexplorer.ie4.mschat`
Help on the Exchange	`news://msnews.microsoft.com/microsoft.public.`
Chat server	`mcis.chatserver`

You can find other newsgroups that focus on chat and IRC issues on Usenet. Use your newsgroup reader (Outlook Express, for example) to connect to your Internet service provider's news server and then search for *irc*.

You'll find a couple of FAQs about these two chat clients at the previously listed Microsoft chat newsgroups.

Summary

We show you how to get your chat client up and running, how to change your world, and how to keep from being pestered.

▶ Shows you how you are identified to others on the chat rooms.

▶ You can use some of the standard IRC chat commands with Microsoft Chat.

▶ You can find additional resources and help with Chat.

Chapter 35

Publishing on the Web

In This Chapter

Windows comes with a Web page editor and the ability to ship Web pages and graphics to your Web server. Having a Web presence is actually pretty cool, and if you're a business, it can actually make you some money. We provide some add-ons and tweaks to make this a little more possible.

▶ Why not make it easier to get to Notepad when you want to edit an HTML file?

▶ Download Programs for HTML development

▶ Use Microsoft's FTP built into Internet Explorer to copy your Web pages up to your Web server

Working with HTML

HTML is the language of Web pages. That is, HTML is the programming language used to create documents that Web browsers like Internet Explorer can then display as Web pages.

Edit HTML Files with Notepad

Secret

Sometimes Notepad can be the perfect little HTML editor, even if you usually use FrontPage or another fancy WYSIWYG editor. While it is always possible to use Send To to "send" an HTML page to Notepad, you can also just add a command to the HTML context menu that enables you to right-click the HTML file and edit it with Notepad.

One way to do this is to insert the following text into a text file, save the file and rename it Notepadhtml.reg, right-click the renamed file, and click Merge. This creates a new command called Notepad, which shows up on the HTML context menu when you right-click an HTML file.

```
REGEDIT4
[HKEY_CLASSES_ROOT\htmlfile\shell\notepad]
@="&Notepad"
[HKEY_CLASSES_ROOT\htmlfile\shell\notepad\command]
@="c:\\windows\\notepad.exe %1"
```

Thanks to Yannis Pantzis for this secret.

Change Your Text Files to HTML

If you want a quick and dirty way to convert your text files into HTML format, you should check out Text2Web at `http://virdi-software.com/`. It's not beautiful, it's not sophisticated, and it's not real clever, but it will create tables and lists from your text.

You can insert text from the Clipboard or from a text file. You can set the font, font color, and background color of the resulting HTML page, as shown in Figure 35-1. Text2Web will convert HTML and mailto addresses to hyperlinks.

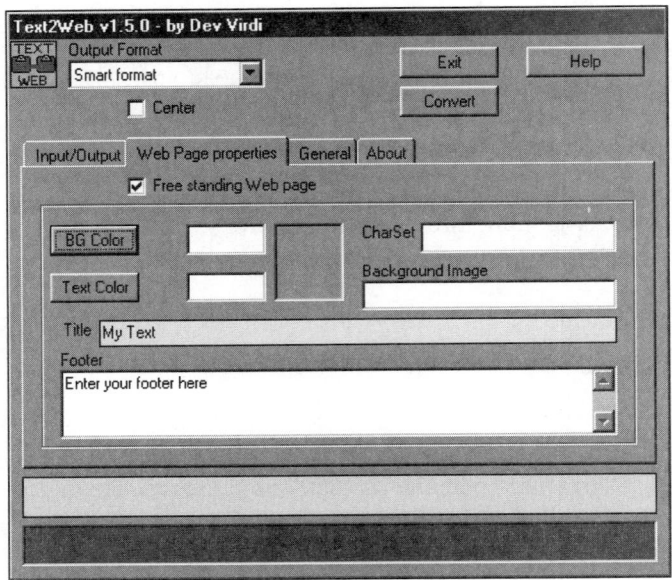

Figure 35-1: You need the Pro version of Text2Web to set the font, font color, and background color.

Thanks to Chris Pirillo at `http://www.lockergnome.com`.

Prettify or Compress Your HTML Code

If you use FrontPage, you'll notice that your underlying HTML source code doesn't look all that readable. The indents aren't in the right places, the line lengths can get pretty long, and you'll wonder why there aren't any carriage returns. This may even be true if you are editing your own code straight in Notepad.

<PRETTY>HTML (that's the name of the product) will read through your HTML source and put in the proper indents, add comments at the beginning

of headers and tables, and set the line lengths so that you don't have to scroll to the right. We tried it on a number of our HTML files, and it did a beautiful job, as you can see in Figure 35-2. This makes it much easier to actually edit the HTML source document.

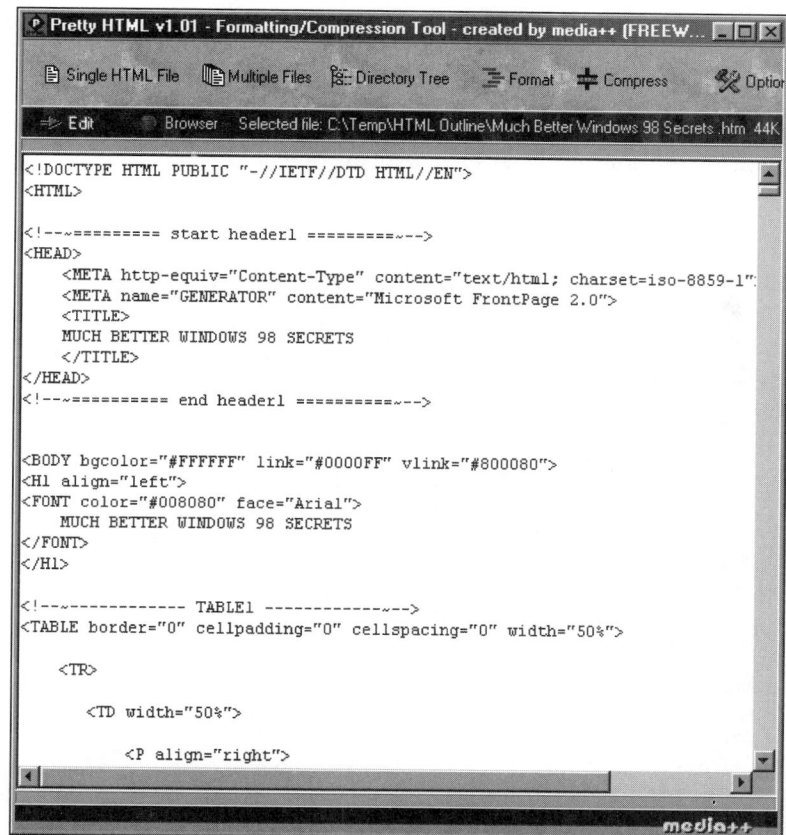

Figure 35-2: This HTML document has been processed by <PRETTY>HTML.

You can also use <PRETTY>HTML to compress HTML files, however they were produced. This actually uglifies the HTML file but makes for a quicker download. We saw about a 20 percent reduction in the size of HTML files. This will make your Web site seem a bit zippier.

You'll find <PRETTY>HTML at http://www.mpp.at. There is a freeware version, and there is also a professional version with a few more features.

Buttonz! and Tilez!

These two programs, which work separately but come together in the same zipped package, are just as cute as can be. They do exactly what their titles say they do.

Buttonz! helps you make sophisticated button icons that you can activate on your Web pages. Associate the button image with an action, a link to another Web page, whatever.

With Buttonz!, you can easily create the bevels, gradients, textures, lighting, colors, captions, size, and shape of all kinds of buttons, as shown in Figure 35-3. Output your buttons as JPEGs, BMPs, or in a number of other standard graphical formats.

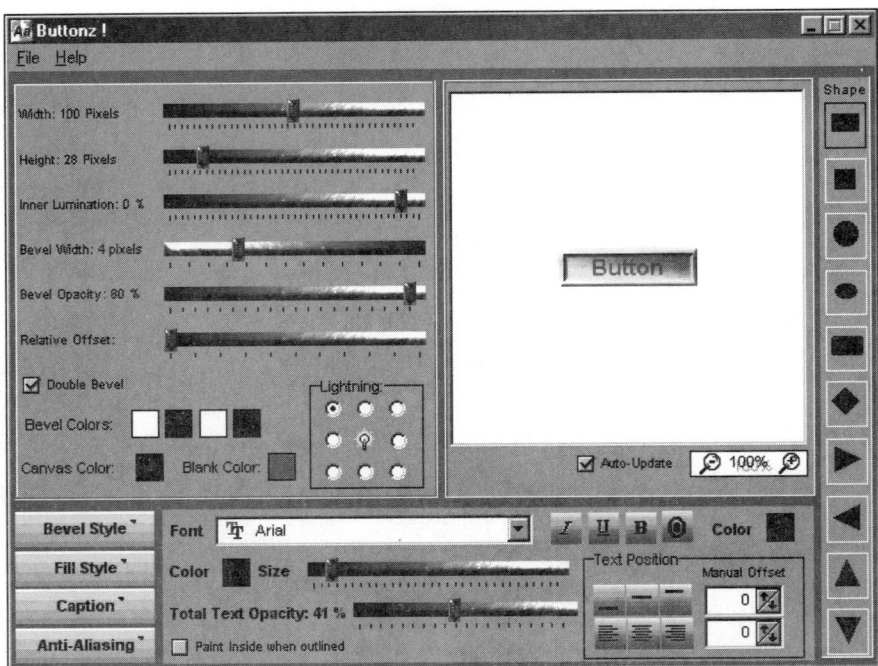

Figure 35-3: The Buttonz! user interface with a button in progress

Tilez! is a dedicated tile painter. Put the tiles together to create a background for your Web pages or folder views in your Explorer. Tilez! uses three layers to create its effects, as shown in Figure 35-4. You can insert various images into any of the layers.

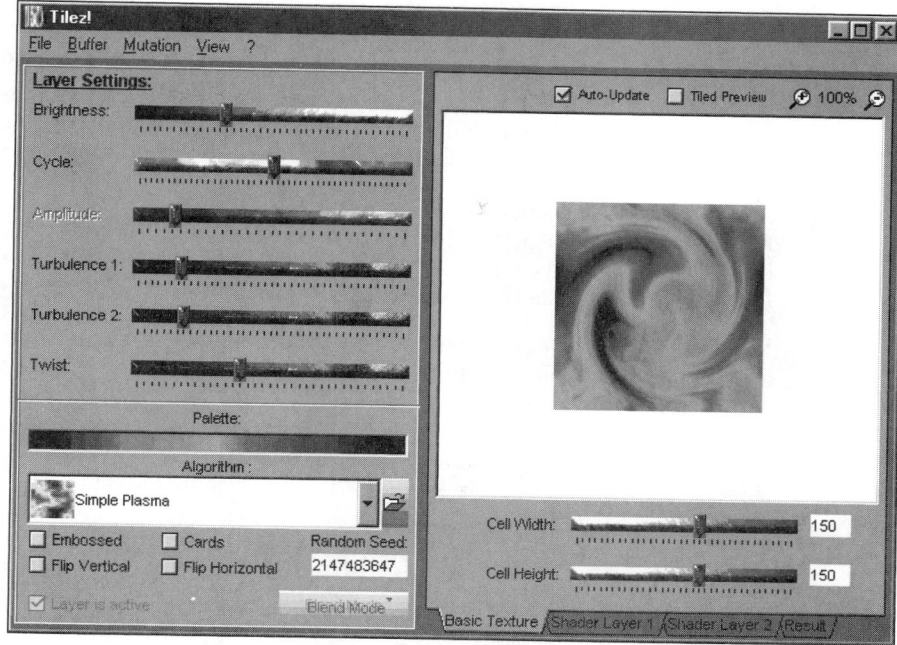

Figure 35-4: The Tilez! interface with one layer of a tile displayed. You switch to the other layers by clicking tabs along the bottom of the window. A fourth tab lets you see the result.

Both of these very cool programs are free, and you'll find them at http://www.listsoft.ru/eng/programs/pr1020.htm .

Special Cursors for Your Web Site

You can insert code into your Web pages that will change the cursor displayed on the computer screens of the folks who visit your site. They'll need to download a little browser plug-in, but you can easily send them out to get it.

You'll find the plug-in and a set of cursors at LiveCursors at http://www.livecursors.com. When you select a cursor to use at your Web site, you'll be presented with the HTML that you can then copy and paste into your Web pages to display that cursor.

Thanks to Chris Pirillo at http://www.lockergnome.com.

Watermark Your Graphics Files

If you'd like to put a unique mark in your graphics files to dissuade others from appropriating them and using them on other Web sites, check out the freeware program Stash. You can use one of five data hiding techniques on gif, pcx, bmp, png, and tiff images (although not jpeg).

A number of programs allow you to do this, but this one is free. To watermark a graphics file, Stash simply encodes data (text from a text file) into the graphics file. If you are checking out a graphics file, it decodes the data from the graphics file (creates a text file from the text).

In the Stash window (see Figure 35-5), you need to first browse to a graphics file, then to a text file, and finally to an output file. You have to actually browse to an existing output filename.

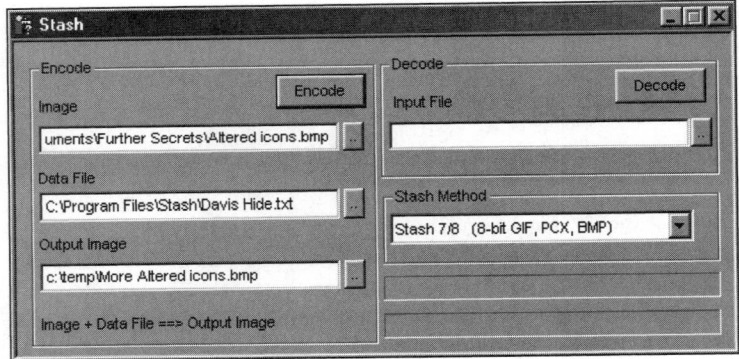

Figure 35-5: You have to enter the path and name of an existing output image file in the Output Image field.

You find Stash at http://www.smalleranimals.com/stash.htm.

Create HTML Applications

If you can write HTML documents, you can write HTML applications that use underlying Internet Explorer functions to display and operate. They'll work on any computer running Internet Explorer version 5 and later.

Here's a sample of a very simple application:

```
<HTML>
<HEAD>
<TITLE>Simple HTML Application</TITLE>
<HTA:APPLICATION ICON=x.ico borderStyle=Raised sysMenu=no>
</HEAD>
<BODY>
```

```
This is a simple HTML application.
<BR>
<BUTTON onclick="self.close()">Exit</BUTTON>
</BODY>
</HTML>
```

Save this text in a text file. Rename the extension `hta`. Click it, and you'll have an open application window. All of the tags above are standard HTML tags, except `<HTA:APPLICATION ICON>` and `<BUTTON>`. These have been added to allow for HTML applications.

Publishing Your Pages on the Web

The Web really is a great equalizer. Anyone can publish their own Web site with very little effort.

Publish on Your Own Web Domain

On the Web, no one knows you're a dog, at least not unless you make it painfully obvious. You can publish all the painful details on your own Web site.

Internet service providers have been providing Web site hosting to their dial-in accounts for a number of years. It was quite easy for them to add your user name to the end of their World Wide Web address and give you a Web address. For example, the Windows Secrets site, which has been up since the release of *Windows 95 Secrets* in August of 1995, was initially under the Web address `http://www.halcyon.com/davis/secrets.htm`.

Not all ISPs offered a Web hosting service. MSN was a conspicuous bad example of this lack of service. Other companies decided that there was a business in providing only Web hosting (and POP3 e-mail receiving service on the side) without having to go to the considerable expense of providing direct dial-in access ports.

The companies who just wanted to provide Web hosting services only needed to provide a Web server connected to a fast Internet backbone; they left it up to you to find a way to get on the Internet.

There are now many companies providing Web hosting services with all kinds of business models. You can get free Web hosting services, which include the insertion of advertising sold by the Web hosting company either into or on top of your Web page. You can also get cheap Web hosting that includes a link to the Web hosting service in your Web pages.

To find an index of sites that offer free Web hosting, go to `http://wsindex.hypermart.net/`.

If you are willing to pay, you can get Web hosting at all levels of sophistication, from mere HTML page serving to full e-commerce transaction processing, including credit card payment verification.

Web hosting can include a virtual domain name. As one of its services, a Web hosting company may interface with InterNIC and other registrars for you. (InterNIC is the first organization that provided domain names, but several dozen competing companies now offer this service. See `http://www.DomainBuyersGuide.com` for an impartial comparison.)

Once it has secured your domain name, the Web hosting company will make sure that your domain name is associated with your directory on its Web server.

Now you'll find the Windows Secrets site at `http://www.davisstraub.com/secrets`.

You can find out more about the various Web hosting companies (where else but) on the Web. Their presentation on the Web gives you a pretty good idea of their capabilities. If their own Web site is slow, yours will be, too.

You might check out `http://www.pair.com` or `http://www.websolo.com`.

Your own ISP may also be able to match the deals available from dedicated Web hosting companies. Check the Web page of your own service provider to see what they have available.

Your Own Dynamic IP Address and Static Domain Name

If you dial up your ISP, chances are you are assigned a dynamic IP address from its pool of available addresses. That address is yours for the length of your connection, but as soon as you hang up, your service provider can give the address to someone else. Without a static address, you're a hard man (or woman) to find.

There are a number of ways around this problem. You can set up your Web site on a Web server that is permanently connected to the Internet with a static address. Your ISP or a dedicated Web hosting company can provide this service. Still, this is only an address for your Web page, and doesn't give you a static address for NetMeeting, game playing, and other Internet applications. For example, you might need a static address to telnet into a server with a security firewall where you work.

You can also sign up for DSL with your local telco. You are going to be on 24 hours/day, so they might as well assign you a static IP address.

Another option is to use a *dynamic DNS* service, which takes your current IP address and assigns it to your static domain name. You can then have your clients or friends contact you through the dynamic DNS server using your domain name, which doesn't change. Of course, you have to be online, and your computer has to use an applet to send the server your latest IP address.

Your domain name is unique to the dynamic DNS service, and is not part of the standard Internet domain naming service. The service charges a yearly fee to provide this static-domain-name-to-dynamic-IP address service. ICQ, MSN, and AOL, through their "buddy" systems, all provide the ability to associate your dynamic IP address with your registered name for their format, but they don't provide a domain name that is associated with your dynamic IP address.

You can find this service at TZO at `http://www.tzo.com`. Check out their FAQ at `http://www.tzo.com/tzomanual.html`.

Microsoft FTP

You can use an FTP client either to access FTP sites, or to access Web sites using FTP protocols. This second function lets you see the files making up a Web site instead of their HTML content. It is very handy if you are maintaining your own Web site.

Microsoft has significantly enhanced the FTP (File Transfer Protocol) capabilities of the Internet Explorer and partially integrated FTP into the Explorer interface. This has been a long time coming, and we've long since gotten used to other FTP clients that provide much more power than what Microsoft has given us now. Still, we want to be fair about what Microsoft has offered, so that if it meets your needs you won't have to find a third-party application.

We wrote about Microsoft FTP late in the process of writing this book, because we kept hoping that the bugs would be driven out of the FTP module and that the capabilities we sought would be added. In the end, we had to write about what was actually there. If you've discovered that Microsoft has made some improvements since we wrote this, please go to our Web site to review the updates we've made to our discussion of this capability (`http://www.davisstraub.com/secrets`).

Type **ftp.microsoft.com** in your Address toolbar (you are using the Address toolbar, aren't you?), and press Enter or click the Go button. If you're not already online, you soon will be. Up will pop an Internet Explorer window that looks something like the one shown in Figure 35-6.

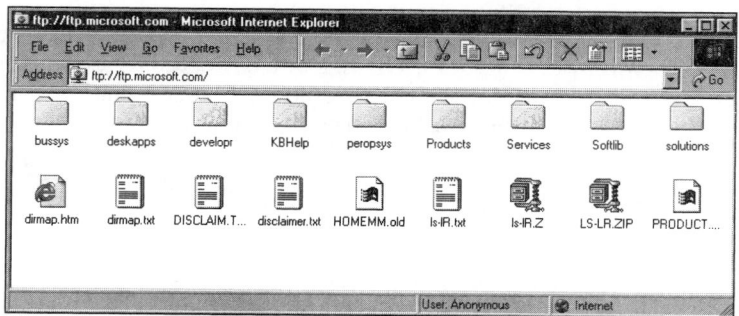

Figure 35-6: The Microsoft FTP window looks a lot like the Explorer.

The Microsoft FTP window gives you a single-pane view of the FTP site. Instead of a Web site view, you get a folder view of a remote computer. It's sort of like the classic folder view associated with the original Explorer File Manager in Windows 95, but now you get a classic view of a remote computer, perhaps even a UNIX box.

Right-click the client area of this view and click View ⇨ As Web Page, and you'll be rewarded with the FTP server's notice, as shown in Figure 35-7.

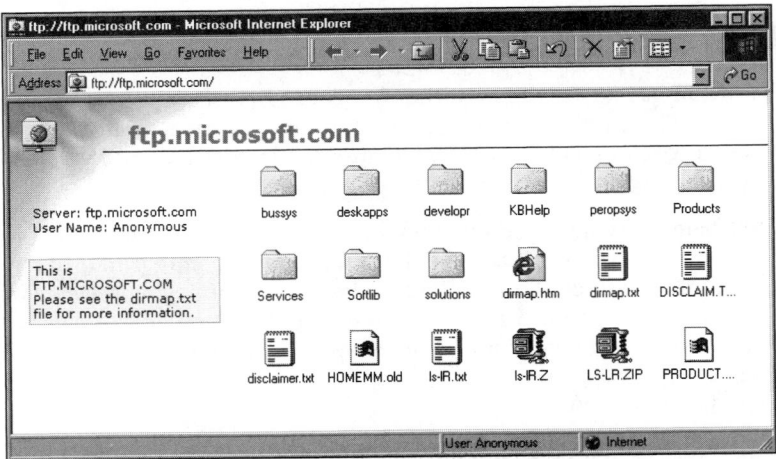

Figure 35-7: You can use Web page view with an FTP window, too.

The names of FTP sites don't necessarily start with *ftp*, just as WWW site names don't necessarily start with *www*. If you want to invoke the FTP window on your computer, you might have to type **ftp://** before the name of the FTP site.

You can drag and drop files from your Explorer into the FTP folder window. You can't go the other way. You can right-click a file or folder in the FTP folder window, click Copy To Folder, and navigate to the folder that will be the repository of the file or folder you're downloading from the FTP site.

You can turn the FTP folder window into an Explorer view, just by clicking View ⇨ Explorer Bar ⇨ Folders. The FTP site is treated as a branch of the Internet Explorer, just as a Web site would be. Folder icons with globes on them distinguish FTP sites from Web sites, as shown in Figure 35-8.

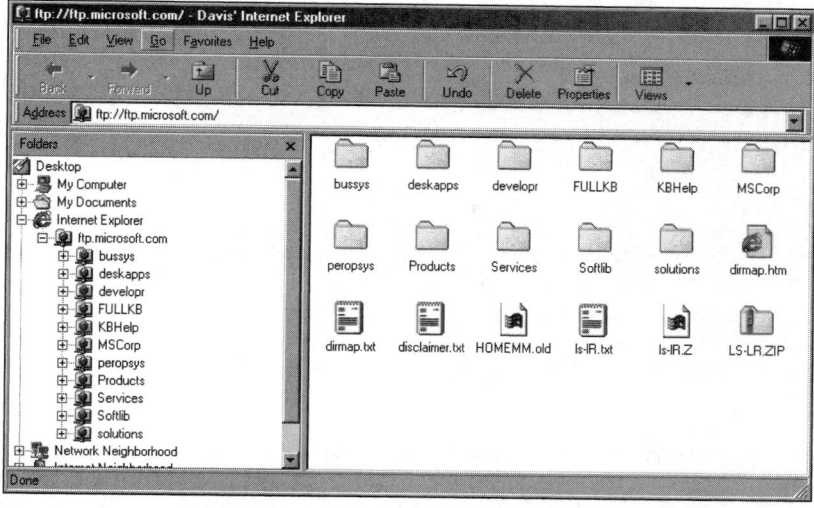

Figure 35-8: The Explorer view can be helpful for navigating around an FTP site.

Clicking View ⇨ Explorer Bar ⇨ Folders does seem to have a bit of a bug; we found that other windows such as My Computer would then open in Explorer view. This wasn't consistent, so it was hard to say what caused it.

The FTP site icons shown in Figure 35-7 are as transient as any Web site icons attached to the Internet Explorer icon in the Explorer window. Open up another Explorer window, and you won't find them there at all. Close the first Explorer window and open a new one, and all visual indication of the Web sites or FTP sites will be lost (except to the History folder).

If you've got FTP sites that you use all the time (such as your own Web site), you won't be able to go back later and find them in the Explorer. To be able to repeatedly access an FTP site, you'll need to create a shortcut to it in the Favorites folder.

There are thousands of FTP sites that enable you to download files. They are set up as file repositories, and anyone can log onto them to find the files that they want. Microsoft FTP assumes an anonymous logon when you type in an FTP address, so it will log you onto the site with the user name *anonymous* and the password *yourusername@yourisp.com*.

If you need a personal user name and password to log onto an FTP site, perhaps your own Web site, and you try to log on to the site without providing this information, you will be prompted for it. If the FTP site has an area that allows anonymous logon, you will be logged onto that area without being prompted for your user name and password, which would enable you to go to your personal area.

Microsoft FTP will not, of its on accord, save your password for the selected site — although it will remember your user name. Your user name will then be appended to the FTP address and displayed in the Address field.

If you weren't prompted for your user name and password, you can force an FTP logon with your user name and password by choosing File ➪ Login As in the FTP folder window.

Secret

If you want to save your user name and password for an FTP site, you'll need to click Favorites ➪ Add to Favorites, and then save the FTP site in one of your Favorites folders. You might want to create a separate folder under Favorites for FTP sites. You can't right-click the FTP folder window and click Save as Shortcut to save a shortcut on the Desktop. But you can move the shortcut from the Favorites folder or subfolder to the Desktop or wherever you like.

You'll have to add the password to your shortcut. Right-click the shortcut to your FTP site, click Properties, type a colon right after your user name in the URL field, and follow that with your password, as shown in Figure 35-9. Click OK.

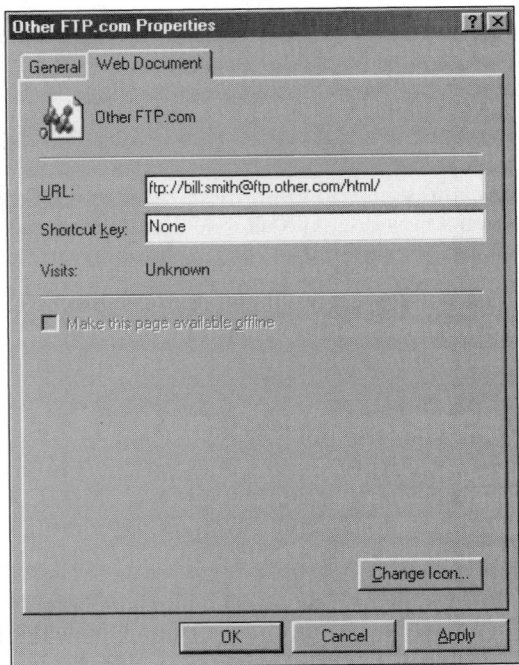

Figure 35-9: Insert your password right after your user name, and before the @ sign.

Now, whenever you click the Shortcut icon, it will log on with your user name and password to the FTP site. Unfortunately, your user name and password are also now quite visible in the Address toolbar of the FTP window.

Internet Neighborhood, an FTP Alternative

What's very good about Microsoft's FTP client is that it doesn't look like a client at all. It is integrated right into the Internet Explorer, which is integrated right into the Explorer. You have to learn how to use it, but you don't have to learn a lot.

Internet Neighborhood, from KnoWare, is an attractive alternative to Microsoft's FTP client for the very same reason: It is an extension of the Explorer. This means that the FTP sites hang as branches off the Internet Neighborhood icon in the Explorer, as shown in Figure 35-10. Internet Neighborhood and Microsoft FTP can happily coexist.

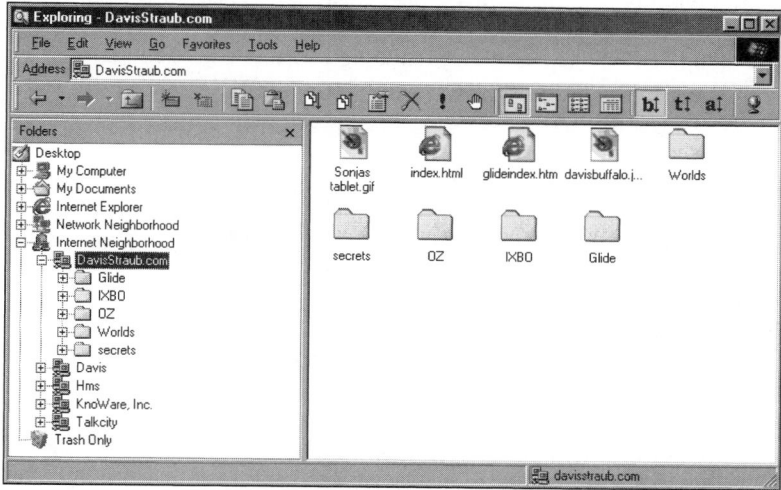

Figure 35-10: FTP sites are displayed under the Internet Neighborhood icon in the left pane; their contents are in the right pane.

Internet Neighborhood FTP icons are static. Once you create a connection to an FTP site, it remains a branch under the Internet Neighborhood icon until you delete it. While you can create shortcuts to the Internet Neighborhood, you can't create shortcuts to the FTP sites that branch off from it.

To access a new FTP site, highlight the Internet Neighborhood icon in the left pane of your Explorer and click FTP Site Wizard in the right pane. Type the name of the FTP site, as shown in Figure 35-11, and the user-friendly site name and site description are created automatically. You can specify an initial directory on the remote computer.

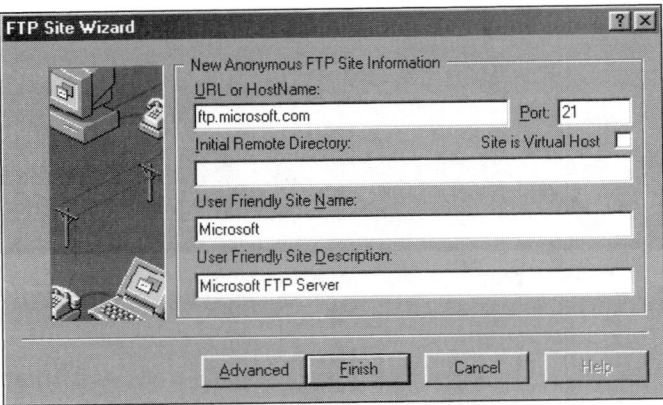

Figure 35-11: Fill out this dialog box in the FTP Site Wizard to add a new site.

You can enter all of the properties associated with an FTP site by clicking the Advanced button in the FTP Site Wizard. You can also change them by right-clicking an FTP site icon, and clicking Properties. The information about your FTP site is stored in the various tabs of the FTP Site Information dialog box, as shown in Figure 35-12.

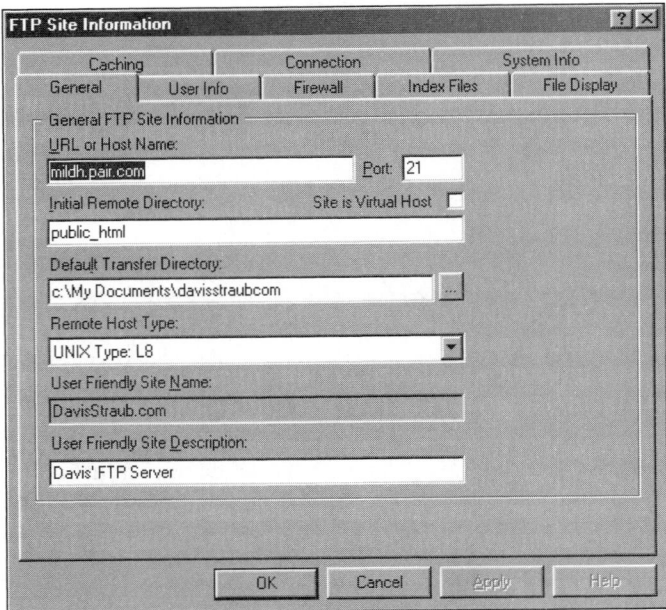

Figure 35-12: The General tab of the FTP Site Information dialog box for a particular Web site

You can drag and drop files and folders in either direction. Sites appear in the Explorer under their user-friendly names (not necessarily the combination of FTP site name and initial remote directory). You can set a user name and password for a site, and the password will be hidden behind asterisks. If your FTP site requires an account name, you can enter that also.

If the FTP site maintains an index file of the files at the site, you can specify its filename; the file descriptions will then appear next to the filenames in the Internet Neighborhood Explorer window. You can cache FTP directory listings so that you don't have to go online again to check over the filenames and descriptions. This makes it quite a bit easier to see what files are on the FTP or Web site without having to be online at all times.

Internet Neighborhood is also significantly faster than Microsoft's FTP client. Really, you've got to wonder about just who wrote this thing at Microsoft. It works, but it's a dog.

You can download Internet Neighborhood from `http://www.knowareinc.com/in32.html`. Once you install it, be sure to right-click its icon in the Explorer and click Online Help. You can download the help file as a compiled Windows Help file. We wonder why this help file doesn't get downloaded in the original file.

FTP Between FTP Sites

Neither Microsoft's FTP client nor Internet Neighborhood will let you cross-load between FTP sites. You have to download to your hard disk first and then upload to another FTP site.

Not everyone needs to move files between FTP sites, but if you do need this ability it's great to have a tool that can accomplish the task. Flash FXP is just the tool for the job. In the example in Figure 35-13, we've copied `disclaimer.txt` from `ftp.microsoft.com` to `davisstraub.com`.

To use Flash FXP, click Site ⇨ Site Manager ⇨ New. Enter the FTP site's name, address, your user name and password, if necessary, the complete pathname of any folder on the remote computer in which you want to start, and the local folder for downloading. Click Save. Do this for two sites. Double-click each site name in the Site Manager, and you're connected to both.

You can download Flash FXP from `http://www.flashfxp.com/`. It's donationware.

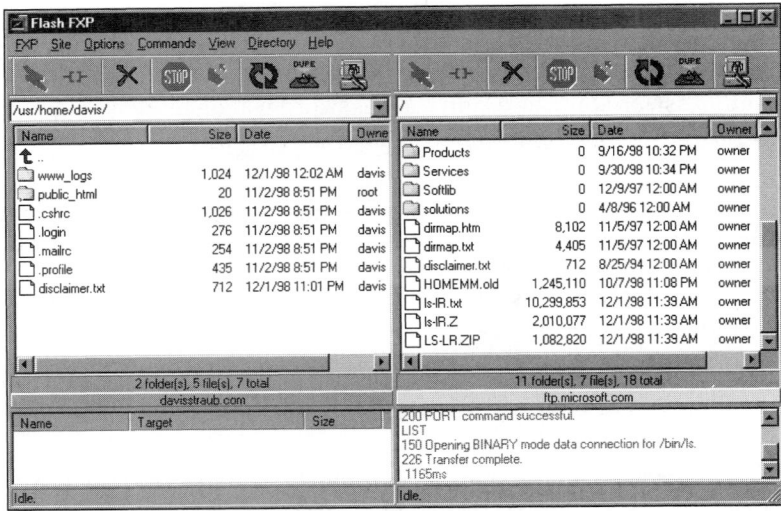

Figure 35-13: In this illustration, disclaimer.txt appears in the directories for both FTP sites.

Web Publishing Wizard

The Web Publishing Wizard is a front end to some of the Windows FTP functions (Start ⇨ Programs ⇨ Accessories ⇨ Internet Tools ⇨ Web Publishing Wizard). FrontPage Express uses these same functions to upload files to the Web server. If you feel comfortable using the Microsoft FTP client or a third-party FTP client, then we suggest ignoring the Web Publishing Wizard.

One function that the Web Publishing Wizard tries to carry out undercover is translation from an HTTP address to an FTP address. For example, to copy a file to your Web site, you only have to give the HTTP address of the Web site (see Figure 35-14), and the FTP address will be substituted. Sometimes this works, and sometimes it doesn't.

Of course, the Web Publishing Wizard is a one-way deal. You can't use it to delete files from your FTP site or Web site. You also can't use it to see what files are up on the site — sort of like the Wizard of Oz when it comes to packing much of a punch.

Tip

If you are using the Web Publishing Wizard and having problems, try not typing the name of a folder on the server when prompted to enter one. The server-side software should be able to determine the correct folder name from your user name and password. If you are logging in as anonymous, then do enter a folder name if you want to navigate to that subfolder.

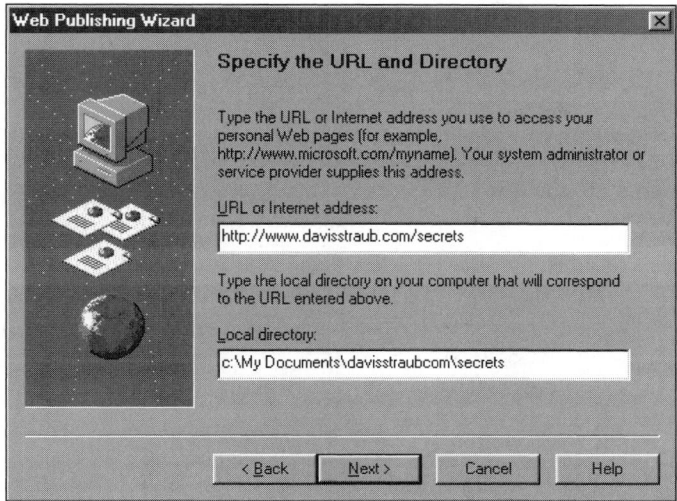

Figure 35-14: You don't need to know the FTP address to use Web Publishing Wizard.

Once you've put in an address that doesn't work out, there is no user-friendly way to get rid of it. You'll need to use your Registry Editor if you want to get rid of an old or incorrect URL. Here's how:

STEPS

Deleting Old URLs in Your Web Publishing Wizard

Step 1. Start your Registry Editor.

Step 2. Navigate to HKEY_USERS\ .Default\ Software\ Microsoft\ WebPost\ Sites. Double-click this key in the left pane of your Registry editor.

Step 3. You'll notice a number of keys under this key. Each of these keys is a placeholder for an FTP or Web site address (see Figure 35-15).

Step 4. To delete old or incorrect addresses, right-click the key corresponding to the old or incorrect address in the left pane and click Delete.

Step 5. To change the FTP or Web server name, right-click the corresponding key and click Rename. To change a URL, double-click DestURL in the right pane. To change a subfolder of the URL, double-click Subfolder in the right pane.

Continued

STEPS

Deleting Old URLs in Your Web Publishing Wizard *(continued)*

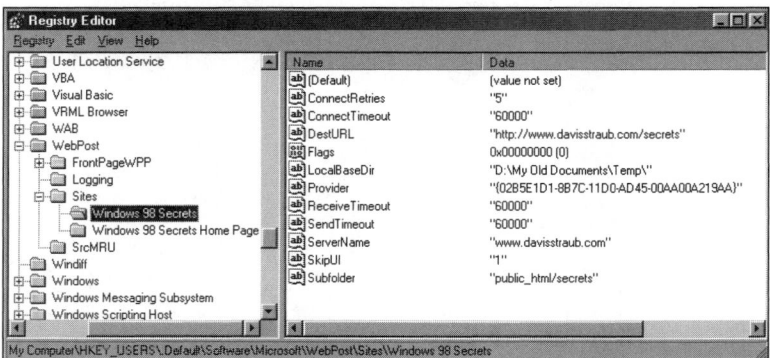

Figure 35-15: Navigate to the key for an FTP or Web site, and you can see the URLs that the Web Publishing Wizard has associated with the site.

The Web Publishing Wizard really is a weak sister, but it's usable once you get the addresses correctly entered and at least one file copied to the FTP site or Web site. A major problem is that the wizard won't record your server setup information until you've successfully transferred at least one file. It can be quite frustrating restarting the wizard time after time, trying to figure out what went wrong.

One way around this, assuming that you've created at least one successful connection, is to export the key of the successful site from your registry, and then reimport it under a new key name. You can then edit the key to try different addresses until you get it to work. All in all, it's not worth the effort given the power of other tools.

Web Folders

Starting with Internet Explorer 5, Microsoft added Web Folders as a special folder type in your Explorer. You can use this folder to store subfolders, which are connections to your Web servers. Unfortunately, the Web servers must support the FrontPage extensions if they are going to work with Web Folders. Web servers that are only accessible through FTP will not do it.

You can get the latest word about how to install and use these folders in "How to Install and Use Web Folders in Internet Explorer 5" at http://support.microsoft.com/support/kb/articles/q195/8/51.asp.

All in One Internet Tool Box

There is one nifty little tool that we use all the time to check up on our Internet and local TCP/IP connections. It's called NetInfo, and it's free.

NetInfo is a collection of standard Internet and TCP/IP utilities. You get Ping, Trace, Finger, and more, all in one window. Just click the tabs to switch among them (see Figure 35-16). In the Ping tab, type in the IP address or server name and click Start to ping a server.

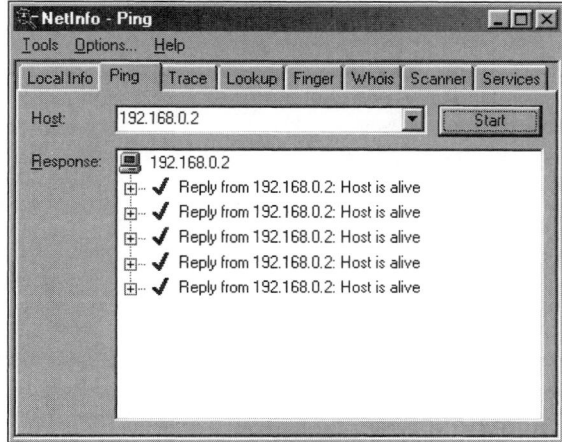

Figure 35-16: You can use NetInfo to ping a server and see if it responds.

You'll find NetInfo at `http://www.netinfo.co.il`. Be sure to check out its FAQ page.

Summary

▶ Use Microsoft FTP to upload Web pages to your Web server.

▶ Prettify or compress your HTML files with third-party add-ons.

▶ Set yourself up on the Web with your own Web domain name.

▶ Use Internet Neighborhood, a third-party add-on, to turn your Explorer into an FTP client as well.

Part IV

Hardware Secrets

Chapter 36

Plug and Play—
Device Management

In This Chapter

Windows Me "captures" your PC hardware. Microsoft provides a raft of 32-bit drivers for almost everything under the sun. We discuss:

▶ What's so great about plug and play?

▶ How Windows works with existing hardware and new Plug and Play devices

▶ Automatic hardware detection during and after setup

▶ Adding new hardware drivers

▶ Untangling resource conflicts

▶ Setting up multiple hardware configurations (profiles)

▶ Why CD-ROMs and sound cards mess with your parallel ports

Peace among the Pieces

Microsoft has made a very big deal about Plug and Play, even adding it to Windows 2000. A consortium of hardware manufacturers and software developers agreed in 1994 to a standard that enables easier installation and tracking of PC hardware independent of the operating system. Windows 95 was the first commercial manifestation of an operating system to completely embrace this standard. Windows Me and Windows 98 have extended and improved it.

Nobody (not even Microsoft) owns the PC's hardware and software standards. Therefore, companies who would like nothing better than to grind each other into the ground have to cooperate with one another to arrive at standards that offer great benefits to the customer.

Everyone knows it is relatively difficult to set up PC hardware (and accompanying hardware drivers), especially when your computer is filled with cards from different manufacturers. The major difficulties are as follows:

■ Assigning hardware interrupts, of which there are only 16 — and some of these are used by the basic computer hardware

■ Assigning nonconflicting I/O addresses so that each add-on card can have its own unique address

■ Assigning direct memory access (DMA) channels (in non-PCI bus cards) so there is no conflict

■ Installing PC Cards (formerly known as PCMCIA cards) that adhere to different standards

■ Setting monitor parameters to automatically work with your video card

■ Making sure there are no memory blocks used (especially by video and network cards) that conflict with memory assignments, particularly in upper memory

■ Recognizing and highlighting conflicts so they can be resolved

■ Gracefully handling multiple hardware configurations for one computer — for example, docking stations with portables

■ Recognizing when the hardware configuration changes, so that the operating system and Windows-aware application software can take the appropriate action

Microsoft realized that many of its support calls had to do with hardware conflicts of the first three types. Hardware manufacturers realized that it was more difficult to sell add-on devices (in particular multimedia kits) when they were so difficult to install.

The first order of business for Plug and Play was to make it easier to install hardware and resolve any conflicts with the hardware interrupts, the I/O address, the memory ranges used, and the DMA channel used, if any. Windows solves most of these problems automatically and gives you the tools to solve the rest.

32-bit Drivers

Windows Me is a 32-bit operating system (for the most part) and one big part of that is its 32-bit drivers. Microsoft has released close to 1,400 new 32-bit device drivers in addition to those that initially shipped with the original Windows 95 operating system. All the 32-bit device drivers get loaded into extended memory so they don't take up conventional or upper memory.

Not only are they 32-bit, but they have lots of new features—features that come about because they have more room to wiggle in extended memory. The Device Manager and the Add New Hardware Wizard install these new drivers for the hardware that they detect. When you run Windows Me Setup, it casts aside 16-bit drivers for the new 32-bit drivers.

Microsoft includes the most recent version of its Windows Driver Library (WDL) in the \Drivers folder on the Windows CD-ROM. This is a good place to look if you need a driver that is not included in Windows by default. Microsoft also maintains the WDL online at ftp://ftp.microsoft.com/softlib.

New 32-bit drivers are available from the Microsoft Windows Update Web site. If you have an Internet connection, click the Start button, point to Settings, and click Windows Update to get the latest drivers for your hardware.

16-bit Drivers

If you need to run 16-bit drivers, you're going to have to use the older installation routines that come from the manufacturers. Only in relatively rare circumstances, however, will you need to run these drivers.

Secret

There is a list in your \Windows folder named Ios.ini that contains the names of the hardware driver files that can be (and are) *safely* replaced by 32-bit drivers in Windows. *Safe* just means that the 32-bit driver implements at least all of the functionality of the 16-bit driver. If you find that your real-mode driver is on the list but provides functionality missing from the replacement 32-bit driver, you can delete it from the list and reinstall the driver.

If you have 16-bit drivers that aren't replaced, you'll find them listed in the Device Manager with a yellow exclamation mark. You can remark out the drivers in Config.sys and Autoexec.bat, install more generic 32-bit drivers using the Add New Hardware Wizard, and reboot your computer. (For details, see "Adding New Hardware Drivers" later in this chapter.)

Plug and Play BIOS and Devices

You may have a computer that doesn't have a Plug and Play BIOS and has no Plug and Play cards. That's fine. Windows does its best to search for and identify the hardware you have installed and then install the appropriate drivers.

You may have a computer without a Plug and Play BIOS, but with some Plug and Play devices. That's fine also. The Plug and Play devices give Windows a little more flexibility in configuring the hardware resource usage to avoid conflicts among the devices.

You may have a computer with a Plug and Play BIOS *and* Plug and Play cards. Great! Windows can work with the Plug and Play BIOS to configure your computer automatically so that there are no conflicts among hardware devices.

Windows enumerates all the Plug and Play devices it recognizes in your computer — including buses such as ISAPNP, PCI, and PCMCIA (PC Card) — each time you start Windows. This also happens when a Plug and Play device sends information that the computer's hardware configuration has changed, and when you click the Refresh button in the Device Manager. This enumeration is different than hardware *detection* (see the next section, "Hardware Detection") because it only applies to Plug and Play devices.

If Windows does not recognize your computer as being Plug and Play, there may be an updated system BIOS available for your particular model that is more fully compliant with the Microsoft Plug and Play standard. Check out your computer manufacturer's Web site.

Hardware Detection

Windows Setup detects installed hardware and drivers for a broad range of pre-Plug and Play hardware as well as the new stuff. Detection happens during Windows setup, and when you use the Add New Hardware Wizard. Windows doesn't run the hardware-detection program each time you start Windows.

Windows creates a hardware-detection log called `Detlog.txt` in the root directory of your boot drive every time hardware detection runs. You can read this to see what hardware is being detected and in what order.

Secret

The installation files contain a database of existing hardware and drivers. This database is stored in specific `inf` files and coordinated by the `Msdet.inf` file. You will find these files in the `\Windows\Inf` folder. (If you don't see the Inf folder, choose View ⇨ Folder Options in the Explorer, and mark "Show hidden files and folders" in the View tab.) The detection routines are noninvasive and do their best to determine just what you've installed over the years from one of a zillion different manufacturers.

Secret

Hardware detection won't be able to determine what monitor you have unless it is Plug and Play compatible, so you'll need to pick your monitor from a list.

Windows may register your modem as generic, so if you know what modem you have, you should go back later and specify that modem. See "Configuring Your Modem" in Chapter 44 for specifics on how to do this. Knowing the right modem assures you that Windows-aware (TAPI compliant) communications software will use the correct initialization string. If you leave the modem in the generic configuration, Windows will use your modem's factory default settings, and you may not be able to adjust some values, such as volume.

Secret

Hardware detection most likely will assign your hard drive, diskette drives, and disk controller cards to the generic category, unless you have specific SCSI controllers. You may have manufacturer-specific hard disk driver software, but you shouldn't use it unless it has been updated for Windows Me—or at least for Windows 95—and is 32-bit.

Older IDE drives that are 1GB and larger often came with software that allowed them to be partitioned even in a computer with a BIOS that doesn't understand drives larger than 524MB. Windows works with Ontrack's Disk Manager 6.03 (and later) and other partition software of this nature.

Detecting non-Plug and Play display adapters is probably the most difficult problem for hardware detection because there are so many. Microsoft has written a series of display drivers, and Windows Setup does its best to install the correct one. If you are installing Windows Me over Windows 3.1x, you may need to install a Windows display driver that doesn't have all the functionality of your previous Windows 3.1x driver. You may be able to download a newer driver for this older hardware from the manufacturer's Web site. You can also install the Windows 3.1x driver (and lose some Windows Me display driver functionality), if you like.

Secret

Hardware detection finds only one keyboard, even if you have a portable with an external keyboard plugged into it. Both keyboards will be live. If your external keyboard is an extended keyboard and the one on the portable is not, you should make sure the extended keyboard driver is installed (or install it if it isn't).

Secret

Windows Setup checks your BIOS to determine if you have Automated Power Management features compatible with the APM 1.0 and APM 1.1 standards. If you do, a Power Management icon will appear in your Control Panel. You can use this icon to adjust the power control settings of your portable.

Lots of portables have a BIOS that is not really compatible with APM 1.0 or 1.1 (as far as Microsoft is concerned). So even if you have control of your power saving configuration through your BIOS settings, you may not have an APM icon in your Control Panel. You just won't have the convenience of power management through Windows. Look in the Device Manager under System Devices for other APM features, which may or may not work on your portable.

Old versions of Windows, such as Windows 3.1x, didn't do a thorough job of checking for APM features in your BIOS. When Win 3.1x didn't find exactly what it was looking for during setup, it didn't install Windows-based APM at all. Windows Me does a better job, but it may still find a BIOS that is incompatible and not add an APM icon to the Control Panel.

Secret

Windows Me can support multiple mice simultaneously. If you have a trackball built into your portable as well as a serial mouse attached to a serial port, Windows Setup will recognize and install two mouse drivers. Both mice should work. If only one driver is installed, you can install the other after initial setup. The mice will most likely be on different interrupts, so you won't have to do any interrupt conflict resolution. If not, see the section entitled "The Device Manager" later in this chapter.

Secret

If you install Direct Cable Connection (DCC), your serial and parallel ports will also be classified in the Device Manager as modems. They aren't really modems, of course, but storing this definition in the modem device type is a convenient way of keeping track of the fact that DCC will work over these ports. DCC finds all available ports when it uses hardware detection to see what is available. You can remove ports from the modems list using the Device Manager, if in fact these ports are being used exclusively for mice or other devices.

Windows Setup installs a Dial-Up Adapter if you direct it to install DCC and/or Dial-Up Networking (DUN). No piece of hardware is itself a Dial-Up Adapter, other than your ports or your modem. Again, this is a convenient label to put on a capability. All of the necessary network protocols and services are bound to this pseudo device. The Dial-Up Adapter is referenced as a network adapter device in the Device Manager.

Hardware detection finds your serial and parallel ports. Serial ports are defined as Plug and Play–compatible devices if they have the 16550A UART or better. If hardware detection finds an extended capability parallel (ECP) port, you will have to configure it after setup. For details, see "Configuring ECP and EPP Ports" in Chapter 44.

During the installation of Windows Me or 9x over Windows 3.1x, CD-ROMs and sound cards are detected first through their signature drivers, which are called from `Config.sys` and `Autoexec.bat`. The calls to these drivers are remarked out and 32-bit drivers are installed instead, unless there aren't any 32-bit drivers for these devices.

Detection after Setup

Hardware detection takes place during Windows setup, but you can also force it to happen later, or you can install a driver for a specific device that may or may not be physically installed yet. You use the Add New Hardware icon in your Control Panel, discussed later in this chapter in "Adding New Hardware Drivers," to install new drivers for your devices.

If you physically install new hardware without using the Add New Hardware icon and the device is Plug and Play compatible, the device will notify Windows that it has been installed, and Windows will install a driver automatically. You will be prompted for the diskette that contains the driver, unless Windows can find the source files on your hard disk or CD-ROM drive.

The Registry of Hardware

Windows keeps information about installed hardware and its drivers in the registry. The original entries are made during Windows setup. You can use the Registry Editor to view the hardware drivers installed on your computer. To see how to invoke the Registry Editor, turn to "Starting the Registry Editor" in Chapter 11.

Secret

You'll find references to your hardware under the HKEY_LOCAL_MACHINE key, specifically under the Enum (enumeration) subkey. It's easy to use the Registry Editor to view the values stored there.

When you start Windows, a dynamic hardware tree is created based on information in the registry. This tree is stored in RAM, and you can view it using the Registry Editor under the HKEY_DYN_DATA\Config Manager\ Enum subkey. Looking at this data is not particularly enlightening, as you will quickly see for yourself. It consists of unique keys that enumerate the installed hardware and its current status.

The hardware tree in RAM is updated every time the hardware configuration changes. Microsoft's favorite example is that the tree updates when you plug your portable into a docking station. We assume they have a lot of these over at Microsoft's Redmond campus.

It is a much better idea to use the Device Manager to manage your hardware configuration. The Device Manager's user interface is a lot more informative and understandable. You should use the Registry Editor only if the Device Manager is not working for you and you understand the effect of the changes that you are making.

Adding New Hardware Drivers

In a perfect world, you would physically install your new device, such as a printer, in your computer (or perhaps plug it into a port). The drivers for that device would be automatically installed and the device activated. If you install a Plug and Play–compliant device, this *almost* happens.

You may need to turn off the computer first so you don't inadvertently cause any electrical damage when you install a card in a slot (although you can plug in PC Cards without turning off your computer). After you turn your computer back on, you may be asked for a diskette or CD-ROM from the device manufacturer that contains the drivers needed to use the device. If the drivers for that device were shipped with Windows, you may be asked to insert the Windows CD-ROM. After Windows installs the new drivers, you'll be able to use your new device.

If the device is pre-Plug and Play, you may need to click the Add New Hardware icon in the Control Panel (as shown in Figure 36-1) to inform Windows that it needs to check for the new hardware and add a new driver.

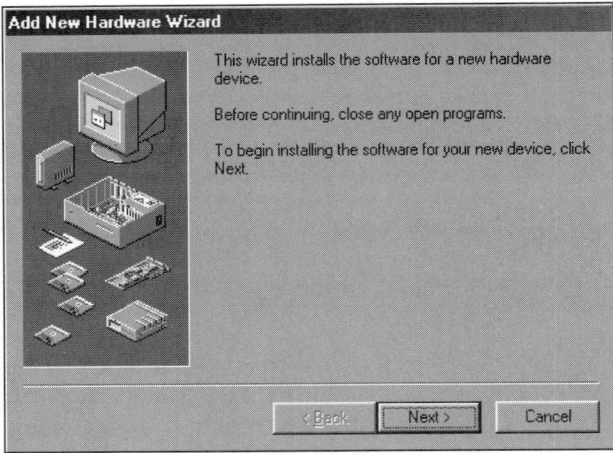

Figure 36-1: The Add New Hardware Wizard. It invokes the hardware-detection routines to find your pre-Plug and Play device.

This wizard will first run through the Plug and Play enumeration process to make sure that this isn't a Plug and Play device. You can then have the wizard attempt to automatically detect your installed hardware (and thereby find the device that you just installed). Alternately (or afterward if your hardware is not detected), you can direct the wizard to install a specific driver by providing it with a manufacturer and model designation or by pointing it toward an installation diskette from the manufacturer (see Figure 36-2).

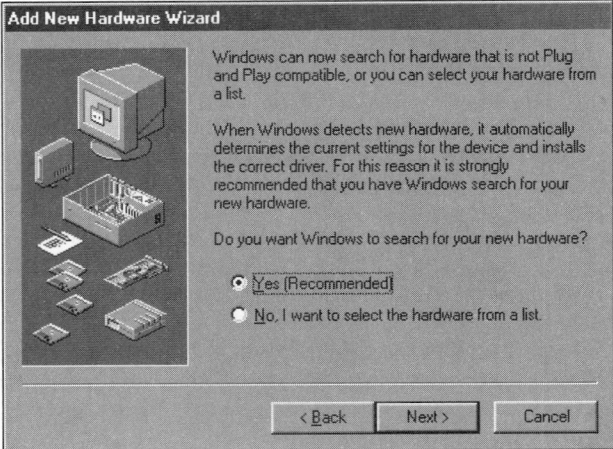

Figure 36-2: You can have the wizard attempt to automatically detect your hardware. If you know what driver you want installed, you can pick the manufacturer and model yourself.

Getting the Settings Right

Windows can resolve potential conflicts between Plug and Play devices, setting their IRQ, I/O, memory address, and DMA channel requirements so all these devices can cooperate. It needs your help to do this for pre-Plug and Play devices (which Microsoft insists on calling *legacy* devices).

We know this is not how Plug and Play is supposed to work in a Plug and Play operating system, but Windows has to encompass the past. Pre-Plug and Play cards and devices can't be configured automatically. You may need to move some jumpers or run a hardware-specific DOS-based configuration program that changes the settings on a given card. You can do this before running the Add New Hardware Wizard or after you determine the conflicts.

Secret

After the Add New Hardware Wizard finds your hardware, or after you direct it to install a driver for a specific device, a dialog box detailing the settings specified for that device appears (see Figure 36-3). The driver settings have been configured by the wizard not to conflict with any existing settings for other installed hardware. *But these settings may have nothing whatsoever to do with the actual settings or available settings for your device.*

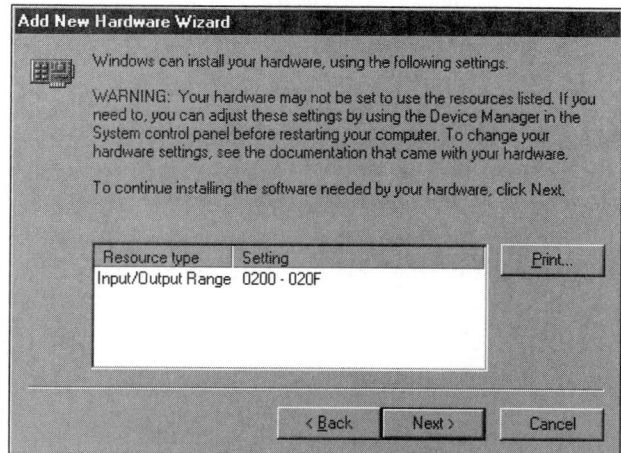

Figure 36-3: The Add New Hardware Wizard's resource settings dialog box. The wizard has determined the settings that it would like to see you set your device to. You may not be able to do this, given the limitations of your device. These settings will not conflict with any other existing hardware that you have installed. Don't try to change them just yet.

You cannot change these driver settings at this time, even if you know they don't match the actual device settings. The wizard did not interrogate your device to see what settings you actually have or what settings are possible (unless it's a Plug and Play device). Understand that the wizard is not so smart at the moment. You are going to have to provide the smarts to get this process completed.

Secret

Continue with the Add New Hardware Wizard, clicking the Finish button in the last dialog box. The drivers for the new device are now installed. You will find them in the Device Manager, as described later in this chapter, if you care to look for them. *Don't use the Device Manager to change the settings at this time, because it will do no good.* We'll get to that in a minute.

You can now physically reconfigure your device to match the driver settings just assigned to it, change your device to other settings that don't conflict with the driver settings for other hardware, or leave your device settings as they are and change the driver settings for your device in the Device Manager. The actual settings for your device might be determined by jumpers or by device settings stored in ROM on the device. If you need to make changes on your device, you might need to turn off the computer to set jumpers or run a DOS application that enables you to change the device's ROM settings.

You can use the Device Manager, as described in the next section, to make sure that the actual settings for your device do not conflict with existing hardware drivers. If they do, you are going to have to change them. Remember, we are talking about the *actual* device settings, not the driver settings that the Add New Hardware Wizard just assigned to your device, which it *took from those available.*

If you need to change ROM settings on the device, open a DOS window and run the device-specific configuration routines on the manufacturer's diskette now. Change the settings on your device so there is no conflict with existing hardware drivers. When you are done, you are ready to shut down Windows 98.

If you need to change jumpers on a device, shut down Windows and turn off your computer. If you change jumpers, be sure the new device settings don't conflict with existing hardware drivers. For details, see the next section, "The Device Manager." Restart your computer after you have made the changes.

Your device may have a limited range of choices allowed for the various resource settings. Limiting the number of IRQs available to a device is one way that a manufacturer can reduce its price, but this practice causes high user dissatisfaction when conflicts become irresolvable. Do your best to move device resource usage around to avoid conflicts, and keep in mind that you may not be successful. You might have to purchase an improved device, hopefully Plug and Play enabled.

To get the actual device settings and the driver settings as recorded in the registry in sync, you need to use the Device Manager. Using the Device Manager now — and not before — you will be able to make changes in the resource settings for your new device driver that match the device's actual settings. After you make these changes, you may need to restart your computer once again to get the new values to take hold.

The Device Manager

The Windows Control Panel is filled with icons that let you manage your computer's hardware and drivers. We outline what some of these icons do in "Control Panel Settings" in Chapter 15, and the rest in the many hardware-specific chapters in this book. If you have a question about a specific piece of hardware, turn to the chapter that focuses on that hardware.

The Device Manager, which you access through the System icon in the Control Panel, provides a general view of all hardware installed on your computer. Sometimes the Device Manager and the hardware-specific icons overlap in functionality, and sometimes you can do something only in one and not the other.

The Device Manager is a powerful tool. Nothing like this was available before Microsoft released Windows 95 in 1995, even from third-party software developers that created Windows-specific diagnostic tools. The Device Manager superseded MSD, the MicroSoft Diagnostic tool that came with Windows 3.1x but was never documented by Microsoft. The Device Manager is much easier to use and much more powerful than MSD.

To get to the Device Manager, take the following steps:

STEPS

Starting the Device Manager

Step 1.   Right-click the My Computer icon, and click Properties.

Step 2.   Click the Device Manager tab in the System Properties dialog box. The Device Manager is shown in Figure 36-4.

Devices are listed in the Device Manager. Click the plus sign to the left of a device type to see the installed devices. Double-click a particular device name to display its Properties dialog box. You can also highlight a device and click the Properties button.

If you mark the "View devices by connection" option button, the devices are displayed hierarchically by their hardware connection to the motherboard.

To get your computer to reidentify the Plug and Play devices on your computer, click the Refresh button. This button also tells your computer about any SCSI devices that have been newly plugged in.

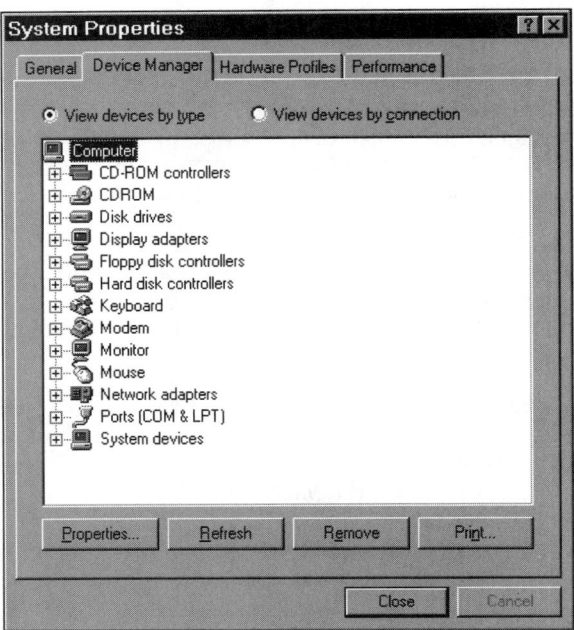

Figure 36-4: The Device Manager. To print your system configuration, highlight Computer and click Print. To view the installed devices of a particular type, click the plus sign next to the type (or double-click the type). To view the properties of a specific device, double-click the device.

If there is a yellow exclamation mark over a device name, it means that there is a problem with the device driver. This mostly likely indicates a resource conflict. You may need to set different jumper settings on a non-Plug and Play device. Use the Device Manager to track down these conflicts.

If you have to hunt for the source of a problem, highlight the Computer icon in the Device Manager and then click the Properties button. In the View Resources tab of the Computer Properties dialog box, successively click the option buttons to check for interrupt, I/O, memory, and DMA channel conflicts.

The yellow exclamation mark may also indicate a missing device that was previously installed, or a removable device (such as a Zip drive). You can remove the device permanently (until you reinstall it) by highlighting the device and clicking the Remove button.

If there is a red X over your device, the Device Manager is telling you that this device isn't functioning. You may need to install 32-bit drivers, or it may be working with 16-bit drivers and you'll have to just leave it that way.

Click the Print button to generate a report of the devices in the computer. You can specify a summary report, a report on a specific device, or a report for all the devices. The report lists your devices, their properties, and the resources they use. You can print any of these reports to a text file. Be sure to first install the Generic/Text Only printer driver (using the Printers icon in the Control Panel) and then assign it port FILE.

IRQs, I/O, Memory Addresses, DMA Channels

If you double-click Computer in the Device Manager (or highlight it and click the Properties button), you get a wonderfully powerful dialog box that shows all the hardware interrupt request settings for your computer, (see Figure 36-5). You now know just what hardware is using just which interrupt. You'll see which interrupts (between 0 and 15) are available.

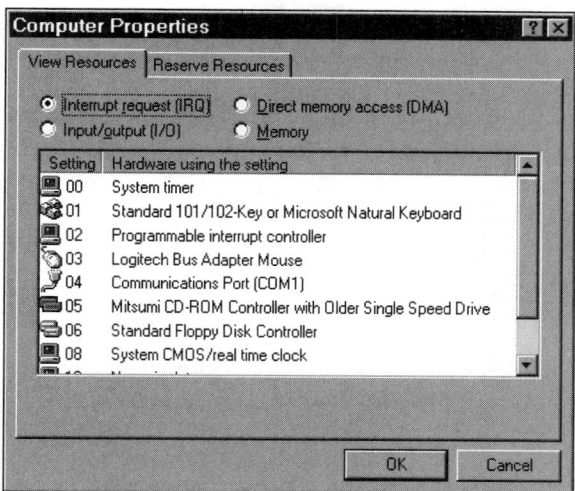

Figure 36-5: The View Resources tab of the Computer Properties dialog box. You can't change anything here, but you do get a consolidated view of interrupt usage.

You can view other resources by clicking the option buttons at the top of the View Resources tab. These buttons let you view consolidated I/O, memory addresses, and DMA channel usage — very helpful.

The Reserve Resources tab lets you set your resources so that Windows won't assign them to a Plug and Play device.

Specific Device Drivers

The device drivers installed in your computer are by default displayed by type in the Device Manager. Clicking the plus sign next to a device type displays the device drivers installed. Double-clicking a device driver's name displays its Properties dialog box, as shown in Figure 36-6.

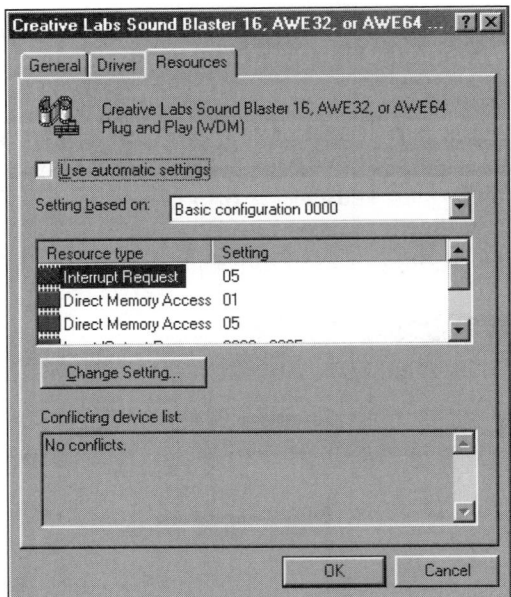

Figure 36-6: The Resources tab of the Properties dialog box for the Creative Labs Sound Blaster. (These values are actually incorrect so don't use them.) You can change them in the Device Manager.

Changing Device Driver Settings

If you have Plug and Play devices, you should usually let the hardware-detection routines in Windows determine what the resource settings should be. If you set them manually, the settings become fixed and Windows can't adjust them to avoid conflicts. You can, however, change the resource settings for Plug and Play as well as non-Plug and Play devices.

To change the resources assigned by Windows to a device in order to match the actual settings for that device and avoid any conflicts with other devices, take the following steps. If your device driver settings don't match the device's settings, the device driver entry in the Device Manager will have a yellow exclamation sign on it.

STEPS

Changing a Device's Resource Settings

Step 1. Double-click the specific device in the Device Manager.

Step 2. Click the Resources tab in the Properties dialog box for the device.

Step 3. Double-click a resource type in the Resource Settings field (or highlight a resource and click the Change Setting button). If the "Use automatic settings" box is marked, you'll need to clear it first.

If this resource can be changed, you'll see a dialog box to let you adjust its settings (see Figure 36-7). Use the spin arrows in the Value field to change the values of the resource requested.

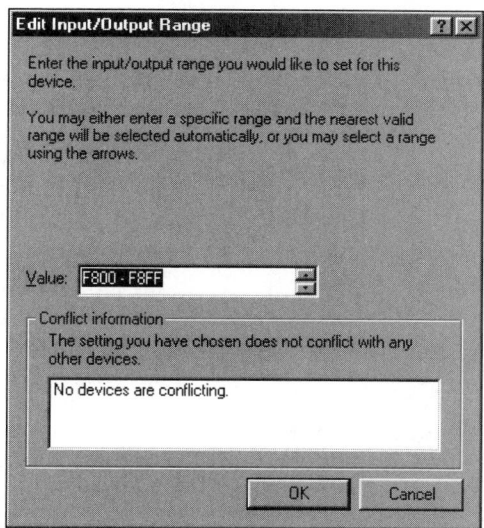

Figure 36-7: The Edit Input/Output Range dialog box. This dialog box is specific to changing an I/O resource. Other resources display different dialog boxes.

Your device driver may allow different basic configurations, which in turn allow for different resource values and the ability to change some resources in one configuration but not in another. In the Resources tab, display the "Setting based on" drop-down list to see if there are other configurations. If there are, you can try them to see what difference this makes in allowable resource values.

Continued

STEPS

Changing a Device's Resource Settings *(continued)*

Step 4. Click OK in the Resource Settings dialog box to accept the changes that you have made, and then click OK again in the Properties dialog box.

Step 5. You may be asked to restart your computer to allow the new resource settings to take effect.

Throughout this process, be sure you haven't introduced any new resource use conflicts. If you printed a copy of the system summary, you will have a ready reference on resource use. Also, the Device Manager will track conflicts and warn you when you have created them.

If you have changed settings in the driver for a non-Plug and Play device, you need to make the same changes to the hardware itself. You may now need to go back and either change the jumpers on the device to match the settings that you just made or, if the hardware device is software configurable, run the manufacturer's software to reconfigure the hardware. This may require opening a DOS window to run the hardware configuration software.

Remember, the previously detailed process just changes the device driver settings, and not the actual hardware itself (if it is not Plug and Play).

IRQ Conflicts

Windows lets two physical devices share the same interrupt request line (IRQ) under certain circumstances. Many Peripheral Component Interconnect (PCI) devices are capable of sharing IRQs through the use of *IRQ steering* (see the next section), and this can be a big help if you have lots of devices fighting for resources. However, it doesn't work for two devices that are used at the same time, such as a modem and a mouse. Devices that are not used at the same time, such as a scanner and a modem, are much better candidates for sharing IRQs. A non-PCI device can't share an IRQ with a PCI device. Each device still keeps a different I/O address.

IRQ sharing should happen automatically when you install new hardware. You can also set the interrupts for a given piece of hardware using the Device Manager. Double-click a specific device in the Device Manager, click the Resources tab, clear the "Use automatic settings" checkbox, and change settings as described in the previous section.

If you have problems with IRQ sharing on an older computer, you may need to upgrade its BIOS. You can get an upgraded BIOS from a third-party supplier, or you can go to your computer manufacturer's Web site.

You can also disable a device to eliminate an IRQ conflict. You have to disable it physically first (check the documentation that came with the device to find out how) and then disable it in the Device Manager. If the device is an integrated device that resides on your motherboard (such as a serial port), you also have to disable it in the BIOS. If you don't do this, the next time you power up Windows, the Plug and Play enumeration process will notice the difference, restore the device, and assign resources to it. To completely disable a device and reclaim its resources, follow these steps:

STEPS

Disabling a Device in the Current Configuration

Step 1. Right-click the My Computer icon, click Properties, and click the Device Manager tab.

Step 2. Click the plus sign next to the type of device you are looking for, and then double-click the device you want to disable to open its Properties dialog box.

Step 3. Click the General tab, and then click the "Disable in this hardware profile" checkbox. Click OK. (If you have multiple profiles, this will only apply to the current one.)

Step 4. Restart your computer.

Step 5. If you are disabling a device that is not integrated on your motherboard, you are finished. If this is an integrated device, you must now disable the device in your computer's BIOS settings. The exact steps for doing this vary from one computer to the next. In general terms, you need to press a key during your computer's power-on self test to enter your BIOS's setup program, and then set the value in that program to disable the device.

If your computer has a specialized port — for a PS/2 mouse, for example — you may see that device listed in your Device Manager even if you don't have one connected. Sometimes just having the capability on your motherboard to support such a port is enough to make it show up, even if you don't have a physical port. Disabling the device using the steps above may free up these resources, but not in every case.

IRQ Steering

Windows Me (along with Windows 98) supports a feature called *IRQ steering* that allows devices to share interrupts. With IRQ steering, Windows can catch messages sent to an interrupt request line (IRQ) and reroute them to the next available IRQ. This is useful for PCI bus devices in laptops with docking stations. As hardware is added and subtracted (when docking occurs), PCI devices can be dynamically reconfigured to work together. In addition, if two PCI cards are sharing an interrupt, IRQ steering "steers" the request to the correct card. It can also determine if a PCI card needs an IRQ at all (many don't). If IRQ steering is not enabled, the BIOS handles this routing instead of Windows.

IRQ steering is not enabled by default. For this reason, a PCI device may display "Error Code 29" as its status when viewed in the Device Manager. Assuming the device is not physically disabled for some reason, you can correct this error by enabling IRQ steering. To do this, follow these steps:

STEPS

Enabling IRQ Steering

Step 1. Click the Start button, point to Settings, click Control Panel, and click the System icon.

Step 2. Click the Device Manager tab, expand the System Devices branch, and double-click PCI Bus to open its Properties dialog box. Click the IRQ Steering tab.

Step 3. Mark the "Use IRQ steering" checkbox to enable it.

Step 4. You will see a list of four routing tables with checkboxes (see Figure 36-8). Windows searches for these tables in the order shown, and uses the first marked table that it finds, ignoring the others.

Ordinarily, the first, second, and fourth tables are marked. Use these default settings unless you have a problem with a PCI device. If you do have a problem, clear the first table and mark the third one. When you have finished, restart your computer.

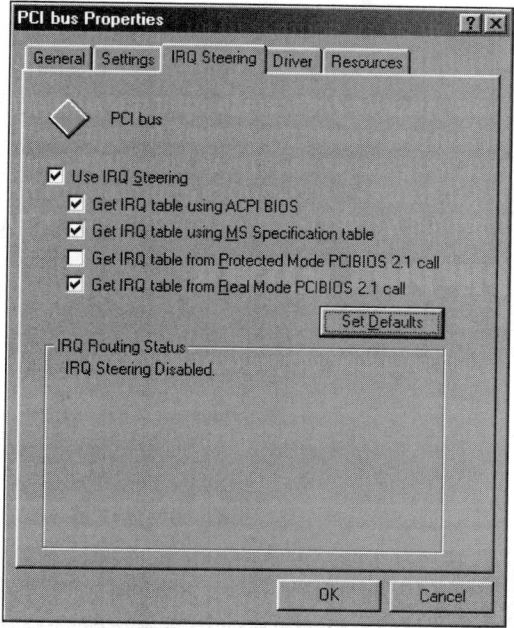

Figure 36-8: IRQ Steering tab of the PCI Bus Properties dialog box. Use this tab to enable IRQ steering.

Forced Configurations

You can manually assign IRQs, I/O addresses, and DMA channels, and direct Windows to use the ones you assign. Once you manually assign a specific configuration to a device, Windows is no longer free to change that configuration if new hardware is added later. This is true even if the device that you configure is Plug and Play compatible.

It is best to allow the Windows hardware enumerator to assign resources to all your Plug and Play devices. This gives the enumerator maximum flexibility to reconfigure Windows if new devices are added. If you have a Plug and Play BIOS and you force a configuration, Windows will also change the BIOS to match your forced settings if those settings are available to the BIOS.

PC Cards

PC Cards, previously known as PCMCIA cards, are most popular in laptops. They let you swap devices (such as a modem or floppy drive) "on the fly," without turning off your computer. Windows supports many of these products, including many that are not Plug and Play compatible.

Plug and Play-compatible PC Cards won't automatically be detected unless you first run the PC Card Wizard. If you install Windows Me or 98 over Windows 3.1x, the wizard remarks out the real-mode drivers in the `Autoexec.bat` and `Config.sys` files, and enables 32-bit support for your PC Card socket. To run the wizard, click the PC Card (PCMCIA) icon in the Control Panel. (If clicking the icon displays a Properties dialog box instead of the wizard, PC Card support has already been enabled.)

You can use the real-mode PCMCIA card drivers instead if you need to, but you won't have Plug and Play capabilities. Also, you can't mix and match real-mode drivers with Plug and Play—all of your devices must either use one mode or the other.

After you install your PC Card socket driver using the PC Card Wizard, check the Device Manager for a PC socket listing to verify that the socket is installed properly. If you don't see it, use the Add New Hardware Wizard to indicate the manufacturer and model you are using. (To start the wizard, click the Add New Hardware icon in the Control Panel.) If your model is not listed, click the Start button, point to Settings, and click Windows Update to download a driver for it (if one is available).

If you have trouble installing or using PC Cards, you can access the Windows PC Card Troubleshooter by clicking Help in the Start menu, clicking Trouble-shooting in the Contents tab, clicking Windows Troubleshooting, and clicking PC Card. This document is also maintained online at `http://support.microsoft.com/support/tshoot/w98pcmcia.asp`.

Updating Device Drivers

You can install new device drivers over existing ones for some devices by using the Device Manager. You may want to do this when you get a new driver from your hardware manufacturer, or to see if Microsoft has made new drivers available on its Windows Update Web site.

You could, of course, install the new device driver by using the Add New Hardware Wizard. However, this wizard is primarily designed to search for new hardware and install the corresponding driver. If you haven't installed new hardware and just want to update a driver, the Device Manager provides a semantically friendlier starting point.

STEPS

Installing an Updated Device Driver

Step 1.   Double-click the specific device in the Device Manager.

Step 2.   Click the Driver tab in the Properties dialog box for the device, if it has one. If there is no Driver tab, you can't update the driver.

Step 3.   Click the Upgrade Driver button to launch the Upgrade Device Driver Wizard, and then click Next.

Step 4.   The wizard offers to search for a better driver than the one you have or let you select the driver from a list. If you ask the wizard to search for the driver and click Next, you can tell the wizard where to look, including the Microsoft Windows Update location online (see Figure 36-9).

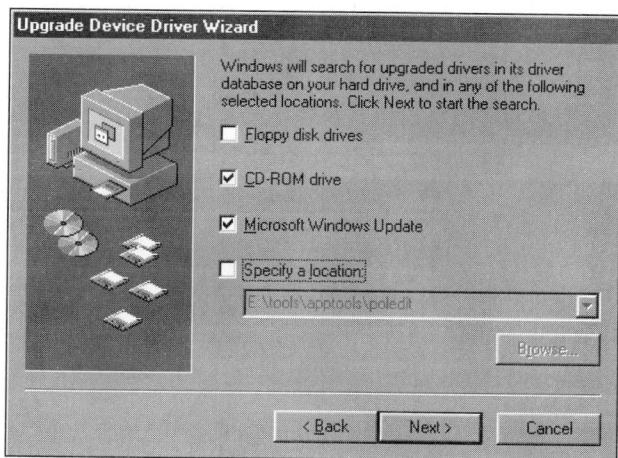

Figure 36-9: The Upgrade Device Driver Wizard offers to search for a better driver, and asks you where to look. If you select Microsoft Windows Update, the search will include Microsoft's driver library on the Internet.

Step 5.   If you told the wizard that you wanted to select the driver in the previous step, it will display a list of the drivers for that device type (modems, for example) that came with Windows. By default, the list is set to "Show compatible hardware"; you will see only the drivers that Windows knows are compatible with your device. To see a complete list of available drivers for your device type, select the "Show all hardware" option. You can choose one of the drivers on the list, or you can click the Have Disk button if you have a new driver on a diskette, a CD-ROM, or your hard drive.

Continued

STEPS

Installing an Updated Device Driver *(continued)*

Step 6.   When you've answered all of the questions in the wizard, click the Finish button, and then click OK in the Driver tab of the Properties dialog box.

Step 7.   Restart your computer to allow the new driver to take effect.

Resolving Resource Conflicts the Easy Way

There is another way to resolve resource conflicts. Windows Help contains a Hardware Conflict Troubleshooter. It gives you a little background on resource conflicts and then promptly leads you to the exact same places that we just covered. It's kind of cute, though.

STEPS

Starting the Hardware Conflict Troubleshooter

Step 1.   Click the Start button, and then click Help.

Step 2.   Click the Contents tab, and then click Troubleshooting.

Step 3.   Click Windows Troubleshooters, and then click Hardware Conflict.

Step 4.   Follow the suggestions and shortcuts to the Device Manager.

Hardware Profiles

We have *hardware profiles* for different hardware configurations on one computer, *user profiles* for different users on the same computer, and *Windows Messaging profiles* (if you have Windows Messaging installed) for different mail services. Windows presents us with quite a prolific world.

You don't need hardware profiles if you have a Plug and Play computer with Plug and Play devices, except as noted in "TCP/IP Conflicts Between the LAN Card and the Dial-Up Adapter" in Chapter 25. Windows can automatically load the hardware drivers that it needs based on the hardware it detects and stores in the hardware tree in RAM. Change the configuration (by pulling the portable from the docking station, for example), and Windows reconfigures itself dynamically.

The static hardware profiles are a bit of a kludge. A menu comes up in DOS full-screen text mode before the Windows Desktop appears and asks you to choose your current configuration.

Tip

You have to set up the hardware profiles manually. You install all the drivers for all the hardware configurations for all the profiles, and then assign the proper set of drivers to each profile. The hardware doesn't have to be installed at the time that you install the drivers. You can just install the drivers, and then make any necessary changes later if there is a difference between the device settings and the resource settings that you chose.

To create multiple hardware configurations, take the following steps:

STEPS

Creating Multiple Hardware Configurations

Step 1. Use the Add New Hardware Wizard to install all the drivers applicable for all your configurations. Tell the wizard what to install if you don't have all the hardware physically installed at the moment. You can run the Add New Hardware Wizard in each hardware configuration and have it search for the installed hardware if you like. This will also build up a base of installed hardware.

Step 2. Click the System icon in the Control Panel, and then click the Hardware Profiles tab. Original Configuration (or Undocked if you have a portable) will be highlighted.

Step 3. Click the Copy button and then type a name for the new profile in the Copy Profile dialog box, and click OK. You may want to use the Rename button to give "Original Configuration (or Undocked)" a more descriptive name as well.

Step 4. Click OK, close the Control Panel, and restart your computer. Before the Windows Desktop reappears, you will see a text menu showing the profiles you have set up. Select a profile by typing its number (in this case, choose a profile you have just created). Windows will start up in that profile.

Step 5. Open the Control Panel, click the System icon, and click the Device Manager tab. Double-click each applicable device to display its Properties dialog box, and in the Device Usage area of General tab, mark or clear checkboxes to disable or remove the device from the profile you are currently in. Figure 36-10 shows the Properties dialog box for a Dial-Up Adapter.

Continued

STEPS

Creating Multiple Hardware Configurations *(continued)*

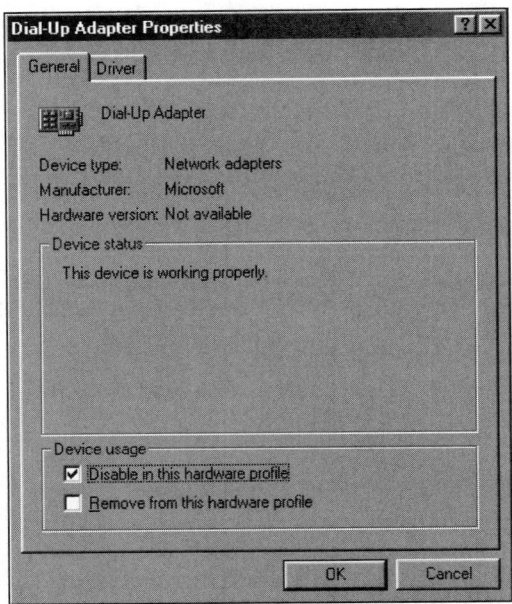

Figure 36-10: The Properties dialog box for a Dial-Up Adapter. Mark the "Disable in this hardware profile" checkbox to disable the adapter in your current profile. You may have more or fewer checkboxes available, depending on the individual device.

Step 6. After completely defining the hardware available for this hardware profile, repeat steps 4 and 5 for each hardware profile you have created. You must restart your computer each time for the changes in the profile configuration to take effect.

For some devices, you will have an additional option in step 5 between the checkboxes "Remove in this hardware profile" and "Disable in this hardware profile." If you remove a device from one of your profiles and then need to restore it later, the Add New Hardware Wizard may not detect it. Instead of removing a device in the Device Manager, you should normally disable it. To restore a device that was accidentally removed from one profile, you'll need to remove it from all the profiles. Then run the Add New Hardware Wizard to reinstall the device, and use steps 4 and 5 detailed previously to restore the device to each profile.

LCDs and External Monitors

Perhaps you have a portable that uses its built-in LCD screen in one configuration and uses an external monitor in another. You can choose a different monitor for each of the two separate hardware configurations. If the portable is not Plug and Play compatible, you will probably want to do this. Portable computers that aren't Plug and Play compatible can have problems with the Windows video drivers supplied by Microsoft (and developed in cooperation with the video chip and card manufacturers). The video chips inside many portable computers can drive external monitors to greater resolutions than the LCD screen can handle. In some cases, the older generic video drivers that come with Windows are not sophisticated enough to be able to handle the switch between a lower-resolution LCD screen and a higher-resolution external monitor.

Problems occur when you're attempting to view Windows on the LCD display (or after you've set the portable to feed the video signal to both the external monitor and the LCD display). If the Windows video drivers are set for a resolution above the resolution supported by the LCD display, Windows displays an error message indicating that the video driver settings need to be changed. The Windows Desktop is then displayed at the lower LCD resolution (640 × 480) and at a reduced color depth of 16 colors.

You can make up for some of the lost functionality of the older, generic Windows video drivers for non-Plug and Play portables. It takes a bit of doing, but you can configure your computer and Windows to let you manually switch between the LCD screen and the external monitor at bootup time in a manner that will eliminate the Windows video error message, set the proper resolution, and retain 256-color depth.

The first step is to set your portable's BIOS to output to the external monitor. You need to do this because the Windows video drivers determine the maximum video resolution based on the display that's currently set to receive the video signal, and they will drop to the lower resolution if the video signal is set to feed to the LCD screen or (in some cases) to both screens.

How you change your computer's BIOS settings varies among BIOS manufacturers. For example, if your portable has a Phoenix BIOS, press the F2 key when prompted during bootup to display the BIOS setup screen, and use the menus to set the primary display to CRT.

After you've changed your BIOS settings, you need to create two Windows hardware profiles. Unless you have a Plug and Play external monitor and Plug and Play video chips in the portable, the Windows hardware-detection routines won't be able to tell that you have two displays, so you're going to have to force the issue.

STEPS

Creating Two Windows 98 Hardware Profiles for Two Monitors

Step 1. Click Start ⇨ Settings ⇨ Control Panel. Click the System icon, and then click the Hardware Profiles tab.

Step 2. Your original hardware profile should be highlighted. Click the Copy button to make a copy of it.

Step 3 Enter a new name for the new profile — perhaps "External Monitor (800 x 600)" if the original profile has the LCD screen as the display. (If the original profile has the external monitor as its display, name the new profile "LCD Screen (640 x 480).")

Step 4. Highlight the original profile and click the Rename button to rename the original profile, perhaps to "LCD Screen (640 x 480)." Click OK.

Step 5. Shut down Windows normally. Restart Windows. You will be given the choice between two hardware profiles, as shown here. Choose the new profile.

```
Windows cannot determine what configuration
your computer is in:
Select one of the following:
       1.     External Monitor (800x600)
       2.     LCD Screen (640x480)
       3.     None of the Above
Enter your choice:
```

Step 6. Open the Control Panel and click the Device Manager tab. Click the plus sign next to the Monitor icon and double-click the attached icon for your current display. At the bottom of the General tab of the Properties dialog box, clear the "Disable in this hardware profile" checkbox. Click the OK button, and then click OK again.

Step 7. Right-click the Desktop and choose Properties. Click the Settings tab. Change the color depth (select it from the Colors drop-down list), and change the resolution (drag the Screen Area slider bar) to match the new display and the new hardware profile.

Step 8. Click the Advanced button, click the Monitor tab, and click the Change button. The Update Device Driver Wizard will launch. Install a display driver that corresponds to your second configuration in the Select Device dialog box. Click OK, click Close, and then click OK again.

Step 9.   Click Start ⇨ Settings ⇨ Control Panel. Click the Device Manager tab. Click the plus sign next to the Monitor icon and double-click the attached icon for your other display (the one that doesn't apply to this new profile). Make sure the "Disable in this hardware profile" checkbox is checked. Click the OK button, and then click OK again.

You have now created two hardware profiles. When you restart your computer, you will be given the choice between them just after the Windows splash screen is displayed and just before Windows starts up.

Just because you have two Windows hardware profiles doesn't mean you've correctly configured your hardware to work with them. Your BIOS has been set to direct the video feed to the external monitor. You need to be able to flexibly override this BIOS setting to direct your internal video hardware to send its signal to the external video port, to the LCD display, or perhaps to both.

Often you can accomplish this with a small utility (or set of utilities) that the portable computer manufacturer supplies. You can run these utilities in a batch file to switch the video hardware output between displays. You still need to use these utilities to correctly set the video feed to correspond with the hardware profile you choose during bootup.

Hot Swapping and Hot Docking

A Plug and Play–compatible computer can notify Windows when the connection with a docking station is made or broken. This will trigger a reconfiguration of the hardware tree, which in turn makes Windows aware of the new hardware.

Secret

You can plug a device into your SCSI controller card (if you have one), and then use the SCSI device (for example, a SCSI-based Zip drive) without having to restart Windows. Unfortunately, Windows doesn't automatically check that you've installed a new device. You need to give it a hint. To do this, open the Device Manager (click the System icon in the Control Panel and click the Device Manager tab), choose the "View devices by connection" option button, highlight Computer, and click the Refresh button.

Look for the new device by opening up the branches in the Device Manager and looking for your SCSI host adapter. Check to see if the new device is connected to it.

Autorun

Windows can automatically start CD-ROMs and audio CDs when you insert them into your CD-ROM player. In order for a CD-ROM to start automatically, it needs to have a file named `Autorun.inf` in its root directory.

You can turn off Autorun in the Device Manager. Highlight your CD-ROM drive, click the Properties button, click the Settings tab, and then clear the "Auto insert notification" checkbox.

AutoEject

AutoEject, a free utility by Kevin Marty, solves a big problem for users of Jaz, Zip, and CD-ROM drives whose eject mechanisms are under software control. With these drives, you're not really supposed to power down the system with media in the drive. If you forget, on startup Windows may treat a removable drive as a hard drive and assign it a letter. This can make your `C:` drive look like a `D:` drive, and so on, wreaking havoc with programs that expect to find stuff on certain drives.

AutoEject is a good solution to this problem, although it won't work on removable drives with stupid mechanical latches, such as SyQuest drives and floppies. Placed in your StartUp folder, AutoEject will automatically eject any or all removable media when Windows is shut down. You can download AutoEject from `http://www.visi.com/~kmarty/software.html`.

Sound Cards, CD-ROMs, and LPT Ports

Secret

Windows doesn't flag interrupt conflicts between devices such as sound cards and CD-ROMs and the LPT1 and LPT2 ports. LPT1 and LPT2 use interrupts 7 and 5 respectively. Many sound cards and CD-ROMs are also set by default to use these very same interrupts. In spite of this conflict, the Device Manager doesn't inform us that it exists.

The Device Manager is silent on this conflict because printers connected to these parallel ports really don't use these interrupts. In some ways, the ports are up for grabs.

The problem is that Direct Cable Connection *does* use these interrupts when it is configured to use a parallel cable. DCC is at its fastest when it uses the parallel ports, and it will slow by a factor of three if it finds a sound card or CD-ROM drive using these interrupts. The only way you notice this is by testing the speed of communication across these ports. If you notice a problem, change the resource settings in the Device Manager so that the LPT port is on interrupt 7 and the sound card or CD-ROM is on interrupt 5. See "Configuring Serial Ports" in Chapter 44 for more on how to do this.

Detlog.txt, Setuplog.txt, and Ios.log

Secret

If you are using any 16-bit drivers, you have three files — the first two are in your root directory and the third is in your Windows folder — that can give you another look at your hardware. Detlog.txt is a record of the hardware-detection process. Setuplog.txt details what files were installed. Ios.log tracks your real-mode drivers.

You can simply read these files with Notepad to get a little added insight into your configuration.

If you inadvertently erase a file that is crucial to the proper running of Windows, you can rerun Windows Setup to verify files and install only those that are missing. If you do this, Windows reviews Setuplog.txt during the setup process to see what you originally installed.

Summary

Microsoft has made a concerted effort to bring a new level of standardization to the PC world. By providing an extensive list of 32-bit device drivers and giving manufacturers a new model for creating new ones, it has improved the stability of Windows.

▶ Windows deals with both existing and Plug and Play hardware, providing a way to track it all.

▶ Hardware-detection routines built into Windows do a robust job of matching your hardware to Windows' needs.

▶ We show you how to add new hardware drivers to match your devices.

▶ The major benefit of Plug and Play is the automatic resolution of hardware conflicts. It isn't automatic with non-Plug and Play hardware, but it is easier.

▶ If you have multiple hardware configurations, you can direct Windows to the current configuration.

▶ You may find a conflict between your sound card and CD-ROM driver and your parallel ports if you use Direct Cable Connection.

Chapter 37

Disk Tools and File Systems

The Real Changes

If you want to look at the changes that have been made to the fundamentals of an operating system, look at how it works with files that are stored on disk drives.

Moving from Windows 3.1*x* to Windows Me

If you are moving from Windows 3.1*x* to Windows Me, you'll notice that most of the changes Microsoft has made to the "disk operating system" (what used to be called "DOS") affect what is under the hood — speeding up access to your hard disk, diskettes, and CD-ROM drive. Microsoft also reduced the amount of user interaction required to set obscure performance parameters — such as permanent swap files and disk cache size — while at the same time improving the performance that tuning these parameters is supposed to provide.

These advances have vastly increased the amount of available conventional memory and improved the responsiveness of your computer to multiple tasks. Compression drivers let you double (more or less) your hard disk (and diskette) space. In this section, we look at the major changes and additions since Windows 3.1x.

VFAT

In Windows for Workgroups 3.11, the Virtual File Allocation Table (VFAT) was called *32-bit file access*. You accessed it through the Enhanced icon in the Windows for Workgroups Control Panel. Starting with Windows 95, it's called the *32-bit protected-mode* VFAT file system. Microsoft released the prebeta version of this code when it produced Windows for Workgroups 3.11. It worked, except for numerous software and hardware incompatibilities. And it sped up read and write operations, at least when you didn't have to turn it off because of these incompatibilities.

Microsoft much improved the code back in Windows 95 and 98, and it now actually works reliably. It provides fast access to files. It improves multitasking by reducing the amount of time that it blocks other tasks. It is compatible with existing DOS partitions — the original FAT — on your disks as well as FAT32 partitions. Because your processor doesn't have to switch to real mode to read and write to the disk, everything gets faster.

In addition to providing 32-bit hard disk access, Windows Me, 98, and 95 use VFAT to implement long filenames.

Vcache

Windows Me comes with a 32-bit protected-mode dynamic cache. It replaces the old, 16-bit, real-mode SmartDrive (`Smartdrv.exe`) that was used in Windows 3.1x. Vcache doesn't take up conventional or upper memory space. It does a much better job than SmartDrive does of caching disk reads and writes. It also caches CD-ROMs and networked drives.

You don't have to specify how much memory should be set aside for Vcache (unlike SmartDrive). It sizes itself based on available free memory and disk read/write activity. (That's the dynamic part of Vcache.)

Direct CD-ROM Support

There's no more messy ducks (the old `Mscdex.exe` file) in your `Autoexec.bat` file or CD-ROM driver in your `Config.sys` file. Windows Me provides another one of its 32-bit protected-mode drivers, CDFS (CD-ROM file system), to support CD-ROM drives. This driver replaces the 16-bit real-mode `Mscdex.exe` that comes with Windows 3.1x and MS-DOS, as well as CD-ROM manufacturers' 16-bit CD-ROM drivers.

You get a dynamic CD-ROM cache that works with Vcache. The driver uses no conventional or upper memory. It isn't an add-on afterthought called by a line in the old `Config.sys` file. CDFS is also quite a bit faster than `Mscdex.exe`.

Long Filenames

You can type filenames up to 255 characters long in Windows Me. The names can include spaces. Windows Me can read and write long filenames supported by other operating systems, such as Windows 2000/NT, NetWare, UNIX, and OS/2.

Files with long filenames also have short filenames that are recognized by applications that can't handle long filenames (including DOS). Windows manages these short names to ensure that only unique names are created.

The unique short filenames consist of the first six characters of the long filename, plus ~1 or additional ordinals. See the section entitled "Long Filenames" later in this chapter for details.

Windows-Based Disk Tools

Windows 3.1x required that you quit Windows and go to DOS if you needed to work directly with your disk drive at a low level. While you can still do this, it's a lot harder to "get out of" Windows Me.

Fortunately, Windows Me comes with very powerful Windows-based disk tools that help you manage and protect your files. ScanDisk finds and repairs problems with your disks. Defrag makes your files contiguous.

Compression Disk Drivers

Windows Me comes with a 32-bit protected-mode compression disk driver that works with both DoubleSpace and DriveSpace disks. Instead of taking 50K of conventional memory, it is loaded into extended memory (except in MS-DOS mode). These drivers enable you to read existing compressed disks, but they do not allow you to create new compressed disks.

Built-In SCSI Hard Disk Support

Earlier versions of DOS and Windows didn't support SCSI drives without special drivers from hardware manufacturers that you loaded in `Config.sys`. Windows Me and 9x have built-in support for SCSI devices.

Installable File System Manager

Both the VFAT and the CDFS are installable file systems managed by the Windows Installable File System Manager. You can add other file systems, and you will if you connect your computer to network servers. Windows can manage multiple file systems, which makes it much easier to connect to many different networks at once.

Windows Me doesn't support HPFS (high performance file system), which is native to OS/2, NTFS 4 (the Windows NT 4.0 file system), or NTFS 5 (the Windows 2000 file system) on local hard disks, but it does have the ability to read and write to these disks over a network.

Dynamically Sized Swap File

Virtual memory no longer requires a permanent swap file for the fastest operation. Windows can dynamically size the required swap file. This cuts down on the user decisions required to optimize Windows. The swap file can even be on a compressed drive without incurring a performance hit.

Support for Enhanced IDE Devices

Windows supports the enhanced IDE (EIDE) specification, so it can handle drives larger than 1GB directly. In fact, Windows supports EIDE hard disks as large as 137GB.

Windows also supports IDE-based CD-ROMs. You can hook these drives to the existing IDE card used by your hard disk without buying a separate SCSI card to support the CD-ROM.

Multitasked Floppy Drive Formatting

No longer does everything grind to a halt while you format a diskette. A Windows 32-bit driver handles multitasked access to your floppy drives.

Moving from Windows 95 to Windows Me

While the file system tools that are supported in Windows Me (many of which first appeared in Windows 98) are less fundamental than those Microsoft first introduced with Windows 95, they are significant, especially for users with larger disks.

FAT 32

Windows Me and 98's 32-bit File Allocation Table (FAT32) allows a single hard drive letter (partition) to be larger than 2 gigabytes in size. (The 2GB barrier was a limitation of FAT16, the 16-bit file system used in previous versions of Windows and DOS.) FAT32 also stores files without the 30 percent or so of wasted space typical of older 2GB FAT16 drives. This is because FAT32 supports cluster sizes of 4K (instead of 32K for 2GB drives) on partitions up to 8GB.

The fixed cluster size of 4K for FAT32 volumes up to 8GB in size results in an average of 4 percent slack. The much higher slack percentages for large FAT16 volumes of different sizes are provided in Table 37-1.

With its typical waste of only 4 percent, FAT32 greatly reduces the amount of slack space on large hard disk drives, relative to FAT16. Now that most hard disk drives are greater than 2GB, Microsoft had to come out with a FAT that could handle the large drives without excessive wasted space.

Table 37-1   FAT16 Partition Size Versus Slack

Cluster Size	Maximum Partition Size (FAT16)	Slack
2K	128MB	2%
4K	256MB	4%
8K	512MB	8%
16K	1,024MB (1GB)	16%
32K	2,048MB (2GB)	32%

DriveSpace

Windows Me adds a higher level of disk compression with its DriveSpace utility for computers with 486 or faster processors. DriveSpace compresses files (quite often at a ratio greater than 2.5:1) to free up more room on your hard disk.

You can use a Windows utility called Compression Agent to schedule compression, error scanning, and defragging to take place during idle times. Compression Agent is a part of the Windows Task Scheduler.

Disk Defragmenter Optimization Wizard

The new Disk Defragmenter Optimization Wizard automatically tracks the programs that you use most often. The wizard arranges program files in the order that they are accessed when a program starts, allowing the program to start more quickly.

Direct Memory Access to Drives

Direct memory access (DMA) for hard drives and CD-ROM drives enables your PC to directly access data on an IDE drive or CD-ROM drive without using CPU time. IDE controllers that support *bus mastering*, the ability to take over traffic control on the hardware bus, have their own processors that can handle most of the work. This makes access times faster and saves CPU time for other multitasking purposes.

Finding Your Disks and the Disk Tools

You've got to be able to find the disk tools if you're going to use them. Fortunately, you can easily reach this collection of programs through several different routes.

The Start Button

The easiest way to find the disk tools is to click the Start button, point to Programs, then Accessories, and finally click System Tools. If you haven't edited your Start menu, the System Tools submenu will contain Disk Defragmenter, ScanDisk, Scheduled Tasks, System Information, and DriveSpace, as well as Backup, System Monitor, and Net Watcher, if you installed them.

A Drive Icon

Another way to display the disk tools that is almost as easy is to click My Computer, right-click one of the hard drive icons, click Properties, and then click the Tools tab. Windows displays the dialog box shown in Figure 37-1. You have access to ScanDisk, Backup, Disk Defragmenter, and Compression.

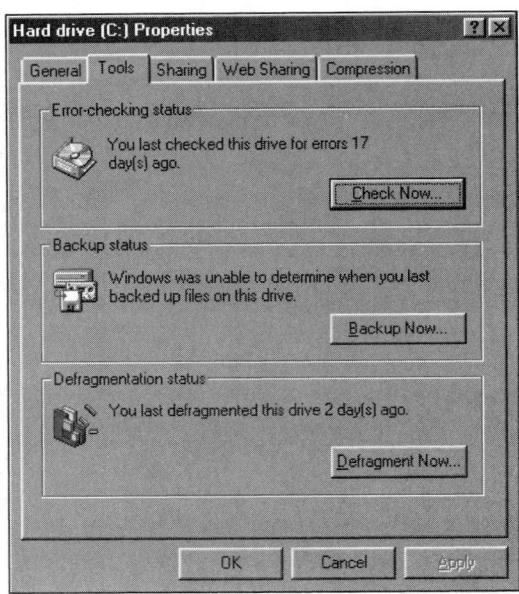

Figure 37-1: The Tools tab of the Properties dialog box for a hard drive. Click Check Now to launch ScanDisk, Backup Now to launch Backup, or Defragment Now to launch the Disk Defragmenter. Click the Compression tab to check or start disk compression.

You can right-click any drive icon in any folder or Explorer window and click Properties to get to this Tools tab.

In a DOS Window

You can type **Scandisk**, **Defrag**, or **Drvspace** in a DOS window. Each of these commands invokes the Windows graphical version of these programs. You can run Windows programs from your DOS window.

Tip If you type **Scandisk /?** in a DOS window and press Enter, you'll see the following instructions for finding the section of the Windows Help system that tells you how to use command-line parameters with ScanDisk:

> For information about the command-line parameters supported by ScanDisk for Windows, look up 'disk errors' in the Windows Help index. Then view the topic 'Checking your disk for errors when your computer starts.'

Device Manager

The Device Manager lets you look at the basic resources used by your devices, including your disk drives and controller card(s). You can get to the Device Manager (a tab in the System Properties dialog box) in at least two ways:

- Right-click My Computer, click Properties, and then click the Device Manager tab.

- Click the Start button, point to Settings, and then click Control Panel. Click the System icon and choose the Device Manager tab.

Once you're in the Device Manager, click the plus signs next to the icons labeled "Disk drives," "Floppy disk controllers," or "Hard disk controllers." Highlight the controller or drive name that is displayed, click the Properties button, and then click the Resources tab. The resources used by an IDE hard disk controller are shown in Figure 37-2.

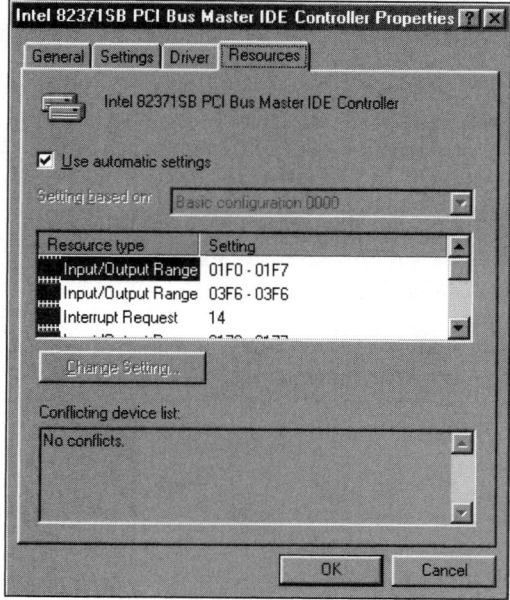

Figure 37-2: The Resources tab for an IDE/ESDI controller

File System Performance

The Performance tab of the System Properties dialog box lets you disable all sorts of 32-bit file access settings as well as optimize your disk-caching scheme.

Use the same steps to get to the System Properties dialog box as described in the preceding section, but click the Performance tab instead of the Device Manager tab. Click the File System button to display the File System Properties dialog box, as shown in Figure 37-3.

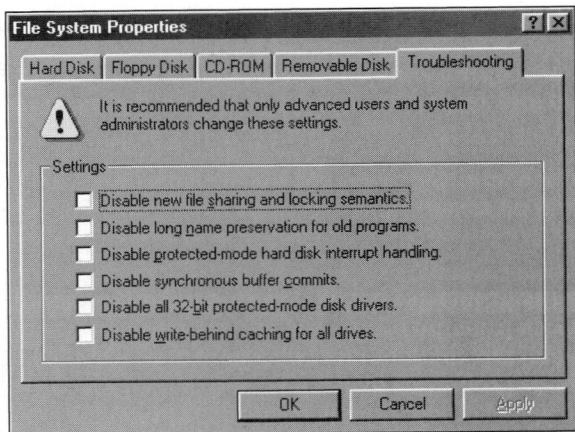

Figure 37-3: The Troubleshooting tab of the File System Properties dialog box

To see how to optimize file system performance, turn to the "Setting Disk-Cache Parameters" section of this chapter.

Virtual Memory Performance

Windows can manage your swap file without any input from you. In fact, it is generally best to leave these settings alone and allow Windows Me to select the best settings. If you want to change its location and set a minimum or maximum size, you can do so.

Use the same steps to get to the System Properties dialog box as described in the earlier section entitled "Device Manager," but click the Performance tab instead of the Device Manager tab. Click the Virtual Memory button to display the Virtual Memory dialog box, as shown in Figure 37-4. See the "Managing Your Swap Space" section of this chapter to learn about changing your swap file size.

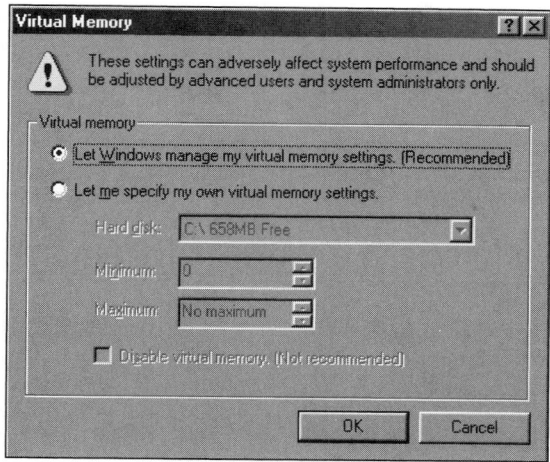

Figure 37-4: The Virtual Memory dialog box

System Monitor

You can use System Monitor to track how your hard disks (or hard disks on other computers on your network) are being used to supply virtual memory to your operating system. You'll find System Monitor in the Start menu.

Click the Start button, point to Programs ⇨ Accessories ⇨ System Tools, and then click System Monitor. It won't be there unless you did a custom installation of Windows and specifically chose to install it. You can use the Add/Remove Programs icon in the Control Panel to add it. Click the Windows Setup tab, and look under System Tools.

STEPS

Using System Monitor to Evaluate Virtual Memory Performance

Step 1. Configure System Monitor to display graphs for allocated memory, disk cache size, Swapfile in use, Swapfile size, swappable memory, and unused physical memory, as shown in Figure 37-5. To do this, choose Edit ⇨ Add Item, highlight Memory Manager, select the six items in the list on the right, and click OK. (To select all of the items at once, click the first one, and then Ctrl+click the remaining ones.) Use Edit ⇨ Remove Item to take out any other graphs. Once you've got System Monitor's six graphs sized the way you want, choose View, mark "Always on top," and then close System Monitor.

Continued

STEPS

Using System Monitor to Evaluate Virtual Memory
Performance *(continued)*

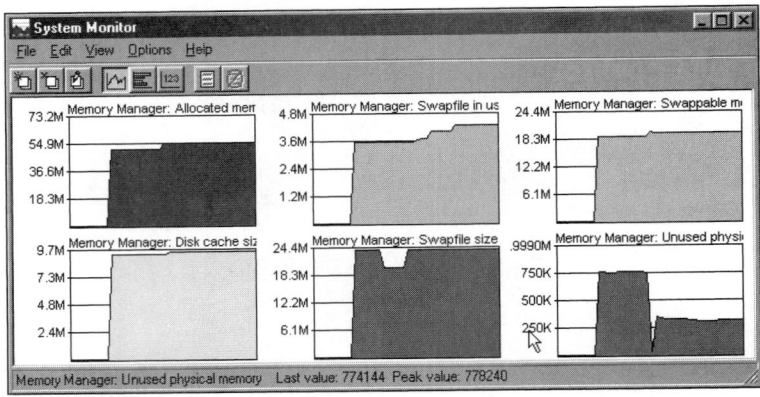

Figure 37-5: The System Monitor showing allocated memory, disk cache size, Swapfile in use, Swapfile size, swappable memory, and unused physical memory.

Step 2.   Temporarily stop unnecessary programs in your StartUp folder from loading at startup. Click your Start button ➪ Programs ➪ Accessories ➪ System Tools ➪ System Information. Choose Tools ➪ System Configuration Utility. Click the Startup tab and clear all the checkboxes of the startup applications. If you really need a certain program to run, don't clear its checkbox. Click OK.

You can also click the Win.ini tab, click the plus sign next to [windows], and see if there are any programs called on the load= or run= lines. You can clear these checkboxes. The same is true for any load= or run= lines in the Autoexec.bat and Config.sys tabs.

Step 3.   Once you've lightened up your StartUp group and other files, click OK, close the Microsoft System Information window, and restart Windows.

Step 4.   Immediately after Windows has finished loading, click Start ➪ Programs ➪ Accessories ➪ System Tools ➪ System Monitor.

Step 5.   After System Monitor loads, start your favorite large application, perhaps your word processor or spreadsheet program, and open a data file within it. Then start another program, and then another. Write down the number of minutes and seconds that elapse while loading these applications and data files.

If you have a certain long routine you often run, such as sorting a database or recalculating a spreadsheet, do that as soon as you have the necessary application running.

Step 6.   Close all of the applications you opened in step 5, and then reopen the same programs and documents again, writing down the elapsed time now that your system's disk cache (usually Windows' own disk cache) contains some of the applications and files.

Armed with these times and the graphs in System Monitor, you're ready to do a little interpretation. Here's how to read what each of the graphs means to your system:

- **Allocated memory** is a combination of free memory, swap file size, and disk cache size, among other uses of memory by applications and DLLs. When this chart rises above the amount of physical memory (RAM) you have installed, you know that Windows is swapping some code or data out of main memory and onto disk storage, which is much slower.

- **Disk cache size** is a visual indication of Windows' dynamic disk cache. Windows tries to determine the optimum size for the cache. (Sometimes a smaller cache can be just as effective as a larger one, because more RAM is available to the operating system for its needs when the cache is smaller.)

- **Swapfile in use** refers to the amount of the Windows swap file that contains parts of programs that have been moved from memory into hard disk space. When swap file in use starts going up, it means that Windows can't hold everything in its faster RAM space. When this happens, your performance will start to go down.

- **Swapfile size** reports on the physical size of the Windows swap file. Not all of this is still being used.

- **Swappable memory** is the amount of memory Windows *can* swap from disk to memory, or vice versa, if it needs to. You should see swappable memory rising as each new application is loaded.

- **Unused physical memory** is memory that isn't currently occupied by a program or data. As you load each program, you should see the unused physical memory reduced, until it approaches zero.

SuperMonitor

Gary Tessler of TNT (Tessler's Nifty Tools) has developed a replacement for System Monitor. It's called SuperMonitor, and it displays different resources in separate windows. You can use it to determine usage by individual applications.

To determine an application's memory usage with SuperMonitor, you start a window on memory and then stop that window's monitoring. (This "freezes" the figures.) Then start your application and open another SuperMonitor window. The difference between the two readings is the amount of memory used by the application or any combination of applications you choose.

SuperMonitor can display continuous, average, or maximum values in different windows. You can set the timing interval SuperMonitor uses, and you can log the figures to a disk file.

You'll find the latest version of SuperMonitor at `http://cbr.nc.us.mensa.org/homepages/NIFTY_TOOLS/subrief.htm`.

Disk Tools

You use ScanDisk and Disk Defragmenter to fix your hard disks, diskettes, and other removable media (not CD-ROMs) when your files get corrupted or are stored in too many pieces. If parts of the surface of your hard disk are bad, ScanDisk marks them so files won't be stored there. ScanDisk also moves the data off these spots if it can.

ScanDisk

ScanDisk does an excellent job of analyzing your hard disk and repairing errors. Microsoft has taken great pains to make sure it works under all circumstances.

ScanDisk reviews and repairs errors on compressed drives as well as on physical drives. It repairs problems with long filenames, the FAT and FAT32, the directory and file structure, the drive surface, and the internal structure of compressed volume files (CVFs). It can find and fix errors on diskettes and hard drives, and, as if you really cared, RAM drives and memory cards that are treated as drives.

ScanDisk can find and repair problems on both DriveSpace and DoubleSpace drives (but not on Stacker or SuperStor drives). The CVFs don't have to be mounted (have a drive letter associated with them) for ScanDisk to work with them, although in most cases they will be.

ScanDisk can't find or fix errors on CD-ROMs, networked drives, or pseudo drives created by using `Assign`, `Subst`, `Join`, or `Interlnk` (all of these are DOS commands).

If one of your applications reports disk problems when reading a file, run ScanDisk immediately to repair the file. If Windows crashes while you are editing a file and the file is damaged, it is very likely that ScanDisk can fix it.

ScanDisk Options

As stated earlier in this chapter, you can start ScanDisk by right-clicking a drive icon in a folder or Explorer window, choosing Properties, clicking the Tools tab, and then clicking the Check Now button. If you do this, you are presented with a ScanDisk dialog box containing buttons labeled Options and Advanced, as shown in Figure 37-6.

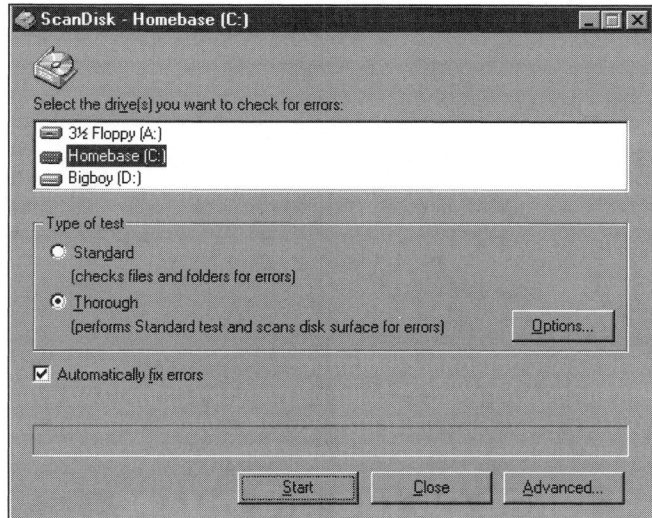

Figure 37-6: The ScanDisk dialog box

To find out what all these buttons do, take the following steps:

STEPS

Exploring ScanDisk Options

Step 1. Start ScanDisk and mark the Thorough option button (see Figure 37-6), and then click the Options button.

Step 2. Right-click any item in the Surface Scan Options dialog box. Click the What's This? button to see what the option really does.

Step 3. Click the Cancel button in the Surface Scan Options dialog box, and then click the Advanced button.

Step 4. Right-click any item in the ScanDisk Advanced Options dialog box, and click What's This? to learn more about what it does. Click the Cancel button when you're done.

One advanced option that doesn't respond to a right-click is "Report MS-DOS mode name length errors." Windows allows paths of more than 66 characters. MS-DOS does not. If you have paths that exceed 66 characters, you will experience error messages when you run any of the other disk utilities discussed in this chapter and they call ScanDisk. The error messages occur frequently if you have set up user profiles, because user profiles automatically create long paths.

Clearing this field allows ScanDisk to automatically correct any problems in any folder, no matter how long the path. Back in the days of Windows 95, you had to manually move the folders in the paths to allow ScanDisk to work automatically without stopping.

ScanDisk Command-Line Parameters

You can run ScanDisk from a Windows DOS prompt. You may want to add some command-line parameters to the command line of the shortcut. (Right-click the shortcut, choose Properties, click the Shortcut tab, and type the command line in the Target field.)

ScanDisk can take the following parameters:

```
Scandisk {x:} {options}
```

or

```
Scandisk x:\drvspace.nnn
```

or

```
Scandisk x:\dblspace.nnn
```

x: is the drive letter for the drive you want to check. It can be the drive letter assigned to a compressed volume file.

ScanDisk can take the following options:

/all or /a	Checks all your local, nonremovable hard disks
/noninteractive or /n	Starts and finishes ScanDisk without user input
/preview or /p	Prevents ScanDisk from correcting errors that it finds
dblspace.nnn	Name of compressed volume file (CVF) to check
drvspace.nnn	Name of compressed volume file (CVF) to check

Hidden CVFs reside on host drives and are named by their type of compression (DoubleSpace or DriveSpace) and a number (*nnn*) as the file extension. If you want to scan an unmounted compressed drive, include dblspace.*nnn* or drvspace.*nnn* on the command line. The drive letter in this case would be the host drive letter.

Running ScanDisk from DOS

Secret

There are really two ScanDisk programs, Scandskw.exe and Scandisk.exe. The Windows version is Scandskw.exe, an executable stub, which calls code located in the dynamic link libraries Shell.dll and Dskmaint.dll.

Scandskw.exe is called when you click the Check Now button in the Tools tab of the Properties dialog box for a hard drive, or ScanDisk in the System Tools submenu of the Start menu. It is also called when you type **Scandisk** at a DOS prompt in a Windows DOS session. You can also type **Scandskw** at the command prompt in a Windows DOS session.

Scandisk.ini

Secret

Scandisk.ini, the ScanDisk configuration file, is stored in your \Windows\ Command folder. This file works only with the DOS version of ScanDisk and is not used if you run ScanDisk from Windows or from a Windows DOS session.

Scandisk.ini is internally well documented, and you can edit it to change the way the DOS version of ScanDisk operates. In Windows, just click it to open it. In MS-DOS mode, open it with Edit.com, and you will find plenty of documentation explaining how to change ScanDisk's parameters.

ScanDisk and Your File Allocation Tables

Secret

The DOS version of ScanDisk always uses the primary copy of your File Allocation Table (unless it finds a physical disk error). The primary File Allocation Table replaces the backup File Allocation Table when ScanDisk repairs errors.

The Windows version of ScanDisk checks both of your file allocation tables, and, if they are out of sync, determines which File Allocation Table is "better" and uses that one.

ScanDisk and Setup

ScanDisk is run automatically when you run Windows Setup. If ScanDisk finds problems with your hard disk, you can fix them before you continue with the setup process.

Setup runs ScanDisk to put everything in order and to cut down on the number of variables before you install this very complex operating system. ScanDisk is discussed in more detail in "Running ScanDisk" in Chapter 2.

Defrag, the Disk Defragmenter

As you probably know, DOS and Windows (all versions) don't necessarily keep the contents of your files stored in contiguous sectors of your hard disk. Your files become more fragmented as they are rewritten, and fragmented files take longer to read and write. You can speed up disk access by occasionally defragmenting the files on your hard disk.

You can run Defrag while you are running other programs. Disk reads and writes interrupt the defragmentation process, but Defrag is always operating and continues to defragment where it left off, after the read or write is complete.

Tip

If you find that Defrag is restarting often, you may be running another program that is making frequent writes to the disk. Try quitting other programs while Defrag is running. If you are running the Microsoft Office Find Fast utility (which indexes files in the background), you may need to pause Find Fast while Defrag runs. To do this, click Start ⇨ Settings ⇨ Control Panel, and click the Find Fast icon. From the Index menu, select Pause Indexing.

Defrag in Details View

Defrag is a fun program to watch if you put it into Details view. Here's how:

STEPS

Running Defrag in Details View

Step 1.   Click the Start button, point to Programs ⇨ Accessories ⇨ System Tools, and then click Disk Defragmenter.

Step 2.   In the Select Drive dialog box, display the drop-down list to show the available drives. You can defrag your floppies if you want to (but why?). Highlight the hard drive that you want to defragment (or select All Hard Drives to defragment all of them), and click OK.

Step 3.   Click the Start button in the Disk Defragmenter dialog box, click the Show Details button, and then click the Legend button. The Defrag Legend dialog box appears on top of the Defragmenting window, which contains rows and rows of little colored squares that represent disk clusters (see Figure 37-7).

Showing details slows down the defragmentation process a little, but what you lose in speed you make up for in visual interest.

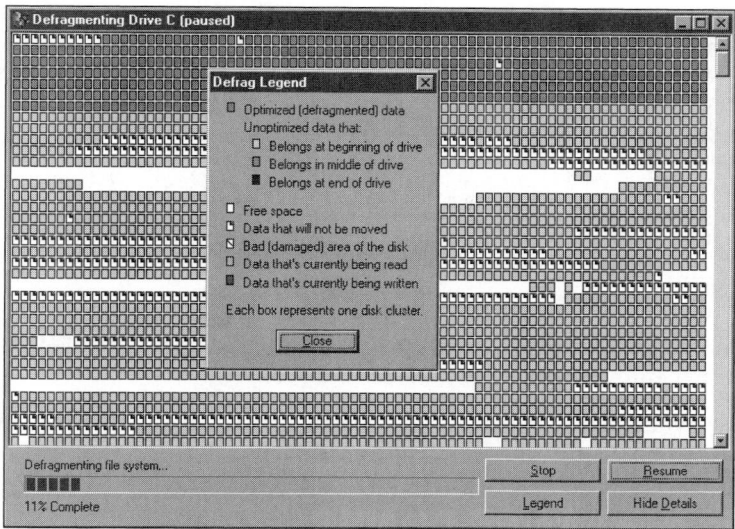

Figure 37-7: The disk defragmenter in Details view with the Defrag Legend showing

Before you click the Start button in the Disk Defragmenter dialog box, you can choose how extensive you want the defragmentation process to be. To see these options, click the Advanced button. To find out what each option does, right-click the text next to each option and click the What's This? button.

Disk Defragmenter Optimization Wizard Settings

The Disk Defragmenter Optimization Wizard is a Windows Me feature that first appeared in Windows 98. Task Monitor is automatically loaded when you start Windows. Task Monitor checks which programs you are running and directs Disk Defragmenter when it defragments your disk to place the most used programs in the spot on your hard disk where they will get loaded the fastest.

To access the few settings available for this wizard, click the Settings button in the Select Drive dialog box.

Data that Will Not Be Moved

Secret

You may notice that some or many sectors on your hard disk are marked "Data that will not be moved" in the Details view of the Defragmenting window. Defrag doesn't move files that are marked *both* hidden and system. Some copy protection schemes put a file or two in certain locations and mark them as both system and hidden. If they are moved, the copy protection scheme fails.

Defrag takes the conservative approach. In reality, almost all files that are marked both system and hidden are, in fact, not related to any copy protection schemes. Windows marks many of its files as both system and hidden. Of course, they are easy enough to see in a folder or Explorer window, so they are not really all that hidden.

If you have a CVF (Compressed Volume File, the "real" file that contains a compressed drive letter) on a host drive, it will probably appear as a large block of contiguous sectors and will be marked as "Data that will not be moved." If you view the compressed drive itself, you'll see that data in these clusters can indeed be moved. Both views are right.

The CVF shouldn't be moved, and you can defragment the files within it by defragmenting the compressed drive directly.

Secret

Your dynamically sized swap file is also marked as unable to be moved, but it doesn't have the hidden or system attribute.

You can have Defrag move the files marked both system and hidden by changing their attributes. You (not Defrag) are taking the responsibility for the consequences.

To remove the system and hidden attributes from a file, type the following command at any DOS prompt:

```
attrib -s -h {drive:\pathname\filename}
```

Unfortunately, the Windows Find dialog box doesn't let you collect all the files that have a certain attribute turned on (or off). If it did, you could search for all the files with the attributes system and hidden, and decide for yourself whether to turn these attributes off for each file displayed in the Find dialog box.

If you want to find out more about the attrib command, type **attrib/?** at the DOS prompt.

It's very important to reset any CVFs back to hidden and system so that they are not moved by Defrag. To do this, type the following command at the DOS prompt:

```
attrib +s +h c:\Drvspace.nnn
```

or

```
attrib +s +h c:\Dblspace.nnn
```

In the preceding command line, *nnn* is the number of the CVF volume.

Never use earlier versions of Defrag from MS-DOS 6.*x* because they will destroy long filenames.

Tip

The disk defragmenter will not work with Stacker or SuperStor compressed drives. If you have these types of compressed drives, get a third-party disk defragmenter program, such as the one included in Symantec's Norton Utilities for Windows. You also can't use Defrag over a network. It has real trouble with CD-ROMs, which are read-only. Don't try it on drives that are created by `Assign`, `Subst`, or `Join`.

You can run Defrag on the host drive and/or on the compressed drive if you have DoubleSpace or DriveSpace drives.

Defrag Command-Line Parameters

If you run Defrag from a DOS prompt, from the Run dialog box (Start ⇨ Run), from a batch file, or from a shortcut, you can change the way it runs by adding command-line parameters.

```
Defrag {x: or /all} {options} {/noprompt} {/concise or /detailed}
```

The command-line parameters are as follows:

`x:`	Drive letter designator for drive to be defragmented
`/all`	Defragment all local, nonremovable drives
{*options*}	
`/f`	Defragment files and free space
`/u`	Defragment files only
`/q`	Defragment free space only
`/noprompt`	Do not display confirmation message boxes
`/concise`	Don't show the Details view (this is the default)
`/detailed`	Show the Details view

Disk-Related Functions

Numerous commands and functions affect the drive performance and file-access speed.

Disk Space

When you select a folder in the left pane of the Explorer, the status bar displays the total size of the files stored in the folder. It also lists the amount of free space available on the drive partition that contains the highlighted folder.

Another way to find the size and available disk space on a particular drive is to take the following steps:

STEPS

Displaying Disk Size

Step 1. Click My Computer.

Step 2. Right-click a drive icon, and then click Properties.

These steps display the General tab of the Properties dialog box for the selected drive, as shown in Figure 37-8.

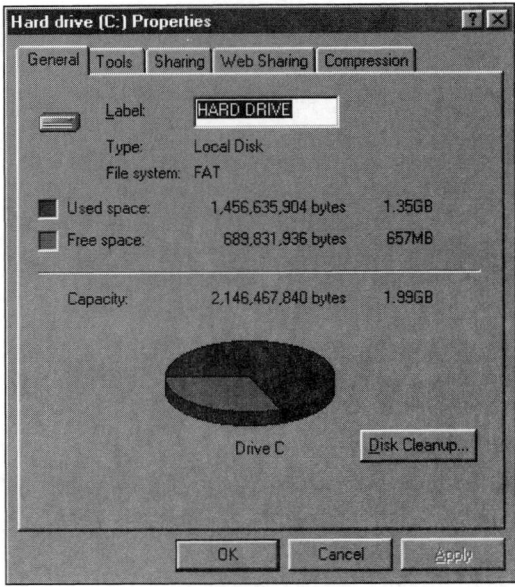

Figure 37-8: The General tab of the Properties dialog box for a hard drive. You can type a new name for the disk in the Label field.

If you are viewing your folder or Explorer window as a Web page (right-click the client area, and click View ➪ As Web Page), you can place your mouse pointer over a hard disk icon to display the disk size and amount of used and free space.

Click the Disk Cleanup button to access a few utilities that identify files you can delete from your hard disk.

Disk Cleanup

Disk Cleanup adds up the space that you could reclaim by deleting some temporary files. After it searches your disk for these files, it displays the Disk Cleanup tab of the Disk Cleanup dialog box. Just mark the checkboxes for the categories that you want to remove.

Click the More Options tab to find other ways to access the Drive Converter (SFAT32) and the Add/Remove Programs utility.

File Size and Attributes

The status bar of the Explorer (or any folder window) tells you the size of the files you have highlighted or, if you have highlighted a folder in the left pane, the number and total size of all the files in the folder.

Right-click a file in an Explorer or folder window and click Properties to display the General tab of the file's Properties dialog box, as shown in Figure 37-9. This tab tells you the size of the file as well as its attributes (Read-only, Archive, Hidden, System).

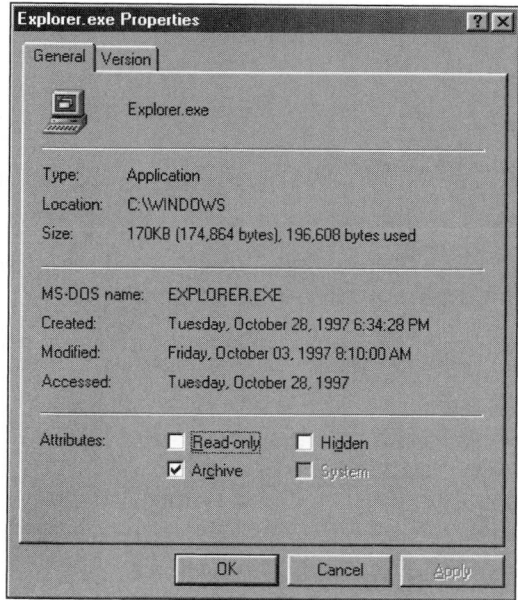

Figure 37-9: The General tab of a file's Properties dialog box. You can change a file's attributes by marking or clearing the Attributes checkboxes.

If you select a folder, or a group of files and then right-click the group (or the folder icon) and choose Properties, the General tab shows the total size of all the files. This is handy if you are dragging these files to your floppy disk drive. The total size of the selected files is also displayed in the status bar of the Explorer or folder window.

Secret

Do you want to know the total size of all the files on a hard disk? Take the following steps:

STEPS

Finding the Total Size of All Files on a Disk

Step 1.   Highlight a drive icon in the left pane of an Explorer window.

Step 2.   Highlight the top entry in the right pane.

Step 3.   Scroll down the right pane, and Shift+right-click the last entry.

Step 4.   Click Properties.

The total number of files and their accumulated size will be displayed. It may take a few seconds to count all the files.

Format

You can format a hard disk, diskette, or other removable media by right-clicking the icon representing the drive in either a folder or Explorer window and choosing Format from the context menu.

Secret

You can't format a compressed diskette in this manner. If you try to format the compressed volume or the host drive, you'll receive error messages. If you want to format such a diskette, you'll need to uncompress it first (which may require that you erase the files on it).

You can format a compressed drive using DriveSpace. See the "DriveSpace" section in this chapter for details.

Thankfully, clicking Format in the context menu does not immediately begin the formatting process. You're given the opportunity to determine some format parameters. If you accidentally click Format after you right-click your boot drive, you will have a chance to back out.

Diskcopy

Tip

Do you want to make a copy of a diskette? Put the diskette in the diskette drive, click My Computer, right-click the diskette drive icon, and then click Copy Disk.

Sharing

If you are on a network (even if you just have Direct Cable Connection installed), you can give other computers access to files on your disk drives. To share access to all the files on a drive, right-click the drive icon in a folder or Explorer window, and click Sharing in the context menu to display the Sharing tab shown in Figure 37-10.

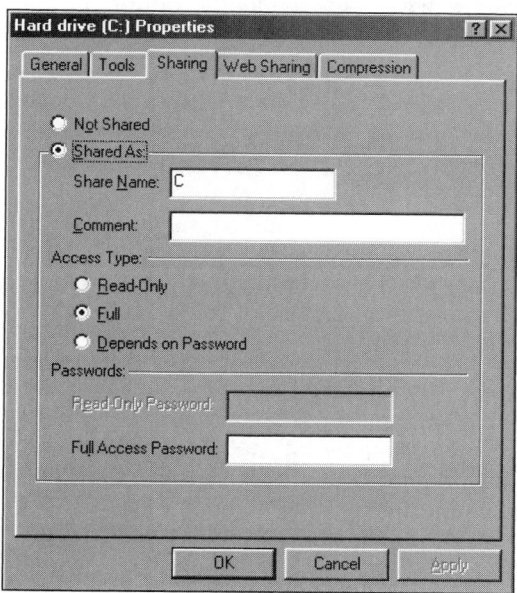

Figure 37-10: The Sharing tab of the Properties dialog box for a hard disk drive. Choose the Shared As option button to share your drive with other computers on the network.

Secret

If you place a $ as the last character in a folder's share name, you create a hidden share. The remote user must know the full UNC name for the hidden folder in order to access it.

Recycle Bin Size

Just because you delete a file doesn't mean it is gone. The files sit in your Recycle Bin, taking up disk space until you empty it. The free space on your disk doesn't increase until you empty the trash. (An exception to this is if you right-click the Recycle Bin on the Desktop, choose Properties, and mark the checkbox labeled "Do not move files to the Recycle Bin. Remove files immediately when deleted.")

If you like, you can adjust the maximum amount of space the Recycle Bin can occupy on your drive(s). By default, the maximum size is set to 10 percent of each drive. To change this setting, right-click the Recycle Bin on the Desktop and choose Properties. If you want to use the same size setting on each drive, mark the "Use one setting for all drives" option button, and drag the slider on the Global tab. If you prefer to set different maximum sizes for each of your drives, mark the "Configure drives independently" option button, and then use the tabs for each drive to configure the maximum Recycle Bin size on each drive individually.

Testing Direct Memory Access to Drives

In order to take advantage of direct memory access (DMA), your computer must have a bus-mastering IDE drive. However, not all IDE drives are compliant with bus mastering. To see if yours is, set your browser to a Microsoft document at `http://support.microsoft.com/support/kb/articles/q159/5/60`. Run the test recommended in this article to see if your IDE components support bus mastering. You must have the Windows drivers for IDE controllers installed.

Once you've determined that your hardware supports DMA, you must turn this feature on with a little-known switch in the Control Panel. Click the System icon, click the Device Manager tab, and then click the plus sign next to Disk Drives. Select the drive for which you want to enable DMA, click Properties, and then click the Settings tab and mark the DMA checkbox. You must restart Windows for the change to take effect.

If your system doesn't support DMA or you aren't using the bus-mastering drivers that are included with Windows, the DMA checkbox won't appear. Some third-party drivers that enable bus mastering also don't display a DMA checkbox, because DMA is always on and can't be disabled.

Chkdsk /f

Chkdsk (Check disk) is an outdated DOS command that deletes bad files when you specify the /f parameter. It doesn't work anymore in a Windows DOS session, and you should instead use ScanDisk to fix files or the DOS command Mem to give you a memory usage breakdown.

Troubleshooting Disk Access

Even though the 32-bit disk and file access provided by Windows Me is much better than what came with Windows for Workgroups 3.11, there may still be incompatibilities. You can turn off various portions of the disk driver to track down problems with disk access. To get to these troubleshooting options, take the following steps:

STEPS

Troubleshooting Disk Access

Step 1. Right-click My Computer. Choose Properties and click the Performance tab.

Step 2. Click the File System button.

Step 3. Click the Troubleshooting tab.

Disk Compression

Windows 98 included DriveSpace and the Compression Agent, which gave you even higher levels of compression, as well as control over which files are compressed to what levels when. Windows Me, however, does not fully support disk compression. Specifically, Windows Me can only read existing compressed disks, but cannot create them, nor can it adjust the settings on existing compressed disks.

Disk Caching

Windows Me's Vcache dynamically adjusts the size in memory of your disk cache. Older disk-cache programs that made you manually adjust this size are obsolete.

Vcache caches on a per-file basis, unlike the older SmartDrive from Windows 3.1x, which cached on a per-contiguous-sector basis. If your hard disk is fragmented, SmartDrive wouldn't store your files together (in contiguous sectors). Vcache is much smarter when it comes to caching a complete file.

Vcache can read-cache removable media, such as Zip disks, although it can't cache their disk writes.

Setting Disk-Cache Parameters

You can give Vcache a few suggestions about how to optimize caching the file system on your hard disk and, separately, on your CD-ROM.

Secret

You have three options that affect how fast Windows displays filenames and folders: Desktop Computer, Mobile or Docking System, and Network Server. If you choose Network Server, Vcache caches 64 directory paths and 2,729 filenames in memory. If you choose Desktop Computer, it caches 32 paths and 677 files. The Desktop Computer setting uses 10K of memory as cache and the Network Server setting uses 40K. You can mostly likely spare the additional 30K to speed up access to your files and folders.

To modify your file system cache, take the following steps:

STEPS

Modifying Your Hard Disk File System Cache

Step 1.   Right-click My Computer. Choose Properties to display the System Properties dialog box, and click the Performance tab.

Step 2.   Click the File System button to display the File System Properties dialog box.

Step 3.   In the Hard Disk tab, choose from among the options in the "Typical role of this computer" field.

Secret

A historical note: The Windows 95 registry stored the wrong values of the cache sizes for the mobile and network servers in the registry at HKEY_ LOCAL_MACHINE\ SOFTWARE\ Microsoft\ Windows\ CurrentVersion\FS Templates. Microsoft fixed these values in Windows 98, and they're correct in Windows Me, too.

To optimize caching the CD-ROM, click the CD-ROM tab in the File System Properties dialog box, and specify both a cache memory size and the CD-ROM drive's speed. This cache should be sized like this:

Your Computer's RAM	CD-ROM Speed	Cache Size
8MB	Single	64K
8–12MB	Double	626K
12MB or more	Quad or more	1,238K

The Windows memory manager wants to page your loaded applications to the hard disk and manage your RAM for caching the latest applications and data. You can restrict its ability to assign your RAM to cache by fixing the size of the cache. If you want to do this, take these steps:

STEPS

Fixing the Size of Your Cache

Step 1.   Click System.ini in your \Windows folder.

Step 2.   Add the following two lines to the [vcache] section (add the section if it's not there):

```
MinFileCache=4096
MaxFileCache=4096
```

Step 3.   If you have more than 16MB of RAM, set the above values to about 25 percent of your installed RAM.

Step 4.   Save the edited System.ini file and restart Windows.

You are restricting the amount of RAM that Windows is allowed to use for disk caching.

Managing Your Swap Space

You don't need to create a "permanent" swap file, as under older versions of Windows, because Windows Me (like Windows 98) dynamically sizes your swap file space.

Windows Me manages your dynamically sized swap space for you, so you don't have to assign the volume or minimum and maximum size parameters. If you want to change these parameters, take the following steps:

STEPS

Managing Your Swap Space

Step 1.   Right-click My Computer. Choose Properties, and click the Performance tab.

Step 2.   Click the Virtual Memory button to display the Virtual Memory dialog box (shown in Figure 37-11).

Continued

STEPS

Managing Your Swap Space *(continued)*

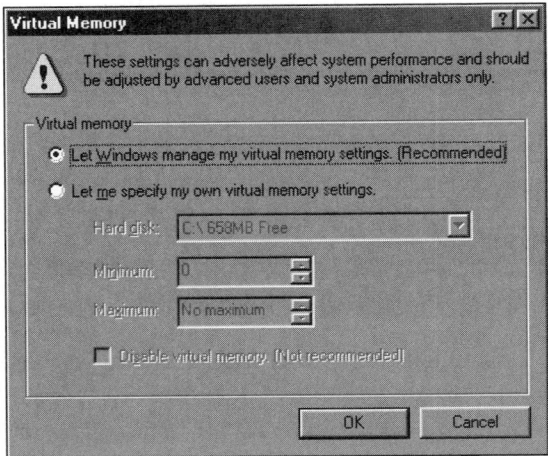

Figure 37-11: The Virtual Memory dialog box. You decide where to place your swap file, and its minimum and maximum size.

Step 3. Choose "Let me specify my own virtual memory settings."

Step 4. Choose volume and size parameters.

If you go back to the Virtual Memory dialog box after restarting Windows, you'll see that the option is set back to "Let Windows manage my virtual memory settings." This is normal. It's managing using the settings you specified earlier.

When you let Windows manage your swap space and your memory, it will take every opportunity to page your loaded applications to the swap space on your hard disk. It uses the freed-up RAM to cache your data and most recently used application code. You might find your hard disk chattering away as this paging occurs in the background.

You can reduce this paging and caching by fixing the size of your swap space. To do this, first defragment your drive to set up a contiguous area on your hard disk big enough for your fixed-size swap space. See the "Defrag, the Disk Defragmenter" section of this chapter for instructions on how to do this.

Next, set the swap space at 2.5 times the size of your total RAM. To do this, set the minimum and maximum size to the same value in step 4 above, choosing a value in megabytes that is 2.5 times the size of your RAM in megabytes.

Swap Space on a Compressed Drive

Your swap drive can be on a compressed drive (CVF). It is stored in an uncompressed form on the compressed drive to ensure that writing to the swap space will never fail.

A swap file is not particularly compressible, so it doesn't hurt to write it out in an uncompressed form. There is an advantage to putting the swap space on a compressed drive. You don't have to set aside enough unused uncompressed disk space for the maximum amount of space that the swap space might occupy, because much of the time this space will never be used.

Virtual File System

Starting with Windows for Workgroups 3.11, Windows significantly reduced its use of DOS for disk/file access. In WFWG 3.11, the file access subsystem was called *32-bit file access*. In Windows Me, it is called the Virtual File Allocation Table (VFAT).

VFAT is compatible with the existing DOS file allocation system. All DOS disks that were partitioned and formatted as FAT partitions can be read and written to by VFAT. This includes hard disks and removable media, including diskettes.

VFAT was implemented to handle the new long filenames that were first introduced by Microsoft in Windows 95.

Lock and Unlock

All disk access is directed through VFAT, so you don't normally access the disk directly or through DOS or your BIOS. If you have programs — usually old, pre-Windows-95 disk utilities — that access the hard disk directly (using interrupts 25 and 26), Windows Me prevents them from accessing the disks.

You can use the Lock command to allow direct disk access. After you are done, you use the Unlock command to prevent direct disk access again. You can do this in batch files or at the DOS prompt. You can't access the disk directly even in MS-DOS mode unless you use Lock and Unlock. No access by other programs is allowed when a drive is locked.

If you have a DOS program that requires direct disk access (see "Undelete and Unerase" in Chapter 13), create a batch file that runs Lock and Unlock around the program. Caution: It is not a good idea to run pre-Windows Me disk utilities because they can destroy long filenames. You should update your disk utilities to ones that are compatible with Windows Me.

Disk utilities provided with Windows Me (including Defrag and ScanDisk) use the Microsoft-developed *volume locking* API. The commands in this application programming interface lock and unlock the disk drive. All third-party disk utilities should use this API.

Real-Mode Disk Drivers

You may have a hard disk drive that requires a 16-bit driver. Microsoft has made a special effort to provide 32-bit protected-mode drivers for almost all disk drives available, but it didn't cover all of them.

You may be tempted to keep your 16-bit driver because some disk manufacturers boast that they shipped "fast" 16-bit drivers. These drivers are not as fast as the 32-bit drivers from Microsoft. Comment them out of your Config.sys file.

You can check if your hard disk is running in MS-DOS compatibility mode (16-bit) by clicking the System icon in your Control Panel, and then clicking the Performance tab. If File System is listed as 16-bit, you may be able to upgrade to 32-bit mode.

Microsoft provides a troubleshooting guide to determine how to fix this problem. You'll find it in the Knowledge Base at http://support.microsoft.com/support/kb/articles/q130/1/79.

Long Filenames

The VFAT file system can handle long filenames — up to 255 characters. Every file has two names, the new long filename and a short filename that is compatible with the FAT file system. The backward-compatible short filename complies with the 8.3 filename rules.

You see the long filename in Explorer and folder windows. If you open a DOS window, you see both names. VFAT creates a short filename using the long filename as a template, and it makes sure that all of the short filenames in a folder are unique.

Valid Filenames

A filename that obeys the 8.3 filename rules can contain any alphanumeric character, any ASCII character greater than 127, and these special characters:

$ % ' - @ ~ ` ! { } ( ) ^ # & _

In addition to these characters, a long filename can contain spaces, and it can also contain the following characters:

+ , ; = [ ] .

A null (one of the ASCII control characters) is included at the end of the long filename, so the total length of the filename, including the null, can be 256 characters. With DOS 6.22 and previous versions, the maximum length of a path and filename combined was 80 characters. It is now 260 characters, including the null. Filenames and folder names obey the same rules.

You can mix case throughout the filename. Filenames are not case sensitive, but the case you choose is preserved and displayed on screen. However, if you type a filename of eight letters or less in all capitals *and* you type its extension in all capitals, Windows "corrects" your typing to sentence case (for example, JUNK.TXT becomes Junk.txt). Windows 95 used to *always* correct names with all capitals, but Windows Me and Windows 98 only do this if the extension is all capitals, as well as the filename. Long filenames are not changed.

You can display uppercase filenames if, in your Explorer, you click View ➪ Folder Options ➪ View ➪ "Allow all uppercase names."

You can't have two files in the same folder with the same name except for the case of the letters. For example, ToDo.txt and TODO.txt are seen by VFAT as the same filename.

The double quote mark is not a valid character to use in a filename. You use double quote marks to denote long path and/or filenames that contain spaces. For example, if you want to copy a file that has spaces in the filename from the DOS prompt, use this format:

```
Copy "File with a long name" "A new name for the long name file"
```

DOS Commands and Long Filenames

Secret

The DOS commands that come with Windows Me have been updated to handle long filenames (and the short filenames that must go with them). If you use versions of these commands from DOS 6.22 or earlier (from an old diskette, for example), you lose the long filenames. If the long filename and the short filename are the same, it doesn't matter.

If you copy files from a Windows Me computer to a diskette, take that diskette to a computer running DOS 6.*x* or Windows 3.1*x*, and then edit those files on the diskette, the long filenames are preserved when you copy those files back to the Windows Me computer. If, on the other hand, you copy the files off the diskette onto the hard disk of the DOS computer, edit those files, and then copy them back onto the diskette, you will lose the long filenames. Only the short 8.3 filenames will be preserved.

Long Filenames Across the Network

The 32-bit network clients in Windows Me/9*x* give you long filenames over the network if the server supports them. Earlier 16-bit real-mode network clients can only provide short filenames. This includes NetWare NETX and VLM drivers. You'll need to use Microsoft's Client for NetWare Networks or a 32-bit client provided by Novell instead if you want to support long filenames.

Other file systems on the servers create different short filenames from the long filenames. No big deal. They are still compatible with Windows Me.

You have to configure NetWare servers to use the LONG namespace in order for Windows Me to see long filenames on them.

To configure the NetWare server to use the LONG namespace, take the following steps:

STEPS

Enabling Long Filenames to Be Seen on a NetWare Server

Step 1.   On the NetWare server, type these commands at the prompt:

```
load long
add name space long to volume xxx
```

Step 2.   Add this line to the file Startup.ncf:

```
load os2
```

Step 3.   Shut down the NetWare server.

Step 4.   Reboot the NetWare server.

Changing Drive Letters for Removable Media

Unlike your floppy and hard drives, you can set the drive letter designator for your CD-ROM, Zip, Jaz, or Syquest drive. You must be using the native Windows Me 32-bit drivers for this to work. (Older CD-ROM drives may still be using 16-bit Windows 3.1 drivers, even under Windows Me.) Here's how to change your drive letter if you are using a 32-bit driver:

STEPS

Designating Your Drive Letter

Step 1.   Right-click My Computer, choose Properties, and click the Device Manager tab.

Step 2.   For your CD-ROM, click the plus sign next to CDROM, highlight
your CD-ROM drive, and click the Properties button. For Syquest
and Zip drives, click the plus sign next to Disk Drives, highlight
your Zip or Syquest drive, and then click the Properties button.

Step 3.   Click the Settings tab.

Step 4.   Select the letter you want for this drive in the "Start drive letter"
and "End drive letter" fields (choose the same letter in both
fields).

Step 5.   Click both OK buttons. You will be prompted to reboot your
computer.

Disk Drive Partitioning

You have to partition physical drives before you can format them into FAT16
or FAT32 volumes. A physical drive can have just one partition, in which case
the partition must be bootable, or it can have multiple partitions, including
one bootable partition. You assign a drive letter to each partition, and refer
to each one as a *drive*.

Windows works with third-party disk partitioning schemes, including Disk
Manager, SuperStor, and Golden Bow. These schemes were created to let
you partition hard drives that were larger than what earlier versions of Fdisk,
which Microsoft supplies, could handle. Windows also works with Fdisk-
partitioned drives on removable media.

Windows Me comes with an updated Fdisk, which you can use to partition
your drives. In most cases, the computer manufacturer will have already set
up disk partitions on your hard drive when you get a new computer. You can
use Fdisk.exe to change these partitions, but you will lose any files stored
on them unless you back them up first.

You shouldn't use Fdisk if your hard disk is already partitioned with a third-
party scheme. Use the third party's tools instead. You can determine if
your hard disk was partitioned with a third-party product by examining
Config.sys. You are using a third-party disk partitioner if you find
references to the following files: Dmdrvr.bin, Sstor.sys, HarDrive.
sys, or Evdisk.sys.

If you want to change the partition structure on your hard disk and you'd
rather not go through the pain of redoing your Windows and software
installation, you'll need to get Partition Magic. You'll find it at http://
www.powerquest.com.

Booting from a Zip Drive

Zip drives from the Iomega Corp. are an increasingly popular removable storage medium. With $15 disks that are only slightly larger and thicker than a 1.44MB floppy disk, Zip drives let you store about 100MB in a convenient package. A newer, higher-priced Zip 250 drive can use more expensive 250MB Zip disks, as well as also reading and writing the original 100MB disks. But Zip 250 drives aren't yet as prevalent among Windows users as Zip 100 drives.

Not only can you use Zip drives for large data files, but you can also install on them whole programs that are bulky and infrequently used. A Zip drive installed on an IDE or SCSI controller is comparable to a hard drive in access time. People who can't spare an IDE or SCSI connection can use a version of the Zip drive that operates off a parallel port (these drives are quite a bit slower).

With all its similarities to a floppy drive, however, a Zip drive (no relation to PKZIP compression software) doesn't work well as an A: or B: floppy drive. That's too bad, because many people have vacant B: drives and could use a removable disk drive there. And if a Zip drive could be configured as drive A:, you could boot from a 100MB removable drive, making it easy to switch between different configurations or entire operating systems. (Your data files could reside on a hard drive and continue to be accessible from whichever configuration you were currently using.)

Fortunately, there is a shareware utility that allows you to boot from a Zip disk in the same way many people boot from different floppy diskettes. Benedict Chong has developed two related programs: Z-pA works with IDE/ATA Zip drives, while ZppA works with parallel-port Zip drives.

You have an IDE/ATA Zip drive if it is mounted internally (like a floppy drive) and has a 40-pin connector at the back of the drive. A Zip drive that requires an external AC adapter is not an IDE/ATA drive. A SCSI Zip drive, of course, has a cable that plugs into a SCSI controller. (Some SCSI adapters already allow devices 5 and/or 6 to be configured as bootable devices. Check your documentation.)

Both versions of Chong's program will reside in the master boot record (MBR) of your C: drive. They run before the operating system is loaded, and detect a Zip drive whether or not a disk is present in the drive.

When Z-pA detects a Zip drive, it configures it as the letter A: or B:. A Zip drive configured as drive A: can boot up just like a floppy drive configured as drive A:. And if you designate your Zip drive as drive A:, you can right-click files in the Explorer and use the Send To menu to copy files to the drive. The command to "Send To drive A:" appears automatically when you install Windows.

Windows is a particularly hospitable environment for Zip drives. It supports "floppy drives" over 100MB, while previous versions of DOS and Windows only supported floppies up to 32MB.

Z-pA and ZppA are available for download in 30-day trial versions from a Chong's Web site. Z-pA is at `http://www.blueskyinnovations.com/zpa.html`. Use the same URL for ZppA, but change the filename at the end to `zppa.html`. You should also read the FAQ at `zpafaq.html`.

Bigger and Better

Hard disks always get bigger, and BIOes have to catch up with them.

What's a Gigabyte?

In the physical world, a kilo is 1,000. But in the computer world, a kilo is 1,024, or 2 to the 10th power. Still, it doesn't stop there. The mega, as in a megabyte, is 2 to the 20th power, or 1,048,576 — a bit more than a million. To keep things straight, we use this convention: KB is kilobytes in the sense of 1,024 bytes, and MB is megabytes in the sense of 1,048,576 bytes.

When it comes to gigabytes and hard disk sizes, things may be not quite as they seem. Windows uses this convention: A gigabyte, GB, is 1,073,741,824 bytes. You can see this in Figure 37-12 if you compare the two capacity figures for the hard drive. (Actually, the GB amount shown should have been rounded up to 2.00GB, because it is equal to 1.995GB.)

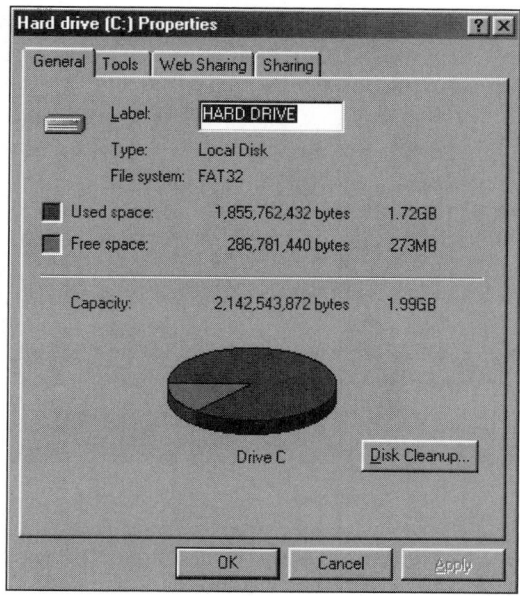

Figure 37-12: The Properties dialog box for this 2GB hard disk illustrates the convention that "GB" equals 1,073,741,824 bytes.

We've summarized all of this in Table 37-2.

Table 37-2:	Size Designations
Physical World	*Computer World*
k = 1,000	K = 1,024
m = 1,000,000	M=1,048,576 (1,024 × 1,024)
g = 1,000,000,000	G=1,073,741,824 (1,024 × 1,024 × 1,024)

Hard disk manufacturers, on the other hand, like to make their gargantuan hard disks look even bigger. They declare that one billion bytes equals a gigabyte. So what do we care?

Windows Me using FAT32 can handle 2 terabytes (2 times 1,024 times a gigabyte, or 2 to the 41st power) of hard disk space. But many older computer BIOSes can only handle 7.8GB hard disk drive partitions. This is due to an incorrect implementation of their interrupt 13 (INT 13) extensions. You should get a newer BIOS or upgrade your older one. Or, if for some reason you have to purchase a drive that fits just right at 7.8GB (as all but the hard disk manufacturers define it), you'll want to buy an 8.4GB drive.

Of course, you can buy bigger drives, but you'll need to partition the drive into partitions no larger than 7.8GB partitions unless you have a more recent or an upgraded BIOS.

FDISK

Microsoft provides FDISK, a utility that partitions hard disks into logical volumes that can then be formatted. It also writes the master boot record.

If you want to learn a bit more about how it works and some of its version history, check out "Notes on DOS FDISK Command" at http://www.firmware.com/support/bios/fdisk.htm and "Undocumented FDISK" at http://www.lyngsoe.com/fdisk.

Windows Takes On the Big Drives

Windows Me can handle a single hard disk partition of 2 terabytes (2 to the 41st power bytes). Even with hard disk storage values doubling every year, this book will probably be out of print by the time (2005) you can purchase such a drive for your personal computer.

However, it is quite possible to purchase hard disks that are greater than 8.455GB (decimal GB, as used by hard disk manufacturers), which translates to 7.874GB (binary) under Windows. If your computer's BIOS "fully" supports the interrupt 13 extensions, you can install a drive bigger than 8.455GB (decimal) and create a primary partition on it greater than 7.874GB (binary). The Microsoft Knowledge Base article that pertains to this issue is "Hard Disk Limited to 8-GB Partition," found at http://support.microsoft.com/ support/kb/articles/q153/5/50.asp.

When you start your computer, Windows tests your BIOS to make sure that it has all the interrupt 13 extensions required to support drives larger than 8.455GB. If it doesn't find them, then that is the limit.

Any computer you buy today will no doubt have a BIOS that supports partitions much larger than 8GB. In case you're working with an old computer, however, the next three sections outline what three disk drive manufacturers had to say about this issue when FAT32 first came out.

Seagate

This quote comes from the Seagate Web site at http://www.seagate.com/ support/disc/faq/8point4.shtml:

> The 8.4-Gbyte constraint is based on an obscure method of causing the PC to perform a disc drive operation called an interrupt (INT). When the BIOS wants to get data onto or off the hard disk, it must send a software interrupt. The key storage interrupt is INT 13h. Older versions of BIOS do not support this interrupt on disc drives larger than 8.4 Gbytes. Like the rest of PC architecture, this interrupt has been enhanced to accommodate the larger capacities required in today's systems.
>
> There are three solutions for adding INT 13h Extensions to existing systems: upgrade system BIOS, add an intelligent host adapter card with new BIOS on the board, or use Seagate's DiscWizard software. The new BIOS is a hardware solution that will allow the system to recognize greater than 8.4-Gbyte capacity as a native function, and the DiscWizard software bundle, utilizing Disk Manager, will create a new layer of software that will translate to accommodate greater than 8.4-Gbyte capacity.

Continue reading the Seagate Web page for more clues on how to set up your BIOS and get a correct reading on your hard disk capacity.

Maxtor

This quote comes from the Maxtor Web site at http://www.maxtor.com/ technology/q&a/qa610017.html:

> The maximum parameters at the 8.4 GB barrier are 16,383 cylinders, 16 heads and 63 sectors for a capacity of 8.455 GB. To go beyond this boundary, a new extended INT 13 function is needed from the BIOS as

a support feature for the drives. The BIOS listed below are all "CORE" BIOS. Even though a BIOS is dated correctly or is the current version, it may not be able to support extended interrupt 13 because of modification done to the "CORE" of the BIOS from the motherboard manufacturer.

If the BIOS is believed to fall within the following guidelines but does not support the drive, contact the system or motherboard manufacturer for a potential upgrade to their product.

- **American Megatrends INC. (AMI):** BIOS versions with a date of January 1, 1998 or newer.

- **Award:** BIOS versions dated November 1997 or newer. Award recommends Unicore (800-800-2467 or http://www.unicore.com.

- **Phoenix:** Version 4 Revision 6 or newer. If the BIOS is revision 5.12, it does not support extended interrupt 13. All Phoenix BIOS are Version 4, so 5.12 is an older release than 6. Phoenix recommends Micro Firmware (877-629-2467 or http://www.firmware.com/support/index.htm).

Quantum

This quote comes from the Quantum Web site at http://www.quantum.com/src/whitepapers/8.4barrier.html:

Addressing more than 8.4GB of capacity on a hard disk drive is a problem for most PCs because of BIOS limitations. The best way to solve the problem is to use a BIOS that utilizes Interrupt 13 extensions and an LBA (logical block address) method of addressing. If a system's BIOS can't be upgraded, OnTrack Disk Manager driver software (available on Quantum's World Wide Web) can be used to move beyond the 8.4GB limitation.

Check if Your BIOS "Fully" Supports the INT 13 Extensions

You can use Sandra, a shareware package discussed in "Add to Your System Info" in Chapter 23, to check to see if your BIOS "fully" supports the interrupt 13 extensions. Double-click CPU & BIOS Information. Scroll down to System BIOS Properties. If Supports Enhanced Disk Drive has a green checkmark (it does not in Figure 37-13), your BIOS "fully" supports interrupt 13 extensions.

ExtBios, a small freeware utility, can also provide some help. You'll find it at "The BIOS IDE Harddisk Limitations" page at http://web.inter.nl.net/hcc/J.Steunebrink/bioslim.htm.

ExtBios interrogates your BIOS and uses a couple of functions from the interrupt 13 extensions to provide version information and drive parameters, as shown in Figure 37-14.

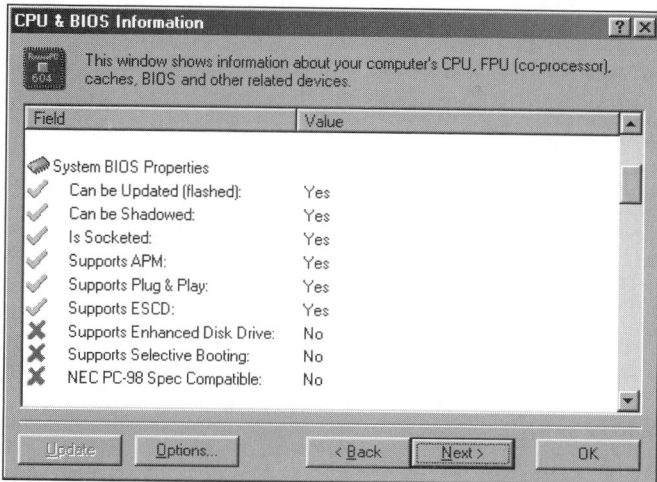

Figure 37-13: Sandra shows that this computer's BIOS does not support hard disks larger than 8.4GB.

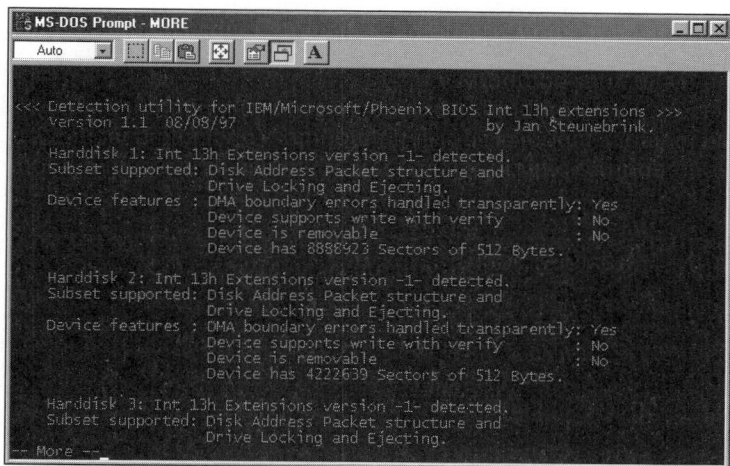

Figure 37-14: Some of the results from running ExtBios

An easy way to use this utility is described in these steps:

STEPS

Running ExtBios

Step 1. After your have downloaded `Extbio11.zip,` extract its contents to a new folder.

Step 2. Display the contents of the folder that contains the extracted files.

Step 3. Click Start ➪ Programs ➪ MS-DOS Prompt.

Step 4. Drag the file `Extbios.exe` from the open folder to the DOS window and drop it there.

Step 5. In the DOS window, at the end of the command line type | **more** and press Enter.

If the results displayed by Extbios indicate only version 1 support for interrupt 13 extensions (as shown in Figure 37-14), your BIOS doesn't "fully" support the extensions. You won't be able to create a hard disk partition greater than 7.8GB unless you take some additional steps.

You can choose one of these solutions:

■ Upgrade your system BIOS, if possible

■ Install a new hard disk controller card, assuming that your card isn't built into your motherboard, or that if it is, you can disable it

■ Upgrade the BIOS on your hard disk controller card

■ Use one of the translation packages offered by the hard disk manufacturers

The version of FDISK that comes with Windows Me can partition a drive bigger than 8.4GB. You can limit the partition size to 8.4GB by using the /x switch. You can run FDISK from a DOS window or from a real-mode DOS command line.

FAT32X for Drives over 8GB

On a FAT32 hard drive larger than 8GB, Microsoft uses FAT32X (X as in *extended*). A FAT32X partition supports hard drives with more than 1,024 cylinders, the maximum number supported by many computers' BIOS routines.

Disk utilities adapted to FAT32X partitions soon after it was introduced by Microsoft. For example, version 4.0 of Partition Magic, the premium third-party partitioning software, was the first version to support FAT32X drives. Partition Magic supports conversions both ways between FAT32 and FAT16. It also includes the Boot Magic utility, which allows a single drive to multiboot between Windows, Windows 2000 or NT, Linux, and so on. For more information, see http://www.powerquest.com.

Does Your Hard Disk Have Overlay Software Installed?

Disk drive manufacturers include overlay software with their big hard disks just in case your BIOS can't handle the large hard drive. If your hard disk came bundled with the computer, the odds are that the BIOS can address all of the hard disk, but that isn't always true.

Computers whose BIOSes cannot handle hard disks greater than 7.8GB can be made to work with bigger drives using EZ Drive, DiscWizard, Disk Manager, or one of the other overlay packages. If you later upgrade your BIOS to handle larger drives, or if you move this drive to a new computer, you'll want to remove this overlay software.

If you didn't set up your computer, or if you've forgotten whether or not you loaded overlay software, you can check if it's there. Microsoft provides a Knowledge Base article that gives you a number of ways to do this. You'll find "How to Tell If Drive Overlay Program Is Installed in Windows" at http://support.microsoft.com/support/kb/articles/q186/0/57.asp.

Add a New Hard Drive

In Chapter 2, we tell you how to copy all your Windows Me files to a new hard disk. It involves a great many steps, but no additional software purchases.

If you'd like to install a new hard disk in your computer and move Windows Me to the new (hopefully bigger and faster) drive, then you might want to check John Hildrum's "Add A New Hard Drive" Web site. He'll take you through each step, and when you're done installing your new hard drive, he'll show you how to transfer Windows onto it.

There is software that makes this process easier, and Microsoft includes a batch installation wizard in its *Windows Resource Sampler Kit*, which you'll find on the Windows CD-ROM. You can find out more about the other software packages at John's site.

You'll find John's instructions at http://www.hildrum.com/harddriveadd.html.

You should also check out Seagate's "Installing a Second ATA (IDE) Hard Disk" at `http://www.seagate.com/support/disc/faq/www96009.shtml`. You also might review "Adding a second hard drive" at `http://204.191.245.9/1996/Feb96/HardDriv/2ndHD/2ndHD.html`.

Add a Second SCSI Hard Drive

If you've got a SCSI hard drive in your computer, it is a simple process to add a second hard drive—or at least it can be. In the previous section, we pointed you to a number of articles that discuss how to add a second hard drive, transfer the Windows operating system to the second drive, and make this the boot drive. Those articles concentrate on EDI drives, which are both more common and also a bit more difficult to reconfigure than SCSI drives.

If you buy a second drive, it is most likely going to be bigger than the first drive, if only because the price per megabyte of the new drive will be much less than the previous drive. If the new drive is bigger, it makes it that much easier to copy everything, or almost everything, from the old drive.

Tip

Adding a new drive increases the power draw on the power supply and adds to the heat load of your cabinet. Most computer manufacturers supply a power supply that is adequate to handle the hard disk addition. But to keep the new hard disk cool enough to be within specs, you'll want to make sure that there is adequate air flow over it. Most cases are designed to allow airflow over two hard disk drives. You can always put a temperature probe on your new hard disk after the fact and make sure that the temperature of the air around it is within spec.

Get Ready to Plug in Your New Drive

You only have to do two things before you plug the new SCSI drive in. First, pull off the jumper that activates the terminator. We're assuming, at least for now, that this drive won't be the last drive on your SCSI cable. You may have to move a jumper (instead of just pull it) to accomplish this task, or even pull the terminator. Bare SCSI drives come configured as if they were going to be the only drive in the computer (true in most cases), and as if they were going to be at the end of the SCSI cable (also true in most cases). In your case, you don't want the SCSI cable to be terminated before it reaches the existing SCSI drive at the end of the cable.

Second, arrange the jumpers on the drive so that this drive gets identified as number 1—or perhaps another number between 1 and 6, but some number that is not being used to identify another SCSI device. SCSI ID 0 is normally used for the boot drive, which is usually at the end of the SCSI cable. SCSI ID 7 is normally used for the SCSI adapter, which is at the other end of the SCSI cable. There may be other devices on the SCSI cable (a CD-ROM and/or Zip drive perhaps). If you know those SCSI IDs, be sure to set the SCSI ID of the new hard disk to a different number.

You can find out the SCSI ID numbers of the other devices (and the boot device) using the Device Manager. Navigate to the Disk Drives branch, highlight each hard disk or Zip drive, click Properties, and then click the Settings tab. You'll see the SCSI ID in the Target ID field, as shown in Figure 37-15. Also check in the CD-ROM branch.

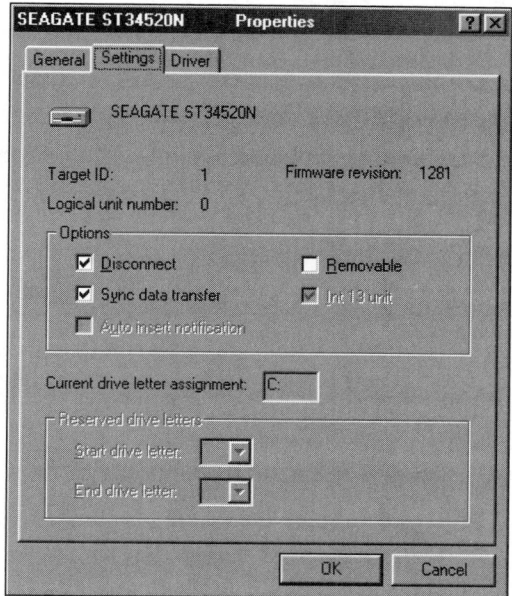

Figure 37-15: The Target ID for this SCSI drive appears on the first line under its name.

If your SCSI adapter has been set to use SCAM (SCSI Configured Auto Magically), you don't even have to set the SCSI ID number on the new hard disk—but at this point you may not know whether this is the case or not. To find out, boot your computer, and during power-on self-test, you may be given the opportunity to access the SCSI BIOS. The Adaptec AHA 2940 SCSI controller is accessed by pressing Ctrl+A, for example.

If you are able to access the SCSI card's BIOS, you may be able to set the SCSI adapter to SCAM mode, or at least determine if it is already in this mode. You may also be able to later change the boot drive's SCSI ID—if so, this will come in quite handy, because you will be able to easily designate which drive is the boot drive.

Plug in Your New Drive

Now you're ready to turn off your computer and plug in your drive. Most consumer personal computers that include SCSI drives use the standard 50-pin SCSI cable. When you purchase a SCSI drive, make sure that it has this interface. Narrow SCSI drives use the 50-pin interface.

There are a couple of other interfaces — 68-pin and SCA 80-pin. Unless you're building servers and doing hot Plug and Play with hard disks, you won't need to purchase these types of SCSI drives. It is possible to buy small adapter cards that let you plug drives of this type into 50-pin cables, but unless you get a real good deal, this is not the best choice.

You hope that your computer manufacturer has laid out the SCSI cable so that you can just plug in the SCSI drive. Hopefully there is an empty 3 1/2-inch bay just above the last drive that has a 50-pin connector. If so, you're in luck because you can just attach the new hard disk to the metal clamp built into the bay, plug in the SCSI cable, and then plug in the four-line power cable.

Turn on your computer and let it restart Windows. If your computer hangs trying to identify your new hard disk, you've probably set the SCSI ID of the new hard disk to a value that is already being used. Turn off the computer, and reset the SCSI ID of your new drive.

Use FDISK to Partition Your New Drive

Once you are up in Windows, click Start ⇨ Programs ⇨ MS-DOS Prompt. Type **fdisk** at the DOS prompt and press Enter. Press Enter again to allow the hard disk to be formatted (later) in 32-bit FAT format, as shown in Figure 37-16.

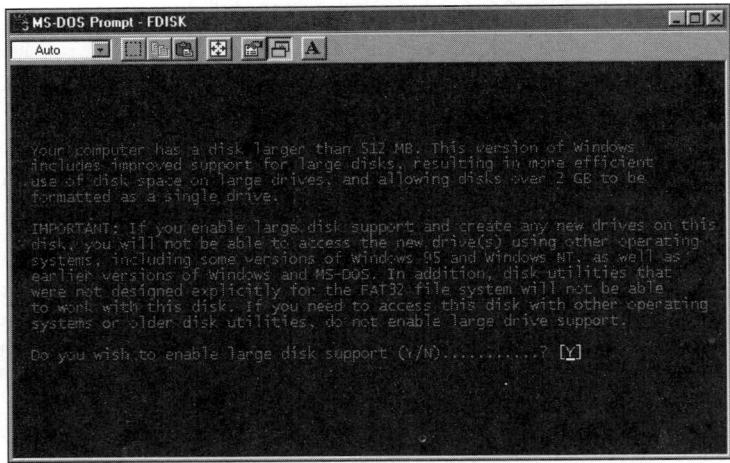

Figure 37-16: Press Enter to answer Yes to this question.

Press **5** to change the current fixed disk drive (see Figure 37-17), and then press Enter. You are going to format the second drive, your new drive, and you want to be sure that you don't format the first drive. Then press **2** (to format the new drive) and press Enter.

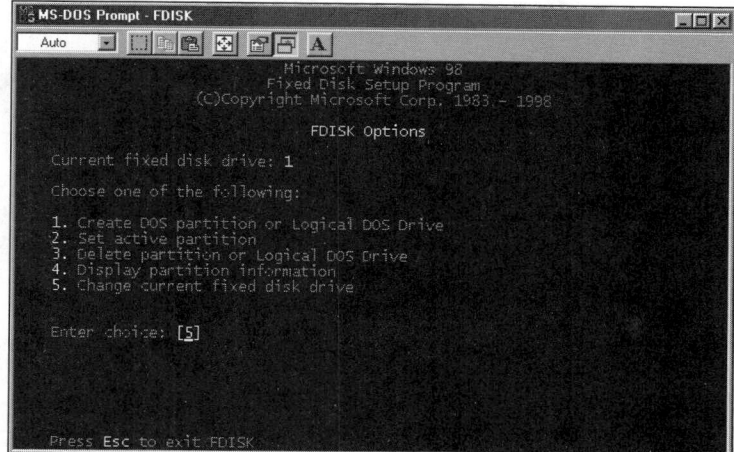

Figure 37-17: Enter **5** to choose the last option.

Press **1** and then Enter to create a DOS partition on drive 2, as shown in Figure 37-18.

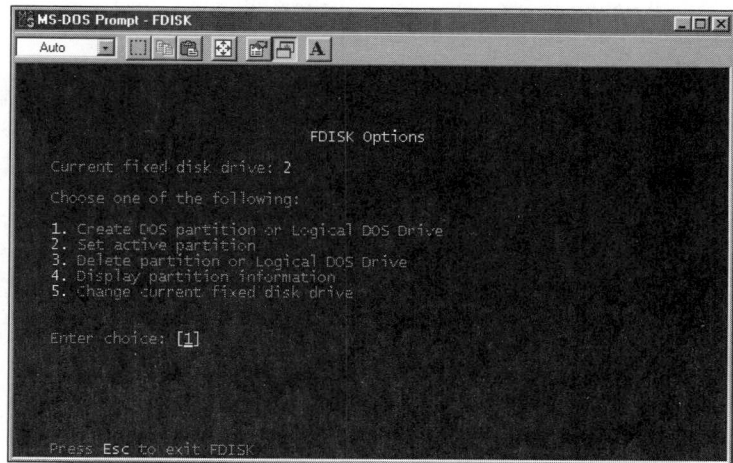

Figure 37-18: Press **1** to select the first option here.

Press **1** again, and then Enter to create a primary DOS partition, as shown in Figure 37-19. You want to create a primary DOS partition to allow this partition to become the bootable volume, the C: drive.

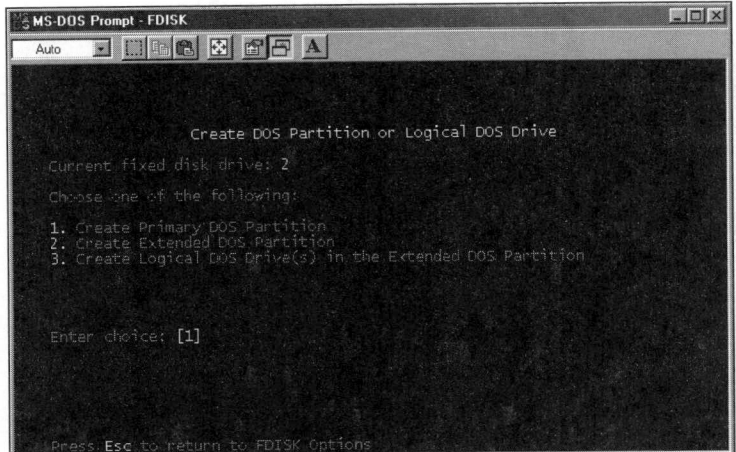

Figure 37-19: Your choice here should be **1**.

Press Enter to use the maximum available size of your new hard disk for the primary DOS partition. All drives less than 8GB will use 4K clusters for file storage. You might as well format the whole drive as one primary partition unless you have criteria other than optimal file storage space efficiency for dividing the drive. Press Esc to end FDISK.

Now restart Windows, and your new hard disk will be recognized as drive D:. The second primary partition is assigned the drive letter D:.

Format Your New Drive

You now need to format the new drive. Right-click the D: drive icon in your Explorer, select Format, mark the Full and "Copy system files" options in the Format dialog box (see Figure 37-20), and click the Start button. Alternatively, you can click Start ⇨ Programs ⇨ MS-DOS Prompt, type **Format D:/s**, and press Enter.

Copy Files onto Your New Drive

After the formatting is complete, you now have a hard disk that is ready to accept files. You can click its icon in your Explorer and see that there are currently no files on it.

It's quite easy to copy everything over to your new hard disk from the old hard disk. If you are going to make the new hard disk the boot drive, you'll definitely want to do this.

Using your Explorer, drag all the files in the root directory on C: to D:. We assume that you've set Explorer to display all files (View ⇨ Folder Options ⇨ View ⇨ "Show hidden files and folders"). Drag and drop all of the folder icons that branch off the root directory of your C: drive to your D: drive, except your C:\Windows folder.

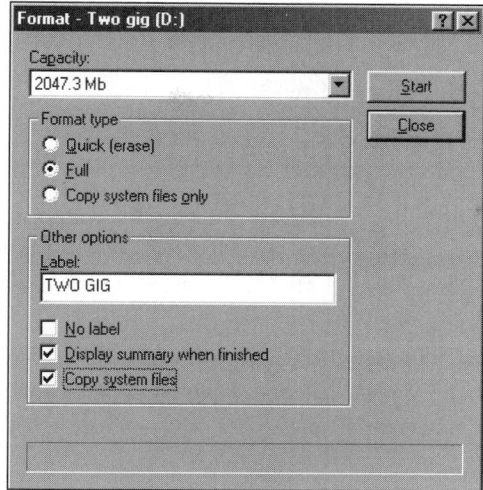

Figure 37-20: Select the Full and "Copy system files" options.

Highlight your D: drive icon in the left pane of your Explorer, right-click the right pane, and click New ⇨ Folder. Change the name of this new folder to Windows, assuming that is the name of your Windows folder on your C: drive.

Drag and drop all the subfolders of your C:\Windows folder onto your D:\Windows folder. Drag and drop all the files in your C:\Windows folder onto your D:\Windows folder *except*, and this is crucial, your Win386.swp file. This is the Windows swap file; it is dynamically created and sized when you run Windows. It will be created automatically when you reboot later.

Swap Drive Assignments and Designate Active Partition

Now that you have copied everything other than the Windows swap file from C: drive to D: drive, you are ready to turn the D: drive into the C: drive, and vice versa. If you can use your SCSI adapter BIOS to specify which SCSI ID number is associated with the boot drive, then you'll be able to leave the drives alone and switch them around logically.

If your SCSI adapter does not have this capability, you'll have to change the SCSI ID values for the drives by pulling them out of their bays and moving jumpers. You'll want to change the SCSI ID of your new disk to 0 and the SCSI ID of your older disk to 1 (or whatever the new disk was previously).

You are going to need a Windows Startup diskette for the next few steps. You may have created one when you first installed Windows. You can create one now by clicking Start ⇨ Settings ⇨ Control Panel ⇨ Add/Remove Programs ⇨ Startup Disk. You can also create one by using the method we discuss in

"Creating a Windows Boot Diskette" in Chapter 16. If you don't have one, create one now.

Insert your Windows boot diskette in drive A:.

If you can change the boot disk assignment in the SCSI BIOS, click Start ⇨ Shut Down ⇨ Restart ⇨ OK. Go into your SCSI BIOS during the power-on self-test, and change the designation of the boot drive from 0 to the current SCSI ID for your new drive. Escape from your SCSI BIOS, and continue your power-on self-test. If you can't change the boot disk assignment in the SCSI BIOS, click Start ⇨ Shut Down ⇨ Shut Down ⇨ OK. Make the changes in the drives while the computer is off, and then turn it back on.

Your computer will boot up to the MS-DOS prompt on drive A:. Type **fdisk** and press Enter. You are now going to designate the primary DOS partition on your new hard disk as the active or bootable partition. Press **2** and Enter, as shown in Figure 37-21.

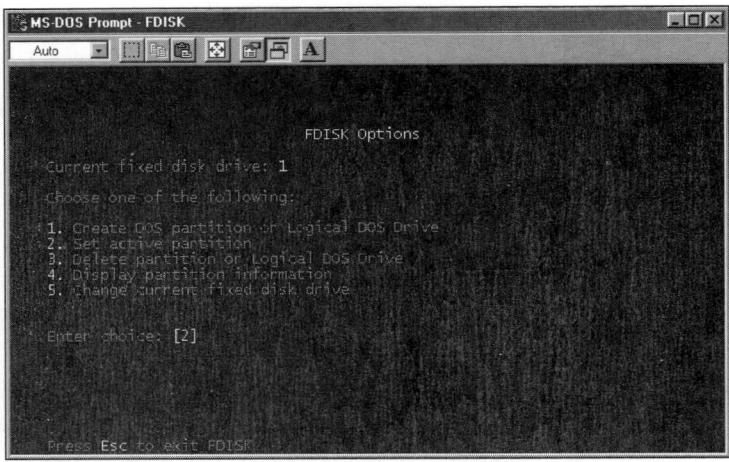

Figure 37-21: Select option 2 in this list.

Press Esc, and remove the Windows boot diskette from your floppy disk drive. Restart your computer. It should now bring up Windows on your new hard disk. You can erase the now-redundant files on your D: partition at any time.

Get Internet Explorer Straightened Out on Your New Drive

Secret

You will find that Internet Explorer doesn't seem to know where the Internet Explorer executable file is, even though logically it is in the same place, C:\Program Files\Internet Explorer. Click the Internet Explorer icon on your Desktop, click the Locate button in the Program Not Found dialog box (see Figure 37-22), and then browse down to C:\Program Files\ Internet Explorer\Iexplore.exe.

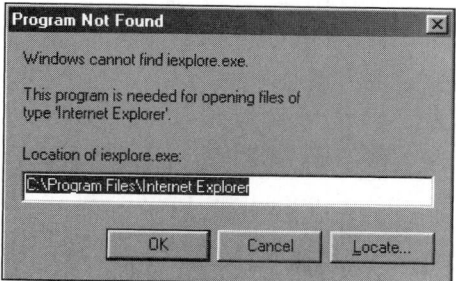

Figure 37-22: Click the Locate button to point to Internet Explorer's executable file.

Internet Explorer won't be able to remember what's in the Temporary Internet Files folder. Your history Web page names will still be there, but they won't know that the associated files are still stored on your hard disk. The same is true for your offline Web pages. You'll have to synchronize again.

You may also find that when you click a link in your e-mail client, it doesn't always bring up your Internet Explorer window and access the indicated site. You can always right-click the link, click Copy Shortcut, and then paste the URL into your Address field, either in the Internet Explorer window or in the Address toolbar.

You might reinstall Internet Explorer and Outlook Express, if you have downloaded these from the Microsoft Web site, or have a separate setup file for them.

Secret

You may also find that you can no longer invoke Internet Neighborhood (a third-party FTP client) in the Explorer. You'll have to reinstall it. The FTP sites that you've configured under Internet Neighborhood will still be there after you reinstall. You can use the Registry Crawler or the Registry Editor to go to HKEY_USERS\ .Default\ Software\ KnoWare\ Internet Neighborhood\ FTP-Sites to see which FTP sites you've registered.

Where can you purchase a bare drive to install in your computer? There are lots of places to buy them. We recommend Dirt Cheap Drives at http:// dirtcheapdrives.com. They treated us right.

Moving to FAT32 from FAT16

If your PC has a hard disk larger than 2GB, Windows Me will probably be installed using FAT32, which can format drives larger than 2GB as a single, large drive letter.

However, if you are trying to install Windows Me on an older PC with a hard disk that is smaller than 2GB, you may wind up with one drive letter (or several drive letters) that use the older FAT16 format. If that is the case, and you want to upgrade a drive from FAT16 to FAT32, we include here some information about pitfalls and tricks you may need to know.

The newer FAT32 file system supports drive partitions much larger than 2GB in size, but 8GB is currently the optimum size partition. This is because the FAT32 file system stores files less efficiently (with more cluster waste) on partitions larger than 8GB. The 8GB size is also the absolute limit for IDE and SCSI hard disk controllers that do not support interrupt 13 extensions. Without support for these extensions, which implement a feature called *logical block addressing* (LBA) that FAT32 needs, you cannot create a partition larger than the default LBA limit of 7.9GB. A disk controller needs a BIOS chip upgrade if it doesn't support interrupt 13 extensions.

Speaking of LBA, there were reports when Microsoft released Windows 98 in 1998 that FAT32 wouldn't work at all on some laptops and 486-class systems with BIOS chips that don't support LBA. You should check with your hardware manufacturer to make sure you can run FAT32 before reformatting your hard disk.

To find out how your hard disk is currently configured (FAT16 or FAT32), click My Computer, right-click the drive, and select Properties. The File System field indicates whether a drive is FAT or FAT32.

Windows Me comes with a program called Drive Converter (FAT32), which lets you convert your hard disk to FAT32 without losing all your data and programs. You can access the Drive Converter by clicking Start ⇨ Programs ⇨ Accessories ⇨ System Tools ⇨ Drive Converter (FAT32), or by clicking Cvt1. exe in your \Windows folder. After the conversion, you will need to run Defrag; be prepared for that part of the operation to take up to several hours.

You can also convert to FAT32 by running Fdisk on any drive over 512MB. It will ask you whether to enable *large disk support*. If you answer yes, any partitions you create that are over 512MB in size will be marked as FAT32 partitions and will be formatted as such. Fdisk will destroy any programs or data on that drive, so back them up first.

Do not use FAT32 on any drives that you need to access from older operating systems that you plan to dual boot. This includes Windows NT, the original version of Windows 95, and earlier versions of Windows or MS-DOS. If you need to dual boot one of these operating systems with Windows Me, they won't be able to read data stored on a FAT32 drive. You *can* share FAT32 drives across a network, just like any other FAT drives.

If you have antivirus software enabled when you convert to FAT32, it may intercept the request to update the partition table and/or the boot record and ask whether to allow them to be updated. You should answer yes. After you've finished the conversion and rebooted your computer, your antivirus software may detect that the partition table and/or boot record has changed and offer to "repair" it for you. *Do not* allow the antivirus software to restore the boot record or partition table, or your drive and all of the data on it will become inaccessible.

Windows does not give you a way to go back to FAT16 after you have made the conversion to FAT32. However, a third-party utility called Partition Magic http://www.powerquest.com does let you go back and forth between FAT16 and FAT32 without destroying your setup.

Convert to FAT 32?

To see how much additional space you'll gain by converting a FAT16 drive to the FAT32 file format, you should check out diskSpace Explorer. It not only shows you what percentage of disk space each of your folders and files currently consumes, it also lets you compare wasted space under multiple formatting options, as shown in Figure 37-23.

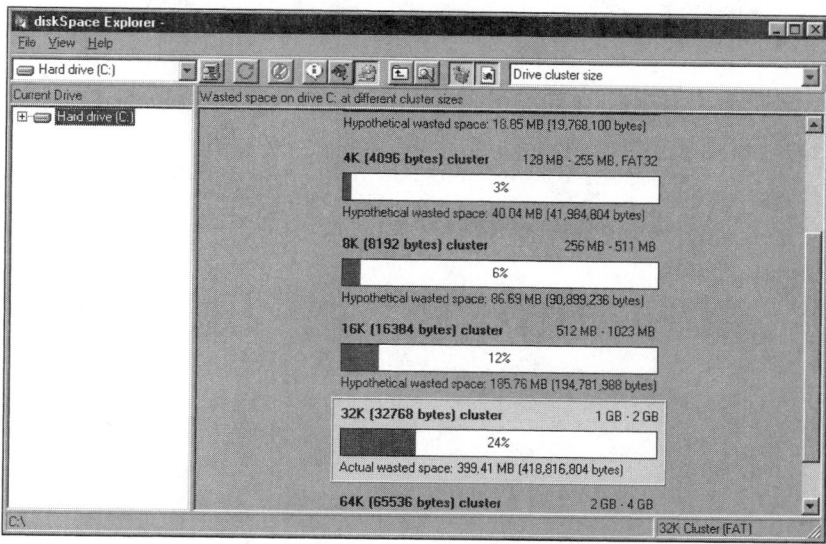

Figure 37-23: Comparisons of wasted space for a hard disk, as performed by diskSpace Explorer

You'll find diskSpace Explorer at http://www.east-tec.com.

A freeware disk statistics program, Stats 99, shown in Figure 37-24, is available at http://www.contactplus.com/index2.htm. It gives you a different set of measures of your hard disk space usage, such as use by file type, date, modification date, and so on.

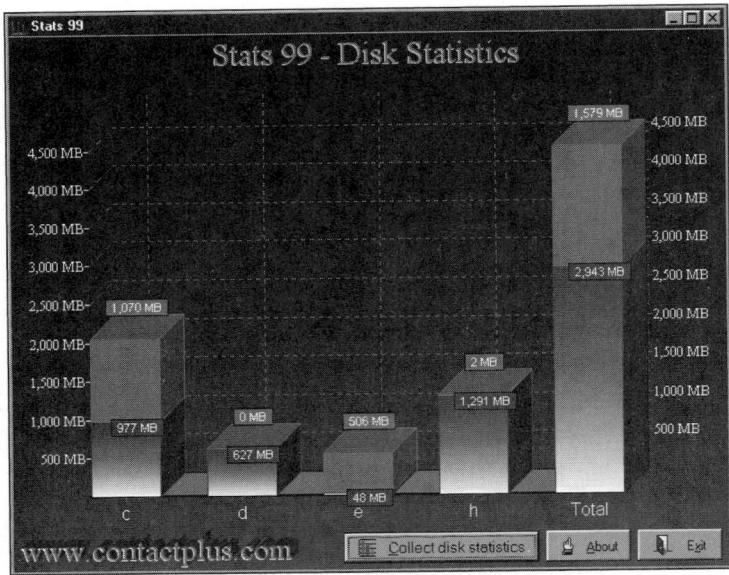

Figure 37-24: A different comparison, illustrated by Stats 99

Like diskSpace Explorer, Stats 99 can give you an idea of how much you would gain by converting your FAT16 formatted hard drive to FAT32, as shown in Figure 37-25.

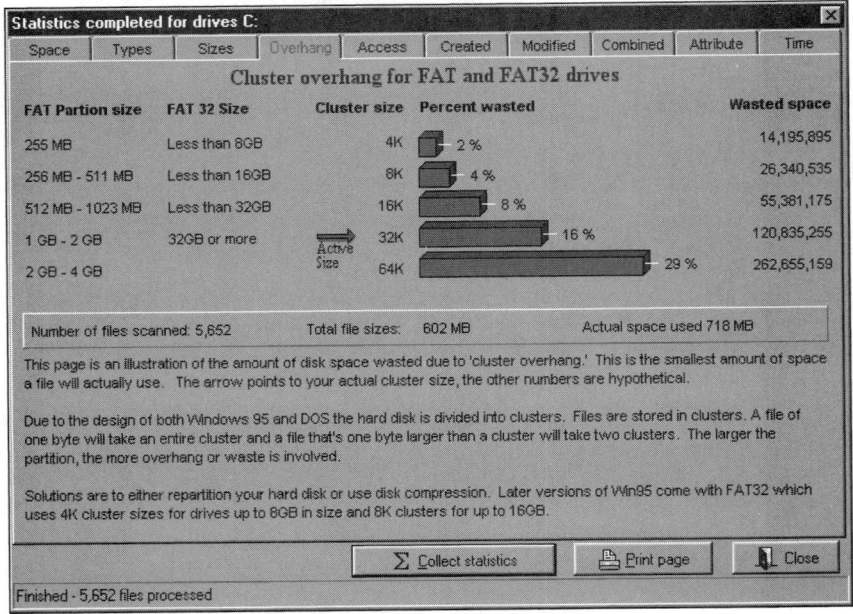

Figure 37-25: The Stats 99 analysis of wasted space on the same disk

Yet a third tool, one that gives somewhat different results, is available right on your Windows CD-ROM. You'll find it in \tools\reskit\config. It's fat32win.exe. If you run the setup program in \tools\reskit, you'll install this program and all the rest of the 26 *Windows Resource Sampler Kit* programs. You can then access them by clicking Start ⇨ Programs ⇨ Windows Resource Kit ⇨ Tools Management Console.

The Tools Management Console, shown in Figure 37-26, is a common interface that consolidates a bunch of utilities and network management functions, helping you remember where all these little critters are hiding out.

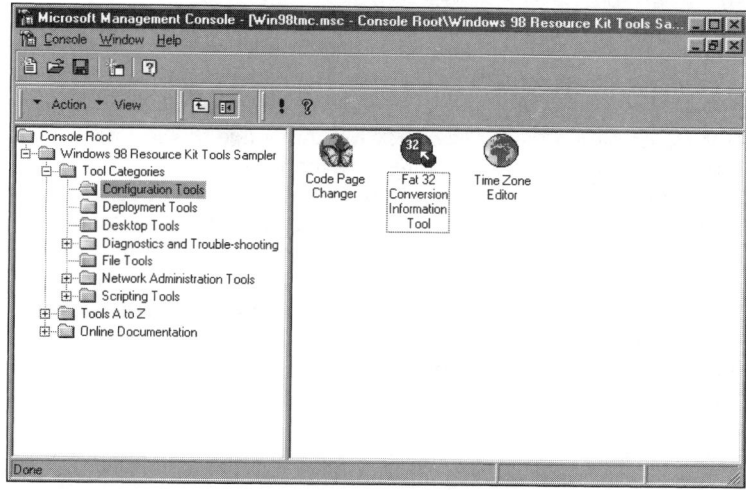

Figure 37-26: The Tools Management Console. Look in the Configuration Tools folder to find the Fat32 Conversion Information Tool.

Fat32 Conversion Information Tool gives quite a bit higher number than the two previous tools, but in our tests, its estimate appeared to be just about right.

If you'd like to learn more about FAT32, you can read the Microsoft Knowledge Base article "Description of the FAT32 File System" at http://support.microsoft.com/support/kb/articles/q154/9/97.asp.

Also, the Seagate FAQs are quite good. Check out these two:

■ "FAT32 Basics" at http://www.seagate.com/support/disc/faq/win98_fat32_light_faq.shtml

■ "Windows 98 and FAT 32 File systems" at http://www.seagate.com/support/disc/faq/win98_fat32_faq.shtml

Bad Sector Problems

You may have tried to convert a FAT16 volume to FAT32, only to find that the Microsoft FAT32 Converter refused to do the job because your hard disk had a bad sector. It appears that Microsoft has erred on the side of caution with respect to whether to convert a hard disk when ScanDisk reports a bad sector. Here is what Don Lebow, a Microsoft MVP, had to say on the Windows98 disk general newsgroup when FAT32 became widely available:

> Piecing together some conversations I've had with MS folks, I think it goes something like this...
>
> Their approach is conservative. The thinking seems to be that if a bad cluster is spotted, there may be problems with the disk (may or may not be true, as we know). And such a problem could mess up something else in the data conversion process. Data loss is the Big Scary. They wanted to cut the possibility of that happening to the absolute bare minimum. So they felt that since this is a basic OS tool, they'd rather "err" on the side of caution.
>
> The same thinking went into why they don't offer a FAT32-FAT16 conversion, which again Partition Magic does. The process itself is more complicated than converting the other way, due to disk space considerations and such. Their internal testing indicated that it couldn't be made as bulletproof as they wanted. So they decided not to offer it.
>
> If you think about it, from their point of view it's probably better to have some "issues" with the conversion program not working, rather than a big splash box on http://www.news.com saying "Windows 98 Users report Scrambled Disks."

So what do you do if you want to convert a hard disk to FAT32 and you've got a bad sector or two? You can do a number of things, according to Attila Szabo (aka MrScary) also a Microsoft MVP.

First, you can check out "How to Cause ScanDisk for Windows to Retest Bad Cluster" at http://support.microsoft.com/support/kb/articles/q127/0/55.asp.

Be aware that the method detailed in the Knowledge Base article does nothing more than tell ScanDisk to ignore the bad sector mark and recheck this area to determine if it really is bad or not. If it is bad (pretty likely), ScanDisk will leave it marked as bad, and you will have made zero progress.

Also, the method described states that you should change the fourth value found at HKEY_CURRENT_USER\ Software\ Microsoft\ Windows\ CurrentVersion\ Applets\Check Drive\ Settings from 00 to 04. Other users have stated that this is incorrect—you should instead add 4 to whatever value you find there. Then run ScanDisk.

Second, use a third-party application that converts with the errors present (such as Partition Magic).

The Partition Magic Web site, http://www.powerquest.com, doesn't give any indication that Partition Magic can indeed convert a hard drive with bad sectors from FAT16 to FAT32, but Don Lebow mentions:

As far as Partition Magic goes, the evidence I've seen has been anecdotal (i.e., "CVT.EXE wouldn't do it, but Partition Magic would"). I suspect that the program just takes note of any (presumably mapped) bad clusters and ignores them.

Seems reasonable to us.

Finally, use a third-party package that reliably recovers the bad clusters, such as Gibson Research Center's SpinRite 5.0. Attila states, "Personally, SpinRite has been my choice and it has had a perfect record (so far) in recovering the clusters, allowing the intended MS Converter to run successfully."

SpinRite is the ticket. It can determine what spare sectors are available from the hard disk spare sector table and remap them to remove the bad clusters from the purview of Windows ScanDisk and FAT32 disk drivers. Here's what Steve Gibson, the author of SpinRite, had to say, after following our little discussion on the Windows98 disk general newsgroup:

> *Question*: After upgrading my Windows 95 system to Windows 98, when I tried to convert to FAT32, it said I had bad cluster marks and it refused to do it. Sure enough, when I did a thorough ScanDisk, it said I had 32,768 bytes in bad sectors, and when I was defragging my hard drive, I saw a bad cluster in the details. When I wrote the Windows 98 newsgroup with this problem, a bunch of people there suggested SpinRite. But since I'm not a computer expert, I have a few questions I would like to ask before I try it out: (1) What potential negatives could SpinRite do to my hard drive? (2) Is it easy to use? (3) Is this the right product to fix this problem?
>
> 1. What potential negatives could SpinRite do to my hard drive?
> SpinRite is more than ten years old, and it's been used with complete safety in every imaginable situation and configuration. It's bullet proof and is the most widely known and recommended hard drive utility in the PC industry. You can use it with total confidence.
>
> 2. Is it easy to use?
> Yes, embarrassingly so. Sometimes "techie folks" who LOVE SpinRite's power want more options and features and more "power stuff" ...but we have always steadfastly refused to do that since we believe that such "power features" would bog it down and make it more complex. We really did write SpinRite for YOU, not for some propeller head (even though we very much appreciate their support!).
>
> 3. Is this the right product to fix this problem?
> Apparently so, since we're selling many copies to people for exactly this reason. Since SpinRite is able to inter-operate with the drive's internal defect systems, it's able to "unmark" bad sectors in the system's FAT, and then have the drive replace those bad sectors with brand new spare sectors (from the drive's internal spare sector pool). It thus gives Windows and its FAT32 Converter a "perfect" drive to convert after having moved the defects from "external" management to "internal" management. It works like a charm!"

SpinRite 5.0 worked just fine for us. You'll find it at http://www.grc.com.

SpinRite is able to replace the bad sector with a good one from the drive's spare sector table. It remaps the new sector to appear as though the new sector is in the same location as the bad sector. You should run SpinRite at level 5 the first time you use it to repair bad sectors, which can easily be the first time you run it on your computer. It defaults to a lower level to test the disk and recover data, but it doesn't do bad sector remapping at the lower level. Because this process can take many hours (let it run overnight), you'll want to go to level 5 first if bad sectors are your problem.

SpinRite doesn't indicate in its onscreen messages that it is repairing the bad sectors by using good sectors from the spare sector table. In fact, it indicates that it is testing the bad sector at a very deep level and checking if it is okay, and if it is, then unmarking the sector as bad.

Well, this wouldn't cut it, because if the sector is bad it needs to be replaced in order for the Microsoft FAT32 conversion to work. This replacement is in fact what is going on, so realize that SpinRite is not telling you the whole story.

BIOS Problems

If you still have problems, it may be because you have a setting in your BIOS that protects the boot sector on your hard disk. This feature keeps viruses from editing these files and corrupting your computer.

You'll need to press the indicated key during the power-on self test to go to your BIOS setup and turn off this feature.

Don't Let the Help Confuse You

The FAT32 Converter help file (click the Details button in the FAT32 Conversion Wizard) states the following:

Once you convert your hard drive to FAT32 format using Drive Converter, you cannot return to using the FAT16 format unless you repartition and reformat the FAT32 drive. If you converted the drive on which Windows is installed, then you must reinstall Windows after repartitioning the drive.

Secret

Don't be confused by the poor wording here. You don't have to reinstall Windows if you convert your drive to FAT32. Also, you can use Partition Magic (http://www.powerquest.com) to convert a FAT32 partition back to a FAT16 partition without having to reformat the partition. All your data, including Windows itself, will be saved.

Wasted Space

Secret

You can use DOS to give you an idea of how much space you might be wasting by putting small files into large clusters. This method will also tell you how much less you're wasting after you move up to FAT32 with 4K clusters.

Click Start ➪ Programs ➪ MS-DOS Prompt. At the DOS prompt, type **cd** and press Enter. Then type **dir /a/s/v** and press Enter. You'll see your whole hard disk flash before your eyes.

After a minute or so, you'll see something like what we show in Figure 37-27. The difference between the value for "bytes" and the value for "bytes allocated" is the amount of space not used by the files, but allocated to the clusters that store those files. To convert this to megabytes, divide the difference by 2 to the 20th power.

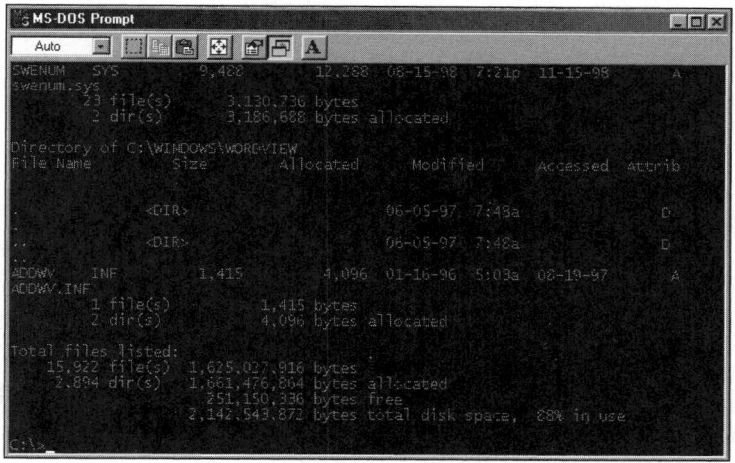

Figure 37-27: Subtract bytes from bytes allocated to determine your wasted space.

In the example shown in Figure 37-27, 1,661,476,864 bytes allocated minus 1,625,027,916 bytes equals 36,448,948 bytes, or 34.76MB wasted.

What if Your Computer Hangs After You Convert to FAT32?

Secret

If you have a SCSI drive and your computer won't boot once you've converted your hard disk to FAT32, it may be because the BIOS on your SCSI card does not fully implement the interrupt 13 extensions. You need to update your SCSI card's BIOS.

If you have an Adaptec 2940 or 3940 series SCSI card with a BIOS version prior to 1.23, you'll need a new BIOS. You can determine the version of your Adaptec BIOS by pressing Ctrl+A when prompted to do so during the power-on self test.

To upgrade your Adaptec SCSI BIOS, contact Adaptec at `http://www.adaptec.com/advisor/index1.html`. You can download the latest BIOS and update your onboard SCSI BIOS yourself.

If you are updating your BIOS to version 1.34.3, you'll probably be downloading the file `aful343a.exe`, although there may be a newer version of the BIOS update by the time you read this.

After you update your SCSI BIOS (following the instructions from Adaptec) you'll want to reset your SCSI parameters (press Ctrl+A when prompted during the power-on self-test) to their defaults. This gets rid of previous erroneous values for the hard disk size. You can then change the values to the ones that are right for you.

You'll also want to update your SCSI driver, as discussed in the next section.

Thanks to Bill Drake for help with this secret.

Upgrade Your Adaptec 29XX and 394X Series SCSI Driver

If you are experiencing any problems with your Adaptec SCSI cards, you might want to download the latest drivers for these cards. You'll find them at `http://www.adaptec.com/support/overview/windows98.html`. Download the `7800w9x.exe` file. This file includes all of the drivers for the 29XX and 394X cards, and they supersede the ones that came on the original Windows 98 CD-ROM.

After you have downloaded the file, click it to unzip the drivers.

Thanks to Attila Szabo for this update.

FAT32 for Windows NT 4.0

While Windows 2000 (formerly known as NT 5.0) supports FAT32 formatted partitions, NT 4.0 does not. If for some reason you need to dual boot between Windows Me and NT 4.0, there is a shareware program that lets NT 4.0 read from and write to FAT32 drives.

It won't create a FAT32 partition, nor will it convert existing FAT16 or HTFS-formatted partitions to FAT32. You'll need Windows or Partition Magic to accomplish that task. Also, the NT 4.0 boot drive cannot be formatted as a FAT32 partition.

You'll find FAT32 for NT at `http://www.winternals.com/products/fat32.shtml`.

Better Performance from Your Hard Disk

So many things can keep your hard disks from doing their best.

Stop Thrashing!

Almost as annoying as your computer dialing your modem on its own is your computer thrashing about without any input from you. The hard disk just takes off, and after a while the racket gets a bit unbearable. Besides the noise, you'd rather the computer waited patiently for your commands, and didn't find something irritating to do on its own.

Actually, if the computer did some useful things on its own, but did them unobtrusively, it wouldn't be nearly so bad. But hard disk thrashing can be a signal that the computer is having a difficult time handling its memory, and this can be a cause for alarm.

If you're off the computer and you hear the hard disk start up and continue, it's probably because a background application has started. These applications are meant to do useful work while you're not demanding all of the computer's resources through your interactions. Unfortunately, some of them can be installed without you ever being aware of their existence. Not a pleasant thought, actually.

Stop Indexing

If you've installed Microsoft Office 97 or 2000, you may find that it likes to maintain an index of all the words in your Word document files. While you're not at the computer, a program called Find Fast starts up and searches through your hard disk to find your Word documents and build or update its index based on what it finds. It's out there on its own reading and writing. (Microsoft Office 2000 sets up Find Fast as an "install on demand" component. You'll find its icon in the Control Panel. When you click the Find Fast icon for the first time, the feature is installed.)

The System Configuration Utility lets you prevent Find Fast from loading when you first start Windows. It won't build an index for you if it never loads, so that's the trade-off. Personally, I only used the results of Find Fast a couple of times, and after that I turned it off.

Turning Off Find Fast

Step 1. Click Start ⇨ Programs ⇨ Accessories ⇨ System Tools ⇨ System Information ⇨ Tools ⇨ System Configuration Utility.

Step 2. Click the Startup tab. Clear the checkbox next to Microsoft Fast Find.

Step 3. Click OK.

You'll need to restart Windows if you want this setting to take effect immediately. You can get the indexing to stop in the short term by clicking Start ⇨ Settings ⇨ Control Panel ⇨ Find Fast ⇨ Index ⇨ Pause Indexing.

Your Screen Saver

If you have a screen saver activated, the screen saver may be reading files from your hard disk. This would be especially true if it displays lots of different graphics files.

You can check this by right-clicking your Desktop ⇨ Properties ⇨ Screen Saver ⇨ Preview. Listen to your hard disk to see if it is making a racket.

Scheduled Tasks Are Being Performed

Your Task Scheduler may be scheduled to perform its maintenance chores whenever you leave the computer for a while, or at certain times whether you are working on the computer or not. The Task Scheduler has plenty of flexibility built in, and if you, or someone who has access to your computer, have used this flexibility to schedule tasks at inopportune times, you'll hear about it.

Open your Explorer and highlight Scheduled Tasks in the left pane. Review the schedule of tasks in the right pane. If you see one that might be the cause of the problem, double-click the offending task.

You can click the Schedule tab to rearrange the task schedule for a more appropriate hour or day. Click the Settings tab and see if the task is told to begin only if there is a break in your use of the computer. See if "Only start the scheduled task if computer is idle for [ ] minutes" is marked (see Figure 37-28).

If this checkbox is cleared, then the scheduled task could start up as you use the computer. If that's what is happening to you, mark this checkbox.

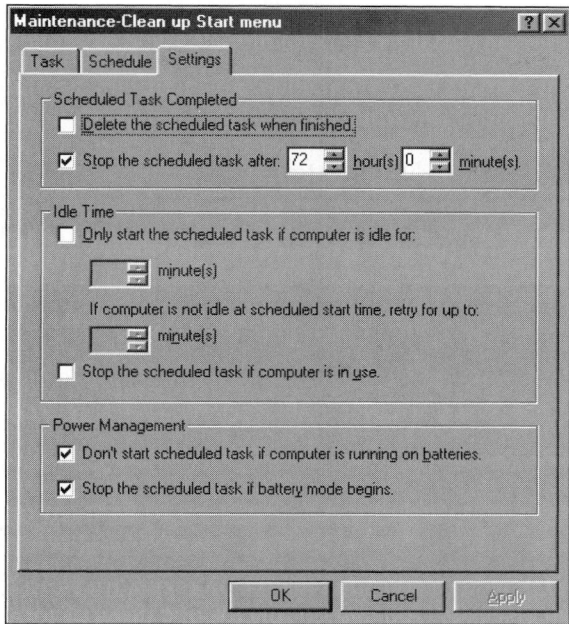

Figure 37-28: Because the checkboxes in the Idle Time area are cleared, the Clean Up Start Menu task will start whether or not the computer is in use.

Swapping from Memory to Disk

Windows includes a virtual memory manager that makes its own decisions about when it should write the contents of memory to the hard disk and free up space to be used for other purposes. Usually this happens when you load a program, so you're not going to notice that Windows is both reading and writing to the hard disk within the same short time interval. There will be times, though, when the memory manager moves stuff out of memory onto the hard disk by itself.

The amount of memory swapping and writing to the hard disk is minor at these times, so it should not be a major source of irritation.

Quit Checking for a CD-ROM

If you have enabled the "Auto insert notification" option in the Properties dialog box for your CD-ROM drive, Windows looks for a CD-ROM in the drive every few seconds. You're not going to notice any disk thrashing, but you may at least notice the CD-ROM light flashing every couple of seconds. The hard disk light may also flash on if both devices are on the SCSI bus.

You can turn off "Auto insert notification" by taking these steps:

STEPS

Turning Off Auto Insert Notification

Step 1.   Press Win+Pause/Break (or right-click the My Computer icon and click Properties), and click the Device Manager tab.

Step 2.   Double-click the CD-ROM (right at the top of the devices list), and then double-click your installed CD-ROM device.

Step 3.   Click the Settings tab and clear the "Auto insert notification" checkbox, as shown in Figure 37-29.

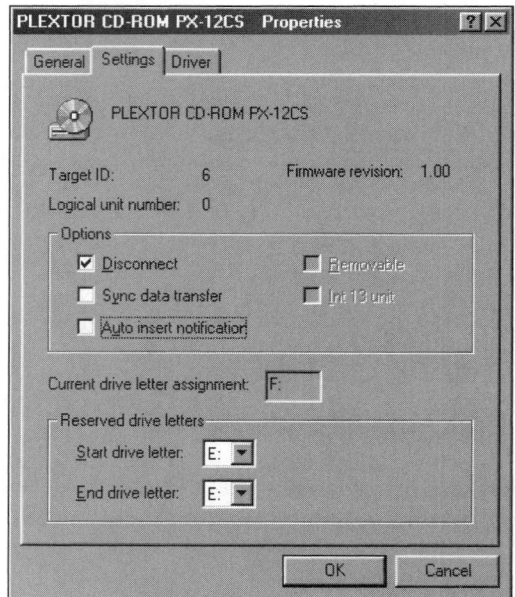

Figure 37-29: The "Auto insert notification" checkbox is selected, but has been cleared.

Step 4.   Click OK. Click Close. Restart your computer when prompted.

Hitting the Disk Lightly

Do you notice that even after you've done everything we've discussed here, your hard disk light flickers on briefly every half second? The disk is being hit ever so lightly. If so, it's because you have a SCSI hard disk. The disk (or maybe just the SCSI bus) is being interrogated to make sure that everything is still there.

Defrag Before Anything Else Runs

The Disk Defragmenter utility is very picky. If any other application changes the contents of the hard drive while it is running, it restarts. Sure, you can use your computer while Defrag is running, but just don't write a file to the hard disk. Also, screen savers are a constant irritant. Defrag stops as soon as they come on.

You may have programs in your StartUp folder that interfere with the operation of Defrag. You can force Defrag to start before anything else. In your \tools\mtsutil folder on your Windows CD-ROM, you'll find the defrag.inf file. Right-click it and click Install. The next time you restart Windows, it will run Disk Defragmenter before anything else starts.

If you want this to happen again, you'll need to right-click this file and install it again. You won't need to issue any command when you restart Windows to start Defrag.

You can find out more about this utility, and lots of other handy utilities, by reading the mtsutil.txt file in the same folder.

Unfortunately, while Defrag starts first, all of the other applets that normally run at startup also get started. Because Defrag can have problems when other programs are running, it is best to close down everything that you can before you run Defrag.

You can start Disk Defragmenter in two ways: Start ⇨ Programs ⇨ Accessories ⇨ System Tools ⇨ Disk Defragmenter, or right-click a hard disk icon in your Explorer, click Properties, click the Tools tab, and then click the Defragment Now button. When you use the first method, the Disk Defragmenter begins by displaying the Select Drive dialog box. Clicking the Settings button in this dialog box brings up the Disk Defragmenter Settings dialog box (see Figure 37-30), which lets you change the way Defrag works. When you use the second method, the Select Drive dialog box doesn't appear automatically. To get to it, click Stop ⇨ Select Drive ⇨ Settings.

The first checkbox optimizes your hard disk so that your most heavily and recently used programs start faster. You probably want to leave this setting marked, but defragmenting can take significantly longer when it's enabled, especially if you haven't defragmented in a while.

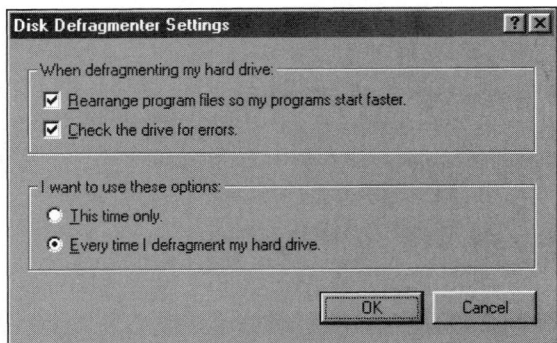

Figure 37-30: Whether the Disk Defragmenter Settings dialog box appears automatically depends on the method you use to start the Defragmenter.

Stop Everything Else to Run the Defragmenter

You can set up the Disk Defragmenter to run before anything else gets a chance, as we detailed in the previous section. Another option is to stop everything else and let it run by itself.

The Disk Defragmenter restarts when something is written to the disk. When this happens, it quickly sees that a bunch of the hard disk has been defragmented and soon catches up with itself and continues defragmenting. Unfortunately, if some application keeps writing to the disk, the Defragmenter starts over and over again, and ends up getting nowhere fast. If this is happening to you, then it's best to stop everything else and let the Disk Defragmenter run the show.

To ensure that everything has stopped, take these steps:

STEPS

Quieting Down the Computer to Run the Defragmenter

Step 1.   Close all running programs. Right-click any taskbar buttons and click Close. Right-click any icons in the system tray, and click Close, Exit, or an equivalent command. Press Ctrl+Alt+Delete, highlight a task other than Systray and Explorer, and click End Task. Repeat this process until only Systray and Explorer are left open.

You can ignore system tray icons that don't have Close, Exit, or equivalent commands.

Step 2. Right-click the Desktop and click Properties, and then click the Screen Saver tab. Display the Screen Saver field, scroll up to the top, and highlight (None). Click OK.

Step 3. Click Start ⇨ Settings ⇨ Control Panel ⇨ Power Management. For both "System standby" (if you have it) and "Turn off hard disks," choose Never. Don't worry about "Turn off monitor." Click OK. If you want to save these settings, click Save As, and name the settings **Defrag**. Click OK.

Step 4. Click Start ⇨ Programs ⇨ Accessories ⇨ System Tools ⇨ Disk Cleanup. Choose which disk, and click OK. Mark the checkboxes for the files that you will delete, and click OK.

Step 5. Right-click your Recycle Bin, click Empty Recycle Bin, and Yes. You don't need to do this if you emptied the Recycle Bin as part of the disk cleanup.

Step 6. Click Start ⇨ Programs ⇨ Accessories ⇨ System Tools ⇨ Disk Defragmenter ⇨ OK. Let 'er run.

If you have installed Microsoft Office, you might find that the background program Find Fast, which builds an index of words in Word documents, is running without being obvious about it. Find Fast interferes with the Disk Defragmenter and makes it restart when it updates its index.

Before you run the Disk Defragmenter, you'll want to stop Find Fast. To do so, click Start ⇨ Settings ⇨ Control Panel ⇨ Find Fast. Click Index ⇨ Pause Indexing ⇨ OK.

Tip If you have a power management setup in your BIOS, you may need to disable it there so that your computer doesn't go into Standby mode or wind down the hard disk. See "Let Windows Do Power Management" in Chapter 46.

Turn Off Your Screen Saver Automatically Before Defragmentation

While you still have to deal with your power management settings, you can run an applet that will automatically stop your screen saver if it notices that a disk maintenance utility has started up. If you run ScanDisk and Disk Defragmenter from the Task Scheduler, it is nice to be able to automatically close down your screen saver so that it doesn't interfere.

Tray Widget 98 has this automatic feature. Run it when you start up, and it sits in your system tray. Double-click it to bring up the menu shown in Figure 37-31. This menu lets you suspend your screen saver, disable it, or let Tray Widget stop it automatically.

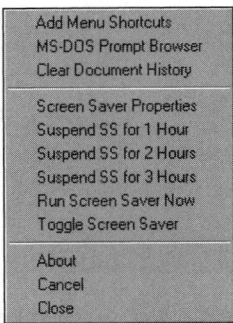

Figure 37-31: The Tray Widget menu gives you several options for suspending your screen saver.

You'll find this shareware utility at `http://www.windowspc.com/ TrayWidget98/`

Take Advantage of New Hard Drive Technology

Progress marches on, and progress brings us new technologies. One technology that keeps changing is hard drives. As computers have gotten faster, hard drive controller manufacturers have tried to keep up by supporting ever-newer standards.

In the old days, when the IBM PC/AT sported a 16-bit bus, manufacturers developed the 16-bit ATA (or AT Attachment) standard for hard drive controllers. This standard is better known today as IDE (or Integrated Drive Electronics).

A new standard, ATA-2 — also known as Fast ATA or Enhanced IDE — introduced better direct memory access (DMA) modes. These modes speed up disk reads and writes.

The latest IDE drive standard is variously called Ultra ATA, ATA-33, DMA-33, Ultra DMA, or simply UDMA. Ultra DMA theoretically can support a maximum burst mode transfer of 33.3 megabits per second (Mbps). (*Burst mode* is a nonsustained transfer rate over a very short period of time.)

This is an improvement over the 16.6Mbps maximum rate for DMA transfers under the original IDE standard, although you won't actually hit these ideal speeds in real-life usage. For more information on these standards, see `http://www.pcguide.com/ref/hdd/if/ide/std-c.html`.

We used HD Tach, a utility that reports on hard disk performance, to test two hard drives, both with and without DMA enabled. One drive improved its read burst speed from 8.4 Mbps to 11.9. The other improved from 8.3 Mbps to 11.2. More important, the CPU utilization dropped from 83 percent to 29 percent on one drive, and from 61 percent to 20 percent on the other. Lowering the CPU utilization of a drive allows a computer to process more data or serve more users at the same time as disk files are being transferred.

HD Tach is available at `http://tcdlabs.simplenet.com/hdtach.htm` The trial version of HD Tach tests your drives' read performance; the $49.95 registered version also tests write performance.

If your system's BIOS, chip set, and hard disk support UDMA, Windows Me and 98 are supposed to automatically load driver support and enable bus-mastering DMA transfers when it is installed. If your system is DMA/UDMA capable but has not been configured to take advantage of DMA/UDMA, you may be able to improve your hard disk performance by enabling it.

We asked Microsoft for a definitive answer about whether Windows does or does not automatically enable DMA. It turns out that the Windows DMA drivers, when installed for the first time, do *try* to enable DMA but may disable it if your system fails certain tests. Specifically, the drivers query the motherboard chip set, query the drive itself, and then test a short pattern of disk reads and writes to see if they are reliable at DMA speeds.

Microsoft spokesman Frank Kane put it this way when we first asked about this in 1998:

> On a machine that is upgraded to Windows 98, we retain the DMA settings (or lack thereof) of the previous state. If it was Windows 95 Gold, DMA will be off. But if a user had an OSR2 [Windows 95B] machine and had turned on DMA, it will remain on in Windows 98...
>
> When users check the DMA box in Device Manager, sometimes it appears unchecked after the system reboot. In such a case, we have determined that at least one of the three criteria mentioned above have not been met, so the system is not suitable for DMA.

To test for yourself whether a drive supports DMA, see "Does Your System Support DMA?" later in this chapter. You can also run `\tools\reskit\help\rkbook.chm` on the Windows CD-ROM. Search on **PIO mode 4** and read the resulting topic.

Remove Your Intel IDE Driver

While Windows Me and 98 come with drivers to support DMA capability, Windows 95 did not. If you downloaded an Intel Bus Master IDE driver from the Intel Web site and installed it under Windows 95, when you update your computer to Windows Me or 98, you'll probably run into problems. You'll find corrupted files due to improper timing of the DMA transfers. The Intel Bus Master IDE driver is not needed and doesn't work under Windows Me or 98. You'll want to use the one supplied by Microsoft.

If you did install the Intel Bus Master IDE driver, you'll find that you can't remove it under Windows Me or 98. In order to remove it, you'll need to download the latest version of the Intel Bus Master IDE driver. The installer program that comes with it allows you to uninstall the older version and replace it with the Microsoft driver. You'll find the new version at `http://developer.intel.com/design/chipsets/drivers/busmastr/index.htm`. You can find a discussion of this issue at `http://www2.ldd.net/scribers/griz/intelbus.htm`.

You'll also find drivers and an overview of the bus master problem at `http://www.bmdrivers.com`.

Does Your System Support DMA?

How can you tell if your computer will support DMA transfers to the hard disk? Intel claims that their 430 and 440 chip sets support DMA transfers via bus mastering of the IDE drives. Of course, if you have SCSI hard disks (as opposed to IDE drives), this doesn't apply to you.

You can check to see if you have this chip set by using a system information program such as Sandra. We discuss Sandra in "Add to Your System Info" in Chapter 23. If you have installed it, just double-click the Mainboard Information icon, as shown in Figure 37-32.

Figure 37-32: The Sandra user interface, with the Mainboard Information icon highlighted

Scroll down in Mainboard Information window to display Chipset Information, as shown in Figure 37-33. If you find a listing under System Chipset whose last three numbers start with 43 or 44, then you have an Intel 430 or 440 chipset.

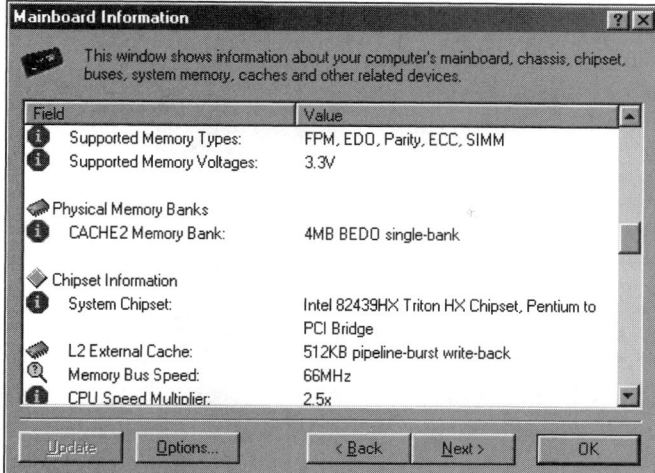

Figure 37-33: The chip set information appears about halfway down Sandra's Mainboard Information window.

One knowledgeable writer on the Microsoft support newsgroups, Jain Sandeep, claims that Intel 430TX or later chip sets are required to support DMA transfers, but this conflicts with Intel statements. We didn't resolve the conflict in our limited tests.

You'll need IDE hard disks that support DMA. If you have the manuals for your drives, you can see if the manufacturers bothered to inform you of this capability. You can check whether your drives support the *multiple-word DMA protocol* (that's what Microsoft calls it) by following the steps in the Microsoft Knowledge Base article "DMA Check Box Does Not Remain Checked" at http://support.microsoft.com/support/kb/articles/ q159/5/60.asp.

You'll also need a computer BIOS that is Bus Master IDE aware. The BIOS should be in sync with the Intel chip set, and if the chip set supports bus mastering, so should the BIOS. You can check your BIOS settings to see if there is any indication of Bus Master or DMA support for IDE.

You can mark the DMA checkbox if you have one, as shown in Figure 37-34. To find it, press Win+Pause/Break (or right-click the My Computer icon and click Properties) to open the System Properties dialog box, click the Device Manager tab, click the plus sign next to Disk Drives, highlight your hard disk name, click the Properties button, and click the Settings tab. After you mark the checkbox and click OK, restart Windows.

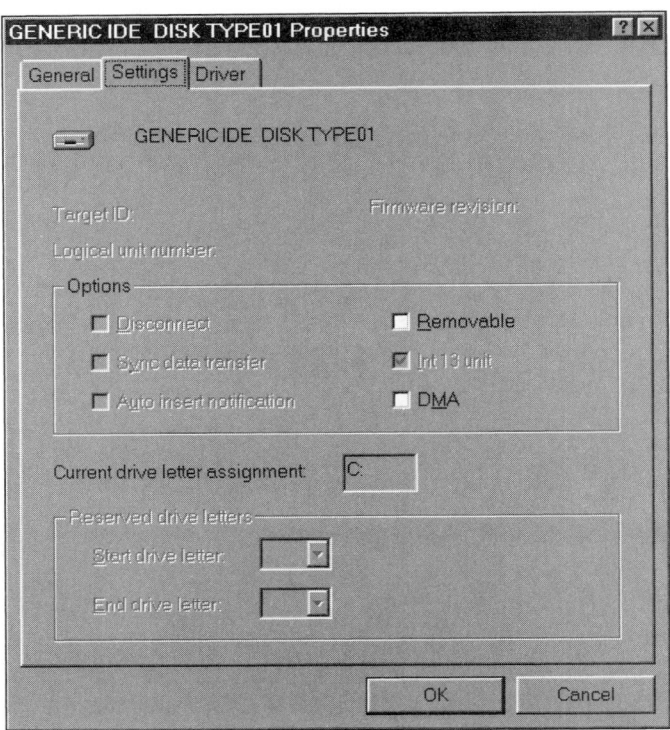

Figure 37-34: The DMA checkbox is in the Options area of the Settings tab in your hard disk's Properties dialog box.

You can look for one more reassuring sign that your computer can do DMA transfers to IDE devices. Open up your Device Manager, click the plus sign next to "Hard disk controllers," and look for Intel 82371XX Bus Master IDE Controller, where XX is replaced by AB, EB, SB, and so on, as shown in Figure 37-35. If you find this, then you know your computer can do DMA transfers. If you see an entry such as Intel 82371AB/EB PCI Bus-Master IDE Controller, you have a UDMA-capable system. The entry Standard Dual PCI IDE Controller means you do *not* have bus-mastering drivers loaded.

To Mark or Not Mark the DMA Checkbox

If you want to reduce the load on your processor due to hard disk reads and writes, then you want your hard disks operating in UDMA or DMA mode. Of course, you have to have hard disks, BIOSes, and hard disk controllers that support this.

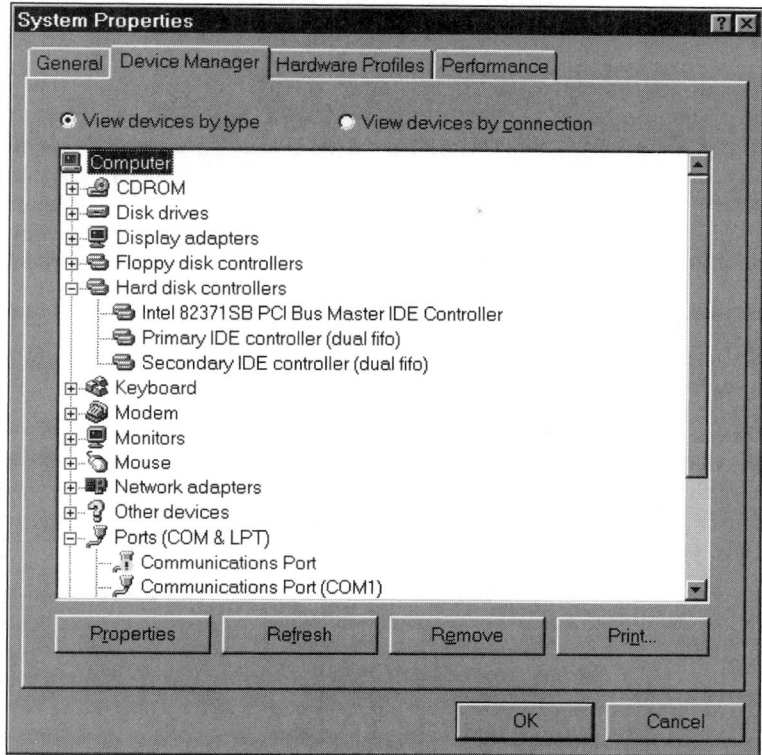

Figure 37-35: This computer is equipped with a UDMA-capable hard disk controller.

While there seems to be continuing disagreement over whether marking the DMA checkbox is necessary to activate UDMA or DMA operation, given that your computer has this capability, you can test it yourself. When you install Windows Me or 98, they are supposed to test your computer to see if it can use DMA, and implement it if it can. These versions of Windows are supposed to leave the DMA checkbox cleared if your computer can't do it.

If Windows correctly identifies your IDE hard disks, and determines that they can't support DMA, you may find that you do not have a DMA checkbox at all.

If you press Win+Pause/Beak (or right-click the My Computer icon and click Properties), click Device Manager, double-click "Hard disk controllers," and see that you have bus mastering installed, then Windows Me and 98 should set up the drivers to handle UDMA and DMA. You can mark the DMA checkbox by double-clicking Disk Drives in the Device Manager, highlighting a hard disk drive, clicking Properties, clicking the Settings tab, and then marking the DMA checkbox.

You'll want to use a hard disk performance-testing program such as HD Tach to compare how much of your processor is used when the DMA checkbox is marked versus cleared.

Microsoft's Take on Enabling IDE DMA

Microsoft provides a few paragraphs of help regarding implementing DMA with IDE drives under Windows. Their method calls upon the user or OEM to edit an `inf` file, remove the enumerated and detected IDE devices from the Device Manager, and then mark the DMA checkbox. You are supposed to do this after you determine that your computer and hard disks can manage DMA. You'll find "Enabling IDE DMA on Windows-based Systems" at `http://www.microsoft.com/hwdev/devdes/idedma.htm`.

Bill Drake, a regular contributor to the Microsoft technical support newsgroups, looked further into the issue of updating `inf` files and the subsequent changes to the registry. He concluded that revising the `inf` file is not enough to change the registry, and that redetection of the hardware is required. Here is what he had to say about this subject in 1998:

> If the entries detailed in the "Enabling IDE DMA on Windows-based Systems" article properly exist in mshdc.inf — with the proper values to enable DMA/UDMA mode — then the file is correct as is. However, if the value-data has changed (for whatever reason), the actual info is not incorporated into the Registry until the hard disk controller entries are removed from the hardware tree and redetected.
>
> *Inf* info is not used by Windows 98 directly. When an *inf* entry is updated, the only way to make Windows 98 aware of the change is to delete/redetect that item.
>
> When you update a hardware item in Windows 98, that change often results in changes to that particular hardware device's *inf* file entries. The changes to the *inf* file usually occur as part of a device driver update. However, to make the *inf* changes effective, the modifications must be incorporated into the Windows 98 Registry itself.
>
> To incorporate the change, Windows 98 must be forced to "see" that the hardware has changed. This will ensure the *inf* database is updated — and then the new data in the *inf* database will be consulted when the new piece of hardware is actually incorporated into the Registry.
>
> When you change an item in the hardware tree, and an *inf* file has been updated, you will see a dialog box with a progress-bar that says "Building Driver Information Database." At that point, you are building (or rebuilding) two files called DRVDATA.BIN and DRVIDX.BIN, which live in your C:\WINDOWS\INF folder along with most of your Windows 98 *inf* files.
>
> The *bin* files are what Windows 98 actually consults when fiddling with hardware. The *inf* files are simply the raw "input" files that are compiled into the *bin* data files. If you have updated something, and you do not see the "Building Driver Information Database" item, then as

far as Windows 98 is concerned, the *inf* entries have not changed since the last time the *bin* files were compiled/updated.

Consequently, if you know that something has changed, and you don't see the "Building" dialog, that update will not be reflected in your Windows 98 hardware tree until such time as the "Building" dialog is forced to appear.

Updating the *bin* files is normally driven by an "Add New Hardware" request — either manually through Control Panel or automatically through PnP. However, if you are not sure whether the *bin* files have been properly updated or not — you can go to the *inf* folder and manually delete the DRVDATA.BIN and DRVIDX.BIN files. This will force Windows 98 to recompile those files in their entirety the next time a request to update any driver is made.

Once you are sure you have a current copy of the *bin* data files, then the way you move the data from the *bin* files into the W9x Registry itself is to remove/redetect the piece(s) of hardware whose *inf* files were changed. This is the only way that improvements which require *inf* changes can be incorporated into the Windows 98 Registry itself.

Changing the *inf* or recompiling the *bin* files does not update the Registry, and only the Registry changes actually result in changes to the operation of that particular driver.

Bill goes on to say:

I puzzled out the *inf* methodology originally by zeroing the archive attributes in the *inf* folder and seeing what happened when an *inf* update went in. This was years ago, shortly after the W95 Gold release — when I was investigating just exactly what goes on during one of US Robotics' notorious modem *inf* updates.

Since then, I have investigated the methodology used for the various Intel chipset *inf*-compatibility updates for Windows 95, the various Adaptec SCSI Host Adapter *inf* updates for the 154x, 284x and 294x DMA bus master Host Adapters. Also, I've investigated the continuing US Robotics Sportster and Courier Modem *inf* updates, which have occurred through the development of X2 and now V.90, and finally the Intel and Microsoft DMA bus master updates for EIDE hard disk controller chipsets.

By comparing the similarities and differences between the various manufacturers' approaches — along with each manufacturer's specific installation instructions, I was eventually able to narrow down the common threads in each update procedure, and figure out what I thought was really going on. I then did a bunch of tests on my own system to establish what *inf* changes are reflected in the Registry, and when.

Since then, info released by US Robotics Technical Support has confirmed the specific methodology required to ensure an update is actually propagated into the Registry, but this was common knowledge in my technical support community long before USR posted their details.

Furthermore, continuing improvements to the algorithm used to detect changes to *inf* file contents in the *inf* and INF/OTHER folders has removed the necessity to manually delete the DRVDATA.BIN and DRVIDX.BIN files to "force" an update in the vast majority of cases.

However, when Microsoft is having a problem with compatibility (and the Windows 98 hard disk drivers are having a problem with this) it is common to find uncrossed t's and undotted i's in install procedures, which force the need for manual housekeeping of stuff that should be automatic.

There were similar compatibility problems with the early Windows 95 hard disk drivers. Microsoft went through several versions of the REMIDEUP.EXE patch as they found and fixed problems with the Windows 95 hard disk drivers, which eluded the original beta testers.

Furthermore, my experience has also shown me that the current Windows 95 REMIDEUP.EXE patch fixes many more problems than Microsoft officially admits in the Knowledge Base.

I expect a similar evolution for the Windows 98 hard disk drivers. We'll see this as developments in the DMA/UDMA implementation by hard disk manufacturers make it obvious that there is a need for better "bulletproofing" in the Windows 98 drivers to catch sloppy DMA/UDMA/ATAPI implementation in hard disk/CD-ROM/tape drive/Zip/LS-120 hardware.

Add to the above the relative "youth" of the Windows 98/NT driver model as well as the ACPI specification—and the three issues mentioned combine to create interactions the original driver designers could not anticipate (or find and fix) without extending the beta testing period into infinity.

Personally, I think Microsoft should have waited until they got the ACPI support working properly before releasing Windows 98. In my opinion, then they would have had time to find and bulletproof against the vast majority of the DMA/UDMA hard disk and EIDE controller bugs which are plaguing so many Windows 98 users. However, the above is not an absolute guarantee that the Windows 98 hard disk drivers would have been bulletproof from the get-go.

Microsoft admitted that there was a problem with getting the information in inf files incorporated into the registry, at least for older versions like Windows 95, in the Knowledge Base article "Hardware List Not Updated After Installing New .inf File" at http://support.microsoft.com/support/kb/articles/q139/2/06.asp.

Ultra DMA Drives May Have Difficulties with Windows

Most UDMA drives, perhaps the great majority, work fine under Windows. But there seems to be a discernable minority of UDMA drives that have been installed in systems that aren't quite capable of supporting the maximum speeds that UDMA can produce. Problems can be caused by electromagnetic interference on the system bus, poor flow control in hardware or firmware, or inferior circuitry on the drive itself. In such cases, a drive can "time out," slowing the system and/or corrupting data files.

If you have a UDMA drive in a system that isn't quite up to speed (so to speak), you may experience one or more of the following difficulties when upgrading from Windows 95 to Windows Me:

- Windows Me fails during the Plug and Play process and won't complete the installation.

- After a successful installation, Windows Me will only start in its very limited Safe mode.

- When transferring files, a drive appears to slow way down, and then speed up again. This may also pause or hang software or your keyboard and mouse.

- You start missing perfectly good files, or you lose the ability to access your hard drive at all.

- Windows shutdown takes much, much longer than normal.

Of course, these symptoms can be caused by many other problems. One of the frustrating things about UDMA difficulties is that they may be intermittent and hard to diagnose.

If your hard disk controller identifies itself as an Intel Bus Master IDE Controller, you should read http://developer.intel.com/design/ chipsets/drivers/busmastr/dwnlod.htm. You may need to switch drivers — see "Remove Your Intel IDE Driver" earlier in this chapter.

Seagate Technology has prepared a fix for three early production versions of its Medalist Pro 7200 RPM hard drives. If a drive controller had been configured for UDMA support with these drives in Windows 95 or NT, and then Windows 98 was installed, the Windows 98 installation crashed. This also occurs with some other manufacturers' drives, and Seagate is to be commended for publicly posting on its Web site the exact model numbers affected, and for offering a fix. See http://www.seagate.com/support/ disc/faq/medpro_dma.shtml or call Seagate technical support at 405-936-1200.

Microsoft reports that an old Windows 95 driver can cause computers to crash while accessing a hard drive using UDMA if a hardware error is encountered. The driver may also read or write incorrect data when a hard drive is recovering from a "suspend" state. You can correct both of these problems and others with an updated driver, available from http:// support.microsoft.com/support/kb/articles/q171/3/53.asp.

Mark Stapleton, a mechanical engineer with Georgia Tech Research Institute, has done extensive research on this subject. By far the most frustrating problems, according to Stapleton, are intermittent crashes or data errors caused by UDMA transfers at speeds that are not quite reliable. He and others point to the old IDE cable that many PC manufacturers still use to connect drives to the motherboard. The cable is not shielded against electrical interference, which can be a problem at high transfer rates. The Circuit Assembly Corp. sells a special ATAS cable for $12.99 plus shipping that is well grounded and may solve this kind of trouble. See `http://www.ultracable.com`.

Trouble with IDE

Some Windows users have noted performance problems with their IDE hard drives after they have installed new motherboards in their computers. Windows apparently doesn't detect the presence of some of the new hardware correctly, and could use a little help.

Check your IDE drive interface by pressing Win+Pause/Break (or by right-clicking the My Computer icon and clicking Properties). Click the Device Manager tab. Under "Hard disk controllers," check if there is an exclamation point in a yellow circle for the primary and secondary IDE channels (if they are listed). If there is, click the Performance tab, and check if File System and Virtual Memory might be set to something other than 32-bit (see Figure 37-36).

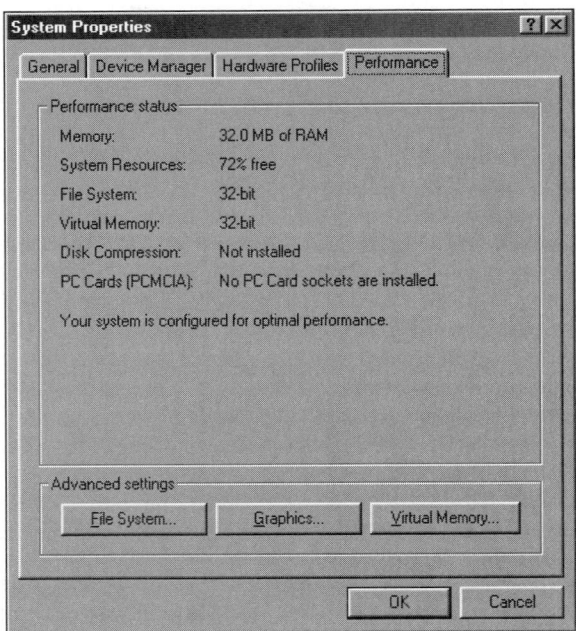

Figure 37-36: On this computer, the Performance tab indicates 32-bit for both File System and Virtual Memory. If you have different settings, it could indicate an erroneous registry entry.

Secret

If you are experiencing both of the symptoms discussed in the previous paragraph, and you have IDE hard disk drives, it is likely the case that a NOIDE drive entry was placed in your registry when Windows first unsuccessfully attempted to initialize the 32-bit hard disk driver.

To remove this entry, use your Registry Editor to navigate to HKEY_LOCAL_ MACHINE\ System\ CurrentControlset\ Services\ VxD\ IOS. Remove the "NOIDE" string in the right pane, exit the Registry Editor, and restart Windows.

You can learn more about this issue in these three Knowledge Base articles:

- "Compatibility Mode Problems with PCI-IDE Controllers" at http:// support/microsoft.com/support/kb/articles/q159/5/60

- "Troubleshooting MS-DOS Compatibility Mode on Hard Disks" at http:// support.microsoft.com/support/kb/articles/Q130/1/79.asp

- "Secondary CMD Controller Not Recognized at Startup" at http:// support.microsoft.com/support/kb/articles/q159/5/56.asp

Front End for Disk, File, and Directory Caching

Windows sets aside chunks of memory for saving the current list of file and directory names. You can set how much memory is used for these tasks by pressing Win+Pause/Break (or right-clicking the My Computer icon and clicking Properties), clicking Performance ⇨ File System, and then choosing one of the options in the "Typical role of this computer" drop-down list. The Network Server option uses the largest amounts of memory (about 40K) for this task.

There is another tool you can use to set these values and cache an even larger number of file and directory names. Cacheman, a disk and filename cache utility, lets you incrementally determine the number of filenames and directory names you will cache.

You use the lower two sliders to set the Name Cache and Directory Cache values, as shown in Figure 37-37.

The Cacheman settings are not displayed in the File System Properties dialog box (see the first paragraph in this section), but the fact that the Cacheman settings are being used is. Cacheman adds its key to the HKEY_LOCAL_ MACHINE\ SOFTWARE\ Microsoft\ Windows\ CurrentVersion\FS Templates branch of your registry so that it can tell Windows to set different values for these cache settings.

You can also use Cacheman to set disk cache or vcache settings that are normally set in System.ini, if you set them at all. Windows normally uses its dynamic memory to cache its disk reads. When this memory fills up, it swaps the oldest disk reads out to the hard disk swap file.

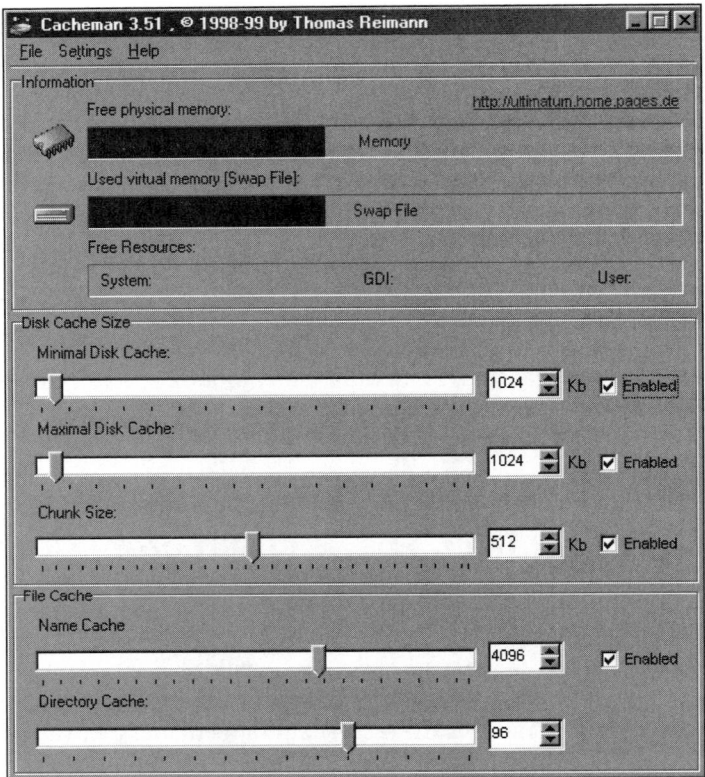

Figure 37-37: The number of file and directory names cached are displayed in the lower two right-hand boxes.

You can limit how much memory Windows uses for disk caching so that all of the rest of your dynamic memory is managed by Windows for its other functions without bothering about disk caching. Depending on your usage, this can increase your computer's performance.

The top three sliders in Cacheman enable you to set the disk-cache minimum and maximum size, as well as a memory chunk size, which has a minor effect on system performance. Cacheman lets you choose from a list of performance settings based on your usage, and then sets the slider values for you. You can then manually move the sliders if you don't care for these values.

Cacheman writes the results of your changes (if you click File ⇨ Save) to the System.ini file. They take effect the next time you restart Windows.

You'll find this freeware program at `http://members.xoom.com/ultimatum`. Thanks again to Chris Pirillo at `http://www.lockergnome.com`.

Speeding Up Caching and Swapping

The best way to speed up the performance of your computer is to add memory. This allows you to switch among already loaded programs and data much more quickly, because they will be more likely to be in the memory cache if they have been swapped out to the hard disk. Windows uses additional memory for caching what it swaps out, so with more memory, Windows will find your programs and data in the memory cache and won't have to go to the hard disk to find them.

If you have two or more physical hard disks (not hard disk partitions or logical drives), you can get some additional performance by moving your Windows swap file and your Internet Explorer cache folder to the other drive. This assumes that the other drive is little used, and pretty much dedicated to swapping and caching. The additional performance comes about because the other hard drive circuitry can handle some of the data transfer independently and not interfere with those data transfers happening on the primary drive.

To change the Windows swap file location, follow these steps:

STEPS

Managing Your Swap Space

Step 1. Right-click My Computer, choose Properties, and click the Performance tab.

Step 2. Click the Virtual Memory button to display the Virtual Memory dialog box.

Step 3. Choose "Let me specify my own virtual memory settings," as shown in Figure 37-38.

Step 4. Choose volume and size parameters. Click OK, click Yes when you see the warning about not letting Windows manage virtual memory automatically, and click Close.

Step 5. Restart Windows.

Continued

STEPS

Managing Your Swap Space *(continued)*

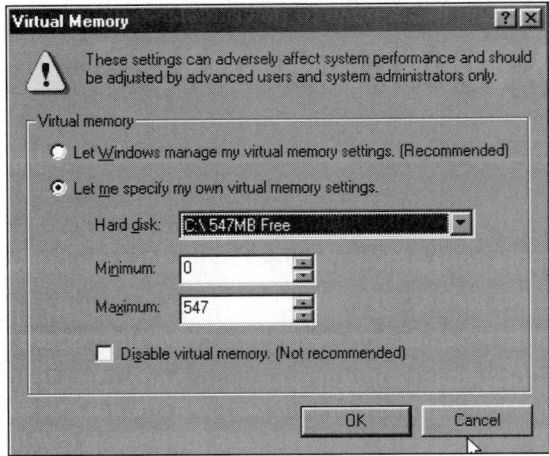

Figure 37-38: After you mark the second option button, you will be able to change the settings below it.

To change your Internet Explorer cache location, follow these steps:

STEPS

Changing Your Internet Explorer Cache Location

Step 1. Right-click the Internet Explorer icon on your Desktop, click Properties, and click the Settings button.

Step 2. Click the Move Folder button shown in Figure 37-39. This lets you specify a new folder on the second hard disk. You will lose all of your temporary Internet files and all of your offline Web pages. You'll need to resynchronize your offline Web pages again later.

Step 3. Choose a new folder on your secondary hard disk. Click OK, click OK again, and then click Yes when asked if you want Windows to restart and finish moving your Temporary Internet files folder.

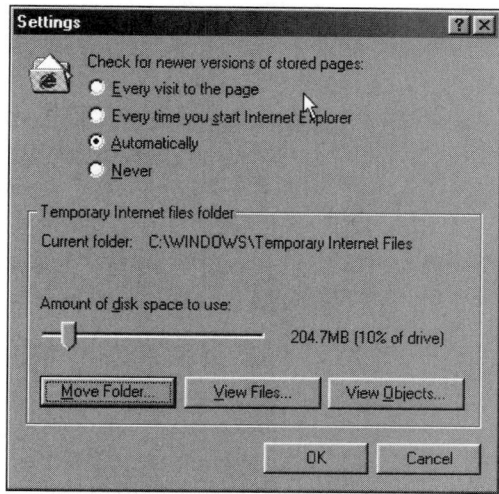

Figure 37-39: The Move Folder button lets you move your Internet Explorer cache.

Setting Aside the Swap File and the Temporary Internet Files Folder

Windows is quite happy to manage your swap file and your Temporary Internet files folder without any interference or guidance from you. The only recommendation that Microsoft makes is that if you have a spare drive that is faster than your main drive and you aren't using it for anything else, you might think of putting the swap file there. We'll just bet that not too many of you are in this situation.

One option for speeding up Windows and its associated applications is to cut down on the hard disk fragmentation that develops between defragmenting sessions. One way to do this is to stick the swap file in its own partition and put the Temporary Internet files folder in another partition. If each of these folders is in its own partition, they won't place parts of themselves in every momentarily free portion of your main hard disk.

It's not worth the effort to repartition your hard disk with FDISK because it wipes out everything, but you can use Partition Magic to set up a couple of 200MB partitions that you can use to store these files. If you're setting up a new computer with a multigigabyte hard disk, you might consider setting aside a mere 400MB for these files.

You'll need to configure Windows to use these additional partitions. To set the location of your swap file in the Virtual Memory dialog box, press Win+Pause/Break (or right-click the My Computer icon and click Properties), click the Performance tab, and click the Virtual Memory button. Mark "Let me specify my own virtual memory settings," and then select the hard drive partition by volume name in the "Hard disk" drop-down list (see Figure 37-40). Click OK, click Yes, click Close, and restart Windows.

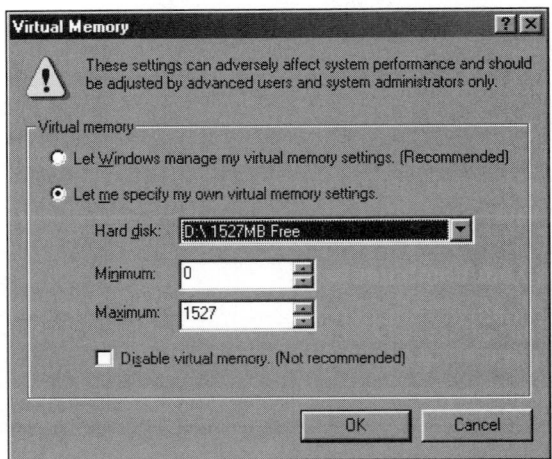

Figure 37-40: Select a partition from the "Hard disk" drop-down list.

To change the location of the Temporary Internet files folder, follow the "Changing Your Internet Explorer Cache Location" steps in the previous section.

Not Enough Room on a Hidden or Host Drive?

You may receive messages that you are running out of space on a host or hidden drive, but when you run the Disk Cleanup utility, there are no files to clean up. Makes you wonder just what is going on.

You'll have a host drive if you've used disk compression (say, DriveSpace) to create a compressed drive or a compressed volume file (CVF). The host drive, which can be and often is hidden, can be sized so that it has only a couple of megabytes free at most. The rest of its space is used by the CVF, and is given a different drive designator.

Secret

The Windows Disk Cleanup utility may incorrectly and automatically find that the available space on the host drive is below a certain threshold percentage and ask you to run the utility to delete certain files. When you run Disk Cleanup, you'll see that there are no files marked for deletion. And after you run it, you'll find that the free space on the drive hasn't changed.

This often happens after you install new software. What we think is going on here is that Disk Cleanup is incorrectly calculating the space that the temporary setup files used, and is assigning that space to the host drive instead of to the CVF. This reduces the amount of the free space on the host drive as seen by Disk Cleanup, and as a result it is automatically triggered to run.

You can stop this erroneous behavior by taking these steps:

STEPS

Taming Disk Cleanup

Step 1. Click Start ⇨ Programs ⇨ Accessories ⇨ System Tools ⇨ Disk Cleanup.

Step 2. In the Select Drive dialog box, select the host drive in the Drives drop-down list (see Figure 37-41), and then click OK.

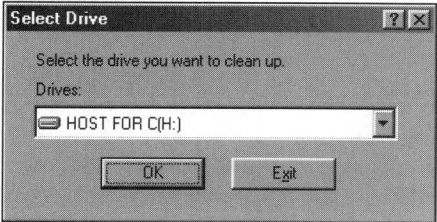

Figure 37-41: Select the host drive in the Drives field.

Step 3. Click the Settings tab, and clear the checkbox (see Figure 37-42).

Step 4. Click OK, and click Yes.

Continued

STEPS

Taming Disk Cleanup *(continued)*

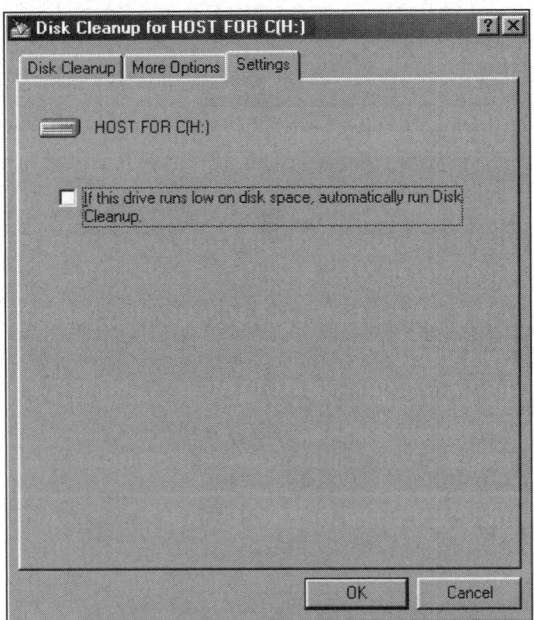

Figure 37-42: Clear the checkbox in the Settings tab.

Now you won't get any spurious messages about low disk space on a drive to which, in fact, you don't actually add any software or files.

About a month after I discovered how to solve this little problem, Microsoft posted a Knowledge Base article that gave the same answer. Always nice to have them come in second and back up my original idea.

Disable Low Disk Space Notification

You can disable low disk space notification altogether by eliminating the broadcasting of the message. You can do this for one drive or for a set of specific drives. You'll need to edit the registry by taking these steps.

STEPS

Stopping the Low Disk Space Message

Step 1. Click Start ⇨ Run, type **regedit**, and press Enter.

Step 2. Navigate to HKEY_LOCAL_MACHINE\ System\ CurrentControlSet\ control\ FileSystem. Highlight this key in the left pane of your Registry Editor.

Step 3. Right-click the right pane, and click New ⇨ DWORD Value.

Step 4 Rename the DWORD value **DisableLowDiskSpaceBroadcast**.

Step 5. Double-click DisableLowDiskSpaceBroadcast, and enter a value from Table 37-3 to correspond with the disk drive whose low disk space message you want to stop.

You can add the values to come up with a unique value for a set of drives. For example, a value to turn off the low disk space warning for drives C: and D: would be 12 (because 4 + 8 = 12).

Step 6. Exit the Registry Editor.

Table 37-3   Disk Drive Data Values

Drive Letter	Data Value	Drive Letter	Data Value
A	1	N	8192
B	2	O	16384
C	4	P	32768
D	8	Q	65536
E	16	R	131072
F	32	S	262144
G	64	T	524288
H	128	U	1048576
I	256	V	2097152
J	512	W	4194304
K	1024	X	8388608
L	2048	Y	16777216
M	4096	Z	33554432

Completely Clear Your Hard Disk

Secret

Apparently, the DOS command FDISK, used to partition your hard disk, does not completely update a disk partition after the first time it is used. You can force FDISK to completely start over. This is useful in removing Disk Manager, EZ Drive, or other nonstandard disk partitioning schemes. You can also use it to remove any boot sector viruses.

You'll need to run a little debug script or a compiled program that incorporates the script. You can find such a script at http://www.firmware.com/pb4ts/hdclear.htm.

Thanks to Attila Szabo for getting this program written and Robert M. Whitworth for writing it.

You can completely clear the partition information in other ways as well. After further discussions with Attila, he came up with a list of Web sites that speak to these issues and a list of URLs for other programs that provide this kind of service. Attila states, "I've used these three programs before, and they produce the same results in a roundabout way as the debug script or clearhd.com. I included the start Web pages just for reference."

- IBM hard drive support at http://www.storage.ibm.com/techsup/hddtech/hddtech.htm. The Utilities link on this page leads to Zap at http://index.storsys.ibm.com/hddtech/utility/ZAP.ZIP.

- Western Digital hard drive support at http://www.wdc.com/support/. The WD Diagnostics link on this page leads to Wd_Diag (which replaced Wd_clear, it seems) at http://www.wdc.com/support/ftp/wddiag/wd_diag.exe.

- Quantum hard drive support at http://support.quantum.com/. The Software and Utilities link on this page leads to Zero Fill Utility at http://support.quantum.com/software/ZDISK101.EXE.

CD-ROMS and Removable Drives

These types of drives have been slowly integrated into the Windows world, but often with a few rough edges. We show you how to tweak some of the unlisted settings.

Increase Your Look-Ahead Buffer for Fast CD-ROM Drives

Secret

If you use your CD-ROM drive extensively, it could be worth it to increase the amount of RAM memory that you allocate to the buffer (often referred to as the *prefetch buffer* or *look-ahead buffer*) for reading data from the drive. Windows lets you indirectly set the size of the buffer, but you can edit your registry to increase the size of the cache and the buffer to correspond to faster CD-ROM drives.

Your CD-ROM drive needs to use the Windows CDFS (32-bit Compact Disc File System) for this to be worthwhile. If your drive runs in MS-DOS compatibility mode, none of these changes will do anything useful. To determine whether your CD-ROM drive is using the CDFS driver, right-click your My Computer icon, click Properties, and click the Device Manager tab. If CD-ROM is listed directly below Computer at the top of the device list, then Windows is using the CDFS driver.

To see how you normally change the size of the CD-ROM cache and prefetch buffer, take these steps:

STEPS

Changing the CD-ROM Cache and Pre-Fetch Buffer Size

Step 1. Right-click your My Computer icon and click Properties (or press Win+Pause/Break), and click the Performance tab.

Step 2. Click the File System button, and click the CD-ROM tab.

Step 3. Move the "Supplemental cache size" slider to the left and right, and read off the amount of cache that corresponds to each position, as shown in Figure 37-43.

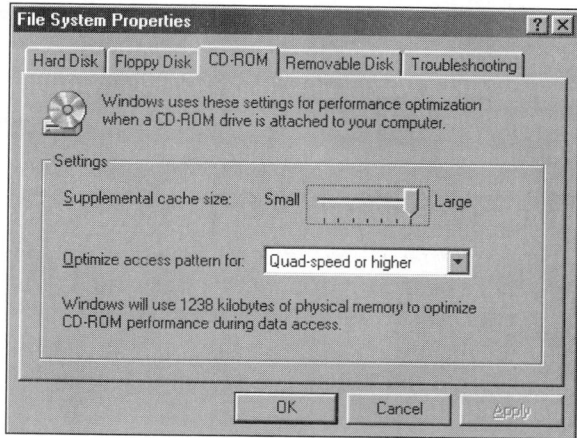

Figure 37-43: As you move the slider bar from Small to Large, the corresponding cache size is listed at the bottom of the Settings area.

Continued

STEPS

Changing the CD-ROM Cache and Pre-Fetch Buffer Size

(continued)

Step 4. Display the "Optimize access pattern for" drop-down list to change the size of the prefetch buffer corresponding to the speed of your CD-ROM drive. Notice that it doesn't go any higher than quad speed. Newer CD-ROM drives are 32*x* speed.

Step 5. Click Cancel twice to close the dialog boxes.

While the File System Properties dialog box enables you to change these values within a restricted range, you can edit your registry (or merge in a `reg` file) to directly change the values to correspond to your hardware. Larger values for the buffer and cache will take larger chunks of memory, so make sure that you have plenty to start with, and then test your configuration after restarting Windows.

STEPS

Editing CD-ROM Cache and Prefetch Buffer Size in Your Registry

Step 1. Start your Registry Editor. Navigate to HKEY_LOCAL_MACHINE\ System\ CurrentControlSet\ Control\ FileSystem\ CDFS.

Step 2. Double-click the value in the right pane of your Registry Editor that you want to change, and then edit the value in the Edit DWORD Value dialog box.

Step 3. Depending on whether you upgraded Windows 95 to Windows Me or started with a clean or new computer, you will have either hexadecimally formatted or decimally formatted DWORD values (see Figure 37-44). Notice that the decimal value is in parentheses.

Step 4. To change your cache value, double-click CacheSize and type the value in the "Value data" field of the Edit DWORD Value dialog box, using Table 37-4 as a reference.

Step 5. To edit the value for your prefetch buffer, double-click Prefetch and make the change, using Table 37-5 as a reference.

Step 6. Click OK to close the Edit DWORD Value dialog box, close the Registry Editor, and restart Windows to see how the changes affect your CD-ROM speed and memory use.

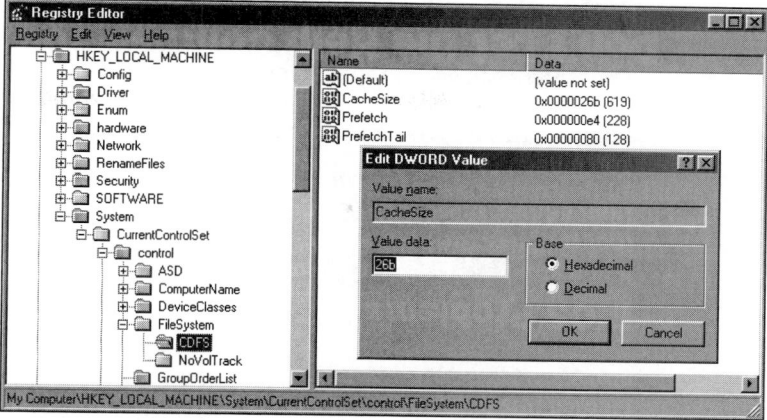

Figure 37-44: The Edit DWORD Value dialog box shows whether the data is in hexadecimal or decimal format.

Table 37-4   CacheSize Registry Values

Cache Size	Decimal	Actual Cache Size (KB)	Hex
[Default]	619	1,238	26b
Medium	1,238	2,476	4d6
Large	2,476	4,952	9ac

Table 37-5   Prefetch Buffer Registry Values

CD-ROM Speed	Decimal	Hex	DWORD
4x [Default]	228	e4	000000e4
8x	448	1c0	000001c0
16x	896	380	00000380
24x	1344	540	00000540
32x	1792	700	00000700

You may find speed improvement when playing video clips (avi, mov, mpeg), running multimedia apps, or copying large files from your CD-ROM. This may not be the case with graphics-intensive games because most games use their own disk read-ahead technologies, which work independently from the Windows prefetch buffer and cache values.

Thanks to Anthony Kinyon for pointers on this secret.

DMA, UDMA, and CD-ROM

DMA, direct memory access, allows quicker access to hard drives and CD-ROM drives. Not all hard disk or CD-ROM controllers support DMA.

Secret

UDMA CD-ROM drives seem to conflict with DMA. Users have reported that with both UDMA and DMA operating, UDMA CD-ROM drives work but cannot play audio CDs.

If you turn off either DMA or UDMA, the problems disappear. To turn off DMA, right-click your My Computer icon, click Properties, click the Device Manager tab, double-click your CD-ROM driver, click the Settings tab, and clear the DMA checkbox if you have one (see Figure 37-45).

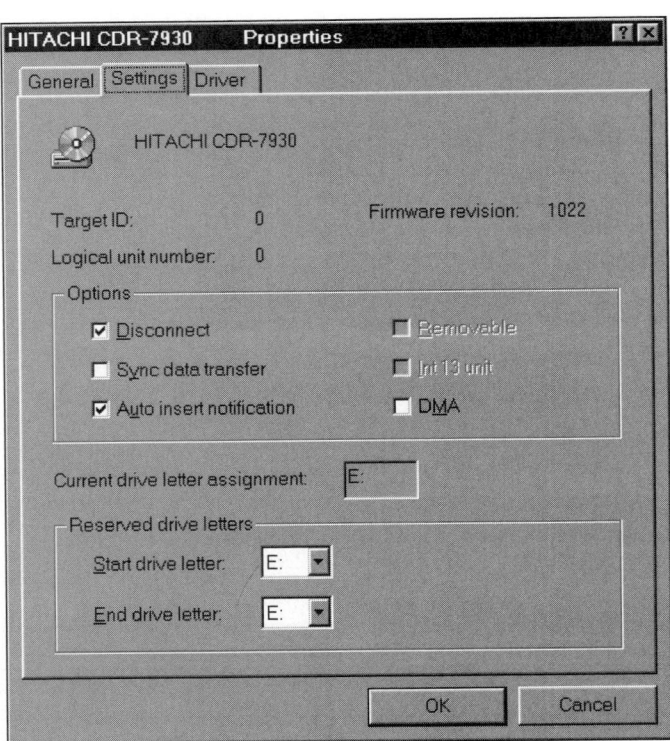

Figure 37-45: The DMA checkbox in the Settings tab has been cleared.

Thanks to Don Lebow for giving us guidance on this secret.

Copy Files from 'Foreign' CD-ROMs

Secret

It is possible to read files on CD-ROMs that were written by other operating systems, as long as they were written to the ISO standard. Some of the filenames on the CD-ROM may not be compatible with the Windows or DOS standard. However, even if this is the case, you can still copy the files from the CD-ROM to your hard disk.

Using the method detailed in these steps, you can copy all the files whose names comply with the standard using one command. Then go back and individually copy those files whose names don't comply, one at a time.

STEPS

Copying Files with Xcopy

Step 1.   Click Start ⇨ Programs ⇨ MS-DOS Prompt.

Step 2.   Type the following command, making changes to match your CD-ROM letter designator and the target folder on your hard disk:

```
Xcopy /c d:\*.* c:\targetfolder
```

The /c switch allows Xcopy to continue after encountering a bad filename.

Step 3.   Copy individual files from the CD-ROM using the Copy command to rename them one at a time. For example:

```
Copy d:\badfilename c:\targetfolder\goodfilename
```

Thanks to Matthew Berryman for pointing out this tip.

Learn About CD-ROM Drives

Would you like to know more about CD-ROMs before you purchase a computer or CD-ROM drive? If so, check out "18 Questions to Ask Before Purchasing a CD-ROM" at the Plextor site. You'll find the page at http://www.plextor.be/english/18qie.htm.

Test Your CD-ROM Drive

If you have a CD-ROM drive, why not test it to be sure that you're getting all the performance that you've paid for? You can download a very nifty testing tool, the CD-ROM Drive Analyzer, shown in Figure 37-46.

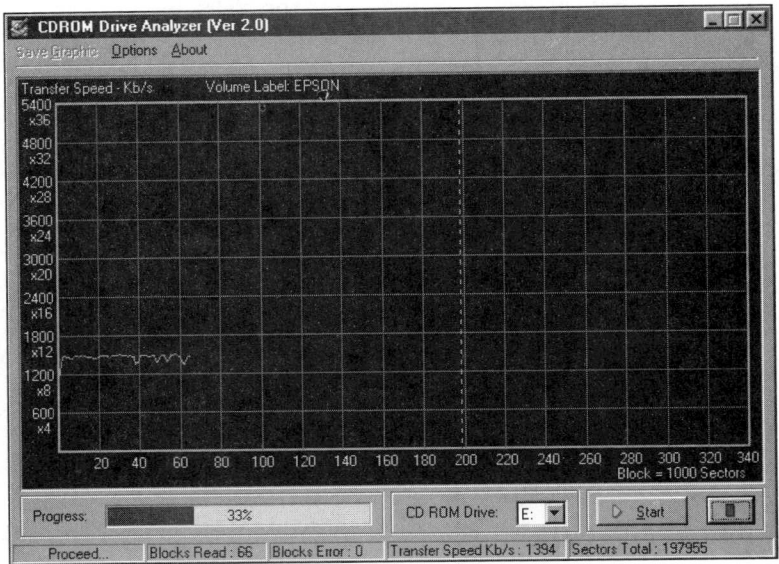

Figure 37-46: This chart displays the results of the CD-ROM Analyzer's performance tests.

Let the CD-ROM Analyzer run for a few minutes to build up a graphical record of its results. You'll find it at http://www.geocities.com/Research Triangle/Lab/1228/cdan_e.html.

Trouble with Zip and Jaz Cartridges and Drives?

Secret

Does your Zip or Jaz drive emit a series of clicking sounds when you first insert a cartridge or when you attempt to read or write data? If so, you may be experiencing the "Click of Death," a symptom of future serious problems with your drive and/or cartridge. This is caused by a manufacturing problem Iomega had with several batches of drives before it was corrected.

According to Steve Gibson:

Iomega Zip and Jaz drives cause Click of Death by incorrectly writing to their removable media. This miswriting can damage the user's data, the factory-written low-level formatting, the head's positioning servo information, and the proprietary "Z-Tracks" that are used internally to manage and maintain the Zip and Jaz drive's cartridge data.

The clicking sound itself is nothing more than the sound of the heads being retracted from the cartridge into the drive and then immediately reinserted. This deliberate strategy is employed by the drive when it is having trouble locating, reading, or writing any of the cartridge's data. This removal and reinsertion of the heads recalibrates the head positioning mechanism, "scrubs" the heads to remove excessive oxide deposits, and eliminates electrostatic charge build-up on the heads.

There have been extensive discussions of this problem. You can follow them and check out many of the Web sites dedicated to the subject by first going to Steve's site at `http://www.grc.com/clickdeath.htm` and following the links to "What Else Has Been Written About the Click of Death?"

If you are experiencing this problem, Steve has a couple of answers for you. You can download a freeware Zip and Jaz drive and cartridge-testing program with a cute name, Trouble In Paradise (TIP), from his site. Use this program to see if your drive is damaging your cartridges (see Figure 37-47). If it is, you'll need to replace your drive before you can attempt to recover lost data. (Apparently Iomega will replace your drive even if it is not under warranty if you are experiencing these problems.)

Trouble In Paradise will also check to see if you have the latest ASPI (Advanced SCSI Programming Interface) driver. These drivers are used by Zip and Jaz drives, as well as SCSI CD-ROMs, tapes, scanners, and other devices.

If you have damaged Jaz or Zip cartridges, and you've replaced your malfunctioning drive, you can use SpinRite 5.0 (here's where the money comes in) to recover the data from the damaged cartridges. This is all discussed at Steve's site, and you can decide for yourself whether this is what you need to do.

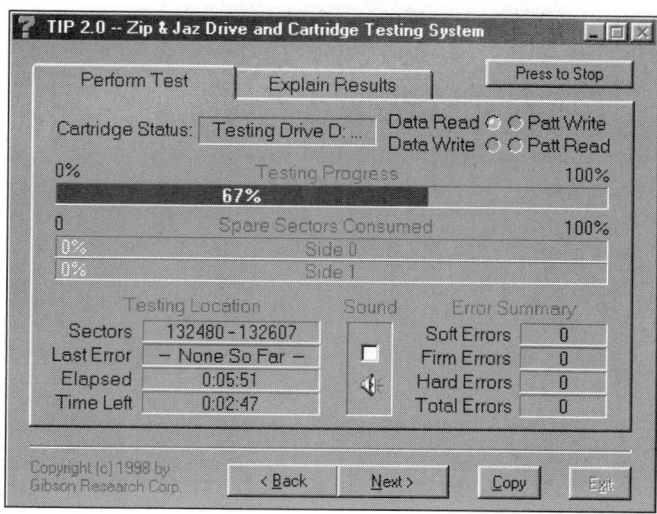

Figure 37-47: Trouble In Paradise in the process of testing a Zip drive

Summary

The people staffing the Microsoft support lines want to quit hearing from you about problems with your disk drives. Windows provides you with a set of tools to keep everything in working order.

▶ We show you how to find all the disk tools in all the little corners of Windows.

▶ We explain how to take advantage of the FAT32 file system, and what to watch out for in converting to FAT32.

▶ We show you how to repair your disks when you experience a problem, and how to keep an eye on your disks to prevent trouble.

▶ Microsoft includes a great little disk defragmenter that can speed up disk access. We show you how to get the most from it.

▶ Do you want to double your hard disk space at little or no cost in disk access speed? Try DriveSpace.

▶ We show you how to create super-high-density diskettes.

▶ Help Windows run the big drives, convert to FAT32, use UDMA, speed up your programs, defrag your drive, and cut down on wasted space.

▶ Fix Windows configuration problems with UDMA, DMA, and IDE drives.

▶ Put your swap file and Internet cache files in other partitions to cut down on fragmentation.

▶ Get rid of the bogus low disk space notification.

Chapter 38

Managing Hardware

In This Chapter

We place all sorts of secrets about pieces of your computer here, including ones related to input devices, the display, the CD-ROM drive, and so on. Most importantly, we discuss how to deal with interrupts, the bane of any Windows power user.

▶ Getting more interrupts for your plug in cards

▶ Controlling USB ports

▶ Finding basic BIOS information

▶ Upgrading your hardware

▶ Finding useful upgrade information online

Interrupts

There are never enough of them.

Grab Interrupts for New Peripherals

It is most unfortunate that we still have only the 16 defined interrupts that came with the original IBM AT hardware. PCI architecture does add interrupt sharing, and Windows supports IRQ steering, which allows the interrupts to be shared. Still, there may be times when you could use a few free interrupts.

It is possible to free up hardwired interrupts with a bit of rewiring, or at least reconfiguring, on your part.

If your computer has COM2 enabled, but you are not using this port for a modem or a serial connection, you can disable it. You can do this either in your computer's BIOS or by rearranging jumper connectors on your computer's motherboard or peripheral card. The same is true of any other COM port that is available to be freed up.

Newer computers allow you to disable the serial device in the computer's BIOS. You'll need to restart Windows and press the designated key during power-on self-test to enter the BIOS setup program. Then navigate within the setup menus to find the menu in which you can disable the serial ports. The designated key and the menu structure are different for every BIOS.

If you have an older computer or a card that is configured with jumpers, you'll need to refer to the manual to correctly change the jumper settings.

After you disable the serial port, you'll want to remove it from your Device Manager. Restart Windows after making the changes in your BIOS or jumpers, and press Win+Pause/Break (or right-click the My Computer icon and click Properties). Click the Device Manager, highlight the disabled communications port under the Ports (COM & LPT) branch, and click the Remove button (see Figure 38-1). The port that you have disabled should be marked with a yellow exclamation point.

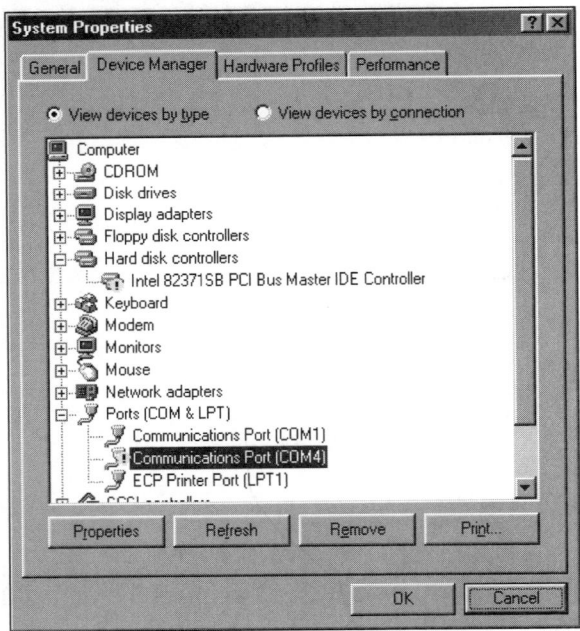

Figure 38-1: In this example, COM4 is the one we want to remove. Note the yellow exclamation point.

Some motherboards and BIOSes (in particular AMI BIOSes) still let Windows see the serial ports even if they have been disabled in the BIOS. In these cases, our recommendations won't work.

If your computer has a dual PCI IDE controller used to control only one device (most likely your hard disk), then it is possible to free up one half of the dual controller and thereby free up interrupt 15. You will need to do this in your computer's BIOS.

Be sure that your computer isn't using the second IDE controller. While your hard disk may be on the first controller, your CD-ROM drive could be on the second. If it is, don't do this. The Device Manager won't tell you directly, nor will Microsoft System Information. You'll have to check in your computer's BIOS and use your hardware manuals.

After you disable the second controller in your computer's BIOS, restart Windows and go to your Device Manager. The Secondary IDE controller will be marked with a yellow exclamation point. Highlight the device and click the Remove button. Click OK.

Finally, you can free up interrupt 7 (or perhaps interrupt 5) by disabling LPT1, your parallel port (again, in your computer's BIOS or with jumpers), and then removing it from the Device Manager. You'll be able to do this and still print to your printer if your parallel port hardware supports ECP (see the following steps).

STEPS

Freeing Up IRQ 7 or IRQ 5

Step 1.   Start your computer. During the power-on self test, press the designated key to enter your BIOS setup. Disable your LPT1 parallel port. Exit the BIOS setup, saving your changes.

Step 2.   Start Windows. Press Win+Pause/Break (or right-click My Computer and click Properties). Click the Device Manager tab. Click the plus sign next to Ports (COM & LPT) and highlight your LPT1 port. Click the Remove button, and click OK.

Step 3.   Click Start ➪ Shut Down ➪ Shut Down ➪ OK.

Step 4.   Turn off your computer and install the device that is configured to use IRQ 7 (or IRQ 5).

Step 5.   Turn on your computer, and let Windows install the new device, using drivers either from the Windows CD-ROM or from the device manufacturer's diskettes. Go to the Device Manager and make sure that the device is installed. If it is, shut down Windows.

Step 6.   Reenable LPT1 in your BIOS before restarting Windows. Windows should automatically find the LPT port when it restarts.

Step 7.   Check in the Device Manager to see if Windows indicates a conflict. Even if there is an exclamation mark next to the LPT1 device, it may work fine.

Continued

Step 8. If your parallel port can operate as an ECP port, you can define it to take advantage of these characteristics, and then remove the conflicting LPT1 port. Use the Add New Hardware control panel applet to manually add the ECP port, and then follow the remaining steps.

Step 9. Using the Device Manager, click the LPT1 port, click the Properties button, click the Resources tab, and write down the Input/Output Range memory values. Click Cancel, and then remove the original LPT1 device by clicking the Remove button and OK while the LPT1 port is highlighted.

Step 10. Click the ECP port in the Device Manager, click the Properties button, and click the Resources tab. Clear the "Use automatic settings" checkbox, and display the "Setting based on" field. Choose a setting (if possible) that matches the previous LPT1 Input/Output Range with no Interrupt Request. Click OK.

Step 11. Shut down Windows and restart. Windows may redetect the LPT1 port. If this happens, you can most likely ignore the yellow exclamation point in your Device Manager regarding the LPT1 port.

With Plug and Play BIOSes, other devices may grab interrupts before your newly installed device has a chance to get the ones that you just freed up. That's fine; there should then be others available and you can use them.

Thanks to John Helms for help with many of these steps.

Need to Share an Interrupt, but Can't?

Secret

If you find that you can't get your IRQ steering to work with your PCI bus, it may be because you don't have the latest patch for your VIA chip set. Of course, this is only true if your motherboard uses the VIA chip set.

The symptom: IRQ steering is disabled, even though the Use IRQ Steering checkbox is marked in the PCI Bus Properties dialog box (see Figure 38-2). To get to this dialog box, press Win+Pause/Break (or right-click My Computer and click Properties), click the Device Manager tab, scroll down to System Devices, open up this branch, double-click PCI Bus, and click the IRQ Steering tab.

If the "Get IRQ Table from Real Mode PCIBIOS 2.1 call" checkbox is dim and clear (it is not in this figure), you may be able to fix this with the patch that corrects the IRQ routing table. You can use Sandra (see "Add to Your System

Info" in Chapter 23) to check if you have the VIA chip set. Click the Mainboard Information icon, and then scroll down to Chipset Information.

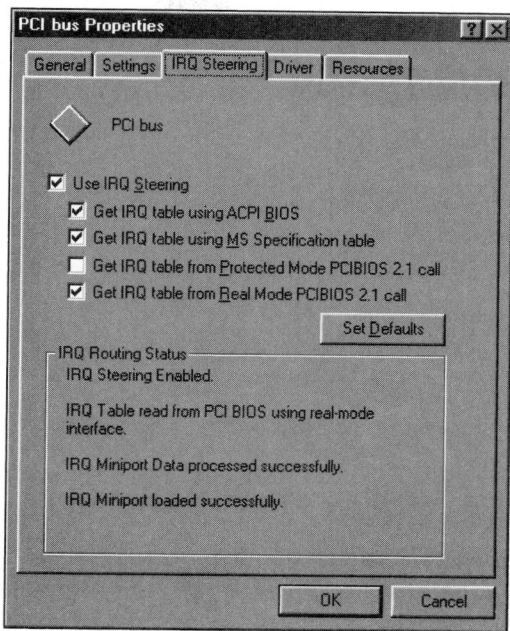

Figure 38-2: The IRQ Steering tab of the PCI Bus Properties dialog box. Use IRQ Steering has been marked.

Download the VIA IRQ routing miniport driver from http://www.via.com. tw/drivers/.

Thanks to Atilla Szabo for pointing out this secret.

Disable PCI Interrupt Steering

If you have two PCI devices that are having a conflict, you may have to disable PCI interrupt steering to work out the problem. To do this, take these steps:

STEPS

Disabling PCI Interrupt Steering

Step 1.   Press Win+Pause/Break (or right-click My Computer and click Properties). Click the Device Manager tab.

Continued

STEPS

Disabling PCI Interrupt Steering *(continued)*

Step 2. Double-click System Devices at the bottom of the Device Manager and then double-click PCI Bus. Click the IRQ Steering tab.

Step 3. Clear the Use IRQ Steering checkbox (see Figure 38-3).

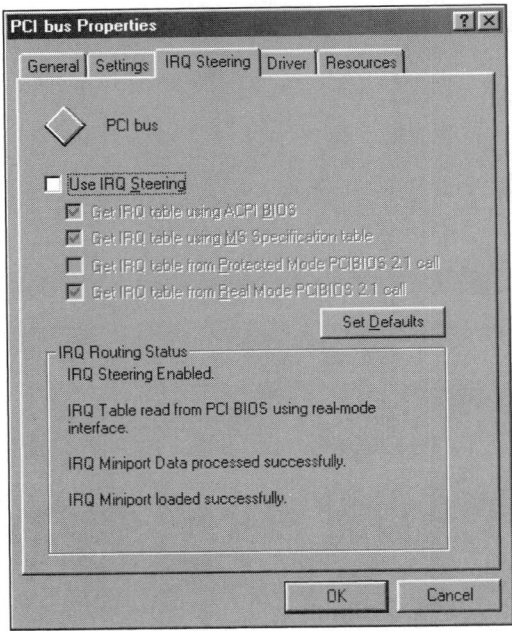

Figure 38-3: The IRQ Steering tab of the PCI Bus Properties dialog box. The first checkbox is the one to clear in this instance.

Step 4. Click OK, and then click Yes to restart your computer and have this new setting take hold.

You may find that you also have to disable PCI steering in your computer's BIOS. Press the indicated key during the power-on self-test to enter your BIOS setup program, and then hunt around for the option that lets you disable it (this will vary depending on your BIOS).

PCI steering only works if you have a mixture of PCI devices — some Plug and Play, and some not. PCI steering sits in front of the non-Plug and Play PCI device and handles requests for device configuration values. This stops a

Plug and Play PCI device from stealing an interrupt that a non-Plug and Play PCI device must use. It sort of makes non-Plug and Play devices look like Plug and Play devices to the lower-level Windows device drivers.

PCI steering doesn't affect interrupt sharing. If the PCI devices can share interrupts, PCI steering supports it.

You still have to have a sufficient number of interrupts in your computer to support all of your devices, PCI or not. You'll need to check the Device Manager to determine what available interrupts you have, and then make changes in your BIOS or other areas, as described in the previous section.

You can find out more about this issue by viewing "How to Disable PCI BIS IRQ Steering in Windows" at http://support.microsoft.com/support/kb/articles/q182/6/28.asp. Also, click *Interrupts* or *Interrupt sharing on PCI-devices* in the "Windows Networking FAQ" at http://www.helmig.com/j_helmig/faq.htm.

Thanks to Jeff Richards for insights on these issues.

Get Enough Interrupts for Your PCI Cards

Secret

If you have only PCI cards, and not ISA cards, you want to be sure that all the interrupts are available to your PCI bus. If you have only Plug and Play PCI cards, you'll have no need for PCI steering. Make sure that your BIOS allocates all of the available interrupts to your PCI bus. This prevents them from being used by Plug and Play ISA cards (we are assuming you don't have any).

You'll have to go to your Plug and Play BIOS setup by pressing the indicated key during the power-on self-test. Navigate through the menus until you find the interrupt setup screen that enables you to nominate which interrupts are assigned to the PCI bus.

Secret

After you have configured your Plug and Play BIOS, install one PCI card at a time, and then confirm in the Device Manager that an interrupt has been assigned to the card. If you have two PCI cards that allow for interrupt sharing, install them last if you have only one interrupt left.

Secret

If any of your PCI cards are not Plug and Play, you may need to enable PCI steering. Use the steps in the previous section to enable PCI steering, marking the Use IRQ Steering checkbox instead of clearing it. If none of your PCI cards will share an interrupt, install your non-Plug and Play PCI cards last, and you won't have to enable PCI steering. If you have PCI cards that can share interrupts, and you have non-Plug and Play PCI cards, you will have to enable PCI steering.

Thanks to Jeff Richards for help with these secrets.

USB

The Universal Serial Bus isn't universal yet, but it's available on most new computers.

Turn Off USB if You Don't Use It

If you don't have a USB (Universal Serial Bus) device attached to your computer, you can turn off USB support in your BIOS and save the time required to load the USB drivers in Windows. You'll have to get to your BIOS setup menu before Windows starts (hold down the indicated key during the power-on self test), and then find the USB IRQ setup and disable it.

If later you decide to install a USB device, enable this feature in your computer's BIOS. Windows will then automatically detect and install USB functionality.

To see if you have a USB port, open your Device Manager and see if the Universal Serial Bus Controller is listed under Computer.

Thanks to David Bradford for pointing us toward this tip.

Want to know more about the Universal Serial Bus? Check out the USB Web site at http://www.usb.org.

USB – Adding on to Get Add-ons

Most computers produced since late in 1998 include a Universal Serial Bus port. Some include two. These ports provide a new way to connect a device to your computer, and may allow you to connect a device without having to use one of the limited IRQs.

The USB port will probably allow you to connect only one device, not the vaunted 127. If you want to connect more than one device to the USB port, the device either has to incorporate a USB hub (most don't) or you'll have to purchase a USB hub.

The power provided from the computer's USB port will probably not be enough to support more than one device. If you want to add multiple devices, make sure that the hub you purchase can be powered by an AC adapter.

You'll find an example of such a hub at http://usb.belkin.com/html products.html.

Tip

You should also confirm that your computer's BIOS fully supports USB peripherals. Some computers that include USB ports don't have a BIOS that recognizes USB peripherals — including keyboards and mice — on startup. You can go to the support area of your computer manufacturer's Web site to check on its BIOS updates.

Thanks to Bob O'Donnell at InfoWorld for these words of caution.

Debug Your Universal Serial Bus

The Universal Serial Bus Viewer is a part of the *Windows Resource Sampler Kit*, which you'll find on your Windows CD-ROM. If you've installed all the applets, then you can go to the Microsoft Management Console to find the Universal Serial Bus Viewer.

Click Start ⇨ Programs ⇨ Windows Resource Kit ⇨ Tools Management Console. In the left pane of the Microsoft Management Console, expand Windows Resource Kit Tools Sampler, then Tool Categories, and then Diagnostics and Troubleshooting. Double-click USB Viewer in the right pane.

Otherwise, you'll find the Universal Serial Bus Viewer under \tools\reskit\ diagnose\usbview.exe on the Windows CD-ROM. You can run it from there or right-drag and drop a copy of it to wherever you like.

If you have an early version of the Intel 82371SB PCI to USB universal host controller chip set, you may have problems with your USB port. If this is the case, you're going to need an update to your motherboard.

STEPS

Determining Whether You Have an Early Chip Set

Step 1. Press Win+Pause/Break (or right-click My Computer and click Properties). Click the Device Manager tab.

Step 2. Double-click the Universal Serial Bus Controller.

Step 3. Double-click Intel 82371SB PCI to USB Universal Host Controller, and then click the General tab.

Step 4. If the Hardware Version field states that the USB controller is 000, then you definitely have the early version of the chip set. Problems have also been noted with version 001.

Other Hardware Issues

We came up with a few other hardware matters that deserve mention.

Is Your Computer Compatible with Windows Me?

To find out, turn to the Windows compatibility list at Microsoft's Web site at http://www.microsoft.com/hwtest/hcl/. Click the Advanced link, clear all of the checkboxes under Operating System but the one for Windows Me, and click the Search button.

Thanks to Scott Schnoll for pointing us toward this site.

GenuineIntel?

Secret

Ever wonder what was up with the single word *GenuineIntel* in the General tab of your System Properties dialog box (right-click My Computer, click Properties)? Couldn't they have put a space between *Genuine* and *Intel*? Maybe there is a secret code?

To find out if there is, take these steps:

STEPS

Checking Out Your Processor

Step 1. Open your Registry editor and navigate to HKEY_LOCAL_MACHINE\ hardware\ DESCRIPTION\ System\ CentralProcessor\ 0.

Step 2. Double-click VendorIdentifier in the right pane of the Registry Editor to display the Edit String dialog box and put a space between *Genuine* and *Intel*, as shown in Figure 38-4. Click OK, and close the Registry Editor.

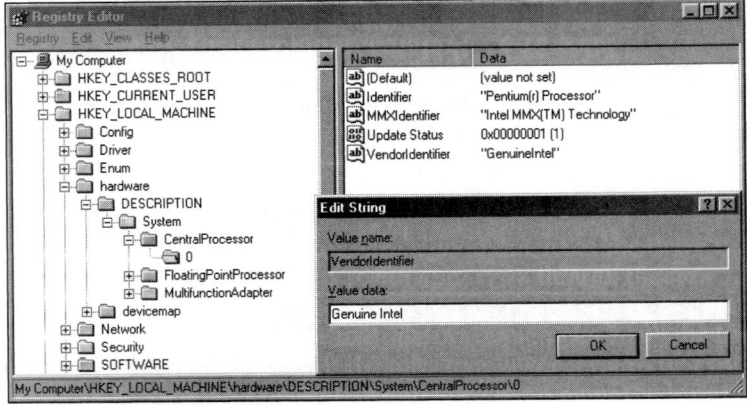

Figure 38-4: Edit the "Value data" field to add a space.

Step 3. Right-click My Computer, click Properties, and notice that if you have an Intel processor (something similar appears for other processors), you will see additional information under Genuine Intel, such as "x86 Family 5 Model 12 Stepping 12."

The next time you restart Windows, this reverts to GenuineIntel, and the additional information disappears. Strange.

Thanks to Anthony Kinyon for help with this secret.

Basic BIOS Info from Your Registry

Secret

Windows stores your BIOS name, version, and date in your registry. If you don't see this information during the power-on self test, you can get to it by opening your Registry Editor and navigating to HKEY_LOCAL_MACHINE\ Enum\ Root\ *PNP0C01\ 0000, as shown in Figure 38-5.

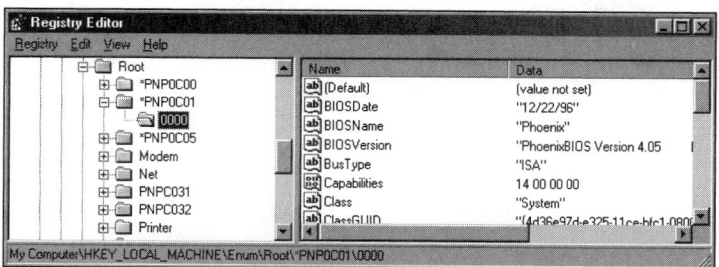

Figure 38-5: This branch of the registry lists basic information about your BIOS in the right pane.

Add More Memory

If you have empty memory sockets on your motherboard, you can add additional memory—SIMMs or DIMMs—to your computer. The first thing you want to do is take a peek at your motherboard and confirm that you do have some empty memory sockets. If you don't know what they look like, pull out the manual for your computer (or any computer's manual) or check out the support pages at your computer manufacturer's Web site. If neither of these resources is available, review the diagram of a (typical) motherboard at http://support.micronpc.com/faq/mbdfaq/images/ts00838.html. (The memory sockets are labeled SIMM BANKS in the diagram.)

Most computers built in the last few years use either SIMM modules (single inline memory modules) or DIMM modules (dual inline memory modules). Check out your computer's manual to see which kind of memory modules you have in your computer.

You also need to know what type of memory chips you have on the modules — EDO, FPM, and so on — and whether they are nonparity checking (very likely) or parity checking (maybe in a server). You can use Sandra (see "Add to Your System Info" in Chapter 23) if you can't find out from your manuals. In Sandra, click Mainboard Information, and scroll down to Supported Memory Types to see if you have SIMM or DIMM modules, as shown in Figure 38-6. Scroll further down to Logical Memory Banks to see what type of memory you have installed.

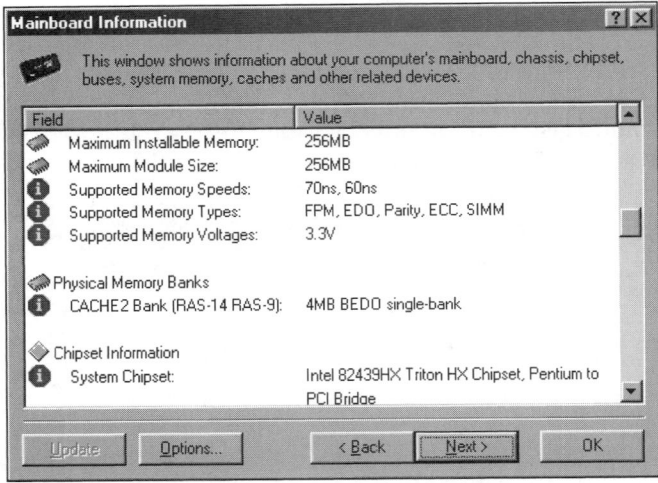

Figure 38-6: The computer in this example uses SIMM modules.

Your computer may also display your memory chip type during the power-on self-test. You may be able to see it then, and you might be able to press the Pause/Break key to pause the display and confirm what it says.

Next, you need to know how much memory you can install and how much you are willing to pay for. If you have a couple of banks for SIMM sockets available, you will probably be able to install anywhere from 8MB (what's the point) to 64MB (whoa, big fella) of memory. Check your computer manual for a chart of possible memory sizes and combinations.

Now, if you have a couple of banks of memory sockets available, you know your memory type and module type, and you know how much you can install, it's time to spec out the memory modules to purchase. You don't necessarily need to purchase the memory from your computer vendor, unless you want to put a little extra change in their pocket.

For example, SIMMs are for the most part packaged in 72-pin modules (although older computers may use 30-pin SIMMs) using EDO nonparity-checking chips. A single module at 16MB would be labeled 4×32. The 4 stands for 4×4, in other words 16MB. The 32 means non-parity-checking memory. The other option would be 36, which stands for parity-checking memory. You can read more about this nomenclature as it is applied to SIMMs and DIMMs at Micron's general memory explanation site, http://support.micronpc.com/faq/topissues/ts16531.html.

It is a rare personal computer that uses parity-checking memory. If, for example, you want to add 32MB to your computer, and you have two banks of SIMMs available, you'll want to purchase two 16MB modules (two 4×32 72-pin SIMMs), as shown in Figure 38-7.

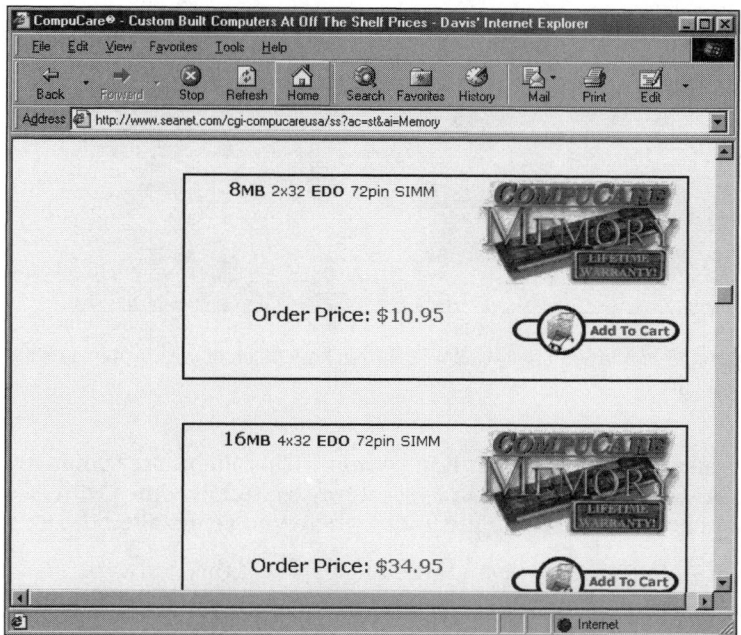

Figure 38-7: In this page from an online store, the second entry is the kind of memory we want. We want to purchase two of these.

Once you've purchased the memory modules, putting them in couldn't be easier. The main issue is keep your hands off of anything but the insulated material. Your computer manual should supply you with instructions on how to push in the new modules. If not, you can check out Micron's support site at http://support.micronpc.com/faq/mbdfaq/specs/ts00315.html.

Cool Down Your CPU

You can send software commands to your CPU to shut down portions of it that aren't doing any useful work. If those portions are idled, then they aren't producing heat. This cuts down on the overall heat production of your CPU, thereby putting less stress on the components. Laptop users may find it simply makes working with the computer in your lap more comfortable.

Waterfall Pro is a little shareware utility, shown in Figure 38-8, that sends HLT commands to idle portions of your CPU. You can find it at http://cpu. simplenet.com/leading_wintech.

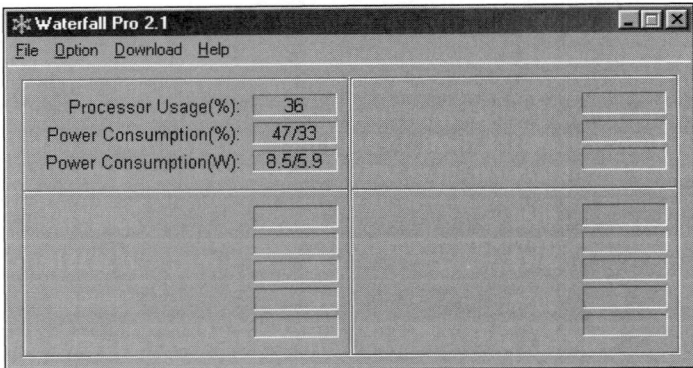

Figure 38-8: The Waterfall window tells you how much of your system is shut down to cool off.

Installing Waterfall places it in your StartUp folder. After you restart Windows 98, its icon appears in your system tray. Waterfall comes with an uninstaller. Just click Setup.exe in the folder where you've installed the utility.

Thanks to Robert Sullivan for telling us about this software.

Force Windows to Rebuild Your Hardware Driver Set

Secret

Windows may have detected your hardware incorrectly and installed the wrong driver. You may find that you have a "ghost" driver for a piece of hardware that isn't installed. You can often remove these bad hardware drivers using the Device Manager. Right-click My Computer and click Properties, click the Device Manager tab, highlight the offending hardware driver, and click the Remove button.

If this doesn't work, you can force Windows to reinstall all of your hardware drivers. This secret is for advanced users only. Don't use it unless you are willing to reinstall Windows and all of your software and drivers if it doesn't work for you.

STEPS

Reinstalling Your Hardware Drivers

Step 1. Restart your computer and hold down the Ctrl key during the power-on self-test.

Step 2. In the Windows Startup menu, choose the third menu item, Safe mode.

Step 3. Click Start ⇨ Run, type **regedit**, and press Enter.

Step 4. Navigate in your Registry to HKEY_LOCAL_MACHINE, right-click the Enum folder, as shown in Figure 38-9, and click Delete. Close the Registry Editor.

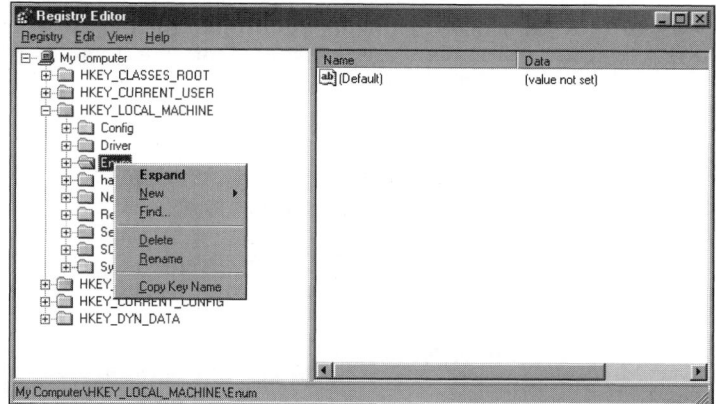

Figure 38-9: Delete the Enum folder from the Registry Editor.

Step 5. Click Start ⇨ Shut Down ⇨ Restart ⇨ OK.

Step 6. Windows should automatically detect your hardware and rebuild the Enumeration tables. If it does not, click Start ⇨ Settings ⇨ Control Panel ⇨ Add New Hardware ⇨ Next ⇨ Next. Let Windows search for all the hardware and install the correct drivers.

Thanks to Serge Paquin for help with this secret.

Wake Up Your SCSI Devices

If you forget to turn on SCSI devices such as your scanner or Zip drive before you start Windows, there's no need to do a restart to get Windows to detect the devices. After you turn them on, hold down the Alt key as you click My Computer, click the Device Manager tab, and click the Refresh button. Windows will now detect your devices.

Thanks to Bill Schneider for pointing out this tip.

Real Information Online about Computer Hardware and Software

No Web site does it all, and you have to search around the Web to get answers to your specific questions. We did find one site though, PC Mechanic, which concentrates on the kinds of questions that people building or buying personal computers need to ask. The site contains lots of good information about drive types (buy EDI and forget SCSI), memory, motherboards, video cards, networking, and monitors. It's definitely geared toward the buyer who wants to specify every component in his or her new purchase.

PC Mechanic also has a nice section on setting up a small network and connecting the network to the Internet. You'll find it at http://www.pcmech.com. The networking article starts at http://www.pcmech.com/networking.htm.

Behind the Dell Inspiron

One of the great things about the Web is that computer users can put up their own sites and tell the world about the computers that they use. If there is a newsgroup to help gather the impressions of a wide range of users of a particular model, the Web site author can provide a great resource to everyone using that computer by interacting frequently with the newsgroup. Turns out, this kind of Web site is also very useful for people looking to buy a computer.

If you are looking at a particular model, use the search engines to find Web sites that specialize in the computer model that you are interested in. Chris Pirillo at http://www.lockergnome.com pointed out a great site that deals with the Dell Inspiron portable. You'll find it at http://www.edgeworld.com/notebook/i7main.htm.

Summary

There is hardware, and then there are hardware drivers. Sometimes they just don't get along.

▶ How to get the fonts back when they've all gone away.

▶ Install only Plug and Play PCI cards — dealing with PCI steering and interrupt sharing.

▶ USB, still on the bleeding edge.

▶ Figure out what kind of memory to add to your computer.

▶ Force Windows to recognize your hardware.

▶ Find out more about your computer online.

Chapter 39

Configuring Memory

In This Chapter

Memory is an issue of our common DOS heritage. If you use DOS programs that demand large amounts of conventional memory or expanded memory (DOS games perhaps?) you will do well to study this chapter. We discuss:

▶ Determining whether you need to be concerned about memory

▶ The six most important memory issues

▶ Getting more conventional memory for your DOS programs

▶ Using Mem to see your memory use

Why Worry About Memory?

Why should end users have to be concerned about the issue of how memory is configured or used on their computer? After all, you should be able to just buy enough memory to run your programs and leave it at that. The fact that it hasn't been that way has made Windows just that much more difficult to use.

Windows Me does a significantly better job of dealing with memory issues than Windows 95 did. Most of the fixes are under the surface, and you won't have to worry about them.

But if you are losing memory and performance under Windows Me, read on.

When to Worry About Memory

There are six major memory issues with Windows:

■ Configuring your memory so you can run DOS programs that require large amounts of conventional memory and/or expanded memory

■ Having enough hard disk space so the Windows swap area for virtual memory is large enough to handle all your active applications as well as the Windows components

■ Running out of Windows resources when you have a number of Windows applications open

- Windows applications that can (and often do) spring memory leaks, eating up resources until they are all gone

- Windows programs that use significant amounts of conventional memory, which is always limited

- Unrecognized memory address conflicts between video and network cards in upper memory

In this chapter, we devote several pages to concentrating on the first issue, configuring memory for running DOS programs. So let's take a minute look at the other issues first.

Hard Disk Space for Virtual Memory

To get the full story on virtual memory, turn to "Managing Your Swap Space" in Chapter 37. Windows uses your hard disk to "swap" programs and data out of RAM when it needs this memory to accomplish your more pressing tasks. Unlike previous versions of Windows, Windows Me doesn't ask you to create a "permanent swap file" for maximum performance. It handles swapping automatically.

It is a very good idea to let Windows have plenty of room on your fastest hard disk for swap space. Depending on the amount of RAM that you have (more RAM calls for more hard disk swap space — see "Setting Disk-Cache Parameters" in Chapter 37), it is best to have at least 20MB of unused hard disk space available.

If you don't have enough hard disk space and the swap file takes up every bit of it, you will get an error message about not being able to write User.dat, a file that is part of the registry. Windows produces information about the state of the machine dynamically and every so often writes it out to User.dat in the background. If you don't have enough hard disk space, it can't write the information to disk.

Again, turn to "Managing Your Swap Space" in Chapter 37 for more information on swap space.

Windows Resources

Old versions of Windows, such as Windows 3.1x, often ran out of resources and displayed error messages that blamed limited memory as the problem. This was very frustrating to users who had just purchased multiple megabytes of memory and were quite willing to yell back at their machines that they had plenty of "memory."

If you received such a message when using Windows, what was really happening was that one of your applications asked for more system resources and Windows ran out of them. You may have had plenty of unused memory (RAM) and plenty of swap space left, but you just couldn't use them because of a limitation in the ability of Windows to assign system resources.

Resources are essentially lists (referred to as *heaps*) of memory. The lengths of the lists under Windows 3.1*x* were quite small. The lists can be much longer with Windows Me. The lists point to areas of memory where user interface elements (and other items) are stored — things like dialog boxes, windows, and so on.

System resources under Windows 3.1*x* employed four 16-bit heaps. Three of the heaps were part of the User resource, which managed the user interface portion of Windows. One was the Graphic Device Interface (GDI) resource, which managed drawing objects to the screen. Because these lists were 16-bit heaps, they could address only 64K of memory each — a total of 256K of memory to store the objects used in the user interface and displayed on your screen.

If one of your applications asked Windows 3.1*x* for more objects and one of the heaps had already allocated all the memory on its list, Windows generated the out-of-memory message.

Windows 95 greatly expanded the lists for the GDI and User resource areas. George Moore from Microsoft has reported that, "In addition to all of the things in User and GDI that were moved to the 32-bit heap, Device Contexts and Logical Font structures in GDI are moved to the 32-bit heap. This means that the old system-wide limit on the number of Device Contexts has been raised from around 150–200 to over 10,000. In addition, you can now also easily load many, many more TrueType fonts than you ever could under Windows 3.1."

In Windows Me and 9*x*, the three heaps in User have been replaced by one 32-bit heap with the ability to address 2GB of memory — probably enough for the next couple of years. Microsoft maintained the 16-bit heap for the GDI for compatibility reasons. Essentially, some programs managed this heap directly without going through the Windows application program interfaces (APIs), and changing it to a 32-bit heap would break these programs. Some of the elements that were in the GDI heap have been moved to the 32-bit User heap, as George Moore points out.

Table 39-1 shows how system-wide resources have increased in Windows Me.

Table 39-1   System-Wide Resources Then and Now

Resource	Windows 3.1	Windows Me
Window/menu handles	About 299	32K (each)
Timers	32	Unlimited
Listbox items (per listbox)	8K	32K
Listbox data (per listbox)	64K	Unlimited
Edit control data (per control)	64K	Unlimited
Regions	All in 64K	Unlimited
Physical pens, brushes, and so on	All in 64K	Unlimited
Logical fonts	All in 64K	750–800
Installed fonts	250–300	1,000
Device contexts	200 (best case)	16K

16-bit Windows 3.1x Programs Spring Memory Leaks

Many 16-bit applications, written for Windows 3.1x, had the unfortunate habit of asking for system resources and then not giving them back after they quit. The longer you ran Windows 3.1x, the fewer resources you had until you finally ran out of resources and were forced to start Windows again.

These same programs will have the same problems running under Windows Me, but Windows Me has two defenses. First, with greater system resources, the problems will show up less frequently. Second, Windows Me cleans up after Win-16 applications (those written for Windows 3.1x), making sure that the resources they were allocated get back in the common pool.

It can do this only after all Win-16 applications (excluding those that have been specifically tagged as "Windows 98-aware") have quit. Windows must wait to clean up resources because Win-16 applications can share the same resources. Therefore, you have to be sure that you quit all your old Win-16 applications every now and then to get the resources back.

Windows Me always cleans up the resources used by today's 32-bit applications, even if they don't do it properly themselves.

Piggy Windows Programs

Some Windows programs, 16-bit drivers, and even 32-bit protected-mode video drivers use up lots of conventional memory. If you tried to run a couple of these oinkers, you would soon see the error message saying you were out of memory when, again, you had plenty of memory. In this case, you ran out of conventional memory.

The problem here is poor programming. The writers most likely included fixed memory segments in their programs, which under Windows 3.1*x* have to be allocated out of the limited pool of 640K of conventional memory. Microsoft has fixed most of this problem in Windows Me and 98 by loading these structures in extended memory instead of conventional memory. Windows Me automatically provides a good deal more DOS memory than Windows 3.1*x* because it substitutes 32-bit protected-mode drivers for the 16-bit drivers that work with Windows 3.1*x*. These 32-bit drivers reside in extended memory. In many cases, you have to check your `Config.sys` and `Autoexec.bat` files, and if you haven't done so yet, remark out the 16-bit drivers.

Under Windows Me, these piggy programs will have more conventional memory available to them. Given that portions of the programs that were previously loaded in conventional memory are now loaded in extended memory, they should be less of a problem than under Windows 3.1*x*. You should upgrade your applications if this continues to be a problem for you. Just because the program is a newer version doesn't mean its authors have fixed the problem.

In this chapter, we concentrate on increasing conventional memory for DOS programs that require much more than even these piggy Windows programs, although any increases in conventional memory will also help these Windows programs work better.

Conventional Memory Tracker, a component of Microsoft's Kernel Toys, lets you find out which programs and drivers are using a portion the lower 640K of your memory. Download Kernel Toys from .

You'll find additional memory tracking tools at `http://www.windows98.com/apps/system-analyze.html`. Also see "Using Mem to Determine Available Memory" later in this chapter.

Memory Conflicts

Windows Me will correctly identify most, if not all, potential memory conflicts. These occur when a video, network, or some other card uses a memory address between A000 and FFFF without revealing that address to

Windows. This used to cause serious configuration difficulties for Windows 3.1*x*. Windows Me is much better at spotting these cards and not using the forbidden memory addresses.

The Device Manager will highlight any detected memory-use conflicts. You can also use the Device Manager to reserve memory address ranges for use by hardware devices.

Memory conflicts are discussed in detail in the "Troubleshooting Memory Conflicts" section near the end of this chapter. The Device Manager is revealed in all its glory in "The Device Manager" in Chapter 36.

Fatal Exception Errors

If you receive error messages in the form of "Fatal Exception Error 0x:xxxxxxxx," it probably means that you have a bad physical memory chip in your computer. The first thing you can do to try to get rid of these errors is to turn off your external (L2) cache. You can often do this by restarting your computer and pressing a key when prompted to bring up your BIOS setup screen. You then need to follow the instructions on your screen to see how to disable this cache.

If this is not the problem, you can also try increasing the number of memory wait states in BIOS.

If neither of these methods works, you are in the position of replacing SIMMs. You can test RAM using a RAM drive configuration. To see how, check out the following article in Microsoft's Knowledge Base: http://www.microsoft. com/kb/articles/Q142/5/46.htm.

The Short of It — More Conventional Memory

Before we go into all the gory details, we want to give you some quick tips on how to get the most conventional memory possible if you need it to run your DOS programs or if your Windows programs are running out of conventional memory.

The PC Memory Map

Before we continue with the issue of configuring memory to run DOS programs, here's an overview of how memory is structured on personal computers. If you already understand this structure, then go right to the next section.

Figure 39-1 shows a memory map that applies to most 386, 486, and Pentium computers with 16MB of memory. 16MB equals 16,384K of RAM. The first 640K of the first megabyte of RAM is addressed from 0–640K (0000h–9FFFh), and the next 384K is addressed starting at 1,024K (10000h). The rest of RAM starts at 1,408K (16000h) and continues through 16,768K (106000h).

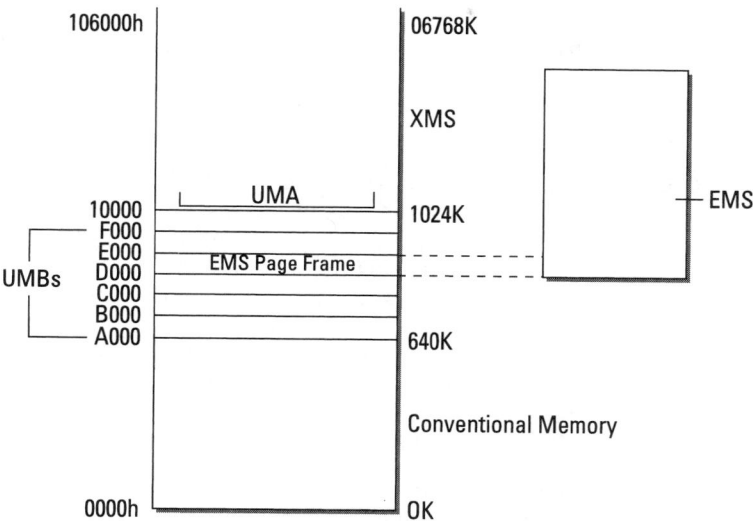

Figure 39-1: This diagram shows a PC with 16MB of RAM (640K of conventional memory plus 15,744K of extended memory = 16,384K plus 384K of UMBs, for a total of 16,768K). EMS memory is taken from the extended memory by using EMM386.exe or another third-party memory manager, or is given to DOS programs running in Windows DOS sessions by Windows 98 itself.

The Windows Device Manager uses a slightly different memory address notation than is standard for DOS and Windows 3.1x. For example, the address A000 (the notation used in DOS) is shorthand for 000A0000 (the notation used by the Device Manager).

The first notation recognizes the fact that we were concentrating our attention on a small range of memory below 1MB, so it ignores anything smaller than a paragraph (16 bytes). Therefore, it drops the three higher digits and ignores the first digit.

The second notation points out the fact that Windows can address FFFFFFFF (4,294,967,295) bytes of memory using its flat-memory, protected-mode model. All eight places are used, as in 000A0000. We use the notations interchangeably.

You should be concerned with six types of memory: *conventional memory,*
UMBs, and *extended memory* are the first three. You can load portions of DOS
into the *high memory area,* the fourth type. DOS applications also use a fifth
type of memory, *expanded memory. Virtual memory,* the sixth, is a combination of RAM and swap space on your hard disk.

- *Conventional memory* is the first 640K of memory in your PC. DOS
  applications run in this memory. Windows also uses this memory when
  it switches to V86 mode in order to access some DOS device drivers
  and PC hardware. Some Windows programs use significant amounts of
  conventional memory. Windows can put some (or all) of its translation
  buffers in conventional memory.

- *UMBs* (upper memory blocks) are memory addresses where hardware
  devices and software drivers may be accessed by DOS and Windows.
  Exactly 384K of memory addresses are reserved for UMBs, and it is
  always located just above the first 640K of conventional memory. Much
  of this memory can't be used to relocate 16-bit drivers and DOS TSRs
  from conventional memory, because it is used by the ROM on your
  video card and/or network card and the system ROM. The 64K EMS
  page frame, if any, is located here. The 16-bit drivers and DOS TSRs
  can use UMBs if the parameter *ram* or *noems* is present after EMM386.
  exe in your Config.sys file.

- *Extended memory* (also called XMS, for eXtended Memory Specification)
  is the memory above conventional memory and the UMBs. It begins at
  the 1MB line, which is the same as 1,024K (640K plus 384K). If you have
  16MB of RAM in your system, the first 640K is conventional memory, and
  the rest begins at the 1,024K line and is counted upward from there.

- The *high memory area* (HMA) is the first 64K of extended memory (minus
  16 bytes), and it is used by DOS, Windows, and a few other programs. No
  more than one program can be loaded into HMA, which is typically a part
  of DOS. Loading DOS in HMA saves about 46K in conventional memory.
  The DOS buffers also get loaded here.

- *Expanded memory* (also called EMS, for Expanded Memory Specification)
  is a special type of memory that requires at least 64K of address space
  in the UMBs. On a 386 and higher, expanded memory is usually provided
  by an expanded memory manager, a program that converts extended to
  expanded memory as required. Expanded memory requires a 64K page
  frame somewhere below the 1MB line in order to function.

- *Virtual memory* is the combination of RAM that can be addressed by
  Windows and the dynamic swap file space on your hard disk. Windows
  manages this combined memory to enable you to load a significant number
  of applications at once without running out of physical (RAM) memory. The
  programs that are actually doing something are in RAM, while those sitting
  idly are swapped to the hard disk.

UMBs from A to F

You can think of the 384K of UMBs as six separate areas, each of which is 64K in size. These six blocks are known as A, B, C, D, E, and F. This is because the address of the first byte of memory in the A block is A000 (pronounced "A thousand") in hexadecimal numbering.

The A block is used for the addresses of the RAM on your VGA or higher video board. When the board is in graphics mode (as opposed to text mode), the 64K of address space at A000 is used by Windows to write information into the RAM on the board. No matter how much RAM is physically installed on the board, the same 64K block is used to write to all video memory.

The B block is used for two purposes. The first 32K, which begins at B000, is used when a VGA or higher resolution video board is in monochrome graphics mode. These memory addresses would be used, for example, if you were using a monochrome monitor and the Windows VGA monochrome driver. The second 32K, from B800 to C000, is used for VGA or higher text mode. A portion of this address space is used when you are at a DOS prompt and type a command. The DOS output is written to B800, where it appears on your screen as text characters.

The C block is used for the read-only memory (ROM) chip that is present on all VGA and higher video adapters. This chip always begins using address spaces at C000. From that point, the chip may claim 16K, 24K, or more, depending on the complexity of the adapter and how many video modes it supports.

The D block has no reserved function, but it is often claimed by memory managers for the 64K page frame required to use expanded memory.

The E block is often unused on AT- and EISA-bus machines, but it is usually claimed by machines with a Micro Channel Architecture (MCA) bus. MCA machines include a unique set of ROM chips that reside at addresses starting at E000 and continue toward F000. These chips contain instructions in ROM that are used when OS/2 is running. For those people who are not using OS/2, many memory managers can claim these addresses for other purposes.

Finally, the F000 block is reserved on all PCs for the ROM chips that hold the basic input-output system (BIOS) — instructions that run low-level functions, such as writing to disk drives.

Knowing the purpose of each UMB can help you claim more conventional memory for both Windows and DOS applications running under Windows.

Stack Pages

In Brian's Windows Manager column for *InfoWorld Magazine* back in 1994, he dealt thoroughly with a mysterious setting called MaxBPs=768. This setting, added to the [386Enh] section of a Windows 3.1 System.ini file, reduced crashes by setting aside an extra 4K of extended memory for Windows "break points" or BPs.

Windows Me, by contrast, dynamically allocates break points, which are 10-byte chunks of memory used to track virtual device drivers (VxDs). As VxDs use more memory, Windows Me simply assigns more memory to break points as needed. The MaxBPs line, therefore, is no longer necessary in Windows Me.

The MaxBPs=768 setting does still work in Windows 3.11 and Windows for Workgroups 3.11, but it is not needed in Windows Me.

Windows Me has its own setting to deal with a similar but different kind of program crash. This setting deals exclusively with 32-bit software.

The problem that afflicts 32-bit software affects stack pages. *Stack pages* are 4K blocks of memory that Windows sets aside for 32-bit device drivers to use as a stack. (A *stack*, in this case, refers to a scratch area of memory used by programs. This entire discussion of stack pages, by the way, is unrelated to the Stacks= command found in Config.sys, which is used by 16-bit DOS drivers.)

If a 32-bit device driver exceeds 4K of memory for its stack, the program causes an error, but Windows can recover. This is because Windows, by default, maintains two extra memory pages known as *spare stack pages*.

If you have a bug-ridden device driver, you may get the following error message:

```
There are no spare stack pages. It may be necessary to increase the
setting of "MinSPs" in System.ini to prevent possible stack faults.
There are currently 2 SPs allocated.
```

The typical user, facing this message, could be forgiven for having a blank look. What's a "MinSPs" and what should it be increased to? Looking in Windows doesn't reveal anything that looks like "MinSPs."

The solution is to add a MinSPs (minimum stack pages) line to the [386Enh] section of your System.ini. Start with a value of 4, which doubles the spare stack pages, and restart Windows. If that value doesn't resolve the problem, try 6, and then 8. Each spare stack page consumes 4K of extended memory.

Add the setting to your System.ini file like this:

```
[386Enh]
; Increases stack pages from 2 to 4.
MinSPs=4
```

You can make this change using the System Configuration Utility.

STEPS

Editing Your System.ini File

Step 1. Click Start ⇨ Programs ⇨ Accessories ⇨ System Tools ⇨ System Information.

Step 2. Click Tools ⇨ System Configuration Utility.

Step 3. Click the System.ini tab, highlight [386Enh], and click the New button.

Step 4. Type **MinSPs=4**. Click OK.

Step 5. Click Start ⇨ Shut Down ⇨ Restart ⇨ OK to have the changes take effect.

How Windows Uses Upper Memory

Windows looks for space in UMBs for two different purposes:

■ It places an expanded memory page frame, 64K in size, in an unused area above 640K.

■ Windows claims another area, approximately 16K in size, for DOS translation buffers. These buffers are used by Windows to transfer data to and from any real-mode devices you may still have, such as disk drives. If there is not enough space left in UMBs, Windows takes the equivalent amount of space out of conventional memory.

Windows doesn't need any separate memory manager to accomplish these tasks. It has its own built-in expanded and UMB memory manager.

Memory for DOS Programs

You can run DOS programs in a Windows DOS session after Windows starts. Windows provides each DOS program in a Windows DOS session with a "virtual machine." The memory available to the virtual machine is determined by settings in the program's Properties sheet and elsewhere. Windows provides protected-mode drivers that are used by DOS programs running in Windows DOS sessions.

No Config.sys or Autoexec.bat

With no `Config.sys` or `Autoexec.bat` — typical of Windows Me — you ordinarily don't have any real-mode drivers or DOS TSRs. You will find that on a representative computer, a Windows DOS session has about 604K of conventional memory available.

Troubleshooting Memory Conflicts

Windows Me relocates some extended memory from addresses above 1MB to UMB addresses between 640K and 1MB. Problems occur when Windows relocates memory into a block that is also used by a device such as a video board or a network adapter. Boards such as these require some address space between 640K and 1MB to operate. Windows attempts to identify all UMBs in use, but this attempt may not always be successful.

You can check for memory conflicts between different devices by using the Device Manager. Windows highlights known conflicts in the Device Manager.

STEPS

Checking for Memory Conflicts

Step 1. Click the Start button, point to Settings, and then click Control Panel.

Step 2. Click the System icon in the Control Panel. Click the Device Manager tab in the System Properties dialog box.

Step 3. At the top of the tree, Computer should be highlighted. If not, highlight it.

Step 4. Click the Properties button to display the View Resources tab of the Computer Properties dialog box.

Any memory conflicts that Windows detects are displayed in this dialog box.

The addresses between 640K and 1MB that Windows relocates memory into are referred to in the Device Manager in hexadecimal numbering as 000A0000 to 000FFFFF.

Using Mem to Determine Available Memory

If you type **Mem /c/p** within a Windows DOS session, you see something like Table 39-2.

Table 39-2 Results Produced by Mem

Modules Using Memory Below 1MB:

Name	Total		Conventional		Upper Memory	
SYSTEM	18,736	(18K)	11,056	(11K)	7,600	(8K)
HIMEM	1,168	(1K)	1,168	(1K)	0	(0K)
EMM386	4,320	(4K)	4,320	(4K)	0	(0K)
DBLBUFF	2,976	(3K)	2,976	(3K)	0	(0K)
WIN	3,712	(4K)	3,712	(4K)	0	(0K)
vmm32	75,408	(74K)	1,392	(1K)	74,016	(72K)
COMMAND	7,456	(7K)	7,456	(7K)	0	(0K)
IFSHLP	2,864	(3K)	0	(0K)	2,864	(3K)
Free	623,024	(608K)	623,024	(608K)	0	(0K)

Memory Summary:

Type of Memory	Total	Used	Free
Conventional	655,360	32,336	623,024
Upper	84,560	84,560	0
Reserved	393,216	393,216	0
Extended (XMS)	32,421,296	140,720	32,280,576
Total memory	33,554,432	650,832	32,903,600
Total under 1MB	739,920	116,896	623,024
Largest executable program size	623,008 (608K)		
Largest free upper memory block	0 (0K)		
MS-DOS is resident in the high memory area.			

Mem tells you which programs and drivers are loaded in memory, how big they are, and where in memory they are loaded (conventional or UMBs). You can see how much conventional memory is available, the size set aside for UMBs, and how much is used. Reserved memory is the memory between 640K and 1,024K ($384 \times 1,024$ bytes).

Mem has a number of command-line parameters that alter its behavior as follows:

```
MEM {/CLASSIFY /DEBUG /FREE /MODULE modulename} {/PAGE}
```

/CLASSIFY or /C	Classifies programs by memory usage. Lists the size of programs, provides a summary of memory in use, and lists largest memory block available.
/DEBUG or /D	Displays status of all modules in memory, internal drivers, and other information.
/FREE or /F	Displays information about the amount of free memory left in both conventional and upper memory.
/MODULE or /M	Displays a detailed listing of a module's memory use. This option must be followed by the name of a module, optionally separated from /M by a colon.
/PAGE or /P	Pauses after each screenful of information.

Mem is invaluable for determining how well you are doing in placing 16-bit drivers and DOS TSRs into UMBs.

Windows and DOS Games

So let's finally get to the real point of this chapter. How can you get your games to work under Windows Me?

Many games written for PCs were originally written for DOS. This is because doing so gives the game's author access to the hardware and therefore the best chance at getting the best performance. Since the games market is highly competitive and very technically sophisticated (compared to the business market), game authors really have to know how to deal with the hardware.

Until Microsoft introduced DirectX, games that relied on Windows suffered. Game makers didn't care if their programs even worked with Windows in Windows DOS sessions. They figured that their clients would just exit Windows (or not even start it) to run the game. DOS games often have memory managers that conflict with the Windows memory-management specification.

Microsoft is of course very interested in having games work in Windows and with Windows. It is embarrassed that this "technical" part of the market considers Microsoft and Windows a stumbling block to performance.

Consequently, Microsoft programmers have worked hard to make sure that Windows Me can run DOS games in Windows DOS sessions. That doesn't mean they have always succeeded. Of course, the fact that it is more difficult to get to DOS in Windows Me than it was in Windows 3.1x makes Microsoft committed to getting DOS games to work in Windows DOS sessions.

Three lists of DOS games that have special considerations in MS-DOS under Windows are provided in the Microsoft Knowledge Base. You'll find them at:

```
http://support.microsoft.com/support/kb/articles/q132/9/94
http://support.microsoft.com/support/kb/articles/q132/9/95
http://support.microsoft.com/support/kb/articles/q132/9/96
```

Summary

When we combined previous versions of Windows with existing DOS programs, we learned to be very careful about how we configure memory. In a lot of cases, it was way too difficult.

▶ We show you how to see if you are suffering from afflictions that could be caused by memory problems.

▶ We give you a lot of ways (and show you the quick and dirty ways) to give your DOS programs more conventional memory.

▶ We also show you how to get more upper memory so you can get more conventional memory.

Chapter 40

Displays

In This Chapter

We placed all sorts of secrets here regarding one of the most important pieces of your computer: the display.

▶ How to get a bigger picture

▶ How to quickly change your display resolution and number of colors

▶ Learning the best settings for your display's refresh rate

▶ Restarting Windows isn't a requirement to change your monitor properties

▶ How to get control of your monitor and video card

▶ Using two monitors effectively

The Display

Microsoft provides some tools for manipulating your display, but they are pretty limited. We give you access to quite a few more.

Getting a Bigger Picture

Microsoft provides a nifty little magnifier with Windows Me that has the unfortunate habit of moving your Desktop icons. Takes forever to get them back into place!

You can get to the Microsoft Magnifier by clicking Start ➪ Programs ➪ Accessories ➪ Accessibility ➪ Magnifier. You may not have installed it, so it may not be there. If it's not, click Start ➪ Settings ➪ Control Panel ➪ Add/ Remove Programs ➪ Windows Setup ➪ Accessibility ➪ Details, and then mark Accessibility Tools in the Accessibility dialog box, as shown in Figure 40-1.

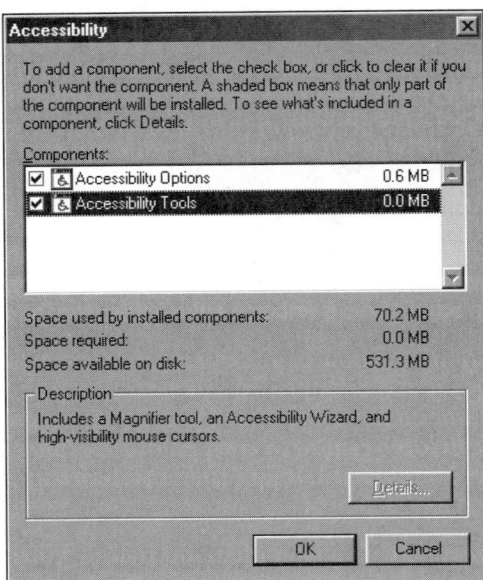

Figure 40-1: Mark the Accessibility Tools checkbox to install Microsoft Magnifier.

To start the Magnifier, click Start ⇨ Accessories ⇨ Accessibility ⇨ Magnifier. If you don't have this Start menu item, you can also start the Magnifier this way: In your Explorer, click Help ⇨ Help Topics ⇨ Index, type **mag**, double-click Magnification level, and click Click Here. Up comes the Magnifier.

One thing that is neat about the Microsoft Magnifier is that it shows the mouse pointer. Sure would be nice if it didn't take up the whole top of the screen, though.

Screen Loupe is a shareware screen magnifier that is quite a bit more advanced, although it doesn't show the mouse pointer, as you can see in Figure 40-2.

With lots of options, as shown in Figure 40-3, this clever and well-programmed little goody is for Windows spies who want to see exactly what is going on in those pixels.

Screen Loupe will let you capture a view to the Clipboard so that you can save it as a graphic, it displays your mouse pointer position even while minimized, and you can lock a view so that it is displayed while you still move the mouse pointer.

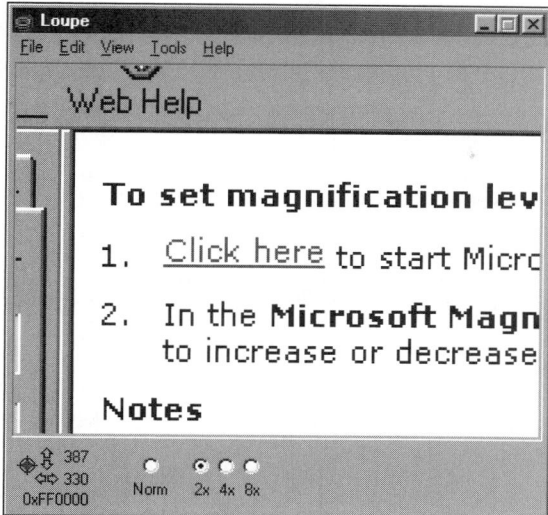

Figure 40-2: A sample Screen Loupe view, magnified to 2x

Figure 40-3: The General tab of Screen Loupe's Options dialog box shows some of its capabilities.

You can display horizontal and vertical pixel rulers at any position and length across your Desktop (see Figure 40-4) to determine the size of any visual element. You can also pop up a window of ASCII codes or Windows error codes, and display the current level of resources.

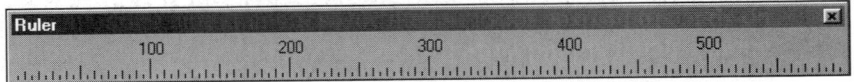

Figure 40-4: Screen Loupe lets you display a ruler like this one on your Desktop.

You'll find Screen Loupe at http://www.execpc.com/~sbd.

Quickly Change Your Display Resolution and Color Depth

The Quick Res utility that originally came with the Windows 95 PowerToys has been incorporated into the standard Windows Me package. Now you can quickly change your display resolution and color depth by clicking a system tray icon and choosing from among the values shown in Figure 40-5.

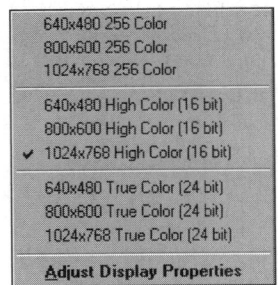

Figure 40-5: You access this context menu via the Display Settings icon.

What if you don't see this icon in your system tray? You can turn it on by taking these steps:

STEPS

Turning on the Display Settings Icon

Step 1.   Right-click the Desktop, click Properties, and click the Settings tab.

Step 2.   Click the Advanced button to display the Display Properties dialog box, shown in Figure 40-6.

Step 3.   Mark the "Show settings icon on task bar" checkbox. Click OK.

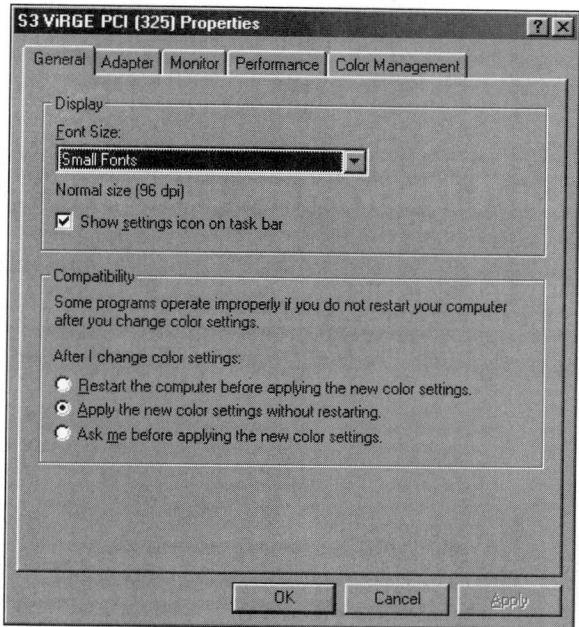

Figure 40-6: The Display Properties dialog box

Set Your Display/Video Adapter Refresh Rate

If you have a Plug and Play video adapter and monitor, then Windows can set the optimum video refresh rate for your combination of card and display. You may be able to check what Windows has selected and choose from a limited range of other options. To do so, take these steps:

STEPS

Changing the Video Refresh Rate

Step 1. Right-click the Desktop, click Properties, and click the Settings tab.

Step 2. Click the Advanced button to display the Properties dialog box for your display, and click the Adapter tab, as shown in Figure 40-7.

Continued

STEPS

Changing the Video Refresh Rate *(continued)*

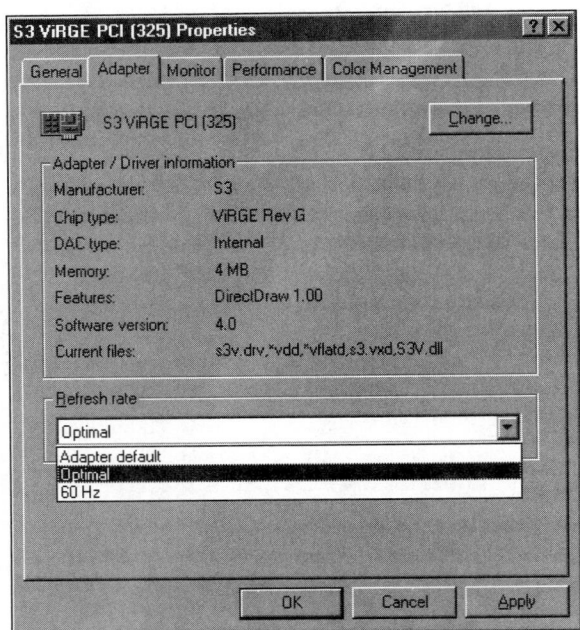

Figure 40-7: The Adapter tab shows the settings for your display adapter.

Step 3.   See if you have a Refresh Rate drop-down list. If you do, you can continue on to step 4. If you don't, you won't be able to adjust this setting.

Step 4.   Display the Refresh Rate drop-down list and pick a refresh rate. Click Apply. Your screen will now go black and then come back as the refresh rate is adjusted. You can choose to keep the new refresh rate if your Desktop looks good.

As you'll notice in Figure 40-7, the Adapter tab may not give you any indication of what your actual refresh rate is. Since the refresh rate of a monitor is a big selling point, it might be nice to know if you are getting what you paid for.

PowerStrip, described later in this chapter in "Get Control of Your Monitor and Video Card," tells you what your current refresh rate is and lets you choose a specific value for the refresh rate. If PowerStrip correctly detects your video card and monitor model, it will display the supported refresh rates. To choose a specific refresh rate with PowerStrip, take these steps:

STEPS

Changing the Video Refresh Rate with PowerStrip

Step 1. Click the PowerStrip icon in the system tray, and then click PowerStrip Configuration.

Step 2. Check the "Refresh rate" displayed at the bottom of the PowerStrip Configuration dialog box, as shown in Figure 40-8. This is your current refresh rate. Click Cancel.

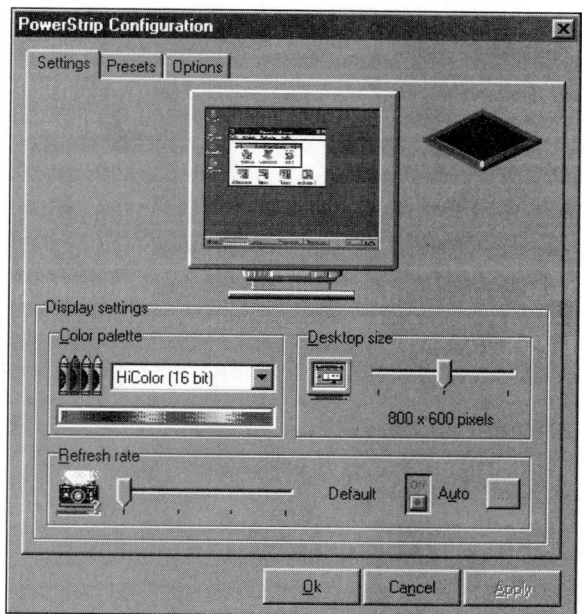

Figure 40-8: The "Refresh rate" area is in the lower part of PowerStrip's Settings tab.

Step 3. Click the PowerStrip icon in the system tray and choose Advanced Options ⇨ Graphics System Information.

Continued

STEPS

Changing the Video Refresh Rate with PowerStrip *(continued)*

Step 4. Scroll down the "Display modes supported" list to see a complete list of the display modes supported by your video card/monitor combination (see Figure 40-9). Choose a supported refresh rate, resolution, and color depth by double-clicking one of the values in this list. Click Close.

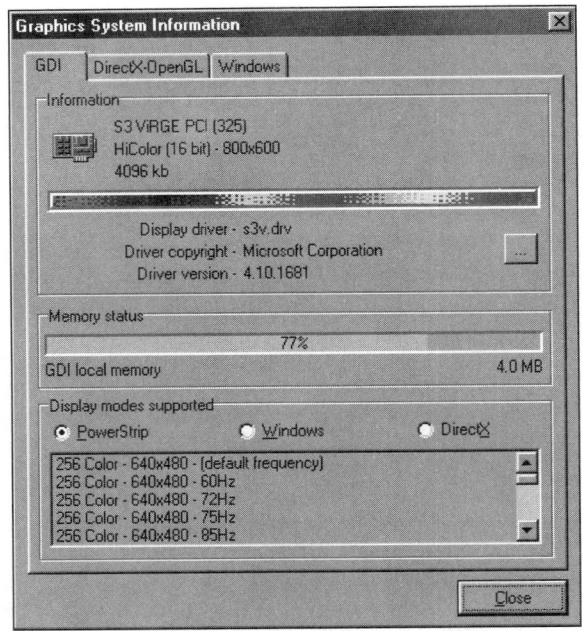

Figure 40-9: Select a display mode from the list in the Graphics System Information dialog box.

Don't Restart Windows When You Change Your Monitor Properties

Some changes in screen properties request a restart of Windows before the changes take effect. You may be able to get your computer to make the changes without restarting Windows.

STEPS

Making Monitor Changes Without Restarting Windows

Step 1. Right-click your Desktop, click Properties ⇨ Settings ⇨ Advanced ⇨ and Performance.

Step 2. Mark the "Apply the changes without restarting" checkbox.

Step 3. Click OK. Click OK again.

You may not have this checkbox in your Performance tab. If you don't, you won't be able to make this change. Also, older analog monitors do not support this capability.

Thanks to Penelope Baker for help with this tip.

Get Control of Your Monitor and Video Card

Sometimes the Display Properties dialog boxes just don't provide enough control and feedback about the capabilities of your video card and monitor combination. EnTech Taiwan produces a truly super utility that lets you control your monitor and video card from the Desktop. It appears that most of EnTech's income is from sales to video card and monitor manufacturers who want to give customers a powerful tool for controlling their products.

PowerStrip is a very professional package with a great online overview that runs automatically the first time you start it. The overview highlights PowerStrip's capabilities — easy access to resolution, font size, and refresh rates settings. PowerStrip's features include display power management for Windows 2000/NT, hot keys to switch display resolutions, screen adjustment controls (such as those under your monitor bezel), custom refresh rates, color calibration, and TV controls for video cards with NTSC/PAL codecs on the chip. In addition, PowerStrip offers optimization of DirectX and OpenGL parameters, 3D accelerator support, multimonitor support, and PCI diagnostics. And that isn't all.

PowerStrip sits in your system tray. Right-click it and click Show PowerStrip to display the toolbar shown in Figure 40-10.

Figure 40-10: The PowerStrip toolbar

PowerStrip is not limited to the buttons in the toolbar. It offers numerous other functions as well, including screen adjustments, redefining the mouse pointer, and power management (see Figure 40-11).

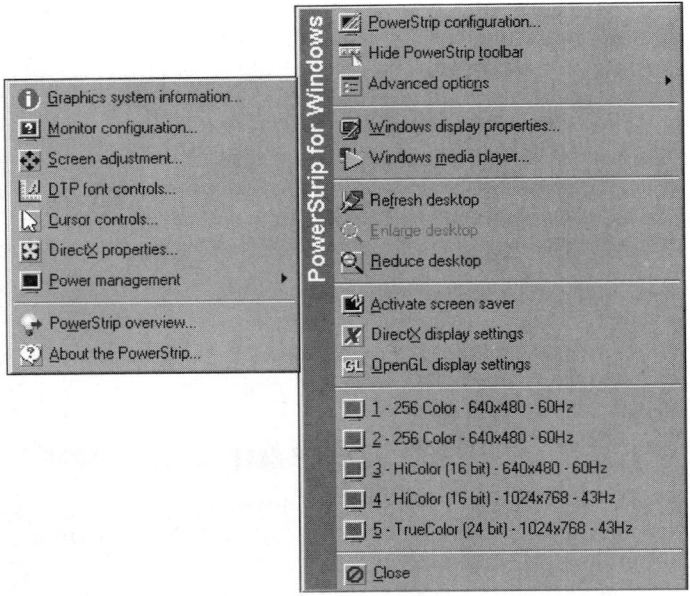

Figure 40-11: Double-click the PowerStrip icon in your system tray to select from this menu.

You'll find PowerStrip at `http://www.entechtaiwan.com/`.

What's the Point of Two Monitors?

Somebody must want this feature, because Microsoft used an awful lot of resources to make it available. Here's something you can do with the second monitor if you have a constant connection to the Internet.

Use the second monitor as a real-time monitor. Right-click the Desktop on the second monitor, click Active Desktop, and View As Web Page. Place active components on the Desktop, such as stock tickers, timely updated news Web pages, and so on.

Drag over your e-mail client and have it check for e-mail periodically. You'll be able to read your e-mail or check the stocks while you are working on your other monitor.

If you are doing development work, set the resolution of the second monitor at a different resolution than your primary monitor. You can check your Web pages or dialog boxes on the lower- or higher-resolution monitor to see how they look.

Thanks to Jamie Sanchez for pointing us toward these tips.

Which Monitor Is Which

Once you spread your Desktop across multiple monitors and hook them up to various video cards (which actually determine which is which), you might forget what's connected to what. Here's how to get back to where you started:

STEPS

Make the Monitors Identify Themselves

Step 1. Right-click the Desktop, click Properties, and click the Settings tab.

Step 2. You'll see icons representing multiple monitors. You can move these icons around to reflect the physical location of the actual monitors. But, that is what you are trying to remember. So...

Step 3. Right-click one of the monitor icons and click Identify. A number will appear on the monitor.

Thanks to Steve Ellmore for help on this tip.

Summary

Since you look at your display almost 100 percent of the time you're using your PC, it's pretty important to use it as effectively as you can.

▶ You can get a bigger picture with Microsoft Magnifier.

▶ You can quickly change your display resolution and number of colors.

▶ Your display's refresh rate can be tweaked to get the best settings for your hardware's capabilities.

▶ You may be able to change your monitor properties without restarting Windows.

▶ You can get control of your monitor and video card with some simple tools.

▶ You can use two monitors effectively, with capabilities that Microsoft went to some effort to incorporate into Windows.

Chapter 41

Printers

In This Chapter

We look at the Windows print subsystem, the software that drives physical printers. We go over the significant features and discuss:

▶ Using the Printers folder to install, configure, and manage your printers

▶ Dragging and dropping documents to any of your printers

▶ Making the feature, drag and drop to a printer icon, do anything you want it to

▶ Printing TrueType fonts correctly on PostScript printers

▶ Printing to a printer that isn't physically connected to your computer

▶ Troubleshooting printing problems

▶ Automatically installing network printer drivers

Printing Features

The Windows printing subsystem has not changed radically since 1992. Windows printer drivers continue to be based on a universal driver that gives printer manufacturers a big head start toward producing specific drivers for their printers.

But many incremental improvements in Windows Me, Windows 98, and Windows 95 before it have increased configuration flexibility and provided faster and more stable printing. And Windows Me now includes drivers for approximately 1,000 printers, in addition to new ones that may appear.

The 32-Bit Printer Driver

Like all the other drivers that come with Windows Me, the printer driver has entered the 32-bit world. This means that it spools print jobs as threads, which Windows can preemptively multitask. The 32-bit driver gives the print subsystem more control over the printing process, including bidirectional communication with the printer.

Each printer has its own print queue. You can have multiple printers connected to different ports, all printing at the same time and all managed by a different print-queue manager.

The print-queue managers do a better job of spooling print jobs to the printers than earlier versions of Windows did. They are aware of when the printer is ready for more data, and they don't send it until it is.

Image Color Management

Windows includes Image Color Management (ICM), a utility designed to produce more consistent color among displays, and between your display and your printer. The latter has been a big challenge in desktop publishing, because the way your eye perceives color emitted from a monitor is very different from the way it perceives color reflected from a printed page. Programmers of individual applications, such as Adobe's PhotoShop, must include calls in their programs to implement ICM.

The initial ICM version that shipped with Windows in 1995 only supported RGB color, and it was designed to be invisible to you as a user. New versions have more powerful features and support more color models, including CMYK (cyan-magenta-yellow-black, the standard for printing on a commercial press). It also lets you set the *rendering intent*—the way you ultimately want the image or document to be seen—from within the application you use to create the document or image.

To set the rendering intent, select Color Management from the program's File menu. Windows offers a choice of four rendering intents:

- Perceptual matching—best for photographic images
- Saturation matching—best for graphs and pie charts
- Relative Colorimetric matching—best for logos and artwork in which a few colors must be matched exactly
- Absolute Colorimetric matching—best for creating idealized, device-independent images, such those on Web sites

Universal Print Driver

The universal print driver communicates between printer-specific minidrivers and the rest of the operating system. It supports higher-resolution laser printers, and it can download TrueType outlines to printers that support the PCL language (the HP LaserJet printer control language). This lets the printer rasterize fonts without using the resources of the computer.

The universal print driver also supports Hewlett-Packard's HPGL/2 plotter language, so CAD and similar applications can send their HPGL output to a printer instead of to a plotter.

Unified Printer Control Interface

In Windows Me, printer configuration, installation, and the print-queue management functions are combined and associated with the individual Printer icons in the Printers folder. Each printer has an icon representing its own print-queue manager and printer driver properties. You set the configuration information for each printer individually, and manage each print queue separately and simultaneously.

Spooling EMF, Not RAW Printer Codes

When you print a document, the document file has to be translated into the printer's codes that instruct the printer on how to print each character. Microsoft refers to these printer codes as the RAW data. (We capitalize raw as RAW here because Microsoft does so in order to contrast it with EMF, or *Enhanced Metafile Format.*)

In Windows Me, both the translation to RAW data and the print spooling are done in the background. You don't have to wait for the lengthy translation to RAW data to finish before you can continue working with your application. Your document is instead translated to EMF, which is a much higher level and more compact format than the RAW data. This reduces the initial translation time and returns you to your application more quickly.

The temporary EMF file is spooled and translated as it is sent to the printer. EMF is built into the Graphic Device Interface (GDI) module of Windows. If you run into problems spooling EMF files, you can switch to the old way of spooling RAW data files instead. We show you how later in this chapter in the section entitled "Details."

PostScript printer drivers spool PostScript files to the PostScript printer. There is no EMF translation available for PostScript printers. PostScript is already a high-level page description language like the Enhanced Metafile Format, so there is little or no benefit in translating first to EMF and then from EMF to PostScript. The PostScript printer driver translates your document to a temporary PostScript file, spools this file, and starts sending it to the printer as the driver creates the temporary file.

DOS and Windows Printing Work Together

The Windows print subsystem spools DOS print files, so you can print from any DOS application and let the operating system handle the printer. The printer ports are virtualized, which makes the DOS application think it is printing to a real port, when in fact it is printing to the Windows print subsystem. You can turn off DOS print spooling.

DOS print files are not translated into EMF print files. Rather, the translation occurs as the files (as RAW data files) are spooled. This still releases the DOS application faster than it would be without a spooler.

Offline Printing

If you don't have a printer currently hooked up to your computer, you can still create print files. They will be printed automatically the next time you get connected to a printer and use the queue manager to put the printer back online. To do this, you must first install on your computer a printer driver that references a printer connected to a network server or to another computer over a peer-to-peer network. This network can be as simple as the Direct Cable Connection (DCC) program, which lets your laptop computer connect to your desktop computer.

Secret

Offline (or *deferred*) printing is useful whenever your computer is not connected to a network printer. Unfortunately, offline printing works only for printing to nonlocal (network) printers. You can't use it with a local printer that, for whatever reason, is not currently connected to your computer. You can pause printing while you reconnect your local printer, if for some reason it was offline when you started printing, but pausing does not save the print jobs for later printing.

Bidirectional Communications

For years, users couldn't have cared less what a printer had to say to them. Now we all realize that things are a lot easier when the printer can talk back.

Plug and Play printers can give the Windows printer installation routines all the information they need to set up the printer, without requiring you to answer any questions about manufacturer, model, and so on. Many Plug and Play printers can send status reports to the printer driver reporting such things as "paper jam" or "out of paper." This helps if the printer is down the hall. And some sophisticated Plug and Play printers can supply even more detailed status reports.

Support for Enhanced Parallel Port

The EPP and ECP specifications for parallel ports permit higher speeds and improved bidirectional communication. This is most evident when you use devices that can deal with these higher speeds. See the section in Chapter 44 entitled "Configuring ECP and EPP Ports."

PostScript

Adobe and Microsoft jointly developed the PostScript printer driver for Windows. The fact that Microsoft is willing to credit Adobe with joint development speaks volumes about Adobe's role in PostScript, and Microsoft's desire to have a well-respected printer driver.

The same PostScript printer driver is used for all PostScript printers. Windows uses a separate spd (Simplified PostScript printer description) or ppd

(PostScript printer description) file to modify the driver to reflect the features of each PostScript printer. These files are stored in the `\Windows\System` folder. The filenames are shortened versions of the printer name.

The Windows PostScript driver includes PostScript Level 2 support as well as numerous incremental upgrades to better handle more complex PostScript documents.

If you have a PostScript printer and are using Adobe Type Manager (ATM), you'll want to make sure you have a fairly recent version of the ATM software. ATM versions 3.01 and earlier do not support Windows' Image Color Management, and this incompatibility can cause your system to crash when you try to print.

Printer Shortcuts

Because each printer has its own associated icon in the Printers folder, you can place shortcuts to each printer driver on your Desktop (or in any other folder). When you want to print to the printer, drag and drop your document file onto the shortcut.

If you drag a Printer icon from the Printers folder, Windows assumes you want to create a shortcut when you drop the icon. You don't need to hold down the Ctrl+Shift keys.

Print Without Installing Printer Drivers First

You may have installed a local printer by installing its driver on your computer. You can always print to that printer. If you want to print to another printer on your network, you don't necessarily have to install the driver beforehand. You do need to have a driver for that printer installed on your computer, but the installation process can be automatic. This comes in handy, because there could be all sorts of printers on an extensive network, and it would be a bit of a pain to manually install drivers for all of the 1,000+ printers that Windows supports.

If you print to a shared printer on your network that's on a computer running Windows Me, Windows 98, Windows 2000/NT, or Novell NetWare, Windows Me automatically installs the printer driver for that printer on your computer. Microsoft calls this *point and print*.

If the network printer is connected to a Windows computer, all the information about the printer and the location of the files associated with it is stored in the registry of that computer. Point and print uses this information to change your registry, copy the appropriate files from the other Windows computer, and install the printer driver on your computer.

See the section later in this chapter entitled "Point and Print" for details on how to set up your computer to use and share this capability.

Network Printer Management

Both Digital Equipment Corporation and Hewlett Packard provide printer server software that eases the job of managing printers that are connected directly to NetWare, Microsoft, and Digital networks. A Windows 98 computer using this software becomes a network print-management station.

No Need for Logical Port Redirection

Windows 3.1*x* required that you assign a network printer to a specific logical port if you wanted to print to it. This is not necessary in Windows Me, as long as your network supports the universal naming convention (UNC) for naming its server, folders, and printers. When you install a network printer, Windows retains its UNC name and uses it to direct the output to the correct printer — for example, \\Billserver\Laser.

If your network doesn't support UNC (the 16-bit networks that worked with Windows 3.1*x* do not), you can still redirect printer output to logical ports LPT1 through LPT9 through the Capture Printer Port button (in the Details tab of the Properties dialog box for your printer). Some DOS programs may require that you print to a logical port and not to a printer through a UNC port name.

The Printers Folder

You'll find that most printing functions in Windows are consolidated in the Printers folder. You can get to the Printers folder in four ways:

1. Click the Start button, point to Settings, and then click Printers.

2. Click My Computer, and click the Printers folder icon.

3. Right-click My Computer, click Explore, and click the Printers folder icon in the left pane of the Explorer.

4. Use any of the above methods, but click the Control Panel folder instead of the Printers folder, and then click the Printers folder in the Control Panel.

Your Printers folder window will look something like the one shown in Figure 41-1. You won't have any icons other than the Add Printer icon in this folder until you install some printers (or have them installed for you). Each installed printer driver has its own Printer icon in the Printers folder.

You can use the Printers folder and the icons in it for a variety of purposes. Click the Add Printer icon to install a new printer. Click a Printer icon to view its print queue. Right-click a Printer icon and click Properties to view a printer driver's properties, or click Set As Default to change the default printer. Right-click the client area of the Printers folder window and click Capture Printer Port to redirect a logical printer port to a network printer.

Figure 41-1: The Printers folder window. This folder contains the Add Printer icon and icons for each of your installed printers.

You'll find most everything to do with printers in the Printers folder. You can:

- Install new printer drivers
- Delete printer drivers you are no longer using
- Change the characteristics of your printer driver
- View and manage the print queues (pause and purge print jobs)
- Set the default printer
- Give LPT*x* names to printers connected to networked servers (redirect logical printer ports to network printers)

Printer driver installation and configuration and print-queue management are combined in Windows to make it easier to get at the important printer functions. So what is outside of the Printers folder that relates to printing?

- The Fonts folder, where you'll find the fonts that are installed on your computer. (See "Where Are the Fonts Installed?" in Chapter 21 for details on fonts.)
- Printer and communication port configurations, including the new enhanced parallel port, which you will find in the Device Manager under the System icon in the Control Panel.
- The Add New Hardware icon in the Control Panel, which you can use to run the Add Printer Wizard. (You can also run this wizard from the Printers folder by clicking the Add Printer icon.)
- The Network icon in the Control Panel, which lets you enable printer sharing.
- Shortcuts to Printer icons. (You can't drag a Printer icon out of the Printers folder, but you can drag to create a shortcut to the Printer icon on the Desktop.)
- The Print Preview capability, a system-wide dynamic link library (DLL) that developers can incorporate into their applications. (An example of this type of Print Preview is found in WordPad.)
- The common Print dialog box, which developers can use in their applications. (An example of this dialog box is found in WordPad.)

- Shared printers attached to servers on your network. You can view shared printers by clicking the servers' icons in the Explorer; they also appear in your Printers folder if you print to them, drag and drop them to the Printers folder, or click them.

- Network printer management tools from DEC and HP.

Tip

The Device Manager tracks most of the hardware attached to your computer, but it doesn't track your printers. The Properties dialog box associated with a particular printer is the only place that displays the parameters of that printer driver stored in the registry. The Device Manager does track the printer port parameters.

Drag and Drop to a Printer Icon

You can drag and drop a File icon from a folder window, the Explorer, or the Desktop, to a printer's icon or its queue window. The printer's icon could be a shortcut on your Desktop, or it could be an icon in the Printers folder. With this action, you are telling Windows to invoke the application associated with the print command for this file type and then execute the application's print command.

If you want to quickly print a file or a group of files, this is an easy way to do it. The associated application starts, and you may see the document in the application window on the Desktop while the document is spooled to the printer. The application is closed as soon as the document is completely spooled.

This is the same thing that would happen if you right-clicked a document file and chose Print from the context menu. The actions listed at the top of the context menu are the ones defined for the file type in the registry and listed in the File Types tab of the Folder Options dialog box. We discuss file types in detail in "Associating Actions with File Extensions" in Chapter 12.

If you drag and drop a file to a Network Printer icon in a shared folder, and your computer doesn't have that printer's driver installed, you are instructing Windows to start installing the driver on your computer.

You can define an action named Print for a given file type, and then associate that action with a specific application's print command. This connects the user action of dragging and dropping a file of that type onto the Printer icon with the specified application's print command. You define the Print action using the method detailed in "Creating and Editing File Types and Actions" in Chapter 12.

Secret

You can define the "Print" action to be something other than Print, if you like. This will let you drag and drop a file to a Printer icon to invoke a different action. For example, you can define the Print action to invoke a file translator that converts the specified file type into another file type. If you do this, you can convert files of the specified type by simply dragging and dropping them onto any Printer icon.

The Print action is defined by default for many file types. This happens when you install the Windows application associated with the file type (after you've installed Windows).

Installing a Printer Driver

Windows documentation often refers to *installing a printer*. That really means *installing a printer driver*—in other words, installing software. This is confusing, because the intuitive meaning of installing a printer is to physically place a printer next to a computer and connect them with a printer cable. You'll have to do a little translation in your head when you see the words *install a printer*.

If you have a new computer running Windows, or if you get a new Plug and Play printer, chances are you won't have to install a printer driver at all. After you physically connect the printer to the computer, turn on the printer and start Windows, your system will detect the new printer, and will attempt to identify and install it. Especially with newer equipment, that should be all there is to it.

On the other hand, you may want to install drivers for printers you don't own. Perhaps your work will be printed at a service bureau, for example, or on a specialized printer at your office. You can use the Add Printer Wizard to easily install drivers for printers that are not connected to your computer.

If you install Windows Me into a directory with an existing, previous version of Windows, Windows Millennium Setup automatically installs the printer drivers for the printers that you previously installed. On the other hand, if you install Windows Me into a *new* folder on a computer running a previous version of Windows, you will be asked during setup to install a new printer. You'll see the Add Printer Wizard, and you just need to answer the questions.

After Windows is installed, if it does not detect your new printer on startup, you can invoke the Add Printer Wizard (to add a new printer driver) by opening the Printers folder and clicking the Add Printer icon. If your printer is Plug and Play compatible, the Add Printer Wizard can communicate with it, find the correct printer driver, and install the correctly configured printer driver itself.

Otherwise, the Add Printer Wizard asks you for the manufacturer's name and printer model before it proceeds to find the correct files from the Windows CD-ROM. To do this, it uses the inf files Msprint.inf and Msprint2.inf in the \Windows\Inf folder. (This folder is only visible if the "Show hidden files and folders" option button is selected in the View tab of the Folder Options dialog box, which you display by choosing View ⇨ Folder Options in any Explorer or folder window.)

If you have a printer that isn't covered in these two inf files and you have a printer setup diskette from your printer manufacturer, you can click the Have Disk button in the Add Printer Wizard. This diskette has to include an inf file for the new printer.

The Add Printer Wizard will ask you to choose a port if it can't detect a connection (see Figure 41-2). If this driver is for a printer you can't physically connect to a port, choose FILE. If the printer is connected to a serial port and is not Plug and Play compliant, indicate the correct serial port. The wizard will let you change the port's baud rate, and so on. The wizard also lets you choose a meaningful name for your printer, so if you share it on a network, others will know where to find their output.

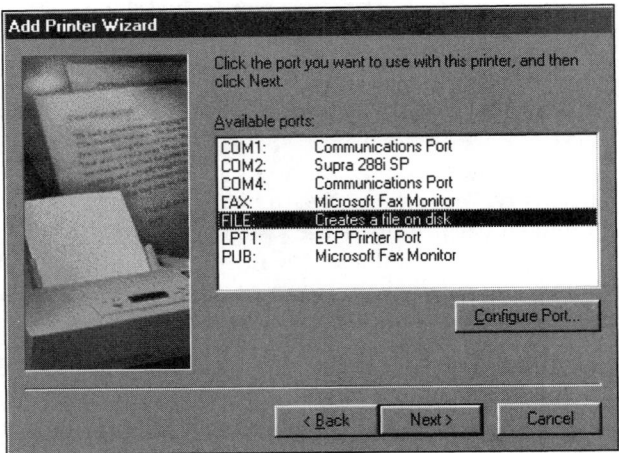

Figure 41-2: The Add Printer Wizard will ask you to choose a port for a printer if it's not currently connected to your computer. It might be across town at a service bureau, for example.

When the Add Printer Wizard has finished installing the driver, it asks if you want to print a test page. You should do this if you're setting up the printer for the first time. Printing a test page lets Windows check out the printer, and if Windows finds a problem, it leads you to a Windows Help-based print troubleshooter. The troubleshooter asks you questions to help you track down glitches in your printer driver configuration.

You can also invoke the print troubleshooter from the Contents tab of the Windows Help window. Click the Start button, click Help, click the Contents tab, click Troubleshooting, click Windows 98 Troubleshooters, and then click Print.

You can install a printer driver for a network printer in the same manner that you install a driver for a local printer. The only difference is that you will be asked for the server and printer name. Type the name using the UNC. Your network must support this convention if you install a network printer this way.

You can install a printer driver on your computer for a printer on a network in a few other ways, a couple of which are a little more automated. See the section entitled "Point and Print" later in this chapter for details.

It goes without saying that new printers are constantly coming onto the market. If a driver for your printer is not included with Windows, you may want to check Microsoft's Hardware Compatibility List (HCL). This list is constantly updated with the latest available drivers, as well as other information. You can search the HCL for your printer: Go to `http://www.microsoft.com/hwtest/hcl/`, select Printer in the Category list, choose your manufacturer, and click the Search button. The search will tell you the compatibility level of your printer, and whether a driver is available for download. You may also want to visit the printer manufacturer's Web site to see if you can locate the proper drivers.

To get the latest update, you can click the Start button, point to Settings, and click Windows Update. This connects to Microsoft Windows Update site, which will interrogate your computer to see if you have the latest drivers.

Printer Driver Properties

Each printer driver has its own icon in the Printers folder. Attached to each printer icon is a Properties dialog box containing numerous properties that you can customize for that printer.

Properties that were previously global for all printer drivers have been moved to each printer driver's Properties dialog box. For example, you can determine for each printer whether to print directly to the printer or through a print queue.

Getting to a Printer's Properties

You get to a printer driver's properties by right-clicking its icon in the Printers folder and clicking Properties in the context menu. You can also highlight a Printer icon in the Printers folder and choose File ⇨ Properties. If a printer's Print Queue window is open, you can choose Printer ⇨ Properties in that window.

You can't get to a printer's properties by right-clicking a shortcut icon for the printer on your Desktop and clicking Properties (unless you have installed Target, a utility in Microsoft PowerToys). This will just get you to the properties of the shortcut. You need to click the shortcut icon and then choose Printer ⇨ Properties in the Print Queue window.

You can also get to some of a printer's properties through the printer setup options in your application, usually through the Print or Print Setup command in the File menu. The 32-bit applications can use the common Print dialog box `dll` to get to the printer properties. The properties you access through your applications will not exactly match the ones connected to the printer's icon in the Printers folder. Settings that you make in the application — the number of copies, for example — will override any settings you make in the printer's Properties dialog box, or physically on the printer itself.

Basic Printer Properties

There are too many printer properties to go through all of them in this book. Besides, we want to focus on the undocumented aspects of printer drivers, not those features that are obvious.

You can find out what the various option buttons and fields in the Properties dialog box do by right-clicking them and then clicking the What's This? button that appears. You can also click the question mark in the upper-right corner of the dialog box and then click an area of interest.

Here, we'll go over a few of the options in the Properties dialog box to give you an idea of the range of things you can set. After that, we give you some guidance on how to deal with some of the less well-explained printer driver properties.

The Graphics tabs of the Properties dialog box for a LaserJet compatible printer and a PostScript compatible printer are shown in Figures 41-3 and 41-4. The specific graphics properties depend on the features available in the printer and the printer driver.

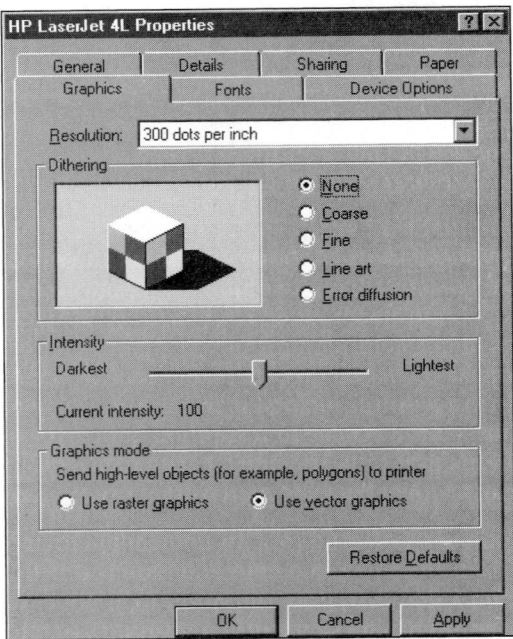

Figure 41-3: The Graphics tab of the Properties dialog box for a Hewlett Packard 4L printer. You get to determine the quality of the graphics output (traded against time to produce the output and per-sheet costs). Resolution doesn't affect text unless you print the text as a graphic (a setting on another tab).

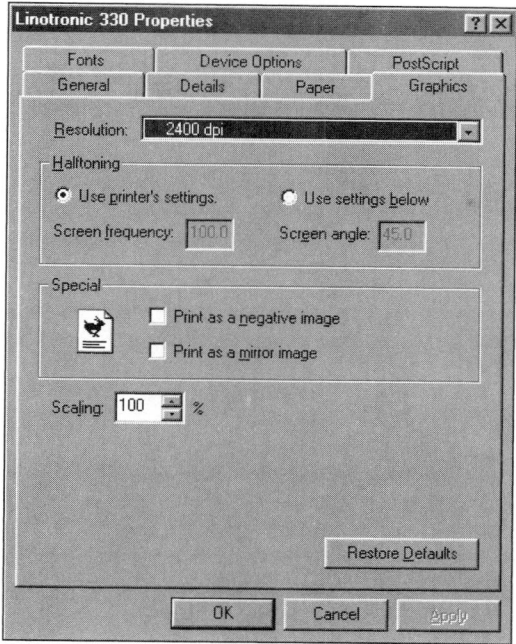

Figure 41-4: The Graphics tab of the Properties dialog box for a Linotronic 300. The Linotronic is often used at service bureaus to produce film and other high-end output. You send PostScript from your application to a file using this driver, and then send the file to the service bureau. If you're printing to film, you can use the two checkboxes in the Special area to flip or reverse the image.

Separator Page

The General tab of the Properties dialog box is the same for all printers. One of the options on it lets you print a separator page between print jobs so that you can easily separate them. Separator pages are useful if many different people print to one printer.

The separator page can be blank, or it can contain a graphic that more easily identifies it. The graphic needs to be in the Windows Metafile format. Files of this type have the extension wmf.

Secret

Microsoft doesn't ship any applications with Windows that can produce Windows Metafile files. You have to purchase an application that creates such files if you want to be able to create a separator page with a graphic on it. Paint Shop Pro, a shareware program available at almost every shareware site on the Internet, enables you to create wmf files or convert other types of graphics files into wmf files.

After you turn off separator pages, you may still get them when you print from MS-DOS-based programs. This happens when the program is printing to a UNC printer name instead of to a port. To stop the extra pages, capture a specific port for this printer (see "Logical Printer Port Redirection" later in this chapter).

Details

All Windows printer drivers have the same Details tab, which is shown in Figure 41-5. Use the "Print to the following port" drop-down list to change the port to which you are printing (after you physically reconnect your local printer) or to print to a file.

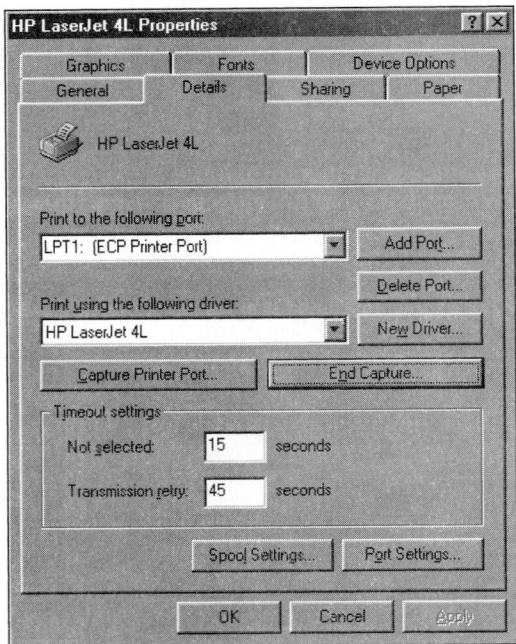

Figure 41-5: The Details tab of the Properties dialog box

Click the Capture Printer Port button if you want to redirect output from a named LPT port to a network printer. Use the Port Settings button if you need to turn off the spooling of DOS print jobs. You can even switch to the properties of one of the other printer drivers by using the "Print using the following driver" drop-down list (this overwrites your existing driver). You can also update your printer driver from a diskette using the New Driver button.

Secret

If you change the "Print to the following port" field to a network printer path, and that printer is of the same type as the printer whose properties you are currently viewing and editing, you will switch the current printer to the network printer as soon as you click Apply or OK. This is probably not what you want to do, as you lose your driver to your current printer. It's better to add a separate driver for the network printer than to switch connections in this field.

If you move the network or local printer, you can use the Add Port button to specify the new path to the printer.

You can adjust the time interval that your applications wait before Windows reports a printer time-out error. Change the number of seconds in the "Not selected" field to a higher value if you find that you continually get the "Windows will retry in 5 seconds" message box when you try to print.

Logical Printer Port Redirection

The Capture Printer Port button lets you redirect output from a named LPT port to a network printer. You can set up nine redirections (LPT1 through LPT9) and specify if they will be valid the next time you reboot your computer. If you do, Windows connects to the servers where these printers are located every time you restart your computer while connected to your network.

Add a Port

If you want to connect to a different printer, or if your network printer has moved, click the Add Port button. The network path to your already installed network printer will be shown in the list of ports. You can type the path to a network printer for later use.

DOS Print Spooling

You can use the Port Settings button to turn off DOS print spooling. Most of the actual port settings (including the I/O address and IRQ setting) are found in the Device Manager.

Printing Directly to the Printer with No Spooling

If you want to turn off spooling and print directly to the printer (with no intermediate temporary file), click the Spool Settings button to display the Spool Settings dialog box, and mark the "Print directly to the printer" option button. You can also use the "Spool data format" drop-down list to choose the RAW or EMF format. If you turn off spooling, the format has to be RAW.

If you are printing to a file, the bottom third of the Details tab will be grayed out. These properties are not used when you're printing to a file instead of to a physical printer.

Spooling and Speed

Print speed is measured in two ways in Windows. One is the length of time it takes to regain control of the system after you issue the Print command (called the *return to application* or RTA speed). The other is the time from when you issue the Print command to when your finished page drops into the printer's paper catch (called *page drop speed*). Both of these speeds are affected by the spool settings in Windows.

You can affect each of these times by setting options in the Spool Settings dialog box (click the Spool Settings button in the Details tab of the Properties dialog box).

For faster RTA speed, mark the "Start printing after first page is spooled" option button. If this is not a PostScript printer, choose EMF as the spool data format.

For faster page drop speed, mark either the "Print directly to the printer" option button or the "Start printing after last page is spooled" option button.

Fonts

Almost all of the printer drivers have a Fonts tab in the Properties dialog box. Unlike the Details tab, each type of printer has different options on the Fonts tab.

If you are printing to an inkjet printer at a lower resolution (75–150 dpi), or if you are using the Generic/Text Only printer driver, you will probably find that TrueType fonts are not available.

TrueType Fonts on PostScript Printers

Tip

It's easy to use TrueType fonts and print them to a PostScript printer or a PostScript file that you will take to a service bureau. In almost all cases, unless you are doing a quick draft document, you should mark the "Always use TrueType fonts" option button on the Fonts tab, as shown in Figure 41-6. (This is not the default setting.)

You should also click the Send Fonts As button and choose Outlines in the "Send TrueType fonts as" drop-down list, shown in Figure 41-7. If you don't do this, the output you see on your screen may not match the output from the printer.

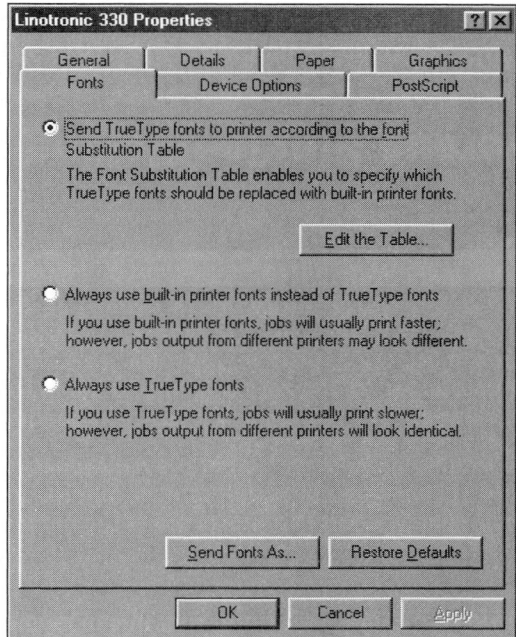

Figure 41-6: The Fonts tab of the Properties dialog box for the Linotronic 300. Mark the "Always use TrueType fonts" option button, and then click the Send Fonts As button.

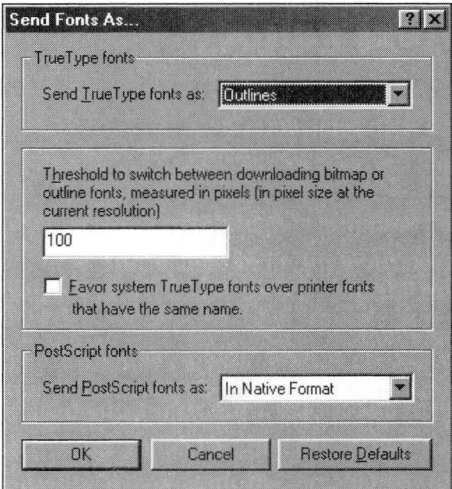

Figure 41-7: The Send Fonts As dialog box. Choose Outlines from the "Send TrueType fonts as" drop-down list.

If you treat TrueType fonts in this manner, the printed version of your document should match the one you see onscreen. The spacing and line breaks won't shift because the PostScript printer won't substitute the TrueType fonts with PostScript fonts, as it would if you did not mark the "Always use TrueType fonts" option. However, if you are using a fancy font or a font designed for use in headlines, you may want to test it before printing your final output.

Sharing

Tip

You can use drivers for printers that you don't actually have — no problem with that. For example, if you want to create a PostScript file for a Linotronic 300 that is many miles away in a service bureau, you install a printer driver for it on your computer and then print to a file. You can then ship the file through your modem to the bulletin board at the service bureau for printing later that day or overnight.

One thing that you can't do with a printer driver that is configured to print to a file is share the printer (because there isn't any printer there to share). If you have an actual printer connected locally and you've enabled print sharing (using the Network icon in your Control Panel), you have a Sharing tab in the printer driver's Properties dialog box that lets you specify whether or not to share the printer.

You can also get to the Sharing tab by right-clicking a local printer's icon in the Printers folder and clicking Sharing in the context menu. For more details, see the section later in this chapter entitled "Sharing a Printer."

PostScript Properties

The PostScript driver has its own PostScript-specific tab, as shown in Figure 41-8. The Advanced options let you do such wonderful things as getting rid of the Ctrl+D at the beginning or end of your PostScript output so you don't have to manually edit them out if you run over a UNIX network to a PostScript printer.

You can choose among several PostScript output formats. The default format, "optimize for speed." is fine for local printers. If you're printing to a file for offsite printing, you might want to try "optimize for portability – ADSC." (ADSC stands for Adobe Document Structuring Conventions.) Choose Encapsulated PostScript (EPS) if you're printing to a file that will be incorporated into another file.

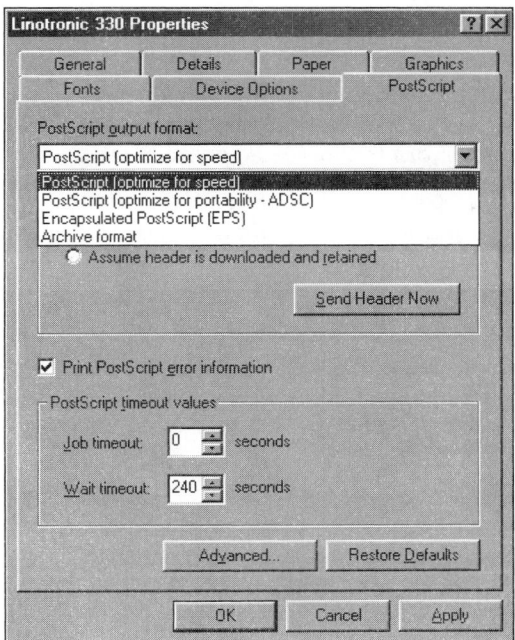

Figure 41-8: The PostScript tab of the Properties dialog box. Use the "PostScript output format" drop-down list to specify an output format, and click the Advanced button for more options.

Defining Your Own Printer

If you have installed the Generic/Text Only printer driver, you can define escape sequences (printer commands) that control your specific printer and set the various font sizes and types. In most cases, you don't have to do this, because Microsoft has included printer drivers for hundreds of different printers with Windows. But the capability is there if you run into a new one.

Use the Device Options and Fonts tabs associated with the Generic/Text only printer driver to define the printer codes for your particular printer.

Tip Installing the Generic/Text Only printer is a great way to produce text-only output from applications that don't have an option to save unformatted text-only files.

Managing Print Queues

You can change the order in which documents will be printed by changing their order in the print queue. To do this, open the Printers folder, click the Printer icon to open the Print Queue window, and simply drag the documents into the order you want. You can only do this for documents that haven't started printing yet.

Windows doesn't let you move documents from one printer's queue to that of another. This is because the documents have already been translated into RAW format for that specific printer. Instead, you must remove the document from the old queue and print it again to the other printer.

You can use the Purge Print Documents command in the Printer menu of a queue to remove all documents from the queue (and not print any of them). However, you cannot use your computer to remove documents from the print queue of a network printer.

The print spool folder is `\Windows\Spool\Printers`. This is where the translated documents are held while they wait to be printed. You can't move this folder without reinstalling Windows, and there's no good reason to do so.

Deferred Printing

You can print documents using a printer driver for a network printer that isn't currently connected through the network to your computer. The print jobs will be spooled, and you can print them later when you reconnect to the printer through the network. The print jobs are tracked in the print queue for that printer, and when you put the printer online, they are automatically printed. Deferred printing will not work if you have turned off spooling in your printer properties (as described in "Printing Directly to the Printer with No Spooling" earlier in this chapter).

One way you can use deferred printing is to create documents on a portable, print them to the print queue, and then print them later when you connect your portable to a computer with a printer (perhaps your desktop computer). The portable has to have a printer driver for the desktop's printer installed as a network printer, and the two computers need to be connected with Direct Cable Connection (DCC) or through another network connection. If you use a docking station, the files you send to the queue while undocked will be printed automatically when you redock. See "Connecting Two Computers" in Chapter 17 for more on connecting laptops and desktops.

You can also use Dial-Up Networking (DUN) to phone in from the portable to the desktop computer and print your documents at the office while you are on the road or at home. You need to have the desktop computer configured as a DUN server. (See "Setting Up Your Windows Computer at Work as a Host" in Chapter 19.)

If you are on a network and printing to a network printer and you lose the connection to that printer, your print jobs will be spooled until the connection is reestablished and you place the printer online. The printer driver for the network printer will display itself as offline as soon as the network connection is broken.

Even if you are presently connected to the network printer, you can take it offline (for you) by right-clicking its icon in your Printers folder and clicking "Use printer offline."

Secret

If you take a network printer offline by right-clicking its icon in the Printers folder and clicking "Use printer offline," the icon in the Printers folder is ghosted. If you have a shortcut to that icon on your Desktop, however, it is not ghosted when the printer is offline. If you click the shortcut icon on the Desktop, you will see a message stating that the printer is offline in the title bar of the Print Queue window. To turn the printer back online, click the "Use printer offline" command again.

Printing with the Task Scheduler

One approach to deferred printing that works on a local printer is to use the Windows Task Scheduler (previously called System Agent) to schedule your print job. You can set it up to print on an as-needed basis, or on a regular schedule — to print your modem log every night, for example. Follow these steps to set up a print job in the Task Scheduler:

STEPS

Scheduling Unattended Printing

Step 1. If you have the Task Scheduler icon in your tray, double-click it to open the Scheduled Tasks window. You can also open the window by clicking the Scheduled Tasks icon in the My Computer window, or by clicking Start ➪ Programs ➪ Accessories ➪ System Tools ➪ Scheduled Tasks.

Step 2. In the Scheduled Tasks window, click the Add Scheduled Task icon to start the Scheduled Task Wizard, and then click Next.

Step 3. From the wizard's list, select the program you used to create the document you want to print — or click Browse if you don't see the one you want. Click Next.

Step 4. Give your task a name, such as **Print Weekly Status Report**, and indicate when you want the task to run, as shown in Figure 41-9. If this is the only time you want to print this file, mark the "One time only" option button. Click Next. If you choose one of the last two options ("When my computer starts" or "When I log on"), skip to step 6.

Continued

STEPS

Scheduling Unattended Printing *(continued)*

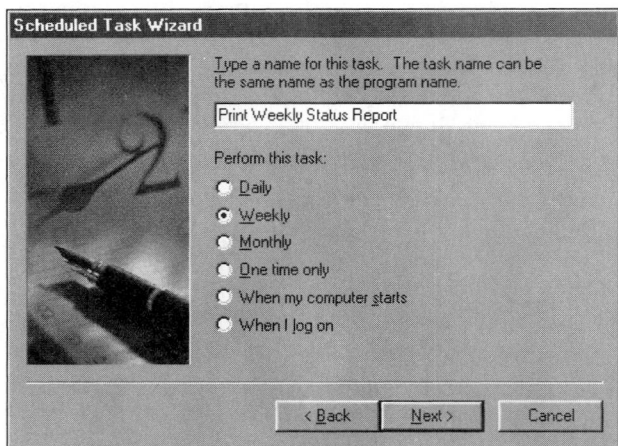

Figure 41-9: The Scheduled Task Wizard lets you name your task and indicate how often it will run.

Step 5. Enter the time and date when the task should run, and click Next.

Step 6. Mark the "Open advanced properties for this task when I click Finish" checkbox. Click Finish.

Step 7. The Task tab of the Properties dialog box for this task will open. In the Run field, add a space after the path for the program you have chosen, and then type the command to print a document, using this syntax:

```
/p "drive:\foldername\filename"
```

You must use the quote marks if any of your files or folders have spaces in their names. As the example in Figure 41-10 shows, the command to print a report you wrote in WordPad might look like this:

```
C:\Program Files\Accessories\Wordpad.exe /p "C:\My
Documents\Report.txt"
```

Step 8. Click OK, and then close Task Scheduler.

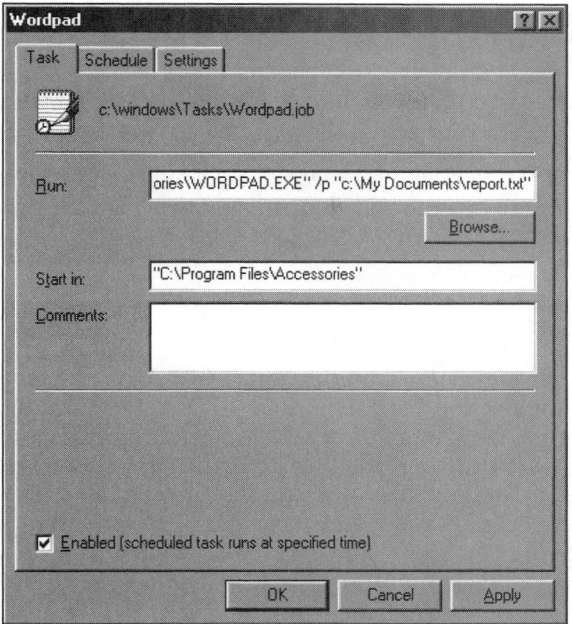

Figure 41-10: Type **/p** after the program's filename in the task's Properties dialog box, followed by the path and name of the file you want to print.

Although the /p switch for printing is quite common, it is by no means universal. Microsoft Word and Excel are two noteworthy exceptions. (Word uses /x and Excel uses /e.) The switch is defined for an application by the developers. If you have trouble getting the Task Scheduler to work for your document, you can check the application's syntax for printing. In the Explorer, choose View ⇨ Folder Options, and click the File Types tab. In the list there, highlight the file type that you want to use and click Edit. Highlight Print in the Actions list, and click Edit. Look at the contents of the "Application used to perform action" field. After the filename of the application (probably ending in exe), you'll see the appropriate characters needed to carry out the Print action. Use these characters instead of /p in the steps above. For a more complete discussion of actions associated with file types, see "General Actions on Any File Type" in Chapter 12.

If you want to get back to the Properties dialog box for a task, simply right-click the task in the Scheduled Tasks window and click Properties in the context menu. You can temporarily disable a task without deleting it by clearing the

Enabled checkbox on the Task tab. To change your task's schedule, go to the Scheduled tab and change the contents of the fields there. On the Settings tab, you'll find additional ways to constrain your task — for example, the Power Management settings let you avoid running a task if you're on battery power, or let you tell your computer to "wake up" for tasks that run late at night.

The Task Scheduler also keeps a log, which can be handy if you're trouble-shooting. To see the log, click Advanced ⇨ View Log in the Scheduled Tasks window.

Printing to a File

Tip

You can always create a print file for a specific printer and manually send this file to the printer later. To do this, change the "Print to the following port" field in the Details tab for that printer's driver from a specific port to FILE. When you print your document, you can use all the settings available for that printer, including the paper tray and the number of copies to print. A new file will be created that contains the document formatted with the printer codes for that specific printer. You will be prompted by your application to choose a name and location for the file. The default extension for a print file is usually ps or prn, depending on whether the printer driver you're using is PostScript or not.

Printing to a file can be a very effective way to work with a service bureau, since they don't have to have your application or your fonts to print your file. Printing to a file also lets you design a document at home, and then print it on a specialized PostScript printer at the office or a copy center. Keep in mind that the file you produce will often be considerably larger than your original document, especially if you include imported images or print color separations. Perhaps the biggest drawback is that you cannot edit the print file after you create it. If your service bureau finds a mistake, or you don't want that paper tray after all, you must go back to your original document and print to a new file.

When you later have access to the printer whose driver you chose, you can copy the file to the printer port. You actually need to use the DOS Copy command. You can't drag and drop the print file to the Printer icon. This method would make the most sense (visually), but it doesn't work.

Secret

You can run the DOS Copy command from the Run dialog box if you like (click the Start button, and click Run). Assuming that the name of your print file is File1.hp, you would type the following command in the Run dialog box:

```
command /c copy /b file1.hp lpt2:
```

This copies the file of print commands to the second parallel port (which could also be redirected to a network printer). The /c parameter tells Command to execute the following command and then return to the DOS prompt. The /b parameter tells Copy to copy the file in binary mode. For some trickier approaches to printing files, turn to the "Printing to an Offline PostScript Printer" section coming up next.

Note that if you use this method for a network printer, you'll need to capture a printer port to make it work.

Some people print to a file to generate ASCII text reports — from a database application, for example — which they can read on their computers as well as print. To do this in Windows, make sure to set "Spool data format" to RAW before you print. (Click the Spool Settings button in the Details tab of the printer's Properties dialog box to check this setting.) For the most readable results, install the driver for a generic printer (by choosing Generic/Text Only in the manufacturer list of the Add Printer Wizard) with FILE as its port. Then target that printer in your application when you print the report.

The whole point of deferred printing is to get around this tiresome technique of manually copying print files to the printer port. Unfortunately, deferred printing works only for network printers and not for local printers that are presently offline.

Printing to an Offline PostScript Printer

You can also use the technique described in the previous section to print to an offline (off-premises) PostScript printer. First install a PostScript driver on your computer for your target PostScript printer. Then use the PostScript driver to print the document to a file. Transfer this file via diskette or over the phone lines to the location with the PostScript printer. Finally, use the DOS Copy command to print the PostScript file on the target printer.

Printing PostScript Files

You can create a print file of PostScript output on a computer that doesn't have a PostScript printer connected to it (or to the network that the computer is connected to). You then take this PostScript output file, which usually has a ps extension, to a computer with a PostScript printer and copy the file to the printer. (The PostScript output file is just a series of ASCII commands and parameters.)

Copying a file to the printer is a DOS-based function, but we can configure Windows 98 to carry out this function without using the Start ➪ Run dialog box or opening a DOS window and issuing the DOS Copy command.

Secret

There are two ways to do this. First, you can create an association between the ps file extension and a command that copies the file to the printer. Second, you can create a batch file (and a shortcut to it) that consists of the DOS commands to send the file to the printer. Then you can place the shortcut to the PostScript printing batch file in the SendTo folder. Because the batch file is generic, it will send any file to the printer, not just PostScript files.

To create an association to the ps file type, take the following steps:

STEPS

Create a Print Command Associated with a PostScript Print File

Step 1.   Open your Explorer, choose View ⇨ Folder Options, and click the File Types tab.

Step 2.   Click the New Type button.

Step 3.   Type **PostScript Print Output File** in the "Description of type" field, **ps** in the "Associated extension" field, and **PostScript Commands** in the Content Type (MIME) field.

Step 4.   Click the New button, and then type **Copy to Printer** in the Action field and **C:\Windows\Command.com /c Copy /b %1 Lpt1:** in the "Application used to perform action" field. Click OK.

You can replace Lpt1: in this command line with another printer port designator, or with the UNC name of a network printer.

Step 5.   Click the Choose Icon button, and browse to find an appropriate printer-type icon. Click OK.

Step 6.   Click OK, and then click Close.

You can now click any file with a ps extension to print it on your PostScript printer. Unfortunately, the DOS window will flash briefly when you use this method.

To create a batch file and an accompanying shortcut that will print any file (and not flash a DOS window), take the following steps:

STEPS

Create a Print Batch File

Step 1.   Click Edit.com in your \Windows\Command folder (if you haven't already made a shortcut to this nifty DOS editor).

Step 2. Type **C:\Windows\Command.com** /c Copy /b %1 Lpt1:

Step 3. Choose File ⇨ Save As, and save the file as **Ps.bat**.

Step 4. Right-drag and drop Ps.bat to your Desktop to create a shortcut to it. (You could also try another method to create a shortcut on your Desktop. Right-click Ps.bat, and click Create Shortcut. Right-click the shortcut, which appears in the same folder as Ps.bat, and click Cut. Then right-click the Desktop and click Paste.)

Step 5. With the new shortcut on the Desktop highlighted, press F2, rename the shortcut something like **Print Files**, and press Enter.

Step 6. Right-click the shortcut, choose Properties, and then click the Program tab.

Step 7. Choose Minimized in the Run drop-down list, and mark the "Close on exit" checkbox. Click the Change Icon button and find an appropriate icon for this shortcut that prints files. Click OK.

Step 8. Right-click a PostScript print output file in a folder or Explorer window, and click Copy in the context menu.

Step 9. Right-click the new shortcut on the Desktop and click Paste. The PostScript file will be copied to the PostScript printer. A button will appear briefly on the taskbar as the file is copied.

The file is treated as a DOS file, and it will be spooled to the printer if you haven't turned off DOS print spooling.

You can place this shortcut in the \Windows\SendTo folder. If you do this, you can right-click the PostScript (or text) file, point to Send To in the context menu, and then click the shortcut in the Send To submenu to copy the file to the printer.

Troubleshooting with Windows Help

If you are having trouble printing, you can use the Print Troubleshooter section of the help system to track down the problem. Windows Help is no longer just a semi-meaningless collection of statements of the obvious; it is actually useful in the real world. The print troubleshooter can pinpoint a problem for you, as long as you answer the questions correctly.

To get to the print troubleshooter, click the Start button, click Help, click Troubleshooting, click "Hardware & system device problems," click "Hardware, memory, & others," and then click Printing Troubleshooter.

You should also check a file called `Printers.txt`, located in your `\Windows` folder. It contains information about problems and workarounds for specific printers.

There is an online troubleshooter in the Microsoft Knowledge Base called "Solving Problems with Printing in Windows," which is located at `http://support.microsoft.com/support/tshoot/w98print.asp`. You can also search the Microsoft Knowledge Base for articles related to your particular printer or problem; the address is `http://support.microsoft.com/support/`.

Other Troubleshooting Strategies

If you are having trouble printing, and have established that the printer is connected properly and that its properties are set correctly, try these strategies to isolate your problem:

- **Make sure you have enough disk space for spooling.** You should have at least 3MB free on the logical disk drive that contains your `\Windows\Temp` folder. Although the temporary files in this folder are supposed to be automatically deleted when you shut your computer down, sometimes (after a crash, for example) they remain on your disk and cause problems.

- **Try printing from a DOS prompt.** Restart your computer in Safe mode, open a DOS session and then try printing a test file to LPT1 (or whichever port you've assigned your printer). To do this, type **copy c:\boot.ini lpt1** (or **copy c:\Windows\System\testps.txt lpt1** if you have a PostScript printer) and press Enter.

   If `boot.ini` (or `testps.txt`) does not print, the problem may be with the port, the cable, or the printer. If it does print, the problem may relate to the spool settings or bidirectional communication. Click the Spool Settings button in the Details tab of your printer's Properties dialog box, and mark the "Print directly to the printer" option button. If your printer supports bidirectional communication, mark the "Disable bidirectional support for this printer" option button.

- **Try printing from Notepad or WordPad.** If you can't print from these two applets, check to make sure the port is set up correctly, and that there are no resource conflicts. To do this, open the Control Panel, click the System icon, and click the Device Manager tab. Click the plus sign next to Ports (COM & LPT), Double-click the port you have assigned to this printer, and click the Resources tab. Look at the "Conflicting device list" box. If there is a resource conflict, Windows will tell you what the conflicting device is, and which resource the two devices are fighting over. You can change the port's resource setting in this tab; see "Configuring Serial Ports" or "Configuring Parallel Ports" in Chapter 44.

If you *can* print from Notepad or WordPad, click the Spool Settings button in the Details tab of the printer's Properties dialog box, and try different combinations of spool settings and bidirectional support until you find a combination that works in your other applications.

- **Try disabling the Enhanced Capabilities Port (ECP port) if you have one.** Open the Device Manager, find the ECP port, and double-click it. On the General tab in the Properties dialog box for the port, mark "Disable in this hardware profile."

- **Try reinstalling the printer port.** Using the Device Manager, select the port assigned to your printer and click the Remove button. Restart your computer. In the Control Panel, click the Add New Hardware icon and let Windows 98 detect your hardware and walk you through reinstalling the port.

- **Try a different printer driver.** In the Printers folder, click the Add Printer icon and use the Add Printer Wizard to install the Generic/Text Only driver (to determine whether the problem is your driver). If the generic driver works, you may be able to solve the problem by deleting your printer from the Printers folder and reinstalling the driver for your printer's manufacturer and model. If that doesn't work, try installing a driver for a printer that your printer emulates. For example, if you have a PostScript printer, try using the Apple LaserWriter II NTX driver.

Windows Printing System

Microsoft introduced the Windows Printing System (WPS) in December 1992 as a way for printer manufacturers to speed up printing and reduce the cost of printers. WPS is a combination of software and hardware that comes with your printer and lets the translation to the printer's codes take place on the computer, instead of on the printer. There are also several printers on the market that use third-party software to offer similar features, but without the hardware component of WPS. You will need to have the setup disks for this software when you install the printer in Windows.

If you are already running WPS when you install Windows Me, Setup will automatically update several key WPS files. If you install WPS later, Windows will detect this and prompt you to load the Windows CD-ROM to update these files.

Windows changes some of the ways WPS works. For example, separator pages are now handled in the printer's Properties dialog box. If you're on a network, you need to capture a logical port for the printer, rather than using a UNC name. And you should enable bidirectional communication even if the port you are using is not bidirectional. (To do this, click the Spool Settings button in the Details tab of the Properties dialog box for your printer and mark "Enable bidirectional support for this printer.")

Sharing a Printer

You can share your printer over your network so that others can use it to print their documents. There are two basic ways to do this. The first is to configure your computer as a server (either a file server, a print server, or both), as described in the next section. Your computer can become a file and print server on a peer-to-peer network such as Microsoft Network, or on a server-based network such as a Novell NetWare or Windows NT network.

Unlike Windows 2000/NT or Novell servers, the Windows Me file and print server doesn't have a database that can track users and maintain user-level security. If you want the kind of security that allows users to use your resources by group or user name instead of by password, you'll need to use these other servers.

Enabling Print Sharing

If you want share your local printer with others on a network, you must first enable print sharing. To do so, take the following steps:

STEPS

Enabling Print Sharing

Step 1. Click the Start button, point to Settings, and then click Control Panel.

Step 2. Click the Network icon. Click the Add button.

Step 3. Highlight Service in the Select Network Component Type dialog box, and click the Add button.

Step 4. Highlight Microsoft in the Select Network Service dialog box. Then highlight either "File and printer sharing for Microsoft networks" or "File and printer sharing for NetWare networks." If you are installing print sharing for another network and you have a diskette from the manufacturer, click the Have Disk button instead, select the correct diskette drive, and choose the appropriate service. Click OK.

Step 5. Click the File and Print Sharing button.

Step 6. In the File and Print Sharing dialog box, shown in Figure 41-11, mark "I want to be able to allow others to print to my printer(s)."

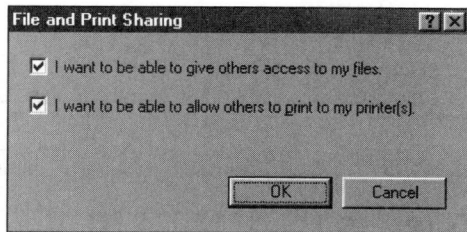

Figure 41-11: The File and Print Sharing dialog box. Mark the checkboxes next to the resources that you want to share.

Step 7.   Click both OK buttons.

You have to restart your computer so that the changes you made can take effect.

Actually Sharing Your Printer

To share a printer, take the following steps:

STEPS

Sharing a Printer

Step 1.   Click the Start button, point to Settings, and then click Printers.

Step 2.   Right-click the icon of the printer that you want to share, and then click Sharing in the context menu.

Step 3.   You'll see the Sharing tab of the Properties dialog box for the printer, as shown in Figure 41-12. Mark the Shared As option button.

Step 4.   Fill out the three Shared As fields.

Step 5.   Click OK.

Continued

STEPS

Sharing a Printer *(continued)*

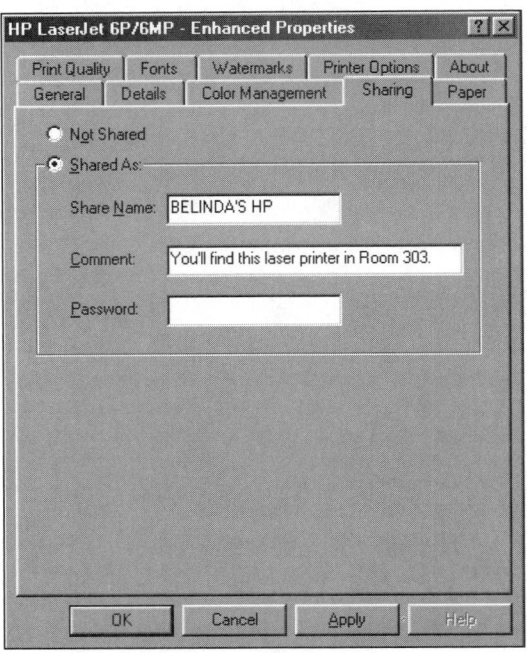

Figure 41-12: The Sharing tab. Click Shared As to allow your printer to be used by others. You can give a useful comment and name to help others decide if they want to use your printer and determine where to find the output.

Your computer is now a full-fledged print server. If you are using a NetWare network, you can use the Windows computer as a complete print server and off-load the extra resource use from your NetWare server.

If you are using a Windows 2000, NT, or NetWare server to provide user-level security, you won't see the Password field that appears in Figure 41-12. The users who can access your printer will be determined by the database of users to whom you have granted access to your resources. This list of groups and users is kept on the Windows NT or NetWare server.

To specify which server the list of users is kept on, take the following steps:

STEPS

Specifying User-Access Control

Step 1.   Click the Start button, point to Settings, and then click Control Panel.

Step 2.   Click the Network icon. Click the Access Control tab.

Step 3.   Click the "User-level access control" option button.

Step 4.   Type the name of the server that has the list.

A Shortcut to a Shared Printer

If you create a shortcut from your Printer icon in the Printers folder, that shortcut will only work on your computer. You cannot e-mail it to someone else on your network and have it work for them. Here's how to make a shortcut that you can send to your coworkers:

STEPS

Creating a Shortcut to a Shared Printer

Step 1.   Click My Network Places on your Desktop and locate the print server.

Step 2.   Click the print server to view its resources.

Step 3.   Right-click the Shared Printer icon, and click Create Shortcut in the context menu.

Monitoring Shared Printer Use

If you have a shared printer or other resource on your computer, you may want to see who is using it. If you have installed Client for Microsoft Networks as a networking protocol, you can use the Net Watcher utility to perform this and other network housekeeping functions.

To start Net Watcher, click Start ➪ Programs ➪ Accessories ➪ System Tools ➪ Net Watcher. If you don't find Net Watcher, use Add/Remove Programs to install it. (Click the Add/Remove Programs icon in the Control Panel, click the Windows Setup tab, highlight System Tools, click the Details button, and mark the Net Watcher checkbox.)

Slow Network Printing with MS-DOS Programs

If you print a document from a DOS program or press the Print Screen key while in a DOS window and it takes from 60 to 90 seconds for the printing to begin, the DOS program might not have closed the printer port. The Windows default setting is to wait 45 seconds after the DOS program stops sending information to begin printing if the printer port isn't closed by the DOS program, so this can mean some rather long waits.

To solve this problem, add the following lines to your System.ini file:

```
[Network]
PrintBufTime=10
[IFSMGR]
PrintBufTime=10
```

If these lines aren't already in your System.ini file, create them in the appropriate sections after the [386Enh] section. They set the print buffer time at 10 seconds (instead of the default 45 seconds). If you experience problems, you should try increasing the values.

Point and Print

You can, of course, install a printer driver on your computer for a network printer in the normal (non-point and print) fashion by using the Add Printer Wizard. Just click the Add Printer icon in the Printers folder.

When you do this, the wizard finds the printer driver files necessary to install that printer driver. You need to know exactly what kind of printer you are installing so you can tell this to the Add Printer Wizard, and you need to have the printer driver source diskettes or CD-ROM handy.

You can install printers that are shared on networked Windows Me, Windows 98, Windows NT, and NetWare servers with point and print. If you are printing to a Windows print server, all the information about the printer drivers and the drivers themselves are stored there. You don't have to do anything to allow the drivers to be transferred to the client Windows computer. The Windows printer server must be running file and printer sharing for NetWare networks or file and printer sharing for Microsoft networks.

Automated Printer Driver Installation

A better way to install a printer driver for a network printer is to have Windows install the driver automatically. You can do this in three ways: Drag and drop a document icon to the network printer's icon in its Shared Folder window, drag and drop the network printer's icon to your Desktop or your Printers folder, or click the network printer's icon in the Shared Resources folder window of the server.

Drag and Drop a Document to a Network Printer Icon

When you print a document by dragging and dropping it to the icon of a network printer that you haven't yet installed, you invoke a version of the Add Printer Wizard.

STEPS

Installing a Network Printer by Drag-and-Drop Printing

Step 1. Open a folder window containing a document file or a shortcut to a document file.

Step 2. Make sure you have the Shared Resources folder window open for the server whose printer you are going to install.

Step 3. Drag and drop the Document icon to the Printer icon in the Shared Resources folder window. The message box shown in Figure 41-13 will appear.

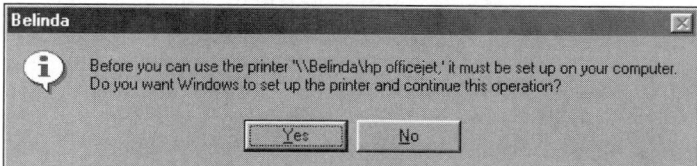

Figure 41-13: A message box telling you that you have to set up the printer driver on your computer

Step 4. Click the Yes button. The Add Printer Wizard (network printer installation version) appears, as shown in Figure 41-14. If you want to assign a logical printer port to your network printer, click the Yes option button to indicate that you want to print from MS-DOS programs, and then click the Next button. (MS-DOS programs often require that you print to an LPT port.)

STEPS

Installing a Network Printer by Drag-and-Drop Printing *(continued)*

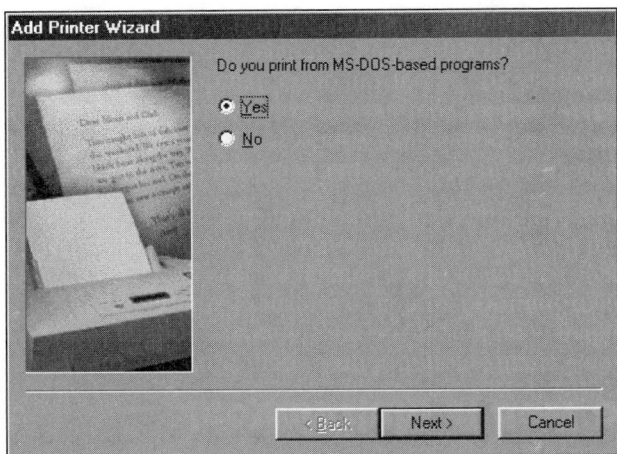

Figure 41-14: The network printer installation version of the Add Printer Wizard. If you don't want to capture a printer port, click Next. Otherwise, click the Yes option button, and then click Next.

Step 5. Finish answering the Wizard's questions. Give the printer a name that reminds you which one it is when you print to it. When you click Finish, the wizard will copy the printer drivers from the network server and install them on your computer. While the wizard is running, you may see a message that a dll file needed for this printer is in use by another program. If so, exit any other applications you may be running (Microsoft Word, for example), and click the Retry button.

If the printer has trouble printing your file, the print troubleshooter will automatically start and lead you through a troubleshooting process.

The printer driver for the network printer is now installed. When you open your Printers folder window, you'll see an icon for the network printer.

Secret

Now that you have installed the network printer, you can drag and drop documents to either of its icons to print documents. The network printer's icons in the shared resources folder and in your local Printers folder behave in the same way. Click either and you will see the same Print Queue window. One minor difference is that only the icon in the Printers folder is ghosted if the network printer is offline.

Drag and Drop a Network Printer Icon

The Network Printer icon should be visible to you in the Explorer or in a Shared Resources folder window that is focused on the network server computer. You can drag and drop the network printer's icon from the Explorer or folder window to your Desktop or to your Printers folder window or Folder icon, creating a shortcut to the network printer.

Now follow steps 4 through 5 in the "Installing a Network Printer by Drag-and-Drop Printing" steps in the previous section. After the wizard is finished, the network printer's icon will appear in your Printers folder as well as in the place where you made the shortcut.

Secret

You have created a shortcut to the network printer, but the network connection must be there for the printer to work. If your network connection is DCC, you can't invoke the connection by clicking the network printer's icon if it isn't already set up. You have to make the connection first before the network printer can be seen.

Click the Network Printer Icon

If you can see the icon that represents the shared printer on the network computer, just click it. The wizard will start, as described in a previous section, "Drag and Drop a Document to a Network Printer Icon," and install the network printer. It copies the shared printer's driver over to your computer and puts the Printer icon in your Printers folder. As an alternative, you can also right-click the network printer's icon and click Install.

Point and Print to a NetWare Server

If you want to be able to have Windows client computers point and print to your printers managed by a NetWare printer server, you're going to need to do a little more work. You have to copy the driver files that are used for each of the printers managed by that server to a directory on the server. It turns out that this is more akin to the Add Printer Wizard than to point and print.

Set Up a NetWare Print Server for Point and Print

If you have administrative privileges on the NetWare server that you are logged onto, you can configure the server to store the needed printer drivers and auxiliary files. Take the following steps to do so:

STEPS

Configuring a NetWare Server to Store Point and Print Files

Step 1. Right-click a NetWare Print Queue icon displayed in the NetWare Shared Resources window. Click Point and Print Setup in the context menu.

Step 2. Click "Set printer model." In the Select dialog box, highlight the manufacturer and model of the printer associated with the print queue on the NetWare server. Click OK.

Step 3. Right-click the same NetWare print queue again, and then click "Set driver path."

Step 4. Type a path and folder name that is valid for the NetWare server and in which you will store the printer driver files for this printer.

Step 5. Open `Msprint.inf` or `Msprint2.inf` in your Inf folder with Notepad. See which files are going to be copied when you install this printer. Extract these files from your Windows CD-ROM cabinet files and copy them into the directory you just created on your NetWare server.

You now have the printer driver source files on your NetWare server. This makes it somewhat easier to point and print to a NetWare printer from a Windows client computer.

Point and Print to a NetWare Printer

Now that you have set up your NetWare server to allow point and print (after a fashion), you can use it to install printer drivers on a Windows client computer. To do this, take the following steps:

STEPS

Installing a Printer Driver from a NetWare Server

Step 1. Log onto a NetWare server from a client Windows computer.

Step 2. In My Network Places on the client computer, click the NetWare server's icon to display a folder window listing the resources of the NetWare server.

Step 3. Drag and drop a Printer icon from the NetWare window to your local Printers folder window. This activates the Add Printer Wizard.

Step 4. Type the name of the new printer.

Your NetWare network printer driver is now installed on your local Windows 98 computer.

Managing Printers

Just a few paperwork items here.

Windows Setup Changes the Values for Your Print Spooler

Secret

The Windows Setup program can change the values of your print spooler settings if they are different than Windows' defaults. If you have more than one printer defined, you'll need to change back the spooler values for each one.

Windows Setup changes the spooler settings for data format to EMF, and for communications support to bidirectional. If those are the settings that you used previously, there is no need to check your current settings. But, if you set your data format to RAW and your communications support to disable bidirectional, you'll want to change them back.

STEPS

Setting Your Print Spooler Values

Step 1. Click Start ⇨ Settings, and click the Printers icon.

Step 2. Right-click a Printer icon, click Properties, and go to the Details tab.

Step 3. Click the Spool Settings button to display the Spool Settings dialog box, shown in Figure 41-15.

Continued

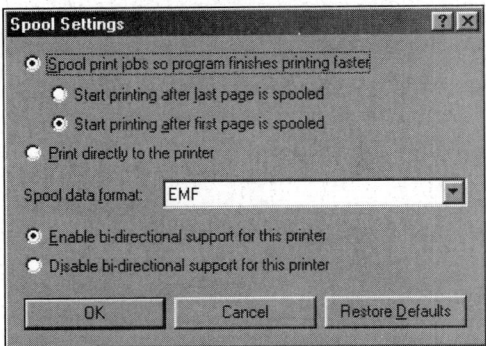

Figure 41-15: The Spool Settings dialog box lets you change the Windows 98 defaults if your printer doesn't support them.

Step 4. Display the "Spool data format" drop-down list to switch to RAW if you so desire.

Step 5. Mark the "Disable bi-directional support for this printer" option button.

Step 6. Click OK. Click OK again.

Step 7. Right-click the next Printer icon and repeat steps 2 through 6 until you have completed them for all of your printers.

Thanks to Dale Grant for help with this secret.

No Fonts in Your Text Editor?

If one day you open up Microsoft Word or another text editor and find that you can't type anything, that the font list only contains one font repeated many times, that most of your fonts are missing, that your characters are scattered all over the page, or that the formatting has gone haywire, don't despair. You could either have a corrupted printer driver, or you may have accidentally chosen a printer driver for a printer that doesn't support your normal array of fonts.

Choose File ⇨ Print in your editor, and see what printer you are defaulted to use. If you normally use another printer, choose it instead. You can also click Start ⇨ Settings ⇨ Printers. The default printer has a checkmark next to it, as shown in Figure 41-16.

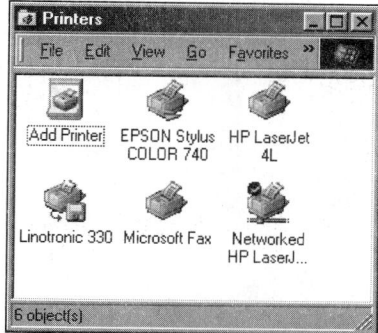

Figure 41-16: In this example, the Networked HP LaserJet is marked as the default printer.

Right-click another printer and set it as the default instead. See if your fonts return.

It may be that all of the Printer icons in your Printers folder are dim. If this is the case, check to see if you have two different hardware profiles. (Press Win+Pause/Break or right-click your My Computer icon and click Properties, and then click the Hardware Profiles tab.) You may have booted your computer into a hardware profile that doesn't have any printers configured for it. This might happen, for example, if you have docked and undocked hardware profiles for a portable computer. Reboot to a hardware profile that contains printers or add printers to the hardware profile without them (click Start ⇨ Settings ⇨ Printers ⇨ Add Printer).

If this doesn't solve your problem, install a new printer, or remove an existing printer and install the same printer again. Click the Add Printer icon in the Printers folder (see Figure 41-16) and follow the steps in the Add Printer Wizard. When asked if you want to set the new printer as the default printer for Windows-based programs, mark the Yes option button.

Complex Graphics on Hewlett Packard Printers

Hewlett Packard LaserJet 4 and 5 models may not print your complex graphical image due to lack of memory installed in the printer. The best way around this problem is to force your computer to use its processor and memory to do the work that the printer can't do.

You can force the computer to get busy (and slow) by taking these steps:

STEPS

Helping Out the Hewlett Packard Printer

Step 1. Click Start ⇨ Settings ⇨ Printers. Right-click your HP LaserJet icon, and click Properties.

Step 2. Click the Details tab, and click the Spool Settings button. Then display the "Spool data format" drop-down list, and select RAW (see Figure 41-17). Click OK.

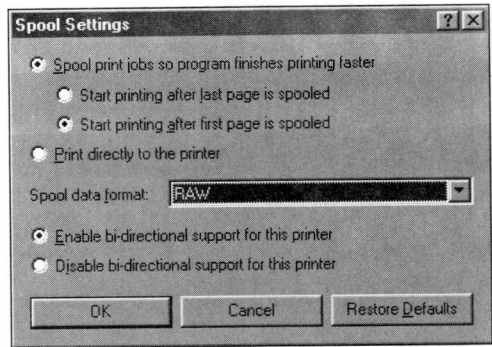

Figure 41-17: The Spool Settings dialog box. RAW has been selected in the drop-down list.

Step 3. Click the Graphics tab. Mark the "Use raster graphics" option button, as shown in Figure 41-18.

Step 4. Click the Fonts tab, and mark "Print TrueType as graphics."

Step 5. Click the Device Options tab, and move the "Printer memory tracking" slider all the way to the right for Aggressive memory tracking, as shown in Figure 41-19.

Step 6. See whether the "Page protection" checkbox is dim. If it isn't, clear it if it is marked, and mark it if it is cleared. Click OK.

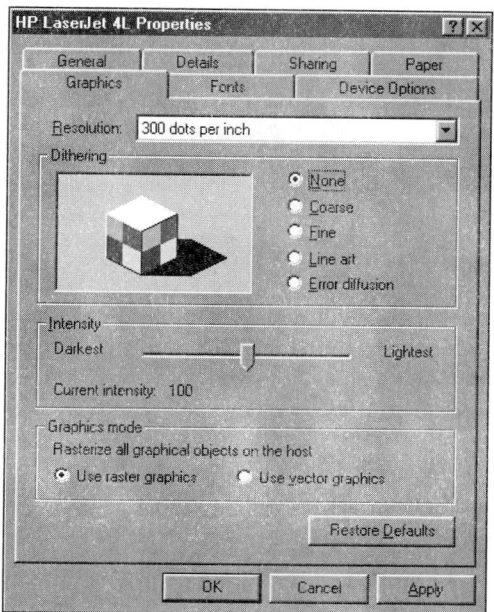

Figure 41-18: The Graphics tab of the Properties dialog box for an HP LaserJet 4 or 5 printer. Mark the "Use raster graphics" option button.

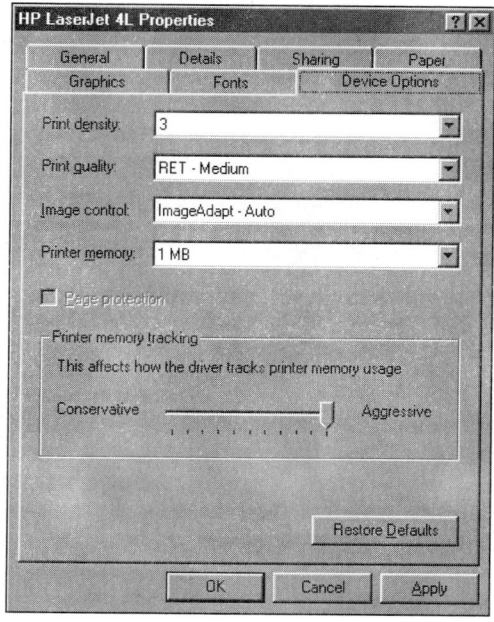

Figure 41-19: The Device Options tab for the same printer's Properties. Adjust the "Printer memory tracking" slider bar.

For a more detailed discussion of how printer memory is managed, see "Spooling EMF, not RAW Printer Codes" in Chapter 29 of *Windows 98 Secrets*.

Different Printers for Different Papers

If you want to quickly switch between different settings for your printer driver, you can create different printer icons in the Printers folder for the same printer. Assign different names and settings for each Printer icon and then print to the printer with the appropriate settings.

Click the Add Printer icon (Start ➪ Settings ➪ Printers) to create a new printer icon. In the Add Printer Wizard, mark "Keep existing driver" to use the same driver that you have already installed for your printer. Give the new printer a name that describes what its settings will be.

Right-click the new Printer icon, click Properties, and change its properties to reflect the settings you desire. For example, if you have an Epson Stylus Color 800, you might want to change the settings for different resolutions and paper type. You might name three Printer icons as follows:

```
Normal paper (360 and 720 dpi)
Photo quality Inkjet paper (720 and 1440 dpi)
Glossy paper (720 and 1440 dpi)
```

Thanks to Marc Arts for help with this tip.

Summary

Windows Me supports an incredible number of different printers, with a number of tricks you can take advantage of. We describe them for you.

▶ We discuss how the new Printers folder unites almost all of the print functions in Windows, making it easier for you to manage your printers.

▶ Because each printer has its own icon, you can put a shortcut to each printer on your Desktop. You can drag and drop documents to the particular printer that you want without having to change the default printer.

▶ You can define drag and drop to a printer to be any possible action, not just printing.

▶ DOS files are, by default, spooled to the printer through the Windows print spooler. This alleviates printer device contention.

▶ We show you how to print TrueType fonts correctly on PostScript printers.

▶ You can print to a print queue and have your files printed later when you actually connect to your printer.

▶ You can have the appropriate printer drivers automatically installed when you print to network printers.

Chapter 42

Keyboards and Characters

In This Chapter

We show you how to type the characters available to you in Windows, how to pick a keyboard layout for easier access, and how to use shortcuts to run Windows from the keyboard. We reveal:

▶ The relationship between fonts and characters

▶ What characters and character sets come with Windows

▶ The five ways to type (or insert) little-used characters into your documents

▶ Modifying your keyboard layout to more easily enter these little-used characters

▶ Creating multilingual documents

▶ Using multilingual e-mail and Web sites

▶ Windows shortcut keys that can speed up your work

▶ Speeding up your keyboard

▶ Changing your keyboard driver if you get a new and different keyboard

Fonts and Characters

There is a relationship (although it is a complex one) between the characters you see on your keyboard's keys and the characters that appear on your screen when you press those keys. For one thing, the appearance of the characters you type depends on which font you are using. For another, you can type characters that may not appear on your keyboard, such as (©), (™), (®), ¼, ½, ¾, é, õ, ä, ¢, £, and ¥.

The characters that are displayed on your screen are stored on your computer's hard disk in font files. Each font file has at least 224 character definitions (known collectively as a *character set*) stored in it. Most of the basic Windows fonts come with 652 character definitions. A *font* is a visual expression of a character set. When you purchase a packet of fonts, the characters come with it at no additional charge (this is a typographer's little joke).

Both TrueType and bitmapped screen fonts ship with Windows. The TrueType fonts consist of font descriptions for each character and the ability to scale the font across a wide variety of sizes. TrueType fonts work with both the screen and the printer. The bitmapped fonts are for display on the screen, and consist of dots on a grid.

For a more complete understanding of fonts, you should read this chapter and Chapter 21.

Windows Character Sets

The fonts that ship with Windows are based on these principal character sets, among others:

- Extended Windows ANSI (652 characters — also called Windows Glyph List 4, or WGL4)
- Windows ANSI, Windows 3.1 version (224 characters — also called ISO-8859-1 or Latin 1)
- Windows ANSI, Windows 3.0 version
- DOS/OEM (also called IBM PC-8 or Code Page 437)
- Symbol
- Wingdings
- Webdings
- Marlett
- Lucida Sans Unicode
- Lucida Console

Five of the TrueType fonts (Arial, Courier New, Tahoma, Times New Roman, and Verdana) use the Extended Windows ANSI character set. This character set, also referred to as *Windows Glyph List 4* (WGL4), consists of 652 characters, including the basic 224 ANSI characters plus support for Baltic, Central European, Cyrillic, Greek, and Turkish alphabets. The extra characters are accessible only when you use the appropriate keyboard driver (see the "Using Multiple Languages" section later in this chapter).

Abadi MT, Calisto MT, Comic Sans, Copperplate Gothic, Century Gothic, Impact, Lucida Handwriting Italic, News Gothic, and OCRA Extended use the 224-character Windows ANSI character set, defined when Windows 3.1

and TrueType fonts were developed, and known more esoterically as the *ISO 8859-1* or *Latin-1* character set. These fonts were formerly part of Microsoft Plus! for Windows 95, but are now included with Windows. Most commercially available English fonts also use this standard.

Five of the bitmapped screen fonts (Courier, Fixedsys, MS Sans Serif, MS Serif, and System) use the earlier Windows 3.0 version of the Windows ANSI character set, which defined fewer characters between positions 128 and 160.

The bitmapped screen font Terminal and the bitmapped DOS fonts used in windowed DOS sessions all use the DOS/OEM character set. This is also referred to as the *IBM PC-8* (which stands for 8-bit) or *Code Page 437* character set. IBM developed this character set when it created the first IBM PC. This same character set is stored in ROM in U.S.-made PCs and used by full-screen DOS programs.

Four additional TrueType character sets ship with Windows — Symbol, Wingdings, Webdings, and Marlett. They have their own particular characters and don't relate to the previously mentioned "standards." Figure 42-1 shows characters from the TrueType fonts Times New Roman, Symbol, and Wingdings with their corresponding character numbers. The Times New Roman characters display the first 255 characters of the Extended Windows ANSI character set.

The Marlett font contains the Windows "furniture." The symbols on the Minimize, Maximize, and Close buttons at the right end of Windows title bars are in this font. Because the symbols in the buttons are fonts, it is easy to resize the buttons. Make sure not to delete this font from your \Windows\Fonts folder.

Lucida Sans Unicode and Lucida Console use subsets of the Unicode character set, and have 660 and 1,738 characters, respectively. They include letters (Latin, Greek, Hebrew, Cyrillic, and so on), symbols, and characters for drawing boxes on a nongraphic terminal. Lucida Console replaces the TrueType DOS fonts that were used with earlier versions of Windows.

Tip

Unicode is a 16-bit character set intended to accommodate all commonly used data-processing characters of all the earth's languages in its 64,000 data points. Microsoft has indicated that Unicode is the direction that fonts and documents in the future will be going. Typically, a font only contains one or more *ranges* or subsets of Unicode, because the entire set is so big.

The Windows TrueType Character Sets

Windows includes three kinds of TrueType fonts: Text typefaces (e.g., Arial, Comic Sans, Lucida Sans Unicode, Times New Roman or Verdana), Symbol and decorative fonts such as Wingdings and Webdings. To access characters that cannot be typed directly from the keyboard use the Character Map applet, use the special keystroke combination difined by your word processor, or:

1) Make sure the Num Lock light is *on*.
2) Hold down the Alt key while typing the appropriate number on the numeric key pad.
3) Release the Alt key.

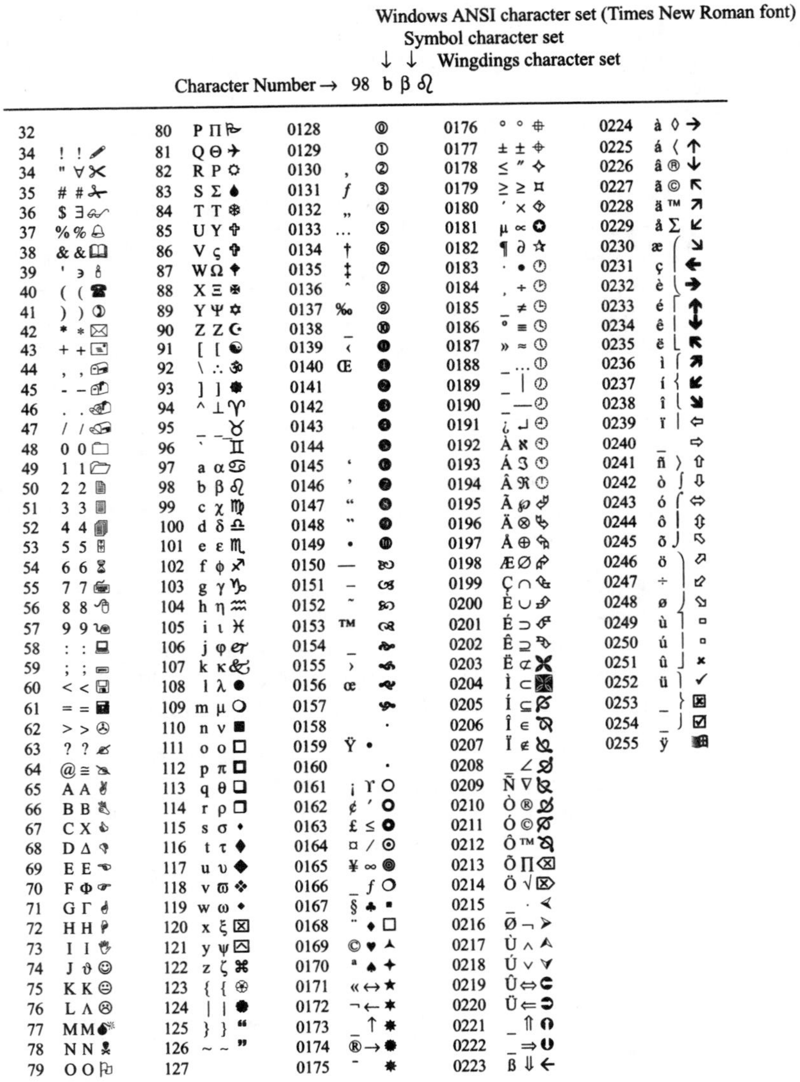

Windows ANSI character set (Times New Roman font)
Symbol character set
↓ ↓ Wingdings character set

Character Number → 98 b β ℒ

#	ANSI	#	ANSI	#	ANSI	#	ANSI	#	ANSI
32		80	P Π	0128	Ⓞ	0176	° ° ⊕	0224	à ◊ →
34	! !	81	Q Θ	0129	①	0177	± ± ✦	0225	á ⟨ ↑
34	" ∀	82	R P	0130	, ②	0178	≤ " ✧	0226	â ® ↓
35	# #	83	S Σ	0131	ƒ ③	0179	≥ ≥ ¤	0227	ã © ↖
36	$ ∃	84	T T	0132	„ ④	0180	′ × ✧	0228	ä ™ ↗
37	% %	85	U Y	0133	… ⑤	0181	μ ∝ ♻	0229	å Σ ↙
38	& &	86	V ς	0134	† ⑥	0182	¶ ∂ ☆	0230	æ ↘
39	' ∋	87	W Ω	0135	‡ ⑦	0183	· • ☉	0231	ç ⟩
40	((	88	X Ξ	0136	ˆ ⑧	0184	¸ ÷ ☉	0232	è ⟨ →
41	))	89	Y Ψ	0137	‰ ⑨	0185	¹ ≠ ☉	0233	é ⌈ ↑
42	* *	90	Z Z	0138	_ ⑩	0186	º ≡ ☉	0234	ê ⌊ ↓
43	+ +	91	[[	0139	‹ ❶	0187	» ≈ ☉	0235	ë ⌊ ↖
44	, ,	92	\ ∴	0140	Œ ❷	0188	¼ … ①	0236	ì ↗
45	- -	93	]]	0141	❸	0189	½ │ ⑫	0237	í ⌈ ↙
46	. .	94	^ ⊥	0142	❹	0190	¾ — ⑬	0238	î ⌊ ↘
47	/ /	95	_ ⎯	0143	❺	0191	¿ ↵ ⊕	0239	ï ⌊ ⇐
48	0 0	96	` ‾	0144	❻	0192	À ℵ ☉	0240	⇒
49	1 1	97	a α	0145	' ❼	0193	Á ℑ ☉	0241	ñ ⟩ ⇑
50	2 2	98	b β	0146	' ❽	0194	Â ℜ ↗	0242	ò ⌡ ⇓
51	3 3	99	c χ	0147	" ❾	0195	Ã ℘ ↗	0243	ó ⌈ ⇔
52	4 4	100	d δ	0148	" ❿	0196	Ä ⊗ ♠	0244	ô ⌈ ⇑
53	5 5	101	e ε	0149	• ⓫	0197	Å ⊕ ♣	0245	õ ⌡ ↖
54	6 6	102	f φ	0150	— ⓑ	0198	Æ ∅ ☞	0246	ö ⟩ ↗
55	7 7	103	g γ	0151	– ⓒ	0199	Ç ∩ ↖	0247	÷ ⌡ ↙
56	8 8	104	h η	0152	˜ ⓓ	0200	È ∪ ♥	0248	ø ⌡ ↘
57	9 9	105	i ι	0153	™ ⓔ	0201	É ⊃ ☞	0249	ù ⌡ □
58	: :	106	j φ	0154	ⓕ	0202	Ê ⊇ ♦	0250	ú ⌡ □
59	; ;	107	k κ	0155	› ⓖ	0203	Ë ⊄ ✗	0251	û ⌡ ✗
60	< <	108	l λ	0156	œ ⓗ	0204	Ì ⊂ ■	0252	ü ⟩ ✓
61	= =	109	m μ	0157	ⓘ	0205	Í ⊆ ✗	0253	⟩ ☒
62	> >	110	n ν	0158	•	0206	Î ∈ ♢	0254	⌡ ☑
63	? ?	111	o o	0159	Ÿ •	0207	Ï ∉ ♦	0255	ÿ ■
64	@ ≅	112	p π	0160	·	0208	∠		
65	A A	113	q θ	0161	¡ ϒ ○	0209	Ñ ∇		
66	B B	114	r ρ	0162	¢ ′ ○	0210	Ò ®		
67	C X	115	s σ	0163	£ ≤ ●	0211	Ó ©		
68	D Δ	116	t τ	0164	¤ / ○	0212	Ô ™		
69	E E	117	u υ	0165	¥ ∞ ◉	0213	Õ Π		
70	F Φ	118	v ϖ	0166	¦ ƒ ○	0214	Ö √		
71	G Γ	119	w ω	0167	§ ♣ ■	0215	· ≺		
72	H H	120	x ξ	0168	¨ ♦ □	0216	Ø ¬ ≻		
73	I I	121	y ψ	0169	© ♥ ▲	0217	Ù ∧ ∧		
74	J ϑ	122	z ζ	0170	ª ♠ ✦	0218	Ú ∨ ∨		
75	K K	123	{ {	0171	« ↔ ★	0219	Û ⇔ ⊂		
76	L Λ	124				0172	¬ ← ✳	0220	Ü ⇐ ⊃		
77	M M	125	} }	0173	↑ ✴	0221	⇑ ∩		
78	N N	126	~ ~	0174	® → ❀	0222	⇒ ∪		
79	O O	127		0175	¯ ↓ ✻	0223	ß ⇓ ←		

Figure 42-1: The Windows TrueType character sets (ISO-8859-1)

The Windows ANSI Character Set

The Windows ANSI characters numbered 0 through 127 are identical to their counterparts in the DOS/OEM (IBM PC-8) character set. (These characters are also called the *ASCII* or *lower ASCII* character set, after the American Standards Committee for Information Interchange, which codified them decades ago.) The next 32 characters, 128 through 159, are mostly punctuation marks, although some character numbers are left unused. Of special interest are the curly single and double quotes. Following these are 32 characters of legal and currency symbols, then 32 characters of uppercase accented letters, and, finally, 32 characters of lowercase accented letters.

One way to access the characters numbered above 127 is to hold down the Alt key, type a zero (0) on the numeric keypad, and then type the three digits of the character's number—0189, for example. This extra zero is already included in the character numbers shown in Figure 42-1. This is the most basic method of accessing these additional characters. Better methods are detailed later in this chapter.

You must add a leading zero when using this method to insert characters numbered 128 through 255 in the Windows ANSI character set because Windows is downward compatible with the IBM PC-8 character set, which is used by DOS applications. The IBM PC-8 character set already uses the Alt+*number* method for its own characters, and Windows allows you to enter characters from this set using the same method.

For example, regardless of whether you're typing in DOS or Windows, Alt+171 inserts character number 171 from the IBM PC-8 character set, the one-half symbol (½). If you type Alt+0171 in Windows, you get character number 171 from the Windows ANSI character set, which is a chevron bracket («). (Windows ignores characters in the IBM PC-8 character set that do not exist in Windows, such as line-draw characters, or converts them into other keyboard characters.)

The difference between the Windows 3.0 ANSI character set and the Windows 3.1 version is that fewer characters between character numbers 128 and 160 are defined in the older version. Because this character set is not used for TrueType fonts, you don't need to be concerned about it when you're creating documents. In Figure 42-2, the Windows 3.0 ANSI character set is shown in MS Sans Serif.

	!	"	#	$	%	&	'	(	)	*	+	,	-	.	/	0	1	2	3	4	5	6	7	8	9	:	;	<	=	>	?
@	A	B	C	D	E	F	G	H	I	J	K	L	M	N	O	P	Q	R	S	T	U	V	W	X	Y	Z	[	\	]	^	_
`	a	b	c	d	e	f	g	h	i	j	k	l	m	n	o	p	q	r	s	t	u	v	w	x	y	z	{	|	}	~	.
.	.	.	.	.	.	.	.	.	.	.	.	.	.	.	.	'	'	.	.	.	.	.	.	.	.	.	.	.	.	.	.
	¡	¢	£	¤	¥	¦	§	¨	©	ª	«	¬	-	®	¯	°	±	²	³	´	µ	¶	·	¸	¹	º	»	¼	½	¾	¿
À	Á	Â	Ã	Ä	Å	Æ	Ç	È	É	Ê	Ë	Ì	Í	Î	Ï	Ð	Ñ	Ò	Ó	Ô	Õ	Ö	×	Ø	Ù	Ú	Û	Ü	Ý	Þ	ß
à	á	â	ã	ä	å	æ	ç	è	é	ê	ë	ì	í	î	ï	ð	ñ	ò	ó	ô	õ	ö	÷	ø	ù	ú	û	ü	ý	þ	ÿ

Figure 42-2: The Windows 3.0 version of the Windows ANSI character set, used by the current bitmapped screen fonts. It is shown in MS Sans Serif.

Font designers are supposed to base their TrueType fonts on the Windows ANSI (Windows 3.1) character set or on the Extended Windows ANSI 652-character set, which includes the previous 224 Windows 3.1 ANSI characters. That is, their fonts are supposed to be an expression of the same characters as those defined by the Windows ANSI character set. Font designers generally stick to this standard unless they are designing a special-purpose font such as Wingdings.

It is important that font designers use the Windows ANSI character set. As computer users, we are interested in easily accessing the ANSI characters no matter what text font we are using. If the copyright symbol is displayed when we use Times New Roman, we would like that to also be the case if we are using Coronet. This will be true only if the copyright symbol is present in the Coronet font, and if it has the same character number as it has in Times New Roman.

The Five ANSI Accents

One reason that many English-speaking computer users aren't more familiar with the accented letters in the ANSI set is that these letters seem to be a jumble of random, unrelated symbols. Actually, all of the accented letters in the ANSI character set fall into one of five types:

1. Characters with an acute accent:

    Á É Í Ó Ú _ á é í ó ú _

2. Characters with a grave accent (*grave* rhymes with "Slav" or "slave"):

    À È Ì Ò Ù à è ì ò ù

3. Characters with an umlaut (also called a *dieresis*):

    Ä Ë Ï Ö Ü ä ë ï ö ü ÿ

4. Characters with a circumflex (also informally called a *hat*)

    Â Ê Î Ô Û â ê î ô û

5. Characters with a tilde, or an Iberian or Nordic form:

    Ã Æ Ç _ Ñ Õ Ø ¡ ¿ ã æ ª ç ñ õ ø º ß

These accented characters largely occupy the positions numbered 192 through 224—the uppercase letters start at 192, while the lowercase versions are exactly 32 positions higher. On non-U.S. keyboards, the accented characters that are common in the national language are assigned to keys, so that pressing, say, the ñ key on a Spanish keyboard automatically inserts ANSI character 241 into the document.

When you use accented characters in your documents, they still sort correctly in alphabetical order. Windows applications use the "sort value" of each letter, not the numerical ANSI value, so characters are sorted *a, á, b, c*, not *a, b, c, á*, as their numerical value might suggest. The actual sort order is deter-mined by the sort rules associated with the locale that you set in the Regional Settings Properties dialog box (which you access by clicking the Regional Settings icon in the Control Panel).

The DOS/OEM Character Set

The number of total characters possible under the Windows 3.1 ANSI standard is the same as under DOS — 224. (You can form 256 characters by using all possible combinations of an 8-bit byte, which is used in both character sets. The first 32 characters are nonprinting "control" characters, which leaves 224 that can be used for printing characters.) However, more international characters and symbols are available in Windows because the ANSI set eliminates the line-drawing and math characters that are part of the IBM PC-8 set.

Because it moved IBM's math characters into a new Symbol font and deleted the line-draw characters entirely, Windows has room to add several accented letters needed in various languages, as well as copyright and trademark symbols, and the like. (Most Windows word processing applications can draw lines without having to use text characters.)

The IBM PC-8 character set is shown in Figure 42-3. In the U.S. keyboard layout, the main keyboard provides keys for each of the alphabetic characters and punctuation marks, numbered 32 through 127. You access the other characters (number 128 and up) by holding down the Alt key, typing the appropriate character number on the numeric keypad (with the Num Lock light on), and then releasing the Alt key. Alt+157, for example, produces ¥, the Japanese yen symbol. Notice that if you use this method with the DOS/OEM character set, you don't need to type the additional zero for the characters above character number 127, as you would for the Windows ANSI characters.

Although the IBM PC-8 character set seems to be a chaotic jumble of letters and signs, there is a natural order of sorts (no pun intended). For instance, the first 32 characters are control codes (including tab and carriage return characters), the next 32 are punctuation and numerals, the next 32 are uppercase letters, and exactly 32 places above that are the lowercase letters.

CTRL & PUNC:		ALPHABETIC:		ACCENTS & LINE DRAW:			MATH:
0 ■	32	64 @	96 `	128 Ç	160 á	192 └	224 α
1 ■	33 !	65 A	97 a	129 ü	161 í	193 ┴	225 β
2 ■	34 "	66 B	98 b	130 é	162 ó	194 ┬	226 Γ
3 ■	35 #	67 C	99 c	131 â	163 ú	195 ├	227 π
4 ■	36 $	68 D	100 d	132 ä	164 ñ	196 ─	228 Σ
5 ■	37 %	69 E	101 e	133 à	165 Ñ	197 ┼	229 σ
6 ■	38 &	70 F	102 f	134 å	166 ª	198 ╞	230 µ
7 ■	39 '	71 G	103 g	135 ç	167 º	199 ╟	231 τ
8 ■	40 (	72 H	104 h	136 ê	168 ¿	200 ╚	232 Φ
9 ■	41)	73 I	105 i	137 ë	169 ⌐	201 ╔	233 Θ
10 ■	42 *	74 J	106 j	138 è	170 ¬	202 ╩	234 Ω
11 ■	43 +	75 K	107 k	139 ï	171 ½	203 ╦	235 δ
12 ■	44 ,	76 L	108 l	140 î	172 ¼	204 ╠	236 ∞
13 ■	45 -	77 M	109 m	141 ì	173 ¡	205 ═	237 φ
14 ■	46 .	78 N	110 n	142 Ä	174 «	206 ╬	238 ε
15 ■	47 /	79 O	111 o	143 Å	175 »	207 ╧	239 ∩
16 ■	48 0	80 P	112 p	144 É	176 ░	208 ╨	240 ≡
17 ■	49 1	81 Q	113 q	145 æ	177 ▒	209 ╤	241 ±
18 ■	50 2	82 R	114 r	146 Æ	178 ▓	210 ╥	242 ≥
19 ■	51 3	83 S	115 s	147 ô	179 │	211 ╙	243 ≤
20 ■	52 4	84 T	116 t	148 ö	180 ┤	212 ╘	244 ⌠
21 ■	53 5	85 U	117 u	149 ò	181 ╡	213 ╒	245 ⌡
22 ■	54 6	86 V	118 v	150 û	182 ╢	214 ╓	246 ÷
23 ■	55 7	87 W	119 w	151 ù	183 ╖	215 ╫	247 ≈
24 ■	56 8	88 X	120 x	152 ÿ	184 ╕	216 ╪	248 °
25 ■	57 9	89 Y	121 y	153 Ö	185 ╣	217 ┘	249 ∙
26 ■	58 :	90 Z	122 z	154 Ü	186 ║	218 ┌	250 ·
27 ■	59 ;	91 [	123 {	155 ¢	187 ╗	219 █	251 √
28 ■	60 <	92 \	124		156 £	188 ╝	220 ▄	252 ⁿ
29 ■	61 =	93]	125 }	157 ¥	189 ╜	221 ▌	253 ²
30 ■	62 >	94 ^	126 ~	158 ₧	190 ╛	222 ▐	254 ■
31 ■	63 ?	95 _	127	159 ƒ	191 ┐	223 ▀	255

Figure 42-3: The IBM PC-8 character set. In addition to nonprintable control codes, punctuation, and alphabetic characters, the PC-8 character set includes accented characters, line-draw characters, and math symbols. You access these last three types of characters using the Alt key and the numeric keypad.

Easily Typing the Less-Used Characters

As you saw in Figure 42-1, Windows provides a broad array of characters that do not appear on your keyboard. These characters include fractions, footnote superscripts, copyright and trademark symbols, and many others. Even if you are using a French, German, or other European-style keyboard, you only get a few different characters defined on your keyboard, mostly for the accented letters.

One standard (but awkward) method of inserting characters that don't appear on the keyboard is to use the Alt+*number* method. You turn Num Lock on, hold down the Alt key, type a number on the numeric keypad, then release the Alt key. For example, typing Alt+0169 inserts the (©) symbol.

Another (somewhat awkward) method is to use the Character Map applet that comes with Windows (Start ➪ Programs ➪ Accessories ➪ System Tools). In the Character Map window, you select a symbol (or several symbols), copy it, and then switch to your word processing program and paste it into your document. Note that if you are using multiple languages, you must use the Character Map's Select and Copy buttons, not the keyboard shortcuts or context-menu versions of these commands.

This method is cumbersome because it requires that you switch between applications, but you might find it useful at times because it lets you preview all of the 224 available characters in a font before you actually insert them in your document. They do look pretty small on high-resolution monitors, but clicking a character lets you see a magnified view of it.

If you're using the Character Map to view a font that uses the Extended Windows ANSI character set, you will still see only 224 characters at one time. Display the Font drop-down list, and you'll see that Windows divides up the font into language groups, such as Arial, Arial Baltic, and Arial Greek. If you switch among fonts for different languages, the first 96 characters stay the same, while the other characters change with the language group. You must have installed Multilanguage Support in order to see these additional characters; see "Using Multiple Languages" later in this chapter to find out how.

In addition to using the Alt+*number* method and the Character Map, Windows provides four other more efficient ways of inserting characters that don't appear on the keyboard. If you install the U.S.-International keyboard layout (see the "U.S.-International Keyboard Layout"), you can type characters such as (©) into text in any Windows application by pressing a simple two-key combination.

In the "Switching Between Keyboard Layouts in One Language" section, you learn how to type nonstandard characters using only one or two keystrokes. You can switch this ability on and off at any time (by switching between keyboard layouts), and you can use it in conjunction with the Character Map applet or the Alt+*number* method whenever you wish.

If you have a full-featured word processing program such as Microsoft Word or WordPerfect, you can also insert many special characters using keyboard shortcuts defined in those programs. See the section entitled "Accessing Unusual Characters in Word for Windows" for details about typing these characters in Word.

Finally, the "Accessing More Hidden Characters" section introduces you to a typeface that comes with Windows that contains hundreds of symbols. You also learn about the typefaces from Microsoft and third-party vendors that contain literally thousands of other special characters you can use in your documents.

The U.S.-International Keyboard Layout

One way of inserting additional characters is to use the U.S.-International keyboard layout. Most Windows users, in the U.S. at least, use the plain United States 101 keyboard layout with the English (United States) language. This layout corresponds with the keys on typical U.S. keyboards. Each key inserts a lowercase letter and an uppercase letter, and that is it. There are no keys for extra symbols or accented letters, such as the *é* in *café*.

There are five keyboard layouts associated with the U.S.: 101, Dvorak, LH Dvorak, RH Dvorak, and International. The LH (left hand) and RH (right hand) Dvorak layouts are relatively new to Windows.

When you switch to the U.S.-International keyboard layout, most of the keys on a regular U.S. keyboard gain a third or a fourth meaning. The C key, for example, lets you insert the copyright symbol (©) and cent sign (¢), as well as the normal uppercase C and lowercase c.

You don't need to have a U.S. keyboard to use the U.S.-International keyboard layout. Any of the keyboard layouts provided by Windows work with any of the U.S. or European keyboards. The only problem with using a keyboard layout for one language with a keyboard designed for another is that the character that you see on the keyboard may not be the character that appears onscreen when you press a key.

Secret

There are two problems with the U.S.-International keyboard layout: Shift+ Tab doesn't do a back tab, and you have to resolve conflicts with your word processor regarding Alt+Ctrl key redefinitions.

Installing the U.S.-International Keyboard

To switch to the U.S.-International keyboard layout, take the following steps:

STEPS

Installing the U.S.-International Keyboard Layout

Step 1. Open the Control Panel by clicking the Start button, pointing to Settings, and then clicking Control Panel.

Step 2. Click the Keyboard icon.

Step 3. Click the Language tab.

Step 4. Double-click the first (and most likely only) entry in the Language and Layout box (or highlight it and click the Properties button) to display the Language Properties dialog box (see Figure 42-4).

Step 5. Display the Keyboard Layout drop-down list, and choose United States-International.

Step 6. Click OK to close the Language Properties dialog box.

Step 7. Click OK to close the Keyboard Properties dialog box. You will be asked to insert your Windows CD-ROM.

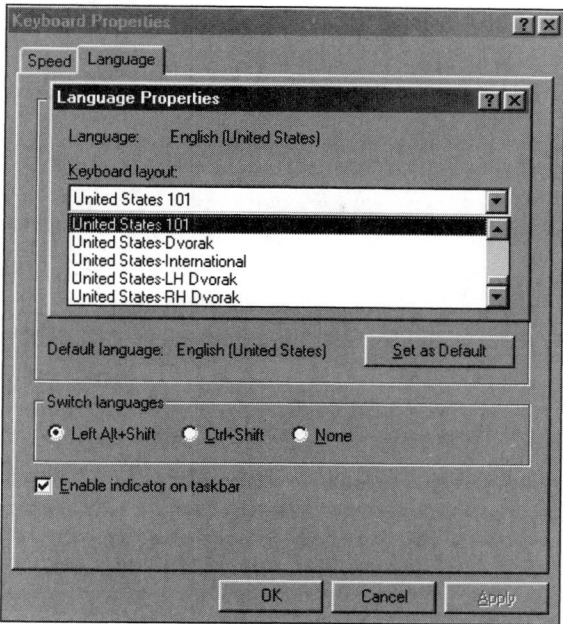

Figure 42-4: The Keyboard Properties dialog box somewhat covered over by the Language Properties dialog box

The change is available immediately in all applications.

While the U.S.-International keyboard layout is in effect, the *right* Alt key on your keyboard turns into an "Alternate Character" key. When you hold down this key (alone or with the Shift key), most of the keys on your normal U.S. keyboard gain new meanings.

We refer to this Alternate Character key as AltChar. The location of this key on extended 101-key keyboards and the meaning of each of the keys in the U.S.- International keyboard layout are shown in Figure 42-5. When you're using the U.S.-International keyboard, the AltChar key is the same as Ctrl+ Alt. This can cause conflicts if any Ctrl+Alt key combinations are redefined in your word processor.

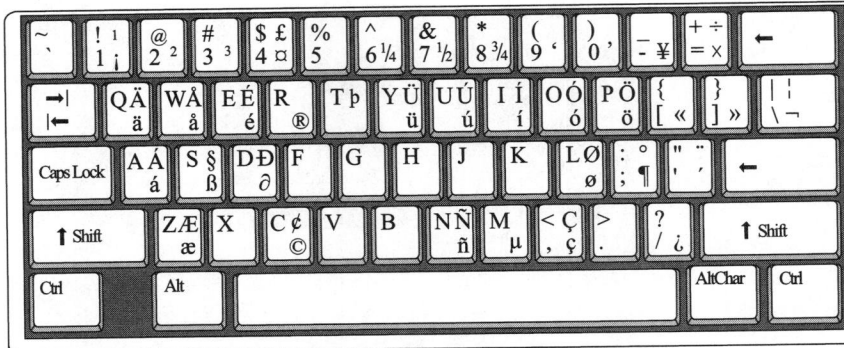

Figure 42-5: The U.S.-International keyboard layout

The normal character is shown on the left of each key, and the character inserted when you hold down AltChar or Shift+AltChar is shown on the right.

Unusual Characters on the Keyboard

You gain access to many characters by switching to the U.S.-International keyboard. For clarity's sake, we break them into the following categories:

- Legal characters, such as the copyright symbol (©), the registered trademark symbol (®), the section mark (§), and the paragraph mark (¶) used by lawyers.

- Currency symbols, such as the British pound (£), the Japanese yen (¥), the cent sign (¢), and the international generic currency symbol (€).

- The fractions one-fourth (¼), one-half (½), and three-fourths (¾), and the degree symbol (°), useful when typing addresses, such as 1201/2 Main St., or recipes (300°).

- Superscripts from one to three (123), useful for inserting footnotes into a page of text, or for expressions such as $x2$. Windows doesn't offer superscript numbers higher than three, but Windows NT provides a full set of superscript and subscript numbers, from 0 to 9.

- True multiplication and division symbols (÷), so you don't have to use a lowercase x and a forward slash (/) in your documents.

- Open and closed quote marks (' '), also called "smart quotes," which look like the quote marks used in professionally typeset magazines and newspapers.

- Accented characters, so you can correctly spell words such as *résumé* and *mañana*.

The U.S.-International keyboard actually provides two different ways to insert accented letters into your documents. This ability is becoming more important as more Americans have names that include accented letters, such as Frederico Peña, Secretary of the Department of Transportation.

The first way to insert accented letters is to hold down the AltChar key and press one of the letters on your keyboard that has an accented alternate character. For example, AltChar+E produces the accented *é,* while AltChar+N produces the accented *ñ.*

The second way is to use what are called *dead keys.* These are keys that do nothing until you press another key on the keyboard.

On the U.S.-International keyboard, five keys are converted into dead keys. These are as follows:

- The circumflex or "hat" over the 6 key (^) — Used in words such as *crêpes Suzette*

- The back quote (`) — Produces a grave accent in words such as à la carte

- The tilde (~) — Used in words such as jalapeño

- The apostrophe (') — Produces an acute accent in words such as exposé

- The double quote (") — Produces an *umlaut* (or *dieresis*) in words such as *naïve*

When you press one of these dead keys, Windows shows nothing on your screen until you press another key. If the second key you press is a letter that has an accented form, such as most vowels, the appropriate accented letter is inserted into your document. If a letter doesn't have an accented form, the letter *t* for example, both the accent and the *t* are inserted, one after the other. If you want to insert just the accent itself, press the corresponding dead key followed by the spacebar.

This behavior produces a small irritation when you're using the apostrophe and double-quote key on your keyboard. When you press the apostrophe, which is common in contractions such as *don't* and possessives such as *Brian's,* you don't see the apostrophe until the second letter is typed. But you don't get an apostrophe at all if you type an unusual contraction, such as Hallowe'en. With the U.S.-International keyboard, pressing the apostrophe and then *e* produces the letter *é,* unless you remember to press the spacebar after the apostrophe.

This is a very minor problem, because most English contractions end in *s* or *t,* not in vowels. But it is a more serious problem with the double-quote key, which you use to begin sentences that are quotations, such as "Are you there?" Sentences often begin with *A, E,* and other vowels, and you must remember to press the spacebar after the double-quote key when typing any such sentence.

If you often use symbols or accented characters, the advantages of using the U.S.-International keyboard far outweigh the slight disadvantage of remembering how to use the apostrophe and double-quote key. But because it *is* irritating, we wish Microsoft hadn't used the apostrophe and double-quote key as a dead key. Instead, they should have used the colon (:) and the semicolon (;). The colon looks like an umlaut, and the bottom of the semicolon resembles an acute accent mark. Because colons and semicolons are always followed by spaces or carriage returns in normal English usage, you wouldn't need to remember to press the spacebar before pressing a vowel after these keys. If a letter immediately followed a colon or semicolon, you could be sure that it was meant to be an accented letter.

In any case, using the U.S.-International keyboard is usually better for users of U.S. keyboards than switching to an entirely different keyboard layout to type in another language, such as French. You can, of course, use the Keyboard Properties dialog box in the Control Panel to add keyboard layouts in addition to (or instead of) U.S. layout. There are now 67 available keyboard layouts (up from 26 with Windows 95). They range from Afrikaans to Ukrainian. But the non-U.S. keyboard layouts almost always move some alphabetical keys to new positions that are customary in those locales. For example, the top row of alphabetical keys on keyboards sold in France starts out with the letters AZERTY, not QWERTY, as on U.S. keyboards. Unless you're a touch typist who learned to type on keyboards in a different country, it's better to stick with the U.S.-International keyboard.

What If You Don't Have an Extended Keyboard?

For users with older 84-key keyboards (the ones on the original IBM AT, with 10 function keys on the left side), the U.S.-International keyboard provides another way to access alternate characters. This is necessary, of course, because 84-key keyboards do not have two Alt keys and therefore cannot convert one into an AltChar key.

While the U.S.-International keyboard is in effect, you can hold down Ctrl+Alt while pressing a letter as a substitute for holding down the right Alt key (the AltChar key). Shift+Ctrl+Alt does the same thing as Shift+AltChar.

Unfortunately, these parallel methods are in force even if you are using a 101-key extended keyboard. This means that you must take care when using a macro language in your word processor to redefine Ctrl+Alt keys or Shift+Ctrl+Alt keys to run macros. These macro definitions overrule the meaning of letters that have an alternate form when used with the AltChar key. In other words, a macro that you have defined to run when you press Ctrl+Alt+A takes precedence over AltChar+A. Instead of AltChar+A inserting *á* into your document, the macro will execute.

Switching Between Keyboard Layouts in One Language

You can set up two (or more) keyboard layouts and easily switch between them. You can switch back and forth between the U.S. and the U.S.-International keyboard if you like. This can help you avoid the irritation of dealing with poorly defined dead keys (see the "Unusual Characters on the Keyboard" section earlier in this chapter).

Secret

To set up both the U.S. and U.S.-International keyboard layouts, follow the steps in the section entitled "Setting Up and Using Multilingual Identifiers" later in this chapter. Choose the language English (United States) and associate the U.S.-International keyboard layout with it; then choose English (Australian) and associate the U.S.-101 keyboard layout with it. You now have two language identifiers on your taskbar that are in fact the same language (almost) but refer to two different keyboard layouts. You switch between layouts by choosing one or the other language identifier.

The only problem this can cause occurs if you have two spelling dictionaries in your word processor, perhaps one for the U.S. and one for Australia. The text that you type while you are typing Australian English (using the plain U.S. keyboard layout) will be proofed by the Australian spelling dictionary.

Accessing Unusual Characters in Word for Windows

For an example of how a full-featured word processor handles nonstandard characters, see Table 42-1. The elements in this chart were taken directly from the Word for Windows Help files (and edited to improve clarity).

Table 42-1 Shortcut Keys for Inserting Accented Letters in Word for Windows

Character	*Keystrokes*
à, è, ì, ò, ù, À, È, Ì, Ò, Ù	Ctrl+ ` (accent-grave), the letter
á, é, í, ó, ú, ´y, Á, É, Í, Ó, Ú, ´Y	Ctrl+' (apostrophe), the letter
â, ê, î, ô, û, Â, Ê, Î, Ô, Û	Ctrl+Shift+ ^ (caret), the letter
ã, ñ, õ, Ã, Ñ, Õ	Ctrl+Shift+ ~ (tilde), the letter
ä, è, ï, ö, ü, ÿ, Ä, Ë, Ï, Ö, Ü, Ÿ	Ctrl+Shift+: (colon), the letter
å, Å	Ctrl+Shift+@, a or A
æ, Æ	Ctrl+Shift+&, a or A
œ, Œ	Ctrl+Shift+&, o or O

Continued

Table 42-1 *(continued)*

Character	Keystrokes
ß	Ctrl+Shift+&, s
ç, Ç	Ctrl+, (comma), c or C
_'_	Ctrl+' (apostrophe), d or D
ø, Ø	Ctrl+/, o or O
¿	Ctrl+Alt+Shift+?
¡	Ctrl+Alt+Shift+!
(©)	Ctrl+Alt+C
(®)	Ctrl+Alt+R
(™)	Ctrl+Alt+T
... (ellipsis)	Ctrl+Alt+. (period)
' (single opening quotation mark)	Ctrl+` (accent-grave), `
' (single closing quotation mark)	Ctrl+' (apostrophe), '
" (double opening quotation mark)	Ctrl+` (accent-grave)," (double quote)
" (double closing quotation mark)	Ctrl+' (apostrophe)," (double quote)

Word for Windows (6.0 and later) is by default set to replace straight quote marks with the typesetter's quote marks. You won't have to use the last four keystroke combinations in the table if you leave this setting at its default.

Secret

There are some conflicts between the U.S.-International keyboard layout and Word for Windows. The Word team at Microsoft has chosen to redefine a number of the Ctrl+Alt shortcut keys, so many of the AltChar+*letter* shortcuts don't work as indicated. Fortunately, you have a number of options if you want to use the convenient U.S.-International keyboard layout with Word.

First, many of the keys on the U.S.-International keyboard that conflict with a Word shortcut key have a different shortcut key in Word (refer to Table 42-2). You can just use these shortcut keys instead of AltChar+*letter*. For example, on the U.S.-International keyboard layout, you type AltChar+N to get the letter ñ, but Word defines Ctrl+Alt+N as a shortcut for choosing View ➪ Normal. If you're typing in Word, you can use Word's keyboard shortcut Ctrl+Shift+~ (tilde), n to get the letter ñ instead.

Second, you can remove 13 of the 16 keyboard shortcuts in Word that conflict with the U.S.-International keyboard layout. Fortunately, these shortcut definitions are stored in the `Normal.dot` template. You can easily change or eliminate these shortcut key combinations in `Normal.dot` or whatever template you use with Word.

STEPS

Easing Use of the U.S.-International Keyboard with Word

Step 1.   Click your Microsoft Word icon to open Word. Choose File ⇨ New from the menu.

You can make the changes to the Normal.dot template or to a new template. If you create a new template and then decide you want your new template to be the default template, you can use the Explorer to rename Normal.dot to Normal.old, and then rename your new template to Normal.dot.

Step 2.   If you want to make changes to Normal.dot, click the OK button in the New dialog box. If you want to make a new template based on Normal.dot, click the Template option button, and then click OK.

Step 3.   Choose Tools ⇨ Customize, and click the Keyboard tab (or click the Keyboard button in Word).

Step 4.   Select the template that you want to change from the "Save changes in" drop-down list in the lower-right corner window of the Customize (or Customize Keyboard) dialog box.

Step 5.   Choose the categories shown in Table 42-2 in the Categories list, and scroll through the Commands list until you find the ones listed in the table.

Step 6.   In the Current Keys field of the Customize (or Customize Keyboard) dialog box, highlight the shortcut key that you want to remove. Click the Remove button.

Step 7.   Repeat steps 5 and 6 until you have removed all the shortcut key definitions that you want. The changes are made immediately to your new template or to Normal.dot.

Step 8.   If you are creating a new template, choose File ⇨ Save when you are done.

Table 42-2   Word for Windows Shortcut Keys That Can Be Removed

Category	Command	Predefined Shortcut	Alternate
File	FilePrintPreview	Ctrl+Alt+I	Ctrl+F2
Edit	GoBack	Ctrl+Alt+Z	Shift+F5
Edit	RepeatFind	Ctrl+Alt+Y	Shift+F4

Continued

Table 42-2   *(continued)*

Category	Command	Predefined Shortcut	Alternate
View	ViewNormal	Ctrl+Alt+N	
View	ViewOutline	Ctrl+Alt+O	
View	ViewPage	Ctrl+Alt+P	
Insert	InsertAnnotation	Ctrl+Alt+A (Word 6.0 and 7.0)	
Insert	InsertComment	Ctrl+Alt+M (Word 97)	
Insert	InsertEndnoteNow	Ctrl+Alt+E	
Format	ApplyHeading1	Ctrl+Alt+1	
Format	ApplyHeading2	Ctrl+Alt+2	
Format	ApplyHeading3	Ctrl+Alt+3	
Table AutoFormat	TableUpdate	Ctrl+Alt+U	
Window and Help	DocSplit	Ctrl+Alt+S	

The third conflict involves the fact that you can't easily redefine two Word shortcut keys that conflict with the U.S.-International keyboard layout. They are as follows:

Add a command to a menu	Ctrl+Alt+ = (equals sign)
Remove a command from a menu	Ctrl+Alt+ – (minus sign)

Word has defined another keyboard combination, Ctrl+Alt+T, to insert the trademark symbol. You can remove this keyboard shortcut if you so desire. (Choose Insert ⇨ Symbol, choose Normal Text in the Font drop-down list, click the (tm) symbol, click the Shortcut Key button, click Alt+Ctrl+T in the Current Keys field, and click the Remove button.) In Word, you can very easily insert a trademark symbol without using Ctrl+Alt+T. Simply type **(tm)** in your text. As soon as you continue to type, Word's AutoCorrect feature automatically replaces (tm) with (^{TM}).

You can, of course, choose to ignore these three conflicts and choose Insert ⇨ Symbol to pick the (and ¥ characters from Word's built-in character map. (By the way, this character map is the only place we've found that shows all 1,726 characters of the Lucida Sans Unicode character set. Unfortunately, it only works with fonts that Word considers to be symbol fonts.) Another alternative is to define a new AltChar+*letter* shortcut for the three orphan symbols by choosing Insert ⇨ Symbol, highlighting them one at a time, and clicking the Shortcut Key button.

Accessing More Hidden Characters

A little-known benefit of Windows is that it includes two bundled fonts containing numerous clipart-like characters. These fonts are called Wingdings and Webdings, and they can definitely add interest to your documents — once you know what characters they contain. Wingdings has been around for a while and is similar to the Zapf Dingbats font. (*Dingbat* is a traditional printer's term for a piece of decorative type.) Webdings is relatively new in Windows, and it is intended as an aid for Web site designers (though it looks just fine in print).

Every Windows user has access to hundreds of characters that are not visible on any keyboard. And users who previously purchased the Microsoft TrueType Font Pack have access to more than 1,000 additional math symbols, bullets, arrows, and dingbats. (Unfortunately, the Font Pack is no longer available from Microsoft.) We have all this richness of special characters, but there is almost no way for the average person to find out what characters are available.

To be fair, we must mention that Microsoft does provide the Character Map applet with Windows to try to help people access these symbols. When you start this map, it displays 224 characters that belong to a Windows font: the first 96 characters in the font, plus 128 characters that pertain to the language you are using. Unfortunately, the Character Map window is small (and it can't be resized, although you can click on one character at a time to see an enlarged view of each character), so it's difficult to use it to browse through your type collection.

To give you a place to see many of these characters and symbols, we've collected all the characters (other than the extended multilingual fonts) available to Windows users into two charts. Figure 42-1, the Windows 98 True Type character sets, which is at the beginning of this chapter, is for all Windows users, while Figure 42-6, the Microsoft TrueType Font Pack character sets, is for users who have the TrueType Font Pack. You might want to photocopy these charts and tack them on the nearest bulletin board for the next time you need just the right symbol.

You can insert about half of the characters in these figures into a document by pressing a key on your keyboard. Pressing the *w* key, for example, inserts character number 119 into your document. (Refer to Figure 42-1.) If you're using a text typeface such as Arial, the inserted character is, in fact, a *w*. But if you're using Wingdings, the same keystroke inserts a diamond-shaped bullet (♦), and if you're using Webdings, that keystroke inserts a little golf flag (⛳).

The Windows 95 TrueType Font Pack Character Sets

The True Type Font Pack included four TrueType special character fonts: Lucida Bright Math Extension, Math Italic, Math Symbol, and Monotype Sorts. To access characters that cannot be typed directly from the keyboard:

1) Make sure the Num Lock light is *on*.
2) Hold down the Alt key while typing the appropriate number on the numeric keypad.
3) Release the Alt key.

Lucida Bright Math Extension character set
Lucida Bright Math Italic character set
Lucida Bright Math Symbol character set
Monotype Sorts character set

Character Number 64 →

Figure 42-6: Many users are unaware of the nontext character sets in The Microsoft TrueType Font Pack. This product is no longer available, but it still works with Windows if you already have it.

We use many of the higher-numbered special characters in the standard Windows ANSI character set all the time. Windows makes it easy for us to use a long dash for emphasis — like this — by typing Alt+0151. A bullet that you can use to set off paragraphs is at Alt+0149.

The Wingdings and Webdings character sets take these special symbols much, much farther. Many of their characters are pictorial. This includes keyboard and mouse symbols (Alt+55 and Alt+56), and electronic mail symbols (Alt+42 through Alt+47) in the Wingdings font.

Using Multiple Languages

Many North American companies routinely use different languages in their documents. Companies in the southern U.S. often produce documents containing both English and Spanish text, while Canadian documents often include both English and French.

In WordPad, Word for Windows, and other word processors, you can mark text as belonging to a particular language. By default, text in Word documents is marked as the language you have selected using the Keyboard icon in the Control Panel. But you could use the Tools ➪ Language command to mark one section as English (United States), and mark another section as French (Canadian), for example. You can mark text blocks as small as a single word or character as belonging to a particular language.

The ability to mark sections of text for different languages is helpful when you're spell checking, hyphenating, and using a thesaurus in a document with text in multiple languages. If you have installed proofing utilities in another language, Word for Windows automatically uses those utilities when operating on any section of text marked as that language.

This ability to keep track of what text is in what language is part of the operating system in Windows, so many applications can take advantage of this capability. In fact, Windows has added support for many new languages, including Albanian, Belarusian, Estonian, Latvian, Lithuanian, Romanian, Serbian, Slovak, Ukrainian, and Turkish.

In addition, Windows makes it easy to switch among different languages and, if you like, among different keyboard layouts. You can set up a number of different language identifiers and choose among them as you write a multilingual document. You just pick the appropriate identifier to tell Windows which language you're going to use for the next section.

Setting Up and Using Multilingual Identifiers

If you have installed Multilanguage Support, you can write documents using Baltic, Greek, Turkish, Cyrillic, or Central European character sets (and Hebrew in Lucida Unicode). Installing Multilanguage Support installs the Arial, Times New Roman, Tahoma, Verdana, Lucida Console, Lucida Sans

Unicode, and Courier New fonts with the Extended Windows ANSI character set, which contains 652 characters.

To install Multilanguage Support, click the Add/Remove Programs icon in your Control Panel, click the Windows Setup tab, and mark the Multilanguage Support checkbox.

You use the Keyboard Properties dialog box in the Control Panel (under the Keyboard icon) to set up multilingual identifiers. Once you've created the identifiers, they appear in the tray on your taskbar, as shown in Figure 42-7.

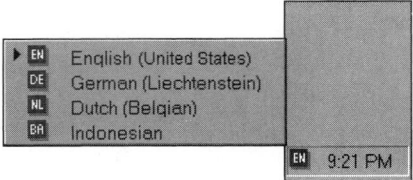

Figure 42-7: Language identifiers in the tray on the taskbar

To create these identifiers, follow these steps:

STEPS

Adding Multilingual Identifiers

Step 1. Open the Control Panel by clicking the Start button, pointing to Settings, and then clicking Control Panel.

Step 2. Click the Keyboard icon.

Step 3. Click the Language tab.

Step 4. Click the Add button to display the Add Language dialog box.

Step 5. Display the Language drop-down list.

Step 6. Pick the language that you want, and click OK. The default keyboard layout for that language or location is now displayed next to the language in the Keyboard Properties dialog box.

Step 7. If you want a different keyboard layout, click the Properties button, and choose a new layout.

Step 8. Repeat steps 4 through 7 until you have added all the language identifiers that you will be using regularly, and then close the Keyboard Properties dialog box.

Once you have set up a list of language identifiers, you can choose among them by picking them from the taskbar. Click the language identifier in the tray (the identifier for the currently selected language). When the list of identifiers pops up, click the one that you want to use.

You can also use the Left Alt+Shift key combination to rotate through the list. You have to release the Alt key before you press the next Shift key.

If you prefer, you can change the Left Alt+Shift shortcut key to Ctrl+Shift, or to no shortcut key at all. To do this, select the desired option button in the Language tab of the Keyboard Properties dialog box.

One language/keyboard layout combination is always set as the default. To designate the default combination, highlight it in the Language tab of the Keyboard Properties dialog box, and click the Set As Default button.

Multilingual Documents

Once you have set up multilingual identifiers, as described in the previous section, you are ready to start typing in a foreign language. Of course, your keyboard keys often won't have the correct characters engraved upon them (check out Greek in Figure 42-8, for example), so you'll need to make up a chart that tells you which characters show up in your document when you type specific keys.

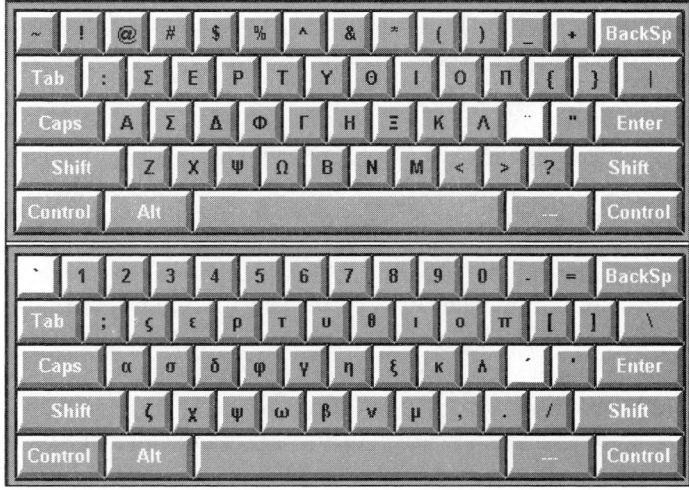

Figure 42-8: The Greek keyboard layouts for unshifted (bottom) and shifted (top) characters

All you need to do to switch among languages and keyboard layouts is press Left Alt+Shift. To test this, start WordPad. Type text and then press Left Alt+Shift to switch your language/keyboard layout to Greek (assuming you set up a Greek identifier). The Font list box in the WordPad Format bar switches from a font identified as Western to one identified as Greek, and Greek letters now appear in your document as you type. If you're using a font that doesn't have the expanded character set, Windows will substitute another font that does, so your readers can still read your text.

You may want to write in a language for which Windows does not provide a keyboard identifier — Hawaiian, for instance. Fonts are available (often as shareware from universities) for a number of languages not specifically supported by Microsoft — but they're pretty cumbersome to use if you have to remember and type a special code for each letter. Fortunately, Janko's Keyboard Generator makes it easy to set up a native Windows keyboard layout for just about any written language with an alphabet (recent examples include Thai and Mongolian). Using a graphical representation of a keyboard, you assign a character to a key simply by dragging it. Janko's Keyboard Generator is shareware; the license fee is $15, and there is no license fee if you use it only on your home computer. You can download the latest version from `http://solair.eunet.yu/~janko/engdload.htm`. Janko also includes a number of links to sites that offer ready-to-use keyboard files built with his generator (as well as fonts), so you may be able to save yourself some work.

Multilingual Proofing Tools

If you find yourself using different languages frequently, you would probably benefit from one or more proofing tools specific to your languages. A Web search reveals a number of proofing tools for single languages; there are a few companies that make a business of offering tools for a variety of languages.

Alki Software Corp.'s Proofing Tools packages are designed specifically to work with recent versions of Microsoft Word. A significant number of languages supported by Windows are represented in their catalog. The manual alone is valuable for its extensive charts showing the location of Windows characters and the layout of every different keyboard language supported by Windows. More importantly, each package provides a spelling checker, thesaurus, and hyphenation utility for the language. You can visit Alki Software Corp. at `http://www.proofing.com`

World Language Resources (`http://www.worldlanguage.com` offers browsers, word processors, spelling checkers, and Office proofing tools for over 400 languages. They also sell translation tools and offer an online translation service.

Microsoft Foreign Proofing Tools from Language Partners International Inc. allows you to check spelling, find synonyms, and hyphenate in over 30 languages, from Basque to Turkish. The company says it uses the same spelling dictionary, hyphenation file, and thesaurus that Microsoft incorporates in its foreign versions of Word. Each package (one language) is $99.95. Call

Language Partners International at 800-222-9242, send e-mail to info@ languagepartners.com, or visit `http://www.languagepartners.com`

Fingertip Software makes keyboards, keycaps, fonts, and utilities for over 20 Slavic and European languages (Cyrillic and Latin characters). Their Cyrillic Starter Kit includes support for KOI8-R, a Cyrillic character set used on the Internet but not supported by Microsoft. Fingertip's 3-D Keyboards are software applications designed to make it easier to type in more than one language. Contact Fingertip Software at 800-209-4063, or visit `http://www. fingertipsoft.com`.

The Web Is Multilingual

Even a small amount of time spent browsing the Web makes it clear that English is no longer the only language spoken there. Windows' Multilanguage Support extends to Internet Explorer, making it easy to read Web pages written in other languages. However, you implement it separately from the Windows Multilanguage Support detailed in "Setting Up and Using Multilingual Identifiers" earlier in this chapter.

If you know in advance that you want to download support for one or more specific languages, use Windows Update. Click Start ⇨ Settings ⇨ Windows Update, and let your system connect to the Internet if you aren't already connected. At the bottom of the Windows Update Web page appear your choices for downloading language support. If you don't have the most current version of Internet Explorer, you will be forced to download the update before you can view the Windows Update page.

If you don't want to bother downloading language support in advance, there's no need to. Internet Explorer and Outlook Express now offer a function called Install on Demand that lets you install what you need when you need it (this includes nonlanguage components such as plug-ins, too). If you go to a Web site that requires support for a different language, the Install on Demand dialog box will appear. Click Download to install support for the specified language before continuing, or click Cancel to just keep browsing in your default language.

Some people find Install on Demand annoying. If you are among them, you can click the "Never install any of these components" checkbox on the Install on Demand dialog box when it appears. You can also turn off Install on Demand by right-clicking the Internet Explorer icon on your Desktop, choosing Properties, and clicking the Advanced tab. In the Browsing section, scroll down to the Enable Install On Demand checkbox and clear it.

Note that many Russian speakers on the Internet use an older Cyrillic character set called KOI8-R. This standard came out of the UNIX computing environment (as did the Internet) and is still widespread, especially among academics, who tend to be UNIX users. KOI8-R is not compatible with

Unicode, and is not supported by Office — but it is supported by Internet Explorer and Outlook Express.

If you find Web sites or e-mail messages that should appear in Cyrillic but do not, choose View ⇨ Fonts in Internet Explorer or View ⇨ Language in Outlook Express and select the KOI8-R character set. KOI8-R fonts are available from some third parties; if you need to communicate in Russian, it's worth a visit to Janko's Web site (see "Multilingual Documents"), or to the KOI8-R Russian Net Character Set site at http://www.nagual.pp.ru/~ache/koi8.html

Multilingual E-Mail

The Internet and many other e-mail systems handle only the lower ASCII character set (unless you are using MIME or UUENCODE). Windows Messaging takes that a step further by letting you send and receive e-mail with the full Windows ANSI character set (224 characters).

Outlook Express supports the full range of both ANSI and Extended ANSI characters, giving you access to the non-Latin character sets. To read messages containing these characters, you must have first installed Multilanguage Support for Windows by clicking the Add/Remove Programs icon in your Control Panel, clicking the Windows Setup tab, and marking the Multilanguage Support checkbox. You must also have installed support for the specific language used in the message, as described in the preceding section.

When you receive an e-mail message, Outlook Express looks in its header to see which character set it should use (press Ctrl+F3 to see the full header information for a selected message). If the message header sufficiently identifies the language of the contents, Outlook Express will either display the message in that language or it will display the Install on Demand dialog box. If you have installed support for this language but the message is not correctly displayed, choose View ⇨ Language (either in the Outlook Express menu bar or in your message's menu bar), and select the correct language for viewing the message.

When you do this, you may see an error message asking if you want to use the character set you have just selected to view all messages whose headers contain the same character set as this e-mail message. You should click Yes. This will affect all messages you receive in the future whose headers contain that character set. If you find you have made this substitution in error (maybe you substituted Greek for English and now *everything* appears in Greek), you can go back. Choose Tools ⇨ Options, click the Read tab, and click the International Settings button. You'll see any substitutions you've set up — highlight the one you want to remove, and click Remove (see Figure 42-9).

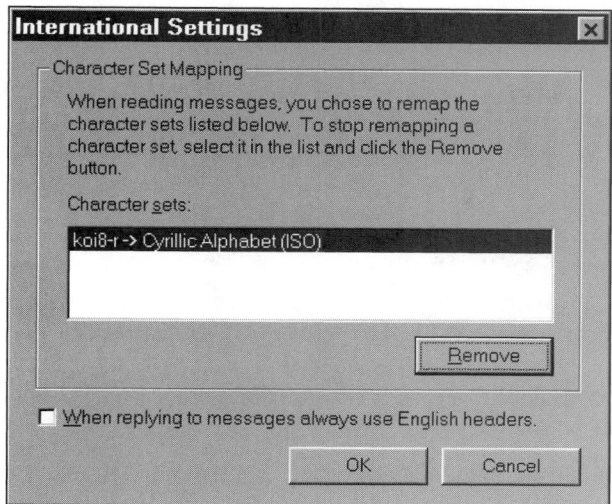

Figure 42-9: The International Settings dialog box. You can see what character set substitutions you have set up, and remove them if necessary.

To send e-mail messages in other languages, you must not only have Multilanguage Support installed, but you must also set up one or more multilingual identifiers for your keyboard, as described in "Setting Up and Using Multilingual Identifiers" earlier in this chapter. In the menu bar of the New Message window, choose Format ⇨ Language, and select the language you want to put in the header of your message. You can still change languages as you type in the body of the message, simply by picking the identifiers from the tray or using the Left Alt+Shift key combination.

When you send a message whose header information is in the Western alphabet, but that contains characters from a different language (Greek, for example), you will see a Message Character Set Conflict dialog box (shown in Figure 42-10). It offers you a choice between sending your e-mail message in Unicode, or sending it as is. For the best results, choose Cancel to go back to your New Message window, click Format ⇨ Language, and choose Greek. The Western characters you have already typed for the address subject will not change.

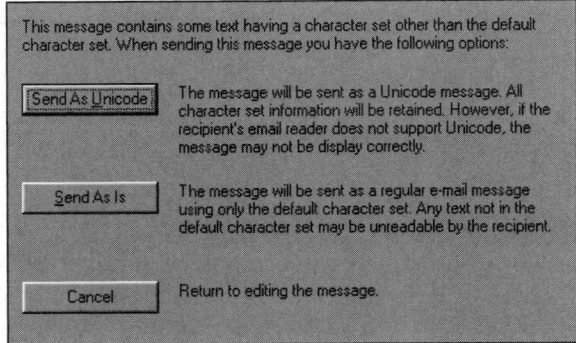

Figure 42-10: The Message Character Set Conflict dialog box

If you prefer to use an English header (perhaps you only quoted one line of Homer and the rest is in English), it's best to format your message using Rich Text (HTML) — you can then send it as is. You can also send using the As Is option by using the UUENCODE and MIME formats; see "UUENCODE or MIME" in Chapter 28 for details on how to set the format for your outgoing mail. If you send a plaintext message in Unicode, your recipient must view the message using the Unicode (not the Greek or Western) character set. Unicode is called Universal Alphabet (UTF-8) in the Outlook Express pull-down menus. If you send your message as is in plaintext, the Greek letters will probably not be readable.

When you reply to a message, Outlook Express attempts to use the same language by default (within the limitations of the character sets you have available). To use a different character set, you must use the Rich Text (HTML) format. Keep in mind that your correspondent must be able to receive whatever format you send. It may take some experimentation to find the combination of formats and characters that your pen pal finds the most palatable.

Using Keyboard Shortcuts

In this section, we examine the many shortcuts Windows and Windows applications assign to key combinations, such as Ctrl+Insert and Ctrl+A. Additionally, we teach you how to redefine key combinations that aren't used by *any* Windows applications in order to support your own macros.

You can specify that you have to press and release the Shift, Ctrl, or Alt keys *before* pressing the letter key of the combination by marking the Use StickyKeys checkbox in the Keyboard tab of the Accessibility Properties dialog box. You'll find this dialog box under the Accessibility Options icon in the Control Panel.

The Most Important (and Poorly Documented) Shortcuts

Despite the ease-of-use publicity about Windows, a novice Windows user is confronted with a bewildering array of new objects to click and shortcut keys to learn. These shortcut keys are difficult to memorize, and some shortcuts are not documented at all. Furthermore, once you've learned these shortcuts, they are hard to remember because many of the key combinations are confusingly similar and do not follow any logical pattern.

Pressing Alt+Esc, for example, switches you from your current application to other applications running under Windows, while Alt+F4 exits the application that is running. Quick—do you remember which is which? Why is the act of exiting assigned to an F4 key combination instead of one based on the Escape key?

As another example, most Windows applications that support multiple, smaller windows (*child windows*) inside their main application window enable you to jump quickly from child window to child window by pressing Ctrl+Tab. But not Word for Windows—Ctrl+Tab actually inserts a tab character inside a document table. To cycle through child windows in Word, you have to press Ctrl+F6.

Despite these inconsistencies, there *are* many shortcut keys that work the same way in all or most Windows applications. We have gathered many of these in Table 42-3. You'll find other shortcut keys in "Hot Keys" in Chapter 10 and "Windows Shortcut Keys" in Chapter 20.

Table 42-3   Windows Shortcut Keys

Key or Combination	Effect
Alt or F10	If you press and release either of these keys without any other keys, it activates an application's menu bar. You can then choose a command from the menu system with the keyboard. Press the underlined letter in the menu name, and then press the underlined letter in the desired command. (You can also press the right and left arrow keys to highlight a menu name, press the down arrow key to highlight the desired command, and then press Enter.)
Alt+*letter*	Activates the menu on an application's menu bar that has an underlined letter corresponding to the letter you pressed. Works the same way if you press and release Alt, and then press the underlined letter.
Alt+Down Arrow	Displays the contents of a drop-down list. This combination is a toggle.
End	Moves to the end of a line (in a word processor).

Continued

Table 42-3   *(continued)*

Key or Combination	Effect
Ctrl+End	Moves to the end of a document (in a word processor).
Enter	Selects a choice that is highlighted on a menu or in a dialog box.
Alt+Enter	Switches a DOS application that is running full screen to running in a window (and back). This doesn't work to toggle a Windows application from a maximized to a restored window and back. If you have highlighted an icon, pressing Alt+Enter is the same as right-clicking and then clicking Properties.
Esc	Closes a dialog box or drop-down menu without taking any action.
Alt+Esc	Each time you press this combination, you switch (in a round-robin fashion) to another application running under Windows.
Ctrl+Esc	Displays the Start menu and the taskbar. The taskbar buttons are covered up by the Start menu if the taskbar is docked on the right or left edge of your Desktop.
Ctrl+Esc, Esc, Tab	After you've pressed these keys, you can use the arrow keys to navigate between taskbar buttons, or use the Tab key to navigate between the Start button, the taskbar, and the Desktop.
Tab or F6	Switches the focus between the Start button, the taskbar, and the Desktop. Focus must first be on one of these items before pressing the key. If the taskbar is set to "Auto hide" mode, pressing either key brings up the taskbar.
Alt+F4	Closes the current application. If the current application is the taskbar, this also exits Windows after you give confirmation.
Ctrl+F4	Closes a child window in multidocument Windows applications (File Manager, Word for Windows, and so on).
Home	Moves to the beginning of a line (in a word processor).
Ctrl+Home	Moves to the beginning of a document (in a word processor).
Alt+Hyphen	Pulls down an application's multidocument control menu from the Multidocument Control Menu icon at the far left end of the menu bar. This menu controls the size and other aspects of the child window. Do not confuse this icon with the System Menu icon, which controls the application itself (see Alt+ spacebar) and is located directly above the multidocument control menu icon.

Key or Combination	Effect
Print Screen	Copies the entire Windows display to the Clipboard. You can then paste the image into MS Paint or another graphics application and print it if you like.
Alt+Print Screen	Copies only the currently active window to the Clipboard. This could be the current application or a dialog box that has the keyboard focus within that application. This may not work on 84-key keyboards and computers with old BIOS chips. If it doesn't, try Shift+Print Screen instead.
Spacebar	Marks or clears a checkbox.
Alt+spacebar	Pulls down the System Control menu, the icon in the upper-left corner of an application window that controls that application's size and position, among other things.
Tab	Moves the selection box (the dotted rectangular box) to the next choice in a dialog box.
Shift+Tab	Moves the selection box in reverse order.
Alt+Tab	Switches to the application that was the current application before the application you are presently in. Switches back when pressed again. This may not work on 84-key keyboards and computers with old keyboard BIOS chips.
Alt+Shift+Tab Alt+Tab.	Switches between applications in the opposite direction as Alt+Tab.
Alt+Tab+Tab	Switches to every application currently running under Windows. Hold down Alt and press Tab repeatedly until the icon of the application you want to switch to is highlighted. Then release the Alt key. This is like Alt+Esc, but it displays only the icon and application names until you release the Alt key. (See the "Alt+Tab+Tab — The Task Switcher" section.) This may not work on 84-key keyboards and computers with old keyboard BIOS chips.
Ctrl+Tab or Ctrl+F6	Jumps to the next child window in a multidocument application such as File Manager. (Use Ctrl+F6 in Word for Windows.)
Ctrl+X	Cuts highlighted item.
Ctrl+C	Copies highlighted item.
Ctrl+V	Pastes a copied or cut item.
Ctrl+Z	Undoes a previous action.

The following keyboard shortcuts work with the Microsoft Natural Keyboard. The Win key is the key with the Windows flag.

Win	Displays the Start menu
Win+E	Starts the Explorer
Win+F	Opens the Find Files dialog box, similar to F3
Ctrl+Win+F	Opens the Find Computer dialog box
Win+M	Minimize All Windows
Shift+Win+M	Undo Minimize All
Win+R	Opens the Run dialog box
Win+Tab	Switches between taskbar buttons
Win+Break	Opens the System Properties dialog box

Alt+Tab+Tab — The Task Switcher

You probably already know two shortcut key combinations that enable you to switch among running applications. Alt+Esc opens a different application every time you press it, and Alt+Tab switches from your current application to the application you previously used, and back.

But the best way to switch among your running applications isn't documented at all. Just *hold down* the Alt key while you press the Tab key several times, pausing slightly between each press. Unlike Alt+Esc, which switches applications and redraws the window for every application in turn, Alt+Tab+Tab switches applications but shows only the application's icon and name. Alt+Tab+Tab is a much faster method than Alt+Esc, because it lets you cycle quickly through all your running applications until you find the one you want. Simply release the Alt key when the desired application's icon is highlighted. The application's window is fully drawn and shifts to the foreground.

Alt+Esc and Alt+Tab+Tab work with both Windows applications and DOS applications running under Windows, whether they are running maximized, restored, or minimized as icons on the taskbar.

The 84-key keyboards and computers with older keyboard BIOS chips may not recognize the Alt+Tab key combination. IBM's BIOS for its enhanced-AT 101-key keyboard was one of the first to accept the Alt key as a way to modify the meaning of the Tab key. Test your keyboard to see which combinations of keys you can take advantage of. If you have a 101-key keyboard, you shouldn't have a problem with Alt+Tab+Tab or any of the other possible combinations.

Using the Humble Shift Key

Behold the lowly Shift key. You hold it down while you type, and all you get is an uppercase letter, right? Not quite. Beneath the Shift key's humble reputation lies a world of undocumented functionality.

Many Windows users know the most basic ways the Shift key has been redefined. One of the first lessons for a new Windows user, for example, is that holding down the Shift key in a word processor while pressing an arrow key actually highlights text, instead of just moving the insertion point. And holding down Shift while clicking in text highlights everything between the insertion point and the place you clicked (in most word processors).

In the Explorer and on the Desktop, holding down the Shift key while hovering over an icon with your mouse pointer selects all the icons between (and including) the previously highlighted one and the one you hover over. (If you want to select multiple icons that aren't adjacent to one another, hold down the Ctrl key while you hover over each one.)

Other functions of the Shift key are much less well known. When you use the straight-line tool in MS Paint and many other drawing programs, for example, holding down Shift forces the line you draw to be perfectly horizontal or vertical. Similarly, when you use the box or oval tools, Shift forces these shapes into perfect squares or circles, respectively.

If you have redefined any application menu items — by writing a Word for Windows macro to modify the File Print routine, say — you can often force the application to revert to the original, built-in procedure by holding down Shift while clicking that menu choice. (To defeat Word's AutoExec macro, however, you must start the application with the command `Winword /m`.)

Another great use of the Shift key involves the `\Windows\ Start Menu\ Programs\ StartUp` folder. If you put shortcuts to applications in this folder, Windows automatically loads the applications every time it starts. But if you hold down Shift when you see the Windows logo — and keep it held down until the taskbar is displayed on your Desktop — the StartUp folder is completely ignored! This is *very* handy if something in the StartUp folder is hanging Windows. You might also use this just to get Windows up and running quickly for some short task.

If you hold down Shift as soon as you see the "Starting Windows" message, your `Config.sys` and `Autoexec.bat` files are ignored. (If you don't see the "Starting Windows" message on your computer, hold down the Shift key during the Windows phase of the bootup process.)

If you are using the File Manager, you can use the Shift key to display subdirectories only when you *care* to see them. For example, clicking the Drive C icon (or pressing Ctrl+C) displays the top-level directories of the `C:` drive. If you instead hold down the Shift key when you click the Drive C icon, you force the File Manager to display all of the subdirectories on that drive.

The Shift key works as a keyboard shortcut, too. When you press Ctrl+Shift+C, File Manager changes to drive C: and displays all subdirectories, and so forth. This (undocumented) feature does not work in the Windows Explorer.

If you mark the Restart option button in the Shut Down Windows dialog box and then hold down the Shift key as you click the Yes button, Windows restarts without a warm reboot. Note: This can disable Automatic Power Management, but APM will be enabled the next time you reboot *without* using the Shift key.

Secret

If you want to open a file using an application that is different than the application associated with its file type, you can hold down the Shift key as you right-click the file, and then choose Open With in the context menu.

Do you want to really delete a file instead of sending it to the Recycle Bin? Highlight the file in a folder or Explorer window, and hold down the Shift key as you press Delete.

If you don't want a CD-ROM to start up automatically when you insert it in your CD-ROM drive, hold down the Shift key for a few seconds after you insert the CD-ROM.

Add a Windows Key to Your Windowless Keyboard

The Windows keyboards are pretty cool because they give you two very useful keys that are well integrated with Windows. If you don't have a Windows keyboard (heck, they're only about $15), you can remap your existing keyboard to include a Windows key and a context menu key.

To do this, use the Keyboard Remap applet, one of a collection of applets in Microsoft's Kernel Toys. You can download Kernel Toys from http://www.microsoft.com/windows95/downloads/default.asp. (Click the link for the Windows 95 Kernel Toys Set.)

STEPS

Remapping Your Keyboard

Step 1. Download the executable file for Kernel Toys (W95krnltoys.exe) into a folder where you store files temporarily (we create our own permanent Temp folder). Click the file to extract its contents into the temporary folder.

Step 2. Right-click the Keyremap.inf file, and click Install. (If you see the Insert Disk dialog message box, click OK. Then in the Copying Files dialog box, click the Browse button, navigate to the folder that contains the downloaded files, click OK, and click OK.)

Step 3. Click Start ⇨ Settings ⇨ Control Panel, and click the Keyboard icon.

Step 4. Click the Remap tab.

Step 5. In the Right-Hand Side area, select Right Alt in the "When this key is pressed" list, and select Windows in the "Act as if this key is pressed" list. Click Apply.

Step 6. Select Right Ctrl in the "When this key is pressed" list, and select Menu in the "Act as if this key is pressed" list. Click OK.

You have now created a Windows key and a context menu key for your Windowless keyboard.

Thanks to Anthony Kinyon for pointing out this tip.

More Win Key Keyboard Shortcuts

Microsoft defines a small set of useful shortcuts that use the Win key.

Winkey! is a keyboard macro programmer that lets you define up to 200 macros that work with the Win key (combined with other keys), as shown in Figure 42-11. It takes 2MB of RAM, but RAM is cheap these days, so if you have plenty, and you'd like to use the Win key to speed things up, this freeware package may be your ticket.

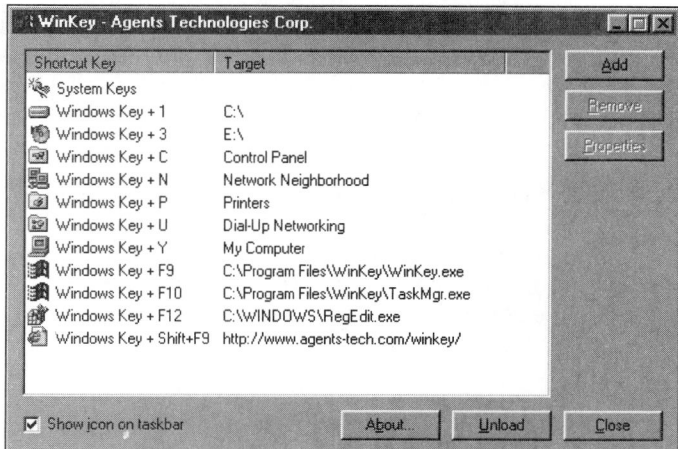

Figure 42-11: Winkey! lets you take full advantage of your keyboard's Win key.

You'll find this not-so-little utility at `http://www.agents-tech.com/winkey/`

Caps Lock Notification

Tip

If you find yourself accidentally hitting Caps Lock, you can provide yourself with a little notification so you won't end up typing something LIKE THIS. You'll need to install the Accessibility options when you install Windows 98 or later using the Add/Remove Programs icon in the Control Panel.

STEPS

Turning on Caps Lock Notification

Step 1.   Click the Start button, point to Settings, and then click Control Panel.

Step 2.   Click the Accessibility Options icon.

Step 3.   Mark the Use ToggleKeys checkbox. Click OK.

You will now hear a tone every time you press the Caps Lock, Num Lock, or Scroll Lock keys. The tone for enabling the key function is different from the tone for disabling it.

Turning Num Lock On or Off at Boot Time

If you have an enhanced keyboard with two sets of arrow keys, you may want the default state of the Num Lock key to be on when you start up Windows. Microsoft didn't see the need to build a switch into Windows that allowed you to set the state of the Num Lock key, so you'll have to use lower-level methods.

You can usually edit your PC's BIOS settings to turn the Num Lock key on or off. When you first boot up your computer, you are usually given a prompt that allows you to go to the BIOS by pressing a key such as Escape or F2 (the actual key depends on your computer). Once you're there, you can hunt around for a Num Lock setting.

DOS National Language Support

When you install Windows, Setup determines whether you are using something other than a standard U.S. keyboard layout and require a character set other than the standard IBM PC-8 to display characters on your computer screen. If it finds the National Language Support calls in these files (lines that refer to the code pages specific to the keyboard layouts used in your country), it keeps them in the new `Autoexec.bat` and `Config.sys` files and chooses the appropriate keyboard layout for Windows.

The Change Code Page tool (`changecp.exe`) on the Windows CD-ROM lets you choose a different code page (character set) for DOS programs when you set up Windows. You'll find it in the `\tools\changecp` folder. If you run Change Code Page after you've been using Windows for a while, it can make some of your filenames unreadable — so use it with caution if at all.

Making the Keys Repeat Faster

If you use your arrow keys a lot (and who doesn't), you'll want your insertion point to rip around your documents at the fastest speed possible. You can set the key repeat rate and the delay time before the key repeats itself in the Speed tab of the Keyboard Properties dialog box.

To change the keyboard speed, follow these steps:

STEPS

Changing Key Repeat Rate and Delay Time

Step 1. Open the Control Panel by clicking the Start button, pointing to Settings, and then clicking Control Panel.

Step 2. Click the Keyboard icon.

Step 3. Move the sliders, as shown in Figure 42-12.

Step 4. Test your settings by clicking in the test field and holding down a key.

Step 5. Click OK.

Continued

STEPS

Changing Key Repeat Rate and Delay Time *(continued)*

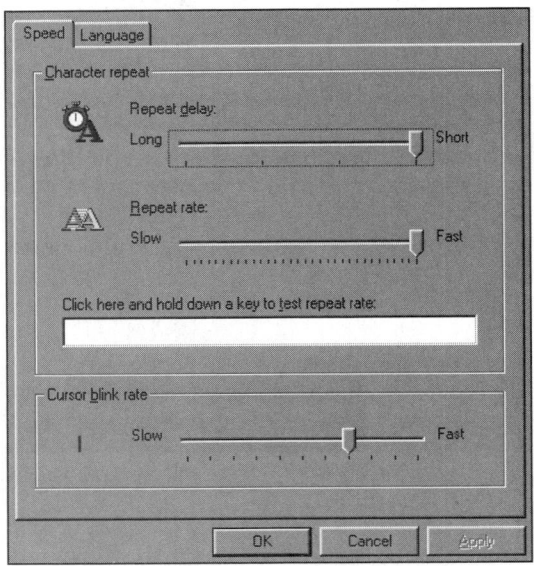

Figure 42-12: The Speed tab of the Keyboard Properties dialog box

The Speed tab of the Keyboard Properties dialog box is part of the user interface to the registry. The actual registry information about the keyboard is stored in the User.dat file in the \Windows folder. It is part of the information that is particular to a given user. This is what the exported ASCII file version of it looks like:

```
[HKEY_USERS\.Default\Control Panel\Keyboard]
"KeyboardSpeed"="31"
"KeyboardDelay"="0"
```

This registry entry states that the repeat delay time is as short as possible, and that the key repeat rate is as fast as possible. We tried entering a number of values greater than 31, and it made no difference. If you set the sliders in the Speed tab of the Keyboard Properties dialog box all the way to the left, the values stored in the registry are 0 and 3, respectively.

Secret

If you have a portable computer and an external keyboard, the speed and repeat rate settings may not be applied to them when you first start Windows. You'll have to open the Keyboard Properties dialog box every time you start Windows and change these settings. You can put a shortcut to the Keyboard Properties dialog box on your Desktop to help with this process. For details, turn to "Creating Shortcuts" in Chapter 10.

If You Get a New and Different Keyboard

Almost all keyboards sold now are based on and compatible with the PC/AT Enhanced Keyboard (101/102-Key) or the Microsoft Natural Keyboard. If you have a different keyboard attached to your computer, when you install Windows, it should detect the keyboard and install the correct keyboard driver. If you change your keyboard or if the hardware-detection procedures in Windows Setup didn't install the correct driver, then you can manually identify the keyboard to Windows and get the correct keyboard driver installed.

Follow these steps to change the keyboard driver:

STEPS

Changing the Keyboard Driver

Step 1.   Open the Control Panel by clicking the Start button, pointing to Settings, and then clicking Control Panel.

Step 2.   Click the System icon, click the Device Manager tab, click the plus sign next to the Keyboard icon, and double-click the icon for your keyboard.

Step 3.   Click the Driver tab.

Step 4.   Click the Upgrade Driver button, click Next, and then mark the option button to display a list of all drivers in a specific location and click Next again.

Step 5.   Mark the "Show all hardware" option button and choose a new keyboard driver from the list, as shown in Figure 42-13.

Continued

Changing the Keyboard Driver *(continued)*

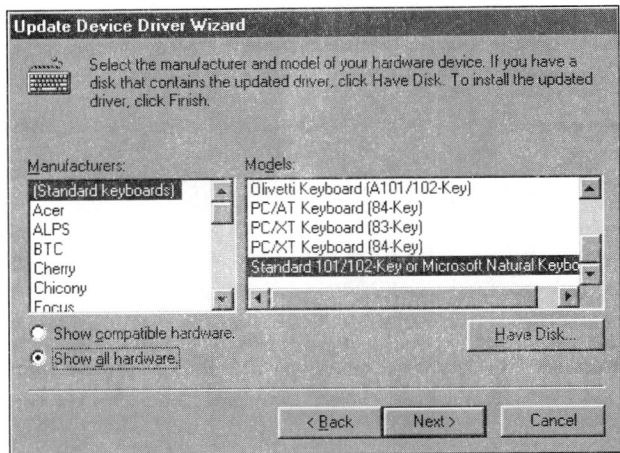

Figure 42-13: The Upgrade Device Driver Wizard. Choose a new keyboard driver here.

Behind the Keyboard Properties

Information about your keyboard type, layout, and language is stored in the registry in the System.dat and User.dat files in the \Windows folder. You can start the Registry Editor and search on *keyboard* to see how it is stored.

You can find other hardware and driver properties of the keyboard by clicking the System icon in the Control Panel, clicking the Device Manager tab, clicking the plus sign next to the Keyboard icon, highlighting your keyboard description, and then clicking the Properties button. There is not much you can change (unless you want to change the keyboard driver, as described earlier in the "If You Get a New and Different Keyboard" section.

Summary

We detail the characters that you can use in Windows and show you how to type characters that are not shown on your keyboard. We also discuss keyboard shortcuts and hot keys. Finally, we tell you how to modify properties of your keyboard driver to, for example, increase the key repeat rate. We provide:

- Lists of the character sets that come with Windows and the fonts they are associated with

- Tables of characters so you can find just the ones you want to spice up your documents

- Four methods of typing characters that don't show up on your keyboard

- Steps for creating multiple keyboard layouts, as well as multilingual documents

- A table of all Windows hot keys

- Instructions on how to fix the Shift key so that it works the way a touch typist would expect it to

- Steps for modifying your keyboard speed

Chapter 43

The Mighty Mouse

In This Chapter

Windows Me builds on the big mouse support improvements that Microsoft introduced with previous version of Windows. With the ability to open by single-clicking (or double-clicking, your choice), your mouse is friendlier and more useful than ever. We describe:

▶ Taking advantage of the new single-clicking capabilities

▶ The power of the right mouse button and why you'll want to use it often

▶ When you still need to use double-click

▶ What's so great about the 32-bit protected-mode mouse driver

▶ Improving your mouse's responsiveness

▶ Turning your mouse pointer into a nifty animated pointer

▶ Turning your middle button into a double-click button

Mouse Basics

In this chapter, when we say "mouse" we don't mean *mouse* exactly, but whatever pointing device you use that acts like a mouse. It could be a trackball, BallPoint, InPort, pen and tablet, or any one of the other devices that are variants on these themes. The purpose of all these devices is to move the mouse pointer about the screen.

The Windows user interface is a point-and-click interface. The mouse is the instrument you use to point and click. Windows Me makes the mouse easier to use by letting you single-click (if you choose) in a lot more situations.

Windows supports, right out of the box, a broad variety of mice from different manufacturers. All Microsoft Mouse–compatible mice, of course, are supported as though they were, in fact, manufactured by Microsoft. Windows specifically names mice manufactured by many companies, including Logitech, Kensington, Compaq, and Texas Instruments (TI). Windows also offers generic support for various "standard" mice.

Among the mouse models that Windows supports are serial mice, bus mice, PS/2 mice, trackballs, the TI QuickPort BallPoint mouse, and the Kensington Serial Expert mouse, as well as all models compatible with these models.

If you're installing Windows Me over Windows 3.1*x,* the old Windows 3.1*x* mouse drivers work as before. When you set up Windows Me, it remarks out calls to the older mouse drivers if the new Windows Me mouse drivers support your mouse. If you have a Windows 3.1*x* mouse driver that provides features not found in the Windows Me mouse driver, you can continue to use it or upgrade to a new Windows Me version if one is available from your mouse manufacturer.

Double-Clicking Versus Single-Clicking

A *click* means a press and release of the left mouse button. A *double-click* is two clicks within a set time interval. A *right-click* is a click of the right mouse button.

Windows Me lets you cut down significantly on double-clicking. We highly recommend that you enable single-clicking. Although it may take a little getting used to, it will be a lot easier on your mouse hand in the long run.

Tip

What is the keyboard equivalent of a double-click (or, if single-clicking is enabled, a single click)? First, use your arrow keys to move the highlight to an icon. When the item that you want to open is highlighted, press Enter.

Clicking to Open

An important feature of Windows is the ability to simply single-click to perform many actions that used to require double-clicking. This is a part of Microsoft's effort to make Windows more "Web-like" in its behavior. Microsoft found that many people have trouble getting the hang of double-clicking.

To set single-clicking as the default, if you haven't already, open the Explorer and choose View ⇨ Folder Options. In the General tab, mark the Custom option button, and then click the Settings button and mark "Single-click to open an item (point to select)." Underneath this option, you're given a choice of when to underline items in the Explorer; choose the one you prefer. Click OK, and then click OK again.

You can now complete many, but not all, actions using a single-click. Double-clicks are still required to initiate actions in some places. For example, you need to double-click in the common File Open dialog box and within many applications. You also need to double-click to open keys in the Registry Editor, and to select devices in the Device Manager. However, on your Desktop and within the Explorer, a single-click will suffice.

Of course, you can continue to double-click as you have in the past. However, we feel strongly enough about the advantages of Web style that this book assumes you are using it. If you are using what Microsoft refers to as Classic style (aka The Old Way), you'll need to mentally adjust the directions you find in these pages.

You can open all icons on the Desktop by clicking them. *Open* has multiple meanings. If the icon is a folder, it means open a folder in a window to display its contents. If the icon represents an application, it means start the application. If the icon represents a document, it means start the application associated with the document and open the document within the application.

Open is often the default action associated with a click, but you can choose or define other actions that will take place instead. For example, you could choose the Explore action, a variation on Open that opens the item in an Explorer window. If you set this action as the default action, then clicking an icon on the Desktop initiates the Explore action. See "Associating Actions with File Extensions" in Chapter 12 for more details.

Clicking a filename or icon in a folder window often opens it. You still need to double-click filenames and folder names in common file dialog boxes (dialog boxes associated with File Open). This opens them within the associated application.

If a folder icon appears in the left pane of the Explorer, you only have to single-click it to open it and display the folder's contents in the right pane.

Hovering to Select

In Windows 3.1*x* and Windows 95, you used to single-click a file, application, or folder icon when you wanted to select (highlight) it without performing an action on it. For example, you might want to select multiple File icons in preparation for moving them to another folder. But if you have single-clicking enabled in Windows Me, clicking will actually open the file — in this case, not what you had in mind.

When single-clicking is turned on, you can select an icon simply by "hovering" your mouse over it for a moment (no clicking needed). The icon becomes highlighted to indicate that it's selected. To select a consecutive group of icons, highlight the first icon by hovering over it, and then hold down the Shift key and hover over the last. To select nonconsecutive multiple icons, highlight the first icon and then hold down the Ctrl key as you hover over each additional one you want to select.

In the common file dialog boxes (associated with File Open in many applications) you'll still need to click to select. This is also true for applications, including RegEdit and the Device Manager.

Other Places Where Single-Clicking Works

Even if you're using the Classic style, you don't have to double-click to open a file because Windows provides an alternative — you can right-click the file and choose an action from the context menu. The first action listed in the menu is often Open.

If an application is active but minimized, you only have to single-click its taskbar button to restore the application to a window.

You can single-click items in the Start menu to open their associated applications.

In the Explorer, you can single-click the plus symbol next to a Folder icon in the folder tree to open the branch.

To display the Task Manager in Windows 3.1*x*, you had to double-click the Desktop. In Windows Me, you can right-click the taskbar to display a context menu that lets you perform similar functions.

In all cases where a double-click was required under the old Windows 3.1*x* for an action, Windows Me lets you instead right-click and then click a command in a context menu.

The Right Mouse Button Stuff

Windows makes extensive use of the right mouse button. This represents a fantastic improvement in functionality and ease of use over the old Windows 3.1*x* user interface, which had no consistent, system-wide use of the right mouse button.

The right-click is not implemented consistently. Programs written for Windows 3.1*x* don't use the right mouse button in the same manner as programs written for Windows Me. However, it rarely hurts an object to just right-click it and see what happens. Ordinarily, you can't start something that you didn't want to with a right-click. (The exception is *context menus,* which are the floating menus that are brought up when you right-click an object. In a context menu, a right-click does the same thing as a left-click. For example, if you right-click a filename, you actually delete it if you right-click Delete on the context menu. Good thing we have the Recycle Bin to help us retrieve things we didn't mean to delete!)

Tip

You can right-click nearly everything that you see on the Desktop, including the Desktop itself. You can right-click anything in a folder window or in the Explorer. Our advice is to right-click anything and everything just to see what happens.

Tip

What is the keyboard equivalent of the right mouse button? Shift+F10.

You can set the speed with which menus cascade from context menus. See "Changing Mouse Menu Speed" later in this chapter.

Right-Clicking My Computer

If you right-click the My Computer icon on the Desktop, you can use commands in the context menu to open a My Computer folder window, open the Explorer, map or disconnect network drives, find files or computers, and bring up the System properties, including the Device Manager (click Properties in the My Computer context menu).

Right-Clicking the Start Button

Right-clicking the Start button lets you:

- Open the Start Menu folder window, which contains the Programs folder icon (and possibly other icons as well)
- Open the Explorer focused on the Start Menu
- Find a file in the Start Menu folder or one of its subfolders

Tip

Right-clicking the Start button and choosing commands from the context menu can be quite useful if you want to make changes in the folders and shortcut icons associated with the Start menu. For example, if you right-click and choose Explore, you can use the Explorer to move folders and shortcut icons in the Start Menu folder or the Programs subfolder. Changes you make in the Explorer will be reflected in the Start menu and the Programs submenu. You may find additional commands in this context menu; they are added automatically when you install some applications, such as WinZip. With Windows 98, you can also right-click menu items and shortcuts in some of the Start menus (including Programs and Favorites) to display appropriate context menus.

Right-Clicking the Taskbar

The taskbar displays buttons for running applications or folders; you single-click a taskbar button to bring the associated application or folder to the top of the Desktop. Right-clicking the taskbar lets you:

- Open or close toolbars
- Cascade the open windows on the Desktop
- Tile the open windows horizontally or vertically
- Minimize all open windows (or undo the previous minimization)
- Edit the properties of the taskbar

Turn to "The Taskbar and its Toolbars" in Chapter 5 for more details on using the taskbar.

Right-Clicking the Time

Right-clicking the time at the right end of the taskbar gives you the same options as right-clicking the taskbar itself, and it also lets you adjust the settings for the date and time.

Right-Clicking a File Icon

Right-clicking a File icon lets you open the file with its associated application, and if a document has an associated Quick Viewer, you can quickly view the document's contents by choosing Quick View (assuming you have installed the Quick View component of Windows 98).

When you right-click a File icon, you can also access all the standard file-management commands, including Cut, Copy, Delete, and Rename.

Shift+Right-Clicking a File Icon

If the file is of a registered file type, Shift+right-click adds the Open With command to the context menu. Open With lets you open the file with an application other than the one associated with that file type.

Right-Clicking a Folder Icon

The context menu for a folder is similar to that of a file. Choosing the Open command in a folder's context menu displays the contents of that folder in a folder window (if the icon is in a folder window) or in the Explorer (if the icon is in the Explorer). You can also use the context menu to move, share, create a shortcut to, rename, or delete a folder, and to bring up its properties.

Right-Clicking a Shortcut

Right-clicking a shortcut brings up a similar context menu to that which appears when you right-click the target of the shortcut. The difference is that the Properties command in the context menu for a shortcut brings up the Properties dialog box for the shortcut itself, not for the target.

However, if you have installed `Target.dll`, the context menu for a shortcut includes an important additional command, Target, that lets you get to the application or document to which the shortcut points. When you point to Target, a submenu appears that includes, among other things, an Open Container command and a Properties command. Open Container opens a folder window with the focus on the target. Properties displays the Properties dialog box for the target.

Target is a component of Microsoft Windows PowerToys. Download PowerToys from http://www.microsoft.com/windows/software/ powertoy.htm.

Right-Clicking the Desktop

If you right-click the Desktop itself (staying clear of icons and the taskbar) you display the Desktop's context menu. This context menu lets you:

- View, update, and customize the Active Desktop
- Arrange (line up) the icons on the Desktop
- Create a new folder, file, or shortcut on the Desktop
- Open the Display Properties dialog box

The last item is the same as clicking the Display icon in the Control Panel.

Right-Clicking the Client Area of a Folder Window

The options you get when you right-click the client area of a folder window are similar to those you get when you right-click the Desktop, with a few differences.

You don't get a Properties command for bringing up the Display Properties dialog box, and you do get commands for changing how the icons are displayed in the folder window: Large Icons, Small Icons, List, and Details. You also get options that let you toggle in and out of Web Page view for the folder and customize the Web Page view. For example, you could add a background photo for the folder.

Right-Clicking the Title Bar of the Active Application

If you right-click the title bar of the application window with the focus, you display the System menu for that window. (The title bar of a window with the focus is blue if you are using standard Windows colors.)

The System menu is programmable, so it can change from application to application. The standard functions that are available in this menu include moving, sizing, and closing the window.

You can also right-click the title bar of a folder window to display its System menu, or right-click a taskbar button to display the System menu for the associated folder or application.

Right-Clicking in a Dialog Box

Dialog boxes are a little different than most windows that show up on your Desktop. You may see common resource dialog boxes used by older, 16-bit Windows applications or common dialog boxes used by 32-bit Windows applications. Many Windows applications also have their own unique dialog boxes.

Many Windows-compliant dialog boxes have a Question Mark button in the upper-right corner. If you click that button and then click an item in the dialog box, you get an explanation of the item. As an alternative to using the Question Mark button, you can right-click an item, and then click the What's This? button that appears.

Right-Clicking in a 16-Bit File Open Dialog Box

Common resource dialog boxes for 16-bit Windows applications include the File Open and Fonts dialog boxes. If you right-click within one of these dialog boxes, a What's This? button appears.

Right-Clicking in a 32-Bit File Open Dialog Box

Right-clicking a filename in a 32-bit Windows common File Open dialog box highlights the filename and displays a context menu with options to open the file and perform other file-management tasks. Right-clicking in other places gives you other context menus appropriate to the item you clicked. In some areas, you get the What's This? button.

Figure 43-1 shows the 32-bit File Open dialog box with the context menu for the first filename displayed.

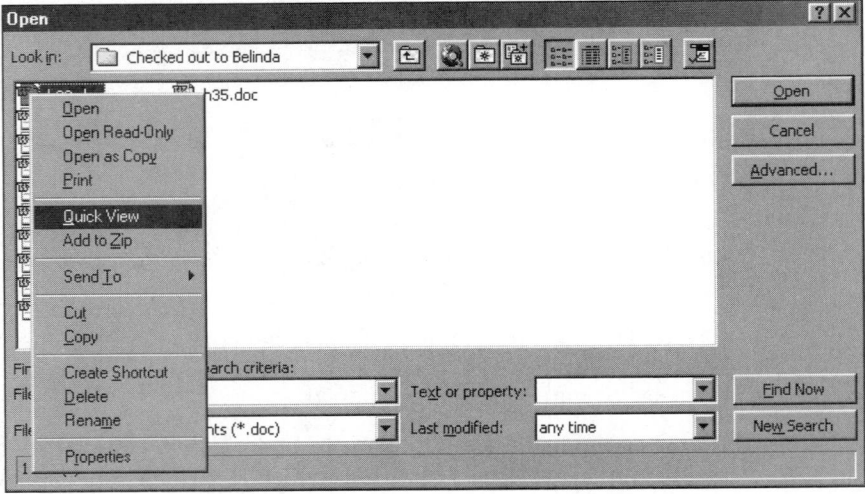

Figure 43-1: The File Open dialog box. Right-click a filename to display its context menu.

Right-Clicking in the Client Area of an Active Application

You can right-click within an application. If the application is Windows-aware, a context menu appears with frequently used commands that are appropriate to the place you clicked. When you right-click a document in your word processor, for example, the context menu might give you commands for copying, cutting, and pasting text.

Disabling the Right Mouse Button

If for some reason you want to disable the right mouse button in Windows, you might try IKIOSK from Hyper Technologies Inc. IKIOSK is designed to let system administrators disable or gray out various features and menus of Windows. You can download a 60-day trial copy from `http://www.hypertec.com`. Disabling features can be somewhat unpredictable, so make sure you have a good system backup, and start slowly.

Driving Your Mouse

The included Windows mouse drivers are 32-bit protected-mode drivers. They take up zero conventional memory, leaving more room for any DOS programs you may run in a windowed DOS session.

The mouse driver supports MS-DOS programs in Windows DOS sessions, in either full-screen or windowed mode. As long as Windows is running and you're running your DOS program in a DOS virtual machine, the mouse works with your DOS program.

You can now connect a serial mouse to any of the four serial ports: COM1 through COM4. Under Windows 3.1*x,* you could only connect a serial mouse to COM1 or COM2.

The current Windows mouse driver supports Plug and Play mice. Windows automatically recognizes and installs these mice during setup. Windows hardware-detection routines can detect pre-Plug and Play mice.

Windows includes an easy-to-use Mouse Properties dialog box with lots of functionality. Mouse manufacturers can still substitute their own Properties dialog box for this one, or add to it.

You can define the middle button of your Logitech three-button mouse to substitute for a double-click.

All along, the mice used with PCs and compatible computers have had at least two buttons, but the right one didn't do anything in Windows 3.1*x* itself. Starting with Windows 95, Microsoft decided to define the behavior of the right mouse button. In Windows Me and in applications designed for them, clicking the right mouse button brings up a *context menu*, a menu of options available for the item you clicked, as we saw in the section entitled "The Right Mouse Button Stuff."

Setting Up Your Mouse Driver

The Windows installation and setup procedures include automatic hardware detection. Make sure your mouse is plugged in when you run Windows Setup, so that the hardware-detection routines can identify your mouse and install the correct driver.

If your mouse isn't detected properly, you can easily add it using the steps detailed later in this chapter in the "Adding a Driver for a New Mouse" section.

If your mouse isn't supported by the mouse drivers that come with Windows, you can still use your existing mouse driver. If you have installed Windows Me in your existing Windows directory without first deleting Windows 3.1*x*, your mouse driver will still be functioning.

Changing the Driver for an Existing Mouse

You can change to a different mouse driver if you find that the one you have installed is incorrect for the mouse you're using, or if an updated driver becomes available. Follow these steps to change your mouse driver:

STEPS

Changing the Driver for an Existing Mouse

Step 1.   Click the Start button, point to Settings, click Control Panel, and click the System icon. Next, click the Device Manager tab in the System Properties dialog box, and click the "View devices by type" option button. Click the plus sign next to Mouse, highlight your mouse, and then click the Properties button. Click the Driver tab, and then click the Upgrade Driver button to launch the Upgrade Device Driver Wizard.

Step 2.   Click the Next button to progress to the second Wizard dialog box. Here you can have the wizard search for a better driver for you, or you can tell it to use a specific driver file. If you want to use a specific driver file, skip to step 5.

Step 3. To have the wizard search for you, click "Search for a better driver than the one your device is using now (Recommended)" and click Next. You will be given a list of places you want the wizard to look for new drivers (see Figure 43-2). Click all the checkboxes that are appropriate. If you select Microsoft Windows Update, your computer will connect to the Microsoft Web site and download the Update Agent to search that site.

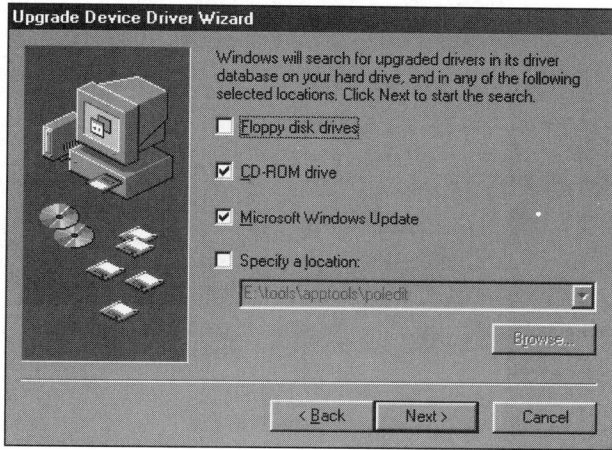

Figure 43-2: The Upgrade Device Driver Wizard asks you where to look for a better driver. If you select Microsoft Windows Update, your computer will connect to the Microsoft Web site and download the Update Agent to search that site.

Step 4. Click Next, and the wizard will carry out its search (this may take a couple of minutes). At the end, the wizard will tell you whether it found another driver for your mouse (see Figures 43-3 and 43-4). If there is more than one driver that would work for your mouse, the wizard will advise you which one is the best (it may be the one you already have). If another driver would be an improvement, you'll have the option of downloading it (if necessary) and installing it. Follow the wizard's prompts to complete the installation.

Step 5. If you have a specific driver you want to use, click "Display a list of all the drivers in a specific location, so you can select the driver you want" in the Wizard's second dialog box. Then click Next and mark "Show all hardware."

Continued

Changing the Driver for an Existing Mouse *(continued)*

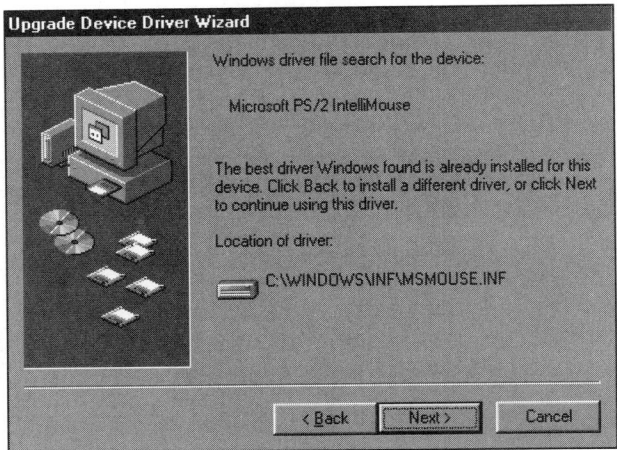

Figure 43-3: The Wizard will notify you if it found a better driver. In this case, it only found the current driver.

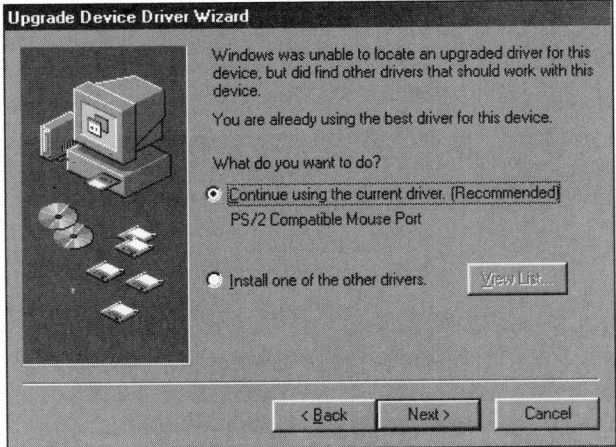

Figure 43-4: If there are other drivers that would work with your mouse, the wizard will tell you whether one might be an improvement. It will let you choose whether to keep the driver you have or install a new one.

Step 6.   Choose a mouse manufacturer and model from the list, as shown in Figure 43-5. (If the mouse you have isn't listed, if you know that it is not compatible with the models listed, and if you have a mouse driver diskette, click the Have Disk button. Put your mouse driver diskette in the disk drive and click the OK button if the correct path to your diskette drive is shown. Otherwise, type the correct path or browse to find it before clicking OK.) Click Next to install the driver you have selected, and then click Finish.

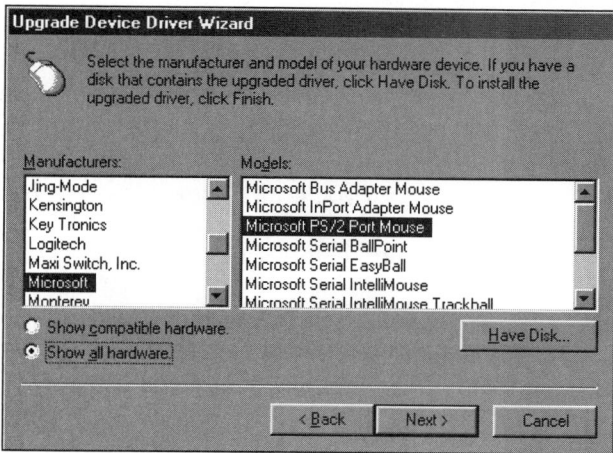

Figure 43-5: Highlight a manufacturer and then a mouse model, and then click Next. You will have to restart Windows after you install a new mouse driver.

Step 7.   Click OK until you have exited all the dialog boxes, and then restart Windows 98 to have the new mouse driver take effect.

Adding a Driver for a New Mouse

If you get a new mouse after you have installed Windows, you probably won't need to do anything but plug it in and restart the computer. Windows should recognize that you have added new hardware and install it automatically.

However, if this doesn't happen, it's easy to install a new mouse driver by following these steps:

STEPS

Adding a Driver for a New Mouse

Step 1.   Click the Start button, point to Settings, and then click Control Panel. Click the Add New Hardware icon. Click Next.

Step 2.   Windows tells you it will now search for new hardware. Click Next, and be prepared to wait for a few minutes while the wizard searches for any new Plug and Play devices.

Step 3.   If it doesn't find any new Plug and Play devices, it displays a dialog box asking if you want Windows to search for hardware that is not Plug and Play compatible. If you see this dialog box, skip to step 5. If the wizard does find new Plug and Play devices, it asks you if the one(s) it found include the one you want.

Step 4.   If the answer is yes, click the mouse you want to install, click "Yes, the device is in the list," click Next to install the driver, and skip to step 6. If your mouse is not on the list, mark "No, the device isn't in the list," and click Next.

Step 5.   Click "No, I want to select the hardware from a list," and click Next. Select Mouse from the list of hardware types, and click Next. Then choose a mouse manufacturer and model. (If the mouse you have isn't listed, if you know that it is not compatible with the models listed, and if you have a mouse driver diskette, click the Have Disk button. Put your mouse driver diskette in the disk drive and click the OK button if the correct path to your diskette drive is shown. Otherwise, type the correct path or browse to find it before clicking OK.) Click Next to install the driver you have selected.

Step 6.   Click Finish.

Step 7.   Restart Windows to have the mouse driver take effect.

You can install mouse drivers that were written for the old Windows 3.1*x* operating system if you don't find one that works with your mouse. Try to install one of the new ones first before you install an older driver. Just because your mouse and the mouse driver don't have the same names doesn't mean one of the new drivers won't work—try a few first.

Secret

To install a Windows 3.1*x* mouse driver or a mouse driver that didn't come with Windows Me, click the Have Disk button in step 5 above. You need to have a diskette with the mouse driver on it. The diskette needs to include a mouse setup file. This file has an `inf` extension and defines how to install the mouse drivers.

Many mice, including newer Microsoft Mice that use Mouse Driver 9.0, will not support what Microsoft refers to as "nonstandard" IRQs and I/O addresses. This means you may only be able to assign this type of mouse to the serial ports COM1 or COM2, not COM3 or COM4.

Configuring Your Mouse Driver Properties

Use the Mouse Properties dialog box to set the properties of the mouse driver. You can use this dialog box to change the responsiveness or speed of the mouse pointer relative to your movements of the mouse. You can switch the function of the right and left mouse buttons for left-handed operation. You can also change the double-click time interval. A longer interval counts two separate mouse clicks that are separated by a longer period of time as a single double-click.

You get to pick from a collection of mouse pointer icons, including animated pointers that correspond to a range of mouse functions. You can turn the hourglass pointer into a spinning world, for example. Since Windows Me uses the same `ani` file format as Windows 2000 and NT, you can select from a wide variety of shareware and freeware animated icons available on online services and the Internet. And if you're using an LCD screen, you can add mouse pointer trails by setting the number of ghost images that get left behind (briefly) at the mouse pointer's former location.

Follow these steps to change the properties of your mouse:

STEPS

Configuring the Mouse Driver

Step 1. Click the Start button, point to Settings, and then click Control Panel. Click the Mouse icon (it looks like a white right-handed bar of soap).

Step 2. The Buttons tab of the Mouse Properties dialog box, as shown in Figure 43-6, lets you switch the "handedness" of the mouse buttons and set the speed at which you have to click the mouse twice in order to get the two clicks to count as a single double-click.

Continued

STEPS

Configuring the Mouse Driver *(continue)*

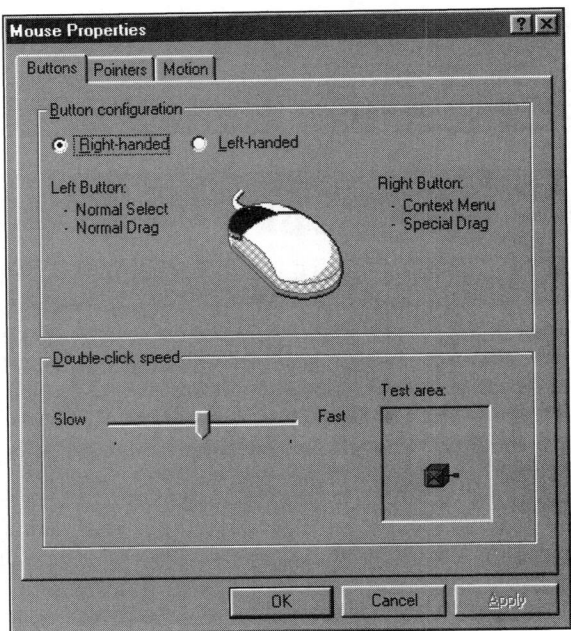

Figure 43-6: The Buttons tab of the standard Mouse Properties dialog box. You can swap the left and right mouse buttons and adjust the time interval between mouse clicks that will count as a double-click. The Properties dialog box for your particular pointing device may look different, depending on your driver.

Changing the Handedness of the Mouse Buttons

Click the "Left-handed" option button to switch the left and right mouse buttons. On a three-button mouse, these are the two outside buttons. If you are left-handed, swapping the function of the left and right mouse buttons lets you use your index finger to single- and double-click when you're controlling the mouse with your left hand.

Changing the Double-Click Speed

Although Windows lets you use a single-click for many actions that used to require a double-click, there are still some times when a double-click is required (selecting a word in text, for example). And if you prefer the old way, you can still revert to double-clicking. To do this, choose View ⇨ Folder Options in the Explorer, and mark the "Classic style" option button.

To adjust how fast you need to double-click, do the following:

STEPS

Changing Double-Click Speed

Step 1. Move the "Double-click speed" slider to the left to increase the time interval allowed between two mouse clicks that are counted as one double-click. Move the slider to the right to increase the speed with which you must twice click the left mouse button (assuming a right-handed configuration) in order for it to count as a double-click.

Step 2. To test your double-click agility, click twice in the test area. If your two clicks count as one double-click, the jack-in-the-box goes up or down.

Secret

The range of the slider is between 900 milliseconds (nine-tenths of a second) at the left end and 100 milliseconds (one-tenth of a second) on the right end. This makes the middle of the slider equal to half a second.

Changing the Double-Click Height and Width

Secret

Windows 3.1*x* enabled you to determine the size in pixels of an invisible box around the location of the mouse pointer where the first click of a double-click takes place. The mouse pointer must be located within this box for a second click to count as part of the double-click. You could insert the variables DoubleClickWidth and DoubleClickHeight in the [Windows] section of the Win.ini file to do this. If you didn't add these variables to Win.ini, the default size of the box was four pixels on a side.

The size of the double-click box is now set in the registry, and the default is two pixels. You might want to enlarge the box if you find that Windows is missing a lot of your double-clicks (because you are moving the mouse a bit between clicks). The easiest way to do this is by using TweakUI. Just open TweakUI in your Control Panel, click the Mouse tab, and increase the number in the Double-Click field. (TweakUI assumes you want a square box.) You can test the sensitivity by double-clicking the Gear icon.

Desensitizing Dragging

If you find that you are often inadvertently moving Folder icons around in your Explorer, you can widen the area that you have to drag an icon before it begins moving. Signs that accidental dragging is a problem for you include folders disappearing when you click on them and error messages stating that you can't move a folder when you weren't trying to move one to begin with.

The default Windows setting for initiating a drag is two pixels. That is, if you highlight an icon, press and hold down the left mouse button, and move the mouse pointer just two pixels, then the icon begins to move. The hand movement required to do this is comparable to a slow left click with a slight movement of your wrist.

You can increase the distance that you have to move an icon before dragging starts by using TweakUI. Open TweakUI in your Control Panel, click the Mouse tab, and increase the number in the Drag field to something like five or ten pixels (see Figure 43-7). Test the setting using the Gear icon. If you're still having problems, increase the size again.

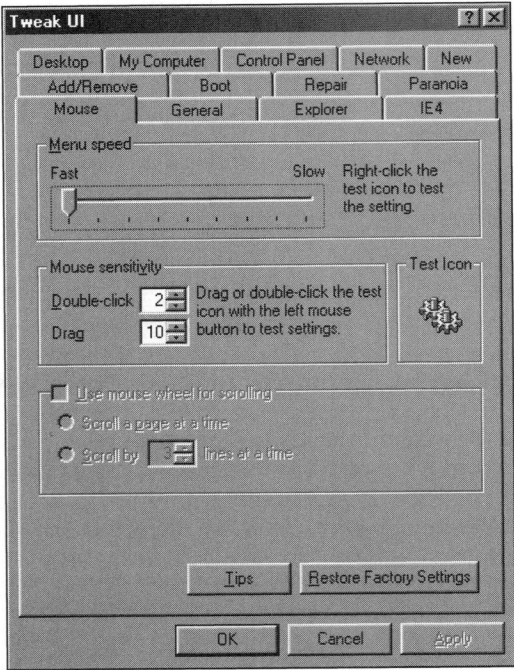

Figure 43-7: The Mouse tab of TweakUI lets you set double-click and drag sensitivity, as well as the speed of some menus.

High-resolution displays with high-density mice are the source of this problem. Microsoft's defaults are for VGA resolution screens. Two pixels is much too small a distance for high-resolution displays, and high-density mice take only the slightest movement to move this far.

Changing Mouse Menu Speed

The Start menu contains submenus. The context menus that appear when you right-click often contain submenus. You can change the speed at which these submenus appear. At the slowest setting, you must right-click again to see the submenu.

You adjust the menu speed using TweakUI. Click the TweakUI icon in the Control Panel, click the Mouse tab, and drag the "Menu speed" slider bar in the desired direction. Click Apply, and then test the setting by right-clicking the Gear icon in the Mouse tab and hovering over a command to display its submenu. When you have the speed adjusted the way you want it, click OK.

Using Different Mouse Pointers

You can (and we feel should) use some of the newer static and animated mouse pointers created for Windows. They are a lot of fun and are often better designed than the Windows standard ones. Only a few animated pointers come with Windows Me; these pointers are stored in the \Windows\Cursors folder.

You must have your display card driver set to at least 256 colors in order for animated cursors to work.

Secret

Some cards that can display 256 colors have video drivers that don't work with animated pointers. You'll need to test your card and driver with one animated pointer to make sure that it works.

Secret

Animated pointers don't work if you use 16-bit real-mode hard disk drivers instead of the 32-bit protected-mode drivers that come with Windows. Your Config.sys file references these drivers if you are using them. You can also check to see if you are using 32-bit hard disk drivers by double-clicking the System icon in your Control Panel, and then clicking the Performance tab. If File System and Virtual Memory are marked as 32-bit, you are not using 16-bit hard disk drivers.

If you did a custom Windows installation, as is our recommendation, or installed Windows Me over Windows 95, you must have installed the mouse pointers initially (as an accessory) in order to have them available now. If you didn't install them during setup, you can click the Add/Remove Programs icon in the Control Panel, click the Windows Setup tab, click Accessories, and mark the "Mouse pointers" checkbox to install them.

Tip

We suggest you create a folder called Ani as a subfolder of your \Windows folder and move your animated cursors into this folder, even the ones currently stored in \Windows\Cursors. This way, you can easily get at the animated pointers with the Browse button in the steps shown here.

STEPS

Changing Mouse Pointers

Step 1. Click the Mouse icon in the Control Panel, and click the Pointers tab, as shown in Figure 43-8. Starting with Normal Select, scroll down the list of pointer functions and their associated pointers. Try clicking different pointers as you go down the list. When you click a pointer, it appears in the gray box in the upper-right corner of the dialog box, and if the pointer is animated, you see what the animation looks like.

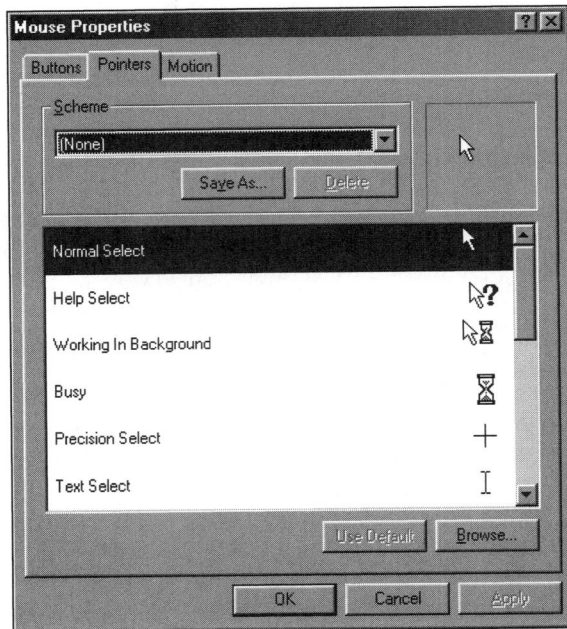

Figure 43-8: The Pointers tab of the Mouse Properties dialog box. Each mouse function has an associated mouse pointer.

Step 2. Click the Schemes pull-down menu in this tab, and you will see various pointer schemes designed by Microsoft. If you have installed any Themes, you will see pointer schemes that relate to those themes. In these pointer schemes supplied by Microsoft, only the Busy and Working in Background pointers are animated. You can use this Schemes menu to choose a new pointer scheme, or mix and match.

Step 3. To use a different mouse pointer for a particular mouse function, click that mouse function and then click the Browse button. In the Browse dialog box, you will see the animated pointers stored in the \Windows\Ani folder (if you have created this folder) or other pointers in the \Windows\Cursors folder. Animated pointer files have the ani extension, and static pointers have the cur extension. When you highlight a pointer file, it appears in the Preview box in the lower-left corner of the dialog box.

Step 3. Double-click the pointer that you want to replace the existing pointer.

Tip

We suggest you do not replace the mouse pointers associated with Normal Select, Precision Select, or Text Select with animated pointers. They will be too distracting. Go ahead and replace the mouse pointers associated with Working In Background and Busy with two animated icons that express waiting.

Table 43-1 describes the mouse pointers associated with the different mouse functions.

Table 43-1   Windows Mouse Pointers

Pointer	Function
Normal Select	This is the normal mouse pointer for selecting items.
Help Select	When you click the ? button in the upper-right corner of a dialog box, you get this mouse pointer. When you see this pointer, you can click any option in the dialog box to get a brief explanation of what the option is for.
Working In Background	Windows or a 32-bit multithreaded application is busy but using a background thread, so you can proceed with something else if you want.
Busy	Windows or an application is busy trying to accomplish some task before it can proceed.
Precision Select	This pointer guides your eye to its center to help you select with precision.
Text Select	This pointer is also called the *I-beam*. You use it in word processors to select text.
Handwriting	This pointer appears when you have switched to a mode that is expecting handwritten or ink input from you (in an application that supports handwriting).

Continued

Table 43-1   *(continued)*

Pointer	*Function*
Unavailable	When you drag a File icon over an area or application that won't accept the file if you drop it there, this pointer appears to remind you of that fact.
Vertical, Horizontal, Diagonal Resize	The double-headed arrow pointers appear when you position your mouse pointer along the edges of a sizable window.
Move	When you click the Move command in the system menu of a window, this pointer appears. When you see it, you can move the window with your arrow keys.
Alternate Select	The only place we've seen this pointer is in the FreeCell solitaire card game.
Link Select	This pointer appears when you hover over a clickable link, whether in the Explorer, in a Help file, or when viewing a Web page.

A very important cursor not included in this list shows the insertion point in text editors and word processors. This cursor, aptly called the *insertion point*, tells you where your text will get inserted if you start typing.

If you use the Display Properties dialog box to change the background color of your windows to something other than the default stark white, you'll need to set the color of the insertion point so that it shows up well on top of the background color.

View the Animated Cursor Schemes Web site at `http://www.islandnet.com/~wwseb/cursors.htm` to see more animated pointer themes.

Changing Mouse Pointer Speed

Secret

Speed is a bit of a misnomer. What you are determining is how much *faster* the mouse pointer moves (the rate of acceleration) as you move the mouse faster. This is a semicomplicated multiplier of the already-set ratio of mouse pointer movement to mouse movement.

The ratio of mouse pointer movement to mouse movement has already been set by your mouse and video driver. The pointer speed values multiply this ratio so that the mouse pointer moves even faster if you move the mouse faster. Each one of the tick marks in the "Pointer speed" slider, shown in Figure 43-9, corresponds to a different set of values for Mouse Speed, MouseThreshold1, and MouseThreshold2. These values are shown in Table 43-2.

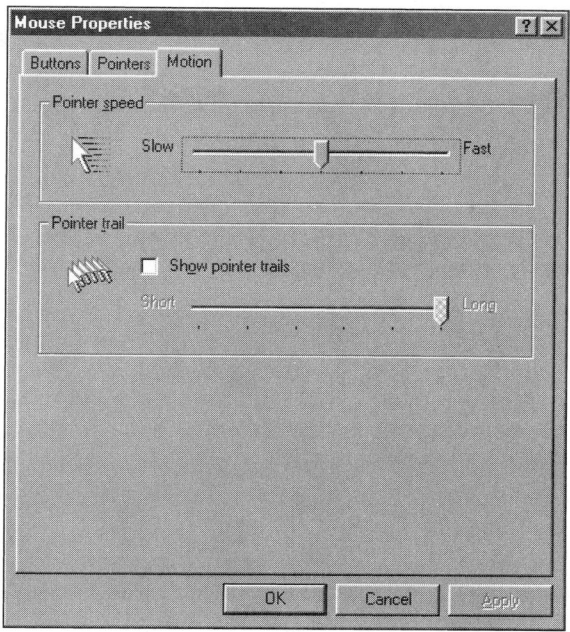

Figure 43-9: The Motion tab of the Mouse Properties dialog box. Change the responsiveness of the mouse pointer to movements of the mouse. Add trails to the mouse pointer on LCD screens. The units for MouseThreshold1 and 2 are pixels.

Table 43-2   The Pointer Speed Values

Slider Position	1	2	3	4	5	6	7
MouseSpeed	0	1	1	1	2	2	2
MouseThreshold1	0	10	7	4	4	4	4
MouseThreshold2	0	0	0	0	12	9	6

If you move your mouse slowly, the mouse pointer moves slowly. If you move the mouse quickly, the mouse pointer moves even more quickly if the MouseSpeed is greater than zero.

Windows compares the number of pixels the mouse pointer has moved during the time interval between mouse interrupts against the mouse thresholds. The mouse sends out interrupts periodically. If you move the mouse quickly, the mouse pointer movement exceeds the number of pixels of one or both of the mouse thresholds.

If the MouseSpeed is set to 1 and the mouse pointer movement exceeds the number of pixels given by the value of MouseThreshold1, the mouse pointer speed is double the normal rate. If the MouseSpeed is set to 2 and the mouse pointer movement exceeds MouseThreshold2, the mouse pointer speed is quadrupled. If it exceeds MouseThreshold1, it is doubled, the same as if MouseSpeed is set to 1.

Play with this "Pointer speed" slider a bit to see what you are comfortable with. The optimal setting will vary depending on whether you have a trackball or a mouse, among other things.

Tip

Think your computer is "too slow"? Try this: Set all your mouse speed settings to the maximum speed. Allow about half a day to get used to this, and see if it doesn't make your PC feel a lot faster. Many "slow" computers are merely suffering from a "molasses mouse." It may turn out that the default settings were way too sluggish for you, or the mouse settings may have been made slower than is appropriate for you at some point. If you don't like having your mouse set to the maximum speed, you can always back off a bit later.

STEPS

Changing the Mouse Pointer Speed

Step 1. Click the Motion tab in the Mouse Properties dialog box. Move the "Pointer speed" slider to the left to decrease the travel of the mouse pointer across the screen relative to the speed of travel of the mouse across the mouse pad. Move the slider to the right to increase the responsiveness of the mouse pointer movement on screen to the speed of mouse travel on the mouse pad.

Step 2. You won't be able to test the speed difference unless you click the Apply button. You might want to try a few different speeds and click the Apply button after each change. When you've found a setting you like, click OK.

Changing Mouse Speed Values in the Registry

Secret

You may wonder how we figured out what values are set by the "Pointer speed" slider. They turn out to be the same values as those set by the mouse driver in Windows 3.1x. But to determine the actual values, we looked in the registry. The way we did it is generally quite useful and bears detailing:

STEPS

Seeing Your Registry Values Change

Step 1. Display the Motion tab of the Mouse Properties dialog box. (Click the Mouse icon in the Control Panel and click the Motion tab.)

Step 2. Also display the Registry Editor by opening Explorer and clicking `Regedit.exe` in your `\Windows` folder.

Step 3. Open the Registry editor to HKEY_CURRENT_USER \Control Panel\Mouse. Highlight Mouse, as shown in Figure 43-10. If you don't see this Mouse branch in the registry, check the Secret at the end of this section.

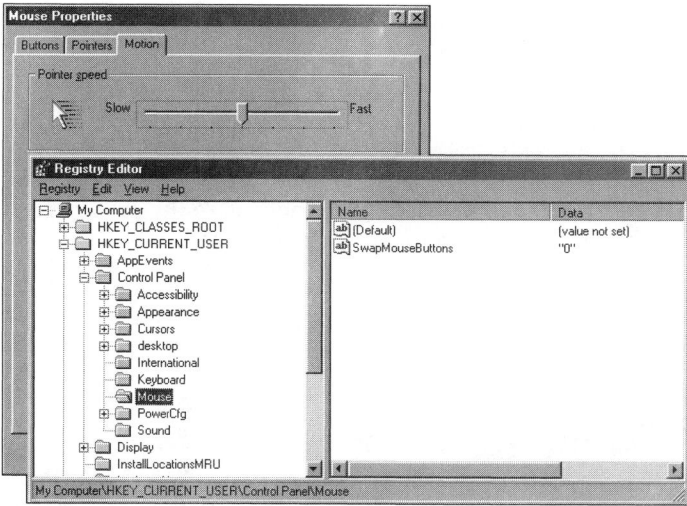

Figure 43-10: The Motion tab of the Mouse Properties dialog box and the Registry Editor working together

Step 4. Click the Motion tab of the Mouse Properties dialog box. Move the "Pointer speed" slider. Click Apply.

Step 5. Click the Registry Editor and press the F5 key. You will see the values of MouseSpeed, MouseThreshold1, and MouseThreshold2 change.

Step 6. Repeat steps 4 and 5 to check all the values assigned by the "Pointer speed" slider. You can do the same thing with the "Double-click speed" slider (in the Buttons tab).

Step 7. Exit the Registry Editor.

Secret

The values set in a user interface to the registry (in this case the Mouse Properties dialog box) are immediately reflected in the registry, and used by the applications that rely on them.

Secret

You can also edit the values directly in the registry. If you use this method, the mouse doesn't use these new values until you restart Windows. Until you do, the mouse uses 0, 0, 0 instead, meaning no acceleration.

If you have user profiles enabled for your computer, there is a separate mouse setting for each user. If you edit these values in the registry, you need to change them in the branch that applies to the particular user.

Secret

You have to make some changes in your mouse speed values (through the Mouse Properties dialog box) before the Mouse branch will show up in the registry. You may need to make these changes and quit Windows 98 before you see the branch, because it takes Windows a while to write these changes back out of memory to the disk files that contain the permanent copy of the registry.

If you have made changes to mouse speed, you will find the Mouse branch in HKEY_CURRENT_USER, as well as in HKEY_USERS. If you have disabled user profiles in the Passwords Properties dialog box (under the Passwords icon in the Control Panel), these branches are the same. The HKEY_CURRENT_USER branch is an alias for the current user found in the HKEY_USERS branch.

Numerous values are not stored in the registry unless they are different than the default values. For example, if you don't make any changes in the mouse double-click speed, you won't find an entry for it in the registry.

Changing the Pointer Trails

Pointer trails, which leave "ghosts" of the mouse pointer in the mouse pointer's former position, are really useful only on LCD screens where the mouse pointer is hard to find. Otherwise, they are just a distraction. (The default is no pointer trails at all.) Here's how to modify them:

STEPS

Changing the Number of Pointer Ghosts

Step 1. On the Motion tab of the Mouse Properties dialog box, click the "Show pointer trails" checkbox and then move the "Pointer trail" slider to the left and right. You will see the effect immediately.

Step 2. To apply the change that you have made to the mouse pointer trails, click OK.

Creating Your Own Mouse Pointers

Windows comes with a number of static and animated mouse pointers that you can assign to different mouse pointer functions. More are available online.

You can edit these mouse pointers to create your own pointers, or you can create your own static and animated pointers if you still have your old Windows 95 CD-ROM (or can borrow one). It contains two programs, Imagedit.exe and Aniedit.exe, that help you create pointers and string pointers together to create animated pointers. Unfortunately, they are not included on the Windows Me CD-ROM. Use both programs to look at existing animated and static pointers to get an idea of how they are created.

These programs are stored in the \Admin\Reskit\Apptools\Aniedit folder on the Windows 95 CD-ROM. You can copy them to your \Program Files\Accessories folder (or any folder you like) on your hard disk. They have an accompanying setup (inf) file, so you can use the Add/ Remove Programs icon in your Control Panel to "install" them if you like. Use the Windows Setup tab, click the Have Disk button, and then browse to the folder on the hard disk that holds these applications. (Installing sets up an association of Aniedit.exe with the file type cur.)

You can have even more fun tracking the distance that your mouse has traveled with Odometer for Windows. You'll find it at http://www.winfiles.com.

Built-In Trackballs and Mice

Secret

If you have a built-in trackball in your portable, you can use a plug-in serial mouse along with it without having to disable the trackball. Both devices are detected by Windows and both are functional at the same time.

If you add a serial mouse later or enable the internal trackball (using your BIOS setup) after Windows is installed, you have to force Windows to detect the "new" hardware (unless these are Plug and Play devices). Use the Add New Hardware icon in the Control Panel, and follow the steps in the section earlier in this chapter entitled "Adding a Driver for a New Mouse."

A generic built-in trackball is most likely supported by the Microsoft PS/2 Port Mouse or Standard PS/2 Port Mouse drivers in Windows.

The Mouse in a DOS Box

If you have a DOS program that is mouse-aware — that is, it can accept and use mouse movements and mouse button presses — Windows automatically allows you to use your mouse with the DOS program in a DOS Windows session. You don't have to do anything special to let it know you're using a mouse. Windows passes along mouse movements and button presses to the DOS program.

You have two options for modifying how the mouse works with your DOS programs while running in a Windows DOS session. You specify both options in the Misc tab of the Properties dialog box for a given DOS application or for your general DOS Windows sessions. (To display the Properties dialog box, right-click the shortcut icon for a specific DOS program or, if you want to change these options for all DOS Windows sessions, right-click the Dosprmpt shortcut in the \Windows folder. Then click Properties.)

First, you can select the QuickEdit option, which disables the mouse functions of the DOS program (if it has any) and dedicates the mouse to marking, copying, and pasting between the DOS program and Windows programs or other windowed DOS programs. This is particularly useful if the DOS program is not mouse-aware. Second, you can choose the Exclusive Mode option to force the mouse to work only within the DOS client window area and only under control of the DOS program. Turn to "Misc Properties" in Chapter 20 for more details on how to set these options.

Double-Clicking with the Middle Mouse Button

Many of the mouse drivers that come with Windows Me include middle button options in the Mouse control panel. If your mouse has a middle button, you may be able to use these options to make a middle-click act like a double-click or other actions. On the other hand, if you have a three-button mouse and the driver you're using doesn't let you customize the middle button action, you may still be able to turn it into a double-click with the following trick.

Logitech builds and sells more mice than Microsoft (although not more at retail) and most of its mice (and trackballs, for that matter) have three buttons. If the mouse that came with your computer has three buttons, it is very likely a Logitech mouse. Look on the underside of the mouse for a label.

Logitech sells a piece of software—the Mouse Control Center—that lets you define, among other things, the function of the middle button as well as the right button. The default setting for the Logitech middle button is double-click, and we prefer to use this button rather than double-clicking the left mouse button. Even though there's a lot less double-clicking in Windows Me, it hasn't been eliminated entirely.

Secret

You can set the middle button of the Logitech mouse to double-click even if you don't have Logitech's Mouse Control Center. By editing the registry, you can define this mouse behavior using only the Logitech mouse driver that Microsoft ships with Windows:

STEPS

Making the Middle Mouse Button Double-Click

Step 1. Install the Logitech mouse driver that comes with Windows first. See the steps in the earlier section entitled "Setting Up Your Mouse Driver."

Step 2. Use the Explorer to find `Regedit.exe` in the `\Windows` folder. Click it to start the Registry Editor.

Step 3. Click the plus signs to navigate to

HKEY_LOCAL_MACHINE\SOFTWARE\Logitech\MouseWare\ Current Version

Figure 43-11 shows the Registry Editor at this location for a particular mouse (in this case, the Logitech MouseMan).

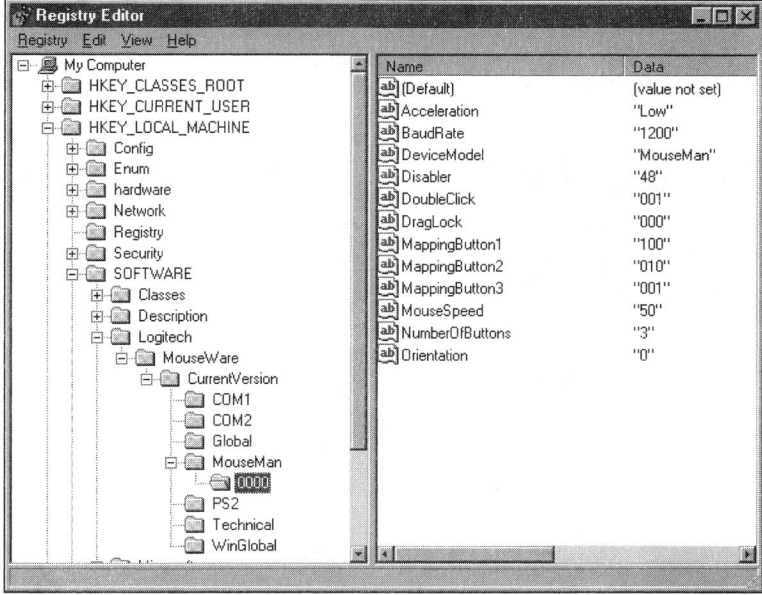

Figure 43-11: The Registry Editor. Edit the DoubleClick value in the right pane by double-clicking it. To get the middle key to be a double-click, change this value to 001.

Continued

STEPS

Making the Middle Mouse Button Double-Click *(continued)*

Step 4.   Click the plus sign next to your Logitech mouse type. Click the 0000 key in the left pane.

Step 5.   Double-click the DoubleClick key in the right pane. Change the value from 000 to 001.

Step 6.   Exit the registry and restart Windows to have this change take effect.

Tip

This double-click definition doesn't work with Microsoft Edit — the character-mode editor for text files.

Secret

This double-click definition also doesn't work if you have configured the mouse to be a left-handed mouse.

Placing the Mouse Icon on the Desktop

Tip

You can have ready access to the properties controlling the way your mouse behaves if you place a shortcut to the Mouse Properties dialog box on your Desktop:

STEPS

Putting the Mouse Icon on the Desktop

Step 1.   Click the Start button, point to Settings, and then click Control Panel.

Step 2.   Right-drag the Mouse icon to the Desktop.

Step 3.   Drop the Mouse icon on the Desktop and click Create Shortcut(s) Here.

Step 4.   Press F2, type a new name for the shortcut to the Mouse Properties dialog box, and press Enter.

If you have a Logitech mouse and want to have Logitech's purple mouse icon on your Desktop (Microsoft provides only the soap-bar-like icon in the Control Panel with its Logitech driver), you can change the shortcut icon you just created. Here's how:

STEPS

Putting the Logitech Purple Mouse Icon on the Desktop

Step 1. Right-click the Mouse shortcut on the Desktop. Click Properties, and click the Shortcut tab.

Step 2. Click the Change Icon button. Click the Browse button and search for the folder for your old Logitech driver (Lmouse, perhaps?).

Step 3. Look for a Logitech executable file in this folder, such as Wmousecc.exe. When you find it, double-click it.

Step 4. Choose the mouse icon you want, click OK, and then click OK again.

Your Mouse in the Device Manager

If you click the System icon in your Control Panel and then click the Device Manager tab, you'll see an entry for Mouse, and one for Ports. These two entries list the driver files for the mouse and serial ports, and they display the characteristics of the serial ports.

The Ports section of the Device Manager stores the address and interrupt of the serial port to which your mouse may be attached. If there are conflicts between these assignments and other port hardware in your computer, they will be highlighted. For details on dealing with ports, turn to "Changing Serial Port Settings" in Chapter 44.

Whipping Your Mouse Clicks into Shape

Microsoft sells a special $80 mouse called IntelliMouse with a wheel between the left and right mouse buttons, designed to let you scroll up and down Web pages without using the vertical scroll bar. However, an inexpensive utility called Scroll from Pointix Corp. lets any mouse do the same thing by adding a "drag" function to your right mouse button. You can drag the entire contents of your browser window (or any other window for that matter).

This is a lot more fun to do than it is to describe. With Scroll installed, right-clicking works as expected: a context menu pops up. If you hold down the right mouse button and move your mouse a little bit, though, you start scrolling the contents of the window in the direction of your move. It's very easy to control the action. Sliding up and down in long Web pages and navigating long documents and spreadsheets is a breeze. When you reach the point in the window you want, just let up on the mouse button and the movement stops. (If your mouse has a middle button, you can use that for the scrolling action instead of the right button, if you prefer.)

Scroll adds four other powers to your mouse that bring up various Windows functions or utilities. These functions appear when you slide your mouse rapidly in one of these directions: side to side, up and down, clockwise, or counter-clockwise. The four unique motions, which Pointix calls *glicks* (for *slide clicks*, or actions that are executed by a certain kind of glide), are patented technology known as *Ergopoint*. Pointix also makes Engine 2.6, a set of utilities that work with Scroll to enhance these four functions.

Pointix's Scroll and Engine are available in a 15-day free trial version from the company's Web site, `http://www.pointix.com`. Scroll 1.0 sells for $9.95 by itself, or for $24.95 packaged with Engine. When installed, Engine takes up about 3MB of hard disk space. Contact Pointix Corp. at 888-POINTIX.

If you already have an IntelliMouse, you'll want to try Flywheel, a $10 shareware utility available from Plannet Crafters Inc. (`http://www.plannetarium.com`). Flywheel lets the mouse's tracking wheel work with all software applications, not just those that offer IntelliMouse support, and it offers two new ways of using the wheel. Contact Plannet Crafters at 770-667-1278, or e-mail info@plannetarium.com.

Scrolling with a Three-Button Mouse

Windows supports ordinary, two-button mice as well as two-button mice with scrolling wheels. It also supports a three-button mouse, turning the middle button into the equivalent of a scrolling wheel.

Move your mouse so that your pointer is near the middle of your screen. Click the middle mouse button once. A special panning pointer appears and remains at this original spot.

Now move your mouse up or down and the screen scrolls in the direction that you have moved your mouse. The further away from the panning pointer you move the mouse pointer, the faster the screen scrolls.

Thanks to Randy Linden for telling us about this tip.

Mouse Left-Handed

Have you ever thought of switching? We did, and have never looked back. You can imagine that it takes a bit of mousing around to write four books, plus respond to lots of e-mail from our readers. The old right hand gets plenty sore, and way overworked. Switching to left-handed mousing completely cleared up all of our repetitive stress problems. It took about two days to get used to using the left hand, but it soon became totally natural. Of course, if you're left-handed, you'll have even less trouble switching.

So you say that you have a mouse that is designed for the right hand? No worries, we've found that the ones that we've tried work great in your left hand. Check it out for a few days and see for yourself.

To switch to a left-handed mouse, click Start ➪ Settings ➪ Control Panel ➪ Mouse, go to the Buttons tab, mark "Left-handed" (see Figure 43-12), and click OK. Your index finger on your left hand will now click the number-one button.

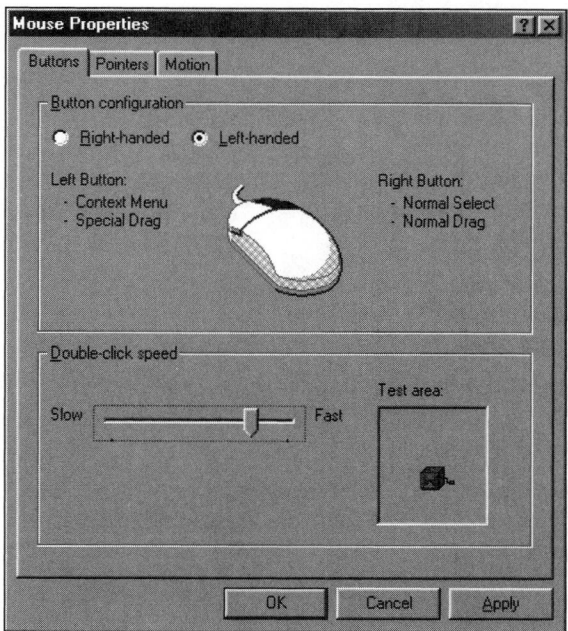

Figure 43-12: The Buttons tab of the Mouse Properties dialog box makes it easy to switch the "handedness" of your mouse, and tells you what each button does.

Use Number-Pad Mouse Keys Together with the Mouse

Under Accessibility Options in your Control Panel, Microsoft offers the option of using the numeric keypad to control your mouse pointer. What's cool about this is that you can use it in conjunction with your mouse. Turn your mouse into a left-handed mouse, and now you're controlling the mouse pointer with two hands.

If you don't find the Accessibility Options in your Control Panel, click Add/Remove Programs in the Control Panel. Click the Windows Setup tab, double-click Accessibility, and mark Accessibility Options to install them.

You can choose whether the numeric keypad controls the mouse pointer when NumLock is on or off. You can also turn this capability on or off using the MouseKeys shortcut, which appears in your system tray (see Figure 43-13).

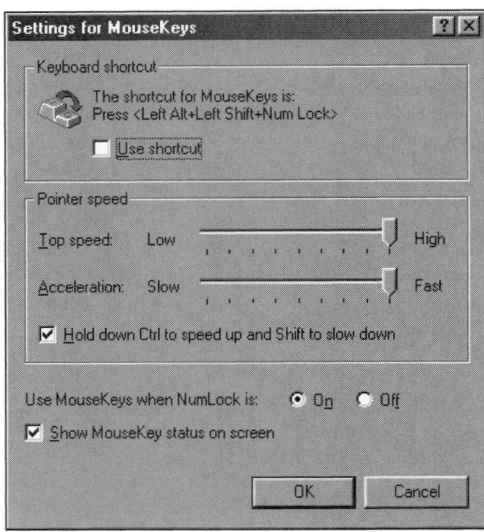

Figure 43-13: The options at the bottom of the Settings for MouseKeys dialog box let you change the way the numeric keypad interacts with the mouse pointer.

Click Start ➪ Settings ➪ Control Panel, click the Accessibility Options icon, and click the Mouse tab. Mark the Use MouseKeys checkbox, and click the Settings button to display the dialog box shown in Figure 43-13. You can now use the slider bars to set the pointer speeds. If you use your numeric keypad for data entry, mark the Off option button. If you use it for navigation keys, mark the On option button.

Now you can use the mouse keys and your mouse at the same time to control the mouse pointer.

Left-Handed Mouse Pointers

We use the mouse with our left hand all the time, even though we're right-handed. Placing your mouse to the left of your keyboard really helps keep the work spread evenly between both hands.

Ever notice that the arrow mouse pointers point to the upper-left corner? Left-handed pointers would point to the upper-right corner. You could edit your pointers to point in the right direction, or you can download some from http://www.stanback.net/

These pointers at this Web site are very basic. If you are interested in editing pointers, animated pointers, or icons, then an icon editor and a library program, widely available on the Internet, are the answer. Library programs search through all of your files that contain icons, including pointers, and create a library so that the icons are easy to get to (see the next section).

Animated pointers are made up a series of individual frames, each of which must be edited. Changing a pointer from right-handed to left-handed just involves a mirrored flip. This is a simple one-step operation in an icon and pointer editor. For example, we used IconEdit Pro to flip the pointer arrow shown in Figure 43-14.

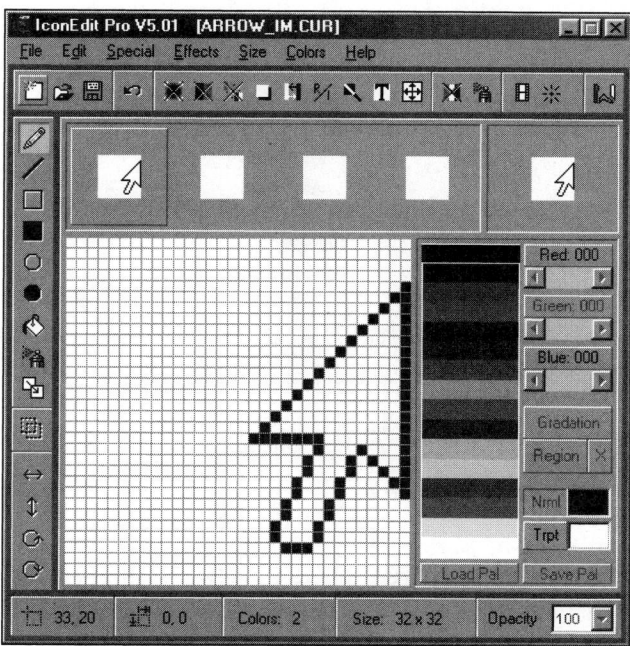

Figure 43-14: The mouse pointer, viewed in IconEdit Pro

You'll find IconEdit Pro at http://rainbowpcm.com/icon_edit_pro.html.

Icon Library Generator

If you are going to edit icons as well as pointers, you will need an icon library generator that can gather up all of the existing icons on your hard disk and place them in an easily accessible library or libraries. Pointers, both static and animated, are much easier to find than icons because they exist in standalone files with recognizable extensions.

EasyIcons generates icon libraries and includes Icon Easel, which you can use to edit icons, static pointers, and animated pointers. You can drag and drop a folder onto EasyIcons, and it will search all of the files in the folder and subfolders for icons. It then places the icons in a library, as shown in Figure 43-15.

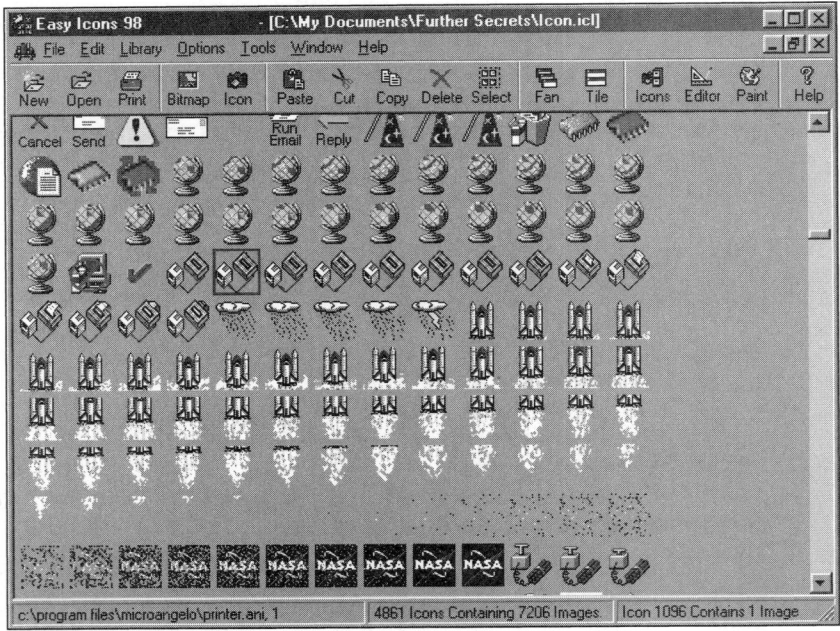

Figure 43-15: An icon library created with EasyIcons

You'll find EasyIcons at http://www.easyapps.com. If you put a few thousand icons into one library, it will take a while to save them — quite a while. You might think about breaking up the libraries into smaller chunks.

Left-Handed PenPartner

Wacom makes a wonderful and inexpensive digital tablet, the PenPartner, which lets you draw (and mouse) with a stylus. I find it very difficult to drag with a mouse, and I much prefer using the stylus. The stylus acts as a mouse also, so you can run any program with it (although not as easily as with a mouse).

The PenPartner is powered off a PS/2 or keyboard port, but it also connects to a serial port. If you have a portable computer, it may not put out enough power to power both the PenPartner and the keyboard. Other more expensive tablets are available from Wacom that have their own power supplies.

The PenPartner can work in conjunction with a mouse, and you can plug in both at the same time, using the stylus in one hand and the mouse in the other. Well, almost. The PenPartner driver won't let you run the mouse in left-hand mode and the PenPartner in right-hand mode. This is crucial for a stylus, because the left mouse button on a stylus is the pen point. If you have configured your mouse for left-handed use (our recommendation), the stylus works as a right mouse button. Not good.

Wacom provides drivers for some of its other, more expensive, tablets that allow for left-handed mice and right-handed pens, but not for the PenPartner. This seems a bit shortsighted to us. Of course, they don't tell you about this in any of their literature or on their support Web site.

You can check out the PenPartner at `http://www.wacom.com`.

No Joy from Your Joy Stick

If you're getting no response from your joystick, you might check out the Microsoft Knowledge Base article "How to Troubleshoot a GamePort Joystick" at `http://support.microsoft.com/support/kb/articles/q141/8/54.asp`.

Summary

In Windows Me, using the mouse is a lot less work than in older versions of Windows. You need to know how to customize your mouse, and how to take advantage of its power.

▶ A Mouse Properties dialog box lets you easily change the responsiveness of the mouse pointer to mouse movements.

▶ You can do a lot more with a single-click.

▶ You can use animated pointers in place of some of the duller mouse pointers.

▶ You can turn the middle button on your Logitech mouse into a double-click button.

▶ The right mouse button is a powerful tool.

Chapter 44

Modems, Serial Ports, and Parallel Ports

In This Chapter

Modems and ports (serial and parallel) are communications devices. Windows automatically detects them and helps you set them up. We discuss:

▶ Configuring your modem driver

▶ Getting behind the configuration routines and changing modem driver parameters

▶ Manually controlling which ports can be used by Direct Cable Connection (DCC) and adding ports that were inadvertently removed

▶ Configuring your modem settings to work with DOS applications communication programs

▶ Configuring your serial and parallel ports

Hello, World

When the personal computer was envisioned and designed, the focus of its communication facilities was the monitor, the keyboard, and the printer — the electronic typewriter model. Serial ports and modem communications were peripheral considerations, so to speak. This legacy has hung on.

Computer-mediated communication is now the major reason to own a personal computer. The widespread use of laptop and portable computers in business has increased the demand for reliable, easy to use, fast communications links. Inexpensive high-speed fax/modems, the advent of commercial Internet service providers (ISPs), and the adoption of graphical user interfaces for online services all speak to a popular interest in electronic communications.

Windows 3.1x was not up to the task of effectively handling these communications demands. High-speed communications (over 9,600 bits per second, or *bps*) required third-party replacements to the Windows 3.1x serial port driver (`Comm.drv`). Personal computers required a new chip, the 16550A Universal Asynchronous Receiver/Transmitter (UART), to keep up with the data flow through the serial port or modem.

When Microsoft began designing Windows 95, it was already clear that the operating system's communications capabilities had to be much stronger than they were in Windows 3.1*x*. At the minimum, a new communications driver was required. Ideally, communications would be seamlessly integrated into the basic functionality of the operating system. Windows Me has taken this integration even further, into the user interface.

Windows 98 Communications

Microsoft had to make changes to the basic operating system to reduce the frequency and duration of time intervals during which the CPU can't deal with data coming into the serial and parallel ports. The CPU can't handle incoming data when it is switching between 16- and 32-bit mode. The 32-bit protected-mode drivers that come with Windows Me have reduced the amount of mode switching required of the processor.

The designers of Windows have provided a way for applications to determine which one gets to use the modem or port without having to unload one of the applications. By defining a common modem interface, all communications packages can communicate with the modem at a high level.

Windows uses a virtual communications driver, VxD, in combination with Unimodem, the universal modem driver, to provide high-level services that developers can employ to make their communications packages easier to use and more cooperative.

In addition, some modems, called *Windows modems* (also referred to as *WinModems* or *controllerless modems*), now rely on VxD for many functions that used to be handled by the hardware. Because WinModems require VxD in order to operate, they will not work in DOS mode. These modems are usually bundled with new computer systems; they are rarely sold separately.

Unimodem supports a variety of new data/fax/voice modems (also called *VoiceView* modems). These modems are designed to support new telephony applications such as Microsoft Phone.

One Modem for All Communications Software

You have to configure your modem only once, and communications packages that are supported by Windows don't have to know how to configure the modem themselves.

Communications packages built for Windows don't have to know which command strings to send to get the modem moving. They can send higher level, more general, and more abstract commands that work on any modem Windows recognizes. Communications software providers can turn their resources to other more fruitful areas of product design.

Windows ships with many modem-mediated communications facilities built in. These include Phone Dialer, Dial-Up Networking (DUN), HyperTerminal, Internet Explorer, Outlook Express, NetMeeting, Personal Web Server, Web Publisher, NetShow, MS Chat, remote network administration (Net Watcher), online registration, CompuServe e-mail, MSN, System Monitor, and others. All of them operate through the interface that defines the capabilities of your particular modem.

Windows 3.1x Communications Support

Old Windows 3.1x communications applications will still work with Windows Me because the old communications driver (Comm.drv) hasn't changed and is still used by these applications. Although Comm.drv thinks that it's talking directly to the hardware, it now talks to the new communications driver.

Only one Windows 3.1x-style communications application can have access to the modem at a time. But Windows Me-style communications applications can share the modem. For example, Microsoft Fax can be active and set to wait for a fax while you use Internet Explorer to connect to a Web site. While the phone line is off-hook, Microsoft Fax can't answer an incoming call, but you don't have to unload the fax software while you connect to the Internet.

Some applications replaced Comm.drv with their own communications port drivers. These applications will still work with Windows Me. The replacement communications drivers work with the virtual communication VxD instead of directly with the communications hardware.

DOS Communications Support

You can still run DOS-based communications software in a DOS window (see Chapter 20 for more on DOS). When an MS-DOS-based or Windows-based communications program requests the use of a serial port, Windows checks to see if the port is in use. If the port is available, Windows gives the program access to the port.

However, after you are finished running the DOS program, Windows by default does not give the serial port back to your Windows-based programs until the DOS window is closed. If a Windows-based program attempts to use the serial port before the DOS window is closed, you receive an error message such as, "Another program is using the selected Telephony device" or "Cannot initialize port."

This is different from Windows 3.1x, which by default released the port after two seconds of inactivity. Microsoft changed this for compatibility with some of the Windows Me and 9x tools that have an automatic answering capability, such as Microsoft Fax and Dial-Up Networking Server.

If you need "hot-swapping capability" between an MS-DOS-based communications program and a Windows-based communication program, you can change the default behavior by editing the System.ini file.

STEPS

Enabling "Hot Swapping" Between DOS- and Windows-Based Communications Programs

Step 1.   You'll find System.ini in your \Windows folder. Make a backup copy before you start editing.

Step 2.   Click the Sysedit.exe icon in \Windows\System.

Step 3.   Add this line to the [386Enh] section of System.ini:

COM<n>AutoAssign=0

where <n> is the number of the serial port, such as 1.

Step 4.   Save System.ini, shut down, and restart Windows.

The default COM<n>AutoAssign setting in Windows is –1. This setting causes Windows to not release a serial port previously used by a non-Windows-based program running in a DOS window until that program's DOS window is closed.

The default value for this setting in Windows 3.1x was 2, causing Windows to grant access to the port after two seconds of port inactivity. However, if you set this value to 2 on a Windows Me computer, you should not run a 32-bit communications program (such as HyperTerminal) and then attempt to run an MS-DOS-based communications program. Because of the way the 32-bit program controls the port, the MS-DOS-based program will be unable to access it and may cause your system to hang (stop responding).

Setting the value to 0 allows an MS-DOS-based application to hand off a "hot port" to a Windows-based program with no delay. Keep in mind that this configuration can cause problems or instabilities because two programs will be able to send commands to the modem at the same time. Unless you have a pressing need and are willing to live with some instability, we recommend that you keep the default setting of –1.

Install Microsoft Fax

Windows includes Microsoft Exchange Client and Microsoft Fax. This combo allows you to keep a fax phone number list and send and receive faxes.

If you have installed Outlook 98 or higher, you can combine Outlook with Microsoft Fax. You can't use Microsoft Fax alone; it requires a full MAPI messaging client such as Exchange (Windows Messaging) or Outlook.

If you want to combine Outlook with Microsoft Fax, check out the instructions at the Exchange Center at http://www.slipstick.com/exchange. You'll need to install the corporate version of Outlook to connect to Microsoft Fax (even if you're not a corporation).

There are third-party fax programs that you can use with Windows applications. You might check out MightyFAX at http://www.rks-software.com. This is a shareware package that you can try out for a limited number of times. It basically runs as a printer driver.

Stop Dialing!

You may find that your computer wants to dial into your ISP unbidden. This may happen when your computer first starts up, on a regular schedule, or at odd hours during the day and night. It can be quite annoying, especially if it is running up costs on its own, without accomplishing any useful work.

Add in the irritating sound of the modem at work, and the fact that you feel yourself at war with your computer, and the annoyance factor of this behavior can get quite high. We'll show you how to put the computer in its place.

In the section "Stop Your Modem from Dialing When You Start Windows" in Chapter 3, we discuss how to get the Personal Web Server to stop dialing in when you first start Windows. You've also got to be on the lookout for other software that will try to dial the modem.

Synchronizing Offline Web Pages

If you have configured offline Web pages to update on a schedule, possibly on a schedule determined by the channel publisher, then Internet Explorer will, if properly configured, cause your modem to dial into your ISP. You need to get to your offline Web pages to stop this behavior. We show you how to set up easy access to them in "Easy Access to Your Offline Web Pages Folder" in Chapter 26.

Once you've opened the Offline Web Pages folder window on your Desktop, right-click an offline Web page name and click Properties. Click the Schedule tab to see if the offline Web page has been scheduled for updating, as shown in Figure 44-1.

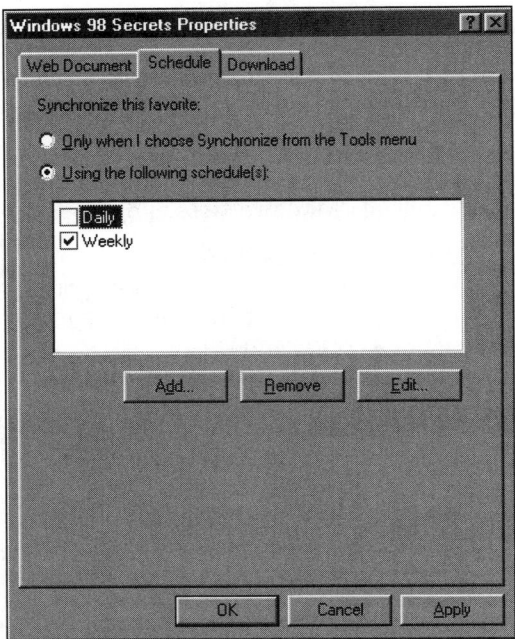

Figure 44-1: The Schedule tab for this offline Web page is set to synchronize weekly.

You need to add a schedule if there aren't any listed and you do want your offline Web sites updated. If there aren't any schedules listed in the Schedule dialog box (whether marked or unmarked), you know that none of your offline Web pages have been updated automatically and your modem hasn't been invoked to call up your ISP.

If you see a marked schedule, highlight it and click the Edit button. Click the Synchronization Items tab. You get to see a list of offline Web pages, as shown in Figure 44-2. Notice the checkbox at the bottom of the dialog box ("If my computer is not connected...).

If this checkbox is marked, it is pretty clear what is going to happen. Whenever the schedule calls for a specific Web page to be updated, Internet Explorer will invoke its Dial-Up Connection dialog box (a connection manager), which will in turn send the command to your modem to dial up your service provider.

You can either clear this checkbox or click the Schedule tab and reschedule the offline Web page updates to a time less bothersome to you. Also, you can decide to synchronize the offline Web pages upon your command by marking the "Only when I choose to synchronize from the Tools menu" checkbox (refer back to Figure 44-1).

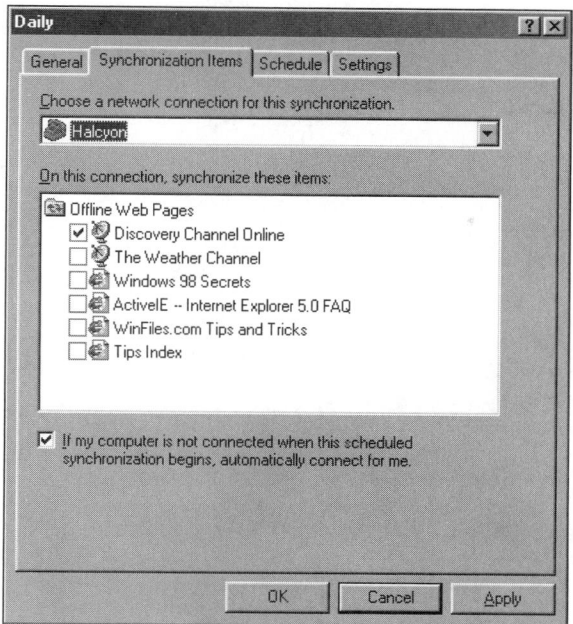

Figure 44-2: The Synchronization Items tab for this schedule shows which offline Web pages will be updated.

You can also turn off the capability to synchronize offline Web pages on a schedule. In the Internet Explorer, click Tools ⇨ Internet Options, click the Advanced tab, and clear the "Enable offline items to be synchronized on a schedule" checkbox.

Outlook Express Dials in to Gather Your E-Mail

If it turns out that offline Web page synchronization isn't causing your computer to dial up, perhaps it's dialing because Outlook Express is trying to download your e-mail. Click your Outlook Express icon on your Desktop. Click Tools ⇨ Options, and see if you've marked "Check for new messages every [   ] minute(s)" in the General tab, as shown in Figure 44-3.

If you have selected "Connect only when not working offline" or "Connect even when working offline" in the drop-down list under Send/Receive Messages, then Outlook Express will dial up your Internet service provider based on the interval you've chosen.

Outlook Express will also try to connect to your service provider if you have marked "Send messages immediately" in the Send tab, as shown in Figure 44-4.

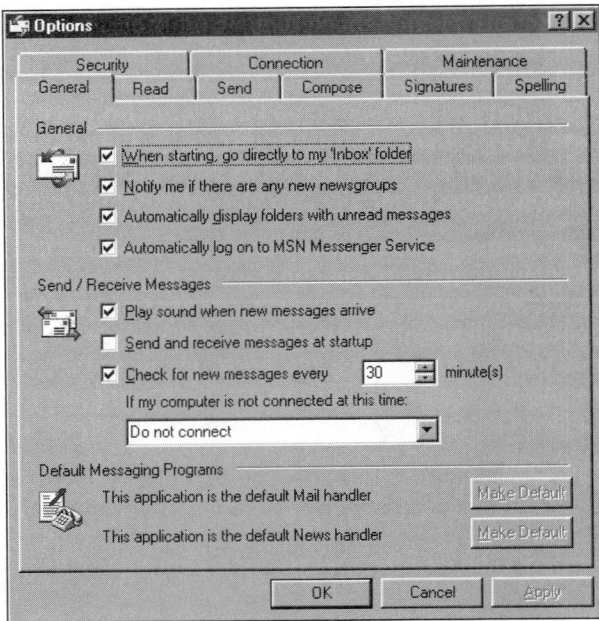

Figure 44-3: In this example, the computer will dial up every 30 minutes if necessary to send and receive mail.

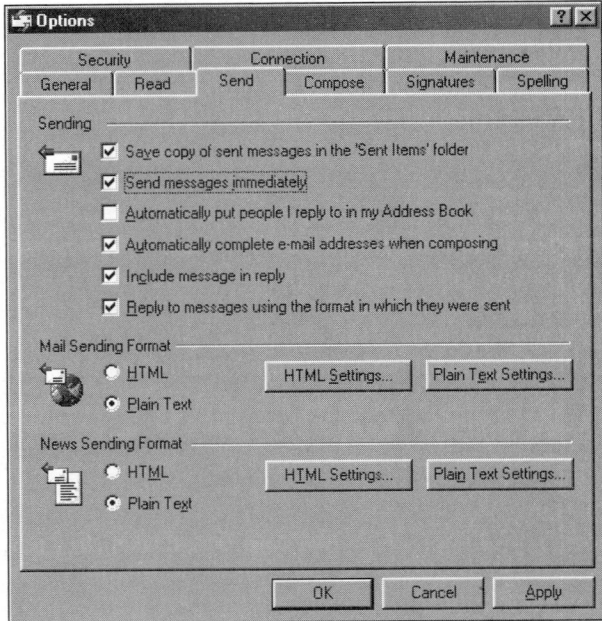

Figure 44-4: The "Send messages immediately" checkbox is marked, so Outlook Express will dial a connection every time you send a message.

When you start Outlook Express, it will also ask if you want to connect to your service provider if you have marked the "Send and receive messages at startup" checkbox in the General tab (see Figure 44-5).

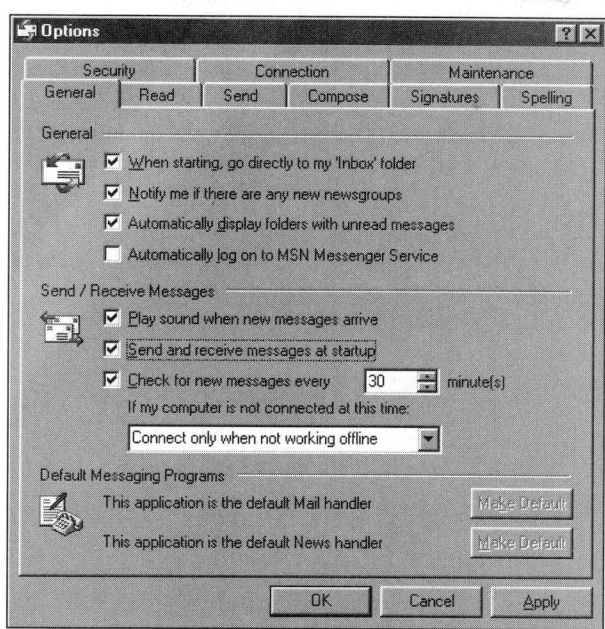

Figure 44-5: Because the "Send and receive messages at startup" checkbox is marked, Outlook Express will ask whether to dial up every time it starts.

Click the Change button in the Connection tab of the Options dialog box to see if Internet Explorer and Outlook Express are configured to always dial your default connection, as shown in Figure 44-6. If they are, then they will in fact dial into your service provider.

You can stop Internet Explorer from dialing into your ISP by marking "Never dial a connection." This will stop the offline Web page synchronization feature and the Task Scheduler from forcing Internet Explorer to dial into your service provider.

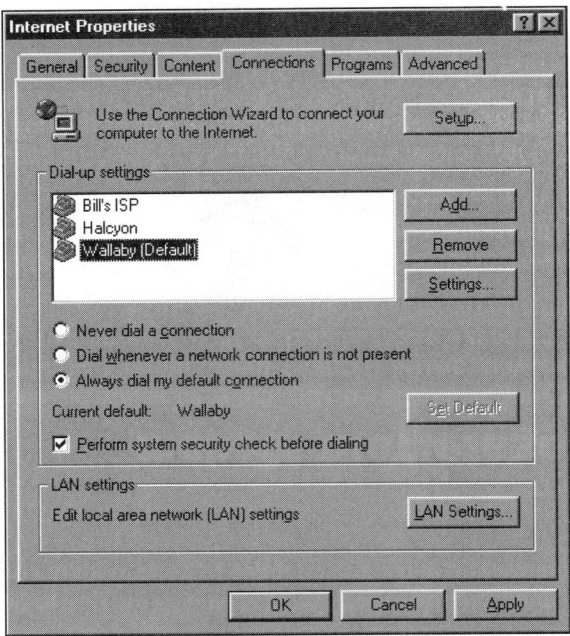

Figure 44-6: When you click the Change button on the Connection tab, the Internet Properties dialog box appears, set to its own Connections tab.

The Task Scheduler Schedules a Task that Dials Your Modem

The Task Scheduler uses the same scheduling functions as offline Web page synchronization. If you have a scheduled task that dials up your modem, that could be the source of your problem. You can easily check this out.

Open your Explorer, and highlight Scheduled Tasks in the left pane. Check the Next Run Time column to see if there are any tasks that appear to call your modem. Right-click such a task, and click Run. See if it does dial or not. If so, you can remove it from your Scheduled Tasks folder, or set a less bothersome schedule.

Take Your DUN Connectoids with You

Windows provides Dial-Up Networking services that allow you to connect your computer to your ISP, to a Dial-Up Server on another Windows computer, to a Windows 2000 or NT RAS server, or to another communications server.

You can create a new connection by clicking Start ➪ Programs ➪ Accessories ➪ Communications ➪ Dial-Up Networking ➪ Make New Connection. You can also just click the Dial-Up Networking icon in your Explorer and then click Make New Connection.

Your existing dial-up connections are displayed as icons in the Dial-Up Networking folder. To activate a connection — that is, to dial into your server — just click any of your connection icons (DUN connectoids).

Each DUN connectoid maintains the settings required to successfully make a modem-to-modem connection with a particular server. It's easy to transfer your connectoids to other folders on your computer or to other computers. Here are some situations in which you might want to do this:

- You use multiple computers

- You travel to different locations and use other people's computers

- You want to install the e-mail connection on a department full of computers

- You want to e-mail your connection information to someone else

- You want to save your DUN connectoids in your My System or other folder so that you can recover them if you have to reinstall Windows or you lose your Windows installation

The DUN connectoids are front ends for registry settings. Right-click a connectoid and click Properties. You'll find the server's phone number and, in the Server Types tab, various server connection settings.

To transfer these registry settings as a package, all you have to do is drag and drop the DUN connectoid, just as though it were a file (it has a DUN extension). You can drop it onto your Desktop, into any (real) folder on a computer on your network, onto a diskette, into an e-mail message, into a document — whatever. You won't be able to drop it on another computer's Dial-Up Networking folder (although it will in fact show up there later), Control Panel folder, Printers folder, or Scheduled Tasks folder, because these aren't actually folders.

If you carry your DUN connectoids with you on a diskette, you can drag and drop them onto the Desktop of any Windows computer. Click the connectoid, and the computer will dial up your server. You'll notice that the DUN connectoid also shows up in the Dial-Up Networking folder after you click it once.

There are some caveats. Your user name and password are not included with the connectoid. You'll have to type these in yourself. If the computer's Dial-Up Networking connection settings are set to not prompt you for information before dialing, you won't have an opportunity to enter these values. To get that opportunity, click the Dial-Up Networking icon in the left pane of the computer's Explorer window and choose Connections ⇨ Settings. Mark the "Prompt for information before dialing" checkbox, then click OK.

The DUN connectoid includes the name of the modem on the source computer. This points to all the parameters that define the modem and its serial connection. If the target computer doesn't have the same modem, you can change the modem that your connectoid uses. To do so, right-click the connection and click Properties. Then display the "Connect using" drop-down list, and choose the installed modem.

You may not have to do this. Just click the connectoid and see if it dials the target computer's modem. It may work just fine. If you right-click your transferred connectoid on the target computer in the Dial-Up Networking folder and click Properties, you will be notified if the modem it names isn't installed. Follow the steps in the previous paragraph to associate the installed modem with this connectoid.

There are numerous pieces of shareware that enable you to do what we've just detailed. You couldn't do this using earlier versions of Windows 95 with the earlier version of Dial-Up Networking. Windows Me solves these problems, and renders the shareware unnecessary.

Take Your Calling Card or Long-Distance Provider with You

We have to confess that we think that Windows has the weirdest telecom interface. If we knew of a way to access the Dialing Properties dialog box directly, we would tack a little icon on it and put it on our Quick Launch toolbar. Barring this, you can choose between clicking the Modems icon in your Control Panel and clicking Dialing Properties, opening the Phone Dialer (Start ⇨ Programs ⇨ Accessories ⇨ Communications ⇨ Phone Dialer) and clicking Tools ⇨ Dialing Properties, or any of a myriad of other indirect ways. We just wish there were one overall console that let you deal with all the Windows communication issues.

The Calling Card button in the Dialing Properties dialog box brings you to the calling card creation interface shown in Figure 44-7. We extensively discuss how to set up specific long distance carriers and other calling cards in Chapter 45.

Secret

Once you set up a new calling card, you will want to make a copy of this vital information so that you can take it to other computers, or restore it if you ever lose your Windows configuration. You can do this by exporting the relevant portion of your registry.

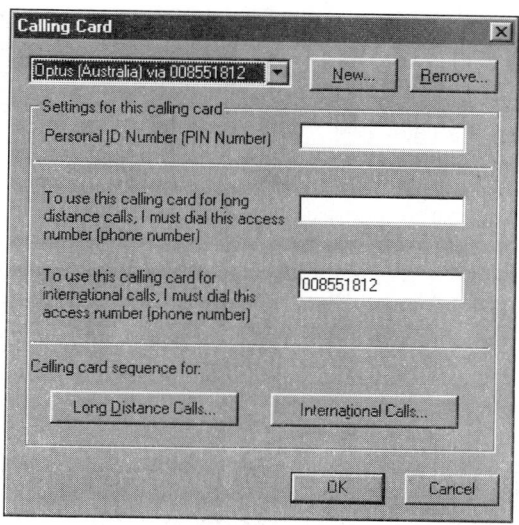

Figure 44-7: Click the New button to begin creating a new calling card. Click the Long Distance Calls button to set up the dialing rules for the card.

STEPS

Saving Your Calling Card

Step 1. After you have set up a card using the steps in Chapter 45, use Registry Crawler (see "Crawl Through the Registry" in Chapter 11) to search your registry for your calling card name or long-distance provider name. You can also just use your Registry Editor to navigate to the following branch of your registry (see Figure 44-8):

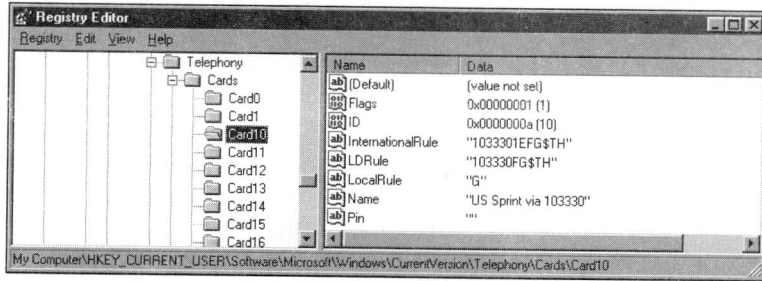

Figure 44-8: Each card has a card number as shown in the left pane. Your latest entry will be the highest card number.

Continued

STEPS

Saving Your Calling Card *(continued)*

HKEY_CURRENT_USER\Software\Microsoft\Windows\
CurrentVersion\Telephony\Cards

Step 2. If you've just entered a new card, it will have the highest number. Highlight the card you want to save in the left pane of your Registry Editor, click Registry ⇨ Export Registry File. Give the file the same name as your calling card, and save it in your My System folder or another appropriate folder.

In the exported card's reg file, your PIN number will be encrypted and the phone number will be phony. You'll have to reenter your PIN and phone number after you merge this information to another registry.

Step 3. To import this calling card entry into another registry, you have to make sure that you don't overwrite an existing entry. Navigate to the location shown in step 1 in the new registry, and check and see what the highest Card# is in the left pane.

Step 4. Edit the following line in your exported card reg file so that the Card# shown at the end of the line is one higher than the highest card number in the new registry:

[HKEY_CURRENT_USER\Software\Microsoft\Windows\
CurrentVersion\Telephony\Cards\Card24]

Step 5. Right-click your exported card reg file, and click Merge to merge it into the new registry.

Step 6. Highlight the Cards key in the new registry. It's just above the Card# keys (refer back to Figure 17-8).

Step 7. Double-click NextID in the right pane of your Registry Editor. Click the Decimal option button (see Figure 44-9) and increase the number in the "Value data" field by 1. Click OK. You have to do this because in step 5 you just added one card to the list of cards stored in the registry.

Step 8. Double-click the NumEntries variable in the right pane of your Registry Editor, click the Decimal option button, increase the number in the "Value data" field by 1, and click OK. You've added one card to the number of cards stored in the registry.

Step 9. Highlight your card number key in the left pane of your Registry Editor. Double-click the ID variable in the right pane. Click the Decimal option button. In the "Value data" field, enter a value that's one less than the current NextID value, which you set in step 7. Close the Registry Editor.

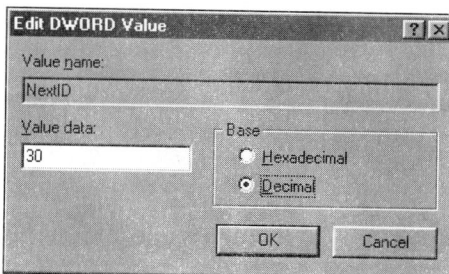

Figure 44-9: You've inserted one calling card, so you need to increase the NextID data value by one.

Step 10. Click Start ⇨ Settings ⇨ Modems ⇨ Dialing Properties ⇨ Calling Card. Enter the correct value for this card's PIN in the Personal ID Number (PIN Number) field. Click OK.

This would all be too much work if it weren't for the fact that remembering the dialing rules and the calling card dial-in numbers is even more work.

Tip

You don't have to merge the exported card reg file. You can just keep it for reference, and look at it if and when you have to create a new entry using the standard user interface. If you follow the discussion in Chapter 45, you may even be able to figure out the abbreviations for the dialing rules stored in the registry file.

Tip

Here's another option. Instead of just exporting the branch for your particular calling card, export the whole Cards branch. When you want to merge it into another registry, just be sure that the number of cards in the new registry is equal to or less than the number in the saved branch. The entries in the registry of the target computer will be overwritten.

Speed Up Modem Dialing

Ever notice how fast your modem dials into your ISP? Just turn up the volume on your system tray a bit and listen to the touch-tone tones as your modem spits them out. You may have to click the Modems icon in your Control Panel, highlight your modem, click Properties, and move the Speaker Volume slider over to the right to hear the modem.

The phone company's equipment can interpret the tones much faster than your modem is likely putting them out. If you want to speed up your dialing, you can send a command to your modem.

STEPS

Speed Up Your Modem Dialing

Step 1. Click Start ⇨ Settings ⇨ Control Panel, and click the modems icon.

Step 2. Highlight your modem and click the Properties button.

Step 3. Click the Connection tab, and then click the Advanced button.

Step 4. In the "Extra settings" field, type **S11=35** (see Figure 44-10). Click OK, click OK again, and click Close.

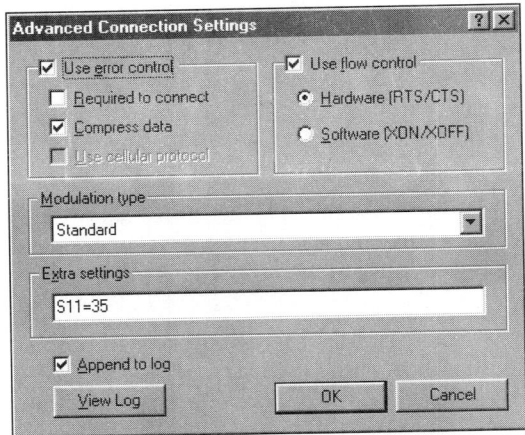

Figure 44-10: The "Extra settings" field in this figure contains the setting for modem dial speed.

Secret

The S11 setting is the setting for modem dial speed. Some modems can't go this fast, so you can drop back to S11=50. With your volume up, you should be able to hear the difference before and after you make these changes.

If your modem can't dial this fast, you may get the error message shown in Figure 44-11. If you do, then you'll know that you have to either back off on the dialing speed or not use this setting at all.

Some modems are not fully Hayes compatible, and for them this modem string will have no effect. You can hear the difference quite clearly if the modem string does take effect, so you'll know right away whether or not your modem supports it.

Thanks to Greg Miller for pointing out this tip.

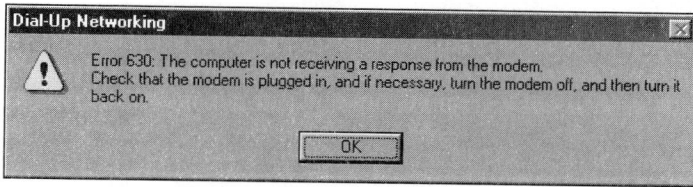

Figure 44-11: You may get this error message if your modem can't dial the phone number as fast as you want it to.

Don't Let Your Modem Fall Back Too Far

Modems fall back to lower communication speeds if they encounter line noise that is too intense. But they can fall back too far without making additional efforts at maintaining the higher speed. While your modem manufacturer may claim that your modem is Hayes compatible, it may not set certain modem registries to the correct default values that allow for these more aggressive efforts at maintaining high speeds.

Secret

If you have your modem manual handy, you can check the default values for the crucial modem registries. You'll want to check the S10 and S36 registry default values, which should be 50 and 7, respectively. If these are not the default settings, you can add these values to the modem initialization string:

STEPS

Keeping Your Modem from Slowing Down Prematurely

Step 1. Click Start ⇨ Settings ⇨ Control Panel, and click the Modems icon.

Step 2. Highlight your modem and click the Properties button.

Step 3. Click the Connection tab and then click the Advanced button.

Step 4. In the "Extra settings" field, type **S10=50** and **S36=7** (see Figure 44-12). Click OK, click OK again, and then click Close.

Continued

STEPS

Keeping Your Modem from Slowing Down Prematurely *(continued)*

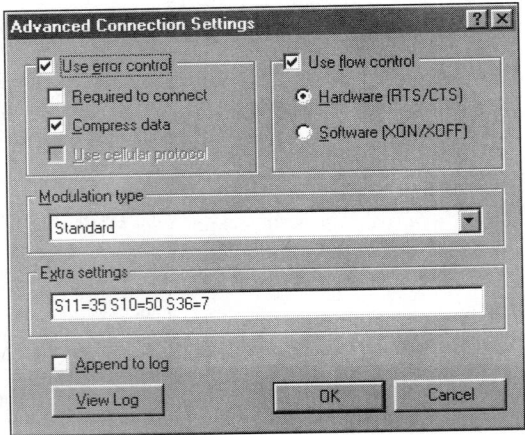

Figure 44-12: Add these modem settings to the "Extra settings" field.

Thanks to Anthony Kinyon for help with this tip.

STAC Compression

Microsoft has added the STAC (http://www.stac.com) compression
algorithm to its modem communication drivers. You may remember back
in ancient history when Microsoft added disk compression to Windows
that competed with STAC's disk compression algorithm. Later, it paid STAC
a bunch of money and bought a chunk of stock in the company.

Secret

If your ISP supports STAC compression on their end, you could get dramatically increased performance. One Internet service provider claims up to
four times the download speed, or 13 Kbytes/second with a 33.6 modem.

You can check with your ISP to see if they support the STAC protocol. Perhaps
they advertise this feature on their Web page. Service providers who use
Livingston PM3 units and support 56K access are likely candidates.

You have to configure your Dial-Up Networking connectoid and your modem
driver to take advantage of this capability. Here's how:

STEPS

Configuring Your DUN Connectoid and Modem Driver to Use STAC

Step 1. Click your My Computer icon, and then click the Dial-Up Networking icon.

Step 2. Right-click the connection icon for your ISP, click Properties, and then click the Server Types tab.

Step 3. Mark "Enable software compression." The other checkboxes under Advanced Options can be cleared, as illustrated in Figure 44-13.

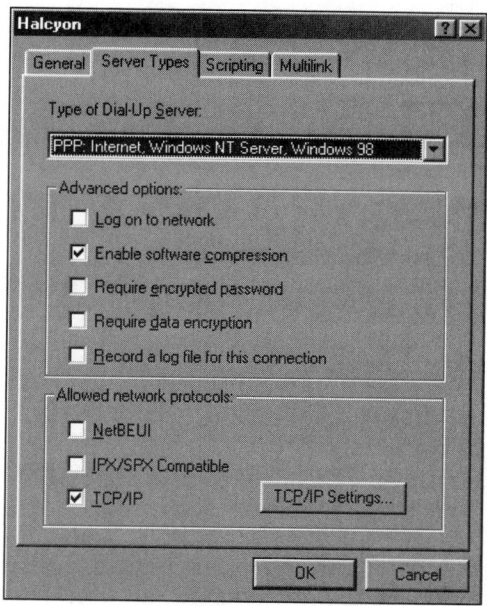

Figure 44-13: Mark the "Enable software compression" checkbox on the Server Types tab of the Properties dialog box for your DUN connectoid.

Step 4. Click the General tab, and click the Configure button to open the Properties dialog box for the modem associated with this connectoid. Go to its Connection tab, and click the Advanced button.

Continued

STEPS

Configuring Your DUN Connectoid and Modem Driver to Use STAC *(continued)*

Step 5. Clear the "Compress data" checkbox, as shown in Figure 44-14. Make sure that you have marked "Use flow control" and "Hardware (RTS/CTS)." Click OK, click OK again, and click Close.

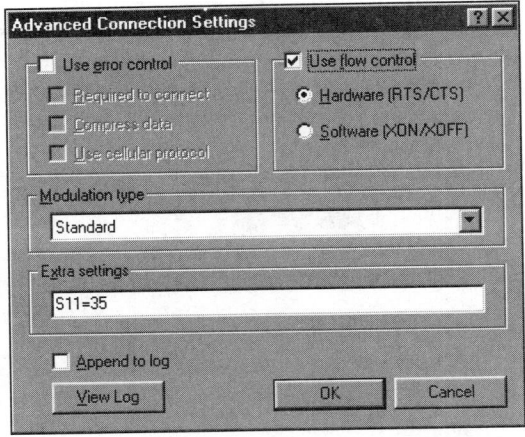

Figure 44-14: The Advanced Connection Settings dialog box for the modem associated with this DUN connectoid

To check whether STAC compression is being used, connect to your ISP by clicking its DUN connectoid. After the connection is made, double-click the Modem icon in your system tray, and click the Details button to expand the Connected To dialog box (see Figure 44-15). This dialog box indicates whether you are using STAC compression.

If you are sure that your service provider supports STAC, and you don't see it in this dialog box, go once again to the Advanced Connection Settings dialog box and mark "Use error control."

Thanks to Penelope Baker for help with this secret.

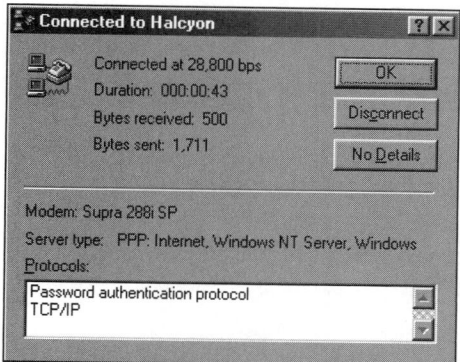

Figure 44-15: If you are using STAC compression, it will be listed under Protocols in the Connected To dialog box. In this example, there is no STAC compression.

Speed Up Download on Cable or DSL Modems

Unlike Windows 95, Windows Me has an automatic mode that is supposed to reset your IP packet size depending on the speed of your Internet connection. You can read more about this in the Microsoft Knowledge Base article "Description of the Internet Protocol Packet Size Setting" at http://support.microsoft.com/support/kb/articles/Q183/4/37.asp.

If you've got a fast and noise-free connection to your ISP, you can enjoy the benefits of cutting down on the overhead of continuous error detection and correction. If you increase the size of your IP packets, you will decrease the percentage of extra error-checking characters that are sent with your data.

Secret

If you are using a cable or DSL modem, you might check to see if the automatic mode is right for you. One user we heard from found that changing the IP packet size from Automatic to Large sped up large file downloads by a factor of three.

STEPS

Changing Your IP Packet Size

Step 1.   Click Start ➪ Settings ➪ Control Panel, and click the Network icon.

Step 2.   Highlight Dial-Up Adapter, click Properties, and click the Advanced tab.

Step 3.   Select IP Packet Size, display the Value drop-down list, and highlight Large (see Figure 44-16).

Continued

STEPS
Changing Your IP Packet Size *(continued)*

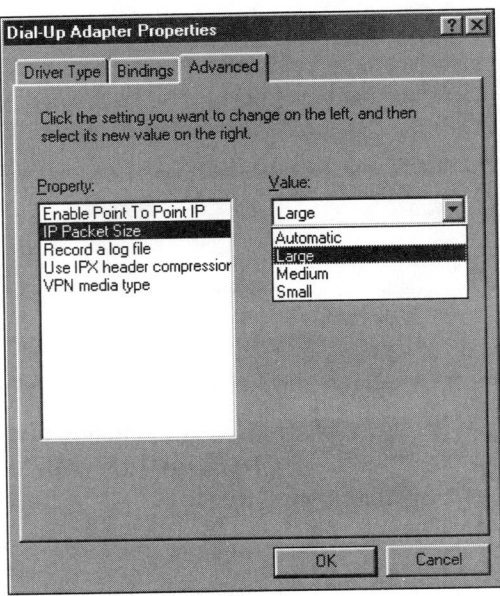

Figure 44-16: Select IP Packet Size in the Property list, and then display the Value drop-down list and select Large.

Step 4.   Click OK, and click OK again.

This is the same as increasing the MTU size to 1,500.

Thanks to Scott Sizemore and Dustin Miller for insights on this issue.

Test Your Download Rate

A number of variables affect your file download speed from your Internet service provider. All of these values get set in the registry, pretty much behind the scenes or at best in Advanced dialog boxes, as shown in the previous section. A clear view of these variables and their effects on the speed of communication would be helpful.

A perfect little piece of freeware for doing just that is iSpeed. It displays all of the relevant variables and lets you adjust their values, either one at a time or as a set based on your connection type (see Figure 44-17). You can then test the settings and decide for yourself which ones provide the best file download rates. You'll find iSpeed at `http://www.hms.com`.

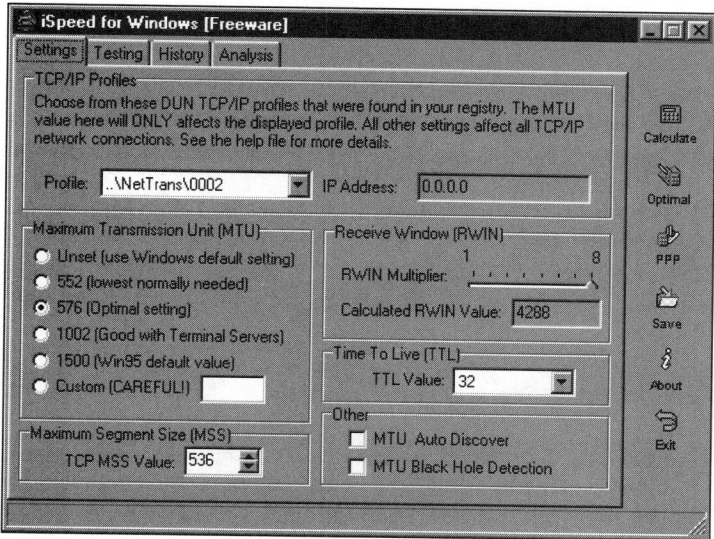

Figure 44-17: The Settings tab in the iSpeed window lets you test different combinations of communications settings.

All of the Windows TCP/IP settings that you can add to the registry are listed in the Microsoft Knowledge Base article "Windows TCP/IP Registry Entries" at `http://support.microsoft.com/support/kb/articles/Q158/4/74.asp`. Don't make these additions unless you are thoroughly familiar with TCP/IP protocol issues.

The Microsoft Knowledge Base also contains an interesting article on an old Winsock bug that was not fixed until Winsock 2.0 was released for Windows 95. Windows Me and 98 come with Winsock 2.0 or higher as factory-standard equipment. The bug in Windows 95 kept a registry entry that modified the search order for DNS servers and kept them from making any difference. You'll find the article, "Windows 95 Service Provider Priority Values Not Applied," at `http://support.microsoft.com/support/kb/articles/Q170/6/19.asp`. This article contains links to many other Knowledge Base articles that pertain to Winsock, DUN, and TCP/IP issues.

Medical Care for Your Modem

Modem Doctor, shown in Figure 44-18, is one neat little shareware package for checking over your modem and learning a little bit about how it operates. The shareware version doesn't do all of the tests, but it does enough. Register it and you get the rest of the tests.

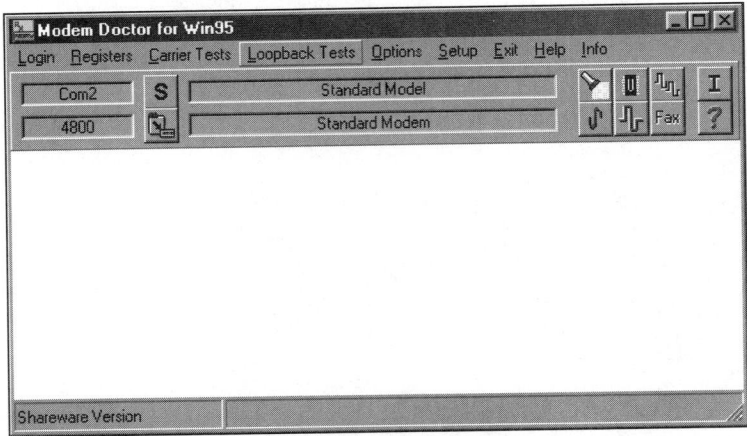

Figure 44-18: The Modem Doctor user interface

Modem Doctor checks all of your serial ports for modems, and tests your serial ports and modems by sending out commands and waiting for answers. You can do loopback tests with the registered version. Modem Doctor also works with Windows to call up the modem, Dial-Up Networking, and Internet configuration dialog boxes.

You'll find it at http://www.modemdoctor.com

Can't Save Your Dial-Up Networking Password

Of all Windows communications problems, this one has probably plagued the largest number of people. You are unable to save the password that you use to log on to your Internet service provider, or to any other network that you dial into.

A number of different factors can cause the DUN connectoid or the connection manager not to display your password in asterisks in the Password field, and to dim the "Save password" checkbox. We discuss these factors and how to fix the problem in "Saving Your DUN Connectoid Passwords" in Chapter 25.

Additional information is available in the article "Dial-Up Networking Password Is Not Saved" at `http://support.microsoft.com/support/kb/articles/q148/9/25.asp`.

You can follow the steps detailed in these documents, or you can download a shareware package that saves the password for you. Affirmative Action DUN saves the password itself and integrates with the Windows dialer. We recommend that you just solve the problem, but if you want a quick fix, this is it.

You'll find AA DUN at `http://www.nadalia.com/aadun`.

HyperTerminal Update

HyperTerminal, a smart terminal communications program, comes with Windows Me — but Microsoft doesn't have it on the Windows Update Web site. You can get the latest version of HyperTerminal, updated since the latest release of Windows, at the Hilgraeve HyperTerminal Private Edition Web site: `http://www.hilgraeve.com/htpe.html`.

Configuring Your Modem

If you are installing Windows and its hardware-detection program identifies an internal or external modem, you'll be automatically prompted to configure it. If you install a modem later, Windows should detect it automatically and start the Install New Modem Wizard. If this doesn't happen, or if you declined to configure your modem during initial setup, you can engage the Install New Modem Wizard from the Control Panel.

Before installing a pre-Plug and Play modem in your computer, you may need to physically configure it by setting the jumper switches; read the modem's documentation to see what to do. If your computer has a Plug and Play BIOS, the modem may not require any configuration on your part; Windows' hardware-detection modules may be able to configure your modem for you automatically. For a Plug and Play modem, this should all be set in the modem itself, so all you have to do is insert it according to the manufacturer's guidelines.

If you are not sure whether Windows has configured your modem, click the Start button, point to Settings, click Control Panel, and click the Modems icon. If your modem has already been configured, you'll see it listed in the General tab of the Modems Properties dialog box. If your modem has not been configured, you can do it now by following these steps.

STEPS

Configuring a Modem

Step 1.   Click the Start button, point to Settings, and then click Control Panel. Click the Modems icon. If you have already installed a modem, you'll see the General tab of the Modems Properties dialog box, as shown in Figure 44-19. Click the Add button to start the wizard, and skip to step 3. (If a modem is already listed, you can optionally remove it before installing another modem by highlighting it and clicking the Remove button.)

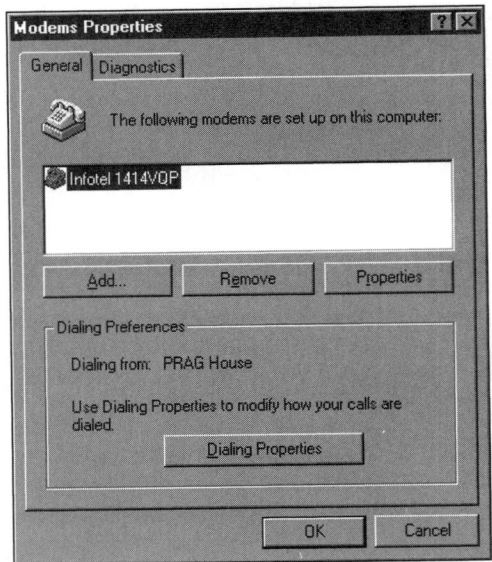

Figure 44-19: The General tab of the Modems Properties dialog box

Step 2.   If you haven't yet configured a modem, the Install New Modem Wizard automatically starts. You can have the Windows hardware-detection routines look for your modem or, if you do not have a Plug and Play BIOS, you can select it from the list of explicitly supported modems. You can change the selection during this configuration process, so it doesn't hurt to let Windows try to detect your modem. Make sure you are not running any communications programs, because they won't allow the detection routines to access the modem. If you do not have a Plug and Play BIOS and want to specify the modem yourself, mark the checkbox labeled "Don't detect my modem; I will select it from a list" (see Figure 44-20); if you have a Plug and Play BIOS, you do not have this option at this point (you will later). Click Next.

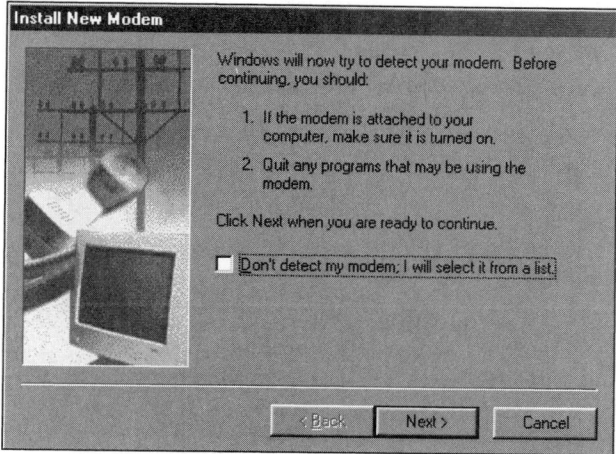

Figure 44-20: Choose whether to have Windows detect your modem.

Step 3. If you choose to have Windows detect the modem, it will take a few seconds to query the modem to determine its type and which communications port it is using. Windows can't detect all modems. The fallback position for the detection routines is Standard modem at a certain speed, such as 14,400 bps. Click Change if you don't think the modem that has been detected is correct or you think you can do a better job.

Step 4. If you are choosing your own modem, or if you clicked Change, you will see a list of modem manufacturers in the next Wizard dialog box, as shown in Figure 44-21. Select your modem's manufacturer in the list on the left, and select the model of your modem on the right. Click Next.

If you have a diskette or CD-ROM from a modem manufacturer that includes a Windows setup routine for the modem, click Have Disk instead. Modems manufactured after the release of Windows 95 may have these diskettes. Microsoft also publishes setup files for new modems on its Web site.

Step 5. If your modem is not listed, select Standard Modem Types (but only for the time being—you'll change it later) and specify your modem's speed, if you know that value. Click Next.

Step 6. If you choose the modem from the list yourself, and it's not Plug and Play, you need to tell Windows which port it is connected to. Most modems are serial modems, so you have a choice of COM ports. Choose the port based on how you have physically configured the modem, or the manufacturer's recommendations. If you have a parallel modem, you should choose an LPT port. After highlighting your port, click Next.

Continued

STEPS

Configuring a Modem *(continued)*

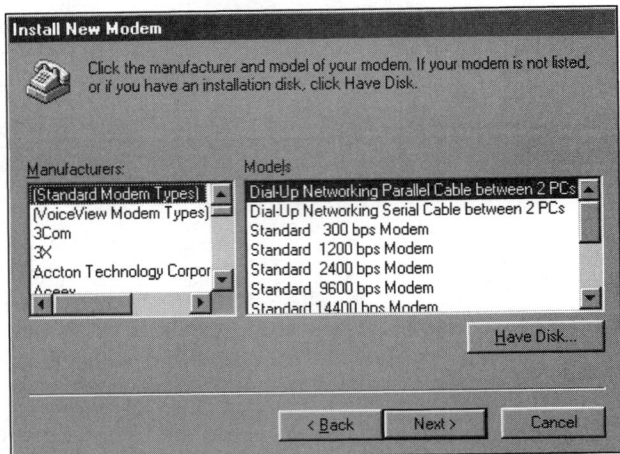

Figure 44-21: The modem selection dialog box in the Install New Modem Wizard

Step 7. The first time you set up a modem, you will be asked for your area code, the number required to get an outside line (if any), whether you are using tone or pulse dialing, and your country code. This information defines the location you are calling from and how the modem should make the call. See "Where Am I Calling From?" in Chapter 45 for more on telephony issues.

Step 8. Click Finish. The modem name now appears in the General tab of the Modems Properties dialog box.

As mentioned in step 3, if Windows identifies your modem as Standard and you have a better idea of what your modem is, go ahead and set the driver to your best guess. You can always replace the driver if it doesn't work correctly.

Secret

If your modem doesn't show up on the list of supported models, try selecting a model similar to yours from the same manufacturer. You don't want to use the Standard modem setting if you can help it because this setting doesn't support data compression and correction, so you won't be able to run your modem at its highest speed. It is much better to choose a modem model similar to yours, even if you can't find one from the same manufacturer. (This may take some guesswork on your part.)

Tip

If your modem is unnamed — generic as far as you can tell — try setting it as a Hayes, U.S. Robotics, Practical Peripherals, or Microcom modem. If you have a generic 28.8Kbps modem, try the Boca Research Bocamodem 28.8Kbps V.34bis Data-Fax modem.

When you select a particular modem model, you're telling Windows about the initialization string and the various other strings that control basic modem functions. These strings do vary from one modem to the next, but they often have enough in common that strings for one modem will frequently work with another.

Testing Your Modem Configuration

Tip

You can test whether your modem configuration is the right one by calling the Microsoft Network. Simply click the MSN icon on your Desktop. You can also test your modem with HyperTerminal. Click the Start button, select Programs ▷ Accessories ▷ Communications, and click HyperTerminal. HyperTerminal comes already set up for connecting to several bulletin boards. Click one of the icons and click the Dial button when the Connect dialog box appears. If your connection is successful, you will see a message in the HyperTerminal window from the computer you called. Choose Call ▷ Disconnect to end your call.

Tip

If you have an external modem and the hardware-detection routines did not find it, you may have an incorrect cable connecting your serial (or parallel) port to your modem — either that or your port may be incorrectly set up.

Whenever you have an active modem connection, the Modem Status icon, which looks like two connected computers, appears in your tray. When data is being transferred, the two computer screens in the icon blink. Right-click this icon and click Status to see the current status of your modem connection.

Changing Basic Global Modem Settings

You can adjust some of the properties associated with your modem by highlighting your modem driver and clicking the Properties button in the General tab of the Modems Properties dialog box.

STEPS

Changing Modem Driver Settings

Step 1. Click the Start button, point to Settings, and then click Control Panel. Click the Modems icon. Highlight your modem in the list.

Step 2. Click Properties to display the General tab of the Properties dialog box for your modem, as shown in Figure 44-22 (note that some modem manufacturers may add tabs that let you access your modem's special features).

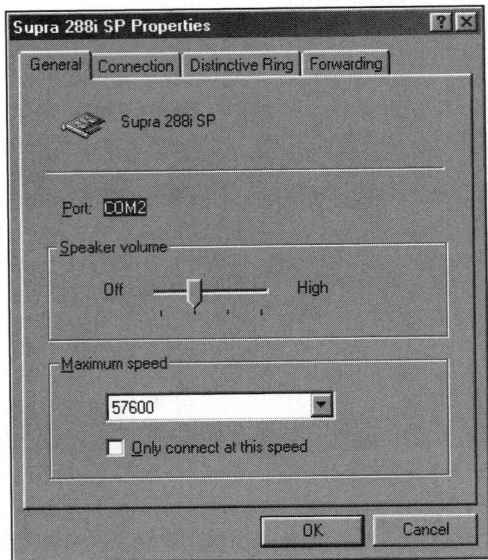

Figure 44-22: The General tab of the Properties dialog box for a modem. You have already selected the port, so unless you move the modem, you shouldn't change that. You can set a global volume for the speaker and the maximum speed your computer/modem combination can handle.

Step 3. An alternate and equivalent way of carrying out steps 1 and 2 is to click the System icon in the Control Panel. Then click the Device Manager tab, click the plus sign next to the Modem icon, click the icon associated with your modem, click Properties, and click the Modem tab.

Step 4. If necessary, change one or more values in your modem's General tab. The maximum speed at which your modem can receive data from your computer depends on what kind of error correction protocol it has and the speed of your CPU. For instance, if you have a 28.8Kbps modem (it talks to other modems at a rate of 28.8Kbps), it may be able to sustain 57.6Kbps or higher with compression. If you find your communications applications are reporting high error rates, reduce this maximum value.

Changing the Basic Modem Connection Properties

Each connection — each bulletin board, ISP, friend with a computer and a modem, or server at work that you connect to using your modem — requires unique connection settings. You can follow these steps to set the default choices that your modem will use until you modify them for a given connection:

STEPS

Setting Modem Connection Properties

Step 1. Carry out steps 1–3 in "Changing Modem Driver Settings" in the preceding section. Click the Connection tab to display the connection properties for the specific modem, as shown in Figure 44-23.

Step 2. The values of 8, None, and 1 for data bits, parity, and stop bits are probably just fine. Change them only if you are attaching to a new service that regularly calls for other values.

Step 3. By default, Windows waits for the dial tone before dialing. If you are calling outside the U.S., you should clear the checkbox labeled "Wait for dial tone before dialing" to turn off this U.S.-specific behavior. You may also need to clear this checkbox if you purchased a modem in a country other than the one you are presently calling from.

Step 4. You can adjust how long you're willing to wait for the connection to be made by marking the checkbox labeled "Cancel the call if not connected within [　] secs" and entering a number of seconds.

Continued

STEPS

Setting Modem Connection Properties *(continued)*

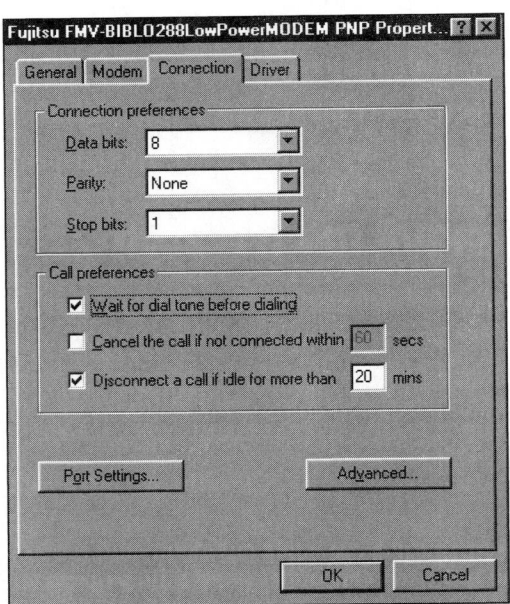

Figure 44-23: The Connection tab of the Properties dialog box for a modem. You can set global default values for the data bits, parity, and stop bits.

Step 5.   To disconnect the phone after a set time of idleness, mark the checkbox labeled "Disconnect a call if idle for more than [   ] mins," and enter a number of minutes.

Step 6.   Click OK.

You can customize these values for each connection, so you should only change the default settings if you are creating new connectoids that regularly use values different from the defaults created by your Windows Setup.

Tip

In addition to the global modem settings, each Dial-Up Networking connectoid has its own Modem Properties dialog box. To find it, click the Start button, choose Programs ➪ Accessories ➪ Communications, and click Dial-Up Networking. Right-click the icon for the connectoid whose properties you want to change, and choose Properties. Then click the Configure button on the General tab, next to the "Connect using" field. The settings you make here will be in effect for all applications (such as Internet Explorer, Outlook

Express, and Microsoft Fax) that use this particular DUN connectoid. HyperTerminal has its own connectoids, which are displayed when you open the HyperTerminal folder. To display the modem settings for the connectoid, right-click the connectoid icon, choose Properties, click the Connect To tab, and then click the Configure button.

When you create a new DUN connectoid, the modem defaults are set to the global modem settings. But once you have created a connectoid, you must change the settings within the connectoid itself, because the connectoid no longer uses the global settings. See "Setting Up Your Computer at Home as a Guest" in Chapter 19 for more about setting up connectoids.

If you can't open the Modems Properties dialog box, or if the Configure button is not available in a DUN connectoid's Properties dialog box, the Modemui.dll file may be missing or damaged. This file should be in your \Windows\System folder. If it's there, rename it to something like Modemui. xxx and extract a new copy from the cab files in the \win98 folder of your Windows CD-ROM. (To learn how to locate the correct cab file, see "Missing Files" in Chapter 15.) Once you've found the correct cab file, just click it in the Explorer window, locate Modemui.dll, and drag a copy of it into your \Windows\System folder.

Your particular modem may offer additional tabs besides General and Connection in the Modems Properties box. For example, you may be able to take advantage of distinctive ringing on your phone line, and designate a different ring pattern for fax, voice, and data. Or you may be able to enable call forwarding—a handy feature if you use telephony software such as Microsoft Phone. These tabs are put there by the manufacturer of your modem at the time you install it, and are not part of Windows.

Changing More Advanced Connection Settings

Your communications software can set specific connection settings (referred to as *connectoids*) that override the default connection settings. The Windows modem driver sends the command strings that are associated with the default settings to the modem when it is first initialized. A communications package can ask the modem driver to send to the modem other command strings that override these values.

Tip

The "Extra settings" field in the Advanced Connection Settings dialog box (available through the Advanced button in the Connection tab of the Modems Properties dialog box) lets you enter a specific command string that you want the driver to send to the modem along with the initialization string. You normally use this field to put the modem into a debug mode in order to track communications errors. Don't use it unless you are familiar with your modem's commands.

STEPS

Setting Advanced Connection Properties

Step 1. Carry out the "Changing Modem Driver Settings" or "Setting Modem Connection Properties" steps in the two previous sections to change driver settings or connection properties as appropriate.

Step 2. Click the Connection tab in the Modems Properties dialog box for your modem, and then click the Advanced button to display the Advanced Connection Settings dialog box, as shown in Figure 44-24.

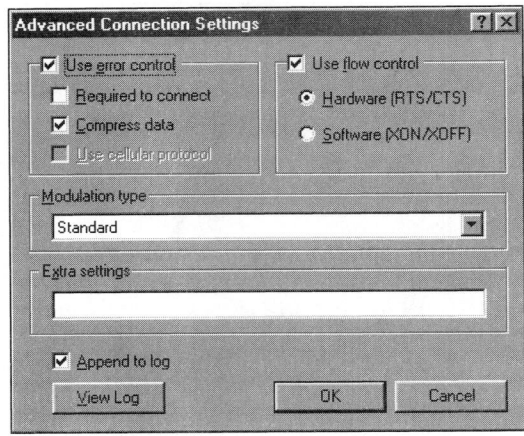

Figure 44-24: The Advanced Connection Settings dialog box

Step 3. The Advanced Connection Settings dialog box lets you add to the string that Windows normally sends when initializing your modem (preparing it for communication) by typing additional strings in the "Extra settings" field. Do not type the attention (AT) command. It is sent automatically by the modem initialization string.

Step 4. Mark the "Use error control" and "Compress data checkboxes if you are sending data to modems or services that support these functions. Some, such as CompuServe, do not. If you are using software compression (for example, compressed SLIP with your Internet service provider), enabling hardware compression here (by marking the "Compress data" checkbox) might cause conflict. One sign that you have conflict between two types of compression is if your communications are very slow. You can turn off either software or hardware compression. (You should only mark the "Compress data" checkbox if you are using an external modem and the serial port is faster than the modem port.)

Don't mark the "Required to connect" checkbox if you have a SLIP or PPP account. If the modems can't negotiate error control, TCP/IP will handle it.

Step 5. Choose "Use flow control" (*handshaking*) if you are running at 9,600 bps or better, and if you have an external modem and the modem cable has the RTS and the CTS lines. You have to use hardware flow control if you have a SLIP account because SLIP requires it, and hardware flow control also works with PPP. You'll most likely never need to use software flow control. (One situation where it might be useful is described just after these steps.)

Step 6. If you are using a cellular modem, mark the "Use cellular protocol" checkbox to reduce errors over multiple cellular connections. This box is only enabled if you're using a CDPD (Cellular Digital Packet Data) modem and the TCP/IP protocol.

Step 7. The default setting in the "Modulation type" drop-down list is Standard. This is the fallback low-speed communications standard if two modems can't communicate at a higher speed. If you experience trouble while trying to communicate with a given site at 300 and 1,200 bps, switch from Standard to Non-standard (Bell, HST).

Step 8. Mark the "Append to log" checkbox if you want to keep a log file to help with debugging a connection. The file, Modemlog.txt, will be in your \Windows folder.

If you enable the log file, Windows adds to it whenever a TAPI-enabled communications programs (such as DUN, HyperTerminal, or Phone Dialer) connects through your modem. The entries are in sequential order, stamped with the date and time of the connection. The Modemlog.txt file will continue to grow as long as you have this option turned on, so you'll need to delete it periodically, or use this feature only when you are troubleshooting.

Step 9. Click OK.

Windows 3.1*x* used software flow control (XON/XOFF) by default. Starting with Windows 95, and continuing with Windows Me, Microsoft turned on hardware flow control (RTS/CTS) by default because it results in better modem performance. If you have installed Windows Me over Windows 3.1*x* and are using an external modem, however, you may find that your serial cable or switch box will not work with hardware flow control. While your modem can send data just fine, it can't receive anything. Ideally, you should replace the connecting device (not the modem itself, just the cable or switch). But you may be able to get around this by configuring your modem for software flow control. If you are using a 16-bit communications program, you have to do this in the application itself.

Secret

You may notice that the Modemlog.txt file masks out the phone numbers you dialed (so they look like ATDT#######, for example). This is an intentional security measure, designed to protect calling card numbers. But you can disable it (for troubleshooting purposes only) by typing **E1** in the "Extra settings" field of the Advanced Connection Settings dialog box. Be sure to change it back when you're done troubleshooting.

Better Serial Ports

Over the lifetime of PC-compatible architecture, the UART chip that controls serial ports has evolved. It began in the IBM PC as the 8250. In the AT class machines, it was upgraded to a 16540. The current chip of choice in Intel 486 and Pentium-based PCs is the 16550A.

Secret

The 16550A has two advantages over its predecessors. First, it incorporates a 16-byte buffer. By buffering incoming and outgoing data, the 16550A UART can accumulate characters without losing them while waiting for its interrupt request to be serviced by the CPU. Second, the 8250 and the 16540 UARTs send an interrupt to the CPU whenever they receive a character. The 16550A can send one interrupt to service all the characters in the buffer.

By accumulating characters while waiting for the CPU to be available, the 16550A greatly enhances the reliability of high-speed communications, which is a very important feature, given our increased usage of the serial port as a networking device.

Secret

Windows 3.1x didn't take much advantage of this buffering capability of the 16550A UART. It didn't use it to transmit data and used only a single byte of the buffer in the receive mode. This allowed third-party software developers to find a niche in the market by creating additional COM port drivers to replace Comm.drv.

Windows 98 takes full advantage of the 16650A UART, enabling the full 16 bytes of the receive and transmit buffers.

Testing Your Internal Modem for a 16550A UART

You can test whether your internal modem includes a 16550A UART.

STEPS

Testing an Internal Modem

Step 1. Set up your modem driver, as described in the steps in the "Configuring Your Modem" section elsewhere in this chapter.

Step 2. Click the Start button, point to Settings, and click Control Panel. Click the Modems icon.

Step 3. Click the Diagnostics tab. Highlight the port with your modem attached. Click More Info. The More Info dialog box will tell you which UART you have.

Changing 16550A UART Settings

If your serial port uses a 16550A UART, you have the option of adjusting the size of its receive and transmit buffers. You might want to do this if you are dropping characters during transmissions or if you want to increase your throughput. To change these settings, click the Port Settings button in the Connection tab of the Properties dialog box for your modem.

The same Port Settings button is associated with each DUN connectoid. To verify this, right-click a connectoid in the Dial-Up Networking folder. Then click Properties, click the Configure button, click the Connection tab, and there it is. Each connectoid can have its own Advanced and Port Setting values. You can also do this for HyperTerminal connectoids. However, to find the Configure button in a HyperTerminal connectoid, you must go to the Connect To tab after you right-click the connectoid and click Properties.

Changing Any Modem Settings

The file Modems.inf and the files starting with Mdm in the \Windows\Inf folder contain the modem manufacturer and model information displayed when you click the Have Disk button in the Install New Modem Wizard. (The Inf folder is only visible if you have chosen View ⇨ Folder Options in an Explorer or folder window and marked "Show hidden files and folders" in the View tab.) Modem manufacturers can ship a file on a diskette with their modem that provides equivalent information about their new modem. Plug and Play modems contain the pertinent information on a ROM chip.

Secret

Each modem model has an associated initialization string or set of initialization strings that are defined in the modem setup files. Additional strings for hanging up the modem, setting it in auto-answer mode, turning on or off the speaker and setting its volume, data compression, tone or pulse dial, and so on, are provided in the modem's setup, or inf, file.

You can edit the information in these files if you want to change the values Windows uses when you configure a modem. You do this by changing the inf file before you add the particular modem driver. From the Explorer, click the inf file that has a name resembling the manufacturer of your modem. You can then edit it with Notepad, but be sure to make a backup file first.

After you have added a modem driver to your Windows configuration (using the associated inf file), you can change any of the settings associated with the modem by using the Registry Editor. This is a bit easier than editing the esoteric inf file directly. Turn to "The Registry Editor" in Chapter 11 if you are not familiar with how to edit the registry.

Go to this branch of the registry:

HKEY_LOCAL_MACHINE\System\CurrentControlSet\Services\Class\Modem

There may be a number of modems specified on this branch, each designated as a branch and starting with the branch key numbered 0000. This area of the registry is shown in Figure 44-25.

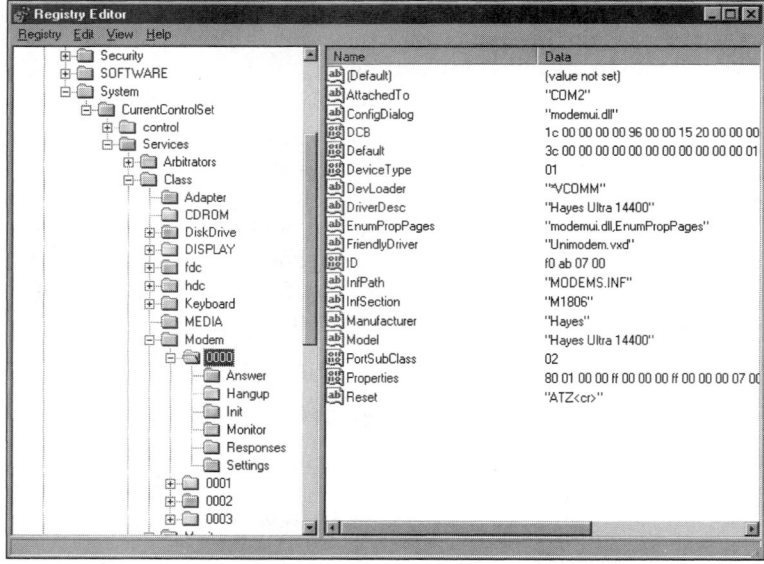

Figure 44-25: The Registry Editor displaying the area of the registry that contains the modem configuration information. Click the plus signs next to the names in the branch to get to this area. (The names on the branch now have minus signs in front of them.)

Find the branch that corresponds to your modem driver by checking the DriverDesc field (in the right pane of the Registry Editor) for its familiar name as you highlight each key, starting with 0000. If you have set up DCC, you will see modems in the DriverDesc field labeled Serial Cable Between 2 PCs.

Expand the branch for your modem by clicking the plus sign in front of its designated number to see the keys that you can edit.

If you want to change the initialization string for your modem in the registry, click the Init folder for your modem in the left pane of the Registry Editor. The initialization string is displayed in the right pane. Double-click the 2 in the right pane and edit the string. You might want to edit the Answer, Hangup, Fax, and Settings values. (You may see other values and variables as well, depending on what items your modem manufacturer chose to place in the registry.)

It's a good idea to make a copy of System.dat and User.dat in your \Windows folder before you make any changes to your modem configuration in the registry.

Test and Interrogate Your Modem

You can find out if your modem is working and what values are stored in its registers. To do this, you can use Terminal, the Windows 3.1*x* communications package, because it makes it easy to talk directly to your modem. Alternatively, you can configure HyperTerminal.

If you upgraded over Windows 3.1*x*, you'll find Terminal.exe still in your \Windows folder. Otherwise, you may need to retrieve it from your Windows 3.1*x* diskettes.

Click Terminal.exe in a folder window or in the Explorer. To check if the modem is working, type the command string **atz** or **ath** or **ate1m1v1**. (Check your modem manual to see which one you should use.) If the modem returns OK, then it is there and listening to you.

Next, send the **ati?** command, replacing the **?** with the numbers **2** through **9**, one at a time. This should tell you what kind of modem you have.

You can send AT commands to your modem using HyperTerminal. Just follow the steps detailed next. You can also send AT commands from a terminal window associated with a particular connection. If you have created a connectoid for HyperTerminal, take the following steps:

STEPS

Sending AT Commands in HyperTerminal

Step 1. Right-click a HyperTerminal connectoid. Click Properties, and choose the Connect To tab.

Step 2. Click the Configure button, and then click the Options tab.

Continued

STEPS

Sending AT Commands in HyperTerminal *(continued)*

Step 3. Mark the "Bring up terminal window before dialing" checkbox.

Step 4. Click OK. Click OK again.

Step 5. Click this connectoid. Click the Dial button in the Connect dialog box.

Step 6. The Pre-Dial Terminal Screen appears on your Desktop. Type the AT commands and see what response you get.

Step 7. Press F3 to cancel the attempted connection when you are done.

Step 8. Click Cancel in the Connect dialog box, and then close the HyperTerminal window.

You can invoke a modem diagnostic dialog box by clicking the Modems icon in the Control Panel, clicking the Diagnostics tab, highlighting the port to which your modem is attached, and then clicking the More Info button. Windows sends various AT commands to your modem and reports the responses in the dialog box, as shown in Figure 44-26. It's not too interesting unless you know from looking in your modem's manual what the correct responses are supposed to be.

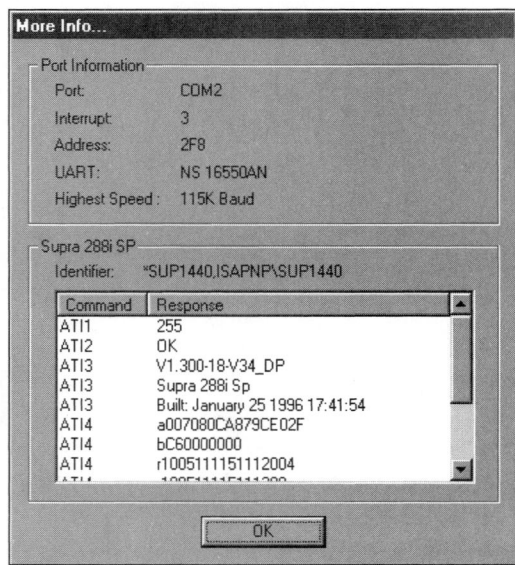

Figure 44-26: The More Info dialog box

Bruce Pennypacker shared this tip for testing the COM port and modem configuration. Because this test doesn't use any TAPI applications, it helps you make sure that your hardware is set up properly. In a DOS window, type the following at the command prompt:

```
echo ATDTnnnnnnn > COMx
```

Here, *nnnnnnn* is a number to dial and *x* is the number of the COM port. This should cause the modem to go off-hook and dial the number. To disconnect, type:

echo ATH > COM*x*

When you're finished, type **exit** to close the DOS window.

Modem Speed

After you have made a modem connection, right-click the Modem Status icon in your tray and click Status. If you are using a 32-bit communications program designed for Windows, you'll see a box that displays the status of the current connection, including the *line* speed (also known as the *data link* speed or *data circuit-terminating equipment (DCE)* speed). This is the speed between your modem and the modem you are connected to. In other words, it's the speed at which data is transmitted over the telephone line.

Most 16-bit communications programs that are designed for Windows 3.1*x* report the *port* speed (also known as the *serial port connection* speed or *data terminal equipment (DTE)* speed) in the status box. The port speed is the speed between your modem and your computer. More precisely, it's the speed between the serial port that your modem is connected to and your computer. The port speed is typically faster than the line speed, causing 16-bit programs to report a faster speed than 32-bit programs (for example, 57,600 bps instead of 28,800 bps or less). Most people are interested in knowing the line speed, which changes depending on the connection.

Here is a way to make your 16-bit applications report the line speed instead of the port speed:

STEPS

Making 16-Bit Applications Report the Line Speed

Step 1.   In Control Panel, double-click the Modems icon.

Step 2.   Click your modem, and then click Properties.

Step 3.   In the Connection tab, click the Advanced button.

Continued

STEPS

Making 16-Bit Applications Report the Line Speed *(continued)*

Step 4. In the "Extra settings" field, type **S95=0**, and then click OK.

Step 5. Click OK and then Close to return to the Control Panel.

If the S95=0 setting doesn't work for you, check your modem documentation to see if it specifies another character string for this.

Tracking a Dial-Up Connection with System Monitor

While the modem status box (which you display by right-clicking the Modem Status icon in the tray when you are connected and choosing Status) shows you the line speed at which the modem is connected, the line speed is not necessarily a true indicator of the rate of data transfer. A modem can be running at its full capacity of 28.8Kbps, but the online service to which it's connected might be sending out information at a fraction of that rate. Whether the server is overloaded with too many users, or you have a bad telephone connection that's slowing down the signal, a utility called System Monitor (Sysmon.exe) can tell you whether you're getting the throughput you expect.

In order to view modem performance statistics in System Monitor, you must be using a 32-bit communications program, and you must have marked the "Append to log" checkbox in the Advanced Connection Settings dialog box (see "Changing More Advanced Connection Settings" earlier in this chapter).

You may have installed System Monitor when you installed Windows; if so, it should be in your \Windows folder. If not, you can retrieve it from the Windows CD-ROM. Click Add/Remove Programs in the Control Panel, click the Windows Setup tab, highlight System Tools, click the Details button, and mark the System Monitor checkbox.

Start System Monitor, either by clicking its icon in the Explorer or by clicking Start ⇨ Programs ⇨ Accessories ⇨ System Tools ⇨ System Monitor. In the System Monitor, choose Edit ⇨ Add Item. The Dial-Up Adapter should appear in the Categories list. Highlight it, click Bytes Received/Second and Shift+click Bytes Transmitted/Second (to select them both), and click OK. Then log on to a Web site with lots of graphics and see what happens (as in Figure 44-27).

When you add Bytes Received or Bytes Transmitted to your System Monitor window, you'll want to configure the applet to show a meaningful period of time. A rapid update interval of 1 second or 3 seconds should give you an accurate indication of the real throughput you're getting from your online connection. To set this parameter, choose Options ⇨ Chart and move the slider bar to the interval you prefer.

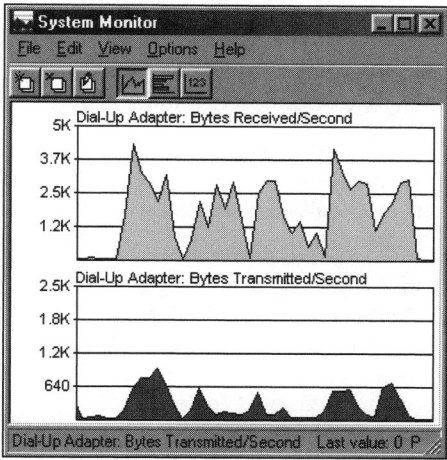

Figure 44-27: System Monitor is set up to show the data transfer rates through the Dial-Up Adapter. In this case, the update interval is every three seconds.

If you check your throughput from various servers at various times of the day, you may find that your online provider is the cause of slowdowns in your data throughput. If you get close to the rated speed of your modem when connected at midnight, but a much lower number during the business day, you've just found some peak hours to avoid—unless your service provider can be shamed into upgrading his or her lines and modems.

If you have a 56K modem, you'll notice that the charts for Bytes Received and Bytes Transmitted show quite different transfer rates. The rate for bytes received is probably much higher than for bytes transmitted. There's nothing wrong with your modem; this is normal. These modems take advantage of digital technology to push more information over the phone lines than they theoretically should handle. They count on the fact that your service provider's server can generate a digital signal directly, without using a modem at all. This data can travel faster over the phone lines. Data sent from your modem, however, regardless of the modem's quality or speed, cannot be sent faster than 33.6Kbps. Too much "noise" is created when the modem converts your digital data to analog for transmission on your local phone loop (the telephone system then reconverts it to digital for further transmission). Of course, your actual speed will vary, depending on the quality of your connection to the phone company and other factors.

Using a Modem with DOS Programs

Some people still want to be able to run their modems with DOS programs. This might be especially important if you like to play DOS games online. However, it may be difficult to get the application to even see that your modem is there.

Because DOS programs do not support the newer TAPI standard, they cannot "share" a modem with any other programs — even if they aren't connected at the moment. So make sure that any other communications programs (such as Microsoft Fax or HyperTerminal) are completely shut down.

If the DOS program still fails to locate the modem, you may have one of the newer WinModems. These modems depend on the Windows VxD driver, and probably won't work with your DOS software at all. If you have a WinModem, you're stuck with a decision between giving up the DOS applications and replacing your modem.

If you don't have a WinModem and you can't get DOS to locate your modem, you probably have a Plug and Play modem that has been configured to a setting that older DOS programs have problems with. The easiest way around this is to manually configure your modem port to settings familiar for DOS programs. In the Control Panel, click the System icon, click the Device Manager tab, click the plus sign next to Modem, and double-click your modem. Look in the Modem tab of the Properties dialog box to see which COM port your modem is configured to use. Click OK, click the plus sign next to Ports, and then double-click the port assigned to your modem. In the Resources tab of the port's Properties dialog box, clear the "Use automatic settings" box. Depending on the resources available on your computer, change the setting for this port to one of the settings listed in Table 44-1 in the "Configuring Serial Ports" section later in this chapter. Try to stick to COM1 or COM2.

Two Modems

Some people need to use two modems — one for a fax line and one for Dial-Up Networking, for example. It is entirely possible to set this up, as long as each modem has its own COM port and its own interrupt (IRQ). This might be easier said than done, however, since COM ports share interrupts. You should look for modems that allow you flexibility in setting the IRQ value and COM port. If you can't find this type of modem, you can try freeing up an IRQ by switching to a nonserial mouse.

A different problem can occur if the two modems are the same model. When you install them, Windows will give them the same "friendly" name, which is the name you see in the Modems Properties dialog box (accessed through the Modems icon in the Control Panel). Especially if the friendly name is long, Windows may not use the right modem for a given communications program. If the modems are identical and are installed as the same model, both modems will appear in the Modems Properties dialog box. The solution is to remove the second modem and then reinstall it as a different model. To do so, follow these steps.

STEPS

Re-Installing a Second Modem

Step 1.   In the Control Panel, click the Modems icon.

Step 2.   Click the second modem, and then click Remove.

Step 3.   Click the Add button to launch the Install New Modem Wizard, mark the "Don't detect my modem; I will select it from a list" checkbox, and then click Next.

Step 4.   In the Manufacturers and Models lists, choose a manufacturer and a model that is compatible with your modem. If your modem is not compatible with another modem, choose Standard Modem Types at the top of the Manufacturers list and select the model that matches the speed of your modem in the Models list.

Note that if you choose one of the standard modems, you may not be able to use some of the advanced features of your modem. For example, the option to use data compression may not be available.

Step 5.   Click Next. Click the appropriate port for the modem, and then click Next again.

Step 6.   Click Finish.

Serial and Parallel Ports as Modems

In Chapter 17, we discuss Direct Cable Connection (DCC), which lets you hook two computers together using a serial or parallel cable.

DCC keeps track of your serial and parallel ports as though they were modems. When you first click DCC, hardware-detection routines determine which serial and parallel ports are available. They create modem designations for each of these ports and allow you to choose between Serial Cable on COM*x* and Parallel Cable on LPT*x*. The modem descriptions and properties of each port are stored in the registry in the area referred to in the "Changing Any Modem Settings" section of this chapter.

These are not real modems, but the Modems area of the registry is a convenient place to keep track of the fact that these ports are available to be used by DCC. These port connections do not show up on the list of modems when you click the Modems icon in the Control Panel.

There are two ways to see which ports the hardware-detection routines have found. You can click the Start button, point to Programs ➪ Accessories ➪ Communications, and then click Direct Cable Connection. If you click the Change button and then click Next, you'll see a list of ports available for DCC.

The other way to see the list of ports is to click the Start button, point to Settings, and then click Control Panel. Click the System icon, and then click the plus sign next to the Modem icon. A list of all "modems" will appear, including your serial and parallel cables on ports if you have previously run DCC.

If you use this second method, you can remove certain ports that you won't be using with DCC — perhaps ports that are being used only by your mouse, for instance. If you remove a port/cable that you decide later to use with DCC, you must restore it manually.

To add back a removed port, take the following steps:

STEPS

Adding a Removed Port

Step 1. Click the Start button, point to Programs ⇨ Accessories ⇨ Communications, and finally click Direct Cable Connection.

Step 2. Click the Change button, and then click Next.

Step 3. Click the Install New Ports button.

Cable Modems

Modems that connect to your television cable instead of the phone line are becoming available, and cable companies in most parts of the country have begun to offer this service. The cable modem connects to your computer through an Ethernet card, so it doesn't use a COM port at all. Instead, you select the Network option from within your application. There's no need for dial-up, because you're always connected. Early users have reported much faster performance than telephone lines can provide.

Configuring Serial Ports

You can change a serial port's settings as well its address and interrupt values. You make all changes to serial and parallel ports through the Device Manager, found under the System icon in the Control Panel.

Changing Serial Port Settings

The functions of ports are configured in the Device Manager. You can use the Device Manager to change a serial port's speed, data bits, stop bits, parity, and flow control (handshaking). If you are using this serial port for a connection, the settings for that particular connection override these settings.

STEPS

Changing Serial Port Settings

Step 1. Click the Start button, point to Settings, and then click Control Panel. Click the System icon to display the System Properties dialog box, and click the Device Manager tab.

Step 2. Click the plus sign to the left of the Ports icon in the Device Manager. You will see a listing of all the serial and parallel ports connected to your computer.

Step 3. Highlight the serial port you want to change and click the Properties button. Click the Port Settings tab.

Step 4. Using the options in this tab, shown in Figure 44-28, you can change the values for speed, data bits, stop bits, parity, and flow control (handshaking).

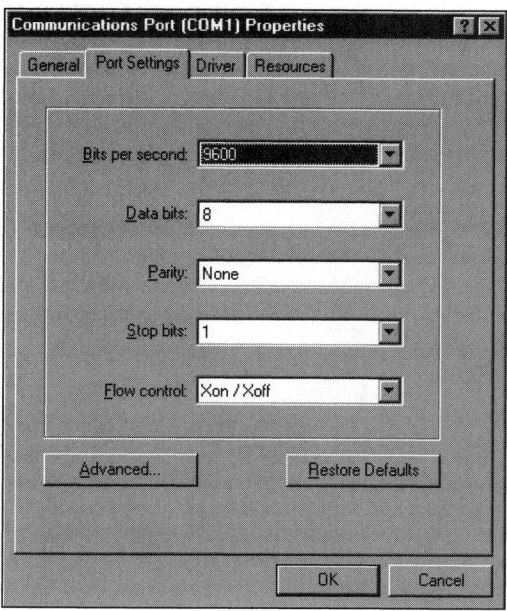

Figure 44-28: The Port Settings tab in the Communications Port (COMx) Properties dialog box

These port settings are similar to the basic global connection settings for a modem. You should set these settings only when you use the port with a device, such as a scanner, a printer, or even a mouse. The specific software that uses the port — a communications package or a connectoid (whether HyperTerminal or DUN) — can have different settings, and these settings override the serial port settings.

In Windows, after you install a modem, the serial port that the modem is configured to use may not be listed in Device Manager. To determine which serial port the modem is configured to use, click the plus sign next to Modem in Device Manager, highlight your modem, click Properties, and go to the Modem tab.

During setup, Windows recognizes the serial ports that are already installed in your computer. Serial ports in personal computers with ISA buses (not MCA or EISA) have default values for addresses and interrupts. Table 44-1 lists these values.

Table 44-1   Default Address and Interrupt Values

Port	Address	Interrupt
COM1	03F8h	4
COM2	02F8h	3
COM3	03E8h	4
COM4	02E8h	3

Years ago, some Windows 3.1x users had problems with internal modems set to COM4, which failed to operate if there was no COM3. Other users had trouble with serial mice on COM2 if COM4 was present but COM3 wasn't. These problems have been fixed, starting with Windows 95 and continuing through Windows Me.

You'll notice in Table 44-1 that COM1 and COM3 share the same interrupt. The same is true for COM2 and COM4. If you have devices on the higher-numbered COM ports, they will conflict with devices on the port they share the interrupt with. You can't use both devices at the same time if they share an interrupt and you are using a computer with an ISA bus.

If one device is, say, a scanner and the other is a modem, then it is unlikely that you will use them both at the same time, so sharing an interrupt is okay. If one is a mouse and another is a printer, your mouse will go haywire when you are printing. You can change the interrupts so there is no conflict.

You can determine a serial port's I/O address with Debug, a DOS program used for troubleshooting problems with your system setup. See "Finding a Serial Port I/O Address Using Debug" in the Microsoft Knowledge Base at http://support.microsoft.com/support/kb/articles/q78/6/04.asp.

Changing Serial Port Addresses and Interrupts

You can configure your serial port addresses and interrupts to avoid conflicts between devices that can't share the same interrupt. You can have a modem on COM3 and a mouse on COM1 and use different interrupts for each device. Your serial port hardware must support the new interrupt number and you must change the configuration switches on the (pre-Plug and Play) hardware to match the interrupts that you choose in Windows.

Secret

The address and interrupt information for each port is stored as a *basic configuration* (which is just a grouping of resource settings). Only one basic configuration is active at any one time for a given port. Depending on your BIOS, you can set each serial port to use one of either four or nine basic configurations, as we show in the steps in this section. A computer with a Plug and Play BIOS will only show four basic configurations, and they will not be editable (since the BIOS should take care of the configuration for you). The default basic configuration of the COM1 serial port is basic configuration 0 (shown as 0000 if you have a Plug and Play BIOS). For the COM2 serial port, it is basic configuration 2 (or 0001 for a Plug and Play BIOS).

If you have a non-Plug and Play BIOS, serial port basic configurations 0, 2, and 4 are noneditable. You can change the interrupt in basic configurations 1, 3, 5, 6, 7. You can change either the serial port address or the interrupt in basic configuration 8.

Basic configurations 0 and 1 are designed for COM1, 2 and 3 for COM2, 4 and 5 for COM3, and 6 and 7 for COM4.

Use the Resources tab of the Communications Port (COM*x*) Properties dialog box to choose which basic configuration to use for each port.

STEPS

Changing Serial Port Addresses and Interrupts

Step 1. Click the Start button, point to Settings, and then click Control Panel. Click the System icon. Click the Device Manager tab.

Step 2. Click the plus sign next to the Ports icon in the Device Manager. You will see a listing of all the serial and parallel ports connected to your computer.

Step 3. Highlight the communications port that you want to change and click the Properties button. Click the Resources tab to display the resource properties for the communications port (see Figure 44-29).

Continued

STEPS

Changing Serial Port Addresses and Interrupts *(continued)*

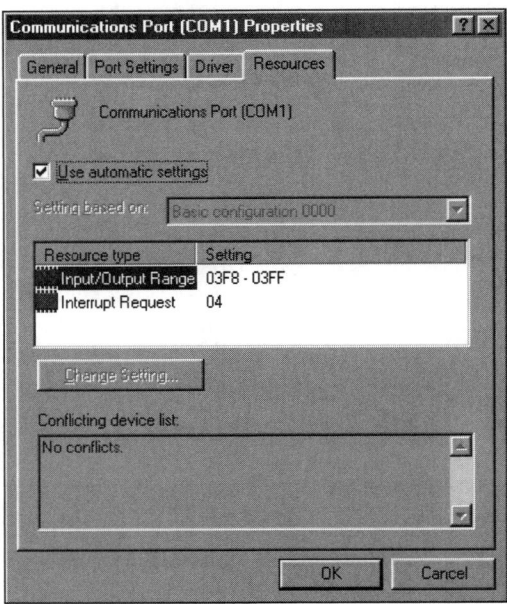

Figure 44-29: The Resources tab in the Communications Port (COM*x*) Properties dialog box

Step 4. If you have a Plug and Play BIOS, you can only change the basic configuration. Clear the "Use automatic settings" checkbox so that you can change the default settings. Display the "Setting based on" drop-down list, and highlight a basic configuration. You are warned if there is a conflict with another hardware device driver. Once you have selected a new basic configuration, go on to step 9.

Step 5. If you have a non-Plug and Play BIOS, you can change the Input/Output Range or the Interrupt Request settings. Highlight either Input/Output Range (the address of the serial port) or Interrupt Request. Click the Change Setting button. If you get a message stating that this setting can't be changed, try another configuration. Basic configurations 0, 2, and 4 are not editable. Basic configurations 1, 3, 5, 6, and 7 have editable interrupts. Basic configuration 8 has editable address and interrupt values.

Step 6. If the address in the currently selected basic configuration can be changed, when you highlight Input/Output Range and click the Change Setting button, you'll see the Edit Input/Output Range dialog box, as shown in Figure 44-30. You can give the port a new address if the documentation for the port hardware indicates support for the new address.

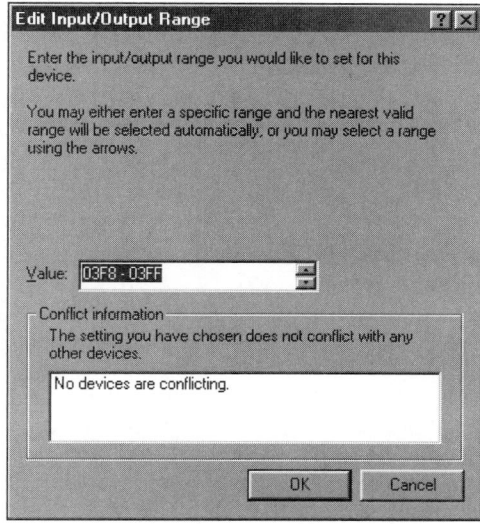

Figure 44-30: The Edit Input/Output Range dialog box for a computer without a Plug and Play BIOS. Change the value of the port address by scrolling through the available addresses. The lower field reports whether a hardware device driver is already using this address.

Step 7. Scroll through the various available addresses to set a new address for this port. You are warned if there is a conflict with another hardware device driver.

Step 8. If the interrupt in the currently selected basic configuration can be changed, you can highlight Interrupt Request in the Resources tab, click the Change Setting button, and then change the interrupt value in the Edit Interrupt Request dialog box. You will be warned if there is a conflict.

Step 9. Click OK. Click OK again.

Step 10. Restart Windows 98.

If you disable a COM port for any reason, you should also make sure you remove it in the Device Manager. Otherwise, you'll see a yellow warning symbol in the Device Manager, indicating that the port is not working or not configured in the way Windows expects.

Infrared Communications

Using infrared (IR) devices and the Microsoft Infrared Communications Driver, you can use wireless infrared links instead of serial and parallel cables. For example, instead of using a serial or parallel cable to exchange files using DCC, you can use an infrared link. You can also print to infrared-capable printers without the need for cable.

While some computers (mostly notebooks) have built-in IR ports, you can also buy IR adapters that connect to serial ports. The IR devices simulate serial connections, and require that you assign them a COM port on installation. Make sure you find out in advance what the correct COM port is for your device; if you assign an incorrect COM port, the device will not be able to recognize other IR devices.

Configuring Parallel Ports

The Windows user interface for configuring parallel ports is almost the same as that used for serial ports. As with the serial port settings, the number of basic configurations available for a parallel port depends on your BIOS. However, for parallel ports there are fewer configurations: two if you have a Plug and Play BIOS, and four if you do not. Both of the Plug and Play basic configurations have interrupts; for non-Plug and Play, basic configurations 0 and 2 do not.

Tip

Windows Me, by default, does not assign an interrupt to a parallel port. The interrupt is rarely needed for printing. The previous standard in Windows 95 and earlier was to assign interrupt 7 to LPT1 and LPT3, and interrupt 5 to LPT2. Here's how to change addresses and interrupts:

STEPS

Changing Parallel Port Addresses and Interrupts

Step 1. Click Start, point to Settings, and click Control Panel. Click the System icon to display the System Properties dialog box. Click the Device Manager tab.

Step 2. Click the plus sign next to the Ports icon in the Device Manager tab to see a listing of all serial and parallel ports connected to your computer.

Step 3. Highlight the parallel port that you want to change, and click Properties. Click the Resources tab.

Step 4. If you have a Plug and Play BIOS, you can change the basic configuration. Clear the "Use automatic settings" checkbox, and display the "Setting based on" drop-down list to see the possible basic configurations (0000 or 0001 in this case). Highlight a basic configuration and go on to step 8.

Step 5.   If you do not have a Plug and Play BIOS, you can change the Input/Output Range or the Interrupt Request settings. Highlight either Input/Output Range (the address of the parallel port) or Interrupt Request. Clear the "Use automatic settings" checkbox to allow settings other than the default ones. Display the "Setting based on" drop-down list to see the possible basic configurations (0, 1, 2, or 3). Highlight a basic configuration and click the Change Setting button.

Step 6.   If you highlighted Input/Output Range in step 5, you can change the port address setting with the arrow buttons.

Step 7.   If you highlighted Interrupt Request in step 5, you can change the interrupt value. You will be warned if there is a conflict. There isn't an interrupt displayed with every basic configuration.

Step 8.   Click OK. Click OK again.

Step 9.   Restart Windows.

Configuring ECP and EPP Ports

Windows Setup detects whether you have an *extended capabilities port* (ECP) or an *enhanced parallel port* (EPP), but it won't set up the port for you. Both of these port types provide you with high-speed and bidirectional communication capabilities. If you want high-speed communication, you have to enable ECP or EPP support yourself. Here's how:

STEPS

Configuring ECP or EPP Support

Step 1.   First make sure that the ECP or EPP port is implemented in your computer's BIOS (usually it won't be if it's coming right from the manufacturer). Restart your computer, and during power-on self-test, press the key indicated on your display to get to the BIOS setup screen (this may happen fast, so be ready). Once you are in the setup screen for your particular BIOS, look for the place where you change the parallel port (this will be different for every BIOS manufacturer). Most likely the BIOS will assign a configuration for your port. Once the port is configured, save your changes and continue with the Windows boot up process.

Step 2.   When Windows starts it will do a hardware search. Windows should find your ECP or EPP port and configure it.

Continued

STEPS

Configuring ECP or EPP Support *(continued)*

Step 3. If Windows doesn't find your port, click the Start button, point to Settings, and then click Control Panel. Click the Add New Hardware icon to start the Add New Hardware Wizard. The wizard will first search for new Plug and Play–compatible hardware. If the wizard doesn't find your port, click the "No, I want to select the hardware from a list" option, and click Next.

Step 4. Double-click Ports in the list that appears. Double-click ECP Printer Port in the next list, click Next to accept the configuration settings, and click Finish.

Step 5. If you need to change the configuration your port has been assigned, follow the "Changing Parallel Port Addresses and Interrupts" steps in the previous section.

How Many Serial and Parallel Ports?

The old Windows 3.1*x* operating system could handle up to four serial ports and nine parallel ports. The four serial ports shared two interrupts.

Windows Me can logically address up to 128 serial and 128 parallel ports — the same as previous versions of MS-DOS. Most computers come with far fewer actual serial and parallel ports. Some manufacturers sell add-in cards that give you additional ports. These are useful for handling such tasks as answering multiple modems or collecting data from laboratories.

Port Values Stored in Win.ini

To maintain compatibility with existing Windows 3.1*x* applications, Windows Me stores port information in the Win.ini file. If you make changes to the serial port settings, they are reflected in changes to the settings in Win.ini as well as the registry. Therefore, you shouldn't edit Win.ini directly. Use the Device Manager (double-click the System icon in the Control Panel) and make changes in the Port Settings tab of the Communications Port (COM*x*) Properties dialog box for the desired serial port. The changes will show up in both places.

Printer port information — what printer drivers have been set up and which ports they are connected to — comes from the Printers folder. It is stored both in the registry and Win.ini.

Table 44-2 shows a typical set of entries for port information in your Windows 98 Win.ini file.

Table 44-2   Port Information in Win.ini

Entry	Explanation
[Ports]	Ports section heading
LPT1:= LPT2:= LPT3:=	Possible parallel ports
COM1:=9600,n,8,1,x COM2:=9600,n,8,1,x COM3:=9600,n,8,1,x COM4:=9600,n,8,1,x	Serial port settings. 9,600 bits per second, no parity, 8 data bits, 1 stop bit, xon/xoff
FILE:=	Print to a file
FAX:=	Print to a fax
PUB:=	Fax rendering
\\OurServer\hp=	Network printer

```
[Devices]
Linotronic 300 v47.1=PSCRIPT,FILE:
HP LaserJet 4L=HPPCL5MS,LPT1:
Microsoft Fax=WPSUNI,FAX:
Rendering Subsystem=WPSUNI,PUB:
Server's HP=HPPCL5MS,\\OurServer\hp

[PrinterPorts]
Linotronic 300 v47.1=PSCRIPT,FILE:,15,45
HP LaserJet 4L=HPPCL5MS,LPT1:,15,45
Microsoft Fax=WPSUNI,FAX:,15,45
Rendering Subsystem=WPSUNI,PUB:,15,45
Server's HP=HPPCL5MS,\\OurServer\hp,15,45
```

The [Devices] section, which lists the available printers, is useless and is necessary only for compatibility with Windows 2.*x* applications.

The [PrinterPorts] section lists again the available printers, the ports they are attached to, and their time-out settings in seconds. The first time-out is how long to wait for the printer to report that it is alive. The second is how long to wait for the printer to respond to an attempt to communicate with it before reporting an error. See "Printer Driver Properties" in Chapter 41 for further discussion of printer issues.

Previously, the base I/O port address and the IRQ values were stored on the COM*x*BASE and COM*x*IRQ lines (where *x* is a number between 1 and 4) in the [386Enh] section of the System.ini file in the \Windows folder. These lines are no longer operative. If you want to edit your System.ini with Notepad, you can remove these lines.

Null Modem Cables

If you are going to use Direct Cable Connection across serial ports, you should use null modem cables to connect two Windows computers. When you ask for a *null modem*, sometimes the sales people at the computer store will know what you're talking about, and sometimes they won't. This is not exactly a brand name. It's easier to pick these items out of a mail order catalog. If you need to be specific, Tables 44-3 and 44-4 describe the connections for null modem cables.

Table 44-3   Serial 9-Pin to 9-Pin Null Modem Cable

Signal	Host serial port pins	Guest serial port pins
Transmit Data	3	2
Receive Data	2	3
Request to Send	7	8
Clear to Send	8	7
Data Set Ready and	6, 1	4
Data Carrier Detect		
Signal Ground	5	5
Data Terminal Ready	4	6, 1

Table 44-4   Serial 25-Pin to 25-Pin Null Modem Cable

Signal	Host serial port pins	Guest serial port pins
Transmit Data	2	3
Receive Data	3	2
Request to Send	4	5
Clear to Send	5	4
Data Set Ready and	6, 8	20
Data Carrier Detect		
Signal Ground	7	7
Data Terminal Ready	20	6, 8

Summary

Windows gives you a great deal of control over your ports and modems:

▶ You can change the address and interrupt values for serial or parallel ports to avoid conflicts with other hardware devices.

▶ You can configure your modem once, and this configuration will be used by all Windows-aware communications software.

▶ You can determine whether your internal modem has an advanced serial port (UART) chip.

▶ If your Internet service provider has the right stack of modems, you can speed up your access.

▶ The freeware program iSpeed tells you how to get optimum performance from your Internet connections.

▶ The doctor is in for medical care for your modem.

Chapter 45

Telephony

In This Chapter

Windows provides a powerful resource to aid in telephone communications. Among other features, TAPI (Telephone Application Programming Interface) indicates to TAPI-compliant communications applications the characteristics of the location you are dialing from. We show you how to use the Dialing Properties dialog box for:

▶ Entering the numbers that you have to dial to get an outside line or a long-distance line

▶ Automatically using calling cards to bill calls correctly from out-of-town locations

▶ Defining alternative dialing methods for unusual situations

▶ Formatting phone numbers so you can dial them from anywhere

▶ Designating the first three digits of a phone number in your area code as requiring long-distance dialing

▶ Setting up speed dialing with Phone Dialer

Where Am I Calling From?

Microsoft provides a resource in Windows for keeping track of where you are. What problem are they trying to solve?

Consider for a moment your garden-variety communications package. You know that it keeps track of the phone numbers of the computer services that you use. That is, it keeps track of the area codes and local numbers. It also knows that if you place an area code in a phone number, it has to dial a 1 to make a long-distance call.

If you stay in one place (say, your office) and have your calls billed to one number (most likely the number you are calling from), your communications software only needs to know the number that you are dialing. It knows how to complete the call because the billing and other information required are implicit.

If, on the other hand, you and your computer travel around at all, your computer needs to know not only where you are calling *to,* but also the special features of the phone system you are dialing *from.* In addition, you need to be able to easily choose the long-distance carriers that handle your calls and determine how they will bill you.

Different locations have different means of accessing outside lines or long-distance carriers. For example, calling from the office may require that you preface your phone numbers with a 9, while calling from home does not. If you call from a hotel, you might have to use a credit card and dial into a specific long-distance carrier. A phone number may be local when you call from home and long distance when you call from the office. Some phones have only pulse dialing services. Some locations require special calling methods.

You can handle all these situations with the Dialing Properties dialog box.

Preliminary Location Information

The first time you set up your modem (see "Configuring Your Modem" in Chapter 44 for details) you encounter the Location Information dialog box as part of the Install New Modem Wizard (shown in Figure 45-1). At this point, all you need to do is type your area code.

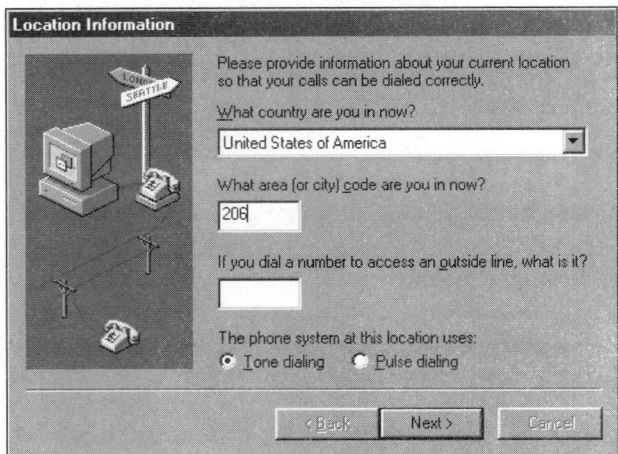

Figure 45-1: The Location Information dialog box

You have the option of changing the country code, typing a number required to get an outside line, and choosing whether or not to use pulse dialing. You can change all these values later in the Dialing Properties dialog box.

Dialing Properties

The Dialing Properties dialog box (shown in Figure 45-2) lets you define the characteristics of the (perhaps numerous) locations you will be calling from. You will most likely define your office and/or home location right away. Define others as you need them.

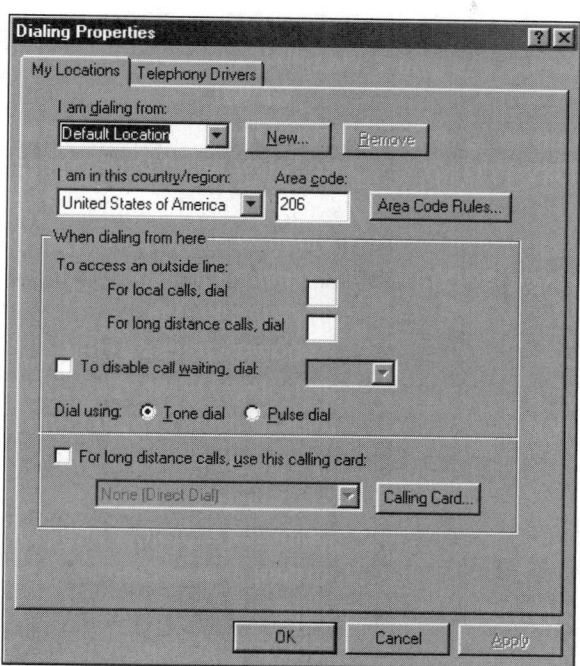

Figure 45-2: The Dialing Properties dialog box

One fast way to display the Dialing Properties dialog box is to click the Telephony icon in the Control Panel. If you access this dialog box frequently and want to create a shortcut to it, just drag and drop the Telephony icon from the Control Panel onto the Desktop.

Perhaps an even easier way to get to Dialing Properties is through the Telephony Location Manager (\Windows\System\Tlocmgr.exe), now an integrated part of Windows. Put a shortcut to this applet on your Desktop, or better yet in your \Windows\Start Menu\Programs\StartUp folder, and you'll have immediate access to the Dialing Properties box, your list of location names, and the Phone Dialer. We talk more about this in the "Telephony Location Manager" section later in this chapter.

You can also access the Dialing Properties dialog box through the Modems icon in the Control Panel or in these Windows-aware communications programs: Phone Dialer, Dial-Up Networking, HyperTerminal, and Microsoft Fax. Here are the specific methods for each program:

- Phone Dialer (Start ⇨ Programs ⇨ Accessories ⇨ Communications ⇨ Phone Dialer) — Choose Tools ⇨ Dialing Properties.

- Dial-Up Networking (Start ⇨ Programs ⇨ Accessories ⇨ Communications ⇨ Dial-Up Networking) — Click a connectoid and click the Dial Properties button in the Connect To dialog box. (Make sure the "Prompt for information before dialing" option is enabled under Connections ⇨ Settings.)

- HyperTerminal (Start ⇨ Programs ⇨ Accessories ⇨ Communications ⇨ HyperTerminal) — Click a connectoid and click the Dial Properties button in the Connect To dialog box. (Make sure the "Prompt for information before dialing" option is enabled under Connections ⇨ Settings.)

- Microsoft Fax — Open Windows Messaging, click Tools ⇨ Services, select Microsoft Fax, click Properties, click the Dialing tab, and click the Dialing Properties button.

The Dialing Properties dialog box is independent of the application that you use to call it up. It works the same for all Windows TAPI applications. All of the features discussed in this chapter are applicable to any TAPI-compliant communications software.

Setting Up a New Location

The particular characteristics of each location are stored by location name. Location names can be anything: Grandma's house, Home Office, HO with ATT, Michigan - direct, Timbuktu - pulse. When you set up a new location, choose a name that is unique and meaningful to you.

A location name stands for a location and for the unique dialing sequence used to make a phone call from there. This includes whether you use a calling card, have to dial a number to get an outside line, and so on. If the number you're dialing is in the international format (see the section later in this chapter entitled "Format for the Numbers That You Dial Out"), the information stored in the location is used to create the sequence of numbers needed to place the call correctly.

Click the New button to define a new location, and click OK when you are informed that a new location was created. Then in the "I am dialing from" field, type over the default name (New Location) with the location name you want to use.

Each location should have an area code. The "Area code" field can accommodate a number up to 29 digits in length, but your entry will most likely be no more than 5 digits in length. A location should also have a country code, since each country has its own set of rules for dialing local, long-distance, and international calls. The drop-down list contains more than 200 country codes, so you'll probably be able to find yours. However, if your country code or dialing rules have changed recently or your country is not on the list, you may need to edit your `Telephon.ini` file to correct this. See the "Telephon.ini" and "Changes in International Dialing Access Codes" later in this chapter.

You can set up rules for how to use the area code in dialing. Click the Area Code Rules button. In the Area Code Rules dialog box, mark the "Always dial the area code (10-digit dialing)" checkbox if your location always requires you to dial the area code first.

You'll also see a box under "When calling within my area code" for entering prefixes (the first three digits after the area code) that are in the area code for your location but are long distance and therefore require you to dial 1 first. Click New to the right of this box to enter these prefixes. You may also need to dial other area codes from your location that are not long distance, and therefore don't require you to dial 1 first. Click the New button next to the box under "When calling to other area codes" to enter these area codes.

Defining How to Dial Out

Your location may require that you enter a number to get an outside line. You might also have to enter a long-distance access number to get a line that is used for special billing purposes. You may have multiple such billing numbers at work. If this is the case, you could set up separate locations for each billing number.

Tip

Call waiting can interfere with modem access. If the line you are using at a given location has the call waiting feature, you need to turn it off for the duration of your call when you are using a modem. In the U.S., you normally disable call waiting by dialing *70, 70#, or 1170. These three choices are displayed in the drop-down list to the right of the call waiting checkbox.

You have the choice of pulse or tone dialing with your modem. If the local telephone office can handle only pulse dialing, you need to mark that option button.

Credit Card Calls

The procedures for making credit cards calls (or for using a specific long-distance carrier) are uniform enough in most cases for you to automate them. Windows includes specific phone numbers for some long-distance carriers (AT&T, British Telecom, MCI, U.S. Sprint, and others), and you can add more to the basic list. Information on long-distance carriers and calling card numbers is a part of the location definition, so you can have different location names for the same physical location but with different calling cards.

To specify a specific long-distance carrier, or to bill calls from the location that you are defining to a calling card, mark the "For long distance calls, use this calling card" checkbox, and then click the Calling Card button. The Calling Card dialog box appears, as shown in Figure 45-3. Click this same button if you need to change the settings for a calling card.

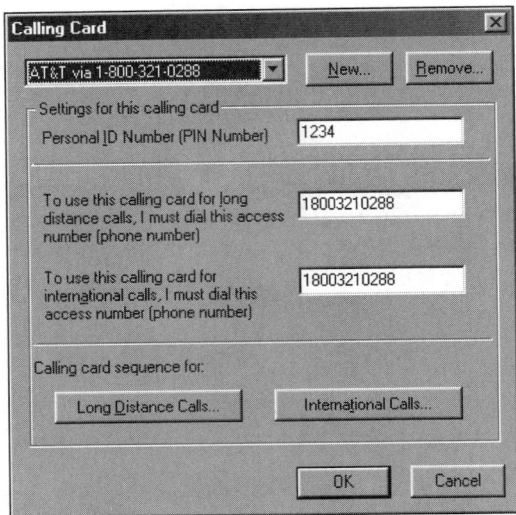

Figure 45-3: The Calling Card dialog box

The drop-down list at the top of the dialog box by default contains 23 calling card numbers from numerous long-distance vendors, including AT&T, British Telecom, Carte France Telecom, MCI, Telecom Australia, U.S. Sprint, and others. If the list includes the long-distance carrier that you want to use, select it and enter your PIN number. Then check to make sure that the access numbers shown for your card are correct, and change them if necessary. Your card number will be encrypted when it is stored on your hard disk in the `Telephon.ini` file and the registry. If you want to add a calling card that's not on this list, see the next section.

Adding a Long-Distance Carrier/Method to Your List

If your long-distance carrier is not on the list in the Calling Card dialog box, or if you want to access your carrier through another method, you can use the steps below to create a new carrier listing. You can also use these steps to define another dialing method to match your situation. The Calling Card Sequence dialog box is not only useful for entering information about calling cards and accessing long-distance carriers, you can also use it to dial a string of numbers that you need for other purposes.

STEPS

Adding a New Long-Distance Carrier

Step 1. Click the New button in the Calling Card dialog box to display the Create New Calling Card dialog box. Type a name to identify a carrier or a method. Click OK. Click OK again when you see a message box informing you that you must enter dialing rules in order to use this calling card.

Step 2. In the Calling Card dialog box, enter your PIN and the access numbers (phone numbers to dial) for long-distance and international calls.

Step 3. Now click the Long Distance Calls button at the bottom of this box. The Calling Card Sequence dialog box appears, as shown in Figure 45-4.

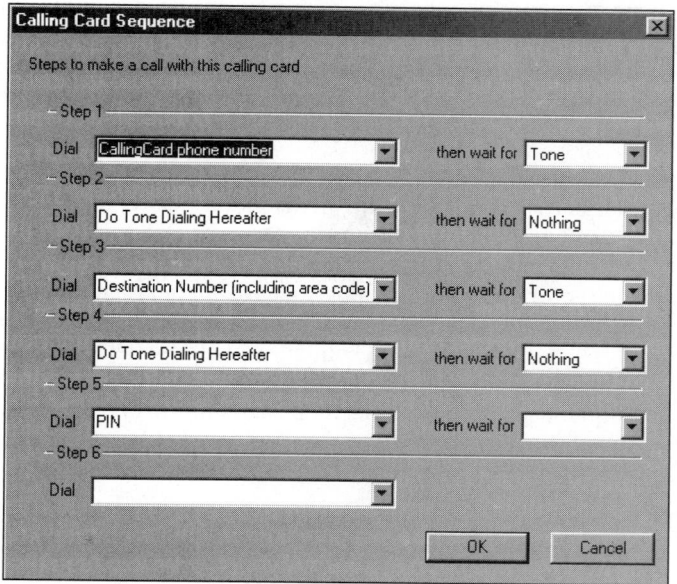

Figure 45-4: The Calling Card Sequence dialog box. When you first display this dialog box, the fields contain a suggested sequence of steps, which you can change using the drop-down arrows.

Step 4. You use the Calling Card Sequence dialog box to enter the steps you must go through to make a long-distance call. Windows starts you out with some suggestions in the first three fields. You can click the drop-down arrow for each field to select from a list of choices for that step, or you can type a number if necessary.

Continued

Step 5.   When you have finished entering the dialing sequence for long-distance calls, click OK. Now click the International Calls button in the Calling Card dialog box and enter the dialing sequence for international calls as you did in step 4. Click OK.

Step 6.   Click OK in the Calling Card dialog box, and then click OK again to exit the Dialing Properties box. You have defined the properties of a given location as well as a new long-distance carrier.

The Dialing Rules

Each of the long-distance carriers/methods has a set of three templates of dialing rules: local, long distance, and international. You can add a long-distance carrier to your list and edit the dialing rules to match those required by that carrier. The templates are not associated with particular long-distance carriers; you can use them to define any dialing method.

The templates of dialing rules are a series of numbers, letters, and punctuation marks that you type in the fields in the Calling Card Sequence dialog box. When a number is dialed, these rules are read and carried out. When you use the drop-down lists in the Calling Card Sequence dialog box, Windows adds these characters to your `Telephon.ini` file and registry for you. You don't need to know what the template really looks like; you just describe the steps. However, if you need to indicate a sequence of steps that is not covered by the drop-down lists, you can also enter the template manually in the Calling Card Sequence box. Select Specified Digits in the desired drop-down list, and then type the characters you need. You can type entries in some fields and use the drop-down list in others.

You can also create new dialing rules by entering these number and character sequences in your `Telephon.ini` file. The registry will update itself based on the `Telephon.ini` file. We discuss how to edit `Telephon.ini` later in the "Telephon.ini" section. Here is an example template of dialing rules:

```
1 - (800) 674-7000 $TH$T01EFG
```

This is a variation on the template for international dialing shown in Figure 45-4 in the previous section. The rules in this template are as follows:

1. Dial the number 1 - (800) 674-7000.

2. Wait for the "bong" tone ($).

3. Using touch tone, send the calling card number (TH).

4. Wait again for the "bong" tone ($).

5. Using touch tone, send 01 (T01).

6. Send the country code, area code, and local number (EFG).

Spaces, hyphens, periods, and parentheses are ignored.

The dialing rules shown in Table 45-1 let you complete a phone call throughout much of the world.

Table 45-1   Dialing Rules

Code	Represents
0-9	Number to be dialed
#	Touch tone pound sign
*	Touch tone star
!	Hook flash
,	Pause for two seconds
@	Wait for a ringing tone followed by five seconds of silence
$	Wait for the calling card tone — the "bong" tone
?	Prompt user for input
E	Country code
F	Area code
G	Local phone number
T	Dial the following number using touch tone
P	Dial the following number using pulse dialing
W	Wait for a second dial tone
H	Your calling card number

Waiting for the "Bong"

Secret

Your modem may not support the option of waiting for the "bong" tone. If it doesn't, it will ignore the $ and dial your calling card number before the phone company is ready to receive it.

If this happens, try substituting the @ symbol for the $ in your version of the dialing rules. Your modem may respond to this. If not, you can also substitute four commas (,,,, instead of $) to force an eight-second wait until the calling card number is sent.

Suppressing the 1 Prefix

Your company's phone system may dial the prefix 1 for you when you dial long-distance numbers. You can use the Calling Card dialog box to create a set of dialing rules that suppresses the prefix 1 for all of the calls you make from work:

STEPS

Creating Dialing Rules to Suppress the 1 Prefix

Step 1. Click the Start button, point to Settings, and click Control Panel. Click the Telephony icon to open the Dialing Properties dialog box.

Step 2. Click the New button, click OK, and then type a name that describes your office location and phone system.

Step 3. Mark the "For long distance calls, use this calling card" checkbox. Click the Calling Card button. Click the New button, type a description for the dialing method used at your office (perhaps a name that describes the dialing rules), and click OK.

Step 4. Click the Long Distance Calls button. In the Step 1 Dial field, select "Destination Number (including area code)" from the drop-down list, and click OK.

Step 5. Click the International Calls button. In the Step 1 Dial field, select Specified Digits from the drop-down list, type **011**, and click OK. Then fill in the four fields listed here, choosing the indicated options from the drop-down lists:

Field	Option
Step 1 Then wait for	Nothing
Step 2 Dial	Destination country/region
Step 2 Then wait for	Nothing
Step 3 Dial	Destination Number (including area code)

Step 6. Click OK three times.

Format for the Numbers That You Dial Out

Windows-aware communications applications use certain styles to designate numbers that can be dialed out. The most flexible style is the international style:

+CC (AC) LocalNumber

The plus sign, spaces, and parentheses are all required elements of this format. CC is the country code, which in the U.S. is 1. AC is the area code. There is a space between the country code and the area code and a space between the area code and the local number. The local number can have hyphens in it.

If you enter a number in this format, you can call it from anywhere. If you are calling it from the same area code in the same country, TAPI-compliant software won't use the area code and country code (unless you specify to dial this number as a long-distance number — see the next section).

If you want to dial a number such as 911 or an extension number within your company, you shouldn't put the number in the international format. Just type it as is.

You can type phone numbers in Phone Dialer, as shown in the section entitled "Setting Up Speed-Dial Numbers" later in this chapter.

Secret

Dial-Up Networking and HyperTerminal connectoids automatically format phone numbers in the international format. You can change this by clearing the "Use area code and dialing properties" checkbox in any connection's Properties dialog box. To get to this checkbox, right-click the appropriate connectoid in the Dial-Up Networking or HyperTerminal folder window and click Properties.

If you clear the "Use area code and dialing properties" checkbox, the software sends only the phone number as you have entered it. It doesn't use any of the location properties from the Dialing Properties dialog box to format the sequence of numbers sent when you make this call.

Which Local Prefixes Require Long-Distance Dialing

Secret

Windows-aware communication applications assume that all phone numbers with the same local area code as your location's area code are local numbers; that is, they can be reached without dialing a 1 followed by the area code. This may not be the case, however, so you need a way of telling applications which numbers are not really local to a given location.

Windows allows you to indicate which prefixes (the first three numbers of a local phone number) are long-distance numbers with respect to a given location. It assumes that any local number you enter with one of these prefixes requires the long-distance dialing rules.

To tell Windows which prefixes in the area code of a given location require long-distance dialing, click the Area Code Rules button in the Dialing Properties box to display the Area Code Rules dialog box, as shown in Figure 45-5. Click the New button under "When calling within my area code." Enter a prefix that requires long-distance dialing, and click OK. Repeat this process for each of the prefixes you need to dial that require long-distance dialing. You can indicate whether the area code is required in addition to a 1, by marking the "Always dial the area code (10-digit dialing)" checkbox.

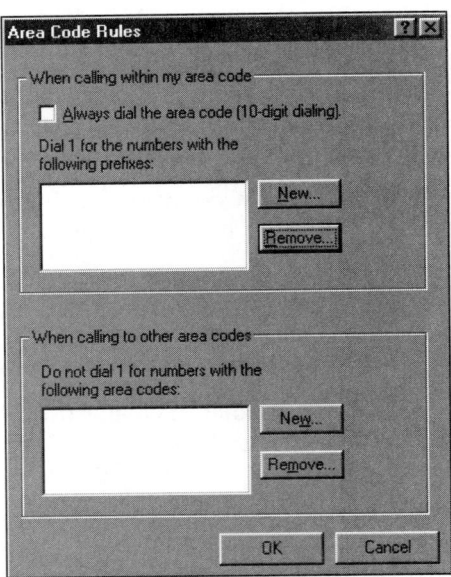

Figure 45-5: The Area Code Rules dialog box. Use it to specify prefixes that require long-distance dialing.

Now whenever you call from that location, TAPI-compliant applications will automatically dial phone numbers with these prefixes as long-distance calls. The list of prefixes that require long-distance calls is stored in the [Locations] section of the Telephon.ini file. See the section entitled "Telephon.ini" later in this chapter to find out how to read this file.

Ten-Digit Phone Numbers

You may live in an area that requires you to dial the area code and the phone number even to make a local call. In these areas, the prefix 1 is not used, and local calls may have different area codes. Go to the Dialing Properties box and click the Area Code Rules button to get to the Area Code Rules dialog box. At the top of the box, mark the "Always dial the area code (10-digit dialing)" checkbox to enable this option.

If there are some area codes that do not require you to dial 1 first, you can enter them in the "When calling to other area codes" section in the lower half of the Area Code Rules dialog box. Click New to add an area code, and then click OK.

Using a Prefix Other Than 1 to Dial Long Distance

Perhaps in your location you use a number other than 1 to begin a long distance call. To configure Windows for this situation, follow these steps:

STEPS

Using a Number Other Than 1 to Begin a Long-Distance Call

Step 1. Click the Start button, point to Settings, and then click Control Panel. Click the Telephony icon to open the Dialing Properties dialog box.

Step 2. Click the Calling Card button. Click the New button. Type a description for the dialing method that describes these dialing rules. Click OK.

Step 3. Click the Long Distance Calls button. In the Step 1 Dial field, choose "Specific digits" from the drop-down list. Type the long-distance prefix for your phone system (this could be a whole string of digits if necessary—your office security code, for example) and click OK. In the Step 1 "then wait for" field, choose Nothing from the drop-down list.

Step 4. In the Step 2 Dial field, choose "Destination Number (including area code)."

Step 5. Click the OK button three times.

Phone Dialer

If ever there was an application that is in fact an applet, it is Phone Dialer. This program uses your modem to dial your phone for you. You then pick up the phone and speak with the person whose number your modem dialed. Of course, the phone and the modem must be on the same phone line for this to work.

Microsoft didn't intend Phone Dialer to be a serious application. It is just an example to developers of how they can use the facilities provided by Windows to create full-fledged communications applications. Unless you have a shortcut to Phone Dialer on your Desktop so that you can get at it quickly, or you have to dial a long string of numbers to place a call (as you might if you're using a calling card), you won't use Phone Dialer, because it is more work than just dialing the number on your phone.

Phone Dialer uses the information in the Dialing Properties dialog box to make phone calls. It can store up to eight phone numbers on its speed-dial buttons, and it keeps a record of the last 20 numbers you called. It can prompt you to keep a record of the phone numbers of calls coming in and/or going out. Phone Dialer is shown in Figure 45-6.

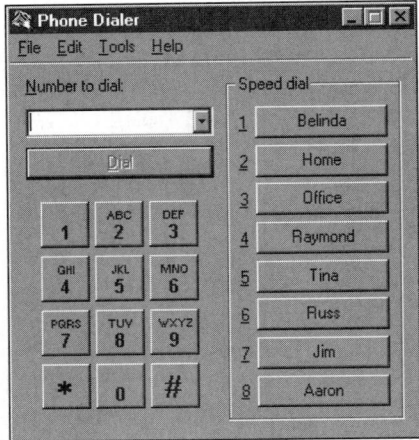

Figure 45-6: Phone Dialer. Click a speed-dial button, and Phone Dialer will dial the number for you if your modem is hooked up to your phone line.

Setting Up Speed-Dial Numbers

You can define the eight blank speed-dial buttons to dial a number when you click the button, just like on a real phone. This is the productivity benefit of Phone Dialer.

STEPS

Setting Up the Speed Dialer

Step 1.   Click the Start button, point to Programs ➪ Accessories ➪ Communications, and then click Phone Dialer.

Step 2.   Choose Edit ➪ Speed Dial.

Step 3.   Click the button that you want to define in the Edit Speed Dial dialog box. Type the person's name and phone number. Repeat this step for all the buttons that you want to define.

Step 4.   Click the Save button when you are done.

Step 5. If you want to quickly define a single blank button in Phone Dialer, just click the button, enter the person's name and phone number in the Program Speed Dial dialog box, and click Save or Save and Dial.

When you're entering numbers for the speed-dial buttons, use the international style if you want the numbers to be dialed correctly from any location.

Secret

The speed-dial phone numbers and the last 20 phone numbers you have dialed with Phone Dialer are stored in the `Dialer.ini` file in the `\Windows` folder. You can edit this file with Notepad if you like. `Dialer.ini` also stores the position of Phone Dialer on the Desktop and log book information.

Telephony Location Manager

A handy applet for changing dialing locations as well as getting to Phone Dialer and the Dialing Properties dialog box is the Telephony Location Manager (`\Windows\System\Tlocmgr.exe`). When you click `Tlocmgr.exe`, it puts itself in your tray until you shut down your computer. If you would like it to always be in your tray, put a shortcut to `Tlocmgr.exe` in your `\Windows\Start Menu\Programs\StartUp` folder.

When you click the Telephony Location Manager icon in the tray, a list of your dialing locations appears to let you change your location without opening the Dialing Properties dialog box. When you right-click the icon, a context menu appears with options to start Phone Dialer or open the Dialing Properties box. If you are using a laptop with a docking station, this context menu may also include a HOTDOCK Properties command for changing locations automatically when you dock or undock.

Telephon.ini

The `Telephon.ini` file is stored in the `\Windows` folder. It stores data about your locations and calling cards, as well as pointers to applications that use the telephony services provided by Windows. Windows updates the registry based on what it finds in `Telephon.ini`.

In Windows 95, there were no telephony keys in the registry; all telephony was managed by `Telephon.ini`. We think `Telephon.ini` is still probably easier to edit. However, if you prefer to edit the registry directly, the relevant keys are HKEY_CURRENT_USER\Software\Microsoft\Windows\CurrentVersion\Telephony and HKEY_LOCAL_MACHINE\SOFTWARE\Microsoft\Windows\CurrentVersion\Telephony.

If you don't have any stored locations or calling card data, you may have a damaged or missing `Telephon.ini` file. You can create a new one (which will be missing your special edits) by clicking the file `Tapiini.exe` in the `\Windows\System` folder.

The sections in `Telephon.ini` of interest to us are the [Locations] section and [Cards] section.

Locations Section

Here is an example of a line in the [Locations] section:

```
Location1=1, "Home," "9","","206",1,0,0,1,"357,847",0," "
```

Here is how to interpret the line:

```
Locationx=ID, "location name", "# (number) for outside line", "#
(number) for long-distance line", "area code", countrycode, card ID,
previous card ID, use area codes, "LD prefixes"
```

These and other variables are listed in Table 45-2.

Table 45-2   Location Variables

Variable	Stands For
x	Ordered sequence of location numbers.
ID	The location's identification number.
location name	Your name for the location.
# for outside line	The prefix you have to dial to get an outside line.
# for LD line	The number you have to dial to get a long-distance line.
area code	Area code.
countrycode	Country code.
card ID	If a calling card is used, this is its ID; otherwise, it is 0 for direct dialing.
previous card ID	The previous calling card ID before its last modification.
use area codes	If 1, then dial local phone numbers with prefixes listed in the LD prefixes (next variable) using the area code. This is true only in North America, only if the country code and the area code for the number being dialed are the same as the current location, and only if the prefix of the number being dialed is listed in LD prefixes. If 0, then don't include the area code before the local call number.
LD prefixes	List of prefixes that are long-distance calls from Locationx.

Cards Section

The [Cards] section stores the data about the calling card methods. These methods don't have to be calling cards exactly, but they can include any alternative dialing methods that can use a special phone number and/or a user code number. You can define these calling methods yourself using the methods detailed in the "Adding a Long-Distance Carrier/Method to Your List" section. Here's an example:

```
Card12=1, "AT&T Direct Dial via
10ATT1","55041111938112","102881FG","102881FG","10288011EFG",1
```

The format of this line is as follows.

```
Cardx=ID, "card name", "encrypted card", "local call", "long-
distance", "international", hidden
```

These and other variables are shown in Table 45-3.

Table 45-3	Card Variables
Variable	**Stands For**
x	Ordered sequence of card numbers
ID	Card ID
card name	Your dialing method name
encrypted card	Your card number encrypted
local call	The dialing rules for making a local call
long-distance	The dialing rules for making a long-distance call
international	The dialing rules for making an international call
hidden 0,1,2,3	Whether or not this calling card method is displayed as an available dialing method
0	Not hidden
1	Not hidden — values can only be set up by an application
2	Hidden
3	Hidden — values can only be set up by an application

Changes in International Dialing Access Codes

Between the original version of Windows 95 and the release of Windows 98, the international dialing access codes (codes you dial to access international long distance) changed for 40 countries. Even more have changed since then, and it seems reasonable to expect that more country codes will change in the future. You can revise them by editing your Telephon.ini file or your registry.

The rules for how to dial local, long-distance, and international calls from any given country are also constantly changing. Windows Me comes with updated sets of rules for the countries that have changed recently. When you install Windows Me, the updates are automatically written into the [CountryOverrides] section of your `Telephon.ini` file, and consequently into your registry. If the dialing rules change for the country you are dialing from, you will need to edit them in `Telephon.ini`.

Microsoft maintains a Knowledge Base article that lets you easily update your `Telephon.ini` file to incorporate changes in the country codes and country dialing rules. You can find it at `http://support.microsoft.com/ support/kb/articles/Q142/3/28.asp`. Check the date on the Knowledge Base document to make sure it is more recent than what you already have, then copy the last part of the article into your `Telephon.ini` file, which is stored in the `\Windows` folder. You can't just add one country, since the number sequence is important; paste in the whole section instead.

Summary

We focus on how to work with the Dialing Properties dialog box to define the properties of each location you dial out from. The Dialing Properties dialog box is used by all Windows-aware communications applications.

▶ We show you how to define each of your dialing locations.

▶ We describe how to use calling cards or alternative dialing methods with your modem or voice calls.

▶ We show you how to tell communications applications just which local phone prefixes require long-distance dialing.

▶ We show you how to use Phone Dialer as a speed dialer.

Chapter 46

Power Management

In This Chapter

Power management has always been a hit and miss item, with Windows and BIOSes not quite on the same page. You can come to a provisional détente, but don't expect total victory.

▶ If you want to schedule a task to run when your computer is suspended (it has to wake up), you might be able to. We tell you how.

▶ Windows and the BIOS fight to see who is in charge of power management. You can put Windows in charge, most of the time.

▶ If you've set your BIOS to enable power management, you can force Windows to reinstall power management.

▶ Will it all work out in the future? Maybe.

Schedule Tasks to Start When Your Computer's Asleep

You may have, knowingly or unknowingly, configured Windows' Maintenance Wizard to set up a schedule of tasks to be run late at night. The wizard assumes that this is when you'd like these housekeeping tasks to occur. But if you turn your computer off at night, none of the essential mopping and dusting ever gets done, until you are forced by system slowdowns to do it yourself during billable hours.

To check your existing schedule of tasks, open your Explorer and click Scheduled Tasks under the Control Panel under My Computer. You'll see a list of tasks and their scheduled times and dates, as shown in Figure 46-1.

You can reschedule any task for a more appropriate date and time by right-clicking it, clicking Properties, and clicking the Schedule tab.

You'll want to make sure that at least the tasks originally scheduled by the Maintenance Wizard are carried out. If you let your computer run WinAlign (referred to in Scheduled Tasks as Tune-Up Application Start) and Defrag, your most heavily used applications will load faster and your data files will also load more quickly because they are more likely to be contiguous. Again, this is only going to happen if you let it.

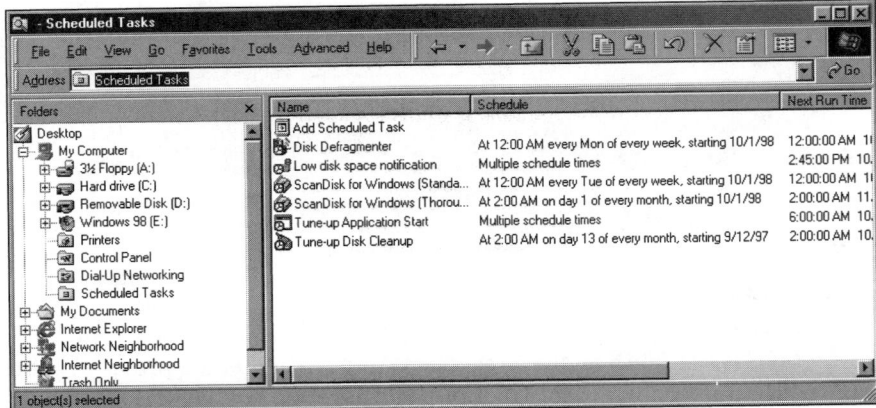

Figure 46-1: Scheduled Tasks is a special Explorer folder that keeps track of all the tasks you have scheduled.

If you have a computer whose BIOS supports at least Advanced Power Management (APM) 1.2, you'll be able to let your computer go to sleep at night, and it will wake up at the scheduled times to take carry out the scheduled tasks. We often turn off our computers because they are wasting electrical power, because the fan is noisy, or because turning it off creates less wear on the hard disk. Letting the computer go to sleep solves these problems. As long as it will wake up to take care of its nighttime duties, then we've got the best of both worlds.

To check what level of power management your computer can support, take these steps:

STEPS

Checking Your Level of Power Management Support

Step 1.   Press Win+Pause/Break (or right-click My Computer and click Properties).

Step 2.   Click the Device Manager tab.

Step 3.   Scroll down to System Devices, and click the plus sign.

Step 4.   Click Advanced Power Management Support, and click the Properties button.

Step 5.   Click the Settings tab to see your level of Advanced Power Management support, as illustrated in Figure 46-2.

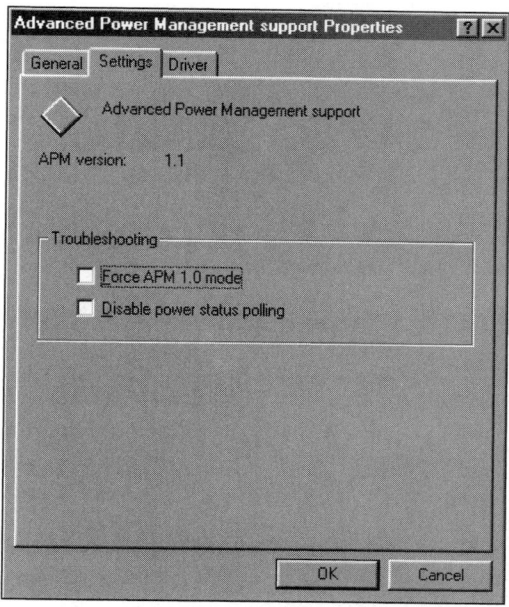

Figure 46-2: The computer in this example can support only APM 1.1 or lower.

If your computer can support at least APM 1.2, you'll find the "Wake the computer to run this task" checkbox in the Settings tab for each individual task, as shown in Figure 46-3. (Click the Scheduled Tasks icon in your Explorer, right-click a task, click Properties, and click the Settings tab.)

Mark this checkbox if you want the computer to be woken up to carry out this task. This is the default action.

A Microsoft Knowledge Base article states that this checkbox may exist even if your computer doesn't support at least APM 1.2. However, it won't work unless your computer does support APM 1.2. You'll find the article " 'Wake the Computer to Run This Task' Feature May Not Work," at http://support. microsoft.com/support/kb/articles/q188/6/24.asp.

Tip

If your computer doesn't support APM 1.2, you might think about letting it stay on overnight once a week or once a month. Schedule all of the tasks for that night, in order (ScanDisk first) and about an hour apart (see "Reschedule Maintenance if Your Computer Doesn't Stay Up All Night in Chapter 14).

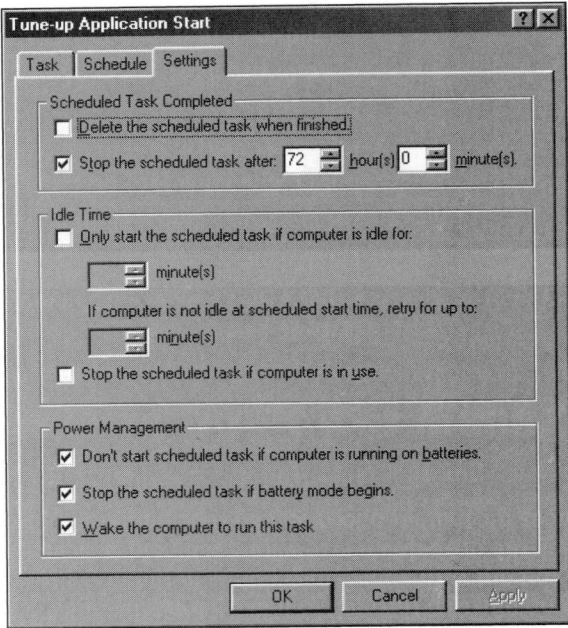

Figure 46-3: The power management settings for APM 1.2 or higher include the additional setting "Wake the computer to run this task."

Let Windows Do Power Management

If you have a new computer that fully and completely supports the Microsoft-defined Advanced Configuration and Power Interface (ACPI), then you can fully control your computer's standby, disk spin down, monitor turnoff, and power management features. All you have to do is go to your Control Panel and click the Power Management icon.

If you have an older computer whose BIOS supports Advanced Power Management, either APM 1.1 or APM 1.2, you may find that controlling the power management settings is not quite so easy. Your computer's BIOS and the Windows Power Management control panel are fighting to see whose settings should be used. Because you can set the power management features in either location, your computer doesn't know whom to believe.

If you want to control your computer's power management features through the Windows 98 Power Management control panel, you'll need to reset the values for power management in your BIOS. To do this, click Start ➪ Shut Down ➪ Restart ➪ OK.

When your computer restarts (reboots), press the indicated key that allows you to set up your BIOS. Sometimes computers are configured so that you aren't given any indication on the screen of what this key is. You'll need help from the person that set up your computer in this case. Try pressing Esc or F2 during the power-on self-test.

In the BIOS setup window, go to the power management features menu. Make sure that APM is enabled. Now, disable the power management mode—not power management itself, but all the timing settings, if you have any. If there are timing settings in the BIOS that are not reflected in similar settings in your Windows Power Management control panel, do not disable power management mode for them. Instead, customize the values for each of these settings.

For those BIOS power management settings that are replicated in the Window Power Management control panel, either disable their settings in the BIOS or set them to the largest value available. You can then use the control panel to set these values. The unfortunate consideration here is that the terminology used in these BIOS settings may not be reflected in the control panel, so it is sometimes difficult to understand which setting is which.

The Power Management control panel for APM 1.1, shown in Figure 46-4, has only two settings: initiate system standby and turn off monitor. APM 1.2 has an additional setting for spinning down the hard disk. When you configure your power management settings in your BIOS, be aware that these are the only settings that you can control in the Windows Power Management control panel, if your BIOS only supports APM and not ACPI.

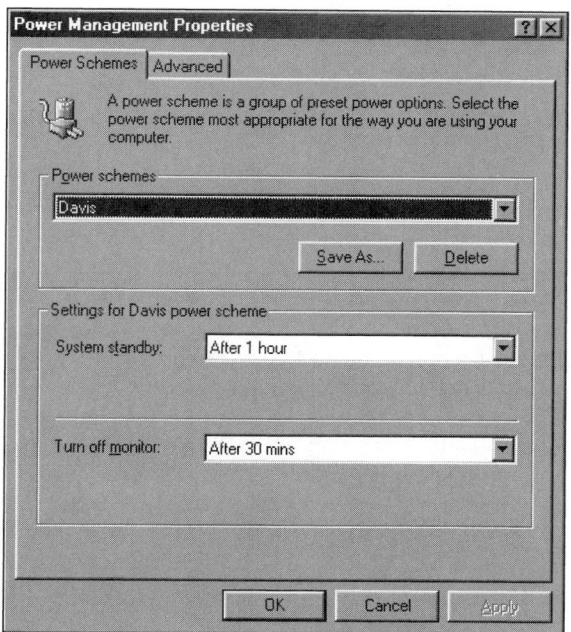

Figure 46-4: The Power Management Properties dialog box for APM version 1.1 has only two settings. If you have version 1.2, you'll see an additional setting.

Advanced Configuration and Power Interface

When you set up Windows Me or 98, ACPI is installed only on those systems that Microsoft had certified as ACPI compliant at the time of the release of that version of Windows. Your computer may not have been on the list when your copy of Windows was released.

Secret

If you are sure that your computer is ACPI compliant and you want to give this version of power management a try, you can force the ACPI driver to be installed. Here's how:

STEPS

Forcing ACPI Installation

Step 1. Click Start ➪ Run, type **regedit**, and press Enter.

Step 2. Navigate to HKEY_LOCAL_MACHINE\ SOFTWARE\ Microsoft\ Windows\ CurrentVersion\ Detect. Highlight this key in the left pane of your Registry Editor.

Step 3. Right-click the right pane, and click New ➪ String Value.

Step 4 Rename the string value **ACPIOption**.

Step 5. Double-click ACPIOption in the right pane, type the value **1**, and click OK. Exit the Registry Editor.

Step 6. Click Start ➪ Settings ➪ Control Panel ➪ Add New Hardware. Click Next twice, and have the wizard search for new hardware.

You can remove ACPI support by changing this value to **2** and running the Add New Hardware Wizard again.

A more detailed discussion of this process can be found in the Microsoft Knowledge Base article "How to Enable ACPI Support in Windows" at http://support.microsoft.com/support/kb/articles/q195/2/18.asp. You can also keep track of the latest developments in the slow progress toward OnNow technology by reviewing Microsoft's "Update on Windows Retail Upgrade for ACPI System" at http://www.microsoft.com/hwdev/desinit/retailup.htm. (OnNow is a Microsoft initiative that is supposed to provide standards that let computer manufacturers put their computers into a sleep state, and then restore your last configuration and state of your work almost instantly when the computers are revived.)

Get Stand By Back in Your Shut Down Windows Dialog Box

You'll find the Stand By option in your Shut Down Windows dialog box if your computer supports Automated Power Management (APM) or the Advanced Configuration and Power Interface (ACPI). It's possible to lose this option if there are some problems with your Standby mode.

You will lose the Stand By option if you received the following message in a dialog box and answered yes: "The last few times your computer went on standby it stopped responding. Would you like to prevent your computer from going on standby in the future?" You will also lose this option if your computer stopped responding while in Standby mode two times in a row.

If you have changed the APM configuration in your BIOS, or if you never had it properly configured, you will not have the Stand By option in your Shut Down Windows dialog box.

Secret

If you previously had the Stand By option and now it is gone, and if you haven't changed your BIOS, you can take these steps to get it back:

STEPS

Retrieving Your Stand By Option

Step 1.   Start your Registry Editor (\Windows\regedit.exe).

Step 2.   Navigate to HKEY_LOCAL_MACHINE\ System\ CurrentControlSet\ Services\ VxD\ VPOWERD.

Step 3.   In the right pane of your Registry Editor, you should see entries for Flags and SuspendFlag, as shown in Figure 46-5.

Step 4.   Double-click the Flags value and verify that its value is greater than or equal to 200. If it is, subtract 200 from its current value and type the new value. Click OK.

Step 5.   If the SuspendFlag value is not already 0, double-click SuspendFlag and enter the value **0**. Click OK.

Step 6.   Exit the Registry Editor and restart Windows.

Continued

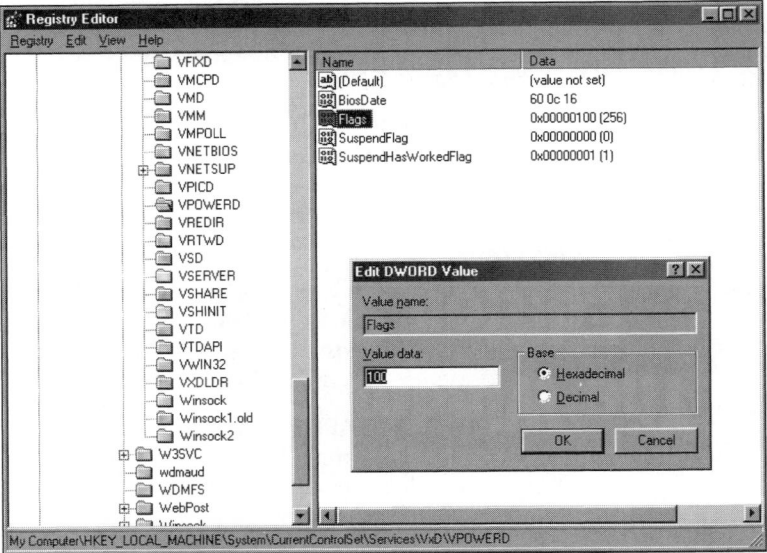

Figure 46-5: The registry entries for Flags and SuspendFlag should appear in the right pane.

If you never had the Stand By option or if you lost it after making changes to your computer's BIOS, you need to make sure that you have some form of power management built into your computer and operating. Otherwise, you can't go into Standby mode.

Reinstalling Power Management

You can restore Standby mode without editing your registry by removing Advanced Power Management from your Device Manager and then forcing Windows to autodetect all of your hardware once again (thereby reinstalling APM). You may need to use this method if you lost APM after making changes in the power management area of your BIOS.

STEPS

Reinstalling Advanced Power Management

Step 1. Reenable power management in your computer's BIOS if you have disabled it.

Step 2. Right-click your My Computer icon, click Properties, and click the Device Manager tab.

Step 3. Click the plus sign next to "System devices," as shown in Figure 46-6, highlight "Advanced Power Management support," and click Remove. Click OK.

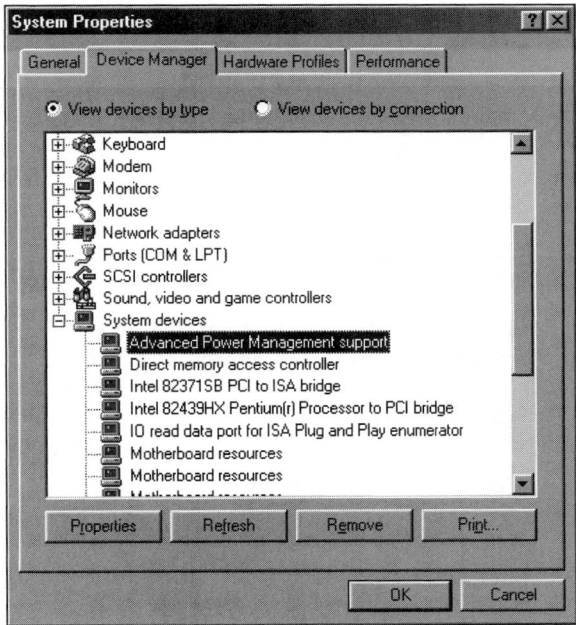

Figure 46-6: The Device Manager tab of System Properties. Click the plus sign to expand the list of system devices, and then remove "Advanced Power Management support."

Step 4. Click Start ⇨ Shut Down ⇨ Restart ⇨ and OK.

Step 5. Click Start ⇨ Settings ⇨ Control Panel ⇨ Add New Hardware ⇨ Next ⇨ and Next.

Step 6. Assuming that power management is enabled in your BIOS, Windows 98 will find it and reinstall it.

You should now have a Stand By option in your Shut Down Windows dialog box. If this is not the case, then there are probably incompatibilities between your computer's BIOS and Windows. See the next section, and look for further details in this Microsoft support article: "Standby Missing From Windows Shutdown Dialog Box" at http://support.microsoft.com/support/kb/articles/q188/1/34.asp.

Problems with Power Management

Windows' support for power management is not 100-percent foolproof, to say the least. Microsoft has had to write code that interfaces with code written by the BIOS manufacturers, and there has been little agreement in the past about how power management should be implemented.

You may have to update your BIOS to get it to work with the Windows power management features.

One of the more common problems is that Windows power management may prevent a PC from going into Standby mode because some driver or application is not ready. A different problem you may encounter is that your computer enters Standby mode normally, but you can't get out of Standby.

Microsoft has a Web page to help you troubleshoot such problems. The Advanced Power Management Troubleshooter for Windows is at `http://support.microsoft.com/support/windows/tshoot/apm98`.

The tool that is most commonly recommended by this page to determine the source of driver conflicts with power management is called `Pmtshoot.exe`. Download this 161K file from Microsoft into a temporary folder, and then run it once to install a background monitor. This monitor analyzes your next attempt to suspend or resume your computer. It can detect a driver or other program that is interfering with Standby.

Windows ships with a version of this file on its CD-ROM. You can run the file `\tools\mtsutil\pmtshoot\pmtshoot.exe` to install the monitor. However, we recommend you use the version of Pmtshoot downloadable from the Web because it is likely to be a later version with the ability to fix some problems by itself.

You can get `Pmtshoot.exe` from the Knowledge Base article "Description of the Power Management Troubleshooter Tool" at `http://support.microsoft.com/support/kb/articles/q185/9/49.asp`. Anyone who has questions about power management under Windows should read this article.

The following PC manufacturers have special issues with Windows power management. If you've upgraded or may be upgrading to Windows Me and own one of these machines, you should read the relevant information on the Web:

- **Toshiba**. With some older Toshiba notebooks, you need to update the BIOS before you install Windows Me. Although Windows Me will work, installing it before your laptop has a BIOS that explicitly supports ACPI makes it problematic to update the BIOS later. If Windows does see the updated Toshiba BIOS when installing, it will record a variety of registry settings that it would not write if you hadn't yet updated the BIOS. See `http://www.csd.toshiba.com/tais/csd/support/issues/98070001.htm` for details.

- **Gateway**. SoundBlaster audio may cause Gateway computers to lock up after resuming from Standby. Go to http://www.gateway.com/support/techdocs/software/windows/30682.html#PM.

- **Dell**. A variety of older Dell models should have a BIOS upgrade before installing Windows Me. See http://www.dell.com/98upgrade, and then click the name of the Dell product you have.

- **Compaq**. A document describing a number of quirks with Compaq hardware can be found at http://www.compaq.com/athome/international/en/win98/1215.html.

Continuing Problems with Power Management

If your computer's BIOS only supports APM, and not ACPI, then you may continue to have power management difficulties if you are unable to get a BIOS update. Computer manufacturers will volunteer the fact that earlier models don't completely support Windows Me because of this very problem. While 99.99 percent of Windows Me works just fine, power management may not.

The problems occur when your computer goes into Standby mode. It may not return from Standby, or it may return but with "flaky" behavior. Even if the Advanced Power Management Troubleshooter does not indicate a problem, that doesn't mean that there isn't one. You can follow the troubleshooting methods detailed at the Microsoft Web site given in the previous section, but they may not pertain to your problem.

If you have installed Windows Me on a computer that doesn't support ACPI, be cautious about using Standby and other power features. If they don't work for you, chalk that up to a bit of system incompatibility and just assume that you don't have that feature (in spite of what the Windows dialog boxes indicate).

USB and Standby Mode

Users have reported that their computers won't go into Standby mode if a peripheral device is plugged into their USB port. The USB port is supposed to be integrated with Windows power management. If the device is causing the problem, it may be because the device driver is not written to account for the power management modes.

You'll need to get on the Web and track down the device manufacturer's home page and see if you can download a new driver.

OnNow, ACPI, and Smart Batteries

Power management has definitely been a bear, as you can see from some of the topics discussed earlier in this chapter. The solutions to power management problems have been around for a while, but it takes time for everyone to implement them. Successful implementation requires support from the operating system (Windows Me does), the drivers (some do, some don't), and the BIOSes.

Tip

If you are looking for a new computer, especially if it is a portable, make sure that it supports the OnNow, ACPI, and Smart Batteries power-management features. To learn more about them, start at http://www.microsoft.com/hwdev/desinit/ONNOW1.HTM and http://www.microsoft.com/hwdev/desinit/wakeup.htm.

FAT32 and Suspend to Disk

Some computers have a suspend-to-disk function that allows the computer to write the current contents of memory to the hard disk and go into a Suspend mode. When the computer wakes up, it writes the previously written memory content back into memory. This function can be handled by the computer's BIOS, independently of the operating system's power management facilities.

The BIOS can write the current contents of memory to the disk and recover it without using any operating system resources. Unless the BIOS is of recent origin, though, it most likely won't be able to write to a FAT32 formatted hard drive. The BIOS expects to find a FAT16 formatted drive.

If you find that your computer can't suspend to disk after you've converted your hard disk to FAT32, you may be able to get a BIOS upgrade from your computer manufacturer — but the odds aren't good. Navigate to the manufacturer's support Web page and see what their story is.

Summary

First there was Advanced Power Management, but that relied on the BIOS to manage power. Then there was ACPI, but that relied on the BIOS to support it. Someday we'll have the operating system, the drivers, and the BIOS in sync.

▶ If your computer is ACPI compliant, you can force it to be installed.

▶ If you lose the Stand By option in your Shut Down Windows dialog box, you can get it back.

▶ Each computer manufacturer has its own unique problems with power management.

▶ Your computer may have a suspend-to-disk feature, but it may not understand FAT32.

Chapter 47

Multimedia

In This Chapter

Sounds, video, CD-ROM players, MP3 players, and worldwide radio tuners. The computer is an entertainment machine.

▶ Make sure you can get the full range of 3D sounds

▶ Find the wav file you are looking for

▶ Microsoft provides a cool CD player with Windows

▶ Surround yourself in 3D video on the Web

▶ Web-TV and the Web are integrated, so you can type channels in your Address bar

▶ Make sure that you have the right driver for your ATI card

▶ Use handy shortcuts for Web-TV

▶ MP3 and Winamp — play that downloadable CD-ROM music

Enable Surround Sound

Just because you have the speakers set up for surround sound doesn't mean that your computer is set up to deliver it. You can check to make sure it is by using the Multimedia icon in your Control Panel.

STEPS

Enabling Surround Sound

Step 1. Click Start ⇨ Settings ⇨ Control Panel ⇨ Multimedia.

Step 2. Click the Advanced Properties button in the Playback section of the Audio tab.

Step 3. Display the Speaker Setup drop-down list, scroll down to the bottom, and select Surround Sound Speakers, as shown in Figure 47-1. Click OK.

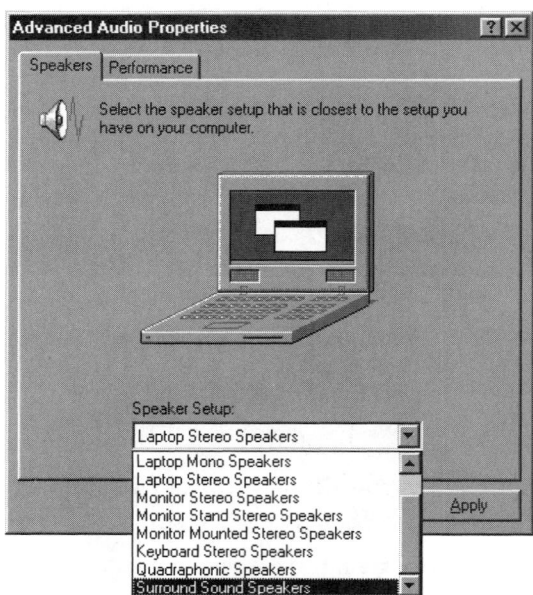

Figure 47-1: The Speakers tab of the Advanced Audio Properties dialog box lets you select the kind of speakers you're using.

Thanks to Adam Vujic for pointing out this tip.

Find That Special Sound File

Now that you have 3D surround sound and a 45-watt subwoofer, maybe you should have the coolest wav files to attach to each and every Windows "event." One of the earliest uses of the Web, after it became accessible to ordinary people, was to swap wav files. Now that the Web is all grown up, you can still use it to download wav files.

Check out the king of all wav sites, The Daily WAV at http://www.dailywav.com.

Windows Software May Render Audio CDs Increasingly Obsolete

Windows software is making big changes in the way we buy, store, and play back music in our offices and homes. The force behind this change is a music compression standard known as MP3 (Moving Pictures Experts Group 1

Layer 3). With the growth of the Internet, musicians around the world who haven't negotiated a contract with a recording label are converting their best tunes to the digital MP3 format and distributing them free as a method of promotion.

Thousands of such songs are now available on the Web. Anyone can play these selections on any multimedia computer equipped with speakers and software such as the Windows Media Player that comes with Windows.

This underground music movement might have remained unknown to most consumers if it weren't for a lawsuit filed at the beginning of the MP3 craze by the Recording Industry Association of America (RIAA). The suit, filed against Diamond Multimedia Inc. of San Jose, California, was an attempt to stop Diamond from distributing a $200 pager-sized MP3 player called Rio.

Using a parallel port adapter (with a pass-through for a printer), you downloaded MP3 files from a PC into Rio's memory. The device then played an hour or two of music through headphones or speakers. It was, at that time, the ultimate in portable music enjoyment. Unlike portable audio CD players, vibration has little or no effect on the Rio's playback. It's a lot smaller than portable CD players, too.

Special Windows software bundled with Rio units is a major factor in MP3's popularity. MusicMatch Jukebox is a shareware program that enables users to convert tracks from any audio CD into the MP3 format. Once you've converted your audio CD collection, you can use Jukebox to play songs in any specified order (or in random order) on your multimedia PC. Or you can download the songs you want onto your Rio and go anywhere with them.

Around the time of the RIAA lawsuit, Brian interviewed the owners of MusicMatch, husband and wife Dennis Mudd and Pamela Evans, at their office in a Portland, Oregon, suburb. They see an explosion of new music that multimedia PCs have made available. Their Web site, `http://www.musicmatch.com`, is a haven for international musicians who have contributed one or more songs in exchange for the ability to sell their homegrown CDs through MusicMatch.

The "fair use" provisions of copyright law allow any buyer of copyrighted music or other media to make a copy for his or her own personal use. For example, you can copy a chapter of a book to read on the bus. But what about sharing songs with others who aren't buyers of the original CD? Many of the songs found on "pirate" Web sites are pure copyright violations.

Mudd and Evans say pirate sites are quickly shut down by music-industry lawyers — and in any event there's plenty of good music to choose from that bands *want* you to share. There are now thousands of MP3 tracks to download, and lots of places to look for them.

To find music to suit your personal taste, start at `http://www.mp3.com`, a Grand Central Station for digital music. You'll also find a collection of software there, including the Nad MP3 Player (free) and the popular Winamp (see more on Winamp in the next section).

Audiofind is a useful index of music sorted by title, artist, and genre, found at http://www.audiofind.com. There are 30 different genres listed, so you're bound to find something that suits your tastes. If the alphabetical listings don't meet your needs, you can search on any word in a title or name. Audiofind also helps you buy regular audio CDs.

For a listing of dozens of other music sites, go to http://www.hot100.com/music. This Web page sorts music sites by popularity, leading you to commercial and independent sources of audio CDs, MP3 files, and much more.

If you're noticing that it's a lot of work to download all these songs one by one, you'll want to automate the process. You can do this with MP3-Wolf, a shareware program that searches the Web and downloads the type of music you like. MP3-Wolf — available from Trellian Australia, which makes several good Internet search tools — starts from a site such as Audiofind and a keyword you enter, perhaps **rock** or **jazz**. It then downloads from links that point to MP3 files with your particular emphasis.

MP3-Wolf can't listen to the songs for you and pick out the ones you'll like, of course. But it's a lot easier to choose music by listening to the files the program has downloaded for you than by downloading them individually. You can obtain MP3-Wolf from http://www.trellian.com. The free version is limited in the number of links it can index. The $25 registered version has unlimited indexing and it can download from 20 different Web sites simultaneously, using a single Internet connection.

Winamp — Computer as Music Box

Winamp is a nag-free shareware music player. It will play a wide variety of sound files, but its raison d'être is its ability to play CD-quality MP3 files. This is not the only MP3 player out there, but it is definitely one of the most sought after and respected.

The MP3 sound format is a standard used to compress and replay CD-quality sound. Microsoft has built it into Windows Me (in its Windows Media Player). So you can already play MP3 sound files without Winamp. It's just not as much fun.

Winamp comes with a CD player user interface, as you can see from Figure 47-2. You can download an MP3 music file from their site, or from one of the many provided as links within Winamp (click the icon in the upper-left corner of the Winamp player, and choose Winamp, Links). Winamp is a music front end to the MP3 portions of the Internet.

After you download an MP3 file, click the play button, and you're playing CD-quality audio recordings. Click the EQ button on the right side of the Winamp CD player to display the equalizer and control it with a slider bar.

Figure 47-2: Winamp looks like a CD player on your screen.

Want to put a new face on Winamp? Download a new "skin." For example, you might like the Earth Tone version shown in Figure 47-3. The "skin" sites are all linked in Winamp. Need an updated list of "skin" and "music" sites? Click the Update button on your Winamp CD player, and the list will be downloaded from the Winamp site.

Figure 47-3: Give your CD player a different look by changing its "skin."

Want to have a visual display of the music, as shown in Figure 47-4? Download a visual plug-in, and then download a visual plug-in player.

Figure 47-4: One of Winamp's visual plug-ins

All of this and more is available at http://www.winamp.com. Winamp is a portal to the world of Internet music.

If you develop an interest in encoding MP3 files from your music CDs or other sources, you will find shareware encoders as well as commercial converters at http://www.mp3.com and other linked sites. They also offer a CD-ROM containing a wealth of players, utilities, and the astounding number of over 1,000 freeware Winamp skins. (Some Web users have too much time on their hands.)

Because MP3-formatted music files are downloaded over the Internet (this is not a streaming audio format unless you've got a fast connection), recording companies are concerned that their copyrighted material may be stolen. You can read more about this issue at http://www.mp3.com.

EarthTuner

As we write this, we're listening over an old K modem to Australian Broadcasting System's Triple J Radio, originating in Sydney, Australia. We found Triple J by rotating the globe shown in Figure 47-5 and clicking New South Wales. Up popped a list of Australian radio and TV stations broadcasting on the Web and organized by format.

EarthTuner keeps a database of available broadcasting sites and gives you easy access around the world to the stations' Web sites (if available) and their streaming audio and video servers. With 12 preset push buttons, you can store your favorite Internet radio channels for easy retrieval.

EarthTuner uses the Real Networks RealPlayer streaming audio and video control, no doubt causing Microsoft a bit of heartburn. It will ask if you want to make it the default media player when you install it.

You'll find EarthTuner at http://www.earthtuner.com.

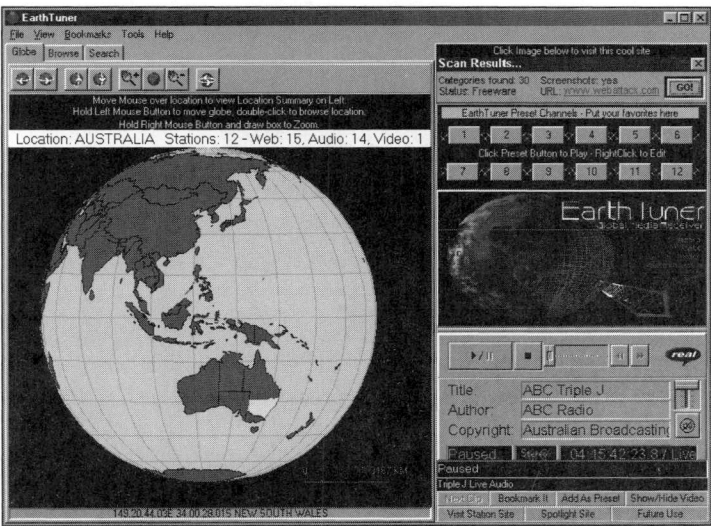

Figure 47-5: Rotate the EarthTuner globe to select a locale for radio stations that broadcast on the Web.

Built-In Radio Toolbar

Internet Explorer comes with its own radio toolbar. To access Internet Explorer's radio features, invoke the toolbar by right-clicking the Internet Explorer or Explorer toolbar and marking Radio. To display Microsoft's radio station guide, click the Radio Stations toolbar button and click Radio Station Guide.

The Speaker icon on the Radio toolbar is a general mute button. The radio volume control adds another volume control to the six already available. It appears to act as an additional control on the volume at which wav files are played.

Because the radio volume control and the wave volume control are configured so that radio volume is on top of wave volume, you'll find it quite difficult to keep the volume of Windows events low, but the volume of the radio up. To check this out for yourself, right-click your Volume Control icon in your system tray (or click Start ➪ Programs ➪ Accessories ➪ Entertainment ➪ Volume Control), and click Open Volume Controls. Then adjust the radio volume control in the Radio toolbar in your Internet Explorer and the wave volume control in the Volume Control dialog box (see Figure 47-6).

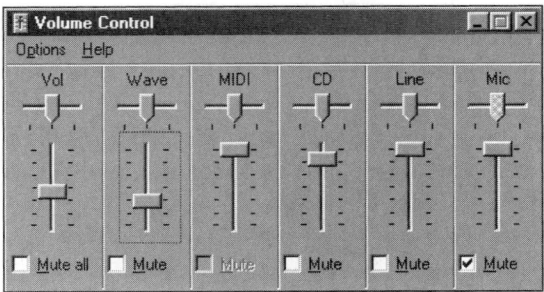

Figure 47-6: The Vol and Wave controls in the Volume Control dialog box control the volume of the radio, as does the radio volume control in the Radio toolbar. Are three volume controls enough? As it turns out, they aren't. You can't set the wave volume separately from the radio volume.

Find Your Video, Sound, Image, Icon, Midi, Wave, and Mouse Pointer Files

Your multimedia files are spread all over your computer. Wouldn't it be great to have a multimedia explorer that would seek them all out and give you quick access? Multimedia Xplorer does just that, and a lot more. This is great Estonian software.

Open Multimedia Xplorer and you'll see a version of the familiar Windows Explorer interface (see Figure 47-7). Click a filename in the lower-right pane to view the image or images or play the sound within it.

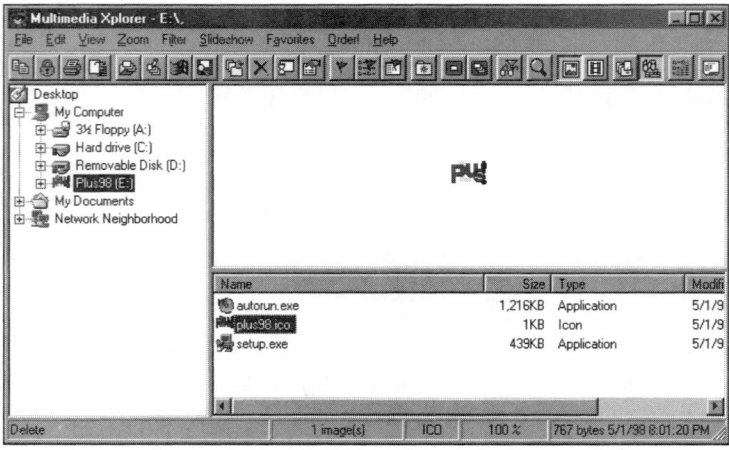

Figure 47-7: Multimedia Xplorer looks similar to the Windows Explorer, but it lets you view or play the multimedia files as you browse.

Click the Multimedia Detective toolbar button (the eighth from the left) to gather up a hierarchical list of all the files that contain images, sounds, videos, midi music, icons, or mouse pointers, as shown in Figure 47-8. Click any of the filenames listed in the Multimedia Detective to display or play its multimedia content.

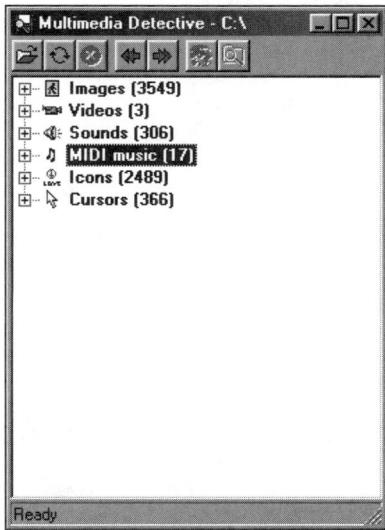

Figure 47-8: Multimedia Detective organizes your multimedia files hierarchically for easy previewing.

With Multimedia Xplorer, you can convert bitmap images (bmp, jpeg, gif, png, tiff, pcx); play sound files (wav, mid, rmi, aiff, au, snd, mp2, mp3, mpa, ra); play video (avi, mpeg, mov, rm); extract icons; display animated mouse pointers; change your startup, shut down, and power-off Windows logos; produce slide shows; and set up wallpaper. It uses the Windows Media Player to display all the files that it finds.

It is great to have this much power over your multimedia files. Multimedia Xplorer is shareware, and you'll find it at http://www.moonsoftware.com/.

Extract Sound Schemes from Desktop Themes

Desktop Themes usually come with a whole set of sounds that are assigned to various Windows events, such as Maximize, Minimize, Close Window, Exit Windows, and so on. All of the sounds taken together, along with their assignments to these Windows events, constitute a Windows sound scheme.

Secret

You can save sound schemes from Desktop Themes and invoke them whenever you like, even if you don't care for the rest of the Desktop Theme. You can edit any set of sounds and their assignments to create sound schemes.

If you haven't already loaded some Desktop Themes from the Windows CD-ROM, or from various sites on the Internet, you'll need to get them first. To copy some themes from the Windows CD-ROM, click the Start button ⇨ Settings ⇨ Control Panel ⇨ Add/Remove Programs ⇨ Windows Setup ⇨ Desktop Themes. You can pick which themes you want to install.

To use only the sounds from a theme, clear all of the checkboxes except the "Sound events" checkbox, as shown in Figure 47-9. Click OK to make those sounds the current sounds.

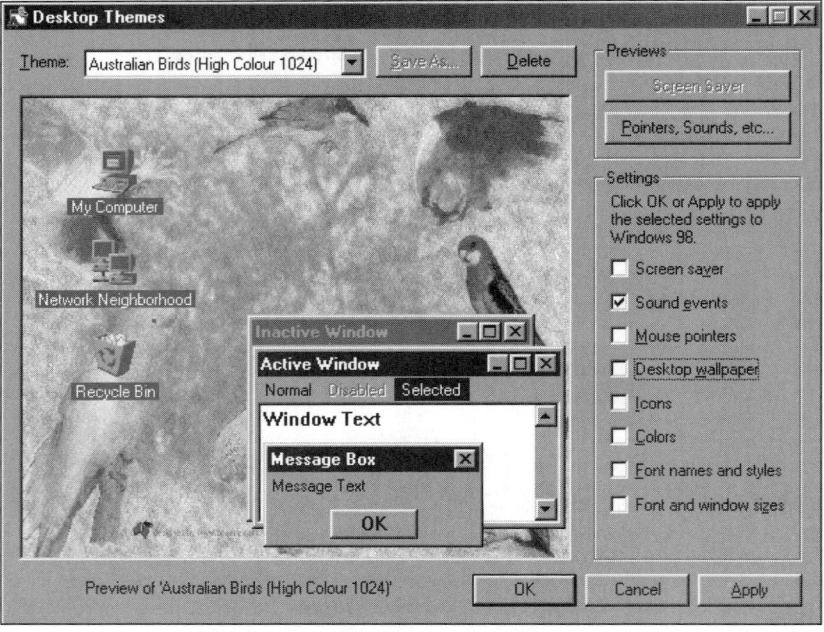

Figure 47-9: The Desktop Themes dialog box lets you choose which settings from a theme you will use. In this example, only the sounds are selected.

Now that you have a set of current sounds taken from a theme, click Start ⇨ Settings ⇨ Control Panel ⇨ Sounds. Click any of the Windows events, as shown in Figure 47-10. To hear the sound, click the Play arrow to the right of the Preview box.

To save the current sounds as a sound scheme, click the Save As button, enter a name in the "Save this sound scheme as" field, and click OK.

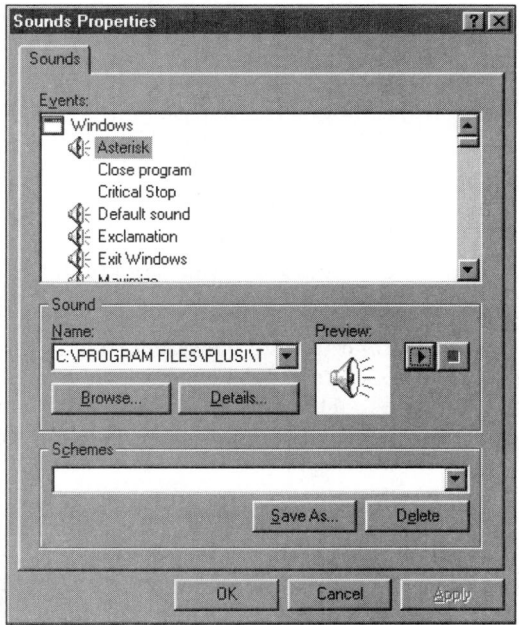

Figure 47-10: The Sounds Properties dialog box lets you hear a sound.

You can use the Browse button to browse for any other wav files that you want to assign to Windows events. Other programs that use sounds will also appear in the Events list, so you can scroll down to them and assign new sounds to their events.

A good way to find wav files and other multimedia files is to use the Multimedia Xplorer. We discuss it in the previous section, "Find Your Video, Sound, Image, Icon, Midi, Wav, and Mouse Pointer Files."

Panoramic Views

The Surround video viewer is seamlessly installed when you install Internet Explorer and/or Windows. It provides the user with a way of viewing properly formatted panoramic and rotating object views. To get an idea of what this means, you can check out a couple of Web sites that use Surround video.

A good place to start is Black Diamond Consulting, the original authors of Surround video. They have a number of links to Web sites that use this technology. You'll find the links at http://www.bdiamond.com/products/live.htm.

The MSN Carpoint site makes good use of Surround video, both for 360-degree interior panoramic shots of new cars and trucks, as well as for walk-around views of new cars (actually, the car appears to rotate). These are the two modes for Surround video, so you get a good idea of how to use this technology. You'll find the gallery of car panoramas at `http://carpoint.msn.com/gallery`. To see the Toyota Tacoma interior, visit `http://carpoint.msn.com/Gallery/Inside/142800`.

A particularly interesting site is Strolling.com at `http://strolling.com/` You'll be able to click a map to get a number of views of London, Paris, and New York.

Surround video is not the only format used to view panoramic and object pictures. Many producers use the Apple QuickTime VR format, and sometimes combine it with QuickTime movie to allow you to walk between panoramic views. You can check out a 360-degree panoramic view of a hang-gliding launch site on Maui at `http://www.maui.net/~drex/sixmile.html` or `http://www.infographicdesign.com/vr/sixmile/html`. We've included a sample of the view in Figure 47-11.

Figure 47-11: A portion of the 360-degree pan of the hang-gliding launch halfway up Haleakala. The complete pan took 18 shots.

In order to view this panoramic picture, you'll need to download the 7MB Apple QuickTime viewer `http://www.apple.com/quicktime/`.

To see how you can integrate panoramic views with pseudo walkthroughs, go to Apple's campus for a virtual tour at `http://www.apple.com/quicktime/samples/interactive-mm/vac/vacdemo.html`. QuickTime movie is used to simulate walking from one panoramic viewpoint to the next.

As you will see from these sites, this video format is not actually a form of VR (virtual reality), in spite of Apple's hyped up name for it. Both Surround video and QTVR do essentially the same thing—allow the author to create and you to view panoramic and surround-object pictures.

I wrote to the author of the Maui panoramic view, cartographer Bob Franklin, and asked him what he thought about this technology. Here's what he had to say:

> Creating a view from one position is a file size and production issue. QTVR also has a mode for object views such as those in the rotating car. These are more difficult to produce, and file size resources are costly.
>
> There are pseudo walkthroughs available in QTVR, either as teleportation or a streaming view, as you move from one panorama

node to another. VRML would choke at the resources and production required to give an immersive experience in a real scene.

QTVR is a subset of QuickTime, arguably far more sophisticated and powerful than any other media format. The metaphors can easily mix with other aspects of QuickTime (straight audio, straight video, sprites, and so on), so the sky's the limit to create any level of virtual experience. Most people deploy panoramas, mainly to give a better sense of being somewhere else — academia, real estate, entertainment, interactive games, and so on. The object part of QTVR is used less frequently, due to production and file size issues, but it is typically used to show products in online catalogs.

Production issues are very complex, storage file size can go ballistic very quickly, and download bandwidth can go exponential. The ability to present "seamless" viewing experiences is more related to decompression technologies than to processor speeds.

The "one viewer position" issue is actually driven by the need to "stitch" multiple images together, because lenses just won't go beyond about 160 degrees. Most of the software designed to process these multiple images focus on automating the process. In fact, if you begin to put these images together, you'll discover that you need to keep the camera exactly centered vertically on the horizon and exactly aligned with the horizon. Furthermore, you need to make the shots centered at compass increments evenly divisible into 360 degrees.

To that end, a mini industry has developed to produce tripod heads with detented positions, some automated by electric motors, and universal leveling mechanisms. Look at http://www.kaidan. com. Bogen also makes them. Other issues related to creating these images have to do with lens focal lengths vis-à-vis number of shots, and maintaining exposures to a constant standard — in other words, a manual camera set to a fixed aperture and shutter speed.

My scene was done with a Polaroid PCD 2000 digital camera with no built-in compression (artifacts), but I had to correct the exposures after the fact (in PhotoShop), so that color and contrast matched. The lens was a 38mm, so it required 18 shots. A 20mm lens might only need 10. The best shots with an automatic camera would be done with the sun directly overhead. This is not usually possible. Also, you don't have to take shots sequentially. You can wait for part of the scene to get more interesting before shooting it. Doing this with a digital camera would require some expertise in PhotoShop or the like.

The concept and viewing technology was introduced by Apple through QuickTime four years ago. Since then, there have been a number of players in on it and, as you pointed out, there are a few technologies that can be implemented as browser plug-ins, or standalone apps, including viewers based on Java. There are many composing programs as well. IPIX at http://www.ipix.com is another major player on the technology end.

IPIX has an image format that is infinitely zoomable (well, almost) and serves the portion of the image that the viewer requires on the fly.

I believe they also have a Java player. Some other companies have various proprietary cameras and such, all aimed at making production easy. The Surround video technology is not available for Mac. In general, I disdain any technology that is not cross-platform — my major beef with Microsoft. User share on other platforms is still quite high, and ah, well, I'm one of them.

One of the issues with the technology of this "viewing experience" is that the image is not displayed pixel for pixel as it is stored. The idea is that at each point of view (360 per zoom level), whatever is displayed in the window is displayed in a perspective consistent with the viewing window's command. This requires compression for storage and a very rapid decompression on the fly as the viewer pans around, zooming in and out. There are quite a few licensors of codecs (compression/decompression) out there who have algorithms that do a fair to excellent job in this vein, jpeg being the most famous.

You can create a panorama in two ways, no matter which technology you use to store and display it. First, you can manually "blend" the collected frames together in a raster image editor such as PhotoShop. Second, you can use software that is "smart" enough to do the blending for you, assuming that the photographer has given the software mathematically consistent images to start with (hence the specialized tripod heads). If you use this second method, you also need a software tool to store the resultant data in a form easily reassembled. There are many, and fortunately for me, most use QuickTime.

Thinking about this then, one could imagine that "looking out" from a central position to a surrounding environment is fundamentally different than "looking in" at an object. "Looking out" has the potential for "interpreting" raw raster data in an infinite way, because the data are "stitched" together so that there is no start or finish. For each microscopically incremented viewing position, there is a version of the data that can be viewed and made sense of, visually.

My scene of the six-mile launch is infinitely interpreted from data that are (roughly) 300 pixels high by 2800 pixels wide, or 840,000 total pixels. Let's take a finite example of "looking in" where, say, we look at a car from 360 positions. Extrapolating, my window for viewing the scene was 300 pixels high by 400 wide (120,000 pixels). To look in at an object from a finite 360 compass points would require a storage source file containing 43,200,000 pixels. Quite a difference. As a result, *object views*, as they are called, are often sampled from 15 to 30 degree compass points, and they often don't have that smooth look.

To carry the extrapolation a little farther, imagine the production, storage requirements, and access speeds necessary to "move" the panorama a finite distance in some singular direction, let alone give the viewer an infinite choice of directions! What would the "grain" of the movement have to be so that the movement would seem at least a little bit "seamless"? You can see this would be impossible under today's technology, except for some small demonstration project.

VRML has tried to address this issue by "re-creating" the environment as data, rather than "recording" it, as QuickTime has. Obviously this has its own limitations, but as rendering speeds increase, I would imagine that sophisticated production techniques will allow some pretty cool viewer experiences.

Meanwhile, the technologists in the immersive video world have deemed the "scene" to be the lowest common denominator. A scene is a collection of nodes. (The term *node* refers to the place where the user "stands.") Each node can consist of a panoramic view (looking out) or an object view (looking in). The user moves from node to node within a scene by clicking hotspots within his or her current view. This leads to an experience not unlike some interactive games, such as Riven or Myst, as opposed to Tomb Raider, which is really VRML. Thus the rudiments of a VRML experience can be approached in immersive video, but not duplicated.

For me, I find the interaction to be the fascination here. We do not experience the world in real life as the viewer of a movie being directed and shown by another, but as something we glance at, do double takes on, stop and focus on, return to and move on, and so on. This technology allows this type of interaction, and the net experience is one of being there.

I have found that producers of this sort of content do panoramas. Object movies (looking in) require a quantum leap in production effort to produce a good quality result. Ironically, automobiles have been a big exception to this. It turns out that auto shows often have the cars on giant turntables, which allows for very exact image sampling.

Some more ambitious attempts at scenes produce linear video between different panorama or object nodes. You are here, click on this hotspot, and you are transported (as on a moving sidewalk) to the next viewing spot, all the while watching your progress, as opposed to the usual "teleportation" metaphor.

When Voyager landed on Mars, a QuickTime VR was produced from the telemetry, showing a 360-degree view. It is posted on NASA's site `http://mars.jpl.nasa.gov/MPF/vrml/qtvr.html`. I have found that academia is a big user of this technology, archeology (panoramas) and medicine (objects) in particular. Real estate is a big market too, as are travel, destination resorts, and so on.

I have seen an object movie (looking in) that was produced with 3 degrees of freedom. Imagine an object in motion as a loop (repeating movement, as a piston cycling). There is a user-selectable viewpoint, which not only moved around the object, but also moved around it from multiple views in the Y-axis. And all the while the object was in temporal movement. The limitation here was bandwidth. Only 8 percent of the possible three axis views were produced, with two seconds of temporal dimension, but it took 2.3MB of compressed data at 180×240 pixels to view in real time!

The real attraction is that quite a lot of information (in its larger sense) is storable in pretty low bandwidth data. While other developers have been attacking this venue in a strong way, Apple's QuickTime has a big head start in many aspects, probably due to its longevity in multimedia playback in general.

I use QuickTime because it has more production tools available; it is cross platform; it supports all media formats; and, in one technology, it will read virtually any audio or video format (including streaming with 4.0). On top of that, it licenses and distributes all major (and minor) audio and video codecs as part of QuickTime. This means that quality is extremely high. It is the only media player that mixes media, supports multinode scenes, and offers advanced animation and infographic tools.

Web-TV

Will the computer and the TV merge? Our feeling is that the computer/ Internet experience will overpower TV within ten years.

Web-TV Through URLs

Your Web-TV channels are accessible from your Address bar. You can use the Address bar in an Internet Explorer, Explorer, or My Computer window, or the Address toolbar on your Desktop. Simply type the TV prefix and enter the channel number type — for example, **tv://12**. This is just like entering **http://** to get to a Web address or **file://** to get to a folder or file.

If Web-TV isn't running, you can launch it and go right to your desired channel by clicking Start ⇨ Run, and entering the TV URL. If you type the TV URL in the Address bar and Web-TV isn't already running, it will start up.

You can also create a Start menu folder and insert shortcuts for your favorite TV channels:

STEPS

Creating a Folder of TV URLs for Your Start Menu

Step 1. Navigate with your Explorer to your My System folder (hopefully you created one previously). Right-click the right pane of the Explorer, click New ⇨ Folder, and rename the new folder **TV Channels.**

Step 2. Right-click the TV Channels folder and click Explore.

Step 3. Right-click the right pane of the Explorer, and click New ⇨ Shortcut.

Step 4. Type **tv://12**, or whatever channel you want, in the "Command line" field (see Figure 47-12). Click Next.

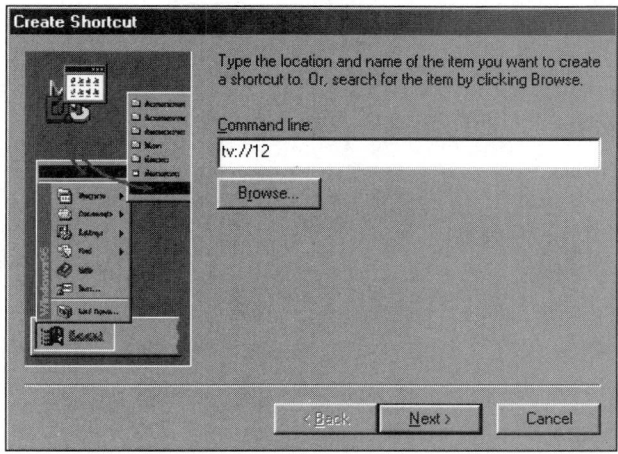

Figure 47-12: Type the "address" of the channel in the "Command line" field.

Step 5 Rename the shortcut to a familiar name for the TV channel. Click Finish.

Step 6. Drag the TV Channels folder to the Start button and drop it there. A shortcut will appear on the Start menu.

Web-TV with ATI All-In-Wonder Cards

If you have the ATI All-In-Wonder card (which includes a TV tuner) you might run into trouble when you set up Web-TV. If you find that Web-TV appears to be configured correctly, but you still aren't able to set up your TV channels — and hence cannot watch TV on your computer — you'll want to check out your video drivers.

Windows may misidentify your display adapter as the ATI Rage II+ [mach_64]. This setting allows you to run your All In Wonder card at various color depths including up to True Color. This may mislead you into thinking that your display adapter is set up properly.

While the Mach_64 drivers correctly drive the ATI display adapter for most everyday tasks, these drivers don't include the files required to view Web-TV. To install the proper video driver, take the following steps:

STEPS

Installing the Proper Video Driver for the ATI Card

Step 1. Right-click your Desktop, click Properties, click the Settings tab, and click the Advanced button.

Step 2. Click the Adapter tab, and click the Change button. In the Update Device Driver Wizard, click Next.

Step 3. Mark the option to display a list of all the drivers in a specific location, and click Next.

Step 4. Mark the "Show all hardware" option button. Select ATI Technologies under Manufacturers, and the All-In-Wonder [ati_m64] driver under Models. Click Next.

Step 5. Restart Windows when asked.

Thanks to Dave Adams for help with this tip.

Web-TV Control Keys

It's not a remote control, but you can use the keyboard shortcuts listed in Table 47-1 to control Web-TV.

Table 47-1   Web-TV Keyboard Controls

Key	Action/Result
F10	Displays the Web-TV menu
F6	Toggles between full-screen and windowed display
0–9	Changes channels (cannot use keypad numbers)
Windows+Ctrl+Shift+Z	Program Guide (starts Web-TV if not running)
Windows+Ctrl+Z	Starts Web-TV or toggles between windowed and full-screen display if running
Windows+Crtl+V	Turns volume up (this works even if Web-TV isn't running)

Key	Action/Result
Windows+Shift+V	Turns volume down (this works even if Web-TV isn't running)
Windows+V	Mutes Master Volume (this works even if Web-TV isn't running)
Windows+Crtl+Alt+Z	Increases channel by one
Windows+Crtl+Alt+Shift+Z	Decreases channel by one

Thanks to Michael Grant for pointing out these tips.

Summary

Let's hear and see and feel it for Windows multimedia. Make that ugly computer do something a lot more fun.

▶ MP3 audio threatens the music industry. Download the threat to your computer.

▶ Tune into radio stations around the world and bring back audio memories of your vacations abroad.

▶ Search for all your multimedia files and only multimedia files.

▶ Mine the themes for sounds.

▶ Find panoramic views on the Web.

▶ Create your own folder of Web-TV shortcuts.

▶ Use keyboard shortcuts to control your Web-TV.

Appendix

The Windows Me Millennium Edition Secrets CD-ROM

The CD-ROM that accompanies *Microsoft Windows Me Millennium Edition Secrets* contains the entire book in a machine-readable format. You can search the text to find topics of interest. You can also print out sections if you need to refer to them separately.

Reading or Installing the E-Book from the CD-ROM

To read the e-book from the CD-ROM or install the e-book on a hard drive, run Setup.exe from the CD-ROM. On most PCs, Setup.exe will start automatically when you insert the CD into the CD-ROM drive. It's also easy to uninstall the e-book if you wish to do so (see the following instructions).

To run the setup program, follow these steps:

1. Insert the CD into your CD-ROM drive, such as D:.

2. The Windows Me Secrets e-book setup should start automatically. If your system is configured so the setup procedure does not start automatically, click Start ➪ Programs ➪ Accessories ➪ Windows Explorer. In Windows Explorer, double-click the file Setup.exe on your CD-ROM drive.

3. After the setup program begins, you will be given the choice of installing the e-book on your hard drive, or only installing small DLL files that allow the e-book to be read from the CD-ROM.

4. If you chose to install the e-book, you can run it at any time by clicking Start ➪ Programs ➪ Windows Me Secrets ➪ Windows Me Secrets.

Once the e-book is open:

- You can read the book by opening any chapter in the left pane and selecting any topic.

- You can jump to any topic by clicking the Index tab.

- You can search for any word or phrase by clicking the Search tab.

To uninstall the e-book, follow these steps:

1. Click Start ⇨ Settings ⇨ Control Panel ⇨ Add/Remove Programs.

2. Select Windows Me Secrets and click the Remove button.

3. You will receive the choice of two options: Automatic or Custom uninstall. The Automatic uninstall option removes all signs of the e-book. The Custom uninstall option allows you to remove individual features of the e-book.

Index

Continued

Continued

Continued

Continued

DISCARDED